History of the Office of the Secretary of Defense

THE MCNAMARA ASCENDANCY
1961-1965

HISTORY OF THE OFFICE OF THE SECRETARY OF DEFENSE
Alfred Goldberg, *General Editor*

Volume I: Steven L. Rearden, *The Formative Years, 1947-1950* (1984)
Volume II: Doris M. Condit, *The Test of War, 1950-1953* (1988)
Volume III: Richard M. Leighton, *Strategy, Money, and the New Look, 1953-1956* (2001)
Volume IV: Robert J. Watson, *Into the Missile Age, 1956-1960* (1997)

HISTORY OF THE OFFICE
OF THE
SECRETARY OF DEFENSE

Volume V

THE
MCNAMARA
ASCENDANCY
1961-1965

Lawrence S. Kaplan
Ronald D. Landa
Edward J. Drea

Historical Office
Office of the Secretary of Defense
Washington, D.C. • 2006

Published by Books Express Publishing
Copyright © Books Express, 2011
ISBN 978-1-780394-13-8

Books Express publications are available from all good retail and online booksellers. For publishing proposals and direct ordering please contact us at: info@books-express.com

Foreword

This is the fifth volume in the history of the Office of the Secretary of Defense. It covers the first four and one-half years of Robert S. McNamara's term as secretary of defense, an exceptionally important and fateful time in the history of the United States and the Department of Defense (DoD). These were years of great international challenges for the United States and of much change in DoD. The volume begins with the efforts by President John F. Kennedy and McNamara to establish more effective management of the military establishment and ends with the full commitment of President Lyndon B. Johnson's administration to the war in Vietnam.

Robert McNamara was the longest-serving secretary of defense, the most controversial, and arguably the most successful in administering the Defense Department. The strong leadership he exerted benefited markedly from his personal relationship with and support from Presidents Kennedy and Johnson. He remained a prominent and often dominant figure through more than seven years in the two administrations.

The period from 1961 to mid-1965 witnessed strenuous efforts by McNamara to establish greater control over the DoD budget and to make the department function more efficiently and economically. He regarded the budget as central to conceiving and implementing policy and viewed it in the broader context of national security, embracing policy in its many aspects—the national economy, strategic planning, technology, force programming, collective security, military assistance, and resource allocation. McNamara had a deep understanding of the relationship between programs and budget and the need to rationalize the process that linked them. His dynamic approach and aggressive style contributed to problems with the military and Congress, both of which on occasion took exception to his innovations and practices.

Despite sometimes bitter resistance, McNamara succeeded in effecting large and important changes in the way DoD did business. He moved the department toward greater centralized direction, greater cohesion, and greater joint effort and mutual support by the military services. Progress in this direction was made possible by the exercise of personal control and coordination by the secretary, using powers strengthened by legislative and executive actions. This improved unification occurred at the expense of growing disaffection by the military.

Like the previous volumes in this series Volume V seeks to present a broad and analytical account of U.S. national security that necessarily includes in considerable detail the policymaking roles of the president, National Security Council, State Department, and Joint Chiefs of Staff. Much of the volume is devoted to OSD participation in the critical international events of the period. While the focus is properly on Washington decisionmaking, the international background of foreign policy decisions is thoroughly explored.

This is a scholarly, readable, and informative account. An exhaustive history of DoD for these years is not possible in a one-volume study, especially for a period as eventful as McNamara's first term. Given the scale and purpose of the book, it was necessary to be selective and discriminating in choosing topics. Accordingly, such important subjects as intelligence, logistics, and research and development, though touched on, did not receive the attention they undoubtedly would have merited in a larger work.

The authors are eminently qualified. Lawrence S. Kaplan holds the Ph.D. from Yale University. He has been Distinguished Professor of History at Kent State University, where he was director of the Lyman L. Lemnitzer Center of NATO Affairs, and is currently adjunct professor at Georgetown University. He is the author of many historical works, including *A Community of Interests: NATO and the Military Assistance Program, 1948-1951*, and is a former president of the Society for Historians of American Foreign Relations. Ronald D. Landa, author of the five budget chapters and contributor to others, received his Ph.D. in history from Georgetown University, edited volumes of the *Foreign Relations of the United States* for the State Department, and in the OSD Historical Office made an invaluable contribution to research and editing of this volume and to the editing of previous volumes in this series. Edward J. Drea wrote the chapters on military assistance and "The Search for Savings" and helped with other chapters. A Ph.D. graduate of the University of Kansas, he has had a long and distinguished career publishing studies of World War II, including *MacArthur's Ultra*. He is the author of Volume VI in the OSD series, which will cover the period 1965-69.

Interested government agencies reviewed Volume V and declassified and cleared its contents for public release. Although the text has been declassified, some of the official sources cited may still be classified. The views expressed are those of the authors and do not necessarily represent those of the Office of the Secretary of Defense.

ALFRED GOLDBERG
Historian, OSD

Preface

The term "revolution" is often too loosely applied to political or bureaucratic change, but it aptly describes the transformation that Robert S. McNamara wrought in the Department of Defense. Even before the president of the Ford Motor Company took office as secretary of defense on 20 January 1961 he set in motion plans to reshape the management of the department in the way he had helped restructure the operations of an automobile company in distress after World War II. McNamara's insistence on examining every aspect of the Defense establishment in the pursuit of efficiency and economy produced new methods of linking the budget to programs. His emphasis on eliminating waste and containing costs, at least initially, won over normally resistant constituencies. In his first years in office he shook up the Pentagon, bringing to it an energy and intelligence that would make him the most successful manager in the history of the department up to that time as well as its most controversial secretary.

Crises in Cuba, Berlin, Laos, and Vietnam inevitably intruded on the progress of McNamara's plans to reorganize and energize the military establishment. Rising costs in military assistance to Southeast Asia, the demands of maintaining troop strength in Europe, and conflict with NATO partners over strategy and the role of nuclear weapons affected the secretary's efforts to control the direction of the nation's defense programs. The challenge was compounded by growing opposition inside the Pentagon and friction with Congress over policies that elevated missiles at the expense of aircraft, increased emphasis on conventional forces and deemphasized reliance on nuclear weapons, and attempted to synchronize weapon selection and procurement. After four years in office McNamara was vulnerable to criticism at home and abroad. Difficulties notwithstanding, the secretary could claim success in coping with the Soviet adversary and in retaining the loyalty of the White House.

The volume covers a wide range of subjects in varying degrees. Appropriately, the first chapters deal with the reorganization of the Defense Department and the instruments by which it was achieved. The budgets for the Kennedy years, treated in Chapters III-VI, reflect the changes sought by the McNamara team.

Of the 20 chapters total, 11 deal with the engagement of DoD with the outside world—the Soviet Union, Southeast Asia, Cuba, and the NATO allies. Among those, six center on the military crises that developed between 1961 and 1965.

Many chapters are essentially monographs in themselves, requiring research into topics seemingly distinct from each other and separated by time frame as well as subject matter. The task of the authors was to weave them together into a coherent whole that was both narrative and analytical. It is fitting that in an enterprise of this magnitude the writing of the book was a cooperative effort. I provided a first draft that subsequently underwent thorough revision and rewriting by others to yield this final version.

In listing the names of collaborators I hardly do justice to the contributions they have made. First is Ronald Landa, whose expertise is manifested in the budget chapters. He has written the five chapters covering the budget issues for the period and contributed extensively to the research and writing of other chapters. Edward Drea, author of Volume VI in this series, wrote chapters XVI and XVII with his typical care and insight and shrewdly reviewed others.

Fellow historians in the OSD Historical Office John Glennon, Max Rosenberg, Roger Trask, and Nancy Berlage read and re-read chapters, contributing text, making needed corrections, verifying citations, and adding skillful editorial touches that help to make the book more readable as well as more accurate. Colleagues in the Office of the Historian, Department of State, Edward Keefer, Louis Smith, Erin Mahan, and John Carland, offered useful comments on several chapters. Elaine Everly not only brought order to my disordered files but also provided an unusually close reading of the chapters and checking of the notes. The greater part of the typing burden was borne by Ruth Sharma with her usual superb skill and keen eye. Her contribution through numerous complicated drafts was invaluable. Floyd Stewart and his talented production staff in OSD Graphics, notably Colleen Wiatt, worked their usual wonders.

Several archives and libraries were essential to the completion of this project. At the Pentagon Library Yolanda Miller, Debbie Reed, and Barbara Risser reliably directed us to pertinent materials in its collection. Susan Lemke and Richard Montgomery were always responsive to requests for documents in the Lemnitzer and Taylor Papers at the National Defense University Library, as were Jesse McNeal and Sandra Meagher of the Directives and Records Division, DoD-Washington Headquarters Services, in providing materials from the Suitland, Maryland, Records Center of the National Archives and Records Administration. At Suitland Mike Waesze and Elizabeth Sears were unfailingly helpful. We also appreciate the courtesies accorded us at the National Archives, College Park, Maryland, by Will Mahoney, Clifford Snyder, and Jeanine Swift of the Modern Military Division and by Milton Gustafson, formerly chief of the Diplomatic Branch. Kathy Lloyd of the Naval Historical Center, Fred Graboske of the Marine Corps History and Museum Division, and Daun van Ee of the Library of Congress greatly facilitated research in their respective collections. Finally, Deborah Shapley shared her insights as well as papers gathered for her biography of McNamara.

Outside the Washington area the John F. Kennedy Library in Boston and the Lyndon B. Johnson Library in Austin were indispensable resources. The archivists of both libraries, especially Steve Plotkin and Michelle DeMartino of the Kennedy Library and John Wilson, Regina Greenwell, and Linda Seelke of the Johnson Library, not only were hospitable during visits but always responsive to telephone requests. In the early years of this project Robert T. Colbert and Ruth Alexander in the Defense Contract Administrative Services office at the Federal Building in Cleveland were careful custodians of documents sent from the Pentagon for my use as well as gracious hosts during my many visits to their facility.

The Historian and Deputy Historian deserve special mention in this preface. No matter how thoroughly an editor might parse a text, errors never can be fully eradicated. To the extent they have been, the endeavor owes a particular debt to Deputy Historian Stuart Rochester, as gifted an editor as he is a writer, for shepherding the manuscript through the several redraftings, substantially revising Chapter XV, and effectively recasting many others. His impressive skills, sound judgment, and exacting standards markedly improved the final product.

As for the general editor, Alfred Goldberg, head of the OSD Historical Office, his impact was felt at every stage of this project. He originated the series of which this volume is a part, critiqued every one of the 1,000 draft pages, and made significant changes in each of the chapters. His encyclopedic knowledge of most of the issues confronting the McNamara Pentagon served the writing of this book in ways rarely offered by general editors. Were it not for his official position pride of authorship should be his.

LAWRENCE S. KAPLAN

Contents

I.	**MCNAMARA AND THE NEW FRONTIER**	1
	The McNamara Appointment	3
	McNamara's Team	6
	On a Fast Track	10
II.	**SHAKEUP IN THE PENTAGON**	16
	The Symington Report	17
	The Vance Task Force	19
	Defense Intelligence Agency	22
	Defense Supply Agency	24
	Civil Defense	29
	Counterinsurgency	35
	The Space Mission	43
	LeMay's Reappointment, Anderson's Departure	47
	A Balance Sheet	49
III.	**EXPANDING THE FY 1962 BUDGET**	52
	Eisenhower's FY 1962 Budget	53
	Congress Defers Action	55
	A Quick Look by DoD and BoB	57
	28 March Amendment	62
	26 May Amendment	64
	The Berlin Crisis and the 26 July Amendment	67
IV.	**THE FY 1963 BUDGET: INTRODUCING THE PPBS**	72
	Antecedents	72
	Organizational Framework: Getting Started	75
	BoB's New Approach to the Spring Preview	78
	The Requirements/Planning Phase	79
	The Programming Phase	80

viii Contents

   The First Draft Presidential Memorandums (DPMs) 83
   The Budgeting Phase 85
   White House Decisions 87
   A Lasting Impact 91

 V. CONGRESS AND THE FY 1963 BUDGET 96
   McNamara at Center Stage 97
   Rebellion over the RS-70 100
   Vinson's Walk in the Rose Garden 104
   Furor over Army National Guard and Reserve Reorganization . .107
   The Senate Weighs In 110
   Finessing the Controversies. 112

 VI. THE FY 1964 BUDGET 118
   White House Expectations 119
   Shrinking the Service Estimates 122
   Final Decisions 125
   The Ups and Downs of the Authorization Bill 131
   Calls for Substantial Cuts 135
   The House Shaves the Appropriation Bill 136
   Averting Deeper Cuts in the Senate. 137

 VII. BERLIN: THE WALL 143
   Berlin in the Eisenhower Administration 143
   Indecision, Spring 1961 144
   The Acheson Initiatives 147
   The Vienna Summit 150
   Toward the Berlin Wall 151
   The Wall 156
   "Poodle Blanket" 162
   Confrontation at Checkpoint Charlie 165
   Aftermath: Clay vs. Washington 166
   Toward a Soviet-GDR Treaty 169

 VIII. THE BAY OF PIGS FIASCO 172
   The Eisenhower Legacy 172
   Road to "Trinidad" 174
   The JCS Role 175
   The Civilian Leadership Role 180
   Invasion 183
   The Taylor Report 186

	Recriminations	188
	Repercussions	192
IX.	THE CUBAN MISSILE CRISIS	195
	Supporting Cuban Exiles	196
	Operation Mongoose	198
	Contingency Plans	199
	Prologue: September–16 October	203
	Act I: 16-21 October	206
	Act II: 22-28 October	209
	Epilogue: 29 October–20 November	214
	Impact on Berlin	218
	Withdrawal of Jupiter Missiles from Turkey	220
	Cuba after the Missile Crisis	223
X.	LAOS	228
	Responding to the Eisenhower Warning	231
	Divisions within DoD	239
	Geneva: May-June 1961	243
	The Phoumi Burden, 1961-1962	247
	Geneva Again: June-July 1962	254
XI.	VIETNAM: RELUCTANT ENGAGEMENT, 1961-1963	260
	Kennedy and Counterinsurgency, January-April 1961	262
	The Gilpatric and Staley Reports	266
	The Taylor-Rostow Mission	270
	McNamara's Initiatives, December 1961-July 1962	274
	The Strategic Hamlet Program	277
	Comprehensive Plan for South Vietnam, July 1962-May 1963	281
	The Buddhist Rebellion and the Fall of Diem	283
XII.	FLEXIBLE RESPONSE	293
	Basic National Security Policy (BNSP)	296
	The "Missile Gap"	298
	The Acheson Report	303
	The Athens and Ann Arbor Addresses	305
	Counterforce and Flexible Response	309
	SIOP and Command and Control	316
	Assured Destruction	319

XIII.	**THE LIMITED NUCLEAR TEST BAN TREATY**	323
	Initiatives under Eisenhower	324
	Establishment of ACDA	325
	Proposing a Test Ban Treaty	327
	End to the Moratorium	331
	Search for Compromise, March–November 1962	335
	Seizing a Window of Opportunity	340
	Harriman's Mission to Moscow	345
	Debate over the Treaty	351
XIV.	**NATO RELATIONS: TRANSATLANTIC DIFFERENCES**	357
	NATO Strategy in 1961	358
	NATO Force Requirements for the 1960s	362
	France and the Force de Frappe	370
	Germany: Nuclear Aspirations?	373
	Skybolt	375
XV.	**MLF: A NOTION TOO FAR**	385
	Birth of a Concept	386
	JFK and the Ottawa Signals	388
	Defense Reservations, 1961–1962	390
	Athens and After	396
	Impact of Nassau	402
	The Merchant Team	405
	Slowing the Pace	410
	Johnson and the MLF	412
	Demise	415
XVI.	**THE EMBATTLED MILITARY ASSISTANCE PROGRAM**	421
	Adjusting the FY 1962 Budget	421
	Latin America	426
	The Kitchen Steering Group	427
	The FY 1963 Program	429
	Troubles at AID	431
	The Clay Committee	432
	The Shift to Military Sales	433
	The FY 1964 Program	435
	The FY 1965 Program	439
	Preparing the FY 1966 Request	443

XVII.	THE SEARCH FOR SAVINGS	447
	Balance of Payments	447
	The Cost Reduction Program	453
	Base Closures	462
	The TFX and Cost Effectiveness	466
XVIII.	TIGHTENING THE BUDGET: FYs 1965 AND 1966	475
	The Kennedy Administration and the FY 1965 Budget	476
	Kennedy's Assassination: Johnson Takes the Reins	479
	The FY 1965 Authorization Bill	484
	The FY 1965 Appropriation Bill	487
	Preparation of the FY 1966 Budget	489
XIX.	VIETNAM: INTO THE VORTEX	498
	McNamara in Saigon–December 1963	499
	The Khanh Coup	502
	Toward Escalation: Spring 1964	504
	The Other Players: Laos and Cambodia	515
	The Tonkin Gulf Resolution	517
	Crisis in Saigon	524
	Back to the Drawing Board	527
	"McNamara's War"	531
XX.	CONCLUSION	535
	LIST OF ABBREVIATIONS	550
	NOTES	555
	NOTE ON SOURCES AND SELECTED BIBLIOGRAPHY	630
	INDEX	650

CHARTS

1. Department of Defense, 9 March 1961 21
2. Department of Defense, 1 August 1964 50

TABLES

1. Eisenhower Proposed FY 1962 Budget (NOA) 54
2. Eisenhower FY 1962 Budget 55
3. FY 1962 Appropriations (NOA) Enacted 69
4. Military Services' Program Estimates for FY 1963 and
   Secretary of Defense 22 September 1961 Guidance 83
5. January 1962 Budget Estimates for FY 1963 Program 92
6. TOA and NOA by Program, FY 1962-FY 1964 130
7. Selected Country Programs (MAP), FY 1964 438
8. Military Assistance Program Comparison of NOA Request
   with Actual Funding, FY 1961-FY 1965 446
9. Financial Summary by Program, FY 1961-FY 1966 495
10. Comparison of Active Forces, 1961 and 1965 496

Photographs follow pages 198 and 390.

History of the Office of the Secretary of Defense

The McNamara Ascendancy
1961-1965

Chapter I

McNamara and the New Frontier

The New Frontier, like the New Deal, was rarely troubled by efforts to define it. Suffice to know that it signified youth, vigor, pragmatism, and impatience with the legacy of the previous administration. The new president, John F. Kennedy, personified these traits in full measure. Of all the New Frontiersmen brought into his administration after 20 January 1961, 44-year-old Secretary of Defense Robert Strange McNamara came closest to the archetype, and he would become the most influential member of the Kennedy cabinet. As George W. Ball, undersecretary of state in both the Kennedy and Johnson administrations, observed: "In any group where Robert McNamara was present, he soon emerged as a dominant voice. I was impressed by his extraordinary self-confidence—based not on bluster but on a detailed knowledge of objective facts."[1] His personality intimidated his colleagues, to the extent that others had difficulty in sustaining opposing views.[2]

Dominance, however, imposed special burdens. When the New Frontiersmen lost their way, as they did in the Bay of Pigs debacle less than three months after entering office, a leading figure like McNamara assumed a responsibility for the results, deservedly or not. McNamara had the strength and self-assurance to accept blame for the misadventure even though he had little to do with the planning or execution of the operation. In an interview 25 years later, he expressed his deep regret over his acquiescence in the invasion of Cuba.[3] This confession represented less an act of contrition than a form of noblesse oblige—taking responsibility for errors others had committed but which leaders must acknowledge as their own. For the failures in Vietnam, McNamara would deliver at length a more personal mea culpa.

The term New Frontier itself was as vague as historian Frederick Jackson Turner's broad reference to the frontier as the wellspring of American exceptionalism. The inspiration for Kennedy's adoption of the image came at a Cambridge cocktail party in June 1960, when Walt W. Rostow, an economic historian at the Massachusetts Institute of Technology, suggested to the Massachusetts senator that he call his program "the New Frontier."[4] The phrase became part of the litany of Kennedy's presidential campaign after his moving acceptance speech at the Democratic convention in Los Angeles in July 1960. "We stand today," the nominee declared, "on the edge of a new frontier—the frontier of the 1960s, a frontier of unknown opportunities and paths, a frontier of unfulfilled hopes and threats." The speech included also a reference to "uncharted areas of science and space, unsolved problems of peace and war," issues central to the concerns of McNamara's Pentagon in the years ahead.[5]

Kennedy filled out the top ranks of his administration with a mix of old and new. Patriarchal cold warrior Dean Acheson acted as the president's chief adviser on the North Atlantic Treaty Organization (NATO), septuagenarian W. Averell Harriman became an adviser on Laos as well as a general troubleshooter in the State Department, while members of the Republican establishment Arthur H. Dean and John J. McCloy held key positions in disarmament negotiations. Commitment and energy mattered as much as experience or pedigree in the appointment of the cabinet and recruitment of staff. Whether youthful World War II veterans moving into Washington for the first time or reinvigorated New Dealers and Fair Dealers returning from eight years in the political wilderness, perhaps the unifying element among the new men lay in confidence that their contributions could make a difference, that accomplishments would be measured by their performance rather than by ideology. They did not aim at fundamentally reshaping America as the New Dealers of the 1930s had, nor did they need new agencies to achieve their objectives. McNamara made clear his efforts to exploit hitherto untapped powers of his office rather than urge Congress to pass new legislation reorganizing the Department of Defense.

There was little aura of the impassioned reformism that characterized the New Deal of the 1930s. Indeed, many in Kennedy's inner circle might have taken offense at being described as idealists; they considered themselves tough-minded pragmatists. Arthur M. Schlesinger, Jr., a New Frontiersman and Harvard historian, later wrote that he and his associates never really thought that "the world was plastic and the future unlimited. . . . At bottom we knew how intractable the world was . . . . The President knew better than anyone how hard his life was to be. Though he incited the euphoria, he did so involuntarily, for he did not share it himself." Recognizing Kennedy's invocation of the New Frontier in public speeches, Schlesinger noted, "I think he regarded it with some embarrassment as a temporary capitulation to rhetoric."[6] Despite such caveats the Kennedy administration exuded an unusual air of excitement and a willingness to confront old problems with fresh approaches.

Among the many legacies of the Eisenhower administration that demanded attention, national security loomed large. The putative inadequacy of the outgoing administration in managing the nation's defenses was a major theme of the

Democratic election campaign in 1960. National security policies at the end of Eisenhower's second term were depicted as mired in uncertainty and disarray. Nuclear capabilities in particular gave cause for concern as the aftershocks of Sputnik, the dramatic 1957 Soviet space launch, continued to unsettle the country. Soviet technological achievements invited the charge of a missile gap, made all the more serious by increasing doubts about the viability of the strategy of massive retaliation and the reliability of the U.S. nuclear commitment to Europe's defense.

Europe was not the only critical arena in the nation's contest with the Soviet Union. Closer to home, the increasing hostility of Fidel Castro's Cuba added still another test. And in Southeast Asia the crisis in Laos raised the possibility of U.S. military intervention in a distant, unfamiliar place. Innovative approaches to all of these challenges became a high priority for the new administration; in Secretary McNamara the Defense Department had a leader willing to experiment with new programs and new techniques.

From one perspective the weighty defense agenda overwhelmed the new secretary, a self-described political naif, who embarrassed the administration when he discovered, and then seemingly admitted to the press, that the missile gap did not exist.[7] The Castro irritant, which he had to confront immediately on taking office, still remained when he departed seven years later. Nor did European allies accept his rationalizations for increasing conventional forces or for limiting NATO's nuclear options. His management of the Pentagon gained initial support but also won him enemies among some of the military chiefs and their allies on Capitol Hill. His proposed solutions for resolving conflict in Southeast Asia led ultimately to a widening of the war and his departure from office.

The foregoing, however, is too bleak and one-sided a picture of McNamara's record, for his long and eventful tenure saw the introduction of a host of pathbreaking institutional changes, including cost containment techniques and a new planning-programming-budgeting system, that served to make the nation's vast military machine more efficient. And achieving a better balance between nuclear and conventional forces, though resisted in NATO, in the eyes of the administration increased the credibility of America's defense posture.

The McNamara Appointment

McNamara came to Washington with a Harvard degree, World War II military experience, and, some would say, a hardheaded approach to problems. A Californian who graduated from the university at Berkeley with a Phi Beta Kappa key in 1937, he went on to an MBA degree in 1939 at Harvard Business School, where he taught from 1940 to 1942. In the Army Air Forces during World War II he attracted the attention of Robert A. Lovett, then assistant secretary of war, later secretary of defense under Truman, through his innovative contributions to management techniques called "statistical control." After the war a number of young colleagues from the Army Air Forces, including McNamara and led by Charles (Tex) Thornton, who had headed statistical control during the war, promoted themselves as a team to serve industry in the manner they had served government. These so-called "Whiz Kids" went from Washington to the Ford Motor Company, then in transition under the inexperienced Henry Ford II, grandson of the founder. McNamara served as comptroller of Ford from 1949 to 1953, rose to vice president in 1955, and to president on 9 November 1960, one month before his appointment as secretary of defense.[8]

With the kind of mind that Kennedy admired—quick, confident, incisive—McNamara had reason to believe that what he had accomplished in the Army Air Forces and in industry he could do as well in the higher reaches of government. He observed from the outset that the "mechanism of decision-making" in DoD was faulty. "We were *too slow* to develop the alternatives and the decisions as to the numbers and types of forces we *really needed*." But as Roger Hilsman noted later, McNamara liked "to concentrate on what could be quantified—money, men, guns, and ammunition." Conceding McNamara's intelligence, Hilsman doubted mastery of numbers constituted a sufficient entree into the subtleties of international politics.[9]

McNamara's previous career was fashioned in the Midwest, not in Washington or Boston. The auto business honed his skills and burnished his reputation. Robert Lovett, who declined the Defense post when offered him by Kennedy, was the most prominent of those who brought McNamara's name to the attention of the Kennedys. Lovett remembered the young officer from his World War II Pentagon days as the brightest of the management group that he had brought down to Washington from the Harvard Business School. He told Clark Clifford, another veteran of the Truman administration, that he saw McNamara as "the prize of the lot, and the Kennedy people ought to consider him for either the Treasury or Defense." A Republican, McNamara had contributed to Kennedy's campaign; it does not seem that Kennedy knew this.[10]

Early in December 1960 McNamara received phone calls from Washington, including one from Robert Kennedy, whose name "didn't mean a great deal to me." He did agree to Kennedy's request to meet with Sargent Shriver, the president's brother-in-law. Shriver immediately flew to Detroit to offer him either the Treasury or the Defense position. He felt unqualified for Treasury and immediately declined the offer. Uncertain about his qualifications for Defense, he was in no hurry to accept. Although he obviously relished the challenge, he pointed out that only weeks before he had been chosen president of Ford and wondered about the propriety of leaving the post so soon after taking it.[11] Understandably, he also expressed concern about the financial sacrifice entailed; he needed to consult with his wife and children before accepting an annual salary reduction from $410,000 to $25,000. As he noted in an interview years later, he was not yet wealthy but on the way to becoming so.[12]

McNamara met the president-elect in Washington on 8 December at Kennedy's home on N Street in Georgetown, where each man impressed the other. Almost every biographer has told the story of McNamara's initial refusal to accept because of his lack of preparation for the position and Kennedy's response that he was not aware of any school for either cabinet members or presidents. McNamara later claimed that his "refusal was based solely on the grounds that I did not feel qualified to handle the responsibility." These doubts did not last long. Kennedy recognized the qualities that McNamara would bring to the post and accepted the terms that he had written down in advance of the interview. The secretary-designate insisted on appointing whomever he wanted without being subject to political pressures.[13]

McNamara saw himself as a "working" secretary. His secretaryship would be marked by rigorous probing of problems, getting advice, and then acting. As he pointed out, the secretary of defense could follow either of two broad philosophies of management: "He could play an essentially passive role—a judicial role. In this role the Secretary would make the decisions required of him by law by approving recommendations made to him. On the other hand, the Secretary of Defense could play an active role providing aggressive leadership—questioning, suggesting alternatives, proposing objectives, and stimulating progress. This active role represents my own philosophy of management."[14]

Aside from initial uncertainty about his readiness for the position, McNamara had a high regard for his immediate predecessor, Thomas S. Gates, and his instinct was to suggest that Kennedy keep Gates in office. An active manager, Gates had worked closely with the Joint Chiefs of Staff and had put to use the expanded authority of the secretary of defense resulting from the Department of Defense Reorganization Act of 1958. There were those who regarded Gates as "the first of a new breed of secretaries of defense."[15] McNamara recognized these qualities when he met the outgoing secretary and came away with the feeling that Gates should remain in office even though he was a Republican. Kennedy shared this view for a time, and briefly thought of keeping him on for a year, with his brother Robert as deputy secretary. But as Arthur Schlesinger later noted, Kennedy's advisers felt that it would be embarrassing to retain Gates after having made such an issue of defense inadequacies during the recent campaign.[16]

Once McNamara had made up his mind he acted quickly, accepting the position on 13 December 1960. The press took notice of his hard-driving style and quickly identified him as a potential strong man in the Kennedy cabinet. Could the other cabinet members, men of considerable distinction themselves, stand up to the forceful personality of the secretary of defense? The secretary of state in particular might have difficulty in holding his own against the aggressive new defense secretary. Dean Rusk, with long experience in the State Department under George Marshall and Dean Acheson, was in many ways a fine choice as the principal foreign affairs adviser to the president. But he may have been appointed partly because the president intended to exercise active direction of foreign affairs himself and to use other foreign policy experts, such as the special assistant for national security affairs, McGeorge Bundy, to provide him with a range of opinions for decisionmaking. Rusk certainly possessed executive capabilities but not the force to stand up to McNamara or the president—or so it seemed in 1961. The president, according to Theodore Sorensen, preferred that Rusk be more assertive and propose alternatives to Pentagon plans, but this restraint was the price Kennedy would have to pay for the type of person he had chosen for State.[17]

The contrast between the two secretaries was stark. McNamara demanded and received freedom to choose his own men. Rusk did not have that option. Kennedy intended to shape his own foreign policy but left McNamara much leeway in defense matters. Moreover, Rusk had competition not only from a president who thought of himself as his own foreign minister, but also from White House intellectuals who often had Kennedy's ear before Rusk could be heard. The Joint Chiefs never provided such competition for McNamara, who maintained firm control of the relationship. When General Maxwell Taylor served as military adviser in the White House, he no more upstaged the secretary of defense than he did as chairman of the JCS when he succeeded General Lyman L. Lemnitzer in 1962.[18]

Still, McNamara's influence had limits. Sorensen's loyalty to the president may have accounted for his claim that Kennedy "was impressed but never overwhelmed by McNamara's confident, authoritative presentations of concise conclusions." Kennedy also felt certain that U.S. presidents knew more about press and congressional relations than did automobile company presidents.[19]

McNamara's Team

Whatever the accuracy of Sorensen's judgment, McNamara's freedom, rather than deference to the chief executive, characterized his actions in Washington in December 1960 and January 1961. From the moment he accepted the responsibility of office he went right to work. Within a few days of accepting the position he moved into the Ford suite at the Shoreham Hotel and labored until he had put his team together: "I just stayed on that damn phone until I had the people I wanted."[20] Faced with having to hire people he did not know personally, McNamara called on veteran insiders such as Sen. Henry Jackson, chairman of the Subcommittee on National Policy Machinery of the Senate Government Operations Committee and a member of the Senate Armed Services Committee. He also reached out to such institutions as the Rand Corporation and the Lawrence Livermore Radiation Laboratory in California.[21]

McNamara had his team lined up by 20 January 1961, Inauguration Day. It turned out to be a group remarkable both for its compatibility with the secretary's leadership style and for the quality of its individual administrative talents. They were a mixture of experienced officials and pragmatic intellectuals, younger versions of the band of Whiz Kids that McNamara himself had been a part of 15 years before. Collectively they infused great energy and broad intelligence into the department. Their presence, however, caused considerable dismay among many of the military, especially older hands like General Lemnitzer, chairman of the JCS, who could not refrain from expressing his annoyance over the brash self-confidence of youthful civilians moving into areas generally untouched by the secretary.[22] In essence they were an extension of the secretary's own personality and of his insistence on mastering all aspects of the department, including even the realm of the Joint Chiefs.

Once McNamara found the right person, he would use him in a variety of offices. Paul H. Nitze, for example, began service in 1961 as assistant secretary of defense for international security affairs, became secretary of the Navy in 1963, and finally deputy secretary of defense in 1967. Harold Brown similarly went from director of defense research and engineering, beginning in May 1961, to secretary of the Air Force in 1965, while Cyrus R. Vance moved from general counsel in 1961 to secretary of the Army in 1962 and to deputy secretary of defense in 1964. Able and versatile, they served McNamara well and went on to distinguished careers in their own right.[23]

Chief among his appointees was Deputy Secretary Roswell L. Gilpatric, a former assistant secretary and under secretary of the Air Force in the Truman administration who had helped prepare the Rockefeller Brothers report of January 1958 on shortcomings of U.S. defenses and served on the Symington Committee in December 1960. Ten years McNamara's senior, he was a polished and able advocate for the secretary's policies, his "alter ego," as both men recognized. They worked well together; the age differential posed no barrier to their collaboration. Gilpatric had won a reputation as a perceptive critic during his service with the Air Force. While his angle of observation was close to McNamara's, his style was different. As a sophisticated member of the New York establishment his smooth manners and his long experience with defense contractors and congressmen could leaven McNamara's abrasiveness. As journalist Clark Mollenhoff judged, "The 'Bob and Roz' team appeared to be one of the most effective combinations created by the Kennedy Administration." Gilpatric later judged the relationship to have been "extremely close" and that they had "become very close friends."[24]

Other leading appointments looked equally impressive. McNamara sought out and found people who would stand up to the Pentagon brass. He felt that in one way or another the JCS had dominated his predecessors. "It was not that I didn't have respect for the Chiefs," he claimed. "I have a tremendous regard for them."[25] But he perceived them as hidebound by their service traditions. The young physicist Harold Brown had been director of the Livermore Laboratory. Nitze, a Wall Street banker, had succeeded George Kennan as chairman of the State Department's policy planning staff in the Truman administration. From the Rand Corporation, McNamara picked Charles J. Hitch to be his comptroller, and with Hitch came a group of young management analysts. While he did not know Hitch personally, McNamara knew of his book *The Economics of Defense in the Nuclear Age* and recognized that Hitch's interest in basing budgets on program planning fitted precisely his demand for a quantitative understanding of how to match funds with programs.[26] This formidable first team boasted strong assistants who revived the sobriquet of Whiz Kids, most notably represented by Alain Enthoven, a young economist educated at Stanford and Oxford.

Despite their relative youth the new Defense leaders had more federal government and national security experience than those who had come in with Eisenhower eight years before. McNamara, unlike Charles E. Wilson who retained only two members of his predecessor's staff, intended to keep a half dozen members of the Gates administration, including Herbert F. York as director of defense research and engineering (until Harold Brown would take office in May 1961) and Air Force Under Secretary Joseph V. Charyk.[27]

McNamara determined to be as thorough in his search for appropriate choices of service secretaries as for his OSD aides. He chose Eugene M. Zuckert, former assistant secretary of the Air Force in the Truman administration and his own former colleague at the Harvard Business School, as secretary of the Air Force, and named Elvis J. Stahr, Jr., president of West Virginia University and former Rhodes scholar, as secretary of the Army. John B. Connally, Jr., a Texas lawyer, became secretary of the Navy.

McNamara helped each of the new departmental secretaries select assistants who would go along with the changes he intended to make in DoD. To Connally and Zuckert he observed that "the Secretaries Offices of the three Military Departments—Army, Navy, and Air Force—have not heretofore followed a consistent pattern of organization." The Navy had no assistant secretary for financial management, while the Army had no assistant secretary for research and development. He urged the departments to establish three assistant secretary positions: one for financial management, another for materiel, and still another for research and development.[28] To Stahr and Connally he noted that Hitch, the new comptroller, could help find candidates for the financial management position.[29] Gilpatric later commented almost offhandedly that the role of the service secretary diminished progressively in the McNamara years, "in the sense that they were primarily supply officers . . . . They did not get brought into major policy issues."[30]

This reduction of authority of service secretaries did not signify a McNamara revolution. The ground had been well prepared in the Eisenhower period, particularly with the Defense Reorganization Act of 1958, which eliminated the service secretaries from operational channels that ran from the president and secretary of defense through the Joint Chiefs.[31]

On a few occasions McNamara exercised the appointment prerogative that Kennedy had accorded him. While Kennedy promised McNamara a free hand, the promise did not preclude presidential advice. Kennedy wanted Franklin D. Roosevelt, Jr., to serve as secretary of the Navy, partly as a sentimental gesture; President Roosevelt's rise had begun as an assistant secretary in the Navy Department under Woodrow Wilson. More practically, the appointment would reward Roosevelt's important political service in West Virginia when Kennedy was struggling early in the presidential primary campaign.

The president-elect had advanced Roosevelt's name before McNamara had a candidate in place. This information appeared in the *New York Times*, but McNamara admitted that he had missed the significance of the story when he saw it. Although willing to meet personally with Roosevelt, he still would not accept him for the position. "He was a very nice person," McNamara remembered, "but inexperienced in managing large organizations." Kennedy then conceded gracefully: "I guess I'll have to take care of him some other way."[32]

The successful candidate, John Connally, a close ally of Vice President Lyndon B. Johnson, had strong political credentials also. McNamara made this selection independently, but at Kennedy's advice he spoke with Johnson, who was obviously delighted to clear the Connally nomination.[33]

The appointment of an assistant secretary of defense for manpower became a more public issue than had any of the others. On the morning of 13 December 1960, the day he named his new secretary of defense, the president-elect had breakfast with AFL-CIO president George Meany, who suggested that the Defense Department should have a leading labor official as assistant secretary for manpower because of the importance of labor matters. Meany claimed he left the breakfast table convinced that the secretary of the International Brotherhood of Electrical Workers, Joseph Keenan, an AFL-CIO vice president and Kennedy supporter, would get the position. When McNamara learned of this prospect, he rejected Keenan's candidacy for lack of qualifications. Kennedy accepted the veto.[34]

Inevitably, the rejection of Meany's choice raised a storm of protest, beginning with Meany himself, who felt betrayed. Offering Keenan an ambassadorship to New Zealand no more appeased Meany than did the intervention of Secretary of Labor-designate Arthur J. Goldberg. Meany felt sure that McNamara had rejected Keenan solely because of his position as a union chieftain. The matter didn't end there. At hearings on McNamara's nomination, Sen. Margaret Chase Smith (R-Maine) pointedly asked about restrictions against the appointment of labor leaders to Pentagon positions. In denying any such discrimination, McNamara evaded a direct answer as to why he did not accept Keenan. He asserted that he did not veto the nomination, but that Keenan's was one of many names not chosen: "I do not think it appropriate to say that I vetoed the suggestion any more than I vetoed the appointment of 150 other men whose names I considered for the top posts in the Department." He never did reveal specific reasons for rejecting Keenan.[35]

As he prepared to enter office McNamara appeared to have gotten the men he wanted. Even when facing the formidable Georgian combination of Sen. Richard Russell, chairman of the Senate Armed Services Committee, and Rep. Carl Vinson, chairman of the House Armed Services Committee, he managed to win. When newspaper rumors surfaced of pressure by Russell and Vinson to name Georgia Gov. Ernest Vandiver as secretary of the Army, McNamara went to Capitol Hill with an offer to say publicly that neither legislator was importuning him on this issue. Apparently, Russell and Vinson were pleased with McNamara's deference and let the matter drop. The legislators understood McNamara's message and Vandiver remained governor of Georgia.[36]

On a Fast Track

McNamara had a running start that propelled him into office in high gear. On 3 January 1961 he moved into an office in the Pentagon near that of Gates, where he and his deputy-secretary-designate, Gilpatric, gained insights from Gates and Deputy Secretary James Douglas. Not long intimidated by the challenge of his new position, McNamara intended to shake up the department and introduce new ways of operating its machinery; inevitably, his presence led to rumors about his intentions. While the press abounded with stories of his style and authority, the Pentagon waited uneasily. If the service secretaries had been gradually losing power during the Eisenhower administration, McNamara's advent seemed to augur a quickening of the pace.

The most immediate question involved the secretary's relationship with the Joint Chiefs. McNamara painstakingly sought to reassure the JCS and their supporters that he would maintain a close and respectful working relationship. He claimed to approve Secretary Gates's practice of meeting regularly with the Joint Chiefs and expected to follow that precedent. With as much force as he could muster, McNamara expressed admiration for the abilities of the military leaders, particularly for the character of their chairman, General Lemnitzer. While promising not to act before listening to the advice of the JCS, he never said he would necessarily follow it. On the contrary, he felt that the Joint Chiefs' unwieldy organization limited their ability to participate in the formulation of national security policy. Moreover, in retrospect he observed that civilian experts, such as the "Rand intellectuals," helped keep the secretary from "becoming a captive of the Joint Chiefs and the services."[37]

At his first meeting with the Joint Chiefs on 9 January, McNamara elicited a favorable reaction from Chief of Naval Operations Arleigh Burke, who sized him up as "a sharp, decisive individual." Clearly impressed, Burke told his staff that the secretary-designate "is going to be very decisive and he is going to be very quick. He catches on very fast. He may be extremely good . . . . He is alert . . . . He is going to get impatient . . . . You have got to know your stuff." Before Burke left office on 1 August 1961, this accurate appreciation of McNamara's leadership qualities had given way to a strong negative view of the secretary, particularly because of his often crosswise relationship with the military.[38]

General Lemnitzer, always correct in his references to the secretary's professions of consultation, at the same time could not conceal that McNamara's arrival brought a "drastic change" not wholly to his liking. Gates, for example, did not involve himself in details, but McNamara did. It was not the details that disturbed the chiefs; it was the secretary's insistence on participating in, even controlling, strategic planning. As Lemnitzer put it later, "When we would work long and hard to resolve some of the issues between the services and produce a final document to get to the Secretary of Defense," it was a disappointment to find that the secretary would turn over their work to a systems analysis group, "with no military experience at all," to approve or modify the document.[39]

Given the aura that surrounded the new secretary it came as no surprise that the Senate confirmed his nomination with little difficulty. The potential rift with organized labor barely ruffled the surface. Nor did he have a problem with Sen. Leverett Saltonstall's queries about possible major changes in the Defense Department organization. McNamara's categorical response that he proposed "to make no major changes in the organization of the Department until I have had an opportunity to study it fully" seemed to satisfy his questioners.[40]

The one area of controversy turned on McNamara's personal arrangements for placing his investments in trust. This should have presented no serious problem; Eisenhower's secretary of defense Charles E. Wilson had been the head of General Motors when nominated, and he managed to solve the issue. Wilson's solution should have provided a precedent for McNamara. It did not. While Wilson had sold his stock in General Motors, McNamara put his financial holdings into a trust. The Senate Armed Services Committee members, however, objected that his holdings would not be in an irrevocable trust. McNamara then agreed to have the trustee supply the committee with reports and to deny himself the right to alter the agreement without notifying the committee in advance. This arrangement satisfied the committee members.[41] The Senate confirmed McNamara's nomination by voice vote on 20 January 1961.

Some scars remained. More than six months later, in testifying before the Jackson Subcommittee, McNamara commented on two difficulties he had encountered in recruiting his Pentagon team. The lesser was the level of salaries for his upper-echelon officials—they were much below those with similar responsibilities in the private sector. The more important obstacle arose from the matter of conflict-of-interest. Although he would support the strictest possible standards, he found the regulations currently in place unrealistic and not accomplishing their purpose. He proposed not divestment but full disclosure as a far better protection of the public interest.[42]

Acting on the ideas he had been considering since the president offered him the position, McNamara had the benefit of the president's special attention to defense matters outlined in his inaugural address. In that message Kennedy supplied what seemed an open-ended opportunity for the secretary of defense to take major initiatives.[43] More specifically, in his State of the Union address on 30 January Kennedy instructed the secretary of defense "to reappraise our entire defense strategy—our ability to fulfill our commitments—the effectiveness, vulnerability, and dispersal of our strategic bases, forces and warning systems—the efficiency and economy of our operation and organization—the elimination of obsolete bases and installations—and the adequacy, modernization and mobility of our present conventional and nuclear forces and weapons systems in the light of present and future dangers."[44] Kennedy wanted preliminary conclusions on what actions should be taken presented to him by the end of February. Previously, the president had instructed McNamara to undertake the appraisal "without regard to arbitrary or predetermined budget ceilings."[45]

Undaunted by the enormity of the demands, McNamara relished the opportunities they offered. His readiness to implement the president's requests evoked both awe and disbelief from Chairman Carl Vinson of the House Armed Services Committee. Testifying on 23 February, McNamara told Vinson that he expected to submit recommendations before the end of that month. The chairman could hardly believe that in such a short time span the Defense Department could have studied and presented a detailed statement of requirements for missiles, aircraft, and vessels. Stewart Alsop observed that McNamara's three crisp "yes, sir" answers to questions suggested that he had mastered the machinery of the Pentagon even before entering fully into the obligations of his office.[46]

The president spelled out in his State of the Union address three particularly worrisome issues requiring immediate attention: First, the need to enhance the capability of conventional forces "to respond, with discrimination and speed, to any problem at any spot on the globe at any moment's notice." This required additional air transport forces. Second, the president wanted rapid acceleration in Polaris submarine production and deployment by using currently unobligated shipbuilding funds and thereby advancing the original schedules by at least nine months. Third, he directed the secretary of defense, pending completion of the overall DoD appraisal, to reexamine the missile program, improving its organization and "cutting down the wasteful duplications and the time-lag that have handicapped our whole family of missiles."[47]

The department stood ready to act on all of these fronts. The pace of the secretary's activities, particularly with respect to missiles, could have been set back by his statement of 6 February, as reported in the press, that the celebrated missile gap of the 1960 presidential campaign was more myth than reality. Given that the Democrats had campaigned vigorously against the failure of the Eisenhower administration to cope with Soviet superiority in missile production, McNamara's purported admission at a background briefing session with newsmen over cocktails came as a shock. Later, when questioned at a hearing of the House Armed Services Committee, he denied that he had said there had been no missile gap and maintained that he had said there was no "destruction gap" or "deterrent gap."[48]

In any event, the flap over the missiles failed to keep McNamara from considering development of a deterrent nuclear force so great that the Soviets would not dare to risk an assault. The mix of bombers, missiles, and submarines would have sufficient counterforce capabilities to survive a first-strike attack and still be able to retaliate and destroy the enemy's strike forces. This impressive buildup would go beyond the concept of a massive retaliatory strike, which had been at the heart of the Eisenhower policy. It would send a message to the Soviets that emphasized deterrence rather than a second strike.[49]

At the same time, McNamara's planners felt concern that this approach carried with it many of the problems associated with the strategy of massive retaliation. To respond to lesser challenges, they took steps toward what would later be called "flexible response." The buildup of missiles or bombers could have little effect on the so-called wars of liberation in the Third World to which Soviet Premier Nikita Khrushchev devoted so much attention. The traumatic failure at the Bay of Pigs in April 1961 and the continuing failure to overthrow the Castro regime focused unwelcome but very urgent attention on the means to cope with non-nuclear challenges. In the competition for the allegiance of the newly independent Third World countries, the Soviets seemed to enjoy all the advantages. Nuclear superiority did not mean much in dealing with problems of new nations. A better strategy would link economic and political actions with counterinsurgency programs and so confront communist subversion or guerrilla warfare in Asia, Africa, and Latin America. Long before flexible response became official doctrine, its principles were in place. In a special message to Congress on 28 March 1961 the president observed that "we must be able to make deliberate choices in weapons and strategy, shift the tempo of our production and alter the direction of our forces to meet rapidly changing conditions or objectives at very short notice and under any circumstances."[50]

To effect the host of changes he felt necessary for successful defense of the United States, McNamara introduced the most unsettling of all his innovations in the spring of 1961, namely, the reshaping of the budget process.* In the hands of Comptroller Charles Hitch, it seemed a mini-revolution. In essence, civilians, for the most part young iconoclasts from the Rand Corporation and the academic

---

* See Chapter IV.

community, moved in to examine and sometimes override the judgments of the Joint Chiefs in shaping military policy. They engaged first what they considered the shocking inefficiency of the traditional process stating requirements and programs wherein the individual services drew up lists of needs with little reference to interconnections between them. Duplication and waste, they believed, accompanied the rivalry for money among the services.[51]

The waste and inefficiency that so distressed such young aides as Alain Enthoven derived not only from rivalry among the services and the inability of the JCS to harmonize their needs, but also from structural change in the American military economy as the armaments industry moved into newer fields of technology. Consequently, there developed a pressing need for a more rational system of management for the future. This might not achieve a reduction in costs; indeed, the administration asked for more money, not less, in maximizing the FY 1962 budget. But according to the new managers, the worth of the added costs could be measured by an increase in effectiveness of the nation's defense efforts. The new system would apply financial management to the decisionmaking process for force structure and weapon systems. That relationship would be established and maintained through budgetary control and accountability for performance, under the awkward name of the planning-programming-budgeting system (PPBS).

The speed with which the secretary established task forces to examine the major problems of the department deepened the sense of ferment. Within three days of taking charge at the Pentagon he had four task forces undertake the following missions: (1) provide requirements for strategic forces and continental defense; (2) explore the conduct of limited war; (3) review the entire field of research and development; and (4) consider the effectiveness and usefulness of foreign and domestic bases and installations. The *Washington Post* called it a "crash reappraisal" that cut across service lines. Representatives from the Joint Staff, the military departments, and the Office of the Secretary of Defense all participated in these task forces. They had extremely short deadlines: 13 February for the first two task forces and 20 February for the other two. McNamara wanted their final revised studies in hand by 25 March.[52]

McNamara followed the activity with a barrage of specific questions that eventually grew to more than a hundred in number directed at individual officials. They ranged from queries about base closings to the rate of missile production acceleration to the appropriate organizational placement of DoD space research. No office escaped the secretary's scrutiny or the extensive list of numbered questions originating from him or Deputy Secretary Gilpatric. For example, General Lemnitzer had to provide by 15 May a statement of quantitative requirements for strategic nuclear weapon delivery vehicles based on target analyses and survivability factors—number 12 on the list. Number 14 required Secretary of the Air Force Zuckert to submit data on operating plans, costs, and total effectiveness of the proposed B-70 program. Number 6 tasked Director of Defense Research and Engineering Herbert York to report on command and control of operational, particularly strategic, forces. Ranking did not indicate magnitude of the issue or urgency of the problem. Although numbers 1 and 2 concerned revision of the basic national security policies and controlled response in the event of a thermonuclear attack, respectively, the sensitive questions of Minuteman ICBM expansion and Titan II squadron reductions were numbered 20 and 21.[53]

The first few months left a paramount and unmistakable impression of the intent to fundamentally shake up the Pentagon—its familiar patterns, its accustomed habits, and its ways of doing business. Encrusted procedures would yield to altered management techniques and to such new organizations as the Defense Intelligence Agency. Not least apparent already was the larger role of civilian responsibility.

Whether the consequences of these changes would measure up to the claims made by the McNamara team remained to be seen over the long term. Through 1961 the resistance of the military services to both the manner and substance of the changes, combined with such early tests as the Bay of Pigs episode in April and the Berlin Wall crisis in August, fueled doubts. But regardless of the long-range verdict, from the outset the McNamara Pentagon had boldly embarked on far-reaching reforms, some built on procedures and structures established under earlier administrations, others McNamara's own contribution.

Chapter II
Shakeup in the Pentagon

Two days before the inauguration of President Kennedy, Secretary of Defense-designate McNamara met with his future deputy secretary, assistant secretaries, and service secretaries to discuss how he envisioned their roles and relationships. He wished "to integrate the Service Secretaries into the Defense operation as an arm of the Secretary of Defense" instead of having them "function only as an advocate of their own Military Departments."[1] Army Secretary-designate Elvis Stahr suggested that McNamara's concept "entailed a fundamental change in the traditional responsibility of a Service Secretary." McNamara agreed but felt the change "was consistent with the Defense Reorganization Act of 1958." Perhaps to reassure his listeners, McNamara stated that "he was under no obligation to make any major changes in organization without complete personal study." Organizational change, McNamara seemed to suggest, was secondary to a change in attitude and procedure.[2]

The difference would sometimes be hard to discern. To be sure, in light of the reforms that followed, McNamara's cautious response here, as in that to his congressional interrogators in his military posture briefing on 23 February 1961, appears somewhat disingenuous. He told congressmen that it would take time "to determine the changes in organization, methods, and procedures,"[3] but his impatience showed early and often. A year later he claimed that "the efficient organization of the Defense Establishment is a never-ending task." Indeed, he regarded the defense effort as a dynamic activity subject to constant change and requiring continual adjustments.[4] Although he had a study made of the matter, he had no detailed plans for comprehensive structural reorganization largely because he deemed them unnecessary. He could implement his ideas and disarm potential critics by citing the Department of Defense Reorganization Act of 1958 as his authority. This act represented President Eisenhower's response to DoD's organizational deficiencies evidenced by the persistence of interservice disputes that had plagued the department from its inception. It had been conceived with the clear intention of accelerating the trend toward centralization of authority under the secretary of defense.*

After 1958 the expanded powers of the secretary gave him the authority, should he choose to exercise it, of transferring, reassigning, abolishing, and consolidating functions "to provide in the Department of Defense for more effective, efficient, and economical administration and operation and to eliminate duplication." He could designate one or more of the services to develop and operate new weapons or he could establish new agencies to handle supply and service activities common to more than one department, all without going to Congress for approval.[5] The Defense Reorganization Act of 1958 did not permit the secretary to (1) merge departments; (2) appoint a single chief of staff for all the armed forces; (3) prevent a service secretary or member of the Joint Chiefs from presenting to Congress, on his own initiative, recommendations relating to the Defense Department; or (4) transfer or abolish any statutory functions or agencies of DoD without congressional review. The short but significant list of constraints set boundaries but still left McNamara ample powers to make changes.[6]

McNamara's predecessor, Thomas Gates, had taken considerable advantage of his increased powers, a fact that the new secretary occasionally acknowledged. Initiatives by Gates included the establishment of both the Defense Communications Agency in May 1960 and a major joint activity, the Joint Strategic Target Planning Staff, in August 1960. And even as the Eisenhower administration was coming to an end in January 1961, Gates contemplated placing OSD—not the military departments, as JCS Chairman Lemnitzer noted with displeasure—in charge of all intelligence activities. This prepared the foundation for the creation of the Defense Intelligence Agency by McNamara that soon followed. Lemnitzer cautioned himself to watch his blood pressure at this time; no doubt it continued to rise under McNamara.[7]

The Symington Report

During the presidential campaign, in September 1960, Kennedy appointed a Committee on the Defense Establishment, consisting of six influential civilians and headed by Sen. W. Stuart Symington† of Missouri, the first secretary of the Air Force (1947-50), to study the administration and management of the Department of Defense and recommend necessary or desirable changes. By 5 December the committee had drawn up a plan for broad revisions of the military establishment, proposing fundamental changes in both the composition and conduct of DoD. By comparison with this proposed reorganization, probably the most

---

* See Watson, *Into the Missile Age*, ch IX.

† The others were Clark M. Clifford, Thomas K. Finletter, Marx Leva, Fowler Hamilton, and Roswell L. Gilpatric.

far-reaching ever officially advanced for the Defense Department, McNamara's innovations would seem like minor variations.

The committee offered five major recommendations that would radically reorganize the Defense Department: (1) greater centralization of full power in OSD, with all appropriations made to the secretary rather than to the military departments; (2) abolition of the JCS, replacing it with a chairman of a joint military staff presiding over a new military advisory council chosen from senior military officers permanently separated from their services; (3) abolition of the separate military departments and their secretaries, undersecretaries, and assistant secretaries; (4) retention of individual military services and their chiefs of staff, but with responsibility only for logistics and administration and reporting directly to the secretary of defense; and (5) replacement of existing unified commands by four new ones—a strategic command, a tactical command, a defense command, and a command in charge of National Guard and Reserve elements, with responsibility for civil defense.

The committee wanted to replace the seven assistant secretaries of defense with two under secretaries, one for administration and one for weapon systems. It also made a gesture to mollify the Navy—arguably the principal loser in the proposed changes—by placing the strategic command under its leadership. The Army would control the tactical command, and the Air Force, continental defense. Although the Joint Chiefs of Staff would be eliminated, a chairman would direct an enlarged Joint Staff and serve as the principal military adviser to the president and the secretary of defense. Additionally, a special assistant to the secretary of defense would perform arms control duties and provide liaison with the State Department and other involved agencies. This appointee, in Symington's opinion, might have "the most important job in the Government with the exception of the President."[8]

The president-elect and his secretary of defense-designate certainly recognized the deficiencies identified in the Symington report, but Kennedy gave no specific endorsement to the committee's remedies, stating that he would take them under advisement.[9] He never implemented the recommendations. McNamara later offered a number of explanations for not acting on them, ranging from his need to study more closely the problems of the department to a conclusion voiced some years later, to wit: "It seemed to me, when I took office ... that the principal problem standing in the way of efficient management of the Department's resources was not the lack of management authority—the National Security Act provides the Secretary of Defense a full measure of power—but rather the absence of the essential management tools needed to make sound decisions on the really crucial issues of national security."[10]

But no matter how much distance the president and secretary of defense attempted to place between themselves and the report, their demurrals did not reassure those who saw their organizations endangered by the proposed structural changes.[11] McNamara never identified himself as a supporter of the Symington report. He did say that he would review the proposals but continued to delay any formal response until he had become fully familiar with the current organization. Given evidence that he seemed very much disposed to make organizational changes in DoD, those suspicious of McNamara's intentions plainly had grounds for concern.[12]

McNamara's selection of Roswell Gilpatric, a prominent member of the Symington committee, as his deputy raised questions during the Senate hearings on Gilpatric's nomination. Sen. Styles Bridges (R-N.H.) referred to this connection when he asked the deputy secretary-designate if he believed that the Kennedy administration would implement the report. Admitting that he agreed with the report's conclusions, Gilpatric qualified his position by stating that "before I accepted designation for the Deputy Secretaryship of Defense, I fully understood both the views of the President-elect and of Mr. McNamara, as they have publicly expressed them, including Mr. McNamara's statement here today." Gilpatric still believed that changes would be made in light of rapid advances in weapons technology.[13]

The tone of the hearing seemed to convey a disposition in Congress, as indicated by the queries of Senator Bridges, not to support a major reorganization, and this signal no doubt helped to bury the report.[14] McNamara, reflecting a generation later, claimed he never doubted that he could "get control of that Department without the organizational changes that had been proposed by the Symington Committee. I thought that could be done by recruiting the proper kinds of people, by laying out the approach to formulation of security policy—i.e., integrating foreign policy, security policy, military strategy, force structure, and budgets—and by developing the tools to apply that set of intellectual concepts."[15]

The Vance Task Force

At the beginning of February McNamara assigned General Counsel Cyrus Vance to assist him in reviewing existing practices and in planning necessary changes. Vance set up the Office of Organizational and Management Planning to oversee the in-house review. It proved its worth in helping to chart the organizational adjustments that occurred during McNamara's tenure.

Under task number 81,* the general counsel was to "review the activities of the total military establishment and identify those operations which can be organized to serve all services"; in number 82 he was to "undertake a comprehensive study of alternative long range organizational structures for DoD." Both assign-

---

* See Chapter I.

ments, directed on 8 March 1961, carried a completion date of 1 September 1961.[16]

During his first year in office, McNamara made two major organizational changes under the authority of existing legislation. One, the establishment of the Defense Supply Agency (DSA), effective 1 October 1961, occasioned controversy that erupted into the public arena. Given the tensions arising from the intelligence lapses in the Bay of Pigs operation, the other change, creation of the Defense Intelligence Agency (DIA) in August 1961, might have provoked greater reaction within and outside DoD, but this proved not the case. No matter the differences in their public reception, the two agencies shared the distinction of being the first of many institutional additions to OSD by McNamara. The precedent of previously established agencies reporting to the secretary of defense—Defense Communications Agency (DCA), Defense Atomic Support Agency (DASA), and National Security Agency (NSA)—eased the way for these new agencies. Secretary Gates had created DCA on 12 May 1960 as the single manager for all military communications, integrating separate service elements into a single system.[17] It served as a model for the two McNamara additions.

Changes of lesser moment took place within OSD. On 29 January 1961 a new assistant secretary of defense (installations and logistics) replaced the two assistant secretaries overseeing installations and logistics. And on 31 January the assistant secretary (health and medical) had his functions transferred to the assistant secretary for manpower. These two changes freed up two assistant secretaryships for assignment to other functions. Thus, two new staff offices came into being in 1961: an assistant secretary for research and engineering* and an assistant secretary for civil defense.[18]

In some respects, McNamara made his strongest impact in areas where he created no new structures or agencies. The need to exercise greater control over military operations became clear to McNamara shortly after taking office. On an inspection trip to the Strategic Air Command's headquarters in Omaha on 4-5 February 1961 the secretary became alarmed by the rigidity of the Single Integrated Operational Plan (SIOP). He came away haunted by what he saw as inadequate control of the strategic forces by civilian authority. The danger of missiles being fired off accidentally or without the sanction of the White House required immediate attention. He devoted much effort during 1961 to ensuring proper control of the nuclear forces.† To redress this situation, McNamara established a committee under retired Air Force General Earle E. Partridge. Although the Partridge Committee report did not satisfy the secretary, it initiated the creation of a mechanism for increased OSD control over future SIOPs.[19]

---

* From 19 May 1961 to 15 July 1965, this assistant secretary served also as deputy director for defense research and engineering. The position of assistant secretary carried statutory rank.

† See Chapter XII.

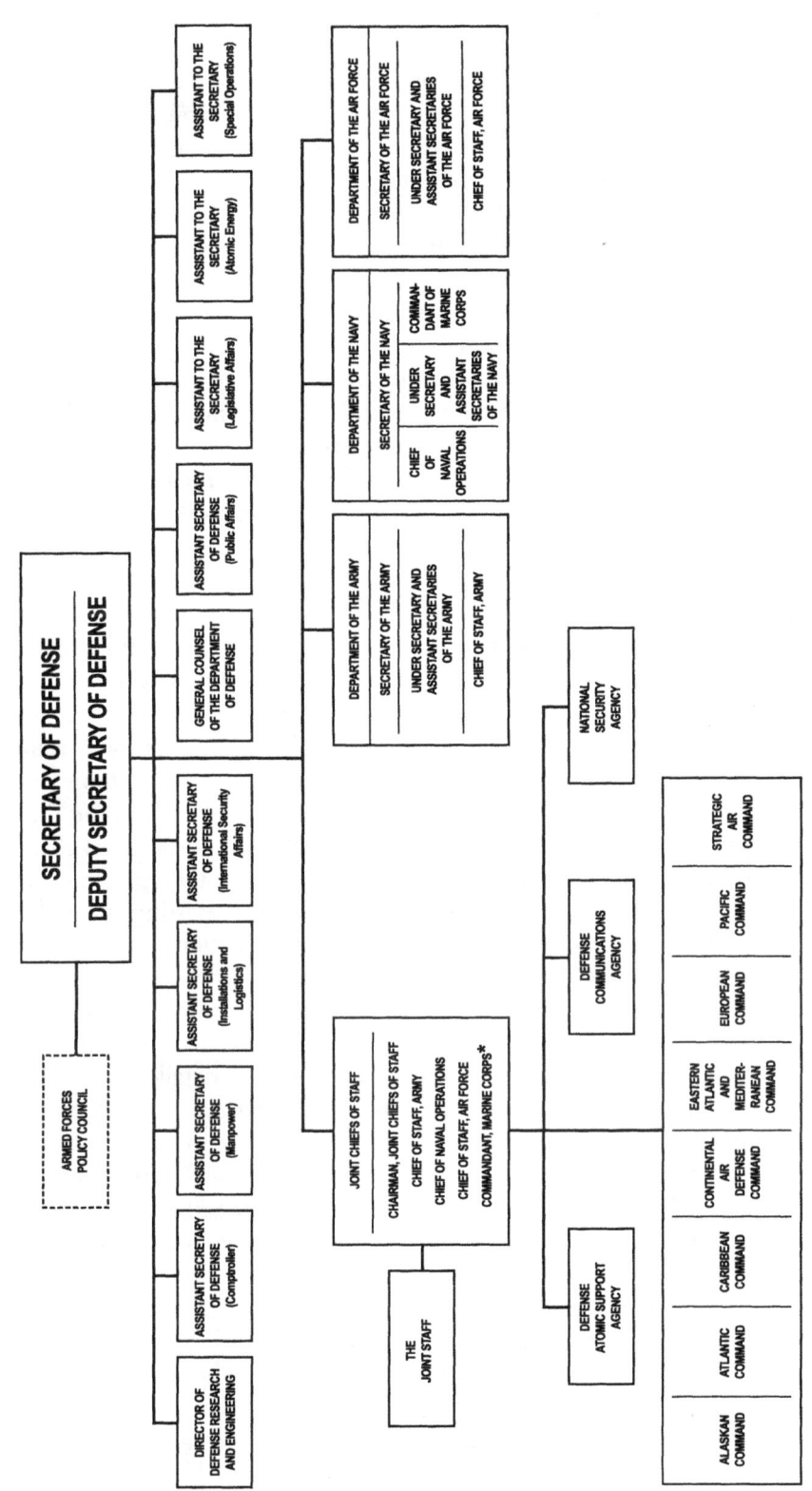

CHART 1
DEPARTMENT OF DEFENSE
9 MARCH 1961

Also accomplished without reorganization, the secretary's decision in DoD Directive 5160.32 on 6 March 1961 to assign responsibility for space research, development, and engineering to the Air Force had major consequences for the services in terms of defining their respective roles and missions.[20] Given the potential significance of military activities in space, the distress of the Army and Navy was understandable. Here, as elsewhere, the volume of queries that McNamara hurled at his staff, the JCS, and the military services threw potential adversaries off balance. He moved so fast that he gave little time for effective coalitions to form. To carry out his decision to place all research and development space activities in the hands of the Air Force, the Vance team acted swiftly. They knew that interservice rivalry and stratagems could derail proposed changes even in a mission as important as the space function. McNamara directed that no one could undertake a new space project beyond the preliminary research stage without the approval of the secretary or deputy secretary.[21]

Defense Intelligence Agency

The twin objectives of increasing the control of OSD and enhancing efficiency inspired the establishment of the DIA—the first new agency formed under McNamara's aegis.

On 8 February 1961, McNamara informed the JCS that the National Security Council "on the recommendation of the Joint Study Group on Foreign Intelligence Activities of the United States Government requires the Department of Defense to effect a wide variety of organizational and procedural changes in its military intelligence activities." In response, the secretary proposed to establish a defense intelligence agency "which may include the existing National Security Agency, the intelligence and counter intelligence functions now handled by the military departments, and the responsibilities of the Office of the Assistant to the Secretary, Special Operations." Accordingly, he asked the JCS to draft an initial directive for such an integrated agency within 30 days.[22]

The Joint Chiefs responded on 2 March with a detailed plan for a "Military Intelligence Agency" to achieve "maximum economy and efficiency." They had pronounced views on how the agency would relate to the JCS and OSD and pointedly chose the title "Military Intelligence Agency" rather than "Defense Intelligence Agency." To assist and advise the director, they wanted to establish a military intelligence board, chaired by the director, with service intelligence chiefs, the Joint Staff J-2, and the director of the National Security Agency as members. They made a point of emphasizing inclusion of the National Security Agency within the scope of the new agency. Moreover, they maintained, the Joint Chiefs should have direct operational control of the agency.[23] The JCS plan never materialized. The Bay of Pigs fiasco in April and strong endorsements from General Maxwell Taylor, the president's military adviser, and Dr. James R. Killian,

Jr., who had been Eisenhower's science adviser, for a unified Pentagon intelligence agency helped ensure that the secretary's intention to place the new agency under OSD would prevail.[24]

The final directive on 1 August placed authority for the DIA under the secretary rather than the JCS. The National Security Agency remained untouched. The chain of command ran from the secretary of defense to the director of the DIA "through the JCS." While the director would be guided by both the JCS and the secretary, the directive noted that the chiefs would act "under the authority and direction of the Secretary of Defense, and the United States Intelligence Board." Plans for a consolidated budget confirmed the judgment of a DIA historian years later that the result was "a union—not a confederation of Defense intelligence and counterintelligence activities," as the JCS would have preferred. The triservice leadership of the agency, however, suggested some appreciation of the sensitivities of each of the military services as well as the qualifications needed for the posts: its first director was Air Force Lt. Gen. Joseph F. Carroll; his deputy was Maj. Gen. William W. Quinn, Army chief of information; and the chief of staff was Rear Adm. Samuel B. Frankel, deputy chief of Navy intelligence. The agency became operational on 1 October 1961.[25]

Congress and the military services expressed concern about the enhanced authority acquired by the secretary. The very act of consolidation meant that the Army, Navy, and Air Force intelligence offices would come under close OSD supervision. With service intelligence policymaking removed from their jurisdiction they would have limited activities and would have to function under constraints never experienced before. The Joint Chiefs transferred their residual intelligence functions to the DIA in June 1963 when the secretary announced the "disestablishment" of the Intelligence Directorate (J-2) of the Joint Staff.[26]

To counter negative views of their intelligence operations and cast doubt on the effectiveness of the new agency, the services fed fears in the press and in Congress that monolithic intelligence findings might emerge from OSD's centralized office, with legitimate criticism stifled and service intelligence officials tempted or coerced into tailoring their findings to the prejudices of the secretary of defense. The assurances of DIA officers allayed some of this criticism. General Quinn, deputy director, emphasized to the Senate Subcommittee on Appropriations on 15 May 1962 that the "DIA represents the culmination of intensive studies of Defense intelligence activities by the Joint Chiefs of Staff and other components of the Department of Defense." Thus, DIA was in no sense solely an OSD venture.[27]

When the question of additional costs for the new agency inevitably surfaced in Congress, General Quinn anticipated savings but only in the future.[28] When asked whether the new agency would duplicate CIA activities, Quinn acknowledged some inevitable but unimportant overlap. The purposes of the DIA involved only military intelligence, and, though the Army, Navy, and Air Force had representatives with the CIA, the DIA could provide better than the CIA what the services required. When asked if he thought CIA appropriations should be reduced if the DIA took over part of its workload, Quinn demurred, saying "I would not want to address myself to that one."[29]

Unspoken but hovering above all discussions about intelligence lingered the failure of the CIA at the Bay of Pigs.* Fairly or not, the president blamed first that agency, and then the military chiefs. McNamara's relative ease in achieving the desired centralization owed much to a recognition of these criticisms. By the time of the Cuban missile crisis of October 1962 the DIA had become a key source of intelligence.[30]

An assistant director for scientific and technical intelligence, appointed on 30 April 1964, reflected expansion of those activities. In the course of 1964 DIA coordinated and shared relevant intelligence with NSA in the new Defense Special Missile and Astronautic Center. It also assumed overall management supervision of a worldwide special intelligence communications system designed to serve the secretary of defense, the JCS, the military departments, and unified commands.[31]

Defense Supply Agency

By contrast with DIA, establishment of the Defense Supply Agency should have occasioned little uproar. While logistics constituted a central concern of the services, jurisdiction over supply did not normally cause great debates. Also, the governing principle for DSA—one agency to purchase common supplies for all the services—had precedents before McNamara entered office. In 1961 some 11 common supply categories operated under the single manager system,† but under the aegis of a military service. The McCormack amendment to the DoD Reorganization Act of 1958, Sec. 202c(6), had specifically stated: "Whenever the Secretary of Defense determines it will be advantageous to the Government in terms of effectiveness, economy, or efficiency, he shall provide for the carrying out of any supply or service activity common to more than one military department by a single agency or such other organizational entities as he deems appropriate."[32] Despite ample precedent and the deliberateness with which McNamara proceeded—it took almost six months before the secretary made his final decision—DSA aroused more opposition than had any of the other agencies previously established. Indeed, only the jurisdictional battle over space research and development elicited greater passions.

---

* See Chapter VIII.

† The single manager system stemmed from the 1955 Hoover Commission recommendations that called for the secretary of defense to appoint one of the three service secretaries as single manager for a selected group of commodities or common services.

Ironically, the situation seemed made to order for the secretary's intervention in 1961. The military services had accepted the single manager system as a way of responding to persistent congressional pressures for efficiency and reduction of duplication. Such categories as subsistence, clothing and textiles, medical supplies, petroleum products, construction supplies, and automotive supplies had been integrated under a single manager system to avoid congressional insistence on a new agency to effect unified procurement. But despite these advances, disagreements continued over what to classify as common-use supplies as well as over development of more uniform procedures of distribution.[33]

To devise a "long-term blueprint for managing common supply and service activities," McNamara appointed a committee headed by Vance on 23 March 1961. Vance worked with the services' assistant secretaries for installations and logistics to weigh the advantages and disadvantages of continuing the existing system of single managers, establishing a new agency under the secretary of one of the military departments, or creating an agency under the secretary of defense.[34]

The committee presented its findings on 11 July 1961 after an exhaustive examination of the alternatives. The committee valued all DoD properties in the supply systems at $42 billion, and at $68 billion for currently used equipment (ships, aircraft, etc.). Production equipment in use amounted to $5 billion, as did storage and excess/surplus awaiting transfer or disposal. Overall, the committee estimated the Defense inventory at $120 billion.

Concern centered primarily on the $42 billion investment in the supply inventories, which had a gross number of 4.2 million items cataloged, of which fewer than 20 percent belonged in the "common use" classification, that is, identical items used by two or more services. The committee determined that in such broad categories as general supplies or automotive supplies many items did not fit into the responsibilities of the single manager. Some of these would have to remain within the jurisdiction of individual services. Any increase in the number of single managers would produce more duplication and a greater variety of procedures.

The prospect of consolidating all supplies under one military department seemed equally uninviting. It could exacerbate tensions between the services and make the chosen one susceptible to charges of favoritism. Moreover, the confusion and the likely bitterness attending such a reorganization might make any new system less responsive to combat requirements.

As noted above, the committee's third alternative consolidated supply services in a separate agency under the aegis of the secretary of defense. The military services would retain management of their weapon systems as well as their own retail supply distribution systems and facilities, as in the past, while the new agency would take over wholesale management of common supplies within the continental United States. The chief drawback to this alternative stemmed from the danger of it becoming a "control" rather than a "service" agency.[35]

At hearings on the Defense Supply Agency in May 1962, a member of the subcommittee of the House Committee on Government Operations noted that someone had facetiously remarked that the "DSA was a single manager for the single managers." Facetious or not, this was a description with which the agency's first director, Lt. Gen. Andrew T. McNamara, a former Army quartermaster general, appeared comfortable. He observed that his authority would total that now existing on several levels, and "I have a clear path to the Secretary of Defense. That gives me an opportunity, as you know, to manage quickly, perhaps more so than they [single managers] had."[36]

The final plan for the agency differed from the Vance committee's version in two respects. Under the committee's proposal, a defense supply council, which included the chairman of the JCS and the deputy secretary of defense, would have supervised DSA operations. But Secretary McNamara preferred to have the council serve in a strictly advisory capacity, with the director possessing broad authority to run the agency. He did not limit the agency head to a military figure, although the first director was indeed an officer. The director would report to the secretary of defense, a decision taken after the JCS indicated an unwillingness to take on responsibility for DSA activities.[37] In this important respect, the DSA differed from the Defense Communications Agency and the Defense Intelligence Agency, which reported to the secretary of defense through the JCS.

In a news release of 31 August 1961 announcing his intention to establish the agency, the secretary claimed that if all the items under consideration came into the integrated management inventory of the new agency, the total value could amount to $21 billion—more than five times as much as the existing integrated inventory of $3.7 billion—resulting in a potential inventory reduction of 2 to 4 billion dollars. The new agency would create a stock fund to finance procurement of supplies.[38]

In DSA's first annual report, for fiscal year 1962, General McNamara made a special point of noting how swiftly, after coming to a decision, the secretary acted to launch the agency. After announcing its establishment on 31 August, on 12 September the secretary had called the newly selected director back from Korea "post-haste" to take charge. On 1 January 1962, when DSA became operational, it took control of six major Defense Supply Centers to which it added three more by 1 July. Although these actions dealt only with soft goods, not with weapon systems, they marked one of the biggest steps toward unification in DoD's history. And with an open-ended charter the scope of DSA's operations did not stop with plans for 1962.[39]

In the short run, at least, a dramatic reduction occurred in the 13,000 written reports required by the service and supply organizations of the new agency. These reports had covered such items as the number of fire hydrants on a military base. As General McNamara put it, "Somebody years ago apparently wanted to know how many fire hydrants there were on the base and asked for a report.

They've been grinding them out regularly ever since." The agency director probably understated his judgment when he said there was room for "drastic" improvement in this area.[40]

Not simply would this change result in savings of hundreds of millions of dollars in procurement costs, it would bring the nation's most creative business management talent and methods to bear on procurement issues, just as military operational planning and weapon research had benefited from such research groups as the Rand Corporation and Massachusetts Institute of Technology's Lincoln Laboratories. A similar breakthrough, the secretary told the president in September 1961, could come in logistics management, "where we spend half of the Defense budget." He observed that 60 percent of procurement dollar expenditures went into single-source procurement. Where source competition existed, prices went down from 30 to 60 percent. To support this initiative, he proposed to establish the Logistics Management Institute as a "non-profit, fact finding and research organization, guided by a group of trustees of national reputation and supported by a contract with the Defense Department." The institute, established late in the fall of 1961, would provide a wide range of advice: simplifying specifications, increasing competitive defense buying, and encouraging incentive-type contracts that would link cost with performance.[41]

Predictably, the euphoria that followed the establishment of the DSA dissipated before the end of 1962. In June and July 1962 a House special subcommittee on defense agencies, after a long and hard look at the activities of DSA and its powers, now concentrated under the secretary of defense, roundly criticized what it saw as excessive centralization at the expense of the military services. Numbers alone told some of the story. The subcommittee learned that DSA as of 28 February 1962 had 10,129 personnel—9,487 civilian and 642 military—and by 30 June 1963 the projected total would reach 23,057—22,025 civilian and 1,032 military.[42] DSA's work force came mainly from personnel transfers that created commensurate personnel decreases in the military departments. This did not carry the intended message to the committee but rather seemed to confirm charges of excessive power in OSD, an apparent preoccupation of this congressional subcommittee.

Its chairman, Rep. Porter Hardy (D-Va.), expressed the widespread concern that McNamara was implementing his hitherto masked master plan to unify all defense activities in his office and include a general staff of the kind Congress long had opposed. "The Defense Supply Agency," Hardy charged, "in effect, could become the J-4 for the Department of Defense. The Defense Intelligence Agency could become the J-2 for the Department of Defense; and in fact, it may be it probably is. The Joint Chiefs of Staff, if divorced from their service responsibilities, could become the J-3."[43]

In this light critics interpreted DSA as a bypassing of the single manager system, instituted by the Eisenhower administration specifically to ensure the efficiency that Secretary McNamara now claimed could come only through his plan. The secretary spoke positively on this issue: "I think we can prove that we will save men and money and material through the Defense Supply Agency that were not saved under the single management concept." He did not budge in the face of congressional skepticism.[44]

Continued criticism from the military services reinforced suspicions about McNamara's ultimate designs for DoD. To them, the DSA symbolized the erosion of the authority that the military services and the JCS had formerly enjoyed. Secretary of the Army Elvis Stahr shared these views, even though he couched them in diplomatic language when he left office in 1962. While he viewed the secretary of defense as "certainly the ablest man I have ever been closely associated with," he also noted that "there just are not enough McNamara's." The job McNamara was trying to do was too big for one man.[45]

The subcommittee registered its reservations in its report in mid-August 1962. McNamara's protests notwithstanding, the subcommittee equated DSA with the creation under OSD of a fourth system of supply, if not a fourth military department:

> There is almost unanimous opposition among military personnel to the creation of a fourth service of supply or an independent logistic department. The Joint Chiefs of Staff are in unanimous agreement that there should be no fourth service of supply. Informal discussion with other highly respected military personnel completely support the subcommittee's position that each service must have complete control over its own logistical support function. This, of course, would include distribution of supply beyond the wholesale level; yet according to the former General Counsel of the Department of Defense, there is nothing in the law that would prevent the assignment to the Defense Supply Agency of the responsibility for the distribution of supply to the military services.

Therefore, the committee concluded, "there is an inherent danger in the Defense Supply Agency that cannot be overlooked . . . . It could well be the forerunner of a fourth service of supply."[46]

The subcommittee's report challenged the statutory authority under which McNamara had authorized DSA, but refrained from stating explicitly that the McCormack amendment* was illegal. It sought a new amendment to the National Security Act that would validate the actions taken by the secretary through a particular date in 1963, but would state that "no activity or function being conducted or performed by any military department or military service on the effective date of this act will be transferred, consolidated, or assigned to any agency heretofore created under the authority of this section." Given the sever-

---

* See above, p. 24.

ity of the House subcommittee's judgment about DSA's authority and the issues the report raised, surprisingly the panel's recommendations evoked little response, outside of newspaper comments.[47]

In contrast to the House subcommittee, the Senate seemed to look benignly on the DSA's needs, without much regard for the potential dangers the new agency posed. Sen. Leverett Saltonstall paved the way in hearings before a subcommittee of the Senate Appropriations Committee in May 1962, eventually bringing about the passage of the final appropriation for supply operations requested by OSD.[48]

When the House Committee on Government Operations reported on 20 September 1962 on its study of the DSA, it took into account the Armed Services Committee's mid-August report and its subcommittee's objections to the DSA and dismissed them almost out of hand. For one thing, Armed Services Committee Chairman Carl Vinson had agreed to the McCormack amendment, including the broad authority granted to the secretary of defense. Moreover, the secretary had authority independent of the McCormack amendment to establish the DSA. Most significantly, a decided congressional majority wanted leadership from the secretary of defense and favored the action taken in this instance. In brief, Congress saw no need for a modification of the 1958 act or of the McCormack amendment.[49]

The promise of vast savings, more than the logic of Secretary McNamara's arguments, won the day and allayed congressional concerns over the statutory legitimacy of DSA. As the new agency demonstrated an ability to meet or exceed its stated goals—for FY 1963-65, DSA reported direct annual cost savings of $61.8 million, $99 million, and $197 million[50]—Congress took notice. A model of how efficiency could affect costs, the agency represented an irresistible combination: reduction of waste without reducing security. The reality, of course, fell short of perfection, challenged regularly on every front,[51] as vested interests felt threatened and errors of judgment became evident. But DSA's acceptance in 1962 permitted further consolidation of competing units within DoD.

Civil Defense

Acquisition by transfer of a function new to DoD—civil defense—required the establishment of another assistant secretary of defense position in 1961, a major organizational change. Civil defense had remained a stepchild in the national security family during the whole decade before the advent of the Kennedy administration in 1961. Little more than $500 million—an average of $54 million per year—had been spent on civil defense from 1951 through 1959. During the same period, Congress slashed an average of more than 80 percent from appropriation requests for civil defense.

Until 1958 the Federal Civil Defense Administration (FCDA) had responsibility for the function. Although the question of greater Defense involvement arose during the 1950s, when the Soviet Sputniks in 1957 triggered a wave of apprehension in the United States the Eisenhower administration did not turn to DoD but chose in 1958 to merge the FCDA and the Office of Defense Mobilization (ODM), creating a new Office of Civil and Defense Mobilization (OCDM).[52]

Efforts during the Eisenhower years to initiate an extensive civil defense program found little support in the White House. The Security Resources Panel of the ODM Scientific Advisory Committee (Gaither Panel) in its report of November 1957 recommended a five-year program to shelter the civilian population at a cost of $25 billion. The president did not choose to act on this and other recommendations of the panel for protection against bomber and missile attack.[53]

Public concern about civil defense mounted rapidly during the early months of 1961 as the expanding Soviet missile threat, the Bay of Pigs disaster, and the worsening Berlin crisis provided daily grist for the mills of the news media. Within the new Kennedy administration studies and discussions pointed toward greater emphasis on civil defense and assignment of the function to the Department of Defense. In December 1960 the Symington Committee had recommended placing civil defense under DoD. Secretary McNamara supported increased funding, particularly for fallout shelters. Forced to take cognizance of growing pressure from Congress and forceful criticism from the Republican governor of New York, Nelson D. Rockefeller, President Kennedy, on 25 May 1961 in his Special Message to the Congress on Urgent Needs, delivered in person to a joint session, outlined a plan to shift responsibility for civil defense to the Department of Defense and to greatly increase expenditures. He followed through with Executive Order 10952 on 20 July, which transferred OCDM's civil defense function to DoD. He pledged that the function would remain civilian in nature. He proposed also to reconstitute OCDM as a small agency, the Office of Emergency Planning, to provide staff advice to the president and assist in the coordination of civil defense functions.[54]

In his report to the country on the Berlin crisis on 25 July, the president detailed the changes he proposed to bring about in the civil defense program. He mentioned most prominently the assignment of basic responsibilities to the secretary of defense and his request to Congress for a $207 million appropriation. The emphasis would be on fallout shelters.[55]

It has been suggested that a prime reason for shifting civil defense to DoD was to remove it from the jurisdiction of the Independent Offices Subcommittee of the House Appropriations Committee to the Department of Defense Subcommittee. Chairman of the Independent Offices Subcommittee Rep. Albert Thomas (D-Tex.) was notoriously skeptical about civil defense and cut its appropriation regularly. More sympathetic, the chairman of the Defense Subcommittee, Rep. George H. Mahon, also of Texas, steered the FY 1962 supplemental appropriation for civil defense through the House in August 1961. Unfortunately for civil defense, in January 1962 the chairman of the Appropriations Committee, Rep. Clarence Cannon (D-Mo.), reassigned the function to Thomas's subcommittee.[56]

Civil defense imposed an additional task on OSD. Even though he recognized the relationship between civil and military defense, civil defense management was not an assignment that a burdened secretary had actively sought. Predictably, McNamara insisted on having responsibility for the whole civil defense program, not merely the shelter program as OCDM proposed. Once accepted, McNamara devoted the same energy to this responsibility that he brought to everything else. In rapid order on 31 July 1961 he appointed Special Assistant Adam Yarmolinsky as the interim civil defense head and followed up on 31 August by creating an assistant secretaryship for the function. The first and, as it turned out, the only assistant secretary for civil defense, Steuart L. Pittman, a Washington attorney, assumed office on 20 September. Before the end of the year he had available the services of some 1,100 employees transferred from OCDM.[57]

To secure money quickly, the administration included civil defense in the third amendment to the FY 1962 budget. Congress promptly approved $207.6 million on 10 August which, McNamara pointed out in testimony before a House subcommittee on 1 August, would go chiefly for a public shelter identification and marking program ($93 million) and for stockage. Transfer to DoD of a prior appropriation of $49.2 million to OCDM raised the total available for civil defense to $256.8 million. At the same time the secretary reassured the congressmen that the effort would remain under civilian control but that it would be "integrated with all aspects of military defense against thermonuclear attack." In keeping with his commitment to cost effectiveness, he pledged to seek maximum protection at the lowest possible cost.

In his statement the secretary pointed out that protection against fallout from nuclear explosions was much less costly than protection from the effects of blast. Moreover, the expensive blast shelters would be competitive with antimissile defenses such as the Nike-Zeus while fallout shelters would be complementary rather than competitive. An effective missile defense system would diminish the need for blast shelter. Meanwhile, effort would go toward developing a greater fallout protection system to serve some 50 million Americans.[58]

During the summer and fall of 1961, when the civil defense fever reached its apogee, the White House supported a large civil defense program but it did not go all out, probably because of the large costs the commitment would entail. Still, in his draft memorandum to the president in October McNamara proposed that the major portion of the $400 million he wanted for civil defense in FY 1963 go for a major fallout protection program. Secretary of State Rusk suggested an even larger effort, "substantially beyond the modest increase proposed in the FY

'63 DoD budget." The president's brother, Attorney General Robert F. Kennedy, opposed the fallout shelter program, later calling himself "a minority of one."[59]

At a meeting with his advisers on 24 November, the president decided in favor of a public shelter program rather than a private one. He settled on a civil defense program of $700 million annually for five years at a total cost of $3.5 billion. This represented a compromise between proposed $400 million and $900 million programs. He and McNamara agreed to the preparation of a statement of the National Civil Defense Program detailing the roles of federal, state, and local governments and private citizens. They also planned to meet with congressional leaders and state governors to discuss proposed programs and organizational and communications arrangements. Sensitive to the need to inform a nervous public, they also promised preparation and nationwide dissemination of a booklet on fallout protection by the end of the year.[60]

By mid-December the civil defense program had evolved sufficiently for Deputy Secretary Gilpatric to unveil it in a press conference. He announced that DoD would request civil defense funds "in the neighborhood of $700 million" for FY 1963. Priority would be on providing 20 million spaces in community fallout shelters in the next fiscal year, for which the federal government would provide financial incentives to states and localities, which would have to play an important role.[61]

As the worry over nuclear attack waned during the early months of 1962, so did support for the federal program. Still, in hearings before congressional committees in January and February McNamara remained firm in his support of the $695 million he actually requested for civil defense. He maintained that the proposed program represented his own personal convictions and those of President Kennedy. The greater part of the money—$460 million—he pointed out, would pay for incentives to educational institutions, hospitals, and welfare institutions to provide shelter spaces. He balked at providing shelter for the total U.S. population of 180 million people, which the Atomic Energy Commission estimated would eventually cost $25 billion. He calculated the cost of DoD's proposed shelter program over the next four years at more than $3 billion, of which the federal government would pay $1.8 billion. Members of the congressional committees voiced disapproval and skepticism about the cost and extent of the shelter program.[62]

Observers noted the mercurial rise and decline of national concern about civil defense in the span of a year. In April 1962 one journalist recalled that in December 1961 he had heard a top Defense Department official declare that "the whole thing jumped from apathy to hysteria before we had a chance to catch our breaths." Four months later, he found that "the same official and his associates are anxiously trying to determine whether interest has slipped back into apathy." Assistant Secretary Pittman was acutely aware of the change in the interim: "Public interest was at an extraordinarily high pitch last fall, following the Berlin crisis. It is now rather quiet. Whether this quiescence is disinterest or a very sensible 'wait-and-see' attitude is difficult to analyze."[63]

By this time the home shelter building boom that had flourished during the fall and early winter had collapsed. Moreover, of the 35 million pamphlets on fallout protection deposited in post offices for pickup by the public, 4 million still remained. The booklet appeared at a time (late December 1961) when the near-hysteria over civil defense was still close to a peak. In its final form the booklet had already shed much of its alarmist tone.[64]

Congressional action or inaction mirrored the fluctuation in public interest and concern. In essence, the reversal of support for the heart of the program— shelter-building—reflected a public sense that a truly effective civil defense program that could protect the population of the country lay beyond the nation's capacity, not only financially but militarily, especially in the event of a first nuclear strike against the United States. Congress did not complete its work on the FY 1963 civil defense appropriation until late September. It gutted the shelter program and provided a mere $113 million for all of civil defense.[65]

The prospect for vigorous support of a large civil defense effort grew dimmer even though the Cuban missile crisis in October 1962 caused President Kennedy to inquire into the progress of the program and to alert civil defense authorities in the southeastern states to possible danger. Thereafter the administration kept paying lip service to civil defense, even as the program continued to sink into near-obscurity. Pittman must have seen the handwriting on the wall when McNamara proposed in February 1963 to reduce the position of assistant secretary of defense for civil defense to director of civil defense.[66]

In spite of the support of the president and the Governors' Conference during the summer of 1962 for full funding of the shelter program in the FY 1963 appropriation request, Congress had chosen to provide only a portion. For FY 1964 DoD asked for $346.9 million for civil defense, but received only $111.6 million.[67] Supported by his staff and scientific experts, Pittman fought valiantly for the fallout shelter program in appearances before congressional committees. He succeeded with the House of Representatives, securing authorization in August 1963 for $175 million for shelter incentives. The Senate Armed Services Committee did not act on the House authorization bill, which led to the resignation of the dispirited Pittman on 31 March 1964. The same day Secretary McNamara, in a further signal of loss of interest in civil defense, transferred the civil defense function to the secretary of the Army, who assigned the responsibility to a director of civil defense. The official explanation was that the operational responsibility for civil defense belonged in the Army.[68]

A disillusioned Pittman believed that McNamara confined his support to shelter survey, marking, and stocking and gave little more than token backing to the vital shelter incentive proposals. Although McNamara continued to tell Congress that fallout protection was the most cost-effective damage-limiting measure against nuclear attack, this had to be understood, Pittman subsequently observed, "in the context of his growing hostility toward ABM [Anti-Ballistic Missile] and commitment to the doctrine of 'mutual assured destruction.'"[69]

For FY 1965 DoD requested $358 million, from which Congress deleted the greater part, intended for the fallout shelter program. The final appropriation was $105.2 million. Civil defense fared no better in FY 1966, receiving only $106.8 million against a requested $193.9 million. Thereafter appropriations for civil defense declined still further.[70]

Although presidents from Truman to Johnson asked for large sums of money for civil defense, Congress responded consistently by slashing the appropriation requests. The sticking point throughout seems to have been the shelter program—providing money for shelters in public buildings and providing incentive money for shelters in private buildings. Most of the funding approved seems to have gone for stockage of supplies, shelter survey and marking, education and training, a warning system, communications systems, and technical guidance and assistance to state and local civil defense agencies. These did not require the huge sums that a national fallout shelter program would have required.

The organizational demotion of civil defense in DoD paralleled the decline in public and congressional concern and in money allocated for the function. McNamara and Secretary of the Army Stephen B. Ailes tried to put the best face on the downgrading, but there could be little doubt of its true meaning. Although occasional bursts of interest in civil defense occurred thereafter, and McNamara continued to ask for money for civil defense, it never again elicited from any administration or the country the level of attention reached in 1961-62.

The author of the official history of the U.S. civil defense program, Harry Yoshpe, concluded that "the record provides little evidence of Presidents, other than Kennedy, perhaps, making a serious effort to get the Nation and the Congress to face up to the civil defense problem." And even Kennedy may have come to consider his effort overdone. According to presidential assistant Arthur Schlesinger, "Kennedy feared overexciting people about public issues, as he came to believe that his call for an air raid shelter program had done during the Berlin crisis of 1961."[71] Many factors in addition to high cost contributed to the failure to develop a viable national civil defense structure—public apathy and fatalism, secrecy, the quarrels over civilian vs. military control, and the absence of a legislative base. The Kennedy administration apparently expected that placing civil defense under the Defense Department would give it an aura of military necessity and facilitate securing greater support from Congress. After a promising beginning the program reverted to its accustomed minor role in national defense. It seems most probable that the Kennedy/McNamara policy of relying on offensive nuclear forces to deter attack rather than on a defensive strategy based on an anti-ballistic missile capability and civil defense sealed the fate of the latter. In competition with other DoD high-priority programs sponsored by the JCS and the military services, civil defense, a newcomer in DoD, could not hope to compete without the strong support of an effective political constituency. Somehow, in all the years after World War II, such a constituency did not emerge and civil defense remained a nagging yet marginal concern.

Counterinsurgency

Unlike civil defense, from the very beginning of the Kennedy administration the counterinsurgency mission had a powerful constituency—the president and the secretary of defense—and received continual and close attention and support from this highest level of authority. Kennedy and McNamara engaged themselves with much intensity in developing an organization to direct counterinsurgency policy and the forces to perform the mission.

Their disposition to create forces to counter insurgencies was greatly fortified by an address on the likely future of war and peace among the nations of the world given by the leader of the Soviet Union, Nikita Khrushchev, on 6 January 1961, just two weeks before Kennedy became president. In his speech, which the State Department titled "The Communist Doctrine of Wars of Liberation," Khrushchev forecast diminished likelihood of global and conventional local wars but an increase in "national liberation wars"—uprisings of peoples against their imperialist or colonial oppressors. "The Communists," he went on, "fully support such just wars and march in the front rank with the peoples waging liberation struggles."[72] Kennedy subsequently described the address, to a convocation of Communist party organizations in Moscow, "as possibly one of the most important speeches of the decade" and considered its content a "pattern of [Soviet] military and paramilitary infiltration and subversion which could be expected under the guise of 'wars of liberation'."[73]

The president's views about wars of national liberation and U.S. responses were also influenced by Brig. Gen. Edward G. Lansdale's report of his 2-14 January visit to South Vietnam at the request of outgoing Secretary of Defense Gates. Lansdale, who had made his reputation as a counterinsurgency expert in the Philippines and was currently deputy assistant to the secretary of defense for special operations, asserted that the Communist Viet Cong's expanding control over much of the country had made them confident of victory in 1961. He listed numerous actions that the South Vietnamese should take with U.S. support; otherwise the probable Communist victory would result in the quick loss of the rest of Southeast Asia and constitute "a major blow to U.S. prestige and influence . . . throughout the world."[74] Kennedy reviewed Lansdale's report on 26 January and was so impressed that he directed that a 28 January meeting of his top officials—Vice President Johnson, Rusk, McNamara, Lemnitzer, CIA Director Allen W. Dulles, and others—scheduled to discuss the planned Cuban invasion, be broadened to include South Vietnam, and that Lansdale attend.[75]

Still another significant document at this time influenced the president's views on counterinsurgency—a Pacific Command-initiated study eventually titled "Basic Counterinsurgency Plan for VietNam," begun in early 1960 and finally completed on 4 January 1961, with inputs from the U.S. country team in Saigon and concerned Washington departments and agencies. It called for extensive South Vietnamese political, military, economic, and psychological actions, with U.S. advice and assistance, against the Viet Cong insurgency. The president may have first learned of the plan's contents at the 28 January meeting.[76]

Several days later, at his initial meeting with the National Security Council on 1 February, Kennedy directed McNamara in consultation with other interested agencies to "examine means for placing more emphasis on the development of counter-guerrilla forces." Special Assistant McGeorge Bundy formalized the request on 3 February in National Security Action Memorandum (NSAM) No. 2, adding that the White House wished to be informed "promptly of the measures which it [DoD] proposes to take."[77]

Thereafter, until his untimely death in November 1963, the president maintained extraordinary interest and participation in all phases of expanding U.S. counterinsurgency activities in underdeveloped Asian, African, and Latin American nations undergoing communist pressures. These included not only overt and covert military operations, but local police training, civic action programs (school, health, and political), agricultural improvements, riot control, and psychological and propaganda activities.

Since the counterinsurgency effort was so broad, it involved many governmental agencies, including the Defense, State, and Treasury departments as well as the CIA, the Agency for International Development, and the U.S. Information Agency, none of which had overall responsibility. Following the Bay of Pigs disaster of April 1961, the Cuba Study Group concluded that future Cold War operations "should be planned and executed by a governmental mechanism capable of bringing into play, in addition to military and covert techniques, all other forces, political, economic, ideological, and intelligence, which can contribute to its success."[78]

The initial attempts to centralize responsibility were not successful. On 8 December 1961, however, a special NSC Counter-Guerrilla Warfare Task Force,* noting the "magnitude and urgency" of indirect communist aggression and the lack of a "single [U.S.] high-level locus of authority and responsibility" to

---

* The task force included Richard M. Bissell, Jr. (CIA), Lansdale from DoD, Walt Rostow (White House), and Henry C. Ramsey (State). They served as individuals, not as representatives of their agencies. See editorial note, *FRUS 1961-63*, VIII:229.

respond with the "vitally needed concerting of inter-agency resources," proposed the organization of such a body. General Taylor agreed and had so recommended to the president.[79]

After several weeks of discussion over its composition, organizational form, and placement, on 18 January 1962 Kennedy directed the establishment of the Special Group (Counterinsurgency)* "to assure unity of effort and the use of all available resources with maximum effectiveness in preventing and resisting subversive insurgency and related forms of indirect aggression in friendly countries." Its membership consisted of the president's military representative (General Taylor) as chairman, Attorney General Robert Kennedy, Deputy Under Secretary of State U. Alexis Johnson, Deputy Secretary of Defense Gilpatric, General Lemnitzer (the JCS chairman), new CIA Director John A. McCone, presidential special assistant McGeorge Bundy, and AID Administrator Fowler Hamilton. Initially, the president listed Laos, South Vietnam, and Thailand as the nations for which interdepartmental programs should be prepared and conducted to prevent or defeat subversive insurgency.[80] In mid-June, he added eight others to the group's purview: Burma, Cambodia, Cameroon, Iran, Ecuador, Colombia, Guatemala, and Venezuela.[81] Thereafter, some of these were deleted but others, chiefly from Latin America and Africa, were added.

The Special Group (CI) met weekly for about two hours. The members, not substitutes, were expected to attend; they could bring no support staff (thereby necessitating prior agenda preparation). As departmental or agency heads or deputy heads, members were expected to ensure timely responses to proposed actions. Attorney General Robert Kennedy's presence obviously served as an additional inducement to attend and act. General Taylor chaired the group until October 1962, when he became the JCS chairman. He remained a group member, but State's Alexis Johnson replaced him as group chairman and NSC's Michael Forrestal became the White House representative. Early in April 1963, when W. Averell Harriman became the under secretary for political affairs, he replaced Johnson as the group chairman. By then, much of the intense activity and attention that marked the group's early days had passed—innovation and introduction of ideas and plans had given way largely to their implementation. When President Kennedy first introduced the counterinsurgency effort, he intended it specifically as an anticommunism measure; in 1963 and after, this meant that U.S. actions, particularly in Latin America and Africa, supported friendly but not necessarily democratic or popular regimes in many countries.

---

* What eventually would popularly be known as "counterinsurgency" initially included many other terms—sublimited war, counter-guerrilla operations, guerrilla warfare, covert aggression, special operations, and numerous others. The first general use of "counterinsurgency" within the government apparently occurred with PACOM'S Basic Counterinsurgency Plan for Viet-Nam, frequently cited as the CIP. However, the term seemed not to have gained widespread use until after the Special Group (Counterinsurgency) was established in January 1962. It was generally referred to as Special Group (CI).

President Johnson abolished the Special Group (CI) early in 1966 and transferred its functions to the newly established Senior Interdepartmental Group.[82]

Implementing counterinsurgency policy proceeded rapidly in response to the president's initial formal directive of 3 February 1961. McNamara tasked the Joint Chiefs and the assistant secretary for international security affairs "to examine the means for placing more emphasis on the development of counterguerrilla forces." Kennedy met with the JCS on 6 and 23 February, asking detailed questions and requesting reports on actions they were taking. He indicated an interest in every facet of the subject: What was the size of the force and the number of men in training at the Army's Special Warfare Center at Fort Bragg, North Carolina, and at the two subordinate centers, in Germany and Okinawa? What was the rank of the Fort Bragg center's commander? How many Military Assistance Advisory Group personnel in Vietnam and those training Laotian troops had received guerrilla training? What types of equipment and training were being supplied to these troops and to those of such other nations as Iran, Congo, Ecuador, Colombia, etc.? What was the DoD's specific role in training the Cubans being readied for the forthcoming Bay of Pigs invasion? And within the 66 current MAAGs, what proportion of their effort was devoted to counterinsurgency training and to teaching the operation of American-supplied military equipment? He directed that "the JCS make 'a sort of analysis' of what we can do *around the world* in building anti-guerrilla forces," asking the chiefs for comment regarding *each* Latin American country. It seemed that any and all details of a counterinsurgency program were of interest to the president.[83]

The military services responded variously to the president's intense interest—the Army and Air Force quickly and enthusiastically, the Navy somewhat less, and the Marines far less. Almost immediately, the Army increased its Special Warfare School manning by 500 spaces while McNamara proposed another 3,000 men and $19 million in the amended FY 1962 budget request to double the size of the Special Forces and allow establishment of a fourth unit, in Panama. Kennedy included these requests in a message to Congress on the Defense budget on 28 March.[84] In his 25 May summons to the legislature on urgent national needs, the president informed Congress that he had directed McNamara to reorient additional forces for "sub-limited or unconventional wars" and have the services place "new emphasis . . . on the special skills and languages which are required to work with local populations."[85]

Late in 1961, Congress on its own added $7.5 million to the Army budget specifically for the development of new Special Forces weapons and equipment. Even earlier, on 5 September 1961, McNamara directed that the MAAG in South Vietnam also serve as an experimental command for the development of organizational and operational procedures in the "conduct of sub-limited war." The next month, in a memorandum to the president, the secretary proposed $100 million in Army R&D funds for each of the next five years for "remote area limited warfare" to improve what he termed "an existing situation that is very unbalanced."[86]

The Army, as the likely major participant in counterinsurgency operations, responded aggressively to the numerous presidential recommendations and also took many steps on its own. It opened the Panama center in mid-1961 and enrolled increased numbers of foreign students there and at Fort Bragg; it enlarged the breadth and scope of its training and educational courses and increased enrollment; it began to send likely flag officer candidates to Vietnam for short-term, on-the-spot training; and it established a special course at Fort Bragg for officers and/or enlisted men going to appropriate MAAG and attaché posts. At the president's firm suggestion, the Army accorded members of the Special Forces a unique headgear—the green beret—even though several years earlier it had responded negatively to a similar proposal. And, again on Kennedy's recommendation, the Army raised the rank of the Special Forces Center's commander to flag-officer level. To much fanfare, on 12 October the president visited Fort Bragg where, in addition to 82d and 101st Airborne Division demonstrations, the Special Forces Center executed judo, guerrilla, and other counterinsurgency tactics in response to orders given in foreign languages including Russian and Czech. One trooper with a small rocket engine attached to his back ascended 30 feet and flew some 200 feet, landing near the president, an impressive feat indeed.[87]

The presidential interest in counterinsurgency also caused the Air Force to move quickly, with major impetus coming, surprisingly, from then Vice Chief of Staff Curtis LeMay, the very embodiment of "strategic" doctrines and operations. At his direction, in mid-April 1961, the Air Force activated the 4400th Combat Crew Training Squadron (code named Jungle Jim) at Eglin AFB, Florida, with 352 men and 32 B-26, C-47, and T-28 aircraft—all of World War II vintage—to devise techniques for supporting counterinsurgency operations. Following the Army example, LeMay authorized a unique uniform featuring an Australian-type bush hat, fatigues, and combat boots.[88]

In September the squadron became operational, coincidental with McNamara's decision to use Vietnam as a U.S. military experimental laboratory. The president approved on 11 October a proposal to deploy a segment of the 4400th to Vietnam "for the initial purpose of training Vietnamese forces." The detachment, code-named Farm Gate and consisting of 155 men and 16 aircraft, arrived in Vietnam during November-December 1961. Deeming the 4400th and its Farm Gate contingent a success and in accord with the president's counterinsurgency objectives, the Air Force in January 1962 expanded the squadron to group level, and three months later established the Special Air Warfare Center with two groups (the 1st Air Commando and 1st Combat Applications). The Air Force enlarged its special forces to 3,900 men and 184 aircraft in 6 squadrons by 30 June 1964 and planned for 10 squadrons, 5,800 men, and 253 aircraft a year later. Moreover, in support of the Army's Special Forces, elements of these USAF units took up station in Panama, Europe, and the Far East for the training of indigenous forces and to conduct contingency and combat operations in Vietnam and elsewhere as necessary.[89]

At best, the Navy initially responded lukewarmly to the president's calls for counterinsurgency measures. Although it considered several measures during 1961, the Navy took no organizational action until 1962 when it authorized 60-man SEAL (*Sea-Air-Land*) teams, one each for the Atlantic and Pacific fleets, with a mission to "develop a . . . capability for sabotage, demolition, and other clandestine activities conducted in and from restricted waters, rivers, and canals" and to provide training for this purpose to Allied personnel. Under the existing circumstances, Vietnamese requirements received initial attention, and the first major SEAL operations occurred in Vietnam in April 1962.[90]

The other early naval counterinsurgency measure proposed but also kept on hold during 1961 involved the organization of SEABEE technical assistance teams (STATs) to provide developing countries with "technical training, engineering support, and construction assistance in their nation-building efforts." In February 1962, the Navy directed establishment of four 13-man teams; however, mission and funding questions delayed operational status until late January 1963, when the first team arrived in Vietnam for six months of "nation building" in support of remotely located Army Special Forces. Thereafter, during the remainder of the advisory years, more than a dozen STATs served in Vietnam both as trainers and as construction workers.[91]

The Marines considered themselves natural counterinsurgency warriors and therefore believed they required no special training. When the president early on questioned service commanders on what steps they had taken or proposed, Marine Commandant David Shoup stated that his troops were ready to go in and act as guerrillas, not serve as trainers to indigenous forces. Kennedy wryly commented that the countries in question would have to do their own guerrilla and anti-guerrilla combat, adding that he realized that "this would disappoint the Marine Corps, but that into each life, some disappointment must fall." Some years later, Marine Lt. Gen. (then Maj. Gen.) Victor Krulak described the Marine Corps attitude: "The Marines knew it [counterinsurgency] was going to go away. Hell, we've been to Nicaragua, we know all about that jazz . . . . They [only] paid the President of the United States lip service." Actually, the Marines did introduce counterinsurgency subjects into their school curricula, embarked on language training, and sent representatives to the DoD- and government-wide training courses. And in the spring of 1962, HMM-362, a Marine squadron of helicopters, was dispatched to Vietnam for combat support of the Vietnamese.[92]

Although DoD appeared to have made major progress in 1961, Kennedy on 11 January 1962 stated that the capability was inadequate to meet the "threat of Communist-directed subversive insurgency and guerrilla warfare . . . ." It should, he added, duplicate preparations for conventional warfare—doctrinally, organizationally, and functionally. He wanted the Army to appoint a general officer immediately under the chief of staff "as the focal point for Army activities directed at this problem" as well as another flag officer to serve similarly in the Joint Staff. He left it to McNamara to decide whether comparable appointments were needed in the other services; the secretary opted for additional-duty assignments there.[93]

Two days later, McNamara informed the president that the Army had appointed Maj. Gen.-designate William B. Rosson with the title of special assistant to the chief of staff for special warfare; shortly after, in mid-February, General Krulak became the Joint Staff's special assistant for counterinsurgency and special activities. Both generals met with the president on 5 March, at which time he expounded that counterinsurgency was "the most pressing war either at hand or in prospect." Krulak would soon become DoD's top counterinsurgency official, "always being sent for by the Secretary of Defense, the Chairman of the Joint Chiefs of Staff, or the President," as he later recalled. "It turned out," he also recalled, "that when McNamara went somewhere, he took me with him."[94]

In his 11 January directive, the president also called for extensive training programs from the service academies through the National War College level to insure that all officers were properly instructed about subversive insurgency. He directed that his requirement for Army officers to serve in Vietnam for short periods of training under actual guerrilla conditions be expedited and broadened to include the other services. Moreover, officers being sent as attachés or to MAAGs in nations where communist insurgency was likely should undergo a pre-assignment period of training at the Army's Special Warfare Center. Kennedy expected DoD "to move to a new level of increased activity across the board. I expect to direct similar action in other departments which have a part to play in this matter."[95] McNamara followed the president's lead. On 14 February he reported to the Senate Subcommittee on Defense Appropriations on the buildup of "specialized guerrilla warfare forces." He followed this up with a speech on countering wars of liberation that would "require some shift in our military thinking."[96]

To further impress the importance that he attached to the subject, the president in March 1962 proposed that specific counterinsurgency training or experience be a mandatory prerequisite for promotion to flag-officer rank. McNamara and Gilpatric dissented here, arguing that such training or experience "should be included among the criteria bearing on, rather than made a prerequisite for, selection . . . ." They believed that a blanket requirement would inject "an undesirable degree of inflexibility into the promotion and assignment system."[97]

Kennedy also continued to emphasize the non-military aspects of counterinsurgency. At the West Point commencement on 6 June 1962, the president declared that the role of the new officers far exceeded their military duties; it included political, economic, and social matters. He called the armed forces "an arm of our diplomacy," emphasizing that their role was "to deter war as well as to fight it." Three months earlier, on 13 March, he had issued detailed instructions for the training of all officer-grade personnel and the establishment of the National Interdepartmental Seminar, a special joint-agency school under State's Foreign Service Institute, for both military officers and civilian officials being assigned to underdeveloped countries. The school graduated its first class on 3 July 1962 and the president met the graduates at the White House and emphasized their importance in nation-building and forestalling communist takeovers in the developing countries of Latin America, Africa, and Asia.*[98]

On 24 August 1962, after more than 18 months of piecemeal policy guidance, including numerous and conflicting drafts prepared primarily by the State Department and JCS, Kennedy approved a document entitled U.S. Overseas Internal Defense Policy and distributed it widely as NSAM No. 182. As indicated by its title, the 30-page doctrinal statement plus three annexes spelled out in detail the roles and missions of the several governmental agencies involved in attempting to avert or combat communist-inspired insurgencies in affected nations by taking timely political, economic, social, cultural, and military actions. Although DoD's list of tasks was extensive, a major stated objective, no doubt with an eye to the increasing Indochina entanglement, was to "minimize the likelihood of direct U.S. military involvement in internal war by maximizing indigenous capabilities."[99]

Thereafter, counterinsurgency became more a normal day-to-day function rather than a special program. Kennedy did not let up in his abiding interest in the activity, as when upon his return from a June 1963 trip to Europe, he praised the Special Forces unit garrisoned in Germany but told McNamara it could be better employed by "demonstrating and training all over the underdeveloped world where the guerrilla actions are rising in intensity."[100] General Taylor informed the president that joint mobile training teams were currently in 9 Latin American countries and plans called for 91 teams in 12 Latin American countries during FY 1963. In Asia, teams were now in six countries as well as in two African nations. Army Chief of Staff General Earl Wheeler added that a limiting factor to the number of deployed teams was often the opposition of the U.S. ambassador.[101] The president then directed Secretary Rusk to address this problem with his ambassadors. When the joint State-DoD message was judged insufficient, he instructed that the ambassadors be given "a real sales job on why it is going to be so helpful to them, what a good face forces can put on our nation, and how inspiring they are." A joint follow-on message of 2 December 1963, some six pages in length, urged the use of Special Forces elements in underdeveloped or newly developed nations.[102]

---

* By the beginning of 1965 about 1,000 had completed the course.

Certainly, by the time of Kennedy's death in November 1963, the role of counterinsurgency within DoD operations had in large measure met the administration's stated goals. In personnel, funding, and weapons, it would never compete with the other major DoD missions, but for the intended purpose of combating and defeating the spread of communism in underdeveloped or developing countries, it had acquired, with McNamara's strong support, the degree of commitment and promise of success that Kennedy had intended.

The Space Mission

Inevitably, space research and development became a prime issue among the military services in the early 1960s. The Soviet Union's successful launching of the Sputnik satellite in October 1957 and others thereafter set off shock waves that had still not subsided at the time the Eisenhower administration left office. Sputnik had galvanized a drive within the United States to upgrade university education, as federal funds poured into crash programs ranging from intensive study of foreign languages to expanded research in physics. It also inspired plans to catch and overtake Soviet space exploration. With the passage of the National Aeronautics and Space Act of 1958 and the establishment of the National Aeronautics and Space Administration (NASA) shortly thereafter, the nation had taken a giant step toward a fuller exploitation of its space resources.

The spectacle of Soviet satellites circling above American skies gave way to even greater embarrassment when the Soviets successfully placed the first man into orbit in April 1961. These achievements dramatized to the world the apparent superiority of the Soviets in science and technology, not excluding military technology.

Given the attention that space pioneering attracted, there existed ample incentive for intense competition among the services for the military application of space technology. Each service had an expensive agenda to push as the Kennedy administration entered office. Prior to this time no clear division of service responsibilities nor any definition of their respective jurisdictions existed, posing the first of two space issues that McNamara faced after taking office.

The other issue related to jurisdictional boundaries between NASA and DoD. Although the latter had conducted virtually all space activities in the immediate aftermath of the 1957 Sputnik panic, NASA took over the major portion after its establishment in 1958. Confusion over boundaries persisted, however, particularly when NASA had to depend on and borrow so much from the military to advance its Mercury man-in-space project. The 1958 act had intended to address this problem through the creation of the National Aeronautics and Space Council, but the council had not yet succeeded in clarifying all relations between NASA and DoD, particularly for the development of launch vehicles.[103]

McNamara concentrated his attention more on interservice than on civil-military competition over control of space research. On 6 March 1961 he issued DoD Directive 5160.32, declaring that "research, development, test, and engineering of Department of Defense space development programs or projects, which are approved hereafter, will be the responsibility of the Department of the Air Force." This paragraph received the most notice from the press and military departments, although two other paragraphs may have had equal significance. One of them required submission of proposals for research and development of space projects beyond the preliminary stage to OSD's director of defense research and engineering for evaluation. The other made clear that proposals submitted to DDR&E had to receive approval from the secretary of defense or the deputy secretary before they could go ahead. The Air Force may have achieved the status of primus inter pares, but its primacy went no further than the military departments. Control would reside in OSD. The directive did not preclude preliminary research on the part of other services.[104]

The swift reaction within the Pentagon had less to do with the accretion of the secretary's powers than with his choice of the Air Force as the controlling service. The latter's leadership, understandably elated over McNamara's decision, made a not wholly successful effort to contain its satisfaction. Before a congressional committee on 18 March Air Force Chief of Staff General Thomas D. White disavowed any intention of taking over any project currently under way: "I might say I pontificated, again, to my commanders . . . the Air Force would bend over backward to meet the requirements of the Army and the Navy as prescribed by the directive."[105]

General White's gracious response did little to calm feelings in the other military departments, which perceived not only the preemption of a vital mission by the secretary of defense but also equally peremptory follow-up actions that appeared to reinforce the Air Force position. McNamara had already announced a sweeping reorganization within the Air Force that, in part, would facilitate its new role. Most of the changes that followed, the Air Force had contemplated for some time. A new organization, the Air Force Systems Command, headed by General Bernard A. Schriever, would take over the responsibilities of the Air Research and Development Command, as well as weapon system procurement and production functions formerly under the Air Materiel Command (redesignated Air Logistics Command). An independent Office of Aerospace Research would promote and monitor basic research. Schriever's new command would begin functioning on 1 April 1961.[106] This whirlwind of activity fed rumors that the Air Force intended to take over civilian as well as military space programs. White and Schriever even admitted to considering the possibility, though not advocating it. Under questioning by the House Committee on Science and Astronautics in mid-March both backed off, Schriever noting, "I see no reason why we cannot work shoulder to shoulder in the most cooperative manner and there is plenty to do for both, I can assure you."[107]

But to the Army, whose plans for the Nike-Zeus antimissile system seemed in jeopardy, General Schriever's apparent deference to NASA still left an impression that the Air Force would function as the exclusive custodian of the military's interests in space. In the same committee hearings, Assistant Secretary of the Army for Research and Development Richard S. Morse saw in the assignment of development responsibilities to the Air Force a step toward ultimate operational control of whatever developed from research. He viewed McNamara's directive as a management tool "which really tends to then control an ultimate role and mission" of the armed services.[108]

In mid-February, even before McNamara had issued his directive, the point man for the Army's opposition to the Air Force, Lt. Gen. Arthur G. Trudeau, chief of Army research and development, had testified to the House committee that "the military use of space is too vital to be entrusted to any one service," expressing preference for a unified military space agency to one controlled by an individual service.[109] Conceivably he might have seen things differently had the Army gotten the powers given to the Air Force. Trudeau's views represented the Army position. Even General Lemnitzer joined the criticism, although circumspectly, in his role of JCS chairman. A generation later he made clear his feeling that the JCS had had little say on the 6 March directive and spoke more bluntly, claiming that the Army was better prepared for the space research job than any other service, with the help of "Wernher von Braun and his people that we had brought over from Peenemunde."*[110]

Desirous of expanding its air defense mission beyond its point defense role, the Army particularly suffered distress because it believed itself on the verge of a breakthrough with the Nike-Zeus antimissile missile that would convert it into an antisatellite weapon with a much broader mission than originally anticipated. If space connected to air, it also connected to earth. The Army had a variety of capabilities for carrying out a requirement to push into space.[111] Army leaders had no neologism like "aerospace" to gain attention, but they could point to a solid, well-advanced program of space research accomplishments.

The continuing drumbeat of criticism of the March 1961 directive forced OSD into a defensive position, but it did not retreat from the substance of the decision in favor of the Air Force. Gilpatric conceded in testimony before the House Committee on Science and Astronautics on 17 March that the order had not been referred to the JCS for consideration, but presumably the views of the individual chiefs were included in the comments of the service secretaries. Gilpatric made no apologies for the speed of OSD's actions and for the short-

---

* The German research center in World War II that developed the V-weapons.

cuts employed: "A major criticism of the Department of Defense, which has been made for many years both in the Congress and elsewhere, has been the slowness of the decision-making process within the Department." He and Secretary McNamara believed in prompt, firm decisions. The alternative would be equivocation and compromise that watered down directives and ultimately satisfied no one: "You can't change anything in the Pentagon without stepping on somebody's toes."[112]

That Gilpatric and not McNamara expressed these sentiments had significance for those whose toes were stepped on. Some inferred that Gilpatric's service as under secretary of the Air Force in the Truman administration and more recently as chairman of Aerospace Corporation, a non-profit company supporting Air Force space and missile work primarily, might have biased his outlook.

In reality, the Army challengers should not have experienced shock at McNamara's directive, particularly since President-elect Kennedy had appointed a special task force to recommend solutions to the space jurisdictional questions and the panel had come to much the same conclusion. Under the chairmanship of Jerome B. Wiesner, his chief science adviser, the Ad Hoc Committee on Space on 12 January 1961 recommended that Kennedy centralize control of all military space development. Gilpatric noted later that the Air Force already had responsibility for "over 90% of the total defense effort in space development activities."[113]

Within a week of the issuance of the March directive, the JCS and all but one of the military secretaries fell in line. The exception, Army Secretary Stahr, remained unhappy with the order as well as with the downgrading of the civilian secretaries. Eventually, 15 months later, for other reasons as well, he resigned at the end of June 1962.*

Service opposition came from the Navy also. Even before McNamara issued his directive on 6 March, Vice Adm. John T. Hayward, the Navy's top research director, had joined General Trudeau in opposition to issuance of the order. Service dissent caused McNamara to ask Vance: "Is there evidence in the testimony that either Trudeau or Hayward . . . acted in any way contrary to instructions which I have given that 'once a decision has been made, I expect all members of the Department to support it fully?'"[114] The query implied that he might take disciplinary action against what he regarded as insubordination, but this did not happen. Within the year the charge of muzzling dissent would arise again, but for the moment McNamara's strong language silenced critics within DoD.

Only three weeks after McNamara issued his directive, the president informed Congress that the administration would ask for an increase of $125.67 million for NASA for a FY 1962 total of $1.23 billion. Whether the military

---

* See p. 93.

would receive what they considered an appropriate share of these funds caused anxiety in all the services, especially the Air Force.[115]

Although the military may have had worries about NASA's role, from the OSD perspective sharing authority with NASA seemed readily acceptable. DoD held responsibility for space activities "peculiar to or primarily associated with the development of weapons systems, military operations, or the defense of the United States"; its portion of the national space program would complement the work of NASA. McNamara and NASA Administrator James E. Webb jointly reviewed the total program and agreed to maintain close cooperation through constant exchange of information. Defense personnel as well as missile boosters and tracking facilities stood ready to support NASA space experiments. For FY 1963 the Air Force had NOA (new obligational authority) of $1.1 billion for space research, development, testing, and evaluation, more than double the amount in the FY 1961 budget.[116]

President Kennedy infused the space program with new power and purpose in his Special Message to Congress on Urgent National Needs on 25 May 1961. Directing attention to the space competition with the Soviet Union, he made his famous proposal for "landing a man on the moon and returning him safely to the earth." To help make it possible he asked for additional funds to accelerate development of rockets and satellites. This daring concept did, indeed, require close cooperation between NASA and DoD; the latter had been supportive of NASA from the beginning of the U.S. commitment to space exploration, and the new administration, as it expanded the program, reaffirmed that partnership.[117]

LeMay's Reappointment, Anderson's Departure

By 1963 McNamara had decided that changes in military leadership were needed to reinforce his organizational changes. McNamara found himself increasingly at odds with two of the chiefs—General Curtis E. LeMay and Admiral George W. Anderson, Jr.—both of whom had entered office on McNamara's recommendation in 1961 (LeMay became Air Force chief on 30 June 1961, and Anderson took over the Navy on 1 August that year).

During the House Armed Services Committee's consideration of the FY 1964 authorization bill in the spring of 1963, it appeared that the committee's provision of extra funds for the RS-70* was energizing LeMay's supporters in Congress to urge his reappointment in June to another two-year term as Air Force chief of staff. Because LeMay had a high and generally favorable public profile, his supporters believed a challenge would ensue if he were replaced. Moreover, they felt that the president, given other difficulties on Capitol Hill, would not risk angering the many congressmen who supported LeMay and his ideas. Some in

---

* See Chapter VI.

the press saw LeMay's reappointment as a test case of whether the president and McNamara were willing to tolerate differing views from the military.[118]

On 6 May the president announced that he was extending LeMay's term, but by one instead of the customary two years. At the same time he made the unexpected announcement that he was replacing Admiral Anderson as chief of naval operations. To avoid anticipated criticism Gilpatric and Navy Secretary Fred H. Korth visited key congressional members a few hours before the announcements and assured them that the decisions did not stem from any disagreements the two officers had with administration policy. In a later interview, Gilpatric recalled that when the president, McNamara, and he discussed DoD personnel matters, the subject of LeMay's tenure frequently came up. According to Gilpatric, LeMay rubbed the president the wrong way: "Every time he had to see LeMay he ended up in sort of a fit." The general "couldn't listen" and "would make what Kennedy considered perfectly . . . outrageous proposals that bore no relation to the state of affairs in the 1960s." Everyone was aware of the problem, but the alternatives seemed "so much worse" that "we just resigned ourselves to living with him." The president extended his tenure by a year, according to Gilpatric, because "it would be rougher with him out than with him in."* The press speculated that behind the decision lay fear that simultaneously removing LeMay and Anderson, both popular officers, would cause a tremendous uproar.[119] The LeMay decision, then, probably represented a tactical choice by the administration to avert a confrontation.

The decision not to retain Anderson for another term came as a surprise. At a press conference Kennedy denied a charge that he was replacing him as a warning to other naval officers to toe the line and expressed the highest confidence in Anderson, who, he pointed out, was being offered another post in government. Anderson subsequently accepted the position of ambassador to Portugal. Although the president made it appear a routine change, unnamed Defense Department officials explained to the press that Anderson had not "handled his job as was expected," citing, among other things, the contretemps with McNamara during the Cuban missile crisis† and his public criticism of McNamara's TFX decision.‡ One press account, however, stressed Anderson's differences with Secretary Korth, particularly over a planned Navy reorganization, as the major reason for his removal.[120]

---

* Subsequently, in mid-1964, President Johnson reappointed LeMay for another seven months, until 31 January 1965. Speculation about this unusual appointment suggested that it was to permit him to complete 35 years of service. Perhaps even more likely, his retirement would occur after the 1964 election and thus would preclude his waging public criticism of administration policy during the campaign.
† See Chapter IX.
‡ See Chapter XVII.

A Balance Sheet

If it did not have the formal or overarching, integral quality of other major DoD reorganizations, McNamara's drive to transform the department during these early years of his tenure between 1961 and 1964 nonetheless produced significant and sweeping changes. Change on such a large scale, inevitably, was a product of many factors—unrelenting Cold War pressures, rapidly shifting technological and bureaucratic demands, and a strong-willed temperament. Above all, the inspiration for McNamara's action came from his pragmatic ethos. To achieve maximum efficiency in management, with concomitant savings to the taxpayer, was a special point of pride with McNamara. He entered office with the belief that he could solve management problems that had overwhelmed his predecessors. A joint agency such as the Defense Intelligence Agency, and the Air Force as a single management agency for space research under OSD supervision, exemplified what could be accomplished by realignment and consolidation.

There always existed the political need to assure Congress and the public that the emphasis in the proposed changes on cost containment and on centralizing authority would result in greater security for the nation. The secretary saw himself as an educator, convinced that the public would respond favorably if only it could understand his aims. He encountered opposition from all sides—from the military services, from Congress, and occasionally from the White House. He tried to placate or disarm opponents with broad assurances, as with the space function. But his retreats were tactical and his compromises minimal. In the Kennedy years he managed, for the most part, to face down his critics and carry through his plans.

Centralization of power in OSD, the most visible change, and so much a product of a steady progression from the beginning of the department, required no new legislation or radical reorganizational scheme. (See Chart 2.) The Kennedy administration's handling of the Symington Committee's findings underscored this conclusion. Gilpatric openly confirmed the direction that McNamara was taking in a speech he delivered in Monterey, California, on 2 May 1962. Referring to aerospace activities, he observed:

> Generally speaking, these steps have had a common design, namely, to bring together and establish more centralized control over functionally alike activities in the military establishment . . . . The effect of most of the changes and the other steps that I have outlined will leave you with one impression, and that is that there has been a tendency, a very pronounced tendency, to centralize more authority in the Office of the Secretary of Defense—a trend that has given rise to considerable skepticism and criticism in a number of quarters. Ten years ago, I myself, would have shared those doubts. Now I see no alternative to this centralization.[121]

CHART 2
DEPARTMENT OF DEFENSE
1 AUGUST 1964

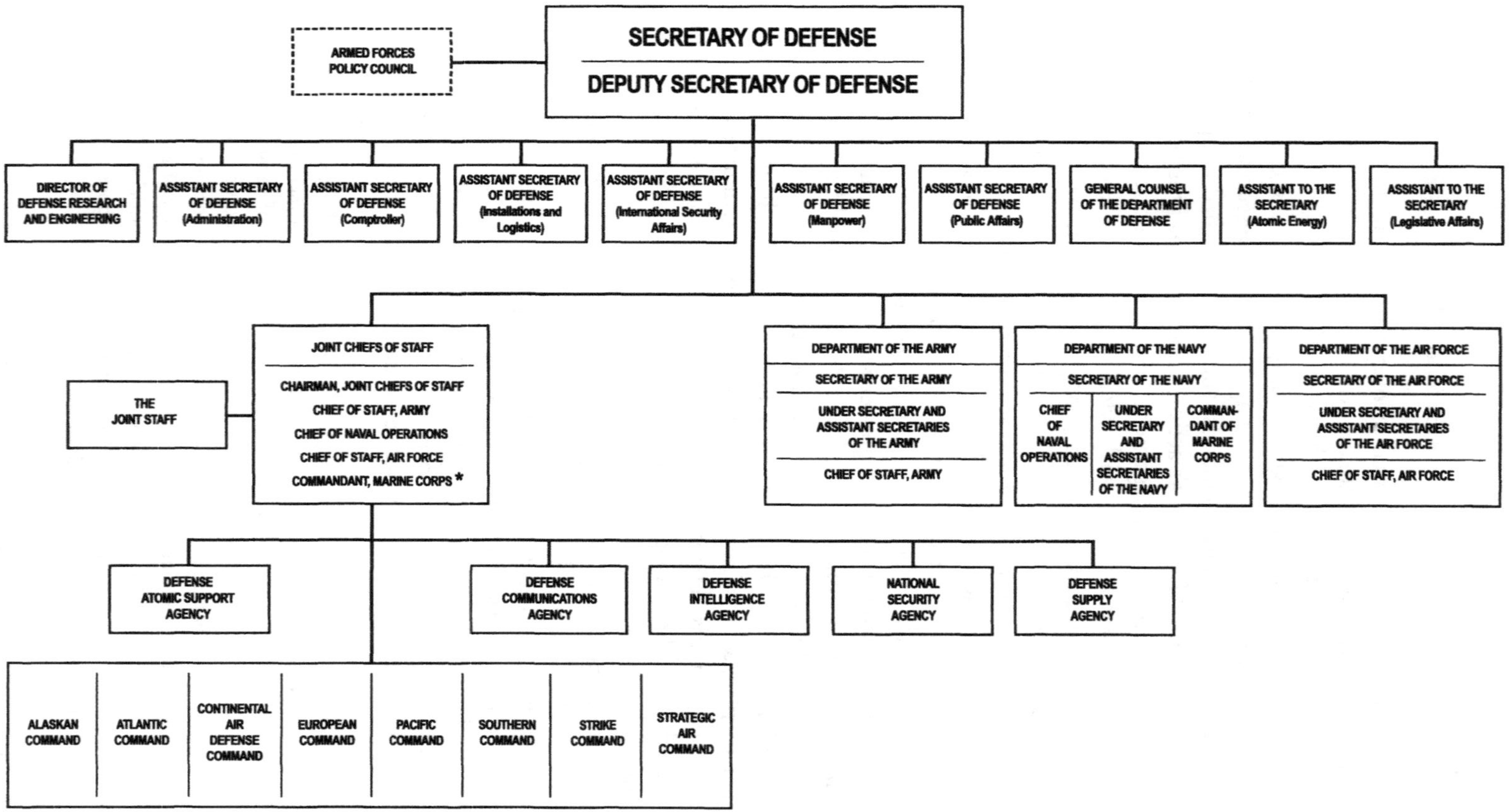

SECRETARY OF DEFENSE
DEPUTY SECRETARY OF DEFENSE

- ARMED FORCES POLICY COUNCIL

Offices reporting to the Secretary of Defense:
- Director of Defense Research and Engineering
- Assistant Secretary of Defense (Administration)
- Assistant Secretary of Defense (Comptroller)
- Assistant Secretary of Defense (Installations and Logistics)
- Assistant Secretary of Defense (International Security Affairs)
- Assistant Secretary of Defense (Manpower)
- Assistant Secretary of Defense (Public Affairs)
- General Counsel of the Department of Defense
- Assistant to the Secretary (Atomic Energy)
- Assistant to the Secretary (Legislative Affairs)

Department of the Army
- Secretary of the Army
- Under Secretary and Assistant Secretaries of the Army
- Chief of Staff, Army

Department of the Navy
- Secretary of the Navy
- Under Secretary and Assistant Secretaries of the Navy
- Chief of Naval Operations
- Commandant of Marine Corps

Department of the Air Force
- Secretary of the Air Force
- Under Secretary and Assistant Secretaries of the Air Force
- Chief of Staff, Air Force

Joint Chiefs of Staff
- Chairman, Joint Chiefs of Staff
- Chief of Staff, Army
- Chief of Naval Operations
- Chief of Staff, Air Force
- Commandant, Marine Corps *

- The Joint Staff

Defense Agencies:
- Defense Atomic Support Agency
- Defense Communications Agency
- Defense Intelligence Agency
- National Security Agency
- Defense Supply Agency

Unified and Specified Commands:
- Alaskan Command
- Atlantic Command
- Continental Air Defense Command
- European Command
- Pacific Command
- Southern Command
- Strike Command
- Strategic Air Command

* WHEN PERTAINING TO MARINE CORPS MATTERS

McNamara would not always have his way. Errors of judgment about new weapon systems would raise obstacles in the path of reorganization. His critics correctly claimed that McNamara had intended that his changes would enhance OSD's authority. That he encountered opposition to his efforts is hardly surprising. What is surprising is the extent of his achievements in the Kennedy years, at a time when Congress frustrated such other programs as military assistance, civil defense, and the proposed reorganization of the National Guard and the Reserve. The secretary's success suggests that the idea of more centralized command had a wide appeal, particularly when combined with the rhetoric of a forceful personality who promised—and seemed to deliver—impressive savings in the operation of the vast Defense machine. The positive image of a man in charge helped to win support, often hesitant and wary but in the end admiring, for many of his reorganization plans.

CHAPTER III

Expanding the FY 1962 Budget

Just as the Eisenhower administration transformed the Defense budget inherited from the Truman administration, Kennedy and McNamara imposed their own imprint on Eisenhower's final budget. In each instance the difference was dramatic. Where Eisenhower in the name of fiscal responsibility cut Truman's FY 1954 Defense budget of $41.3 billion by some 15 percent, the Kennedy administration added almost 12 percent to Eisenhower's proposed budget of $41.8 billion for FY 1962.

As the Korean War wound down in 1953, the Eisenhower administration embraced a strategic concept of massive nuclear retaliation popularly characterized as "a bigger bang for a buck." This involved greater reliance on nuclear forces, permitting Eisenhower throughout his tenure to submit DoD budgets leaner than Truman's final one by cutting conventional forces. Only the very last Eisenhower budget reflected the growing realization by the president and his advisers that changing world conditions required increased conventional war capabilities.[1]

The Kennedy team came into office convinced that the United States needed even greater conventional capabilities than provided in Eisenhower's proposed budget. Looming crises in Laos, Vietnam, Cuba, and Berlin seemed more likely to require non-nuclear forces. Kennedy took a strong personal interest in the concept of counterinsurgency—using specially trained personnel to prevent and combat subversive insurgency and other forms of indirect aggression in friendly countries. For an overall strategic concept, the new administration adopted the idea of flexible response—the ability to respond at levels ranging through the whole gamut of military force, from counterinsurgency to massive retaliation.* The need for more resources, including enhanced major weapon systems, to provide this range of capabilities occasioned a blizzard of budget-related activity in the early months of 1961.

---

* For the Kennedy administration's emphasis on counterinsurgency and its adoption of the concept of flexible response, see Chapters II and XII, respectively.

To obtain additional funds the Kennedy administration submitted to Congress amendments to the FY 1962 budget rather than attempting a wholesale revision. The administration put forward three sets of amendments—in March, May, and July—that together proposed adding more than $5.6 billion. To further fine-tune and accelerate desired changes, it also sought supplemental appropriations to the FY 1961 budget, though in smaller amounts.* This incremental approach allowed the Kennedy White House and the new DoD leadership time needed for deliberation on the complex Defense budget issues, although the July amendments represented a necessarily hurried response to the worsening situation in Berlin.

Eisenhower's FY 1962 Budget

In his State of the Union message on 12 January 1961, a week before leaving office, Eisenhower displayed a measure of satisfaction with the nation's defenses, dismissing the so-called bomber gap as "always a fiction" and contending that the missile gap "shows every sign of being the same." However, in presenting the FY 1962 budget to Congress on 16 January, he acknowledged that "the advent of nuclear-armed intercontinental ballistic missiles in the hands of a potential adversary has confronted this Nation with a problem entirely new to its experience." To provide a deterrent against attack and ensure survival of adequate retaliatory forces should an attack occur, he urged continuation of the Navy's highly mobile Polaris submarine-launched ballistic missile and the Air Force's Atlas, Titan, and Minuteman intercontinental ballistic missiles (ICBMs), most of them encased in concrete-hardened silos. Eisenhower also observed that the emergence of the ballistic missile threat required extensive revamping of U.S. air defense forces. Accordingly, he had begun efforts to improve warning time in both land- and space-based detection systems, as well as to strengthen manned and missile air defense systems.[2]

The Eisenhower budget proposed $41.84 billion in new obligational authority (NOA),† more than three percent above the preceding year's request of $40.577 billion. The expenditure estimate of $42.91 billion was almost five percent higher

---

* During its last months in office the Eisenhower administration obtained from Congress two supplemental appropriations to the overall FY 1961 federal budget. The Kennedy administration obtained a third supplemental, enacted on 31 March 1961, which included $264.9 million for various Defense functions. On 29 May it requested a fourth supplemental that contained $15 million for retired military pay and $40 million for Army personnel. The House and Senate approved $14.5 million for retired military pay, but rejected the $40 million for Army personnel. Because it was so late in the fiscal year, the Senate Appropriations Committee recommended that the $40 million item be included in the FY 1962 appropriation bill.

† New obligational authority is the amount appropriated by Congress, including cash and new contract authorization, minus appropriations to meet previously unfinanced contract authorizations falling due during the fiscal year.

than the estimate for FY 1961 ($40.995 billion).* Both increases exceeded the inflation rate and represented a gain in real terms.

TABLE 1

Eisenhower Proposed FY 1962 Budget (NOA)
by Appropriation Category
($ billions)

Military personnel	12.266
Operation & maintenance	10.842
Procurement	13.378
RDT&E	4.349
Military construction	.985
Revolving & mgt funds	.020
Total (military functions)	41.840
Military assistance[a]	1.800

[a] Military assistance was not a part of the Defense Department budget but was customarily shown in connection with it.

Source: *The Budget of the United States, FY 1962*, 482.

The NOA request for the Army—$10.406 billion—reflected a greater emphasis on conventional warfare capabilities, although the number of divisions remained at 14. The Army would receive $1.8 billion for procurement as compared with $1.6 billion in 1961 and $1.4 billion in 1960, an increase of 29 percent over the three-year period. The Navy's budget of $12.23 billion allowed it to build 30 ships, 10 more than in the previous fiscal year, but the total number would remain the same. Eisenhower requested funds for procurement of long lead-time components for 5 additional Polaris submarines, bringing the number of authorized Polaris vessels to 19. The Navy would have 817 vessels, including 14 attack carriers. The Air Force budget—$17.856 billion—completed the funding of 13 Atlas and 14 Titan squadrons and anticipated completion of 12 Minuteman squadrons by June 1964. For the first time in 25 years no money would go for procurement of manned bombers; B-52 and B-58 production would be terminated on completion of current production schedules in the summer and fall 1962. The 84 Air Force combat wings—4 fewer than the year before—would include 34 strategic wings.[3] All told the armed forces would have 2,492,900

---

* Budget submissions also contained estimates of expenditures for the fiscal year. These estimates might be more or less than NOA and were subject to congressional change.

members, with 870,000 for the Army, 625,000 for the Navy, 175,000 for the Marine Corps, and 822,900 for the Air Force. These numbers were identical with those for FY 1961.[4]

TABLE 2

Eisenhower FY 1962 Budget
Planned Composition of Armed Forces

	30 June 1961	30 June 1962
Army		
Divisions	14	14
Battle groups	9	9
Navy		
Warships	381	381
Other	436	436
Attack carrier air groups	16	16
Marine divisions	3	3
Marine air wings	3	3
Air Force		
Combat wings	88	84
Strategic	37	34
Air defense	19	19
Tactical	32	31

Source: *The Budget of the United States, FY 1962*, 486.

Congress Defers Action

Congressional consideration of the FY 1962 budget was unusual in two respects. For one thing, work on the budget marked the beginning of a greatly enlarged role for the House and Senate armed services committees in authorizing appropriations. Previously these committees had authorized funds only for military construction. However, in the Military Construction Act of 1959, PL 86-149 (Sec. 412(b)), Congress stipulated that "no funds may be appropriated after December 31, 1960, to or for the use of any armed force of the United States for the procurement of aircraft, missiles, or naval vessels, unless the appropriation of such funds has been authorized by legislation enacted after such date." The armed services committees now had to authorize funds for the procurement of aircraft, missiles, and naval vessels—a sizable chunk of the overall DoD budget—before the funds could be appropriated. Congress approved Section 412 in the face of DoD's contention that it was unwise and unnecessary and despite the understandably cool attitude of members of the appropriations committees who felt it encroached on their turf.[5]

A second departure from custom was that the House and Senate put off substantive budget hearings for a month or more to allow the incoming administration time to reconsider the budget. Prior to Kennedy's inauguration, Director-designate of the Bureau of the Budget David E. Bell informally notified McNamara that he had worked out with the chairmen of the House and Senate appropriations committees a timetable for submitting amendments to the FY 1962 budget. Because the defense appropriations subcommittees expected to delay their hearing schedules, Bell feared that the delay, if prolonged, might set back passage of appropriation bills well into the new fiscal year. He therefore asked that proposals for revising the FY 1961 or 1962 budgets be submitted to the White House by 20 February, so that BoB and the president, after reviewing them, could formally submit amendments to Congress by 15 March. Two days before the inauguration, in a meeting with his designated key advisers, McNamara assigned tasks based on the timetable Bell had furnished, although he mentioned 1 April (not 15 March) as the target date for submitting amendments to Congress. The schedule, said McNamara, allowed them "very little time," and he did "not yet have clearly in mind the political requirements on which are based the military requirements which in turn generate the specific Defense programs."[6]

Knowing that the Eisenhower administration's authorization bill of over $10.5 billion would undergo revision, the House Armed Services Committee, chaired by Carl Vinson, decided to conduct hearings in two phases. The first, beginning with testimony by McNamara on 23 February and ending on 28 March after other DoD officials had testified, focused entirely on the U.S. military posture, the kind of overview the committee had traditionally received from the Department of Defense at the beginning of each legislative session. The second phase was to deal with the authorization bill once the new administration determined the amount of the revised authorization request.[7] Until that time the Senate Armed Services Committee also delayed its hearings.

A similar lag characterized the appropriations committees' handling of the appropriation bill ($40.804 billion)* submitted by the Eisenhower administration. On 16 February the Defense Subcommittee of the House Appropriations Committee, chaired by George Mahon, opened hearings on the bill. McNamara, however, appeared only briefly, as the subcommittee adjourned to show respect for the memory of one of its members who had recently died. The next day McNamara did not return, and JCS Chairman General Lyman Lemnitzer testi-

---

* The appropriation bill of $40,804,345 covered only funds for military personnel ($12,235,000); operation and maintenance ($10,841,945); procurement ($13,378,000); and research, development, test, and evaluation ($4,349,400). The amount in the bill for military personnel was slightly less than that proposed in Eisenhower's FY 1962 budget. Military construction and military assistance were each dealt with in separate legislation.

fied. For the next several weeks the subcommittee took testimony solely from the military services' representatives regarding their individual submissions under Eisenhower's proposed budget, focusing on military personnel and operations and maintenance. This initial phase of House subcommittee hearings concluded on 21 March.[8] Testimony by the service secretaries and other JCS members, and a return appearance by McNamara, would await the administration's decisions on the amendments it wanted to propose to the appropriation bill. Also awaiting submission of budget amendments, the Senate Defense Appropriations Subcommittee did not conduct any hearings at all in February or March on DoD appropriations.

A Quick Look by DoD and BoB

At the outset the new administration made clear that DoD programs would undergo urgent review and identified those areas where it would take immediate action. In his State of the Union address on 30 January, Kennedy announced that he had instructed McNamara to reappraise defense strategy, operations, organization, forces, and weapon systems, and to come up with preliminary recommendations by the end of February. The president would then determine, based on these recommendations, "whatever legislative, budgetary or executive action is needed." In the meantime he had directed an increase in airlift capability to assure that forces would respond "with discrimination and speed, to any problem at any spot on the globe at any moment's notice." The president had also directed acceleration of the entire missile program, including the use of unobligated shipbuilding funds to construct and place on line additional Polaris submarines at least nine months earlier than planned. Eisenhower's Polaris program called for construction of 14 submarines and the procurement of long-lead items to build 5 more. Kennedy's directive pertained to the five submarines for which long-lead procurement had been approved.[9] By focusing on airlift capability and Polaris submarines, Kennedy could achieve immediate results, in large measure because the infrastructure already existed.

Much of the administration's first meeting of the National Security Council on 1 February focused on the DoD budget, with BoB Director Bell discussing weaknesses in the existing system of budget preparation and McNamara describing actions being taken with regard to the FY 1961 and 1962 budgets, including the increase in airlift capacity and the acceleration of Polaris production. McNamara stated that he had ordered a "complete re-appraisal" of the FY 1962 budget based on reports by four task forces that were examining strategic weapons, limited war requirements, weapons research and development, and requirements for bases and installations.[10]

McNamara took prompt action in February and March to increase airlift capacity, a relatively easy and popular change. He increased procurement of Lockheed C-130E extended-range turboprop aircraft from 50 to 99 and advanced delivery of the first 50 aircraft to March instead of September 1963.[11] DoD also selected a contractor for the future C-141 jet aircraft. Like the C-130, it could perform long-range strategic and short-range tactical assignments, but it would require fewer refuelings, need less tanker support, and cost less to operate.[12]

Taking into account a Department of State paper on foreign policy considerations bearing on the Defense budget and after consulting with White House staff, McNamara submitted on 20 February the report the president had requested. This hasty review, which addressed "only the most urgent and obvious problems," drew on studies prepared by three of the four task forces. It did not cover bases and installations, on which McNamara planned to report separately, because he believed any actions taken in FY 1962 to close installations would have little effect on expenditures in that fiscal year. Overall McNamara proposed an addition of $2.008 billion to the FY 1962 budget, more than half of which would be for strategic forces and continental defense. Some 50 pages of attachments provided details on specific proposals; a separate annex tabulated the positions taken by the JCS members, most of them unanimously.[13]

Defense officials discussed the recommendations with Bureau of the Budget representatives, and on 10 March McNamara and Bell, in a joint memorandum to the president, put forward those they agreed on (discussions had produced some adjustments in specific amounts), and indicated those few areas, six in all, where they differed. For FY 1962 the BoB revisions totaled $159.5 million more than DoD's.[14]

Kennedy apparently had expressed concern about increasing the size of the military budget. His special assistant for national security affairs, McGeorge Bundy, thought the president was right in thinking it important, "but wrong in thinking that it is all-important." Bundy felt that any proposed increase in new obligational authority for FY 1962 would be less than press reports had been hinting. Moreover, "the state of the country, the state of the world, and the state of the Congressional mind" persuaded him "that that there will not be great trouble on this point."[15]

DoD and BoB had indeed sought ways to contain the additional funding. The handful of disputed areas reflected disagreements about manner and timing of funding as well as amounts. One disagreement involved Defense's proposal to use $330 million of FY 1962 funds as an increment to begin work on an additional 10 Polaris submarines, over and above the 19 already programmed, in what was termed a "second acceleration." BoB did not contest building 10 more submarines, rather the manner of funding. It proposed adding $778 million to the $330 million in FY 1962, making a total of $1.108 billion for full funding of construction of the submarines. Congress, according to BoB, would probably criticize partial funding "as a dodge" aimed at reducing the total amount of the budget revisions. Moreover, partial funding "would be an unfortunate precedent from a management standpoint." In DoD's view, full funding seemed unnecessary, but it indicated it would not object to inclusion of the additional funds. In the end Kennedy accepted BoB's recommendation.[16]

The wider spectrum of Air Force strategic weapons posed more numerous issues than did naval vessels. On two of these DoD and BoB differed slightly. One was how rapidly to accelerate the transition from the older liquid-fuel Atlas and Titan intercontinental ballistic missiles to the new solid-fuel Minuteman. The Atlas and Titan systems had proved costly, difficult to launch, and vulnerable to enemy attack. BoB wanted to cancel the last four of the planned eight-squadron Titan II program in order to reduce the anticipated increases in the FY 1962 budget. Defense wanted to cancel only two squadrons, expressing uncertainty about the reliability of Minuteman. A DoD White Paper noted that "approximately 100 Minuteman missiles dispersed and hardened" could come from the money saved by the elimination of the last two Titan squadrons. Although McNamara expressed willingness to accept BoB's position, Kennedy decided to cancel only two squadrons.[17]

Another Defense-Budget disagreement concerned the B-70 bomber under development, which the Air Force saw as the weapon of the 1970s. Perhaps because of high expectations surrounding the effort to realize the many possibilities claimed for the B-70—multiple weapon capacity, Mach 3 speed, high-altitude capability, and use as an intimidating visible deterrent—research and development of the plane had run into serious trouble by the late 1950s. Between 1958 and 1962 it underwent half a dozen major design changes and two development stoppages. Projections of its ultimate cost mushroomed. Moreover, the aircraft would not enter the inventory until Polaris and Minuteman had already become integral parts of the strategic retaliatory force. In light of these factors the Eisenhower administration opposed development of a complete weapon system. It included $354 million in the FY 1962 budget for developing only one or two B-70 prototypes, a skeletal aircraft without any combat capability.[18]

McNamara and his aides displayed perhaps even greater skepticism about the B-70. Improving Soviet air defenses, particularly surface-to-air missiles, brought into sharper question whatever virtues the B-70 might possess. Vulnerable on land and not designed to carry the air-to-surface Skybolt missile under development,* the B-70 would have to fly at subsonic speeds in low-level attacks. Gilpatric later recalled that he and McNamara, before they took office, concluded that "the B-70 was a turkey."[19]

As a result of its review Defense proposed reducing the FY 1962 funds for B-70 development to $250 million. BoB, however, recommended that the president consider canceling the entire program, in view of the "doubtful need" for such

---

* Regarding the Skybolt program, for which the Kennedy administration added $50 million in FY 1962, see Chapter XIV.

an aircraft and its extremely high projected cost. Here the president decided to continue the program, but to scale it back a little further than McNamara had recommended, to $220 million in FY 1962.[20]

The Bureau of the Budget agreed with Defense's other recommendations regarding Air Force strategic weapons, including some which curtailed or canceled important programs. One concerned the relative emphasis to be placed on the two versions of Minuteman, the fixed-site version dispersed in hardened silos or the more technically complex mobile Minuteman to be mounted on railway cars whose eventual deployment lay even further in the future. Convinced that the mobile Minuteman would incur costs incommensurate with the benefits, McNamara recommended, with Bell's concurrence, the deferral of three mobile Minuteman squadrons and the substitution in the FY 1962 budget of an equal number of fixed-site squadrons.[21]

One Air Force bomber fell victim to the quick review. McNamara and Bell recommended accelerating the already scheduled retirement from the inventory of the medium-range B-47. Under Eisenhower's FY 1962 budget the 900 operational B-47s in 1961 would have declined gradually to 720 in 1962, 675 in 1963, and 450 in 1964. McNamara proposed to reduce the 900 to 180 by 1964. The savings in FY 1962 would be relatively small, $35 million.[22]

DoD and BoB did not offer any new proposals regarding the Air Force long-range B-52 and B-58 bombers. Separately, however, McNamara decided to uphold the Eisenhower administration's decision to halt their production in calendar year 1962. OSD analysts concluded that the B-52 or any other manned aircraft, unless airborne, might not survive ICBM or bomber assaults on bases. In a choice between procuring an additional B-52 wing or putting the same resources into the less vulnerable Minuteman or Polaris, the B-52 could not compete.[23] Yet the B-52 had certain advantages: it could carry large payloads and deliver them with high accuracy. Even more persuasive, unlike Minuteman and Polaris, it could be recalled from a mission. Although B-52 and B-58 production was scheduled to be terminated in 1962, both bomber forces would remain substantially intact at least until 1970. If needed, DoD could always order more manned bombers, but not without incurring a financial penalty.[24]

The Army's Nike-Zeus anti-ballistic missile (ABM) system prompted different recommendations from Defense and Budget. The program, whose development began in November 1956, had a dubious test record. In test firings (22 in all) after August 1959, only 8 could claim partial success; 5 failed completely.[25] In December 1959 Secretary of Defense Neil H. McElroy withheld $137 million tentatively allocated for preproduction. Major continuing technical problems, high projected production and deployment costs, and a low expected rate of success all played a part in his decision.[26]

Anticipating the need for a vigorous offensive, the Army made a preemptive strike even before the new DoD team took office, claiming in a memorandum to Deputy Secretary-designate Gilpatric on 17 January 1961 that Nike-Zeus would provide early warning and an active defense in urban areas against Soviet submarine-launched ballistic missiles. Moreover, the very existence of an ABM weapon would establish "a stable and creditable deterrence." Although the Eisenhower budget provided no funds for production, the Army recommended a limited production and deployment using $73.3 million in FY 1961 funds and an additional $313.5 million for FY 1962.[27]

The JCS divided on the Nike-Zeus issue. Terming ABM "an indispensable element in deterrence," Chairman Lemnitzer won support for limited production from Admiral Arleigh A. Burke and, of course, Army Chief of Staff General George H. Decker. But he failed to persuade Air Force Chief of Staff General Thomas White, who maintained that progress in building ICBMs and their warheads was running several years ahead of ABM developments. He speculated that Nike-Zeus might have already reached its maximum technical growth. If so, the race had really ended before it started. He preferred instead developing sophisticated offensive warheads that could readily penetrate Soviet defenses.[28]

Director of Defense Research and Engineering Herbert York supported White's critique, but without the burden of service interest that the Air Force chief of staff carried. In response to McNamara's request for a "complete reassessment" of ABM activity, York estimated that at the end of FY 1961 expenditures on Nike-Zeus would reach $2.4 billion without reasonable prospects of achieving any effective urban defense. York saw no grounds for believing that the situation would change appreciably. Soviet ICBMs, he maintained, would more than counter any improvements made in the ABMs. Moreover, without a viable U.S. shelter program the Soviets could destroy populations by radioactive fallout even if opposed by a more effective antimissile defense system.[29]

McNamara did not recommend the full amount the Army wanted. Instead he proposed an additional $82.8 million in FY 1962 funds for Nike-Zeus to provide the capability for and to begin production of long-lead items. This would allow completion of the first Nike-Zeus installations about October 1965. BoB opposed the extra $82.8 million, arguing it would entail a decision to be made in the fall of 1962 about the necessary follow-on funding of $550 million in FY 1963 without the benefit of much additional development data. In accordance with the BoB recommendation, Kennedy decided to defer a decision on beginning Nike-Zeus production.[30]

All these decisions were the product of what one scholar has called a "quick and dirty look," without the benefit of systems analysis and program budgeting that would characterize McNamara's later approach to the budget.[31]

28 March Amendment

McNamara's and Bell's recommendations provided the basis for the special message on the Defense budget that Kennedy delivered to Congress on 28 March detailing a series of proposed amendments for FY 1962. The president announced his decisions to increase the number of Polaris submarines from 19 to 29, cancel the last two Titan II squadrons, defer work on the three mobile Minuteman squadrons that had been funded in Eisenhower's budget and replace them with three fixed-site Minuteman squadrons, reduce the B-70 development program by $138 million (to $220 million), terminate development of a nuclear-powered aircraft (while transferring some of the related research aspects to the Atomic Energy Commission), and accelerate the phaseout of a number of B-47 wings. Among the various proposed changes he mentioned the requirement for additional airlift funds, the need to improve air and ground alerts, and strengthening forces for limited and anti-guerrilla warfare. Altogether the changes represented an additional $1.954 billion in NOA.[32]

Congressional consideration of the Defense budget now resumed in earnest, with April and May unusually busy months for the pertinent committees and DoD officials. The administration submitted a revised authorization bill of $11.9748 billion for procurement of aircraft, missiles, and naval vessels. Of the nearly $1.5 billion added to the initial bill, $1.09 billion was for naval vessels, reflecting the major Polaris increase.[33] The Senate Armed Services Committee took up the bill on 4 April, the House Armed Services Committee on 11 April. Concurrently, the appropriations committees began hearings on an amended appropriation bill, now enlarged by nearly $2 billion. Mahon's House subcommittee hearings resumed on 6 April, and the Senate Defense Appropriations Subcommittee, under Chairman Dennis Chavez of New Mexico, began hearings on 18 April.

Inevitably questions came up that reflected the discomfort of the military services with decisions affecting their particular interests, with the Army's Nike-Zeus and the Air Force's bomber programs receiving much attention. At hearings on the authorization bill, McNamara told Sen. Strom Thurmond (D-S.C.) that he opposed production of the Nike-Zeus at the time. Thurmond expressed disappointment that the secretary was not pursuing Nike-Zeus as a "great deterrent toward an attack on this country."[34] Before the House Defense Appropriations Subcommittee, McNamara acknowledged that Nike-Zeus was well along in development and "progress has been quite satisfactory." But he had doubts about deploying the system because of technical, operating, and vulnerability problems, and Nike-Zeus was "a very expensive system in relation to the degree of protection that it can furnish." McNamara held firm that DoD would continue the weapon's development, testing, and evaluation phase, but for the present not approve production and deployment.[35]

Mahon questioned how the decisions had been reached on key strategic and defensive weapons. "I know that the decision on the NIKE-ZEUS was not written by the Army. I know the decision on the B-70 was not written by the Air Force, so who made these decisions?" McNamara answered that the president had made the decisions, "based on recommendations which I made to him, and the recommendations were my personal recommendations."[36]

McNamara defended forcefully his decision to stop full-scale development of the B-70. While nominally keeping it alive with severely reduced development funding, he left no doubt in anyone's mind that the strategic retaliatory weapon of the future was the ICBM, not the manned bomber. Sen. Clair Engle (D-Calif.) challenged the diminished funding for the B-70, suggesting instead the spending of the putative savings of $138 million "so we can look at it a year earlier, and then make the decision as to whether or not we ought to either buy it or postpone it." When pressed further about whether he wanted to develop and test the B-70 "at the earliest possible time," McNamara spoke directly: "I definitely do not. I definitely do not. I don't want any misunderstanding on this point. I think it would be a serious waste of this Nation's resources to pursue that program."[37]

Although an important factor, cost by itself did not drive DoD decisions on weapon systems. Rather, DoD weighed cost against lead time of production, reliability of performance, anticipated effectiveness, and the availability of alternative weapons. At a Senate Defense Appropriations Subcommittee hearing on 18 April, Senator Saltonstall asked McNamara to account for the anomaly of asking for more fixed-site Minuteman missiles even though he agreed that the mobile Minuteman mounted on railway cars was a more survivable alternative. The secretary replied that the fixed-site missile could be developed and deployed more quickly and so should proceed while the development of the mobile version continued. But cost was clearly important, too. DoD Comptroller Charles Hitch told Mahon's subcommittee that deferral of three mobile Minuteman squadrons would save some $80 million, given the difference between the $220 million for mobile and $140 million for three fixed-site Minuteman squadrons.[38]

The secretary's emphasis on ICBMs as the offensive weapon of the future deeply troubled the Air Force and its congressional supporters. Concern for the future of manned bombers, repeatedly expressed during the hearings of the armed services and appropriations committees, became the focal point of congressional differences with the administration's amended budget. After the House Armed Services Committee completed its hearings, McNamara met with Chairman Vinson and other members on 28 April to discuss specific changes the committee advocated in the authorization bill, particularly with respect to manned bombers and nuclear-powered frigates. The changes included the addition of one wing each of B-52s and B-58s at a cost of $525 million and $485 million, respectively; and the addition of $138 million for the B-70 in FY 1962.[39] McNamara felt he had persuaded the committee to back down on these possible changes. In return, he promised to make a statement of "full agreement" with the committee that a strong heavy-bomber force would be maintained at least through 1970, until full development of the missile systems. The secretary also accepted the committee's plan to substitute two nuclear for the three conventional frigates the administration had proposed. All told, he believed he had reduced the committee's additional authorization recommendations from $1.2 billion to $39 million.[40]

The secretary's expectations were not borne out. During a freewheeling, occasionally raucous committee markup of the bill on 2 and 3 May, Vinson was unable to persuade his fellow members to accept all the agreements worked out with McNamara. In a subsequent press release, Vinson noted that the committee would propose an additional $393.2 million, $337 million of which would be "only" for the continued production of B-52 and/or B-58 bombers. The committee "found that the Kennedy program will permit an orderly development of the B-70, and will provide an opportunity to find out a great many things about the B-70 which must be known before the final decision on its complete development can be made." The committee's report on the authorization bill supported the administration's position of continuing B-70 development without commitment to a full-scale weapon system.[41]

Both houses wanted to provide more money to allow production of B-52s and B-58s to continue beyond 1962; they differed only a little in the amounts to be provided and the phrasing of the proposed legislation. The Senate on 15 May approved an authorization bill of $12.5 billion, including everything the president had requested and an additional $525 million earmarked for continuing production of long-range manned bombers. On 24 May the House unanimously approved a somewhat smaller bill ($12.368 billion), providing an additional $337 million designated specifically for the B-52 and B-58. By voice votes on 12 June both houses approved a conference committee bill of $12.571 billion which, among other things, retained the Senate's earmarking of $525 million for long-range manned aircraft without specifying the type of aircraft. As Vinson explained, the House conferees had easily accepted the Senate language since the only bombers being produced were B-52s and B-58s. Vinson also acknowledged that "little, if any" of the extra money might be spent, "but the authority is there if it is found necessary to keep these assembly lines going." The president signed the bill on 21 June.[42]

26 May Amendment

With congressional action on the authorization bill nearing completion, Kennedy on 25 May, a week before leaving for Vienna to meet Soviet Premier Khrushchev to discuss the building tensions over Berlin, among other issues, delivered a special message to a joint session of Congress. The message dealt with "urgent national needs" the president felt required further overall budget increases for FY 1962. The additional money would serve both Defense and other governmental purposes. The most eye-catching proposal was expansion of the U.S. space program with the aim of putting a man on the moon within 10 years. Other proposals were to bolster the conventional warfare capabilities of the Army and Marine Corps, strengthen civil defense, increase foreign aid, and lower domestic unemployment. The president also indicated that he was directing McNamara to begin a reorganization and modernization of the Army,* which, he said, was developing plans "to make possible a much more rapid deployment of a major portion of its highly trained reserve forces." The new plans called for the mobilization for operations of two combat-equipped reserve divisions and supporting elements—89,000 men—within three weeks in an emergency. Eight more reserve divisions could be ready for deployment in less than eight weeks.[43]

The following day, 26 May, the White House submitted to Congress further amendments to the Defense appropriations bill in the amount of $237 million. The largest share, $138 million, would go for additional equipment for the Army and Marine Corps; another $22 million would help increase Marine personnel strength by 12,000 and provide a trained nucleus for a fourth Marine division.[44] Since none of the new requests pertained to procurement of aircraft, missiles, or ships, congressional consideration of the authorization bill was unaffected.

The amount of the requested additions was not great, the purposes uncontroversial. But the president's call for reorganization of the Army and Reserve touched a congressional nerve. Congress viewed the whole reserve issue with great political and budgetary sensitivity. On several occasions the Eisenhower administration had recommended a 10 percent reduction in the number of National Guard units and Army Reserve personnel receiving pay. It failed in each instance.[45] The prickly reserve issue came to McNamara's attention even before he took office, in a letter from Theodore Sorensen, the president-elect's assistant. Sorensen noted that Kennedy had a particular interest in the Reserve and National Guard and wanted

---

* McNamara subsequently called for an overall study of Army organization and recommendations for appropriate changes. Secretary of the Army Stahr formed a committee of military and civilian personnel headed by Deputy Comptroller of the Army Leonard W. Hoelscher. By January 1962 the secretary of defense and the president had approved the report of the Hoelscher committee with modifications.

The main features of the committee's wholesale Army reorganization plan included creation of a Materiel Development and Logistic Command and an Army Combat Developments Command; assignment of responsibility to the U.S. Continental Army Command for all individual and unit training, except for highly specialized training such as at the U.S. Military Academy and the Army War College; transfer of certain operating functions of the Army General Staff to new commands and agencies; establishment of an Office of Personnel Operations; realignment of the Army Special Staff and Operating Agencies; and the elimination of several statutory officers (the chiefs of the technical services—Ordnance, Signal, Quartermaster, Chemical, Transportation, and Finance) and transfer of their functions to other elements of the Army. This far-reaching reorganization became effective on 16 February 1962, but not until December 1964 was it fully completed. See Hewes, *From Root to McNamara*, 316-65.

McNamara to consider "whether these units have ceased to have a major role in our military posture."[46]

The president's speech did not lay out in full the long-term expectations for reorganized ground forces, active and reserve. But it did open the way. As an immediate objective in reorganizing the Army Reserve and National Guard, DoD sought to achieve maximum strategic mobility by concentrating on more and better training for 2 divisions and 18 separate combat battalions. A more flexible organization would facilitate early readiness of the divisions and integration of the separate reserve battalions into regular Army units when needed. In McNamara's words, "the 'One Army' concept must become a reality as well as a slogan."[47]

Congressional questions about that "reality" followed immediately. South Carolina Democrat Rep. John J. Riley wondered how reservists could find time for the required enhanced training while trying to earn a living at the same time. Since it presumably took six to nine months to bring a unit up to combat readiness, he doubted if any could be ready in the three weeks time McNamara had in mind. In response, McNamara stressed that the reserves would have 48 paid drills a year, at least two weeks of full-time training, and sometimes three weeks. Besides, unlike in the past, many reservists had active military experience. Riley remained unconvinced, as did Pennsylvania Democrat Rep. Daniel J. Flood, who asserted that McNamara could not be serious: "You are going to give me two Reserve line divisions in 2 weeks?"[48]

The appropriation bill worked its way through the House, with Mahon's subcommittee winding up its hearings 1 June, but not before grilling McNamara about the future of long-range bombers. The secretary emphasized that terminating production of B-52s in 1962 did not mean the end of the B-52. He thought it "too early to conclude that we will not need manned bombers in substantial numbers at the end of this decade, and therefore I conclude we must be prepared to maintain in our operational force substantial numbers through 1970."[49] He called attention to the more than 700 B-52s and B-58s that would still be operational at the end of FY 1966. "Should it be decided later," he noted in a subsequent letter to Mahon, "to maintain this level of heavy bomber aircraft beyond FY 1966, the request for appropriations can be made several years from now. There appears to be no need to make such a decision before mid-1963 at the earliest." To show the thoroughness that had gone into the decision, McNamara noted plans to preserve B-52 tooling following the completion of production so that restarting would pose no problem.[50]

On 23 June the House Appropriations Committee reported an appropriation bill of just over $42.711 billion. This included additions of some $758 million to the budget request as amended, with $449 million designated for manned bombers. It also represented cuts of $527 million elsewhere, including a flat two percent cut in procurement funds. In a unanimous vote on 28 June, the House approved the bill unchanged.[51]

The Senate Defense Appropriations Subcommittee, which had suspended hearings on the appropriation bill in June, resumed them on 10 July to hear DoD's reclama to the House bill. Under questioning Gilpatric stated that the administration took a very grave view of the Berlin situation and that the president had requested Defense and other agencies to reexamine "our needs" to deal with the situation, a point McNamara reiterated in a statement released later that day. During the hearings the new Air Force chief of staff, General Curtis LeMay, made a last effort to win support for the Air Force's manned bomber program. In a memorandum to Secretary of the Air Force Zuckert on 13 July, McNamara declared he was "shocked and embarrassed" to read in the *New York Times* that the Air Force, and particularly LeMay, was preparing to launch a vigorous campaign in Congress on behalf of greater investment in and continued production of bombers. Noting that the decision on heavy bombers had been made only after thorough discussion with Air Force civilian and military officials, he informed Zuckert that he expected "every civilian and military leader of the Air Force will support my decision and that of the President. Please make sure they understand this."[52] Yet LeMay, exercising his prerogative to offer unfettered congressional testimony, aired his criticisms of the Defense budget before the Senate subcommittee less than a week after McNamara sent his pointed memorandum to Zuckert.[53]

The Berlin Crisis and the 26 July Amendment

In June and early July tensions over Berlin steadily mounted, causing the Kennedy administration to begin planning for various military contingencies there, including the possibility of war.* Additional military forces would clearly be needed, requiring still further increases to the FY 1962 budget.

Seeking former President Eisenhower's views on the developing crisis, CIA Director Allen Dulles and General Lemnitzer joined McNamara in a visit to Eisenhower's farm in Gettysburg, Pennsylvania, on 15 July. They received a mixed message. On the one hand Eisenhower seemed willing to support additions to the Defense budget, but he also wanted actions based on "the decisions of the professionals, particularly the Joint Chiefs." On the other hand, he "would impound every nickel of non-military expenditures that didn't have to be spent." In his report to the president McNamara expressed fear that Eisenhower might use a request for additional funds as a reason for "still another attack" on non-military programs.[54]

---

* See Chapter VII.

With decisions reached on the size of the necessary military buildup, Kennedy, in a somber mood, went before the nation in a televised address on 25 July to press for further resources to deal with the situation in Berlin. On the heels of the address, the administration submitted the next day an amendment to the Defense appropriation bill, much larger ($3.454 billion) than the first two. Intended to build up limited war forces, the money requested was considerably less than the Joint Chiefs and McNamara had proposed. The Joint Chiefs had asked for an increase of 559,000 military personnel and $6.9 billion in NOA. McNamara had scaled this down to 480,000 personnel and $4.343 billion.[55] By excluding costs of mobilizing Army and Marine divisions and naval reservists, the president arrived at the eventual figure of $3.454 billion, which included $207.6 million for civil defense and encompassed expansion of Army forces, an increase in tactical air forces, improvement of airlift and sealift capabilities, and procurement of weapons and equipment for non-nuclear forces.[56]

Because procurement was involved, the authorization bill had to be amended. In an atmosphere bordering on national emergency, the process proceeded rapidly. On 27 and 28 July, respectively, the Senate and House armed services committees authorized an additional $958.57 million, adding this sum to the $12.571 billion previously authorized. Their consensus permitted quick passage of the bill by unanimous vote in both houses and its enactment into law on 3 August 1961.[57]

On 4 August the Senate approved by a vote of 85-0 the Senate Defense Appropriations Subcommittee's recommendations for an appropriation of more than $48.848 billion, including the full amount of $3.454 billion the president had requested the week before. The bill also provided money for military construction, civil defense, and revolving and management funds. In introducing the bill the subcommittee's acting chairman, A. Willis Robertson, noted that three times in his lifetime despots had miscalculated the strength of American determination to protect freedom in the world. Senate passage of the bill would "put Premier Khrushchev on notice" that the United States intended to safeguard that freedom "at whatever cost." The Senate's approval included $525 million specifically earmarked for B-52 and B-58 production, as well as $228.84 million more than the $220 million the administration had requested for development of the B-70. The day before, the Senate soundly rejected, by a vote of 87-4, an amendment proposed by William Proxmire (D-Wis.) to delete from the measure the extra money for continued B-52 and B-58 production. Proxmire referred, with little apparent effect, to recent correspondence with McNamara in which the secretary had reiterated his conviction that the extra money for the long-range bombers was unnecessary. Strongest criticism of the Proxmire amendment and defense of the additional funds came from Sens. Barry Goldwater, Stuart Symington, and Henry Jackson.[58]

The Senate bill differed in several important ways from the House bill approved at the end of June. On 9 August a conference committee resolved all the differences save one. The conferees slightly pared the additional amounts the Senate had voted for long-range bombers from $525 million to $514.5 million (reflecting the House's across-the-board two percent cut on procurement) and for the B-70 from an additional $228 million to $180 million (making a total of $400 million instead of $428 million). The only item still in dispute was the additional money the president had requested to start a fallout shelter program, which the Senate but not the House had accepted.[59]

Final agreement came quickly. On 10 August, only two weeks after receiving the president's request, both the House by unanimous roll-call vote and the Senate by voice vote approved the conference version of the bill. In separate action earlier in the day the House also approved the additional fallout shelter funds. The final bill, signed into law by Kennedy on 17 August, provided $46,662,556 billion, an amount almost $6 billion higher than the original Eisenhower bill.[60]

TABLE 3

FY 1962 Appropriations (NOA) Enacted
by Appropriation Category
($ billions)

Military personnel	12.805
Operation & maintenance	11.731
Procurement	16.675
RDT&E	5.244
Civil defense	.207
Total	46.662

Source: *Congressional Record*, 10 Aug 61, 14394-95.

The day before the president signed the bill, McNamara recommended against spending the extra money appropriated for the long-range bombers, the B-70, and the space glider Dynasoar. Kennedy did not act on the recommendation. In early October, however, McNamara repeated the advice, indicating that he was taking into account a recent Senate Preparedness Committee report and a review just completed of the Defense program for the next several years. Kennedy now approved the recommendation, a decision McNamara announced on 27 October.[61]

Given the public warnings that the extra money for long-range bombers would not be spent, the announcement came as no surprise. Critics of McNamara's buildup of missile forces, seemingly at the expense of manned bombers, now shifted their focus to the administration's withholding of the additional funds to speed development of the B-70, and the Air Force sought to make the aircraft more appealing by altering its design and augmenting its capabilities. The main lines of the bomber vs. missile argument in 1961 thus set the stage for a major controversy over the B-70 and a possible variant, the RS-70, which took place the following year.[62]

Also lingering prominently in the minds of many congressmen were concerns about the planned reorganization of the Army Reserve and National Guard. Earlier, in the spring of 1961, McNamara seemed convinced that he could reduce the strength of the Reserve, improve its overall efficiency, and bring selected units to a higher state of combat readiness. The Berlin crisis scrambled the Pentagon's planning for the Reserve reorganization, shifting the goal from a gradual and orderly change to an accelerated buildup in the summer and fall. Extending the enlistments of regulars and calling up reserve forces provided the additional strength to help meet the crisis. The chronic reserve issue would continue to receive its full share of attention in the next session of Congress.

As with any new administration, the McNamara OSD at the beginning of 1961 undertook to reshape the budget it inherited. The first amendment to the FY 1962 budget in March, formulated under tight time constraints, primarily reflected external threat perceptions and provided additional means to address them. Many of the changes involved acceleration of production programs, such as Polaris submarines and sea and airlift transport; Congress received them well. But McNamara encountered strong opposition to his emphasis on intercontinental ballistic missiles and the consequent deemphasis of armed bombers. He also found many whose belief in the eventual effectiveness of the Nike-Zeus ABM program greatly exceeded his own. The modest second amendment in May had as its chief rationale effecting a more efficient organization of the Army.

Prior to the summer of 1961, even while twice increasing the FY 1962 budget, OSD could pursue a policy of cost containment that McNamara had made a basic element of his program. But the third amendment in July underscored how external events—in particular, the growing crisis over Berlin—could shape the size of the budget. A potential conflict in Europe thus altered McNamara's plans by requiring more funds than anticipated for accelerated development and procurement of weapon systems that in other circumstances would have proceeded more slowly and at less cost. Demands for more manpower and the associated equipment constituted another growth factor in the financial equation OSD sought to solve.

The centrality of the budget in all DoD planning and programming became quickly apparent to McNamara during his first year at the helm. In the upcoming year Congress would severely test the secretary's willingness to compromise as he unveiled a new system for preparing the Defense budget for FY 1963, a budget that would bear entirely his imprint. The same issues that had caused contention within DoD and in Congress—intercontinental missiles, bombers, the B-70, Nike-Zeus, civil defense, the Reserve and National Guard—would be reprised.

CHAPTER IV

The FY 1963 Budget: Introducing the PPBS

Major alterations of organizational structures and the creation of new agencies wrought important changes in the Department of Defense throughout the McNamara years, but the core element of the McNamara revolution was the new methodology introduced at the very beginning that later came to be known as the Planning-Programming-Budgeting System (PPBS). First applied fully to preparation of the FY 1963 budget, it represented not only a different way of looking at budgets, but a different way of thinking about the functioning of the military establishment. It also provided a frame of reference intimately connected to another concept, systems analysis, intended to help the secretary of defense make decisions on a cost-effective basis using quantified data. Over time, the PPBS would permeate every area of Defense responsibilities, from the preparation of the budget to conceptions of strategy, from the composition of military forces to choices of offensive and defensive weapons.

Antecedents

Contrary to the impression some writers have left, McNamara's new approach to budget preparation did not appear "as Aphrodite from the sea, full-blown, fresh, beautiful, and topless." Its main elements—program budgeting, systems analysis, cost-benefit analysis, and multi-year costing—had deep roots in both business and government. Even the name was not entirely new. A book published in 1953 had a chapter entitled "Plans, Programs, and Budgets" in which the author called for the military services to adopt "systems of integrated planning, programming, budgeting, and operation."[1]

During the 1950s budgeting innovations worked their way into the Pentagon as the result, in part, of pioneering work done at the Rand Corporation in Santa Monica, California, for its main client, the United States Air Force. The Air Force started to make use of Rand's cost analysis and fiscal planning methods, including

The FY 1963 Budget: Introducing the PPBS 73

program budgeting, though "with something less than complete enthusiasm."[2] It also began to arrange its components along functional lines, such as strategic, air defense, tactical, and airlift forces, and to project program costs for several years.[3]

The entertainment of a new approach to defense budgeting went beyond the Department of Defense. By the end of the decade, the Bureau of the Budget, in preparing its own analyses of the DoD budget, broke it down both by traditional budgeting items and by functional categories—strategic retaliatory, continental defense, ground and sea, and supporting forces. This helped BoB discern any duplicative or overlapping expenditures in the service budgets by focusing on "the uses to which the expenditures would be put rather than the unit by which they would be used."[4]

For some observers these efforts did not go far or fast enough. Criticisms of defense budgeting focused on several lingering systemic weaknesses. One was the imposition of arbitrary budget ceilings at the beginning of the annual budgeting cycle by the White House and the secretary of defense for the guidance of the military departments and agencies. A second was the reliance on traditional budget categories—military personnel, operation and maintenance, procurement, research and development, test and evaluation, and military construction. Sensible as these groupings may have been, they gave little guidance in the vital matter of harmonizing the costs of the military programs with JCS plans and objectives.[5]

Another widely-perceived flaw was the parochialism inherent in the process. The military services devised their programs and budgets to serve their own interests regardless of whether they duplicated what another service did. No matter how much esprit de corps interservice rivalries might foster, they sometimes reached absurd and even dangerous lengths. In an especially egregious display of parochialism, an Army general shouted to President Eisenhower immediately after the Vanguard rocket engines blew up in the nation's first attempt to orbit a satellite in December 1957: "This is a great day for the Army!" Why? Simply because the Vanguard was a Navy creation, and its failure seemingly opened the way for the Army to be first in launching a satellite—its own competitive Explorer I—into orbit.[6]

A severe, persistent critic of budgeting along service lines and by traditional budget categories, former Army Chief of Staff General Maxwell Taylor, who became President Kennedy's military representative in July 1961, lambasted these practices in his autobiographical account, *The Uncertain Trumpet*, and in testimony before Congress. In 1960 he told one congressional committee:

> In spite of the fact that modern war is no longer fought in terms of a separate Army, Navy, and Air Force, nonetheless we still budget vertically in these service terms. Yet, if we are called upon to fight, we will not be interested in the services as such. We will be interested rather in task forces, these combi-

nations of Army, Navy, and Air Force which are functional in nature, such as the atomic retaliatory forces, overseas deployments, continental air defense forces, limited war expeditionary forces, and the like. But the point is that we do not keep our budget in these terms. Hence it is not an exaggeration to say that we do not know what kind and how much defense we are buying with any specific budget.[7]

Knowledgeable members of Congress, too, called for change. Toward the end of the Eisenhower administration Rep. George Mahon, chairman of the House Defense Appropriations Subcommittee, urged that the DoD budget be formulated in terms of major military missions, with appropriations categories pertaining to weapon systems, personnel, etc. grouped and costed according to their mission. Preliminary efforts to break down the budget into the categories Mahon had specified were not promising. The Navy "did not think it could be done, the Air Force doubted that it could be done, and the Army thought it could be done and submitted the best figures." As a result OSD concluded it would be quite difficult to come up with figures that Defense could stand behind in its testimony to Congress, and the initiative was dropped.[8]

Prior to his appointment as secretary McNamara had been generally aware through hearsay of the deficiencies in DoD budgeting practices. He was no stranger to innovation in financial management from his prewar classes at the Harvard Business School and application of those lessons in the Army Air Forces and at Ford.[9] Given his background and aggressive managerial style, it is not surprising that he undertook the overhaul of the Pentagon's budget machinery.

To carry out the task McNamara chose as his assistant secretary (comptroller) a 51-year-old, soft-spoken economist, Charles J. Hitch. A Rhodes scholar and veteran of the Office of Strategic Services (OSS) during World War II, Hitch went to the Rand Corporation in 1948 to organize and head its new economics division. In 1960 he became chairman of the Rand Research Council that planned Rand's research. That year he co-authored a book entitled *The Economics of Defense in the Nuclear Age*. The book, which McNamara read (apparently after selecting Hitch), criticized current budgeting practices and advocated a new program-based budget with multi-year projections. While skiing at Aspen, Colorado, during the week of Christmas, McNamara came across Hitch's name among the three-by-five index cards he had assembled of candidates to fill positions. McNamara knew what qualities he wanted in a comptroller but was having difficulty finding the right person. When he first telephoned Hitch to offer him the job, Hitch refused. Having married late in life, he and his wife had just had a child, and he was reluctant to move from the Los Angeles area. However, after the two men later met in Denver, Hitch changed his mind.[10]

At his confirmation hearing, Hitch admitted that inexperience in the budgetary field had perhaps left him unqualified for the job. Before accepting the position, he had shared his reservations with both McNamara and Wilfred J.

McNeil, the former OSD comptroller, who convinced him that the job primarily required "leadership and policy guidance," qualities they felt he had. When needed, he could turn to people on his staff with the desired budgetary experience. At the hearing a senator pointed out that McNeil, who was generally considered to have done a fine job, similarly had no accounting background.[11]

Organizational Framework: Getting Started

The new director of the Bureau of the Budget, David E. Bell, had also heard, from informed old BoB hands, about the inadequacies of the budgetary system then used in the Defense Department, which shortcomings he communicated to both McNamara and the president. Discussions among them in January and February would lead to changes in the Defense budget process that involved a longer time span—five years—and with categories organized by purpose or output of the function or mission of the military forces—the "program packages."[12]

As authority for instituting the new methodology, McNamara frequently invoked two directives from President Kennedy that he had received upon taking office: (1) to develop a force structure to meet U.S. military requirements without regard to arbitrary budget ceilings, and (2) to procure this force at the lowest possible cost. In fact, the decision to introduce the new system came during the transition period before the new administration took over. At a meeting with top aides on 18 January 1961, McNamara accepted in principle Hitch's recommendation to institute a systematic programming approach to budget preparation.[13]

Beginning the project, however, suffered delay when Hitch contracted pneumonia toward the end of January. During a discussion of Defense budgetary matters at the Kennedy administration's first meeting of the National Security Council on 1 February, Budget Director Bell focused on the weaknesses in the current system. McNamara described the immediate actions he was taking with regard to the 1961 and 1962 fiscal year budgets and indicated that during the spring the Department of Defense and the Bureau of the Budget would be developing new guidelines for preparation of the FY 1963 budget. Later that day he sent a memorandum to Hitch asking him to outline in writing the steps needed to accomplish this task, emphasizing the development by 1 July of the "guidelines and assumptions" on which to base the FY 1963 budget. Hitch wrote back on 6 February that on returning to the Pentagon the following week—an apparent allusion to the pneumonia that had hospitalized him—he would immediately start preparing the guidelines.[14]

Once back at work, Hitch moved quickly. By the end of February he established a new office of programming headed by a deputy assistant secretary to augment the existing three offices for accounting, budgeting, and management. The 31 positions initially allotted to the new office represented a small slice of the 200 some employees in the comptroller's office. To head the office Hitch selected Hugh McCullough, then involved in managing the Navy's Polaris program. It had two directorates, one for systems planning under John W. Dixon and the other for weapons systems analysis (later renamed simply systems analysis) headed by the 30-year-old Alain C. Enthoven, a former colleague of Hitch's who had left Rand the previous year to work at the Pentagon in the directorate of defense research and engineering. Enthoven had written a 45-page appendix for Hitch's book about the application of differential calculus to military choices entitled "The Simple Mathematics of Maximization."[15]

The brilliant, brash Enthoven and a number of other young analysts—a new generation of "Whiz Kids"—according to some observers came to Washington with a certain disdain for the military, not averse to asserting "their youthful civilian power." Enthoven recalled that before going to the Pentagon he had thought of writing a book about the management of the Defense Department. What distressed him as much as anything else was the "absurd notion" that the comptroller should not have anything to do with weapons, forces, and strategy. Moreover, Enthoven considered the JCS staff bureaucracy part of the problem, not part of the solution, and felt that the JCS had become a "great big political logrolling affair."[16] To Chief of Naval Operations Admiral Arleigh Burke many of the newcomers seemed arrogant and overbearing. They apparently thought that "all civilian officials of the Department of Defense were superior to all military officers, including the Joint Chiefs of Staff."[17]

On his own immediate staff Hitch had three assistants, of whom the most important may have been Henry E. Glass, his economic adviser and speechwriter. Glass provided Hitch detailed institutional memory. He had worked in the comptroller's office since 1953 and drafted the annual budget statements beginning with FY 1955. Outgoing Secretary of Defense Thomas Gates and Deputy Secretary James Douglas told McNamara and Gilpatric that Glass was "one of the most knowledgeable, competent, and helpful men on the staff," and Glass proved especially valuable during the transition period. Although Glass had a staff of three analysts, he sometimes found himself stretched by his responsibilities. Not only did he serve informally as a special assistant to McNamara and prepare the secretary's annual posture statement to Congress, but for a short time Glass also wrote speeches for Gilpatric, until he realized this additional burden was more than he could handle. Hitch came to rely on Glass as an indispensable resource. At a press conference a few years later, Hitch tried to field a particularly difficult question by at first talking in circles. Displaying a fine sense of humor, he suddenly stopped, thought briefly, then turned to Glass, "Henry, am I dodging a question to which we have an answer?"[18]

While new administrations often reflexively reject their predecessor's ways, Hitch seemed alert to the danger of exaggerating the differences with previous practice. In public speeches and congressional testimony, perhaps reflecting

The FY 1963 Budget: Introducing the PPBS 77

Glass's influence and that of another staff member who had advised him not to oversell the new system's anticipated benefits and not to break too quickly with the past, he took care to recognize and pay homage to the accomplishments of McNeil, who had served as comptroller from 1947 to 1959. In one early speech, he made a strong case for instituting change, but also stressed his intention not to discard what had been accomplished in the financial management field. "Quite the contrary," he declared, "most of what we have remains useful and necessary."[19]

Hitch knew that the job of putting together the new system would be difficult and time-consuming, telling McNamara in early March that it would take many months and perhaps years. He intended to contract immediately with the Rand Corporation, because of its expertise in systems analysis, and later with other research centers.[20]

But McNamara and Hitch differed as to how quickly the changeover should occur. McNamara, who—as Hitch put it—felt "keenly the need for this analytical tool" and wanted quick results, asked him to apply the new procedures insofar as possible to the preparation of the FY 1963 budget. Hitch recalled a detailed presentation he and his staff made to McNamara in the early spring of 1961, probably in March. Hitch wanted to apply the new procedures only to strategic forces and to phase them in over a year's time. At the end of the presentation, McNamara, who had remained unusually quiet, banged his hand on the table and announced to a stunned audience, "That's exactly what I want," but "do it for the entire defense program. And in less than a year." In 1965 Hitch recalled he recommended taking 18 months to phase in the system but McNamara shortened the timetable to six.[21]

The hurried spadework began to bear fruit in April. Having received suggestions from each service on how to improve the budget preparation process, Hitch informed the services' assistant secretaries for financial management that he and his key programming people would soon meet with them and their staffs to discuss the introduction of the new system. Setting forth his objectives and sketching the various steps envisioned in the process, he stressed the importance of identifying all major programs on a "program package" basis. His programming office, together with the services and Joint Staff, would begin immediately to define as many of these packages as possible.[22]

Hitch formally presented the new procedures to the service secretaries and Joint Chiefs of Staff, as well as to McNamara, Gilpatric, and other OSD officials, on 17 April. His programming office would try to integrate the planning, programming, and financial management functions in order to provide better tools for decisionmaking by the secretary of defense and his military advisers. The system would be keyed to continuous program decisionmaking, not just to the annual budget cycle. The most important innovation would be the programming arrangement, an examination of the major activities of the Department of

Defense grouped by functions or missions, such as Central War Offensive Forces, Central War Defensive Forces, General Purpose Forces, Sealift and Airlift, and Reserve and National Guard Forces, among others. These functions or missions would represent "program packages," interrelated groups of elements that could be considered together because they supported or were close substitutes for one another. Hitch hoped to complete the programming phase by the end of September, at which time the tentatively approved packages would form the basis for submission of the budget to the president in December.

McNamara confirmed that each major weapon system development program and all basic and applied research programs would be examined at their inception as well as at the time of production decision. He intended to examine the entire plan on paper—key elements such as the number of units, deployment schedule, estimated kill probabilities, and total estimated cost. Admiral Burke quipped that this sounded like "program birth control."

A major feature of the new approach was the development of five-year projections, expressed in forces and dollars, to serve as a basic official plan, subject to modification whenever necessary. McNamara wanted to have the multi-year plan in place by the end of the summer, but definitely no later than the beginning of 1962.

Acknowledging that some "arbitrary" budget decisions would likely be made, McNamara stressed that he wished to minimize these and to increase the number of instances where logic provided the basis for decision. As examples of previous arbitrary budgeting, he cited the amounts that in the past had been fixed in advance for military assistance and the Army Reserve and National Guard. Finally, McNamara cautioned his listeners not to get "mired down in complexity" but to "keep an eye on the broad issues and not worry too much about refinement." In principle, he said, never "build into refinement of financial data more than that required to make a decision."[23]

BoB's New Approach to the Spring Preview

Changes instituted at the Bureau of the Budget early in the Kennedy administration complemented the budgeting reforms McNamara began at Defense. For at least a decade the bureau had conducted with each federal government agency a spring budget preview for the upcoming fiscal year. The preview had produced "target figures" or "budget ceilings" within which the agencies were required to submit their fall budget estimates. The problem, as BoB Director Bell saw it, was that the bureau and the president—in both the spring and the fall—had to make detailed decisions, "resulting in unproductive effort and premature freezing of positions." To avoid this, Bell secured Kennedy's approval in April 1961 for a more flexible approach. Beginning with the FY 1963 budget preparation, the spring preview was to focus on major issues and trends for five fiscal years, not just the upcoming one. Moreover, the bureau, not the individual agency as before, would prepare the projections for the president's subsequent guidance to the agencies. The agencies were not to feel bound by the preliminary figures when submitting their estimates in the fall, so long as they included "a plan showing their recommended priorities for expenditure *within the planning figure.*" When Bell informed agency heads of these departures from past practice, he pointed out that they should consider the new procedures "somewhat experimental" and subject to refinement.[24] During the BoB-Defense preview in early May of the FY 1963 budget, Hitch used members of his own budget office, but also encouraged the military services to contribute personnel to assist in the work. Hitch emphasized that involvement would not commit the services to whatever recommended projections BoB made to the president.[25]

The government-wide spring preview resulted in overall estimated expenditures of some $86 billion for FY 1962, rising to more than $104 billion for FY 1966. The projection for FY 1963 was roughly $92.6 billion, a figure Bell thought could be reduced by one or two billion dollars, but not much more without scaling back commitments already made. He recommended that the president set the preliminary expenditure target at $91 billion. For Defense Bell recommended a preliminary figure for FY 1963 expenditures of just over $45.3 billion.[26]

In mid-June Bell informed McNamara of the bureau's preliminary projections for Defense, including new obligational authority (NOA) for FY 1963 of around $47 billion. Bell furnished McNamara a list of policy questions regarding major weapon systems and problem areas, as well as managerial and organizational issues, to serve as the basis for their discussion of Defense budget guidelines with the president. He also sent McNamara a list prepared by bureau staff indicating areas for saving money, showing specific amounts of anticipated savings. On 20 June DoD and BoB officials set a planning figure of $45.75 billion (NOA) for FY 1963. After further discussion the president reduced the target for Defense to $44.8 billion.[27] The figure, while not representing a ceiling as in the Eisenhower administration, nevertheless narrowed DoD's flexibility in preparing the budget.

The Requirements/Planning Phase

Installation of the new budgeting system in Defense capitalized on another of McNamara's innovations already under way. In March 1961 DoD components, at the secretary's request, had begun a series of studies—dubbed McNamara's "96 trombones" (the number subsequently grew to well over a hundred)—of the most critical military requirements. These were not requirement studies in the traditional military sense but rather military-economic or cost-effectiveness studies, comparing alternative ways of achieving a wide range of national security objectives, involving costs as well as objectives. The secretary assigned specific projects to the Joint Chiefs, the military departments, and members of OSD dealing with such difficult issues as attempting to estimate the forces and weapons the United States would need over the next decade to carry out the strategic retaliatory mission.*28

While many of these studies were still in preparation, Hitch issued general instructions on 13 May to the military services providing guidance on developing and submitting their program packages to his office. Specific dates for submission ranged from 3 July to 31 August. The packages included: I—Central War Offensive Forces, II—Central War Defensive Forces, III—General Purpose Forces, IV— Sealift and Airlift Forces, V—Reserve and National Guard Forces, VI—Research and Development including "Space," VII—Service-wide Support, VIII—Military Assistance Projects, IX—Classified Projects, and X—Department of Defense.†29 Soon thereafter Hitch sent detailed, supplemental instructions to each service that applied specifically to their respective program package submissions.30

How did the services react to the new system? Although Hitch's book had gained wide currency within OSD circles, he recalled that "a lot of resistance" to his ideas developed among the military. "You find lots of military people who think that costs are irrelevant and who refuse to look at the alternatives." Glass had a similar recollection. Much information, he said, "about what was in the budget was exposed by shredding it out by program. It was also a big job for them; they had to come up with the initial figures. . . . They had to increase their staffs to handle it." Admiral Burke believed that the Navy's weapon systems did not easily fit into functional or program categories and that the new framework would effectively dismantle the Navy's existing flexible approach to planning. Furthermore, for financial managers and budget officials on all the service staffs, the imposition of quantification tools and the wresting away of decisionmaking by OSD seemingly impugned their objectivity.31

The Programming Phase

The really innovative phase, the formulation of programs meant to bridge the gap between military planning and formal budgeting, came second in the process. After the military services in July and August submitted their program proposals, the comptroller's office spent approximately two weeks consolidating, analyzing, and preparing a summary of each package. The directorate of defense

---

* See p.14. Major studies included acceleration of the ballistic missile effort, defense against ballistic missiles, adequacy of air- and sealift capabilities, modernization of ground and naval forces, and the proper mix of missiles and bombers in the future.

† Subsequently some of these titles were changed. Among the changes, Central War Offensive Forces became General War Offensive Forces and later Strategic Retaliatory Forces. Further refinements in the titles and number of program packages occurred over time.

research and engineering, not the comptroller's office, had primary responsibility for reviewing submissions regarding research and engineering programs.[32]

Hitch set up a work room (also called a monitoring center or program room) in the Pentagon. All information was put on viewgraphs for projection on huge floor-to-ceiling screens. This allowed changes to be made in the projected figures that showed their effect on the overall packages. Computers were limited in use early on, but the plan was to rely heavily on them once the system became more developed. Because members of Congress, particularly the appropriations committees, were accustomed to working with the old budget categories, McNamara and Hitch decided to prepare the FY 1963 budget in both traditional and new formats. The traditional titles would be used for presenting the budget to Congress, the new program format primarily for planning and internal use within DoD. To transfer data back and forth between the two formats, the comptroller's office developed a "torque converter" to serve as a link between program and budget; the comptroller also employed the new concept of total obligational authority (TOA)—the full cost of a program for a fiscal year regardless of the year in which the funds were authorized, appropriated, or expended. Hitch thought that high-speed computers in the future would be well suited to this task.[33]

Despite the newness of the procedures and the press of time, the services, according to Hitch, submitted "surprisingly complete and thorough" information. The weakest submissions concerned General Purpose Forces, where the services, with some exceptions, concentrated on describing weapon systems and combat units instead of analyzing their effectiveness. "To some extent," Hitch observed, "Army and Navy problems here are tougher because they have more complex force structures." By the end of August, when all the submissions were in, service proposals, including military assistance but not civil defense, totaled almost $64 billion (TOA). Although the work was conducted during the height of the Berlin crisis, the deadline for finishing this program review was pushed back by only one week—to 22 September.[34]

On completion, the comptroller's office transmitted each program package summary to McNamara and Gilpatric. With the help of both civilian and military advisers, the two men went over them in great detail in light of the missions to be accomplished, the cost-effectiveness of the various options for achieving the goals, and the latest intelligence data on the capabilities of the Soviet Union and its satellites. A section that defined the issues for decision facilitated their task. Hitch felt this necessary—at least in the initial year—because so great was the number of issues that without this information, the work would be unmanageable. Hitch admitted that the definition of issues had been "tricky." "I am sure that we didn't define them to the satisfaction of everybody concerned. We tried to do it in a neutral way, and we tried to give the pros and cons wherever we could see pros and cons on the issues." Little criticism arose about definition of the issues. "In fact, all of the reviewing agencies simply accepted our definition of the issues and gave their advice on those issues as defined."[35]

On 11 September McNamara provided the service secretaries, Joint Chiefs, and OSD staff a status report and a timetable for remaining actions on the budget. In doing so he strongly suggested the need for substantial trimming. Already he had completed his review of the Offensive War Forces package, had briefly gone over research and development issues, and had the Sealift and Airlift Forces package currently under review. He definitely planned to examine the important General Purpose Forces package before 23 September, the date when he would send the services the assumptions for use in preparation of their budgets. But he implied that he might not be able to review all the packages by then.

During the last week in September McNamara thought he might discuss with the president "tentative financial levels," since Kennedy had already received from the Bureau of the Budget, the Council of Economic Advisers, and the Treasury Department estimates regarding the government's general revenue situation. As for the DoD budget, McNamara did not want "dollar limits" to be the basis for budget decisions. "Nevertheless," he added, "we must consider the resources of the country." The submissions of nearly $64 billion (TOA), he felt "offhand," were too high. He called attention to the fact that they had already added $6 billion (NOA) to the FY 1962 budget through amendments. His preliminary review of the service submissions for FY 1963 had revealed many items "where we don't receive value for the costs involved." Moreover, many items seemed "out of balance internally within the Services and between the Services."

In any event the services would have a month—until 23 October—to submit their budgets. Hitch's staff and BoB analysts would then take about five weeks to try to isolate fundamental issues and controversial items. Prior to submitting the final budget to the president on 1 December, McNamara hoped to have a full series of discussions with the service secretaries and the Joint Chiefs. In the past the chiefs, he understood, had taken part in only some of the budget discussions. This year he wanted to include them in all the discussions.[36]

On 22 September, conceding he had not had as much time as he would have liked, McNamara sent the services and the chiefs his tentative decisions. The total for all programs was just under $54 billion (TOA), a substantial reduction from the nearly $64 billion originally requested by all DoD elements. His estimates, the secretary admitted, were approximate and in many instances still high, but they would receive further scrutiny once the budget review began. Since the major objective during the Berlin crisis looked to building up combat power, McNamara highlighted the importance of cutting back in areas that contributed little to combat strength, adding, "I have dealt severely in the program review with all programs I so identified."[37]

TABLE 4

Military Services' Program Estimates for FY 1963
and Secretary of Defense 22 September 1961 Guidance
(TOA $ billions)

Program	Services' Estimates	McNamara's 22 Sept Guidance	Reduction
General war offensive forces	10.39	8.93	-1.46
General war defensive forces	3.61	3.03	-0.58
General purpose forces	22.12	18.81	-3.31
Sealift and airlift forces	1.48	1.27	-0.21
Reserve and National Guard	2.46	1.80	-0.66
Research and development	7.14	5.42	-1.72
Service-wide support	13.03	11.06	-1.97
Department of Defense	0.74	0.68	-0.06
Retired pay	1.01	1.01	0
Military assistance	1.70	1.70	0
Total	63.68	53.71	-9.97

Source: Compiled from draft memo McNamara for Kennedy, 6 Oct 61, *FRUS 1961-63*, VIII:160. In his own guidance estimates, McNamara also included an additional $500 million in a miscellaneous category and projected reductions of $3 billion to be obtained from refining cost estimates and eliminating non-essential items.

The First Draft Presidential Memorandums (DPMs)

The five-year projections proved a difficult task, in part because of disagreements between the Joint Chiefs, as might be expected, on several issues, notably the relative merits of individual weapon systems. In July the chiefs tried to produce a corporate opinion on force levels for fiscal years 1963-67, but failed, disagreeing on virtually all the important weapon systems. The new Air Force chief of staff, General Curtis LeMay, stood at the center of the discord. He urged replacing aging B-52 bombers with newer models and producing larger numbers of Skybolt, Titan, and mobile and fixed Minuteman missiles than the other chiefs would accept. Except for the occasional backing of JCS Chairman General Lyman Lemnitzer, LeMay found little support among his colleagues. Since LeMay considered Minuteman more cost-effective than Polaris, he favored producing additional Minuteman missiles rather than enlarging the Polaris force. All the other JCS members, however, wanted the Polaris program to continue beyond the authorized 29 boats. Although they felt that production of fixed Minuteman missiles should continue beyond the 600 authorized for FY 1964, it was too early to set the ultimate force level. Despite a request from McNamara that they reconsider their positions, the chiefs advised him on 15 August that each one had reaffirmed his previous stance. Given this lack of agreement, McNamara turned to his own staff to assemble the projections for long-range nuclear delivery systems.[38]

Sometime during the summer of 1961 McNamara developed a method, which he would employ throughout the remainder of his tenure as secretary, to pull together for the president's consideration a wide variety of information on important strategic and budgetary matters and to stimulate discussion, however contentious, on what was needed. The idea of a draft presidential memorandum (DPM) emerged during work by OSD staff members, including Enthoven, on a paper for the president examining the strategy of massive retaliation and U.S. nuclear weaponry through testing the implications of different assumptions. The suggestion was made that such a review should be extended to other areas. McNamara had these draft memoranda prepared initially by the OSD staff so they would be written "without compromise or bargaining with other interested parties." He also conceived of the DPM as a "device to get the views of appropriate departments for my own review" and insisted that each interested party comment. By circulating them back and forth between himself, the service secretaries, and the Joint Chiefs, McNamara felt he could "force the divergent views to the surface." [39]

Preparation of the first several DPMs supported and supplemented the review of certain program packages in the FY 1963 budget being conducted by the comptroller's office in late August and early September. On 29 August McNamara circulated to the service secretaries and Joint Chiefs the first DPM, which contained his recommendations for long-range nuclear delivery forces during the period 1963-67. Having received their comments, he followed this up with a revised version on the same subject dated 23 September. In the meantime, he also circulated a DPM on sealift and airlift forces on 1 September.[40]

It is not clear whether McNamara discussed his tentative budget decisions with Kennedy late in September, as he said he might do. However, he did send to the president on 6 October three draft presidential memorandums. The covering DPM of that date summarized his preliminary budget recommendations for FY 1963 and projected costs and force structures for four subsequent years. He appended to it the revised DPM of 23 September on long-range nuclear delivery forces and a DPM dated 30 September transmitting his recommendations regarding the Nike-Zeus antimissile system.[41]

In the covering DPM, McNamara noted that the service and related proposals for the program packages averaged about $15 billion more per year over the period FY 1963-FY 1967 than his own recommendations. The budget estimates had been based on the assumption that the Berlin crisis would ease by the beginning of FY 1963. His recommendations for that fiscal year, which came to almost $10 billion less than the services had asked for, also called for fewer combat

The FY 1963 Budget: Introducing the PPBS   85

units and at manning levels lower than those the services proposed. Among his more significant recommendations on specific weapon systems: disapproval of an Air Force proposal to purchase additional F-106 interceptor aircraft to replace F-102s; continuation of the B-70 bomber only as a development program without approving it as a full weapon system, as the Air Force proposed; deployment of Nike-Zeus missile defense for six cities; and construction of a conventionally powered attack aircraft carrier (the Navy wanted it to be nuclear-powered).[42] While the White House pondered McNamara's DPMs, the Pentagon proceeded with the budgeting phase.

The Budgeting Phase

If the new procedures worked as hoped, Hitch expected the final phase that took place each fall—the traditional budgeting exercise—to proceed smoothly and quickly.[43] Within the comptroller's office this work fell to the deputy assistant secretary of defense (budgeting), Joseph S. Hoover, and his staff. The first time around with the new procedures, however, it proved more complicated and drawn out than Hitch may have anticipated.

The services and other DoD components submitted their formal budgets on 23 October, accomplishing in a month what had usually taken five months.[44] Their proposals, not including funds for civil defense and the military assistance program, totaled $52.734 billion (TOA), some $1.122 billion more than McNamara's guidance ($51.612 billion). A large portion of the additional amount, $586 million, pertained to classified projects, an area for which McNamara had provided no guidance. All three services came in under the amount set for General Purpose Forces. The largest increases in percentage terms were those for the Sealift and Airlift Forces package, where the Air Force requested an additional $278 million, nearly a 23 percent increase over what McNamara had tentatively decided. For Central War Offensive Forces both the Navy and the Air Force requested additional sums, but relatively modest as a percentage of the total amounts.[45]

What followed proved in large measure a reenactment of the customary hectic process of finalizing the DoD budget under tight deadlines, but with certain new features. The deep involvement of the secretary provided the major new element, although refinement of the services' budget proposals took place on several levels within DoD. The OSD comptroller's budgeting staff, together with BoB representatives, conducted a detailed review of the service budgets, after which they presented their recommendations to the secretary for decision. A second level of scrutiny involved another intensive review by McNamara. On 7 November he informed the service secretaries and JCS Chairman Lemnitzer that during the next two weeks he would be making decisions on the budget proposals, written notice of which they would receive on a day-to-day basis. If they desired reconsideration, they were to bring their appeals to his attention within three days.[46] McNamara later said that he and Gilpatric shared the review responsibilities, but a random check of the decisions indicates that McNamara made the overwhelming majority of them. The two men went over some 560 individual items, transmitting their judgments back to the service secretaries and to the Joint Chiefs in the form of subject/issue sheets that came to be called "snowflakes."[47]

Still another level of review involved responding to the service appeals or reclamas. For example, McNamara rejected the Air Force appeal regarding the B-70 aircraft—for $398.3 million in FY 1962 funds and $675.8 million in FY 1963. On DDR&E's recommendation, in late November McNamara upheld his earlier decision that no additional FY 1962 money be spent and that only $171 million be spent in FY 1963.[48]

In the meantime, McNamara's invitation to the service secretaries to comment on the long-term projections contained in his draft presidential memorandums produced a mixed reaction. Only one, Navy Secretary John Connally, expressed general satisfaction with the recommended force levels. While indicating that higher levels than those McNamara had proposed would bring significant advantages, Connally did not believe them "absolutely essential" to national security. The Navy response may have been influenced in part by McNamara's decision a few days before to increase Navy manpower levels. Although McNamara had initially set Navy strength at 640,600, Connally and new Chief of Naval Operations Admiral George Anderson persuaded him that the Navy needed at least 28,000 more men. "I have thought for some time," McNamara noted in agreeing to the increase, that "the Navy has exercised tighter control over its personnel than either the Air Force or the Army."[49]

On the other hand, Air Force Secretary Eugene Zuckert and Chief of Staff LeMay submitted detailed memorandums taking exception to the strategic force levels. "I cannot urge too strongly" a reconsideration of decisions concerning long-range nuclear delivery forces, Zuckert told McNamara. He felt McNamara had rejected the strengths needed for "a credible option to pre-empt in general war. This rejection is by choice, not through necessity." Zuckert recommended raising the levels to those proposed in the Air Force budget submission for FY 1963. Obviously unimpressed, McNamara wrote in the margin of the memo, "After repeated requests the AF has failed to supply any quantitative analysis of the deficiency in the force we propose or any such analysis in support of the AF recommendations."[50]

The Army, too, had trouble with spending and force levels. Army Secretary Elvis Stahr continued to urge more funds for procurement of Army equipment and ammunition and to argue for an Army force structure of 16 divisions with a strength of 1,055,700 men, rather than the 14 divisions and 929,000-man level McNamara had proposed. Stahr cautioned against assuming that a lowering of tension over Berlin would justify reducing U.S. military might. "If there were no

Berlin threat," he stated, "I am convinced that we still would have a requirement to maintain at least our current level of combat readiness for the indefinite future. The Communist threat is a constant one, and one that we must be prepared to challenge in its varied forms at any time and on any front."[51]

At a meeting with McNamara on 13 November, all the chiefs except Army Chief of Staff General George Decker agreed that 14 divisions "were sufficient to support our tactical and strategic plans, and that in any event 14 divisions should be properly equipped before new divisions were added." Noting that he and Gilpatric shared the view of the majority of the chiefs, McNamara thought it wise, in order to permit the earliest possible deactivation of two reserve divisions, to provide in the budget for sufficient funds and personnel to permit activation as rapidly as possible of two additional regular Army divisions. He authorized Stahr to increase the Army's budget proposal by an amount necessary to accomplish this objective and to increase Army strength from 929,000 to 960,000. McNamara asked Stahr to prepare a detailed plan and time schedule for establishing the new divisions and bringing them to a combat state of readiness.[52]

White House Decisions

Concurrent with the various levels of budget review within the Department of Defense the White House staff also examined McNamara's tentative recommendations to the president. Reviewers included Military Representative Taylor, Special Assistant for National Security Affairs McGeorge Bundy, Special Assistant for Science and Technology Jerome Wiesner, Special Counsel Theodore Sorensen, and Budget Director Bell. In a memo to the president on 13 November, Bell spoke for them all in praising "the enormous advances in concept, clarity, and logic" that McNamara had introduced into the planning and budgeting process and the "literally revolutionary" changes evident in the preparation of the FY 1963 budget compared with its predecessor. Among the major issues causing disagreement among the White House advisers were the overall size of the strategic retaliatory force, the level of conventional forces, and specific weapon systems such as Minuteman and Nike-Zeus. Although the military services, particularly the Air Force, as well as the JCS had proposed force levels higher than McNamara's, Bell felt McNamara's "impressively logical analysis" of the relative capabilities of U.S. and Soviet forces had persuaded the White House staff that higher force levels were not needed. Nevertheless, it seemed to most of them that McNamara's proposed force levels still looked higher than "purely military grounds" would justify. However, Bell recognized that the U.S. public might have difficulty accepting a slowing down of missile development programs. As for specific weapon systems, the White House advisers agreed that spending $1 billion for development and procurement of 100 mobile Minuteman missiles appeared "questionable."[53]

On the key issue of increasing Army personnel and the number of regular Army divisions from 14 to 16, which Bell did not directly address, the Army received strong backing in the White House from General Taylor. According to Glass, the additional two divisions were "rammed down" McNamara's throat because of Taylor's influence with the president.[54]

The decision on the number of divisions came over a period of days. On 20 November McNamara told his staff of general agreement on the overall force structure for all the services, but not the cost of operating these forces. He believed costs could be cut by an additional $3 billion "without adversely affecting or reducing the force structure." During the next week he would be sending out daily decisions on budget matters, which he urged them not to appeal if they could live with them. Some programs would not be canceled, but simply deferred. One of the many changes discussed with the president the previous week, he noted, concerned the addition of two regular Army divisions. To effect this change required a careful plan to adjust tours of duty and dependency travel and to return two National Guard divisions to reserve duty once the Berlin crisis abated.[55] At a meeting at Hyannis Port, Massachusetts, over the Thanksgiving weekend, the president reportedly "took the initiative in arguing for a higher level" of Army manpower, directing McNamara "to take another look at the numbers implications." Expectations, however, were that McNamara would go no higher than 980,000.[56]

A second major issue relating to Army manpower centered on a proposal under study since the spring of 1961 to reorganize the National Guard and Reserve. Over the years efforts had periodically been made to cut the size of the Guard and Army Reserve but had been defeated by strong public and congressional opposition. Not only had the Berlin crisis during the summer of 1961 diverted attention from the Army reorganization planning the Kennedy administration had initiated, but the problems encountered in the subsequent partial mobilization had shaken assumptions on which the administration had begun to consider reorganization. The Army produced 19 revisions of the plan before submitting it in mid-November to the OSD comptroller's office.[57]

McNamara forwarded the plan with some changes to the president on 7 December. The secretary's memo focused on the details of the reorganization and how to present it to the public, not the cost. To meet contingencies requiring rapid limited mobilization, McNamara contemplated a smaller reserve force but at a higher state of readiness. He wanted to reduce the combined authorized strength for the Army National Guard and Reserve from 700,000 to 670,000 and eliminate 10 divisions, but did not specify how the cut would be allocated. The overall 30,000-man reduction, he pointed out, would be offset by the addition of the two active Army divisions. Six reserve divisions, along with nine brigades and the non-divisional units needed to reinforce the active Army, would have priority and would receive about two-thirds the amount proposed for the entire reserve program. They would receive increased manning and equipment as well as more full-time technicians than the current priority units.

And readiness would be increased. By the end of 1964 the readiness objectives for the new priority divisions would be five to eight weeks, a marked improvement over the current four to six months for deployment of priority divisions. The Army wanted to eliminate only 8 instead of the 10 Reserve and National Guard divisions recommended by McNamara, on the assumption that a smaller reduction might lessen political opposition to the proposed reorganization. Nevertheless, McNamara had discussed his recommendations with Stahr, who told him that he and General Decker considered them "militarily acceptable." McNamara had asked the Army to prepare a detailed plan for implementing and explaining the program, portraying it "not as a device for reducing the role of the Army Reserve Components but rather as an effort to enhance the capability of these components to meet the present day military needs." Presented in this way, McNamara told the president, he felt the plan "should be acceptable to reserve leadership, Congress, and the public."[58] But when a summary of the plan leaked in the *New York Times* a week later, intense opposition quickly developed and persisted until completion of congressional action many months later.[59]

Toward the end of the budgetary review, probably during the first week in December, McNamara and Bell met to resolve remaining differences over the main issues. Previously, the secretary of defense or the OSD comptroller had gone to the Bureau of the Budget office for this final discussion. McNamara changed this. He had Bell and his staff come to the Pentagon and assemble in the secretary's dining room, perhaps the first time that a department head had not conducted this final reconciliation on Budget's home turf. As Glass recalled, "McNamara sat at the head of the table, as the judge.... He would take the role of the President, in other words, reconciling the differing points of view." He proposed "to reduce to a minimum the number of issues which the President had to resolve."[60]

On 7 December McNamara sent Bell his final recommendations calling for almost $50.77 billion NOA for military functions of the Department of Defense, including $692.5 million for civil defense.[61] Amid reports that a balanced overall federal budget still had not been reached, the president returned to Washington from Palm Beach, Florida, on 9 December to meet with Bell and McNamara. At this meeting, also attended by Gilpatric and Hitch, the conferees decided on the general dimensions of the DoD budget. Afterward Hitch reported to the service secretaries, chiefs, and OSD staff that McNamara appreciated how "rough" the budget review had been and that it had produced a "tight budget," so tight that DoD had to make clear to Congress that any additional cuts would have serious repercussions. Gilpatric reminded everyone that he and McNamara had taken seriously the "responsibility of not operating under a fixed budget ceiling."[62]

The budget was finally "put to bed" at a White House meeting on 11 December, with the president deciding in favor of 100 extra fixed Minuteman missiles to bring the total to 200, as McNamara had recommended, but deleting from the budget funds for the mobile Minuteman and canceling that program. Still unconvinced of the wisdom of eventually deploying Nike-Zeus, Kennedy decided against procurement of the weapon in FY 1963. Bell had been recommending that $48.5 billion represent an expenditure target for Defense, and throughout December he insisted on further cuts. Although the press speculated that some last-minute budget decisions reflected efforts to stay under budget ceilings, DoD sources "scrupulously" insisted that no ceilings had come into play.[63]

Despite continued pressure from the Air Force to increase the numbers of fixed Minuteman missiles even more, McNamara, as well as the president, held firm. On 23 December Gilpatric received a briefing from LeMay summarizing a new study confirming the Air Force's earlier conclusions on the need to proceed immediately on production of the B-70 and to budget for a considerably larger hardened and dispersed Minuteman force of 900 missiles plus long lead-time construction of additional missiles in FY 1963 in order to preserve the option to go to a larger force later. LeMay planned to present the same argument to the president the following week, but White House Deputy Special Assistant for National Security Affairs Carl Kaysen urged Kennedy to avoid giving him a definite response on the B-70 since a decision could be postponed at least until the end of 1962. Kaysen pointed out that "no one outside the Air Force now foresees going ahead beyond the three prototypes to a procurement program for a variety of reasons, including high cost ($50 to $100 million per aircraft) and doubt as to whether the design proposed can perform the missions envisioned for the B-70." Kaysen also thought LeMay would raise the need to increase the number of fixed Minuteman missiles, noting that the Air Force wanted 2,600 by 1967, while SAC officers informally were talking about 8,000 or 10,000 by that time. Again he pointed out no need for an immediate decision.[64]

On 3 January 1962 the president met with the Joint Chiefs, McNamara, Vice President Johnson, and others in Palm Beach to review the Defense budget. The Air Force remained unresigned to certain decisions. Vice Chief of Staff General Frederic H. Smith, Jr., attending in LeMay's absence, while gratified that the budget included five additional fighter wings for the Air Force and increased airlift capacity, reiterated strong Air Force concerns about what it considered deficiencies in strategic nuclear weapons in the period after 1965. Among other things, Smith called for funding an additional 100 Minuteman missiles in FY 1963 and "at the very least" proceeding with development of the B-70 as a full weapon system. Kennedy expressed a willingness to hear LeMay make another presentation on the force structure, but he stressed that the Air Force should be ready to show how additional forces would enhance overall U.S. military strength versus that of the Soviet Union. Both the president and McNamara emphasized that the strategic force levels had not been "dictated by availability of funds or other budgetary considerations."

The other chiefs went along. General Decker remarked that the Army had "done well by" the budget, although the personnel ceiling remained rather tight. He reiterated the Army's support for proceeding as soon as possible with Nike-Zeus production. The reorganization of the reserves had "military advantages," but Decker recognized the difficulties that would be encountered in cutting the number of National Guard or Reserve divisions. Like Decker, Admiral Anderson expressed general satisfaction with the budget—it would support a "better Navy" and the Navy could "live with" it—but he thought maintenance and personnel funds would be tight. Anderson also made the case for the new carrier included in the budget and went over the rationale for giving it conventional rather than nuclear propulsion. Marine Corps Commandant General Shoup declared that preparation of the FY 1963 budget had been superior to any he had witnessed in the past seven years.[65]

On 9 January McNamara briefed congressional leaders of both parties, whom the president had invited to the White House, on the new budget.[66] Right up to the last minute Kennedy and BoB, in consultation with McNamara, made about a dozen changes, apparently seeking to attain an overall balanced budget. The new revisions, mostly cuts, accounted for a further net reduction of some $600 million from the figures McNamara had submitted in early December.[67]

Notwithstanding all the trimming, DoD still took a huge chunk of the budget Kennedy formally presented to Congress on 18 January 1962. Estimated overall expenditures came to $92.5 billion, about what Bell had projected the previous spring. DoD expenditures, including military assistance, totaled $49.7 billion, considerably more than Bell's spring projection. The $51.6 billion (NOA) for the Department of Defense represented the largest peacetime defense budget in history. Even though an increase had been expected, it exceeded expectations.[68] The breakdown by program is shown in Table 5.

The budget rested on two optimistic assumptions. The first, which directly affected the Defense portion and on which McNamara had all along based the budget preparation, posited that the Berlin crisis would not extend into FY 1963. The second, more general, anticipated continued robust economic recovery from the 1961 recession, permitting the president to project an increase in receipts of $10.9 billion over the previous fiscal year and an operating surplus of as much as $4.4 billion.[69]

A Lasting Impact

Though it had drawbacks and detractors, the Planning-Programming-Budgeting System the Department of Defense hurriedly inaugurated during 1961 proved extremely durable. Constantly modified, it continued to serve as the

Table 5

January 1962 Budget Estimates for FY 1963 Program
($ billions)

Strategic retaliatory forces	9.4
Continental air and missile defense forces	2.1
General purpose forces	18.4
Sealift and airlift	1.3
Reserve forces	1.9
Research and development	5.7
General support	12.8
Civil defense	.7
Military assistance	1.5
Proposed legislation	.2
Total obligational authority	53.9 [a]
Less prior year funds	2.3
New obligational authority	51.6

[a] Discrepancy due to rounded figures.

Source: *The Budget of the United States, FY 1963*, 58.

---

foundation for budgeting procedures within DoD and spread elsewhere in the federal government. In August 1965 Kennedy's successor, Lyndon Johnson, favorably impressed by the results at Defense, mandated its adoption by all federal agencies. Some, like the Department of State, tried but had difficulty making it work. Perhaps PPBS was better suited to agencies with program-oriented activities. Or, as one writer has observed, perhaps "PPBS works best for an aggressive master; and where there is no master, or where the master wants the machinery to produce his decisions without his own participation, the value of PPBS is likely to be modest and, depending on the people, may even be negative."[70]

Certainly McNamara was an aggressive master. Hitch has pointed out that PPBS gave the secretary of defense the necessary tools for exercising his authority to unify the activities of the military services. And McNamara forcefully used these tools. But the new system not only provided him greater control over the budgeting process, it also demanded more time, requiring that the secretary familiarize himself with the details and relative merits of a multitude of proposals. When Hitch unveiled the new system in the spring of 1961, a member of the Joint Staff remarked, "Good. From now on, whenever the Secretary of Defense wants to cut the Army's budget, he will have to name the units."[71]

McNamara was aware of criticism that he and his staff ignored the advice of the professional military men. He therefore went to great lengths to consult with the Joint Chiefs of Staff and even had a compilation made of the number of his meetings with the chiefs regarding the FY 1963 budget—18 in all—which Lemnitzer later mentioned in his congressional testimony.[72] He also made sure that the service secretaries, as well as the chiefs, received and were encouraged to comment on the budget submissions of all parties involved.

In one sense, all this represented a broadening of participation in the budget preparation. Viewed from another perspective, however, PPBS represented a concentration of power in McNamara's and OSD's hands, for they conceived and inaugurated the system, provided the fiscal guidance, defined the controversial issues, drafted the memorandums to the president, made the final budget recommendations, and accepted or rejected the services' reclamas.

Some saw in the greater concentration of power a danger that lower-level doubt and dissent would be stifled. Since the new system reduced bargaining between OSD and the services, it might tempt OSD "to ignore or simply not to hear things it would rather not hear—other beliefs about technological change, different estimates of costs and gains, conflicting views of the contingencies and uncertainties." Thus Defense programs might become "more nearly tailored to one estimate of the future and to one cost-benefit calculus than in a period when decision-making was less centralized."[73]

Others feared that the new system diminished the roles of the service secretaries. Dissatisfaction with the preparation of the FY 1963 budget, no doubt, contributed to the resignations of Navy Secretary Connally and Army Secretary Stahr, as well as to the near-resignation of Air Force Secretary Zuckert. Just before Christmas 1961, Connally, upset with McNamara's handling of the airlift and sealift portion of the FY 1963 budget, announced his intention to return to the state of Texas to seek the gubernatorial nomination. He was the first Kennedy appointee to leave the administration. Stahr stayed on until the following June, when he left to become president of Indiana University. In an interview he praised McNamara personally, but decried the over-centralization of decisionmaking in the hands of the secretary and his aides. As an example, Stahr cited McNamara's personal review of each of the hundreds of subject/issues in the final stages of the budget preparation, some dealing with millions of dollars but others with much smaller amounts. While he thought this reflected admirable dedication on McNamara's part, it also represented a kind of "overreaching" for personal control.[74] McNamara's involvement in every detail of the budget process was so great that it prompted concern among some DoD officials as to what would happen if he became incapacitated. They doubted whether a substitute or a successor would have his capacity for handling such a large volume of work.[75]

Rather than resign, Zuckert decided to adapt to McNamara's way of operating. He had thought about leaving as a result of mounting frustration over a series of clashes with OSD, but instead convened a meeting of key advisers in December 1961 at Homestead Air Force Base in Florida. He told them that the Air Force had been losing to McNamara on budget issues and needed to improve the quality of its position papers and briefings, which had failed to impress McNamara and others in OSD. Zuckert, having first met McNamara in 1940 when they were on the faculty of the Harvard Business School and having maintained contact with him after the war, may have known him better than anyone in the administration. He later observed that McNamara, "as I had learned from long association, is pragmatic and basically unsentimental about his work. He believes simply that if what you are asking is not in harmony with what he wants you to do, he should reject your proposal, and he should not feel sorry for you."[76]

Notwithstanding the criticism, the new procedures accomplished much of what McNamara had hoped for. He took special pride in the avoidance of the arbitrary budget ceilings formerly employed. Constraints, of course, did come into play, but of a different nature. By an "arbitrary" budget ceiling, Hitch carefully noted in January 1962, "I mean one that has been decided in advance independently of the job to be done or the program approved—not the use of ceilings on particular programs as a management tool to enforce financial discipline."[77]

For McNamara, renunciation of budget ceilings became a matter of doctrinal rectitude. Adhering too rigidly to President Kennedy's instruction on the matter, he was reluctant to admit they could intrude in any form into the budget calculations. When speaking of constraints he seemed to avoid even using the word "ceiling." According to Glass, McNamara "insisted on maintaining to the bitter end that this country can afford whatever defense program it needs . . . that we start with the program, and whatever that program costs, that's what we ask for." Glass pointed out that McNamara obviously "had to keep in mind the overall federal budget and fit the Defense program into that"—and some of the secretary's private comments during the FY 1963 budget preparation reveal his recognition of this need. But McNamara's way of reviewing a program allowed him to "keep working it over until he got it within the necessary bounds. . . . This is what he had in the back of his mind, even though he would not acknowledge it." McNamara refused to "acknowledge that he had to fit the Defense program into the total federal budget, so we had to keep that policy line going in everything having to do with him."[78]

Pressures in the other direction, such as the need to satisfy Congress of the adequacy of the proposals, may have also been at work. A story has been told that at some point in 1961 several White House aides tried to arrest the growth in the number of U.S. missiles. The United States had 450 missiles, McNamara wanted to increase the number to 950, and the Joint Chiefs wanted 3,000. The White House staffers had learned, however, that 450 missiles were just as effective as twice that number. When the president addressed the issue, the following exchange reportedly took place with McNamara:

"What about it, Bob?" Kennedy asked.

"Well, they're right," McNamara answered.

"Well, then, why the nine hundred and fifty, Bob?" Kennedy asked.

"Because that's the smallest number we can take up on the Hill without getting murdered," he answered.[79]

Another source of pride was the adoption of five-year force projections, a feature, like PPBS, that became permanent not only in the Department of Defense but throughout the federal government. Hitch realized that only the planning for FY 1963 had much validity and that the initial long-term projections for FYs 1964-67 were of necessity "very, very crude and rough." For that reason he and McNamara decided not to use them in their presentation to Congress on the FY 1963 budget. Hitch marveled, however, at McNamara's persistence and foresight in developing the multi-year projections. "It just meant a hell of a lot of quick, arbitrary decisions," Hitch said, "but I've never seen a man so hard to discourage; and, in the end, he was right."[80]

Hitch remained as comptroller until 1965 when he returned to academic life. His own quiet persistence—as well as his gentlemanly demeanor, balanced explanations of the new system, and clear vision of what he hoped to accomplish—may have contributed as much or more to the successful launching of PPBS than McNamara's forceful managerial style. In any event McNamara highly valued Hitch's contributions, recalling him to be a "superb" comptroller, not so much in an accounting sense, but more in the area of strategic planning and the derivation of force levels from that planning.[81]

However much the introduction of PPBS constituted a positive, far-reaching achievement for McNamara, Hitch, and others in OSD, it came at substantial cost, too. Not only did the new process leave service sensibilities bruised, particularly the Air Force's, but the resulting budget provoked major controversies with Congress, in part because of perceived shortcomings in the way it had been prepared.

Chapter V

Congress and the FY 1963 Budget

Congressional consideration of the FY 1963 Department of Defense budget presents something of a paradox.* On the one hand, although the requested amount of $47.907 billion was the largest since the Korean War, the appropriation bill—in the words of one scholar—"slipped through Congress almost unnoticed."[1] Floor debate evoked little partisanship despite the congressional elections scheduled for the end of the year. On the other hand, two intense controversies erupted during committee hearings. They centered on the issue of legislative versus executive powers, specifically (1) whether Congress could force the administration to spend money appropriated to develop the RS-70 aircraft, and (2) whether it could prevent the administration from reducing the overall strength of the Army National Guard and Reserve.

The chief opposition to administration plans came from members of the president's own party, including 78-year-old Carl Vinson, the powerful chairman of the House Armed Services Committee; Virginia Sen. A. Willis Robertson, acting chairman of a subcommittee of the Senate Committee on Appropriations; and Louisiana Rep. F. Edward Hébert, chairman of a House subcommittee on reserve affairs. Only timely intervention by President Kennedy in the RS-70 dispute and Secretary of Defense McNamara's promise to study that matter further, plus a carefully crafted compromise with Congress regarding the National Guard and Reserve reorganization, avoided more serious rifts. The disputes, however, marked the beginning of what would increasingly become a strained relationship between McNamara and Congress.

---

* Treated here and in other chapters on DoD budgets is consideration only of the appropriation bill for major military functions, which did not include military construction and housing. Regarding the separate bills for military assistance, see Chapter XVI. Funds for civil defense were included in the DoD appropriation bill for FY 1962 after the president in July 1961 transferred responsibility for civil defense from OCDM to DoD. However, in subsequent years beginning with FY 1963, civil defense was also funded by a separate appropriation bill.

McNamara at Center Stage

Although McNamara had testified before congressional committees in connection with the FY 1962 budget and other matters, his basic presentation (known as the posture statement) and the budget for FY 1963 marked the first that he and his staff had developed on their own. Presenting them to Congress involved intensive effort. During a three-week period from late January through mid-February 1962, he spent all or part of 13 days appearing before the armed services committees on procurement authorization, which came to $12.4811 billion, as well as the appropriations subcommittees regarding the appropriation bill.

McNamara held firm views regarding the nature of the presentation. For one thing, he favored a lengthy, comprehensive statement. "I don't care if it takes a thousand pages," he told Henry Glass, who prepared the statement. "I want to get into the details of the programs and give the pros and cons." Glass advised against this because of DoD's not infrequent adversarial relationship with Congress: "We make our case and let them make their case." In the end Glass drafted the statement the way McNamara wanted, though this kind of elaboration gradually disappeared from subsequent renditions.[2]

The finished statement came to 167 pages and included 38 tables, an introduction describing the preparation of the budget, a survey of the international situation and its bearing on military policies and programs, and a review of the major defense policy problem areas. Subsequent sections corresponded rather closely to the program packages. The discussion of foreign policy represented an innovation, something McNamara felt provided the necessary intellectual foundation for military strategy, force structure, and the budget. McNamara recalled that Secretary of State Dean Rusk had supported its inclusion, but others at the State Department saw it as a usurpation of the responsibility of the secretary of state.[3]

How much of the statement to read to the committees posed a problem. A drawn-out presentation risked losing the attention of committee members, a point about which Sen. Margaret Chase Smith of the Senate Armed Services Committee felt strongly. Committee members, she observed, became restless and disinterested if they had to wait a long time before asking questions. McNamara's assistant for legislative affairs, Norman S. Paul, therefore suggested that the secretary enter into the record a classified comprehensive statement at the beginning of his testimony. He then could read a shorter classified version, perhaps no longer than 45 minutes, which would allow time for questions. Both the long and short classified statements could have complete sets of tables attached. Finally, an unclassified version of the longer statement, with tables, might be given to the committee for release to the press.[4]

When McNamara led off the authorization hearings before the Senate Armed Services Committee on 19 January 1962 and its House counterpart on 24

January, he employed a somewhat different method for condensing the presentation. Each committee member received a copy of the entire classified statement. But in reading the statement the secretary skipped over less important portions that had been lined in blue in the margin. He intended to pause at three or four points so committee members could raise questions on matters covered to that point.[5]

The plan worked better with the House than the Senate committee, whose members, as Senator Smith had predicted, grew restless. After listening to McNamara read about the first quarter of the statement before asking questions, the senators frequently interrupted the rest of his reading. On the other hand, the perhaps more disciplined House committee under Chairman Vinson confined most of its questioning to just two periods, allowing McNamara to read virtually without pause during the entire mornings of 24 and 26 January and a good part of the latter afternoon.[6]

McNamara did not accept Paul's advice in another respect. Paul had wanted the secretary to present a detailed accounting of the savings that had occurred as a result of his organizational changes. Since it was an election year and with authorized spending and expenditures projected to rise significantly, Paul thought committee members would raise probing questions about cost savings. When the subject did come up during the Senate hearings, McNamara explained why he had said nothing about it in the posture statement. First, he pointed out that savings from some changes were difficult to quantify in dollars and cents. Second, and perhaps more importantly, the timing was not right. As McNamara admitted, "I did not wish to embarrass myself or the members of the committee by coming in here asking for $8 billion more for 1963 than the original submission for 1962, and at the same time trying to prove I had saved X amount of dollars." Pressed nevertheless by Stuart Symington to provide figures on how much money he had saved by adopting new procedures, the secretary responded that he would try as time permitted to come up with this information.*[7]

McNamara and Joint Chiefs of Staff Chairman General Lyman Lemnitzer spent three full days before the Senate committee, with a majority of the 15 members present at each session. The pace of the hearings then quickened—perhaps in part because committee participation waned. On some days as few as two or three members joined Chairman Richard Russell, who conducted most of the questioning of the service secretaries, including newly appointed Secretary of the Navy Fred Korth, and their principal military advisers. On 2 February the committee wrapped up its hearings and awaited completion by the House Armed Services Committee of its hearings and House action on the authorization bill.

McNamara's performance astonished his audiences, including his own staff. In the past, after rather brief opening remarks, secretaries had often relied on

---

* Regarding the announcement by McNamara in July 1962 of a Cost Reduction Program, see Chapter XVII.

subordinates when they needed to delve into details. It quickly became apparent to Glass that McNamara "didn't need us, because he had, in addition to the statement, a set of backup books, each of which had to be an inch thick. No matter how I would arrange these backup papers—we would develop a hundred or more—he would rearrange them to suit his presentation. He could immediately turn to the right backup paper in the right book to supplement what was in the statement."[8] According to one newspaperman, who must have received his information from someone present at the closed sessions, McNamara's statement not only exceeded in length all previous presentations by secretaries of defense, but was "possibly the most reasoned and well-constructed." This same press account indicated that the secretary had displayed thorough understanding of the subject and had spoken almost with "relish."[9]

Although a new administration had prepared the budget and posture statement employing untried procedures and under the pressure of the Berlin crisis, congressional committee members were unstinting in their praise. Russell called the presentation "a new peak in our hearings" and "an encyclopedic statement." Sens. Leverett Saltonstall and John Stennis also commended McNamara. Symington termed the statement "unique" and thanked the secretary for giving the committee "a great deal more justification for this tremendous amount of money than has been presented before."[10] Vinson, who had served in the House since 1914, said it was a "magnificent" presentation, "the most comprehensive, most factual statement that has ever been my privilege to have an opportunity to receive from any of the departments of Government." Especially impressed with McNamara's evenhandedness, he said, "you dealt with both sides of the problems. When you reach a decision, you set out the reasons why you reached that decision. You point out why—it probably could have been done the other way, but the other facts were superior and therefore you followed the method you did."[11]

In neither armed services committee did McNamara face sharp questioning. Granted he had to respond to criticisms of the manner in which the National Guard had been activated during the Berlin crisis and to explain the reasons behind some of the key weapon systems decisions, such as the increase in the number of Polaris submarines, the limiting of the number of fixed Minuteman missiles, and the request of only $171 million for the RS-70 development program, but much of the questioning focused on technical aspects where he could demonstrate his mastery of detail.

During the House hearings inquiries about the administration's decisions the previous year not to spend funds appropriated for certain weapon systems certainly revealed annoyance. Vinson asked McNamara to place on record an explanation of why, "after the President signs the appropriation bill and it becomes the law of the land, and after Congress makes the money available, then you say notwithstanding all of those facts, 'I do not think that I should spend the people's money for these things.'" Massachusetts Republican William H. Bates was worried about similar situations in the future: "I just wondered what kind of position we are going to find ourselves sometime in if we really want something. What do we have to say then—that we mean this or what? Just how would we accomplish the will of the Congress? Because this is an authority contained in the Constitution for the Congress." In response to Bates's question as to his authority for not carrying out the provisions of a law, McNamara asserted that a series of precedents existed for such action, that appropriations represented only a ceiling for expenditures, but that "it might be different when the Congress wishes to mandate an action and indicate the action in the law itself." The matter was dropped, and he subsequently provided the committee a more detailed statement on executive prerogatives in the spending of appropriated funds.[12] But the expressed concerns gave warning of difficulties ahead.

Rebellion over the RS-70

Stretching the hearings out through the end of February, the House committee took testimony from the military service representatives in two separate phases—the first focusing on general military posture and the second on the specifics of the authorization bill. During the first phase in mid-February Air Force Secretary Eugene Zuckert and his military aides said little about the RS-70.* The Air Force indicated it had recently submitted an alternate proposal to the Office of the Secretary of Defense regarding the aircraft, but had not yet received a reply. Zuckert was joined—as he had been during the Senate committee hearings—by Vice Chief of Staff General Frederic Smith, because Chief of Staff General Curtis LeMay was just returning to work after recuperating from an illness.[13]

By the end of the month LeMay was making his views known. On 26 February, in the second phase, Air Force representatives expressed to Vinson's committee their unhappiness over the limited RS-70 program during a detailed briefing—at the committee's invitation—by Col. David C. Jones, deputy chief of the Strategic Division of the Air Force's Directorate of Operations. Jones reported that during the past week OSD had rejected the Air Force's recent proposal. That proposal called for three additional prototype aircraft in the development program by using $80 million of the $180 million of impounded FY 1962 funds and $491 million in new FY 1963 funds. LeMay supported Jones's presentation and framed the issue largely in terms of bombers versus missiles, pointing out the desirability of a mix of both manned and unmanned weapons systems but contending that manned systems could perform more missions and had greater flexibility than missiles.[14]

---

* The Air Force proposed to develop the RS-70 (the "RS" for Reconnaissance-Strike) as a more versatile aircraft than the B-70, which was a bomber designed to drop bombs on designated targets. The RS-70, carrying air-to-surface missiles and yet-to-be developed reconnaissance radar, would survey damage following an attack and strike surviving targets it could find.

More openly chafing over the previous year's unspent money than before, committee members sought a way to show support for the Air Force's new RS-70 proposal and considered amending the authorization bill. Such action posed a practical problem. If the committee approved the amendment and the additional money were later appropriated, one member wondered "how in the world are we going to implement that and get the Defense Department to follow the Congressional recommendations? . . . . And they flaunted us and slapped us in the face on this B-70 program this year, and I am just thinking that we ought to rise up, Mr. Chairman, and let the Defense Department and the administration know that we are not at all in favor of their actions on this matter."[15]

An amendment of this kind raised a jurisdictional problem, too. The administration had requested research and development funds, so it remained uncertain whether the Air Force proposal for additional funding properly fell within the purview of the Armed Services Committee's procurement authority. Air Force representatives argued that the proposal envisioned using $180 million of the $491 million for the three additional prototypes; the committee should therefore consider that amount as production funds. Vinson accepted this interpretation and indicated that the committee would amend the authorization bill accordingly.[16]

The next day, 27 February, LeMay let loose a vigorous defense of the Air Force's desire for more funding of both the RS-70 and the Minuteman missile in open session before the Senate Defense Appropriations Subcommittee, chaired by A. Willis Robertson. What especially worried LeMay was the administration's heavy emphasis on increasing limited warfare capabilities and the projected downward trend in spending on strategic weapons, whether missiles or bombers, from about 18-20 percent of the total defense budget to approximately 8 percent in some four years. "I do not think you can maintain superiority in this field with that sort of program," he said. Newspaper accounts called his comments the first major dissent within the administration on defense policies.[17]

A second bombshell quickly followed when Vinson's committee, having concluded its hearings on 28 February, unanimously reported an authorization bill with six amendments that raised the total amount to nearly $13.066 billion. News of the committee's action appeared even before formal issuance of the report. Although McNamara was clearly the intended target, the key amendment "directed" the secretary of the Air Force to spend $491 million during FY 1963—about three times the amount the administration had requested—to develop the RS-70. The committee also proposed to broaden its authority by adding a provision to Sec. 412(b)* that would require authorization of funds not only for procurement, but also for research and development of the RS-70. The committee's discontent went beyond the immediate issue to what it perceived as

---

* See Chapter III.

the diminished role of Congress in shaping national policy. It posed the question whether Congress's function was "solely a negative one in that it can withhold authority or funds and *prevent* something from being done? Or can it exercise a positive authority and by affording the means *require* something to be done?"[18]

McNamara professed public surprise at the committee's action. During his appearance in January, the committee had seemed to him satisfied with the administration's approach on the RS-70. Moreover, it had not asked him to return to discuss the issue and had made its decision without further testimony from him. Given the importance of the issue, McNamara said he welcomed an opportunity to appear again before Vinson's committee or any that would hear testimony on the issue. He subsequently learned that a statement attributed to him about the committee's seeming lack of interest in the RS-70 had infuriated Vinson.[19]

Faced with a major political test of wills and possible constitutional crisis, President Kennedy sought advice on how to deal with the committee's challenge. McNamara wanted him to contest the wording of the proposed amendment. However, his special assistant for legislative affairs, Lawrence F. O'Brien, warned the president that he would lose any floor fight with Vinson, thus weakening his position in future confrontations with Congress. Finally, White House lawyers counseled him simply to ignore the language, if it became law, since the Constitution's separation of powers accorded him the ultimate authority.[20]

The president adopted a two-track policy: he stood solidly behind McNamara while at the same time extending an open hand to Congress. Asked at a press conference on 7 March about the controversy, he emphasized his heavy reliance on and great confidence in McNamara, but also acknowledged congressional authority and competence. Kennedy expressed the hope that the administration could talk it over with both the armed services and the appropriations committees of both houses so "we can get a better judgment as to what the language will be at the end." A week later, he advocated waiting until all the committees and the full Congress had acted before determining what he would do, but expressed confidence that the matter would be resolved satisfactorily.[21]

McNamara sought advice. In a meeting on 5 March he asked the Joint Chiefs whether their views on the RS-70 had changed from the previous fall and whether the budget should be readjusted as Vinson's committee had indicated. LeMay remained the only supporter of additional funding. McNamara made clear his continuing opposition to imposing arbitrary dollar limits or ceilings on programs, but he and the president had concerns that the overall cost of the RS-70 program might reach $10 billion and have a detrimental effect on the rest of the Defense program.[22] So convincing was the secretary in his professed open-mindedness that Chief of Naval Operations Admiral George Anderson left the meeting worried that he might be considering cutting back the Polaris program as a way to free up funds to accelerate development of the RS-70.[23]

The secretary also met with key aides to develop a plan of action, including tactics for presenting DoD's case to Congress and the public. He very much wanted to avoid a public fight with Vinson over the constitutional question of legislative-executive powers, a fight that might appear to be a clash between civil and military authorities.[24] Seeking to head off support for Vinson in the Senate, he planned to meet with individual senators and small groups. But Paul, in light of press reports suggesting that Russell and his committee intended to support the House committee's proposed bill, urged McNamara to meet with the entire Senate Armed Services Committee. Paul felt the Senate committee at this point would likely go along with any substantial increase for the RS-70, but that a majority of its members could be persuaded otherwise "if they get a full briefing on the facts."[25]

McNamara received another opportunity to present his case, but not before Russell's committee. On 14 March, at Vinson's invitation, he appeared in executive session before the full House Armed Services Committee. Paul advised him to say something at the very beginning about the partnership between the legislative and executive branches on Defense matters. Calling attention to Vinson's recent statement that he did not want to run the Department of Defense but only to "sit at the table" and make a point now and then,[26] Paul also remarked, "We all know that this represents a slight understatement of the Chairman's position, but some reference to the wisdom and farsightedness of his Committee would be in order." McNamara did just this. But his blend of deference to the committee and its chairman, plus his detailed exposition of the reasons for limiting the development of the aircraft, brought no apparent softening of Vinson's position.[27]

Having failed to persuade the committee to change its mind, McNamara held a press conference the next day and released a 2,500-word statement—an unclassified version of his statement the previous day—detailing his reasons for opposing full development of the aircraft. He surprised reporters by singling out Air Force Chief of Staff LeMay as the only JCS member who had opposed the administration's position.[28]

Hopes for a compromise grew. In a joint television interview, asked who would win in any showdown, Hébert foresaw a clear-cut congressional victory, but Henry Jackson of the Senate Armed Services Committee predicted a compromise "in which both sides will give," a prediction which Assistant Secretary of Defense for Public Affairs Arthur Sylvester pointedly drew to McNamara's attention. Elsewhere on Capitol Hill and at the Pentagon others spoke in a conciliatory vein. "These aren't the kind of people who're going to annihilate themselves in a bloody political brawl," commented a Vinson aide. "Surely," remarked one Defense official, "men of good will can find some middle ground for agreement."[29]

Fueling the hopes was the perception that Vinson's support in the House was waning. In particular, members of the House Appropriations Committee resented what seemed an invasion of their turf. Chairman George Mahon and other members of his Defense Appropriations Subcommittee informed Vinson they would fight any move to direct the president to spend the additional money before it was appropriated, because this was "impractical and improper." Moreover, the language of the amended authorization bill made it seem that the Armed Services Committee was directing Mahon's committee to appropriate money. Mahon himself visited the White House to convey these views to the president.[30]

Vinson's Walk in the Rose Garden

Aware that McNamara had been unable to persuade Vinson to change his mind but that Vinson's support in Congress was weakening, President Kennedy moved to defuse the crisis. On the morning of 20 March, the day before the scheduled House floor debate on the authorization bill, he told Speaker John McCormack (D-Mass.) and other Democratic Party leaders that he wanted to talk the matter over with Vinson. McNamara joined them that afternoon at the White House and brought information the president had requested about the administration's actions on items Congress had added the previous year to the FY 1962 budget. The secretary pointed out, "We have utilized the funds for the purposes for which Congress appropriated them in 18 instances. Only in 3 cases—the B52 Wing, the B70, and Dynasoar—have the funds been 'impounded by the Executive Branch.'"[31]

At the White House meeting Vinson in effect—as McNamara recalled—told the president: "You're a young President, I'm a senior member of Congress; but I have tremendous respect for you as President and for the office of the President. I understand the constitutional conflict that lies beneath the surface here. I don't want to surface that. You don't want to surface it. I led my troops up that hill, I was the leader of the B-70, I'll put them in reverse, and I'll lead them down the hill."[32]

According to a detailed newspaper account, Kennedy expressed willingness to send Vinson a letter outlining a compromise. When Vinson immediately produced a draft letter from his briefcase, Kennedy, amid laughter, remarked, "That's where you got the name 'Swamp Fox.'" Vinson wanted the president to sign the letter, but they decided that McNamara would sign it and that a second letter from the president would accompany it. While McNamara and one of Vinson's aides—Philip W. Kelleher—hammered out the language of the first letter, the president, apparently growing impatient, invited Vinson for a walk in the Rose Garden. By the time they returned, the text of the letter had been agreed on.[33]

After the meeting McNamara and Kennedy's special counsel, Theodore Sorensen, drafted the second letter, which Sorensen and O'Brien took to Vinson's office for approval. O'Brien recalled that one of Vinson's aides participated in the meeting. "I at least, and I think Ted shared that view, realized that the staff representative, and I can't even remember his name [Philip W. Kelleher?], who was a very key staff fellow with Vinson, was the adamant one . . . . And even as Vinson talked, this fellow would move into the conversation in very strong protest. In fact, almost to the point where I didn't appreciate it. His views were unequivocal and there was no way of compromising [them]. Frankly, after a lengthy conversation, Vinson started to debate with his own staff fellow . . . . Vinson overruled the staff member, said that he found this acceptable and we would shake hands on it."[34]

Some contemporary and later accounts have conveyed the impression that the president persuaded Vinson to change his mind *during* their walk on the White House grounds.[35] But it seems evident that both men, eager to compromise, had decided to do so before then. What became known as the "Stroll in the Rose Garden" was thus not so much a sweet-talking presidential exercise as it was icing on the cake.

On the House floor the next day, 21 March, Vinson read the letters from the secretary of defense and the president, both couched in extremely polite terms. In his letter McNamara said that "we are anxious to work with you, your committee and the Congress in the spirit which a Government of divided powers such as ours must maintain in order to function successfully." McNamara indicated that he was initiating a new study of the RS-70 "in the light of the recommendations and representations of the Armed Services Committee" that would "give full consideration to the magnitude of the committee program and the depth with which the committee has emphasized this." He also promised that if some of the technology developed more rapidly than anticipated, "we will wish to take advantage of these advances by increasing our development expenditures; and we would then wish to expend whatever proportions of any increases voted by the Congress" these advances would warrant. Kennedy's letter drew attention to McNamara's willingness to reexamine the RS-70 issue, but focused primarily on the constitutional issues raised by the committee's recommendation. "I would respectfully suggest," wrote Kennedy, "that, in place of the word 'directed,' the word 'authorized' would be more suitable."[36]

Asking his House colleagues to accept the president's suggestion, Vinson—in a bit of self-congratulation—maintained that insertion of the language directing the president to spend the additional money had forced the administration to compromise. He contended that his committee "had to raise a good ruckus and a good fuss" to make its point. According to Vinson, McNamara had not only been worried that he would lose in any showdown with Congress but that also he might be wrong about the RS-70.[37]

By voice vote the House accepted Vinson's motion to substitute "authorized" for "directed" in the provision regarding the RS-70 and that day passed a $13.066 billion authorization measure, 403 to 0. On 2 April the Senate Armed Services

Committee recommended a slightly smaller authorization bill of $12.9693 billion, but also including $491 million for the RS-70. On 12 April the House by voice vote concurred in the Senate version, which then became law on 27 April.[38]

A brief flap occurred when a Pentagon spokesman announced that the study McNamara had promised was already in progress, implying that no new study would be undertaken. McNamara quickly released a statement expressing annoyance at this implication. The Air Force, he pointed out, had issued instructions on 21 March for a new study to be conducted by a military-civilian team headed by Air Force Under Secretary Joseph Charyk. On the floor of the House Hébert took great satisfaction at McNamara's clarification. All this signified, said Hébert, that "Mr. Vinson has not capitulated, the Committee on Armed Services has not capitulated, the House of Representatives has not capitulated, and Secretary McNamara boldly and firmly stands behind his agreement to take a new look at the RS-70 program and if found feasible to proceed with its production as authorized."[39] In the end, not only did most of the press reject congressional victory claims, but some of Vinson's colleagues privately said he had emerged from the skirmish with "something less than flying colors."[40]

Vinson's motivation remains puzzling. He either changed his mind quickly or did not feel as strongly about the issue as it seemed. His challenge to the administration may have served more as a ploy to gain support from his colleagues on the RS-70 issue and less a reflection of his concern about congressional impotence. As one veteran southern senator noted at the time, Vinson "usually runs with the man in the White House." Soon after working out the compromise, Vinson remarked to O'Brien, "I feel good about this, Larry, because I really want to help the President." Months later, having perhaps forgotten the zeal with which he had pursued the matter, Vinson informed Gilpatric that his aim had been "simply to relieve Congressional frustration and pressure within his Committee."[41]

Neither Kennedy nor McNamara gloated over the outcome. Expressing high regard for Vinson but dispelling any notion that he had changed his mind, McNamara expressed the hope that Congress would eventually come round to his position. He conceded Vinson's great wisdom and experience in military matters as a result of his service in Congress "since two years before I was born." McNamara believed that the Armed Services Committee had not received all of the information about the RS-70 decision until his special appearance before it on 14 March.[42]

The confrontation further damaged McNamara's relationship with his friend, Air Force Secretary Zuckert, who in a personal letter took sharp issue with some of McNamara's public statements. To one journalist it had seemed that McNamara had gone out of his way to castigate General LeMay as out of step with the other chiefs. The press had even speculated that LeMay might be fired for publicly supporting the RS-70, and Zuckert resented the implication that his chief of staff had shown disloyalty to the administration's programs. He also told McNamara that his statements had created "unfairly in the public mind an undeserved lack of confidence in the Air Force and its leadership."[43]

Furor over Army National Guard and Reserve Reorganization

No sooner had the administration sidestepped one controversy over the RS-70 than another surfaced in the appropriations subcommittee hearings over the proposed reorganization of the Army National Guard and Reserve. Like the dispute over the RS-70, it did not emerge until well after McNamara's opening testimony.

When Mahon's House Subcommittee on Department of Defense Appropriations began hearings on the Defense budget on 15 January, the reorganization proposal was not complete, despite much speculation and controversy already developing in the press. Mahon therefore acceded to OSD's request to postpone questioning witnesses about the proposal until completion of the plan.[44]

McNamara had submitted to the president on 13 January a slightly modified version of the plan put forward in December 1961. The new plan still called for reducing the combined authorized strength from 700,000 to 670,000, but proposed the elimination of 8 (4 each from the Reserve and the National Guard) instead of 10 divisions. It had "the obvious advantage of disturbing fewer states and individuals" and would hopefully "moderate to some extent the opposition of the reserve component leadership." But the proposal still lacked specifics, and by law it had to go to two advisory bodies—the General Staff Committee on National Guard and Army Reserve Policy, and the Reserve Forces Policy Board—as well as to the state governors, prior to implementation.[45]

In testifying before Mahon's subcommittee at the end of January and beginning of February and then in mid-February before Robertson's Senate subcommittee, McNamara did less reading of the posture statement than he had done before the armed services committees and more answering of questions. Nevertheless, he received similar accolades from the members, one of whom called him "a veritable walking encyclopedia." Florida Democrat Robert L. F. Sikes, who chaired a few sessions in Mahon's absence, called McNamara's presentation "one of the finest demonstrations of knowledge of the subject and willingness to cooperate and work with the committee that I have seen in my time here." Sikes later marveled that the secretary never "had to refer to a backup witness for information with which to answer committee questions. This is almost unbelievable. As a matter of fact, he left such a complete picture in the minds of his listeners that he nearly killed the rest of the hearings. Much that followed was anticlimax."[46]

Regarding the reorganization plan, McNamara pointed out to the subcommittee that the 100,000-man increase in the size of the Active Army lowered the requirements for the Army National Guard and Reserve. Despite the planned reduction in combined reservist strength from 700,000 to 670,000, however, "there would be no parallel reduction in costs or in our appropriations request for fiscal year 1963 since these reserve components will be maintained at higher levels of combat readiness." McNamara cautioned that it was "quite possible that in fiscal year 1963 the Army reserve components will not be able to maintain even the 670,000 strength level," a development mostly attributable to the suspension of the six-month training period the previous fall to help the Active Army buildup.

The reorganization plan met a solid wall of opposition from the General Staff Committees on National Guard and Army Reserve Policy at their meeting with Army Under Secretary Stephen Ailes and McNamara on 26 January. With McNamara's and Ailes's concurrence, the committees established an ad hoc group, which met during the period 7-15 February, to try to find ways to minimize disruption to the readiness status, organization, and programs of the reserve components. The full committees met on 16 February and, on the basis of the group's findings, again rejected the plan. Meeting on 24 February, the Reserve Forces Policy Board, the secretary of defense's advisory group on reserve affairs, also opposed realignment of any divisions and any reduction in the number of drills.[47]

The plan therefore underwent further revision. Not until the end of March did the Army submit to McNamara a still more refined proposal, one which Ailes felt achieved "the necessary objectives, within the funds made available under the past and presently proposed budgets." It would further reduce the paid drill strength but provide for two additional brigades, so that each of the eight realigned divisions would have a brigade, a feature Ailes believed would make the plan much more acceptable. Another major change from the previous plan reduced the net loss of units from about 700 to 450.[48]

On 30 March Ailes finally brought the plan, with its 642,000 strength level, before Mahon's subcommittee then winding up its hearings. Ailes pointed out that it still targeted eight divisions, but he preferred using the word "realined" rather than "eliminated" because a skeletal division headquarters would remain and eight brigades would be created in place of the eliminated divisions. Ailes would not yet reveal, at least for the record, the affected units, since the plan still required acceptance by the state governors. Ailes took considerable heat for his reluctance to do so. One committee member emphasized how unreasonable it was to submit a plan "showing a cut of eight units, and to believe officials of the department are not going to be expected to make a statement as to what they expect to cut. I do not understand how you can keep from informing the public. I do not see how the Secretary can put off talking to the Governors until June, when this budget will be on the floor within 2 or 3 weeks." Ailes admitted having a list of the eight divisions, but thought it would be unfortunate if the governors received the information through the newspapers instead of in a face-to-face discussion with Defense officials. Rep. Gerald R. Ford (R-Mich.) asked, "What is the use of a presentation or discussion of the plan if it is a nebulous plan that may not go into effect?" Ailes's testimony concluded on a sour note when Mahon told him that he really was not ready to make a presentation to the committee.[49]

The House subcommittee's response to Ailes jolted the administration into action. On 2 April the White House submitted to the House of Representatives several proposed amendments to the appropriation bill, most importantly the further reduction in the Army Reserve by 28,000 from the 670,000 in the administration's original budget estimate. Two days later, on 4 April, the Army announced the details of the plan, including the units slated for realignment, and thereby set off a storm of controversy.[50]

Reservists, their organizations, and state governors vociferously denounced the plan. The public furor included a sharp letter from former President Truman to Kennedy, in which he extolled the history of the 35th National Guard Division composed primarily of Missouri and Kansas men, one of the units designated for elimination, and asked the president to reconsider breaking up the division. Truman and many of his family had served with the division, including a first cousin who became its commanding general during World War II.[51]

In Congress, with the House Appropriations Subcommittee having finished its hearings, the focus shifted to the Senate side. On 6 April Ailes—along with Maj. Gen. Donald W. McGowan, chief of the Army's National Guard Bureau, and Maj. Gen. Frederick M. Warren, chief of Army Reserve and ROTC Affairs—discussed the plan with Robertson's subcommittee. Boasting that he graduated cum laude in Latin from a small Virginia college and therefore knew the meaning of the prefix "re," Robertson chided Ailes for using the word "realinement": "I know what to realine the front wheels of my car means," he declared, "but when you realine the four divisions of the National Guard, are they being put back in line or have you abolished them?" Ailes explained that the plan involved both "cancellation" of obsolete units and "addition" of new ones.

The subcommittee's main concerns, however, focused not on semantics but the plan's origins and cost. The senators wanted to make sure that it originated in the Army for military and not political reasons and that it was not imposed by the Office of the Secretary of Defense. "Did the plan come from the Army and go up to the throne," Robertson asked, "or come from the throne down to the Army?" Ailes replied that it originated in the Army to meet military requirements. He provided the information that though the paid drill strength would fall to 642,000, the amount requested—some $780 million—remained the same as the previous year. Committee members asked how much more it would cost if DoD retained the 700,000-man strength and received the answer that it would be $61.3 million more.

When Robertson and Senator Saltonstall asked for his views, McGowan equivocated, saying that "within the strength and budgetary guidelines the Army staff has produced the best possible plan." When Robertson asked what the guidelines were and whether McGowan had meant that "you cannot go above certain money figures," the general replied, "That is one guide. It always has to be." Warren stated that he opposed the reduction.[52]

Still another congressional participant entered the fray. Representative Hébert had asked McNamara to postpone implementing the plan until a House armed services subcommittee on reserve policy, which he headed, could hold its own hearings.[53] McNamara did not appear before Hébert's subcommittee, which began hearings on 16 April amid "a lot of fanfare and publicity." The task of defending the plan fell to Assistant Secretary of Defense (Manpower) Carlisle P. Runge, who underwent some "rough going" but "held up manfully," in Paul's view, and to Army Under Secretary Ailes.[54]

In the meantime, the House Appropriations Committee, based on the Mahon subcommittee recommendations, had reported out on 13 April an appropriation bill of $47.839 billion. It differed from the president's recommendations in only a few significant respects, one of which was that it added $58.8 million for the Army National Guard and Reserve to maintain the strength at 700,000. In an additional major change it added $223.9 million for the development of the RS-70, but with no stipulation directing that this money be spent. The two-day House floor debate, often lacking a quorum, seemed uncharacteristically subdued, what one representative called a "love feast." Just before departing Washington for the Easter recess, House members on 18 April rejected several minor amendments, and by a vote of 388-0 passed a Defense appropriation bill providing the same amount reported out by the Appropriations Committee.[55]

The Senate Weighs In

The House-approved appropriation bill next went to the Senate for consideration. Robertson's subcommittee resumed hearings in mid-May on the OSD reclamas to it. Within days of the House's action, McNamara made up his mind that, breaking with tradition, he personally would present the appeal. In the past the deputy secretary or the OSD comptroller had done so. In this case Gilpatric submitted a written reclama to Robertson that reflected McNamara's determination, when he appeared in person, to accept the increased amounts the House had voted for the RS-70 and the reserves on the understanding, as Gilpatric told the staff, that "we will use the flexibility given."[56]

In his appearance on 15 May, McNamara focused on those items the House wanted to cut, mostly, he acknowledged, in the interest of saving money and encouraging managerial efficiency, objectives that he shared. He was willing to accept as many of these as possible, even though some might cause difficulty, but not those items he felt would seriously interfere with the proper running of the department. The controversial items in the bill, of course, involved amendments that increased funding levels—for the RS-70 and for maintaining the Army

Reserve and National Guard at 300,000 and 400,000 strength, respectively. On these and other increases, McNamara made a gesture of concession. "How much of the additional funds provided for each of the items could profitably be utilized during the coming fiscal year has yet to be determined," he stated. "Recognizing the strong congressional interest in these matters, we will want to restudy each of them in much greater detail. Accordingly, I recommend that the additional funds appropriated by the House be retained in the bill."[57]

The questioning covered many areas, but Robertson made a special effort to pin down McNamara regarding the RS-70. "You are now going to restudy this and, if you do not want to spend it, you are not going to do so. Is that what you mean?" McNamara replied, "If there is no military requirement for the expenditures, I don't believe that I should recommend to the President that they be spent, and I don't believe you would wish me to spend it."[58]

McNamara had another fight on his hands. The president of the National Guard Association, Maj. Gen. William H. Harrison, Jr., sent him a telegram alleging errors in his 15 May testimony. Contrary to what McNamara had claimed in describing obsolete and inefficient units, Harrison said that the Army National Guard had no 90-mm. antiaircraft units and had had no veterinary-type units since World War II. Harrison charged that providing "misleading information" to Congress and the public only harmed the national defense effort and asked McNamara to issue a public correction. McNamara's response corrected a number of Harrison's assertions and offered no concessions.[59]

On 8 June the Senate Appropriations Committee reported a bill providing $48.429 billion, some $590 million over what the House had approved. It included $491 million for the RS-70. While accepting the House language to maintain Army National Guard and Reserve strength at 400,000 and 300,000 respectively, the committee also added $6.7 million for the Air Force Reserve and $4.17 million for the Navy Reserve. Faced with the committee's action, McNamara showed a willingness to compromise. If Congress passed the measure, he would not proceed with the plan to cut the National Guard and Reserve. On the RS-70 controversy, he noted that the additional funds "probably can be advantageously spent" for research and development of advanced radar.[60]

On 14 June the Senate passed the appropriation bill, 88-0. The Senate version stipulated that Army Reserve end-strength reach no less than 300,000, with Army National Guard strength programmed to attain an end strength of 400,000. Because the House bill did not contain mandatory strength levels, these differences in language, among others, needed to be resolved in conference committee.[61] As the beginning of the fiscal year approached on 1 July 1962 without passage of new appropriation bills, Congress passed continuing resolutions to permit the functioning of federal agencies, including DoD, into the new fiscal year.

Finessing the Controversies

In his own mind McNamara went back and forth on the desirability of compromise. After many state governors had protested to the White House sharply criticizing the reserve reorganization plan, he asked one of his aides, "Is this the right thing to do?" "Yes," the adviser replied, "but it's sure going to stir up a helluva fuss and offend a lot of people." "Well, we're going to do it," declared McNamara. "I'm not in this job just to please."[62]

At the urging of the president, concerned over the growing opposition, McNamara agreed to address the annual Governors' Conference in Hershey, Pennsylvania, on 2 July. In the speech McNamara explained how elimination of some units would be carefully arranged so as to minimize turbulence and asserted that "far from diminishing the role of the reservist, it will give him a new and even more important part in the Nation's defense." Afterwards the secretary met behind closed doors with the governors' National Guard committee for about an hour and a half. He asked them to study the plan and provide comments and suggestions and also offered to meet with them as a group or individually. Later he had the new secretary of the Army, Cyrus Vance, send individual telegrams on his behalf to each of the governors politely reiterating his willingness to work with them. The private session, however, only hardened the opposition.[63]

The next day, by voice vote without dissent, the governors adopted a resolution opposing the plan. They wanted the National Guard to maintain its strength at 400,000 and requested that McNamara restudy the question. They also urged no action in any state until the National Guard advisory committee had time to go over the details of whatever new plan would emerge. The governors' resolve in spite of the arguments he had mustered may have surprised McNamara. Years later he recalled that "not a single governor would support the elimination of the National Guard divisions, even though every one of them knew the divisions were hollow."[64]

OSD settled the disagreement with Congress over the reorganization plan through an artful compromise worked out with Senator Robertson and Representative Mahon. In long, detailed letters sent to the two men on 20 July, McNamara recapitulated the history of the dispute, reiterated Defense's belief that 642,000 men were all that would be needed to support current military plans, but acknowledged that the current fiscal year would be "a period of unusual change and that a somewhat higher strength may be required to ease the transition from the present structure to the one required." If the conference committee would drop the mandatory language about end strengths in the Senate bill, DoD would authorize and program a strength of 400,000 for the National Guard and 300,000 for the Army Reserve in FY 1963, subject to three conditions: (1) all units would have to maintain at least 90 percent of personnel qualified in their military specialties; (2) reserve components would have to apply the same recruiting standards as the Active Army; and (3) no units would be permitted to exceed their authorized strength except those specifically authorized excess strengths to accommodate reservists on drill pay status who would be displaced by the realignment.[65] These conditions were much more stringent than the language of an earlier draft, wherein McNamara had agreed, if Congress dropped the mandatory language, to authorize and program a drill pay strength of 400,000 for the National Guard and 300,000 for the Reserve without condition. The draft simply recognized, as McNamara had cautioned in the posture statement in January, that "it will probably not be possible actually to attain the strengths in an orderly and efficient manner."[66]

The tougher conditions virtually ensured that the higher strength levels would not be reached. By one assessment, the Department of Defense found a way "to exploit the executive's institutional advantages." It was difficult for Congress and Guard supporters to take exception to these conditions "without seeming to flout the public's interest in well-prepared reserve forces." The Department thus "succeeded in achieving indirectly what it failed to achieve directly through reduced appropriations for the Guard."[67]

The conference report, approved by voice vote in the House on 26 July and in the Senate on 1 August, called for total appropriations of $48,136,247,000. The amount seemingly represented $229 million more than the administration had requested, but it was actually $285 million less because it included reappropriation of an unspent $515 million from FY 1962.[68] The bill included an extra $58.8 million for the Army National Guard and Reserve, as well as the conditions proposed by Defense and accepted by Robertson and Mahon. The conferees also approved a compromise amount of $362.6 million for the RS-70. The amounts in the FY 1963 budget proposed and approved for the RS-70 varied considerably, as follows (in millions):

Budget Estimate	$171.0
Passed House	223.9
Passed Senate	491.0
House/Senate Conference Action	362.6

The president signed the bill into law on 9 August.[69]

Congressional opinion varied as to DoD's likely courses of action. Representative Ford thought the extra money appropriated for the RS-70 would not be spent—McNamara seemed as adamant as ever—and that "under the criteria which have been used for the National Guard and the Reserves, criteria which I think are sound—I have doubts that as a practical matter they can attain a strength of 700,000." On the other hand, Senators Saltonstall and Robertson believed that the legislative language would preserve the 700,000-man reserve force and that Defense would indeed spend the extra money on the RS-70.[70]

Not until after final congressional action on the appropriation bill did the Hébert committee release its report (17 August) regarding the reorganization plan. Predictably, the report came out strongly against realignment. It not only opposed the proposed cuts but also chastised McNamara for failing to give consideration to individual state requirements in the event of local or national disasters. The report reminded the secretary of defense that "Congress, having enacted such legislation, has the power to repeal any legislation which in its opinion hinders and defeats the purpose and intent of the Congress." This clear warning to the Pentagon against flouting the will of the legislators was underscored by the sarcastic remark that neither "the Constitution nor our Creator has endowed these experts in the Pentagon with the cloak of infallibility." Noting the unchanging amount of $781 million budgeted for the reorganized reserve components as the plan passed through its later versions, the report contended that the subcommittee "would be naïve indeed to accept testimony from Defense and Army witnesses to the effect that budgetary guidelines were not an overriding consideration" in the plan's formulation. Hébert told a reporter, "I don't think the White House realizes how serious the schism is between McNamara and the Congress." Certain provisions in the Hébert report, however, assisted McNamara in carrying out the plan. Despite suspicions of executive aggrandizement, the subcommittee did agree to eliminate obsolete and unnecessary reserve units. While insisting that deactivation of the eight Army Reserve and National Guard divisions was premature, it did not specifically rule out such action.[71]

Following extensive consultation among Defense officials, members of Congress, reserve organizations, and governors, McNamara and Secretary of the Army Vance unveiled the final reorganization plan on 4 December. How much had the plan been modified? One reporter felt it was "substantially unchanged" from the original proposal, another that it contained few concessions to critics. Yet the opposition had lessened, in part because of Pentagon explanations of the military necessity for reorganization and the patient, ongoing discussion of the issue that "blunted early charges" that McNamara was "ramrodding his ideas through without seeking advice of Congress." Hébert announced his support because of "significant revisions" and because Defense had followed the consultative procedures recommended by Congress. The National Guard Bureau withdrew its opposition, although a few governors remained unpersuaded. In announcing the final plan, the administration regarded reorganization as an accomplished fact and a major victory. The anticipated shortfall in strength did in fact occur. By 30 June 1963 (end of the fiscal year), Army National Guard paid drill strength stood at 360,700 and Army Reserve paid drill strength at 237,000, a total of 597,700. Although Defense had programmed for 400,000 and 300,000 end strengths, respectively, unusually high turnover rates kept the numbers down.[72]

Patience, persistence, and the passage of time also served McNamara well in the RS-70 controversy, as the promised restudy of the matter dragged on through the summer and fall of 1962. On 1 June the Air Force study group submitted a preliminary report, giving three alternate development plans, all envisioning a substantial program for the RS-70. Later that summer LeMay and Zuckert indicated their preferred options, and in early September Zuckert submitted a new proposal calling for eight experimental RS-70s that would require $591.4 million in NOA in the FY 1964 budget.[73]

McNamara again put the question to the JCS. On 29 September the chiefs recommended reorienting the B-70 to the RS-70 concept and suggested that McNamara approve those parts of the Air Force proposal needed to demonstrate feasibility of the RS-70 and its associated subsystems. But the previous day, before the JCS recommendation reached him, McNamara had decided to disapprove the Air Force proposal, noting in a memo to the chiefs that costs would likely come to about $3 billion more than the $8.2 billion the Air Force had estimated, that the plane's claimed technical performance "cannot be supported by the current state of the art," and that the RS-70 would not significantly enhance U.S. capabilities to deter or wage thermonuclear war. He advanced four alternate approaches: (1) complete the manufacture and testing of the three prototypes with total cost not to exceed $1.3 billion; (2) continue to develop radars and related equipment that might prove useful; (3) consider alternative applications of manned aircraft; and (4) begin development of a new aircraft—the RBX, which, because of its post-strike reconnaissance mission, would prove less costly than the RS-70. He estimated that 50 RBX aircraft would cost $1.4 billion.[74]

A major personnel change worked in McNamara's favor. On 1 October General Maxwell Taylor succeeded Lemnitzer as JCS chairman. That day McNamara met with the chiefs—and their new chairman—and suggested they reconsider their endorsement of the RS-70 concept. The drawn-out process tested congressional patience. Rep. Leslie C. Arends (R-Ill.) wrote McNamara urging him to report to Congress, indicating he had heard rumors that the promised study would not be released until Congress went home prior to the congressional elections in November. He charged that McNamara intended to kill the program by a process of "study and re-study, and re-study of the studies." A DoD spokesman commented that the Joint Chiefs were looking into the issue and would probably make a recommendation to the president within a month.[75]

During the month of October 1962 the Cuban missile crisis occupied much of the time and attention of high U.S. government officials, including McNamara and the JCS. After a series of exchanges among themselves, the chiefs on 6 November put forward a compromise proposal calling for the manufacture of five prototype RS-70s to test the aircraft's effectiveness, while deferring a decision on the production of additional aircraft. General Taylor, however, agreed with McNamara on halting the RS-70 program and advocated directing efforts toward development of a purely reconnaissance aircraft. All the various arguments—those initially advanced and subsequently modified by the Air Force, the views of the Joint Chiefs and their new chairman, and McNamara's analysis and recommendations—were laid out in a 36-page draft memorandum McNamara sent the president on 20 November. In the meantime the program's prospects received a setback when the Air Force announced on 15 November that the first prototype test flight, scheduled for December, would be delayed three or four months because of problems with sealing the aircraft's fuel cells.[76]

At a meeting at the Kennedy home in Hyannis Port, Massachusetts, on 20 November with McNamara and other key advisers, Kennedy approved McNamara's recommendations as supported by Taylor. Two days later McNamara announced the Department of Defense's intention to add $50 million in FY 1963 funds to the RS-70 development program. No public mention was made of the decision to go ahead with the new reconnaissance aircraft or the disposition of the rest of the $362.6 million Congress had appropriated for the RS-70. The announcement did indicate, however, that the Department would make a full presentation on the results of the restudy of the RS-70 program to the armed services and appropriations committees during hearings on the FY 1964 budget.[77] Congress would make one last, relatively feeble effort the following year to revive the RS-70 program, but for all practical purposes the program was dead.

Congressional approval of the FY 1963 budget, along with the subsequent realignment of the Army National Guard and Reserve and the virtual cancellation of the RS-70, represented major triumphs for McNamara. Notwithstanding grumbling and snide remarks about the arrogance of McNamara's "Whiz Kids," he could also take heart from the general congressional acceptance of the new planning and programming methods used in preparing the FY 1963 budget.

Early in 1962 McNamara was indeed riding high. As one seasoned Washington journalist observed, "If Robert McNamara were a man whose head could be turned by a compliment, he might find himself hard put to keep eyes front amid the widespread tribute" coming his way. Not only was the president telling visitors that McNamara was the "most satisfactory" cabinet member, but Capitol Hill veterans, after listening "in undisguised awe to McNamara's precise analyses of force requirements," were calling him the greatest ever secretary of defense.[78] The first few months of 1962 probably marked the zenith in McNamara's relations with Congress.

Thereafter these relations deteriorated and caused concern within OSD. During the year Hill staffers had told officials in the office of McNamara's assistant for legislative affairs that Congress, recognizing McNamara's administrative abilities, at first "gave him his head," hoping that he would bring efficient organization to Defense. However, by the time members of Congress realized how quickly he had accomplished this task, it was too late to assert themselves because McNamara "was too far ahead of them." A study prepared within the legislative affairs office in October 1962 forecast an effort by Congress in 1963 to reassert its authority relative to the department, with more outspoken and pointed criticism, some of it personal, directed at the secretary. These criticisms would probably involve his alleged "disregard of human or morale factors," "disregard of military professional opinion in favor of civilian experts," and his "predilection" for quantitative solutions. To counter the anticipated criticisms the paper suggested, among other things, that McNamara "warm his public image" by stressing his interest in human factors and concern over morale and, most importantly, that he establish a pattern of consulting Congress in advance of his major actions.[79]

CHAPTER VI

The FY 1964 Budget

The Kennedy administration's proposed Department of Defense budget for FY 1964 reached a level surpassed only in FY 1952 during the Korean War. This occurred despite rigorous efforts by Secretary of Defense McNamara to control spending, including cancellation of the Skybolt missile system under development for use by U.S. and British aircraft,* and reservations by the president and White House advisers about the need for a sizable strategic force. Presented to Congress in January 1963, the budget request totaled some $49.314 billion in new obligational authority (NOA) for military functions, $1.4 billion more than the amount sought the previous year.

For the first time the administration encountered strong public and congressional pressures to reduce military spending. While certain members of Congress again tried to add funds for various projects, they generally failed, lacking the broad support and enthusiasm that had characterized past efforts. Though Congress spurned calls for drastic cuts, budget trimming proposals carried the day and resulted in an appropriation bill of just over $47.22 billion enacted late in the session in October 1963. Defense appropriations leveled off in FY 1965, only to be followed by sharp increases in subsequent years due primarily to the greatly expanded U.S. military involvement in Southeast Asia.[1] The approved FY 1964 and 1965 budgets, with Congress holding the line, thus represented significant pauses in the upward trend in military spending.

The timetable for preparing the FY 1964 budget resembled that of the preceding year, with the planning and programming phases occurring during late spring and summer and submission of estimates by the military services at the beginning of October 1962. The new procedures instituted the previous year,† by now generally considered a success, remained in place, but with a few refinements. One was

---
* The decision in fall 1962 to cancel Skybolt and the ensuing controversy in Anglo-American relations is covered in Chapter XIV.
† See Chapter IV.

the adoption of a Five-Year Force Structure and Financial Program (FYFS&FP) to serve as the base for budget projections. Begun toward the close of the FY 1963 budget cycle, this document underwent revision early in 1962 and received McNamara's approval on 16 April.[2] Two days earlier, another procedural modification, the Program Change Proposal (PCP) process, allowed the services at any time to submit proposals to alter programs. Approved changes were to be continually incorporated into the FYFS&FP to keep it up-to-date.[3]

White House Expectations

Notwithstanding his demonstrated drive for improving efficiency and reducing costs, McNamara faced pressure from the White House through the summer and fall of 1962 to lower spending even more. The high cost of strategic weapon systems remained a major concern. In April, responding to President Kennedy's expressed desire that costly major weapon systems should meet design objectives and operational requirements "under realistic conditions," the secretary replied that except for a few revolutionary, unique weapon systems that filled an urgent national need, he wanted to ensure that "the component development and then the system development is carried out before production is started." This would apply to "even very important" new systems and "especially very complex and expensive ones."[4]

DoD Comptroller Charles Hitch elaborated on this idea in a public address in September 1962. Before committing to development of a large weapon system, he noted, "we should be reasonably confident that, if technically successful, the contribution of the system to our overall military capabilities" would be worth its "full cost." In some instances OSD might want to commit only to the development phase and postpone a decision on production and deployment. "To the greatest extent possible," Hitch stated, "we want to do our thinking and planning before we start 'bending metal.'"[5] Such promised scrutiny did not augur well for expensive weapon systems under development, such as the RS-70 aircraft* and Skybolt missile, that were nearing a decision on whether to go ahead or not.

From the start, during the government-wide budget preview, the Bureau of the Budget made clear its desire to cut defense spending. The preview began with a request from BoB Director Bell to McNamara and other cabinet heads in early April 1962 for a brief statement of each department's major goals, as well as program changes anticipated through FY 1967 that would have a significant effect on the budget. On 23 May McNamara submitted projections totaling $55.26 billion in NOA for major military functions in FY 1964, including $1.5 billion

---

* Regarding McNamara's decision in November 1962 not to spend additional FY 1963 funds Congress had appropriated for development of the RS-70 and instead to maintain a limited development program, see Chapter V.

for military assistance. In July BoB listed both possible upward and downward adjustments. It recommended that prior to the budget decisions in the fall DoD update its strategic force projections in light of more recent intelligence estimates and perhaps look at "somewhat lower U.S. force objectives."[6]

These recommendations formed the basis of a discussion on 17 July that McNamara, Deputy Secretary of Defense Gilpatric, and Hitch held with Bell and his staff. McNamara, who had read the BoB comments, seemed "quite receptive," promising to deal promptly with the questions the bureau had raised and to discuss its proposals with DoD officials. BoB suggested that the Skybolt program, because of rising cost estimates, undergo a thorough review before McNamara decided to commit the weapon system to production.[7]

BoB's hopes that further review within Defense might lead to generally lowered force projections proved unfounded. Perhaps as a result of the meeting with Bell and his staff, McNamara the following day asked the Joint Chiefs of Staff and the services to review the adequacy of the overall military posture as represented in the FYFS&FP and give special attention to appropriations for FY 1964 programs. Several weeks later the Joint Chiefs and the individual service secretaries replied, indicating—not surprisingly—that they required more forces than the just approved FYFS&FP had shown.[8] Since the spring the chiefs had been at odds over force structures while drafting the latest Joint Strategic Objectives Plan, JSOP-67. JCS Chairman General Lemnitzer eventually worked out a number of compromises regarding the JSOP which he forwarded to McNamara on 27 August, including a proposal to increase the number of Army divisions from 16 to 17 in FY 1965 instead of the 18 desired by the Army in FY 1964. His reply a few days later to McNamara's request for a review of the overall military posture confirmed the force levels Lemnitzer and the chiefs had recommended for the JSOP.[9]

As the White House explored ways to reduce the federal budget, broader budgetary and political considerations came into play. Kennedy and his advisers wanted very much to keep overall federal expenditures for FY 1964 below $100 billion. Coming in under this figure, which had considerable symbolic value, would increase the chances that fiscally conservative members of Congress would support the president's planned tax cut proposal. During the spring budget preview, federal government expenditure projections had reached $108 billion, which BoB staff reduced to $102 billion. Bell and Deputy Director Elmer B. Staats felt that $101 billion would be an appropriate minimum, and even that would require "a tight, strongly held, budget policy."[10] Following meetings with cabinet heads during the summer, BoB presented a memo to the president at the end of August calling for FY 1964 expenditures of about $100.4 billion, including $50.4 billion for military functions, not including military assistance, and emphasizing the difficulty, especially in the area of defense, of cutting spending further.[11]

At the beginning of October Kennedy met with Bell, Treasury Secretary C. Douglas Dillon, and Chairman of the Council of Economic Advisers Walter Heller to discuss the memo and whether to keep estimated expenditures under $100 billion, as the president put it, for "the political argument of the tax thing." Some, including Special Counsel Theodore Sorensen, urged that the estimates be lowered well below the $100 billion mark, to around $98.4 billion. If the amount fell barely under $100 billion, Sorensen thought the mark would definitely be exceeded the following year, which—in an apparent allusion to the 1964 elections—was "a worse year to do it." In defense spending, Skybolt emerged as a possible candidate for cancellation, but the president appeared inclined to continue the program because of the British involvement. Bell pointed out the difficulty of finding areas for further reduction, given the large built-in increases in both defense and space programs. The president nevertheless asked Bell and Dillon to study ways to reduce the overall estimates by about $2 billion.[12]

A few days later Dillon suggested to Bell that among other things DoD might reduce expenditures further by phasing in military pay increases in two steps, immediately canceling both Skybolt and the Mobile Medium-Range Ballistic Missile (MMRBM), and by keeping research and development at the FY 1963 level. These steps would cut $525 million from the overall budget. Bell believed they should stress to the president the "very strong upward pressures" on the budget, for example, the lack of provision so far for production and development of Nike-Zeus, additional Minuteman missiles, or an expanded military space program, all of which Bell noted were under active consideration within DoD.[13] Although McNamara did not participate in these late summer and early fall discussions, Bell probably informed him of their basic thrust. In any event the White House concerns gave McNamara little upward flexibility in shaping his budget.

Other factors complicated the process. As had happened in 1961 with the building of the Berlin Wall, an international crisis—this time over Cuba—added strains and distractions to what was, even in the best of circumstances, an intensive and time-consuming process involving DoD, BoB, and the White House. The Cuban missile crisis undoubtedly slowed work on the budget, especially during the hectic days at the end of October, and may have caused the president and other top officials to give insufficient attention to some key budgetary matters.

However, well before that, on 22 September, McNamara acknowledged that OSD was falling three to four weeks behind in preparing the early versions of draft presidential memorandums (DPMs) on the RS-70, strategic nuclear forces, Nike-Zeus, and other key programs.[14] As Hitch saw it, flaws in the programming timetable and the new PCP procedures were the major reason for the delay. In May OSD sent the services a schedule for review by the secretary of submission of certain important programs, but did not impose penalties for late submittals.

Indeed many proved tardy. Moreover, the services took advantage of the new flexibility to propose changes wherever and whenever they wished. As a result the comptroller's office was "flooded with program change proposals—too many, too large, and too late." By late September it received PCPs recommending additions of $6.7 billion to McNamara's spring projections for FY 1964 and even larger additions for subsequent years. The office did the best it could to review and process them, but Hitch realized his staff could not complete the work by 1 October, which would delay the ensuing budget review.[15]

Shrinking the Service Estimates

OSD faced the awkward task of reconciling the White House desire for substantially lowering already tight preliminary spending projections with military service recommendations for huge spending and NOA increases. Inherent in the budgetary process, the problem was nothing new. But the FY 1964 gap between White House expectations and service estimates turned out to be extraordinarily large. Final estimates for military functions, which the services submitted on 1 October, totaled $61.034 billion (NOA).[16]

During October and November OSD reduced the estimates by examining closely a large number of specific items, however small in cost, and by cutting several major programs. In a memorandum on 24 October McNamara informed all DoD principals that he soon would begin making tentative decisions, based on staff evaluations, on remaining issues. Appeals had to be made within three days. He exhorted the services to "ruthlessly eliminate all activities, the cost of which is not commensurate with their contribution to our national defense." Finally, he promised that he would judge their appeals "predominately from the standpoint of critical military necessities." Of some 600 proposed items, OSD made cuts in about 400. The services appealed 73 of these cuts; OSD eventually granted only about a third of the appeals. These actions resulted cumulatively in downward adjustments of $12.5 billion and upward adjustments of $1.4 billion, a total net reduction of $11.1 billion (NOA). In mid-November OSD released the text of McNamara's 24 October memorandum and informed the press about the huge service budget requests and the "economizing" drive in the Pentagon intended to soften the impact of an anticipated federal budget deficit in FY 1964.[17]

McNamara also tackled major issues in his DPMs, preliminary versions of which he circulated for comment to the service secretaries, the Joint Chiefs of Staff, and White House staff. The majority focused on program packages, such as strategic retaliatory forces and general purpose forces, but a few dealt with specific programs such as the RS-70 and the Nike-Zeus antimissile system. Aware of criticism by some members of Congress that he paid little attention during the preparation of the budget to the views of the uniformed military, McNamara encouraged the chiefs to express their views and provided assurances that he would fully and fairly convey them to the president. In a meeting on 15 October, McNamara told the chiefs and the service secretaries that he would send them, in addition to two DPMs recently circulated, similar papers that would require a "tremendous amount" of their time and attention. He wanted their "personal judgments" on these matters, although he acknowledged he might not always accept them. Before submitting a final memorandum to the president, McNamara wanted to understand clearly any split views among the Joint Chiefs so he could discuss the disagreements in the memorandum.[18]

The major disagreements that arose between McNamara and the Joint Chiefs concerned strategic retaliatory forces, as well as deployment of an anti-ballistic missile defense system. The service chiefs opposed McNamara's recommendations to cancel the Skybolt missile; only General Taylor, who had replaced Lemnitzer as JCS chairman on 1 October, sided with McNamara on its cancellation.[19] On the Minuteman missile, however, the chiefs' joint position was much closer to McNamara's than the Air Force's. The gap between OSD and the chiefs on the one hand, and the Air Force on the other, was most striking in the long-range projections:

	1965	1966	1967	1968
Air Force				
Minuteman	900	900	850	750
Improved Minuteman	----	300	800	1200
Total	900	1,200	1,650	1,950
OSD				
Minuteman	800	800	800	800
Improved Minuteman	----	150	350	500
Total	800	950	1,150	1,300

While the chiefs jointly supported the Air Force request for 900 Minutemen in FY 1965, they wanted 1,050 in FY 1966 and 1,200 in FY 1967, only 100 more in FY 1966 and 50 more in FY 1967 than McNamara but 450 fewer than the Air Force for FY 1967.[20]

White House advisers took altogether different positions on the budget from those of the services and the Joint Chiefs. Both Deputy Special Assistant for National Security Affairs Carl Kaysen and Science Adviser Jerome Wiesner thought the strategic retaliatory force levels too high, however much they represented drastic reductions from the service estimates. Kaysen suggested slowing down the Minuteman buildup more than McNamara wanted. McNamara's arguments seemed to him "more a defense against service demands for a bigger force than justification of the forces he has requested." Kaysen also suggested cutting naval general purpose forces by $1 billion and using the money either to reduce the budget or to increase Air Force and Army logistical support. In a memorandum to the president on 4 December, Wiesner, more forceful in his criticism, thought the recommended force levels "greatly in excess of those required to maintain a secure deterrent." Moreover, he said, "the very rapid build-up of our missile forces will almost certainly intensify the arms race." Wiesner offered two alternatives to McNamara's recommended levels, the more severe stabilizing the number of Minutemen at 800 in FY 1966 and holding the number of Polaris submarines at 35 in FY 1967 instead of increasing it to 41.[21]

Nike-Zeus remained controversial, although the debate within the administration was perhaps not as sharp as the previous year. The Army proposed deploying the Nike-Zeus system beginning in 1967 and a more advanced Nike-X system in 1969. McNamara recommended that no deployment of either system be decided on. Instead he wanted to reduce the Nike-Zeus test program, develop fully only the Nike-X system, and delay a decision on deployment of the latter until mid-1964. The Army proposal, he felt, would cost an additional $2.7 billion and provide only limited protection under Nike-Zeus during the 1967-69 time frame. Another reason for delay, as Harold Brown later explained, was that "once you start deploying something, it is very, very hard to change. All of the effort would have gone into getting the bugs out of Nike Zeus, and there would have been very little effort left over for developing Nike X."[22]

Nike-Zeus proponents received a boost from a National Intelligence Estimate (NIE) issued in early July, indicating that the Soviet Union was placing greater emphasis on forces for both retaliatory and preemptive action, on nuclear-powered submarines, and on forces for intercontinental attack, particularly ICBMs. To report on the implications of the estimate for U.S. military policy, the president established an interagency committee chaired by the Department of State, with Assistant Secretary of Defense (ISA) Paul Nitze representing Defense. While the committee's report submitted in late August called for no major changes in U.S. retaliatory forces, it concluded that the Soviet Union's rapid strides in developing anti-ballistic missile defenses and its initial deployment of such systems might give it a propaganda advantage that the United States would have to counter with its own anti-ICBM systems. Although Nitze—with McNamara's backing—had demurred, earlier, at the end of July, the committee favored reconsideration, "with due weight given to the political considerations favoring deployment as quickly as feasible at least on a limited scale."[23]

A longtime advocate of Nike-Zeus, General Taylor, then serving as the president's military adviser, told the president in August of deficiencies he perceived in the report, including the failure to describe clearly enough the encouragement to aggressiveness by the Soviets, especially in Western Europe, if "they beat the U.S. to an effective ABM while the U.S. remains unprotected." Taylor urged an immediate decision on Nike-Zeus deployment, but the matter was put off until the fall budget deliberations. Subsequently, in November, Secretary of State Dean Rusk weighed in with McNamara, making essentially the same argument as the committee report and Taylor. He declared that a decision not to deploy, in light of the Soviet Union's apparent deployment of an anti-ballistic missile system, had "immense political and psychological implications" for U.S. national security for a decade to come.[24]

The Joint Chiefs of Staff divided over Nike-Zeus, with Chief of Naval Operations Admiral George Anderson backing the Army position and Air Force Chief of Staff General Curtis LeMay essentially supporting McNamara's. Taylor, of course, supported the Army. An NSC staff member reported that Taylor felt so strongly about Nike-Zeus that he "deliberately and sharply split" with the secretary of defense on the issue.[25]

At a meeting in Hyannis Port over the Thanksgiving holiday, on 23 November, the president reached several tentative budget decisions, generally accepting all of McNamara's recommendations. He approved a force level of 950 Minuteman missiles for FY 1966, of which 150 would be the improved version. He also decided to cancel Skybolt, subject to discussions with the British on possible alternatives, and to add 6 Polaris submarines, bringing the total to 41. After McNamara summarized the arguments on Nike-Zeus and Taylor spoke in favor of the Army proposal, Kennedy again deferred a decision on deployment until the conclusion of the budget process, but decided to go ahead with McNamara's reduced development program.[26]

Final Decisions

As budget preparation drew to a close, McNamara erected defenses against criticisms—some that he then faced from the White House and others he anticipated from Congress—that portrayed his recommended force levels as either unnecessarily high or dangerously low. With the former, he marshaled a number of arguments to persuade Wiesner and others, including Kennedy, of the inadvisability of further reductions. As for Congress, he asked the chiefs to agree to inclusion in the final budget memorandum of a statement that they had provided him "continuing counsel and assistance" in developing the budget and that although the force structure did not include everything the services had recommended, the chiefs believed the proposed program would "further increase our combat effectiveness and provide powerful forces in a high state of readiness for defense of the security interests of the United States." But the chiefs balked, preferring instead alternate language Admiral Anderson proposed, stating that the secretary's program did not include "all the forces, modernization and improvement" they had recommended.[27] On 3 December McNamara sent a slightly modified memorandum to the president recommending total Department of Defense NOA, including military assistance and civil defense, of $54.4 billion. He inserted a footnote explaining that the chief of naval operations, the Air Force chief of staff, and the commandant of the Marine Corps had "certain reservations, particularly as regards the rate of modernization and the growth in combat effectiveness of certain US forces in relation to the Sino-Soviet threat."[28]

At a White House meeting on 5 December that lasted nearly two hours, attended by presidential advisers, top OSD officials, and General Taylor (but not the Joint Chiefs), McNamara carefully went over his memorandum, focusing on the large gap between service estimates and his own recommendations. Differences over strategic retaliatory forces, besides the RS-70 and Skybolt, centered on the number of Minuteman missiles. He noted that the chiefs had recommended more such missiles than he, and they "felt fairly strongly on that point."[29]

In response to a question from the president, McNamara stated that approval of the Army's requested additional division, which he opposed, would cost about $1.5 billion over five years in equipment, support forces, and operating expenses. But he pointed out, and Taylor concurred, that neither the Joint Chiefs collectively nor Army Chief of Staff General Earle Wheeler separately wanted to press for an additional division at present. McNamara thought more necessary a substantial increase in PEMA (Procurement of Equipment and Munitions for the Army). For FY 1964 he proposed spending $3.3 billion on PEMA, whereas in previous years it had been well below $2 billion.[30]

As for the Navy, McNamara mentioned that the differences centered on the shipbuilding and conversion program, with the Navy requesting about $2.2 billion and McNamara recommending approximately $500 million less for FY 1964. Over several years his recommendations would save $2-3 billion. Disagreements involved both the amount of money and how to use it. The Navy wanted to phase in nuclear submarines earlier than McNamara did and also to replace conventional frigates with nuclear-powered ones. In scaling back the Navy estimates, the secretary recognized that shipbuilding was "a very popular issue with certain members of Congress and I anticipate great controversy on it." McNamara concluded his presentation by drawing attention to the chiefs' views as described in the memorandum and asked Taylor to say more on the subject. Taylor remarked that the secretary had made a "very fair" presentation. The Army, he said, appeared quite happy with the budget, especially with the extra procurement money. The Navy concerned itself primarily with modernization and what it considered a declining aircraft inventory. The Air Force, the "most unhappy" of the services, was upset that strategic capabilities were not keeping pace with the increasing Soviet threat.[31]

The president then spoke at length, questioning the need for the "awful lot of megatonnage" in U.S. strategic weapons, and remarked, "I don't see quite why we are building as many as we're building." Taylor said he always felt "we probably have too much and I think if we were starting from scratch I would still take that position." However, at the present time, there were "too many imponderables for us to back away and go back to a very small force." Kennedy continued probing the justification for the strategic force levels and cited Wiesner's recent memorandum calling for reductions in the number of Minutemen from 950 to 800 and Polaris submarines from 41 to 35. In countering Wiesner's arguments, McNamara dwelt on the many uncertainties in U.S. estimates, particularly the questionable effectiveness of Hound Dog missiles and an "archaic" B-52 force. He responded unequivocally to the president's queries about further reductions: "I would say that my recommendation to you on our strategic forces is to take the requirement and double it and buy it. Because I don't believe we can under any circumstances run the risk of having too few here. . . . I think it's money well spent." When the president asked whether the proposed force levels would deter the Soviet Union, McNamara replied that their purpose was principally to deter, but they also gave the United States and its allies "the confidence that we have that deterrent power."[32]

McNamara admitted that the total number of Minuteman missiles projected for FY 1968 was certainly open to argument, but he saw "no room for argument" about the 150 now under debate. He worried that a decision against the additional missiles would lead to the charge that the administration was changing the nation's fundamental military policy by not procuring the weapons needed to destroy the Soviet Union's nuclear capability. The Air Force, which had been substantially cut, felt strongly about this issue and would make it public.

McNamara also thought he would be unable to rebut a second anticipated charge, namely that cuts in the number of Minutemen missiles and Polaris submarines would "lead us to a position where the Soviets have more megatonnage and more warheads." He feared that a myth like the "missile gap" could easily develop, fanned by deep emotions beginning to surface in the Pentagon. "I don't mean to say that Curtis [LeMay] is emotionally biased, but he is saying that the program that I am presenting is endangering the national security. And he believes it." When Bell suggested that needlessly high force levels might nurture the opposite myth, namely indefinite U.S. nuclear superiority, McNamara replied, "I can fairly state today that that is the national policy, Dave. I'm also prepared to recognize it may not be the right policy, but I don't think we ought to change it in the fiscal '64 budget. . . . In a minute we have to say that our policy is to maintain nuclear superiority. Now, maybe we can change that someday but we can't change that today without seriously weakening the alliance." Wiesner finally conceded McNamara's point by admitting that "we have to face the whole issue of what we're trying to accomplish and we can't do it in three days and a budget." In the end, Kennedy came out for more air- and sealift forces and requested that more attention be paid by the Air Force to "indirect warfare." After a brief discussion on Nike-Zeus, the president expressed the desire to postpone that decision a little longer.[33]

In mid-December, in a formal address in New York City as well as in a national radio and television appearance, Kennedy endeavored to prepare public opinion for the upcoming record budget, with its high deficit and his tax cut proposal, and to clarify some key defense issues. One was Minuteman. The first 20 Minuteman missiles, stored in silos near Great Falls, Montana, had been declared operational on 11 December. Pointing to this initial capability, the president stressed McNamara's belief that as Minuteman became available in large numbers, defense expenditures would "peak off." In remarks that appeared to doom Nike-Zeus, the president also said he saw no sense, because of the high cost involved, in deploying an anti-ballistic missile system until it was perfected. He drew attention to the technical difficulties in trying to "shoot a bullet with a bullet" and asserted that "if you have a thousand bullets coming at you, that is a terribly difficult task which we have not mastered yet." But he did not think the Soviet Union had either.[34]

As he had the previous year, the president invited the Joint Chiefs to his Palm Beach, Florida, residence over the Christmas holiday, 27 December, to hear their views on the budget. The most critical was Admiral Anderson, whose relations with McNamara had become strained after a verbal confrontation with the secretary during the Cuban missile crisis. Anderson cited inadequacies in Navy personnel and in funds for operations, spare parts, and maintenance, and urged that the Navy have more say in these areas. In general he asked for more Navy authority and more attention given to "professional judgement." He also voiced disappointment that the Navy had asked for eight additional nuclear attack submarines and received only six.[35]

In contrast, General Wheeler pronounced the budget "most satisfactory" to the Army and repeated a comment McNamara had made in one of his DPMs that the Army would be in its best shape since the Korean War. Still, the Army was not happy with its personnel level of 960,000 and with postponement of the decision to deploy Nike-Zeus. During a sporadic discussion regarding Nike-Zeus, the president stressed that a $9 billion deficit projected for the next fiscal year made the system too expensive a proposition at the time. The president queried both Wheeler and McNamara on the cost difference between the Army's Nike-Zeus proposal and McNamara's more modest development program. Kennedy subsequently said he had decided to stay with McNamara's recommendation on Nike-Zeus.[36]

Although the Air Force probably fared the worst of the services in the budget decisions, General LeMay observed that "in his five years of budget planning this had been the best with the greatest amount of agreement among the Chiefs and the best feeling of support from their civilian superiors, including the President, that the Joint Chiefs had ever had." LeMay had misgivings about inadequacies in Air Force assault forces, the slow rate of modernization of tactical fighters, and insufficient funding of air defense. His major concern, however, related to the strategic forces, where he discerned a trend toward an all-missile force. He had presented his arguments to McNamara and had been "properly heard," but his strong concerns remained. General David Shoup, commandant of the Marine

Corps, believed that the budget's procurement funding would leave the Marine Corps "the best they had ever been in peacetime." The president then expressed concern about sea and air transport and fighter aircraft and requested further study on these matters. Kennedy reminded the group of the huge amounts of money the administration had spent in the last two years on defense and of the various international crises it had had to deal with. He felt quite certain about the need for more dollars rather than fewer in the future, and envisioned at least as many troubles worldwide, and in Latin America probably more. While the chiefs should be "constantly mindful" that "we are doing enough," he also wanted them to remember that he faced a hefty budget deficit.[37]

After a discussion of future policy toward Cuba, Taylor put forward a Joint Chiefs proposal concerning testimony before Congress, which was approved. The proposal read: "Provided the Chiefs are on record with a corporate position, the official queried may state that position indicating it is unanimous or split as the case may be, without identifying the views of an individual chief or service. Under such circumstances, any member of JCS may explain his personal position in accordance with usual procedures bearing on testimony before Congress." McNamara said that in accordance with the proposal, only he, Gilpatric, and the chiefs would disclose any positions or decisions taken by the chiefs.[38]

Admiral Anderson, disappointed with the meeting, recalled that as he went over his areas of disagreement with McNamara, neither the secretary nor Gilpatric said anything. At the end of the meeting, Kennedy "thanked us all, we left, and there were no changes made." This was not quite true. Afterwards McNamara and Gilpatric continued the discussion with the president alone and agreed on no further changes in the sealift and tactical airlift portion of the budget. However, they did decide to add 72 C-130 transport aircraft, causing an adjustment in the NOA estimate to reflect the change but leaving the expenditures estimate unaltered.[39]

In his message to Congress on 17 January, the president proposed a federal administrative expenditures budget of $98.8 billion and NOA of $96.1 billion. Kennedy acknowledged that the economy's performance in 1962 had not met expectations. To stimulate growth he was including in the budget a tax reduction and reform proposal, although its initial effect would be a revenue loss. This had contributed, he said, to his decision to limit proposed expenditures severely, except in national defense and space programs. He characterized Defense programs as essentially continuing the emphases of previous years on strengthening strategic retaliatory forces, improving air and missile defenses, increasing the strength and flexibility of conventional forces, and bolstering counterinsurgency forces.[40] In fact, funds for strategic retaliatory forces, Table 6 shows, declined rather sharply from the administration's FY 1962 estimates.

The final DoD estimates in the president's budget message amounted to $49,314,237,000 NOA for military functions. The addition of military assistance, military construction, civil defense, proposed supplementals, and a separate new appropriation title (Family Housing, Defense—as required by the 1962 Military Construction Act) brought the overall Defense estimates to $53,960,637,000, the largest military budget since the Korean War. Use of $300 million in transfers from prior year balances reduced this to $53,660,637,000.[41]

TABLE 6

TOA and NOA by Program, FY 1962-FY 1964[a]
($ billions)

	FY 62 (Original)	FY 62 (Final)	FY 63 (Current Est.)	FY 64 (Budget Est.)
Strategic retaliatory forces	7.6	9.1	8.5	7.3
Continental air and missile defense forces	2.2	2.1	1.9	2.0
General purpose forces	14.5	17.5	18.1	19.1
Sealift and airlift forces	.9	1.2	1.4	1.4
Reserve and Guard forces	1.7	1.8	2.0	2.0
Research and development	3.9	4.3	5.5	5.9
General support	12.3	12.7	13.7	14.6
Civil defense	-----	.3	.2	.3
Military assistance	1.8	1.8	1.6	1.6
Proposed legislation	-----	-----	-----	.9
Total obligational authority [b]	44.9	51.0	52.8	55.2
Less financing adjustment	1.2	1.6	1.5	1.5
New obligational authority	43.7	49.4	51.3	53.7

[a] Numbers do not add in all instances due to rounding. Figures exclude cost of warheads.
[b] Total Obligational Authority (TOA) was usually larger than NOA because it included elements not part of NOA, such as transfer of unobligated balances, reappropriations, and net offsetting receipts (collections from the public).

Source: Table 1, Financial Summary, House, Subcommittee of the Committee on Appropriations, *Hearings: Department of Defense Appropriations for 1964*, 88 Cong, 1 sess, 109.

Congressional reaction to the budget by both parties was negative. Republicans denounced it quite harshly; Senate Minority Leader Everett Dirksen (R-Ill.) called it "incredible" and "a mockery of the Administration's brave talk of letting the taxpayer keep more of his money through tax reductions." J. William Fulbright (D-Ark.), chairman of the Senate Foreign Relations Committee, said that on first impression the budget, especially for defense, looked "extraordinarily high." Another prominent Democrat, House Appropriations Committee Chairman Clarence Cannon, termed the budget "entirely too big" and promised that Congress would "look for and find places to cut it substantially without impairing national security."[42]

The Ups and Downs of the Authorization Bill

Concurrent with the president's budget message to Congress, DoD submitted to the House and the Senate a draft of proposed legislation authorizing some $15.358 billion for procurement, research, development, test, and evaluation of aircraft, missiles, and naval vessels. During the previous year's clash over the RS-70, Congress had amended its procedures to require authorization of funds not only for procurement but also for research, development, test, and evaluation. As a result of the broadened scope of their responsibilities, the armed services committees planned to hear testimony not only from McNamara, the service secretaries, the JCS chairman and service chiefs, but also from Harold Brown, director of Defense Research and Engineering.[43]

Despite concern within OSD over the antagonism some members of Congress had displayed toward McNamara the previous year, Hitch remained upbeat in the fall of 1962 about prospects for the FY 1964 budget. Some observers, however, predicted acrimonious confrontations with Congress, particularly over the reduced funding for the RS-70 and cancellation of Skybolt. Certain congressmen promised strong protests about Skybolt, in part because of a feeling of betrayal, since they regarded continuing administration support of Skybolt as the price paid for their acceptance of the diminished RS-70 program. Others simply desired a greater voice in shaping defense policy, an attitude that promised closer scrutiny of McNamara's policy decisions than they might otherwise have invited from a technical point of view.[44]

Assistant for Legislative Affairs David McGiffert believed that the previous year's controversy over National Guard and Reserve reorganization would not be revived. Yet he foresaw continuing difficulties regarding the RS-70 and possible tough questioning, especially in the Senate, over Skybolt. He also anticipated pressures to accelerate the shipbuilding program, a favorite cause of House Armed Services Committee Chairman Carl Vinson, who was understood to have raised the issue recently with the president. In fact, Vinson asked a congressional staffer to obtain from the Navy a list of ships it had requested but which McNamara had rejected, plus a prioritized list of approximately 10 ships the Navy would like to have included in the budget if Congress were to amend the appropriation bill. At the top of the latter list were the two additional nuclear-powered attack submarines.[45]

When McGiffert discussed with Vinson the upcoming posture hearings, the chairman said he wanted McNamara to read his entire statement, even though it would take a substantial period of time. He expected the secretary to cover

Skybolt and the RS-70, although he would wait to receive an explanation for Skybolt's cancellation before deciding whether to hold separate hearings on that subject.[46]

Longer than the previous year's, the posture statement, prepared by Henry Glass of Hitch's staff, came to 221 pages, including 40 pages of tables. McNamara spent 17 hours (30 January through 4 February 1963) presenting and discussing the statement with the House Armed Services Committee, during which he devoted considerable time the first morning to a discussion of the Cuban missile crisis and its aftermath. To McGiffert it seemed that the committee questioned McNamara "exhaustively, frankly, and in some respects, caustically" about the key issues, whereas the previous year his appearance before the committee was "all sweetness and light." In particular, the questioning on the RS-70 revealed a strong majority feeling that the manned bomber program should continue. However, Vinson told McNamara privately that he felt the RS-70 as proposed was not desirable.[47]

Following McNamara's appearance, Representative Hébert revealed in a radio-TV interview that the committee had learned that the secretary had overridden a majority of the Joint Chiefs of Staff on both the RS-70 and Skybolt decisions. These decisions, the congressman declared, did not raise questions of civilian control over the military, but dealt with weaponry matters where "military judgment should be given full consideration." Hébert believed that Congress had probably furnished the secretary of defense too much power. The question for Congress now was whether "we want to take back that power."[48]

During subsequent testimony Hébert sharply pressed Brown regarding his recommendations on the RS-70 and Skybolt, as well as how much military advice he had received on these matters. But Brown declined to name the military members of his staff he had consulted. Hébert also questioned General Wheeler and Admiral Anderson as to McNamara's consultations with the chiefs and to what extent they had directly advised the president. McGiffert believed that the Louisiana congressman was serving as "Vinson's stalking horse" in pursuing this line, but Vinson had lost his zest for the kind of confrontation that in 1962 had raised serious constitutional questions. When a committee member inquired whether the chiefs should be asked to divulge the number of times McNamara had reversed or changed their unanimous decisions, Vinson maintained it would be improper to do so long as Congress desired civilian control of the military.[49]

At the conclusion of the hearings, the committee met on 25 February to prepare its report and unanimously approved by show of hands an amendment to provide $134 million for two additional nuclear-powered attack submarines. It also added $363.7 million for two more prototypes of the RS-70. Feelings ran especially strong on the RS-70. A colleague asked Vinson if he "would entertain consideration of legislation to clip the Secretary of Defense's wings just a little bit?" Again reflecting a less strident position, Vinson replied, "I am not hot enough on any legislation to take away from the Secretary and the President the authority in military matters. I cannot do that and the Congress won't do that. That won't be a sensible thing." On 6 March the committee unanimously reported a bill of $15.856 billion authorizing everything the administration had requested, as well as the additional funds for the RS-70 and attack submarines.[50]

During two days of House floor debate on the measure, 12-13 March, McNamara became the object of biting criticism. Rep. Leslie Arends and Hébert delivered slashing attacks, while insisting their comments were not personal. Arends used the word "monarchy" to describe McNamara's management style. On 13 March the House approved the additional funds for the RS-70, but by an unexpectedly close vote, 224 to 179. To some degree, McGiffert felt, the nay votes may have reflected cost-consciousness, but the vote indicated "much greater support than last year for our position" and "more willingness to express dissent." Proponents of budget reduction lost another key vote. By a margin of 245 to 149, basically along party lines, the House defeated a Republican amendment to cut $800 million from the bill. The committee version thus remained intact, and on 13 March the House passed, 374 to 33, an authorization measure of $15.856 billion.[51]

Unlike its House counterpart, the Senate Armed Services Committee aimed primarily at reducing expenditures, but it too gave McNamara a thorough, albeit more deferential, grilling. Although Chairman Richard Russell expected McNamara's' testimony to take at most two days, the secretary spent four days (19-22 February), more than 20 hours in all, before the committee. As in the previous year committee members frequently interrupted his testimony with questions on both minor details and broad issues. They even raised several questions before he began reading the posture statement on the first day, 19 February, instead of waiting for breaks at certain points. At the outset Russell pressed McNamara to describe his conception of the role of Congress in providing for the defense of the country, asking whether the secretary believed "Congress is entitled to play more than merely a passive role in reviewing decisions of strategic policy." McNamara responded that Congress's role was to authorize forces and appropriate funds, but that it needed also to properly understand the strategy underlying the administration's proposals.[52]

On the second day, Margaret Chase Smith submitted to McNamara 36 questions regarding the unclassified version of the posture statement, a few of which she discussed verbally with him. Following testimony by Brown, the service secretaries, and their military aides, the committee concluded its hearings on 8 March, having covered a host of issues without giving much indication of what kind of bill it would report.[53]

Following House action, the Senate committee on 9 April reported an authorization bill of only some $15.147 billion, about $709 million less than the House measure and $211 million less than the administration request. The reductions resulted essentially from a three percent uniform cut in research, development, test, and evaluation; a three percent cut in certain support areas, e.g., spare parts; and reduced procurement quantities of some aircraft, missiles, and ships. And the committee eliminated funds the House had voted for the two extra attack submarines. On the other hand, it approved without change the House's increased amount for the RS-70. By a 9 to 8 vote, at the urging of Senator Thurmond, it added $196 million to begin procurement of Nike-Zeus.[54]

Much of the Senate floor debate centered on the Nike-Zeus amendment. In an extraordinary move, on 11 April the Senate agreed to Thurmond's proposal to consider the matter in executive session, the first time it had taken such action since 1943. Thurmond argued the need for Nike-Zeus to keep up with the Soviet Union's development of an antimissile system that reportedly could shoot down Polaris missiles and possibly even Minuteman missiles. However, supporters of the administration's position, led by Russell, carried the day. Following a nearly four-and-a-half-hour secret session, the Senate approved, 58 to 16, Russell's amendment to remove the funds for Nike-Zeus. A tragic event influenced the Senate's deliberations. The day before, a *Thresher* submarine and its entire crew were lost in the North Atlantic. Citing the disaster, Russell and his supporters defeated an amendment to restore the funds for the two additional attack submarines, which were of the *Thresher* type, on the grounds that the submarine's loss was reason for putting additional money, if any, into Polaris submarines. Later that day the Senate passed by voice vote an authorization bill of about $14.951 billion.[55]

OSD informed the two committees that it opposed all the Senate cuts except the elimination of the additional funding for two more submarines and the three percent across-the-board reduction in R&D funds. To provide ammunition for the House conferees in deliberations with their Senate counterparts, Vinson asked McNamara to furnish him a statement, signed by the secretary, the JCS chairman, and each member of the Joint Chiefs, regarding the effect of the proposed Senate cuts on U.S. military capabilities. The response spoke of the reductions' "deleterious effect on our ability to maintain the required degree of offensive and defensive capability." Separately, the military services provided detailed comments to the armed services committee chairmen.[56]

These efforts had a mixed result. The conferees reinstated only half of the Senate cut but eliminated the funds for two additional attack submarines approved in the House version. They also retained the additional money the House voted for the RS-70. On 13 May the conference committee reported an authorization bill of over $15.314 billion, merely $44 million less than the administration had requested. The bill, approved by voice vote of the Senate on 13 May and the House the following day, became law on 23 May.[57] Below is a comparison of the requested and approved amounts through the key stages:

Administration Request	$15,358,691,000
House Armed Services Committee	15,856,391,000
House	15,856,391,000
Senate Armed Services Committee	15,147,491,000
Senate	14,951,481,000
Conference Committee/Enactment	15,314,291,000

Calls for Substantial Cuts

The criticism of excessive fat that had greeted the federal budget, and especially the defense portion, upon its presentation to Congress in January 1963 became more pointed and widespread as congressional hearings unfolded in the spring and summer. Some criticism had a partisan edge, but other proposals for budget reduction came from the president's own party.

Talk of steep cutbacks by prominent Republicans and a number of Democrats put the administration on the defensive. In light of the projected $11.9 billion deficit, Maurice H. Stans, former Bureau of the Budget director under President Eisenhower, suggested to Republican members of the appropriations subcommittees how the FY 1964 federal budget could be cut by $10-15 billion, which party leaders formally announced as a goal. Kennedy challenged them to indicate specifically where the cuts should come and "whose life is going to be adversely affected by those cuts." Eisenhower joined the fray, claiming the budget could be reduced by $13 billion without jeopardizing national security and especially questioning the large amounts budgeted for space exploration. In response Kennedy ridiculed the competence of Stans, whom the former president had cited as an authority, and dismissed talk of wholesale spending cuts, which, he said, would cut "the heart out of the military budget." Among Democrats, A. Willis Robertson, a member of the Senate Appropriations Committee, urged a $6 billion overall reduction, including $1.258 billion in defense, and said he would support the president's tax cuts only if they were accompanied by corresponding spending reductions.[58]

Wanting to respond in greater depth to Eisenhower's charge, Kennedy asked McNamara to prepare "an analysis of what our military strength was in 1961 if there had been a call for military action at that time, what is available to us today, and what will be available next summer." McNamara's response took sharp issue with Eisenhower's claim, "in view of the many critical deficiencies and vulnerabilities present in our defense posture in 1960 and 1961," which necessitated subsequent large increases in defense spending. As a prime example of the weakness that the Kennedy administration had inherited, McNamara maintained that "if we had continued our forces and readiness at the 1960-1961 level, we would not have had enough forces to carry out a successful invasion of Cuba if that should have proved necessary in the missile crisis of October 1962."[59]

Concurrently, the White House asked DoD to analyze the effect on the U.S armed forces of a $7.756 billion cut in FY 1964 new obligational authority, with the cuts allocated among the services in proportion to the amounts of their budget requests to Congress. Using the individual services' estimates of how they would absorb such cuts, Gilpatric forwarded to the White House the requested figures, with the caveat that OSD had not had sufficient time to determine whether, if the budget were to be reduced by that amount, the cuts should come in the areas indicated by the services.[60]

Academic voices joined the debate. In a pamphlet entitled *A Strategy for American Security*, Seymour Melman, professor of industrial management at Columbia University, and several Columbia colleagues decried the unnecessarily large military budget and its effects on American society, and the U.S. "overkill" nuclear forces capability. The defense budget, they claimed, could be cut by $16-24 billion. On 29 March Rep. William F. Ryan (D-N.Y.) sent the pamphlet to McNamara and asked the secretary to respond to Melman's recommendations. In a detailed commentary on the pamphlet Alain Enthoven concluded that it generally represented "very poor scholarship and analysis" and was "full of inaccuracies, contradictions and unsupported allegations." His remarks formed the basis of OSD's reply to Ryan, which Melman rebutted in a letter to Ryan. The congressman then made public all three letters.[61]

Melman mailed the pamphlet to McNamara and asked for an opportunity to discuss it with him and OSD staff. On the secretary's behalf, Hitch replied that many in OSD had read the pamphlet. He knew that Melman would "not be surprised to learn that we completely disagree with most of its major conclusions." However, Hitch did invite Melman to the Pentagon for a talk, where the two men, joined by Enthoven and Henry Glass, met on 7 June, without any apparent meaningful result.[62]

The House Shaves the Appropriation Bill

The gathering momentum in favor of budget cuts produced dramatic results during House consideration of the appropriation bill. During McNamara's lengthy testimony (6-13 February), as well as the subsequent testimony of General Taylor, the Joint Chiefs, and the service secretaries, the Subcommittee on Department of Defense Appropriations, chaired by George Mahon, gave little indication that it would slash defense spending. Members like Gerald Ford seemed more interested in identifying instances in which McNamara had denied or reduced military service requests for funds, particularly on the RS-70 and Skybolt, or overridden the recommendations of the chiefs, lines of inquiry that pointed to congressional restoration of funds taken out of the budget. After nearly four months, which included testimony from Melman and other advocates of budget reductions, the subcommittee concluded the hearings on 20 May obviously in a different frame of mind.[63]

A month later, on 21 June, the House Appropriations Committee accepted the subcommittee's recommendations and reported a bill of only $47.092 billion, approximately $2.2 billion less than the administration request. It did not include the extra funds for the RS-70 that the armed services committees had authorized. McNamara immediately issued a statement indicating pleasure at the committee's action regarding the RS-70, but also protesting the reduced funding for procurement of Air Force tactical aircraft and for military personnel, which he said would necessitate a manpower reduction of 60,000. Mahon indicated privately that he thought the cuts excessive but that "he had to go as far as he did to prevent a split with the Republicans on his subcommittee."[64]

In presenting the bill on the floor of the House Mahon delivered a strong endorsement of McNamara, who was, he said, "on top of the job" and "devoting his enormous talent and energy to the public interest and deserves the respect and the admiration of the American people." On 26 June the House passed the bill, with minor amendments, by a vote of 410 to 1. Vinson was absent during the floor debate and no House member offered an amendment to restore any of the funds removed from the bill. Democratic leaders may have thought it wiser to seek restoration of some of the funds when the Senate took up the measure.[65]

Averting Deeper Cuts in the Senate

The sizable House cuts posed difficult questions for OSD in determining which to appeal to the Senate. The cuts hit the Air Force, which had less budget flexibility than the Army or Navy, especially hard. Brown pointed out to McNamara the difficulty in requesting restoration of the three percent across-the-board cut in research, development, testing, and evaluation. The Senate, Brown felt, would likely respond that OSD had already accepted a three percent cut imposed by the armed services committees on aircraft, missiles, and ships, presumably the most important part of the program. The question might well be asked as to why it would then contest a three percent cut on the remainder. Instead Brown recommended that McNamara indicate "what the specific impact" of the cuts would likely be. Heeding the advice, McNamara sent Defense Appropriations Subcommittee Chairman Russell a letter of reclama on 12 July, describing in detail the effects of the cuts DoD was appealing—a total of about $437.2 million, less than a quarter the amount the House had pared. McNamara expressed the department's willingness to accept the three percent blanket cut in research, development, test, and evaluation, except as it pertained to military space programs and the Air Force's classified programs.[66]

Despite congressional passage of continuing resolutions to ensure funding of federal programs beyond 1 July into FY 1964, McNamara expressed concern at the slow pace that legislation worked its way through Congress. McGiffert predicted that the current session might stretch even into November or December. McNamara therefore asked the service secretaries and others to provide him descriptions of the impact on military programs caused by the delays so that he could discuss the matter with Russell and other key members of Congress. When McGiffert pointed out that Russell's support during the upcoming weeks of anti-civil rights legislation might divert his attention from defense legislation, McNamara replied that Russell was "quite familiar with the effect on Defense of delays. If we can lay out the facts of our situation, I am sure he will place our national interests first." However, neither McNamara nor McGiffert had hopes for a sizable restoration of the House cuts, which was one reason, as McNamara explained, that he did not appeal more of them.[67]

New advocates for a DoD spending reduction—two young, recently elected senators—now entered the debate over the size of the budget. George McGovern (D-S.D.), a 41-year-old former director of Kennedy's Food for Peace program who had served two terms in the House of Representatives, and Gaylord Nelson (D-Wis.), a 47-year-old former governor of Wisconsin, both urged deep budget cuts. In July 1963, McGovern and Nelson sent a letter to McNamara complimenting him on his congressional budget presentations, but pointing out that testimony of other DoD officials had raised "serious doubts" in their minds about U.S. military programs, particularly the continued stockpiling of nuclear weapons. Through correspondence and meetings with OSD officials, they probed the justifications for various aspects of the budget. In a major speech on the Senate floor on 2 August, McGovern decried the "overkill" capability of U.S. defense forces and tentatively proposed cuts of $4 billion in the Defense budget and $1 billion in the Atomic Energy Commission budget. Other senators, mostly junior members, indicated they planned to speak in the same vein in the near future. McGovern and others had talked with Melman, who apparently had tried to win them over to his position. But McGovern's proposed cuts fell far short of the $16-24 billion called for by Melman.[68]

McGovern wrote to McGiffert thanking him for the cooperation that OSD had shown him and Senator Nelson, and expressing the hope that nothing in his speech would be "detrimental in any way to the best interests of the country." In his dealings with OSD officials, McGovern adopted a reasonable, courteous tone, indicating he trusted that DoD leadership would understand he was not "another Melman." He essentially wanted to promote a public debate on defense matters and the budget in particular that would strengthen rather than weaken the defense program.[69]

Prior to the Senate Defense Appropriations Subcommittee hearing to consider Defense's reclama on the House bill, Russell confided that he expected about 30 votes in favor of drastic cuts as a result of the efforts by Melman and McGovern. He would report out the bill only when he could get it on the calendar quickly in order to prevent any buildup of sentiment to reduce the DoD budget further. McGiffert thought Russell was overestimating such sentiment and that the number of senators favoring deep cuts would amount to 15 at most.[70]

DoD sent a large delegation to Capitol Hill for the hearing on 20 August, including Gilpatric, Brown, Generals Taylor, LeMay, and Wheeler, and other high-ranking military officials. Gilpatric and Taylor did virtually all the testifying. In arguing for the restoration of funds, Gilpatric stressed that the limited test ban treaty* signed the previous month with the Soviet Union had not altered "our assessment of the military threat confronting us now or likely to face us in the future." Asked to comment on proposals for slashing the Defense budget, Gilpatric said that Melman had "grossly oversimplified the problem" and that even the $4 billion cut McGovern advocated "would eliminate over one-half of the entire segment of the 1964 budget that supports strategic retaliatory forces." Taylor concentrated on debunking the "overkill" thesis, assuring the subcommittee that McNamara had "required the military authorities in the Pentagon to justify every strategic weapon supported by this budget" and that every one of these weapons had the "unanimous support" of the Joint Chiefs. These were vigorous arguments against further cuts, but, because DoD had accepted so many of the House cuts, one writer called the reclama "an unprecedented retreat."[71]

Nevertheless, the presentation had some effect. On 17 September the Senate Appropriations Committee, in reporting an amended bill, made a series of changes that restored $289.4 million of the amount the House had cut. This included $60 million for the Mobile Medium-Range Ballistic Missile, a restoration DoD had not requested. McNamara, however, had assured key senators that if the money were restored, he would proceed with the next phase of the weapon's development and would not reprogram the funds.[72]

Floor consideration of the measure on 24 September followed the vote earlier in the day, after a month-long Senate debate, to approve the limited test ban treaty, and discussion of the treaty carried over into the debate on the appropriation bill. Russell may well have arranged the schedule with this in mind, knowing that the Senate would be unlikely to approve even a slight reduction in Defense spending on the heels of approving the treaty. As expected McGovern offered an amendment to reduce procurement and R&D funds by 10 percent or about $2.3 billion. In lengthy remarks he argued that excessive military spending was leading to "the neglect of other vital sources of national strength." Russell, an opponent of the test ban treaty, declared that because the United States enjoyed only a slim margin of superiority over the Soviet Union the amendment would invite war by reducing U.S. strength. He warned against "an unjustified spirit of optimism as to the future designs of Soviet Russia" based on the test ban treaty. Russell's and even McGiffert's more cautious estimate a month earlier regarding Senate support

---

* See Chapter XIII.

for deep budget cuts proved wide of the mark. The Senate rejected the McGovern amendment, 74 to 2, with only Jennings Randolph (D-W.Va.) joining the South Dakota senator. It also narrowly voted down, 45 to 43, an amendment by Leverett Saltonstall to cut procurement funds by about $158 million and another, 72 to 5, by William Proxmire to delete the $60 million the Appropriations Committee had added for the MMRBM. The Senate then passed the bill, 77 to 0.[73]

Although Russell had been in the minority on the test-ban treaty vote, the Senate's actions on the appropriation bill represented not only a triumph for his views, but also a testament to his legislative skills. In a personal letter, Gilpatric praised "the masterful fashion in which you brought the debate on the Bill to the optimum conclusion. This country is indeed fortunate in having you at the leadership helm of the Senate on national security matters."[74]

Following a conference report that split the differences between the House and Senate versions, the House on 3 October approved, 335 to 3, an appropriation of slightly more than $47.22 billion (NOA). The Senate gave its approval later that day by voice vote, and the bill became law on 17 October.[75] The amount was about $2.1 billion less than the administration had requested:

Administration Request	$49,314,237,000
Passed House	47,092,009,000
Passed Senate	47,339,707,000
Conference Committee/Enacted	47,220,010,000

Subsequent additional appropriations for military construction, family housing, and civil defense and a deficiency appropriation for military personnel brought the total to $49,929,659,000.

White House and Department of the Treasury interest in reducing federal spending, plus McNamara's own cost reduction program and cautious approach in approving production of major new weapons systems, clearly exerted strong downward pressures on the FY 1964 Defense budget. It is ironic, however, that the secretary, who labored hard to tighten the budget, had to defend it from public and congressional calls for further reductions.

It must be noted, too, that budget cutting did not focus solely on DoD. Large projected deficits and the president's tax cut proposal provided ample reasons for Congress generally to rein in federal spending. In the fall of 1962 administration officials began using terms like "fiscal responsibility" in a way that reminded one observer of the Eisenhower administration's approach to the budget. In light of the administration's own recognition of the altered economic realities, little wonder that Congress subsequently reduced the overall federal budget for FY 1964 by $6.5 billion.[76]

Calls for defense spending cuts had other roots, too, including partisanship, though Democrats ranked among the strongest proponents of cuts. Yet the motivation behind proposals for across-the-board cuts by McGovern and others may have derived in part from frustration among the rank and file in both houses in dealing with the complexities of the Defense budget, along with an unwillingness to follow the lead of senior members of the armed services and appropriations committees. Moreover, in the immediately preceding sessions, Congress had only reluctantly, and essentially for constituency reasons, cut military spending. In effect it had tried to maintain a balance of power with the executive branch by increasing military spending. In this session it may have occurred to some members that withholding appropriations constituted a more effective way of exercising power. Finally, the relaxation in tension with the Soviet Union following the signing of the limited test ban treaty, plus the growing perception of U.S. military strength as so vast that substantial cuts could safely be made in defense spending, also helped contribute to the trimming of the administration's budget request.[77]

Some of the motivation reflected resentment of McNamara, who increasingly became the object of criticism, in part because of his brilliance, forcefulness, and self-assurance. The working over that Sen. John L. McClellan (D-Ark.) and the Senate Preparedness Investigating Subcommittee gave McNamara during the TFX hearings that spring further diminished his standing with Congress.* "There's no doubt about it," an anonymous Democratic senator was quoted as saying in March, "the Congressional honeymoon with Bob McNamara is over." The press made much of the worsened relationship. Some saw the reason primarily as McNamara's personality and management style.[78]

That the FY 1964 DoD budget did not suffer even more is attributable in large measure to the general support for the administration's programs by Mahon and Russell, as well as to Vinson's less contentious attitude that allowed another effort to increase funding for the RS-70 to fizzle out. Russell, who helped defeat the Thurmond amendment to add funds for Nike-Zeus during consideration of the authorization bill, played the key role. As a biographer has noted, Russell, a consistent supporter of Kennedy's defense buildup, often found himself out front of the administration on military spending matters. Chairman of both the Armed Services Committee and the Defense Appropriations Subcommittee, he presided, as one Senate colleague remarked, "over the spending authorization and substantive law for about half the government as far as money goes." Yet the Kennedy administration deserves credit, too. It took the movement for defense spending reduction seriously and responded to it pragmatically.

Although McNamara expressed public indignation during the spring of 1963 over the cuts made in the budget, the administration at the same time signaled

---

* See Chapter XVII.

that it might itself initiate deep cuts in DoD spending in upcoming years, in part to offset the balance of payments deficit.[79] The hints came as the Pentagon began preparing the FY 1965 budget, a task started under Kennedy that would have to be completed by his successor, Lyndon B. Johnson.*

---

* See Chapter XVIII.

CHAPTER VII

Berlin: The Wall

A grave crisis in Berlin in the summer of 1961 shook the twin pillars of Department of Defense policymaking—strategic planning and the budget—and displaced Laos and Cuba as the central foreign policy focus of the new Kennedy administration. Soviet Premier Nikita Khrushchev's renewed threat to turn control of access to West Berlin over to the government of East Germany forced the administration to augment further the FY 1962 Defense budget, with a third amendment in July 1961, and to confront the limitations of available U.S. military options and larger questions of overall national and Allied security strategy.

As an immediate consequence, the crisis required the calling up of reserves, reorganizing the National Guard, and increasing the number of Army divisions. In the larger scheme these measures heightened Pentagon awareness of the value of conventional alternatives to nuclear forces. Deputy Assistant Secretary of Defense for International Security Affairs Henry Rowen later observed, "The Secretary of Defense quickly realized during the Berlin crisis that he didn't want to use nuclear weapons and that the options he had with existing forces and plans didn't look good."[1] Berlin thus presented the administration with both an early foreign policy test and a seminal opportunity to apply the still evolving concept of flexible response.

Berlin in the Eisenhower Administration

Berlin remained a potential Cold War flash point after the 1948-49 Berlin blockade and airlift, but almost a decade passed before it flared up. Although petty harassment in the form of delays and "administrative" difficulties periodically plagued individual passengers traveling to Berlin in Allied military convoys, there was no direct challenge to the status of the city until 10 November 1958, when Khrushchev asserted that the Soviet Union would "hand over to the sovereign German Democratic Republic [GDR] the functions in Berlin that are still exercised by Soviet agencies." Two weeks later the warnings became explicit. On 27 November the Soviet Union sent the three Western powers a note calling for an end to Allied rights in West Berlin and the conversion of West Berlin into a "free city." The Western powers were given a grace period of six months to follow suit, failing which the Soviet Union would carry out the planned measures through an agreement with the GDR.[2]

Khrushchev's action was a calculated effort to achieve several goals. As one White House official remarked, "If Khrushchev could force the west to grant East Germany legal recognition, he would not only secure the status quo throughout Eastern Europe but would demoralize the West German government in Bonn, disrupt NATO, stop the momentum of western unification and regain the European offensive."[3] Such potential benefits seemed to justify the threat, even at the risk of precipitating a crisis, but strong Western objections caused Khrushchev to back off. The grace period gave him time to maneuver, as he claimed the six months was "fully sufficient to provide a sound basis for the solution of the questions connected with the change in Berlin's situation."[4] He committed himself to no particular date. Initially, vehement Western reaction denounced not only the unilateral Soviet action but also the idea of West Berlin as a neutralized "free city." Washington responded that there would be no negotiations "under menace or ultimatum." Further discussions on Berlin would have to take place within the wider context of a settlement of the German problem and European security.[5]

The Soviet Union agreed to discuss Berlin with the Western allies at the Geneva Foreign Ministers Conference in May 1959, signaling it would allow the treaty deadline to elapse. For their part, U.S. leaders showed some flexibility, proffering token concessions so long as the accommodation would not interfere with Allied rights in West Berlin. Secretary of State John Foster Dulles himself had appeared willing in 1958 to allow East Germans to serve as Soviet deputies for such nominal administrative tasks as stamping documents or issuing passports.* This approach did not appeal to West Germans, and its appearance of appeasement may have figured in Khrushchev's reviving the Berlin crisis when another opportunity presented itself. That opportunity would not come during the remainder of the Eisenhower administration, however, and Khrushchev seemed willing to postpone a resolution until a new administration took office.[6]

Indecision, Spring 1961

In his memoirs, the Soviet premier claimed that he awaited the outcome of the presidential election in 1960 before taking any further step. The new president, young and untested, may have appeared to Khrushchev as a more malleable

---

* An ailing Dulles was succeeded by Christian A. Herter, Jr., on 22 April 1959. Dulles died on 27 May, the day the six-month deadline expired.

negotiating partner than Eisenhower. The Soviet Union lowered the rhetoric as the Kennedy term began but left no doubt about its intentions regarding Berlin. Even if the United States did not stand ready to give formal recognition to an East German government or accept West Berlin as a demilitarized entity, it should at least join with the Soviet Union in removing the outdated occupation status in Berlin. This was the suggestion of Mikhail Menshikov, Soviet ambassador to the United States, in conversations with Adlai Stevenson weeks after the presidential election.[7]

The fragile truce prevailing in late 1960 did not last long. Even before the inauguration Khrushchev sounded a harsh note in a speech voicing Soviet support for wars of national liberation. He emphasized that the West was "particularly vulnerable" in West Berlin to a separate treaty between the Soviet Union and the GDR.[8] Six weeks later, on 17 February 1961, a strongly worded aide-memoire to the Federal Republic made it clear that if the West did not participate in a peace treaty in the future, a separate arrangement would end "the occupation regime in West Berlin with all the attendant consequences."[9]

Why the seeming mixed signals from Moscow? Perhaps fearing China's growing nuclear capability, the Soviets initially sought a rapprochement, a collaboration of convenience with the West, as Averell Harriman's discussions in November 1960 with Menshikov hinted. The resumption of Khrushchev's bluster may have come as a response to Chinese leader Mao Tse-tung's assertion of Soviet softness toward the United States.[10] Possibly, and more likely, the deterioration of East Germany through increasing loss of population to the West was not simply draining the GDR's resources but its morale as well. Shoring up the East German position would entail a more aggressive attitude toward the West.

The renewed tension may have stemmed from actions on the U.S. side as well, even if misread. Kennedy speculated later that the March and May amendments to the FY 1962 Defense budget may have provoked the Soviet Union. Moreover, Harriman's statement in Moscow in March 1961 that "all discussions in Berlin must begin from the start" may have come across inaccurately as Kennedy's repudiation of concessions made under Eisenhower. Nevertheless, these explanations failed to take into account that Khrushchev had manifested truculence before Kennedy moved into the White House.[11]

The revival of the long-simmering Berlin issue forced the new administration to confront the possibility of a crisis, probably in the near future. Initially it seems to have hoped that the tensions would dissolve short of violence, as had happened in the past. The Soviet Union had backed down before and might do so again. Any confrontation should come clearly from the Soviet side, not from any hasty action by the United States. Significantly, Kennedy's State of the Union address on 30 January 1961 made no mention of an impending crisis over Berlin.[12]

The president's failure to mention Berlin caused concern in West Germany. At a meeting with Foreign Minister Heinrich von Brentano on 17 February, Kennedy stated then and repeated in the following month to West Berlin Mayor Willy Brandt and in April to Chancellor Konrad Adenauer that the United States remained fully engaged and would not retreat from its pledge to preserve freedom in West Berlin.[13]

White House reassurances to German leaders represented more than cosmetic efforts to calm an anxious ally's fears. In fact, Washington had no illusions about the fragility and tentativeness of the lull in Soviet-American relations over Berlin. Preparations were well-advanced on scenarios to deal with anticipated troubles. Some dated back to the Soviet challenge in 1958 to turn Berlin into a "free city" and involved Britain and France as the allies most affected by changes in Berlin. Of special importance was LIVE OAK, a tripartite planning group established by the United States, Britain, and France on 4 April 1959 under U.S. Commander-in-Chief, Europe (USCINCEUR) General Lauris Norstad to deal with the military implications of any Soviet action that might threaten Allied access to Berlin. As of June 1960 Norstad had assumed responsibility for all LIVE OAK planning and execution, including planning for coping with any attempted closure of ground access to Berlin.[14]

As part of the preparation, on 7 October 1960 the State Department had asked Defense to suggest from a wide-ranging checklist measures that might be accorded discussion priority or given early implementation. At OSD's request later in October, the Joint Chiefs, on 26 January 1961, six days after Kennedy's inauguration, proposed several actions, including public relations and economic measures, for unilateral tripartite implementation. More importantly, they proposed the holding of a tripartite military exercise that would "demonstrate determination to maintain U.S. legal rights in Berlin." In forwarding the JCS recommendations to Secretary of State Rusk, Assistant Secretary of Defense for International Security Affairs Paul Nitze did not favor the military exercise "at this time" but wanted to establish a tripartite operations staff (in addition to the existing planning staff) under Norstad. Nitze made it clear that the capability to respond quickly and effectively to a Berlin contingency "should be carefully timed and executed to achieve the maximum benefits."[15]

Divisions among the allies and within the U.S. defense establishment compounded the difficulties DoD faced as it assumed an increasing role in the planning for Berlin contingencies. LIVE OAK was a case in point, as differences developed over the utility as well as the size of a probe along the autobahn to Berlin to test Soviet intentions. The Europeans believed that NATO conventional ground forces were no match for the Soviets, who vastly outnumbered the allies in weapons and troops. The Joint Chiefs and Norstad agreed, convinced that defense of the West, including Berlin, remained anchored to a low nuclear threshold, which had been the prevailing assumption of the previous administration. In contrast, during the spring and early summer of 1961 McNamara and Nitze insisted to Norstad that strong probes down the autobahn and other conventional responses should be looked at.[16]

At issue were fundamental doubts the McNamara team had about the views of Norstad, the chiefs, and the allies on the role of conventional forces in Europe and the mindset—inherited from the Eisenhower years—that maintained whatever action took place on the conventional level would quickly escalate to the nuclear and that in any case Soviet aggression could more effectively be deterred playing the nuclear card. The reservations extended not only to the strategic philosophy inherited from the Eisenhower White House but to the inherited machinery as well. Kennedy's national security team did not dismantle existing organizations such as the U.S. Coordinating Committee on Contingency Planning for Germany and Japan; it simply bypassed them. Ad hoc policy studies and special investigations took their place until the Berlin Task Force, headed by the State Department's Foy Kohler, was established in July 1961. Planning for the defense of Berlin fell into a larger framework of NATO policy, with Nitze having taken responsibility for a full-scale review of the situation.[17]

The Acheson Initiatives

As Soviet pressures mounted and U.S. military planning proceeded fitfully, the president turned to former Secretary of State Dean Acheson for advice on the developing crisis. In a special report on Berlin on 3 April 1961 Acheson warned the president that the Soviets "more likely than not" would provoke a crisis later in the year. He concluded that short of a mutually acceptable reunification plan for all of Germany, no solution to the problems of West Berlin appeared in sight. But if every course of action were "dangerous and unpromising," inaction would be "even worse." In this circumstance, he declared, "a bold and dangerous course may be the safest." Acheson's admonition came through as nothing less than a thinly veiled recommendation that the West should be prepared to go to war over Berlin if necessary. Economic and political measures would not suffice by themselves. Significantly, Acheson believed that a buildup of conventional forces would reinforce nuclear deterrence.[18]

Acheson's belligerent warnings stood in stark contrast to an earlier study prepared by the State Department in March entitled "The Problem of Berlin," which aired the possibility of an arrangement allowing for a limited East German role in controlling access to West Berlin without sacrificing the West's basic position. Such negotiations, State said, ought to be preceded by a strong warning to the Soviets that an act of aggression would result in mobilizing U.S. forces as massively and effectively as the invasion of South Korea did in 1950. However, further detailed contingency planning would prove difficult, if only because "the governments concerned, particularly the British, are reluctant to commit themselves to rigid courses of action on a purely hypothetical basis and thus to deprive themselves of freedom to exploit any opportunity for new diplomatic approaches which might present themselves as the situation develops."[19]

OSD found State's conclusions unsatisfactory. ISA's policy planning staff expressed concern that the State paper "does not deal with the situation which would arise if the Soviets increased pressures for a Berlin settlement and we decided to initiate existing contingency plans as a response . . . . Thus the paper gives an impression of a readiness to make concessions which ISA should oppose." In brief, ISA complained that "the paper has a pessimistic, defeatist tone which, though possibly justified on factual basis, seems inappropriate as a setting for discussions with the British or any other country." ISA recommended a more positive view of contingency measures.[20]

In the short run, at least, Acheson's advice determined the administration's approach during British Prime Minister Harold Macmillan's visit to Washington in early April. Although Acheson never claimed that his proposal had become administration policy, his dominant personality conveyed that impression to Macmillan. His recommendation created alarm: In the absence of an agreement on Berlin, the allies should be prepared to take military countermeasures, including sending a division down the autobahn, if routes were blocked. The British and many in the White House circle believed in pursuing negotiations, while Acheson and Nitze, the latter speaking for OSD, saw only futility and frustration in that course. Yet Acheson, for all his belligerence and irritability with those who disagreed with him, may well have been less adamant than he sounded.[21]

Whether or not the Acheson April initiative was less rigid than its rhetoric, it opened a round of intense examination of U.S. and NATO preparedness in the event of a new crisis over Berlin. Previously, in March, McNamara asked the Joint Chiefs again for countermeasure suggestions against Soviet aggressive action. The chiefs responded before the end of April in two reports. On the positive side they found no fault with U.S. contingency planning, but they cited "important deficiencies" in the tripartite planning. To give the Soviets pause would require considerably more Allied troops in place in Europe, and the allies should attempt no probe of ground access until that time. In a third report on 4 May, they responded to Acheson's recommendations, which they found for the most part "a realistic analysis of a complex politico-military problem." They recommended modifying his proposed division-size probe by shifting it to a later stage in the confrontation process. Since a battalion-size force might conceivably open the autobahn, a larger force would come into play only if the smaller probe should fail. The JCS reports supported vigorous efforts to restore ground access to Berlin before trying an airlift. On the other hand, the chiefs believed that because Berlin was ultimately indefensible against overwhelming Soviet ground forces, resorting to a general war, involving nuclear weapons, might be preferable to engaging in a conventional conflict. The JCS apparently judged that a low nuclear threshold should remain a primary objective.[22]

This assumption, clearly a legacy of the Eisenhower era, disturbed OSD and focused the debate on the continuing relevance of the Eisenhower strategy. While the JCS reliance on rapid progression from conventional to nuclear response may have been thinkable in 1958, Nitze viewed it as much less so in the current situation. He wanted the president to have more flexibility in decisionmaking and encouraged "new policy guidance which would facilitate development of military plans for graduated, intermediate military actions between small conventional operations and general nuclear war, and also for possible U.S.-West German military actions as an intermediate step between U.S. unilateral and tripartite or NATO military actions."[23]

McNamara, too, found Acheson's views more persuasive than those of the JCS. The idea of having to move directly to nuclear war after only token ground action he found repugnant on moral as well as logical grounds. But given the chiefs' concern, his report to the president on 5 May 1961 incorporated their views without accepting either their doubts about the defensibility of Berlin or their inclination to rely on the nuclear option. McNamara envisioned among other factors an East German uprising that might be supported by the new special U.S. forces being created. He asked Nitze on 19 May to draft a revision of NSC 5803, "U.S. Policy Toward Germany," that would raise the nuclear threshold by providing for use of "substantial conventional military force" to reopen the way to Berlin; concurrently, he asked the JCS to address the same matters. Moreover, he urged Nitze to work with the chiefs and the State Department in arranging for the participation of the West German government in Berlin contingency planning.[24]

The JCS response was cool but correct. They found the phrase "substantial conventional military force," for example, too vague, and told the secretary that they had initiated action to secure estimates of the forces that would be needed to reopen access to Berlin. The chiefs also expressed concern about limiting use of nuclear weapons to general war measures.[25]

Norstad provided little comfort for the McNamara views. The NATO commander saw no virtue in a large probe not found in a smaller probe, if the objective were just to smoke out Soviet intentions. Should the East Germans or the Soviets block access to Allied traffic, they could frustrate a probe of any size; "the greater the force used the greater the embarrassment which would result from failure." Nor did he see any advantage in using West German troops to reopen the autobahn. Moscow would perceive such a step as a West German invasion of the GDR, and a calculated escalation of hostilities.[26] Norstad's pessimism may have derived from his close association with the NATO allies, specifically with the British and French principals in Berlin, who were reluctant to support a bolder policy.

The meeting of the North Atlantic Council in Oslo in early May underscored the lack of agreement on firm collective action. The key questions concerning economic countermeasures and steps to be taken to increase manpower in the event of blockage of access to Berlin were not answered at that session. Seeking to resolve uncertainties, on 29 May Deputy Secretary of Defense Gilpatric asked for JCS advice on temporary reinforcement of U.S. forces in Europe as a way of demonstrating the seriousness with which the United States regarded Soviet threats.[27]

The Vienna Summit

Allied differences over Berlin policy were far from resolved by the time of the Kennedy-Khrushchev meeting in Vienna on 3-4 June. As late as 3 June, Thomas K. Finletter, U.S. permanent representative to the North Atlantic Council, was still emphasizing the need for the council to understand and confront the serious nature of the problem posed by the threat to Berlin.[28]

The president's encounter with France's President Charles de Gaulle in Paris on 31 May was one more unhappy augury of the future. De Gaulle's blessing for the Vienna session came cloaked in condescension. Kennedy had no problem with de Gaulle's flat statement that any acceptance of interference with Allied access to Berlin would lead to the loss of Germany and the serious weakening of NATO in all parts of the alliance, but he parted company over the French president's contention that existing contingency plans for probes at any strength were worthless. Since the West could not match Soviet power in Berlin, the only appropriate riposte, de Gaulle asserted, was to threaten general war at the outset of any aggression. Still, they agreed at least that Kennedy would inform Khrushchev that the West would not accept any change to Berlin involving the use of force.[29]

The meeting in Vienna proved to be as tense as anticipated, with Khrushchev alternating between smiles and scowls in a pattern that had become familiar over the past half dozen years. To one of his staff, Kennedy depicted the man as "a combination of external jocosity and 'internal rage.'" Khrushchev was unnerving in his apparently sudden changes of moods. The two leaders could not even agree on what constituted the status quo in Berlin. Khrushchev had the advantage of having won from Eisenhower an admission in 1959 that the status of divided Berlin was "abnormal." The Soviet premier's behavior at Vienna suggested that he expected to win more concessions from Kennedy. The president, though, held his ground on a unilateral change of status in West Berlin. His parting comment to Khrushchev, that "it would be a cold winter," clearly implied that a difficult time lay ahead.[30]

When the meeting adjourned Khrushchev made it clear that he intended to sign a treaty with East Germany unilaterally and confirmed this in an aide-memoire on the same day as his final position. Whatever the United States and its allies might do, the Soviet Union would sign a treaty by December.[31] Although Kennedy described the talks as serious, he made a point in a public address of saying that there were "no threats or ultimatums by either side." By glossing over the critical differences, he made possible a cooling period that at least minimized the danger of a rash decision.[32]

A delay of the official U.S. response to the Soviet aide-memoire for some weeks may have provoked Khrushchev into revealing publicly on 15 June his intention to solve the Berlin problem his own way by the year's end. These public threats were followed by a protest against a West German plan to have the Bundestag meet in Berlin. East German leader Walter Ulbricht contributed to the tension by warning that Tempelhof airfield might be closed when West Berlin became a free city.[33]

Within the national security community the events at Vienna accelerated the planning begun prior to the Kennedy-Khrushchev meeting. On 25 May, a week before going to Europe, the president delivered a special message to a joint session of Congress on meeting urgent national needs, among them the Army's plans to accelerate deployment of its reserve forces. When fully implemented, the president said, these plans would provide two combat-equipped divisions and their supporting forces, a total of 89,000 men ready for operations on three weeks' notice and 10 divisions deployable with eight weeks' notice. "These new plans will allow us to almost double the combat power of the Army in less than two months, compared to the nearly nine months heretofore required."[34]

On 6 June the Joint Chiefs answered Gilpatric's query of 29 May about what kinds of temporary reinforcements would become available in the event of a crisis. The deployment of two airborne battle groups along with 224 aircraft to major training areas in Germany could occur within two to three weeks. Deployment of an airborne division of 11,555 men could take place on a crash basis within nine days. The chiefs preferred to use one of 27 National Guard divisions scheduled for training exercises in the summer of 1961 and extend the term of service by 30-60 days. The mobilization would be accompanied by a presidential declaration of a national emergency and the calling up of more reserve troops as well as more national guardsmen. Such action would send a message to Moscow and to the American people about the seriousness of the emergency.[35]

Toward the Berlin Wall

In the disarray following the Vienna summit the president turned again to Acheson, whose earlier report provided a coherent view along with specific action recommendations that had obvious appeal to Kennedy. Acheson's response, in a long report submitted on 28 June, advocated both a buildup of U.S. conventional forces and preparations for general nuclear war. The Soviets had to be convinced, he asserted, that the United States would go to war—even nuclear war—in defense of Western interests in Europe. This perception was indispensable if the Soviet Union was to be deterred. By reducing the issue to simple terms Acheson played a pivotal but not conclusive role in determining U.S. policy on Berlin.[36]

Both State and Defense gave Acheson's report a mixed reception. Those whom Acheson labeled as soft-liners behaved according to form. Many of these "soft-boiled eggheads," as journalist Joseph Alsop called them, were from the White House—Schlesinger, Kaysen, Wiesner; no doubt he had in mind also some State Department officials. In OSD McNamara and Nitze generally favored Acheson's approach, but McNamara did not agree with the pace and scale of the proposed mobilization. Within the White House staff the report elicited the approval of Taylor and Rostow, but they were in the minority compared with such opponents as Sorensen and McGeorge Bundy. The reservationists feared that Acheson's advice was aimed "in the main to escalate the crisis, intensifying it to the brink of war."[37] Even Acheson's longtime friend Harriman was disturbed by the report's seeming hawkishness. He wondered aloud to Schlesinger: "How long is our policy to be dominated by that frustrated and rigid man? He is leading us down the road to war."[38]

The president himself remained undecided. Immediately following an inconclusive National Security Council meeting on 29 June, at which Acheson made his case, Kennedy had Bundy request departmental recommendations for preparatory measures in support of possible future actions. On 6 July the JCS submitted to McNamara a proposal for mobilizing 559,000 military personnel, supported by 40,000 civilians, at a cost of $13.9 billion for FY 1962 and $17 billion for FY 1963. It included a breakdown of manpower and equipment for the three services.[39]

The large increase in forces and the staggering costs projected by the Joint Chiefs may have had an adverse effect on the president, perhaps making him more sensitive to a memorandum Schlesinger presented on 7 July that was critical of Acheson's approach and emphasized instead political rather than military means of coping with the Berlin problem. On the following day Rusk, McNamara, and Taylor met with the president at Hyannis Port to discuss strategy.[40] Recognizing that the United States was not in a good position to negotiate, they agreed to fashion specific political and military approaches to dealing with Berlin. While Rusk would move ahead with negotiating strategies, McNamara was to produce a military plan centered on conventional resistance to Soviet or East German aggression at a level that would permit the United States to demonstrate both its determination to fight if necessary and its willingness to allow the Soviets an opportunity to negotiate. Kennedy could then raise the risks of conflict without letting them get out of control.[41] Given their doubts about the effectiveness of conventional forces, the JCS supported partial mobilization measures as long as they would be ancillary to the "main reliance" on nuclear response.[42]

While the president accepted Acheson's position against early negotiations, he opposed the latter's recommendation for a declaration of national emergency. Countering the former secretary of state's assertion that such a declaration was essential to deter Khrushchev from going too far, Rusk exposed inconsistencies in Acheson's position on 13 July when he cited the report's stated "need for keeping early steps in a low key." At NSC meetings on 13, 17, and 19 July, McNamara in each instance maintained that a declaration of national emergency was not immediately needed and could wait until the situation required it. The secretary of defense had the backing of the president's economic advisers, who had previously warned Kennedy that a proclamation could set off a surge of panic buying and send prices sky-high. The Acheson plan for a proclamation of national emergency "was allowed to die a quiet death" at the meeting on 19 July, when Acheson finally agreed to McNamara's flexible timetable.[43]

On 14 July, while discussions were still underway, McNamara sought information from the JCS on the timetable for deploying reinforcements absent a national emergency.[44] Their recommendations, costed out at $4.3 billion, yielded to the president's decision three days later on a lower estimated cost of $3.2 billion. On 24 July the president directed preparation to deploy to Europe up to six Army divisions and supporting air units after 1 January 1962.[45]

These decisions opened the way for the president to lay down a clear American position in a radio and television address, in which the initiative for once would come from the administration, not Khrushchev. Kennedy's speech of 25 July focused on Berlin because there, in Kennedy's words, "our solemn commitments . . . and Soviet ambitions now meet in basic confrontation." Recognizing the Soviet Union's historic and legitimate concerns about its position in Central and Eastern Europe, Kennedy offered "to consider any arrangement or treaty in Germany consistent with the maintenance of peace and freedom, and with the legitimate security interests of all nations." With some passion he made clear his wish to avoid having "military considerations . . . dominate the thinking of either East or West . . . . Now, in the thermonuclear age, any misjudgment on either side about the intentions of the other could rain more devastation in several hours than has been wrought in all the wars of human history."[46]

Kennedy's speech provided ample grounds for raising rather than lowering voices over Berlin. While refusing to accept Acheson's advice to declare a national emergency, he proposed steps somewhat short of a full-blown mobilization, including a large increase in the draft, and requested congressional authorization of extension of terms of service and recall to active service of selected reserve units and individual reservists. He asked for a buildup of military forces, especially the Army, beyond the modest increases represented in the March and May amendments to the FY 1962 Defense appropriation bill. The Army would grow from 875,000 to approximately one million men, an increase considerably more than the 50,000 figure the Army had earlier requested. Navy and Air Force authorized strengths would increase by 29,000 and 63,000 men, respectively.* To pay for the buildup the president asked Congress to appropriate an additional $3.454 billion† for FY 1962.[47]

The sense of crisis engendered by the president's address persisted as the administration submitted its request to Congress on 26 July for authority to order to active duty ready reserve units and individual reservists for one year, and to extend tours of duty. Responding quickly, Congress granted the personnel authority on 1 August and approved the thrice amended FY 1962 budget on 10 August. The president signed it into law a week later.[48]

Presidential adviser John J. McCloy, after visiting Khrushchev at his summer home on the Black Sea on 26-27 July to discuss disarmament, reported on the Soviet leader's strong reaction to Kennedy's address. Khrushchev insisted on regarding it as a declaration of "preliminary war"; he intended to treat it as an ultimatum that must be met both by a Soviet peace treaty with East Germany and by new preparations for war. Ominously, he observed that while the superpowers might survive such a war, all of Europe would be destroyed.[49] On 11 August, two days before beginning of construction of the Berlin Wall, Khrushchev announced publicly what he had told McCloy privately: If the West initiated war in response to a separate peace treaty, the Soviets would strike at NATO bases wherever they were to be found.[50]

Perhaps the real danger in the escalation of the Berlin confrontation lay in the storm Khrushchev could whip up if, after years of threatening, he concluded a separate peace treaty with East Germany. A peace treaty that legitimized the German Democratic Republic would change the status quo if East Germany joined in negotiations between the major powers. This prospect could not help but agitate U.S. planners and inspire grim scenarios of what would follow from a separate Soviet treaty.

Despite the growing tension, during August DoD made only limited progress toward a military buildup on the scale requested by the president and approved by Congress. Aside from 3,000 troops earmarked for three European-based divisions, reinforcements for Europe remained on a contingency basis and even this was limited to planning. OSD assumed that the Soviets would undertake no serious action until after September and possibly not until the end of the year. Any possible deployment of Army divisions could not occur, as the president had directed, until 1 January 1962.[51]

---

* The growth of the services is reflected in the active duty personnel as of 30 June 1962, totaling 2,807,819—Army, 1,066,404; Navy, 666,428; Marine Corps, 190,962; and Air Force, 884,025.
† This included $207.6 million for civil defense.

The restraint that held back military preparations suggested a piecemeal operation, or at least some uncertainty over objectives. In August the number of U.S. Army personnel in Europe increased negligibly. This accorded with McNamara's memorandum of 2 August to the secretary of the Army, when he spoke of the tentative character of the plans to send two additional divisions to Europe. While recommending advance shipment of supplies and equipment for them, McNamara suggested that these forces be part of the normal rotation unless the Berlin situation worsened.[52]

The administration's preparations, although consistent with a strategy of graduated response, may have appeared so tentative as to have undermined the sense of determination that Kennedy intended the action to convey. Conceivably, full rather than partial mobilization and the dispatch of troops to the scene on a crash basis rather than mere intensification of the planning process would have produced more restraint on the other side.

In determining the pace and scale of U.S. mobilization, the president had to be mindful of the position of the NATO allies and his own Joint Chiefs. Any change in the status of occupation forces in Berlin affected France and Britain as much as it did the United States. The group of intimately concerned powers included West Germany, which became part of quadripartite planning in July; the question of responding to the Soviet Union also involved General Norstad in his dual capacity as USCINCEUR and Supreme Allied Commander, Europe (SACEUR). The views of all these parties reflected a mixture of skepticism and apprehension over the possible consequences of the U.S. initiatives enunciated by Kennedy.[53]

While Lemnitzer admitted that partial mobilization might display Western determination and might even push back the timetable for a planned Soviet operation, he had also warned McNamara on 12 July that 559,000 additional military personnel (half of them for the Army) would not alter the basic strategy of either the United States or NATO, which, by JCS reckoning, remained anchored to a nuclear response.[54] A low nuclear threshold also remained fundamental to Norstad's conception of the defense of Europe. McNamara gathered from a conversation with Norstad on 23 July that SACEUR could not envisage NATO waging a "non-nuclear war and, at the same time protect the nuclear storage sites and NATO's nuclear capabilities." Norstad also objected to any conversion of NATO-dedicated, nuclear-capable aircraft to non-nuclear use. He could not separate the problem of Berlin from his larger responsibilities as SACEUR. As Nitze later observed, Norstad "was from the old school of 'massive retaliation' . . . totally at odds with the flexible response approach that McNamara and I agreed was preferable."[55]

The difficulties U.S. officials encountered in bringing the allies over to their position became apparent in conversations between Acheson and West German Defense Minister Franz Josef Strauss on the weekend of 29-30 July at Nitze's home in southern Maryland. While Strauss recognized in principle that the three occupying powers would have to take the initiative in maintaining their position in Berlin, he had trouble focusing on just what should or could come next. He liked the idea of economic sanctions, or of naval action to close the Baltic or Black Seas, but he seemed unhappy about alternatives should those actions fail. The prospect of conventional warfare on German soil so distressed Strauss that he preferred to evacuate the entire population of West Berlin rather than accede to Soviet pressure. This agitated statement came after midnight. In the brighter light of the morning he disavowed any implication that Berlin was not worth fighting for or that it should be evacuated rather than become a casus belli. He thought that the West was not ready for confrontation but he was also unable to recommend what the West should do when it became ready to act.[56]

Differences among the allies soon became public. The *New York Times* pointed out British indignation over the charge of softness at the same time that British leaders worried about public apathy. The French echoed these concerns when, according to the *Washington Post*, they used the term "saber rattling" to characterize U.S. behavior at the end of July. While de Gaulle spoke of the need for firmness in Berlin, the French cautioned against sweeping military preparations. In West Germany, Brandt, seeking to unseat Adenauer in forthcoming elections as chancellor of the Federal Republic, called for a Western peace conference over Germany, which Adenauer promptly denounced.[57] On 5 August, a week before the Wall went up the foreign ministers of the tripartite powers met in Paris, without any noticeable effect on Berlin policy except for a decision to invite West Germany to join the tripartite Washington Ambassadorial Steering Group.[58]

The Wall

The flight of East Germans to the West became a flood—30,000 in July and additional thousands in the first 12 days of August 1961. To stop this hemorrhage that was seriously weakening the GDR economy Khrushchev and his East German surrogates chose to act. Citing a Warsaw Pact declaration that called on the GDR to establish control around West Berlin, GDR leader Ulbricht blamed West German provocateurs for the exodus and set in motion border controls. The "Berlin Wall," a barricade of barbed wire erected suddenly in the early morning hours of 13 August, was subsequently augmented by concrete construction after pavement and streetcar tracks were torn up.[59] The gradual construction of the Wall suggests that Khrushchev may have been testing Western reaction. If so, he won his gamble, never a particularly risky one given Western disarray prior to 13 August. The onus for a response now fell squarely on the West.

The Wall seemed to come as a "complete tactical surprise." The timing could not have been better from the Communists' standpoint. Many Western leaders were away from their desks—Kennedy in Hyannis Port, Macmillan on vacation in Scotland, and French officialdom presumably at the Riviera. It was August, after all. Although Ulbricht had talked about a "wall" prior to 13 August, its actual construction was not anticipated. Every scenario floated by U.S. planners centered on a crisis growing out of a Soviet peace treaty with East Germany and consequent interference with access to West Berlin. Perhaps, as has been suggested, amid the heated exchanges of June and July, Ulbricht's reference to a wall became "lost in the background noise."[60]

Berlin, August 1961

The Soviet-East German action caused both apprehension and relief in U.S. and Allied circles. Western observers had increasingly worried over the refugee flow and its impact on the health of East Germany; a barrier wall might at least inhibit an East German revolt as its economy worsened. Rusk's public statement on 13 August certainly evidenced a sense of relief. "Available information," he announced, "indicates that measures taken thus far are aimed at residents of East Berlin and East Germany and not at the allied position in West Berlin or access thereto." His additional comments to the effect that limitation on travel in Berlin violated the status quo represented little more than the usual protest.[61]

What seemed to be a passive response on the part of the three occupying powers caused a deterioration in morale in West Berlin and West Germany. Washington considered imposing restrictions on East Germans traveling to the West but U.S. officials deemed such a step both trivial and inappropriate. Although the administration also considered reinforcing the Berlin garrison, McNamara did not think it desirable and no action was taken. From Lemnitzer's perspective as chairman of the JCS, "everyone appeared to be hopeless, helpless, and harmless."[62]

OSD's stance did not depart significantly from the State Department's at this juncture. McNamara had made known his thoughts on the crisis at congressional hearings two weeks before the Wall went up. He gave considerable credence to the belief that Khrushchev's position showed "a marked change and a much firmer line today than existed" in 1958. At the same time he cautioned against a panicky buildup in response to this change: "We should not rush to increase our forces and then rush to tear them down." The peaks and valleys of an adversarial relationship, he stressed, should not deter the Defense Department from a steady course of planning.[63]

The Wall changed neither McNamara's rhetoric nor his reasoning, at least not in the initial stage of its construction. On 14 August, he assured an interviewer of "Western determination to defend the freedom of Berlin and to defend the Allied rights in Berlin . . . [and] to build up the military power, to provide a more effective deterrent, as well as to insure an increased capability for military action in the event the deterrent fails." While this reiteration of policy reflected admirable consistency, it did not respond concretely to the crisis at hand. McNamara declared that "the recent move to blockade East Berliners . . . is unrelated to any action we have taken. It does, of course, violate the treaties which we are parties to and I understand that a strong protest therefore will be submitted against the action that has been taken."[64]

Only after Berliners themselves, notably Mayor Brandt, demanded stronger protests did the United States take any action. Brandt released an urgent letter that he had sent to President Kennedy on 16 August in which he asked, among other things, for dispatch of U.S. troops to Berlin as an earnest of America's continuing intention to remain in the city.[65] In response, the president sent two high-level figures—Vice President Lyndon Johnson and retired General Lucius Clay—to visit Berlin and hopefully raise its inhabitants' morale. The former represented political authority while Clay symbolized the spirit of 1948-49 when he commanded the forces that kept the Berlin Airlift going. Johnson, in an address to the West Berlin parliament on 19 August, invoked the language of the Declaration of Independence, assuring Berliners that Americans had pledged "our lives, our fortunes, and our sacred honor" to the survival of Berlin.[66]

The president considered making Clay the U.S. military commander in Berlin, but refrained from acting on the appointment largely because both

Lemnitzer and McNamara feared that such a move would strain relationships with the command structure already on the scene. They had recommended naming Clay as chief of mission with the rank of ambassador, thereby relieving Ambassador Walter C. Dowling in Bonn of his duties as chief of the Berlin mission. On 30 August the president instead appointed Clay as his personal representative in Berlin, effective 15 September.[67]*

At the direction of the president, over the objections of McNamara and Lemnitzer, the dispatch of a Seventh Army battle group of 1,500 men on 20 August demonstrated another effort to impress the Soviets and the West Berliners alike with the seriousness of America's support. The convoy proceeded along the autobahn to Berlin unchallenged, an action interpreted as a successful riposte, even if belated, to the construction of the Wall. Its success demonstrated, as McNamara adviser William W. Kaufmann observed, that Soviet leaders "were not all that interested in a showdown." The battle group entered Berlin in triumph, greeted by Vice President Johnson in person.[68]

A disquieting incident connected with the move conveyed a different message. The convoy's commander unwittingly set a precedent that the Soviets subsequently used against future troop movements from West Germany to West Berlin. As the convoy arrived at the checkpoint on the approach to the city shortly after dawn on 20 August, a Soviet officer had some difficulty counting the number of soldiers on the trucks. The U.S. commander then ordered the troops to dismount and so expedite the count. While counting was an accepted practice, not so dismounting from trucks. It set a precedent that showed among other things just how vulnerable the tripartite powers were to Soviet/GDR interference with their access to Berlin.[69]

Aside from providing a temporary boost in morale to the beleaguered city, the combination of highly visible troops and high-level U.S. visitors on the scene in fact accomplished little, as the Soviet leadership gave no signs of being intimidated or even impressed. They continued to extend the Wall, and on 22 August issued new regulations curtailing movement of West Berliners into East Berlin. No Western outcry followed this change.[70]

Nor did the allies show any significant reaction to the ending of the quadripartite status of East Berlin. The Soviets reinforced the symbol of the Wall by terminating all occupation agencies in East Berlin. They gradually reduced the number of entry places to one—Checkpoint Charlie at Friedrichstrasse—a concession they probably would not have made had they not wanted reciprocity in West Berlin. Before the year ended the U.S. commandant denied himself entry into East Berlin when GDR officials insisted on processing documents of U.S.

---

* The significance of Clay's role in Berlin did not go unrecognized in Moscow. Khrushchev later claimed that he chose Marshal Ivan Konev to be the Soviet commander in East Berlin to signify how seriously the Soviets regarded the situation. See *Khrushchev Remembers*, 459.

civilian personnel entering with him. This self-denial severed formal official relations between the four-power commandants.[71]

Soviet behavior during the last half of 1961 suggested that the publicized U.S. troop convoy of 20 August amounted to a kind of empty bravado, and certainly not the deterrent to further aggression that Kennedy intended. The building of the Wall without evoking stronger action from the United States and the allies seemed to embolden Khrushchev to more overt challenges. The accusation on 23 August that the Western powers were abusing the access agreements of 1945 by transporting "all kinds of revanchists, extremists, saboteurs, and spies" from West Germany into West Berlin by air prompted only a warning by the United States against any interference with the aircraft of the Western powers in the air corridors.[72]

Still, Khrushchev may have pushed too far. Presidential Assistant McGeorge Bundy later speculated about Khrushchev's "rigidity of . . . performance as a negotiator." A little more flexibility, some modest compromises on the Soviet side, Bundy thought, might have created a breach between the United States and its NATO allies. Indeed, U.S. planners gave signs of compromise pointing "toward acceptance of the GDR, the Oder-Neisse line, a non-aggression pact, and even the idea of two peace treaties." Bundy reported these ideas to the president on 28 August, but Khrushchev made no compromise gesture that would merit any of these concessions.[73]

The president, painfully aware of the situation Khrushchev had forced on him, knew he had to do more than simply show the flag. Kennedy spurred the secretaries of state and defense to accelerate countervailing political and military preparations. He won agreement for a "fundamental reappraisal" of the July decisions "for restrained, gradual military strengthening." Although opposing the 20 August convoy decision, McNamara asked the services on 18 August what they could do to advance the deployment date for up to six divisions and associated air units from 1 January 1962 to 15 November 1961.[74]

In Europe LIVE OAK, the tripartite planning group in being long before the crisis erupted, still was in no position to act. It had not even settled the matter of coordination between the three LIVE OAK powers—the United States, Britain, and France—and the other NATO nations. NATO Secretary General Dirk Stikker complained to Norstad on 3 August about the failure of the tripartite group to keep him informed of their preparations. As late as 26 August the Washington Ambassadorial Group could offer at best only an expression of hope by the U.S. representatives that "instructions would go forward to General Norstad to have Live Oak planning take account of NATO implications."[75]

If Allied coordination lagged, a major reason lay in the indecision and lack of clear direction in Washington. Rusk and McNamara sought assistance through the joint State-Defense Berlin Task Force, established in July. Once the task force

Berlin: The Wall   161

got under way in August meetings became regular and the link between the leaders—Kohler and Nitze—became firmer.[76]

For all McNamara's initial agreement in principle with Acheson on the advisability of a general mobilization and a buildup of conventional forces, he continued to proceed deliberately. He wanted to reorganize ground forces and overhaul what he saw as the current inefficient management and operation of Reserve and National Guard contingents. The Berlin Wall crisis brought to the foreground what McNamara had been trying to avoid: namely, the necessity to increase expenditures that would ensue from declaration of a national emergency before he had completed these and other changes. In this context his reluctance to commit funds for more contingency planning takes on greater understanding. In the end he yielded to the imperatives of the moment. On 24 August he listed for the president the reserve units of the Army, Navy, and Air Force that DoD planned to call to active duty. This callup of over 76,500 men would not necessarily mean deployment of troops to Europe, only preparation for it; until September no final commitment to significant overseas reinforcements occurred.[77]

The White House also continued to move cautiously. On 31 August, after much debate, the administration authorized Norstad as CINCEUR to deal with possible impediments to air access to Berlin by replacing civil aircraft with military if necessary and by permitting fighter planes to take "aggressive protective measures," such as immediate pursuit to deflect harassment. The White House denied Norstad authority to direct fighter planes to take action against antiaircraft and missile attackers because the allies refused to delegate this authority to Norstad. The hitch revealed the continuing state of uncertainty in Washington and among the allies over appropriate measures to take against Soviet encroachments.[78]

Arguably, Soviet resumption of atmospheric nuclear testing on 30 August, rather than the building of the Wall, finally pushed the administration to more decisive action. Persuaded of the need for more aggressive measures, on 7 September McNamara proposed ordering elements of four National Guard divisions to report for duty between 15 October and 15 November. He also proposed an increase of 37,000 military for the European Command, deployment of the 4th Infantry Division, and dispatch of an aircraft carrier and supporting ships for the Sixth Fleet in the Mediterranean. Two days later the president approved the sending of 37,000 men to augment the Seventh Army in Europe, but delayed decision on the other proposals.[79]

The buildup of conventional forces did not impress the NATO allies or allay their fears, nor did it appear to impress Moscow. It was time to play the nuclear card that most of the Europeans considered the strongest gambit available to the allies. Obviously speaking as the administration spokesman, in a public interview on 28 September McNamara forcefully proclaimed that "we will use nuclear weapons whenever we feel it necessary to protect our vital interests." He drove the message home: "Our nuclear stockpile is several times that of the Soviet Union and we will use either tactical weapons or strategic weapons in whatever quantities wherever, whenever it's necessary to protect this nation and its interests." Weeks later, on 21 October, Deputy Secretary Gilpatric, also speaking with full administration approval, echoed the message—U.S. nuclear retaliatory power was so great it would be self-destructive for an enemy to attack. U.S. power was so much greater than that of the Soviet Union he was confident Moscow would not "provoke a major nuclear conflict."[80]

In November 1961 OSD prepared for use in discussions in NATO a detailed paper on NATO military policy in the Berlin crisis intended to assure the allies, particularly West Germany, that U.S. nuclear preponderance was great enough to deter Soviet aggression.[81] For a German reaction McNamara read the OSD paper to Defense Minister Strauss (who followed the text he held in his hand) after dinner at McNamara's home on 26 November, in the company of Nitze and Gilpatric. Nitze impressed Strauss by emphasizing that in light of their "general war inferiority, the Russians could rationally only conclude on discontinuation and restoration of our rights of access to Berlin." Strauss reacted favorably, but that led to discussion of the uses of nuclear weapons and the consequences.[82]

"Poodle Blanket"

Statements about using nuclear weapons if necessary were declaratory, intended to reassure the NATO allies and warn the Soviet Union. The operational policy continued to emphasize the buildup of conventional forces, although now with greater urgency. Early in September, on the 8th, the president raised a number of probing questions about added deployment of non-nuclear forces, to which McNamara responded on 18 September, laying out the risks but concluding: "While a conventional build-up alone would be unlikely to convince him [Khrushchev], the absence of a build-up would probably increase his doubt of our determination." That same day the president withheld approval of sending to Europe the six divisions that Lemnitzer and Army Chief of Staff General George Decker had recommended (the other chiefs opposed sending any divisions at the time), instead approving callup of an infantry division, an armored division, and supporting forces, a total of 75,000 men.[83]

The result was further acceleration of a process that had been under way since spring. The term "horse blanket" applied to the long list of proposals for action from a State-Defense team headed by Nitze and Seymour Weiss, special assistant to the secretary of state. Nitze and Weiss had principal responsibility for stuffing as many potential responses to Soviet provocations as they could, from small-scale military probes to general war, under the horse blanket.[84] By the fall of 1961 the Berlin Task Force had reduced the horse blanket to a "poodle blanket" covering a short but still robust set of options and permitting formulation of much more specific responses to Soviet actions than the horse blanket.

Under the poodle blanket, in an exercise developed largely by Nitze's International Security Affairs office, Allied measures fell into four progressive phases calibrated to the degree of Soviet provocation and Allied success at the various levels of force. Soviet interference with access to Berlin, but well short of permanent closure, constituted the first phase and warranted probes of platoon strength on the ground and fighter escort in the air, counteractions that incurred small risk of general war. The second stage, continuing and significant Soviet-East German blockage of traffic, would be met with "such non-combatant activity as economic embargo, maritime harassment, and UN action" along with NATO mobilization of forces and reinforcement from the United States. A third stage called for a naval blockade or some similar global action, or non-nuclear air action and non-nuclear ground advance in division strength or greater into East Germany. Lastly, if none of these efforts led to termination of Soviet provocations, nuclear weapons would be employed, initially in selective attacks for purposes of demonstration and proceeding through use of tactical weapons to a general nuclear war.[85]

On 13 October the Joint Chiefs offered their own approach, emphasizing the importance of securing maximum NATO participation and placing on the Soviets the onus for initiating an attack. From the White House, Taylor advised that any non-nuclear ground advance not be confined to the autobahn. So long as East Germans constituted the resisting force, the allies should not be held back from extending their operations. The tenor of the JCS and Taylor comments suggested State-Defense general approval of the poodle blanket program of actions.[86]

In response to these recommendations, on 18 October the president authorized the U.S. commandant in Berlin to send two or three tanks to Checkpoint Charlie to demolish any illegal barrier. The tanks would then withdraw from the border and park just inside the Western sector. This aggressive posture derived from an agreement by State, OSD, and JCS on policy guidance for Norstad in which the president specifically endorsed the principles of the poodle blanket, namely that the United States should be in a position to undertake "a sequence of graduated responses to Soviet/GDR actions in denial of our rights of access." The president further made clear that he wanted as much emphasis placed on the capacity to fight with non-nuclear forces as on efforts to enhance the credibility of the nuclear deterrent. The poodle blanket plan with its four phases received NSC approval and became NSAM 109 on 23 October 1961.[87]

As plans went forward during the summer and fall the U.S. assumption that the British and French would support the American initiatives was not borne out. Their discomfort over what they still construed as U.S. impulsiveness added to Norstad's unease over policies flowing from Washington. He worried about when he could act independently without excessive and time-consuming consultation with his superiors. To visiting representatives of State and Defense in late

September he expressed doubt about NATO's willingness to use nuclear weapons *"under any contingency."*[88] Norstad had reason for concern. There existed no consistent administration policy to guide SACEUR at lesser levels than full-scale conflict. The Joint Chiefs advocated granting him advance authority to respond unilaterally to Soviet or GDR ground-to-air attacks in the Berlin Corridor. But given French and British hesitation, OSD demurred. After a White House meeting on 13 September the president decided that Norstad would be given approval if the British, French, and West Germans agreed. McNamara expressed to Rusk his doubt that the allies were prepared to go along.[89]

Publicly, U.S. planners had to hide their frustrations, but behind the closed doors at White House and NSC meetings they vented fully. When the president asked at a meeting on 20 October about relations with the allies, Acheson responded, *"We need to tell them."* This seemed to be one time that Acheson's hard line had the full backing of his colleagues. But this shared sentiment had to remain behind closed doors.[90]

The reluctance of the allies to approve strong actions proposed by the United States might have complicated planning but did not prevent the administration from preparing to substantially increase U.S. forces in Europe. Previously, on 10 October, McNamara had secured the president's approval to deploy, beginning 1 November, 11 Air National Guard fighter squadrons and a tactical control group. At the same time, seven Tactical Air Command fighter squadrons would return from Europe to the United States. Additionally, the Army would preposition in Europe equipment for one armored division and one infantry division. The president also agreed to the rotation of five battle groups of the 4th Infantry Division, thus making available at least two combat-ready battle groups in Europe at all times for an indefinite period. All these measures were supplementary to the augmentation of the Seventh Army by 37,000 personnel and the deployment of the 3rd Armored Regiment from the United States to Europe. For the most part these actions resulted from the recommendations offered by the Berlin Task Force in early October. On 23 October Norstad judged that instead of the rough equivalent of 16 combat divisions in the center, NATO would have approximately 24 combat divisions by the end of the year, most of them effectively manned.[91]

The channels of diplomacy were never closed. Kennedy announced on 13 September, one month after the erection of the Wall, that he would agree to Rusk meeting with Soviet Foreign Minister Andrei Gromyko at the forthcoming UN General Assembly session late in September.[92] The Gromyko-Rusk talks afforded Khrushchev another opportunity to scrap his timetable for a separate treaty. In a speech to the Soviet Communist Party Congress on 17 October, he claimed that Gromyko's talks with Kennedy and Rusk in the United States gave the impression that the Western powers were showing "a certain understanding of the situation and are inclined to seek a solution for the German problem and the West Berlin issue on a mutually acceptable basis." Consequently, he stood ready to concede that "we shall not insist that the peace treaty be signed . . . before Dec. 31, 1961."[93]

Confrontation at Checkpoint Charlie

Whatever the reason for Khrushchev's postponement of the deadline, there followed almost immediately the most serious confrontation in Berlin since the Berlin blockade of 1948, not as dramatic as the Wall but potentially more explosive. On 27 and 28 October, at Checkpoint Charlie, an entryway between East and West Berlin, U.S. tanks faced Soviet tanks.

The confrontation may have been a reaction to what the Soviets interpreted as provocations, specifically the behavior of General Clay, the president's special representative in Berlin. Immediately on his return to Berlin from Washington on 19 September, Clay ostentatiously increased patrols on the autobahn. His aggressiveness was not only a personal gesture on behalf of worried West Berliners but perhaps also a calculated departure from the White House's management of the Berlin crisis. As McNamara had worried, Clay's status made an intricate command relationship in Germany even more convoluted. Maj. Gen. Albert Watson II, the senior U.S. officer and commandant in Berlin, reported in his political capacity to Ambassador Dowling in Bonn and in his military role to Norstad in Paris through General Bruce Clarke, commander of the U.S. Army, Europe in Heidelberg. Additionally, a State Department mission in Berlin headed by E. Allan Lightner, Jr., reported both to Dowling and Watson as well as directly to Washington.[94]

As it happened, Lightner was en route with his wife to the opera in East Berlin when he was stopped at Checkpoint Charlie on the evening of 22 October and asked to show identification. Up to this time a display of civilian automobile license tags had sufficed to permit passage. The United States held that the requirement to show personal identification served to erode the right of the occupying power to travel anywhere in Berlin. When Lightner refused to show his identification to the GDR officer, there ensued a few hours of tense face-offs that ended with the diplomat reentering East Berlin accompanied by a squad of U.S. military police with loaded rifles.[95]

On the following day Ulbricht issued a decree requiring Allied personnel in civilian dress to identify themselves before entering East Berlin. Two days later U.S. armed patrols again accompanied civilian officials across the line and Clay asked Watson to deploy tanks at Checkpoint Charlie. Clay's reaction alarmed the allies, particularly the British, who had never objected to showing their passports when asked. Concern grew when Marshal Konev, Soviet commander in East

Berlin, intervened to send tanks to the city. This new display of strength induced Clay on 27 October to move U.S. tanks to the demarcation line, after which the Soviets deployed tanks within 100 yards of them.[96]

After some 16 hours Khrushchev ordered the tanks pulled back and in his self-serving account of the event claimed victory. According to the Soviet premier the encounter at Checkpoint Charlie was part of a Western plot to exploit the Soviet 22nd Party Congress as well as an occasion to bulldoze the border installations. Forewarned through intelligence channels, Soviet tanks had stopped the U.S. tanks in their tracks. Khrushchev boasted: "I proposed that we turn our tanks around, pull them back from the border, and have them take their places in the side streets . . . . I assured my comrades that as soon as we pulled back our tanks, the Americans would pull back theirs." Having provided a face-saving formula for retreating, he observed that the United States responded within 20 minutes. So he claimed "it was a great victory for us, and it was won without firing a single shot."[97]

Much of this bluster was a cover for Khrushchev's retreat. The Soviet Union had provoked a crisis, worried over its escalation, and relented before it got out of hand. Although it could take satisfaction in the fact that East German officials continued to reject U.S. civilians who would not show their identification documents, Americans circumvented the inspection by entering East Berlin by subway rather than by automobile.[98]

Aftermath: Clay vs. Washington

The United States was as anxious as the NATO partners—and obviously the Soviets themselves—not to go to war over as minor an issue as the passport contretemps. The more critical point remained to prevent the East Germans from forcing the United States to accept their sovereignty over East Berlin before signature of a treaty. And to achieve this objective, the administration had already determined to take commensurate risks. Ambassador Dowling felt that it was vital that the United States make continuing efforts to exercise the right of entry into East Berlin by sending in new probes.[99]

Clay shared these general views. Rather than making him more cautious, the Lightner incident at Checkpoint Charlie may have persuaded him of the need for strong actions; he saw tank deployments at the checkpoint as the only practical approach. In his judgment, Ambassador Llewellyn Thompson's protests in Moscow served no useful purpose and might "indeed force hardening of Soviet backing of East German action." Rather than wait for a Soviet response, likely in any event to be a rejection, Clay recommended that the United States seize the initiative and pressure the Soviet Union until the harassment ceased. There should be no negotiations, he felt, until the Soviets relented.[100] The Joint Chiefs, for their part, sympathized with Clay, but preferred to pursue "minimum procedures at present and reserve stronger measures for use if needed as result of further Moscow talks." In this State concurred.[101]

Clay's apparent inability to live with uncertainty and ambiguity separated him from his colleagues. Macmillan thought him "a public danger." Rumors that he was in trouble with Washington gathered currency when he returned home in November and again in January 1962 for consultations with the president and officials at State.[102] Meanwhile, the foreign ministers of France, Britain, West Germany, and the United States met in Paris on 10-12 December in advance of the North Atlantic Council meeting. Recognizing that any appearance of dissension would embolden Khrushchev to engage in more provocations, the NAC communiqué on 15 December announced the intention to resume five-power talks in the hope of producing a negotiated settlement. The united front notwithstanding, questions about the timing of and basis for negotiations occasioned much discussion and proved extremely divisive. Stikker noted that as a result of continuing disagreements during the drafting of the communiqué, the Council "came as near in my memory it has ever come to a public breakdown over a major issue."[103]

A State Department draft of a modus vivendi of 6 March 1962 dealt not only with Western access to Berlin but also with reaching a mutual understanding that force would not be used to "change the external borders of Germany or the demarcation line inside Germany." Such an understanding, subsequently approved by the president for talks between Rusk and Soviet Foreign Minister Gromyko, would give the West unimpeded access for civil and military traffic.[104]

In the absence of Soviet agreement, harassment of U.S. aircraft continued along the corridor between the Federal Republic and West Berlin throughout February and March 1962. Such tactics as excessive limitations on the space Allied aircraft could use did not stop U.S. military aircraft from flying at altitudes the Soviet Union was trying to reserve for itself. Before this latest test of wills ended, MIGs were flying into the path of Allied aircraft, buzzing civilian flights to Berlin, and dropping metal chaff to interfere with Allied radar facilities. On one occasion, 14 February, they buzzed the plane carrying the British ambassador to Bonn. But the West persisted, and both civilian and military aircraft continued their missions.[105]

Ultimately, U.S. patience was rewarded with some success. Although the Rusk-Gromyko conversations on Berlin, which had begun on 11 March, terminated without agreement on 27 March, the two ministers noted that they would resume contact at an appropriate time. Three days later Soviet flights at the disputed altitudes ended as abruptly as they had started. In April both Clay and Konev, the two most visible antagonists, retired from their positions in Berlin.[106]

By May the worst causes of friction had much diminished. Clay confirmed the existence of a new mood in Berlin when he testified in executive session before the Senate Foreign Relations and Armed Services Committees on 15 May.

After making clear that the British and French had strong differences with the thrust of U.S. policy, he observed that "at the present moment . . . our situation vis-a-vis the East German and Soviet Governments is one of returning to the status which existed prior to the construction of the wall. At the time that I left there, there were no harassments; the Soviet guards on the Autobahn were being very polite, very circumspect, and even the East German policemen were behaving properly. I think that this may continue, because their efforts at harassment did not destroy the morale of the West Berliner." Clay felt justified in taking some credit for the calm that had returned to Berlin, acknowledging that the weakness of the East German economy contributed to the softening of the Communists' position.[107]

Clay could not have foreseen that the Soviets were preparing a new tactic to force the West's hand on Berlin; namely, the construction of a ballistic missile base in Cuba to use as a bargaining chip in negotiations over the status of West Berlin. Conceivably, some of the saber-rattling that occurred in Berlin in late summer and early fall of 1962, such as using armored carriers to transport Soviets to their war memorial in West Berlin, was intended at least in part to divert U.S. attention from the Cuban venture.

Soviet indications of going ahead with a treaty with the GDR and turning over travel control to GDR authorities required the administration to offer repeated assurances of U.S. steadfastness. To help allay West Germany's continuing anxiety over seeming contradictions in the administration's position and to impress on the Soviet Union U.S. resolve, McNamara emphatically stated at a press conference on 28 September 1962 that the crisis in Berlin was the "most serious that we have faced since the end of the Korean War" and that the United States would use "whatever weapons are required to defend our vital interests." Although the Cuban threat would soon overtake the Berlin problem, these statements were in the context of Berlin and possible resort to nuclear weapons. The House and Senate both responded with a concurrent resolution promising to use "whatever means may be necessary" to defend Allied rights in West Berlin. The House passed it on 5 October by a vote of 311-0, and the Senate adopted it by voice vote on 10 October.[108]

Had the Cuban missile crisis* that followed within a few days taken a different turn, perhaps removal of missiles might have occurred as an exchange for U.S. concessions in Berlin—an obvious linkage. As Berlin observer John Ausland noted, "Just as Cuba was in America's backyard, so Berlin was in Khrushchev's. Whereas Kennedy had the advantage of being in a position to control movement to Cuba with naval power, Khrushchev was able to control travel to Berlin with land power. Besides, talk of blockading Cuba inevitably evoked memories of the Berlin blockade."[109] In settling the Cuban missile issue the superpowers made

---

* See Chapter IX.

mutual concessions as both backed away from a general war; but these did not include an acceptance of East German control of access routes or a conversion of West Berlin into a free city.

Toward a Soviet-GDR Treaty

Flare-ups over Berlin continued sporadically throughout 1963, most of them petty but still agitating. In late October 1963 Moscow provoked another incident when it required U.S. troops traveling in convoys to dismount. The purpose seemed to be more to annoy than to make any substantive statement, and the episode actually generated more static within the U.S. military ranks than it did between the rival powers. When Norstad blamed the autobahn incidents in part on U.S. soldiers at the checkpoint, Lemnitzer, who succeeded Norstad on 1 January 1963, challenged Norstad's claim in a message to Taylor, defending the conduct of U.S. military personnel as "exemplary" in that duty. General Paul Freeman, commander in chief, U.S. Army, Europe, had wired Lemnitzer from Heidelberg of his displeasure over interference by a "high military member of a sister service" in a matter that had caused the officers in charge of the checkpoints enough grief as it was.[110] Another old issue that resurfaced concerned air safety in the Berlin air corridors. As late as the last week of May 1964 the Soviets were harassing Allied controllers with demands for flight plans without sufficient advance notice.[111]

Even such occasional provocations ceased when the Soviet Union finally signed a Treaty of Friendship, Mutual Assistance, and Cooperation with East Germany on 12 June 1964. After six years at the center of the tension over Berlin the treaty came as an anticlimax. What counted in the pact was what was left unstated. The rhetoric of traditional statements of friendship and collaboration between the two countries ignored any reference to Allied troops in West Berlin or to their right of access to the city. Only two brief mentions of West Berlin appeared in the document.[112]

The Soviet Union tacitly gave up its demands. The U.S. position stayed exactly as it was in 1958. To confirm this, the three Western powers announced on 26 June that "any agreement which the Soviet Union may make with the so-called 'German Democratic Republic' cannot affect Soviet obligations or responsibilities under agreements and arrangements with the Three Powers on the subject of Germany including Berlin and access thereto." Moreover, they pointedly observed that "West Berlin is not an 'independent political unit.'" Frontiers could be fixed finally only when a final peace agreement was concluded for the whole of Germany. Ironically, while the Soviet-GDR treaty had nothing to say about the issues that Khrushchev had raised with such regularity over the preceding six years, it specifically accepted the agreement reached at Potsdam in 1945 that had divided Berlin into Allied occupation zones.[113]

The West achieved its major objective, namely, to hold the line in Berlin against unilateral Soviet actions that would jeopardize the Allied position. Moscow could claim some success as well. By stopping the flow of people from east to west it had secured some stabilization within East Germany.[114] Nevertheless, the overall impression was that U.S. policy had triumphed over Soviet designs despite often bitter divisions among the allies and acrimonious differences between U.S. planners. The long, drawn-out Berlin crisis had finally ended. Berlin's significance diminished in the next few years as other flash points dominated the Cold War scene.

The Berlin affair provided McNamara with an early lesson in the complexity of formulating national security policy in the context of European politics and multilateral decisionmaking. His ability to fashion a consistent policy during the extended crisis suffered from difficulties in reaching consensus, first of all, within DoD, particularly agreement between OSD and the Joint Chiefs. In Europe Norstad, understandably sensitive to the concerns of the allies, had continuing doubts about the doctrine of flexible response and McNamara's and Nitze's emphasis on conventional forces. Outside the department, McNamara had to cope with pressures from White House agents, especially Acheson and Clay, who would have used conventional forces more aggressively than Defense preferred and from allies who regarded flexible response as not only an insufficient deterrent but an excessive demand on their resources. The threat to Berlin raised a host of questions that defied easy answers much less concurrence on the part of the several stakeholders—when and whether to enter negotiations, the number of troops to be mobilized, when and how to deploy them, and the relationship between the conventional and nuclear options, including the range of alternatives within the nuclear spectrum and when to resort to tactical vs. strategic weapons.

Nevertheless, for all the pitfalls, the Berlin crisis afforded the Pentagon a larger role in shaping U.S. foreign policy. While Defense was nominally a junior partner of State in the process, the military nature of the Berlin crisis broadened the influence of McNamara and Defense, as reflected in the dramatic increase in DoD funding in the third amended budget of FY 1962, the enlargement of conventional forces, and employment of the Reserve and National Guard forces. Defense emerged from the Berlin crisis at center stage in the formation and management of national security policy.

Further, the crisis afforded an opportunity to test in practice the flexible response doctrine. A product of slow and unsteady evolution, to be sure, its introduction here nevertheless created a foundation of experience for application of the concept in future crises, of which the next, Cuba, followed in short order in 1962. The Berlin test reinforced McNamara's belief in the wisdom of flexibility and in the futility of reliance solely or primarily on the nuclear option. For flexible response to be credible ultimately required a buildup of not only U.S. but NATO conventional forces and the centralization of nuclear weaponry under U.S. control, realizations of which remained elusive and debatable and posed challenges in some ways as daunting as coping with the tempest over Berlin.

Chapter VIII
The Bay of Pigs Fiasco

Of the three major international crises the Kennedy administration confronted in 1961, Berlin was the only one where the United States and its allies found themselves face to face with the Soviet adversary. In the other two areas—Southeast Asia and Cuba—the Soviet Union had surrogates serving its interests.

In Cuba, the Kennedy administration inherited a major dilemma and a controversial enterprise. Conceived by the CIA and advanced secretively in the last year of the Eisenhower administration, the Bay of Pigs invasion in April 1961 grew out of a felt need to respond forcefully to events in Cuba that increasingly identified its leader, Fidel Castro, as a threat to the United States and other countries in the Americas.[1]

The Eisenhower Legacy

The initial flush of enthusiasm following the overthrow of the repressive Batista regime in January 1959 gave way before the end of the year to U.S. disenchantment with the behavior of Castro, Batista's charismatic successor. Castro quickly cast the United States as the enemy, proclaimed himself a communist, and turned to the Soviet bloc for support. During Eisenhower's last year in office Castro hounded into exile thousands of middle-class Cubans and rounded up, imprisoned, or executed hundreds more as enemies of the new state. The break with the United States appeared irrevocable as Castro expropriated the property of U.S. citizens and laid plans to export Havana's brand of communism throughout Latin America.

The United States effectively cut off U.S. oil to Cuba in October 1960 and denied Cuban sugar to the American market in December, major economic blows to the new regime.[2] It is doubtful that a less hostile U.S. stance might have turned the Castro revolution away from Soviet influence, given the symbolic and ideological importance of Yankee imperialism to the Cuban revolution. A break with the United States more likely provided vital cement for the new dictatorship.

The United States severed relations with Castro on 3 January 1961, 17 days before Kennedy's inauguration.[3] An American public that had become increasingly appalled not only by the blatant anti-Americanism of Castro's rhetoric but also by his brutal treatment of opponents lent the move strong support. The flood of embittered exiles pouring into Florida helped create an environment that could and would nurture a clandestine operation against Communist Cuba.

The Eisenhower administration had initiated planning early in 1960 for a guerrilla operation to overthrow the Castro government. By the summer of 1960 the CIA undertook to form and train a strike force of 200-300 exiles supported by a small air unit of B-26s. As the planned covert operation grew into a paramilitary operation, Defense and State only gradually became aware of the details. When State learned of the CIA intention to establish Cuban assault training in Florida, it opposed use of any American-controlled territory for the purpose; the CIA then moved the training camps to Guatemala. In the Pentagon the JCS had been giving considerable thought to ousting Castro but had not yet been presented with an action plan.[4] Chief of Naval Operations Admiral Arleigh Burke, a leading figure in voicing opposition to Castro, attended the relevant NSC meetings in March 1960, and in November he suspected that "something was cooking" when Navy intelligence provided information on the Cuban exile-training base in Guatemala. But as late as January 1961 many specifics of the CIA planning remained unknown to the JCS. General Lemnitzer, the chairman, absorbed himself in other problems, such as the crisis in Laos, which seemingly had higher priority in the winter of 1960-61. While the JCS felt concern over the safety of the Guantanamo naval base in Cuba, Army Chief of Staff General George Decker later reflected that he never considered it to be "a strategic necessity in any sense of the word."[5]

The Cuban undertaking remained firmly in the hands of the CIA, under the direction of Richard M. Bissell, Jr., deputy director for plans. Bissell and CIA Director Allen Dulles briefed President-elect Kennedy on 18 November 1960 about the plan to overthrow Castro.[6] By then the scheme had developed into a full-blown scenario, with the attack set for March 1961 and the town of Trinidad on Cuba's south central coast as the assault site. Some 60 to 80 lightly armed invaders would stage an initial landing, followed by 600 to 750 men equipped with heavier weapons. Air strikes from Nicaragua-based bombers flown by Cuban exile pilots would support the landing. If all went well, this operation would spark a general insurrection and the establishment of a provisional government with the blessing of the United States. Should the plan miscarry, the guerrillas would disperse into nearby hills to resume their campaign from there.[7]

Eisenhower maintained his general interest in the project, endorsing the new paramilitary concept on 29 November 1960. While there is no evidence that the 5412 Committee, which supervised covert activities, ever formally approved the invasion plan during his administration, at a White House meeting on 3 January 1961, the date on which diplomatic relations with Cuba were severed, the president charged the Joint Chiefs with finding means of training Cuban exiles in preparation for an invasion. No doubt, in Eisenhower's view this program had the status of a contingency plan, but he had given no specific operational approval. He later claimed, according to General Maxwell Taylor, that he had never seen specific plans for an invasion of Cuba, although, at the same time, he made known his belief that Castro was a real and present danger to the United States. In a meeting between Eisenhower and Kennedy on the eve of the inauguration the outgoing president asserted that his administration was "helping train anti-Castro forces in Guatemala" and that the effort should be "continued and accelerated." Moreover, in the long run the Castro government must not be allowed to continue in Cuba.[8]

Road to "Trinidad"

The new administration had little time to assess the situation. Although Kennedy repeatedly expressed doubts about the feasibility of the CIA invasion plan, he did not crystallize his reservations. The ambiguous message of Eisenhower, whose military credentials he could not hope to match, seemed to imply acceptance of an assault on the island. The civilian advisers that Kennedy brought with him to the White House, along with his major appointees in State and Defense, were not yet familiar with each other. Most of them seemed reluctant to challenge the judgment of men who had helped win World War II, not only Eisenhower but key members of the Joint Chiefs and the CIA.[9] The president personally admired Bissell, whose easy Ivy League manner permitted him to move comfortably as well as confidently in the presidential circle. As a Democrat with professional credentials that went far beyond Yale, Bissell stood in line to succeed Dulles as director of the CIA. His service in the Truman and Eisenhower administrations along with his role as prime mover in the U-2 operation had earned him the support of the new administration, even when his briefings appeared elliptical and more advocative than informative.[10]

Theodore Sorensen later thought that Kennedy fell victim to a variety of pressures. Would he be willing to liquidate well-laid plans, leave Cuba free to subvert the hemisphere, and betray idealistic young Cubans, who, as Dulles put it, "asked nothing other than the opportunity to try to restore a free government in their country?" Moreover, even if Kennedy wanted to back away from such an operation, he faced imperatives that made it necessary to act immediately. The Cuban brigade had attained a peak of preparation and could not stay much longer in Guatemala. There was the danger that the Guatemalan government, increasingly unhappy over public exposure of the training sites, would move to shut them down if the plan were put on hold. What would be the political fallout from a disbanded force loose in the United States to spread its discontent among Republican opponents of the administration? Furthermore, the president had to consider that if he delayed a decision, new Soviet arms and Soviet-trained pilots could make Cuba impregnable to an invasion by an exile army.[11]

In fact, Kennedy had contributed to the rush to judgment. As a presidential candidate he had known in a general way of preparations being made for the liberation of the island in 1960 and made Eisenhower's seemingly half-hearted progress toward that goal a campaign issue. He contrasted the vigor that his administration would display in office with what he represented as Eisenhower's hesitant behavior and promised to help Cubans fight Castro at home and abroad. This brought forth a denunciation by the Republican candidate, Richard M. Nixon, who called it "the most shockingly reckless proposal ever made in our history by a presidential candidate during a campaign." In claiming that Kennedy's policy would violate many U.S. treaties and lose all America's friends in Latin America, Nixon overreached, for the record suggests he intended to follow the same policy if and when he entered the White House. After the election Kennedy couched his public statements in rhetoric that unmistakably portended strenuous efforts to remove the Castro regime. In a press conference on 25 January 1961, he made clear that he would not resume relations with a nation whose revolution had been seized by "external forces."[12]

Given these conditions and circumstances, the setting left little room to cancel Operation Trinidad, the invasion plan named for the debarkation point. The president knew when he took office that the Cuban brigade of some 1,000 men, scheduled for a 50 percent increase, was training in Guatemala. As previously planned, the brigade would go ashore near Trinidad, on Cuba's south coast, far from the main centers of the island, and hold the area until the anticipated uprising took place. Castro's army would require time to engage the liberators. By that time Cuban-exile pilots flying B-26 bombers from Nicaraguan fields would destroy Castro's small air force on the ground and secure the beachhead from air attack. Even if the effort failed the worst-case scenario would have the invaders melt into the nearby Escambray mountains where they would join other resisters in guerrilla warfare against the Castro regime.[13]

The JCS Role

While the Joint Chiefs had knowledge of these preparations, the CIA's tight security kept from them essential information needed to provide informed judgments on the feasibility of invasion plans. The incoming administration first addressed the Cuban issue on 22 January 1961, when Secretary Rusk met with McNamara, Attorney General Robert Kennedy, General Lemnitzer, CIA Director Dulles, and other senior officials to discuss the subject. This marked the first occasion the JCS had to consider formally the Trinidad operation; they clearly were frustrated by their outsider role, even as the military had been asked to provide limited support for the mission. The previous fall Admiral Robert Dennison, commander of the Atlantic Fleet, had been informed of a CIA request for a large landing ship, the USS *San Marcos*, in addition to smaller landing vessels, but not told about their intended use. When Dennison called Lemnitzer about the request, the latter promised him that he would receive a CIA briefing, but at year's end they were still in the dark.[14]

Despite having incomplete information, in anticipation of being asked for their opinion, General Thomas White, Air Force chief of staff, had already submitted an assessment of the Cuban situation and a review of possible options to his colleagues on 10 January. He compared the small number of guerrilla groups in the Escambray mountains with Castro's army of 32,000, police force of 9,000, and people's militia of some 200,000, all being steadily reinforced with Soviet military equipment. For an invasion to succeed, help would have to come from outside and could require surveillance support, an economic blockade, or even military intervention by U.S. forces. At a meeting with President Kennedy on 25 January, Lemnitzer, speaking for the Joint Chiefs who were present, made clear that if a successful landing occurred, "at that point we would come in and support them."

These meetings were followed by another at the White House, on 28 January, where the president, joined by Rusk, McNamara, Lemnitzer, Dulles, and Vice President Lyndon Johnson, heard Dulles's report and reached decisions that lent further impetus to the invasion plan. Kennedy authorized "increased propaganda, increased political action and increased sabotage," and he specifically approved continued overflights of Cuba for these purposes. He directed DoD and the CIA to "review proposals for the active deployment of anti-Castro Cuban forces on Cuban territory" and asked for prompt report of the results.[15]

The Joint Chiefs presented another paper, on 27 January, prepared under the direction of Brig. Gen. David W. Gray of the Joint Staff, that more forcefully contrasted the increasing military capabilities of the Castro government and the weaknesses of the forces being assembled by the CIA and expressed further JCS concerns. The chiefs remained particularly troubled by the absence of any follow-up measures should the initial assault fail. The Gray report, forwarded to McNamara by Lemnitzer, urged that an interdepartmental planning group develop detailed plans with specific tasks assigned to participating executive agencies. The objective was to have "continuous evaluation of the situation as a basis for determining U.S. course of action," and also to establish "command relationships for implementation of each course of action."[16]

On 3 February the chiefs pronounced the proposed beachhead "the best area in Cuba" to accomplish the mission of the Cuban task force. If estimates of Castro's air defense capabilities proved correct, the invaders' planned air operations appeared to be "within the capability of the Air units and should be successful." No overt U.S. involvement need follow if operations proceeded as currently planned. But even with this note of measured optimism, the chiefs expressed misgivings that if a problematic Cuban uprising did not occur in the wake of the landings the Cuban army could eventually wipe out the beachhead. On balance the JCS judged that "timely execution of this plan has a fair chance of ultimate success and, even if it does not achieve immediately the full results desired, could contribute to the eventual overthrow of the Castro regime."[17] This evaluation had a Delphic ring, particularly over the meaning of "fair chance of ultimate success."

At least one military interpretation of "fair chance" might have led to the cancellation of the invasion had it come to the attention of the president or his civilian advisers. General Gray calculated "fair chance" to be "thirty in favor and seventy against," a figure that Lt. Gen. Earle G. Wheeler, director of the Joint Staff, did not present to Lemnitzer when he reported the military evaluation to the JCS chairman on 1 February. The chiefs' hesitation also could have been discerned in their significant suggestion that an "independent evaluation of the combat effectiveness of the invasion force and detailed analysis of logistics plans should be made by a team of Army, Naval, and Air Force officers, if this can be done without danger of compromise of the plan."[18]

During these deliberations, the JCS had to keep in mind other considerations, among them the security of the Guantanamo base, a by-product of the Spanish-American War and an important base for Caribbean defense. They had misgivings about granting the Cuban brigade support from or retreat to the base, given an unpredictable Castro reaction in the event of the invasion's failure. The chiefs in January had rejected Rusk's proposal to include the Guantanamo base in the planning process.[19]

Given the reservations expressed, the JCS position on the original Trinidad plan should have been seen by Kennedy and McNamara as plainly contradictory. As Arthur Schlesinger observed, "there was plainly a logical gap between the statement that the plan would work if one or another condition were fulfilled and the statement that the plan would work anyway." The most convincing explanation for the apparent "sloppiness in analysis" was the chiefs' assumption that once the invasion had begun U.S. involvement would become inevitable.[20] With the United States fully and visibly involved, the enterprise had to succeed; the nation would not accept failure. This obvious but misguided reasoning lay behind the hopes of the Cuban exile leaders as well as the CIA invasion managers.

More forthright communication at this crucial juncture would have revealed the extent of the chiefs' reservations. They gave vent to their misgivings, but privately among themselves rather than to the president, or so they claimed. Marine Corps Commandant General David Shoup reportedly asserted, "If this kind of an operation can be done with this kind of force, with this much training and knowledge about it, then we are wasting our time in our divisions; we ought to go on leave for three months out of four." Admiral Burke saw the plans, the product of civilian thinking, as "weak" and "sloppy," discounting the chiefs' own lack of firm guidance. Doubts notwithstanding, Shoup and Burke both approved the Trinidad plan.[21] Perhaps they expected the president to veto it eventually, or possibly they hoped that the administration would intervene with U.S. forces at a critical moment to ensure success. They may have preferred to register demurrals within their own counsels without going on record in direct opposition to the commander in chief.

In any case, the president and the secretary of defense appear to have failed to sense the significance of the JCS caveats, embracing the positive vibrations and ignoring the veiled warnings. Bissell made the most of the "fair chance" estimate at a meeting in the White House on 8 February 1961, with McNamara, Rusk, Dulles, Nitze, Bundy, and others in attendance, when he pressed the president for an early decision on the operation. The invasion, Bissell felt, should come no later than 31 March, with the final decision to move ahead made at least 21 days before D-Day. Rusk and Assistant Secretary of State Adolf A. Berle opposed making a decision at the time. Kennedy asked for alternatives to a full-fledged invasion that might require support by U.S. planes and ships. He preferred that the Cuban liberators land gradually and quietly so that the operation would appear to come from the mountains as a Cuban in-house uprising rather than as an outside Yankee-sponsored invasion.[22]

The JCS then sent three officers to inspect the covert force in Guatemala. After visiting from 24 to 27 February 1961, they reported that the visibility of the brigade's activities militated against its chances of a surprise attack. They estimated the chance of achieving surprise, essential to success, at only 15 percent. In the absence of surprise, the operation would fail, they judged, because the Cuban air force could sink most, if not all, the vessels of the invasion force. The JCS informed the secretary of defense on 10 March that a landing could succeed initially, but its ultimate success depended on a popular uprising. The constraints were formidable. As an investigation headed by General Taylor later noted, "This effort to treat as covert an operation which in reality could not be concealed or shielded from the presumption of U.S. involvement raised in due course many serious obstacles to the successful conduct of the operation."[23]

Even though McNamara displayed no special interest in this problem, both Rusk and Kennedy appreciated fully the extent of the political fallout that would occur in Latin America over disclosure of an overt U.S. role in the enterprise. But even greater political costs accrued to aborting the invasion. The push for a decision obscured the plan's fatal flaws. Presidential assistant Richard Goodwin later judged that it "was doomed from start to finish."[24] Hindsight exposed the plan for what it was—not a mere miscalculation but an absurdity that called for sending 1,200 to 1,400* men on an amphibious invasion of a country defended by a

---

*The numbers for the brigade varied over time; the final strength figure was some 1,400.

32,000-man army and a militia of more than 200,000. U.S. World War II experience with island invasions in the Pacific, where John Kennedy had commanded a PT-boat, demonstrated that a successful assault required overwhelming strength. In this instance valiant Cuban-exile invaders faced enormous odds.

Despite the pressures to act, the president continued to temporize over Trinidad. When he asked the CIA for refinements, Bissell promptly provided them. On 11 March Bissell suggested preceding the actual full-force assault with a diversionary landing elsewhere by a force of 160 men to seize a beachhead contiguous to terrain suitable for guerrilla operations.[25] The president still could not accept Trinidad as presented. He continued to explore the feasibility of a night attack that included immediate seizure of a flight strip to support B-26 planes and that would avoid risking the opprobrium of a strike from a U.S. base, thus minimizing the appearance of U.S. involvement.[26]

The JCS took another look at the CIA plans in a memorandum to McNamara on 15 March. The CIA offered three alternative concepts. The first was the original paramilitary plan to launch the invasion near Trinidad. The chiefs now viewed it as doubtful because the change to a night amphibious landing without the support of air strikes and an airborne landing would deprive it of "the psychological impact of the original concept."

A second alternative, considered and discarded, called for a landing on the northeast coast, using an airborne company at "evening nautical twilight," followed by nighttime debarkation of the brigade's main forces. Ships would depart before daylight and planes could begin flying the next day from a captured airstrip. While this scenario met some of the earlier stated concerns, it did not meet those of the JCS. They judged that even if the Cuban volunteer force could land and sustain itself without resupply for three days, logistic support difficulties and the distance from the northeast coast to Havana made this alternative "least likely" to succeed.

The third and most plausible alternative proposed an amphibious landing on the southern coast, specifically the Zapata peninsula that protruded into the Bay of Pigs. Two infantry companies would seize key areas after dark, with the rest of the brigade following before daylight. Aircraft would begin operations from airstrips the next morning. Of the three, the JCS agreed that "Alternative III has all the prerequisites necessary to successfully establish the Cuban Voluntary Task Force, including air elements, in the objective area and sustain itself with outside logistic support for several weeks." The drawback, they recognized, lay in the isolation of the area. Its inaccessibility could limit support from the Cuban public.[27] The chiefs' recommendation of alternative three became a critical factor in the president's decision and one that would have serious repercussions in the postmortem examination of the failed operation.

The Civilian Leadership Role

If the Joint Chiefs appeared to react by turns inconsistently or equivocally to the planning for the invasion, McNamara and his OSD staff seemed even more uncertain and tentative. When the chiefs submitted their recommendations to McNamara, including their reservations, he accepted them without subjecting them to his usual close scrutiny. Preoccupation with other seemingly more pressing matters in his early days in the Pentagon and a deference to military judgment in this instance may have disposed him to go along. What seemed initially a minor role for Defense may also have influenced his judgment of the recommendations. Still, at a meeting on 28 January* with Rusk, Dulles, Gilpatric, and the Joint Chiefs, McNamara stated that the "CIA should be told that their plan is not considered to be a good one" and that there was need for an alternate plan. In retrospect McNamara felt that he had let himself "become a passive bystander."[28]

Paul Nitze, McNamara's chief liaison with the State Department, would be no happier than the secretary of defense with his own role. Nitze had established a division of responsibilities in his international security affairs office in which his assistant, William Bundy, dealt with special issues like Cuba. "So I was really not dealing with Cuba much," Nitze recalled, without excusing himself, more than 20 years later. The particular official assigned to ISA for linkage with the CIA, Brig. Gen. Edward G. Lansdale, "was very able, but a loner and a difficult person to control." When Lansdale complained to Nitze that the Cuban invasion plan would not work, Nitze discussed it with Bundy, who favored the undertaking. "I was busy and left it to them despite my doubts," Nitze concluded.[29]

Hence prominent military and civilian leaders moved ahead with the invasion plan, haltingly and at times skeptically but without sufficient challenge to prompt a fundamental reappraisal. Under Secretary of State Chester Bowles and Sen. J. William Fulbright, chairman of the Senate Foreign Relations Committee, were among the few senior figures in the government to speak out against the plan. In a memorandum to Kennedy on 30 March, and again at a 4 April meeting at State, Fulbright took a strong position against the operation and urged instead a policy of containment.[30] But the doubts of other key participants were resolved either by changes in tactics or by faith in Bissell's leadership. Rusk, although initially opposed, was not inclined to disturb a consensus; once assured the air strikes would come from captured airstrips and not from U.S. bases, he went along. McGeorge Bundy, on 15 March, also approved the revised plan. He told the president that Bissell had accomplished a difficult job of making the landing plan both low-keyed and plausibly Cuban: "I have been a skeptic about Bissell's operation, but now I think we are on the edge of a good answer."[31]

---

*The meeting at the Pentagon followed the one at the White House (see p. 176).

With the president's advisers in early spring still "engaged in learning their jobs and learning about one another at the same time," the magnetic personality of Richard Bissell easily dominated. Bissell's impressive record at the CIA inspired confidence. Many years later, he defended himself by observing that "it is amazing in hindsight that none of those concerned with planning and decision making ever said 'the king has no clothes on' or ever recognized as purely wishful thinking the assumption that official denials of responsibility by Washington would be plausible to anyone, least of all the U.S. press, given the character and scale of the invasion." At the time, however, he had not seen that the force of his own conviction helped to delude reasonable men, including himself. In his memoir, written shortly before his death in 1994, Bissell confessed shortcomings in his understanding of clandestine operations. Despite the air of authority he exuded, he regretted that he had not worked more closely with Richard Helms, the CIA director of plans, who as "a better judge of the agency's limitations" might have persuaded him "to consider cutting back the scope of the operation in some way."[32]

The kinds of questions that McNamara might ordinarily have asked of the CIA planners came from lesser White House civilian advisers whose views could more freely be deflected. Schlesinger had sent memoranda to the president containing his objections, which he admitted "look nice on the record, but they represented, of course, the easy way out."[33] After listening to Bissell explain the details of the invasion plan, Goodwin claims to have rather timidly asked, "How do we know the Cuban people will support the rebels, why do we think they want to overthrow Castro?" According to Goodwin, "without a moment's hesitation," Bissell turned and said to a colleague, "We have an NIE [National Intelligence Estimate] on that, don't we?" If the senior officials around the table could accept this answer as definitive, what could Goodwin possibly do, a young man with no experience in military planning, covert or overt, who had never been involved in such major decisions? "And across the room were the men who had done it all."[34]

Among the more obvious failures in planning were intelligence lapses, including that pertaining to the question raised by Goodwin and summarily dismissed by Bissell. As Deputy Secretary of Defense Gilpatric pointed out some 20 years later: "What went wrong fundamentally was a complete misconception of the situation inside Cuba. You can say that it was an intelligence failure. There was a lack of understanding throughout our government—State, Defense, and the White House—of how much support Castro had among his people."[35] Other intelligence failures stood out as well, for example the lack of knowledge about coral reefs in the Bay of Pigs, or about the barely passable mangrove swamp that blocked the escape route to the Escambray mountains, 40 miles away. Perhaps the switch from Trinidad to Zapata in March, so late in the planning, left insufficient time to explore all the obtainable information.

Such intelligence as the administration did receive filtered selectively through the partisan Cuban community in Miami. On 3 March former U.S. military attachés in Cuba reported from Miami the presence of 60,000 Cubans in the Florida area with more arriving every day: "Most of them are refugees from the Castro regime and almost all are willing to render assistance to the U.S. in order to overthrow that regime. They constitute a valuable potential of continuing intelligence information on Cuba." At the same time the attachés noted that 17 U.S. agencies dealt with refugee matters in Miami, but there existed "no policy agreement or established procedure among all agencies to properly exploit the potential and eliminate duplication of effort. Coordinated and organized methods do not exist which would expedite techniques used for the gathering of intelligence information." The attachés recommended to Brig. Gen. Frederick O. Hartel of ISA, less than seven weeks before the invasion, establishment of a central coordinating board.[36] Three weeks later, at OSD's request, the Army took the initiative to ensure cooperation among the three services and with State representatives to "make possible the timely receipt and exploitation of military intelligence information" and also set up liaison with the CIA and other agencies—this only a month before the invasion.[37]

Lack of coordination as well as inadequate intelligence presaged trouble. The first meeting of the interdepartmental working group, following up on the informal discussions begun in January, did not occur until 22 March. The paper it produced the next day containing agreed tasks for assignment to the various agencies constituted, as Taylor's postmortem report observed, "the first successful action to formalize the interdepartmental coordination which up to this point had depended largely upon ad hoc committees and meetings at Presidential level."[38]

Deficiencies also plagued the propaganda campaign aimed both at stirring up the Cuban public and justifying the activities of the Cuban invasion brigade to the outside world. At the president's behest, Schlesinger cooperated with State Department representatives in producing a "White Paper" on Cuba.[39] Early drafts carried the title of "The Communist Totalitarian Government of Cuba as a Threat to the Peace and Security of America." On 24 March, ISA reviewed a third draft that General Hartel considered a "suitable vehicle for presenting the Cuban matter before the Inter-American Peace Committee" of the Organization of American States.[40] The scattershot publicity effort involved on an ad hoc basis Schlesinger, Dulles, Edward R. Murrow at USIA, Adolf Berle at State, and William Bundy at Defense. It is questionable if any draft of the hurriedly assembled justification of an invasion would have made a difference. The final report on 3 April, little more than three weeks after the president had asked for a White Paper, came just two weeks before the invasion itself.

Of course no amount of propaganda could conceal the fatal flaws in the invasion plans, particularly the assumption of a mass uprising of disaffected Cubans. On 4 April the JCS, in response to a request from McNamara, stated that after the 1,300-man brigade secured the beachhead, the force would grow to 6,000 within the following month and would have accumulated enough equipment to sustain as many as 20,000 guerrillas. These expectations defied reality. During the course of a meeting with his top advisers on 16 March the president had asked Admiral Burke his view on the operation's chance of success. Burke gave "a probability figure of about 50 percent."[41] Both the Cuban Revolutionary Council in Miami and the CIA planners in Washington failed to heed the president's warnings about U.S. abstention from overt involvement. Almost on the eve of the landing Kennedy stated his intent to withhold approval if there arose any danger of compromising the United States. His comment at a press conference on 12 April that "there will not be, under any conditions, an intervention in Cuba by the United States Armed Forces" should have made this point abundantly clear even to the most myopic believer in the Cuban-exile cause.[42]

Invasion

The cumulative weight of the errors of commission and omission created too heavy a burden for an operation so problematic to begin with. Although the emphasis on secrecy may have prevented interdepartmental cooperation within the U.S. government, Castro did not require sophisticated intelligence devices to learn about exile forces training in Guatemala for an imminent invasion. The precise date alone remained uncertain because the administration kept postponing D-Day, from 5 April to 10 April, and finally to 17 April, and the president insisted that he might cancel the operation up to 24 hours before the approved D-Day. He gave formal approval for the landing on 16 April.[43]

A series of preparatory actions had to precede D-Day: air strikes by supposedly defecting Cuban pilots, infiltration of men and weaponry, and a diversionary landing in distant Oriente province. None of them succeeded. The diversionary force, intended to lure Castro's force to the east, failed to land. While the D-2 air strikes of eight B-26s did take place, they destroyed only five of Castro's planes and damaged some.* The clandestine landing at night, with ships to depart by daybreak, aborted. None of the cover stories carried weight. The effort to pass off one of the Cuban-exile pilots as a defector from Castro when he landed a B-26 in Miami was soon exposed.[44] The tale of Cuban pilot defectors lacked all credibility, particularly when an unexpected genuine defector flew his plane to Florida, permitting comparison between a real Cuban aircraft and the bogus CIA planes. Moreover, Cuban Foreign Minister Raul Roa informed a receptive UN audi-

---

*Cuban air strength was estimated variously from as few as 12 planes to as many as 37.

ence that the raid presaged a full-scale invasion organized by the United States. Castro had ample time to round up potential supporters of the expected invading force.⁴⁵

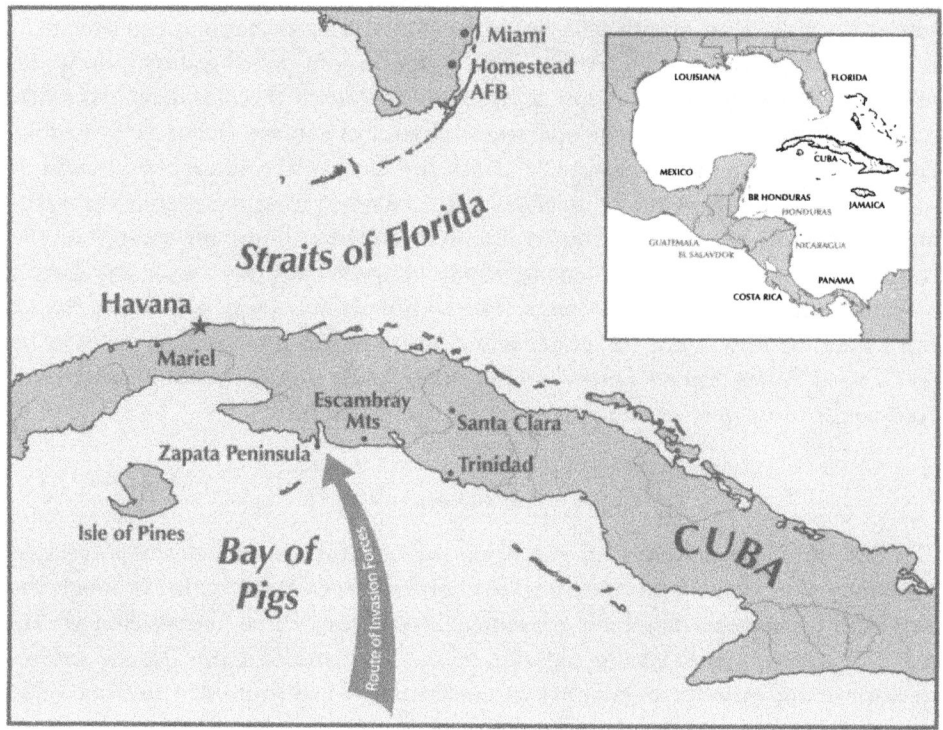

Bay of Pigs Invasion

These opera bouffe events coming on the eve of invasion had a profound effect. Fear of even greater exposure led Rusk, with the president's approval, to cancel a second air strike scheduled for D-Day out of fear of the impact of U.S. involvement on world opinion. CIA Deputy Director General Charles Cabell, filling in for Dulles while the director was out of town, and Bissell tried unsuccessfully to change Rusk's decision that the dawn air strikes the following morning should not take place until they could come from a Cuban airfield. Although Rusk gave them leave to take their case to Kennedy, they chose not to.⁴⁶

In the opinion of both the CIA and the JCS, failure to permit a second strike against Cuban air bases became the major factor in the invasion's collapse. McNamara seemed to offer some support to this view when he claimed that "the decision to cancel some of the D-Day air strikes . . . was made at the only meeting at which neither I nor the Chiefs participated."⁴⁷ The effective Castro air assaults on the landing force, the sinking of the ship supplying munitions, the malfunctioning of radio communications equipment—all traced back to the cancellation of the second strike. One view of the aborted campaign laid responsibility on Rusk and Ambassador Adlai Stevenson for overreacting to United Nations hostility.

Years later Lemnitzer claimed that Castro's air force would have been destroyed had the White House followed the Joint Chiefs' advice and permitted another strike against Cuban airfields. He believed that Stevenson had been receiving such vehement criticism in the UN for the obvious U.S. involvement in the Cuban venture that the ambassador persuaded Rusk and Kennedy to call a halt to the strike without informing the JCS of their decision.[48] For the CIA, the aborted "second strike" became a shibboleth permitting the agency to deflect the inevitable charges directed against its leaders. The influential journalist Charles J. V. Murphy presented the CIA argument in a long article in *Fortune*, in which he claimed that McGeorge Bundy, acting for the president, fatally compromised the invasion by countermanding the air strike at a critical moment preceding the landing.[49]

Arguably, the issue of the second strike got blown out of proportion by its partisans. In refutation, Roger Hilsman, director of State's Bureau of Intelligence and Research, maintained that even if the second strike had gone ahead it would have had limited effect. He pointed out that whatever success the first attack may have achieved, a second strike would have found planes dispersed and protected. The aborted "second strike" explanation, satisfying as it may have been to its proponents, did not take into account the other factors in the failure such as the long stretch of almost impenetrable marshland that separated the invaders from the mountains to the east. Nor did it explain why a single vessel carried all of the vitally needed ammunition. Above all, it did not recognize that the absence of a supportive population, ready to take up arms with the liberators, doomed the enterprise. In this circumstance, as Hilsman observed, "if Castro's air attacks on the beachhead had not crushed the one-thousand-man landing force, the two-hundred-thousand-man army of militiamen that followed would certainly have done so."[50]

The plight of the invaders came as a shock to administration leaders. By 19 April, two days after it had begun, the invasion collapsed. Despite some initial successes on the ground, the 1,400 Cuban-exile liberators proved no match for 20,000 troops and the unopposed Cuban air force. In the waning moments of the disaster the United States could only have its destroyers take survivors off the beach.* If fired upon, the destroyers were authorized to return fire. On the following day, 20 April, at the direction of the president, the JCS directed the

---

* The prisoners taken at the Bay of Pigs remained in Cuban custody until their release to the United States on 25 December 1962.

commander in chief Atlantic (CINCLANT) to conduct patrols off the coast to facilitate the evacuation of survivors, but the ships might fire only in self-defense.[51]

The Taylor Report

Unlike his indecision in the preparatory stages of the operation, the president acted with dispatch after its failure. On 22 April he asked General Taylor to chair an investigation of the disaster. The Cuba Study Group began work on the same day with Attorney General Robert Kennedy, Dulles, and Admiral Burke as the other three members. The circumstances could not have been more depressing. As Taylor noted at his meeting with the president, "I sensed an air which I had known in my military past—that of a command post that had been overrun by the enemy. There were the same glazed eyes, subdued voices, and slow speech that I remembered observing in commanders routed at the Battle of the Bulge or recovering from the shock of their first action."[52] Talking with some 50 witnesses made him all the more aware of the state of confusion that characterized the operation and the semantic problems inherent in the use of the term "fair" chance of success.

The Taylor report, submitted to the president on 13 June, treated the lessons learned judiciously. Such discretion may have reflected the group's composition, as Taylor's three colleagues all had interests to protect. Robert Kennedy was a jealous guardian of his brother's reputation, while Burke and Dulles represented the two agencies under heaviest criticism for their roles in the operation. Taylor, who saw himself as the "sole disinterested member," never implied that the group's composition in any way inhibited the investigation.[53]

The "proximate cause" of the fiasco, according to Taylor's report, lay in the critical shortage of ammunition that led to the surrender of the landing force. While not calling it the most important cause of the failure, the study group concluded that "the Executive branch of the Government was not organizationally prepared to cope with this kind of paramilitary operation." On the question of how close the invasion came to success, the study group produced a mixed verdict: "Had the ammunition shortage been surmounted, which is to say, had the Castro air been neutralized, would the landing force have accomplished its mission? . . . . Under the conditions which developed we are inclined to believe that the beachhead could not have survived long without substantial help from the Cuban population or without overt U.S. assistance." Burke and Dulles felt uncomfortable with the "conjectures in this paragraph." Since the well-motivated and aggressive Cuban expeditionary force fought well enough without air cover and in spite of an ammunition shortage, they thought it "reasonable to believe that if the CEF had had ammunition and air cover, they could have held the beachhead for a much longer time." Such a success "coupled with CEF aircraft overflying Cuba with visible control of the air, could well have caused a chain reaction of success throughout Cuba with resultant defection of some of the Militia, increasing support from the populace and eventual success of the operation."54

Lemnitzer had taken this position in his comments to congressional leaders at the White House on 19 April. The JCS chairman made the point that the Cuban force could get ashore with "reasonable chance of success," but that "ultimate success was considered to be dependent upon the reaction and manner in which it generated disaffection in Castro militia, [and] produced uprisings in Cuba in support of anti-Castro forces."55

The study group did not rebuke Lemnitzer and his JCS colleagues for their ambiguous stance. It recognized that the individual chiefs "did not and probably could not give the plan the same meticulous study which a commander would give to a plan for which he was personally responsible." The group's original draft report used the term "de facto approval," which was deleted in the final report of 13 June. Modification of language did little to mollify the Joint Chiefs. While the Taylor group found fault with civilian leaders, including the secretary of defense, for overlooking the initial JCS preference for Trinidad, it did not exonerate the military leaders for their subsequent acceptance of Zapata. "The record is clear," said the study group, "that the Chiefs subsequently took active part in considering changes to the plan as it developed into final form, did not oppose the plan and by their acquiescing in it gave others the impression of approval."56

The Taylor group recommended a governmental mechanism that would offer more leadership than the 5412 Committee or the ad hoc task forces that had functioned in 1960 and 1961. The group proposed the creation of a permanent committee of under-secretarial rank from State, Defense, and the CIA, with a full-time chairman who would report directly to the president. This new body, with the suggested name of Strategic Resources Group, would replace the 5412 Committee and become the basic coordinator of Cold War strategy for the countries or areas assigned to it by the president for that purpose.57

Burke objected to the proposal, but the main opposition came from the State Department, which resisted any centralization that would undermine its predominance. According to Taylor, "Dean Rusk was less than enthusiastic about an interdepartmental committee reporting to the President with a potentially important role in foreign affairs which might impinge on the traditional responsibilities of the Department of State." State's resistance blocked the recommendation, but Rusk could not prevent the president from bringing management of covert activities into the White House under a new Special Group (Augmented), chaired by Taylor.58

A sense of urgency clearly animated the language and the spirit of the Cuba Study Group's final recommendations. It concluded that while the paramilitary operation may have collapsed, it typified "a form of Cold War action in which the country must be prepared to engage." It was a question then of seeing to it that a future Zapata would have "a maximum chance of success." The report urged upon the president and public a new awareness of the emergency facing the nation: "The first requirement . . . is to recognize that we are in a life and death struggle which we may be losing, and will lose unless we change our ways and marshal our resources with an intensity associated in the past only with times of war." This might include an announcement of a limited national emergency and a review of treaties and international agreements "which restrain the full use of our resources in the Cold War."[59]

The crisis in Cuba posed no more threat to the nation's security than similar troubles in Laos and Berlin, the study group observed, but Cuba remained the primary focus, if only because of "the general feeling that there can be no long-term living with Castro as a neighbor." Ultimately, the study group could see only two solutions: internal discontent that would topple the dictator or active measures on the part of the United States to effect his removal. Neither course appeared feasible in the short run. The power of Castro's police state blocked the first approach and the second, according to the group, could occur only "through overt U.S. participation with as much Latin American support as can be raised." Pessimistically, the group concluded that if the administration chose not to make a decision, in effect it was resigning itself to the passive alternative over which it had less control.[60]

Recriminations

A domestic and international political disaster for the Kennedy administration, the Bay of Pigs led to much soul-searching and postmortem efforts to understand the reasons for the failure. "Victory has 100 fathers and defeat is an orphan," Kennedy remarked immediately after the misadventure. Blame fell most heavily on the CIA's Richard Bissell, who in turn pointed the finger at the president's hesitation to commit U.S. forces. Congressional critics faulted the Joint Chiefs of Staff, particularly its chairman, General Lemnitzer, for not quashing a poorly conceived enterprise and for conveying to the president only vague misgivings. The JCS, in turn, blamed both the CIA and the president, because the agency had failed to consult with military professionals and the president fatally crippled an already flawed operation by canceling a second air strike at a critical moment.[61]

Two major figures—the president and his secretary of defense—ultimately accepted responsibility for failure. The president recognized that his was the final authority. As he told Bissell, if the United States had operated under a parliamentary system, he would have had to resign, but they served under the American system. Only the two CIA leaders, Bissell and Director Allen Dulles, would step down after suitable intervals, though they exited gently.[62]

Publicly, the president and the secretary of defense accepted the blame for the disaster. Characteristically, McNamara seems to have settled on self-recrimination out of a sense of duty and loyalty to the president. At the same time he must have realized that his failure to participate more actively and critically in examining the plan was a grievous mistake. In an interview a quarter century later he acknowledged the error: "I deeply regret that at that time I didn't recommend against it."[63] As for the president, he privately harbored anger and disappointment toward those who had led him down the ill-advised path, including his predecessor, Dwight Eisenhower. Plans for action against Cuba had reached an advanced stage under the previous administration, presided over by a figure of surpassing military experience. Having criticized Eisenhower during the campaign for passivity in the face of Castro's provocations, Kennedy could not disown measures he himself had advocated for Cuban "fighters for freedom."[64] The president recognized his own error in not making clear to his advisers the doubts he had about the operation and his failure to act on those doubts.

At congressional hearings on 19 May Lemnitzer, taking note of press releases implying that responsibility for the invasion failure rested with the JCS, asserted that he and his colleagues had not attempted to rebut their complicity. At the same time, he stated that the chiefs' responsibilities did not extend beyond the armed forces of the United States and their operations. The Department of Defense had no responsibility for planning or conducting covert paramilitary operations in time of peace; those tasks belonged to the Central Intelligence Agency. Lemnitzer admitted that the JCS did evaluate and appraise the plan, offered comments, and assessed that the plan had "a fair chance of accomplishing its limited and initial objectives."[65]

Army Chief of Staff Decker later claimed that the JCS role was to make minimal comments on the plan and then send them on to the secretary of defense. If the operation subsequently miscarried, "it was obvious that somewhere along the line someone had made decisions which adversely affected the success of the operations. Whether these were made by the President or someone else, I do not know. But, at any rate, the operation was caused to fail by the failure of those who were managing it to follow the recommendation that had been made by the Joint Chiefs of Staff.... We were merely on the sidelines as observers and advisers."[66]

Burke owned up to more responsibility than either Lemnitzer or Decker. Years later he claimed that "stupidity, not only of the administration but also of the Chiefs, me included," prevented them from seeing through what they had started. He qualified this admission with a reminder that at "every meeting that the Chiefs had with the President, and we had a lot of them, the President would say, 'This is not a military operation.' We would suggest something, and he would say, 'This is not a military operation, not your operation. We want your advice and your advice only. You have no responsibility for this.' We were told this at every meeting over and over again. It took." Burke's mea culpa suggested that if the invasion had been seen as a military operation the JCS would have demanded more commitment, including the use of U.S. forces to assure victory.[67]

Although McNamara commented to the president that "the operation failed because you acted on faulty advice from your advisors, particularly the representatives of CIA and DoD, including myself," he continued to nurse a grievance against the JCS. He believed that for all their disclaimers they had let the administration down. This message came through clearly in his delayed and then lukewarm response to congressional attacks against the JCS in the press and at the 19 May Senate Foreign Relations Committee executive session hearings.[68]

The secretary's apparent coolness toward Lemnitzer, like the president's, never got on the record. Rather, it showed up indirectly in Kennedy's appointment of Maxwell Taylor as his military representative and in McNamara's obvious disregard for Lemnitzer's judgment. Lemnitzer, equally disenchanted with McNamara, later expressed his frustrations primarily by railing at the secretary's use of the whiz kids in systems analysis to second-guess the JCS. Still, the president retained Lemnitzer as chairman and recommended him to be supreme allied commander in Europe (SACEUR) the following year.[69]

How much of the recrimination that Lemnitzer and his colleagues suffered after the Bay of Pigs invasion resulted from their failure to communicate their doubts more clearly beforehand posed a reasonable question. Their resentment understandably centered on ground rules that left them as advisers without authority and prevented them from staffing the operation appropriately. Their most serious grievance stemmed from their lack of any significant say in or control of the operation. Too many factors related to the success of the mission depended on imponderables such as the scale of a popular uprising or on political issues outside their purview. Moreover, the chiefs found it troubling that assessments of the invaders' combat readiness came from second- and thirdhand reports.

Tennessee Sen. Albert Gore's public call on 20 May for the removal of the Joint Chiefs created a backlash. *U.S. News & World Report*, in particular, came to Lemnitzer's defense, quoting Sen. Francis Case (R-S. Dak.) that he "was flabbergasted that the reputation of the military services of the United States could be laid on the line by persons not in the military establishment." The article gave the impression that if the military chiefs had been properly consulted, the operation would not have gone ahead without appropriate support. The JCS felt unfairly criticized over the debacle but kept official silence and released no self-serving leaks, although in his testimony on 19 May Lemnitzer implicitly blamed the CIA.[70]

The CIA and its partisans had less reticence about finger pointing, which found its way into Charles Murphy's article in the August issue of *Fortune* that blamed the Cuban failure on the administration's meddling in CIA planning. When McNamara read the article, he professed to be "shocked by the general impression left by the story." He proceeded to rebut the author's assertion that political considerations in the end compromised the president's judgment. He objected most strongly to Murphy's claim that the CIA expected U.S. military help during the landing. "At no time during the planning," McNamara told the president, "was I aware of any such assumption. On several occasions before the operation started, you stated categorically that U.S. combat support was not to be provided to the Cubans in the invasion force, and that they were to be told of this decision."[71]

The substance of the article became a public issue when the president commented on Murphy's version of the Bay of Pigs fiasco as it appeared in the *Time* magazine issue of 1 September. Kennedy's expressed annoyance at his news conference on 30 August moved *Time* and *Fortune* publisher Henry Luce to request a meeting with General Taylor in New York. The publisher, worried about damage to his professional reputation, capitulated, with Murphy present. At the end of the discussion Murphy, claiming no malice or rancor intended, extended his regrets for offending the president. He conceded that his sources "may have made honest errors in detail."[72]

While the article raised a storm in the oval office, the president made it clear to Luce that he wanted no public corrections of the piece. "I have felt from the beginning," he wrote the publisher on 12 September, "that it would not be in the public interest for the United States to take formal responsibility for the Cuban matter other than the personal responsibility which I have earlier assumed.... For the present, facing as we do so many difficult problems, I would prefer that we let the matter lie as it is."[73]

Internal feuds within the CIA kept the issue alive for many years. CIA Inspector General Lyman B. Kirkpatrick, Jr., left out of the operation in 1961, faulted his colleagues. He claimed a decade later that the lack of accurate intelligence was responsible for the disaster: "There is no other place to put the blame for that than on the agency mounting the operation." He noted that excluding so many knowledgeable CIA experts from the planning process wasted important expertise.[74]

Other interpretations of the event would continue to circulate, with varying degrees of credibility. Its value as a "lesson of history," however, assured that the Bay of Pigs would resonate in future policy deliberations and political forums as a watershed episode. Schlesinger, for example, had no doubt that the errors of 1961 were translated into success in 1962 during the Cuban missile crisis. Murphy, on the other hand, believed strongly that the debacle at the Bay of Pigs contributed to the growth of communist activity in the Americas. Still others wondered if any lessons were learned, as the Vietnam quagmire soon followed.[75]

Repercussions

The most visible immediate repercussions saw the role of the CIA and to a lesser extent the JCS diminished. Both lost status within the Kennedy administration. Taylor, recalled to active duty on 1 July 1961, shortly after the study group submitted its report, became military representative of the president. He would provide military advice and assistance to the president, but not in competition with the JCS.[76]

The humbling of the JCS was only temporary. Not so the CIA, where the impact of the Bay of Pigs miscalculation had a more lasting effect. The agency would not again control large-scale paramilitary operations. This constituted a victory for the Joint Chiefs. On 28 June 1961, the president directed that in the future "the Department of Defense will normally receive responsibility for overt paramilitary operations. Where such operation is to be wholly covert or disavowable, it may be assigned to CIA, provided that it is within the normal capabilities of the agency. Any large paramilitary operation wholly or partly covert which requires significant numbers of militarily trained personnel . . . is properly the primary responsibility of the Department of Defense with the CIA in a supporting role."*[77]

As for the persisting Cuba problem, on 20 April, even before the dimensions of the disaster had become fully known, Kennedy ordered DoD to prepare contingency plans that involved the use of U.S. forces to overthrow Castro. The charge embraced alternatives ranging from a blockade of Cuba to a landing of U.S. troops. Within six days the JCS prepared a lengthy response for McNamara. They warned that whatever the course taken, any military action should be "swift, sharp, and overwhelming and should present the remainder of the world with a fait accompli."[78] By the end of the month, McNamara and the chiefs gave Kennedy a preferred plan and timetable for an assault on the island. On 1 May, with the president's approval, McNamara asked the chiefs to provide detailed instructions "designed to minimize the lead time required, and maximize security during the period between the decision and the invasion."[79]

Similarly, McNamara charged Nitze with a broad range of responsibilities following an NSC meeting on 22 April 1961. He wanted Nitze to explore with the State Department the political and military implications of recruiting Cuban nationals as part of the U.S. army, possibly under the name of "Freedom Brigade," and consider the possibility of providing unilateral or bilateral security guarantees for Central and South American countries. The secretary also raised the idea of developing some form of Western Hemisphere police force to cope with communist subversion throughout the area. In his instructions to both ISA

---

* The lack of timely and accurate military intelligence as well as concern over CIA support clearly influenced McNamara's decision to establish the Defense Intelligence Agency on 1 August 1961. See Chapter II.

and the JCS, McNamara concluded with a caveat to the effect that contingency plans remained just that and should not indicate that military action against Cuba was probable.[80]

McNamara's cautionary advice reflected the uncertain balance the administration maintained in the aftermath of the debacle. Despite the anger and frustration that fueled support of plans to overthrow Castro, Walt Rostow, deputy special assistant to the president for national security, tried to lower the volume on 21 April when he urged that the momentum of an active foreign policy established in the first months of the administration not become another casualty of the Bay of Pigs. Compared with problems in the Congo, Laos, and Berlin, he saw the setback in Cuba as only a minor affair. Without minimizing the dangers of a communist base in Cuba, or the necessity to prepare for intervention if Castro overplayed his hand, he stressed the importance of not "swinging wildly."[81]

JCS planners probably had little need of McNamara's and Rostow's pleas for restraint. While CINCLANT Admiral Dennison, acting for the Joint Chiefs, prepared a plan that could be implemented on five days' notice, he warned on 19 May that such rapid reactions "could not be maintained indefinitely without reducing readiness, training, and morale." Moreover, there would be loss of secrecy through repositioning of U.S. units, and impairment of ability to deal with emergencies elsewhere in the world. In the following month, the chiefs informed the secretary that "more leeway must be provided in the reaction time," and recommended a reaction time within 18 days from "Execute" to "Assault." In an emergency, a two-division airborne assault could be launched against the Havana area in five to six days.[82]

Even if the chiefs had been disposed to give in to the passions of the day, an NSC action taken on 5 May and approved by the president on 16 May would have cooled their ardor. In its general agreement that U.S. policy should aim at the overthrow of Castro, the council also agreed that none of the aggressive military measures hitherto identified would achieve that result, lacking the endorsement of the JCS and DoD. The NSC preferred to emphasize the positive results that might follow from a close collaboration with Latin American nations in the Organization of American States (OAS). In concert they could initiate such anti-Castro actions as breaking diplomatic ties, preventing arms shipments, establishing a Caribbean security force, and denouncing the Cuban leader as an agent of international communism.[83]

The NSC also discouraged a proposal to organize a separate Cuban military force in the United States for the very reason that its proponents wanted one: A separate exile force implied military action that the administration did not choose to pursue. Drawing on the 4 May findings of the Nitze-led interagency task force, the NSC adopted a policy toward Cuban exiles that echoed the hopes of liberation but posed them in terms of lesser expectations. A proposal to train 4,000 Cubans went too far. Despite the desirability of having a military leadership to take advantage of Castro's overthrow at the right time, the drawbacks far outweighed the advantages. Hostile critics in the UN and elsewhere would question the purpose of this military training. Moreover, such a military contingent would be a "useful, but not an essential, element" in an invasion. The NSC deleted the concept and the emotive language of a "Cuban Freedom Brigade." Instead, it "agreed that no separate Cuban military force should be organized in the United States, but that Cuban nationals would be encouraged to enlist in the U.S. armed forces under plans to be developed by the Secretary of Defense."[84]

Although the Taylor group clearly expressed a preference for national mobilization and covert action against Cuba, the cautious NSC approach prevailed. At the same time, the president and the attorney general, who had a major role in overseeing planning of covert operations, wanted to instill new vigor into efforts to remove Castro. To this end there followed a wide spectrum of activities under the aegis of the Special Group (Augmented) in 1962, including such anti-Castro schemes as Operation Mongoose.*

The Cuban missile crisis of 1962, embodying a frightening fulfillment of the worst nightmares about a Soviet-Castro connection, would intrude soon enough to reprise many of the same questions—and reservations—in a much larger strategic context and with the consequences of failure potentially far graver.

---

* See Chapter IX.

CHAPTER IX

The Cuban Missile Crisis

Conceivably the Cuban missile crisis would have occurred even had there been no Bay of Pigs debacle in 1961. Continuing U.S. efforts to isolate Communist Cuba, the unresolved Berlin problem, and Soviet resentment of U.S. missile bases in Turkey, each or in combination, might have proved sufficient to precipitate a Soviet-American confrontation in the Caribbean in 1962. Yet the disaster at the Bay of Pigs, in strengthening Kennedy administration resolve to overthrow Castro, undoubtedly contributed to growing friction with Castro's chief patron. Khrushchev's mistaken perception of weakness in Washington in the wake of the Bay of Pigs may also have factored in the Soviet decision to transport intermediate-range ballistic missiles to Cuba in the summer of 1962, which in turn seemed to confirm the worst suspicions about the Kremlin's hostile intentions.[1]

Failure at the Bay of Pigs did not signal abandonment of plans for removing Castro or even the possible invasion of Cuba. Within the year and a half between April 1961 and October 1962, the Kennedy administration engaged in a series of provocative actions against the Cuban leader, notably the ouster of Cuba from the Organization of American States, the use of the Alliance for Progress to damage Cuba's economy, military support to anti-Castro Cubans, and, more clandestinely, consideration of assassination schemes against Castro and his aides. By October 1962 it must have seemed almost inevitable to Castro and his Soviet ally that an invasion itself could occur at any moment.

While denying that the United States intended to go beyond any contingency plans and actually invade the island, McNamara admitted 25 years later that he could understand why the Soviet Union and Cuba anticipated U.S. intervention.[2] He himself had presented to the president on 29 April 1961 the Joint Chiefs' recommendation for a swift, overwhelming invasion that would take the island in eight days. There could be little doubt that the Kennedy administration conducted a vendetta after the Bay of Pigs embarrassment or that its objective continued to be the removal of the Cuban dictator from power one way or another.

A shuffling of roles and influence within the administration altered the principals involved and to some extent the choice of tactics but not the overriding goal. Attorney General Robert Kennedy, who had no role in the failed operation, emerged after April 1961 as head of a special group in charge of Cuban affairs and a leading advocate of a more aggressive approach. The two major CIA figures associated with the fiasco, Allen Dulles and Richard Bissell, left office within a year of the event. Their departure did not signify the banning of the CIA from further activities against Cuba. The agency, though tarnished and embarrassed, was too valuable a tool to be left out of the Kennedy plans. It continued to undertake projects designed to subvert or remove Castro through covert action, but it now had to function under appropriate guidance from the White House and closer coordination with DoD. The State Department suffered some diminution of authority as well. From July 1961 General Maxwell Taylor, as military representative of the president and, from 1 October 1962, as chairman of the Joint Chiefs of Staff, carried much weight on Cuban matters. So did OSD in general, even if the JCS (excepting Taylor) never managed to redeem itself in Kennedy's eyes from its putative errors. The personal commitment of Robert Kennedy, the imaginative if sometimes chimerical special operations ideas of Brig. Gen. Edward Lansdale in OSD, and the increasingly assertive voice of DoD, impatient with State's caution, dominated administration planning in Cuban matters after April 1961.

Supporting Cuban Exiles

Even as the Bay of Pigs setback caused them great dismay and considerable disillusionment, the community of Cubans in the United States remained an asset to be cultivated and organized as a pillar of the anti-Castro strategy. The NSC sought to maintain support of the Cuban Revolutionary Council even if it could not recognize it as a government-in-exile. Robert Kennedy, who pressed his brother to remove Bissell from the CIA less for his failure in April than for "sitting on his ass and not doing anything about getting rid of Castro" in the months afterwards, urged the use of exiles for the purpose.[3]

Unfortunately, the Revolutionary Council and other self-styled leaders within the exile community proved almost unmanageable. Their internal feuds alone made it impossible for the United States to mobilize a common front with a common agenda; charges and countercharges, usually involving softness toward Castro, undercut their credibility. Intelligence assessments of one Cuban leader, Reuben de Leon Garcia, a former minister of defense in pre-Castro Cuba, revealed him to be "completely untrustworthy, personally ambitious, and dangerous." The Revolutionary Council under Jose Miro Cardona had a reputation for integrity and selfless devotion to the task of liberating Cuba, but its leaders never forgave the administration for not providing the U.S. military assistance that they believed had been promised during the April 1961 invasion. Proposals to incorporate Cuban exiles into the U.S. armed services as individuals rather than as a unit met with opposition from exile leaders. The council would accept funds for training but not a loss of Cuban identity. Nothing less than a guarantee of an invasion would satisfy them.[4]

Nonetheless, the Defense Department persisted in developing a program for Cuban volunteers in the armed services. Within three weeks of a presidential directive of 5 May 1961, DoD presented a plan for inducting up to 2,000 Cubans between the ages of 18 and 26 "with the clear understanding that they are not being prepared as a combat force."[5] Doubts about the legality as well as the language difficulties of Cuban refugees in the services were brushed aside.[6] Neither concern kept the president from accepting McNamara's program for inducting Cuban volunteers, and the secretary made it clear that he expected implementation "as quickly as possible." Language problems would be avoided by initially inducting only English-speaking refugees; an exception in the Selective Service law allowed enlistment of aliens.[7]

Despite the administration's enthusiasm the program did not succeed. Recruitment numbers alone underscored the problem. For the period 29 July 1961- 31 March 1962, of 898 Cubans processed at the Miami examining station, only 124 qualified for induction, with many rejected for moral or security reasons.[8] Miro Cardona complained about discrimination as a reason for disappointing results. His intervention with Deputy Secretary Gilpatric resulted in changes that established Spanish-language training units and increased the number of recruiting stations.[9]

The heart of the difficulty lay in the refusal of the refugees to join the armed forces unless they could count on fighting against Castro. Military service as a form of refugee resettlement held little attraction for most young Cubans. When the president in September 1962 asked McNamara and the JCS about forming a new Cuban brigade, the Joint Chiefs responded negatively. Based on the experience with Cubans in the army they cited a lack of qualified leadership as well as the continuing evidence of Cuban reluctance to join the U.S. armed forces unless they could serve in separate units.[10]

The administration's inability to harness the energies and ambitions of the exiles to its anti-Castro efforts was symptomatic of its difficulty in moving often dramatic proposals from the planning board to action. Even plans more promising of success than the Bay of Pigs failed to survive the scrutiny of a process that still had to balance competing strategic concerns and weigh short-term benefits and satisfaction against long-term consequences.

Operation Mongoose

Operation Mongoose offered the most extreme example of the administration's determination to undo the damage of the Bay of Pigs episode. Established by the president in November 1961 under CIA auspices, Mongoose came under the general guidance of OSD's General Lansdale, who, as chief of operations, coordinated covert actions within the government against the Castro regime. Robert Kennedy became a member of the new Special Group (Augmented) (SGA), chaired by Maxwell Taylor, to oversee Operation Mongoose. Membership also included Gilpatric (DoD), McGeorge Bundy (White House), U. Alexis Johnson (State), John McCone, who succeeded Dulles as CIA director, and General Lemnitzer (JCS). McNamara and Rusk occasionally attended meetings. Under the rubric of Mongoose, which covered a broad array of programs, the administration at its highest levels attempted to devise means to reverse the Bay of Pigs setback.[11]

Lansdale's primary objective was to foster conditions inside Cuba that would lead to a successful uprising, avoiding the kind of circumstances that had fatally damaged Operation Zapata. Inevitably, there arose temptation to include assassination as a way to solve the Cuban problem. This term per se never appeared in the Taylor report,* although the idea had been discussed in the CIA under the euphemism of "executive action capability" before the Kennedy administration took office. It also apparently came up in a conversation during the summer of 1961 between Kennedy and Florida Sen. George Smathers, but the president firmly ruled out consideration of this approach to removing Castro. The assassination option, however, was revived by the Mongoose planners, the proposed method of execution ranging from enlistment of underworld gunmen to placing a poisoned pill in Castro's food.[12]

According to Richard Helms, later CIA director and in 1962 the agency's deputy director for plans, despite the arcane language that masked assassination plans, the notion not only was seriously entertained but became a priority project. Having been asked "to get rid of Castro," Helms remembered a meeting in January 1962 where "there were no limitations put on the means." Helms felt that the atmosphere legitimized assassination as a tool in the overthrow of the Cuban communist regime. Although sufficient "plausible deniability" existed to protect the attorney general and the Mongoose director from connection with assassination plots, there was also sufficient rage about Castro, as McNamara admitted, to generate an assortment of wild-eyed schemes.[13] Whether assassination or other concepts, actions never seemed to match words. Under prodding from the president, the SGA did develop more plans for sabotage and paramilitary raids, but even before the missile crisis the spirit of the operation was sapped by a recogni-

---

* See Chapter VIII.

Robert S. McNamara, secretary of defense, 1961-68.

JOHN F. KENNEDY LIBRARY

Roswell L. Gilpatric, deputy secretary of defense, 1961-64.

Cyrus R. Vance, secretary of the Army, 1961-64; deputy secretary of defense, 1964-67.

Above: President Kennedy visiting Pentagon in April 1963, accompanied by Secretary McNamara and Deputy Secretary Gilpatric.
Below: Defense budget meeting at Hyannis Port, November 1961.

CECIL STOUGHTON/JOHN F. KENNEDY LIBRARY

McGeorge Bundy, special assistant to the president for national security, 1961-66.

Theodore C. Sorensen, special counsel to the president, 1961-64.

Walt W. Rostow, key presidential aide and State Department policy planning council chairman, 1961-66.

Jerome Wiesner, President Kennedy's science adviser.

Secretary McNamara testifying before the Senate Armed Services Committee, September 1961.

"THE TROUBLE WITH THAT KNOW-IT-ALL McNAMARA IS HE **KNOWS** IT ALL!"

Secretary McNamara with Sen. Richard B. Russell, chairman of the Senate Defense Appropriations Subcommittee.

Key legislators on defense matters, *clockwise from top left*, Reps. Carl Vinson and Otto Passman and Sens. George McGovern and Barry Goldwater.

Top to bottom: Secretary McNamara *(far right)* with President Kennedy at Fort Bragg for counterinsurgency capability demonstration, October 1961; Brig. Gen. Edward G. Lansdale, Pentagon special assistant for counterinsurgency warfare and special operations; U.S. Special Forces soldiers visiting South Vietnam village, 1962.

Paul H. Nitze, assistant secretary of defense for international security affairs, 1961-63; secretary of the Navy, 1963-67.

Harold Brown, director of defense research and engineering, 1961-65.

Charles J. Hitch, DoD comptroller, 1961-65.

Alain C. Enthoven, director of Pentagon's systems analysis office, 1961-65.

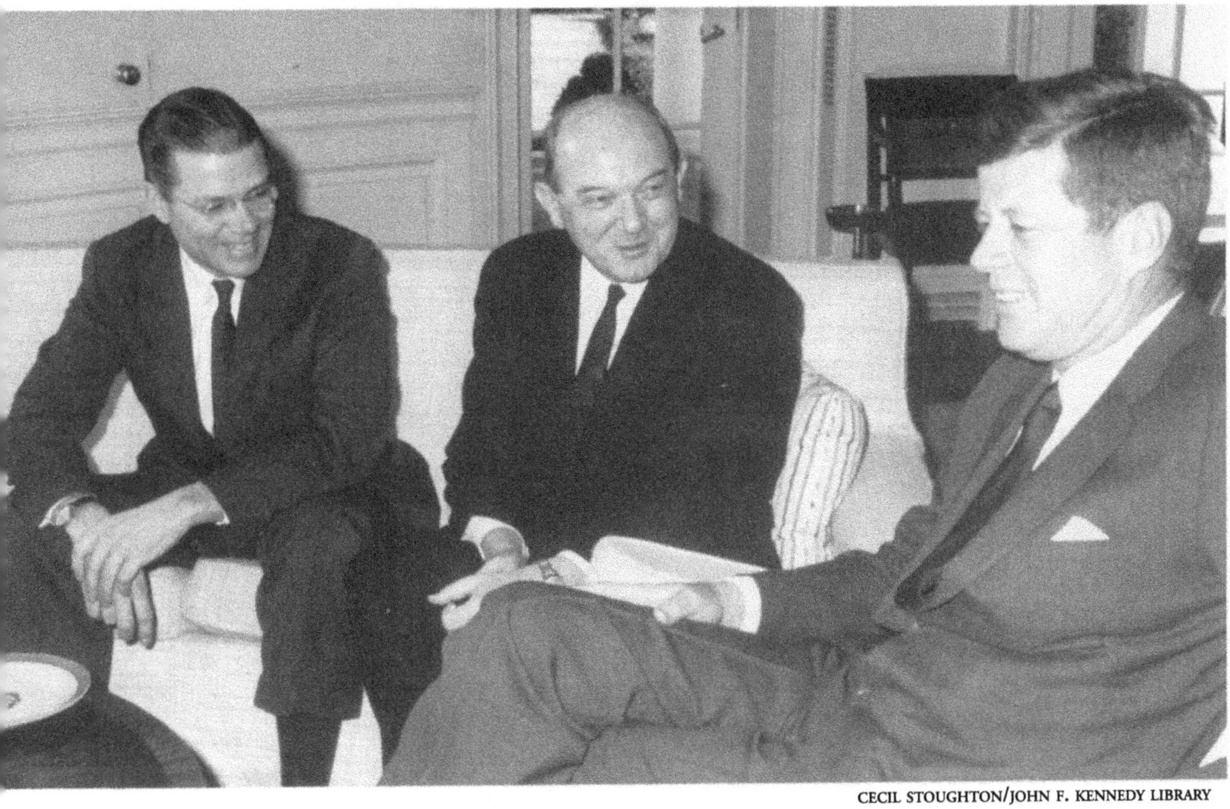

CECIL STOUGHTON/JOHN F. KENNEDY LIBRARY

Above: Secretary McNamara and Secretary of State Dean Rusk meeting with President Kennedy at the White House, December 1962.
Below: President Kennedy with the Joint Chiefs of Staff (*right to left*, Admiral George W. Anderson, Jr., USN, Chairman General Maxwell D. Taylor, USA, General Curtis E. LeMay, USAF, General Earle G. Wheeler, USA, General David M. Shoup, USMC), January 1963.

ROBERT KNUDSEN/JOHN F. KENNEDY LIBRARY

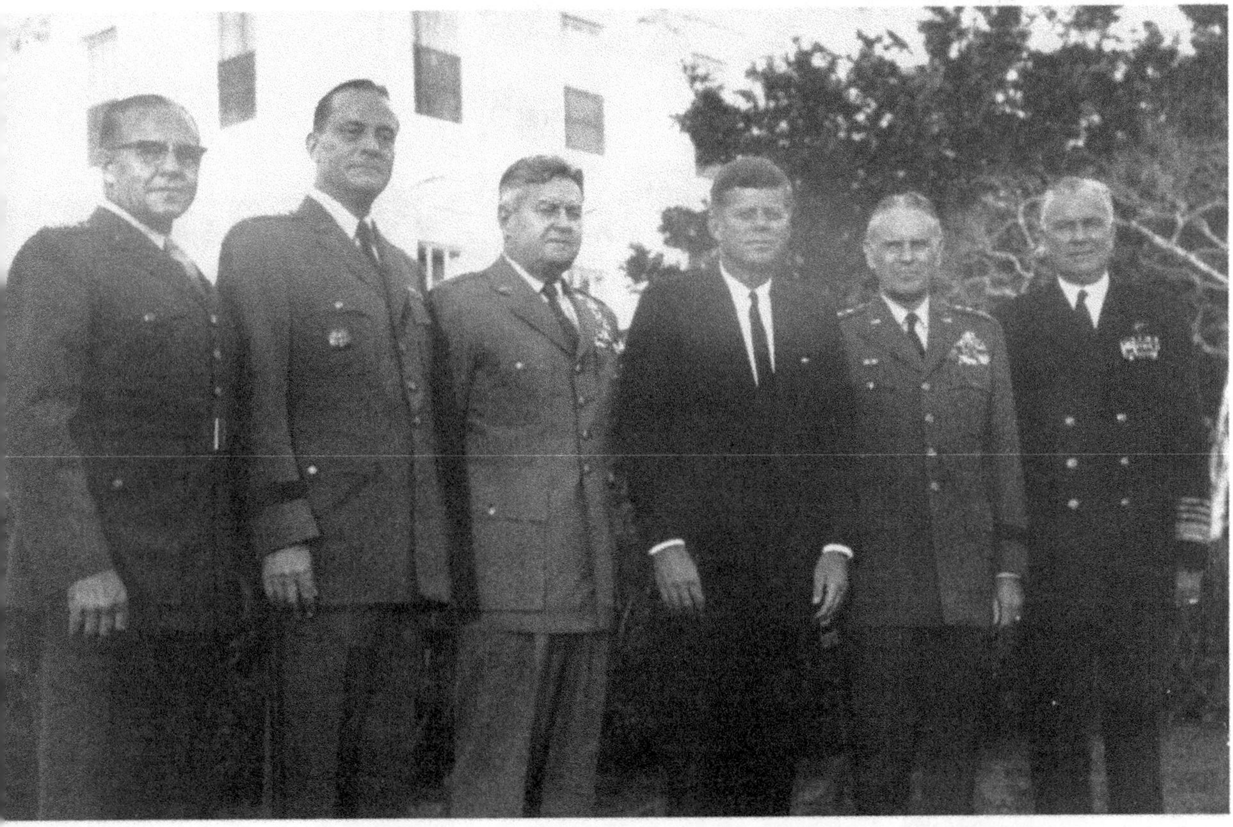

Above: Secretary McNamara at Pentagon press conference, 23 October 1962, discussing Soviet missile buildup in Cuba.
Below: Reconnaissance photo of medium-range ballistic missile site, San Cristobal, Cuba, 23 October 1962.

Left: Soviet Premier Nikita Khrushchev with Cuban leader Fidel Castro.
Below: ExCom meeting on Cuban missile crisis, 19 October 1962.

CECIL STOUGHTON/JOHN F. KENNEDY LIBRARY

Clockwise from top: Undersecretary of State George W. Ball; newly installed U.S.-USSR "Hot Line," August 1963; outgoing and incoming CIA directors Allen Dulles (*left*) and John McCone with Kennedy, September 1961.

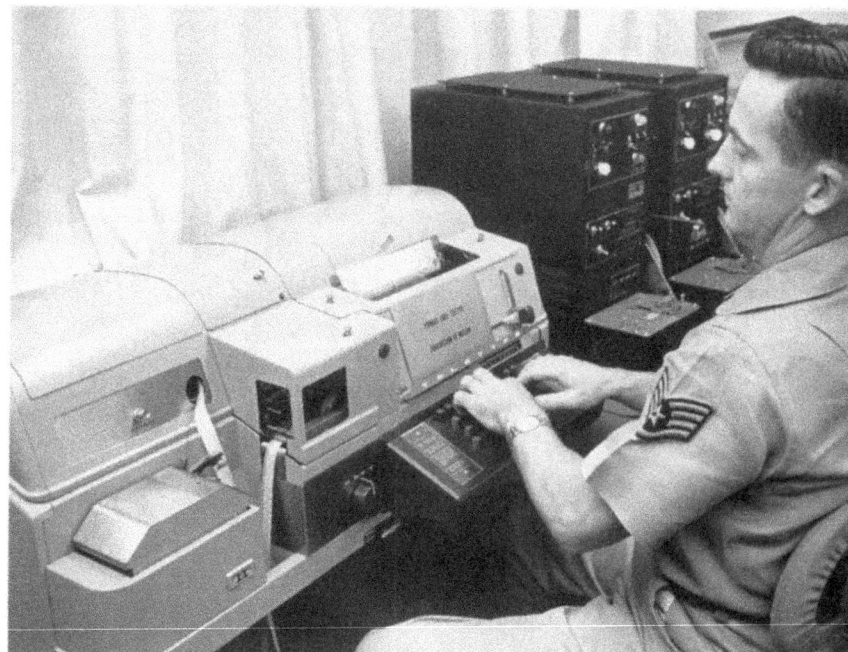

JOHN F. KENNEDY LIBRARY

President Kennedy addresses large crowd in West Berlin, 26 June 1963.

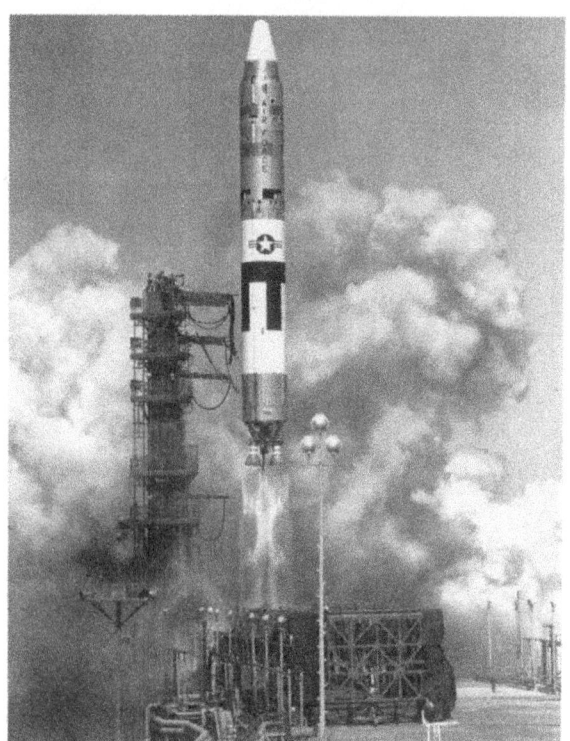

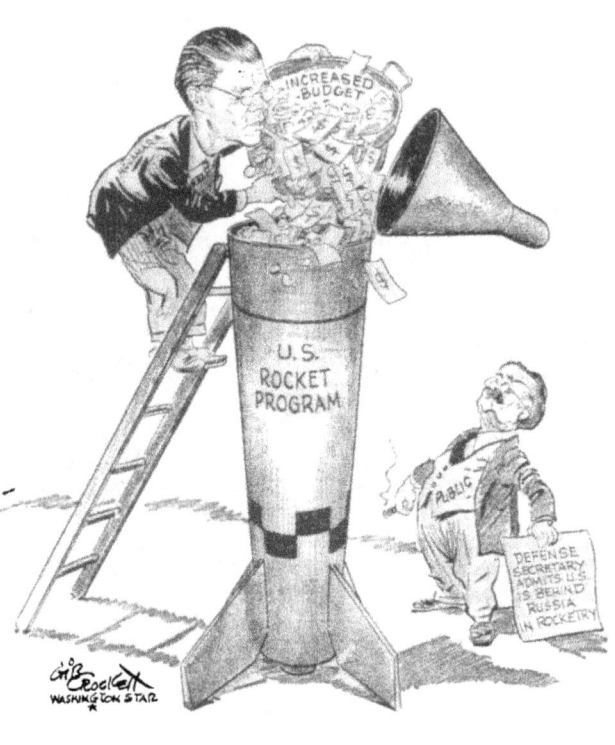

Top left: Launch of Titan II ICBM, 26 October 1962; *right*, 23 August 1962 cartoon showing McNamara trying to close purported "missile gap."
Below: President Kennedy observing launch of Polaris missile, 16 November 1963.

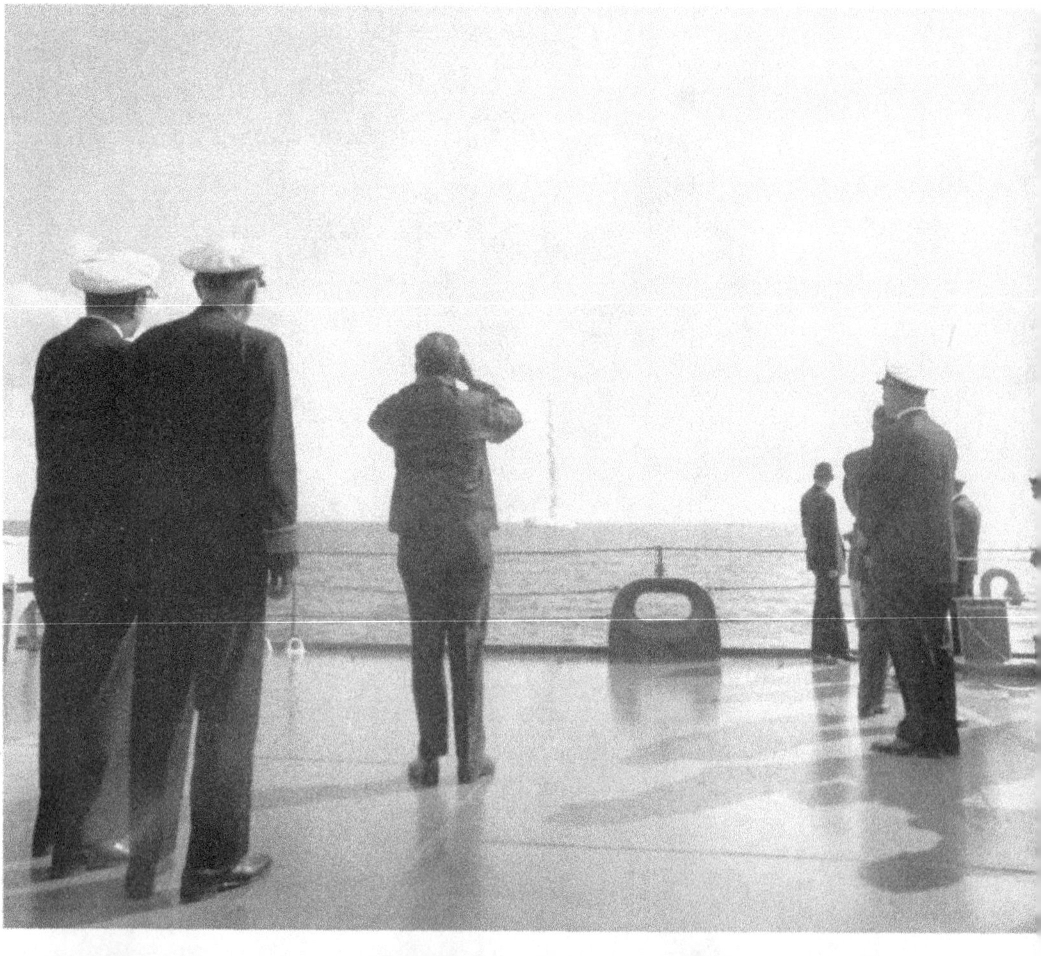

ROBERT KNUDSEN/JOHN F. KENNEDY LIBRARY

ROBERT KNUDSEN/JOHN F. KENNEDY LIBRARY

Above: President Kennedy with Secretary McNamara and General Taylor at the White House, January 1963.
Left: McNamara visited by Laotian Prince Souvanna Phouma, July 1962
Below: U.S. Ambassador-at-Large W. Averell Harriman with Royal Laotian delegation, May 1961.

UPI

Above: U.S. Ambassador Henry Cabot Lodge meets with Ngo Dinh Diem in Saigon.
Below: President Kennedy signing the limited nuclear test ban treaty, 7 October 1963.

CECIL STOUGHTON/JOHN F. KENNEDY LIBRARY

tion that conditions for a popular revolt had not emerged in Cuba and that in fact Castro's grip on the country had become firmer.[14]

Whatever the shortcomings of Mongoose, they were not unique to that operation. Nothing seemed to work well in 1961. A CIA report in November 1961 pointed out that Castro had sufficient internal support to survive in the immediate future. Help from the Warsaw bloc, with $357 million in credits, would compensate for shortages in the economy. Despite Latin American collaboration in ousting Cuba from the OAS early in 1962, Latin America could not be expected to give much energy to further anti-Castro actions. Some nations, such as Venezuela, preferred to postpone collective action until after the Alliance for Progress began functioning. Others, such as Chile, expressed sympathy for U.S. objectives in bringing down Castro but urged delay because of the increase in Castro's strength after the Bay of Pigs.[15]

Prospects for success in 1962 appeared no brighter than in 1961. Differences developed between Lansdale and the CIA over the role of sabotage in the Mongoose program. New guidelines failed to clarify Mongoose's methods, and the "noise level" of activities obviously affected the potential for concealment.[16]

The muddled state of Mongoose in the summer of 1962 became apparent in a memorandum from State's project officer for the program, the deputy director of the Office of Caribbean and Mexican Affairs. He found that the CIA believed a revolution could be mounted by late 1963 but would quickly face defeat if not supported by substantial U.S. military force. Defense claimed it needed 18, or at least 12 days, of preparation, even though some units might get ready in as little as 5 days. State wanted a "virtual civil war situation" before U.S. military intervention could become politically acceptable. The three conditions presented a large barrier.[17]

Not surprisingly, Operation Mongoose went by the board during the Cuban missile crisis in October. Deputy Director of Central Intelligence Lt. Gen. Marshall Carter noted that action against IRBM sites in Cuba "cannot be planned, controlled, and operated through the cumbersome procedures of MONGOOSE and therefore it is not in MONGOOSE channels. . . . The time has long since passed for MONGOOSE-type, Special Group-type consideration." The president and SGA terminated all Mongoose sabotage activities on 30 October 1962.[18]

Contingency Plans

While exploring a range of paramilitary and clandestine options, the administration also conducted more conventional planning to address the Cuban problem. As part of the effort to recast U.S. strategy after the Bay of Pigs, State developed a paper, "Guidelines of U.S. Policy Toward Cuba," in the summer of 1961. Refined repeatedly over the following year, the paper did not satisfy, except in the most general way, the requirements of DoD officials, who in September complained that the initial guidelines, too vague and too passive, failed to come to grips with specific Cuban threats to national security. Not that the State Department's objectives lacked focus. They were indisputable—the reduction of Castro's capability to direct and support subversion, the encouragement of developments in Cuba to separate the country from the Sino-Soviet bloc, and the political isolation of Castro. A proposed four-point shipping program would close U.S. ports to countries whose vessels carried goods to Cuba. Other suggested measures contemplated aid to an anti-Castro rebellion and ultimately the deployment of U.S. forces.[19] Yet the paper conspicuously failed to produce a consensus within the administration about how to implement the objectives. If Defense found State's approach wanting, in November 1961 U. Alexis Johnson, deputy under secretary of state for political affairs, complained to William Bundy of ISA that DoD was "very close-mouthed about exact military plans," intimating that it needed to be more forthcoming in dealings with State over Cuba.[20]

The State Department's effort to establish guidelines for a coherent strategy paralleled work on a more specific contingency plan that the NSC's Task Force on Cuba had begun in April 1961 immediately after the Bay of Pigs venture collapsed. This plan, known as Contingency Plan 1, proposed an invasion force of 60,000 ground troops to secure control of the island. To set the plan in motion would require 25 days from the time of decision to D-Day.[21] On 29 April the president, with the strong support of Secretary McNamara, approved the outline, but wanted the lead time reduced from 25 days to no more than a week. McNamara instructed the JCS on 1 May to fill in the military details of the plan; two days earlier he had indicated interest in five days between decision and execution.[22]

CINCLANT planners submitted an outline plan to the JCS on 1 May that included McNamara's five-day reaction time, but CINCLANT, with the Joint Chiefs' approval, considered the time span unrealistic and recommended a two-track arrangement. OPLAN 314-61, with an 18-day lead time, provided for simultaneous airborne and amphibious assaults, while OPLAN 316-61 provided for deployment of airborne assault forces within 5 days, to be followed by an amphibious invasion 3 days later. Planning continued throughout 1961 and into 1962.[23]

In January 1962, McNamara, dissatisfied with the lead times, wanted the reaction time of 314-61 reduced from 18 to 4 days and the 5 days in OPLAN 316-61 cut to 2 days. Under pressure the JCS produced an air strike contingency plan with a two-day lead time, OPLAN 312-62, independent of either OPLAN 314-61 or 316-61. It could likely be a first step followed by initiation of 314-61 or 316-61. The formidable strike force still would include an attack carrier, a destroyer squadron, two Marine air groups, and 17 Air Force fighter squadrons. Generally, the JCS accepted the secretary's reaction time projections with reluctance, and with assumptions that some advance warning would be available and that some prepositioning would be possible.[24]

Before final adoption of 312-62, new information in July and August 1962 about a Soviet buildup of Cuban air defense capabilities resulted in increased focus on improving air-strike plans. In all of the contingency plans, the most likely scenario precipitating U.S. action was an offshore incident that could expand into a conventional limited conflict. While recognizing that force deployment to the Caribbean would have an impact on military readiness in other parts of the world, the Joint Chiefs showed little concern about its effect on Soviet-American relations.[25]

If Cuban contingency plans evolved in relative isolation from the larger Cold War context, the White House bore some of the responsibility for heeding assurances from Khrushchev and Ambassador Anatoly Dobrynin to Robert Kennedy and Theodore Sorensen (see below). In addition, although they knew of Soviet activity in Cuba, NSC and State Department policymakers expressed doubts about Kremlin involvement, believing that Khrushchev would not presume to participate in any military actions against the United States in the Caribbean.[26] Even so, the State Department informed U.S. embassies in Europe at the end of August 1962 that the Soviet Union was shipping to Cuba large quantities of military materiel, including transportation, electronic, and construction equipment, cranes, and fuel tanks. Beyond reference to sophisticated communications systems, State speculated about the possibilities of surface-to-air missile installations in the Soviet package. Moreover, "this renewed evidence of Soviet willingness to make sacrifices on behalf of Cuban strength is also significant of Soviet interest and willingness . . . to expand its influence in other areas of Latin America." The day before the State message, 29 August, a U-2 mission had discovered surface-to-air missile sites under construction.[27]

Although the State communication did not specify offensive weapons as part of Soviet support for Cuba, the president had already raised the question on 23 August in NSAM 181, asking for an analysis of the military, political, and psychological impact of Cuba-based missiles that could reach the U.S. mainland.[28] In the White House these remained hypothetical questions until the end of August, under the governing assumption that the Soviet leader would not risk a conflict with the United States in an area so distant from Eastern Europe. Further, the administration believed Khrushchev would not dispatch nuclear weaponry to an ally as impetuous as Castro when he had denied it to Warsaw Pact allies under closer geographical control.

Hypothetical or not, Gilpatric sought answers from the Joint Staff on Cuban capabilities for attack against the United States. At a meeting of the Special Group (Augmented) on 10 August, attended by Rusk and McNamara, McCone warned that the Soviets would put medium-range ballistic missiles (MRBMs) into Cuba. On 1 September Gilpatric reported to the president JCS views that while Cuban offensive and defensive capabilities had grown over the summer months, U.S. forces in current contingency plans could meet any new threat, although MIG aircraft could strike targets as far north as Tampa and even farther on a one-way mission.[29]

Still it would require a quantum leap of imagination to move from an expectation of marginal and remote damage from Cuba's existing weaponry to an attack by offensive missiles with the 1,000-mile range of a MRBM, armed with a nuclear warhead, let alone a similarly armed intermediate-range ballistic missile (IRBM) with a range of 2,000 miles. On 12 September CINCLANT notified the Joint Chiefs of "an estimated 3,500 bloc military advisors and technicians engaged in military construction, training and operating newly acquired military equipment." On the same day an agent in Cuba spotted a large convoy with long trailers heading westward from Havana. When his report reached Washington on 21 September, the CIA distributed it with a comment that the agent had probably seen surface-to-air missiles (SAMs).[30] Despite these signs and portents, the Defense Intelligence Agency noted as late as 5 October that reports of Soviets dispatching SAMs to Cuba remained allegations; the weapons had a very short range and, even if the reports were true, there was "no evidence to suggest that the missiles can be used offensively."[31]

The CIA had noted more than two weeks earlier the installation of 12 SAM sites in the western half of Cuba and speculated that more would come to cover the rest of the island shortly, but these missiles had a range less than 35 nautical miles. Similarly, while detecting Soviet MIGs at Cuban air bases in early September, the DIA had considered the MIG to have a combat radius of only 380 miles. Since Iraq, Egypt, and Indonesia now had MIG-21s, it seemed plausible that Cuba had also received them, but U.S. intelligence had no more proof of nuclear warheads being supplied to Cuba than to other Soviet clients.[32]

Both the CIA and DIA based their judgments on empirical patterns of Soviet behavior. Special National Intelligence Estimate (SNIE) 85-3-62 on the military buildup in Cuba, submitted on 19 September, stated the belief that "the USSR values its position in Cuba primarily for the political advantages to be derived from it." As for the Soviet military function, it remained essentially defensive, designed to inhibit the United States from overthrowing Castro. The report concluded that the Soviets would not want to risk U.S. retaliation by excessive provocations, whatever advantage the deployment of offensive missiles or the establishment of a submarine base might give them. Either development "would be incompatible with Soviet practice to date and with Soviet policy as we presently estimate it."[33]

These assumptions received reinforcement from periodic assurances voiced by Soviet leaders in September and early October. Ambassador Dobrynin had told White House Special Counsel Sorensen personally that Khrushchev wanted the president to know he would do nothing to aggravate tensions before the congressional elections in November. In this spirit, McGeorge Bundy assured the American public on television on 14 October, the same day U-2 planes photographed MRBM sites, that the Soviet military presence in Cuba was tolerable, adding, "I know there is no present evidence, and I think there is no present likelihood, that the Cubans and the Cuban government and the Soviet government would in combination attempt to install a major offensive capability." Examination of the film the next day revealed the offensive missile launching equipment.[34]

Prologue: September-16 October

Meanwhile, during September, the JCS had intensified preparations for a possible military confrontation. The president involved himself in these matters when on 21 September he expressed to McNamara his concern over lack of agreement between Air Force Chief of Staff General LeMay and Chief of Naval Operations Admiral Anderson over the extent of losses the United States would incur in attacking SAM sites. Kennedy also wanted assurance that contingency plans were kept up to date, "taking into account the additions to their [Cuban] armaments resulting from the continuous influx of Soviet equipment and technicians."[35] Two weeks earlier, he had asked for McNamara's reaction to formation of a Cuban brigade. Even after the JCS expressed opposition to the idea, Kennedy persisted. In the event of a military operation he felt it essential to have some plan for the brigade's use, whether or not any of its members had "flat feet." McNamara promised a response by 17 October, a promise overtaken by unexpected events.[36]

McNamara offered his own contributions to the contingency preparations. He specified the occasions that would call for military force. After meeting with the JCS on 1 October, he suggested in a memorandum to them the next day that military action could involve not only removal of Soviet weapon systems but also the removal of the Castro regime itself, with the latter objective perhaps a necessary precondition to permanent achievement of the former. While he did not elaborate on the removal of Castro, he did go into detail about provocations that might require military action. He cited six instances: (1) Soviet interference with Western rights in Berlin; (2) evidence that the Soviet bloc was installing offensive weapons in Cuba; (3) an attack against the U.S. naval base on Guantanamo; (4) a serious popular uprising in Cuba leading to a request for U.S. assistance; (5) Cuban armed assistance to communist elements in other Latin American nations; and (6) a presidential decision that the Cuban situation necessitated military action in defense of the nation.[37]

In response to McNamara's pressure for preparation for contingency plans, the JCS reviewed the steps the military might take in the face of different challenges and, just a few days before the discovery of Soviet missiles in Cuba, presented a list that included plans for a blockade, an air strike, and invasion.[38] While these plans covered a wide range of possibilities, they could not cover everything. As long as the exact nature of the threat remained unknown, making the precise fit seemed impossible. For example, while a blockade quickly presented itself as one means of bringing the Cuban economy to a standstill, there was little thought given to a less blunt instrument—a selective blockade or quarantine such as the president actually utilized at the peak of the crisis.[39]

As suspicions of Soviet deception increased and the press and Congress became aware of the expanded threat, a political campaign season brought charges of ineptitude on the part of the administration. Republican Sen. Homer Capehart of Indiana, seeking reelection, as early as 27 August called for an invasion of Cuba to remove the Soviet intrusion. The administration found it particularly difficult to deal with the barrage of criticism from Sen. Kenneth Keating (R-N.Y.), who claimed knowledge from unidentified sources of the presence of MRBMs in Cuba. His accusation that the administration was doing nothing about the threat, uttered in the heat of Keating's own reelection bid, became a divisive issue as election day approached. Keating never divulged his sources, which remained a matter of conjecture a generation later.[40]

Heightened tensions caused Cuba to accuse the United States before the UN General Assembly of a campaign of hysteria in preparation for an invasion. The suspense ended abruptly when two U-2 reconnaissance planes, previously hindered by weather conditions from inspecting the western part of the island, photographed the missile sites on 14 October. The two planes returned to their base without challenge, bringing photographs immediately dispatched to Washington for processing and analysis. The results disclosed the infrastructure at San Cristobal, from erector launchers to radar vans to fueling trucks, for medium-range ballistic missiles.[41]

The next day, two U-2s returned with pictures of an additional launching site. McGeorge Bundy immediately recognized the significance of the pictures when he received them on the evening of 15 October but waited until the next morning to lay them before the president. When Kennedy later asked reasons for the delay, Bundy responded that the information had not become available until late at night and the need for further analysis made a morning meeting preferable. Moreover, if the news had broken that evening it might have disturbed the normal routine of those who, like McNamara, had gone to dinner engagements, from which their early departure would have given rise to public conjecture. Bundy's caution was justified.[42]

Bundy broke the news at the White House at 8:45 a.m. on 16 October, his action beginning the "thirteen days" of crisis. The president immediately summoned his major advisers, a group he formalized on 22 October as the Executive Committee (ExCom) of the National Security Council, with himself as chairman, to take charge and meet each morning until further notice.[43] He deemed the full NSC too unwieldy for rapid response and too large to maintain secrecy. The members of the ExCom came not only from the NSC and the White House staff; at times it included also such experienced and trusted advisers as John McCloy,

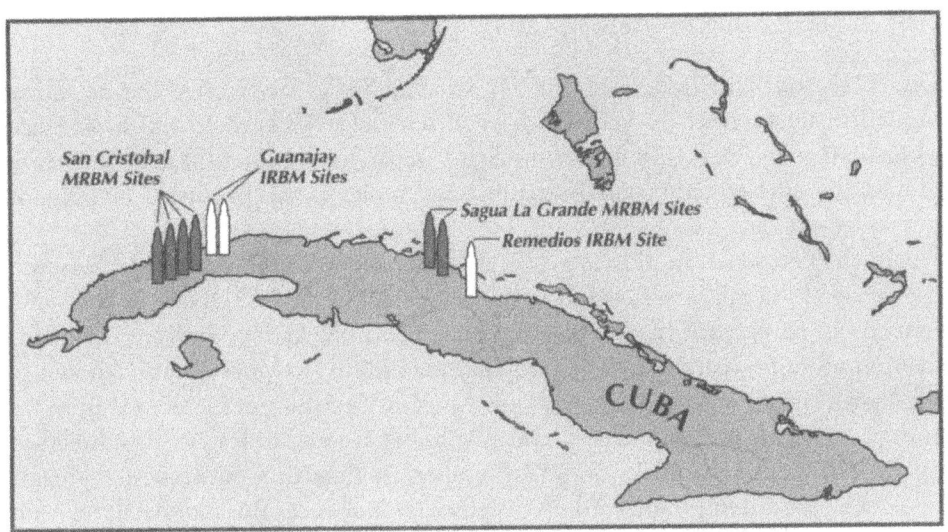

Soviet Offensive Missile Buildup in Cuba, October 1962

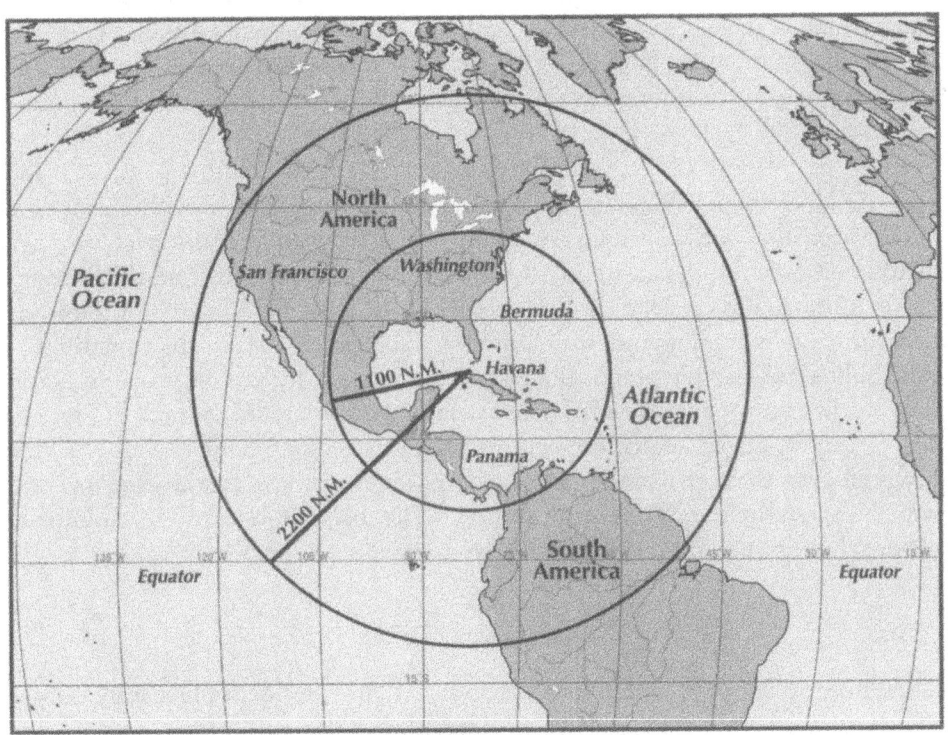

Range of Soviet MRBMs and IRBMs in Cuba

Displayed by Secretary McNamara at Special Cuba Briefing, 6 February 1963. The 1,100 nautical-mile medium-range ballistic missile could reach Washington, D.C., Dallas, and St. Louis; the 2,200 nautical-mile IRBM, almost all targets on the North American continent.

Dean Acheson, and Robert Lovett.*[44] To allay Soviet suspicions, the president himself made an effort to keep his normal schedule. When meetings took place sometimes at the Pentagon and at the State Department rather than at the White House, Robert Kennedy usually attended and spoke for his brother. The guise of normality worked.

In the course of the thirteen days disagreement inevitably occurred between civilians and the military. General Taylor, on behalf of the JCS, spoke in favor of a series of air strikes against offensive weapons and a blockade to prevent the introduction of more weapons.[45] The JCS chairman joined in what became known as the "hawk" position, one he shared with Assistant Secretary of Defense Paul Nitze and, particularly, Acheson. The president himself seemed to lean in this direction in the early meetings of 16 and 17 October. Against this position the "doves" urged a step-by-step program to give diplomacy a chance. Rusk and Ball fell into this category, with Bundy and McNamara also there but for different reasons.[46] McNamara differed most sharply from Taylor over the function of nuclear weapons in a potential conflict. The Joint Chiefs thought that the MRBMs in Cuba changed the strategic balance "substantially"; McNamara believed they changed it "not at all." Many years later he recollected that he had not seen "the problem as a military one, at least not in the narrow sense of the term, but rather as a political problem."[47]

For the purpose of analysis, the crisis may be divided into two phases: the first, 16-21 October 1962, and the second, 22-28 October. Through the middle of October the JCS continued to work on contingency plans even as they discounted much of the accumulating intelligence information. The chiefs designated Admiral Robert Dennison, commander in chief of the Atlantic Fleet, as head of a unified command with primary responsibility for Cuban contingencies. Bulk supplies were prepositioned in Florida, security at Guantanamo Naval Base was increased, and the Air Force assembled a tactical strike force in Florida. The deceptive Soviet stance on sending "defensive" equipment to Cuba, which persisted even through Foreign Minister Andrei Gromyko's face-to-face meeting with Kennedy in the White House on 18 October, inhibited U.S. diplomatic actions, but no such inhibition applied to military activities.[48]

Act I: 16-21 October

Once the Soviet provocation was confirmed, the president's first impulse was to take immediate action, subject to determining the state of readiness of the Soviet missiles and hence their immediate threat to U.S. territory. At the White House meeting the morning of 16 October McNamara stressed that any air strike

---

* The membership included Vice President Johnson, Rusk, McNamara, Gilpatric, Treasury Secretary Douglas Dillon, Robert Kennedy, Taylor, CIA Director McCone, Under Secretary of State George Ball, Ambassador at Large Llewellyn Thompson, Bundy, and Sorenson.

should take place before the missile sites became operational. The secretary went on to include air strikes against airfields and aircraft and all potential nuclear storage sites as well. All this would involve a massive effort.

Changes in position on the major issues occurred among the participants in response to argument and the uncertainty of developing events. If McNamara initially sounded hawkish at this meeting, Taylor approached this second Cuban crisis with some wariness. Worried about timing and the ability to destroy all missiles in a surprise attack, Taylor suggested beginning with reinforcement of Guantanamo, a pause to get ready, followed by concurrent strikes against missile sites and airfields, a naval blockade, and evacuation of dependents from Guantanamo. McNamara's stand on bombing attacks was carefully hedged. Any planned air attack must take place before the missiles became operational. If sites housed launch-ready missiles he would oppose the air attack, deeming the danger excessive in relation to any gain. Moreover, any attack would also have to hit airfields and nuclear storage sites—"a fairly extensive air strike."[49]

This did not represent the considered opinion of the Joint Chiefs. They clearly favored an air strike "even after the missiles were operational," with "no political preliminaries" and against a wide variety of targets, including MIG and IL-28* airfields as well as missile sites. They reasoned that any Soviet military retaliation would be confined to measured steps. One such scenario envisioned a nuclear strike against Johnston Island (a nuclear test site) in the Pacific should Soviet technicians die in a U.S. strike. As for an assault against West Berlin, the chiefs thought that strong military actions would fall "short of direct seizure."[50]

Taylor won support from McCone and Secretary of the Treasury Dillon. McNamara, more concerned with the potentially destructive effects of an attack, was not convinced that the Soviet riposte would be minor and manageable. Nor did he agree with the JCS assertion that the military danger of missiles in Cuba was sufficiently great to warrant attack even after the missiles were operational.[51]

This policy standoff on 16-17 October forestalled a decision to attack, but pressure for action mounted at an ExCom meeting on 18 October when intelligence analysts discovered evidence of fixed IRBMs in addition to the already identified MRBM sites. The IRBMs had twice the range of the MRBMs, and could strike all of the continental United States with the exception of the Pacific Northwest. In light of these new revelations the JCS preference for striking all military targets rather than just missiles and nuclear storage sites gained ground. Concern about the effects of such action on Berlin and Turkey, however, checked ExCom's enthusiasm for the JCS approach as did Robert Kennedy's worry over the damage a first strike would do to "the United States in the pages of history."

---

* When the crisis erupted about two dozen IL-28s had been delivered. Of these, three-quarters were still in their shipping crates.

McNamara subsequently suggested that only two courses of action had emerged in the ExCom discussion on 18 October: "I would call one a rapid introduction to military action. The other is a slow introduction to military action.... The slow introduction is a political statement followed, or accompanied, by a blockade. The rapid introduction is a brief notice to Khrushchev followed by a strike." On 20 October the president decided in favor of a blockade under the less bellicose name of quarantine. It would be accompanied by a demand that Khrushchev remove the missiles or face an air strike.[52]

The outcome of intense exchanges during ExCom meetings accorded with positions the president had always favored: a message, a show of firmness, and options left available for both superpowers. Robert Kennedy, McNamara, and Gilpatric came to share these views. The more they looked at the consequences of a direct strike the more doubts they had. Its potential effect on the Jupiter missiles in Turkey and on the West's position in Berlin stayed in their minds, if not always on the table.[53] The worry that a surprise attack against Cuba would be analogous to Pearl Harbor, "a Pearl Harbor in reverse," to use Robert Kennedy's phrase, can be found repeatedly in Sorensen's notes on the discussions.[54]

McNamara and Gilpatric spent much time together during the days of the crisis and early on engaged in their own version of war gaming, sometimes spending hours playing both sides of the confrontation. Gilpatric believed that during these sessions "McNamara became convinced that this limited form of blockade, quarantine, was the best move.... He never shifted from that ground from that point on."[55]

By a process of elimination the idea of a blockade, refined and presented as a "quarantine," emerged from the ExCom as the preferred course of action. First raised by Taylor in the context of his air strike proposal on 16 October, the idea of a blockade was taken up by Vice President Johnson and then by McNamara as he pondered the uncertainties connected with a preemptive strike. The secretary of defense initially felt that the quarantine alternative "doesn't seem to be a very acceptable one, but wait until you work on the others." An air assault, he projected, would trigger an inevitable Soviet reprisal, followed by massive U.S. mobilization, and then by an invasion force to support an uprising.[56]

Years later Nitze remained convinced that the Soviet Union's strategic inferiority in intercontinental missiles immobilized its leaders. Like Taylor, he had no fears of a major war or of an attack on Berlin or Turkey: "Of course they could, but would they dare do that in the face of the nuclear superiority of the United States at the time? It seemed to me to be improbable that they would, although you couldn't guarantee it." Moreover, the inferior Soviet strategic position in the Caribbean was a critical factor: "In the area of Cuba we had them a hundred to one. They had four submarines in the area and we made every one of those damn submarines surface. So there was nothing they could do in the area."[57]

Nitze and McNamara divided over the latter's concern that the use of nuclear weaponry could lead to a holocaust if escalation of the conflict got out of hand. In this context McNamara's seemingly unequivocal statement to Congress in January 1963 was misleading when he claimed: "We faced that night the possibility of launching nuclear weapons and Khrushchev knew it, and that is the reason, and the only reason, why he withdrew those weapons." Years later Bundy asserted that McNamara had been misunderstood; McNamara was referring not to nuclear superiority but to the common nuclear danger. To an American Legion meeting in September 1964 McNamara made the point that U.S. conventional superiority played an essential role in the outcome of the confrontation.[58]

At the moment of reckoning, how the Soviets would react to U.S. nuclear power, to the danger of nuclear war, or to the superiority of U.S. conventional forces in the area, created a serious division among ExCom members. Nitze and the JCS stood ready to risk a nuclear, or any other kind of Soviet response, confident that none would come. McNamara, Bundy, and the president's closest advisers lacked that confidence. Hence the resort to a quarantine when the military could provide no guarantee that a surgical air strike would destroy all the missiles.[59]

Act II: 22-28 October

In a major address to the American people on 22 October, the president announced that the Soviet Union was installing offensive missiles in Cuba to "provide a nuclear strike capability against the Western Hemisphere." After explaining the characteristics of the power and reach of medium- and intermediate-range ballistic missiles, he pronounced the Soviet action "an explicit threat to the peace and security of all the Americas, in flagrant and deliberate defiance" of numerous international agreements, understandings, and his own public warnings. He also exposed the duplicity of Soviet leaders who had deceived the United States about their intentions. Given the extent of the danger, he announced a number of immediate "initial" actions and ordered "a strict quarantine on all offensive military equipment under shipment to Cuba." All ships containing such equipment would be turned back. If the military buildup continued, he had "directed the Armed Forces to prepare for any eventualities." The president stated that any nuclear missile launched from Cuba against any Western Hemisphere nation would be regarded as an attack by the Soviet Union on the United States and would be met by "a full retaliatory response upon the Soviet Union." Having asserted this firm but measured response, the president requested the OAS and the UN Security Council to help in the dismantling and withdrawal of the offensive weapons under the supervision of UN observers before he would lift the quarantine. Finally, the president called on Khrushchev "to halt and eliminate this clandestine, reckless, and provocative threat to world peace" and to join in a "search for peaceful and permanent solutions." There was no mention of an air strike or an invasion or of attacks on Soviet ships at sea.[60]

The speech fit the Kennedy mold—it kept options open. He followed up with a quarantine proclamation interdicting delivery of offensive weapons to Cuba and listing the specific categories of proscribed weapons. At the same time, he gave the secretary of defense considerable latitude in implementing the proclamation, including taking into custody vessels refusing to identify cargo or to accept search. Moreover, the president signaled continuation of military preparations for an air strike and even a landing force in the event of the failure of the quarantine. He also upgraded the armed forces' alert status to Defense Condition (DEFCON) 3.*[61]

So while the president rallied the nation to a course short of war, the second phase of the crisis opened on 22 October with obvious administration trepidation about the effectiveness of the new quarantine. ExCom members understood fully the absence of any assurance that the quarantine measure would rid Cuba of Soviet bases without major U.S. concessions, such as withdrawal of Jupiter missiles from Turkey or U.S. forces from Guantanamo. Nonetheless, when Gilpatric weighed its advantages and disadvantages, he judged that it offered the best course for controlling the consequences of military action.[62] The president and secretary of defense shared this view.

Recognizing that the next few days would be critical, McNamara set up living quarters in the Pentagon so that he could take full charge around the clock. Beyond the confines of the White House and Pentagon, intense diplomatic activity characterized the week of 22 October. Acheson went to Paris and later to Bonn to inform President de Gaulle and Chancellor Adenauer and elicit their blessing. The two leaders responded positively as did the OAS whose council by a vote of 19 to 0 on 24 October backed the president. In New York, Ambassador Adlai Stevenson worked to create sentiment in the United Nations against the Soviet actions.[63]

Despite the importance of these steps, the focus of ExCom's attention remained on the quarantine—how to establish it and how to enforce it. Soviet ships in the Atlantic en route to Cuba presumably would seek to breach a blockade that the Kremlin immediately labeled as unacceptable. Moreover, low-altitude reconnaissance aircraft determined on 23 October that the Soviet Union was accelerating the missile-site buildup rather than suspending its efforts.[64] By 25 October, however, three of the Soviet ships suspected as missile carriers seemed to be altering course, and the CIA reported that at least 14 of the 22 Soviet vessels ordered to do so had turned back. But the glow of this perceived success was dimmed by news leaked by Rep. James Van Zandt, a Republican candidate for

---

* DEFCON indicates the level of readiness in preparation for hostilities, with DEFCON 5 reflecting normal peacetime readiness and DEFCON 1 being the highest alert posture.

the Senate in Pennsylvania, that the Navy, after challenging but not boarding the Soviet tanker *Bucharest*, had allowed it to proceed to Cuba.[65]

Given the absence of any evidence of a halt in construction, let alone dismantling of sites, and following the downing of a U-2 over Cuba on 27 October (see page 222), the JCS recommended an air strike against those bases no later than 29 October, "unless irrefutable evidence" revealed in the meantime that the offensive weapons were being dismantled.[66] Within DoD the secretary and his military chiefs continued to differ on action that the United States should take against the missile bases. The chiefs stood united in their advocacy of an air strike unless the quarantine served to dislodge the missiles.[67] They accepted, of course, the presidential decision for a quarantine, but their preference for stronger action manifested itself in instructions to SACLANT on 22 October that referred to the "blockade" of Cuba, apparently regarded as a stronger term than quarantine. The message included instructions that "forceful boarding and control of the ship's operation may be necessary. If boarding meets with organized resistance, the ship will be destroyed." With the quarantine set to start at 10:00 a.m. on 23 October, on the preceding afternoon the JCS, with McNamara's approval, instructed CINCSAC General Thomas Power to prepare to go to DEFCON 2, the level before maximum readiness, at the same time on 23 October.*[68]

The chiefs also made known their concerns about other actual and potential limitations on their freedom of action. In often strident terms they opposed Brazil's proposal at the UN for nuclear-free or missile-free zones in Latin America and Africa. Too much attention, they claimed, was paid to world opinion or to "Allied support," as if the United States should wait for the approval of others before taking measures in its own defense.[69]

Not even the softening of the Brazilian proposal satisfied the JCS. The State Department seemed more willing to accept a denuclearized zone that would have the UN set up an inspection system to cover Soviet and Cuban activities in the Caribbean. The chiefs regarded any such zone as a Soviet scheme to entrap the United States. They believed application of any nuclear-free concept to Latin America would inhibit American power with only minimal costs to the Soviets.[70] By contrast, even the hawkish Nitze appreciated the value of at least studying the Brazilian proposal carefully. It contained seeds of a workable formula, "to which the USSR would be more willing to agree than to dismantling in itself."[71]

The JCS sounded equally dubious about offers of military assistance from Argentina and Venezuela. Rather than welcoming this evidence of hemispheric solidarity, the chiefs remained wary of a Latin American role in an enlarged command. If these interested parties pressed for an OAS international command arrangement, the only acceptable compromise would be to encourage OAS members to have their forces report to CINCLANT for operational control.[72]

---

* Allegations that SAC went to DEFCON 1 cannot be verified from official evidence.

Enforcement of the quarantine engaged McNamara's close attention because conventional military procedures might not communicate the political messages that the administration intended the action to convey. Consequently, he insisted on personal management of the operation. What he later called "McNamara's Law"—that there was no way to predict the direction a crisis might take—lurked at the back of his mind. The secretary expressed his anxiety over potential misunderstandings that could easily arise between the U.S. naval challenger and the Soviet respondent, particularly if no Russian-speaking officer was on board a ship doing the search.[73]

The civil-military tension, of course not new to the Pentagon and which had been building almost from the start of McNamara's tenure, reached a dramatic climax in a confrontation between the secretary of defense and the chief of naval operations on 24 October. On that night McNamara went to the admiral's control room, as he did on every night of the crisis, to ask Admiral Anderson to bring him up to date on the events of the day and to brief him on the progress of the quarantine. According to McNamara's account, when the CNO informed him that a Soviet vessel would reach the quarantine line the following day, McNamara asked what he would do when it got there. Anderson responded that he would stop it. When asked in what language he would stop it, Anderson lost his temper: "How the hell do I know? I presume we'll hail it in English." This reply did not satisfy McNamara, who goaded Anderson into saying that the Navy would fire a shot across its bow and if necessary put a shot through the rudder. McNamara remembered Anderson telling him that "you've imposed a quarantine, and our job is to stop the vessels from passing the line." McNamara disagreed: "Let me tell you something. There will be no firing of any kind at that Soviet ship without my personal authority, and I'm not going to give you permission until I discuss it with the President. We're trying to convey a political message, we're not trying to start a war." Gilpatric, who was present the whole time, recollected that Anderson "sort of exploded . . . [and] used some very strong expletive to the effect that, 'This is none of your goddamn business. This is what we're here to do . . . . We're doing this ever since the days of John Paul Jones, and if you'll just go back to your quarters, Mr. Secretary, we'll take care of this.'" After they left the control room McNamara told Gilpatric "that's the end of Anderson . . . . He won't be reappointed."[74] Anderson recalled the encounter as less confrontational and denied that he used much of the language attributed to him by other accounts.[75] The exchange disclosed a fundamental difference between the two men in their understanding of the quarantine's purpose.

McNamara looked at what lay beyond the horizon. His concerns proved justified. There did occur unpredictable events that might have led to disastrous consequences. On 27 October, at the height of the missile crisis, Navy ships forced to the surface a Soviet submarine, B-59, charged with the mission to develop a Soviet naval base at Mariel Bay, Cuba. The vessel carried a nuclear-tipped torpedo. Its commander, fearing that his submarine was under attack, had been tempted briefly to arm the torpedo. He resisted the temptation, but it was not until 2002, at the 40th anniversary commemoration in Havana of the Cuban missile crisis, that the United States learned that Soviet submarines carried nuclear weapons. This incident occurred just a few hours after Soviet surface-to-air missiles shot down a U-2 over Cuba. On the same day a U.S. aircraft on an air sampling mission crossed into Siberian airspace. Although these two incidents aroused fears on the part of both superpowers, they reacted with restraint; both assumed at least for public consumption that errors had occurred. As Kennedy blurted out, "There is always some son-of-a-bitch who doesn't get the word."[76]

In evaluating the contents of the Kennedy tapes made during the missile crisis historians Ernest R. May and Philip D. Zelikow judged in retrospect that McNamara's moderation may have been exaggerated. While giving him credit for reining in the hawks and discouraging precipitous action, they saw him as increasingly concerned with the details of military preparation as the crisis intensified and ready to employ substantial force to remove the missiles. This may be a plausible judgment, but the pervasive uncertainties that affected all of the principals throughout were reflected in the almost daily changes in position taken by most participants in the ExCom meetings.[77]

JCS preparations on 27 October for a massive invasion, assumedly with McNamara's blessing, were evident in the array of forces poised for an attack: two aircraft carriers accompanied by nine escorts and a separate task force of 12 destroyers and cruisers; three Marine battalions that had reinforced Guantanamo, along with a Marine expeditionary brigade en route from California; some 850 Tactical Air Command aircraft in the southeastern states; and four Army divisions assigned to CINCLANT. At the same time, SAC had 52 B-52s airborne with 196 nuclear weapons, and 611 bombers on 15-minute alert.[78]

When the Soviet Union conceded on 28 October, thus ending the crisis, the administration could claim that the carefully calibrated quarantine had prevailed. Khrushchev's behavior from 22 to 28 October displayed a characteristic mix of bluster and deviousness, with just a touch of occasional candor. He angrily denounced the president's address to the nation and then denied the presence of offensive missiles to the United Nations. His willingness, in his response to the UN secretary general, to stop further deployment if the United States ended its blockade may have constituted a sign of reasonableness, as was his order to Soviet ships on 25 October to reverse course. It also may have been a ploy to avoid a confrontation at sea while he accelerated the pace of his preparations on land. His rambling offer in a letter on 26 October to remove missiles in return for a U.S. pledge to lift the blockade and renounce invasion of Cuba was contradicted by a truculent letter of 27 October insisting on the removal of Jupiter missiles from Turkey as the price for Soviet removal of missiles from Cuba. In addition the Soviet Union would pledge not to invade or interfere in the internal affairs of Turkey, and the United States would make the same pledge regarding Cuba.[79]

Robert Kennedy has been credited with solving the problem of the two Khrushchev letters by suggesting to his brother that he respond to the first and ignore the second. This stratagem worked. On Sunday, 28 October, Khrushchev agreed to remove the missiles and accept a "no invasion" pledge without reference to Jupiter missiles. What changed his mind is still a matter of speculation. Was it submission to U.S. nuclear superiority or was it the relative weakness of Soviet forces in the area? Or was it knowledge that the United States was prepared to strike if there was no resolution of the crisis on that Sunday? In his preface to Robert Kennedy's account of the crisis McNamara claimed that President Kennedy conceived a "strategy which applied pressure against the Soviets without ever pushing them to the point where they were forced to an irrational, suicidal, spasm response."[80] In essence, it was the doctrine of flexible response in action.

Acheson did not agree. He removed himself from ExCom deliberations after it became apparent that the president would not follow his advice to destroy Soviet missile sites in Cuba. Reflecting on Robert Kennedy's *Thirteen Days* when it appeared some six years after the event, Acheson contrasted his own lawyer's logic with the intuitive behavior of the Kennedy brothers. Granting that the hundred-to-one shot had paid off, he attributed it "to plain dumb luck." In his view, the administration had survived the crisis because Khrushchev retreated when the military confrontation seemed inevitable.[81] Few members of the ExCom would have supported Acheson's judgment.

The Joint Chiefs were skeptical of Khrushchev's surrender on the suspenseful Sunday in October. Like Acheson and Nitze, they had not shared McNamara's foreboding that the world might be coming to an end. They assumed that Khrushchev was playing for time "to delay direct action by the United States while preparing the ground for diplomatic blackmail."[82] But corroborative evidence of a changed Soviet attitude came when the Cuba-bound Soviet tanker *Grozny*, which had engaged the attention of the ExCom meeting on 27 October, stopped dead in the water on 28 October. Moreover, no other Warsaw bloc ship was entering the quarantine zone. This action not only resolved the question of what steps to take if the ship refused to accept a search, it served as an earnest of Khrushchev's intentions. In a statement later in the day, the president congratulated the Soviet leader on his "statesmanlike decision to stop building bases in Cuba, dismantling offensive weapons and returning them to the Soviet Union under United Nations verification."[83]

Epilogue: 29 October-20 November

Despite the dramatic release from tension after 28 October the ExCom did not exult over Khrushchev's blinking.[84] Fulfillment of the Soviet pledge took three difficult weeks; many loose ends could have unraveled and led to a tragic third act that would have prolonged the crisis. At the 28 October morning meeting of the ExCom, called after receipt of the full *Tass* text of Khrushchev's first letter, the members identified seeds of formidable new difficulties. One concerned the UN role in verifying Soviet compliance; U.S. air reconnaissance would be suspended on the assumption that the United Nations would fly the mission the next day. Second, the president intended to include the IL-28 bomber among the offensive weapons to be removed, although he agreed that the United States should not get "hung up" on this issue.[85]

The most immediate concern, however, was the credibility of the promised Soviet undertakings. For surveillance, on-site inspection was vital; the quarantine would remain in effect until resolution of that issue. Verification depended on Cuba's willingness to admit a UN inspection team into the country. Castro made it clear in his statement of 28 October that permission for this purpose hinged on U.S. abandonment of the Guantanamo naval base, an action clearly unacceptable to the United States. The resulting stalemate made ground inspection impossible. Not even an extended November visit from Soviet First Deputy Premier Anastas I. Mikoyan could budge Castro from what he considered infringement on Cuban sovereignty.[86] The initial solution involved resumption of U.S. air surveillance and overflights of Cuba by U-2s, with the tacit agreement of the Soviet leaders. These measures proved a serviceable compromise for verifying the dismantling of the Soviet missile sites and removal of the missiles by sea, as well as for monitoring Cuban behavior.[87]

Arrangements for dismantling and monitoring the removal of missiles then advanced with relative ease. By 6 November the United States and the Soviet Union had agreed on procedures whereby a Swedish vessel under UN contract would inspect incoming Soviet ships while nine outgoing Soviet merchant ships carrying offensive weapons would accept visual and photographic inspection by U.S. warships.[88]

Missile surveillance issues focused primarily on Cuba and Castro's concerns; the matter of 42 IL-28s centered on U.S.-Soviet understandings. The light bomber did not become a subject of controversy during the missile crisis itself since few were assembled, but it was an offensive weapon system capable of carrying nuclear bombs and reaching key targets in the southeastern United States. After 28 October the IL-28s increasingly represented a further test of compliance with U.S. demands. When the DIA estimated a reasonable time for the Soviet Union to disassemble, load, and transport the missiles, it included the IL-28s in its survey. It believed that of the 33 bombers sent to San Julien airfield, only 13 had been uncrated, of which 7 were flyable. The other 9 of the original 42 remained unassembled at another airfield.[89]

It took three weeks of difficult negotiations to settle the problem of removing the IL-28s. The United States maintained the quarantine and threatened to expand it by including petroleum products. Moscow claimed that the bombers were to be transferred to Cuba and therefore stood apart from the Kennedy-Khrushchev October agreements. Moreover, it said, the planes were really obsolescent, not offensive weapons, and intended only for defensive purposes.[90]

While informal exchanges continued in New York throughout the first three weeks of November, the president ratcheted up the pressure by refusing to state formally that the United States would not invade Cuba. Within DoD General Counsel John McNaughton suggested taking "a serious look . . . at the possibilities of sabotaging the IL-28s."[91] In a letter to Khrushchev on 6 November, the president stresssed U.S. concern about the bombers and unwillingness to accept their continued presence in Cuba. On 7 November Nitze proposed for ExCom consideration even more drastic action. He suggested warning Soviet negotiator Vasily Kuznetsov privately, followed, if necessary, by a public statement, asserting the unacceptability of the continued presence of "an important weapon system capable of offensive use." If this and a presidential assurance that U.S. actions would not include invasion of the island failed to sway the Soviet Union, Nitze proposed an air attack on the bombers.[92] In the meantime, so as not to indicate any softening of U.S. resolve, SAC's alert status remained at DEFCON 2.[93]

News of Soviet implementation of its pledges on missiles, capped by the president's statement on 20 November that "all known" Soviet missile bases in Cuba had been dismantled, served to defer discussion of Nitze's recommendations.[94] Earlier, on 10 November, Ball provided the president with a detailed memorandum on possible U.S. policy alternatives pending a Soviet reply on the IL-28s. After considering a variety of assumptions and possible courses of action, none of which he recommended, Ball observed that the United States would have to decide whether to consider Cuba a puppet of the Soviet Union or accept the Soviet assertion that it could not control Castro. "In that [the latter] event we would tacitly or explicitly accept the fact or fiction (whichever it might be) that Khrushchev had complied to the extent of his ability and thereafter concentrate our pressure on Cuba." Then the United States could refuse to assure that it would not invade the island and, for reasons of U.S. and hemisphere security, not allow Castro to possess offensive weapons. For DoD, Nitze concurred in concentrating pressure on Cuba. He considered agreement on ground inspection more important than the IL-28s. Since the remaining weapons on the island would belong to Cuba, the onus in the event of a U.S. attack would fall on Cuba.[95]

Matters never reached the point of an air strike. In his 12 November reply to Kennedy Khrushchev again emphasized the obsolescence of the IL-28 and that the United States had little to fear since only Soviet airmen flew the planes. He also hinted at the touchy relationship with Castro. In the end he agreed on removal, stating, "We give a gentleman's word that we will remove the IL-28 planes with all the personnel and equipment related to those planes, although not now but later . . . when we determine that the conditions are ripe to remove them." The same evening, at the behest of the president, Robert Kennedy at a Soviet embassy reception informed Ambassador Dobrynin that if the USSR completed IL-28 removal within 30 days the United States would immediately announce an end to the quarantine.[96]

At an ExCom meeting on 12 November, President Kennedy addressed the questions of "continued surveillance and the form of an assurance against invasion," suggesting that "we could set the IL-28s off against the quarantine and our assurances against invasion off against safeguards covering reintroduction of missiles." Nitze, for his part, in a memorandum to the ExCom on 15 November, saw some advantages in the controversy over the IL-28s. "Had the Soviet Union removed both bombers and missiles in the initial withdrawal," he pointed out, "such complete acquiescence might have made it politically infeasible to do more than accept the return to status quo ante." Under the circumstances, however, the United States had an opportunity to use force or the threat of force against the bombers to help effect the "removal of the Soviet presence from Cuba and reorientation of the Cuban regime."[97]

The Soviet Union did not rush to accept the Kennedy proposal. It continued to speak of removing the IL-28s only after lifting of the blockade and would accept UN observation posts in Cuba only if they were also established elsewhere in the Caribbean and the United States. The response coincided with renewed complaints from Castro to UN Secretary General U Thant about U.S. overflights. The Cuban president warned that "any war plane which violates the sovereignty of Cuba by invading our air space can only do so at the risk of being destroyed."[98]

The White House had no intention of accepting Moscow's solution, certainly not an inspection team that would cover the United States without also including Soviet ports. Kennedy so informed Khrushchev on 15 November.[99] Before a new stalemate developed the Soviets granted further concessions, particularly agreement to the completion of the removal from Cuba of 42 ballistic missiles, "the exact number the Soviets claimed were there." Evidence of Soviet good faith prompted Rusk on 17 November to recommend to the president suspension of low-level reconnaissance missions the following day. This was done even though some ExCom members thought these flights necessary to keep up pressure on the Soviet Union.[100]

When Khrushchev finally agreed on 20 November that all of the IL-28s and supporting personnel would leave Cuba within 30 days, the president immediately lifted the quarantine.[101] The administration considered that these actions dropped the curtain on the missile crisis on a happy note. The White House essentially accepted a line of reasoning previously offered by John McCloy on 16 November—that with missiles and IL-28s out of Cuba, the Soviet military on the island would "die on the vine." Other Soviet equipment and troops would also gradually leave because they had lost their mission to safeguard strategic missiles, no longer on the island.[102]

On 28 November the Joint Chiefs advised McNamara that "we are entering a new phase of the Cuban situation" that called for a select relaxation of the readiness posture and a return to a DEFCON 5 alert status.[103] McNamara informed Congress on 30 January 1963 that 42 ballistic missiles had been removed between 5 and 9 November and 42 IL-28s on 5-6 December. He added that all of the bombers and 36 of the missile transporters had been uncovered for photographic and visual inspection aboard the Soviet vessels. The Soviets had had no time, he noted, to construct dummy missiles. Without the missile erectors and fuel and oxidizer trailers, whatever might remain of a missile system would be inoperative.[104]

Nonetheless, there lingered "unfinished business," as the president noted on 7 February, chiefly the continued presence of Soviet forces in Cuba that could pose a threat to the hemisphere.[105] Also, potentially inflammatory loose ends still trailed from the crisis. Cuba never permitted on-site UN inspection of the missiles; no safeguards were ever provided against the reintroduction of offensive weapons. Furthermore, U.S. substitution of its own means of inspection provided a standing invitation for Castro to create an incident by shooting down a reconnaissance plane. Under these circumstances, the termination of the crisis did not lead to an appreciable relaxation of efforts to oust Castro or limit his regime's influence in Latin America. The "unfinished business" mentioned by the president occupied Defense as much as it did State, and indeed the ramifications of the missile controversy ranged far beyond Cuba, involving also the impact of the event on the U.S. presence in Berlin and the fate of the Jupiter missiles in Turkey.

Impact on Berlin

Given the Soviet capability to create trouble in Berlin at any moment, it followed that turmoil in the Caribbean would reverberate in Europe. On 28 September 1962 Khrushchev informed Kennedy that he would take no action on Berlin until after the November elections in the United States, but on 18 October Gromyko warned the president at the White House that the Soviet Union would be "compelled" to sign a treaty with East Germany unless negotiations with the United States provided some positive and rapid results.[106] By that time the administration knew of the missiles in Cuba and recognized that Khrushchev seemed intent on confronting the United States with crises in Cuba and Berlin. After the meeting with Gromyko the president saw no alternative to doing ". . . something. Because if we do nothing, we're going to have the problem of Berlin anyway . . . . We're going to have this thing stuck right in our guts, in about 2 months [when the IRBMs are operational]."[107]

Given this connection, Defense officials had to ask themselves whether Berlin would be held hostage to Soviet freedom of action in Cuba and whether a U.S. assault against the missiles would lead to Soviet aggression in West Berlin.

When Kennedy expressed concern at a meeting on 18 October that military action against Cuba could place the future of Berlin at risk, McNamara "surmised perhaps that was the price we must pay and perhaps we'd lose Berlin anyway."[108] A special national intelligence estimate on 19 October suggested that the Soviet Union would link the two areas and push for negotiations on both Berlin and Cuba. Nitze's office agreed with the assumption that Berlin stood out prominently on Khrushchev's Cuban agenda. Whatever the Soviet interest in the Cuban venture, its investment in Berlin appeared much greater; any settlement on Cuba that compromised the U.S. position in Berlin "would be widely read as a US acceptance of partial defeat in a contest involving significant US interests."[109]

Defense also worried over the impact on Allied solidarity if the Soviet Union responded to a blockade in the Caribbean with a reciprocal response in Europe. The United States could incur blame for creating a casus belli while Moscow might escape criticism if it retaliated with a blockade of its own against the West in Berlin. Yet failure to prevail in an area where U.S. interests "*are seriously involved and those of the Soviet Union are not*" would also destroy faith in U.S. leadership. When ISA planners speculated about the effect of only a partial blockade of Cuba on Soviet behavior in Berlin, they concluded it would make no difference in Soviet calculations. They asked themselves such "hypothetical" questions while recognizing that they might not stay hypothetical for long.[110]

In a memorandum of 19 October McGeorge Bundy saw the dilemma in much the same terms. If the Soviets imposed a Berlin blockade ostensibly in response to a blockade of Cuba, it would "inevitably stir feeling among all Europeans that this crisis was in some measure the fault of the Americans." Bundy feared that morale in Berlin would crack if the United States did not respond further by increasing its military efforts and being "prepared to confront Khrushchev at a very early stage with a bluntly nuclear choice." Even if these signals helped to hold Berlin, Bundy speculated, the USSR probably would not lift its blockade unless the United States did the same in the Caribbean. In such a stalemate Soviet weapons would stay in Cuba and Castro would remain in place.[111]

ExCom's Berlin-NATO subcommittee, chaired by Nitze, at its initial meeting on 24 October opposed taking dramatic initiatives, such as introducing nuclear weapons into Berlin. It viewed the idea of such a diversion to force the Soviets out of Cuba as "not . . . a useful undertaking," at the very least.[112] Nevertheless, the president required a response to his questions about a buildup of forces in Europe. ISA offered an outline of a plan. Starting with a first increment of a corps of three Army divisions, plus one Marine division, and 10 Air Force fighter squadrons along with naval units, Nitze recommended a second large increment of forces from all of the military services, with the hope that the allies in Germany would follow the same incremental framework.[113]

Planning had progressed this far before the crisis ended and fortunately had to go no further. Although the fear persisted that Moscow might use a Cuban settlement to force a negotiated settlement on Berlin,[114] Khrushchev's concessions, beginning on 28 October, moved the administration from a mood of pervasive pessimism over the fate of Berlin to a state of near euphoria. Not only was there an anticipation of greater unity among the allies in response to the successful U.S. stand against the missiles, but ISA wanted to recommend for ExCom consideration that the allies take advantage of the momentum by reducing concessions they had previously been prepared to make over Berlin.[115] Yet it was only after the Soviet Union signed a treaty with East Germany in 1964 that relaxation occurred.*

Withdrawal of Jupiter Missiles from Turkey

Early on the crisis spotlighted the relationship between Soviet IRBMs in Cuba and U.S. Jupiter missiles in Turkey and inevitably inspired the idea of a mutual withdrawal. The United States had 15 Jupiter missiles in Turkey, operational since April 1962, poised to strike at Soviet targets across the Black Sea. Khrushchev equated them with the 42 Soviet missiles in the final stages of readiness in Cuba.[116] Pointing out the Soviet tendency to think in terms of parallels, Ambassador Thompson warned ExCom to be prepared for Soviet pressure to remove the Jupiters from Turkey. In a paper dated 21 October, ISA's William Bundy also reflected about a mutual withdrawal of missiles from foreign bases—the Soviet Union from Cuba, the United States from Turkey and Italy or elsewhere. He noted that "hitherto we have considered the subject of 'foreign military bases' an untouchable subject for negotiation." Even if the exchange made sense from a military point of view, the political impact might be too high.[117]

Thompson's and Bundy's intuition proved correct. A generation later, Fedor Burlatsky, a leading and knowledgeable academic affiliated with the Central Committee of the Communist Party in the 1960s, reported that at a meeting in the Crimea in April 1962 Defense Minister Marshal Rodion Malinovsky emphasized to Khrushchev that U.S. missiles in Turkey could reach Soviet targets within 10 minutes after launch. Conceivably, this information influenced the Soviet leader's decision to deploy missiles in Cuba on the assumption that what was sauce for the goose was sauce for the gander, even though there were significant differences in the respective threats.†[118]

During a meeting with advisers on 16 October, the president observed that the United States had no missiles threatening the Soviet Union in the manner the IRBMs in Cuba threatened America. Bundy reminded him about the Jupiters in Turkey. They may have escaped Kennedy's attention for the moment because

---

* See Chapter VII.
† Jupiter was a liquid-fueled missile with a range of 1,500 miles, deployed only in Italy and Turkey. Very similar to the Thor missile sent to Britain, the Jupiter was nearing obsolescence when it was fielded. By the end of 1963 all Jupiter and Thor missiles would be removed from the NATO area.

he had previously recognized their obsolescence and early in his administration asked for arrangements to remove them from Turkish soil. Essentially they filled no military need.[119]

Other reasons existed to remove the Jupiters. The United States would appear as a peacemaker, displaying sensitivity and flexibility without degrading the nation's strategic position. But the negative impact of such a decision outweighed the positive in the minds of administration strategists. Severe repercussions would follow in NATO. The Turks would see themselves as pawns in a Soviet-American chess game. Turkish soldiers, not Americans, were manning the Jupiters. "Removal of the weapons, in the most real sense," according to an ISA memorandum on 21 October, "is an act of disarming our friend." It would also appear as capitulation to Soviet blackmail, with dangerous consequences elsewhere.[120]

Given these considerations, the JCS opposed a draft presidential order that would have prohibited the firing of Jupiter missiles from Italy or Turkey without further presidential authorization, "even in the event of a selective nuclear or nonnuclear attack on these units by the Soviet Union in response to actions we may be taking elsewhere." They pointed out that regardless of unilateral acts by the United States, Soviet attacks against the Jupiter missiles in Turkey or Italy would constitute aggression and would raise binding NATO obligations to retaliate. New restrictions would undermine the credibility of NATO's defense structure in Europe.[121]

The JCS argument did not persuade the president. At a White House meeting on the morning of 22 October Kennedy expressed concern that General Norstad, Supreme Allied Commander Europe, should fully understand that there would be no reprisal from Jupiters in Turkey or Italy in response to a Soviet attack from Cuba without specific authorization from the White House: "What we've got to do is make sure these fellows . . . don't fire them [Jupiters] off and think the United States is under attack. I don't think we ought to accept the Chiefs' word on that one." Taylor followed this up with a message to Norstad directing that no missiles should be fired from Italy or Turkey without presidential authorization.[122]

The issue moved from the wings to center stage of the missile crisis when Khrushchev presented revised Soviet terms in his second letter (27 October) demanding the removal of Jupiters from Turkey concurrently with recall of Soviet missiles from Cuba. Walter Lippmann had already floated the idea in his newspaper column on 25 October, and the Soviets may have thought he had done so with the president's approval. Lippmann had suggested that the missile systems in the two countries could be dismantled without altering the balance of power.[123]

The reasons for Khrushchev's provocative addition in the second message remain open to question. Whether or not pressure from the Politburo or Khrushchev's own calculations brought Turkey into the picture, it complicated the ExCom's deliberations. Citing Raymond Hare, U.S. ambassador to Turkey, Nitze claimed that it would be "absolutely anathema" to the Turks to pull the missiles out. Next would come a demand for denuclearization of all NATO territory. Explanations about their obsolescence would not mollify the Turks.[124]

Khrushchev had presented the administration with a serious dilemma. If the United States, knowing the Soviet position, now attacked the missiles in Cuba it would stand accused of recklessness. At the ExCom meeting on 27 October the president asked: "Having made it public, how can he take these missiles out of Cuba if we just do nothing about Turkey?"[125] On the other hand, if Kennedy accepted a trade, Turkey, the other NATO allies, and his political opponents as well, would see it as a sellout.

The dilemma deepened as news reached the White House during the meeting that Maj. Rudolph Anderson's U-2 plane had been shot down over Cuba by a Soviet surface-to-air missile. Taylor urged an air strike against the offending SAM site the next day, and McNamara called for a major air strike. If the Soviets responded with an attack on Turkey, the secretary recommended that the United States respond by attacking the Soviet Black Sea fleet. The linkage issue had compounded the crisis. On his way back to the Pentagon that evening, McNamara wondered if he had seen his last Saturday night.[126]

The president sought to find a way to convince Turkish leaders that withdrawing missiles from their country in favor of a Polaris substitute would strengthen rather than weaken their security. He also recognized that he had no time to persuade them of this advantage. At this juncture Robert Kennedy proposed a simple but deft solution—to respond only to Khrushchev's letter of 26 October and ignore the letter of 27 October in which the Soviet premier had cited the missile linkage as a quid pro quo (see page 214). That Moscow did not push the issue of the second letter stemmed in part from the implied assurance Robert Kennedy had given Ambassador Dobrynin in a conversation on the 27th. Even as the attorney general said that the United States would remove the Soviet missile bases if the USSR did not do so, he indicated that the Jupiters would come out of Turkey if the offensive weapons left Cuba. A period of time would have to elapse before action in Turkey would take place; if any leak occurred in the interval the deal would fall through.[127] The arrangement allowed Khrushchev to save face by embracing the carrot rather than the stick. In his memoirs he crowed about his generous behavior as a victor. He not only saved Cuba from invasion but felt sympathy for the distraught younger brother of the president who, he professed to believe, sought Soviet help against the aggressive designs of the U.S. generals.[128]

Quiet diplomacy worked to solve the Turkish question, but it was not a triumph to celebrate publicly. Not until the posthumous publication of Robert Kennedy's *Thirteen Days* did the implicit U.S. promise become public. As Bundy noted 20 years after that revelation, "the assurance on Turkish missiles remains far less important than the stick that Robert Kennedy carried to Dobrynin: a threat of further action within days," unless the Soviet Union agreed by the next day to the demand for withdrawal of the missiles. U.S. preparations for air attacks and invasion had become clearly visible. Whether correctly or not, it seemed to Bundy, Khrushchev deduced that time for further negotiations had run out.[129]

As for Turkish-American relations, fortunately secrecy prevailed. The administration pursued the removal of the Jupiters within a NATO context, unconnected to the Cuban crisis, and based on a need to bring on an effective replacement.[130] In a letter to the Turkish minister of defense in January 1963 about supplying new weapons, McNamara had in mind Turkish sensibilities. He emphasized that while Thor and Jupiter in 1957 were the only strategic ballistic missiles that NATO had ready for operation, rapid technological change had made them vulnerable, to the extent that it was questionable if they could survive a surprise attack. As a replacement for the Jupiters, McNamara directed the JCS chairman on 18 January to assign three Polaris submarines to duty in the Mediterranean beginning no later than 1 April 1963, and to insure dispatch of 14 F-104G aircraft to Turkey in April 1963.[131]

By announcing the Turkish removal as part of a phaseout of these missiles, McNamara effected the transition painlessly, avoiding what might have become an awkward and embarrassing issue for both the United States and NATO. When the question of a deal with the Soviets came up in congressional hearings on 6 February, he replied, "I can say without any qualifications whatsoever there was absolutely no deal, as it might be called, between the Soviet Union and the United States regarding the removal of the JUPITER weapons from either Italy or Turkey." He went on to note that when Khrushchev had brought up an exchange during the missile crisis, "the President absolutely refused to discuss it at that time, and no discussion took place, and certainly there was no agreement to withdraw weapons from any allied nation in association with a response to the agreement of the Soviets to withdraw offensive weapons from Cuba."[132]

Years later McNamara still believed that there "was no 'deal'—no private 'trade' of missiles. I was in the room when the President told Bobby what he wanted from the Soviets. The President said: 'Make it crystal clear, Bobby, that there is no deal.'" The former secretary of defense did admit, however, that Robert Kennedy provided Dobrynin with a "piece of information" to the effect that the Turkish missiles were coming out soon in any event. If this was a distinction without a difference, McNamara did not see it that way. "A piece of information," he claimed, "is a hell of a lot different than a private deal."[133] Whatever its name, the ploy embodied a species of diplomacy by the president and the attorney general that yielded a strikingly successful result.

Cuba after the Missile Crisis

United States relations with Cuba after the crisis afforded none of the satisfaction that the resolution of the Jupiter question gave to the administration. Castro held on to power and his potential for mischief in Latin America remained a threat. Reports of Cuba's intentions to export communism throughout the hemisphere regularly flowed into Washington. The Soviet humiliation in October seemed to embolden rather than discourage Castro and his colleagues.[134] It was hardly surprising then that the president and his brother maintained their preoccupation with eradicating Castro's regime.

Throughout 1963 the secretary of defense and the JCS chairman worked on contingency plans to counter Cuban subversion aimed at fostering instability in Latin America.[135] Continuing overflights of Cuban territory required a careful elaboration of the rules of engagement the United States should follow in the event of a Cuban attack on U.S. ships or aircraft.[136] Provocative as low-altitude overflights of Cuba might have seemed, Castro's refusal to allow on-site inspection permitted no alternative. In spite of its shortcomings, aerial inspection offered a reasonable substitute, one that the Soviet Union and Cuba tacitly accepted, at least for the period immediately following the crisis.[137] The general uncertainty about a situation over which the United States had limited control, however, revived old schemes to undermine the Castro regime and sparked new ones.

The concept of a Cuban brigade took on new life after Castro released more than 100 prisoners seized in the Bay of Pigs episode. It appeared that these veterans could form the nucleus of another possible assault force, underscoring U.S. determination to maintain pressure on Castro. For all the usual reasons, nothing much came of the idea. Indeed, freelancing Cuban volunteers became an embarrassment by initiating unauthorized activities. In March 1963 a hit-and-run raid on a Soviet vessel in the Caribbean evoked public applause for its boldness but also inspired the U.S. Coast Guard to greater vigilance to prevent such incidents in the future.[138] Ambivalence over the use of the volunteers manifested itself in the reaction of the State Department and the United States Information Agency to Robert Kennedy's proposal to send Cuban exile leaders on a speaking tour of Latin American countries. USIA opposed the trip for fear that the exiles would more likely remind an audience of the Bay of Pigs disaster than awaken an awareness of the communist threat.[139]

To coordinate a new set of policies and actions, the president established on 8 January 1963 the Interdepartmental Committee on Cuba with Sterling J. Cottrell, deputy assistant secretary of state for inter-American affairs, as chairman. Secretary of the Army Cyrus Vance and Army Chief of Staff General Earle Wheeler represented OSD and JCS, respectively.[140] Defense soon found itself at odds with State when the latter did not "make the overthrow of the Castro/Communist regime an objective of the U.S." The committee did not appear to have carried much weight or to have provided adequate coordination among the constituent agencies.[141]

At a meeting with Kennedy in February 1963 McNamara persuaded the president to seek from Congress more military assistance keyed to counterinsurgency plans. The discussion covered such possibilities as instigating and staging "selected terrorist incidents in Latin American countries designed to implicate Castro" and arranging "for caches of Soviet-Czech arms to be 'discovered' in selected Latin American countries, ostensibly smuggled in from Cuba." At the same time, as the CIA's William Colby noted, the Kennedy "fury over Castro" led to the appointment of Desmond Fitzgerald of the CIA as head of a special Cuban Task Force to reexamine sabotage and infiltration options and proposals to assassinate Castro. More secret and better able to entertain covert measures than Cottrell's organization, the task force tried to avoid the mistakes of Mongoose.[142]

The Joint Chiefs continued to focus on military plans and objectives. When they met with the president at the end of February, the chiefs made a point of saying that there would be no need to preposition troops in the southeastern United States in advance of any military operation against Cuba. The visible tension preceding such an event would allow them ample time to mobilize forces. McNamara noted in April that the JCS wanted to make sure that "there be no precommitment against an invasion of Cuba."[143]

McNamara assured the president in May 1963 that all contingency plans were being kept up to date. In the face of new deliveries of Soviet T-34 medium tanks and self-propelled anti-tank weapons to Castro's army, the Defense Department had improved its capability for transporting large numbers of troops and heavy equipment at an early stage of an operation. McNamara outlined the time sequence for future strikes: from decision to attack to a full-scale air assault would require 3 days; from landing of troops until all major combat forces were ashore would require another 9 days; and the time from the beginning to the end of the operation would total 27 days.[144]

Despite White House and DoD interest, these activities probably did not amount to much more than rhetorical flourishes, game-playing removed from reality. Given reservations about Cuban exiles and doubts about Latin American allies, did the administration seriously see an invasion of Cuba as the next step after the missile crisis? And what of the non-invasion pledge? Or were military plans conceived less in anticipation of a final blow against Castro than as a means of deterring Castro—and his Soviet patron—from new aggression in the hemisphere to compensate for their defeat in October 1962? It appears likely that the bellicose notes emerging from planning sessions reflected in part sheer frustration over U.S. inability to capitalize on the successful ending of the missile crisis and remove the still dangerous Castro regime from Cuba.

The lack of concrete results from the long anti-Castro campaign took its toll in friction among government agencies responsible for Cuban affairs. State-Defense differences deepened in 1963, with Defense officials repeatedly describing State initiatives directed at Cuban-sponsored subversion in Latin America as too soft. Specifically, Secretary of the Army Vance felt that State plans depended too heavily on limited travel control and propaganda approaches while avoiding more aggressive options such as "non-attributable" actions against petroleum resources, sabotage of Cuban facilities through chemical or biological contamination, or flooding the island with counterfeit currency. If State followed Defense recommendations, Vance said, presumably the Cuban military would have to maintain a high alert and consume supplies and manpower that otherwise would have strengthened the Castro regime.[145]

The pattern of Cuban-American relations remained much the same after Lyndon Johnson became president in November 1963. A stream of reports about Castro's subversive activities in Latin America flowed into the CIA and DIA networks, as they did under Kennedy, without yielding any conclusive way of dealing with them.[146] State prevailed in the rejection of a CIA proposal to attack and cripple the Matanzas power plant, for fear the action might slow down withdrawal of Soviet troops from Cuba or invite another U-2 shootdown. When in February 1964 Castro threatened to shut off the water supply to the U.S. naval base at Guantanamo Bay to protest the U.S. seizure of Cuban fishing boats off the coast of Florida, Johnson ordered the construction of a desalinization facility to convert seawater and make the base self-sufficient. Friction with Panama, fueled by both Cuban assistance to procommunist insurgents and longstanding nationalist resentment towards the United States over U.S. control of the Panama Canal, boiled over into rioting in January 1964 that led to a sealing of the Canal Zone border and evacuation of U.S. military personnel from areas outside the Canal Zone. McNamara, with "solid evidence" of Castro's involvement in the Panamanian unrest, had DoD prepared to implement contingency plans and intervene with infantry and military police should the communists threaten to seize power. Tensions diminished when Johnson offered to renegotiate the 1903 treaty and State and Defense agreed on other concessions that carefully balanced recognition of Panamanian sovereignty with protection of U.S. interests.[147]

Castro outlasted U.S. efforts to eliminate him for reasons that were complex. His survival was not simply a consequence of the U.S. pledge against invasion, nor a result of a calmer atmosphere following the Soviet capitulation. For all the exasperation with Castro, the use of military force to oust him had more appeal than necessity. A nuisance and always a danger as a role model or an exporter of communism to Latin America, Castro nevertheless posed no immediate military or political threat to the United States after the missile crisis. While the quick action in Panama reflected continuing sensitivity to the spread of Castroism, as would the intervention in the Dominican Republic in 1965, Latin America assumed a lesser role in U.S. national security deliberations after 1962. DoD, along with the CIA and State Department, would continue to craft—and discard—scenarios for overthrowing Castro, but diminishing urgency produced a tacit recognition by mid-decade that the nation could live with a non-nuclear communist neighbor.

Further, despite the inability to remove Castro, Kennedy and Johnson established checks against the expansion of his influence and the intrusion of Soviet forces in the hemisphere that mitigated the sense of failure. Kennedy's Alliance for Progress, with its emphasis on social and economic programs, represented a genuine effort to recast hemispheric relations and address Latin America's domestic problems even as it was intended to counter communist influence. Although in the absence of reformed economies, U.S. aid remained limited and primarily military, Johnson could take comfort in positive developments in Brazil, which rejected a move toward a possible communist takeover,* and Venezuela, where the government responded vigorously to Cuban subversion and mobilized hemisphere-wide support for a resolution in the Organization of American States condemning Cuba's "acts of aggression." With the OAS resolution of 26 July 1964, wherein member states voted to impose economic sanctions and sever diplomatic relations with Cuba (all except Mexico subsequently did), the menace of Castro had dwindled to an irritant.[148]

For McNamara the missile crisis confirmed a conviction that nuclear weapons were inherently unusable and that only a flexible response to military challenges made strategic as well as tactical sense. Resorting to force to resolve the Soviet-American confrontation would have involved conventional arms and would have drawn its strength from the military advances that OSD had directed and implemented in 1961 and 1962. Had Khrushchev reneged on his pledge to remove offensive weapons from Cuba, he would have had to face more than 100,000 U.S. troops, many hundreds of aircraft, and scores of ships poised to invade the island.

In retrospect, the favorable resolution of the missile crisis restored U.S. pride and prestige damaged by the Bay of Pigs failure. Cuba in 1962 provided an arena for a crucial Cold War contest in which the United States prevailed. In another arena, Southeast Asia, the combination of political resolve and military might that proved successful in Cuba could not serve as an effective model. There, incremental response and self-imposed restraint failed to achieve a successful outcome against a different enemy and under greatly different circumstances.

---

* In March 1964 Brazilian President Joao Goulart, with the collaboration of the Brazilian Communist Party, seemed bent on seizing dictatorial powers. The JCS dispatched a carrier task group to the area to register the seriousness of U.S., concern, but the crisis passed, with the help of Brazil's armed forces, when Goulart stepped down on 1 April. See Phyllis R. Parker, *Brazil and the Quiet Intervention, 1964*.

CHAPTER X

Laos

A small insular country half a world away, Laos was an unlikely international flash point for the United States in the Cold War. Shortly, neighboring Vietnam would far overshadow it in significance, but in January 1961 Laos briefly eclipsed even Cuba and Berlin as a place of crisis and urgency requiring the incoming administration's immediate attention. At a meeting in the White House on the day before the inauguration of his successor, President Eisenhower, echoed by Secretary of State Christian Herter, forcefully impressed on Kennedy that Laos was "the key to the entire area of Southeast Asia," indeed, "the cork in the bottle." Should Laos fall to the communists, the "free world" would lose the whole region. So dangerous did they view the situation that the United States might have to go in there and fight it out. If the SEATO* allies refused to participate in the struggle, then the United States would have to go it alone.[1]

Paul Nitze remembered Laos as "a smoldering ember, waiting to burst into flames." So pressing did the danger there seem that Vietnam received hardly any mention in Eisenhower's conversation with Kennedy. Press commentary reflected that emphasis. The *New York Times* Index for 1961 devoted only 8 columns to Vietnam, compared with 26 to Laos.[2]

What accounted for the judgments by senior government officials that identified Laos as central to U.S. foreign policy and Vietnam as only peripheral in 1961? The United States had become involved in Indochina as early as 1950 in support of the French struggle to retain their rule over the area against the assault of the revolutionary Viet Minh under Ho Chi Minh. The French failure to prevail led to the Geneva agreements in 1954,† which recognized the independence of

---

* SEATO (Southeast Asia Treaty Organization) was a collective defense pact signed in Manila on 8 September 1954 by the United States, Great Britain, France, Australia, New Zealand, the Philippines, Pakistan, and Thailand.

† These agreements, included in a declaration of 21 July 1954, were the work of the conference held in Geneva by the Soviet Union, China, France, the United Kingdom, Cambodia, Laos, and the Viet Minh. Neither the United States nor the Bao Dai government of Vietnam concurred in the final declaration.

the three States of Indochina—Vietnam, Cambodia, and Laos—but divided Vietnam at the 17th parallel into a northern sector controlled by the Communist Viet Minh and a Western-oriented southern Vietnam pending future nationwide elections. Although Laos was not officially divided, the insurgent Communist Pathet Lao was regrouped in two provinces. The United States refused to sign the accord and established a U.S. presence in place of France in South Vietnam to support the regime.[3]

Laos, the smallest of the three states, had few qualifications for nationhood in the Western sense of the nation-state. Customarily in conflict, the country's four ethnic groups, of which the Lao were only one, had little experience with formally organized armies; those were the creation of the French colonizers and their American successors. An impoverished land with a largely subsistence economy, when not ruled by foreign invaders Laos was dominated by fiefdoms controlled by a few aristocratic families under a weak monarch.

The chief contenders for power in the late 1950s were the weak royal government, the Pathet Lao under Prince Souphanouvong, and a neutralist faction under Prince Souvanna Phouma, half-brother of Souphanouvong. The royal government faction, nominally headed by Prince Boun Oum, was dominated by strongman General Phoumi Nosovan. Into 1960 these remained the chief players in the prolonged contest for control of Laos.[4]

In its closing years, the Eisenhower administration sought to bring about establishment of an anticommunist pro-Western government in Laos. This proved a difficult task in the prevailing circumstances of instability and unpredictability that seemed to be the distinctive features of the country. Governments rose and fell, generals and political leaders came and went, switching sides out of expediency, and uncertainty reigned. The political disarray persisted and seemed acute at the very time the Eisenhower administration departed office. No doubt it gave added insistence to Eisenhower's warning to Kennedy about Laos.

In aiding its preferred faction in Laos the United States violated the Geneva Accords in spirit and letter, as did North Vietnam, which supported procommunist forces even more openly. Complicating the issue was that North Vietnamese supply lines to the Viet Cong insurgents in South Vietnam passed through southern Laos. In providing a purportedly civilian advisory group, under the name Programs Evaluation Office (PEO), that obviously pursued a military training mission, the United States was clearly in violation of the Geneva Agreement on the Cessation of Hostilities in Laos, which prohibited the "introduction into Laos of any reinforcements of troops or military personnel" from outside Laotian territory.[5]

When the United States looked for aid from allies to cope with the situation in Laos it found divided counsels and confused responses. The European members of SEATO—Britain and France—believed that the Boun Oum regime, supported by the United States, would surely fail; they opposed anything resembling

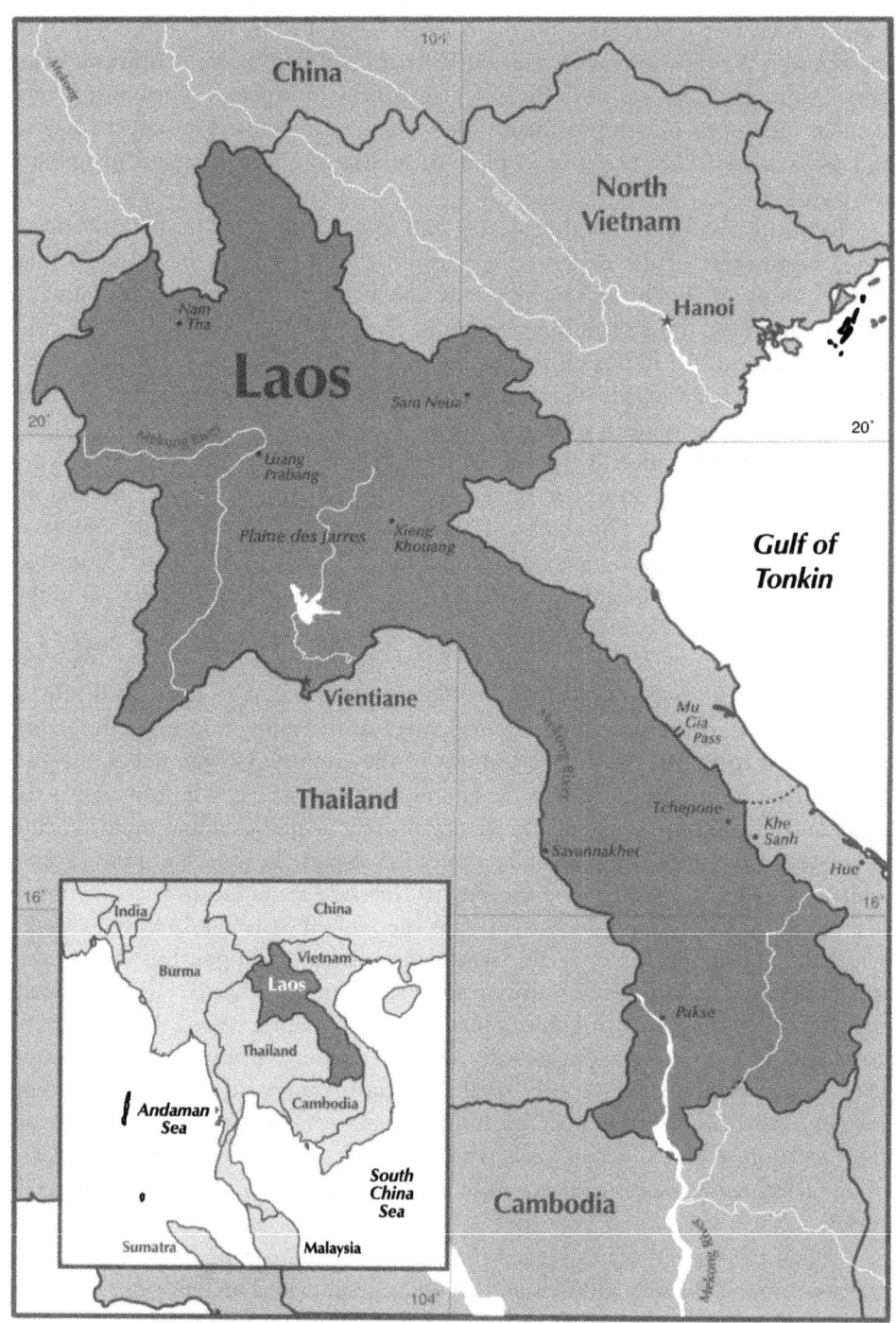

The Key Position of Laos in Southeast Asia

military intervention. As co-chair of the Geneva Conference Britain maintained hopes in a diplomatic solution. France, resentful of growing U.S. influence in Indochina, offered little support for U.S. initiatives, and inclined toward the leader of the neutralist faction, Prince Souvanna Phouma. Prince Sihanouk of Cambodia recommended convening a 14-member international conference to address the problem. Only the Asian allies—South Vietnam, Thailand, the Philippines, and Pakistan—each with a special interest in containing a communist neighbor, urged a vigorous U.S. response.[6]

Tension over Laos ran high in Washington as Eisenhower left office. At a White House meeting on 2 January 1961, Eisenhower and other officials registered frustration over French obstructionism and British caution. Three days earlier, the State Department had issued a statement that "mindful of its obligations under the SEATO Treaty, the United States Government would take the most serious view of any intervention in Laos by the Chinese Communists or Viet Minh armed forces or others in support of the Communist Pathet Lao, who are in rebellion against the Royal Laotian Government."[7]

Only a week before Kennedy's inauguration the Joint Chiefs of Staff had regarded a bilateral agreement with Laos "as a matter of urgency." Given the grip of the domino effect metaphor on the Eisenhower administration it came as no surprise that its leaders, including the president himself, spoke of unilateral intervention to save not just Laos, but Thailand, Cambodia, and South Vietnam as well, if a multilateral approach should fail.[8]

Responding to the Eisenhower Warning

The message that the outgoing president conveyed to his successor on 19 January unquestionably alerted Kennedy to the seriousness of the crisis, but it offered little guidance. McNamara, a participant in the meeting on 19 January, reported that when Kennedy asked what he might anticipate from the Sino-Soviet bloc if the United States or SEATO intervened, Eisenhower's reply "was not completely clear." He implied that the communist bloc could provide more support for the Pathet Lao than the SEATO powers could for the Royal Lao Government (RLG). Nonetheless, departing Secretary of Defense Thomas Gates expressed himself as "exceedingly sanguine" about the U.S. capability to cope with "any foreseeable test," assuming only one limited war situation to cope with at the time.[9]

If an emergency existed in Laos in January 1961, the practical options available to the new administration were few. The prevailing consensus viewed the Boun Oum government, under the controlling Phoumi, as in a near state of collapse that could bring on a communist takeover of the entire country. What should the Kennedy team do in this circumstance? They recognized that other areas of the world occupied a more central place in U.S. foreign policy than did

Laos. But Cuba and Berlin did not yet loom as problems requiring immediate solution, and in Southeast Asia Vietnam appeared to have secondary importance. Laos took priority, requiring tactical if not strategic decisions that would absorb the attention of policymakers for at least a short but significant period. Presidential adviser Theodore Sorensen claimed that Kennedy spent more time on Laos in his first two months than on any other subject.[10]

The president faced the choice of (1) allowing Phoumi to fall, with the hope of minimal consequences; (2) accepting a division of the country similar to that of Vietnam but with an even more difficult frontier to defend; (3) providing military aid to a nation apparently unwilling or incapable of using it properly; or (4) coming up with a diplomatic solution that would secure a genuinely neutral coalition government. The last seemed the most sensible, but it had its pitfalls, not least the likelihood that the North Vietnamese would use Laos as a steppingstone toward the conquest of South Vietnam and the possibility that neutralism would lead to the surrender, not just of Laos, but of all Southeast Asia.

In a lengthy report prepared during the inaugural weekend (21-22 January), a newly formed State-Defense-CIA-ICA* task force listed adverse factors hindering U.S. efforts in Laos: the deteriorating military situation; extensive military support of the Pathet Lao by the communist bloc; virtually a complete lack of backing of U.S.-proposed actions by other SEATO members and South Asia nations as well as their general non-recognition of the Boun Oum-Phoumi government; and finally, "the geography of Laos . . ., a most undesirable place in which to commit U.S. forces to ground action." With little chance of a political settlement so long as a military victory appeared unlikely, and given the currently strong position of the Pathet Lao in northern Laos, the communists might yet establish a puppet state there to use as a springboard against Thailand and South Vietnam.

The task force recommended several military measures in hopes of improving the Laotian position, the more drastic of which would allow Thai planes to attack the communist airlift and ground troops, and commit U.S. aircraft if the Chinese began fighter protection of the Soviet flights. On the diplomatic side, the task force suggested discussions with the Soviet Union and pressure on the Laotian king to seek the creation of a neutral commission that would obtain and supervise a cease-fire, a return of military forces to positions spelled out in the Geneva Accords, and, possibly, free elections.[11]

When the president and his chief advisers discussed the task force report on 23 January, McNamara stated that implementing the military recommendations would be helpful but would not "reverse the unfavorable longer term prospects." Rusk generally favored the military proposals but suggested waiting until the State Department undertook discussions with the Soviet Union. The president

---

* The International Cooperation Administration (ICA) was a separate agency created by the Eisenhower administration to furnish military and technical assistance under the U.S. mutual security program.

expressed alarm at the lack of support from the SEATO partners. He observed that "if the British and French aren't going to do anything about the security of Southeast Asia, we tell them we aren't going to do it alone. They have as much or more to lose in the area than we have." General Lemnitzer demurred, stressing the vital importance of Laos to the security of the entire Southeast Asia area. In the end, the president authorized DoD to prepare for but not actually carry out the task force's military recommendations for support of the RLG forces, pending State discussions with the SEATO allies and with the Soviet Union.[12]

Two days later the president, meeting with the Joint Chiefs for the first time, discussed world problems, of which Laos stood first on the JCS list. In response to Kennedy's observation that he had few viable options, the chiefs stated that a combination of military and diplomatic measures was possible. In the short run, they advocated support of indigenous forces without major U.S. intervention. Given the obstacles the diplomatic approach was encountering among allies and with the Soviet Union, it seemed obvious that time was running out. The White House had no choice but to keep open military options. The steadily deteriorating position of Phoumi's forces required action simply to retain a bargaining position. The president withheld a decision on any military initiative.[13]

The Joint Chiefs, still pained by the Korean War experience, feared having to fight another war in Asia. They informed the president on 6 February that the dispatch of troops to Southeast Asia would initially limit U.S. ability to cope with emergencies elsewhere in the world.[14] This ruled out direct U.S. intervention except as a last resort and placed a premium on such alternatives as increasing material assistance to Phoumi to prop up his forces. U.S. reluctance to deploy troops also sent a negative message to Laos's neighbors, Thailand and South Vietnam.

The shock upon discovering the limitations on U.S. military capabilities in Laos or elsewhere in Southeast Asia caused OSD to set in motion an expanded airlift development and production program to speed long-range deployment of Strategic Army Corps (STRAC) forces. Laos also drew attention to the importance of counterinsurgency units and a new look at limited warfare, which would become an important part of McNamara's agenda in the early years of the Kennedy administration. Brig. Gen. Edward Lansdale, a veteran of antiguerrilla activities in the Philippines and Vietnam and soon to be active in Cuban operations also (see Chapter IX), warned that failure to create a counterinsurgency program quickly would lead to loss of control of the area. A successful program, however, might save South Vietnam as well as Laos by denying the North Vietnamese and Viet Cong a safe haven in Laos.[15]

In the continuing contest between diplomatic and military responses to the crisis, the latter had an advantage. OSD and JCS had empowered the commander in chief, Pacific (CINCPAC) to make some kinds of decisions without reference to Washington, whereas the U.S. ambassador to Laos operated for a time under greater constraints from the State Department and the White House. Although

State served as the primary agent for Laotian matters, failure to delegate authority weakened its position vis-a-vis DoD, where ISA's Laos desk cooperated closely with JCS's Laos Battle Staff.[16] A Laos interagency task force inclined toward the DoD position and built on hopes for a successful Phoumi offensive in February. The task force believed that open but limited support of Phoumi's offensive would underline the seriousness of the U.S. commitment without justifying any increase in Soviet assistance to the Pathet Lao.[17]

The consensus in the administration over the need to shore up the failing RLG and a lack of agreement over the means of doing so posed a genuine dilemma. A possible way out lay in an appeal to the SEATO powers. If the neutral nations of Asia would not lend their help, perhaps the allies in SEATO would support Laos in fulfillment of the SEATO protocol of 1954 embracing the free states of Indochina. Such action might obviate unilateral American intervention. Thailand enthused over this approach and urged joint action to employ the NATO formula for Laos. Adoption of Article 5 of the North Atlantic Treaty, in which an attack against one nation constituted an attack against all, would remedy SEATO's differences over the defense of the RLG. However, though Thailand might have won over the Philippines, both France and Britain were reluctant to accept even the legitimacy of the Boun Oum government.[18]

These divisions within SEATO predictably resulted in ineffectiveness. When the SEATO Council met at the end of March it produced only a toothless resolution that noted a conventional "grave concern" over external communist support of the continuing Pathet Lao offensive in clear disregard of the Geneva Accords. The council then expressed its wish for "an unaligned and independent Laos," secured by negotiations, not warfare, but stated that if these efforts failed SEATO would be prepared "to take whatever action may be appropriate in the circumstances."[19]

With the apparent closure of all other avenues, the administration had nowhere to turn except back to a coalition government that would include both Phoumi and the neutralist Prince Souvanna, a compromise that would appeal to the French and British allies. Even the Soviets might accept an arrangement involving Souvanna, although they wanted an international conference to achieve it. In Washington, Ambassador Menshikov brought up the idea of a Souvanna-led government. U.S. Ambassador Llewellyn Thompson reported early in March that Khrushchev for the first time appeared convinced about the seriousness of the U.S. interest in a neutral status. If the USSR also pressed for a conference, he thought it might be deferring to Chinese views. The new Soviet willingness to negotiate probably meant that they expected the Pathet Lao to win, if not now, then later. Like the Americans, the Soviets faced other issues that held higher priority. As Khrushchev told Thompson, he did not want a confrontation over Laos. "Why take risks over Laos? It will fall into our laps like a ripe apple."[20]

So limited were the administration's policy options that it welcomed anything staving off immediate disaster. While State now looked reluctantly to Souvanna for a political solution, it did not wish it to be at any cost. Souvanna should be pushed into a position in which he would lead a non-communist neutral government. If this came to pass, no international conference need convene. Hopes rested on a meeting between Phoumi and Souvanna in Phnom Penh where Souvanna himself expressed concern about the Soviet-assisted buildup of Pathet Lao forces.[21]

American apprehension at the level of Soviet support notwithstanding, the difficulties of the Phoumi forces did not stem from scanty U.S. aid. The enhanced role of Phoumi in 1960 had accelerated the rate of supply deliveries and transfer of funds. JCS instructed CINCPAC to divert additional emergency monies to Laos from undelivered Military Assistance Program funds targeted for elsewhere. Along with these efforts in February 1961, the PEO, together with the U.S. ambassador, CINCPAC, and the JCS, approved activation of additional Laotian antiguerrilla forces. Military assistance would permit increasing these forces from 20,000 to 29,800, a reflection of their perceived importance. The additional 9,800 would consist of Hmong, the ethnic people in the northeastern mountains most actively engaged in fighting the Pathet Lao. The force level of the regular army (FAL)* would remain at 29,000.[22]

Given the performance of the beneficiaries, DoD had no enthusiasm for throwing more aid at the Laotian army. Even so, in the absence of a modus vivendi between Souvanna and Phoumi, alternatives to more help appeared limited. Accordingly, in February 1961 Defense and State approved additional millions in assistance to help meet expanded military operations. In March the cost of aid rose dramatically as Phoumi's plight worsened. Internal airlift support for the government's forces required an increase in funding. The escalating cost of surrogate fighting in Laos led the president on 28 March to ask the secretary of defense for a tally of military and economic assistance provided Laos since the 1954 Geneva agreements.[23] McNamara found that through 31 December 1960 this had amounted to $277 million, of which only $63 million went for military aid. Another $65 million, programmed or obligated, had not been used by the end of 1960. McNamara added that the data presented "do not adequately reflect a wide variety of emergency actions taken since August 1960 by Department of Defense and other agencies to support operations in the current crisis in Laos."[24]

The administration did seek to assert some control over the use of resources. When General Phoumi wanted to raise six special battalions, the American threat to cut off payments forced him to use the personnel from those battalions to serve as replacements for existing units.[25] This triumph of American efficiency came as a minor victory without much meaning. In reality, assistance to Laos was

---

* Forces Armées de Laos.

as expensive as it was apparently wasteful. Defense officials observed that while the PEO had submitted a preliminary budget of $19.8 million for FY 1962, it did not include two supplements amounting to $4.9 million. And this was just the minimal requirement for supporting Phoumi's army. If hostilities continued on the same scale, another $5 million or more would have to go into the final budget. Therefore, according to an ISA analysis in April, a budget request of $30 million would be more realistic than the original $19.8 million figure.[26]

The rising cost of aid to Laos, the extremely slow diplomatic progress, and the bleak military situation presented a grim outlook. At the end of February Walt Rostow, deputy presidential assistant for national security affairs, had reported to the president that "Phoumi is stuck. In the twenty-one days estimated by our people as required to take the Plaine des Jarres, he has made four to seven kilometers . . . . In addition, the good General has been politicking rather than using his forces to increase our bargaining position in the negotiations ahead." A week later, Rostow saw the situation as close to hopeless. He told the president, "As we have feared, the Communists launched a probing offensive against Phoumi's men. Without much fight our boys fell back, apparently beyond the crucial crossroads."[27]

The same day, 7 March, Rostow's aide Kenneth P. Landon asserted that a decision had to be made immediately. "On the premise that the Soviets regard Laos as a revolving door to Burma, Thailand, Cambodia, and VietNam," he urged the use of forces from other SEATO nations, rushing the necessary weapons into Laos through a massive open airlift, sending Diem's forces in South Vietnam on guerrilla raids into North Vietnam, and making known to the world U.S. readiness to move with its own forces against the communists in Laos.[28]

ISA chimed in with the NSC staff in sounding the alarm. Rather than avoiding escalation, the United States had better risk it. Fears of escalation that tended to paralyze Western response to communist aggression in Laos validated the Chinese Communist argument for stepping up pressure against the West in vulnerable places in Asia and other parts of the world. Should SEATO and the United States now back down from support of Phoumi, the Chinese would have won their argument with the Soviets, namely, that aggression carried no risk of escalation by the other side. For the United States to inform the communists that it had no intention of backing down would impose greater restraint on their actions in Southeast Asia and elsewhere.[29]

In the meantime, on 3 March the president directed General Lemnitzer to prepare a plan for recapturing the Plaine des Jarres, the open grassy plateau in central Laos that occupied a key strategic position, and on 9 March the president and his top advisers considered it. McNamara presented the JCS plan, under the code name of Millpond; more properly a concept, it had 17 preparatory steps leading to recapture of the Plaine starting about 1 April. The JCS envisioned the plan as supporting the CIA and what was primarily a Royal Laotian Army effort.

The only direct DoD involvement called for delivery of supplies to Vientiane in an emergency, placement of a Marine Corps squadron in Thailand to provide helicopter maintenance, and augmentation of the PEO in Laos and the Joint U.S. Military Assistance Advisory Group (JUSMAAG) in Thailand. No consensus for outright military intervention emerged although the president approved the 17 actions proposed by the Joint Chiefs.[30]

There was still no consensus on a hard line. At a meeting of Defense, CIA, and United States Information Agency officials with the secretary of state on 12 March, Rusk spoke of the gravity of the situation. He listed several actions that the United States might take, ranging from a warning to military intervention. More aggressive than either State or JCS, OSD wanted U.S. aircraft to deliver essential military assistance materiel directly to Laos rather than through Thailand. McNamara also wanted to use the T-6 aircraft already in Laos in the possession of Phoumi to bomb military targets. He was convinced that simple propeller aircraft would best serve the fledgling Royal Lao Air Force. The Joint Chiefs equivocated. Lemnitzer felt that T-6s should be employed only after a decision to use the B-26s as well. But he warned that air operations alone would not suffice; to prevail, adequate ground forces would be required. Memories of Korea remained strong.[31]

More meetings with the president on 20 and 21 March brought no decision on action. At the White House meeting on 21 March Rusk spoke of a "two-stringed" approach—negotiation and action. The "two-stringed" approach offered nothing new. If it was not functioning in February, it certainly would not work in an even more precarious military situation in March. It seemed that only Millpond, the program of activities approved by the president on 9 March, offered hope, and the United States could "go on from there." The distance between the long-term covert activities of Millpond and the short-term position of Phoumi's force on the edge of disaster appeared formidable. The only clear decision that won approval was to inform congressional leaders and have the president speak out to the American people—and to the communist world as well—with a warning over the crisis in Laos.[32]

At a televised news conference on 23 March 1961, using three large maps of Laos as a backdrop, Kennedy pointed to areas under communist domination in August 1960 and December, and then to the dramatic Pathet Lao expansion of the next three months. Blaming the North Vietnamese and the large-scale Soviet airlift to the Pathet Lao, he asserted that "if these attacks do not stop, those who support a truly neutral Laos will have to consider their response." While the nation would avoid blundering into a military solution, Kennedy stated that "every American will want his country to honor its obligations to the point that freedom and security of the free world and ourselves may be achieved."[33] The president's language implied that if the communists did not halt their advances they would face massive U.S. intervention. But Kennedy was only bluffing, according to McGeorge Bundy, who said he did not "remember any time when there was a decision to engage in military intervention in Laos—discounting what the undercover boys did." The administration assumed that only through strong language could it achieve its real objectives—cease-fire and a neutral coalition government. Nevertheless, the key to the Kennedy statement lay in the call for "constructive negotiation." By no coincidence, on the same day the British proposed to the Soviets an immediate cease-fire, verification of the effectiveness of the cease-fire by the International Control Commission (ICC),* and reconvening the Geneva Conference after the cease-fire took hold. Moreover, the matter of a neutral Laotian government of national unity would have to be settled as soon as possible.[34]

The administration split between optimists and pessimists over the Soviet role in ending the crisis. Optimists seized on the combination of the president's message and the British bilateral talks with the Soviets to anticipate early action. Even before 23 March the British had discerned signs of Soviet moderation and had evinced interest in asking Prime Minister Jawaharlal Nehru to reconvene the ICC in New Delhi. Llewellyn Thompson from Moscow voiced his belief that the Soviet Union would not take excessive risks in Laos but had adopted an aggressive posture to balance Chinese influence in Southeast Asia. A positive spirit pervaded a meeting between Kennedy and Harold Macmillan at Key West, Florida, on 26 March, although the British prime minister could not offer blanket endorsement for anything but a limited SEATO action in the event hopes for a negotiated settlement collapsed. McNamara was with the pessimists who were skeptical about prospects of Soviet support.[35]

An informed ISA official regarded as "curious" any suggestion that the Soviet Union was experiencing pressure to come up with a prompt settlement in Laos. He found the idea suspect if only because the notion of the Soviets being boxed in came from the Polish ambassador in New Delhi. Interest in negotiations might be just a way of Soviet foot-dragging in conference meetings, recognizing they had nothing to fear from U.S. military intervention as long as talks continued. It seemed that if any party became boxed in by negotiations, it would be the United States. The only alternative seemed a clear determination to use force unless the Soviets met U.S. terms for negotiation.[36]

Initially, the skeptics seemed to have it right. British skittishness about a SEATO role signaled the absence of a concerted SEATO position. At Bangkok the member nations, meeting on 27-29 March, approved talking, not fighting. On 1 April the Soviets resolved SEATO's dilemma by accepting the U.S.-British proposal for a revived Geneva conference.[37] It led to hopes that the Soviets would put their weight behind a meaningful cease-fire.

---

* The group created by the 1954 Geneva Conference to monitor the armistice.

New optimism was sparked by the appointment of the distinguished diplomat, 69-year-old Averell Harriman, as Kennedy's roving ambassador. Harriman had met Souvanna Phouma in India on 21 March and came away impressed with his sincerity and personality. He recommended U.S. support for a government built around Souvanna's leadership, with the Pathet Lao occupying minor roles if necessary. Consequently, Souvanna was invited to Washington on 20 April for a meeting that never took place; Rusk, claiming a previous engagement in Georgia, offended the sensitive prince by his absence from Washington. More likely, the Bay of Pigs crisis on that date would have prevented a meeting even had Rusk been in town.[38]

Although the skeptics at ISA came around at last to considering the possibility of working with Souvanna, they were annoyed by the communist insistence that he was the only legitimate leader, as opposed to the "illegitimate" Boun Oum government. They recognized that Souvanna might provide the key to a solution. As Col. Thomas Wolfe, head of ISA's Sino-Soviet desk, observed: "I don't know whether he can be bought, cajoled or otherwise persuaded to disown the shadow government, but this would certainly seem to be worth working on."[39]

Divisions within DoD

Soviet acceptance on 1 April 1961 of the British proposal for an international conference diverted attention from Souvanna and the nature of the coalition government that might emerge from negotiations. Instead, it focused on the first steps—a cease-fire and means of enforcement. As it became urgent to speed the delivery of U.S. arms and equipment to Phoumi's forces, ISA asked CINCPAC to fill critical shortages as quickly as possible.[40]

Much needed doing before an enforceable cease-fire could take place. Two Canadian officers who had served with the ICC in 1955 and 1956 pointed out to ISA that the requirement of unanimity in the decisionmaking process would make prompt ICC action improbable even if the agency could discover incidents of violation, not likely given the state of transportation and communications within Laos. Moreover, the Hmong, the one Western-backed force serious about fighting, would have become as difficult to police as the Pathet Lao; if they cooperated in disarming themselves, they would need protection against the less compliant Pathet Lao. There was a need, according to the Canadians, for an ICC organizational change that might get information to teams in the field, permitting them to act expeditiously without having to go back to Vientiane for further instructions.[41]

In a report to McNamara on 11 April the JCS agreed with these reasons for the past ineffectiveness of the ICC and objected particularly to the requirement that field inspection teams receive permission from the two warring parties before moving into the area. The JCS paid special attention to the unanimity provision, which they saw as a recipe for paralysis. With the communists represented by Poland, the West by Canada, and the neutralists by India, the latter "reluctant to offend either side," the commission could not operate capably. General Lemnitzer doubted that serious improvements could come about or that the ICC could eliminate covert communist assistance to the Pathet Lao. In this context, the return of the ICC would be contrary to U.S. interests. U.S. efforts to stockpile supplies for the Laotian government forces could be curtailed by the ICC "without slowing up the flow of Bloc assistance to the Pathet Lao." Lemnitzer wanted the United States to insist that the commission limit its functions initially to confirmation of a cease-fire before assuming any other duties. The Joint Chiefs also strongly opposed an informal State Department suggestion to add two more neutralist nations, such as Burma and Cambodia, to the commission.[42]

The defense secretary had received similar advice from his ISA staff. If verification of a cease-fire, a critical issue, could not be satisfactorily arranged, Nitze recommended that the United Kingdom as co-chair of the Geneva Conference demand that the ICC for Vietnam inspect the Hanoi airfield and the main access routes on the North Vietnamese side of the Laotian border. The only drawback to this plan was the likelihood that the Soviets would demand a similar wide-sweeping ICC investigation in Laos "*before* the United States could complete a supply build-up in support of the present RLG." If the Soviets should turn down the proposal, at least aid to Phoumi would continue.[43]

But the Nitze memorandum did not say what good this aid would do if Phoumi's forces could not hold on, no matter the level of aid. Evidence of disaster abounded in April. Phoumi's offensive on 5 April, designed to retake highways critical to the control of the Plaine des Jarres, collapsed within a week as the Pathet Lao strengthened their positions both north and south of the main highway junction.

So discouraging appeared Phoumi's position that the task force on Laos on 10 April had discussed the possibility of a "Lebanon-type" operation, even though U.S. troops flown into a landlocked country could hardly be equated with Americans on the beaches of Beirut in 1958.[44] The task force and the Pentagon were swayed by a report of Lt. Gen. Thomas J. Trapnell, whom McNamara and Lemnitzer had sent to Laos in mid-March to assess the U.S. plan for recapturing the Plaine des Jarres and to judge how well Phoumi had reassigned his commanders. Trapnell reported panic in the government, with little chance for survival, let alone recovery of the Plaine des Jarres at this time. He recommended bombing the Pathet Lao on the Plaine, providing Phoumi with armed helicopters, and raising nine additional battalions. Trapnell also proposed converting the PEO into a full-scale military assistance advisory group (MAAG) and assigning uniformed U.S. officers down to the battalion level.[45]

The administration, believing it had no alternative but to continue providing aid until a cease-fire occurred, accepted some of Trapnell's proposals. At a White

House meeting on 13 April, DoD requested an increase of seven battalions and more than 2,600 replacement and service troops for the Laotian army at additional costs of $330,000 per month in Defense support funds and $1.8 million in MAP monies for their initial equipment.[46] On 19 April, coincident with the Cuban Bay of Pigs debacle, the administration converted the PEO into a MAAG and accepted the creation of seven new battalions. But this flurry of activity did not respond to a more crucial question, the matter of U.S. military intervention, either unilaterally or under a SEATO umbrella.[47]

Pathet Lao columns continued to make advances in northern Laos with minimal resistance from government forces and to consolidate their political control wherever they went. These events accelerated and led to numerous meetings in Washington that produced no firm decisions.[48]

While Kennedy recognized that the communists were stalling on implementing a cease-fire they had agreed to on 17 April and were exploiting the projected conference in Geneva to complete the conquest of Laos, he also had to confront the emergency posed by the Bay of Pigs crisis. If the debacle in Cuba did nothing else, it diminished the credibility of the JCS and the CIA, at least for a time. The president reconsidered the JCS judgments on Laos and found their answers as ambiguous as they had been over the chance of success for the Cuban brigade at the Bay of Pigs. The Joint Chiefs had suggested the unlikelihood of Soviet intervention in Laos, but they were not sure; they spoke of supplying U.S. combat forces by air, but there were only two usable landing strips in all of Laos. According to Sorensen, Kennedy exclaimed several months later: "Thank God the Bay of Pigs happened when it did. Otherwise we'd be in Laos by now—and that would be a hundred times worse." Earlier, Robert Kennedy noted that "if it hadn't been for Cuba, we would have sent troops to Laos." He went on to say those troops probably would have been destroyed, forcing an escalation that might have led to a nuclear war with China and the Soviet Union.[49]

The president made his remark in September 1961, the attorney general in June. Actually, at the end of April and in early May the United States appeared ready to intervene unilaterally. When someone as influential as Harriman, then in Laos with General Lemnitzer, could cable Washington for the deployment of a division-size U.S. force to Thailand, it showed the depth of the crisis.[50] Harriman saw the military situation as out of control. He thought that the Pathet Lao, supported by professionally trained North Vietnamese cadres, could take over the entire country unless the United States or SEATO intervened or a credible cease-fire was arranged. Accepting this urgency, the president on 26 April approved movement of naval forces into the South China Sea and the Gulf of Siam and also approved alerting forces earmarked for movement into Laos under SEATO plans.[51]

More might have been done short of inserting troops. If U.S. troops were not to go into the country, at least the administration might have authorized the use of B-26s to bomb Pathet Lao and North Vietnamese positions. The president's fear of escalation, reinforced by the ultimate hesitations of his military advisers, no doubt contributed to erring on the side of restraint.

In March the JCS had spoken of dispatching a 60,000-man force, claiming that it could match whatever the enemy, including the Chinese and North Vietnamese, might bring to bear. But if no large-scale intervention seemed feasible, they advised staying out. At a critical meeting on 29 April, the military leaders deemed the Laotian situation desperate, but they could not come up with a single coherent solution. Rather, they engaged in the same temporizing that characterized their advice on the Bay of Pigs earlier in the month. When pressed by Robert Kennedy, McNamara expressed his opinion that "we would take a stand in Thailand and South Vietnam," perhaps pointedly omitting Laos. General LeMay observed that airpower could stop the Pathet Lao but still not win the countryside. Army Chief of Staff Decker believed that the United States must hold on to as much of the three Indochinese countries as possible but confessed that he saw no good place to fight in Southeast Asia. Admiral Burke "thought it possible to go in." McNamara continued to manifest his fear of intervention when he made the point that the enemy could easily deny use of airfields needed to move U.S. troops into Vientiane.[52]

The NSC meeting on 1 May reflected conflicting advice from other parts of the administration also and from senior advisers. McNamara proposed using SEATO forces to move into the Laos panhandle, the long narrow southern extremity of the country, "recognizing that if we do we must be prepared to win." He spoke of the possible need to use nuclear weapons to win a war in Southeast Asia. General Taylor opposed the use of U.S. troops in Laos; CIA Director Allen Dulles cautioned about a Chinese response if the United States entered the Laos panhandle. As a result, the NSC continued a holding action and agreed that a final decision should await "further developments in the cease fire negotiations" and a JCS presentation of the military implications of possible actions.[53]

As requested by the NSC, McNamara and Gilpatric provided the president on 2 May with DoD's position on "Alternative Courses of Action in Laos." Attached were memoranda expressing the views of the individual chiefs and two of the service secretaries. One alternative would accept the loss of Laos and compensate for it by introducing U.S. and SEATO forces into Thailand and South Vietnam. After describing Laos as "one of the least favorable places in the world for direct U.S. military intervention," and "weighing the pros and cons," McNamara and Gilpatric favored intervention—the only instance over a period of two years where McNamara departed from his usual hesitation on the subject. They preferred to set a 48-hour deadline for a satisfactory cease-fire in Laos at the existing battle line. If the deadline passed without a satisfactory response, the United States should then move its forces to protect vital centers in Laos and hold them until obtaining a cease-fire. Admittedly, McNamara and Gilpatric observed, should the Chinese and North Vietnamese attack, "at some point, we may have to initiate the use of nuclear weapons in order to prevent the defeat of our forces." Still, they did not believe that the Soviet Union would allow the situation to get to that brink.

Disagreements once again expressed by the Joint Chiefs, and also by the service secretaries, undermined this conclusion. While Lemnitzer agreed with McNamara, Admiral Burke advised deploying troops to Thailand and South Vietnam immediately and into Laos within 48 hours. Air Force Chief of Staff General White called any intervention by ground forces "maldeployment," and recommended the use of U.S. airpower against military concentrations in Laos and against North Vietnam and China if necessary.[54]

At this juncture, Harriman's influential voice lent weight to McNamara's judgment. From Saigon, Harriman gave his imprimatur to Lemnitzer's doubts about the credibility of any cease-fire without direct intervention by SEATO forces to secure the territory in Laos still held by Phoumi's forces. When he learned on 3 May that a cease-fire agreement had occurred in one sector, Harriman warned against the enemy stringing SEATO along with partial cease-fires that would permit the Pathet Lao to consolidate their gains. Such compliance would make the military situation all the more difficult if negotiations broke down.[55]

Despite the combined judgment of Harriman, McNamara, and Lemnitzer, the president remained skeptical of a military solution. The recent Bay of Pigs failure haunted him. Not even Harriman's prestige could turn away doubts raised by the differences among the Joint Chiefs. And the apparent willingness of Lemnitzer and McNamara to entertain the apocalypse that would result from ultimate escalation to nuclear weapons Kennedy could not accept.[56]

Geneva: May-June 1961

The sudden acquiescence by the parties to both a cease-fire and a 14-nation conference in Geneva to implement it relieved the administration for the time being of further agonizing over intervention. The chairs of the conference, the Soviet Union and the United Kingdom, had issued a formal call on 24 April for a meeting, based on a cease-fire in place prior to the event. With the first session scheduled for 12 May, the ICC delay in confirming the reality of a cease-fire and which Laotians should attend caused postponement of the opening until 16 May. By accepting the invitation to stop the fighting on 3 May, the Pathet Lao and their allies resolved the Kennedy administration's doubts over what action to take. Rusk immediately told the U.S. ambassador to advise the Laotian government "to cooperate without raising complicating issues on picayune details."[57]

Why the Pathet Lao agreed to go to the peace table remains obscure. Conceivably, had they continued to stall they might have overthrown Phoumi and taken over the entire country; time seemed on their side. Possibly they feared that the

United States would make good its threat to intervene. By entering into negotiations, the communists could proceed with their conquest of Laos without immediate worry over U.S. military reaction. Possibly, a Soviet decision against excessive involvement also played a large role. Or perhaps the North Vietnamese, in control of the Ho Chi Minh Trail, had no need to press their allies to take over all of Laos.

The U.S. reaction to reconvening the Geneva Conference on the basis of a shaky cease-fire is less obscure. Although suspicions about North Vietnamese good faith in particular remained high, the very act of negotiation appeared to offer some prospect for peace without excessive loss of face or even of strategic positions. The alternative was the loss of Laotian sovereignty to outside communist elements. The negotiations also rested on the assumption, as Deputy Secretary Gilpatric later observed, that the Laotian situation was negotiable, while that of Vietnam was not: "In the case of Laos, you did not have Ho Chi Minh and General Giap, who were determined to take over South Vietnam." Even though both the Soviet Union and the People's Republic of China were involved, Laos remained a localized conflict compared with what Vietnam turned out to be.[58]

DoD planners remained unhappy with the reasoning behind the reconvening of the conference at Geneva. They sympathized with the Thais, who, despairing of any SEATO support, wanted a bilateral defense pact with the United States. Also distressed, Diem in South Vietnam felt that any change that legitimized Pathet Lao and North Vietnamese control in Laos would threaten his nation's survival.[59]

Before departing for Geneva, Nitze, who headed the Defense Department component of the U.S. delegation, made an effort in a memorandum of 9 May to strengthen Harriman's position opposing a "tripartite" Laotian representation at the conference that would separate Souvanna from the Pathet Lao. He wanted those two factions considered as a single entity since Souvanna, in Defense eyes, was as much a spokesman of the Pathet Lao as was his half-brother. If Souvanna's "neutralists" got separate status it would give an automatic 2-to-1 advantage to the communists. Nitze also believed that the U.S. delegation should hold out against complete neutralization or demilitarization of Laos, since any such action would play into the hands of the enemy.[60]

The substance of this message reflected the more aggressive stance of the DoD members of the U.S. delegation to the conference. As expressed by ISA's George Carroll, "we did not think that it was possible to find a purely political solution to Laos, in the sense that we felt that the Communists would not give one inch except in the face of force." At some point in the conference, they believed, the United States would have to make clear that it preferred military action to a communist-dominated Laos.[61]

While this summation did not conflict with the substance of the State Department's scope paper outlining the U.S. approach to the 14-nation conference, the spirit came through as distinctly different. DoD's tone sounded as bellicose as its message. Unlike the generalities of the State views, it identified specific points where military action had to come into play. Any sign of weakness over seating Pathet Lao representatives, over convening in the absence of a genuine cease-fire, or over inadequate powers invested in the reconstituted ICC should trigger an American walkout from the conference. The "proper order of business of the Conference" ought to be, in sequence, a cease-fire, seating of the Laotian parties, empowerment of the ICC, and formation of a coalition government. But, according to Carroll, no such arrangement would occur "without the threat of application of force."[62]

The DoD representatives took some satisfaction in forcing on State a recognition that the communists had no intention of abiding by the terms of the Geneva Accords. This gave little consolation, however, since the U.S. position did not contain a threat of unilateral military action. "The fact that we did not have a firm decision to act," Carroll claimed, "also meant that we would have to watch the faces of the Thai's [sic], the RLG, and the South Vietnamese as they saw us back down from one position to the other. Had we been able to tell Thailand and South Vietnam our intentions to accept defeat in Laos prior to their arrival in Geneva, we would have been on much firmer ground in dealing with them at the Conference."[63]

Whether or not explicit threats of military retaliation would have worked is speculative and doubtful; the existing military situation gave all the advantages to the communists and they made the most of them. On such vital issues as Laotian representation in Geneva, the powers of the ICC, or the credibility of the cease-fire, the Americans repeatedly gave way.

The latter two questions posed immediate interconnected problems. To be meaningful a cease-fire required verification, with appropriate powers vested in the reconstituted ICC, which had no means of inspection. Consequently, the certification of a cease-fire by the Pathet Lao and the North Vietnamese was no more than "wishful thinking." By accepting such certification as valid, Secretary Rusk compromised the U.S. position.[64]

Rusk's opening assertion in Geneva that the United States would continue negotiations only as long as the cease-fire remained in effect lacked credibility. The Pathet Lao continued to attack Meo tribesmen without concern about violations; the ICC had no presence at the scene. Moreover, at the same time, the U.S.-recognized government of Boun Oum initiated negotiations with the neutralists and communists in Laos against the advice of DoD representatives. It refused to take one of the three proposed Laotian chairs at Geneva and be outnumbered by Souvanna and his half-brother. To make matters worse, the Indian chairman of the ICC seemed more interested in giving priority to the issue of a functioning coalition government than to a verified cease-fire.[65]

The West won only cosmetic victories, such as postponing the opening day of the conference to 16 May because the matter of representation remained unsettled. To avoid the seating issue, the British and Soviets proposed to seat as an observer any Laotian group that a conference member requested. Although the United States was prepared to accept the RLG as the only legal government, it agreed to seat other Laotian factions on the understanding that their presence did not confer official recognition. Somewhat lamely, the U.S. delegation explained that it had "no support among delegations in Geneva, with exception of RLG, to hold out on what non-Communist delegations consider to be a trivial point of procedure."[66]

Self-delusion served as a prescription for failure. Some glimmers of hope emerged in the course of the conference, even in the view of a DoD representative, but they came not from a change of fortunes on the battlefield but from Harriman's tactics as head of the U.S. delegation after Rusk's departure on 20 May and from apparent Soviet disinterest in the future of Laos. Harriman was a more influential figure than Rusk in Geneva; the secretary was there only for a few days. The impending summit meeting of Kennedy and Khrushchev in Vienna in early June would offer an opportunity for the president to test the sincerity of Khrushchev's professed wish for a genuinely neutral Laos. Harriman urged the president to make clear to Khrushchev just what "neutrality" meant: first and foremost, the alignment of Laos with neither side and military withdrawal on both sides, including the North Vietnamese and Chinese Communists.[67]

While the two leaders met in Vienna on 3-4 June, a stalemate continued in Geneva. A proposal by the French to implement their military role in Laos, as provided for under the 1954 accords, met with Chinese objections and a consequent temporary adjournment of the conference. The delay provided some breathing space for the West, as members of the conference waited for results of the Kennedy-Khrushchev meeting. The wait seemed worthwhile when the conferees agreed on removal of Laos from the Cold War rivalry under a genuine neutralization of the country. Khrushchev agreed with Kennedy's comment that "Laos is not so important as to get us as involved as we are" and went on to say that "the Soviet Union has no commitment in Laos, has never undertaken any obligations in that area, and will not do so in the future."[68]

But the respite was short-lived. When the conference resumed on 6 June, it did so in the shadow of the fall of Padong in the Meo highlands to the communists, making an obvious mockery of the cease-fire. Both the United States and the United Kingdom decided to boycott the conference. Years later Nitze recalled that Kennedy became so angry at Khrushchev's apparent repudiation of their agreement for a cease-fire and neutralization that he leaned toward DoD's proposal for military action but finally decided in favor of further discussion with the Russians. The Defense Department thereafter publicly described Padong's fall as "a minor engagement which had resulted in few losses to either side, and that the Meo had simply removed to nearby positions"; in no sense was this battle to be a second Dien Bien Phu. Harriman appreciated this press approach and labeled it a strong propaganda victory since even the neutralists vigorously condemned the communists for breaking the cease-fire. A few days later, on 12 June, the U.S. and British delegates returned to the conference table.[69]

Some comfort attended this public relations victory. Even greater satisfaction followed when the three princes—Boun Oum, Souvanna, and Souphanouvong—agreed to meet on 19 June in Zurich. Within four days they had patched together an agreement for the beginnings of a coalition government that promised the establishment of a neutral Laos outside the protection of any military alliance, notably SEATO.[70] But how would the coalition government function, since the balance of power in Laos had not changed? Would not the Pathet Lao, in conjunction with the Souvanna-led neutralists, remove the Boun Oum faction at the earliest opportunity?

The Phoumi Burden, 1961-1962

With this concern in mind, talks had begun between Defense and State and between British and U.S. military leaders about a possible SEATO initiative. Just days before the three princes agreed to form a new government, CINCPAC and his British counterpart discussed the dispatch of SEATO forces into Laos to secure key points along the Mekong River, thus freeing Phoumi's forces to attempt to regain areas lost since early May. CINCPAC proposed rules of engagement to the British for a force of approximately 13,200 troops that would take counterguerrilla action as necessary to protect lines of communication and, barring broad-scale Chinese or North Vietnamese intervention, could resist attacks.[71]

Despite the bold plans for action, conversations in Honolulu, Washington, and London had little result. While the military discussed their plans in Honolulu, they realized that such plans would seriously disturb those SEATO members not participating in the conversations. Phoumi, by contrast, confronted a more realistic situation—the strong sense of superiority displayed by Souphanouvong at the meeting of the princes and how closely he seemed to work with Souvanna. For this Phoumi blamed the ambiguities and uncertainties in the U.S. position and asserted that without strong U.S. pressure a communist takeover would ensue; Souvanna's power he considered fictional, resting wholly on his half-brother's Pathet Lao forces. Phoumi wanted a guarantee of U.S. military involvement if negotiations broke down.[72]

From Vientiane, Ambassador Winthrop G. Brown recommended on 28 June against meeting Phoumi's demands. Whatever the risks of going along with Souvanna, the risks of backing a failed Phoumi were considerably higher. Phoumi's belief that he could establish a military equilibrium without introducing foreign forces had little credibility. Brown believed that intervention would require preparing the nation "to fight at least a Korean type and perhaps a larger war."[73]

One DoD representative in Geneva, however, George Carroll, supported Phoumi's argument. He agreed that "almost the entire grocery store was given away" at Zurich. The communists used the deliberations of the three princes as an opening wedge to fashion a communist-dominated coalition government. Without a U.S. guarantee of the sort Phoumi wanted, the royal government had to give in and accept the three-chair concept in Geneva. Boun Oum was then only one of three equal claimants for legitimacy.[74]

Phoumi took his case on 29 June to Washington, where he met separately with the JCS, McNamara, Rusk, and the president. They encouraged him to believe that even without military intervention the United States remained a firm bulwark of the legitimate royal government. Meanwhile, on 26 June in Paris, Harriman sought to impress on Souvanna the importance of having a strong ICC in place to uphold the integrity of the cease-fire. With this change, the United States could then provide ample economic assistance as an inducement to form an effective coalition government. The ambassador-at-large pursued a two-track diplomacy designed to push Phoumi into a reformed and genuinely neutralist Laos under Souvanna's leadership.[75]

Nitze at ISA also favored this approach. After listening to Phoumi's expectations of military successes by the end of July, Nitze still doubted his ability to produce any satisfactory results. He advised McNamara to pursue a coalition government that might have a reasonable prospect of maintaining its independence. A reformed Souvanna was the key. Nitze also made clear that firmness in support of Laos should not be linked to direct U.S. military intervention.[76]

There was some inconsistency in the U.S. approach to both Phoumi and Souvanna, but the former posed the immediate problem. Phoumi had managed to manipulate the U.S. military in the past and may have believed that he could do so again. Although he received equivocating responses to questions about U.S. military support, Phoumi no doubt left Washington hopeful that he had been successful in winning such support.[77]

In the summer of 1961 military support seemed to consist of reviving SEATO plans for major counterinsurgency activity for defense of the Mekong River cities and particularly for increased military assistance for the Meo (Hmong) tribesmen, willing and committed members of the self-defense corps of the Laotian army. The Hmong would receive "arms, ammunition, and other support" for 7,700 tribesmen, enabling them to play a larger role in the conflict.[78] With all this activity, however, the one element that could have turned the tide in Laos never was approved: the direct deployment of SEATO and U.S. troops. Everything else was peripheral or marginal.

In one of his many memoranda to the president during this period, Rostow on 26 June saw a trap of Soviet devising. In Laos, as in other parts of the world,

Khrushchev had worked out a strategy that followed a regular pattern: "He exerts pressure at some point on our side of the line; by such pressure he creates a situation in which we can only reply at the risk of starting a nuclear war or escalating in that direction; faced with this prospect, we look for compromise; he backs down a little; and a compromise is struck which, on balance, moves his line forward, and shifts us back."[79]

Defense officials subscribed to much of Rostow's thesis. If Soviet activities were not quite as sinister as he perceived, they at least played a significant part in the destabilization of Laos. In his lengthy analysis of U.S. policy on Laos, ISA's Carroll blamed the U.S. plight on the lack of continuity in policy, lack of a clear-cut goal, and inadequate intelligence information. By the time the Kennedy administration recognized the paramount importance of military aid, it came too little and too late compared with the magnitude of help given to the Pathet Lao by the communists. In brief, Carroll attributed much of the failure of U.S. strategy and tactics to idealistic and unrealistic attitudes of the State Department elite. He had a sense that the administration could not make up its mind whether or not Laos was vital to the defense of Thailand and South Vietnam and consequently could not make up its mind about the kind of force needed to save that part of Laos crucial to the defense of the region.[80]

The desultory negotiations for a viable coalition government did little to change DoD judgments. Communist cease-fire violations did not slacken. Supplies poured into South Vietnam via Laos along the Ho Chi Minh Trail. North Vietnam, bolstered as before by Soviet equipment, infiltrated its own troops into and through Laos. In June 1961 McNamara informed the Senate Foreign Relations Committee in executive session that he had evidence that 2,860 North Vietnamese armed agents had infiltrated into South Vietnam by way of Laos over the previous four months and that some 12,000 were active in South Vietnam.[81]

Despite these and other signs of a deteriorating situation the official U.S. policy remained the same: rely heavily on diplomatic moves and rally behind Souvanna on the assumption that he could establish a neutralist government. In July and August numerous tripartite (American, British, and French) meetings considered how best to obtain a genuine cease-fire, a viable ICC, a truly neutral Laotian government, and finally, Soviet agreement so that the Geneva Conference could proceed with some degree of confidence and progress.

At the State Department's behest, George F. Kennan, the U.S. ambassador to Yugoslavia, succeeded early in September in opening a special channel of communication between Kennedy and Khrushchev on Berlin and Laos through the Soviet ambassador in Belgrade. Kennan reported that "the Soviets expected the channel to be . . . a strictly bilateral communication involving no obligation of consultation or information with either side's allies." In response Rusk pressed for an agreement on the removal of all foreign forces from Laos, and he subsequently received from Kennan word that the Soviet ambassador understood that the Soviet Union considered "Chinese and Viet Minh armed personnel as foreign troops to be removed."[82]

Earlier, on 10 August, JCS chairman Lemnitzer briefed Kennedy and top advisers, including Secretary McNamara and General Taylor, on three different plans under consideration. Two of these involved the use of SEATO forces in Laos. A third plan, still being formulated, had the objective of driving the opposition out of southern Laos by employing the combined armies of Thailand, South Vietnam, and Laos, supported by U.S. forces. This plan enjoyed favor since it was believed impossible to save South Vietnam without first securing southern Laos.[83]

Still other proposals received attention at the top. The "Johnson Plan," after Deputy Under Secretary of State U. Alexis Johnson, called for two parallel courses of action: first, a diplomatic attempt to move Geneva negotiations forward to a successful conclusion, and second, military preparations should these negotiations fail. The diplomatic effort would press for a Souvanna neutralist government. Military preparations would include bilateral contacts with SEATO members, an increase of American and Thai military advisers with the Royal Laotian Army, aerial reconnaissance of northern Laos, phased introduction of indigenous troops initially, and then SEATO troops, as required, in support of SEATO Plan 5.[84]

On 29 August the Johnson Plan underwent scrutiny at the White House by Kennedy and high-level officials. The president endorsed continued pressure for a diplomatic settlement with the objective of establishing a neutralist government. McNamara again voiced concern about the requirements of crises in both Laos and Berlin, proposing that "we should make no commitments to undertake military action until we had reviewed the situation in Laos in the light of world problems at the time, especially the situation with respect to Berlin. We would not want to tie down substantial forces in Laos if these forces were required to deal with the Berlin situation."

Kennedy approved the military proposals in part, i.e., continued contingency planning for intervention but no commitment for implementation; increasing American military advisers with the Laotian army to a total of 500, with the Thai army supplying a similar number; outfitting and supporting another 2,000 Hmong guerrillas, bringing that force to a level of 11,000; and conducting aerial photo reconnaissance over Pathet Lao territory twice a week with Thai or "sanitized" aircraft.[85]

The Joint Chiefs, obviously frustrated and discouraged with the president's latest decision to continue down the diplomatic path, vented their dissatisfaction to McNamara on 7 September, asserting that preoccupation with Berlin was diverting attention from Southeast Asia, just as the response to the Berlin Blockade in 1948-49 had led to the loss of China to the communists. In their view, matters in Laos had become so bad that the United States "must take immediate and positive action to prevent a complete communist takeover of Laos and the ultimate loss of all Southeast Asia to include Indonesia." Unless diplomatic progress was immediately forthcoming, before the end of the rainy season (late September or early October) and the resumption of full-scale combat, a communist victory might well happen unless SEATO forces intervened.[86] McNamara did not respond to the Joint Chiefs, perhaps because he recognized that the president's strong preference for the diplomatic approach and his reluctance to intervene militarily reflected the painful lesson of the Cuban debacle five months earlier.[87]

Continuing to plan and push for expanded military preparation should open resumption of hostilities occur, on 29 September the JCS forwarded to McNamara a proposal to restore virtually all of Laos to royal rule. This would require the use of SEATO troops in large numbers initially, and in far greater numbers if North Vietnamese forces intervened and if they invaded South Vietnam also. Should hostilities expand to include a Chinese-North Vietnamese invasion of Laos, the SEATO forces would need 15 divisions and some 278,000 men—of which 4 would be U.S. divisions, 2 from the continental reserve.[88]

Deputy Secretary Gilpatric, speaking for McNamara, replied to this latest plan on 3 October, noting his concerns over the possibility of a crisis in Laos and Berlin at the same time, the effects elsewhere of assembling an air force for Southeast Asia and on U.S. nuclear strike capabilities, and the effect of the deployment of the Seventh Fleet to Southeast Asia on the rest of the Pacific area. And he questioned the viability of any military intervention in this area that involved the use of forces from the continental reserve. Gilpatric concluded his evaluation by stating that "the President's decision on the proposed plan may well hinge on the risks of getting into a serious two-front situation." In reply, the Joint Chiefs observed that only intervention could stem the worsening situation and the subsequent loss of Laos, Vietnam, and the rest of Southeast Asia. Intervention might require mobilizing additional forces and confronting two limited wars, but "we may be faced with such a contingency" anyway.[89]

The administration continued to look toward a diplomatic solution. It found encouragement in the agreement among the three princes on 8 October to have Souvanna as sole candidate for premier and in his willingness to try to form a government of national unity. To further his efforts the United States, Britain, France, and Australia agreed on a general plan for regroupment, integration, and eventual demobilization of the Lao armed forces, with the expectation of creating a new national army no longer based on group affiliation.[90]

Both ISA and the JCS recognized that depending on Souvanna risked not only his being a tool of the communists, it undermined the already precarious defense of the rest of Southeast Asia. In this circumstance, Phoumi remained the only alternative to total disaster. "He is the only driving force in Laos," observed Brig. Gen. William H. Craig of the Joint Staff after an extensive visit to Southeast Asia in August-September, but to make him function successfully "we must begin to get tough with him." Craig wanted to force him to release incompetent officers, whom Phoumi apparently preferred over competent leaders, and to revamp the training program. As a means of effecting change, Craig's team suggested the need of a MAAG-embassy team "of the sort that we had in Greece under Van Fleet and Peurifoy."*[91]

In the absence of such authority, OSD, at the request of the Joint Chiefs, on 19 October asked State and the Agency for International Development for an additional FY 1962 allocation of $4.5 million to fund an increase in Phoumi's regular forces from 38,487 to 46,921 and the irregular troops (auto-defense) from 13,800 to 15,400. Particular effort would go toward expanding training for officers and NCOs. As one ISA official observed, "Since 1954, we have attempted to meet the recurring crises in Laos by increasing the force basis from 15,000 at that time to 62,000 proposed by this action. It is obvious that we are not getting results."[92]

Ultimately, State and AID, which had the responsibility for financing the Laotian troops, rejected the money request on the grounds that Phoumi was misusing funds he already had. In a memorandum to William Bundy in November, U. Alexis Johnson accused Phoumi of integrating poorly trained irregular soldiers into the regular combat units and arbitrarily increasing his force level well beyond authorized strength. "Because of his past record of presenting us with *faits accomplis* and his present reluctance to consult with our military representative in Laos on the organization of the FAR [royal army], approval of your request would constitute . . . funding of these unilateral changes." ICA used much the same language in expressing to ISA annoyance at Phoumi for obligating funds for his own ends "in the full expectation that the U.S. will eventually pay the bill."[93]

Defense recognized the validity of these charges but still clung to Phoumi as the best hope for the survival of a non-communist kingdom. The MAAG chief, Brig. Gen. Andrew J. Boyle, asserted in late December 1961 that Phoumi, for all his faults, occupied a stronger position than he would have had negotiations for a new government been completed in May. He pointed out training improvements as well as the greater aggressiveness among unit commanders.[94] While many of his observations may have been wishful thinking, the one prediction he made came true: a future rift between the Pathet Lao and an ally, Kong Le.†

At this time, DoD seemed to stand alone in its support of Phoumi. Harriman, assistant secretary of state for Far Eastern affairs since 29 November, had reached the limits of his patience and called for punitive action to force the Laotian general to conform to U.S. policy. Phoumi stood in the way of his efforts to test Soviet

---

* Lt. Gen. James Van Fleet headed the American military mission in Greece in 1947–49. John E. Peurifoy was the assistant secretary of state for administration during the same years.
† Kong Le, a 28-year-old captain, led a bloodless coup that for a time seized control of Vientiane in August 1960. Thereafter, he led a faction that sided from time to time with the Pathet Lao or the Boun Oum government.

intentions; the fashioning of Souvanna's coalition government would mark success or failure. When Phoumi demanded two key seats in the Souvanna government as the price of his agreement and then proceeded, though ineffectually, to mount a new offensive against the Pathet Lao, Harriman acted. He recommended stopping the $4 million monthly cash payments to the Laotian government in December 1961. It was resumed the next month only when Boun Oum agreed on 10 January to meet with the other princes.[95]

Convinced that he still had Defense and CIA backing to carry him, much as in 1960, Phoumi's habit of going his own way had not changed. Against U.S. advice he reinforced Nam Tha, a small village 15 miles from the Chinese border, despite recognition that this action would provoke both the Pathet Lao and the Chinese. By moving 5,000 troops into the town before the end of January 1962, he evoked memories of Dien Bien Phu. When Boun Oum rejected further meetings with the other princes, Harriman acted again. This time he held back the money that Phoumi used to meet his troop payroll, effective February 1962.[96]

Phoumi's confidence about rallying his friends in Washington behind him was not misplaced. The Joint Chiefs pressed the MAAG chief to evaluate the effect of sanctions on Phoumi's fortunes and the CIA made a gloomy estimate of the consequences of halting financial and military aid to Laos. Operations could continue for only 45 days and, even worse, "the more opportunistic" of Phoumi's commanders, assuming the abandonment of Phoumi, might rush to an accommodation with the Pathet Lao. The president accepted this appraisal but reacted by authorizing the secretary of defense in April to plan the withdrawal of MAAG training teams located in forward field positions. Moreover, DoD and Phoumi had lost congressional friends, among them Sen. Allen J. Ellender (D-La.), who had returned from Laos in February with a damning report on the status of the country. Ellender judged that the Eisenhower administration had made a grievous mistake when it gave military aid to one faction in what Ellender considered a civil war. The losers had then brought in the North Vietnamese: "It was purely and simply a controversy among the Lao."[97]

Despite these setbacks, Phoumi's American friends did not fail him. Supplies and arms continued to flow into the country; the sanctions amounted to only a part of the aid package. Boun Oum was forced back into negotiations, but only in part because of Harriman's hard line. Phoumi himself remained the single most important cause of his own difficulty, and once more through his failure on the battlefield.

Ironically, the fall of Nam Tha on 6 May 1962 almost achieved Phoumi's objective of entangling U.S. troops in Laos. This latest failure made it impossible for the administration to overlook the Pathet Lao's open breach of the cease-fire. Thailand itself, not just the Mekong Valley, lay in jeopardy. The Joint Chiefs in their report of the defeat to McNamara on 11 May charged that by abandoning the incremental encroachment on RLG territories in favor of a major confrontation, the communists had provided "conclusive evidence" of Souvanna's inability to control the Pathet Lao and also of the futility of relying on him to establish and lead a neutral Laos. They asked for removal of restraints on Phoumi's freedom of military action and for implementation of SEATO Plan 5 if the communists failed to withdraw from their new positions. They neglected to mention that Phoumi's movements in Nam Tha had precipitated the latest crisis. McNamara's marginalia on the JCS memorandum made it clear that he regarded Phoumi as not only inadequate and unresponsive but gravely undermined by his successive misadventures. The secretary's comments reflected his skepticism about the JCS recommendations.[98]

Geneva Again: June-July 1962

What followed seemed in many ways a reprise of the crisis in 1961. The White House felt compelled to publicize a military option that would combine appropriate restraint with such military preparations as the situation required. Still, the president hesitated to do more than dispatch a part of the Seventh Fleet to the Gulf of Siam, as he had done in 1961, until McNamara and Lemnitzer, then on the scene in Southeast Asia, returned to Washington. During May 5,000 U.S. troops arrived in Thailand. On 24 May the president increased pressure by requesting contingency plans involving occupation of northwest Laos by Thai troops and recapture of the southern panhandle by Thai, South Vietnamese, or U.S. forces.[99] In short, what he had disallowed a year before he approved in May 1962.

It still remained unclear how much further the United States would go. An interdepartmental working group, composed of JCS, OSD, and State representatives, on 31 May 1962 recommended occupation of the Mekong Valley. This major objective, if achieved, would deny the north-south road system in southern Laos to North Vietnamese supplying the Viet Cong in South Vietnam.[100]

At a meeting held at the Pentagon on 2 June, McNamara vigorously dissented from the working group's views. He deemed the plan to occupy and control the valley with only 8,000 to 10,000 U.S. troops insufficient without effective assistance—it would require a backup force of about 40,000 U.S. troops, most of them in Thailand, to make it work. Lemnitzer suggested consideration of an amphibious operation to cut across North Vietnam and seal off infiltration routes into Laos and South Vietnam. McNamara wanted a buildup of U.S. forces done quietly and said that an action should occur "only in conjunction with the movement of ground forces forward into the Panhandle." Subsequently, he told the president of his reservations about contingency plans, and particularly his fear of the possibility of rapid escalation of the conflict once embarked on.

On 5 June he told the JCS that he doubted the value of denying the North Vietnamese a north-south road if it had little effect on their supply routes into South Vietnam. He perceived a considerable logistical obstacle in the way of an intervention. The U.S. military in the Southeast Asia area estimated that 2,500-2,600 tons of supplies a day would initially be needed to support combat operations, but at best only 2,000 tons could be transported into Laos by vulnerable air, rail, and road facilities. In further comments on the subject on 12 June, McNamara claimed that while he and the Joint Chiefs shared the State Department's interest in retaining the Mekong River Valley, they felt "it was unwise militarily to introduce U.S. forces for the sole purpose of occupying that valley."[101]

Control of the Mekong Valley also held a psychological dimension. With so much of the country in communist hands, the royal government's control of the valley assumed particular importance for State Department leaders. Should the valley be lost, U. Alexis Johnson concluded, "the political shock effect in Thailand and South VietNam would be severe and would cause internal political repercussions of an adverse nature, the limits of which would be difficult to predict." Moreover, as the valley bordered on Cambodia its loss could lead to a confrontation between Prince Sihanouk and a communist power, which in turn would probably lead to his accommodation with communists.[102]

Fortunately, as in 1961, a deus ex machina—an agreement among the three princes to form a national government—intervened. Phoumi, sobered by his reverses and by the rising hostility of Washington, allowed his relative, Prime Minister Sarit Thanarat of Thailand, to move him to accept a Souvanna-led government on 11 June 1962. On the communist side, U.S. threats of intervention, more credible than in 1961, may have influenced the Pathet Lao. Phoumi would have far less authority in the new government than if he had accepted the proposal of a year earlier. Souvanna would become both prime minister and minister of defense, with Phoumi and Souphanouvong as deputy premiers, each with a veto over cabinet decisions. Phoumi would also serve as finance minister with control over aid funds. Souvanna's neutralists would hold seven seats, with four apiece going to the Phoumists and the Pathet Lao. The remaining four would be given to right-wing neutralists outside Phoumi's circle.[103]

Eager to rid themselves of the Laotian problem and Phoumi burden, administration leaders applauded the new move toward a coalition government, with Souvanna as the repository of U.S. hopes for a neutral Laos. The State Department identified economic assistance as "our chief and perhaps our only effective instrument in helping Souvanna maintain Lao independence." But before taking any specific steps toward reinforcing a new coalition government all parties had to agree on the conditions for neutrality, which meant that the powers of the ICC became the first item on the agenda of the reconvened Conference on Laos at Geneva. Since the ICC lacked the authority to punish cease-fire violations, the

U.S. delegation feared having to withdraw MAAG support within the prescribed 75 days without assurance that the Viet Minh and the Soviets would withdraw their military personnel.[104]

A Laotian statement of neutrality presented by Souvanna on 9 July was accepted by conference members and incorporated into the Formal Declaration and Protocol on the Neutrality of Laos on 23 July 1962. The administration found particularly distressing a statement that the new government would not "recognise the protection of any alliance or military coalition, including SEATO." The arrangement appeared too one-sided, particularly when the ICC checkpoints tallied only 40 North Vietnamese withdrawing from Laos over the 75 days following the signing of the Geneva Accords. Suspicion of communist intentions, ostensibly confirmed by this information, motivated strong opposition by Thailand and South Vietnam, but they signed on.[105]

Rather than retaliate for North Vietnamese behavior, Harriman insisted on having the military advisers withdrawn promptly and urged against any kind of violation by the United States, "neither 'black' reconnaissance flights to confirm whether the North Vietnamese had actually withdrawn nor cloak-and-dagger hanky-panky." He argued, according to Roger Hilsman of the State Department, that blame for the failure of the Geneva agreements would fall exclusively on the communists while the United States would gain international support if U.S. military intervention became necessary. Consequently, the MAAG in Laos was formally dismantled between mid-August and the 7 October deadline, while U.S. troops in Thailand left by November. The CIA's Air America* ceased dropping arms to tribal groups in northeastern Laos although two CIA observers remained in the mountains to monitor Pathet Lao and North Vietnamese activity.[106]

Such precautions suggest a picture of less than complete U.S. compliance with the declaration. While the MAAG disappeared, its residual functions went to an augmented military attaché office. Moreover, CINCPAC recommended the establishment in Bangkok of a nonresident MAAG-Laos, with responsibility for handling all aspects of providing materiel for Laos. The AID mission in Laos would take over such functions as preparing and monitoring the defense support budget with Air America, while DoD provided and arranged for storage of military assistance materiel.[107]

The launching at last of a neutralist regime under Prince Souvanna in July 1962 did not mean that the United States had successfully thwarted North Vietnam's efforts to use Laos in its war against Diem in South Vietnam. The Ho Chi Minh Trail remained open and North Vietnamese control of the Laotian borders of South Vietnam continued largely unhampered. But Laos itself remained intact; both sides recognized that it was not the place to stage a contest.

---

* Air America had operated in Laos since 1960 under a CIA contract in support of Meo tribesmen.

*   *

For eight more years, until 1970, Laos maintained itself as an independent entity, with the United States supplying critical economic aid to Souvanna, and even on occasion—in 1963—mobilizing troops in Thailand in his support. Souvanna, finally recognizing that the primary threat to his survival and to that of his neutralist position came from the Pathet Lao and their North Vietnamese patrons, gladly accepted U.S. aid. So did Kong Le, whose break with the Pathet Lao in 1963 seemed to vindicate CIA activity. In looking back over these events, William Colby, the CIA station chief in Saigon from 1959 to 1962, claimed that the agency's operations in Laos proved that the commission that investigated the Bay of Pigs disaster had wrongly condemned CIA's paramilitary functions. Some 300 to 400 CIA personnel, he asserted, supported more than 30,000 troops in tribal areas and lost fewer than 10 men in the process.[108]

Souvanna himself had moved so far from his anti-American posture of 1961 that in December 1964 he worked out an agreement to permit U.S. planes to attack communist installations along the Ho Chi Minh Trail. With his approval, reconnaissance planes observing North Vietnamese movements of supplies along the trail could get permission to use "suppressive fire." Souvanna reportedly said that "in such a situation, if U.S. and Thai forces are engaged it would only be to defend liberty against Communist subversion in Southeast Asia." The American ambassador reported on 10 December that Souvanna fully supported "the US program of pressures against North Vietnam and believes they should be carried out with deliberate 'sangfroid'." Specifically he requested U.S. aircraft to engage in armed reconnaissance over infiltration routes, which he recognized as meaning that if we "see anything moving on the road, either day or night, attack it." His only caveat was an unwillingness to make public U.S. military action in Laos in violation of the 1962 Geneva agreements for fear of both domestic and international reactions.[109]

If the 1960s witnessed continued de facto division of Laos, at least U.S. fears in 1961 of a collapse, with the communists occupying all of Laos, went unrealized. Although South Vietnam had little reason for satisfaction with the solution, use by the Viet Minh of the Ho Chi Minh Trail alone could not account for Diem's inability to contain the Viet Cong in light of their relatively limited activity in 1961 and 1962. Thailand took more satisfaction in the short-term balance. Diplomacy seemed to have worked. Colby noted that at the end of the 1960s the battle lines remained largely unchanged from the beginning of the decade. Moreover, the Laotian conflict may have produced more of a victory than originally appreciated, he felt, since the 70,000 North Vietnamese troops involved in Laos were "thereby not available to help fight the Americans in South Vietnam." Hilsman was also ready to call the administration's ability to follow a narrow path between full-scale military intervention and complete surrender to the communists "a victory—of sorts." Rather than making Laos an ally in the Cold War and perhaps requiring large-scale military intervention, the long-run interest of the United States, he believed, lay in an accommodation with China in Southeast Asia that would deny the area to the communists.[110]

Rostow interpreted the steady movement of North Vietnamese down the trails through Laos, in violation of the Geneva Accords, as a "firebell in the night." He urged the secretary of state and the president on 28 November 1962 to put pressure on the communists while the situation in both Laos and South Vietnam remained relatively quiet. To the question of whether it was worth risking a major crisis over a continuing but limited flow of men and supplies to the Viet Cong, he said yes. The president, having just survived the Cuban missile crisis, judged otherwise and did not accept Rostow's advice. While sympathetic with the president's position, and with the American propensity to act only when the balance of power was clearly in danger, Rostow felt it a mistaken decision: "With hindsight, . . . I would judge Kennedy's failure to move promptly and decisively to deal with the violation of the Laos Accords the greatest single error in American policy of the 1960s."[111]

Kong Le surprisingly shared some of Rostow's sentiments. In 1964 he noted that the United States had learned in Korea to meet force with force. "More recently, you seem to have forgotten that lesson. No one doubts your great power, least of all the Communists. Yet you seem unsure. Compared to your strength, your policies seem weak in purpose. This is what makes it difficult for us Asians to understand you."[112]

Within the administration, only DoD officials appeared willing to follow the logic of an aggressive posture in Laos. The Joint Chiefs, in particular, counseled preparations for the highest level of escalation, including the use of nuclear weapons, as the only way to guarantee the security of Southeast Asia. They judged that the movement of the Seventh Fleet to the Gulf of Siam in April 1961, and again in May 1962, when the president agreed to deploy combat troops to Thailand, forced the communists to make whatever concessions they made in those years.

But even conceding the accuracy of these conclusions—and communist records supporting them remain unavailable a generation later—they provide no assurance that full-scale warfare, with all the risks involved, would have achieved security. The JCS, more divided than united, agreed on introducing U.S. troops only on condition that the administration be willing to employ nuclear weapons, a risk that the administration, including McNamara, contemplated but would not take. Not only did the White House have to take into account the effect of a major war on the U.S. position throughout the world, but the elements needed for a successful action with conventional means appeared lacking in Laos—access to ports, usable roads, adequate airports, and above all indigenous reliable armies.

If the United States did not intervene militarily in Laos it was not because the administration believed that there could be genuine neutrality in the Cold War, but rather because South Vietnam, with its accessible highways, harbors, and airstrips—and apparently more solid leadership—presented a more appropriate place for a stand against a communist takeover. Intervention in Vietnam eventually proved more of a mistake than it would have been in Laos, if for different reasons. But in the Kennedy years Laos remained intact under a government increasingly more susceptible to Western influence than to that of the communists.

McNamara's role in making or influencing policy on Laos in 1961-62 is not as clear as his record in other international crises such as Cuba and Vietnam. It *is* clear that he was conflicted about whether the United States should intervene and how and to what extent. His views obviously shifted in response to the seemingly ever-changing circumstances in a near-chaotic Laos, but his more consistent positions and instincts appear to have been to stay out and pursue other than military measures. His reluctance to become involved was apparent; he advanced or supported positions on intervention only as a last resort. He warned of grave consequences and probable escalation that might involve China and the Soviet Union. The end result of a great power confrontation over Laos could be a nuclear conflict that would have the direst effect on all concerned. Although more than once he spoke of the possible use of nuclear weapons in Laos, it may be reasonably inferred from his known deeply-felt attitude toward their use that he would not have sanctioned their employment. In this he was at one with President Kennedy.

CHAPTER XI

Vietnam: Reluctant Engagement, 1961-1963

In Indochina, Kennedy faced much the same challenge and dilemma as Eisenhower: how to avert a deeply entangling military involvement while avoiding a negotiated settlement between competing political and ideological rivals that would give the communists an unacceptable foothold in Southeast Asia. Even as U.S. intervention in Laos helped to neutralize communist influence there, Vietnam soon emerged as the graver threat to the containment of communism in Asia and, indeed, a defining battleground in the larger Cold War struggle.

With its sizable population, staunch anticommunist leadership under the Ngo family, and accessible seacoast, South Vietnam, despite its own unsettled conditions, looked defensible in a way that Laos could not be. Neutrality never received consideration in U.S. plans for South Vietnam. Rather, the issue from its creation—like Laos it was a product of the Geneva Accords of 1954—always remained how to protect the new nation, an independent republic by 1955, from the hostile and more powerful communist regime of North Vietnam.

Tempting as it would be to blame the unraveling of South Vietnam on U.S. failure to block the supply routes along the Ho Chi Minh Trail that allowed men and materiel from the North to infiltrate through Laos, more significant was the gathering internal political and social unrest that diminished President Ngo Dinh Diem's standing and effectiveness. Diem, such an attractive figure to his American patrons when he assumed power in 1955—a highly educated Catholic who was both an authentic nationalist and a dedicated anticommunist—increasingly resorted to authoritarian rule and clandestine means to consolidate his fragile position. Achieving control at the price of silencing dissidents and imprisoning or executing many of his critics, the stubborn, aloof mandarin in whom U.S. leaders had placed such high hopes had reduced South Vietnam to a police state by the end of Eisenhower's second term, with the consequence not simply a steady loss of popular support but the attraction of Diem's opponents to the communist cause

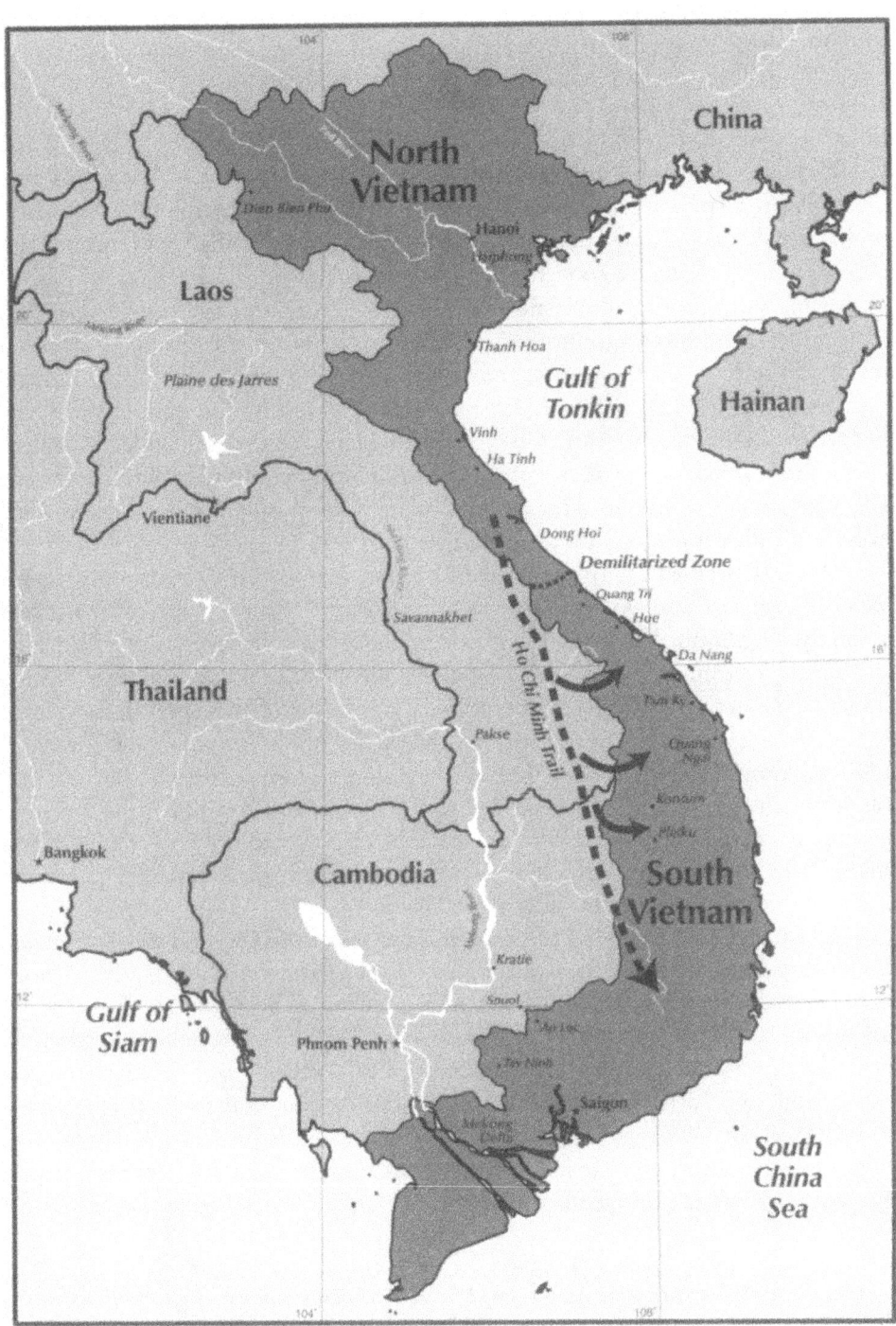

Vietnam (1961)

and the formation of the National Liberation Front (NLF) and its military arm, the Viet Cong (VC).

Kennedy and Counterinsurgency, January-April 1961

Though still a lesser priority than the immediate problem in Laos, that the Diem government was in deep trouble was well established by the time Kennedy took office. Until late in the decade American military advisers had concentrated on preparations to counter a conventional external assault on the South from North Vietnam. With growing domestic opposition to Diem and the rise of the Viet Cong, the Eisenhower administration began to focus on the threat of internal insurgency and took steps to meet the danger by developing in 1960 the Counterinsurgency Plan (CIP), which in 1961 became an important project of the Kennedy administration. In April 1960 Admiral Harry Felt, commander in chief, Pacific, forwarded to the JCS a study on countering communist insurgency in Laos and South Vietnam. This original plan went through a long drawn-out evolution before it reached a final form in January 1961.[1]

The CIP seemed ready for implementation just as the new administration was preparing to take power. The plan postulated a two-track arrangement for strengthening South Vietnam: (1) major political and administrative reforms in the Diem government, including bringing dissident but non-communist elements into the cabinet and dissolving the political apparatus of the Diem family, and (2) increasing the military strength of the Army of the Republic of Vietnam (ARVN) from 150,000 to 170,000 and training and equipping 32,000 of the 60,000-man Civil Guard. To make full use of the enlarged military, the increase would be accompanied by greater delegation of authority to military commanders in the field within a more efficient chain of command that omitted the civilian political leaders at the provincial and local levels.[2]

In January 1961 Secretary of Defense Gates sent Brig. Gen. Edward Lansdale, his deputy assistant for special operations,* to Vietnam on a 12-day inspection trip. Lansdale's report affirmed the conclusions of the earlier CINCPAC study. He saw Vietnam "as a combat area of the cold war." Diem's plight he described as critical, almost hopeless, and 1961 looked to be "a fateful year." Drastic changes must come immediately in the shape of political reform and military assistance. Whether or not Washington approved of Diem, he was "still the only Vietnamese with executive ability and the required determination to be an effective President." Even as it pressured him to make changes, the United States had to assure him of

---

* Lansdale had been instrumental in helping defeat a communist insurgency in the Philippines and during earlier service in Vietnam had become a close friend of Diem. One of the main characters in Graham Greene's 1955 novel, *The Quiet American*, may have been based on Lansdale. He also was the model for the fictional Colonel Edwin B. Hillandale, whom William J. Lederer and Eugene Burdick depicted quite favorably, despite the title, in their 1958 novel *The Ugly American*.

its backing. Regrettably, Lansdale noted, Ambassador Elbridge Durbrow had pressed Diem too hard in the past, and consequently had become almost persona non grata.[3]

The recommendations for reform fit the Kennedy administration's pragmatic approach as well as its still emerging Southeast Asia strategy. No sharp break with the immediate past would occur. Kennedy shared with Eisenhower a conviction that the Moscow-Peking axis had to be confronted everywhere, and that the loss of South Vietnam would presage the loss of all Southeast Asia. Kennedy favored greater flexibility of means to combat the enemy and gave higher priority to counterinsurgency and to the political dimension of the Vietnam problem.[4]

The CINCPAC and Lansdale reports also found a willing audience with their recommendations for increased military assistance. At a White House meeting on 28 January 1961 the president observed that the Lansdale report "for the first time, gave him a sense of the danger and urgency of the problem in VietNam." At its conclusion, he authorized the proposed increase of $28.4 million to expand the ARVN forces by 20,000, and $12.7 million to improve the Vietnam Civil Guard, and confirmed it in writing on the 30th.[5]

The president seemed to consider Lansdale a possible successor to Ambassador Durbrow. No one appeared to fit Lansdale's description of the new ambassador better than Lansdale himself: "a person with marked leadership talents who can make the Country Team function harmoniously and spiritually, who can influence Asians through understanding them sympathetically, and who is alert to the power of the Mao Tse Tung tactics now being employed to capture Vietnam and who is dedicated to feasible and practical democratic means to defeat these Communist tactics." If chosen ambassador he would arrive as Diem's friend.[6]

Though impressed with Lansdale, Kennedy did not appoint him ambassador to South Vietnam. The general's maverick qualities posed only part of the problem. The Defense Department did not want a military "political" man with CIA connections as the head of the country team in South Vietnam. Lansdale's message discomfited the Pentagon leadership.[7] Despite the spadework for counterinsurgency and the eloquent rhetoric on its behalf, the U.S. military mindset that had helped to build the ARVN to withstand a conventional invasion from the North would not entertain such a radical shift in emphasis. If political reform, land distribution, and training of the Civil Guard comprised part of a counterinsurgency program, the military could accept them as long as they did not interfere with the more conventional and still primary military mission.

Even more telling, Lansdale and McNamara lacked personal chemistry. When the general returned from his tour of Vietnam, McNamara asked him for a 10-minute briefing. Lansdale then dumped on the secretary's desk a clutter of VC weapons—rusty knives, swords, pikes, and punji stakes. He did so not to dramatize the primitive weapons used by the enemy, but rather to demonstrate that success rested on "ideas and ideals" rather than on technically advanced arms—

"Let's at least learn that lesson." Instead, Lansdale learned that McNamara had no taste for his dramatic gestures and unconventional methods. As Lansdale put it, "I didn't get along with [him] at all. We were civil to each other, but that's about it."[8]

The disaffection was mutual, but did not prevent McNamara from appreciating the thrust of Lansdale's argument. McNamara kept Lansdale on his staff as an assistant under the supervision of Deputy Secretary Gilpatric and, although Lansdale would later lament that he was never able fully to "educate" the secretary "to understand the real meaning of the war," McNamara was sufficiently persuaded, whatever Lansdale's influence, to move ahead in February and March with plans for implementing a counterinsurgency program.[9]

The military side of the CIP/Lansdale recommendations appeared to get a boost when Lt. Gen. Lionel C. McGarr, chief of the Military Assistance Advisory Group (MAAG), Vietnam, dispatched encouraging reports on the progress of counterinsurgency planning, particularly training of the Civil Guard. By March he expressed conviction that the South Vietnam government (GVN) would accept and implement the CIP military provisions. Moreover, Lt. Gen. Thomas Trapnell's report* of 28 March confirmed acceptance by the South Vietnamese of the military part of the CIP. He strongly supported McGarr's objection to the State Department requirement that military actions be approved by the ambassador prior to implementation. He suggested to the JCS that the MAAG should have the authority to "decide and direct military matters." The Trapnell report implied that McGarr's difficulties in implementing his part of the counterinsurgency plan stemmed from State Department interference as much as from the flaws in Diem's regime.[10]

If Trapnell overlooked the sluggish response of the GVN to its promised reforms, Ambassador Durbrow had not. Earlier, in January, grudgingly admitting that an unsophisticated people had little opportunity to create a democratic two-party system in Vietnam, he deplored Diem's persistent procrastination and put little stock in his professed willingness to take U.S. suggestions "under active consideration." In his view, only if Diem genuinely carried out reforms could South Vietnam diminish the VC threat.[11]

The problem involved more than Diem's intransigence—it included the conflict between the American military and civilian leadership in South Vietnam over the direction of the CIP. The State Department evidently felt that "the military is not sufficiently anti-guerrilla-conscious," while the MAAG resented what it considered oversimplified civilian solutions. McGarr believed that while it was important to have a balance of forces in Vietnam, including an increase in ranger units to combat the Viet Cong, the latter offered no "cure all." Moreover, the American and South Vietnamese governments should not minimize the external threat from North Vietnam. Augmentation of bigger, regiment-size units would

---

* Trapnell, at Secretary McNamara's direction, conducted an inspection trip of Southeast Asia, during which he visited Vietnam on 16-17 March. For his findings on Laos, see Chapter X.

be necessary to protect against that contingency as well as establish control over larger areas where the VC were entrenched. In letters to the Pentagon in February and March, McGarr voiced objections to the ambassador's attempt to insert himself in military affairs, and emphasized the need for a sustained conventional effort that still could entail flexible elements.[12]

State cited Lansdale's recommendation to use more small units, presumably ranger companies, to deal with the VC insurgents and win back the countryside. It suggested that North Vietnam would be deterred from invasion because an act of naked aggression would damage communism's standing before the world and trigger a U.S. and SEATO response that North Vietnam no doubt wished to avoid. These considerations, in State's view, gave priority to beefing up ARVN ranger forces and assigning to MAAG more officers with specialized knowledge of guerrilla warfare.[13]

Using arguments supplied by McGarr, Deputy Assistant Secretary (ISA) William Bundy informed State's George McGhee on 13 March that under the CIP the ranger companies were intended to supplement, not replace, regular units. They could perform vital services only by careful coordination with the operations of larger forces.[14] By determining for the Vietnamese the number of ranger units and how they should be used, the State Department, in McGarr's judgment, undermined the counterinsurgency program. The administration must understand "that neither MAAG or the Ambassador can direct the GVN to follow our recommendations—we can only work through persuasion and advice." Withdrawing or withholding aid from the Diem government based on its compliance with U.S. requirements would only weaken the government's military effort.[15]

The Kennedy administration attempted to straddle conflicting positions with little success. On the one side Durbrow advised no "green light" for Diem until he had complied with his promises of civil as well as military reform. On the other Defense held that excessive pressure on the GVN would prove counterproductive. This standoff between the embassy and the MAAG invited McNamara's attention and possible intervention.[16] As it turned out, the impasse got at least temporarily resolved when Frederick Nolting, the newly-designated ambassador to South Vietnam, met with General McGarr in late April to exchange views about the procedural aspects of their relationship in Saigon. They agreed that in the future they would discuss significant differences on military matters. If unable to reach a joint decision, McGarr could take his case directly to CINCPAC, and the ambassador, if he considered it necessary, would comment on the MAAG views through State channels. McGarr suggested that this arrangement relieved Secretary McNamara from having to take any action at the moment.[17]

Still, this understanding did not go to the heart of the two basic, and related, problems inhibiting progress in the struggle against communism in Indochina: (1) disagreement and ambivalence among U.S. agencies on actions to take in South Vietnam, and (2) the inability and unwillingness of the Diem regime to reform its structure, both military and civil. Differences within and between U.S. departments facilitated Diem's resistance to U.S. demands. Not only could he play off one agency against another, but he could count on occasional sympathy for his position from one or another U.S. advisory group whenever the White House pressed him too hard.

Among the agencies concerned with Vietnam, the CIA was a key player, and it, too, was afflicted with uncertainty and ambivalence. CIA Director Allen Dulles claimed that while his agency had sought to convince Diem to carry out operations against North Vietnam, the South Vietnamese leader consistently diverted CIA-trained units intended for action in the North to cope with VC provocations in the South. But despite Dulles's professions of interest in a campaign against North Vietnam, his enthusiasm was tempered by the reality that the dissident North Vietnamese who might be recruited for sabotage came from areas too far removed from worthwhile geographic targets. Like Diem, he would concentrate agency efforts on the war in the South.[18]

Lemnitzer's 29 March response to McNamara's queries on increased use of helicopter and special warfare units underscored the complicated circumstances and fractured coordination. The JCS chairman relayed McGarr's judgment that the helicopters currently in place comprised all that the Vietnamese could utilize. As for special warfare units, Lemnitzer noted that the MAAG trained the regular Vietnamese forces in counterguerrilla operations, the International Cooperation Administration trained the Vietnamese Civil Guard and police, and the CIA provided training in guerrilla warfare. Although the chairman felt that "during the past year . . . great progress has been made both in the simplification of U.S. responsibilities and in the Vietnamese organization," his response pointed up the difficulty of achieving a coordinated military effort where no one element in the U.S. establishment exercised control and the South Vietnamese ministries themselves lacked integration.[19]

The Gilpatric and Staley Reports

The differences between the CIA and the JCS, between the CIA and DoD, or between the MAAG and the ICA, might not have had serious consequences if the counterinsurgency campaign had shown genuine progress. Despite optimistic predictions and reports from American military observers, excluding Lansdale, the situation in South Vietnam grew worse. The plight of the Diem regime and the failure of military action against the Viet Cong pushed the White House, and particularly McNamara, to inquire further into the progress of U.S. aid to Diem. One mission followed another in the Kennedy administration.

Secretary of State Rusk, regarding South Vietnam as chiefly a military rather than a political issue, initially assumed a passive role, in effect accepting the primacy of military judgment. Consequently, the president took the initiative on 20 April to establish a new task force on Vietnam under Deputy Secretary of Defense Gilpatric, with members from the White House, State, CIA, and USIA.[20] McNamara told Gilpatric that the president wanted an appraisal of the prospects for communist domination of the peninsula and of proposed measures to prevent it from happening. Characteristically, McNamara wanted a plan submitted within a week's time.[21]

Gilpatric designated Lansdale as his chief operations officer. Representatives from DoD, State, JCS, and the CIA met with Gilpatric on 24 April to hear McGarr, visiting from Saigon, identify immediate areas of U.S. concern. It was agreed to prepare a draft plan for the president's consideration.[22]

This was a tall order given the administration's already full plate in late April, what with a review launched that same week of the Bay of Pigs debacle and the continuing preoccupation with Laos. Gilpatric, reflecting on the task force a generation later, spoke of the genuine surprise in Washington over the troubles in South Vietnam and bemoaned "the rise in tensions, the riots, and all the internal problems that came upon us so quickly there in the early part of '61, because President Eisenhower and his advisers had not stressed that area as being as problem-prone as it turned out to be."[23]

The task force provided an opportunity for McGarr to elaborate his thoughts. With 58 percent of the country "under some degree of Communist control or influence," he conceded the government was losing, not winning, that the tempo of the insurgency was increasing, and that "this trend, if continued, can be fatal." While acknowledging the relevance of political and social factors long-term in wresting the countryside away from the Viet Cong, McGarr continued to argue that a military solution had to come first and that "there is absolutely no substitute for adequate military force . . . ." He admitted that although "there is seldom a 'purely military' answer to the domestic unrest in which guerrilla action flourishes," the antiguerrilla action that he advocated was military, but he insisted that conventional organizations at the division and corps level could be adapted for unconventional purposes as well.[24]

Although this view did not square with Lansdale's notion of confronting the internal threat with more specialized unconventional means, the task force could do little to change direction. The task force report of 1 May stressed increased support of the CIP, as approved in January, but with no change in emphasis. The aid program would involve more of the same, but target resources for greater effectiveness. As Gilpatric later expressed it, "The major issue that developed in the task force that I headed was to what extent we would augment the some 1600-man presence that we had in South Vietnam. After many arguments amongst ourselves, . . . we made certain recommendations: not of combat forces, not of uniformed military people from the combat ranks, but enlarging our military assistance personnel, sending out training groups to help the Vietnamese organize their provincial units, the home guards, and the like."[25]

Previously, on 29 April, the president had approved military actions that were incorporated in the task force report, leaving political and economic aspects for later consideration.[26] Consensus remained elusive. The State Department, now concerned about its role, felt that Defense had too large a presence in the plans, and proposed that State officials take the lead. The end result saw the establishment of a new setup under State leadership in which Lansdale was merely the DoD representative.[27]

Lansdale, no longer the group's operational head, reacted indignantly, urging McNamara and Gilpatric to stay out of the new arrangement. "Having a Defense officer, myself or someone else, placed in a position of only partial influence and of no decision permissibility would be only to provide State with a scapegoat to share the blame when we have a flop." The 6 May final version of the task force report represented the State Department's position.[28] Later observers judged that Lansdale's impetuosity, and his apparently unqualified support of Diem, had damaged the initially favorable impression he had made on the White House with his ideas about guerrilla warfare. By this time the president had become as wary of precipitating military action in Vietnam as in Laos.

The Gilpatric task force proposals, approved in part on 29 April and 11 May, produced significant but still incremental changes in U.S. policy. The president authorized additional personnel for the MAAG and asked for a study on "the size and composition of forces which would be desirable in the case of a possible commitment of U.S. forces to Vietnam." In the meantime he confirmed the immediate deployment of 52 Special Forces troops to Vietnam, to be followed by another 350, to accelerate the training of their Vietnamese counterparts. This would involve assignment to remote areas to work with ethnic tribal groups and to accompany them into actual combat operations, although the mission was discreetly termed "combat support." As for the problem of coordination of efforts, a presidential directive to all chiefs of mission on 27 May formally charged them with the oversight and coordination of all the activities of the United States government. But while Ambassador Nolting's authority thus encompassed the MAAG, the directive specified that "it does not, however, include United States military forces operating in the field where such forces are under the command of a United States area military commander. The line of authority to these forces runs from me, to the Secretary of Defense, to the Joint Chiefs of Staff . . . and to the area commander in the field."[29]

To improve morale in South Vietnam, Nolting received instructions to begin discussions with Diem on the possibility of arranging a defensive alliance with the United States and formally rejecting the Geneva Accords. The new round of Geneva talks on Laos, however, raised doubts about the steadfastness of U.S. support both in South Vietnam and Laos.[30] The crisis of confidence in the Diem government required some dramatic action. Kennedy sent Vice President Johnson on a tour of Southeast Asia in May, chiefly to underscore in Saigon the continuing

U.S. commitment to South Vietnam. The visit followed on the heels of a letter from the president to Diem on 8 May that reiterated support for a collaborative effort against communist aggression and suggested that the United States would consider the GVN request for a troop strength increase. Johnson left an impression with Diem that, if he would outline his needs, Washington would meet them. The vice president believed that Vietnam would fall if Diem's position were not bolstered. As the "Winston Churchill of Asia" only Diem, he thought, could check communist expansionism in the region.[31]

Johnson's visit seemed to promise Diem more than the president had intended. New aid would have to await the examination of South Vietnam's economy by a panel of economists headed by Eugene Staley of the Stanford Research Institute. The panel met with Vietnamese officials in Saigon on 23 June to discuss how South Vietnam would finance the costs of expanding both its armed forces and its economic and social programs. Reformation of the country's tax structure was judged vital, and this meant major changes in distributing the burden of the war. The landowning mandarins would have to share the economic load as well as political power to defeat the Viet Cong, helping in the goal to deliver agricultural and social services to rural areas.[32] The Staley report concluded that no military successes could have lasting significance unless accompanied by major societal changes, but then compromised its own advice by recommending large military increases before the proposed reforms could possibly be instituted. Still, William Bundy later characterized the Staley report of 14 July as "a courageous and thoughtful attempt to look to the long term and to put economic measures for the people alongside military action, in more or less equal priorities." Bundy would also recognize that no matter how astute the recommendation, no regime in a developing country, in Asia or elsewhere, could easily embrace a plan that appeared to weaken its power base.[33]

Kennedy reviewed the Staley report and on 11 August issued National Security Action Memorandum 65. He agreed to provide equipment and training assistance for an increase in the Vietnamese military to 200,000 if a review before reaching the 170,000 level showed that the larger number could be met. There was no decision to deploy American troops for direct combat use.[34]

Throughout the process of deepening U.S. involvement in South Vietnam in 1961 the president avoided hard and fast commitment, absent indication of Diem's willingness and ability to carry through his promised reforms. At the same time, he undoubtedly realized that to abandon Diem would open the administration to criticism from political opposition at home, especially after the failure at the Bay of Pigs and the appearance of appeasement in Laos. Both political and military realities constrained the president's ability to pull out of South Vietnam even if the regime refused to comply with U.S. requirements.

The events of the summer afforded the administration little satisfaction. As 1961 wore on Berlin diverted attention for the moment from Southeast

Asia. But South Vietnam could not be ignored for long. The crisis over Berlin, though more intense, abated after the confrontation at Checkpoint Charlie and the callup of U.S. reserves.* Developments in Laos, although still unsettled, at least offered some promise of a neutral government. South Vietnam's situation, on the other hand, worsened in the fall. A sense of impending destruction of the Diem regime in September 1961 derived not from new threats from the North but from spectacular guerrilla gains in the South. When the Viet Cong overran a provincial capital 20 miles from Saigon on 18 September, publicly beheaded the province chief, and captured large supplies of arms without interference from the ARVN, it forced the Kennedy administration to face up to the plight of Diem.[35]

The Taylor-Rostow Mission

By the fall of 1961 the military strength of the Viet Cong had grown to approximately 15,000 men, a five-fold increase in two years. The government's estimate of 1,000 VC losses per month served to underscore the enemy's success in rounding up new recruits, whether by infiltration from the North or by attracting replacements from areas throughout South Vietnam. Moreover, VC units grew bolder, attacking in larger numbers with more sophisticated equipment. Against this reality, the cautiously optimistic reports from the MAAG and the embassy appeared all the more hollow. Long overdue, the time for a high-level U.S. assessment of the problems in South Vietnam had come. Diem's appeal on 1 October for a bilateral defense treaty along with additional aid hastened the reckoning. The president sent his military adviser, General Maxwell Taylor, accompanied by Walt Rostow from the NSC staff and Lansdale, to provide a firsthand report on the threat and recommend steps to cope with it. The announcement of the trip on 11 October immediately drew inquiries from the press corps about the possible employment of U.S. troops, prompted by word of discussions in the Pentagon regarding options for U.S. intervention ranging from a naval blockade to a SEATO border patrol to seal off the Ho Chi Minh Trail. The Taylor mission offered Kennedy a means for necessary fact-finding and to defer decision on what could be a controversial next step.[36]

A day before the announcement, William Bundy noted in a memorandum to McNamara that "the idea of sending US military units in some form was generally in the ascendant." He had expressed to McNamara his personal feeling that "it *is* really now or never if we are to arrest the gains being made by the Viet Cong . . . . An early and hard-hitting operation has a good chance (70% would be my guess) of *arresting* things and giving Diem a chance to do better and clean up." As Bundy ruefully recalled years later, "the breathless character of this memorandum speaks for itself." His advice to McNamara, however, included the estimate of a

---

* See Chapter VII.

30 percent chance that "we would wind up like the French in 1954; white men can't win this kind of fight."[37]

Taylor received his charge from the president on 13 October, and arrived with his party in Saigon on 18 October to begin a week-long high-profile visit to all parts of South Vietnam. The mission intended to signal to Diem how seriously the Kennedy administration viewed the failing struggle with the Viet Cong, and that, as the president told Taylor on his departure, "the independence of South Vietnam rests with the people and government of that country." The group found, according to Rostow, "a vicious circle of bad military tactics and bad administrative arrangements" resulting in "a defensive, reactive military posture which was permitting the Viet Cong to create conditions of frustration and terror, certain to lead to a political crisis if a positive turning point was not soon achieved." Continuing Vietnamese doubts about American commitment and a devastating flood that ravaged the Mekong Delta, the latter leaving thousands homeless, further compounded the problem.

Taylor and his colleagues met with President Diem and the army field commander, General Duong Van Minh, in Saigon. From American advisers they heard firsthand about Diem's isolation from his countrymen and his increasing authoritarianism. After listening to familiar complaints about the lack of a serviceable intelligence system, the absence of a national plan, and the subordination of military leaders to corrupt provincial chieftains, Taylor still recognized that Diem could not be abandoned; there was no suitable replacement in sight. Taylor's group concluded that "we should stick with Diem, hoping to effect improvement by persuasion, by example, and by a larger advisory presence to assist his government and armed forces."[38]

In all these discussions counterinsurgency seemed relegated to a lesser place. Lansdale disagreed with Taylor's approach, particularly when he felt that Taylor disparaged his expertise on Vietnamese matters. He alleged that Taylor sent him afield, "noodling out the defense of the Laotian–South Vietnamese border."[39]

Taylor delivered the report, written in the mountain retreat of Baguio in the Philippines, to Kennedy on 3 November. Years later Taylor claimed that he "had no enthusiasm for the thought of using U.S. Army forces in ground combat in this guerrilla war," expressing doubt that large American units could adapt to the needs of jungle warfare. Diem apparently never raised the issue specifically with Taylor in 1961, though he did so at a private meeting with Lansdale. However, in his report, Taylor did recommend the "introduction of a U.S. military Task Force without delay," a force of 8,000 initially to serve a variety of purposes—render logistical support to flood relief and military operations, conduct combat operations necessary for self-defense and security, and provide backing for the GVN forces if necessary. He doubted if "our program to save SVN will succeed without it."[40]

Almost everything in the report nudged the United States into greater entanglement with the fortunes of South Vietnam. McGarr may not have won U.S. intervention in sufficient strength to tip the balance, but Taylor recommended sending several companies of U.S. helicopters before the end of the year. This deployment accorded with the Kennedy prescription of providing the Diem government "with equipment and with military units and personnel to do those tasks which the Armed Forces of Vietnam cannot perform in time." A small part of the U.S. force Taylor recommended would be combat troops to provide for the defense of the others. Thus the expansion of the U.S. commitment proceeded fitfully but inexorably. Even as the president spoke against dispatch of American troops, he ordered an Air Force Jungle Jim squadron to South Vietnam to instruct the ARVN in simple and adaptable techniques for guerrilla warfare. The Jungle Jim project—code-named Farm Gate—brought U.S.-manned propeller-driven transport and light aircraft to VC-infested areas where they engaged in what were again characterized nominally as combat support operations.* In accepting the thrust of Taylor's findings and guidance, Kennedy bore his share of responsibility for what amounted to a qualitative change in the U.S. stake in Indochina.[41]

It may be that in the absence of a blanket commitment and definitive policy restatement the actions issuing from the Taylor mission marked no break with the past. Yet the report recommended and set in motion a program of U.S. controls of GVN military operations that went beyond advice and training. The United States should support, in Taylor's words, "a limited partnership" in the war, but "limited" belied a more intricate relationship and the partnership envisioned by Taylor made direct intervention more likely. Taylor noted that "if the first contingent is not enough to accomplish the necessary results, it will be difficult to resist the pressure to reinforce. If the ultimate result sought is the closing of the frontiers and the clean-up of the insurgents within SVN, there is no limit to our possible commitment (unless we attack the source in Hanoi)."[42]

The president continued to resist the broad application of the Taylor report recommendations, exercising caution over too precipitate action that might turn the Vietnam struggle into an American war that he neither sought nor intended. By comparison, DoD expressed impatience, believing that the Taylor recommendations did not go far enough. In a strongly worded memorandum to the president on 8 November, McNamara, speaking also for the JCS, judged that a force of 8,000 or so troops in "a flood relief context will be of no great help to Diem." Such halfway measures would not have a decisive impact; rather they would enmesh Americans in an inconclusive struggle. The better alternative would be the dispatch of substantial U.S. forces, along with a willingness to bring the war to North Vietnam. Conceivably this action might trigger Chinese intervention,

---

* See p. 39. McNamara and the Joint Chiefs would finesse the question of whether the squadron's activities constituted a combat role by decreeing that Farm Gate could undertake combat flights so long as a Vietnamese military person was on board for training purposes (Futrell, *The Advisory Years*, 80-83).

a possible danger that would have to be carefully weighed. Some six divisions, McNamara said, 205,000 men, would suffice, without diverting resources from Berlin. The defense secretary and the JCS agreed on no commitment of forces for other than a massive effort to prevent "the fall of South Vietnam to Communism."[43]

Three days later Rusk and McNamara sent the president a comprehensive program for South Vietnam that expanded upon the latter's memorandum and included the introduction of the Taylor-recommended support troops "as speedily as possible." They recognized the seriousness of what they were proposing, that deployment of large combat units would cause sharp domestic and international reaction.[44]

At a White House meeting the same day, 11 November, Kennedy raised a number of questions, without reaching any decisions, about the desirability and practicality of the Rusk-McNamara proposals. In a followup NSC meeting on 15 November the president considered the prospect of Chinese and/or Soviet intervention. After expressing concern about enlisting the support of allies, he decided not to take action on the proposals.[45]

In spite of his skepticism, a week later Kennedy approved the resulting NSAM 111 that called for the United States to pursue "a sharply increased joint effort to avoid a further deterioration in the situation in South Viet-Nam." In return for greatly increased U.S. military assistance, South Vietnam was to undertake military and governmental reform to achieve more effective prosecution of the war.[46] Still, by rejecting the more far-reaching aspects of the DoD-State program for direct intervention—the president stipulated that no U.S. troops would go to South Vietnam to enter combat—Kennedy could portray his own position as a prudent middle course. Prophetically, NSAM 111 was titled "First Phase of Viet-Nam Program."

The White House may have felt relief at emerging from deliberations on the Taylor report with a firm but moderate course of action. At the same time there appeared only a modicum of recognition in the administration that it had traversed a key crossroads on the path to escalation of U.S. involvement. Nor was there appreciation that the evolving concept of "limited partnership" engendered as much resentment on the part of the Vietnamese as it did anxiety among the Americans. The collaboration presumed U.S. superiority and a managing of Vietnamese affairs that was both patronizing and intrusive.[47] Diem had no objection to Americans managing operations of their own uniformed personnel, or in principle to the equipping and training of the Civil Guard and Self Defense Corps to relieve regular GVN troops of static missions, and certainly not to the increased economic aid for flood relief and rehabilitation of the stricken areas of the Delta. But the terms of the NSAM document included specific functions of advisers in every corner of the South Vietnam government. The key demand on the GVN called for "prompt and appropriate legislative and administrative action to put the nation on a wartime footing to mobilize its entire resources," including an "overhaul of the military establishment." It is hardly surprising that these instructions, entailing blatant interference in the internal affairs of the junior partner, aroused resistance.[48]

Among the Taylor report's recommendations the matter of the organization and size of MAAG Vietnam occasioned months of discussion and controversy between the many players involved—the White House, OSD, JCS, State, the U.S. Pacific Command (PACOM), Ambassador Nolting, and the MAAG. The chief issue concerned the establishment of a new U.S. military command in South Vietnam—U.S. Military Assistance Command, Vietnam (MACV)—under a four-star general and the relationship of the command to PACOM, Washington, and especially Nolting, who as chief of mission fought fiercely to retain his authority over the military in the country.[49]

After months of complicated maneuvering, resolution came in February 1962 with the establishment of MACV by CINCPAC and subsequent agreement between DoD, State, and Nolting that the new MACV commander, General Paul D. Harkins, and the ambassador would, in effect, share responsibility. The latter remained the "senior U.S. representative."[50]

McNamara's Initiatives, December 1961-July 1962

The lack of response and reform from the South Vietnamese government and its military to the requirements for change stated in NSAM 111 led McNamara to conclude that he needed "continuous personal contact" to review progress and see what could be done within the framework of existing policy. This judgment resulted in a meeting of Defense officials from Vietnam, PACOM, and Washington in Honolulu on 16 December 1961. The secretary, as always, identified specific tasks to achieve specific objectives, and he expected quick responses. Money, he said, would pose no problem.[51] He continued to criticize South Vietnam's president for failing to live up to his end of the "limited partnership." Training the Civil Guard and the Self Defense Corps moved too slowly, facilities were too limited, and the 5,000-strong ranger force remained mired in rearguard police work. The Honolulu meeting broke up with the uneasy recognition that GVN unwillingness or inability to meet its commitments would place limits on U.S. freedom of action.[52]

Despite the authority he brought to any situation important to him, McNamara in this instance struggled to carry out the innovative ideas that attracted him. Part of the difficulty stemmed from the still-persisting divided command between ambassador and general in South Vietnam, which stood to impact the conduct of American operations. William Bundy accepted it as a fact of life, while

Robert W. Komer of the NSC staff saw in the absence of a single authority the root of U.S. frustration in Southeast Asia. He cited Robert Thompson's* wry commentary that Americans were averse to the appointment of proconsuls even when the situation required it.[53]

To help cope with divided and competing authority in Washington there emerged interagency coordinating committees with overlapping responsibilities, initially the Special Group (Counterinsurgency), established on 18 January 1962. It had a mission to ensure recognition throughout the government that subversive insurgency was "a major form of politico-military conflict equal in importance to conventional warfare," an understanding to be reflected in all U.S. programs, but particularly in South Vietnam, Laos, and Thailand.[54] Less than six months later the secretary of state appointed Averell Harriman to take charge of a new interdepartmental task force for all Southeast Asia. McNamara at first offered his full support, but then qualified it by suggesting that some of its mission could duplicate that of the existing Task Force/Vietnam, which, he feared, would be overshadowed by the new agency.[55]

On such matters as organization of DoD or reordering of the budget process or even the conceptualization of strategic doctrines, McNamara did not hesitate to impose his judgment on the JCS. But, understandably perhaps, he showed the chiefs greater deference when it came to choosing military commanders for the field. While he wanted immediate action to implement the Taylor report, he turned to uniformed colleagues for selection of the new commander of MACV. Accepting the advice of the JCS, to replace McGarr he picked the 57-year-old General Harkins, a protégé of Taylor. McNamara described him to the president as "an imaginative officer, fully qualified to fill what I consider to be the most difficult job in the U.S. Army."[56]

In selecting Harkins McNamara chose a traditional leader rather than one sympathetic to the new ideas of counterinsurgent warfare. His choice bothered both McGeorge Bundy and Roger Hilsman. Bundy observed that the secretary "does not seem to have a personal judgment of General Harkins." It would be, he felt, "little more than a lucky accident" if an officer coming off SEATO duty would be the right man for the Vietnam post. Hilsman thought that in Harkins McNamara had chosen a veteran from a conventional mold and that matters of political warfare, guerrilla operations, and the vitally important social and economic aspects of the conflict lay outside his experience. Diem's secretary questioned the need for a new command and expressed Vietnamese suspicions that the United States would exploit the change to tighten its control over the country.[57] McNamara saw the arrival of a military leader empowered with more authority than his predecessor as a step in the right direction.

---

* See below, p. 277.

Although McNamara deferred to the military in choosing a MACV commander, he did not hesitate to make decisions about policy initiatives such as the defoliation program. Despite his doubts about this form of chemical warfare, it appealed to him as an imaginative antiguerrilla tactic that Defense could quickly implement. The JCS participated in initiating the program; technical aspects came under the director of defense research and engineering. McNamara cautioned the service secretaries that the operation would proceed only after resettlement of affected villages and provision of alternative food sources.[58] On 2 February 1962 he advised the president that the first spraying had occurred on 13-16 January for approximately 16 miles along Route No. 15. He urged extension of the test program largely because the areas already sprayed did not include a sufficient variety of vegetation to permit full evaluation of the use of defoliation techniques before proceeding with a large-scale program. Even as he recognized that the defoliation program by itself would not win a war, he found its possibilities intriguing, particularly its susceptibility to measurement. The president agreed.[59]

As with so much else in the U.S. experience in South Vietnam, the defoliation initiative began with optimism and ultimately ended in disillusion. The hoped-for benefits from increases in military aid of all kinds, particularly helicopters and light aircraft, yielded similar unsatisfactory results. Through the summer of 1962, following the president's guidance, McNamara emphasized U.S. assistance, not direct participation in combat, with the underlying assumption that success would come from the benefits of U.S. training and advice. McNamara asked for rapid responses to the decisions made at Honolulu in December 1961, specifically how many U.S. advisers would be needed at the GVN battalion-and-above level and the schedule to have them in place. The secretary also wanted development of an operations plan whereby the GVN forces would clear a particular province and then have the Civil Guard and Self Defense Corps take over to hold it. In all, he wanted progress reports on some 15 individual actions.[60]

Periodic status reports in 1962 under the rubric "Operation Beef-Up" rarely failed to mention the impressive number of helicopters and light aircraft sent to South Vietnam. Assistance included support of coastal control and surveillance as well. The combined U.S.-Vietnamese Maritime Surveillance Patrol had begun functioning as early as 22 December 1961, and by 9 January 1962 could report successful interdiction of junks carrying weapons and materiel from North Vietnam to the Viet Cong.[61] Such activities could go on, as Nitze advised Sen. Henry Dworshak (R-Idaho), with U.S. personnel restricted to so-called advisory and training roles,[62] even though the administration had to exceed the level of force permitted under the Geneva Accords to achieve its aims.

Despite the continuing efforts to emphasize the limited nature of U.S. combat participation, McNamara pressed for substantial but temporary increases in American military personnel to help with the new tasks imposed on American advisers. The new partnership recommended by Taylor and translated into programs at the December 1961 and subsequent Honolulu meetings brought about major increases in the U.S. military presence.[63] At the sixth Honolulu meeting on 23 July 1962 the secretary stated as his goal a South Vietnamese military that could dispense with American support within three years. Even as the buildup occurred, phased reduction became the key to McNamara's thinking about the future U.S. position in South Vietnam. America's contribution could gradually diminish as the GVN's correspondingly rose. Harkins's belief that a year after ARVN forces became fully operational they could eliminate the VC may have been too optimistic, but McNamara still looked to the end of 1965 as a reasonable date. Conscious of demands elsewhere as well as of budgetary constraints, the secretary looked forward to early reduction of military assistance programs in South Vietnam that had increased from $101.4 million for FY 1961 to $177 million for FY 1962 and $179.4 million for FY 1963.[64] Cost consciousness, while not the driving force behind the DoD approach to South Vietnam, always remained a factor, despite McNamara's earlier observation that money "would pose no problem."

The Strategic Hamlet Program

Despite all the attention being given to advisers and weaponry in 1962, civic action seemed to hold out the most promise for success in that year. The Viet Cong controlled much of the countryside through a combination of terror and promises of economic reform. Consequently, civic action required protection for the Vietnamese peasant and the implementation of promised government reforms.

These two elements came together in the "strategic hamlet" concept, a fortified community consisting of several hamlets combined to form a village, thus contributing to a pacification program designed to remove the influence as well as the presence of Viet Cong in afflicted areas. This involved relocation of populations, not itself a new practice; the French had attempted to establish secure zones in their war with the Viet Minh. But the strategic hamlet program reflected a new approach. It germinated in the course of Vice President Johnson's visit in May 1961, when the United States agreed to help finance the Civil Guard to free regular military units from static defense positions. The Civil Guard and Self Defense Corps (SDC) would protect villages while U.S. specialists worked with Vietnamese counterparts in supporting village-level health and public works measures.

Conversations about developing strategic hamlets did not go beyond that stage in the summer of 1961 as Viet Cong power waxed. They came into focus in the fall following the coincidence of the catastrophic monsoonal flood, which devastated 10 million acres of rice and left behind 320,000 refugees, and U.S. pressure for reforms in the political and military organization of the country following the Taylor visit in October. To address both his civilian and military problems, President Diem gave attention to the recommendations of Sir Robert Thompson, head of the British Advisory Mission in Vietnam, who had applied the strategic hamlet program successfully against communist insurgents in Malaya in the 1950s. The Thompson approach argued that counterinsurgency should give priority to winning the allegiance of rural Vietnamese and depriving the Viet Cong of the infrastructure disaffected peasants had provided—an objective more important than striking at Viet Cong strongholds and killing enemy soldiers. After sweeps of the countryside in the past the GVN forces would withdraw, and too frequently the VC would regroup and return.[65]

The hamlet program, particularly as formally proposed to Diem by Thompson, caught the attention of Hilsman at State, and through him Averell Harriman. Using Thompson's language, Hilsman envisaged "hedgehogs of strategic hamlets, slowly spreading out like an oil blot from the sea toward the mountains and jungle." While one lone hamlet might not have much effect in itself, a series of them, each a compact defensible unit, could give villagers freedom to choose between the Viet Cong and the government. They would make the right choice only if the GVN seriously made an effort to change the peasant's lot in life, and this meant civic action that would include agricultural loans, effective education, and honest administrators. From Hilsman's perspective, the Defense Department should have rallied to the concept. The main source of the enemy's power lay not in the supply line from North Vietnam but rather in the countryside that nourished the guerrillas voluntarily or under duress. By denying the insurgents food and potential recruits from the villages, the GVN would force them into submission through defeat at the hands of troops trained in the tactics of counterinsurgency devised by the U.S. Army.[66]

While the Thompson plan intrigued the State Department, the military exhibited less enthusiasm. In the first place, as McGarr had complained, the British seemed to be poaching on a U.S. preserve. Second, it would undermine the unitary chain of command that both the embassy and the MAAG had been seeking throughout 1961; Diem's provincial chiefs, not the ARVN generals, would supervise the paramilitary and civilian parts of the plan. Third, Thompson urged that the Mekong Delta, a part of the country where VC influence was limited, serve as the initial model for further experiments. Only gradually would the strategic hamlet concept be extended to more dangerous sectors. General McGarr in late 1961 would not have placed the Delta among his priorities.[67]

But the MAAG chief objected particularly that the Thompson plan placed the cart before the horse, putting political concerns above military. McGarr wanted the political and economic phase of the plan to follow military action. Only after clearing the area of insurgents, he maintained, could the SDC assume authority and civic action begin. Yet the hamlet part of the plan most appealed to Diem. Sensible or not from a military perspective, its implementation would permit the Diem government to diminish the authority of the army in the strategic hamlets and invest it in the paramilitary units under the control of the province leaders who owed their powers to the Ngo family.[68] By rallying to the Thompson plan Diem could hope to reduce the power of the generals and at the same time appear responsive to U.S. demands for new tactics in counterinsurgency.

Notwithstanding reservations from McGarr, the Thompson plan interested McNamara, who embraced it as a workable concept promising immediate dividends. U.S. aid increased on every level on the assumption that money would follow, provided a coherent plan existed. Stepped-up military training of the SDC complemented the civilian programs. This took the form of establishing SDC units for the hamlets capable of winning the respect of the rural population and credible enough to relieve the ARVN of police duties.[69]

Statistics seemed to confirm the optimism that the strategic hamlet program inspired, and they particularly impressed the secretary of defense. In Saigon in May 1962, at the end of his first inspection trip to Vietnam, a two-day visit, McNamara observed that "the fortified hamlet and strategic village concept is very sound, that in these areas attacks have dropped off, that SDC training is effective." While it would still take years to clear out the Viet Cong, "progress was good." Even Lansdale, who usually denounced deviations from his own preferred methods, defended the program against critics.[70]

Good news of this kind continued into the summer and fall of 1962. As reports flowed into the Pentagon, General Lemnitzer felt heartened by the "good picture of the slow but steady progress in the strategic hamlet program," particularly after the GVN finally announced a national plan for the hamlets. At last it appeared that the GVN had come around to accepting the importance of planning on a national level, something still sorely lacking when General McGarr submitted his valedictory report to CINCPAC and McNamara in March 1962. Until the summer of 1962, counterinsurgency planning resided in MAAG's Geographically Phased National Level Operations Plan for Counterinsurgency Operations. McGarr reported with some pride on the increasing integration of political, psychological, economic, and sociological activities that accompanied the military role in the countryside.[71]

The trouble with the reports coming from the field and the expectations they generated was that they remained just that, and they reflected as much wishful thinking as solid evidence. The GVN moved too quickly in expanding the strategic hamlets without a well-defined national plan. By mid-November 1962 the government had designated 10,971 for development, with 3,353 reported as completed. The JCS admitted that this rush to build hamlets evidenced "little planning and less coordination." Out of the more than 3,000 hamlets reported functioning, they judged that no more than 600 met the necessary requirements for effective defense. Yet Taylor, now the JCS chairman, could conclude his summary without "modifying the views expressed by General Harkins and Ambassador Nolting regarding the long-term virtues of the program."[72]

A schizophrenic quality pervaded many American official reports on the conduct of the war. The regular status reports told of the number of new hamlets built and Viet Cong killed at the same time that they observed that enemy attacks had increased and that the VC appeared to be winning rather than losing the war. One status report in June 1962 interrupted its celebration of progress with the recognition that GVN's control of the countryside was eroding faster than it was being secured. The Viet Cong still enjoyed an "aura of invincibility."[73] Even in the face of swelling numbers of enemy casualties, Hilsman would ask, "And how do you know if you're winning?" American journalists on the scene repeatedly asked the same question. The answer, too often for the comfort of the U.S. mission in Saigon, held that Diem was losing, not winning. To counter these impressionistic conclusions, Walt Rostow, now in the State Department, recommended the use of sampling techniques in representative areas to "obtain some measure of the way the tide is moving," but getting access to hamlets under even partial VC control would prove difficult. Moreover, if the central government learned about certain hamlets being selected for regular observation, it might act to influence the results of the survey.[74]

Whether or not an accurate assessment could come from statistical techniques remained arguable. No one could dispute, however, that the prospects of defeating communist insurgency in 1962, after a glimmer of hope, grew dimmer. The Diem regime had no intention of allowing the hamlets to develop along democratic lines, or of enacting the genuine political and economic reforms demanded by its U.S. benefactor. For Diem's brother and chief adviser Nhu, "a Rasputin-like nemesis" appointed to head the program, the strategic hamlets offered little more than political opportunity. The more hamlets he could establish, the more he could manipulate to serve the purposes of the Ngo family. Furthermore, the hamlets would not come under the central command structure American advisers deemed critical.[75]

If the Diem government looked to use the strategic hamlets to promote its power against rival generals, U.S. slowness to recognize this, as well as other miscalculations, placed some of the responsibility for failure of the program on the Kennedy administration. While some in the administration understood that forced evacuation alienated the villagers, they wrongly assumed that the benefits to the populace would override short-term disaffection. Even when the regime's intentions became clear, the administration was disinclined to oppose Diem and Nhu openly. As evidence of the shortcomings of the effort became visible, both Nolting and Harkins registered uneasiness about the GVN building hamlets in areas of VC strength.[76]

Comprehensive Plan for South Vietnam, July 1962-May 1963

McNamara, on the other hand, had reason to overlook the self-serving motives of the Ngo family in manipulating the strategic hamlet program. His persistence lay in the high hopes he invested in the Comprehensive Plan for South Vietnam (CPSVN) that emerged from the meeting in Honolulu in July 1962. After a year and a half of piecemeal projects he would finally have a blueprint for victory that would embrace all the earlier plans and give a coherence heretofore lacking. Moreover, the CPSVN would be completed at the same time as Diem's national plan.

MACV completed work on the plan and forwarded it on 19 January 1963 to CINCPAC, who endorsed it and forwarded it to the Joint Chiefs. The plan proposed that within three years the GVN would develop a capability to defend itself against the continuing threat, thus permitting the withdrawal of U.S. military assistance. This would meet McNamara's stated objective of getting out of Vietnam by the end of 1965.[77]

To move the CPSVN from the drawing board to the field would require major adjustments in the military assistance program (MAP), particularly for FY 1964. The South Vietnam national plan would have to be integrated into the CPSVN, adding to its already considerable expense. The MAP would include funds for the Civilian Irregular Defense Group, Montagnard mountain tribesmen whom the United States had been supporting concurrently with the strategic hamlet program. The additional funds became all the more urgent because the program according to McNamara's timetable had to fit into FYs 1963-65.[78]

Terminating most of the U.S. role in South Vietnam at the end of three years would compensate for the high costs of the comprehensive plan. After 1965, with minimal help from U.S. personnel, McNamara thought the GVN ought to complete the counterinsurgency effort. But even before the CPSVN would have run its course, McNamara had his sights set on returning 1,000 U.S. troops by the end of 1963. This scenario of greater cost in the present to produce fewer costs in the future accounted in large measure for his positive reading of conflicting reports from the field. Successes weighed more heavily than setbacks. When a military defeat did occur, Americans and Vietnamese alike refused to recognize it. It fell to skeptical officials from the State Department and White House, such as Hilsman and the NSC's Michael Forrestal, journalists such as David Halberstam and Neil Sheehan, and field officers such as Lt. Col. John Paul Vann to realize that the war was being lost and that nothing being done would likely reverse the outcome.[79]

The battle of Ap Bac on 2 January 1963 dramatically illustrated the difference in outlook between the skeptics and the optimists. Throughout 1962 U.S. advisers had hoped to lure the VC into open combat in sufficient numbers to permit the conventional forces of the GVN to overwhelm them. At Ap Bac, the GVN had an opportunity to meet the VC in a battle that should have led to the enemy's destruction. When GVN forces went after a VC radio station at the settlement of Ap Bac, in the Mekong Delta, they stumbled upon a regular VC battalion. The outcome was not victory, but disaster.[80]

The ARVN had surrounded a force one-fourth its size and emerged with the loss of more than 170 men killed or wounded, among the dead three American advisers, and in the wreckage five U.S. helicopters. Vann attributed the defeat to failures in training, intelligence, discipline, command, and courage. A unit of 350 guerrillas had taken on the forces of a modern army and prevailed. The VC lost 18 men, with 39 wounded. Vann, devastated by the loss, left the Army and leaked to reporters his dark view of the state of affairs in Vietnam.[81]

Yet DoD's reaction was pointedly subdued. Vann's anger and despair found no echo in MACV headquarters, in PACOM, or in the Pentagon. When CINCPAC confirmed to JCS the shooting down of five helicopters, Taylor asked for a strong statement from Harkins rebutting the charge of a crisis and commenting not on the downed helicopters but on the fine fighting qualities of the South Vietnamese soldiers. Harkins reported that ARVN forces "had made a number of errors," but described them mainly "as errors of courage rather than cowardice." Harkins and Admiral Felt downplayed the importance of the battle, blaming the bad publicity on American journalists like Sheehan, who, reporting in the *Washington Post*, called the Ap Bac operation "one of the most costly and humiliating defeats yet on the South Vietnamese army and its United States military advisers." Care to avoid a rift with Diem and his government generally guided the U.S. policy of putting a favorable gloss on even a major military setback.[82]

Such efforts to wish away what the CIA station chief in Saigon, William Colby, later called "a stunning defeat" exacerbated tension between the press and the embassy and, worse, blinded officials to increasingly harsh reality. Rather than regard the incident as a warning about the condition of the GVN forces, the Pentagon preferred to see it as an aberration. On 7 January 1963 the JCS did send out a team, headed by Army Chief of Staff Wheeler, to assess the situation in South Vietnam. The group's appraisal of the U.S. Comprehensive Plan and the GVN National Plan later in the same month ignored the message Ap Bac might have offered. Despite difficulties Harkins had in persuading Diem to listen more closely to MACV advice, the Wheeler team felt that "victory is now a hopeful prospect" and that the three-year plan to phase out U.S. support was sound. No major changes seemed necessary.[83]

The administration in Washington, not well served by such upbeat estimates and disposed itself to take a blinkered view, highlighted the positive and rationalized the negative. Thus in his State of the Union address on 14 January 1963 the president could announce that "the spearpoint of aggression has been blunted in Viet-Nam."[84] Even among the critics none urged abandoning the effort, the prevailing sentiment being to accelerate improvements.

Three months later the CIA presented in NIE 53-63 a more equivocal view of conditions in South Vietnam. On the one hand, the authors believed that enemy progress had been curtailed and that there was improvement in the situation. On the other hand, there appeared "as yet no persuasive indications that the Communists have been grievously hurt." Given an assumption of no great increase in outside support, it appeared "that the Viet Cong can be contained militarily and that further progress can be made in expanding the area of government control and in creating greater security in the countryside." But the intelligence community did not find "that it is possible at this time to project the future course of the war with any confidence." While some signs of promise in resolving political weaknesses showed, it remained "questionable" if military success could be translated into long-term political stability.[85]

An earlier version of NIE 53-63 had displayed more clarity about the prospects for success in South Vietnam and more pessimism. CIA Director John McCone, who reversed his earlier sober judgments and accepted the views of "people who know Vietnam best" (Harkins, Nolting, Felt, Wheeler), dictated the final form. A generation later former CIA official Harold P. Ford cited the revised NIE 53-63 as an example of the damage distorted intelligence could do.[86]

On the strength of a flawed reading of the war's progress CINCPAC and the JCS recommended early in February 1963 increases in GVN paramilitary force levels for FY 1963—from 81,000 to 86,000 for the Civil Guard and from 80,000 to 104,000 for the Self Defense Corps. William Bundy found these figures reasonable and recommended McNamara approve them. Similarly, when CINCPAC asked for a helicopter company plus a maintenance support unit, the secretary and the JCS had no difficulty in approving the request. Confidence in the progress of the comprehensive plan continued sufficiently high to permit the introduction of jet aircraft into the Vietnamese Air Force.[87] Although funding for six jet aircraft had been included in the FY 1962 MAP budget it had been deferred because of its seeming prohibition in the Geneva Accords. But in February 1963 Bundy and his staff could tell the JCS that the Geneva agreement permitted weapon replacements in Vietnam that were not allowed in Cambodia. Admittedly a loose construction, it provided a gloss that State and DoD found convenient.[88]

The Buddhist Rebellion and the Fall of Diem

Spring 1963 presented the administration with another reality check. The Buddhist rebellion of 8 May exposed fatal weaknesses in the GVN, but even before this eruption it became increasingly difficult for even the optimists to overlook the signs of failure: The Viet Cong were growing stronger, the strategic hamlet program was losing ground, and impatience with the rule of the Ngo family was increasing rapidly. American correspondents in Saigon made this information abundantly clear to the world at large.[89]

The delivery of jet aircraft to the Vietnamese became one of the casualties of the changing atmosphere. By the end of April it did not seem worthwhile to challenge the International Control Commission over the issue; American pilots in F-101s could do a better job of photo reconnaissance than Vietnamese pilots in T-33s, according to Hilsman, who remarked, "We don't want to rock the tippy ICC boat more than we have to." Two months before, Bundy might have disregarded this advice, but in May both Bundy and McNamara accepted it.[90]

A more serious jolt to complacency came out of a reevaluation of the CPSVN itself. Almost a year after its encouraging launching, it still lacked significant statistical information for making valid programming decisions. On 20 April Bundy recommended McNamara withhold approval until full review of the military assistance plan for South Vietnam at the meeting in Honolulu scheduled for 6 May. Furthermore, ISA opposed the large increase proposed for the military aid program for FY 1964. The secretary agreed to withhold a decision until he had an opportunity to examine detailed charts on both U.S. and ARVN forces that would let him determine the planned withdrawal of U.S. supporting elements.[91]

Skepticism about the viability of his withdrawal plans bothered but did not daunt McNamara. He felt momentarily buoyed by General Harkins's sanguine comments at the May meeting in Honolulu about the progress of the war, a view shared by "all elements of the Country Team." It still seemed appropriate to anticipate the return of some U.S. units by Christmas. McNamara reminded Hilsman of how bleak things had looked a year and a half before. Harkins's report gave reason for renewed confidence.[92]

CINCPAC inserted a sobering note with reference to the secretary's immediate goal of withdrawing 1,000 men from Vietnam, recommending withdrawal in three or four increments and postponing the decision to implement the move. The Joint Chiefs concurred. Although discussion of details about the impending withdrawal continued through the summer of 1963, the political and religious turmoil in the country froze any action. In fact, the critical need for maintenance personnel called for an increase in U.S. numbers from 16,201 at the end of August to 16,732 by the end of October. The 1,000-man withdrawal goal seemed increasingly shaky.[93]

McNamara was not without his own doubts, which he manifested in complaints about CINCPAC's fiscal projections for FYs 1965-68. He saw the four-year $575 million for MAP as $270 million too much for the South Vietnamese forces to absorb. The equipment provided would be too costly and too complicated for the ARVN to handle. The JCS instructed CINCPAC to rework the proposed program.[94]

Between May and November 1963, when the Diem regime fell, the ARVN's military struggle against the Viet Cong took a back seat to domestic upheaval within South Vietnam. Two days after the meeting in Honolulu adjourned on 6 May, a Buddhist revolt against the Ngo family broke out in the city of Hue. The immediate cause of the uprising was indiscriminate firing on a crowd of Buddhists seeking to fly their sect's flags in public despite a government ban against such exhibitions. The incident, in which several were killed, energized the many factions discontented with South Vietnam's society: Buddhists opposed to the preferential treatment of Catholics, peasants resentful of feudal landlords, a middle class angry at the insufficiency of reforms, and a public impatient with corruption everywhere. While eight or nine people died at Hue, it was the self-immolation of Buddhist monks protesting the regime of Diem and his family that shocked the American public.[95] Amid this disturbing spectacle of civil unrest and violence, the battle against the Viet Cong seemed to recede into the background in the summer and fall of 1963.

Had the government handled the protests with restraint, followed by some reasonable concessions, the outcome might have been different. Instead, the brutal repression of Buddhists, callous remarks by Mme. Nhu, Diem's sister-in-law, and the declaration of martial law in August intensified the opposition and evoked revulsion in the United States and abroad. Diem made a few ineffectual and transparently unenthusiastic promises to investigate the source of the trouble initiated by his brother, but they only added to his difficulties with the American patron. The United States felt trapped between its commitment to win a war against the communists and its identification with an increasingly unpopular regime. Rather than making an effort to alleviate U.S. embarrassment, the Diem government lashed out against the United States. Initially misled by Diem and Nhu, American officials became aware that the ARVN had not carried out the attacks on the Buddhist pagodas on 21 August—Nhu, unknown to the army, had used his Special Forces.

Ambassador Nolting, who had gone out of his way to accommodate the regime, saw the situation as serious, but felt that the GVN would "come through this one slowly," a position not widely shared in Washington and contradicted by the American press.[96] Further confrontation awaited Diem; Nolting's successor as ambassador, Henry Cabot Lodge, possessed a notoriously shorter temper. Appointed by the president in June during Nolting's absence on leave, Lodge planned to take up residence in September. In the meantime, Nolting returned to Saigon in July for one last attempt to influence Diem—too late. En route to South Vietnam, Lodge learned that Diem had imposed martial law after Nhu's Special Forces attacked the Buddhist pagodas in a betrayal of Nolting's understandings with the Ngo family.[97] The steady deterioration of Diem's standing exposed the bankruptcy of the U.S. military's soft line with the GVN. The argument that reprisals against the South Vietnamese president, a strong anticommunist, could have negative effects upon the conduct of the war seemed less persuasive as the year wore on.

Even MACV had lost patience. U.S. military advisers feared that Nhu's efforts to pin the blame for the pagoda assault on the South Vietnamese army would generate loss of public confidence in the army and further undermine the war effort. U.S. reaction in some official circles progressed beyond mere dissociation from the Diem government to sympathy for potential coups planned by disaffected generals. While Lodge doubted the steadfastness of the ARVN generals, let alone the coherence of their plans, he passed along the advice that only Nhu's removal could keep Diem in office. The military leaders needed to know how the United States would react to a coup. From a source as highly placed as Diem's personal secretary of state, Nguyen Dinh Thuan, Lodge learned that "the Army would turn firmly against Nhu if it knew that the U.S. would under no circumstances support a government with the Nhus in control." If Washington held firm, the army would respond, Lodge informed the State Department on 24 August.[98]

State replied promptly the same day, cabling Lodge that the "US Government cannot tolerate situation in which power lies in Nhu's hands. Diem must be given chance to rid himself of Nhu and his coterie." If Diem would not separate himself from his brother the administration would "face the possibility that Diem himself cannot be preserved." The most controversial section of the cable carried the instruction to tell "appropriate military commanders we will give them direct support in any interim period of breakdown [of] central government mechanism."[99]

It is difficult to conceive of a clearer signal to coup leaders than this message contained, and Lodge recognized it as such. The author of the provocative cable was not the president or even the secretary of state or secretary of defense, all out of town at the time, but evidently Assistant Secretary of State Hilsman, with the involvement also, according to Hilsman, of State's Harriman and George Ball and NSC staff member Michael Forrestal.[100] Both Kennedy and Rusk knew of its contents; Gilpatric acting for McNamara, and Maj. Gen. Victor Krulak of the Joint Staff for Taylor, had approved its dispatch. Gilpatric had judged it unnecessary to disturb the secretary's vacation. While Lodge agreed with the substance of the message, he had some doubts about the suggestion that the United States had "only to indicate to [the] 'Generals' that it would be happy to see Diem and/or Nhus go, and [the] deed would be done." The situation had become complicated, and he recommended that "we should bide our time, continuing to watch [the] situation closely."[101]

The cable went out on Saturday, 24 August. By Monday, McNamara and Taylor had returned to Washington; along with CIA Director McCone they felt as uncomfortable with the cable as Lodge. They seemed inclined toward giving Diem one more chance to take action against his brother. On 29 August Rusk instructed Lodge and Harkins to let the generals know that the United States did not plan direct involvement of U.S. forces in an attempted coup but remained willing to bless any coup that had a good chance of success. For the moment, however, information that the coup plans had been called off on 31 August resolved Washington's ambivalence.[102]

Probably more than other components of the administration, DoD gained relief from this development. At a White House meeting on 29 August McNamara had said that he saw "no valid alternative to the Diem regime," even as he recognized that a coup would probably occur. Taylor urged caution in any coup plans. But rebellious South Vietnamese generals forced the U.S. military to look more closely at the political liability that Diem had turned into, and ultimately senior U.S. military leaders were as willing as Ambassador Lodge to accept the overthrow of Diem if carried out with minimal damage to the war effort.[103]

If the Vietnamese generals' decision to call off a coup relieved pressure for the moment, it also permitted differences within the Kennedy administration to surface, as occurred in a high-level meeting at the State Department about the Vietnam situation on 31 August with Vice President Johnson, Rusk and McNamara, General Taylor, former Ambassador Nolting, and others present. Rusk and McNamara spoke out against a coup, particularly one engineered by Washington, McNamara urging the quick reestablishment of communication between the U.S. mission and Diem. In an arresting exchange that followed, Paul Kattenburg, deputy director of State's Southeast Asian Affairs office and recently returned from Vietnam, conveyed Lodge's comment to him that if the United States continued to acquiesce in Diem's repressive regime "we will be butted out of the country within six months to a year." Kattenburg said he had known Diem for 10 years, that there was little prospect of him reforming, and that it would be better "at this juncture" to disengage "honorably" before conditions further deteriorated. Rusk dismissed Kattenburg's take on the situation as overly grim and "largely speculative," saying that "it would be far better for us to start on the firm basis of two things—that we will not pull out of Vietnam until the war is won, and that we will not run a coup." McNamara, according to Krulak's account of the meeting, concurred, with Vice President Johnson getting the last word, stating that he had "great reservations . . . with respect to a coup, particularly so because he had never really seen a genuine alternative to Diem," and "that from both a practical and political viewpoint, it would be a disaster to pull out." "We should stop playing cops and robbers and get back to talking straight to the GVN," Johnson added, and "once again go about winning the war." The session ended inconclusively, but with opponents of a coup d'etat clearly outnumbering those who favored it.[104]

While Washington wrestled with the contradiction between not aiding the coup and wanting to change the regime, the Ngo family refused to yield to American pressure. Nhu even went on the offensive, accusing the CIA of plotting with the Viet Cong and on one occasion suggesting eviction of Americans from South

Vietnam. French President Charles de Gaulle had characteristically added to the confusion by proposing unification and neutralization of Indochina.[105]

From Saigon Lodge offered a clear-cut proposal to demonstrate U.S. displeasure by cutting back on aid. But before accepting Lodge's proposal the NSC in early September wanted to know if the war could be won with Diem. Once again decisions hung fire until another mission could supply answers. McNamara, demanding immediate action, dispatched General Krulak the same day, 6 September, to South Vietnam to determine the potential for military victory. Hilsman, as assistant secretary of state for Far Eastern affairs, picked Joseph Mendenhall of the Bureau of Far Eastern Affairs, and former political counselor at the embassy in Saigon, to examine the political prerequisites for success of a post-Diem regime. McNamara had directed Krulak to leave within minutes of the NSC decision but did allow the aircraft to delay long enough for Mendenhall to join Krulak on the journey.[106]

Krulak visited American advisers in the field—some 87, he claimed—and reported they were making progress at an impressive pace and that the political crisis was only a minor impediment. Mendenhall visited major cities and provincial towns, spoke with Vietnamese he had known in the past, and came away with the perception that civil government had broken down in Saigon and that a religious war between Catholics and Buddhists was pushing the country into chaos. The widespread anger over the brutality of the Special Forces could escalate into a majority preference for the VC over the Ngo family's rule, said Mendenhall. The war could not be won while the Ngos stayed in power. Given these conflicting observations, the president asked the two men on their return: "The two of you did visit the same country, didn't you?"[107]

The sharp differences between Defense and State interpretations of events in South Vietnam underscored the White House's dilemma. In public interviews on 2 and 9 September the president revealed a predilection for the State position, suggesting that Mendenhall's report would carry more weight than Krulak's. Aside from the behavior of the Ngo family toward the Buddhists, the suspicion persisted that Nhu was dickering with the North Vietnamese to seek a rapprochement entailing removal of the U.S. presence from South Vietnam.[108] Yet, frustrated as he may have been with the behavior of the Nhus and with the inability of his advisers to reach a consensus, Kennedy had few options as long as he accepted the "domino" principle. Much as the administration disliked the Saigon regime, it could not move itself to contemplate withdrawal. It had the choice then of living with Diem or finding a replacement.

Seeking "the best possible on-the-spot appraisal of the military and paramilitary effort to defeat the Viet Cong," Kennedy asked McNamara on 21 September to go to Vietnam for the purpose. Taylor and William Bundy accompanied the secretary. Hilsman, pessimistic about the mission, asked "what new questions could be put, what new officials consulted, and what a Washington delegation could accomplish that the Saigon mission couldn't." Domestic political considerations were uppermost in Kennedy's mind, in Hilsman's judgment, as the president had concern about a possible backlash at home from a perceived abandonment of South Vietnam. Kennedy did ask McNamara and Taylor to take into account in their inquiry both political and military factors. But on the long plane ride to Saigon the secretary noted pointedly that his was a military, not a political mission. If it had been political, Rusk and Harriman would have been present.[109]

The mission, in retrospect, was as important a milestone for U.S. policy in South Vietnam as the earlier Taylor mission. Intentionally or not, it set in motion the overthrow of the Diem regime little more than a month later. McNamara and Taylor quickly saw the hopelessness of the situation, stating that they had little confidence in the regime changing its ways: "Indeed, pressures may increase their [Diem's and Nhu's] obduracy. But unless such pressures are exerted, they are almost certain to continue past patterns of behavior." Taylor's JCS colleagues, from their perch in the Pentagon, had other views. Whatever the differences among the Joint Chiefs, they united in their opposition to the removal of Diem. In their judgment no other leader could take his place. As late as 30 October, General Harkins in Saigon also did not want to get rid of Diem.[110]

Despite the reservations, their firsthand experience in South Vietnam disposed McNamara and Taylor to change course. They stood ready to accept Lodge's harsh measures, such as suspending certain loans and terminating financial backing of the Special Forces. These steps would let the Diem government know how seriously the United States regarded political repression in Saigon without giving the matter so high a profile it would have sealed Diem's fate. Moreover, they felt that "a program of limited pressures . . . will not have large material effects on the GVN or the war effort, at least for 2-4 months." Couching a stern message in diplomatic language gave Diem one more chance to reshape his government.

At the same time, on 2 October, the White House announced that McNamara and Taylor had concluded "that by the end of this year, the U.S. program for training Vietnamese should have progressed to the point where 1,000 U.S. military personnel assigned to South Viet Nam can be withdrawn." But McNamara's confidence in his own timetable was clearly eroding. He was skeptical of Harkins's figures that the South Vietnam government controlled 80 percent of the population after observing that its position in the Delta "is weak and precarious. Prove me wrong." He found no answer to his questions about reduction of U.S. forces. He could conclude only that it was necessary to continue to train the Vietnamese to replace U.S. people and let them fight their own war.[111]

Lodge moved quickly to implement the McNamara-Taylor recommendations. He expected that the new policy would force Diem to come to him without closing the door to reconciliation. To make the signal even clearer the ambassador expanded the meaning of the report to include the recall of John Richardson, Colby's successor as CIA station chief in Saigon and intimate of Diem.[112]

In the meantime, the leaders of the aborted military revolt of August were encouraged by the elliptical message from Washington. Although the McNamara-Taylor report did state that "at this time, no initiative should be taken to encourage actively a change in government," the operative word was "actively." Its undertones differed from the message the coup leaders had heard two months before. The embassy knew that they were going to act. It did not have precise information on the timing.[113]

Ironically, almost at the last minute, just before the coup that took the lives of the Ngo brothers, Diem finally appeared ready to approach Lodge. He asked Lodge to accompany him to the opening on 27 October of an atomic energy laboratory. On 1 November, the day of the coup, Diem used the visit of Admiral Felt to request that Lodge make arrangements to discuss exactly what the United States wanted from his government. The next day the Ngo brothers were dead, victims of the generals' rebellion.[114]

The death of President Diem on 2 November 1963, followed so closely by the assassination of President Kennedy 20 days later, ended a seminal chapter in what was to become America's longest war. There can be little argument that the continuing escalation of U.S. involvement that marked the Johnson years sprang inexorably from actions taken during the Kennedy administration.

Of all the agencies in that administration, McNamara's DoD played the largest role in the process. The U.S. ambassador headed the country team that reported to the secretary of state. His military counterpart, first the MAAG Vietnam chief, and then the commanding general of MACV, functioned in a slightly subordinate position. But Secretary Rusk's perception of the war as primarily a military responsibility permitted McNamara quickly to fill the vacuum at the top created by Rusk's deference to DoD. Within State a strong point of view, expressed by Harriman and Hilsman as successive assistant secretaries of state for Far Eastern affairs, objected both to the GVN's conduct of the war and to the increasing military involvement of the United States. DoD benefited from the passive support of Ambassador Nolting, always sympathetic to Diem's problems, and from the active support of influential White House adviser Walt Rostow. Not coincidentally, the important Taylor-Rostow mission of 1961 and the McNamara-Taylor mission of 1963 had as leaders White House or DoD officials, not senior figures in the State Department. In between those visits the regular meetings in Honolulu of U.S. officials involved in aid to South Vietnam took place at CINCPAC headquarters at the invitation of McNamara.

DoD had its own internal differences that contributed to the lack of consensus during these formative years of the Vietnam entanglement. While the JCS and CINCPAC viewed the war as essentially a conflict between the ARVN and guerrillas serving as surrogates for the North Vietnamese military, McNamara had some doubts about this diagnosis and its resulting prescriptions. Earlier, in 1961, even the JCS had had reservations about Taylor's judgment that South Vietnam could not be saved without the introduction of a U.S. task force. When McNamara and Rusk, also in 1961, recommended dispatch of combat forces "only if necessary," Nitze argued that "there was no such thing as being a little bit pregnant, and an open-ended commitment could well lead to an American involvement in another major ground war in Asia under unfavorable political and logistical circumstances."[115] Whatever his qualms, McNamara went along with the Taylor recommendations.

McNamara's concern over waste and excessive costs tempered his aggressive inclinations. He supported such innovative measures as counterinsurgency warfare and defoliation as a way of breaking out of what he perceived as rigid, inefficient, and usually expensive programming by the military chiefs. But he opted for tradition in the choice of Harkins for the MACV post and was never comfortable with Lansdale's more extreme ideas. Increasingly, the costs of the Vietnam war disturbed him. The largest share of the MAP—44 percent—went for the Far East in FY 1963, as it did regularly during this period.[116] Whenever possible he scaled down financial requests that he considered out of line. He accepted the costs as bearable during his first two years in office on the assumption that by the end of 1965 most U.S. forces would have left South Vietnam.

The rush of events and the welter of conflicting advice, normally challenges he met head-on, frequently overwhelmed McNamara when it came to Vietnam. For all his supposed reliance on his civilian Whiz Kids and on his own quick reading of problems, he never quite grasped, or he came to understand too late, the full complexity of the situation in Southeast Asia. David Halberstam noted the oddity of his failing to utilize the talents of his bright young civilian assistants, preferring to move "virtually alone in an area where he was least equipped to deal with the problems, where his training was all wrong, the quantifier trying to quantify the unquantifiable." The mastery he quickly acquired in such areas as civil defense, strategic doctrine, and ballistic missiles was missing on Vietnam, where his preoccupation with body counts and kill ratios overlooked or discounted other, sometimes plainer and more compelling, manifestations of success or failure. His later confessions of error invariably underscored his ignorance of Vietnam, its history, its people, its culture. In this McNamara of course was not alone among the makers of policy. State's Kattenburg recalled the 31 August 1963 meeting with a dozen of Kennedy's best and brightest present—along with the defense secretary were Rusk, Taylor, Bundy, and Colby among others—to discuss what to do about the Diem problem:

> . . . I listened for about an hour or an hour and a half to this conversation before I was asked to say anything . . . and they looked to me absolutely hopeless, the whole group of them. There was not a single person there that

> knew what he was talking about. It simply looked, to me, that way. They were all great men. It was appalling to watch. I didn't have the feeling that any of them . . . really knew . . . Vietnam. They didn't know the past. They had forgotten the history. They simply didn't understand the identification of nationalism and Communism, and the more this meeting went on, the more I sat there and I thought, "God, we're walking into a major disaster."[117]

In the end, McNamara, the consummate manager, failed, as did his generals, to understand how to manage a new kind of conflict. Counterinsurgency meant more than defeating guerrillas with unconventional tactics. In Vietnam, it meant, as Lansdale, Hilsman, and others recognized, a struggle for the allegiance of a discontented and restive populace, winnable only when the government of South Vietnam as well as its U.S. advisers accepted this imperative. Lansdale's vision often seemed blurred by his personal ties to Diem as well as by his self-serving idiosyncratic ideas, yet he seems to have had a clearer perception of some of the underlying realities of the war than did the secretary of defense or the Joint Chiefs. The JCS, under Lemnitzer and Taylor, for their part too narrowly viewed Vietnam through the prism of Korea, despite occasional acknowledgment of differences inherent in a guerrilla conflict. If McNamara's approach was sometimes too analytical, theirs—proceeding from the premise that if the South Vietnamese forces could not cope with the enemy, the United States should commit as much military power as required to defeat the communist adversary in Southeast Asia—was too simple.

Both McNamara and his uniformed colleagues made their share of mistakes in Vietnam. If the military professionals understated their own culpability, McNamara at length may have been overly self-recriminating in his pained mea culpa years after. Although there was enough blame to go around, McNamara eventually would bear most of the burden for the fateful misjudgments—many of them his own—that had their origins in the Kennedy administration.

Chapter XII
Flexible Response

The advent of nuclear plenty in the 1950s created a need for guidelines for the use of nuclear weapons in war. The first clearly enunciated policy on the subject, the massive retaliation doctrine of the Eisenhower years, gave primacy to the maintenance of a powerful strategic nuclear force and looked to it as the answer to conflict at most levels. But its chief objective always was to *deter* conflict, particularly at the nuclear level. Inevitably, the rising nuclear forces of the Soviet Union and the emergence of challenges to U.S. interests in a growing number of areas around the world at relatively low levels of conflict called into question the validity and efficacy of the massive retaliation doctrine.

Kennedy entered office in January 1961 intent on changing the doctrine of massive retaliation. During the presidential campaign he had voiced strong criticism of Eisenhower's strategic policies, implying that he would subject them to a searching review. Within weeks of taking office, McNamara came to share Kennedy's concern about the need to find a more acceptable alternative.

From the beginning, the Kennedy administration struggled to fashion a strategic doctrine that would guide U.S. policy in the desired direction—toward a concept called "flexible response." This term received currency from its use in former Army Chief of Staff Maxwell Taylor's book *The Uncertain Trumpet*, published in 1959. Taylor had taken a strong position against massive retaliation, viewing the use of nuclear weapons only as a last resort. He advanced a strategy of "flexible response," which envisioned waging war with non-nuclear forces at graduated levels of intensity. For deterring nuclear war or fighting it, a force with a few hundred nuclear weapons that could inflict unacceptable damage on an enemy would be adequate.[1] This view came to be known as finite deterrence and had some support from Army and Navy leaders. It was the broader concept of flexible response that attracted the new administration.

The initial tendency by Kennedy and McNamara to minimize the prospects for use of nuclear weapons in conflicts undoubtedly received reinforcement from the international crises of the first two years of the new administration. The Bay of Pigs, Laos, Vietnam, Berlin, and the Cuban missile crisis brought home the recognition that there were circumstances where nuclear weapons should not be employed. A corollary view held that conventional war forces allowed a more proportionate and a more appropriate response and that they should be strengthened and improved to be effective at various levels of conflict. Accordingly, McNamara added to Army strength in particular. The president gave personal attention to the creation of counterinsurgency forces to deal with threats at the lowest levels of conflict. Under the Kennedy administration, conventional war forces reached a higher level of effectiveness than at any time since the Korean War. The existence of these forces at a high level of operational and logistical capability may have influenced in some measure the decision in 1965 to enlarge the U.S. role in the war in Vietnam.

Although conventional force was the preferred response, nuclear force was the absolute weapon and remained paramount in the development of doctrine. Here, too, there could be graduated response because of the availability of tactical nuclear weapons for battlefield use. And even at the higher levels of nuclear warfare there were gradations of strategic nuclear effort that focused on target systems and acquired distinctive names. "Counter-cities" strategy aimed to destroy an enemy's productive resources, urban areas, and populations. The Kennedy administration, seeking to diminish the possibility of general nuclear war, gave serious thought to "counterforce" doctrine—nuclear attack limited to an enemy's nuclear forces. This involved consideration of first strike or second strike and assurance of maintaining a reserve nuclear force capable of absorbing a first strike from the enemy and executing an effective second strike.

Any efforts to alter nuclear strategy had to take into account the reaction of the NATO allies. NATO had occupied a central place in U.S. strategic planning ever since its inception in 1949. In the 1960s the NATO allies had strong doubts about the flexible response doctrine, viewing its emphasis on conventional warfare as too dangerous and too expensive. It evoked specters of World War I and World War II battlefields, killing grounds that had drained the European countries of generations of young men. In addition, raising the nuclear threshold might well encourage rather than deter aggression; the enemy could engage in conventional warfare knowing that the West would be reluctant to escalate to nuclear warfare and even self-deterred from doing so. In a conventional war Europe would be the battleground while the United States and the Soviet Union could refrain from the use of nuclear weapons against each other. And if tactical nuclear weapons came into play Europe would still provide the battle arena. Given this reading of possibilities, the European NATO countries had good reason to cling to the deterrent threat of use of nuclear weapons at the lowest possible threshold as the best strategy.

Despite support for flexible response by OSD and Taylor, the Joint Chiefs and the military were slow to embrace the concept. Massive retaliation had guided the Air Force in its principal mission of carrying out the strategic nuclear offensive and given it primacy among the services. The Army, although it stood to gain from flexible response, remained uncertain about coping with the Soviets in large-scale conventional warfare. The Navy feared that continued emphasis on strategic nuclear forces and greater emphasis on ground forces would diminish the need for its carriers and affect its status within the military establishment. In general, all the services shared the apprehension that McNamara and OSD under the emerging doctrine would exercise greater authority over strategic and force planning.

The strategic doctrine debate hence had important national and international dimensions and involved a prominent array of players involved in discussion and debate, including McNamara and his OSD assistants, the Joint Chiefs, the military services, NATO members, think tanks, and informed observers. Each of the various proposed strategies presented complex theories and rested on necessarily tentative foundations. The lack of firm knowledge about potential enemy capabilities and intentions meant that any strategy was suspect and hypothetical—subject to change and, in the event of conflict, even drastic revision. All of these strategies essentially represented theories that proponents hoped would never be put into practice. Any authority they carried derived from the availability of military forces that might or might not be able to carry them out as intended. Since the actual circumstances of a future conflict could not be predicted accurately and therefore remained problematic, the persistent uncertainty had a strong sobering effect on the deliberations of the strategic thinkers and planners engaged in trying to settle on a consistent strategic doctrine in an unpredictable and inconstant world.

The shifting and complicated nature of strategic thinking during the McNamara years—especially between 1961 and 1964—was reflected in the range and variety of concepts that underwent scrutiny: finite deterrence, flexible response, graduated response, controlled response, counterforce, counter-cities, no-cities, full first strike, first strike, second strike, negotiating pauses, assured destruction, damage limiting. This thinking in the Defense Department and elsewhere spawned a body of ideas, studies, and actions: the missile gap, the Acheson report, the Hickey report, the Partridge report, the Basic National Security Policy document, the Athens and Ann Arbor addresses, draft presidential memoranda, and an enormous volume of papers, memos, and correspondence. Out of this welter emerged not a single overall strategic doctrine but a work in progress—a rational, pragmatic guide based on experience and subject to adaptation as constantly changing circumstances warranted.

Basic National Security Policy (BNSP)

The volatile state of the international scene and unsettled course of strategic thinking no doubt inclined the new administration to question the Eisenhower practice of promulgating an annual Basic National Security Policy (BNSP), despite its apparent flexibility. Eisenhower had used the BNSP as a policy tool, outlining broad national security aims and strategy,* thus providing strategic guidance to State and Defense. The breadth of the strategic guidance permitted a substantial measure of adaptability in determining the military budget and the military force structure, often necessary and useful when Congress failed to provide adequate funds to meet the requirements derived from the BNSP.

From early on, as it pondered changes in strategic policy, the Kennedy administration wrestled with the question of whether to continue the system of issuing an annual BNSP. According to Paul Nitze, "President Kennedy was advised by Richard Neustadt, who was then a professor at Columbia University, in a preinaugural memorandum, that a BNSP document would be used by the departments and agencies to further their pet programs and would reduce and hedge his freedom of action."[2] Indeed, military service contributions to the BNSPs included language designed to favor their own interests, allowing them to do precisely what Neustadt alleged. Moreover, retention of the BNSP did not comport with Kennedy's preference for a more informal system of national security policy decisionmaking. Kennedy eschewed Eisenhower's institutional approach, diminishing the role of the National Security Council and dismantling other aspects of the previous system.

Nevertheless, consideration of continuation of the BNSP occupied the Kennedy administration for almost two years. In DoD the chief proponent for the BNSP was Nitze, who as assistant secretary of defense for international security affairs was properly concerned with it. He argued with McNamara that the Pentagon needed the coherence that the BNSP could supply. McNamara had doubts about obtaining consensus, and the Joint Chiefs seemed to prove his point when they decried as premature any attempt to draft a doctrine that would permit controlled responses according to a range of options. In the spring of 1961, ISA Deputy Assistant Secretary Henry Rowen, acting for Nitze, began a reassessment of the BNSP, completing a draft that delineated a new strategy for controlled and discriminating nuclear response. Deputy Secretary of Defense Roswell Gilpatric circulated it on 5 May and asked for a military assessment of such options as maintaining a ready reserve nuclear force and avoiding initial attacks against industrial, population, and governmental centers. Once again McNamara expressed skepticism about the value of JCS contributions to such a plan and about the BNSP itself as the Joint Chiefs elaborated on the dangers of adopting a variety of strategic

---

* See Watson, *Into the Missile Age*, 36-38.

options. Nuclear planning, they believed, required simplicity of response.[3] Moreover, neither Kennedy nor McNamara wanted to be tied to a BNSP that might, even with its flexibility, restrict their options in dealing with the many contingencies that characterized U.S. defense problems in 1961 and subsequent years. This ISA attempt to delineate U.S. policy died an early death.

Only Walt Rostow's efforts kept the BNSP issue alive into 1963. As chairman of the State Department's Policy Planning Council he produced revised drafts of the BNSP between December 1961 and 7 May 1962, the last an ambitious document 166 pages in length, for consideration by Secretary Rusk, the president, and NSC members.[4] Having examined earlier drafts, the Joint Chiefs persisted in resisting an emphasis on conventional forces and what they perceived as a deemphasis of nuclear forces. According to General Taylor's military assistant, Col. William Y. Smith, they would have accepted the document if "dehydrated and reshaped to incorporate their comments." Without fully endorsing the JCS position, Taylor, as the president's military representative, wanted inclusion of the role of tactical nuclear weapons and statements of policy on the dual capability of military forces, conventional response to aggression, a multilateral NATO MRBM (medium-range ballistic missile) force, and modernization of NATO forces.[5]

Neither the JCS nor Taylor succeeded in modifying the document. Arguably, the nub of their objections came down to the assignment of responsibility for the 19 studies relating to military policy called for in Rostow's document. Only one consigned the principal role to the Joint Chiefs, while the chiefs shared responsibility for six others with ISA. In a memorandum to Taylor on 1 August, Colonel Smith viewed Rostow's BNSP as "noteworthy for its stark portrayal of the loss of influence of the JCS and the concurrent development of a civilian-military general staff in OSD."[6]

On 17 January 1963 the president signaled the end of the debate over the BNSP by rescinding NSC 5906/1, the last Eisenhower BNSP, and directing that policy guidance would come from "existing major policy statements of the President and Cabinet Officers, both classified and unclassified." Gilpatric let the Joint Chiefs know that he had not been "overly concerned at the failure of the Administration to complete the development of a new BNSP." Statements of the president and secretary of defense along with NSC actions would serve in its stead.[7]

McNamara even more pointedly rejected a BNSP, for which he felt no need; his posture statements would suffice to provide the necessary guidance for the fashioning of the SIOPs.* Rowen reported to Rostow in July that the secretary had asked the JCS: "On what problems do you need high level guidance?" The six issues raised by the Joint Chiefs included targeting capability of strategic retaliatory forces and the force levels needed for NATO to contain a Soviet attack by non-nuclear means. McNamara made it clear that answers to these questions did

---

* SIOP stood for Single Integrated Operational Plan. See below, p. 316.

not lie in a BNSP. Rostow had continued to work on a BNSP even after January 1963 but regretfully noted to Rusk in July that "so far as the Pentagon is now concerned the BNSP is dead."[8]

Given their own reservations, the Joint Chiefs accepted McNamara's disregard for the BNSP with equanimity. When they examined an NESC (Net Evaluation Subcommittee of the NSC) report on national planning submitted to them in July 1964, the question of the utility of a BNSP arose once again. Their response, six months later in January 1965, made clear that they did "not lack policy guidance for the preparation of military plans. Necessary guidance is obtained through both face-to-face meetings and a continuing exchange of written memoranda with the Secretary of Defense." Any attempt to "condense this guidance in a single document could result in a paper so broad that it would be difficult to keep meaningful and yet up to date." Moreover, if the document did contain specific guidance, it could impose excessively inflexible restrictions on planning. In brief, the Joint Chiefs agreed that a BNSP was unnecessary; at most, establishment of a "small, high-level interagency group might facilitate the timely initiation and coordination of political-military planning."[9]

Would a BNSP have served a useful purpose during these years? It seems doubtful that any document that might have been adopted could have exercised a significant influence. Given the doubts expressed by the White House, McNamara, and the JCS, any new product likely would have been a lowest common denominator compromise that could not have been the coherent guide such a document was intended to be. The leaders of the administration clearly preferred a mode of national security policymaking different from that of their predecessors.

The "Missile Gap"

While debate over the BNSP went on in the background, the administration grappled with the numerous elements of policy competing for attention and resolution. As a first order of business, it had to address an issue that had gained prominence in the presidential campaign of 1960 and that remained a subject of considerable controversy—the myth of Soviet nuclear superiority. The Democrats had charged the Eisenhower administration with responsibility for permitting a "missile gap" to develop in the 1950s, leaving the United States in a position inferior to the Soviets with respect to missiles. Although the perception played well for the Democrats in the fall election, acceptance of Soviet missile superiority, if left undisputed, could undermine the case for flexible response.

The missile gap controversy, following the shock of Sputnik, the successful 1957 Soviet space launch, engaged an inquiring press and a nervous public over the last two years of the Eisenhower administration. Well-publicized May Day parades and periodic news reports from Moscow dramatizing Khrushchev's boasts about the prowess of Soviet missiles culminated in an announcement by the Soviet premier on 27 January 1959 that the Soviet Union had begun mass production of intercontinental ballistic missiles. Earlier, on 16 January, Secretary of Defense Neil McElroy reportedly admitted at a secret briefing before a Senate committee that the Soviet Union would have a missile superiority of 100 over the United States by 1960. Although McElroy had asserted at a news conference on 22 January that the figure of 300, advanced in the press, was an exaggeration, he confessed in effect that a gap did exist even if its size had been overstated. President Eisenhower confirmed its existence when he informed the public on 28 January that the United States was closing the gap. His assurance did little to calm critics.[10]

Given this background, it came as no surprise that the missile issue provided fodder for the 1960 presidential campaign. In August of that year Senator Kennedy warned about dangerous days as the missile gap loomed "larger and larger ahead." Over the next two months of campaigning he repeatedly demanded a crash missile program to accompany a complete reevaluation of national defense organization. His first State of the Union message, in which he "instructed the Secretary of Defense to reappraise our entire defense strategy," echoed this particular campaign theme. Specifically, McNamara was to reexamine the missile program in light of the gap.[11]

In the midst of an apparent consensus over a missile crisis the secretary of defense made an embarrassing gaffe—revealing that his examination of the problem found that U.S. strategic military power considerably exceeded that of the Soviet Union. The trouble began at a background session with a group of newsmen in his Pentagon conference room on 6 February 1961, where he offhandedly said that "if there was a gap, it was in our favor." To McNamara's chagrin, headlines appeared the next morning describing the missile gap as a myth. Although they did not identify McNamara as the source, the journalists made no effort to disguise the origins of the story. Appearing naive or inexperienced in the ways of Washington, McNamara seemingly failed to recognize the potential ammunition he was giving to the Republican opposition, still smarting over Democratic attacks alleging the existence of a missile gap.[12]

Clearly the administration suffered embarrassment from McNamara's inadvertent disclosure. A disclaimer did not stop further inquiries. Official spokesmen noted ongoing studies had reached no conclusions yet about the missile gap. The president himself hoped that no gap would be found.[13]

General Lemnitzer, chairman of the JCS, later wondered about the figures bandied about. He had thought a small gap possible, but in favor of the United States, "that we were in the lead. The strange thing about it, was that in the campaign, it came out the other way around.... That was the way it ended up in politics." Gilpatric, also reflecting on the question a generation later, claimed that the gap "was not an issue that was fabricated. It was a case of no one on the U.S. side knowing specifically."[14]

The secretary quickly recovered his composure. He explained away the missile flap as simply a matter of emphasis. A missile gap existed only in the sense that the United States lagged behind in the number of ICBMs. Given the small number on both sides, this amounted to little in terms of the overall U.S. strategic posture in the spring of 1961. Technically, the gap had no meaning. What mattered at the moment, he told newsmen at the notorious meeting on 6 February and congressmen two weeks later, was "our total deterrent strength, and I stated there was no destruction gap or no deterrent gap as it related to our present situation." In this context, the United States enjoyed a commanding lead in long-range bombers, while the accelerated production of Polaris and development of Minuteman missiles represented a further strengthening of overall U.S. nuclear superiority. In April he informed another congressional subcommittee that for most of 1963 a small missile gap in ICBMs might exist but by the end of that calendar year the U.S. inventory of ICBMs "may exceed that of the Soviet Union." Confident of his figures, he convinced Congress that this was a foregone conclusion.[15]

In effect, the new secretary of defense confirmed the judgment of his predecessor, Thomas Gates, who had informed senators in January 1960 that while the Soviets probably held the lead in the number of missiles, there was no "deterrent gap."[16] Ironically, Congress and the press construed Gates's characterization as acknowledging the existence of a missile gap, while they concluded that McNamara, expressing much the same sentiments, exposed the gap as a myth. Obviously, enough confusion existed about a gap to permit conflicting interpretations.

Adding to the confusion was the difference between the theoretical capability of the Soviets to produce a missile and their probable rate of production and deployment. The theoretical capability obviously would exceed their probable rate of production. Beyond these considerations questions existed about the reliability and accuracy of the missiles in reaching their targets as well as about the vulnerability of prospective targets. The effectiveness of potential missile defenses would become a factor in measuring relative strength and deficiencies.[17]

National Intelligence Estimates (NIEs) in 1960 and 1961, the period when they would have the most influence on the Kennedy administration, underscored reasons for uncertainty about all aspects of the Soviet missile program. While the findings in the NIE reports were consistent within the limits of available information, what the analysts did not know far exceeded what they did know about Soviet production of missiles, let alone the uses to which they might be put. In May 1960 the CIA admitted that "exhaustive reexamination has failed to establish Soviet ICBM production rates or to provide positive identification of any operational ICBM unit or launching facility other than the test range." Three months later, the analysts noted that they still had "no direct evidence of the present or planned future rate of production. As yet, we can identify no ICBM-related troop training activities, nor can we positively identify any operational launching site, as distinguished from the known test range facilities." In December 1960, at the time of McNamara's designation as secretary of defense, they noted that estimates of Soviet ICBM forces were "highly tentative."[18]

By June 1961, after the controversy over the gap had mostly subsided, the CIA could report that "US intelligence has acquired a considerable body of additional information pertaining to Soviet programs for ICBMs and other ballistic missiles."[19] Credit for more accurate identification of the state of the Soviet missile program went in part to the new spy satellite, SAMOS (an acronym for satellite and missile observation system), which orbited on 31 January 1961 and made some 500 passes before its transmitters were switched off. SAMOS developed its own film, scanned it electronically, and radioed the pictures to ground stations. Not until September 1961 did the satellite produce reliable evidence that Soviet ICBM strength stood at a much lower level than U.S. analysts had assumed—10-25 launchers for ICBMs and 250-300 launchers for MRBMs. Still, it remained clear that of all the Soviet programs, their missile systems remained the most difficult to project.[20]

As McNamara entered office, he had a choice between the figures offered by the CIA and Air Force intelligence; the latter, with a strong interest in higher estimates, regularly dissented from the CIA's findings in this period. The Air Force sought to eliminate the putative gap by increasing the number of missiles and bombers. McNamara fully recognized the self-serving interest in the Air Force estimates. Years later he noted that a copy of Air Force intelligence estimates had been leaked to members of Congress, and this formed the basis of the charges against the Eisenhower administration in the presidential campaign of 1960. The new secretary made it clear that he and his staff judged the CIA estimates more accurate than those of the Air Force.[21]

By January 1961 enough information had emerged to show the early figures as greatly overstated. A downward revision from the estimate of possibly 500 Soviet operational ICBMs in place by 1962, made by the Eisenhower administration in 1959, seemed reasonable, particularly when distinguishing between "ICBMs for inventory" and "ICBMs on launchers."[22]

The success of SAMOS and other reconnaissance satellites in replacing the more vulnerable U-2s for surveillance of Soviet installations raised the CIA's status in OSD's estimation, helping to offset some of the damage to the CIA's reputation from the Bay of Pigs fiasco. The two agencies achieved close cooperation through the easy relationship between Richard Bissell of the CIA and Joseph Charyk, under secretary of the Air Force in the Eisenhower administration, who stayed on for two years under McNamara. Bissell, whose career was shortened by his role in the Bay of Pigs disaster, figured prominently in the building of both the U-2 and the satellite systems. Charyk and McNamara had worked together as Ford officials in the 1950s. This fruitful relationship survived Bissell's departure in 1961, but ended when the Air Force pressed for control over the entire reconnaissance project in 1963.[23]

To reduce potential disputes and sort out lines of responsibilities, Deputy Secretary of Defense Gilpatric and Deputy Director of the CIA General Charles P. Cabell agreed in September 1961 to establish a joint National Reconnaissance Office (NRO), headed by an Air Force official, to finance and control all overhead reconnaissance projects. The Air Force regarded control of the photo satellite program as a basic part of its mission, prescribed by McNamara, to perform "research, development, test and engineering of Department of Defense space development programs or projects."[24]

Another agreement between the CIA and OSD made the secretary of defense the executive agent for the program, with the NRO under his direction and control. Although developed jointly with the CIA, the NRO would operate as a separate entity of DoD. This arrangement did not signal a victory for the Air Force, given McNamara's concern that Air Force dominance could jeopardize his capacity to make independent judgments on weapon procurement and strategic planning. Consequently, he often continued to side with the CIA in opposition to Air Force positions, as he had earlier in assessing the missile gap.[25]

The missile gap disappeared as an issue when Gilpatric provided in a widely publicized speech on 21 October 1961 what amounted to the official interment of the "gap." He noted that "the destructive power which the United States could bring to bear even after a Soviet surprise attack upon our forces would be as great as—perhaps even greater than—the total undamaged force which the enemy can threaten to launch against the United States in a first strike." Gilpatric's confidence in U.S. second-strike capability gained assurance from the CIA estimate in September that the number of Soviet ICBMs on launchers appeared to be between 10 and 25, with no marked increase expected during the immediately succeeding months.[26]

Why did the Kennedy administration engage in a rapid buildup of strategic missiles after it perceived that the United States did not lag behind in a deterrent gap? McNamara's ICBM program did not simply represent an automatic response to a presidential mandate or a submission to political pressures. The secretary appeared to have taken seriously the message of the CIA reports, particularly in late 1960, that considered the relatively low Soviet production schedule a temporary phenomenon, to last only until a new generation of more powerful missiles came on line. Moreover, the CIA noted that the building of an ICBM force "has emboldened the Soviets to challenge the West on a vital issue like Berlin, and has led them to engage the West in other areas around the world formerly conceded to be beyond the reach of Soviet power."[27]

The Acheson Report

Aware from the outset of NATO's uneasiness over the missile gap and any movement away from massive retaliation toward flexible response, the Kennedy administration sought to assuage the allies' worries while trying to make them understand the need to reassess strategic doctrine as Cold War relationships and conditions evolved. To prepare for presentation of changes in guidance at future NATO meetings, Secretary Rusk commissioned former Secretary of State Dean Acheson in early February 1961 to chair an Advisory Committee on NATO. President Kennedy met with Acheson twice in March for discussion of the report, and the NSC made changes in it late in the month.[28]

Acheson also held discussions on major issues with leading OSD officials, particularly Nitze, a former colleague at the State Department and the Defense representative on the committee. They agreed on the importance of addressing NATO's concerns about the appearance of the United States decoupling its defense from its European partners. And they recognized that the change in nuclear doctrine implicit in flexible response would evoke resistance or objections that might be deflected by conceding Europeans a greater voice in nuclear targeting. The JCS expressed itself as generally in accord with the final version of the report but suggested a small number of modifications.[29]

The Acheson report, approved by the president on 21 April as a policy directive entitled "Regarding NATO and the Atlantic Nations," highlighted the virtues of flexible response and helped advance a strategy that Kennedy and McNamara had already begun to develop. The major thrust of the report appeared under the heading "A Pragmatic Doctrine," wherein Acheson urged that the allies give first priority to contingencies short of nuclear or massive non-nuclear assault. To establish a credible deterrent against a subatomic war, NATO should improve its non-nuclear forces to the point where it would have the capacity of "halting Soviet forces . . . for a sufficient period to allow the Soviets to appreciate the wider risks of the course on which they are embarked." The report stressed that nuclear weapons in Europe should be carefully controlled. Moreover, the alliance's vital interest demanded that "the major part of U.S. nuclear power not be subject to veto," although the United States should have veto power and control over the use of nuclear weapons by other NATO countries. The president "should make entirely clear his intention to direct use of nuclear weapons if European NATO forces have been subjected to an unmistakable nuclear attack or are about to be overwhelmed by non-nuclear forces." This reassurance would presumably help make more palatable to the NATO countries the U.S. suggestions for change in doctrine.[30]

The Europeans seemed unimpressed by Kennedy's remarks to the NATO Military Committee on 10 April when he outlined the report's main recommendations and by General Lemnitzer's comments at the same session. Lemnitzer told the Military Committee that it was "imperative for the security of NATO" that America's strategic forces be "sufficiently invulnerable to be able to absorb, if necessary, an initial nuclear attack, and still retain the ability to inflict unacceptable damage on the attacker." The allies responded negatively despite the emphasis on the continued U.S. presence in Europe and pledge to share information on nuclear targeting. The new NATO secretary general, Dirk Stikker, specifically warned against letting the pendulum "swing too far away from massive retaliation."[31]

Lemnitzer spoke as a U.S. member of the Military Committee, but he and the Joint Chiefs were dispatching a different message to the secretary of defense. Like their European counterparts, the chiefs questioned dependence on conventional forces. "While accepting the desirability of 'raising the threshold' . . ., the Joint Chiefs of Staff cannot envisage, now or in the future, a situation in which an attack by as much as 60 divisions could be held by non-nuclear means for a period of possibly weeks." In reviewing a draft of Acheson's report in late March they continued to express reservations, despite claiming to be "generally in accord" with it. They disagreed (as did Supreme Allied Commander, Europe, General Norstad) with the Acheson position that the more likely contingencies—those short of nuclear or massive non-nuclear attack—deserved "first priority." The JCS preferred a less emphatic "priority"—on the grounds that limited war with the Soviet Union was no more likely than a general war.[32] The policy directive issued by the president on 21 April ignored the JCS position.

The Joint Chiefs' skepticism may have impaired the ability of OSD to make effective arguments. In any event, the allies either ignored the call for increased ground troops, or, as the British did, actually reduced their numbers. As for the dangers of an independent nuclear force, the French consciously flouted the U.S. preference by continuing development of their own nuclear deterrent. Franz Josef Strauss, West Germany's defense minister, paid a visit to Norstad at Supreme Allied Headquarters, Europe (SHAPE) to emphasize the error of letting the Soviets think that "there was a clear threshold beneath which conventional forces may be employed."[33] These responses of the NATO allies in 1961 occurred at a time when the United States, energized by the Berlin crisis, materially increased its contribution to NATO's conventional military strength.

Administration officials made repeated efforts to win over the Europeans. Gilpatric denied rumors that the United States would abandon the nuclear option. Nitze, in particular, took the offensive, working with Thomas Finletter, U.S. representative to the North Atlantic Council. Finletter tried to convince the British that an increase in conventional capabilities would not decrease nuclear deterrent capability, while Nitze emphasized to Secretary General Stikker what to him seemed obvious: "We should be prepared for lesser things; the alternative is accommodation to the Russian intentions, for example, a free city of West Berlin, which is not acceptable to Europe."[34]

But as the December meeting of the NATO Military Committee drew closer, U.S. Representative General Clark Ruffner warned that "with the U.S. emphasis on buildup of conventional forces, we have consistently been faced with the feeling among our NATO allies that we are deemphasizing our nuclear capability. The fact that the U.S. has powerful strategic forces and will not hesitate to utilize them when the occasion arises demands constant reiteration."[35] These arguments, no matter how compelling they appeared to Americans, did not convince Europeans.

The Athens and Ann Arbor Addresses

Despite the strong negative reaction of the NATO allies to the proposed policy, McNamara continued to press for it. At the Paris meeting of NATO ministers in December 1961 he made an unsuccessful attempt to sway European critics. Understandably, the substance of his talk centered on the recent Berlin crisis and on the importance of U.S. readiness to meet it on any level. But in advocating the presence of large and diversified forces in the service of NATO, he delivered an ambiguous message that confused his listeners. At the same time that he listed the impressive numbers of strategic ballistic missiles and long-distance bombers, he expressed shock and dismay at witnessing "glaring weaknesses" in NATO's conventional ground forces, with "deficiencies . . . so extensive that both initial and sustained combat effectiveness are inadequate to meet NATO's needs."[36] His alarm over Europe's failure to contribute did not mesh well with the confidence he expressed in the U.S. nuclear contribution. Europeans considered the latter sufficient if the United States really intended to use its nuclear power; by alluding to conventional forces and to the seeming advantage the Soviet Union held in non-nuclear forces, McNamara raised suspicion about the United States' real nuclear intentions. If he had provided accurate information to his allies, why then the alarming demand for more conventional forces from them?

Against this background of skepticism and disagreement, McNamara delivered a major address to the North Atlantic Council in Athens on 5 May 1962 in which he intended to clarify the many misunderstandings that had clouded the meaning of flexible response. And since counterforce seemed one of the most contentious components of flexible response, the Athens meeting offered an opportunity to explain fully its role in nuclear strategy.

The initial draft of the Athens speech was the work of William W. Kaufmann, a McNamara consultant and key adviser on strategic matters. Kaufmann recollected some years later, "I went off into a corner and started to draft the Athens speech at the request of Rowen. I don't recall receiving any guidance on it; it just seemed like a good subject for a speech." He also noted that McNamara encountered difficulty in gaining its acceptance within the administration but finally "bulled it through," with the president's support.[37]

Indeed the president had "read with interest" the draft of McNamara's remarks and suggested changes and emphases. He wanted McNamara "to repeat to the point of boredom that our general war response will come only if our allies are subjected to major attack." He expressed strong concern that the speech be "held within the alliance" and not become available to the Soviets.[38]

The task McNamara set for himself at Athens, to resolve all doubts, was formidable, especially after the cool reception Europeans had accorded most of his initiatives during the past year. He hoped to convince NATO members that nuclear weapons represented no panacea, and that the immediate future demanded a new type of deterrent policy. Perhaps he delivered an overload of information. Kaufmann suggested that the Athens speech tried to convey too many messages to too many audiences.[39] Over the span of one hour, McNamara offered Europeans a detailed exposition of American thought on such major strategic issues as the way in which the United States planned its nuclear operations, the dangers of proliferation of national nuclear forces, the concept of a multilateral NATO MRBM force,* and the changed role strategic nuclear forces would play in the composition of future deterrents.[40]

Counterforce and the imperatives that made it essential as a new NATO strategy emerged in the following passage that highlighted how nuclear technology and weapons had revolutionized warfare since 1945.

> The unprecedented destructiveness of these arms has radically changed ways of thinking about conflict among nations. It has properly focused great attention and efforts by the Alliance on the prevention of conflict. Nevertheless, the U.S. has come to the conclusion that to the extent feasible basic military strategy in general nuclear war should be approached in much the same way that more conventional military operations have been regarded in the past. That is to say, our principal military objectives, in the event of a nuclear war stemming from a major attack on the Alliance, should be the destruction of the enemy's military forces while attempting to preserve the fabric as well as the integrity of allied society. Specifically, our studies indicate that a strategy which targets nuclear force only against cities or a mixture of civil and military targets has serious limitations for the purpose of deterrence and for the conduct of general nuclear war.
>
> In our best judgment, destroying enemy forces while preserving our own societies is—within the limits inherent in the great power of nuclear weapons—a not wholly unattainable military objective. Even if very substantial exchanges of nuclear weapons were to occur, the damage suffered by the belligerents would vary over wide ranges, depending upon the targets that are hit. If both sides were to confine their attacks to important military targets, damage, while high, would nevertheless be significantly lower than if urban-industrial areas were also attacked.[41]

---

* See Chapter XV.

McNamara granted uncertainty that the Soviet Union would follow the U.S. path, but he claimed that it would have strong incentives to do so. He presented figures intended to give comfort to allies. And the conclusions that followed from them he intended should end once and for all doubts about U.S. purposes. "The United States has made clear," McNamara insisted, "that it places the major Soviet nuclear forces threatening Europe in the same high priority category as those also able to reach North America. In short, we have undertaken the nuclear defense of NATO on a global basis. This will continue to be our objective. In the execution of this mission, the weapons in the European theater are only one resource among many."[42]

The secretary placed heavy emphasis on a U.S. nuclear blanket that would cover NATO. Indivisibility of control was a key term in McNamara's lexicon, with unity of planning, decisionmaking, and direction vital in responding to enemy actions. "There must not be competing and conflicting strategies in the conduct of nuclear war," he asserted. "We are convinced that a general nuclear war target system is indivisible and if nuclear war should occur, our best hope lies in conducting a centrally controlled campaign against all of the enemy's vital nuclear capabilities," something not possible if other nuclear forces targeted against cities operated independently. "In the event of war," he was convinced, "the use of such a force against the cities of a major power would be tantamount to suicide . . . . In short, then, weak nuclear capabilities, operating independently, are expensive, prone to obsolescence, and lacking in credibility as a deterrent."[43] It took no leap of imagination for Britain and France to identify themselves as the "relatively weak nuclear forces" that McNamara mentioned.

Aware of the possibility of misinterpretation, the secretary anticipated it by confessing that he realized there were those who believed that "the United States and the Soviet Union might seek to use Europe as a nuclear battleground and thus avoid attacks on one another's homelands. Not only does my government emphatically reject such a view; we also regard it as unrealistic. It ignores the basic facts of nuclear warfare I have described."

U.S. authority would extend to tactical nuclear weapons as well, which would be minimized if not entirely removed in time. McNamara observed that the introduction of battlefield weapons into NATO occurred when its shield was weak and the Soviet atomic stockpile small. Under those circumstances NATO could hope to stop a Soviet advance quickly by use of tactical nuclear weapons. Conceivably, the situation might hold true in the early 1960s, but not for much longer. NATO could not avoid nuclear retaliation in the event it initiated use of nuclear weapons. The secretary warned that "even a local nuclear exchange could have consequences for Europe that are most painful to contemplate. Further, such an exchange would be unlikely to give us any marked military advantage. It could rapidly lead to general nuclear war."

If the use of strategic nuclear and tactical nuclear weapons entailed too great risks, the logical alternative to deterring subnuclear warfare lay in the strength of NATO's conventional troop disposition. McNamara admitted that a conventional forward defense would not necessarily defeat every conceivable mobilization of Soviet power, but in the event of impending defeat nuclear strategy would come into play.[44]

The United States had already done its share to buttress both conventional and nuclear forces. In the wake of the Berlin crisis, it had raised by $10 billion the previously planned levels of non-nuclear defense expenditures for FYs 1962 and 1963, increasing the number of its combat divisions from 11 to 16. And the United States now prepared to do more: exchange detailed information on nuclear forces, consult about basic plans, and commit Polaris submarines to NATO service. The secretary dramatized U.S. priorities by noting that "effective today" he would commit the five fully operational Polaris submarines for NATO use. Beyond these measures, the United States stood willing to discuss with the allies the need for a NATO medium-range ballistic missile force "as soon as possible after this meeting."

While McNamara's optimistic conclusions did foresee difficulties ahead, none were insurmountable. "The question is not one of the ability of the Alliance but of its will. The obstacles are real . . . . However, the brute facts of technology and the realities of military power cannot be denied. They call for us to take common action."[45]

No immediate response came from the allies on the doctrinal issue of counterforce, but they wondered how the proposed MRBM force stood any chance of implementation given the U.S. emphasis on conventional armaments. Both supporters of the multilateral concept and those, such as the British, with a preference for independent national nuclear forces, were left shaking their heads over U.S. intentions and whether any European entity had a role to play in the new scheme. On other subjects the reaction was muted, owing to both the classified nature of the Athens discussion and a need to digest the full import of McNamara's statement, with its mixed signals and wide-ranging scope.[46]

When McNamara covered much of the same ground in his commencement address at the University of Michigan in Ann Arbor six weeks later on 16 June 1962, the allies became more outspoken. The Ann Arbor address, distilling and spotlighting the Athens themes in a public forum, provided an occasion for Europeans to air publicly views they already held—and had articulated in executive sessions—over the past year.[47]

The inspiration for a public version of the Athens speech came from McNamara. His assistant, Adam Yarmolinsky, prepared the first draft, with the help of Rowen and Alain Enthoven of the comptroller's office; Daniel Ellsberg, then an ISA staffer, revised it; Kaufmann merely added some minor touches, although he opposed its presentation because of its broad political implications.[48] McNamara at Ann Arbor unintentionally attracted attention to the more sensitive portions of the Athens pronouncements but omitted the careful reasoning that underlay them. The intricate explanations at Athens became oversimplified at Ann Arbor. Opponents could seize on phrases and recommendations, take them out of context, and shade their meanings. When McNamara asserted that "basic military strategy in a possible general nuclear war should be approached in much the same way that more conventional military operations have been regarded in the past," the concept emerged as a possible first-strike option. When he spoke of the importance of centralized control and of the dangers inherent in the creation of national nuclear forces, he appeared to insult the national pride of both Britain and France.[49] Publicity provoked Europeans into defiant postures; it precipitated the very reactions McNamara's advisers had wanted to discourage and permitted the Europeans to evade the powerful issues that he was trying to convince them to confront.

At no point, for example, did the allies face up to the feasibility of conventional defense in Europe and the possibility of successfully meeting a conventional attack with conventional forces. Although McNamara at Athens had pointed out deficiencies in NATO's non-nuclear forces, he had also pointed out the strengths of the conventional forces at hand, especially that "NATO has more men under arms than the Soviet Union and its European satellites."[50] He deplored the allies' tendency to judge themselves hopelessly inferior in a non-nuclear conflict.* In short, McNamara in great detail at Athens and in broad strokes at Ann Arbor attempted to persuade the allies to his way of thinking about strategic policy. He had asked for an increased commitment, but only a modest one.

Counterforce and Flexible Response

McNamara's strong preoccupation with a counterforce strategy in 1961-62 had its roots in the strategic thinking of the 1950s. By the end of that decade counterforce had emerged as a more humane alternative to the indiscriminate doctrine of massive retaliation because it would allow the United States to target military installations while sparing heavily populated cities. Accompanying the counterforce/no cities policy came an emphasis on damage limitation through anti-ballistic missiles (ABMs) that would help protect U.S. urban areas from the effects of a nuclear war. It attracted attention first among strategic analysts in the Air Force and at Rand but did not receive official policy consideration until the Kennedy administration took office.[51]

The counterforce strategy may have been set in motion early in 1961 at an evening meeting of the secretary with Enthoven, Marvin Stern, a DDR&E offi-

---

* While the Soviet Union had 147 divisions, they were smaller than their Western counterparts and most of them were maintained at much less than full strength. See Chapter XIV.

cial, and Kaufmann. The "no cities" aspect held a special appeal. According to Stern, "McNamara listened for about two hours as Kaufmann gave a very good low-key briefing on counterforce/no cities. He asked no questions during the briefing, and at the end he asked the key question: 'What good is it if the other guy doesn't do the same thing?'" To which Stern offered the answer, educate the Soviets about the mutually destructive qualities of the nuclear weapon.[52] And if their education proved to be incomplete, U.S. possession of a sophisticated satellite system in SAMOS, the capacity to survive the effects of a first strike, and the Strategic Air Command's ability to destroy the enemy's military arsenals could combine to keep deterrence credible.

Kaufmann saw himself chiefly as the explicator of the counterforce concept and maintained that it was Comptroller Charles Hitch, Rowen, and Enthoven who influenced McNamara. He observed that the linking of "no cities" to counterforce signified not only confidence in U.S. power to destroy most military targets, but also to spare civilian lives. Looking on counterforce as "in the nature of controlled response," Kaufmann thought that there were "various ways of implementing it as a strategy." Mass destruction would be avoided. An attack on enemy cities would come only in the final stage of a nuclear war if necessary.[53]

Like Kaufmann, McNamara recognized in counterforce the possibility of a system of controlled response permitting rational choices of the level of warfare to be pursued. To function effectively counterforce required a close management of military operations to a degree not attempted in the past and determination of quantifiable measurements of the number and variety of weaponry needed and the funds to acquire them. OSD would exercise central authority in determining choices of weaponry.

In some key respects OSD and the JCS took adversarial positions on the counterforce subject. When McNamara asked the Joint Chiefs in March 1961 to present a "doctrine" on thermonuclear attack that would permit controlled response and negotiating pauses in the event of a Soviet nuclear attack, they found the concept impractical, at least for the present. As they warned the secretary, national strategy for limited war called for the use of "whatever weapons and forces are required by the military and political exigencies involved in each particular situation and by the national objectives to be attained." They responded formally but more elliptically in April when they said that there was "no significant likelihood" of a nuclear attack against the United States "which would be so executed that it would be to the advantage of the United States and/or its Allies in the current period to respond under a degree of control beyond that provided in current policy, doctrines and strategic plans."[54] In effect, they were saying that the NATO strategic concept of 1957, MC 14/2, supporting massive retaliation, remained valid in 1961. Whether war came by deliberate attack or by miscalculation, NATO could not prevent the Soviets from overrunning Europe unless NATO used nuclear weapons strategically and tactically.

In an accompanying note to McNamara on the same day, 18 April, Lemnitzer underscored this message in stating his personal judgment that "we do not now have adequate defenses, nor are our nuclear retaliatory forces sufficiently invulnerable, to permit us to risk withholding a substantial part of our effort, once a major thermonuclear attack has been initiated." His skepticism about a definitive doctrine notwithstanding, Lemnitzer and the Joint Chiefs remained willing to examine options for controlled attack and response as they made plans for the mid-1960s.[55]

In SIOP-63, the Joint Chiefs made no significant changes from SIOP-62* except for recommending a measure of greater flexibility by withholding attacks against several categories of targets—all attacks against China and satellite states except those essential in suppressing satellite-state air defenses, direct attacks against primary control centers in the Sino-Soviet bloc, and attacks against urban-industrial centers in communist countries. But division occurred over the matter of damage criteria in the JCS report to McNamara on 18 August 1961. A majority of the chiefs opted for a 75 percent expectancy of destroying not only Moscow and Peking but also nuclear delivery forces threatening the United States and other military and industrial resources. Air Force Chief of Staff General Curtis LeMay dissented, asserting that too many major control centers would remain untouched. The Air Force asked for more stringent criteria, with a 90 percent assurance of destroying or neutralizing nuclear delivery forces and essential military installations and 70 percent assurance of inflicting severe damage to critical elements of the industrial infrastructure. McNamara accepted the majority view in general but with reservations that brought the damage criteria closer to those proposed by the Air Force. His position rested on achieving a capability to withhold all attacks except those essential to destruction of nuclear forces and retaining a reserve force that could destroy or neutralize most of the enemy's other assets.[56]

In September 1961, the secretary portrayed the new strategic approach to the president as a two-part program: "in the event of a Soviet nuclear attack, first, to strike back against Soviet bomber bases, missile sites, and other installations associated with long-range nuclear forces, in order to reduce Soviet power and limit the damage that can be done to us by vulnerable Soviet follow-on forces, while, second, holding in protected reserve forces capable of destroying the Soviet urban society, if necessary, in a controlled and deliberate way."[57]

Initially, McNamara found qualified support for counterforce doctrine from the Air Force. Taylor would later note that Air Force leaders at first were unenthusiastic because of their attachment to manned bombers and concern that counterforce strategy focused primarily on ICBMs, but once they perceived that counterforce advanced their long-term interest, the "counterforce extremists ran

---

* See below, p. 316.

out of the ceiling in terms of requirements for missiles and aircraft." And, indeed, USAF leaders recognized that a striking force capable of carrying out counterforce objectives would require a substantial increase in bombers and missiles for the service. The Air Force's conception of counterforce differed from McNamara's by including a possible preemptive strike against Soviet nuclear forces as an intrinsic part of the strategy. SAC Commander in Chief General Thomas S. Power observed later that it would be foolhardy to claim certainty of knocking out the Soviet Union's residual strategic force through a retaliatory attack. Planners must leave open the option of a first strike.[58]

LeMay and his chief planner, Maj. Gen. David A. Burchinal, reacted much the same as Power in a conversation with Gilpatric in December 1961. Assuming the availability of a large, hardened, and dispersed Minuteman force and an "immediate go-ahead on the B-70," they envisioned "full first strike capability." LeMay in July 1962 offered testimony on behalf of counterforce as compelling as anyone on McNamara's staff, but not for the same reasons: "When we speak of counterforce we mean a capability of attacking the enemy's forces and destroying them. There has been a theory advanced by some people in the past that all you required was a force of the necessary size to destroy X-number of his cities, and a threat of having that done would deter him from starting a war."[59]

Air Force views on first strike received little encouragement from OSD. McNamara's focus on an effective and credible second-strike capability helped inspire the early attention he gave to the Polaris seaborne and Minuteman hardened missiles, least vulnerable to an offensive striking force. This became a critical element in OSD's thinking. There would be "no B-70s parked and concentrated on some airfields where they can be knocked out by enemy ballistic missiles," Enthoven recalled. "Instead, our forces would be ICBMs in concrete and steel underground silos, missiles in submarines . . . so that the Soviets wouldn't attack us because we could strike back in retaliation."[60]

But if the Air Force's version of counterforce differed from OSD's, other voices within OSD or closely aligned to it also expressed reservations about the doctrine. Nitze, for example, expressed the view that "to win a war in politically meaningful terms it would be necessary to have a counterforce capability," but he doubted that a counterforce second-strike capability was "technically feasible." And if a true counterforce capability could not be attained, there was a need for a balanced force that could provide more than a second-strike capability. Nitze later pointed to these weaknesses as contributing to the downgrading of the doctrine in 1963.[61] Taylor would point to concern over costs, as the increase in requirements for the Air Force alone "would have been astronomical." Moreover, in questioning whether "counterforce is related to flexible response," he agreed with the Joint Chiefs' position. Responding to a McNamara request in April 1961, the JCS stated that "attempts to implement a strategy including such options [controlled response and negotiating pauses], or declarations of such intent, would at the present time be premature and could gravely weaken the current deterrent posture."[62]

These criticisms did not impress the secretary of defense in 1961. He gave attention to the other side of the coin—the impact that lessening of the danger of nuclear conflict would have on conventional defenses. If the success of a counterforce strategy raised the nuclear threshold so high that strategic missiles would not be deployed by either side, then conventional forces would offer the logical alternative for defense of Western Europe.

Given the greater cost of conventional forces and the perceived imbalance between NATO forces and their Warsaw Pact counterparts, it seemed logical to look to battlefield nuclear weapons to compensate for inferiority in ground forces. But enthusiasm for tactical nuclear weapons had dimmed considerably since the end of the 1950s. Skeptics such as Enthoven considered the placement of these weapons in Europe to be a mistake. He claimed later that no one could ever come up with a credible scenario for use of battlefield nuclear weapons. Instead of rectifying conventional manpower imbalances they would exacerbate them. No matter how resolute the intention to limit these weapons to distinct military objectives, their use would escalate conflict into an uncontrolled and unrestrained exchange of strategic weapons, first in Europe and then between continents. Moreover, pressures in time of crisis would mount to commit these forward-based nuclear weapons before they would fall into enemy hands.[63]

McNamara made plain his impatience with tactical nuclear weapons in a barrage of questions he asked Lemnitzer in May 1962 about their usefulness: "What is the purpose of these weapons? In what contingencies would they be used? And to achieve what objectives? . . . . Is it not at least as plausible that the bilateral use of tactical atomic weapons in Europe would be to our military disadvantage? In any case, is it feasible to defend Europe with such nuclear weapons without destroying it?" These searching questions reflected the secretary's belief that "our posture, doctrine, and understanding of objectives for use of tactical nuclear weapons in ground combat in Europe is in a very unsatisfactory state."[64] At year's end they were still debating the issue. In December the Joint Chiefs used a draft of the State Department's BNSP to observe that "strategic nuclear capabilities required for general war, in which the total resources of the nation are committed, do not of themselves preclude a concurrent military requirement for adequate capabilities to employ appropriate nuclear weapons in the lesser circumstances of limited war."[65] "Appropriate" in this context clearly meant tactical nuclear weapons.

McNamara had spoken with great certainty about the merits of counterforce at Athens and Ann Arbor, but the concept had never been fully accepted within DoD. Differences over many aspects of the strategy, besides the tactical nuclear issue, persisted throughout 1962. Contributing to the concept's demise was the unrelentingly negative reaction to counterforce in Europe.

The special virtue of counterforce that had attracted McNamara—a credible controlled mode of flexible response—received little attention from the Europeans. Instead came a rush to judge the new strategy as evidence of U.S. weakness of will, especially by the French. McNamara's message fitted into a French perception of general U.S. discrimination against France over the years. The United States had repeatedly rejected French requests for aid in developing nuclear weapons. French strategists shared with President de Gaulle criticisms of the U.S. strategy, which they regarded as a threat to both Europe's security and to France's role in the world. They maintained that a French nuclear capability with enough strength to destroy a number of the enemy's cities would serve to discourage adversaries. France's nuclear *force de frappe* could act as the trigger that would bring, if necessary, U.S. nuclear power to bear, and so serve as a further deterrent to Soviet aggression.[66]

Britain's reaction should have been less negative, since McNamara attempted to make clear that the Athens and Ann Arbor strictures did not apply to the RAF's nuclear force, already integrated into the defense plans of the alliance. When the British press ignored this and made much of his reference to the inability of "relatively weak national nuclear forces" to deter aggression, McNamara responded that he had in mind only nations with limited nuclear capabilities that would be a danger to the alliance if employed independently. "I was therefore not referring to Britain—which is wholly clear to anyone reading the speech in its entirety."[67]

McNamara's clarification did not sit well with a government that intended to use its deterrent power independently if necessary. Prime Minister Harold Macmillan certainly was not appeased. Three days after the Ann Arbor speech he entered in his diary a judgment which his French colleagues could share: namely, that McNamara had foolishly condemned all national nuclear forces except those of the United States.[68] At year's end, Macmillan had to bear the double burden of having McNamara abruptly cancel Skybolt* missile development on which the British had previously pinned their hopes of an additional nuclear capability, and then having former Secretary of State Acheson lecture on Britain's need to face up to its declining world status: "Great Britain has lost an empire and not yet found a role."[69] In this atmosphere it was not surprising that the meanings the United States had vested in counterforce had little chance for an objective hearing from British officials.

While the Germans paid more attention to the specific requirements of counterforce and conventional forces than did their British and French counterparts, they also did not welcome the changes. West Germany regarded itself as the front line of NATO defense, the most exposed and most vulnerable territory in the alliance. Any change from time-tested strategies held potential dangers. Unlike

---

* See Chapter XIV.

the United States, West Germany believed that the crisis over the Berlin Wall did not point to the need to furnish more troops to stop Soviet aggression by conventional means. Rather, the Germans continued to subscribe to emphasis on a low nuclear threshold for nuclear exchange that would quickly rise to a strategic level. The threat of massive retaliation remained the key to deterrence; counterforce that devalued the nuclear weapon could lead to a conflict fought on German soil. Only an assurance of early escalation to the nuclear threshold would assure deterrence.[70]

Resistance by the European allies to non-nuclear alternatives and to counterforce doctrine proved unshakable. Their concern was with the impact on them rather than with the theory and technology of the doctrine that so engaged OSD, the Joint Chiefs, and the services. The higher nuclear threshold implied in McNamara's search for alternatives to massive retaliation required increased contributions of conventional forces and raised the question of U.S. commitment to Europe. Both considerations damaged the credibility of the American will to defend Europe. Additionally, Europeans, as always, not only feared the higher cost of conventional forces but also felt it would be futile to attempt to compete with the Warsaw Pact's perceived superiority in numbers of troops. While the allies might share McNamara's doubts about tactical nuclear weapons on the assumption that they would complicate rather than solve NATO's defenses by putting their civilian populations at risk, they would not agree to increased conventional forces as a reasonable alternative. The very element of flexibility that appealed to OSD lay at the heart of their concern. The only acceptable defense of Europe, in the minds of most allies, continued to be the strategic nuclear weapon employed at the lowest possible threshold in any general war with the Soviet Union. Successful implementation of a counterforce doctrine would raise the nuclear threshold to unacceptable levels.

Although OSD and the JCS continued through 1963 to pursue the possibilities of counterforce through studies, they came to accept that the doctrine was not viable. In addition to the opposition of the NATO allies, such difficult problems as locating and destroying elusive Soviet targets, the cost effectiveness of offensive missiles versus defense measures such as ABM systems and civil defense, and the perception of counterforce as a first-strike strategy, created doubts that could not be overcome.[71]

A generation later McNamara would say that he had held a loose construction of counterforce's significance. He claimed that he did not intend his Athens and Ann Arbor speeches to reflect "a shift to a counterforce doctrine, but rather a statement of policy which we hoped would influence the Soviets, were we and they ever to be involved in a nuclear exchange, to limit severely the initial launches of nuclear weapons in the hope that we would avoid destruction of our societies." His underlying purpose was to accelerate NATO's movement toward flexible response. "I never did believe in a counter-force strategy per se. What I was trying to suggest without labeling it as such was a damage-limiting strategy, premised on attacking military targets as opposed to population centers. It was only appropriate, I think, if it ever was appropriate, to that limited period when they had so few weapons relative to ours."72

SIOP and Command and Control

An essential element of U.S. nuclear strategy, especially under a counterforce scenario, was a reliable and effective command and control system. This indispensable need had long engaged the attention of DoD's leaders and planners. The Eisenhower administration had previously made an effort to address the absence of a clear command structure with the aid of a report prepared under Lt. Gen. Thomas F. Hickey. In 1959, NSC's Net Evaluation Subcommittee, chaired by Hickey, took on the task of determining targets to be destroyed and the weapons required for the purpose. The Hickey study group quickly encountered the dilemma over whether to give priority to destruction of nuclear delivery forces over the targeting of governmental, industrial, and communications centers. The former was "counterforce," the latter "countercity," with counterforce needing greater resources to match probable improvements in Soviet capabilities. The Hickey group avoided a choice between the two targeting philosophies in its initial report in November 1959, NESC 2009.73

It remained for Secretary Gates to use the Hickey report as a basis for introducing a major change in coordination and a national target list. The advent of the Polaris submarine missile system projected the Navy onto the strategic nuclear scene and raised important questions about overall coordination and direction of nuclear strategy and forces. Frustrated by the inability of the JCS to resolve these questions, Gates called for a single integrated operational plan, with the Strategic Air Command as the appropriate agency to develop it. Braving criticism from the Army and Navy but with the strong support of President Eisenhower, Gates established the Joint Strategic Target Planning Staff (JSTPS) at SAC headquarters in August 1960. While CINCSAC would direct the JSTPS, he would have a deputy from a different service (the Navy) and a staff drawn from all the services. The National Strategic Target List (NSTL) would also come under the SAC commander. JSTPS managed to produce the first Single Integrated Operational Plan (SIOP-62) before the end of 1960.74 Efforts by the Air Force to acquire command and control over all strategic nuclear forces, including the Navy, did not succeed.

McNamara's assurance about a sure second-strike capability depended on a command and control system above and beyond anything existing. Although Lemnitzer regarded the production of SIOP-62 as the most significant achievement of his tenure as JCS chairman, the new secretary of defense did not share his enthusiasm. In examining the plan, McNamara and his staff saw no clear command structure in place. Reservations about the utility of the SIOP emerged in discussions in the National Security Council less than two weeks after Kennedy's inauguration. As Director of the Bureau of the Budget David Bell observed: "At present the nearest thing to a defense plan is the Joint Strategic Operations Plan [JSOP]* of the JCS, which has not been wholly approved by the Secretary of Defense and is not wholly supported by the budget. In the absence of clear strategic doctrine, a definite defense policy, and an approved implementing JSOP, determinations resulting from budget and program reviews have been in many respects arbitrary." McNamara shared Bell's frustrations. From the outset of his term as secretary he knew full well that the lack of common assumptions among the three military departments on strategic doctrine required immediate attention.[75]

McNamara's doubts about fashioning a coherent consensus out of the customary conflicts and compromises between the services deepened when he visited SAC headquarters in February 1961 and encountered firsthand the rigidity that assumed massive retaliation as the only response to Soviet provocation. General Power's explication of the Air Force's "big bang" strategy only served to exacerbate the secretary's concerns.[76]

Dissatisfied with both Hickey's 1959 report and SIOP-62, McNamara asked the JCS in March 1961 to draft a doctrine that would take into account controlled responses and negotiating pauses. Their reply made clear that options implicit in controlled responses conflicted with their conception of the appropriate use of nuclear weapons. Neither the United States nor the Soviet Union, in their estimation, had secure retaliatory forces capable of conducting such a controlled response as a second strike. To the extent that they contemplated flexible response they saw it as the capability to use nuclear missiles, bombs, and shells deliverable from aircraft, land-based silos, surface ships, and submarines. Nuclear planning, in their judgment, required removal of all limitations "until our forces are endowed with sufficient invulnerability to permit holding a portion in secure reserve."[77]

This JCS response appealed to OSD planners even less than the second Hickey report, which on 1 December 1961 stated that a controlled response strategy could not be implemented until the late 1960s. The report, however, did produce a list of strategic targets and their projected growth over the next 10 years, and an estimate of performance characteristics of planned weapon systems, including the numbers of missiles needed to destroy projected targets. The recommended force posture included 2,000 Minuteman missiles and 40 Polaris submarines. Although they believed that a controlled response strategy was feasible much sooner than the Hickey group envisaged, Hitch and Enthoven appreciated the effort, the latter later calling it "by far the best available on the subject to that date."[78]

---

* JSOP was the product of a JCS directive in 1952 designed to place the planning process on a systematic and regular basis. The proper title was "Joint Strategic Objectives Plan."

But Hitch and his quantifiers found bothersome the reasoning behind the percentages of estimated damage. Why the same figures for both cities and military targets? Why no connection between offensive and defensive forces? Hickey's report suffered further from failure to take into account major changes in intelligence estimates between June and December 1961. Not only had the intelligence community sharply reduced its earlier projection of Soviet ICBMs on launchers, but it also estimated that the Soviets' hardened missiles would not become operational until 1965-66. Hitch rejected the Hickey report's implicit view that all of a list of advanced capabilities had to be achieved "before it makes sense to abandon the spasm war concept."[79]

The persistent question of command and control over strategic forces led to preparation of papers, at the secretary's request, on specific deficiencies in the current system and on areas requiring attention. Despite some differences between the reports of the DDR&E and the chairman of the JCS, they both pointed to the vulnerability of the command center at SAC to nuclear attack and on the need for new, more orderly procedures for devolution of authority in the event of such attack. In particular, the reports emphasized that procedural and physical safeguards against unauthorized use of nuclear weapons required immediate attention. McNamara looked on improvement of command and control capability as of the "highest priority." Consequently, on 24 August 1961 he recommended to the president creation of a command and control task force to "investigate the interrelated organizational, doctrinal, and equipment aspects of the command and control system; [and to] develop and evaluate alternative means by which improvement can be effected."[80]

In September the secretary selected General Earle E. Partridge, recently retired commander of the North American Air Defense Command, as task force chairman. McNamara wanted a proposal for a command structure that would be "compatible with plans for the controlled and flexible employment of forces in the event of nuclear war." The task force completed its assignment on 17 November with recommendations for organizational changes that called for acquisition of equipment and for centralization of authority over the unified commands.[81]

The Partridge committee's report, which recommended a consolidation of command and control under a commander in chief, disappointed McNamara. As the secretary reported to a congressional committee in June 1962, "the Partridge report has not been implemented, because it was an advisory report, and it contained many suggestions, for example, which neither the Chiefs nor I thought deserved implementing." When pressed for more detail, McNamara did not conceal his irritation with the panel's work. Its recommendations included a "certain consolidation of control either within the Joint Chiefs of Staff or relating to the unified commands. And I will tell you quite frankly, I don't know which. I thought it was such an absurd recommendation, I didn't read it." Changes in equipment and doctrine recommended by the Partridge committee did not satisfy McNamara's concerns for centralizing authority in OSD or for advancing "controlled and flexible employment of forces."[82] In later years the SIOPs clearly reflected the centrality of OSD.

Assured Destruction

The command and control problem no doubt contributed to the declining interest in counterforce. By the close of 1963, within the Pentagon, counterforce no longer remained a significant element of flexible response. If any particular event marked a clear break with the doctrine the Cuban missile crisis of October 1962 did. It sensitized McNamara to a deeper awareness of the implications of a nuclear war and strengthened his conviction that the nuclear weapon did not offer a useful tool in the superpower conflict. "One of the reasons why McNamara backed off the no-cities doctrine," according to Enthoven, "is that it was being erroneously interpreted as a theory whereby thermonuclear war could be made tolerable, and therefore fought and won. Gradually he turned against it because it seemed to be getting bent out of shape."[83]

The price of an acceptable counterforce strategy ultimately proved too high. The increase in the potential effectiveness of Soviet offensive forces had reached the point in 1962 where the defensive side of counterforce, that is, the ability of the United States to survive a massive nuclear assault, had become too problematic. Too many lives and too much property were at stake. Even if defenses capable of shooting down a sufficient number of enemy missiles *could* be built, the cost would be astronomical. Most likely, the United States could not buy effective defense at any price. On the offensive side, counterforce whetted the Air Force's prodigious appetite for ever more missiles and manned bombers to achieve its mission. The mission encompassed a dangerous temptation to acquire first-strike capability, a facet of counterforce that the secretary did not welcome and did not consider feasible.

After 1962 McNamara, increasingly convinced of the need to avoid use of nuclear weapons altogether, centered his attention on creating a capability that would suffice to deter attack. During the summer and fall of 1963, in iterations of a draft presidential memorandum, he pursued a new theme he termed "assured destruction" as offering the best prospect for deterrence. In a refined draft on 6 December, "Recommended FY 1965-FY 1969 Strategic Retaliatory Forces," McNamara set forth general nuclear war objectives with the major focus on assured destruction. This objective required the capacity "to destroy, after a well planned and executed Soviet surprise attack on our Strategic Nuclear Forces, the Soviet government and military controls, plus a large percentage of their population and economy (e.g. 30% of their population, 50% of their industrial capacity, and 150 of their cities)." Acquisition of such a capability would give confidence that the Soviet Union would be deterred from attacking. The numbers cited represented an objective rather than reflecting existing capabilities.[84]

McNamara recommended against adding up to 750 Minuteman missiles to reach a total of 1,950 as proposed by the Air Force, because they would not make a significant difference in a nuclear war. He rejected the notion that these additional offensive forces would be cost-effective in reducing damage inflicted on the United States by a Soviet attack. As for a *full first-strike capability* that could render the Soviet Union helpless, he found it not feasible during the projected time period. The forces recommended were sufficient for *assured destruction* and could "accomplish what might reasonably be able to be done" to contribute to "damage limiting."[85]

In the very next month the secretary oddly revived prospects for support of damage limitation in his Senate testimony in January 1964, perhaps inadvertently or possibly to win over congressional skeptics. He ruled out a "cities only" strategy as "dangerously inadequate" and a full first-strike force as "simply unattainable," recommending a "damage limiting" strategy as "the most practical and effective course for us to follow," to destroy the war-making capability of the enemy.[86] In fact, it seems that he merely substituted the term damage limiting for assured destruction; his description of the strategy's objective clearly fit assured destruction. Whatever his intention, he triggered another round of debate over counterforce versus countercity targeting. It provided another opportunity for LeMay to insist during the drafting of the Joint Strategic Capabilities Plan (JSCP-65) that damage limitation should have priority over countercity strategy. A compromise brokered by Taylor, at the time chairman of the JCS, in February 1964 included elements of both counterforce and assured destruction strategies.[87]

The compromise within JCS did not sway McNamara. His downgrading of the civil defense program reflected accurately his views on damage limitation. The combination of an inevitably high death rate in the event of a Soviet attack and the high cost of expanding shelters to shield the public demonstrated convincingly that the number of additional survivors per billion dollars expended would not justify the marginal returns on the investment.*[88]

The same pessimism pervaded McNamara's position on ABMs as revealed in a draft presidential memorandum of 14 November 1963. He lost whatever confidence he might have had initially in the Army's Nike-Zeus because it could not discriminate between real warheads and decoys. And he remained less than enthusiastic about its successor, the Nike-X, which held only slightly more promise as an effective defense against incoming missiles. At most he would recommend a strategic program "to provide the technical and organizational base for later decisions" on such elements as the Nike-Zeus test program. Meanwhile, the Nike-X "would be limited to development work only."[89]

---

* See Chapter II.

In February 1965 the secretary pointed out to the House Armed Services Committee that "over and above the technical problems there are even greater uncertainties concerning the preferred concept of deployment, the relationship of the Nike-X system to other elements of a balanced damage-limiting effort, the timing of the attainment of an effective nationwide fallout shelter system and the nature and effect of an opponent's possible reaction to our Nike-X deployment."[90] In brief, the advances of nuclear technology seemed to render the urban and industrial centers of both the United States and the Soviet Union equally vulnerable, thereby providing a deterrent far more effective than an ABM could offer.

These conclusions derived from a series of studies conducted by Rand, by the Weapons Systems Evaluation Group, and particularly by a task force led by Brig. Gen. Glenn A. Kent, USAF, begun in the summer of 1962. The Kent group completed its study in January 1964, concluding that potent use of U.S. strategic offensive forces against enemy offensive forces could achieve damage limitation that would reduce population losses at lesser costs than defensive measures. In his testimony before congressional committees in the winter of 1964-65 the secretary repeatedly mentioned damage limitation as an important element of assured destruction, but there were limits to the effectiveness of both active and passive defenses. Area defense forces, he noted, could destroy enemy vehicles before they reached their targets, and civil defense programs could reduce the vulnerability of urban centers. But "pervading the entire Damage Limiting problem is the factor of uncertainty." Along with the excessive costs of attempting to solve the problem would be the adversary's ability to "offset any increases in our defenses by increases in their missile forces." The first objective of strategic nuclear forces had to be the capability for assured destruction. This would ensure "with a high degree of confidence" that the destruction of, "say, one-quarter to one-third of its population and about two-thirds of its industrial capacity" should be sufficient to deter an aggressor from attacking. Mutual vulnerability was the path to security. In this context increased damage-limiting measures offered diminishing, marginal returns.[91]

In practice, the Pentagon's shift from counterforce to assured destruction was a logical transition. Assured destruction could be accommodated without significant changes in the SIOP. Targeting of Soviet strategic bases, of course, continued even as cities became prime targets. As new Soviet military targets appeared and were identified they became potential objects of U.S. attack. Enthoven observed in 1968: "Our targeting policy, as reflected in the guidance for the preparation of a targeting plan, has not changed. From 1962 on, the targeting plan has been based on the principle that we should have different options that target strategic forces and cities."[92]

*   *

Semantic nuances sometimes obscured and confused the strategic debate in these years, but the flexibility that McNamara and his colleagues sought went beyond any specific doctrine. Having reached the point where he perceived nuclear warfare itself as suicidal, the secretary wanted a powerful nuclear component sufficient to serve only as a deterrent. The special emphasis on conventional forces as the most viable means of defending Europe provided the necessary non-nuclear component of flexible response. As for what constituted sufficiency on the nuclear side, McNamara asserted that massive retaliation was "useless."[93] The huge numbers of nuclear weapons required would not guarantee U.S. security. At the opposite extreme, finite deterrence, Taylor envisioned that a few hundred nuclear weapons would suffice to deter aggression, but that proposition became less cogent as Soviet nuclear strength rapidly expanded. By contrast with massive retaliation and finite deterrence, McNamara regarded assured destruction, "an actual and credible capability," as having the best probability of deterring attack.[94] It represented the highest level of graduated response under the flexible response doctrine, to be invoked only after the failure of conventional and tactical nuclear responses. Able to survive a first strike against the United States, controlled assured destruction forces could be calibrated according to prevailing circumstances and used incrementally. For all of these strategic concepts the basic question remained the same—how much nuclear weaponry was enough to deter aggression?

The key to DoD's policies, nuclear and non-nuclear, resided in "controlled response," with the "response" as varied and flexible as possible and the "control" firmly in the hands of Washington. This linkage remained intact when assured destruction became the declared dominant nuclear strategic option. Indeed, controlled response had an almost mantra-like ring to McNamara and his circle, as if through appropriate incantations it might solve all manner of strategic issues. In the larger context, "no cities," "damage limitation," and "assured destruction" conjoined as components in the securing of the important objective of establishing firm command and control of nuclear weapons centered in OSD.

Throughout his first years in office, the secretary worked to raise the consciousness of the NATO allies about the need to consider new strategies along such paths as counterforce and assured destruction. A year after the Cuban missile crisis, he publicly dwelt on the need to impress continually on the allies the realization that they no longer lived in a time of Western nuclear monopoly.[95] He admitted in 1994 that, having concluded in the early 1960s that nuclear weapons had no military utility, in long private conversations with both Kennedy and Johnson he "had recommended, without qualification, that they never, under any circumstances, initiate the use of nuclear weapons. I believe they accepted my recommendations. But neither they nor I could discuss our position publicly because it was contrary to established NATO policy."[96] He might have added that such an admission would have raised a storm of protest within DoD and Congress as well as within NATO.

CHAPTER XIII

The Limited Nuclear Test Ban Treaty

That "the best is the enemy of the good" is a saying at least as old as Voltaire. According to an even older adage, "better is half a loaf than no bread." Both characterized the Kennedy administration's bumpy road to a limited nuclear test ban agreement. In an exchange with Sen. John Sparkman a week after the treaty was signed in August 1963, McNamara admitted that "a full and properly inspected comprehensive test ban would in my opinion be more desirable than the limited three-dimensional ban."[1] Even when the celebrants sounded a cautionary note, as in McGeorge Bundy's observation that the treaty marked "a good first step," or in Arthur Schlesinger's recognition that "it was not the millennium," they agreed that it represented, in President Kennedy's words, "a step towards peace—a step towards reason—a step away from war."[2]

Other parties to the debate over the test ban treaty, including members of the scientific community and key elements within the government, questioned not only the efficacy of a limited test ban but the wisdom of any type of ban. The Defense Department especially had its share of dissenters. The generally receptive views of McNamara, and to a lesser degree of General Taylor, first as White House military adviser and then chairman of the Joint Chiefs of Staff, frequently did not reflect the thinking of the Joint Chiefs. Both former and current chiefs of the military services had doubts about the "best" as well as the "good."[3] Limited as well as comprehensive test bans, they believed, endangered the nation's security. Since the latter was impossible to achieve, it was therefore less dangerous; the former troubled them precisely because it could be achieved.

Although a majority of arms control experts looked on a test ban as a useful development in which the relative position of each side, according to one study, "would remain virtually unchanged while the absolute danger to both might be reduced," the chiefs challenged this view; they saw the cessation of testing as a benefit to the other side. From their perspective, even if the treaty did not solidify Soviet superiority in high-yield weapons, it would impede needed research on the

U.S. side. Above all, Soviet cheating in the future, which might be expected, could enhance Soviet nuclear capabilities at the expense of the United States.[4] Thus were drawn the outlines of a dispute that lasted throughout the Kennedy administration and beyond.

Initiatives under Eisenhower

As far back as 1946, efforts had been made to put the nuclear genie back in the bottle. In that year the Acheson-Lilienthal report became the basis of the U.S. Baruch Plan for international control of atomic energy. Ten years later President Eisenhower proposed halting the production of nuclear weapons and encouraging the reduction of stockpiles, and offered variations on this theme during his second term. The early Eisenhower proposals all assumed that some weapons would remain in the atomic arsenal even after disarmament. Toward the end of the decade, however, general and complete nuclear disarmament became the goal.

Machinery for negotiating nuclear arms reduction had existed since the establishment of the United Nations Disarmament Commission in 1952. The U.S. position, as expressed in official policy statements in 1960, assumed that elimination of weapons of mass destruction would proceed in gradual, verifiable stages. The Soviet position entailed both a pledge against first use of nuclear weapons and international inspection to follow (but not before) the renunciation of weapons of mass destruction. On-site monitoring of a halt to nuclear weapon testing and phased liquidation of stockpiles had no place in the Soviet program. Given Soviet superiority in conventional forces and weaponry, the United States was reluctant to accept bans on nuclear weapon testing or production without verification and other guarantees that were unacceptable to the Soviet Union, resulting in a stalemate.

The issue was too important to be left unaddressed. The Geneva meeting of foreign ministers in 1959 established a Ten-Nation Committee on Disarmament—in addition to the two superpowers, it consisted of four members each from NATO and the Warsaw Pact countries—to explore solutions. The committee had made little progress by 1961.[5] Although mutual suspicion hampered the negotiating process, a U.S.-USSR moratorium on testing, begun in 1958, lasted to the end of the Eisenhower administration. Unfortunately, Eisenhower himself provided a pretext for later Soviet resumption of nuclear testing when he prefaced an announcement in December 1959 that the United States would continue the moratorium with the caveat that "although we consider ourselves free to resume nuclear weapons testing, we shall not resume nuclear weapons tests without announcing our intention in advance of any resumption."[6] Whether a comprehensive treaty could have materialized at this time remains a matter of speculation, as the downing of the U-2 over Sverdlovsk on 1 May 1960 chilled the atmosphere. The Geneva Conference recessed on 5 December and did not reconvene until President Kennedy was in office.

Kennedy partisans later accorded Eisenhower grudging credit for initiating negotiations for a test ban, but faulted him for his relative passivity. Eisenhower did establish a high-level Committee of Principals* to coordinate an executive branch review of arms control policy and gave his blessing to negotiations, but McGeorge Bundy dismissed his Atoms for Peace and Open Skies proposals as "substantively trivial." Even Bundy, however, allowed that the president succeeded—and it was no mean achievement—in permanently reversing the presumption fostered in the Pentagon that testing could not be limited or prohibited altogether. In brief, Eisenhower opened the way for Kennedy to make choices that had not been foreclosed by his predecessor's decisions.[7]

Establishment of ACDA

Kennedy indicated his intent to extend the testing moratorium and pursue other means to prevent proliferation of nuclear weapons and escalation of the arms race when he asked in his Inaugural Address that both superpowers ". . . for the first time, formulate serious and precise proposals for the inspection and control of [nuclear] arms . . . ."[8] But first he asked that negotiations be postponed from February to March, until a panel of experts headed by James B. Fisk, president of Bell Telephone Laboratories, had studied technical considerations relating to any agreement on ending nuclear weapons tests. As an earnest of his intentions the president appointed John J. McCloy, the well-regarded former U.S. high commissioner for Germany, as his adviser on disarmament and arms control, to oversee the expanded arms control effort.[9]

McCloy on the whole enjoyed strong support from the leadership of both State and Defense. Dean Rusk years later counted McNamara as a staunch believer in the virtues of arms control, stating that because of his assistance, "I never had to arm-wrestle the Joint Chiefs on this score. McNamara took care of all disputes with the chiefs inside the Pentagon." Rusk may have overstated McNamara's unequivocal support, but the defense secretary was fundamentally committed to the broad principle. Paul Nitze, another dependable champion despite his own occasional qualms, recalled that when he accepted the position of assistant secretary of defense for international security affairs, the president asked him to pay particular attention to arms control. More than willing to comply, Nitze had extensive experience with arms control as head of the State Department's Policy Planning Staff in 1950-53 and as adviser to the U.S. delegation to the Disarmament Conference

---

*The committee, formed in 1958, included the secretaries of state and defense, the CIA director, the chairman of the Atomic Energy Commission, and the White House science adviser. Kennedy expanded the membership to include the chairman of the JCS and directors of USIA and subsequently the Arms Control and Disarmament Agency. See *FRUS 1961-63*, VII:13-14.

in Geneva in the summer of 1960. He subsequently played an important role in the establishment of the Arms Control and Disarmament Agency (ACDA), which emerged from the McCloy review. But for Nitze's influence ACDA might have become an isolated backwater at State, with little connection to other elements of the national security bureaucracy and hence little coordinating authority or clout. "So I testified at length on its behalf," Nitze noted, "and was instrumental in getting ACDA established as an independent agency."[10]

McCloy made an eloquent appeal in August 1961 for a careful delineation of the new agency's bureaucratic relationships when he testified before Congress for the bill establishing the agency. Because responsibility for negotiating disarmament proposals fell within the province of the State Department, he recommended that the director report to the secretary of state. But the director would not be just another bureau chief in the department. The agency would have a "semiautonomous character," with separate budget and annual reports to Congress, and the director an enhanced standing and direct access to the president as principal adviser on disarmament.[11]

Whether or not the credit for creating ACDA belongs to Nitze or McCloy, the new agency was established in September 1961 under the directorship of William C. Foster, a former deputy secretary of defense in the Truman administration.[12] The JCS expressed unease over the jurisdictional arrangement. Asking how a director with the equivalent rank of an under secretary could issue recommendations that would be coordinated at the cabinet level, the chiefs would have preferred just strengthening the existing disarmament bureau within State. OSD registered similar concern when Deputy Secretary of Defense Gilpatric asked for clarification of ACDA's relationship with the NSC; he wanted to be sure that ACDA recommendations would pass through the NSC as well as through State. The designation of Foster, with his prior Defense background, as principal adviser to the president defused much of the DoD criticism, as did the expansion of the Committee of Principals to include the JCS chairman.[13]

JCS dissatisfaction might have had a more significant impact on Congress in 1961 but for the supportive views of Eisenhower and JCS Chairman Lemnitzer. The former president sent a personal note to McCloy on 29 June to let him know that "I heartily concur in your purpose."[14] Lemnitzer testified on 25 August that "the vital interests of the Joint Chiefs of Staff in this area are clearly recognized by all concerned." The chiefs agreed to a centralized direction of arms control efforts. "Arms control affairs," he recognized, were "inextricably intermeshed with military as well as political matters. Necessarily, the Joint Chiefs of Staff have a vital and continuing interest in every facet of arms control as an integral part of their responsibilities for the military security of the United States." Congressional appreciation of Lemnitzer's testimony was reflected in Rep. James O'Hara's response to Lemnitzer: "I think it is news of major importance when the Chief of Staff [sic] comes before the Committee on Foreign Affairs and recommends an agency, the goal of which is the end of arms. I wish that the widest publicity could be given your testimony."[15]

Proposing a Test Ban Treaty

The review of disarmament proceedings begun by McCloy early in 1961 encompassed transcripts from 250 negotiating sessions in Geneva. McCloy focused initially on the sweeping U.S. disarmament plan of 27 June 1960, which called for balanced, phased reductions of forces to minimal levels, with on-site inspection of air and naval bases as well as missile launching pads. U.S. and Soviet force levels would drop from 2.5 million to 2.1 million in the first stage. An international disarmament control agency would monitor each nation's compliance. But the proposal barely met the JCS requirements, let alone Soviet interests. The latter had no intention of allowing the kinds of controls indicated in the U.S. plan. And when the U.S. Disarmament Administration* attempted to revise the 1960 proposal by accepting nuclear-free zones and uninspected bans on transferring nuclear weapons to other nations, the Soviet Union was not appeased and the Joint Chiefs were not satisfied.[16]

In light of steadfast resistance from all sides, not surprisingly the McCloy group settled for pursuing a nuclear test ban rather than embark on the broader and more difficult negotiations over general disarmament. The United States then unveiled on 18 April 1961, in conjunction with its British partner, a compendious draft treaty for a test ban. At the 292nd meeting in Geneva of the Conference on Cessation of Nuclear Weapons Tests the allies presented a detailed text of some 60 pages, proposing inspection machinery that would cost $2.5 billion dollars to install and $500 million each year thereafter. The plan provided for a Control Commission to supervise a worldwide detection system, with equal U.S. and Soviet representation and three neutral observers holding the balance, and an administrator to carry out the commission's policy. To placate the Soviet Union the treaty stipulated strict safeguards against inspectors ranging beyond their immediate assignment; observers from the host country would accompany inspection teams along prescribed routes and would restrict their inspection to areas predetermined by seismic data. The plan proposed to ban all tests in the earth's atmosphere, in outer space, in the oceans, and underground, except those producing signals of less than 4.75 seismic magnitude.[17]

The test ban plainly posed risks for the United States, particularly the possibility of Soviet tests going undetected at high altitudes or underground below the 4.75 seismic threshold. McCloy recognized the gamble implicit in signing such a treaty but felt that other considerations outweighed the risks. In March he had

---

* Eisenhower had established the Disarmament Administration, the predecessor to ACDA, as a unit inside the State Department in 1960.

outlined for the president the benefits that could flow from such an accord. At the very least it would break the deadlock over disarmament and provide experience in superpower cooperation in matters of arms control and inspection, perhaps leading to other avenues of cooperation, such as the exploration of outer space. It would also help halt the spread of nuclear weapons to other nations. And important "political gains" would accrue in the form of enhanced U.S. international stature.[18]

None of these hopes materialized in 1961. The Soviet negotiators refused to join their U.S. counterparts in what the State Department called "a great adventure in international collaboration for peace." If the U.S. side was cautious, the Soviet side was refractory. Instead of the single impartial administrator envisaged in the treaty, a concept Moscow seemed willing to accept the year before, it now demanded a tripartite administrative board—a troika. Additionally, the Soviets insisted on limiting annual inspections in the USSR to three visits (the Western nations sought 20), with all manner of restrictions on staffing and procedures. If no staff could be hired, no control posts established, and no interpretation of seismic data allowed, State noted, the treaty would be a sham. "At almost every stage in the process, there would be abundant opportunity to thwart and block the mechanism of control . . . . The whole purpose of the test-ban treaty is to deter clandestine tests. What deterrence would this Soviet system offer?" For his part, Khrushchev told Kennedy at the June 1961 summit meeting in Vienna that more than three inspections would be "tantamount to intelligence, something the Soviet Union cannot accept."[19]

By the time of the Vienna summit the Soviets had in fact lost interest in a test ban treaty. Having earlier allowed the two issues to be treated separately, Khrushchev now insisted on linking a comprehensive test ban to general and complete disarmament. Only with the latter achieved would he agree to abandon the troika arrangement and accede to external controls. Khrushchev informed Kennedy that "if there were general and complete disarmament there would be no question of espionage because there would be no armaments. Then there would be no secrets and all doors must be open so that complete verification could be ensured."[20] Political commentator Walter Lippmann, speculating about reasons for the Soviet shift, thought Khrushchev may have sought to avoid alienating the Communist Chinese, who had their own nuclear ambitions, or he may have counted on blame for the failure to fall on Washington if the United States rejected a treaty because of objections to the troika. "The question," said Lippmann, "is whether, with a resumption of testing, they will catch up with us, perhaps surpass us."[21]

Of course, the Soviet Union was not alone in the conviction that testing offered definite advantages. The Atomic Energy Commission and Joint Chiefs had their own misgivings about limiting nuclear testing. Assumptions about Soviet cheating only in part explained their hesitation. The AEC worried about the

United States standing pat on its weapons stockpile. "Nuclear weapons development is not a static science," the agency reported to Congress in January 1961. "Our weapons scientists are convinced that further nuclear testing would achieve major advances in weapons design." As for the threat to health from nuclear fallout, the agency noted that testing could be conducted underground or in outer space without causing fallout.[22]

The JCS shared the AEC's reservations along with even deeper suspicions about Soviet behavior during the moratorium. They feared Moscow was conducting clandestine tests even as the United States abided by its self-denying rules. Their overriding worry was that the Soviet Union might achieve a breakthrough at the expense of the United States during the pause. Not until a reliable system of verification was developed and became operational could they accept any prolonged test ban. With the McCloy review still under way, on 11 March 1961 they asked for an immediate presidential decision on resuming testing, maintaining that a continued voluntary moratorium was not in the best interest of the nation. Absent an agreement within 60 days after resumption of negotiations the service chiefs recommended U.S. renunciation of the moratorium. Looking beyond the Soviet Union to the Sino-Soviet relationship, they suggested later in March that should a treaty be concluded and Communist China not accede to it within "a reasonably short time," that, too, would provide grounds for the administration to resume testing. A week later they recommended 1 June as a deadline for concluding an agreement with the stipulated safeguards; if the Conference on Cessation of Nuclear Weapons Tests produced no such accord by that date, the United States should begin testing nuclear weapons as soon as possible.[23]

The draft text of a nuclear test ban treaty that State introduced at Geneva on 18 April thus encountered a lack of enthusiasm if not overt hostility from the JCS. Col. E. F. Black, military assistant to the deputy secretary of defense, dismissed the Joint Staff's cool reception as owing to their understandable reluctance to spend much time analyzing military implications of a nuclear test ban treaty during its interim development. He likened the situation to painting "a moving train," and "now that the train has stopped and the engineer has gotten out to throw the switch on the track ahead" he recommended that the Joint Staff take a careful look.[24]

McNamara himself had already identified some problems with the treaty, but expressed them without the vehemence of the chiefs. At a meeting of the Committee of Principals on 2 March he asked, first, how the United States might disengage itself from a treaty in the event of subsequent actions by other countries, and second, how the administration could extricate itself from the current voluntary moratorium.[25] By 28 July, convinced that the Soviet Union had no interest in a treaty except on terms unacceptable to the United States, McNamara proposed that the president initiate preparations to resume nuclear weapons testing while continuing efforts to negotiate a satisfactory agreement. He had Director of

Defense Research and Engineering Harold Brown notify Jerome Wiesner, White House science adviser, of DoD's belief that in the short run a delay in the resumption of nuclear testing would not have a substantial effect but over the long run "possible Soviet gains from testing must certainly be considered an important military disadvantage to the U.S. Therefore, the position of the Department of Defense . . . is that nuclear weapons testing underground should be resumed as soon as it is politically expedient."[26]

Although the defense secretary had come to share the chiefs' sense of urgency about resolving the issue sooner rather than later, the president was intent on giving diplomacy a wider window and preferred deferring any resumption of testing for six months while pursuing but keeping preparations to a low profile. Kennedy's reluctance to resume testing did not signify any greater faith in Soviet trustworthiness. On the contrary, his patience was wearing thin. He told British Prime Minister Harold Macmillan in May that if there was no progress in negotiations with Khrushchev "the United States should be ready to resume nuclear tests for both seismic research and weapons development." He criticized Khrushchev for rejecting U.S. and British proposals submitted in April despite efforts to accommodate Soviet views. But the president was attempting to sustain, in the words of AEC Chairman Glenn T. Seaborg, a difficult "balancing act."[27] Late in June he announced the formation of an advisory committee, chaired by Wolfgang K. H. Panofsky of Stanford University, to determine if the Soviet Union was conducting clandestine tests, and to what effect. At the same time the panel was asked to weigh the advantages of the United States resuming testing.[28]

In its report to the White House on 8 August, the Panofsky panel concluded that there was no immediate need for the United States to resume testing, for it found no evidence that the Soviets were secretly breaking the moratorium. Granting that self-denial would limit possibilities for some weapons development, the panel envisaged other ways of compensating for the absence of tests. Except for the strong backing of John S. Foster, director of the University of California's Lawrence Livermore Laboratory, the JCS received little support for challenges to both the premises and the conclusions of the Panofsky report. The single concession to the military and to the national weapons laboratories came in the recognition that if the Soviet Union was testing secretly, in the long run the United States would have to abandon the moratorium or risk impairing its military position.[29]

Notwithstanding his frustration with the Soviets the president accepted the judgment of the Panofsky panel and put off any immediate resumption of testing. By midsummer, though, the internal differences within the Department of Defense had narrowed and the Pentagon's civilian and military leadership stood united in their opinion of that decision. Lemnitzer complained about the Panofsky report's "conjectural" conclusions based on unconfirmed or inadequate intelligence estimates. McNamara saw no alternative to testing, and he was joined by the president's military representative, General Taylor. In a memo to Kennedy on 7 August and in a statement the next day before the NSC, Taylor argued the need for the United States to test and develop light strategic warheads and small atomic weapons, including the neutron bomb, in order to have the tactical means to execute U.S. military strategy.[30]

In holding out against these military opinions the president listened to his national security affairs assistant, McGeorge Bundy, who discounted Taylor's views as "subject in a measure to criticism that one can generally apply to estimates from professional soldiers on weapons development: they tend to think in terms of what we can do while minimizing what the enemy can do with the same opportunity." Kennedy evinced skepticism about the Joint Chiefs' analysis in a memorandum to Taylor: "Was it done by one, two, or three men? Was it done outside of the Defense Department by a group of scientists, or what? This is particularly interesting in view of the fact that the Chairman of the AEC seems to find himself 'in general agreement [with] the findings and conclusions of the [Panofsky] report.'"[31]

End to the Moratorium

After 30 August the moratorium critics suddenly had a stronger claim, as the Soviet Union announced on that day that it would resume testing, blaming the West's intransigence for precipitating its action. Two days later, it exploded the first nuclear device in its new test series, providing the president with reason to follow suit. Bundy later wrote that of all the provocations in Soviet-American relations in 1961-62, the Soviet announcement disappointed the president the most. Kennedy's immediate reaction, according to Sorensen, was unprintable. He felt that Khrushchev must have been aware of preparations for resumption of testing when they met in Vienna. Nonetheless, Kennedy countered with what Sorensen characterized as "a controlled and deliberate response."[32]

Several considerations caused Kennedy to postpone a decision. First, he could not be certain that Khrushchev had deliberately deceived him. McCloy gleaned from his discussions in Moscow in late July that Soviet scientists and military men were pressing the Soviet leader to test a 100-megaton bomb, prompted in part perhaps by Eisenhower's veiled threat in his aforementioned December 1959 statement (see page 324). In a White House meeting with Senate leaders on 31 August Sen. Hubert Humphrey (D-Minn.) suggested to the president that a split in the Kremlin may have caused Khrushchev to yield to the protesting hard-line faction against his own inclination. Although Allen Dulles said the CIA discerned no sign of any rift, Seaborg implied in his memoirs that Khrushchev had favored serious arms control negotiations during this period. Further, the United States was simply not ready to resume testing overnight. The absence of equipment in place to undertake major tests posed a practical obstacle to any effective early response to the Soviet action. Even underground testing, Seaborg advised the president, required a level of planning and preparation that exceeded the capacity of existing facilities.[33]

Finally, there was the political factor. Edward R. Murrow, director of the United States Information Agency, urged delay in order to reap propaganda benefits from the Soviet action that would strengthen U.S. international standing. McNamara helped the political case by telling the president he saw no military necessity for bombs of 100-megaton size. If so, Moscow would derive no particular advantage from testing weapons of that magnitude, and the administration could effectively blunt congressional pressure for retaliation. Under these circumstances, it was just as well that the president proceeded slowly.[34]

While Kennedy deferred a riposte, he could not conceal his dismay over the failure of the test ban negotiations. He and his staff hoped that world outrage, spurred by U.S. denunciation of their behavior, might impress the Soviets. The Soviet decision, he asserted, "presents a hazard to every human being throughout the world by increasing the dangers of nuclear fallout." The Soviet government's action exposed "the complete hypocrisy of its professions about general and complete disarmament." Recalling Arthur Dean, chairman of the U.S. delegation to the Disarmament Committee, from Geneva, on 3 September the president, along with Prime Minister Macmillan, proposed an atmospheric test ban without inspections. Expected to further isolate the Soviet Union in the United Nations if it rejected the proposal, the offer allowed Moscow six days to reply.[35]

Unfortunately, the Soviet resumption of tests in the atmosphere did not provoke the anticipated strong international response. A conference of 24 non-aligned nations meeting in Belgrade on 1 September displayed unhappiness with both countries. The neutral bloc asked both Kennedy and Khrushchev to meet again at the summit, but refrained from explicit criticism of the USSR.[36] The Soviet testing continued.

To underscore its rejection of the joint U.S.-U.K. proposal, the Soviet Union conducted two additional atmospheric tests between 1 and 5 September. On 5 September Kennedy announced the U.S. decision to resume underground testing while keeping the deadline open on atmospheric testing. Although, unlike those of the Soviet Union, the tests would be conducted underground and in laboratories, without danger of fallout, the president regretted having to take such a step. He lamented to aides, "What choice did we have? They had spit in our eye three times. We couldn't possibly sit back and do nothing at all. We had to do this."[37]

The JCS were no happier with the decision for underground testing than with the proposed ban on atmospheric testing. The former, limited in yield, served primarily for expensive development of small tactical weapons. The latter, while politically attractive for international consumption, had "profound" implications for the U.S.-Soviet nuclear competition that disturbed others in DoD besides the Joint Chiefs. Even Nitze later conceded that "many of the concerns of the JCS were valid." At a meeting of officials on 2 September, the day before the Kennedy-Macmillan announcement, Gilpatric and Brown observed that such an agreement would preclude the United States from conducting atmospheric tests needed to develop antimissile weapons, to test the vulnerability of missile-launching sites, and to evaluate the impact of electromagnetic radiation on those sites.[38]

The arguments for resumption of atmospheric tests became more compelling in light of continuing Soviet testing activity in the fall of 1961 and the tepid response of nonaligned nations that cast doubt on the political rationale for a test ban. Based on the latest Soviet test series, a Defense White Paper estimated that the "Soviets could have early capability of launching into intercontinental ballistic or orbital trajectories payloads of 50-100 MT."[39] It did not escape attention in the Pentagon that the Soviet military newspaper, *Red Star*, claimed that the USSR possessed nuclear warheads equivalent to 100 megatons and had the missiles to deliver them. In view of these developments, even as he dismissed the utility of the 100-megaton bomb, McNamara gave his "considered opinion that we must continually be prepared to conduct those tests most vital to us and that these tests should be conducted in any environment, upon the approval of the President."[40]

Actually, the president and the NSC approved atmospheric testing in principle as early as 2 November 1961 but hedged the decision with a host of reservations, including assurance that atmospheric fallout from such tests would be kept "to an absolute minimum." Circumstances alone forced a delay in implementing the decision, as reviving the organization and restarting facilities that had been idled during the moratorium involved, as predicted, long and costly preparations. As Lemnitzer noted, firms manufacturing special cables for the test site had stopped production, and it would take months before supplies became available again. Lemnitzer and McNamara remained less committed than the chiefs to full-blown testing, and the general reiterated the conviction that matching development of the Soviet-sought superbomb was unnecessary for U.S. security. The superbomb, Lemnitzer told the Congressional Joint Committee on Atomic Energy, was a "terror weapon" rather than a weapon having any serious strategic use.[41]

While the administration rebuilt the testing infrastructure and negotiated with the British for permission to use Christmas Island, a sparsely inhabited atoll 1,000 miles south of Hawaii, as a site for the new tests, the UN General Assembly stepped up its efforts to move the nuclear powers toward disarmament. An Irish resolution on 4 December 1961 called for an international agreement, with inspection and control provisions, under which nations possessing nuclear weapons would not transfer them to states without weapons. On the same day Sweden sponsored a resolution, opposed by the United States but accepted by the Soviet Union, to inquire into conditions under which non-nuclear nations would agree not to acquire nuclear weapons nor allow use of them on their territories. In December, the Ten-Nation Committee on Disarmament was expanded to an Eighteen-Nation Disarmament Committee (ENDC) in order to press more effectively for negotiations on general and complete disarmament.[42] Within the United States, too, arms control proponents kept up the pressure. In a controversial lecture at Cornell University early in January 1962 Hans Bethe, a Cornell physicist and adviser to ACDA, told his audience, with reference to the superbomb threat, "there is not much difference between 100 and 10 megatons from the military point of view. Ten megatons is enough to destroy nearly any big city . . . . Nothing has been fundamentally changed by the Russian tests . . . nothing fundamental is likely to be changed by any amount of future nuclear testing."*[43]

Such countervailing pressures fed Kennedy's reluctance to make public the time and place of the forthcoming tests. He kept hopes alive in the winter of 1962 of reaching some understanding with the Soviets that would stay the U.S. decision. At their meeting in Bermuda in December 1961, Macmillan played on the president's sensibilities by linking U.S. use of Christmas Island with a promise to make a new effort to achieve an arms control agreement with the Soviets. Kennedy complied by postponing announcement of the tests through the first two months of 1962.[44]

The latest delay threatened to dissolve the administration's fragile consensus on atmospheric testing. Divisions within DoD, never far from the surface, reemerged. The JCS had earlier agreed to the terms of the April 1961 test ban plan but now rejected them. Soviet behavior since April convinced the Joint Chiefs that the Soviets could not be trusted to abide by treaty restrictions. McNamara and Gilpatric did not accept this judgment. Although they recommended moving ahead with the test series, they remained willing to sign a test ban treaty despite risks of Soviet violations. McNamara consistently believed that the United States would suffer no disadvantage if an enforceable treaty could be obtained in 1962.[45]

When the president finally announced the test schedule on 2 March 1962, he again pointed out that the fallout would be far less than the contamination created by the Soviet series, and that U.S. resumption was solely a result of Soviet refusal to accept an enforceable treaty ban. In a lengthy public address he noted that he was acting in advance of the ENDC meeting in Geneva on 14 March, on which he still pinned hopes for accommodation with Moscow. The United States made another overture by offering to eliminate any threshold for underground explosions and to limit annual inspections on Soviet territory to small areas of high seismic activity. When the Soviet Union rejected these conciliatory gestures, again dismissing the inspection plan as an espionage ploy, the United States commenced

---

* Bethe's talk resembled Lemnitzer's congressional testimony on the point of the superbomb and largely mirrored McNamara's position as well, but the disclosure of classified information in a public venue triggered calls for an investigation into an alleged breach of national security and resulted in a White House review of the incident and a reprimand.

its series of atmospheric tests, designated Operation Dominic, on 25 April 1962 near Johnston and Christmas Islands in the Pacific.[46]

The administration exercised care to minimize radioactive fallout. Testing the Polaris missiles with nuclear warheads occasioned little discussion at the White House because those missiles would be fired over water, where a failure would not be catastrophic. But in testing the Atlas missile at Vandenberg Air Force Base, the prospect of a mechanical malfunction and missile abort, with a possible release of radioactive nuclear material requiring decontamination and evacuation of a land area, gave pause. Bundy recommended putting off the Vandenberg testing, telling the president that the psychological and political consequences of a mishap outweighed the advantage of "user confidence" that would result from a successful firing. McNamara's support of the Atlas test was at best thin. If pressed, Bundy felt that he would order its cancellation. Bundy did not rule out a two-kiloton near-surface experiment for late May in Nevada.[47]

The Joint Chiefs, on the other hand, strongly favored continued testing, including at Vandenberg. They especially wanted to learn about the impact of high-altitude explosions on radio communications. But the White House, never comfortable about the atmospheric tests, soon showed impatience. The Atlas, nearing obsolescence, gave critics another reason to justify cancellation of the Vandenberg program. Bundy and the president dwelt on the failures accompanying the tests, one of tracking, another of a missile launching. Unhappy as well over the publicity given to the high-altitude tests, the president looked forward to their early conclusion. As Lemnitzer scribbled in his notes of a 20 June 1962 White House meeting, the president wanted to "get it over."[48]

From differing perspectives, Lemnitzer and McNamara would agree that not enough was gained from the six months of testing between 25 April and 4 November 1962. The JCS chairman appeared to believe the tests not extensive enough, the secretary of defense that the tests could not yield enough to make them worth the effort. By contrast, Seaborg thought the tests—the first U.S. atmospheric tests since 1958—on balance useful. Despite the limitations and difficulties, the Dominic operation, in his estimate, "produced many important successes": vindicating "the elaborate computational and certification procedures which were developed during the moratorium," revitalizing America's nuclear laboratories, and, not the least, "reawakening" the U.S. defense posture.[49]

Search for Compromise, March–November 1962

Though they encountered a stalemate over the testing issue, U.S. officials in Geneva returned to yet more far-reaching discussions by the Eighteen-Nation Disarmament Conference on the subject of general disarmament. As with the test ban proposal, the administration struggled to fashion a set of provisions that could both achieve consensus within the U.S. national security bureaucracy and contain at least some elements acceptable to the Soviets. Even with an agreed set of objectives, gaining concurrence on procedures and formulas for implementing a comprehensive disarmament treaty presented an enormous challenge. Perhaps as a token of goodwill, ACDA adopted the favored Soviet term "general and complete disarmament" as the goal. In a memo for the president on 3 March 1962, ACDA Director Foster specified, however, that any reduction of U.S. power resulting from a treaty should be matched by "equalizing changes elsewhere."[50]

The plan, as approved by the Committee of Principals and based in large part on recommendations that had changed little from the June 1960 U.S. disarmament proposal, sought to secure maximum agreement in such areas as production of fissionable materials and elimination of chemical and biological weapons. At a White House meeting on 6 March the president raised questions about inspection and verification. Foster responded with a proposal for a zonal random sampling system* as the best approach to inspection. With respect to weapon systems, Foster wanted to focus on reduction of strategic delivery vehicles, while the president agreed with McNamara and Lemnitzer that the United States should seek a 30 percent across-the-board reduction of all armaments, with production cutoff deferred until the second stage.[51]

Over the next six weeks the administration hammered out an "outline" treaty, a summary of which it released on 18 April 1962. But the Soviet Union had already presented to the ENDC its own version of a pact on "General and Complete Disarmament Under Strict International Control" a month earlier, on 15 March. Each draft treaty contained three stages. Stage I of the Soviet treaty called for total elimination of nuclear delivery vehicles, abolition of foreign bases, withdrawal of troops from foreign territories, and reduction of Soviet and U.S. forces to 1.7 million with corresponding arms and expenditures reductions. In Stage I of the U.S. plan, all non-nuclear arms and nuclear weapon delivery systems would be cut by 30 percent; production of weapons-grade fissionable material would end; and U.S. and Soviet armed forces would be reduced to 2.1 million men each. The two proposals converged more closely in Stages II and III; under both plans, Stage III would bring general and complete disarmament, with national armed forces retained only for internal order and an international peacekeeping force operating under the UN.[52]

As in earlier iterations of the plan, the JCS had trouble with the 2.1 million troop-strength ceiling under Stage I. They projected a minimum of 2.57 million needed to operate armaments after a 30 percent reduction. Nor did their criticism let up after the Geneva Conference recessed in September 1962. The chiefs complained to McNamara that ACDA's position on disarmament had periodically shifted to accommodate the Soviet Union, while the Soviet position remained essentially unchanged since 1960. Moreover, they claimed that ACDA tended to

---

* Whereby each side would divide its territory into zones for monitoring and verification purposes.

put forth negotiating positions before proper evaluation. The recess, they argued, should be used to stiffen the U.S. stance rather than offer new concessions.[53]

McNamara called the JCS criticism simplistic, noting that in light of ongoing reevaluation "it would indeed have been remarkable had no changes occurred." What mattered, he asserted, was whether such changes served to make reasonable agreements possible: "I believe that they have."[54] ISA, less diplomatic, declared that "the majority of JCS studies are so loaded with caveats as to constitute *unreasonable* measures which the USSR, even should she become desirous of reaching agreements, would not accept." Too many JCS studies, according to ISA, showed how reductions would affect the United States, without considering their effect on the Soviet Union. OSD had to overrule them "on occasions when better studies might have won support."[55]

Despite continuing internal dissension and seemingly irreconcilable differences with Moscow, the administration doggedly pursued the Geneva talks. All during the spring and summer of 1962, even as the Dominic testing program proceeded, the Western delegations searched for a way to engage the Soviet Union. As in 1961, when the goal of "general and complete disarmament" appeared impossibly complicated, the diplomats turned back to a test ban treaty as a more attainable objective. The Soviet and U.S. draft treaties on disarmament both included banning of tests as a natural component of the disarming process. Even though the obstacles, notably on-site inspection, that had doomed general disarmament in the past had also derailed test ban negotiations, a test ban seemed to have a better chance for success than did any other alternative in sight.

The eight new members of the ENDC introduced a compromise test ban proposal just two days before the United States formally unveiled its proposals on general disarmament. To resolve the test ban impasse, the eight urged consideration of (1) establishing a control system by expanding listening posts already in place, (2) having an international scientific commission conduct on-site inspections, and (3) setting in motion regular consultation between the commission and the nuclear powers with respect to significant seismic events. The recommendations were stated broadly enough to permit Soviet acceptance as long as it was understood that on-site inspections would occur only at the invitation of the country in which a suspicious event occurred.[56]

The United States, normally more insistent with regard to the on-site issue, showed itself open to the eight-nation proposal. New technological advances in underground detection by 1962 had made possible a promising replacement for the on-site examinations that prompted a rethinking of the U.S. position. The technological breakthrough came gradually, beginning with seminal work by the Pentagon's Advanced Research Projects Agency (ARPA) under Director Herbert York in 1959. Under the name of Project VELA, DoD inaugurated a program to devise a means to detect more accurately nuclear explosions fired both underground and in space.* By the time the Kennedy administration took office the technology was sufficiently advanced to elicit cautious confidence and continued support. During FY 1962 the total appropriation for VELA was $60.168 million with an estimated $162 million budgeted for FYs 1963-65.[57]

On the strength of the program's progress, conveyed publicly in a DoD report released 7 July 1962, Bundy told the president he believed the recent advances would permit the United States to relent on its demand for on-site inspection and thus open the way for a nuclear test-ban accord with the Soviet Union. Moreover, satellite photography would provide a further means of checking on certain kinds of underground tests.[58] In effect, technology reinforced Bundy's conviction, shared with McNamara, that chances of a profound clandestine breakthrough from new tests were slight compared with the potential benefits of stopping nuclear proliferation.

Not everyone in the administration felt as sanguine over VELA. Rusk emphasized that the VELA findings were preliminary and would require further evaluation "before they could be the basis for any modification of prior U.S. proposals." At a news conference on 12 July he granted that the VELA research offered "some promising signs" but cautioned that it was presumptuous to assume that its implementation could completely supplant control stations within the nuclear nations and on-site inspection. On his arrival in Geneva two days later, Ambassador Dean caused a brief sensation by suggesting that VELA might allow the United States to dispense with detection stations inside the Soviet Union, appearing to contradict Rusk, who issued a statement on 16 July clarifying the administration's position.[59]

Adding to the confusion was an ambivalent 1 July report from the Inspection Study Group, an interagency unit ACDA established in October 1961 to define and evaluate the inspection requirements of arms control plans. The group concluded that while verification appeared theoretically feasible by means of the latest equipment and methodology, more experimentation was warranted as well as improved intelligence capabilities before on-site inspections could be restricted or eliminated.[60]

When the Soviet Union announced the launching of a new series of atmospheric tests on 21 July, pressure mounted on the United States to respond to the latest ENDC test ban proposal. Rumors generated by positive reports on the VELA project and misreading of Dean's remarks convinced some observers that a shift in U.S. policy was underway. In fact, between 26 July and 1 August the White House held almost daily top-level meetings to formulate the U.S. position,

---

*Because there already existed a capability to detect explosions in the earth's atmosphere, the VELA project excluded low-altitude tests. VELA's main challenge was to find a reliable method to monitor underground tests. Success meant developing a long-range detection capability that would obviate the need for on-site inspection. The trick was to distinguish the detonation signals associated with a nuclear test from earth tremors of similar energy caused naturally by an earthquake.

with debate centering on the degree of confidence that could be placed in the VELA results. At one point, Rusk asked whether the United States should support a comprehensive ban assuming "we knew neither side could test." McNamara and Seaborg answered affirmatively, but many of the attendees remained uneasy about the potential for Soviet advantage should VELA prove inadequate. Dean thought that if they were not careful they might be "walking into a Soviet trap." At the 1 August meeting Kennedy read a letter from Macmillan, who two weeks earlier had told the House of Commons that VELA would help to facilitate a final treaty by rendering on-site inspections unnecessary; Macmillan now prodded the president to act. Lemnitzer dismissed the prime minister's importuning as the British having "another fit of weakness," but Bundy noted pressure coming from all over to define the U.S. stance.[61]

Kennedy emerged from the 1 August afternoon session to announce at a press conference that although the United States stood on the verge of a system of detection and verification for underground testing "which will be simpler and more economical," and although "it may be that we shall not need as many as we've needed in the past," an end to on-site inspections would be premature, specifically with regard to the most problematic issue, unidentified underground events. The United States and the United Kingdom formally presented a comprehensive test ban treaty proposal, a revised version of the April 1961 draft proposal, to the plenary session of the Eighteen-Nation Disarmament Committee on 27 August 1962 that spelled out exactly what concessions the administration was prepared to make consistent with what the president had described as "the technical realities."[62]

The terms of the U.S.-U.K. proposal demonstrated the limits of the administration's faith in the new seismic devices even given the risks that arms control advocates like McNamara and Nitze were willing to tolerate. While U.S. negotiators spoke of fewer control stations and inspections, the comprehensive ban adhered to the principle of mandatory on-site inspection. Under the plan, an international scientific commission, much like the body mentioned in the 1961 draft treaty but with an enlarged neutral membership and an executive officer with reduced staff, would report evidence of suspected nuclear tests. The opposite side, not the country being inspected, would determine which of the certified events were to be examined up to an unspecified number annually for each side. Nationals of the suspect party could not serve on the inspection team reviewing that particular incident.[63] Given these conditions, the administration must have realized that the revised treaty would be no more acceptable to the Soviets than the earlier one had been. The president's advisers had in fact anticipated the outcome and had wrestled with the details of a backup proposal.[64]

The submission by the United States and Britain of a second, more limited, treaty proposal on the same day suggested that the comprehensive test ban treaty was a stalking horse for a more serious—and more circumscribed—alternative.

Instead of a treaty banning tests in all environments, the limited plan would end testing only in environments susceptible to monitoring by national means. The ban could then dispense with international verification and on-site inspections. Concomitantly, the one environment omitted from the second draft treaty plan of 27 August was underground, where there still existed no assurance that the new detecting devices could monitor all thresholds. Although Kennedy and Macmillan declared their "strong preference" for the comprehensive ban, they expressed confidence also in the alternative as an accord that would lead to "a definite downward turn in the arms race." In the words of the alternative treaty's preamble, "immediate discontinuance of nuclear weapon test explosions in the atmosphere, in outer space, and in the oceans will facilitate progress toward the early agreement providing for the permanent and verified discontinuance of nuclear weapon test explosions in all environments."[65]

Despite the removal of the on-site inspection requirement, the Soviet Union rejected the more modest version of the treaty almost as strongly as it did the comprehensive proposal. Soviet Deputy Foreign Minister Vasili Kuznetsov charged that the gist of the U.S. position had not materially changed "during all the years of negotiations" and that the United States would derive special advantages from small underground tests effectively "legalized" under the partial ban. Moscow offered to consider a cutoff date, such as 1 January 1963, after which there would be an "understanding" prohibiting testing of any kind. While Kennedy welcomed the idea of a cutoff date to end all testing, he reminded the American public that no moratorium or gentlemen's agreement would suffice. "This is the lesson," he informed the press, "of the Soviet Government's tragic decision to renew testing just a year ago."[66] Once again the disarmament talks ended in stalemate.

Seizing a Window of Opportunity

The ENDC meetings in Geneva recessed on 7 September 1962 amid "a deep feeling of frustration and gloom," with plans to reconvene on 12 November. In the interval the Cuban missile crisis diverted the world's attention from test ban negotiations. But it was only a temporary diversion. Indeed, the crisis served to focus both U.S. and Soviet thoughts on the dangers of nuclear warfare and consequently on the increasing urgency of reaching some kind of agreement. On 4 November, a week after the height of the missile confrontation, the president announced that the offer made in March to stop further nuclear tests "still stands," if the Soviet Union would accept an "effectively verified test ban treaty."[67]

If the United States was sobered by the Cuban crisis, the Soviet Union appeared to have been equally affected. Little more than a week after Kennedy expressed the imperative need to resolve the testing issue, the USSR representative in Geneva recommended to the ENDC on 13 November that unmanned seismic stations be used to supplement existing national detection stations. When the U.S.

side summarily rejected the so-called "black boxes" as an inadequate substitute for personnel on-site, Khrushchev followed up with a letter to Kennedy on 19 December that extended yet another overture. The Soviet premier implied that the two leaders essentially agreed that on-site inspections were not really necessary, but that the president's hands were tied by Senate opposition to cessation of testing; to overcome that obstacle, he professed a willingness "to meet you halfway in this question." Claiming that Dean had informed Kuznetsov on 30 October that two to four inspections on Soviet territory per year would suffice, he offered to accept two to three on each other's soil.[68]

Dean's alleged concession took the administration by surprise. The United States had asked for 20 annual inspections in 1960 and then reduced them in 1961 to a sliding formula of 12 to 20 depending on the actual number of suspicious events taking place. This was the official U.S. stance in December 1962. At the least the United States would agree to 8 to 10 a year, and that was the number Dean advised the president he had mentioned to Kuznetsov. But Dean's conversations seemed to affect the U.S. bargaining position. The ambassador felt it necessary to write a vigorous defense of his discussions with the Soviet negotiators, categorically denying Kuznetsov's assertions in an 11-page letter to William Foster. Dean insisted that when asked if the United States would accept two or three visitations, he had replied "emphatically no."[69]

Dean resigned as chairman of the U.S. delegation to the ENDC on 27 December. Whatever his culpability, the Soviet proffer of permitting two or three inspections per year as a sudden earnest of cooperation seems disingenuous. As Soviet specialists in the State Department recognized, Khrushchev had cited the "three" quota at his meeting with Kennedy in Vienna in June 1961, more than a year prior to the discussions with Dean that supposedly moved him to make the offer. Moreover, Moscow continued to look on arms control as much as a propaganda vehicle as a subject for serious negotiations. Khrushchev's speech to the Sixth Congress of the Socialist Unity Party in East Berlin on 16 January 1963 coupled the "struggle to prevent thermonuclear war" with a call for a German peace treaty as a pre-condition for disarmament.[70]

Throughout his exchanges with the Soviet premier, the president accented the positive and exhorted Khrushchev to go the extra length, as he was himself prepared to do. Kennedy welcomed Khrushchev's tacit acceptance of the principle of on-site inspections—"not just because of the concern of our Congress but because they . . . go to the heart of a reliable agreement." He appreciated the delicacy of the issue of inspections in the vicinity of defense installations and underscored U.S. flexibility by reducing the number of inspections from the 12-20 formula to 8-10; if he refused the Soviet demand for 2 or 3, internally he coaxed 6 from his advisers as a "rock-bottom" position. Further, the administration signaled it would accept five automatic (unmanned) seismic stations if the Soviet Union balked at seven. Kennedy postponed underground tests in Nevada for the duration of the consultations. Confidence-building efforts notwithstanding, progress toward a treaty remained at a standstill. When the tripartite talks in New York and Washington ended in deadlock, the president ordered the resumption of underground testing, which began at the Nevada site on 8 February 1963.[71]

Kennedy's sincerity in seeking accommodation with the Soviet Union on obstacles in the way of a settlement never came into question. He hoped through superpower collaboration on a test ban to diminish the larger danger of nuclear proliferation, and he assumed the Soviet Union shared that objective. He worried in particular about the nuclear aspirations of China—and, to a lesser degree, France. He worried, too, as he told Macmillan, that "some unfortunate press report" might "damage or even wreck the prospects for real agreement" by its effect on the NATO allies. When the time became ripe for a final agreement he wanted to inform the Europeans well in advance of signing.[72]

The failure to achieve the hoped-for settlement in the winter of 1962-1963 stemmed not solely from resistance on the Soviet side. Khrushchev correctly identified opposition to a test ban treaty in the U.S. Senate as a major hurdle. But opposition also came from inveterate skeptics in the U.S. scientific community. One of the most influential critics, physicist Edward Teller, associate director of the Lawrence Livermore Laboratory, had consistently opposed test ban negotiations and now told House Republicans that such a ban as that proposed by the Soviet Union "would be virtually unpoliced. It would endanger our security and would help the Soviet Union in its plan to conquer the world." Even Nelson Rockefeller, the liberal Republican governor of New York, expressed concern over the "apparent weakening" of U.S. inspection requirements. Some of the harshest criticism in the Senate came from Connecticut Democrat Thomas Dodd, who charged in a lengthy tirade on 21 February that the administration invited war by granting excessive concessions to the Soviets. Dodd blasted "an aggressive faction in the scientific community," singling out Hans Bethe, that had given "persistently wrong-headed advice" to both Eisenhower and Kennedy. Prominent Democratic senators Richard Russell, Stuart Symington, and Henry Jackson joined Dodd in opposition to the proposed test ban.[73]

The guardedness of leading legislators and scientists found reinforcement in the longstanding attitudes of the Joint Chiefs of Staff. When Nitze gave the JCS an opportunity on 14 February to comment on ACDA's latest proposition, they disputed virtually the entire range of ACDA recommendations as to what constituted a "reasonable deterrent," including the further relaxation of the on-site inspection quota to six inspections (the JCS had never budged from the 12-20 figure) and the exclusion of sensitive defense installations from inspection, which the chiefs said amounted to a veto. They found particularly disturbing ACDA's continuing overestimation of the capability of seismic devices to distinguish between natural phenomena and nuclear activity and the acceptance of a 4.0 detection threshold, which would effectively institute "an unpoliced moratorium" on underground testing below that level. The JCS wanted assurance that testing below the threshold would be specifically authorized, so that U.S. technical advances from low-yield testing would not be unilaterally halted while the Soviet Union proceeded with undetected clandestine activity. Finally, the chiefs disapproved of a nonwithdrawal clause that prevented any abrogation of the treaty for three years, which they thought counter to U.S. interests if a state not a party to the treaty (notably Communist China) conducted nuclear testing in the interim.[74]

ACDA took into account the JCS concerns but responded with only grudging modifications. For example, as an apparent compromise on the three-year notice before withdrawal, ACDA accepted a two-year period along with a cumbersome fallback provision permitting withdrawal after 60 days if the aggrieved party felt that a test by a non-party had jeopardized its national security and called a conference to present its case. As for the time it would take to detect explosions below the 4.0 threshold, ACDA tried to convince the chiefs that improvements in VELA would enable the United States to detect "virtually all seismic events" inside the Soviet Union within three to four years; given other sophisticated monitoring systems, ACDA considered the risks acceptable. On the veto assertion, if U.S. negotiators did not exclude sensitive defense installations, they could not prevent the Soviet Union from inspecting similar U.S. bases.[75]

Unpersuaded by ACDA's arguments or analysis, the Joint Chiefs conveyed their dissatisfaction to McNamara in a memorandum of 21 March, recommending further review before the United States made such a critical commitment. McNamara had backed the JCS on similar challenges to ACDA in the past, but his greater willingness to accept a less than perfect test ban pact, strengthened by Brown's scientific judgment as director of defense research and engineering, had been clearly laid out in two long memoranda of his own to the president on 12 February. In his customary methodical fashion he weighed the U.S.-USSR military balance with and without a test ban—both comprehensive and atmospheric—as it would affect or not affect both strategic retaliatory and tactical nuclear forces. He concluded that in the larger scheme little of predictable significance would result from continued testing, though he acknowledged an element of risk from unforeseeable developments. The United States in 1963 had "a clear strategic superiority" over the Soviet Union as well as more advanced nuclear technology. Any change in the strategic balance would for the most part come from policy decisions on the composition and character of the forces rather than moderate improvements in warhead efficiency resulting from testing. Even if the relative military position of the United States were diminished by Soviet cheating—and he granted the U.S. position could be "seriously affected" by a prolonged undetected covert Soviet program—the nation's ability to inflict massive civilian damage in a second strike remained a strong deterrent. In brief, McNamara would take risks (where the JCS would not) on the grounds that an enforceable comprehensive test ban would lock in U.S. superiority in nuclear technology, and even if evasions occurred, they would not have a critical impact on national security.[76]

The proliferation issue, addressed in a second memorandum for the president, provided McNamara incentive enough to support a test ban treaty. He foresaw eight countries capable of acquiring at least a few nuclear weapons and a crude delivery system in the next 10 years even without advances in technology. Unrestricted testing could accelerate the trend toward cheaper and therefore more accessible weapons. "It is probably not an exaggeration," the secretary wrote Kennedy, to say that a ban on testing "is a necessary, but not a sufficient, condition for keeping the number of nuclear countries small." Besides limiting diffusion of weapons, cooperation between the two major nuclear powers on a test ban would set an example and precedent for restraining others from testing.[77]

In one important respect the intramural debate within Defense in the winter and spring of 1963 seemed irrelevant. With U.S. and Soviet negotiators unable to move beyond fundamental differences on inspection numbers and procedures, or even which matter should take priority, the two sides remained so far apart that no agreement seemed in prospect. Seaborg observed in his memoirs that any apparent convergence in the two positions and the reduction of the stalemate to one or two bones of contention was an illusion. As Harriman would later testify, even if the United States had accepted Khrushchev's limit of three inspections, the respective sides remained so at odds on the technical details of the inspection protocol that a meeting of the minds seemed out of the question. "When I saw the details of what our experts would demand in the way of the kind of inspection . . ., the large area over which we would have helicopters range, and the number of holes we would have to drill, and that sort of thing . . . I am satisfied they would never have agreed to it."[78]

When asked at a press conference on 8 May about the likelihood of a treaty with the Soviet Union, the president replied: "No, I'm not hopeful, I'm not hopeful. There doesn't seem to be any sense of movement since December on the offer of two or three that the Soviets have made." Instead of drawing closer to an agreement, Kennedy admitted "we seem to be moving away from it," adding with a seeming air of resignation that "perhaps the genie is out of the bottle and we'll never get him back in 'again." Anticipating yet another round of tests in the absence of a treaty, the president said the failure to reach an accord "would be a great disaster for the interests of all concerned."[79]

Despite the somber outlook, in another press conference on 22 May Kennedy vowed to "push very hard" through the spring and summer "in every forum" to revive the stalled negotiations, acutely aware of the dwindling time available to them before the post-Cuba window of opportunity might close shut forever. Previously, on 6 May, he urged ACDA and the Committee of Principals to use the upcoming recess at Geneva for "an urgent re-examination" of possible new approaches.[80]

Through the spring of 1963, then, ACDA continued to draft variations on its basic treaty proposal and the Joint Chiefs continued to register reservations. Divisions within DoD remained as pronounced as earlier, perhaps even more so. In their comments on an ACDA draft of 24 May the chiefs discerned little change and responded with much the same rebuttal. On 14 June McNamara informed Foster that DoD concurred with the revised proposal even as he dutifully forwarded the JCS's separate views for the president's consideration. The depth of JCS disaffection emerged starkly in a conversation between LeMay and McNamara on 24 June. Striving for some degree of harmony, McNamara had suggested a rewording of the chiefs' statement, but LeMay said they rejected any alterations "apart from such of the changes as related to matters of grammar or style." LeMay contested every matter of substance, including the putative technological advantage that the United States had over the Soviet Union. When McNamara asked LeMay to name the technically qualified individuals on whom the chiefs were relying for advice, the general could come up with only one person, Air Force Maj. Gen. Dale Smith.[81]

On 26 June, the secretary circulated to JCS Chairman Taylor, as well as to Seaborg of the AEC and the president's science adviser Wiesner, a request for comment on three "White Papers" related to the test ban that incorporated the facts and judgments that had emerged from the extended series of springtime meetings. The administration obviously felt a need to demonstrate to Congress a coherent position that even if not amounting to a true consensus at least fairly reflected divergent viewpoints. At a key meeting during this period, as the Committee of Principals tried to forge a "broad consensus" and McNamara highlighted the Joint Chiefs' stubborn differences, Rusk professed perplexity over how the chiefs could take a separate stance from that of the president—something he would never do in the foreign policy arena. McNamara explained that the law enabled the chiefs to present their personal opinions directly to Congress and indeed required them to do so when asked.[82]

McNamara had hoped the administration could avert a "head-on collision,"[83] not only with the JCS but also with the AEC and other opposition elements within the Pentagon who were not prepared to dismiss technical evidence of the shortcomings of the new detection devices or discount the effect of Soviet cheating on the strategic balance. The White Papers exercise, however, rather than leaving the impression of essential concurrence on the broad outlines of a test ban treaty, spotlighted the dissent and underlined the lack of consensus within the government.

Harriman's Mission to Moscow

The indispensable partner to an agreement, of course, remained the Soviet Union, not the JCS. Dejection mixed with perseverance during the spring of 1963 as participants on both sides, buoyed by a commitment to establish a direct "hot line" link between Washington and Moscow,* sought a way out of the impasse. Complicating matters was the Kremlin's preoccupation with growing strains in the Sino-Soviet relationship. In April Khrushchev met with Norman Cousins, editor of the influential *Saturday Review* and a peace activist then touring the Soviet Union, at Khrushchev's vacation home on the Black Sea. By turns introspective and agitated, Khrushchev conveyed to the journalist his good-faith intentions, the pressure he was getting from his own dissidents, and lingering unhappiness over the Dean affair, which he believed had squandered a golden opportunity for a settlement. Although Ambassador Llewellyn Thompson advised Rusk on 24 April that internal and external pressures were preventing the Soviet leader from moving on the test ban issue "at this time," Kennedy, pressed by a tenacious Macmillan, proposed to Khrushchev informal high-level discussions aimed at clearing the air and getting the talks back on track. In two long letters dated 8 May and 8 June, the Soviet premier waxed alternately cranky and conciliatory before finally consenting to receive a senior Western delegation, suggesting 15 July for the group's arrival in Moscow.[84]

Hence, what appears to have been a mutual interest in rescuing the test ban negotiations in the aftermath of Kennedy's glum 8 May press conference preceded fitful but steady progress that gave cause for optimism. A major impetus came from Kennedy's historic address at American University on 10 June, two days after Khrushchev's most recent letter agreeing to the new round of discussions. The commencement speech, fashioned by Sorensen, dwelt on the positive aspects of Soviet-American relations, including the claim that "almost unique, among the major world powers, we have never been at war with each other." What the United States wanted, Kennedy declared, was "not a Pax Americana enforced on the world by American weapons of war," but "a just and genuine peace" that in the nuclear age had become "the necessary rational end of rational men." After framing his remarks in a broader context, at length the president turned to the immediate objective, securing agreement "where the end is in sight, yet where a fresh start is badly needed . . . a treaty to outlaw nuclear tests." Heralding the scheduled resumption of superpower talks, Kennedy pledged with "good faith and solemn convictions . . . that the United States does not propose to conduct nuclear tests in the atmosphere so long as other states do not do so."[85]

The speech received ample notice at home, but it had an even more powerful effect abroad, particularly in the Soviet Union, where the leadership reacted favorably to both the tone and substance of the statement. A CIA report claimed that the Soviets felt no head of state would make such a bold commitment to peace and disarmament unless convinced of the likelihood of an agreement. While

---

* This was a teletype link between the two capitals confirmed in a memorandum of understanding of 20 June 1963. See *American Foreign Policy: Current Documents, 1963*, 521-23.

they resented Kennedy's singling out Communist transgressions as "the primary cause of world tension today" (after promising no finger-pointing), the president's message had produced an "excellent atmosphere." Khrushchev later told Harriman that he thought it the best speech by any president since Franklin Roosevelt. More persuasive evidence of Soviet appreciation than the private confidence to Harriman was the reprinting of the entire text in the Soviet press and the unjamming of Western broadcasts of the speech, the first such occurrence in 15 years.[86]

Expectations increased with the appointment of Harriman as the U.S. chief delegate. With his long experience in dealing with Soviet leaders, the veteran diplomat was a natural choice to head the delegation. Despite his commanding reputation, or perhaps because of it, while continuing to occupy important posts at State, he had not been part of Rusk's inner circle and, in Schlesinger's words, had been "rather systematically excluded" from Soviet affairs. Both Schlesinger and John McNaughton, the DoD general counsel who would accompany the delegation, cite Carl Kaysen, Bundy's deputy, as a key figure in engineering Harriman's appointment after another logical choice, John McCloy, turned out to be unavailable. Tapping the accomplished statesman for the assignment invested the delegation with unquestioned authority and stature and confirmed the president's earnestness. "As soon as I heard that Harriman was going," a Soviet embassy staff member told Schlesinger, "I knew you were serious."[87]

The month between the agreement to meet in Moscow and the departure of Harriman as head of the mission proved a busy and ultimately fruitful period, but not without setbacks. By virtue of the president's manifesto, the initiative fell to the United States to set the agenda, yet a truculent Khrushchev, perhaps posturing for the benefit of his hard-liners, again ruled out inspections on Soviet soil and insisted on coupling any test ban treaty with a non-aggression pact between NATO and the Warsaw Pact nations. As the Joint Chiefs and naysayers dug in their own heels at home, Harriman was faced with competing demands and little room to maneuver, the early skirmishing for position threatening to pull the rug out from under him before even arriving at the bargaining table.[88]

Rusk's instructions to Harriman stated as a first objective "a *comprehensive treaty*, with adequate verification of uncertain events underground." This would include some inspections. Only "if the Russians refuse to budge on a comprehensive treaty" would the mission move on to a partial treaty, covering all environments except underground. Harriman was also to make an effort to gain French adherence without making it a requirement, and at the same time press the Soviet Union to convince China to join the fold. A week later further instructions to Harriman once again referred to a comprehensive ban as the primary goal, but specifically mentioned the 27 August 1962 draft that omitted underground testing as a model for a fallback limited test ban agreement. As for the Soviet push for a non-aggression pact between the two blocs, it would have to await the conclusion of a test ban accord.[89]

Harriman's final guidance even touched on general and complete disarmament, partly in anticipation of Foreign Minister Gromyko's wanting to explore a proposal he had introduced in the ENDC regarding first-stage disarmament. Although the United States would not entertain any Soviet desire "to proceed rapidly to complete and general disarmament on terms which we have always found unacceptable," recent movement on the U.S. side on the general disarmament question opened the door to the possibility of a serious discussion on the subject of "separable first stages." In May, Defense had agreed to destroy 30 B-47s each month for two years, 10 of which would come from storage, in return for the USSR following suit with destruction of an equivalent number of its own medium jet bomber Badgers. ACDA recommended initiation of the process beginning 1 January 1964 contingent on adequate verification procedures that included "adversary" inspection.[90]

DoD's flexibility had its limits. At a meeting of the Committee of Principals on 8 July McNamara rejected a 50 to 75 percent reduction in strategic delivery vehicles as damaging the credibility of the West's nuclear deterrent and wasting its superior nuclear power, especially if such deep cuts were not matched by compensatory reductions in the Soviet Union's superior conventional capabilities. The secretary felt that ACDA leaned too far toward accommodating the Soviet position by seeming to accept a symmetrical reduction of forces that ignored the disproportionate advantage the Soviets enjoyed in conventional strength. They could afford to decrease their troop level in East Germany but NATO could not. When Foster interjected that he understood that this advantage in conventional forces had lately diminished, McNamara agreed "we had made substantial progress" but that the West was still clearly behind. In general, McNamara preferred a more gradual approach of an initial 30 percent reduction across the board and additional cuts later, sticking with the same formula he had backed a year earlier. His cautiousness here was supported by Taylor and CIA Director McCone.[91]

Given the differences within the Committee of Principals, they agreed only that Harriman should receive instructions to take no "initiative relating to changes in our position [regarding] strategic delivery vehicles." In skirting any specific recommendation, the committee, besides getting hung up on McNamara's issues, felt that Harriman would have enough on his hands in Moscow in dealing with a test ban agreement without becoming entangled in the thickets of general and complete disarmament.[92]

Before leaving Washington, Harriman had a 45-minute conversation with McNamara on a range of topics that could come up in Moscow. The secretary mentioned the ABM program as one area where both sides could benefit from a mutual scaling back of enhancements and escalating costs that had "no end in sight." McNamara commented on his stance on weapons reduction and identified trade and outer space as two specific fields for possible cooperation. Notably, Harriman left the meeting with the assurance that McNamara not only would "fully support a comprehensive test ban treaty" but believed such a ban was of "grave importance."[93]

Among other matters needing clarification before Harriman met with the Soviet negotiators was the "special" relationship with the United Kingdom, which had functioned harmoniously in the two countries' joint pursuit of a series of disarmament proposals in the first two years of the Kennedy administration but experienced some tense moments on the eve of the mission to Moscow. While Macmillan had always supported U.S. proposals, he often appeared more conciliatory toward Soviet views and more aggressive an advocate of a testing accord than his transatlantic partner. The British seemed to want a test ban at almost any price, McNaughton recalled, and friction over perceived U.S. tentativeness and British impatience, compounded by personality clashes, strained relations during preliminary meetings in London. The appointment of Quintin Hogg, Lord Hailsham, as the chief British delegate to the Moscow talks especially proved an irritant. A State Department profile on Hailsham noted that he combined "a high degree of political and intellectual astuteness, together with political ambitions, with just enough instability (or perhaps better, unpredictableness) to permit occasional impetuous actions and public statements which subsequently cause both him and his party much embarrassment and concern."[94]

Hailsham shortly lived up to his reputation, aspiring to play the role, not of lower-level facilitator, but of mediator between Kennedy and Khrushchev, much as Roosevelt had between Stalin and Churchill. If the British had had their way, another summit would have followed from the negotiations in Moscow. The president discussed this possibility with Harriman on 10 July but expressed reluctance to accept the idea for fear of difficulties it might cause in Germany and France. He would consider doing it "just to sign the test ban treaty." The British also seemed to be insufficiently sensitive to the possibilities of Soviet cheating after the treaty signing. When McNaughton raised the point at the preparatory conference in London the last week of June, the British "pooh-poohed" it. Sir Solly Zuckerman, the chief scientific adviser for the United Kingdom, dismissed the notion by saying, "I suppose they could go out behind the sun and blow up something if they wanted to spend all their natural resources to do it."[95]

As it turned out, once in Moscow the British presence was barely visible. The key player, "the ball carrier," in McNaughton's phrase, was Harriman. With him firmly in command many of the issues that had befogged the atmosphere during prolonged wrangling in the past evaporated over a week of hard but forthright bargaining. To the Soviet demand for the inclusion of France as a signatory the Anglo-American side countered with a demand for China's inclusion. Neither of these powers intended to join, and neither the United States nor the Soviet Union had the means of persuading them. Kennedy and Macmillan corresponded at length on "the special nature of the French problem," recognizing de Gaulle's innate distrust of the "Anglo-Saxons" and France's understandable aversion to subscribe to a test ban at a pivotal point in the country's rudimentary nuclear program. Macmillan hoped that even if they could not get de Gaulle to sign they could prevail on him to grasp "the symbolic importance which such a treaty may have for all of us" and refrain from "destroying . . . the moral effect" of the treaty with "intemperate remarks." As for China, Kennedy assumed probably correctly that Khrushchev was as anxious to abort a Chinese nuclear project as he was, although the Soviet premier always tried to give the impression, as Harriman told McNaughton, of not being greatly concerned. "They're going to have them anyway," Khrushchev reportedly told Harriman, "but they won't have any military capability for several years and in any event it's not going to amount to anything. It'll be like the French capability. Forget it." And, according to McNaughton, Khrushchev implied that "you could forget the British, too."[96] Whether or not Khrushchev believed this, his bravado—or fatalism—helped to remove both France and China as sources of contention between the superpowers.

Khrushchev brought up the subject of a non-aggression pact at the first meeting with Harriman on 15 July and Gromyko broached it almost daily. As McNaughton remembered, "Harriman's position was flat out. We were not negotiating a Non-Aggression Pact, period. Now, he didn't necessarily say it like that but it came out that way." At most, in return for yielding on the linkage demand, Khrushchev won an understanding in the final communiqué that the United States would take up the matter with its allies.[97]

To the surprise of U.S. negotiators, Gromyko objected to a provision sought by the United States (and thought to be supported by the USSR as well) to permit, albeit with stringent controls, nuclear testing for peaceful purposes. The Soviet Union argued that such a loophole would undermine the credibility of any ban. In return for acceding to the Soviet position, the United States extracted a concession that Moscow had resisted previously: namely, the right to withdraw from the treaty if a nation decided its vital interests would be damaged by adherence to treaty provisions. McNaughton said the Soviet government did not want a withdrawal clause on the grounds that "you don't spend your time at the wedding talking about divorce," but relented in exchange for the U.S. striking the peaceful uses provision when Harriman made clear his instructions required him to walk away without the withdrawal protection.*[98]

All the foregoing questions ultimately proved peripheral. The success or failure of the negotiations in Moscow turned on the principle of on-site inspections that had been a barrier to a settlement for years. Seaborg reduced the problem to its "baldest form": "the Soviets were persuaded that the United States wanted to

---

*The withdrawal clause, contained in Article 4, was plainly aimed at China and its ongoing nuclear program. Seaborg later noted the irony that "when the anticipated trigger event for activating the withdrawal clause—a Chinese nuclear test—occurred in October 1964, withdrawal from the [treaty] was not even suggested as an appropriate U.S. response." Nevertheless, had the withdrawal right not been included, the Senate may not have ratified the treaty. See Seaborg, *Kennedy*, 247.

inspect in order to spy; many on our side were convinced that without adequate inspection the Soviets would cheat."[99] The stumbling block was removed by agreement within the first 24 hours to exclude underground testing and limit the ban to atmospheric, undersea, and outer space environments, which could be policed without on-site verification; by dropping underground testing, the problem of inspection disappeared, and the negotiators could concentrate on composing their differences on the remaining surmountable sticking points. The price paid for an accord, which both sides now judged worthwhile, was the abandonment of a comprehensive test ban for a limited test ban.

Debate over the Treaty

The negotiators finished their work on 25 July, and Rusk, Gromyko, and British Secretary of State for Foreign Affairs Alec Douglas-Home initialed the final document, a "Treaty Banning Nuclear Weapon Tests in the Atmosphere, in Outer Space and Under Water," for their respective countries on 5 August.[100] Accompanying Rusk in the U.S. delegation that attended the official signing in Moscow were senior senators J. William Fulbright, chairman of the Foreign Relations Committee, John O. Pastore, chairman of the Joint Committee on Atomic Energy, Democrat Hubert Humphrey, and Republicans Leverett Saltonstall and George Aiken. Conspicuously absent were Democratic and Republican members of the Armed Services Committee, Saltonstall excepted. A bipartisan delegation served not simply to exorcise the unhappy memory of Woodrow Wilson's experience in Versailles in 1919 but also to recognize the opposition the treaty could face in the Senate. Indeed, two days before the initialing of the treaty the president felt that if Fulbright and Bourke B. Hickenlooper, ranking minority member of Fulbright's committee, did not attend, he should scrap the idea of a Senate representation in Moscow. Although Hickenlooper did not join the delegation, the legislative presence sufficed to justify proceeding with the plan.[101]

In submitting the treaty for ratification the president made a point of not claiming too much. He presented it as a first step in reducing tensions, curbing pollution in the atmosphere, and opening the way to further agreements among the major powers. The treaty itself could not end the threat of nuclear war or outlaw the use of nuclear weapons, nor could it substitute for U.S. military power. Progress in developing nuclear technology would continue through underground testing. Continued research on the peaceful use of atomic energy would also continue. And since atomic laboratories were to be maintained, atmospheric testing could be resumed if necessary.[102]

The timing of the treaty's presentation to the Senate received as careful attention as the text itself. Three days elapsed between the signing of the treaty and its delivery to the Senate. Rusk worried that if the administration moved too swiftly, senators would bridle at the slighting of the consultative process. With public opinion strongly favoring ratification, however, the president was in the mood to "hit the country while the country's hot. That's the only thing that makes any impression to these goddamned senators."[103]

Rusk had come away from a July meeting with the Senate Foreign Relations Committee feeling good about the treaty's prospects there, but the Preparedness Investigating Subcommittee of the Senate Committee on Armed Services was another story. Headed by Mississippi Sen. John Stennis and including such notable defense hawks as Henry Jackson, Strom Thurmond, and Barry Goldwater, the committee was as formidable as it was hostile to any perceived weakening of U.S. security. The subcommittee's leading witnesses insured there would be a heated debate. John Foster and Edward Teller of the Livermore Laboratory were longtime opponents of any test ban. The Stennis subcommittee had the greatest interest in the opinions of the Joint Chiefs, whose own reservations members knew from previous testimony, most recently in June before Harriman left for Moscow. Then, Admiral George Anderson, the outgoing chief of naval operations, stated that the Soviet Union could not be trusted to live up to its obligations: "Our previous experience with the Communists makes us acutely aware that their concepts of truth, of ethics, of morals are vastly different from our own." LeMay expressed the view that "to maintain a favorable balance of military power we must have nuclear superiority. To do this I firmly believe we must continue our nuclear weapon development programs and be able to conduct nuclear testing as required."[104]

When LeMay testified again in August, after the signing of the treaty, he did not change his position. But, upon questioning, he conceded that there were political advantages to a test ban. "Balancing the two together," LeMay suggested, "I believe that if we take certain safeguards to reduce the risk in the technical and military field, we could reduce them [the risks] to an acceptable degree so that we could go ahead and approve the treaty and see if these political gains materialize. But only if we take the safeguards." Teller, less equivocal, insisted that "if we sign this treaty we are taking a very great risk. And I think that if the treaty is not ratified, the risk will be less." The physicist's testimony carried all the more persuasion because he came across, as Fulbright told the president, as "John L. Lewis and Billy Sunday all wrapped in one."[105]

On 9 September the Stennis subcommittee reported to Chairman Russell of the Senate Armed Services Committee its judgment that the treaty "will affect adversely the future quality of this Nation's arms, and that it will result in serious, and perhaps formidable, military and technical disadvantages. These disadvantages, in our judgment, are not outweighted or counterbalanced by the claimed military advantages." The committee thus threw up a major but not insurmountable hurdle in the way of ratification. Even the subcommittee's report recognized "the existence of other factors which, while not within the scope of this report, are pertinent to a final judgment on the treaty."[106]

Acceptance or rejection rested ultimately with Fulbright's Senate Foreign Relations Committee where the treaty, as Rusk had anticipated, enjoyed solid support. While Harold Brown encountered withering skepticism as a ratification advocate before the Stennis subcommittee, the Fulbright committee went along with his argument that the treaty would not threaten U.S. strategic superiority. Senators friendly to the administration were quick to seize on his professional judgment as having more authority than that of fellow scientist Teller, given his broad experience and greater access to information and intelligence as director of Defense Research and Engineering. Brown effectively neutralized Teller's opposition, but the military testimony more than the scientific had to be countered for the administration to succeed; McNamara and Taylor undertook this task.[107]

McNamara's voice came across clear and his conclusions unambiguous. He had always believed that the United States held a commanding lead over the Soviet Union in nuclear technology, and he remained convinced that only minimal advances would come from further testing in the atmosphere. The United States, he noted, had demonstrated in Cuba, Vietnam, and Berlin that "our will matches our might," and had done so without resort to nuclear arms. The vast increase in U.S. nuclear forces, "accompanied as it was by large increases in Soviet nuclear stockpiles, has [not] produced a comparable enhancement in our security." Even the Soviet leaders, he believed, had grasped that "sheer multiplication of a nation's destructive nuclear capability does not necessarily produce a net increase in its security." While this, or any other treaty, did not come risk free, the most serious risk was an outbreak of national euphoria, he warned. In sum, "the risks under the treaty are either small or under our control, and the values of the treaty are substantial even if we consider only the military area. The scales are clearly tipped in favor of the treaty, Mr. Chairman. It has my unequivocal support."[108]

The JCS disagreed with the secretary's judgment but struggled to find a comfortable position in the face of personal intervention by the president and what increasingly looked like a losing battle for them. On the eve of the Harriman mission, as it became evident that Khrushchev was amenable to a limited test ban, the Joint Staff had drafted a memorandum for the secretary recapitulating the litany of objections posed in previous assessments and deeming a limited ban "militarily disadvantageous." The draft never went forward to McNamara, as under persistent White House pressure and Taylor's brokering, the chiefs gave a grudging nod to the treaty in the context of overriding non-military considerations. Kennedy had managed to get the chiefs to go on record with at least a qualified embrace of the treaty before the Senate Foreign Relations Committee prior to meeting with Stennis's panel, where the president fretted that in "a much hotter atmosphere" and "under interrogation by Scoop Jackson . . . and Barry Goldwater and Strom . . . these fellows can be taken along a road . . . ."[109]

The chiefs exacted a set of "safeguards" as prerequisites for their approval—the continuance of underground nuclear testing to improve weapons, the maintenance of laboratory facilities to assure continued progress in nuclear research, maintenance of resources to resume testing in the atmosphere if necessary, and improvement of monitoring devices to detect Soviet violations and keep abreast of Sino-Soviet nuclear activity—but these actions had already been committed to by the president and amounted to a face-saving device that gave the JCS a graceful exit and the administration a way to parry the charge of presidential coercion. As Kennedy chuckled to Fulbright, "let them claim they got that out of us."[110]

LeMay indeed pointedly referred to the "safeguards" in his halfhearted endorsement of the treaty before the Stennis committee. When Goldwater in particular scoffed at the chiefs' seeming eleventh-hour conversion, LeMay said that the president had spoken with them as a body and individually, but he did not defend McNamara against Goldwater's insinuation that the secretary of defense had limited their participation and ignored their opinion despite McNamara's claim "under oath" that he had consulted with them "hundreds of times." McNamara in fact had discussed the subject, if not the treaty per se, with the Joint Chiefs on a regular basis, but such resentment as they had against the administration they directed primarily at the secretary. In the end, by indulging the political case for approving the treaty the chiefs showed they were good soldiers while washing their hands of responsibility. On strictly military grounds they never wavered in their negative judgment that the treaty was a liability and a threat. Taylor later professed to be "surprised by the outcome and rather proud of the Chiefs for overcoming their instinctive opposition to a testing agreement with a dangerous, distrusted adversary." Years later, asked to look back on his major achievements as JCS chairman, he offered, tongue in cheek, "my part in persuading Curtis LeMay to support the limited test ban treaty."[111]

Having thus prevailed over the opposition within the military, the administration worried only about a possible crippling reservation or amendment rather than outright rejection. None came. While the Stennis subcommittee opposed the treaty by a 6-to-1 majority, most senators responded to the persuasive power of the president and the overwhelming weight of public opinion. With the JCS out of the fight, the Foreign Relations Committee recommended ratification by a vote of 16 to 1 on 29 August 1963. Even Everett Dirksen, Republican minority leader and articulate critic of the treaty, voted in favor of ratification, along with four other Republicans. The only amendment accepted was a largely pro forma procedural proviso that all future amendments to the treaty would require Senate approval. It did not affect the language of the document. The treaty passed on 24 September 1963 by a majority of 80 to 19; the president signed the ratification document on 7 October in the Treaty Room of the White House before a bipartisan congressional delegation.[112]

*   *

The product of intense debate and stubborn perseverance, the Nuclear Test Ban Treaty was a diplomatic triumph for Kennedy and Macmillan, both of whom considered it a milestone in the thawing of the Cold War and a vindication of their steady determination.[113] Although it held undeniable risks, as the Joint Chiefs never let McNamara forget, on balance there was sufficient reason to believe that the benefits from the accord would have more lasting significance than the drawbacks when the potential impediment to nuclear proliferation, the end to radioactive fallout in the atmosphere, and the spur to superpower cooperation were factored into the equation. Of transcendent importance, the test ban treaty seemed to confirm mutual recognition of the folly of nuclear war and the concomitant need to take measures for eliminating its possibility.

When the most cherished expectations underlying the test ban campaign failed to materialize, some among the treaty proponents and Kennedy faithful attributed the unfulfillment to Kennedy's death less than two months after ratification. Roger Hilsman saw in the treaty a measured step toward détente that would have led to more progress had Kennedy survived. Seaborg lamented Kennedy's death in the fall of 1963 and Khrushchev's fall from power in 1964. Had they lived and remained in office, he speculated almost two decades later, the world might have witnessed advances in arms control that were lost when they passed from the scene. In 1988, on the 25th anniversary of the treaty signing, Wiesner ruefully observed that "we should not only remember what it was but what it could have been." While a salient achievement, it did not lead to a comprehensive ban. Instead, by the 1980s new technologies had made nuclear competition more dangerous than ever.[114]

Regrets over missed opportunities and the settling for a partial nuclear test ban took on greater urgency as global nuclear activity expanded rather than contracted over the next generation. The treaty helped slow but certainly did not stop the spread of nuclear weapons to other nations. Nor did the agreement retard the development of nuclear technology, which introduced new offensive and defensive systems that further complicated the U.S.-USSR rivalry. Weapons became more lethal as an increase in the number of warheads and improvements in the speed, range, and accuracy of missile delivery marked the next two decades. And although atmospheric tests no longer poisoned the air, the reliance on underground testing so eased anxiety over fallout that testing became more routinely tolerated, leading Kaysen to observe that the treaty, contrary to slowing the arms race, might have accelerated it.[115]

Still, if in retrospect the high hopes in the fall of 1963 proved inflated, hindsight should not dismiss the worth of the effort or the value of what was achieved. Although the genie might not have been put back in the bottle, the nuclear menace became more closely monitored and the permissible boundaries of testing circumscribed worldwide, and for this the Kennedy administration deserves much credit.

Doubtless, the test ban cause would have failed in 1963 if the Defense Department had not climbed aboard. Credit for success belongs in large part to the secretary of defense and his close associates, the deputy secretary and the chairman of the JCS, who gave the endeavor their blessing. In a deeply-divided Defense Department where the Joint Chiefs registered articulate opposition, McNamara was not wholly out of sympathy with the services. Along with the JCS, he had favored the resumption of testing in 1961 when the Soviets broke the moratorium. Moreover, he took up the JCS argument against ACDA's occasionally arbitrary actions and overstated technical results. But he still had fundamental differences with the service chiefs in what was in many ways a manifestation of the larger test of wills over his attempts to widen the military's vision of what constituted national security.

By 1963 McNamara had arrived at two conclusions about nuclear testing not shared by the Joint Chiefs. Whatever gains might have come from continued testing did not equal the benefits conferred by cessation of tests; furthermore, whatever gains the Soviet Union might achieve either through cheating in the banned areas or through experimenting underground would be checked by the ongoing U.S. ability to cope with any Soviet nuclear threat through the strategy of assured destruction. In brief, he believed that the military balance, already in U.S. favor, would not be threatened. Despite the troubling uncertainty that would continue to surround nuclear testing in the 1970s and 1980s and the continuing danger and instability stemming from other unfinished aspects of the nuclear arms control agenda, McNamara's judgment here proved essentially correct. The partial test ban treaty of 1963 has rightfully been called "the first concrete achievement in postwar arms control," and, coming on the heels of the peaceful resolution of the Cuban missile crisis, a powerful symbol along the road to East-West détente.[116] Robert McNamara was instrumental in the accomplishment of that limited but nonetheless historic undertaking.

CHAPTER XIV

NATO Relations: Transatlantic Differences

By 1961 the Western alliance had forged an impressive record: as an infrastructure for the economic revival of Europe, as an agent supporting the unification of Europe, and as a defender of its members from external invasion. But in the 1960s serious controversies developed between the United States and other leading members of NATO—France, Germany, and Great Britain—that created unmistakable strains within the alliance. As the decade advanced, some analysts even speculated about the possible end of the alliance. They judged that NATO had outlived its usefulness, had become a victim of its own success, and had "begun to founder," but they clearly misjudged the enduring strength of the ties that held the organization together.[1]

From the perspective of many of the statesmen and soldiers involved in the day-to-day management of the alliance, "success" would not have described NATO's condition, past or present. The Kennedy administration inherited grievances accumulated over a dozen years of NATO's history. While it made an effort to change some of the patterns set in the Truman and Eisenhower administrations, many of the proposed changes exacerbated rather than calmed tensions within the alliance. Had NATO terminated in 1963 or 1964, its dissolution would likely have resulted from the anger and frustration of junior partners rebelling against the dominance of the senior partner.

The record of the Kennedy years discloses a divergence in strategic thinking between European allies who wanted a low nuclear threshold with early resort to nuclear weaponry if attacked, and the United States with its push toward a high nuclear threshold and substantial conventional forces to make a nuclear response unnecessary. The need to recast NATO relations, however, had become evident before the election of 1960. Many of the ideas identified with the Kennedy administration carried over from the last Eisenhower years, including disillusionment with the doctrine of massive retaliation and offering NATO a medium-range ballistic missile (MRBM) force to counter European interest in independent nuclear capabilities. Massive retaliation as a strategy gave way to enthusiasm for a flexible response that placed less reliance on nuclear weapons and more on conventional forces. How to win European allies to this way of thinking held priority in the administration's NATO policy.

Each of the major allies had some complaint involving American leadership: the British felt unhappy with Washington's indifference to the "special relationship" between the two countries nurtured during World War II and carried over to the Cold War period; France resented U.S. efforts to thwart development of its *force de frappe*; Germany chafed at its perceived second-class citizenship in the alliance; and the other nations reflected some of the Gaullist doubts about U.S. steadfastness in the face of Soviet nuclear power. For its part, the United States had its own bill of particulars against its European partners: inadequate appreciation of U.S. responsibilities in Southeast Asia, sluggishness in response to the Berlin confrontation, and a willingness to allow the United States to assume the major burden of their defense despite a growing and worrisome U.S. balance of payments deficit.

NATO Strategy in 1961

Some of the most formidable alliance problems of the early 1960s derived from the launching of Sputnik in 1957 and its portent. Whatever successes Europe had enjoyed under U.S. protection in the past, it now had to deal with the potential consequences of the new power of the Soviet Union to challenge the United States in its own territory with weapons that did not exist in 1949. That containment had succeeded and Soviet efforts to derail Europe's growth had failed did not influence the attitude of the European partners as much as did their concern about the credibility of the U.S. role in European security in the future. This caused NATO to focus in this period particularly on what constituted defense in an age of approaching nuclear parity between East and West.

In this new climate, U.S. leaders stressed the inadequacy of the old nuclear strategy delineated in NATO's 1957 plan MC 14/2, which provided for nuclear response to any Soviet intrusion into the territory of a member nation no matter what the motivation or the scale. Supreme Allied Commander (SACEUR) General Lauris Norstad had made an effort to refine the policy by introducing the notion of a "pause" after a Soviet attack before unleashing a full nuclear response. Although never clearly defined, "pause" did address the possibility that the adversary might have made a mistake and might be granted some time to permit a graceful withdrawal before a full-scale war erupted.[2]

The changed circumstances in the 1960s required something more than the Norstad pause to maintain the nuclear deterrent while reducing danger of nuclear war. The Kennedy administration in general and the McNamara Pentagon in particular put forth plans for revising the composition of U.S. forces in Europe, using assumptions not shared by the European allies. The differences centered on American efforts to emphasize a buildup of European conventional forces to maintain the deterrent and to keep the nuclear war threshold as high as possible.

These judgments, either implicit or explicit, appeared in the report Dean Acheson prepared for the president and the State Department in the spring of 1961 under the title "A Review of North Atlantic Problems for the Future."[*] The revised doctrine aroused uneasy feelings in the NATO allies. Did the abhorrence of nuclear weapons signify U.S. intentions to abandon the nuclear defense of Europe? If not, would the threshold rise so high that the Soviets could take over Europe before it was reached? In speculating about answers to these questions, Europeans perceived sentiments in the United States that could cause it to abandon the alliance, not only discontent with the balance of payments deficit that might lead to withdrawal of U.S. forces, but also a revived American interest in counterinsurgent and unconventional warfare that might signal the displacement of Europe by Southeast Asia in U.S. consciousness. Even before the Acheson report had been commissioned these fears were reflected in a message from Norstad to McNamara asking him to give German Chancellor Adenauer assurance that "we do not intend to withdraw ground forces from NATO."[3]

Some European anxiety about the new administration was justified, and misgivings were voiced in Washington as well. Within the State Department some Europeanists felt that an excessive emphasis on conventional forces ignored the European partners' legitimate concerns over nuclear defense. From a different perspective Norstad was quick to note that conventional forces alone provided an inadequate deterrent. In a letter of qualified support for Acheson's recommendations he expressed his discomfort with assigning the growth of ground forces "first priority." "As you know," he wrote to Acheson, "the idea of an exclusive first priority bothers me considerably, but my reason for raising the subject in this connection is that here again I think we might be introducing controversy which is unnecessary at this stage of the game."[4] Given circulation of these caveats, Europeans might have recognized that the United States had not abandoned all the underlying commitments of the Eisenhower administration, and that, notwithstanding Acheson's report, the nuclear component remained the bedrock of NATO's defense. The president's message to NATO, however, did not buttress the positions of SACEUR or the Europeanists in the State Department. Speaking to NATO's Military Committee meeting in Washington on 10 April he mentioned "reenforcement of the capabilities of NATO in conventional weapons" before getting around to the continuation of "an effective nuclear capability."[5] The day after Norstad wrote his letter to Acheson the president accepted the Acheson report as official policy.[6]

---

[*] The report and the policy changes that ensued are discussed in Chapter XII.

This shift of emphasis implicit in flexible response had an immediate impact on Defense's relations with European counterparts. Soothing anxious allies was primarily State's role. But to plan a buildup of conventional forces required advancing convincing arguments for the Europeans to increase their defense budgets.

A comparison of conventional capabilities of NATO forces on the Central front with Soviet troops in East Germany and Poland revealed an apparently alarming imbalance. A JCS evaluation of NATO M-day* units assigned to the Central Region as of 1 April 1961 emphasized the inadequacy of NATO's conventional strength. From Belgium, the Netherlands, France, Germany, Canada, the United Kingdom, and the United States the organization could count on 22 divisions, of which the United States would furnish 5 and Germany 8. In blunt language the report stated that "with the exception of the US and Canadian forces, all these units have a reduced combat effectiveness because of personnel manning levels, equipment problems, and austere combat and logistics support forces." This pessimistic analysis would have been even more negative had it taken into account, as the report noted, the maldeployment of these units.[7] By contrast, the Soviet Union had 22 ready divisions in East Germany and Poland and another 51 divisions deployed in western Russia. This figure excluded 34 divisions from Warsaw Pact members. Even if reliability of the numbers was in question, the combat advantage appeared heavily weighted in the Soviet favor.[8]

The glaring weaknesses in NATO forces in Europe obviously informed Norstad's wariness about the thrust of Acheson's report. He shared with the SHAPE planners the belief that NATO had a continuing need for nuclear weapons. He did not accept the assumption that the most likely contingency "is one short of nuclear or massive non-nuclear attack." With a nuclear defense still vital, Norstad's preferred solution was for a highly mobile land-based system of MRBMs under NATO auspices, a concept that itself occasioned considerable debate during this period.† In Washington the JCS also had doubts about giving non-nuclear forces first priority.[9] Within ISA Deputy Assistant Secretary Henry Rowen emerged as a minority voice in believing it possible to close the gap in conventional forces without too much difficulty. It would require, he speculated, "perhaps an increase of about 10 to 15 percent in present NATO defense budgets."[10]

In his comments to Acheson, Norstad pointedly noted that the allies regarded any plans that downplayed nuclear warfare as unsatisfactory. The British mounted an effort to water down the U.S. proposals to augment conventional forces, temporizing as much as possible. ISA officials speculated that the primary reasons involved money difficulties and perhaps sensitivity to a retreat from the "special relationship." The argument used by the British centered on a rapid but modest deployment of five to seven divisions over a four- to five-day period, sufficient to

---

* M=Mobilization.
† See Chapter XV.

show NATO's resolve and induce the Soviets to withdraw. The nuclear option would come into play only if the Soviets were not deterred.[11]

From early on the Germans posed more direct opposition to a conventional-force emphasis than the British. Chancellor Adenauer, alarmed at reports in American newspapers about the United States abandoning Europe, regarded as anathema the very notion of replacing a nuclear with a conventional-first strategy. Consequently, senior U.S. officials took pains early in 1961 to assure the Adenauer government that the United States would not weaken the nuclear strike force in Europe. Averell Harriman, the president's roving ambassador, gave this message to German Defense Minister Franz Josef Strauss in Bonn early in March. At ISA, meanwhile, Nitze not only disavowed false reports about U.S. strategy but claimed that "there could be no doubt that the United States would, as in the past, consider an attack upon a NATO country as an attack upon itself and would consider its nuclear deterrent as being as applicable to a nuclear attack upon Europe as upon the United States."[12]

European confusion ensued as much from McNamara's rethinking of U.S. military policy writ large as from the specific question of conventional vs. nuclear forces. The secretary's drive for efficiency, which had as a by-product a change in allocation of NATO costs, could lead to a loosening of U.S. ties to Europe. This was a subject of NATO Secretary General Paul-Henri Spaak's farewell visit to Washington in February 1961. While Spaak agreed that the other NATO countries should pick up more of the defense burden, he insisted that "the U.S. should be more precise in its views as to what it wanted done. U.S. vagueness had appeared to threaten NATO with U.S. withdrawals from Europe." The United States had to clarify its attitudes in clear and unambiguous terms.[13] It seemed to many that the overarching question of American reliability had to be confronted even more urgently than the raising of the nuclear threshold.

Even without transatlantic prodding, U.S. studies of future policy toward NATO had gotten underway, Acheson's only one of many. At a meeting of State and Defense officials on 3 February to discuss the establishment of the Acheson study group, Nitze had enumerated Defense strategic studies currently in preparation for the purpose of coming up with conclusions suitable for budget planning by 20 February. These reviews would give guidance to planners working on NATO force requirements for 1966. Only incidentally did they pertain to special European concerns.[14]

But as the policy review developed, the JCS position seemed closer to Europe's than to the administration's. JCS attention centered on nuclear preparedness. Lemnitzer recommended improvements in conventional armaments to accompany an appropriate mix of sea and land MRBMs for Europe, with special heed to earmarking for NATO U.S. Polaris submarines that could survive a surprise attack. For his part, Norstad agreed on the need for a buildup of ground forces, but he did not want nuclear weapons neglected. He regarded NATO forces in Europe as more deficient in nuclear than conventional strength.[15]

Lemnitzer's and Norstad's judgments accorded with those of the European partners. As U.S. representative on the North Atlantic Council Thomas K. Finletter observed in a message of 19 April, when NATO got down to the "brass tacks" of long-range planning it wanted the pendulum to shift only modestly from a nuclear emphasis. The British expressed concern over potentially unaffordable costs of a buildup; the French turned their attention to the "pause" in the event of an attack, wanting assurance that it would be brief and followed by a decision on a nuclear response.[16]

NATO Force Requirements for the 1960s

These views did not deter Kennedy or the civilian leaders of Defense from sticking with their plans for raising the nuclear threshold and strengthening NATO's capabilities in conventional weaponry, as the president made clear in his remarks before NATO's Military Committee on 10 April 1961.[17] This was not what the allies wanted to hear from Washington. For a decade Europeans, according to former Army Chief of Staff Maxwell Taylor, had accepted "exaggerated claims for the merits of atomic weapons." They now had to cope with American pressure for a drastic change of thinking, and despite sympathy from SACEUR and JCS, as well as expressions of understanding from Acheson and Nitze, the tactics of persuasion were less than subtle. As Taylor observed, "relatively junior officials of both State and Defense, fired with a missionary zeal to reverse or at least reform the nuclear-oriented strategy of NATO, took off for Europe on various pretexts." They succeeded only in deepening European suspicions of U.S. intentions.[18]

Failure to approve SACEUR's recommended increase in nuclear delivery vehicles meant that European forces would remain less equipped proportionately in nuclear delivery units in 1966 than U.S. divisions and air wings in Europe. The United States would have to make a special effort to gain Allied acceptance of the view that the existing level of nuclear weapons, adjusted and modernized, along with U.S.-based and sea-based strategic strike forces, would suffice for Europe's military security. Recognizing Allied discomfort over the elevation of conventional above nuclear defense measures, Nitze suggested supplying Europeans with more information about the extent of the U.S. nuclear capability in Europe.[19]

Secretary General Dirk Stikker, who succeeded Spaak in April 1961, concurred. Disturbed particularly about discrepancies between SACEUR briefings and the new Kennedy administration policies, he felt that in the absence of convincing evidence the European partners would not wish to commit themselves to significant changes in their defense programs. While the Germans could do more on the conventional side, they wanted to go forward with the buildup of nuclear weapons, particularly MRBMs. Belgium "would continue to hide behind the Congo situation and do nothing." Nor would Italy and Norway be inclined to expand their military forces without more compelling arguments.[20]

At a meeting with Stikker on 14 June, Secretary Rusk and Acheson agreed that the United States would have to spell out clearly just what it regarded as vital NATO force requirements for 1966. Stikker believed that in the event of a reduction in some forces and equipment such as MRBMs, Europeans would demand compensation in the form of manned strike aircraft. Deployment of intermediate-range ballistic missiles became especially sensitive in light of the European allies' increasing interest in acquiring their own nuclear capabilities.

On this subject no early meeting of minds ensued. Gilpatric reported to McGeorge Bundy on 15 June about an effort to convince the allies that NATO already had a substantial nuclear capability in Europe. Earlier, in April, State and Defense officials had discussed the commitment of five Polaris submarines to NATO for the life of the alliance.[21] In informing McNamara of this proposed commitment, Bundy requested that DoD undertake to study how many submarines should ultimately be committed to NATO in addition to the first five, whether they should be on "assignment" to a NATO command or earmarked for assignment, and in what areas the vessels should be deployed.[22]

In his response, prepared by William Bundy in ISA, McNamara agreed to the commitment of five submarines to NATO in 1963, but believed that the first squadron of nine Polaris subs, including the initial five, should "be retained in a strategic role under control and authority of the United States." He added that no Polaris submarines in addition to the first five "should be committed to NATO until it can be established conclusively that the U.S. national nuclear strike capability will not be jeopardized by this action." McNamara wanted the submarines sent to NATO but assigned to USCINCEUR and deployed in the Mediterranean, not the Atlantic, because the Europeans would then identify them with continental defense. The submarines would be earmarked for assignment to SACEUR in wartime.*[23]

JCS analysis emerging from the initial studies of force projections for 1966 argued that NATO's conventional defenses could not hold back a Soviet invasion. An enemy possessing both nuclear and non-nuclear capabilities would not likely allow the momentum of a major attack to stop for a significant period by withholding nuclear weapons.[24] An Army study confirmed this judgment. Citing MC 70 it identified for end-1963 a need for 41 2/3 M-day and post-M-day division equivalents anticipated by M+30 days. To reach this figure required assuming the complete fulfillment of British and West German commitments and return of French divisions from Algeria. These forces had to face possibly as many as 215

---

* See Chapter XV.

Warsaw Pact divisions. And even if the Soviet Union could field only 60 divisions in the Central sector, the West would come up with little better than one-third as many matching forces. Including reinforcement capability, a more accurate assessment of NATO forces available by M+30 days showed a little more than 29 divisions, not 41 2/3.[25]

The most significant of the many reports that followed from the Acheson review may have come from McNamara's NATO Working Group established in JCS early in June and headed by Brig. Gen. Edward L. Rowny to evaluate NATO military policy and force structure for the Central Region. In some respects its findings did not differ substantively from others. The task force identified the equivalent of 22 rather than 21 NATO divisions on this front, which it reduced to only 19 division equivalents as compared to the 20 ready divisions the Soviet Union could deploy against the West with minimal difficulty, plus 35 more employable after reinforcement.

Unlike most of the judgments about NATO's military capabilities, however, the final Rowny report, submitted in September, found compensations for weaknesses and offered reasons for some optimism. First, NATO air forces, qualitatively as good as their Soviet counterpart, had an advantage in air-to-air missiles. Second, the report suggested that it would be misleading to accept the number of Soviet divisions at face value. In East Germany the Soviet Union actually had only 20 combat-ready divisions at 70-85 percent strength and they were smaller and less reliable than those of the NATO allies. Third, the report cited the greater potential for growth in future NATO military contributions. The allies, particularly Germany, were building up at a time when the Soviet Union was reducing its conventional strength. A well-prepared defender, it noted, need not match an attacker one-to-one. Sophisticated defense weaponry could blunt an invasion. "We have, in sum, reasons for a qualified optimism about implementing the NSC Directive."[26]

The secretary of defense wanted hard information on the costs involved in building up NATO forces. He showed particular interest in efforts to standardize DoD procedures used in costing NATO force structures. The preliminary report in July could not supply this part of the task, but by September 1961 figures became available. For the years 1961 to 1966 the final revised estimated cost of total NATO forces came to $29.631 billion for the armies, $27.922 billion for the navies, and $26.646 billion for the air forces, a grand total of more than $84 billion in this period.[27]

The Berlin crisis of 1961 increased pressures on Europeans to share the burden of coping with the consequences of the Berlin Wall. When Kennedy announced to the allies on 20 July 1961 that the United States would add 217,000 men to the U.S. armed forces, he asked them to make comparable increases. The needed NATO forces would cost 61 percent more than the current level of NATO military expenditure for the next five years. The steady increase in anticipated expenditures projected in the report of the NATO Working Group reflected this need.[28]

Whatever optimism the working group wished to generate was dissipated by the continuing shortfall of forces and funds in the face of the apparently overwhelming conventional power of the adversary. Without a remedy there would be continued reliance on a nuclear panacea. In the words of one ISA study, "It is this disparity in ground strength that has both dictated—and in turn been influenced by—NATO's basic strategy; to plan on resorting to nuclear war, general war, at the outset of a war with the Soviet Union. The policy has been almost exclusively deterrence oriented, with relatively little regard for the political or military objectives of any conflict that might, nevertheless, occur." The initial European response to this challenge was not encouraging. From a hope that the 19 2/3 effective divisions could be raised to 40, U.S. planners settled for the old figure of 28 1/3 divisions. As of July 1961 only the Low Countries with their contribution of two divisions each had met their quotas. The United States and France were to add two more divisions each, Germany three, the United Kingdom one, and Canada two-thirds.[29]

While the JCS generally agreed on the need to take action on NATO's 1966 force requirements, they were uneasy over a detailed priority list that McNamara and Rusk had proposed to enhance NATO's ground and air capabilities in forward areas. They managed to reduce the high-priority list to a set of useful guidelines;[30] still, there remained a mix of nuclear and non-nuclear power, with the balance tilted toward conventional strength. McNamara continued to emphasize non-nuclear power and to downplay the nuclear dimension of NATO's strategy.

This message came through at the December 1961 meeting of the North Atlantic Council. The secretary of defense stated that "the Allies have available a large and diversified nuclear arsenal which now provides, and will continue to do so for the foreseeable future, a decided advantage in both delivery systems and nuclear weapons of practically every category." But he went on to observe the catastrophic implications of a general nuclear war which made the use of such weapons unlikely. He hoped for non-nuclear forces that could contain an attack long enough to make the Soviet Union think twice, especially in view of the backup NATO nuclear forces.[31]

While Secretary General Stikker said that he had "never before heard such a forceful or important statement in the Council" and Spaak, now Belgium's foreign minister, similarly praised McNamara's address, the Europeans did not take kindly to McNamara's proposals, particularly his strong advocacy of bigger conventional forces. Coming so soon after the Berlin crisis, his words had little appeal, especially to the Germans, who looked to the nuclear shield for their salvation from the Soviet Union.[32]

Moreover, U.S. actions regarding conventional forces stood in marked contrast to reluctant European compliance. Before the end of 1961 the addition of 40,000 troops from the United States brought to full strength the Seventh Army's combat and support units. Given the jump start precipitated by the Berlin confrontation, the United States could claim by 30 June 1962 that it had already responded to the council recommendation of December 1961 in both troop numbers and nuclear weapons. Approximately $15 billion would go to nuclear forces alone during FY 1963, demonstrating that the United States regarded the Soviet nuclear forces posing a threat to Europe as having the same high priority as those that could reach North America. The commitment on 5 May 1962 of the entire operational Polaris submarine fleet—five boats, each with 16 missiles—represented an earnest of the U.S. MRBM nuclear pledge. By the end of 1963 SACLANT would receive double this number. The U.S. Navy had the nuclear submarines fully operational but anticipated a shortfall in both cruisers and destroyers. Plans went ahead to augment SACEUR's ground forces with three mechanized infantry and two armored divisions as M-day units. For 1963 and 1964 the U.S. Air Force planned to provide NATO with 3 missile and 39 aircraft squadrons.[33]

As the Berlin crisis receded in February 1962, it seemed apparent that progress was being made toward "providing a higher plateau of forces." West Germany, affected more than its allies by the Berlin troubles, committed a ninth division to SACEUR and organized three more. Raising the conscription period from 12 to 18 months assured maintenance of these higher force levels. In France, the Berlin crisis triggered the return of two divisions from Algeria, with the possible commitment of two or three more in 1962. Great Britain, on the other hand, was expected to reduce slightly the number of personnel in the British Army of the Rhine but not the number of units. Similarly, the Low Countries increased their NATO forces slightly, but no dramatic changes were anticipated. By contrast, Greece and Turkey raised the manning levels of their M-day divisions to 76 and 91 percent of their respective goals, but both would need considerable U.S. military assistance to sustain the increases. Overall, the prognosis for the growth of conventional forces was favorable, with 24 1/3 divisions in place by February 1962, and hopes high that France and Germany between them would bring the total to 30.[34]

In November 1962 McNamara presented a more sober picture of the military establishments of France, Germany, and Great Britain. A comparative analysis of their respective contributions gave the nine German M-day divisions a combat capability of "fair" to "poor" and the air force, still in a developmental stage, a "fair" rating. Only the German navy earned the status of "good," even though plagued with deficiencies in its shipbuilding program, logistical system, and storage facilities. The British Royal Air Force and Navy received overall "good" ratings. Not surprisingly, the report rated the Navy air arm second only to that of the United States. But the three divisions Britain committed to NATO, rated fair, had inadequate logistical support, required modernization of equipment, and possessed little offensive capability above the battalion level. France's navy and air force received "good" ratings, but its army, with only two divisions yet committed to NATO, had serious problems with supplies, modern equipment, and support units, and received a rating of fair. In terms of GNP (gross national product) devoted to defense, however, France's 7.9 percent came closest to the 10.6 percent of the United States. Britain spent 7.5 percent, while Germany with a larger GNP than either Britain or France devoted only 5.4 percent to defense budgets.[35]

Failure to achieve many of its stated goals may explain the somewhat sour account of NATO country force capabilities that OSD presented a year later, on 27 November 1963, just after President Johnson took office. For every advance, such as an increase in the combat readiness of the Belgian armed forces over a two-year period, there was a corresponding setback; Belgium intended to withdraw four battalions from Germany. Although Canada did increase its forces in Europe in response to the Berlin crisis, its reply to the 1963 triennial review questionnaire suggested that it would reduce its defense contributions over the next few years. France had brought back all its combat forces from Algeria, but would assign only two of its five divisions to NATO. Greece and Turkey were major casualties of reduced U.S. military assistance. And when seven other NATO members pledged contributions of $13.5 million to supplement U.S. aid to Greece, redemptions of the pledges came slowly. Of all the allies, only Germany and Britain appeared to be advancing military posture without stepping backwards.[36]

In May 1963 McNamara presaged this negative evaluation with his own gloomy response to President Kennedy's earlier query about the comparative progress in defense efforts of the United States and its NATO partners. He compared the U.S. Seventh Division combat slice of 24,000 troops (including non-divisional combat units) with those of the principal allies. Denmark came closest to the U.S. model with 21,900. France, Canada, Germany, and the United Kingdom trailed with 19,000, 19,900, 20,500, and 20,900, respectively. Moreover, he noted that current basing and deployment of NATO air forces rendered them "extremely vulnerable to surprise attack." None of the NATO air forces, aside from those of the United States, possessed logistical capability to sustain operations for more than 20 to 30 days. In sum, he told the president that NATO's force composition was badly out of kilter, and "in the event that we cannot induce our NATO allies to build up their conventional forces so that they can have a credible conventional war option, some realignment of the NATO force structure is clearly called for."[37]

By early August the situation had not significantly improved, as McNamara turned his attention to the JCS share of responsibility. He complained to the JCS chairman that "more than ever I am convinced that we have no satisfactory war plans or strategy for the conduct of combat operations between a conventional land and air battle on the one hand and all-out nuclear war on the other."[38]

The NATO ministerial meeting at Paris in December 1963 highlighted U.S. accomplishments in strategic retaliatory forces. In his remarks McNamara observed that ICBMs of all varieties would increase from 488 to 1,717 between 1963 and 1966, while the total number of manned bombers would decline from 1,295 to 710 over the same period. In 1963, he noted, the number of ICBMs (488) represented more than a four-fold increase from 1961. Concurrently, tactical nuclear weapons in Europe had increased by almost 60 percent since early 1961. As for ground forces, the United States had expanded the number of combat-ready Army divisions by 45 percent in the past two years. The strategic reserve had eight Army divisions compared to only three in 1961. McNamara noted that the United States planned to increase airlift capacity by 400 percent by 1968 compared to 1961 in further support of European defense.

The secretary omitted from his statement mention of efforts the Allied powers had made toward the common goal. That he did not consider the efforts satisfactory came through in his comment that "the United States Congress and American public opinion will become increasingly restless about a situation in which the U.S. maintains qualitative standards—manning levels, stocks and force readiness—generally higher than those of our Allies." To underline his point he spoke of the continuing unfavorable balance of payments situation and of U.S. plans to reduce the gross foreign exchange costs of military operations in Europe, which amounted to about $1.7 billion per year. McNamara, however, did not fail to mention those countries—Germany and Italy—which had made substantial efforts to offset U.S. defense expenditures. But his overall evaluation of NATO's progress toward meeting its military objectives was grudging at best.[39]

A reading of NATO's force levels in this period, 1961-63, need not have yielded overly negative judgments. The organization's military strength grew substantially, even if its members failed to move at the rate prescribed by U.S. officials or by the North Atlantic Council. Despite apprehension over the new thrust in U.S. policy, conventional strength moved upward.

Earlier, in March 1963, the two major continental allies, France and Germany, had received qualified praise from McNamara. Along with the sense that the Germans could do more, DoD appreciated the steps they had taken. From 1961 to 1963 the total net annual expenditures for military forces rose from 11.574 billion to 17.856 billion marks (approximately $4 billion to $4.5 billion). Although McNamara wanted the German defense program to proportionately approximate that of the United States in budget and manpower, he saw a defense contribution of about seven percent of the country's GNP as "about the maximum that we can realistically expect the FRG to achieve during the time frame of 1963-67."[40]

The feeling toward de Gaulle's France was more ambivalent. OSD looked unfavorably at de Gaulle's preference for pursuing a national nuclear program instead of increasing expenditures on modernizing the French army. Still, ISA admitted that "the U.S. would be hard put to criticize the extent of the French defense effort at its current level," estimated at 7.7 percent of GNP for 1962 and 7.6 percent for 1963.[41]

Given the uneven conditions of the force structures of most of the allies, McNamara sought new ways of winning support for building conventional forces. At the meeting of the North Atlantic Council at Ottawa in May 1963 he expressed his concern over the imbalance among military forces, military strategy, and defense budgets. By constituting itself as a Defense Planning Committee (DPC) in 1963 the NAC attempted to put into effect a NATO Force Planning Exercise that would examine the interrelated issues of strategy, force requirements, and available resources. However, France's refusal to consider a strategy preparing for limited war on the Central front limited the scope of the new committee, requiring the United States to shift its focus from strategy to force structure and budgets.[42]

NATO commanders responded to the DPC charges in August 1964 by submitting two scenarios based on their experience in planning exercises that could serve a force structure for 1970, but these did not gain acceptance. The two proposed force goals, Alpha and Bravo, would have required costs that the allies felt they could not afford.[43]

In late 1964 McNamara had doubts about the commitment of the Joint Chiefs and SACEUR, supported by the European allies, to building a credible conventional force. SACEUR's Alpha and Bravo goals wanted to preserve "at all costs," according to a State-Defense paper in October 1964, "the ability of ACE [Allied Central Europe] forces to fight a general nuclear war, which is the least likely contingency." Alpha and Bravo conventional forces could make only a marginal contribution to a general nuclear war as opposed to a small-scale nonnuclear conflict.[44]

In this standoff the secretary saw it as his mission to continue to educate the Joint Chiefs, SACEUR, and their European colleagues in the virtues of his version of flexible response. If he failed to convert his adversaries in the force planning for 1966, he could hope for more success in planning a force structure for 1970. To sustain a defense effort that would meet these goals required acceleration of the pace of arms sales that had replaced military assistance to the more prosperous members of NATO.*

While sales of U.S. equipment provided a source of income, they also created some dissension within the alliance. The French, Germans, and British had their own agendas, which did not mesh with those of the United States. Their interest centered not on buying U.S. weapons for conventional warfare, but on acquiring nuclear capability for themselves. Although public rationalization for independent nuclear deterrents derived from the putative loss of U.S. credibility after Sputnik, it was national pride as much as perceived American vulnerability

---

* See Chapter XVI.

and unreliability that motivated France, Germany, and Great Britain and led to confrontations between them and the United States. The disaffected allies' tactics differed but their objectives were much the same.

France and the Force de Frappe

General de Gaulle returned to power in 1958 in a France still bruised by the experiences with the United States in Indochina and Suez. Even before Sputnik (1957)—and the Fifth Republic (1958)—France believed that only a French nuclear deterrent could provide both security and respect. Like the British, but without their expectations of success, de Gaulle's France undertook extensive negotiations with the United States, which ranged beyond the sensitive issues of nuclear arms. They involved base rights and cost-sharing arrangements for U.S. troops in France. In 1960 and 1961, Philippe Baudet, civilian deputy for national defense, led missions to Washington to work out reciprocal purchases of military equipment. Although nuclear weapons technology rarely came up, it always lurked just beneath the surface of any negotiations as a divisive issue.[45]

The U.S. concern about the unfavorable balance of payments with France figured in a proposed plan for reciprocal purchases of military equipment, worked out in May 1961, that provided for U.S. purchase of $25 million worth of materiel in France and French expenditures of $50 million in the United States, primarily for F-100 aircraft and Tartar batteries.* In August William Bundy strongly recommended accepting the agreement, which State also favored. The trade agreement entered into force on 20 December 1961.[46]

Negotiations with France, while never easy, continued and covered a wide range of weaponry, including missiles such as the short-range surface-to-surface Mace. When these proved too expensive, the more advanced Pershing missiles† were substituted in negotiations. From the U.S. perspective this would represent a generous conveyance of missile technology in the form of tactical surface-to-surface weapons, although the package would not include warheads or technical nuclear information. Questions about funding the request for Pershing missiles did not present a major obstacle to the plan. State and Defense authorized Norstad on 3 May 1961 to make a conditional offer of one Pershing battalion to the French, arranged on a cost-sharing basis, with the U.S. share at $20 million out of a total cost of $68 million.[47]

Initiation of negotiations aroused already latent worries in ISA about providing France more advanced types of missiles such as the Pershing. As one official put it: "The French would be given privileged information concerning an inertial

---

* Medium-range naval surface-to-air (SAM) missiles.

† The Pershing-1 ballistic missile was a surface-to-surface, two-stage, solid-propelled rocket suitable for a nuclear warhead and having a range of between 100 and 400 nm.

guidance system which would be almost identical to that used in ballistic missiles. This might be construed to be in conflict with current U.S. policy which prohibits any U.S. assistance which would encourage accelerated development of an independent ballistic missile capability." This sentiment had wide acceptance in Nitze's office. Rowen supported selling the Sergeant instead of the Pershing to the French. "Its maximum range of 75 n. mi.," he noted in a memorandum to Nitze in November, "limits its potential for mischief substantially as compared with the 400 n. mi. Pershing."[48]

Consideration of France's nuclear capability independent of NATO's authority or U.S. control, always a concern, ultimately became the reason for denying France the Pershing missile as well as provision of other technical information that might assist development of the independent French strategic nuclear capability—the *force de frappe*. But this outcome was neither the initial Defense position nor the result of Defense pressures. Indeed, some sympathy for the French position existed within DoD, based on prior U.S. commitments, as well as a recognition that French purchase of U.S. equipment would alleviate the unfavorable balance of payments created by dollars spent in France for U.S. troop support.[49]

Franco-American relations worsened in 1962 as de Gaulle's hostility to U.S. leadership in NATO took more concrete form. In January 1963, soon after de Gaulle's provocative press conference of 14 January, in which he expressed again France's intention to have its own independent nuclear deterrent, OSD informed Norstad that it envisioned no role for Pershings in the NATO nuclear force. "Moreover, in keeping with strong U.S. preference for multilateral over national approach to nuclear problem, resurrection of French (or other country) interest in Pershing system at this time would not repeat not be advisable." This attitude fed even further de Gaulle's conviction of a U.S. conspiracy, abetted by the British, to subordinate France to American imperial design.[50]

At the same time that DoD denied France the weapon, it was actively pressing the president to approve sale of two Pershing battalions to the Germans. The obvious inconsistency of treatment did not go unobserved. In August 1963 the Military Assistance Advisory Group (MAAG) chief in Paris asked for a review of the U.S. position, given the revival of French interest in the weapon. He suggested "the use of this French interest as a bargaining point in our (US) discussions with them." From his perspective, he could not understand the logic of letting the French in principle have other delivery systems such as Honest John and Nike-Hercules, which could also use nuclear warheads, and "yet balk at selling them SERGEANT and PERSHING, which we have already sold to the Germans."[51]

France and the United States appeared heading for a collision course in NATO from early on in the Kennedy administration, and the fallout from the friction appeared in every area of arms sales. But even as the political climate grew colder between the two countries, France still persisted in seeking technical and other assistance from the United States, and some Defense officials, with the notable exception of General Norstad, persisted in supporting French requests. Defense argued that if France could reduce the cost of developing a *force de frappe*, which would occur later if not sooner under any circumstance, it might use the savings to contribute to NATO's conventional forces.[52]

Ambassador to France James Gavin along with General Taylor argued that the nation had earned the same right as Britain to nuclear information under terms of the 1958 amendments to the Atomic Energy Act that authorized transfer of technical information and material to countries which already had made substantial advances in developing atomic weapons. The first French nuclear tests had occurred by the time the Kennedy administration took office, and it seemed only a matter of time before France would join the nuclear club. The most that the United States had conceded to the French under an agreement of 27 July 1961 authorized release of nuclear information for training French NATO forces. However, this agreement did not provide for exchange of information for designing or developing or manufacturing atomic weapons.[53]

Gavin tried to use this opening late in 1961 to have the United States make available to France enriched uranium for military purposes in sufficient amount to enable France to dispense with the construction of an expensive gaseous diffusion plant. He felt that such aid would counteract de Gaulle's steady subversion of NATO by facilitating action the French would do on their own in the long run, but at great cost. He rationalized that failure to help would lead to anarchic development of national nuclear programs or situations where France and Germany might combine their efforts separate from the United States and NATO. Gavin did not convince Rusk, who responded that "upon reflection here I believe that to furnish enriched uranium to France for military applications would lead to other French requests relating to production of nuclear weapons."

Gavin subsequently took his case to the president in March 1962, but without success. While Kennedy did show some sympathy for Taylor's and Gavin's views, he did not challenge the adamant hostility of Rusk, Norstad, and his advisers in the White House.[54]

By the spring of 1962 the NSC had made nonproliferation of nuclear weapons a fundamental article of U.S. policy. Kennedy aide Sorensen later wrote that Kennedy felt that any nuclear aid, in light of de Gaulle's outlook, "would not win General de Gaulle to our purposes but only strengthen him in his." He was probably correct. When the United States offered Polaris missiles (minus nuclear warheads) to France on the same terms given Britain at the Nassau Conference in December 1962, de Gaulle rejected the offer out of hand, stating that it had little immediate practical value for France.*[55]

The surprise in the Franco-American relationship came not from the deadlock over mutual purchasing agreements, but the persistence on the part of Defense,

---

* See Chapter XV.

despite State opposition, to pursue negotiations. Despite de Gaulle's hauteur, in keeping talks alive France always sought to facilitate the completion of its *force de frappe*.[56] The apparent dogged perseverance of French defense officials in exploring all possible avenues of nuclear assistance from the United States suggested the extent of France's needs. But their efforts did not fit the image de Gaulle was fashioning for France in Europe.[57] Given his perceived intransigence, it seemed reasonable for U.S. policymakers to cut their losses with France and concentrate on cultivating the other two major partners—Britain and Germany.

Germany: Nuclear Aspirations?

The repeated conflicts with France had their impact on German-American relations, since there was more common ground between the French and Germans than American leaders were willing to see between 1961 and 1963. Chancellor Adenauer continued to brood over what he considered the inadequate U.S. response to the building of the Berlin Wall. And like the French, the Germans also had strong reservations about raising both conventional force levels and the threshold of nuclear response.

Increasingly, pressure mounted in the Federal Republic for a more active voice in determining the use of nuclear weapons, particularly those stationed on German soil. Defense Minister Franz Josef Strauss, head of the Christian Social Union Party, a junior partner of Adenauer's Christian Democratic Union, loomed as a German Gaullist seeking a share of nuclear power decisions. Strauss, a burly, bluff, and opinionated politician, proposed that any member nation could initiate use of nuclear weapons with the joint recommendation of the supreme allied commander. Speaking at the North Atlantic Council meeting in December 1961, Strauss asked what would be the American reaction to the Soviets achieving parity in ICBMs. He implied that Europe needed its own deterrent against a Soviet threat that would spare the United States in a deal over the heads of Europeans.[58] In essence, de Gaulle seemed to speak for a German constituency as well as for France.

In this context, McNamara's Athens speech in May 1962 and his Ann Arbor speech in June decrying nuclear proliferation as well as disparaging small independent nuclear establishments received as cool a reception in Germany as in France and evoked suspicion of the new Kennedy administration, with its apparent intention to dictate NATO policy in ways very different from those of the Eisenhower team. U.S. inability to empathize with Europe's concerns led to an uneasiness further exacerbated by Strauss's confrontational style.[59]

German suspicion of U.S. intentions emerged in discussions between members of the U.S. and German general staffs at the Pentagon in December 1962. Speaking for the German delegation, General Friedrich Foertsch, inspector general of the German Army, addressed a series of queries, each with a hidden agenda, to the Americans. Why did they want to delay taking action on many issues until the United Kingdom had joined the European Economic Community (EEC)? Would the United States withdraw its troops or change its position on Europe once Britain entered the EEC? Why could the United States not see that the Cuban missile crisis demonstrated that nuclear weapons comprised a vital element in Western defense? At the same time he made an effort to convince the chairman of the JCS that the Germans did not really wish to acquire nuclear weapons. It was not a happy meeting. As Lt. Gen. Andrew J. Goodpaster of the JCS staff noted, continued discontent might push the Germans into de Gaulle's camp, if not into a neutralist accommodation with the Soviet Union.[60]

Strains in the German-American partnership in December 1962 affected not only the military chieftains. A week after the meeting at the Pentagon, the German embassy in Washington raised new questions arising from McNamara's and Rusk's recommendation at the NATO ministerial meeting for a review of the alliance's strategic concept. Once again emphasis on non-nuclear forward defense raised doubts in German minds about the U.S. commitment to nuclear warfare. McNamara's blunt comments at the NATO ministerial meeting in December 1962 on NATO's strength being substantially below the necessary level in equipment, troops, and availability of ready reserves struck a raw nerve. Reports that the Federal Republic should compensate for these deficiencies and raise its manpower contribution to 750,000 further disturbed the Germans. It would mean a 50 percent increase above the current projected level of 500,000. If achieved, the increase would impose more than financial difficulties. As Horst Blomeyer-Bartenstein, first secretary of the embassy in Washington, informed the State Department, "such a large German army would be an irritant not only to the Soviets but also to certain of our Western friends, even to some people in the United States." Furthermore, the Germans wanted clearer answers on the future of the MRBMs before considering an increase beyond the 500,000 level.[61]

The Kennedy administration paid more attention to German dissatisfaction than to French complaints. The White House and State Department, if not Defense, dismissed France as a lost cause. Their expectations did not go beyond isolating de Gaulle and minimizing the damage his government could do to the alliance. Germany, on the other hand, deserved more solicitous treatment. Its location on the edge of the Iron Curtain, the locus of the armies of the NATO partners, placed Germany geostrategically in a more important position. Germany deserved consideration for other reasons, too. Unlike France, the Federal Republic had made no formal effort to acquire a nuclear capability, a particular blessing, because Germany as a nuclear power would present political and psychological implications far more incendiary than France's membership in the nuclear club. The United States, McNamara told Rusk in February 1963, should see to it that frustration over U.S. policies did not reach such a level as to move Germany in

France's direction.⁶² Germany's willingness to make financial arrangements to ameliorate the uneven balance of payments between the two countries also contributed to a positive image of the Adenauer government.⁶³

All these factors lay behind the decision of DoD, with State Department concurrence, to sell Pershing-1 missiles to Germany, under NATO control. In April 1963, Gilpatric informed the president he supported these purchases on political grounds to show U.S. willingness to cooperate with Germany in building up a military establishment that would have the same tactical nuclear capability as that of U.S. forces. To refuse such a sale would damage U.S.-German relations "at a particularly critical moment in the history of the Alliance." The politico-economic argument gained force from the value these new arms sales would have for the defense posture of NATO. In 1964 the Pershing became operational in West German troop units.⁶⁴

Despite the concerns for German sensibilities, U.S. officials, both State and Defense, recognized that with all Europeans the heart of the matter lay in the U.S. deemphasis of a nuclear strategy and the elevation of a conventional strategy. McNamara's understanding of these sentiments of NATO allies found expression in his attempts to reassure them of the continued U.S. nuclear commitment to NATO. Unfortunately, he usually also made references to the apocalyptic consequences of nuclear weapons that would make their use a disaster for friend and enemy alike. Earlier, in looking over McNamara's address before the Athens meeting in 1962, the president anticipated reactions it might evoke and suggested changes to clarify the U.S. position.⁶⁵ Not even the most careful fine-tuning was likely to satisfy the European partners. General Norstad, on the scene in Europe, had understood the limits of verbal persuasion. Consequently, he, too, in 1962 looked for other approaches, including the Strauss proposal to have the nuclear decision made by the country attacked in concert with the SACEUR. He turned over other ideas as well, among them the formal identification of the U.S. president as "executive agent" of the alliance and—more daring—the establishment of a European force armed with its own nuclear weapons.*⁶⁶

Skybolt

Of all the U.S. partners in NATO, the United Kingdom should have been the most secure and the most supportive. Amendments to the U.S. Atomic Energy Act had assisted its role as a nuclear power, and the United States seemed prepared to maintain the special relationship that separated Britain from the Continent as surely as the Channel itself. But although Britain had its own limited nuclear force, this relationship was troubled by the same misgiving harbored by Germany and France—dependence on the United States for nuclear defense. Each nation

---

* See Chapter XV.

reacted somewhat differently, but none with the intensity of feeling of the Anglo-American wrangle over Skybolt.[67]

Though less disruptive to the two countries' relations than the 1956 Suez crisis, the U.S. decision in December 1962 to halt development of the Skybolt missile, whose use was to be shared with the United Kingdom, created doubt and suspicion in each country about the other's motives and trustworthiness. Gilpatric recalled that "just as the British overreacted to the cancellation of Skybolt, we overreacted to their overreaction."[68] Only an agreement hurriedly worked out between President Kennedy and Prime Minister Macmillan in the Bahamas—for the United States to furnish Polaris missiles as a substitute—avoided a serious breach.

Begun in 1959 by the U.S. Air Force, the Skybolt air-to-surface ballistic missile was to have a range of 1,000 miles, carry nuclear warheads for launching from a B-52 bomber, and become operational by the end of 1964. Complex, costly, and of uncertain reliability, Skybolt represented more of a gamble than any weapon the United States had developed. Air Force initial estimates of research and development costs ($184 million) and of procuring 1,000 missiles ($679 million) were unrealistically low.[69]

In 1960 the Macmillan government, after provisionally deciding to end its own expensive long-range missile program (Blue Streak), reached an agreement with the Eisenhower administration to buy Skybolt, *if successfully developed*, for use on the Royal Air Force's Vulcan bombers. British costs would be minimal—for missiles purchased and fitting them to the Vulcans. Each country could terminate its participation in the program after consultation with the other. By extending the life of its V-bomber force, the arrangement would permit the United Kingdom to maintain an independent nuclear deterrent beyond the 1960s, a cherished fixture in the defense policy of Macmillan's Conservative government. Questioning by the Labour Party of the need for an independent deterrent and doubts whether Skybolt would ever materialize only hardened the government's public commitment to and reliance on Skybolt. Secretary of Defense Gates and other OSD officials repeatedly conveyed to the British their concerns about the cost and difficulty of developing the weapon and warned them not to count on successful completion, yet stopped short of recommending cancellation. In the FY 1962 budget submitted to Congress in January 1961, the Eisenhower administration requested no new funds for Skybolt, proposing to stretch out the previous year's appropriation and leave to the incoming administration and a new secretary of defense the decision on its fate.[70]

When he took over, McNamara essentially had three choices: continue the program at Eisenhower's funding level, increase it by $50 million as the Air Force had requested, or stop development. Years later he declared that the weapon had been "a pile of junk." Yet, from the beginning, he gave Skybolt a fair trial. After a quick study that led to McNamara's recommendation to add the $50 million, Kennedy included the amount in his March 1961 budget amendment that Congress subsequently approved.[71] The secretary based his recommendation on technical and strategic grounds, but political considerations no doubt played a part in the president's approval. For Kennedy to stop the program soon after entering office would have appeared a strange about-face, since he had criticized Eisenhower during the election campaign for skimping on the nation's defenses in order to control spending. Then, too, cancellation, occurring when the new administration was accelerating the Navy's Polaris development, would have especially infuriated the Air Force and its supporters.

Less than a month after requesting the additional money, the president approved a policy directive regarding NATO that seemed to diminish Britain's chances of obtaining Skybolt. Declaring that in "the long run, it would be desirable if the British decided to phase out of the nuclear deterrent business," the statement reflected prevailing thought in the administration that British defense spending should be devoted more to conventional forces. Moreover, the directive stated, if Skybolt's development were "not warranted for U.S. purposes alone, the U.S. should not prolong the life of the V-Bomber force by this or other means."[72] A small but influential group at the State Department had contributed to that conclusion with their belief that Britain's independent deterrent encouraged German and French aspirations for national nuclear forces and impeded the creation of a multilateral force (MLF) in Europe.* But the directive ignored the inconsistency of adding money to the budget to develop a weapon that would serve, at least in part, an undesirable purpose.

By the fall of 1961, during preparation of the FY 1963 budget, rising cost estimates, dissatisfaction with the program's management by the primary contractor, the Douglas Aircraft Company, and skepticism within the government about Skybolt's worth compared with other strategic weapons caused McNamara to conduct another reappraisal. In a preliminary report on 31 October DoD's Committee on Strategic Weapons questioned whether the weapon's development should be continued "even if all technical problems are overcome. It does not seem to add any very significantly new type of threat to our arsenal nor to be much cheaper or more reliable than available weapons." OSD Comptroller Charles Hitch made a similar point, arguing that by the time Skybolt became part of the U.S. arsenal both Minuteman and Polaris would have provided the nation with its necessary retaliatory power.[73] To make matters worse, on 21 October the Air Force had submitted a revised program that raised estimated research and development costs to $492.6 million, more than doubling the initial estimate and representing $100 million more than McNamara was told during a visit to the Douglas plant the previous month. In addition estimated production costs now stood at $1.27 billion, a $591 million jump. Despite the dramatic increases, and over the strong

---

* For the MLF, see Chapter XV.

objections of some of the president's advisers, McNamara recommended and the president approved the revised plan. But approval was conditioned on Skybolt's completion on time and at the estimated cost.[74]

The British complaint at the time of Skybolt's cancellation in December 1962 that they had been left in the dark concerning the growing doubts about the program had little merit. On the contrary, the Kennedy administration, like its predecessor, sought to keep them fully informed. In March 1961 DR&E Deputy Director John Rubel, who had monitored the program since its inception, summarized for McNamara the history of the discussions regarding Skybolt and warnings the Eisenhower administration had given about possible cancellation. Rubel concluded: "It is quite important that the British, in eliciting our cooperation on Skybolt, which we are glad to give, should refrain from overplaying this program in the political arena. Our flexibility of action will be compromised if they do that. We should promise no more than we intend—they should not place a lien on our intentions."[75]

Also in March, after the decision to request $50 million more for Skybolt, McNamara told British Minister of Defence Harold Watkinson that the United States intended to continue the program and promised to notify him "if any hitches developed." Watkinson received a mixed message from other OSD officials; Gilpatric stated that "the program was coming along well," while Rubel and others spoke more cautiously about its prospects. In December 1961, McNamara, having just given his conditional approval to a more costly program, told Watkinson that "we were doing everything possible but . . . we still had reservations as to whether all the technical problems could be solved." The following month the president informed British Secretary of State for Air Julian Amery of his doubts whether Skybolt would ever work. "One should not bank on it too much," he said. The remark nearly caused Amery to fall off his chair. The president hastened to assure Amery that everything was being done to make it work.[76]

Moreover, there was little substance to the charge that U.S. officials failed to appreciate Skybolt's crucial importance to the Macmillan government. Only a few weeks after the inauguration, OSD prepared a briefing paper for the White House pointing out that, "because of the political sensitivity stemming from the British Government's decision to cancel the Bluestreak missile and to rely in large measure on the Skybolt to extend the life of their V-bomber force, every indication of technical or funding difficulties for the development of Skybolt has brought prompt expressions of British concern." The British would likely claim, the paper suggested, that the United States made an unqualified commitment to furnish Skybolt, even though it was obligated to do so only "if the missile is successfully developed." In April 1962 the president's science adviser, Jerome Wiesner, prepared a lengthy report for Kennedy focusing on technical problems in the weapon's development, while noting that a recommendation within the Eisenhower administration to halt Skybolt had been "overruled on the grounds that this would be politically impossible in view of the commitment to the British."[77]

The first two Skybolt test firings in the spring of 1962 were unsuccessful and McNamara grew more displeased with still rising cost estimates and the Douglas company's poor performance; a decision had to be made that fall whether to begin production. After the Bureau of the Budget suggested further reappraisal of the program, the secretary asked the comptroller and the DR&E director to examine alternatives. Late in August Hitch and Harold Brown gave him a lengthy memorandum analyzing the program's technical and financial aspects and various courses of action. When the three met on 24 August, Hitch suggested and McNamara agreed that they wait until the fall, then drop Skybolt from the FY 1964 budget during the concluding phase of its preparation.[78]

The effects of cancellation on the British remained a major worry. Brown and Hitch included in their memorandum a section entitled "The British Consideration," which acknowledged the difficulty of predicting British reaction to cancellation. However, they pointed out that in the fall of 1960, when the Eisenhower administration considered ending the program, the State Department feared the Macmillan government might fall if the program ended. An attached paper prepared by ISA's European Regional Office emphasized that the United Kingdom would feel "let down" by and resent termination of the program. The effect on British public opinion "should not be underestimated," the paper warned.[79]

If the United States prior to this time was entirely forthcoming with the British regarding Skybolt, the same cannot be said for McNamara's subsequent meeting with new Minister of Defence Peter Thorneycroft, who had succeeded Watkinson in July 1962. During Thorneycroft's visit to the United States in September, McNamara, obviously constrained because he had not yet recommended cancellation, did not reveal that he was leaning in that direction. He told Thorneycroft that Skybolt's costs "had further gone up," but left his visitor with the impression that the program "would go forward." Thorneycroft, who also talked with Kennedy, recalled that he "went out of my way" to impress on both the president and McNamara Skybolt's importance for the British and that he received from the latter assurances "as categorical as you could get" that the United States would continue the program.[80]

McNamara apparently did not decide to recommend cancellation until toward the end of October, during the Cuban missile crisis. This was when BoB Director David Bell informed McGeorge Bundy that DoD's budget review would likely result in a "firm recommendation" that Skybolt be halted. According to Bell, McNamara and Gilpatric felt cancellation "can and should be considered on its merits without reference to a 'commitment' to the British." If decided on, cancellation was "regarded as consistent with our present policy to favor the phasing out by the British of their strategic nuclear bombing forces."[81]

At the White House's request, the State Department prepared a quick analysis of the consequences of cancellation, which it predicted, among other things, "could be an unmitigated political blow to the Conservatives. The British would certainly feel let down—hard." The decision would have even wider ramifications. If it seemed that the United States was "'double-crossing' our oldest and closest ally—and it might well appear this way—it would be a serious blow to our whole alliance system." Echoing State's concern about the likely impact of cancellation, on 3 November Nitze urged that McNamara offer to dispatch a high-ranking official to London to discuss with Thorneycroft the technical and military aspects of possible cancellation and that the president also immediately inform Macmillan.[82]

McNamara was not ready to notify the British. He wanted first to obtain the views of the Joint Chiefs of Staff. On 5 November he returned Nitze's memo, after writing in the margin: "As we discussed over the telephone, only today did I send my tentative recommendations on Skybolt to the Chiefs. I believe we should hold the message to Thorneycroft until we hear from the Chiefs. We will try to provide for 3 weeks 'consultation' with the British before the 'leak date' of approximately 12/10."[83] The budget would essentially reach completion during the first week of December, and 10 December seemed a reasonable date to anticipate that stories about it might begin appearing in the press.

On the same day, 5 November, McNamara received a message from Thorneycroft referring to British press reports that Skybolt production was about to begin; this forced his hand. Two days later he met with the president, Rusk, Bundy, and Nitze to discuss how he should respond. He and Rusk pointed out that cancellation "would create a very grave problem for the British Government—might even bring it down." In general they thought the British should be provided much advance warning and "a chance to come up with something by way of an adequate substitute." McNamara and Bundy believed that, in the end, the United States would probably have to provide Polaris missiles. They agreed that McNamara should inform Ambassador David Ormsby Gore and Thorneycroft of the likelihood of cancellation.[84] Save for McNamara's understandable lack of complete candor with Thorneycroft in September, his handling of the matter to this point could hardly be faulted.

The meeting with the president led to a flurry of activity. First, McNamara told Ormsby Gore on 8 November that rising cost estimates for Skybolt procurement ($1.4 billion to over $1.75 billion), along with previous increases, had caused the administration to reconsider "the worth of the weapon." He had referred the question to the Joint Chiefs, but did not expect their views for several weeks. He wanted to let the British government know that the United States was "reconsidering the program." In a telephone conversation with Thorneycroft the next day, McNamara repeated what he had told Ormsby Gore and added that the British would have several alternatives to consider, which he would be willing to come to London to discuss. Consultations probably could not take place until after 23 November (when McNamara planned to discuss the defense budget with the president). Thorneycroft said he would have his ministry "consider how the V-bomber force might be operated without Skybolt and what the U.S. and British governments should state to the public in the event the program is cancelled." McNamara gained the impression that the British wanted to consider a submarine-launched missile if it seemed termination of Skybolt would make the V-bomber force obsolete.[85]

After notifying the British of possible cancellation, the administration quickly worked out its policy. McNamara had proposed offering Minuteman and Hound Dog missiles to compensate for Skybolt's elimination. At this point, on 20 November the Joint Chiefs recommended staying with Skybolt; only the new JCS chairman, General Taylor, favored cancellation. On 23 November, at a defense budget meeting in Hyannis Port with the president, McNamara weighed various courses of action on Skybolt and came down in favor of cancellation. The president—apparently after little discussion—approved ending the U.S. involvement subject to consultation with the British. The next day Rusk wrote McNamara that any discussions with the British should be limited to three alternatives: (1) continuation of the program on their own, (2) their use of Hound Dog instead of Skybolt, and (3) their participation in a sea-based medium-range ballistic missile force, i.e. Polaris force, "under multilateral manning and ownership." Rusk stressed the impossibility "of our helping them set up a nationally manned and owned MRBM force."[86] The third alternative, MLF, had strong backing from some of Rusk's subordinates at State who also favored the end of the British independent deterrent.

But McNamara postponed his trip to London, thereby increasing chances that word of cancellation would leak to the press before he arrived. He could have gone as early as 26 November, having received the JCS views, the president's decision, and Rusk's recommendations. That morning White House staff thought he would leave in the evening. By noon, however, he decided to put off the trip, hoping to go later in the week. When he avoided setting a date, Bundy grew concerned and called to advise against delay. An ISA staff member suggested that Nitze and Rubel go as an advance party, but McNamara replied, "I'll take care of it." Not until 6 December did he decide that he would stop in London on the way to Paris, where the NATO Council was meeting on 12 December.[87]

In the meantime, press reports began to appear on both sides of the Atlantic that Skybolt was in trouble and would be canceled. None of the earlier test flights had been fully successful, and news of the failure of the fifth test—the first guided launch—on 28 November only fueled speculation. Moreover, disparaging public remarks about declining British power by Dean Acheson stung British public opinion.[88] A highly charged atmosphere awaited McNamara in London.

According to Under Secretary of State George Ball, McNamara needlessly soured the atmosphere by his airport arrival statement referring to the five unsuccessful tests. Having seen a draft of the statement, Ball telephoned McNamara urging him to omit remarks about technical problems, which would imply that he intended to cancel Skybolt, not consult about its future. McNamara, according to Ball, acknowledged that perhaps he should not make such reference, but he said "somebody had to tell the British people about the deficiencies of this weapon and the British Government wasn't doing so." For Ball, McNamara's unwillingness to heed his advice "illustrated both the strength and weakness of his temperament. Once he had made up his mind something should be done, he would damn the torpedoes and full steam ahead, in spite of any incidental breakage caused by inappropriate timing."[89] Negative press reaction to McNamara's statement may not have been entirely the result of what he said. Ormsby Gore thought that officials within the Ministry of Defence "through sensational leaks to the press . . . sowed maximum distrust of American motives and made the situation as difficult as possible."[90]

In retrospect, far more important than McNamara's delay of the trip to London and disregard of Ball's advice was his failure (later much regretted) to fight the State Department's objections to offering Polaris as a straight replacement for Skybolt. In McNamara's view Rusk did not feel strongly about the matter, but did not wish to fight over it with his zealous subordinates. So McNamara adhered to the line State had established. Just before leaving Washington, in a meeting with the president, Rusk, and Bundy, he said he would present the strongest possible case "for the technical decision which was anticipated." He would offer the three alternatives State had spelled out, but did not believe the British would be happy with any of them. At some stage, he might propose giving them "a more up-to-date weapons system on the condition that the venture become multilateral if and when a multilateral force should be developed," and he mentioned Polaris. The president indicated "his general approval" of McNamara's approach, and said "he was not eager to join in a large share of further development costs for a weapon to be supplied only to the British."[91]

The issue came to a head when McNamara met with Thorneycroft on 11 December. After the secretary read a long explanation of the U.S. position and presented the three options, Thorneycroft quickly dismissed them, launched into a vigorous defense of the British independent deterrent, and pressed McNamara to indicate his willingness publicly to endorse the deterrent, which McNamara obviously could not do. As U.S. officials had foreseen, Thorneycroft suggested that the United States had an obligation to provide Great Britain with a substitute for Skybolt that would permit preservation of the independent deterrent. In Rubel's view, he "evoked images of the most dire betrayal . . . on the part of the Americans who had, in fact, done nothing more than cancel a development that should never have been started, to which the British had contributed nothing, for which the Americans had no real military need, and which the British had identified as *their* 'independent nuclear deterrent.'" The meeting broke up without agreement.[92] Further discussion of Skybolt would have to await the Kennedy-Macmillan summit meeting in Nassau in the Bahamas the following week.

McNamara had expected Thorneycroft to ask specifically for Polaris; he returned to Washington complaining that the British had not done their homework, that they had not given any thought to what they would like as a replacement. The complaint was wide of the mark. After hearing from McNamara on 9 November, Thorneycroft had an interdepartmental group intensively study the matter and prepare a negotiating paper that Macmillan approved.[93] The problem was not British laziness or a breakdown in communication between Washington and London, as some scholars have maintained,[94] but that Thorneycroft wanted what McNamara could not offer.

The denouement occurred at the Nassau summit meeting (18-21 December), where McNamara, Nitze, and Rubel represented Defense, and Ball—Rusk having made a prior commitment—represented State. When the president offered to continue Skybolt development as a joint Anglo-American project on a 50-50 basis, Macmillan pointed out that "although the proposed British marriage with Skybolt was not exactly a shotgun wedding, the virginity of the lady must now be regarded as doubtful." If accepted, the British would have "to spend hundreds of millions of dollars upon a weapon which the President's own authorities were casting doubts, both publicly and privately." He also rejected the offers of Hound Dog and Polaris as part of a multilateral, mixed manning force. The two leaders finally agreed on 21 December that the United States would sell the United Kingdom a still to be determined number of Polaris A-3 missiles (less reentry vehicles), along with their missile launching, fire control, and ship navigation systems. The missiles would be carried on British submarines. The British Polaris forces and equivalent U.S. forces would be made available in any NATO multilateral nuclear force that might be created. The issue of the independent British deterrent was finessed with an ambiguous phrase. When "supreme national interests are at stake," the British forces could be temporarily withdrawn on appropriate notice. The British felt that McNamara played a helpful role at the conference. According to Macmillan, he was "much more reliable than President Kennedy, who makes the facts fit his arguments."[95]

A curious postscript involved another Skybolt test by the Air Force the next day, 22 December—authorized by Gilpatric in McNamara's absence—and the issuance of a triumphant press release with exaggerated claims of the test's success. McNamara had left Nassau for Colorado to spend the Christmas holiday. Kennedy, accompanied by Ormsby Gore, had gone to the president's home in Palm Beach, Florida. There the president received the news of the test and "went through the roof." He could not understand how anyone could have authorized it when he and Macmillan had just decided to cancel Skybolt and, on top of that, then claim a completely successful test. He immediately telephoned Gilpatric, who "got the full fury of the storm." McNamara made known to LeMay his annoyance over the press release, admonishing him that he trusted "that for both our sakes there will be no recurrence of such incidents."[96]

The United States canceled Skybolt for budgetary, technical, and strategic reasons, not because it wanted to eliminate the British independent deterrent, though that had been a leading objective of the MLF supporters at State, who viewed the Nassau agreement to substitute Polaris as a terrible surrender. Although the British considered Nassau a splendid diplomatic triumph that rescued them from a difficult situation, the Macmillan government itself created the predicament by going too far out on a limb in its commitment to Skybolt and the independent deterrent. The episode left Kennedy suspicious of British motives, and McNamara, who had subsequent problems dealing with Thorneycroft, convinced of the defence minister's unreliability.[97]

McNamara may have committed missteps, but short of offering the British Polaris missiles without strings at a very early stage, a crisis of some magnitude could not have been avoided. As Ormsby Gore later observed, however the Americans handled the matter, "there was bound to have been considerable friction."[98] Looking back four months after Nassau, Kennedy wondered whether "Polaris wasn't inevitable as the outcome . . . . Once this sequence started, there possibly was nowhere else for it to stop."[99] As for the MLF, Skybolt was one thread within the larger debate over the sharing of nuclear weapons with the European allies, an issue that would increasingly focus the Kennedy administration's attention.

In the short run, the Skybolt furor revealed two nations with a common language and different understandings. Nevertheless, the breach was healed more quickly than the Suez confrontation six years earlier. It did not destroy the relationship or the alliance: the British received a better missile than they could have expected a few years before; the Americans had the satisfaction of bringing Britain into the projected multilateral force; and the alliance emerged intact, if frayed.

In the longer run, the Skybolt affair underscored the lack of coherence and clarity that characterized NATO policy during much of the Kennedy and Johnson administrations. Britain, no less than France and Germany, became suspicious and anxious about the U.S. nuclear posture. Despite professions of continuing commitment to the nuclear strategic role of the 1950s, Washington's actions often seemed to undercut declarations. On the heels of Athens and Ann Arbor the Skybolt affair did nothing to bolster U.S. credibility as a reliable partner.

CHAPTER XV

MLF: A Notion Too Far

In NATO's history there is a striking similarity in the roles played by the European Defense Community (EDC) in the early 1950s and the Multilateral Force (MLF) a decade later.* Both were experiments in the integration of national forces, which if successful would have served as powerful agents in advancing the cause of a United States of Europe. The EDC aimed to resolve the destructive rivalry between Germany and France and would have facilitated the tapping of German resources for use in NATO. It was also intended as an instrument for keeping West Germany bound to the NATO camp without the Federal Republic becoming a formal member of the alliance. The MLF sought to accomplish still other ends—arm the SHAPE command with medium-range ballistic missiles, discourage independent German and French nuclear initiatives, and reassure European allies of the reliability of U.S. nuclear guarantees.

Both the EDC and MLF failed, in large measure because, however sound the objectives, an array of competing political, strategic, and bureaucratic interests, as well as complicated legal, logistic, and financial issues, made common agreement both at home and abroad impossible to achieve. In both instances an ambitious plan foundered on a host of practical problems and fell victim to unrealistic expectations. Multilateralism's most ardent supporters, a prominent coterie of State Department policy planners led by Robert Bowie, Gerard Smith, and Henry Owen, joined in the Kennedy administration by George Ball and, more guardedly, Walt Rostow, insisted, as with the EDC, that the purpose of the MLF was not just to frustrate the development of national nuclear weapon systems on the Continent or to manage the French and German "problems," but to make Europeans full and worthy partners of the United States. In theory, an MLF could help break down antiquated and dangerous nationalist behavior and pave the way for a united Europe based on the American model as espoused by such reformers

---

*An earlier version of this chapter, written by Lawrence S. Kaplan, appeared under the title "The MLF Debate" in Douglas Brinkley and Richard T. Griffiths, eds, *John F. Kennedy and Europe*, 51-65.

as French economist Jean Monnet. That the MLF idea survived as long as it did, from 1960 to 1965, was a tribute to the devotion of these true believers.

The MLF never won such dedicated adherents in the Defense Department, which tended to regard a multilateral structure that included in its purest form a mixing of crews from different countries as militarily unworkable because of language, cultural, and other barriers. In general, the Pentagon's interest in the MLF centered less on the lofty objective of altering NATO's nationalist proclivities than on the more limited and urgent need to meet alliance security requirements, though both had strategic implications and at times both of necessity factored into DoD decisionmaking.

Birth of a Concept

Through the 1950s Europe's dependency on the U.S. atomic arsenal for the defense of the Continent against a Soviet missile threat contributed to increasing strains in the NATO alliance and underscored the need to involve the Europeans more directly in their own security. For Defense planners in the Eisenhower years the challenge was to bolster European confidence and capability while maintaining adequate control over deployment and use of nuclear weapons.

The nuclear stockpiles the United States had established in Europe in the aftermath of the Soviets' Sputnik launch provided a precedent for having atomic weapons on the Continent. Although the stockpiling put delivery systems in European hands, the United States retained custody over nuclear warheads through a "dual key" arrangement whereby firing could occur only by authorization of the president and under the orders of the supreme allied commander, Europe. To SACEUR General Lauris Norstad, who was instrumental in developing the stockpiling program, this provision offered a satisfactory formula for a NATO missile force under U.S. authority that presented benefits for both Europe and the United States. Beginning in 1958 the United States deployed liquid-fuel Thor and Jupiter IRBMs in Great Britain, Italy, and Turkey, but range and safety issues limited their utility and acceptability from the start and made them poor candidates for an effective deterrent. Norstad believed that installing a new generation of medium-range ballistic missiles on the Continent under the banner of NATO and command of SACEUR could not only achieve greater military security for Europe but at the same time meet the demands for nuclear sharing made by some of the allies and counter nationalist nuclear aspirations in France and Germany.* Norstad's plan presumed the use of a land-based, solid-propellant Polaris system to replace the Thors and Jupiters. The Norstad initiative was a

---

* On French and German nuclear thought during this period, see Chapter XIV. On the French, see also Constantine A. Pagedas, *Anglo-American Strategic Relations and the French Problem, 1960-1963: A Troubled Partnership*, 69-85. John Steinbruner provides an incisive analysis of French and German nuclear thinking in *The Cybernetic Theory of Decision*, 164-68, 214-15.

harbinger of the MLF concept, though the emphasis on U.S. custody and control and a "multinational" (separate national units under a unified command) rather than a "multilateral" (common ownership and mixed manning) system bore little resemblance to the more far-reaching concept championed by the policy planners in the State Department.[1]

Mounting criticism of the liabilities of a land-based system persuaded DoD to reconsider the possible advantages of basing the Polaris at sea. The State Department's Bowie Report in 1960 advocated a submarine-based MRBM force for NATO that Bowie believed stood a better chance of furthering the multilateral concept than basing the weapon on national soil and offered other advantages as well. Although the Army and Air Force backed SACEUR's preference for a land-based missile, citing the higher operational costs, more complex logistics, and lesser accuracy of the seagoing version of the Polaris, they and Secretary of Defense Gates acknowledged that seaborne deployment might make sense initially because of its ready availability and lesser vulnerability and political sensitivity. Putting the missiles at sea would be more acceptable to the NATO allies than putting them on land, where they would be more visible targets and invite intense domestic debate and opposition. Also, Pentagon planners worried that greater vulnerability of the land-based missile to capture could put pressure on NATO to use the weapon before it might be seized.

In August 1960, the submarine concept got a timely assist from Chairman of the Joint Chiefs of Staff General Nathan F. Twining, who, evidently independently of the State Department advocates, became convinced of the merits of a sea-based NATO MRBM force and introduced his own submarine proposal. With Twining's conversion and Gates's own second thoughts about deploying the Polaris on European soil, OSD moved in the direction of the submarine option while the JCS* held out for future augmentation of the force by a land-based program. There remained fundamental disagreements with State over the custody and control issue and the feasibility of mixed manning as well as differences over cost and the linkage between the U.S. and European contribution.[2]

Defense and State representatives worked hard through the fall of 1960 to reconcile the deep-seated conflicts in their respective positions.[3] Each side made concessions on substance and language so that Secretary of State Christian Herter was able to promulgate a broad patchwork "concept" at the NATO ministerial meeting in Paris in December.† Herter recommended that the United States commit to NATO before the end of 1963 an interim MRBM force of five nuclear submarines, armed with Polaris missiles, on condition that the Europeans come up

---

* Twining's support of the sea-based concept had been a personal endorsement rather than a joint recommendation by the chiefs.

† Watson, *Into the Missile Age*, 550n, cites Herter's speech here as containing one of the first express uses of the term "multilateral force," which until then had generally been referred to simply as "NATO MRBM force."

with an acceptable system to manage them. Also, the NATO nations would be expected to purchase approximately 100 missiles to meet NATO's requirement through 1964. Although Herter hoped "such a force would be truly multilateral," he conceded that crews might be mixed only "to the extent considered operationally feasible by SACEUR" and that "a suitable formula" would have to be devised to govern weapon use and procedures.[4]

JFK and the Ottawa Signals

Six weeks after the December 1960 meeting in Paris President Kennedy took office. Between Cuba, Laos, and Berlin, the new administration had a full slate of foreign policy tests to grapple with, along with its overhaul of the Eisenhower strategic doctrine, before it could come to grips with the complexities of fashioning a multilateral nuclear deterrent in Europe. At the same time, the MLF contained too much potential, and too much effort and energy had already been invested, for it to be dismissed without further exploration.

Even absent the preoccupation with pressing decisions on Cuba and Berlin, a program as vague as Herter's concept and as lacking in consensus within the government would have had trouble moving forward. Despite the temporary bridging of differences between Gates and Herter prior to Paris, such was the unsettled state of the MLF in January 1961 that dissension over the next step persisted not only between State and Defense but within DoD between OSD, JCS, and SACEUR. Norstad doggedly pursued his own agenda, accepting Herter's pledge of five Polaris submarines but insisting they could not take the place of mobile land-based missiles. Although the services and OSD joined in opposition to an independently controlled MLF and any erosion of presidential authority over the use of nuclear warheads, another split flared over the primacy of nuclear vs. conventional forces and whether, in light of the administration's shifting strategic priorities, any compelling need existed for a separate European nuclear capability. While Rear Adm. John Lee, director of the ISA Policy Planning Staff, was a key supporter of the missile program, Lee's superior, Assistant Secretary Paul Nitze, was not.[5] At a meeting attended by NATO Secretary General Paul Henri Spaak and U.S. Defense leaders, Nitze expressed doubts about the effectiveness of a European nuclear force. The ISA boss felt that while the United States could look at the nuclear sharing concept, it should "urge that NATO's chief effort go into strengthening conventional forces." McNamara, in full agreement, cited financial as well as military and political considerations as obstacles to an MLF. He regarded the five Polaris submarines offered by Herter as sufficient for NATO's needs and opposed the large number of ballistic missiles indicated in proposed new NATO requirements.[6]

Nor was there complete accord within the State Department, where most of the MLF proponents held forth. Secretary of State Rusk and Under Secretary Ball, much like Herter and his deputy Douglas Dillon before them, often seemed as wary of the zeal of Smith, Bowie, and Owen as they were troubled by the rigidity of obstructionists at DoD. Europeanists at State like Ball may have dragged their feet on the MLF because they were overly "mindful of the lessons of the EDC." Eventually the Bowie-Owen band of activists found allies in Ball, who became their unofficial spokesman, and Deputy Assistant Secretary for Atlantic Affairs Robert Schaetzel, but few senior officials shared their fervid devotion. Although, with a sympathetic Lee at ISA and Rostow at the White House (Rostow moved over to State in December 1961 to head the Policy Planning Council), the true believers constituted an imposing and influential group, in the early days of the Kennedy administration they wielded limited power in the shaping of U.S. NATO policies.[7]

Nor did any groundswell of enthusiasm for the MLF erupt from the intended recipients on the European side. The muted European response to the American initiative may have reflected apprehension over the direction of the shift in U.S. strategic policy toward flexible response. Or it may have reflected the confusion over which of the proposals—Norstad's original land-based concept or Herter's sea-based option unveiled at Paris—represented the U.S. position. Both were presented to the NATO Council in the same year. Spaak complained to McNamara that the U.S. policy was "ambiguous and contradictory." Norstad insisted that France and Germany really wanted the new, extended-range version of the Pershing missile. Norwegian Foreign Minister Halvard Lange guessed the MLF would "lead nowhere." The Europeans clearly disliked the prospect of having to incur larger national expenditures. Herter's suggestion of linkage between the European contribution of 100 additional missiles in exchange for the U.S. commitment of its five Polaris submarines had been disconcerting, as was the inference of the withdrawal of U.S. troops from Europe and withdrawal of the offer of five submarines if the European allies did not pay what Americans considered to be a fair share. The Europeans could not help but notice American concern over a worsening balance of payments deficit.[8]

In these circumstances MLF discussions proceeded fitfully while the administration sorted out the nuances and staff, laden with briefing papers, shuttled between agencies and embassies. At a press conference on 8 February 1961 Kennedy announced the appointment of Dean Acheson to head an advisory group on the future of U.S. NATO policy,* which, the president said in response to a question, would look at NATO possession of nuclear weapons as one of the "central matters of interest to us." Speaking to the Canadian Parliament in Ottawa on 17 May the president formally committed to the NATO command the five Polaris submarines in the spirit of the Herter proposal and went on to say: "Beyond this, we look to the possibility of eventually establishing a NATO sea-borne force,

---

* See Chapter XII.

which would be truly multi-lateral in ownership and control, if this should be desired and found feasible by our Allies, once NATO's non-nuclear goals have been achieved."[9] Despite leaving wide latitude for interpretation, the expansive tone of the president's statement must have heartened MLF supporters and renewed their determination to surmount the obstacles posed by the Pentagon. Few may have known that the "truly multi-lateral" phrase in the speech was the handiwork of Henry Owen, who inserted the words into the draft that White House speechwriter Theodore Sorensen sent him for comment.[10]

The Ottawa message had as much to do with the concept of Atlantic partnership as with European unity, two potentially antithetical ideas whose tension underlay much of the MLF debate and that could coexist comfortably as long as no effort was made to give them real substance. For all the noble sentiment, Kennedy gave no indication he was prepared to weaken U.S. presidential control over nuclear weapons. Encouraging as the Canadian address may have been to believers in the MLF, from abroad there came little sign of positive reaction and within DoD little evidence of quickening activity to justify their optimism. The only genuine appreciation of the president's evocation of the possibility of a multilaterally owned and controlled NATO nuclear force came from Germany. In a memorandum to the State Department, the German government welcomed the idea and wished to help implement it with personnel and money. The Federal Republic hoped that negotiations would begin soon and that the United States would "express its real intentions concerning the degree of NATO control contemplated over the submarines."[11]

German endorsement came as a mixed blessing. On the one hand, Germany's involvement in a collective enterprise was vital to dampening its interest in a national nuclear capability. The promise of a new multilateral force seemed one way of alleviating Bonn's doubts about the direction of U.S. policy. State took pains to assure the Germans that while negotiations might have to proceed slowly, the United States was continuing its active study of the MRBM requirement. On the other hand, so long as Germans were the only Europeans to embrace the Multilateral Force, attention would focus not on a new NATO nuclear entity but on potential German control of that entity, heightening the anxiety of Britain and other countries over that prospect.[12]

Defense Reservations, 1961-1962

The European reaction, although of concern, remained peripheral to resolving intractable internal differences among the several U.S. parties to the debate. MLF realization remained elusive because of the administration's own reservations, not the least the caveat in Kennedy's Ottawa speech that any advancement of the MRBM program would have to await attainment of non-nuclear, conventional force goals—not an incidental aside but a pointed, telling remark, intended

Clockwise from top: Secretary McNamara interrupts conference with Roswell Gilpatric, Paul Nitze, and Adam Yarmolinsky to take phone call; squash with Secretary of Agriculture Orville Freeman; standing at window of Pentagon office. (From Library of Congress *Look* Collection.)

Clockwise from top left: Rollout of TFX; Navy Secretary Korth leaving TFX probe; Secretary McNamara and Assistant Secretary of Defense (I&L) Thomas Morris hold press conference on results of surplus base study.

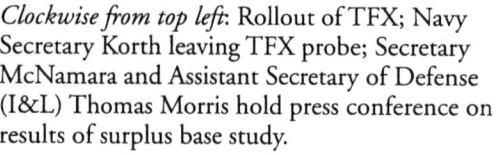

Secretary of the Air Force Eugene M. Zuckert, 1961-65.

John H. Rubel, assistant secretary of defense for strategic weapons, 1961-63.

William P. Bundy, assistant secretary of defense for international security affairs, at swearing-in, November 1963.

Henry S. Rowen, deputy assistant secretary of defense for international security affairs, 1961-65.

ROBERT KNUDSEN/JOHN F. KENNEDY LIBRARY

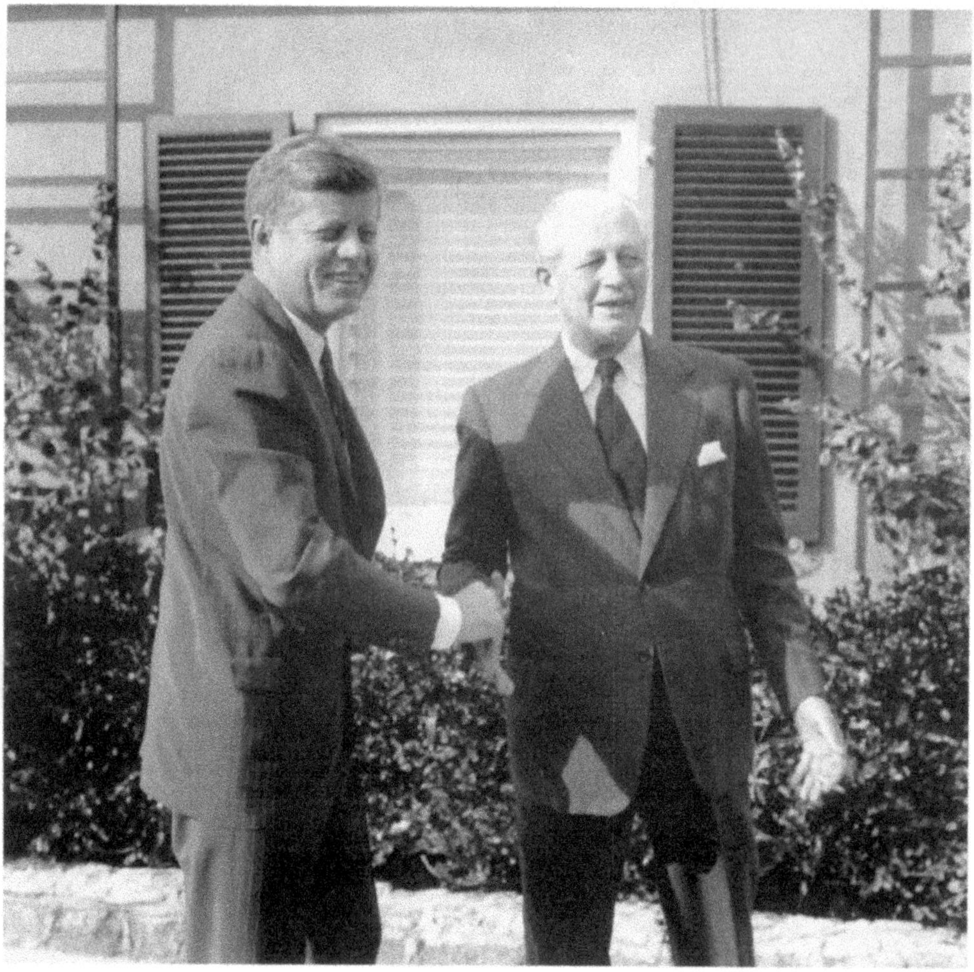

Clockwise from top: President Kennedy with British Prime Minister Harold Macmillan at Nassau, 19 December 1962; Skybolt missiles under the wings of a B-52H; Skybolt cartoon, December 1962.

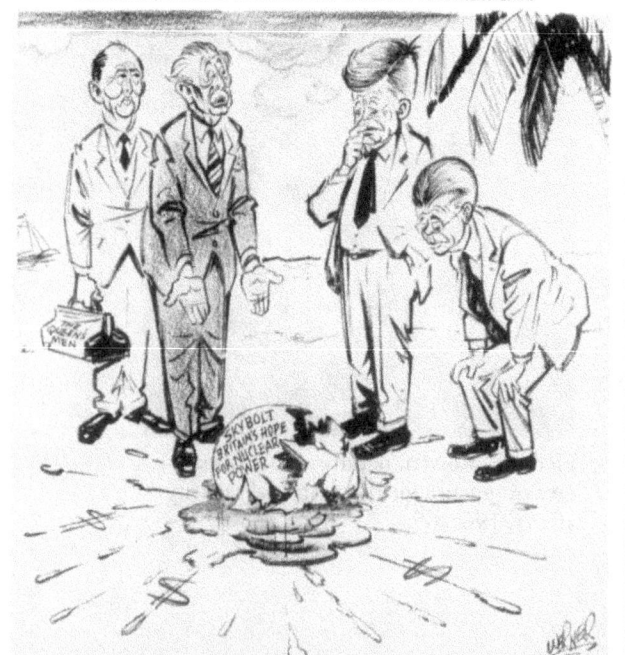

"GENTLEMEN, WE SIMPLY MUST PUT HUMPTY DUMPTY TOGETHER AGAIN."

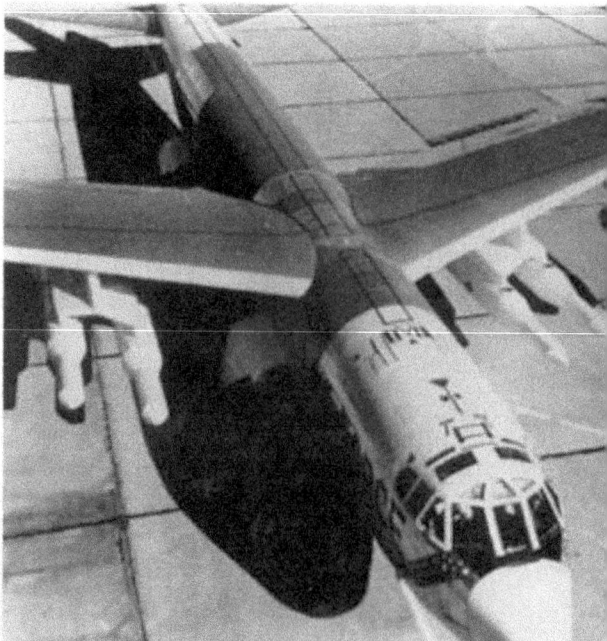

JOHN F. KENNEDY LIBRARY

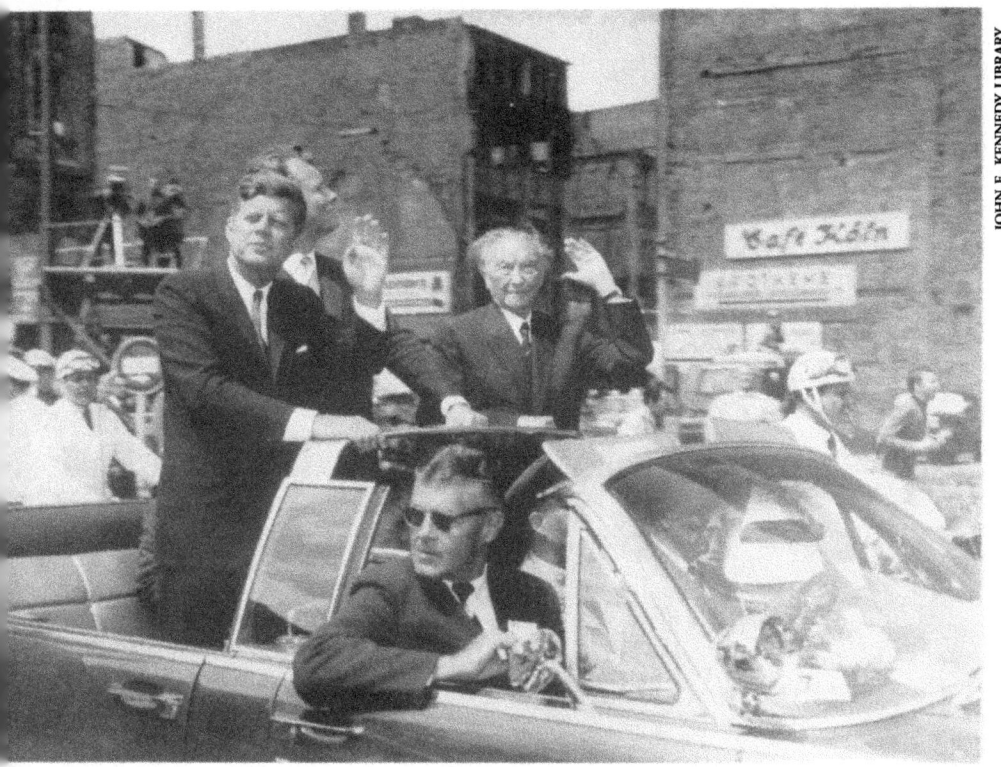

Above: President Kennedy with German Chancellor Adenauer and Berlin Mayor Willy Brandt, June 1963.
Below: Cartoon of NATO tattoo.

JOHN F. KENNEDY LIBRARY

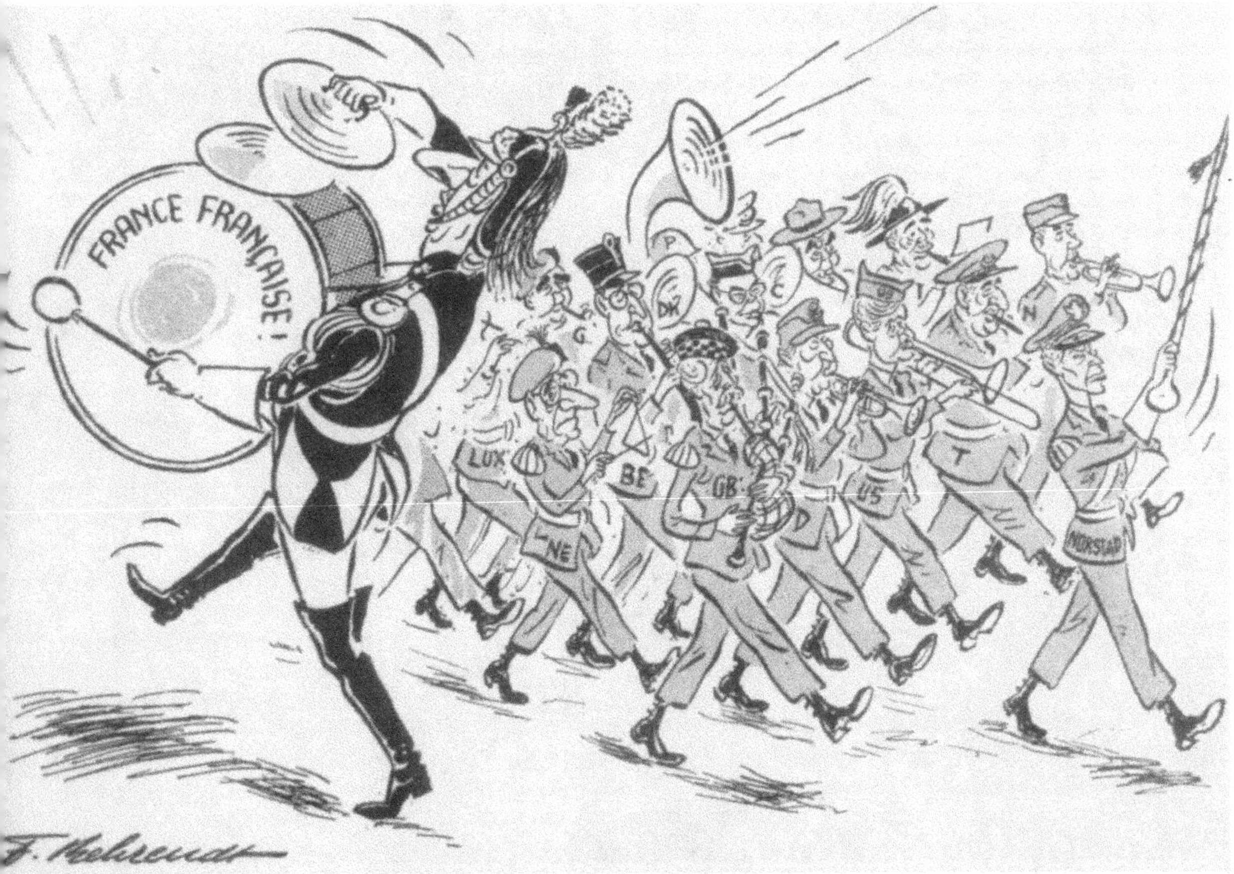

CECIL STOUGHTON/JOHN F. KENNEDY LIBRARY

Above: President Kennedy with Vice President Johnson, September 1963.
Below: President Johnson meets 24 November 1963, 48 hours after Kennedy's assassination, with McNamara and Rusk, Ambassador Lodge, and George Ball.

Clockwise from left: Secretary McNamara departing Pentagon heliport; Secretary of State Rusk with Ambassador Lodge and South Vietnamese General Nguyen Khanh; General Paul Harkins (*right*), head of the MACV Command in South Vietnam, with General Taylor, September 1963.

Clockwise from top left: U.S. Army Special Forces team; U.S. Marine troop transport helicopter squadron in the Mekong Delta; guided missile light cruiser *Oklahoma City*, flagship of U.S. Seventh Fleet, in Saigon harbor, July 1964.

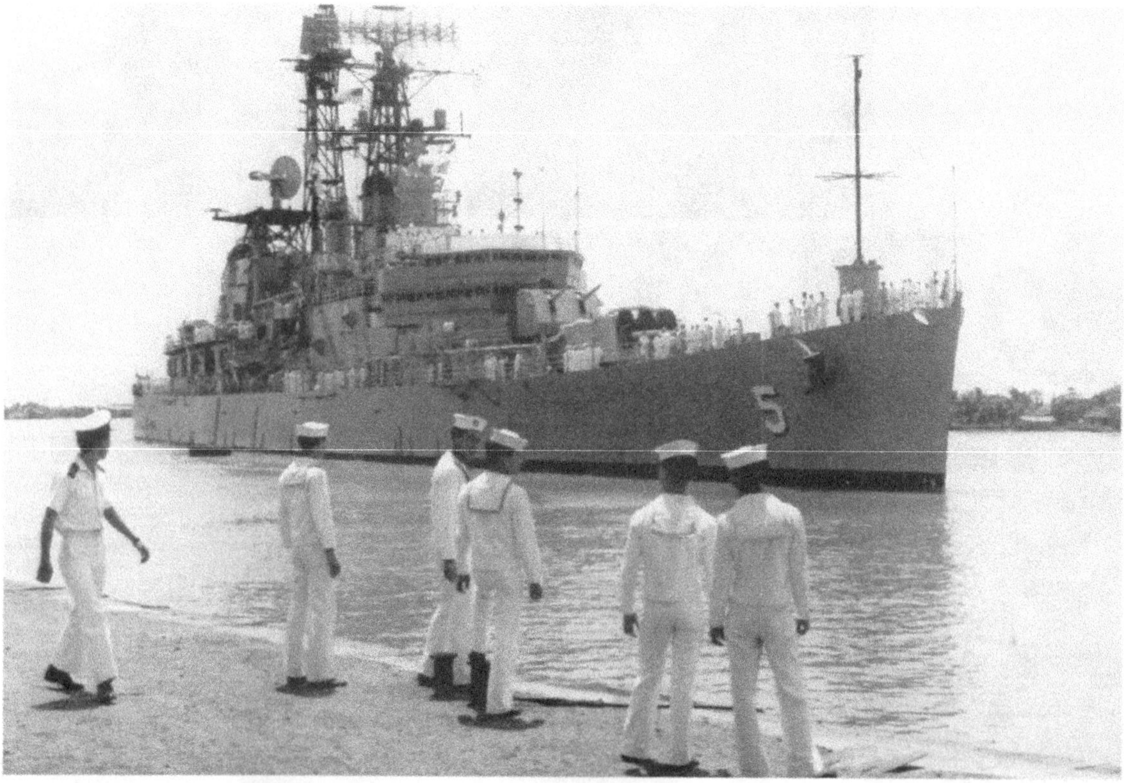

USS *Maddox* operating at sea, early 1960s.

A UH-1B Huey recovers a U.S. helicopter shot down by Viet Cong at Ap Bac, January 1963.

President Johnson escorted by Secretary McNamara on visit to Pentagon Concourse, 21 July 1964.

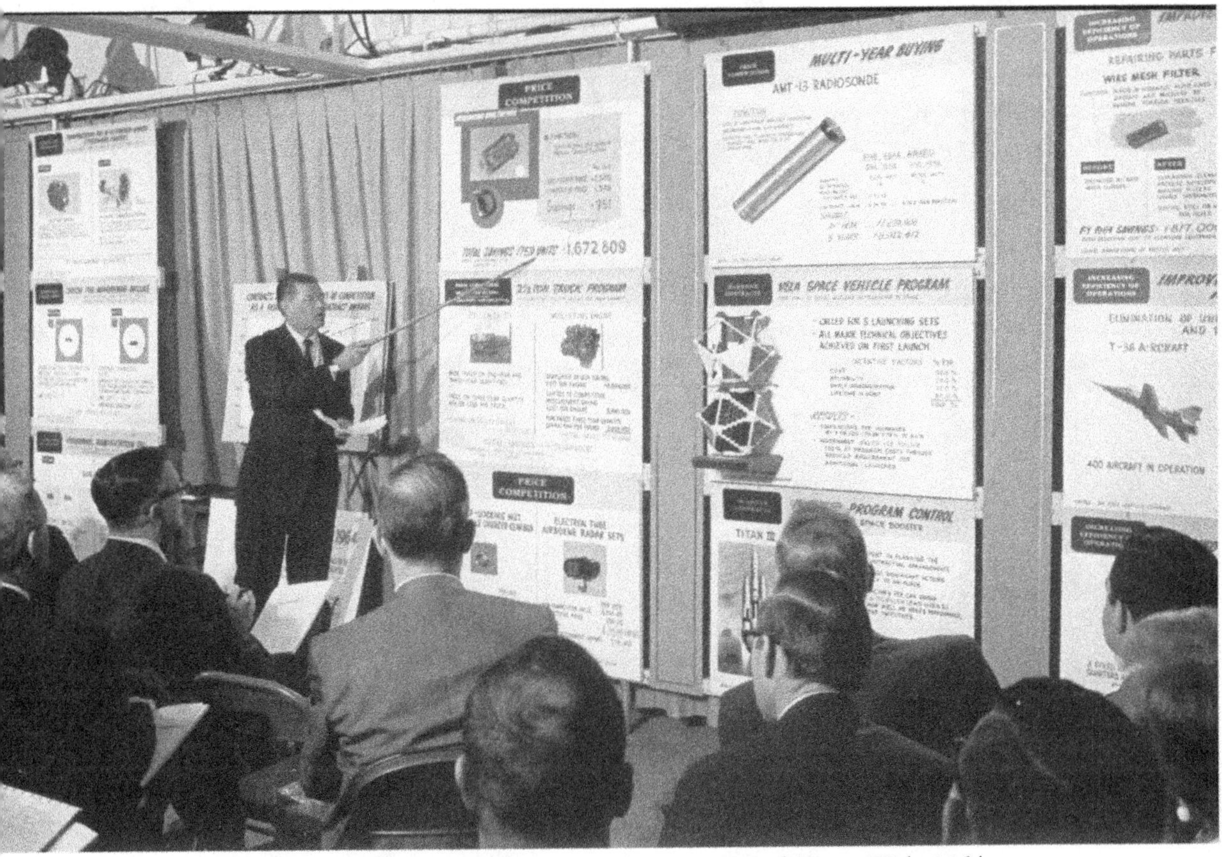

Secretary McNamara reports cost reduction results at press conference, 7 July 1964.

McNAMARA'S BAND

Arthur Sylvester, assistant secretary of defense (public affairs), 1961-67.

Kermit Gordon, director, Bureau of the Budget, 1962-65.

Solis Horowitz, director of DoD organizational and management planning, 1961-64, later assistant secretary of defense for administation.

Henry Glass, economic advisor to the DoD comptroller, 1961-65, later assistant to the secretary and deputy secretary of defense.

Above: Secretary of the Army Stephen Ailes briefing press on proposed reorganization of Army Reserve components, 15 March 1965.
Below: OSD General Counsel John McNaughton (*far left*) and Deputy General Counsel Leonard Niederlehner (*third from left*) with legal staff, April 1964.

Above: President Johnson meeting with Secretary McNamara and the Joint Chiefs at LBJ Ranch, December 1964.
Below: The Joint Chiefs of Staff, April 1965, *left to right*, General John P. McConnell, USAF, Admiral David L. McDonald, USN, Chairman General Earle G. Wheeler, USA, General Harold K. Johnson, USA, General Wallace M. Greene, Jr., USMC.

Above: Vietnam targeting briefing in May 1965 by Lt. Col. Robinson Risner, USAF, who six months later would be a POW in a Hanoi prison.
Below: Left to right, McNaughton, now assistant secretary for international security affairs, Lodge, Sylvester, and General William Westmoreland awaiting Secretary McNamara's arrival at Tan Son Nhut Airbase, South Vietnam, 1965.

Secretary McNamara during a quiet moment in the Cabinet Room of the White House, 28 January 1964.

"LET'S SEE THAT DAMNED COMPASS AGAIN!"

McNAMARA'S WAR

both to remind the NATO partners of the importance of improving conventional defenses and to afford the administration breathing room on the nuclear matter until it could settle on an agreed course of action. The president repeated the point in June to Spaak's successor, Secretary General Dirk Stikker, indicating that "the question of MRBM's was for the fairly distant future."[13]

Acheson's report, delivered in draft to the White House in March and emerging from NSC review on 21 April 1961 as an official policy directive, reinforced the go-slow approach. The former secretary of state advised against an MRBM proposal that could prove divisive, drain resources, and "overshadow" and divert attention from "more pressing tasks" relating to Berlin and "preparing NATO forces for lesser contingencies." Acheson criticized specifically the Norstad plan and its support for land-based MRBMs. But any U.S. MRBM plan, Acheson wrote McNamara in July, "would seem to be the wrong kind of signal to give our allies just when we were trying hard—and for the first time—to persuade them that the path to salvation lies through non-nuclear, rather than nuclear, improvement." He envisaged a destructive internal debate within NATO reflecting British fears of a nuclear-armed Germany as well as French demands for custody over warheads on missiles in France. Further, he did not trust the "paper" commitment to SACEUR as a sufficient safeguard to maintain centralized control and prevent accidental or premature use of an enhanced European nuclear capability. Echoing Kennedy at Ottawa, Acheson concluded that only "after non-nuclear improvements have been achieved" should European participation in the nuclear program be considered—"if this is what our allies want"—and then only if the missile force were seaborne, where it would be "in a safe place . . . in American hands."[14]

In the meantime, Norstad, finding himself increasingly isolated, reluctantly moved toward accepting a seaborne force if a compromise could keep some land-based missiles in the package. Among his other concerns he feared that a nuclear force at sea would enhance the role of the Navy and the Supreme Allied Commander, Atlantic (SACLANT) at the expense of SACEUR and blur their responsibilities. Norstad forwarded to the president SHAPE's views that the Polaris submarines should be assigned to SACEUR and incorporated into NATO's normal command structure subject to SACEUR's direct control. In the communication SHAPE responded to a list of questions about operational guidelines and weapon characteristics, citing accuracy and cost issues raised previously about the sea-based mode. The idea of a mixed crew SHAPE found especially impractical on small vessels.[15]

Acheson's strictures (his widely circulated report came to be known as the "Green Book"), the president's own apparent qualms,[16] and the infighting at Defense stalled any progress on the MLF through the remainder of 1961. Notwithstanding the expectations of the Multilateral Force's supporters, the reality was that three days after his speech in Ottawa the president forbade further dispersal of nuclear weapons for the support of non-U.S. forces until the import of such actions could be studied.[17] In a long conversation with Stikker, Nitze made clear to the secretary general that control over use of nuclear weapons in Europe would remain with the president. Stikker protested that this view contradicted the president's statement at Ottawa, and added that if the president alone could authorize the nuclear decision then the North Atlantic Council had nothing to discuss. The meeting adjourned without any resolution of the question, even after U.S. Ambassador to NATO Thomas K. Finletter tried to find some common ground by suggesting that Nitze and Stikker may have had a simple misunderstanding and Finletter rendered a more flexible reading of the U.S. position.[18]

Nitze's stance on the control issue represented a Defense view that had not materially changed since the nuclear sharing concept was first broached. For McNamara, like Gates, the Polaris submarines offered to NATO betokened a symbol of U.S. commitment, not a first step toward surrendering control over nuclear weapons to a new entity. Not only did McNamara hold firm in that conviction, he insisted that the five submarines pledged to NATO should not be turned over until the United States had a squadron of nine Polaris subs deployed and five additional ones had become available. Given the relative strike capabilities of the United States and the Soviet Union, "it is of the utmost importance," McNamara asserted in December, "that we retain exclusive control of all available Polaris submarines for at least the next 24 months." By the end of the year the DoD stance on the subject of an independent European nuclear force if anything had hardened since the onset of the Kennedy administration. Still, there was enough hint of promise in the president's rhetoric and in the State Department's perseverance to send mixed signals to NATO's International Staff in Paris, which continued to pose questions to which no definitive answers would come.[19]

External geopolitical imperatives had given rise to the MLF and those same pressures now sustained it. As always, Germany occupied the foreground of U.S. concerns about stemming nuclear proliferation within the alliance. When German Defense Minister Strauss spoke with his British counterpart Harold Watkinson near the close of 1961 about Europe needing means of its own to respond to Soviet aggression, he sounded an ominous note in his observation that "there will be a new Germany when Adenauer is gone." Watkinson reported to McNamara Strauss's admonition that he could not "afford to be associated with any proposal which appears to place Germany in a weaker position as a nuclear power than its allies." The message was clear. Willingly or not, Great Britain and the United States had to come up with an arrangement that satisfied German needs for greater equity and nuclear security within the framework of the alliance or face the prospect of Germany going it alone in the post-Adenauer era. Yet the shift underway in U.S. strategic doctrine from "massive retaliation" to "flexible response" meant a more measured, discreet U.S. commitment to the use of nuclear weapons and, implicitly, tighter reins at the helm, making German leaders more nervous—and restive—than ever over dependence on U.S. nuclear striking power. West Germany had looked to Norstad's land-based MRBMs, under SACEUR's control but on German soil, as a way out of the predicament, but with that option having fallen out of favor, one of the few alternatives left to U.S. policymakers seeking German cooperation was a nuclearized MLF under a centralized NATO command structure.[20]

By mid-February 1962, despite persisting friction, most of the key constituencies in the Defense Department had recognized the utility of a NATO MRBM force, albeit with varying degrees of conviction and for divergent reasons. For ISA and the OSD leadership the plan's political value (providing cover for Strauss and comfort for others unsure of U.S. nuclear dependability) had appeal even among those skeptical of the military requirement; for the JCS, unswayed by Acheson's and McNamara's contrary conclusion, the motivation remained what in their judgment was the military necessity to replace aging bombers and outdated Jupiters and Thors. OSD, but not JCS* at this point, was willing to recommend a seaborne force; the "cheapest and quickest means" to get it would be to mount Polaris missiles on surface ships rather than the planned but costly submarines. According to ISA representatives present at a meeting with a State delegation on 21 February, Defense even granted the feasibility of mixed manning. At that meeting, White House Special Assistant Carl Kaysen reported, State and Defense concurred in a preference for a new NATO command distinct from SACEUR and SACLANT for the MLF. But State and Defense could not compose their differences, according to Kaysen, over the extent and terms of European participation and in particular over the paramount issue of U.S. control of the warheads. Whereas Defense, no doubt with strict instructions from McNamara, wanted an explicit, categorical declaration on the U.S. retention of veto authority over use of the weapons, State thought such a peremptory statement up front would have a numbing effect on further discussions with the Europeans. The departments agreed to refrain from an early confrontation on the issue and simply noted "serious obstacles in U.S. legislation and past policy to the creation of a force the use of which is not subject to veto," while professing a willingness to examine the question at a later date.[21]

Stikker had weighed in with his own thoughts on the veto provision and other aspects of the revived MLF debate in a memorandum he handed Finletter in late January 1962. Calling for "an integrated missile force owned and controlled by NATO and placed under the command of SACEUR," the plan to be implemented in stages, Stikker believed it prudent to begin with the establishment of a pilot force of merchant ships equipped with a small complement of Polaris missiles and then proceed to more advanced delivery systems, including surface naval vessels, conventional or nuclear-powered submarines, possibly

---

* Lemnitzer succeeded Twining as chairman of the Joint Chiefs in October 1960; he did not share Twining's interest in the sea-based concept, siding with Norstad instead.

a land-based missile, and perhaps a new missile specifically designed for the new force. He estimated the cost of 80 merchantmen in the initial phase at approximately $1.25 billion including 320 missiles, with maintenance and operational costs of the fleet running up to $250 million a year. Sharing the expense would be governed by the current distribution of payments for NATO's infrastructure, with the U.S. share at 30.85 percent, followed by West Germany's 20 percent. As for control over the warheads, he suggested that pending a final solution "the following procedure could be adopted during the first stage of the establishment of the force. The NATO Council should instruct SACEUR to employ the . . . [force] only when the use of tactical 'atomic battlefield weapons' has been authorized. The United States would then virtually have a right of veto for the time being."[22]

Stikker's penchant for cutting to the chase continued to outpace the still evolving and delicate negotiations within the U.S. government. He was looking far ahead of the Defense Department, where the JCS, and for that matter many of the leaders in OSD, regarded the Multilateral Force as at best a fig leaf to accomplish their respective purposes while sustaining others' illusions. Whether or not the Jupiters and Thors would give way to the Navy's Polaris or to a new mid-range ballistic missile (Missile "X") funded at $100 million for FY 1963 and administered by the Air Force, by fits and starts the chiefs were coming around to concurrence with OSD on the need for action even if it meant under the auspices of an MLF. Still, DoD was not only on a different page but working from a different script than Stikker or the missionaries at State.[23]

Norstad, who had helped plant the idea of the MLF and then seen his version preempted by men he considered misguided ideologues, became increasingly distressed by the direction of both the State Department and his Pentagon colleagues. He objected strenuously to Finletter's proposed statement that accented the advantages of "external" long-range ICBMs and, by implication, denigrated the medium-range armaments Norstad championed. "The enemy threat," Norstad cabled Lemnitzer, "must be considered in its entirety and dealt with through the integrated and intelligent use of all weapons and all forces." He could not have been happy with State's message to Finletter on 16 April that authorized the U.S. ambassador to inform the North Atlantic Council of steps the United States was willing to take toward creating "a genuinely multilateral NATO MRBM Force." They included commitment to NATO of U.S. nuclear forces outside Europe beyond those already committed and, as a second step, should the allies desire, the United States joining in "developing a modest sized (on the order of 200 missiles) fully multilateral NATO sea-based MRBM force." State's guidance provided some of the details the Europeans had long been seeking, including "sufficient degree of mixed manning to ensure that no single nationality is predominant in the manning of any vessel," but stopped short of ceding authority over use of the weapons to the multilateral force. On that sticking point, State demurred:

> . . . US would be prepared to furnish warheads. Ways should be found to safe-guard design data, e.g., US custodians could remain aboard any multilaterally manned NATO vessel with standing orders to release the warheads in case a properly authenticated order to fire was received through agreed channels . . . . A formula which would involve transfer of warheads or procedures for using the force without US concurrence would require amending existing US law and could well entail other obstacles, depending on the character of the arrangements. The US is willing, however, to consider any proposal which is put to it by a clear majority of the Alliance.

That the statement omitted any reference to SACEUR except for a one-line mention that the new force "would come under appropriate NATO commanders' command," and that he had not even been consulted on the MRBM proposal, Norstad took as a personal affront. "Aside from the rudeness involved," he complained to Lemnitzer, "is it tactically wise to make, without any consultation or coordination with me or my headquarters, a statement to the North Atlantic Council dealing with a subject which I proposed in 1957, which I have followed closely since that time, and which bears almost exclusively on my ability to discharge my assigned functions?"[24]

McNamara's reaction to the 16 April cable that so infuriated Norstad was curiously restrained. In a meeting at the White House with Kennedy and Rusk to discuss the statement prior to its release and formal issuance as National Security Action Memorandum No. 147, he conveyed to the president the strong dissent of the JCS and secured deletion of language on multilateral control of the U.S. Polaris submarines assigned to NATO that the chiefs found particularly objectionable. McNamara dutifully communicated the chiefs' views but stated his own belief that no compelling military requirement existed for a European MRBM force. He worried about the cost of such a commitment, which he figured to be as much as $2 billion, a burden that would compete with what he deemed the greater requirement for an increase in Europe's conventional defense capabilities. He went along with Rusk and State, except for insisting on the aforementioned deletion, because of the plan's potential political payoff and because he believed "we must indeed get off dead center in discussion of these issues." Moreover, McNamara was likely less exercised over the statement to NATO than were Norstad and the JCS, or General Maxwell Taylor (currently the president's military representative), because he doubted that the Europeans would accept the "quasi-offer."[25]

After a meeting with McNamara on 18 April, Taylor noted that McNamara was in fact "entirely happy" with the transmittal of the MRBM guidance because it did not give the Europeans the degree of control they wanted and when they rejected it he would then be in a better position to present a counter-proposal: an offer for the United States to provide the weapons and manning personnel at no charge to the allies, in exchange for their agreement to increase their conventional forces. McNamara would not have to wait long to test his scenario.[26]

Athens and After

McNamara seized on the North Atlantic Council ministerial meeting in Athens in May 1962 as an opportunity to elaborate on his strategic views and claim the high ground in an MLF debate that was still nowhere close to resolution. At Athens he would educate the Europeans as to the facts of nuclear life and the problems inherent in the organization and control of nuclear warfare. Prior to the commencement of the formal sessions he arranged for the defense ministers a briefing on "the necessary overall unity of major nuclear operations," especially the need "for positive central direction of the nuclear campaign. The briefing would be part of a program to move our Allies from 'theatre' to 'global' nuclear thinking"—and, left unsaid, away from thinking about either national or independent European nuclear forces.[27]

McNamara dominated the Athens meeting, explaining in great detail the range of technical and other problems associated with a NATO MRBM force, cautioning at one point that "we expect our allies will wish to consider very carefully the full implications of undertaking this venture." While dangling the carrot of the MLF as described in the Finletter proposal and repeating earlier statements that the United States stood prepared to enter into discussions of a multilateral MRBM force if that was what the allies wanted, he spoke of complicated questions, such as whether the force was militarily necessary and how to ease the burden of heavy costs, which the United States had no intention of bearing alone. Above all, he made clear that the emerging U.S. strategy gave priority not only to the indivisibility of control of nuclear weapons but to the elevated importance of conventional weaponry. His bottom line affirmed that national nuclear forces would not be welcome under any circumstances and that a unified European MRBM force could become possible under the right conditions, but it remained secondary to the strengthening of the conventional arsenal, the cornerstone of the new strategy.[28] These themes would not fully resonate and did not receive broad media attention until McNamara restated them in his more publicized Ann Arbor address* a month later, but the thrust of his thinking should have become crystal-clear to the Europeans at Athens.

McNamara's emphasis on conventional armaments effectively sidetracked any serious discussion of the MLF at Athens, and left the Europeans wondering whether the barring of U.S. help to national nuclear aspirants meant implicit support for the multilateral concept, or whether both were being sacrificed on

---

*See Chapter XII.

the altar of a more conventional strategy. The MLF's supporters in the State Department felt let down not just by McNamara's indifference to the European integration objective but by the president's own equivocation and seemingly flagging interest in the initiative despite approving NSAM 147. The continued lack of action on the MLF, State believed, would result in precisely what McNamara had preached against at Athens, a vacuum that encouraged development of national nuclear capabilities along the lines of what the French were doing and what the Germans were intimating.

If State's policy planners felt disappointed by the outcome of the Athens meeting, Norstad must have seethed as he watched McNamara deliver a devastating blow to his MRBM plans, all but ruling out the land-based missile and multinational manning—the heart of his program. Moreover, McNamara had not only challenged the wisdom of the European MRBM deployment but openly discounted the military importance of the medium-range missiles. In so doing McNamara not only provoked Norstad but inadvertently undercut the NATO Military Committee, whose MC 99 paper, prepared without the administration's guidance, reflected Norstad's justification for NATO MRBMs. With Stikker and the committee deferring to Norstad, the United States found itself on a collision course with its alliance partners that both State and Defense officials had so assiduously tried to avoid. To gain control over MC 99 and prevent the NATO Council from "jumping the track" and nullifying the progress achieved in clarifying the U.S. position at Athens, Col. Lawrence Legere recommended to General Taylor that MC 99 could be treated as "expressing 'purely military' views . . . and either placed in cold storage or, if necessary, overruled by compelling political and economic considerations." In the meantime, Legere wrote Taylor on 1 June, Stikker and the council should hold off on approving the draft paper while SACEUR produced detailed documentation for the military utility of the MRBM. McNamara directed the Joint Chiefs to submit a study on this very issue by 31 August.[29]

Little more than a month after the Athens meeting, then, the administration's disarray on the MRBM issue became apparent again, in an embarrassing conflict played out in front of the Europeans between SACEUR, supported by "most all military authorities," according to his staff, and U.S. political authorities over whether or not there existed a military requirement for a ballistic missile nuclear delivery system to modernize his strike force in Europe.[30]

On 15 June the White House sent Finletter on a damage control mission with instructions to amplify the meaning of McNamara's comments at Athens, in particular "to establish with considerable finality the United States position on the military requirement for the MRBM." Straying little from the set piece and mixed message that had become all too familiar to the Europeans since Ottawa, Finletter informed the North Atlantic Council that MRBMs were "not urgently needed for military reasons," as NATO's Soviet targets could be covered by already programmed U.S. nuclear forces, but that the United States remained committed to exploring a multilateral seaborne MRBM force if the allies wished to participate in one—so long as it did not divert resources from "a continuing vigorous buildup of NATO non-nuclear forces" and so long as the allies understood the substantial costs.* The Finletter presentation became widely regarded as a mistake as the double-edged message had already worn thin with the Europeans, and this iteration only compounded European vexation over where exactly Washington was going with it. In a tour of the alliance capitals following the presentation, Rusk stressed that the U.S. purpose was not to kill the MRBM idea or deliver "a mortal blow to the multilateral force," or "put any proposals forward on a take-it-or-leave-it basis." But it did not help that McNamara delivered his Ann Arbor speech on 16 June, repeating and reinforcing his Athens themes the same week that Finletter and Rusk were abroad supplying interpretations that appeared to split hairs and shade meanings for European consumption. At the White House, Taylor warned of navigating rudderlessly, leaving both the allies and Norstad in the lurch: "It is important for us to get our national position aligned both in the ambassadorial and in the military channels."31

Stikker's patience already frayed, the NATO chief blasted the administration for a policy he deemed disingenuous, unintelligible, and lacking leadership. Henry Kissinger, Harvard University professor and a consultant with the National Security Council in the summer of 1962, met with Stikker in Paris on 26 June and came away with the impression that "as Secretary General of NATO, he found it impossible to tell what our objectives were. NATO was being deluged with visitors from Washington, each of them with a slightly different version of United States policy." Between the utterances of Rostow, Rowen, Nitze, Finletter, and Taylor, not to mention Rusk, McNamara, and Norstad, "how could he tell what Administration policy was?" Above all, Stikker expressed exasperation as to how alliance members could possibly entertain a proposal to pay for a missile system whose sponsors considered it militarily useless. Elsewhere, too, the reaction ranged from irritation to incredulity. Italy, Germany, and Greece, among others, found the MLF offer insincere and in any case less likely than ever to see the light of day.32

Of course, McNamara had as his ultimate goal that the alliance members should perceive the futility of pursuing the multilateral force and come to their senses and accept reliance on the Americans' "external" ICBM commitment while devoting their energies and resources to the conventional buildup at home. As Kennedy later recalled the subtext of the administration's apparent seesawing: "It had been the idea—Acheson's to begin with—that we drag out a multilateral force proposal and let the Europeans wrestle with it for a while, until they saw

---

* Henry Rowen, Nitze's deputy in ISA, wrote the instructions and remembered going with Robert Bowie to see Norstad who, furious at again not being consulted, "had them standing while he kept swinging a golf club back and forth 'virtually at our heads.'" See memcon Neustadt with Rowen, 1 Jul 63, fldr Memcons-U.S., box 21, Neustadt Papers, JFKL.

all the bugs in it and decided they'd be better off to leave nuclear forces to us."[33] Neither McNamara nor the president anticipated, however, that the Europeans would become more agitated than resigned, nor that the French and Germans seemed ready to proceed if necessary on their own, possibly in collaboration, rather than abandon the idea of a continental nuclear deterrent. Moreover, as one analyst noted, the European governments found no more agreeable than their U.S. partner the alternative of expanding their armed services to meet increased conventional force requirements.

> In view of this, it should not be surprising if the major European powers seek to base their security on atomic weapons rather than on manpower. They are all subject to acute problems of manpower availability and to the political implications of compulsory service. . . . The idea that the US and UK strategic forces should furnish the firepower while they furnish the cannon fodder is wholly unacceptable. These facts, while not directly related, condition Allied thinking on the need for weapon systems such as the MRBM.[34]

And so whereas McNamara and others in the administration, never comfortable with the multilateral concept, hoped that it would be "disposed of" after Athens,[35] the item remained on the agenda, with the United States and the European principals doing the equivalent of an Alphonse-and-Gaston routine—each side waiting for the other to take the initiative in moving the plan one way or another off dead center. In what amounted to a return to square one in the summer of 1962, the administration again faced the dilemma of risking a splintering of the alliance and proliferation of national nuclear planning—all the more prohibitive under the new "controlling" strategy—or providing the Europeans at least a modicum of theater nuclear security.

With a nod to European dismay, Kennedy took pains in his July Fourth speech in Philadelphia to reaffirm the importance of the transatlantic partnership, declaring that "we believe that a united Europe will be capable of playing a greater role in the common defense" of the free world. He remained vague and his advisers at odds on prescriptions for achieving that unity, but the brief allusion to the Western nations' collaborative role was a forceful signal of United States resolve to stay engaged in Europe and exert what influence it could to promote a unified alliance and cohesive defense. Rusk's special assistant Charles Bohlen (whom Kennedy appointed U.S. ambassador to France in September) told the president he thought it essential that the Europeans understood the United States was not resorting to "any sort of gimmick or scheme" to address their concerns, that it had earnest intentions, and that the solutions were complicated. Still proceeding more by drift and instinct than by direction, the White House appeared inclined to take a serious look at the MLF rather than leave Europe's nuclear fate to the French and Germans. September found McGeorge Bundy, the president's special assistant for national security affairs, in Copenhagen undertaking to persuade the Europeans that "[American] opposition to small national forces should not be read as proof of a general American determination to exclude even a new and united Europe from nuclear weapons." At the same time, Bundy took care not to promise what remained uncertain—the approval of "appropriate agencies" of the U.S. government to the specific custody arrangements and agreement on the financing apparatus.[36]

Sensing a window of opportunity, the MLF faction at State used the summer of 1962 to regroup, corralling new support among those seeking to fill the post-Athens vacuum with a mechanism that, for all its flaws, still had potential as an instrument for unity. Ironically, throughout these years, just as the Multilateral Force's demise appeared near, it would gain a new lease on life because even as a token it continued to serve a useful political purpose, and because for all the barely veiled contempt much of the U.S. national security establishment showed it, an undesirable MLF offered a more palatable option to many than indulging Norstad's multinationalism or de Gaulle's separatism.

Drawing on Ottawa, NSAM 147, and guidance already in place, the MLF lobby resumed the campaign for a multilateral seaborne MRBM force as if the Athens setback had never happened. Bowie, Owen, and Schaetzel deftly cultivated their White House connections with the help of Ball and Rostow. Seymour Weiss, deputy director of State's Office of Politico-Military Affairs, remembered how proficiently Owen's "tight circle" became "a formidable and intimidating machine." Gerard Smith, back at State as a consultant, crisscrossed Europe on a series of trips beginning in August, trying to get the allies back on message. At ISA, Lee worked diligently to head off conceivable Navy resistance to a seaborne force that could involve stationing foreigners aboard U.S. ships. Although Admiral Hyman Rickover was quick to torpedo the notion of manning submarines with crews of mixed nationality, Lee steered the matter to Rear Adm. Frederick Michaelis, a surface-fleet officer (under the supervision of Vice Chief of Naval Operations Claude Ricketts, another surface-fleet officer), an arrangement that promised a more favorable recommendation as well as a felicitous match with the latest thinking to base the MLF on surface naval or merchant vessels. Lee's adroit maneuvering yielded results when Michaelis's report indicated the MLF was manageable from the Navy's standpoint and OSD's director of defense research and engineering, Harold Brown, chimed in with a strong endorsement of the surface-ship mode.[37]

MLF opponents chafed as the multilateral idea regained momentum. Legere, who felt neither McNamara nor Rusk paid sufficient attention to the bureaucratic stratagems of the MLF activists and their capacity to wrest control of U.S. NATO policy, urged Taylor to talk to the president about not getting too far out in front of a still debatable proposition. He grumbled that columnists like James Reston and Joseph Alsop were making too much of the MLF drumbeat, Reston treating the Fourth of July speech and followup press conference "as though they will dwarf the Monroe Doctrine in the history books." McNamara and Rusk, even if they were inclined to weigh in more strenuously, by September had Cuba on their minds.[38]

As for Norstad, he and his staff argued to the end that the physical presence of medium-range missiles in forward areas was vital to deterring limited aggression and that the mobility of the Soviet IRBMs that turned up in Cuba reinforced their case for land-based NATO MRBMs, but even the Joint Chiefs seemed to realize that the best chance for SACEUR to get the weapons lay in anchoring his claim to the seaborne MLF as the only plan in play. When the JCS issued the report requested by the secretary, they accepted a mix of external and theater missiles, with a stated preference for the improved land-based Missile "X" but with a bow to the "almost as good" Polaris. Norstad, allowed to ventilate his frustration, pleaded his case to Kennedy during a visit to Washington in mid-July, but Rusk's and McNamara's briefing notes for the president depict the meeting as more a gesture of courtesy than an occasion for reappraisal.[39]

After months of being marginalized, his visit to Washington in fact proved Norstad's swan song. Had the Cuban missile crisis not intervened in October, his designated successor, General Lemnitzer, would have been SACEUR throughout the fall of 1962. Instead, Lemnitzer did not assume the post until January 1963, leaving both men in Paris uncertain about their respective roles. (Lemnitzer did take over the U.S. European Command while he waited for Norstad to leave.) Despite professions of his "close personal relationship" with Lemnitzer (cited twice in one cable), Norstad fretted about the dangers of a divided command and sought reassurance from McNamara that there would be no change in his overall authority. He never received it. The Kennedy administration looked on Norstad as a troublesome holdover from the Eisenhower era and had been searching for the right moment to move him out of Europe without further rattling the Europeans. The door that slammed shut at Athens reopened for State's multilateral boosters but not Norstad.[40]

As their schedules returned to normal late in 1962 following the Cuban crisis, the secretaries of state and defense turned their attention to NATO business and the MLF matter. McNamara in particular had qualms over the message State's Europeanists were sending the allies* and information Admiral Lee was imparting on his own travels abroad. Smith and Lee were communicating details relating to MLF ownership and operation that McNamara considered premature. The defense secretary may have felt nervous over the interest being generated by the U.S. emissaries and questioned whether the allies fully grasped the extent of their fiscal obligation and that no action would be taken on the MLF without a prior

---

* On 16 November, Ball gave a major speech to a NATO gathering in Paris in which he spoke of the critical challenge of upgrading conventional forces but also allowed, in an unmistakable reference to give-and-take on the nuclear issue, that the Americans had no monopoly on wisdom and, no less than the Europeans, would have to adjust attitudes and habits. See "NATO and the Cuban Crisis," Dept of State *Bulletin*, 3 Dec 62, 831-35.

commitment to expand conventional forces. Although Rusk and Bundy agreed that Smith and Lee had not exceeded their mandate, Rusk believed the allies were still not facing up to the problems of command and control. McNamara was concerned enough about the administration's schizophrenic handling of the MLF—some were selling the concept, others pouring cold water on it, he remarked at a DoD-State conference on 30 November—that he suggested the item be kept off the NATO Council's December agenda. Still not satisfied with the JCS review of NATO MRBM requirements, he asked for additional targeting data while blocking a proposed Mediterranean Pilot Force that would have replaced missiles in Turkey and Italy with a small pilot MLF in the aftermath of the Cuban affair. The year 1962 wound down much as it had begun, with believers and unbelievers seeking to inflate and deflate the MLF balloon as it struggled to stay aloft.[41]

Impact of Nassau

The MLF topic, McNamara made sure, received no formal consideration at the 13-15 December NATO ministerial meetings. Relieved by the successful defusion of the Cuban crisis and buoyed for the moment by the effective demonstration of Western solidarity, the defense ministers were in an upbeat mood and willing to cut the Americans some slack, though worry over the Soviets' next move and the future shape of the alliance inevitably crept into the background. Taylor, who became JCS chairman in October 1962, had warned McNamara that "there would almost certainly be some spill over" of the MRBM subject during the December consultations with the allies.[42] And indeed, the sessions were punctuated with published reports, promptly denied, of behind-the-scenes deliberations in which the United States was said to be contemplating relinquishing veto power over launch of the weapons. McNamara retained an air of confidence, not unlike at Athens, that the Europeans would never accept the American "ifs" and would eventually balk at any MLF plan because of the heavy collateral responsibilities.[43]

Once again, McNamara underestimated the staying power of the MLF, this time his assumptions overtaken by the U.S. decision, in which he had a pivotal role, to cancel Skybolt, the air-launched missile on which Britain counted to maintain its measure of nuclear independence under the "special relationship" it enjoyed with the United States. The Nassau Conference of 18-21 December culminated ostensibly in an agreement with the British government to terminate Skybolt for reasons of cost and production delays,* but in reality ended in a haze of recriminations and ongoing negotiations to clarify what had been decided and how to preserve the special relationship with the British without fatally compromising the administration's larger goal of a unified European security framework.

---

* See Chapter XIV.

With the British insisting on obtaining Polaris as a substitute for Skybolt, the White House faced the challenge of how to calm British nerves and the political furor that followed Skybolt's cancellation (as well as repair the longstanding personal relationship Kennedy and other U.S. leaders had with Prime Minister Macmillan) without incurring French and German resentment and demands for their own "national" Polaris forces. The MLF beckoned again as a facile answer, at least conceptually, to a many-sided problem. The British in effect got Polaris so long as London committed to integrate its allocation into a "multilateral NATO nuclear force," with the face-saving proviso that the British could withdraw their missiles from the organization if and when "supreme national interests are at stake."[44] De Gaulle, offered the same terms, i.e., purchase of Polaris and assignment of French missiles to a NATO command except in a national emergency, rejected the overture as having too many strings attached and enhancing U.S. domination more than French security.[45] The administration, left yet again to reconcile words and actions, had to explain to West Germany and Italy why they should not be proffered the same accommodation and how such "national" dispensations squared with the U.S. commitment to collective solutions to European defense needs.

It was symptomatic of the confusion and ambiguity surrounding the Multilateral Force that in the immediate aftermath of Nassau the concept's most fervent supporters brooded over its prospects having been severely damaged by the bilateral Polaris concessions even as the Nassau bargain appeared to elevate its role and imbue it with an official imprimatur. As always with the MLF, the devil lurked in the details. The Skybolt accord was cobbled together with such vagueness—both by design and as a result of hurried preparation—that, as Richard Neustadt later wrote in his report to Kennedy, each participant could interpret the outcome from his own partisan perspective, "from his own predisposition," and find validation and a mandate for pursuing whatever course he favored.[46] That could mean a resurrection of Norstad's multinationalism, with continuing lip service to multilateralism where expedient, or a deepening genuine commitment to multilateralism as a matter of policy and principle. While Nassau may have narrowed the options available to the president (or placed them in sharper relief), it also accelerated an overdue reckoning on what course U.S. policy should take. The upshot still awaited definition.

As a White House memorandum indicated, two tracks remained open to the administration at the start of 1963 (three if one counted a combination of the two). The first focused on subsidizing British and French (if the latter could be persuaded) national MRBM forces, and entertaining possible requests from Germany, Italy, and others as well, in exchange for a loose commitment to incorporate these forces eventually into an MLF; the second, creating a bona fide multilateral mixed-manned nuclear force open to all NATO members, with a central command and yet to be determined restrictions on control of warheads.

Despite their instinctive misgivings about pursuing the MLF down any track, Kennedy and McNamara, painted into a corner by the Skybolt denouement and fearing most of all a Franco-German nuclear program in the absence of any concrete U.S.-sponsored alternative,* leaned toward the staff recommendation to press ahead with the second track. McNamara remained no less determined to subordinate any nuclear program to the conventional force priority, and indeed, on 12 January 1963, the same day that he and Rusk agreed at the White House to develop plans for the multilateral enterprise, the defense secretary asked the chairman of the JCS and the secretary of the Air Force to continue studies of NATO's capabilities for non-nuclear conflict and conventional force requirements. As for the president, he was willing to go down the MLF road to avoid the alternative of proliferation—as he told a national audience in an interview with the three television networks the evening before the Nassau conference, the worst situation would be having "ten, twenty, thirty nuclear powers who may fire their weapons off under different conditions"—but neither he nor the British were particularly enthused by the post-Nassau construction of what the two governments had seemingly consented to. On the way out of a cabinet meeting, he joked to McGeorge Bundy, "If Macmillan and I had known what we were signing we might not have signed it."[47]

By 19 January an interdepartmental steering committee had already produced an outline of what the Multilateral Force would look like. It proposed assigning to the MLF such national forces as 20 British-based U.S. B-47s, 55 British V-bombers, and three Polaris submarines, which the JCS considered an "overly large . . . initial commitment." The commander of the projected force would report to SACEUR, and its command headquarters would have representatives from each NATO nation. The United States, "at least initially," would maintain custody of the warheads and exercise a veto over their use. Participating nations would contribute a fair share of all U.S. research and development work after 1 January 1963 from which the MLF would benefit, but no single nation would be permitted a share of more than 40 percent of the personnel nor charged more than 40 percent of the cost. U.S. financial participation would depend on the other participating nations raising their defense budgets "by an amount sufficient to cover both their contribution to the multilateral nuclear force and also provide for necessary improvements in their conventional forces." To prove the seriousness with which the United States now viewed the MLF and to hasten its implemen-

---

* On 22 January, de Gaulle and Adenauer signed a Franco-German Treaty of Cooperation. The stunning development was a key factor in the more aggressive wooing of the Europeans in the direction of a full-fledged MLF. De Gaulle's refusal to participate in a NATO nuclear force and France's veto of British entry into the Common Market added a sense of urgency to firming up the MLF effort. See Winand, *Eisenhower, Kennedy, and the United States of Europe*, 333-36. A second factor was Kennedy's decision to remove the Jupiters from Italy and Turkey, which, without the promise of an MLF, would have left the two countries shorn of an auxiliary nuclear role and with the perception of a sudden unacceptable vulnerability. See Steinbruner, *Cybernetic Theory*, 252.

tation, the steering group recommended the U.S. seek approval from the North Atlantic Council for bilateral discussions within the foregoing context and that an individual with the rank of ambassador, assistant secretary, or under secretary head the negotiating team.[48]

Scrambling to assure Bonn that the appearance of a special arrangement with the British was not meant to reduce Germany to a second-class status, State's European bureau wasted no time in instructing the U.S. embassy to emphasize the multilateral language in the Nassau declaration and the integral role planned for Germany in the new scheme: "The point to be stressed with the Germans is that a major new line of policy has been unfolded at Nassau." In a message of 10 January, cleared with OSD's ISA, State wired that "Nassau permits immediate start on multilateral mixed-manned component of nuclear force." In what by any standard was a tortured characterization of the meaning of Nassau, Ball explained to the North Atlantic Council on 11 January that both the U.S. and British governments "had felt grave responsibility to take no steps re Polaris which would be prejudicial to ability of whole alliance [to] mobilize full potential for nuclear defense." Ignoring what remained a contentious issue at the Pentagon, Ball proclaimed that with respect to the mixed-manning feature of the nuclear force, the United States "believes more strongly than ever that this component is essential."[49]

The Merchant Team

The whirlwind of activity in the aftermath of Nassau led to the appointment of a State-Defense negotiating team on 24 January 1963 under the direction of Livingston Merchant, a senior foreign service official, former ambassador to NATO and assistant secretary of state for European affairs during the Eisenhower administration, and a close associate of Bowie. With Smith joining Merchant and Lee, the senior Defense member, at the head of the delegation, its leadership had a strong, experienced pro-MLF background. On 21 February the president instructed the Merchant team to investigate "as a matter of urgency . . . the possibility of an international arrangement" relating to the creation of a Multilateral Force. Merchant, Smith, and Lee, with a large support staff, traveled through Europe from 22 February to 17 March, visiting Paris, Rome, Brussels, Bonn, and London with the goal of completing preliminary agreements with the allies "preferably prior to the Italian elections in April."[50]

The record of conversations at the White House through January and February leaves no doubt that Kennedy gave the Merchant group the green light to proceed earnestly on the MLF negotiations, but he did so hesitantly. At a meeting in the president's office on 18 February, he began by expressing "deep concern" about the endeavor "and particularly the fact that the United States might be tying itself too closely to a project that might fail." Over the next several months as the MLF remained a "hot and cold item" for the president and prospects for successful conclusion of the round of preliminary agreements waxed and waned, there occurred considerable finger-pointing within the administration as to what exactly had been authorized and, if given a green light, how vigorously and explicitly the Merchant team had been instructed to advance the MLF proposition. McNamara later insisted that "the Merchant mission was simply supposed to have been a more intensive, more exploratory, version of the Smith-Lee mission" that had gone abroad in the fall of 1962. "It was supposed to have been bound by the same cautionary limits on non-commitment." Merchant's party, McNamara said, "had a restricted hunting license and they knew it." He blamed the true believers for "capturing" the Merchant operation, Owen and Schaetzel in particular choosing "to hear only the words which licensed them to proceed."*51

In truth, even objective observers had trouble discerning the mixed signals. Rusk, no friend to the MLF advocates even as he gave them a long leash, believed that Nassau represented a turning point, after which the MLF "became a real undertaking for us," whether the British were serious or not about their part of the bargain, which he admitted was never nailed down. Bundy later chided himself for not reining in the "passionate believers" who "pressed the case more sharply and against a tighter timetable" than was prudent. "I myself," Bundy wrote Kennedy in June 1963, "have not watched them as closely as I should have, and more than once I have let them persuade me to support them where I might well have been more skeptical." At the same time, Bundy observed that the administration, of necessity, had to up the ante after Nassau or "we would have left General de Gaulle a free field." McNamara himself conceded that the whole post-Nassau exercise "took on more significance than it otherwise would have" following de Gaulle's threat to polarize the alliance around the nuclear issue. Nitze, who felt McNamara did not adequately keep his top assistants and immediate staff adequately informed as to his thinking, would say in retrospect that the MLF "made sense as an interim measure to get the Germans hooked," and that even the agnostics were aboard in the absence of any other antidote to an independent European deterrent.52

In the end, there was little to distinguish Nitze's position in January 1963 from Ball's assessment that "the only thing we had was MLF. Therefore it was proper to make that the vehicle of all our efforts and to keep it in the forefront

---

* Steinbruner notes that with Ball's help, the MLF coalition at State was able to circumvent Jeffrey Kitchen, head of the politico-military affairs office, William Tyler, Schaetzel's boss in the European bureau, and "other parts of the State bureaucracy which were either unreliable [MLF] advocates or direct opponents" (Steinbruner, *Cybernetic Theory*, 250, 252-55). McNamara traced the problem to Rusk, to whom he was willing to defer as the principal voice on matters of foreign policy but faulted for being temperamentally indisposed to controlling his own staff. McNamara told Neustadt he had "great respect" for Rusk but added that Rusk's "distaste for challenging his people" prevented the secretary of state from disciplining or firing Owen and left the "hatchet work" to him. Owen, whom McNamara described as "Machiavellian," struck Neustadt as "thoughtful, indefatigable," and "capable when roused of dedication bordering on fanaticism" (draft memcon Neustadt with McNamara, 29 Jun 63, 5-6, 13, fldr Memcons-U.S., box 21, Neustadt Papers, JFKL).

of all discussions." For all his private doubts and occasional protests, McNamara was neutralized by the circumstances and up to a point, during this period as at other times, he tacitly supported the MLF while convinced as ever that long-term it would fail. If the Merchant team went about its mission too aggressively, "selling" and "arm-twisting" rather than simply "ascertaining" European interest, it seems to have made little difference—the Europeans weren't buying and as soon as the theoretical concept took on detail and definition the American sponsors, as happened repeatedly, beat a retreat.[53]

As with earlier attempts to reach closure, all the treacherous undercurrents in the MLF debate resurfaced. Even the submarine vs. merchantman quarrel, apparently resolved, reemerged when the Germans expressed uneasiness over the survivability of a surface missile platform and Merchant requested latitude to offer the Europeans the submarine option. Rickover's known hostility to basing the MLF on U.S. submarines for fear of compromising U.S. nuclear reactor technology (Rickover had met with the president on 11 February to convey his concerns directly) and presumed congressional opposition to sharing Polaris submarines with allies—along with the established cost and manning advantages of the surface mode—clinched the argument for basing the missiles on surface vessels.[54]

SHAPE and the Joint Chiefs refused to accept the mixed-manning aspect of the MLF as a given, even after Kennedy enjoined JCS Chairman Taylor and Chief of Naval Operations Anderson to heed the importance of that decision "as Merchant begins his explorations" and to work with their senior counterparts in Europe to win them over to the idea. In a personal note to the two on 21 February, the president acknowledged "there are many professional problems in operating any mixed manned force, and I know also that we have much still to do before we can say that the plan for the MLF is solid all the way through, but if we can get it through the heads of the senior military people in Europe that this is the way to get about a problem they and we share, we shall be more than halfway home." In June Lemnitzer became upset that his speech to the Western European Union Assembly had been construed as outright support for the MLF and advised Taylor that he was only speaking on the subject generally and not taking a position, "other than to indicate that I would welcome any augmentation of ACE [Allied Command Europe] nuclear capabilities regardless of the mode."[55]

New obstacles arose. Foy Kohler, U.S. ambassador to the Soviet Union, warned that the Soviets were "deadly earnest" in their distress over the possibility of eventual German control of nuclear delivery systems that could penetrate the U.S.S.R. The MLF touched a sensitive Soviet nerve, according to Kohler, and even though the nuclear force as proposed would be less menacing than a national German program, the Soviet Union would still react "with considerable alarm and perhaps with specific counter-actions." On the control issue, John McNaughton, DoD general counsel, reminded the White House of the complicated legal issues relating to any transfer of weapons even if the president retained veto authority under an agreed rule of "unanimity" whereby no missile could be fired without the unanimous consent of the participating nations. At the same time that Kennedy insisted he absolutely had no intention of giving up the U.S. veto, he acceded to Smith's and Merchant's entreaty that "the political effectiveness of the proposal would be gravely compromised if there were no modification of our existing practices," i.e., if the U.S. monopoly on ownership and control of the weapons was such that the nuclear-sharing premise became a mere charade. Kennedy, McNaughton recalled, did not fully realize the implications of transferring ownership of the weapons to the MLF, which was "in a sense a corporation owned by a bunch of countries":

> . . . It's one thing to say that we have a veto because the board of directors can't overrule us; it's quite another thing to be sure that the corporation down the line is going to behave completely consistent with our veto. There is also a question that if we have our nuclear weapons in these ships, it's conceivable that someone could compromise the design information. . . . The President would come to a meeting on the MLF and would say something like, "We shouldn't worry about this because of course we'll still own the warheads," and someone would squirm in his chair and say, "Mr. President, the decision you took three weeks ago was that we would sell the warheads to the corporation." There would be a pause while he'd think how he could have made such a decision, then they'd go through the argumentation of how you could protect design information, how you could avoid the unauthorized firing by way of international custodial units, . . . and the like. This happened twice. On each occasion he thought that we were still going to own the warheads.

It remained for Rusk to comment that any diminution of U.S. control over the MRBM force would aggravate the Soviets' "overriding fear that the Germans will somehow manage to obtain control of nuclear weapons which they can fire on their own decision."[56]

Judging from the cool European reception of the Merchant entourage, neither the Soviet Union nor MLF dissenters in the United States had reason to worry about any imminent weapons transfer. Although Merchant on his return notified Rusk that "a substantial element of the leadership of important members of the Alliance wants an MLF—and any doubts on this score in the United States should be set at rest" and a Ball-drafted telegram to the embassy in London relayed that "Merchant's team made gratifying progress" in Bonn and Rome, an unvarnished U.S. Information Agency evaluation based on a monitoring of the European press, and Merchant's own caveats, told a different story. "More doubts were raised . . . than laid to rest as the preliminary result of Mr. Merchant's European trip," read a USIA briefing dated 7 March. "Initial reaction ranged from open antagonism in France, through mounting skepticism in West Germany and Britain to qualified endorsement in Italy and Scandinavia." The Germans continued to push for a submarine instead of a surface nuclear fleet and for clarification of the control mechanism, as did the Italians. Merchant believed he could rely on the Belgians to "scramble aboard the bandwagon" despite their concern over expenditures. "The returns are not yet in," he said, "from The Hague, Ankara and Athens, but none of these will crucially affect the prospects or the outcome.... The Scandinavian countries, Portugal and Luxembourg, I consider out and in my own judgment Canada is dubious." Everywhere there was apprehension over the financial obligations of the participating countries, stemming from Merchant's calculation that the U.S. contribution would be on the order of one-third of the total funding requirement.[57]

Although Merchant felt he had made some headway with the British after a "decidedly tepid" first meeting, and that at the end of the day "the leverage we possess" would "prevent them wrecking our policy," London remained a key impediment to achieving a consensus among the allies. Even before the ink dried on the Nassau agreement, Macmillan had donned blinders and, at the prodding of the Defence Ministry, begun to hedge on the multilateral commitment, viewing the multinational provision as the crux of the document and the multilateral section as a non-binding corollary. While the Foreign Office sought to smooth over the differences with the U.S. interpretation, which emphasized the integral connection between the two and their marriage in another section, the Ministry of Defence panned the MLF as unaffordable, superfluous, and having the potential for mischief in empowering Germany and provoking the Soviet Union. Moreover, as Ball recognized, the British had their own "conditioned reflex against mixed manning."* Minister of Defence Peter Thorneycroft was adamant that the United Kingdom not relinquish its grip on nuclear independence for what seemed a feckless effort to spite de Gaulle and curry favor with the Germans. Thorneycroft derided the MLF as "a remarkably unproductive way of spending £500 million," on another occasion skewering the proposal as "the biggest piece of nonsense that anyone had ever dreamt up."[58]

Merchant put the best possible face on his mission's less than encouraging progress, trumpeting small victories and discounting significant setbacks. In his report to Rusk, followed by a meeting at the White House on 22 March, he concluded that despite sizable hurdles there was "sufficient evidence of European interest to warrant an unconditional endorsement" of a surface fleet multilateral force. He suggested placating German and Italian resistance by expressing U.S. willingness to consider a possible follow-on addition of submarines to the fleet at a later date, and recommended the administration "move ahead vigorously on all fronts" so that the preliminary agreement could be signed and sealed during the

---

* Lord Montgomery, calling the MLF "utter and complete poppycock," asked: "How can a ship fight effectively if a third of the crew is Portuguese, a third Belgian, and a third Danish? . . . You might just as well man a ship with a party of politicians" (J. W. Boulton, "NATO and the MLF," *Journal of Contemporary History*, Jul-Oct 72, 289).

president's visit to Europe in June. Kennedy agreed to write German Chancellor Adenauer and Italian Premier Fanfani seeking their approval and offering cooperation to resolve any lingering issues, but until the administration had a firmer commitment he chose to delay the start of consultations with Congress, which Merchant had urged begin early. Assistant Secretary of State for European Affairs William Tyler left for Bonn and Rome at the end of March with the pledge that "a decision to go forward now with a surface force would not preclude consideration of submarines at a later stage" and that, on the control issue, the United States was not wedded to the unanimity principle if the allies preferred a different arrangement, so long as U.S. concurrence constituted an element of any new formula. The Tyler visit, buttressed by McNamara's dispatch of Admiral Ricketts a week later to convince the Germans of the military soundness and survivability of the surface mode,* succeeded in gaining Adenauer's acquiescence in a provisional agreement with the understanding that the surface ship and veto topics could later be reexamined. With Germany in the fold and the assumption that the Italian government would follow soon after the country's spring elections, the MLF advocates seemed to have turned another corner, sustaining their momentum even though for every stumbling block they eliminated, a new one seemed to stand in the way.[59]

Slowing the Pace

Merchant had hoped that the NATO conference at Ottawa in late May would present an opportunity for putting the final pieces in place to achieve preliminary agreements with the remaining holdouts, principally Britain, and bolstering the president's position before the White House undertook discussions with Congress. But the combination of unrelenting challenges and accumulating doubts finally took their toll and slowed the MLF drive.

Both financing and operability questions increasingly clouded the picture as the allies got nearer the brink. Even the obliging Adenauer raised the money issue in his 2 May letter of assent. McNaughton recalled Kennedy wondering why the Germans would bankroll an MLF with the Americans wielding a veto over its exercise: "He would say . . ., 'If I were a German, I wouldn't be interested in this. What are you giving me that I haven't already got? . . . You're giving me something that I can't fire without the Americans firing it with me. I've already got an American force backing me up.'" The main problem, however, was Britain, whose defiant opposition to the multilateral concept underscored the fragility of the enterprise and whose conspicuous absence from the coalition made the others' participation moot in terms of the credibility and relevance of the organization.

---

* McNaughton accompanied Ricketts to explain the U.S. position on the veto question. The Germans disliked the unanimity idea not because they distrusted the United States but because they believed it gave the other European participants too much power to nullify a concerted action.

British refusal to join the club would reduce the venture to a largely U.S.-German affair and resurrect the same issue that had plagued the MLF startup after Kennedy's maiden Ottawa speech two years earlier. The Ottawa meeting in the spring of 1963 produced a cautious communiqué reminiscent of past vague affirmations. Instead of paving the way for closure on an agreement, it became an occasion for pausing and taking stock. After scrapping Merchant's June deadline, the president's advisers, including MLF staff, determined to work more deliberately toward a draft treaty without any specific timetable.[60]

With the arrival of summer, some in the administration clearly evidenced relief at the interruption in MLF negotiations. The uncertain status of the MLF gave McNamara a pretext for backpedaling on nuclear assistance to Italy, deferring a decision until "we know where we are with the MLF and are better able to judge what effect changes on the Italian political scene will have on that country's attitude toward its force modernization requirements and toward the Alliance in general." In a memorandum to the president on 15 June Bundy advised a switch in the approach to the Europeans "from pressure to inquiry." He enumerated a list of potential snags and warned the president against expending excessive political capital on the program in the face of "only grudging support among the very people in whose interest the force has been designed." Bundy said it would be wrong to abruptly abandon the MLF, that they should seek "to widen the discourse . . . instead of pressing in a somewhat nervous and narrow way for a single specific solution." His portrayal of the troubles ahead must have disposed Kennedy to confront his own doubts about the MLF. Even as the president continued to exhort his troops to stay the course and as he made every good faith effort to give Merchant's mission a chance of success (McNaughton learned that Kennedy himself actually wrote some of the paragraphs to Adenauer "making a solid pitch for the MLF"), he was too intuitive and pragmatic not to, in Taylor's words, "smell a rotten apple."[61]

Still, the MLF idea stayed very much alive in the summer of 1963. Kennedy's inspiring address at the Paulskirche in Frankfurt on 25 June paid a glowing tribute to the interdependence of the Western alliance and spoke of the need to develop "a more closely unified Atlantic deterrent, with genuine European participation." "How this can best be done," he said, "is now under discussion," though, he added, it was "in some ways more difficult to split the atom politically than it was physically." On 28 June McNamara approved Merchant's proposal for an interdepartmental coordinating committee for carrying forward MLF plans, nominating McNaughton and Ricketts as the regular Defense members and Rear Adm. N. G. Ward as Ricketts's alternate. Later in the summer Merchant set about to revive a negotiations schedule with the formation of a working group to address outstanding issues pertaining to financing, ownership, command and control, and operability arrangements. John Steinbruner notes that the will of the MLF proponents "remained undiminished. Like contemporary versions of Sisyphus, they slowly began to roll the rock back up the hill."[62]

In July Kennedy suggested a trial demonstration of the mixed-manning concept and asked DoD for a report on the feasibility of establishing an experimental mixed-manned ship or ships for that purpose. The plan called for using a guided missile destroyer to enable MLF participants to become proficient in the maintenance and operation of complex electronic and other systems and/or a naval auxiliary ship to practice more routine mixed-crew training. The ship(s) would operate as part of the U.S. Sixth Fleet in the Mediterranean and the U.S. Second Fleet in the Atlantic, and participate in U.S. and NATO exercises as appropriate. A U.S. naval officer would command any vessel involved in the project and, while no single nation would have a majority of the crew, the administration thought it desirable that no less than half the personnel on a U.S. ship be U.S. nationals. McNamara had concurred in the demonstration so long as it did not signify any commitment to advancing MLF negotiations or the draft of a treaty. As late as October the president seemed intrigued with the idea as both a test case and an earnest of U.S. sincerity, at little downside cost, that might also buy some time to get the British to come around while keeping the Germans engaged.[63]

Implementation of the mixed-manning experiment, and the fate of the MLF, would fall to Kennedy's successor. With the president's assassination in November 1963, along with dramatic political developments in Germany and Britain that saw Adenauer and Macmillan ousted from office in October, inevitably the MLF campaign slackened during a reevaluative transitional period. Whether the MLF would have continued to evolve and come to fruition had Kennedy lived is grist for speculation, but he did give signs of wearying of trying to rescue a concept that he knew full well—from his own June travels in Europe and Bundy's constant reminders—had little real constituency outside the State Department's European bureau. Neustadt's extensive interviews with White House staff members in 1963 reveal a president who had neither devotion toward nor illusions about the achievement of a shared nuclear force, and by the fall of that year it seemed only a matter of time before he would have lost patience and interest as well. The demonstration project may have afforded a graceful means to keep the MLF "on ice" while Kennedy turned his attention to a test ban treaty and other possibly more attainable goals.[64]

Johnson and the MLF

At a meeting in the White House on 6 December 1963, senior officials briefed the new president, Lyndon Johnson, on the status of the Multilateral Force prior to the semiannual NATO session scheduled for later that month in Paris. Both McNamara and Rusk urged caution, with McNamara repeating his familiar refrain of "no military requirement for the MLF" and Rusk interjecting that they really could not know the nature and extent of future U.S. missile requirements until they analyzed the latest intelligence estimates on Soviet nuclear activity. The importance of continuity in relations with the allies received emphasis in a State Department paper prepared for the conference. State expected MLF would not be a prime topic since "no aspect of this subject [nuclear control in the alliance] is ripe for action at this time" and the "basic problem . . . is still very far from solution."[65]

Johnson had little experience and not much appetite for foreign affairs compared with his cosmopolitan predecessor. Philip Geyelin wrote that for all his robust qualities the provincial Texan "had no taste and scant preparation for the deep waters of foreign policy." Furthermore, he had little in common by temperament or upbringing with the Eastern intellectuals who dominated the New Frontier's inner circle and the party's foreign policy establishment. Yet he felt secure enough to retain members of Kennedy's brain trust, and in the end he relied on their judgment and advice to a greater degree than the more cerebral and introspective Kennedy. In foreign affairs especially the central cast remained much the same, with Rusk and McNamara gaining influence and McGeorge Bundy, while staying on as national security adviser, losing some clout in a White House environment less tight and intimate.[66]

The presence of so many key holdovers promised a smooth transition, but what that portended for the MLF was anybody's guess. Among the older hands there remained both unbowed believers in the multilateral principle like Ball and Rostow, and determined opponents. Even as McNamara and Bundy rode the brake on the multilateral negotiations, the MLF contingent hoped the Johnson changeover might jump-start them.

To some extent MLF proponents had grounds for optimism. The president gave his blessing to the mixed-manning demonstration project in January 1964,* consented to preliminary consultations with Congress that Kennedy had finally authorized shortly before he died, and in April conveyed what sounded like a forthright endorsement of "the establishment of a multilateral nuclear force composed of those nations which desire to participate." At a key meeting at the White House on 10 April attended by Ball, Finletter, Rostow, and Smith (who had succeeded Merchant as the head of the MLF's negotiating team), with McNamara notably absent and DoD not represented, Ball requested intensifying congressional contacts with an eye to drafting a charter and possibly achieving a signed agreement by year's end. Finletter opined that "the U.S. had to stop being diffident about the MLF" and "if the President would give the go-ahead sign, the MLF would be accepted by a number of countries." Johnson directed that State

---

* The U.S.S. *Biddle* (later renamed the U.S.S. *Ricketts* after the death in July of the admiral most closely associated with the MLF) began assembling a crew from six NATO nations and the United States and set sail in October. See Glenn T. Seaborg, *Stemming the Tide: Arms Control in the Johnson Years*, 108.

broaden its discussions with the appropriate congressional committees, but with Bundy registering Defense's "serious reservations" and other complicating factors coming to light, the meeting concluded with not as affirmative a consensus or as committed a commander in chief as the MLF faithful chose to portray.[67]

Still, activity over the spring and summer of 1964 did nothing to dispel the impression that the administration was energetically pursuing a multilateral force objective. McNamara himself endorsed expanding the sharing of nuclear information with the allies (assuming no transfer of weapons) and asked the Joint Chiefs to undertake a comprehensive study of prospective MLF command and control procedures, with particular attention to the prevention of unauthorized or accidental detonation. In August he wrote Rep. George Mahon, chairman of the House defense appropriations subcommittee, professing his "personal support and that of the Defense Department for this important program." Yet the defense secretary designated Nitze, who moved over from ISA to become secretary of the Navy in November 1963, and McNaughton, who took over ISA in July 1964, as his principal representatives on MLF matters—neither of whom was keen on the MLF, or for that matter in the past had masked his disdain for the idea.[68]

Had the European allies become more receptive and given the latest movement some impetus, events might have taken a different course. But with the exception of Germany, not a single country was strongly committed to the plan in the summer of 1964. In Britain, where the Conservative Party had replaced Macmillan as prime minister with Alec Douglas-Home, neither major political party was supportive, and indeed Bundy's assessment a year earlier that "almost no one with any political standing is personally favorable to the MLF" still applied. With scathing sarcasm, the London *Times* defense correspondent observed that "a fleet of missile firing ships, manned by polyglot crews and wearing ensigns of many colours, has begun to stream erratically through the exposed and turbulent waters of Anglo-American relations." Italy continued to demur under a musical-chairs succession of governments. Greece and Turkey expressed a wish to participate but had no funds to spare (Kennedy had characterized them as "waiting only for a complimentary ticket"). The Netherlands showed some warmth toward the MLF, but its decision, like Belgium's, appeared to be predicated on what the British decided. The remaining NATO members, including France and Canada, excluded themselves entirely, with France becoming ever more adversarial and threatening to leave the alliance.[69]

Even German support appeared to waver for lack of evident progress and worry over alienating de Gaulle. Johnson huddled with German Chancellor Ludwig Erhard in Washington in June for a wide-ranging review of the international scene, including a pro forma reaffirmation of the two nations' commitment to produce an MLF agreement by December. But the British then introduced a potential poison pill with the proposal of an alternate concept, an Atlantic Nuclear Force (ANF), that married their preference for a federation of national nuclear forces with a token element of mixed manning. They suggested a mixed-manned force consisting of select strike aircraft and land-based missiles (over time both the Pershing and ICBM Minuteman were mentioned); the latter, of course, were anathema to McNamara even as the land-based MRBM on the European continent appealed to Norstad's disciples at the Pentagon, who relished the opportunity to revisit the land-based option, though minus the mixed-manning provision. McNamara, in an ironic turn as MLF champion, tried as best he could to squash the British initiative, urging German Defense Minister Kai-Uwe von Hassel to "keep the door open" to the British proposal as a "possible add-on" to the surface missile fleet but not permit it to sidetrack the American plan. Nonetheless, with Labour's Harold Wilson succeeding Douglas-Home in October and eagerly embracing the ANF concept as politically advantageous, with the Dutch and Belgians taking their lead from London, and with the French and Germans reacting to dueling propositions that further muddied the nuclear relationships among the allies, there resulted renewed uncertainty over the status of the MLF.[70]

At home, too, the MLF was running into trouble. Leery House and Senate leaders, particularly members of the Joint Committee on Atomic Energy, skeptical of the ability to maintain secrecy and security under conditions of nuclear sharing, postponed scheduled hearings and kept MLF lobbyists at arm's length. Both on the Hill and at the White House, the combination of the long road leading up to the November elections, the momentous civil rights legislation that dominated the U.S. national agenda through much of 1964, and especially the unfolding events in Southeast Asia, shunted the tangled MLF negotiations to the periphery. Protecting Johnson in a way he felt he had not adequately served Kennedy, Bundy finally harnessed State's MLF operatives, whom he deprecated in a blistering memo for the president as free-lancing zealots with a "passionate commitment to their own view of Europe."* Johnson accepted Bundy's recommendation to clear all MLF activity through the White House, including the requirement that all officials traveling overseas on MLF business have specific written instructions and that the secretaries of state and defense designate officials authorized to talk to the press on the subject. With the national security adviser's procedural guidance formally issued as NSAM No. 318 on 14 November, the administration would speak with one voice on the MLF, even if only to deliver an epitaph.[71]

Demise

By the time the Johnson administration refocused on the MLF late in 1964, the plan had lost much of the traction it gained earlier in the year. A coalescing of

---

* Bundy also took a mild swipe at McNamara for paying more attention to sales than statecraft, referring in the memo to the secretary's fretting over the U.S. losing aircraft market-share to the British when helping U.K. business would be good politics: "One of our jobs is to introduce McNamara the statesman to McNamara the merchant and make sure they do not get in each other's way."

circumstances and pressures—congressional coolness, Allied disinterest, French hostility, Soviet anxiety, State and DoD's increasing absorption with Vietnam, and the eleventh-hour diversion created by the British hybrid alternative—proved too inhibiting for even the MLF diehards to overcome.

As part of the retooling in NSAM 318, Bundy recommended the suspension of any end-of-the-year deadline while using the occasion of Prime Minister Wilson's December visit to the White House to take a final stab at softening the British position. Although he, Rusk, McNamara, and Ball all viewed the MLF as "the least unsatisfactory means of keeping the Germans well tied into the alliance," they strongly opposed a mere bilateral German-American pact and felt they had to keep the British "in the game." Bundy appears to have been influenced, or reinforced, by a 10 October memo from NSC aide David Klein advising that if they were not careful, the MLF could weaken rather than strengthen NATO and lead to disintegration rather than unification. Klein also showed sensitivity, as certainly did Bundy, to the effect failure would have on the president's political stature. They had to give Johnson as well as Erhard and Wilson a graceful exit. "The last thing we want to do," Klein wrote Bundy, "is tie this MLF millstone around the President's neck . . . ." They had to broaden the MLF into something Germany and Great Britain could both accept or "tailor . . . tactics so that the amount of broken political crockery will be minimized." Searching to "make the British and the Germans see their common interest in agreement," Bundy was even willing to contemplate "a new name for the enterprise," posing the title "Atlantic missile force" that was barely distinguishable from the British ANF.[72]

Bundy further consolidated MLF responsibility under a small ad hoc committee consisting of McNamara, Rusk, Ball, and himself, with Neustadt, who stayed on after completing his Skybolt report, managing the staff work and directing preparations for the Wilson meeting with Johnson.[73] Whether the ANF represented a serious attempt to resolve the Anglo-American impasse dating to Nassau, as the British maintained,[74] or merely a ploy to abort the MLF in order to cling to the vestiges of a national nuclear deterrent, the proposal of a mixed-manned land-based Pershing or Minuteman force got no acceptance. Minuteman especially was a "non-starter," Bundy said, wiring Neustadt in London at the end of November that "U.S. Congress and military would find security threat in mixed manned Minuteman overwhelming . . . . A surface ship is a very simple machine compared to a silo, and if difficulties of sailing with foreigners trouble the Earl of Burma [Admiral Lord Mountbatten], he should consider living underground with wogs next to a megaton." A few days earlier he told Ball that looking at "a deeply reluctant and essentially unpersuaded Great Britain," "a protracted and difficult Congressional struggle," and increasing strains in the alliance, "the MLF is not worth it."[75]

Wilson's 6-9 December visit to Washington followed a flurry of last-minute memos and conversations anticipating German, British, and French reactions to various scenarios, with the gathering realization that the likelihood of forging a compromise that would satisfy all the principals was close to nil and perhaps not even desirable at this point. A chief concern on the eve of Wilson's arrival was that even if the parties could reconcile the British and German positions, de Gaulle, sensing that the MLF was verging on success, might turn up the heat on the Germans and threaten to wreak havoc with NATO and Franco-German relations. With a lull in the Cold War, a Franco-German nuclear partnership becoming increasingly unlikely as relations between the two countries became more tense, and the prospect of an independent German nuclear initiative in the absence of an MLF also diminishing, the greater danger to some now seemed to lie in the rupture of the alliance and needless provocation of the Soviets over an ill-conceived, awkwardly imposed nuclear arrangement that had more cosmetic value than strategic relevance. To Bundy, the risk of ill-advised action had come to outweigh the risk of inaction. In a memo to the president on 6 December 1964, the day before the meeting of the U.S. and British leaders, he gave Johnson a summation of how "the devil's advocate would state your choices":

> (1) *If* you go full steam ahead, you face a long, hard political fight, a major confrontation with de Gaulle, and a possibility of defeat or delay which would gravely damage the prestige of the President.
> (2) *If* you go half steam ahead, there will probably be no MLF, but it will not be your fault alone. . . . Your wisdom, caution and good judgment will have the praise of liberals, of military men, of the British, of the French, and of many Germans—and you will have freedom to make a different choice later if you wish.[76]

A suddenly engaged Johnson believed the German question still critical and worried that the Germans would not wait long to develop their own separate deterrent if they felt themselves consigned to the role of nuclear outsiders in NATO's power structure. The president and his senior advisers went through "five days of stormy intramural debate," with McNamara somewhat surprisingly joining Ball in arguing for a stronger pro-MLF U.S. stance to break the impasse. The defense secretary may have felt obliged to side with what he perceived as the president's inclination, or he may have feared that in the absence of an agreement a later fallback might entail a land-basing concession. In the end Johnson bowed to political realities and the futility of pressing the case with a Congress every bit as uncomfortable with the MLF's unanswered questions as the European legislatures, and that from long experience he recognized as insurmountably arrayed against the concept.[77]

Johnson chose, then, not to force the issue with Wilson during two days of insubstantial talks, after which the pair distributed a bland communiqué pledging continued cooperation in pursuit of a unified Atlantic strategic nuclear defense. The real message that came out of the anticlimactic summit lay in NSAM 322, issued eight days after the prime minister's departure and spelling out the effective demise of the MLF. It declared that the United States remained committed as ever to the collective, integrated defense of the Atlantic alliance but would leave it to the allies to propose what form the nuclear arrangements should take, on the understanding that under any plan the United States would retain a veto for the foreseeable future over firing of the weapons. Further, the president emphasized, any agreement should take into account the legitimate interests of both Great Britain and Germany and reflect French "opinion and . . . desires" as well. For good measure, the president removed any timetable and placed a gag order prohibiting "any American official in any forum to press for a binding agreement at this time." So deadening was the message that McNamara appears to have made no significant reference to the MLF at the December meeting of the North Atlantic Council, nor did the council communiqué on 17 December give any indication that the subject ever came up for discussion.[78]

To insure that Wilson did not spin the outcome to suggest that the president had tilted toward the British or dropped the MLF for the ANF, or lest the impression result that the United States had succumbed to French or Soviet pressure, Johnson leaked NSAM 322 to James Reston of the *New York Times*, who conveyed the thrust of the document from the White House perspective in an article of 21 December 1964. As Harlan Cleveland, who would succeed Finletter as U.S. ambassador to NATO, observed, Johnson essentially adopted the posture Bundy had recommended to both Johnson and Kennedy, "namely to encourage the enthusiasts to see if they could bring it off, but not get committed to it personally." Although Johnson would remain solicitous to efforts at home and abroad to resuscitate the MLF, announcing, for example, at a press conference on 16 January 1965 that "we will continue to follow the progress of these talks with the greatest of interest," the resignation of Smith (the day of the Reston story) and the dismantling of the State Department's MLF unit by year's end put into sharp relief how fatal a blow had befallen the multilateral concept.[79]

The downhill spiral would continue for another year until the MLF finally expired at the close of 1965. Owen and remnants of the band of true believers stayed on in other capacities, refusing to give up hope completely and seizing the occasional vital sign as a reward for their vigil. Ball and Rostow remained influential advisers who continued to preach the merits of multilateralism but mostly to their own small chorus of followers. McNamara told Bundy in March 1965 that DoD had "already begun to give thought here to some 'more modest possibilities.'" In April the defense secretary, perhaps being polite, conceded to Ball that a new look at the problem "could be quite useful" and asked McNaughton to serve as DoD's representative for a study of both the ANF and MLF. At a NATO defense ministers' meeting in Paris 31 May-1 June, McNamara proposed a select committee on nuclear planning that could provide an organizational means of sharing nuclear responsibility while avoiding physical transfers of the weapons, the consideration of which had caused so much contention. Subsequently, the thrust of the administration's nuclear-sharing deliberations increasingly shifted from hardware remedies to consultation on issues relating to nuclear technology and policy, culminating with DoD's establishment of a NATO Nuclear Planning Group in 1966.[80]

Finletter was gone by September 1965. In October, with all but the last nails in the coffin, a paper probably authored by Bundy, who was as responsible as any member of the Johnson administration for removing the MLF from the nation's agenda, offered last rites and an overblown eulogy with the comment that the MLF had been "one of the best motivated and most imaginative [proposals] that the US has put forward in the last 15 years." As late as 8 November John Leddy, who had become assistant secretary of state for European affairs in June, tried to coax one last gasp with a plea to Rusk to urge the president and McNamara to reconsider a genuine collective nuclear weapons system rather than mere consultative arrangements. The end came, appropriately, with a visit to the White House by Chancellor Erhard in December, almost a year to the date of Wilson's visit and the issuance of NSAM 322. In a sense the other shoe in the Anglo-German standoff now dropped. Prior to the meeting with Erhard, Bundy advised the president that "the Germans no longer really expect that we will support a MLF, and I believe that if you and Erhard could reach a firm agreement . . . that no new weapons system is necessary, the way might be open toward a non-proliferation treaty and toward a new collective arrangement for command control and consultation in NATO." Erhard gamely importuned Johnson on the need to share actual ownership of weapons, but in essence acknowledged in the official joint statement that the time had come to let go and move on. For all practical purposes, the passing of the Multilateral Force occurred with that meeting, on 20 December 1965.[81]

One of the more astute postmortems on the failure of the MLF came from Alastair Buchan, whose early obituary in October 1964 noted prophetically: "It may well be, therefore, that the MLF will in the end prove to have been nothing but an expensive and time consuming detour on the road to a more effective system of political and strategic planning among the Western allies . . . a solution which became blocked by reason of French chauvinism, British hesitations and a series of false American judgments."[82]

John Steinbruner defined the central dilemma among the several inherent flaws that plagued the MLF: "To grant the Europeans some control over nuclear weapons was the politically indicated course of action; to deny any dispersion of control was the militarily indicated course." The conceit was plausible so long as the MLF, in Steinbruner's words, was "carefully wrapped in vagueness." Though McNamara and OSD countenanced the MLF for a time as "a military toy to keep the children quiet," to use Buchan's phrase, they kept it on a short leash when it threatened to deflect funds and priority from the conventional forces or undermine centralized U.S. control of the nuclear trigger.[83]

McNamara, unless one understands that he never bought into the principle, and bestowed or withdrew DoD support for the plan depending on the bureaucratic or political vicissitudes of the moment, appears uncharacteristically equivocal if not sometimes paradoxical in his attitude toward the MLF. For such a rigorous analytical thinker to blow so hot and cold reflected, as Steinbruner explains, the distinct separation in his mind between the political and military dimensions of the issue and his acceptance of the political rationale even when it collided with conviction and logic.[84] Years later McNamara himself would explain simply that he went along with the MLF as a half-baked solution to a political problem if it satisfied the Europeans' need for a greater sense of nuclear security, even if they grossly exaggerated the effectiveness of its deterrent value. "I didn't believe that it was a very satisfactory solution," he said in a 1986 interview, "but I did recognize the [political] problem. If the Europeans were willing to accept the MLF as the solution to the problem, then I was willing to support the MLF, and I did so on that limited basis. It turned out the Europeans weren't willing to support it, and therefore we withdrew it."[85]

Bundy would later say that the MLF drew its nourishment from a hope and a fear: "a hope to turn nuclear weapons into an instrument for advancing the unity of Europe, and . . . a fear that without membership in this shared force, the Germans would be dangerously drawn to the French and British course of national nuclear capability. The hope proved unattainable, and the fear groundless."[86] If on occasion McNamara and for that matter even Bundy seemed to have a kinship with the State Department's more ideologically driven adherents, it was because, however profound the difference in their temperaments and perspectives, they in fact shared an abiding interest in the non-proliferation goal—persuading Germany to forgo an independent nuclear program and, beyond that, preventing the proliferation of national nuclear systems generally. Although with hindsight it became clear that Washington's fear of nuclear proliferation within the Atlantic alliance was as overstated as the Europeans' fear of nuclear isolation, the MLF proved useful in providing an outlet for nervous allies to ventilate and a breathing spell for Washington, too, during a dangerous interval in the Cold War. If the multilateral effort did not foster the grand design, the level of integration that was the enthusiasts' dream, it may have helped avert the disintegration that constituted their worst nightmare by buying time for the alliance to figure out a new paradigm for the West's nuclear arrangements in a world of dramatically changing technologies and strategies. To that extent, the multilateral venture realized some lasting redeeming significance despite its unfulfilled vision and ultimate and mostly unlamented demise.

CHAPTER XVI

The Embattled Military Assistance Program

Military assistance from the United States to its allies began with the huge lend-lease program in World War II that helped Britain, Free France, the Soviet Union, China, and other countries. At the onset of the Cold War, a few short years after World War II, the United States found it prudent to reinstitute military assistance on a global scale to nations threatened by communist aggression. By 1961, after more than a decade of such help, the goal of using economic and military aid to rebuild war-torn nations of Europe and Asia to prevent the spread of communism seemed fulfilled. In the meantime, new challenges raised by what seemed an expanding communist threat made distant corners of the globe appear vital to U.S. security. Soviet Premier Khrushchev's encouragement in January 1961 of wars of national liberation further impelled the United States to assure threatened nations they would receive help from Washington. Yet by the end of the Eisenhower era, congressional and public sentiment was turning against foreign assistance to what some considered ungrateful allies and unworthy recipients.[1] The new administration undertook to reverse that trend and reinvigorate foreign aid. Its initiatives, energetically advanced in the spirit of the New Frontier, sought to overhaul and redirect the Military Assistance Program (MAP) to make it more efficient and responsive.

Adjusting the FY 1962 Budget

Military assistance and economic assistance were the two components of the foreign aid program, under the overall supervision of the International Cooperation Administration (ICA), a semi-autonomous agency in the Department of State. The secretary of defense managed MAP with the help of the assistant secretary for international security affairs, to whom he delegated broad powers for executing the program. The Joint Chiefs and the military departments provided advice and recommendations on all aspects of military assistance. Within DoD there always existed the need to coordinate and balance the military assistance and the military sales programs, which obviously had an important effect on each other.

The proper balance between economic and military assistance programs had long been a contentious issue between State and Defense and in Congress. Both programs were part of the Mutual Security Program (MSP) budget, and transfers of available funds between the two often occurred by mutual consent. Congress had always played a powerful role in determining both the funding and the organization for foreign aid. From one year to the next, funding the foreign aid program remained a prolonged and complex process in both the executive and legislative branches of the government.

From the beginning, Kennedy's transition team considered the MAP process deficient because it did not offer the president alternative budget plans and did not spell out the implications of military aid. State Department planners held that military aid served numerous non-military purposes—securing U.S. base rights, countering communist military assistance, maintaining internal security, sustaining pro-American regimes, and nation-building, which were ICA goals as well. Designing MAP solely on the basis of military considerations would not always best serve U.S. interests.[2]

Intent on continuing foreign aid programs, Kennedy was just as determined to reverse the balance of payments deficit to maintain the integrity of the dollar and a sound U.S. economy. To reconcile these seemingly contradictory policies, one month after taking office Kennedy instructed his staff to develop means "for fair sharing in both foreign aid and military partnership" with the European allies as well as methods to ease the balance of payments deficits. He believed such measures would demonstrate to Congress and the American people the value of foreign assistance.[3]

On 25 February 1961 Rusk, McNamara, Budget Director David Bell, and others met to discuss the FY 1962 MAP budget. ISA Deputy Assistant Secretary William Bundy offered a figure of nearly $2.4 billion in new obligational authority (NOA)* (originally proposed to Eisenhower by State and Defense) as opposed to $1.8 billion agreed to by Eisenhower. He justified the larger amount by pointing to the administration's strong emphasis on coping with conventional and low-intensity conflict and the priority on promoting self-sustaining growth in the underdeveloped countries. Bundy introduced the idea of the United States serving as "the arsenal of the free world," by which he meant greatly expanding export of military equipment and services to developing countries through cost-sharing assistance.[4]

When the ensuing discussion revealed the many obstacles MAP faced, Rusk and McNamara deferred a substantive review because there was insufficient time to work through the issues before the March deadline for submission of the

---

* Unless otherwise indicated, all money figures are NOA.

amendments to the FY 1962 budget. Instead, within the next 10 days McNamara would provide funding levels and other recommendations for State's consideration.[5] These ideas—cost-sharing, the proper mix of military and economic aid, and shifting MAP to the DoD budget—held McNamara's attention throughout his tenure.

Although the Joint Chiefs supported ISA's recommendation to increase the FY 1962 funding to $2.365 billion, McNamara informed Rusk on 7 March that the final figure depended on the amounts requested for military assistance and economic aid, the extent of Allied cost-sharing, and the size of the DoD budget. He suggested to Rusk that they delay a joint recommendation until these matters were settled. The president, however, made his preference clear when he informed Congress on 22 March of his intention to submit a total $4 billion foreign aid request, of which only $1.6 billion was for military assistance. Kennedy also proposed legislation to integrate the separate government aid programs[*] under a single agency.[6]

Meanwhile, on 15 March Rusk proposed to McNamara a joint State-Defense study to determine how best to formulate MAP's future role in promoting U.S. strategic interests. Without awaiting a formal reply,[†] in late March he appointed Charles Burton Marshall of State's Policy Planning Council to begin the study.[7] OSD contributed to the study, but without consulting the Joint Chiefs, the service secretaries, or the unified commands, all of whom had important roles in formulating MAP programs and budgets.[8] Marshall's report, issued on 17 May, recommended long-term military assistance programs to improve forces and thereby reaffirm the resolve of the United States "not just to hold a line but to push on to required achievements in joint security." The cost for this ambitious program, Marshall estimated, would be between $750 million and $1 billion in addition to the $1.6 billion FY 1962 authorization already requested.[9]

McNamara and Rusk pared the figures, and the following day recommended to the president that because of "the gravity of the present international situation" $400 million should be added to the MAP budget. Such action would give substance to the new emphasis on greater and more rapid assistance to threatened countries. But it would require public and congressional support. Rusk had previously advised Kennedy that a bold and imaginative program had a "better chance of Congressional approval and popular acclaim" than more of the same old Cold War military assistance rhetoric. In the end, on 25 May Kennedy reduced the proposed increase to $285 million and justified a total request for $1.885 billion by citing the deepening crisis in Southeast Asia and growing needs in Latin America and Africa.[10]

---

[*] These included the ICA, Export-Import Bank, Peace Corps, Food-for-Peace, and Development Loan Fund.

[†] DoD Deputy Secretary Gilpatric formally concurred with Rusk's recommendations on 29 March. See *FRUS 1961-63*, IX:241.

Perhaps more significant than the revised amount, however, was DoD's accompanying proposed legislation to (1) streamline MSP procedures by sharply delineating between economic and military assistance to allow each program to be evaluated on its own merits; (2) continue the three-year authorization authority to ensure stability in long-range planning; (3) raise the $55 million ceiling on military aid to Latin America to $60 million; and (4) repeal the 1954 prohibition against using MAP funding for internal security purposes in these nations. Finally, OSD recommended authorization for the president to furnish up to $400 million from U.S. military stocks as emergency aid to threatened countries. If used, this would be in addition to the $1.885 billion authorization request. During their early June 1961 hearings, members of the usually sympathetic House Foreign Affairs Committee had little difficulty with the increased funding request, but some bristled at the proposed amending legislation as a threat to their prerogatives and "an expression of no confidence in Congress."[11]

Legislative leaders informed the White House that the foreign aid bill was in trouble with possible cuts of 20 to 30 percent. These estimates proved exaggerated. However, McNamara did encounter tough questions during committee hearings from Rep. Otto E. Passman (D-La.), the irascible chairman of the House Appropriations Subcommittee on Foreign Operations Appropriations, who loathed foreign aid and was determined to kill what he deemed a wasteful program.[12]

Passman insisted that provisions for funding contingencies already written into the budget made the $400 million transfer authority unnecessary. Allowing the president to transfer funds without any congressional approval, Passman remarked, would just be adding $400 million to the MAP budget. McNamara objected that the authority was tightly controlled and necessary for rapid, decisive action at times Congress was not in session. Unimpressed, Passman dryly remarked that based on his 13 years on the committee he had observed that "there is practically always an emergency."[13]

On 4 August the House Foreign Affairs Committee authorized $1.8 billion, a slight reduction of $85 million from the May request, because members remained unconvinced events warranted the additional funds. Their Senate counterparts approved only $1.55 billion. A compromise on the part of the House managers of the legislation authorized $1.7 billion for each of FYs 1962 and 1963 budgets. DoD's legislative proposals fared poorly. Aware of congressional opposition, OSD dropped its request to separate MAP and economic funding. Congress adopted a two-year authorization, not the extended one requested by McNamara. The House and Senate split their differences and authorized $300 million for the controversial presidential authority to draw from DoD stocks for emergency aid. On 31 August both chambers passed the Foreign Assistance Act of 1961, and President Kennedy signed it into law on 4 September.[14]

As requested by Kennedy in his March message to Congress, the 1961 Foreign Assistance Act established the Agency for International Development (AID), which on 3 October 1961 replaced the International Cooperation Administration and the Development Loan Fund.* The secretary of state retained responsibility "for the continuous supervision and general direction of the assistance programs." Guided by the act and the recommendations of a presidential task force, AID took over not only responsibility for foreign assistance but also for coordinating economic and military assistance.[15]

The 1961 authorization act had as its principal objective the shifting of military assistance from grant-aid to sales so that Allied countries, especially those recovered from World War II, would pay for a greater share of their defense. New authority enabled the president to offer investment guaranties to encourage private enterprise initiatives in developing countries by protecting American businessmen from investment loss resulting from war, revolution, expropriation, or confiscation by foreign governments. The law also broadened the president's ability to sell military equipment to friendly nations on credit terms. The administration expected these measures would encourage sales of U.S.-manufactured weapons and equipment by the private sector to friendly countries, thus helping to reduce the nation's balance of payments deficit. Fees charged for credit guaranties and money from sales would be placed in a revolving account established by Congress to finance additional sales until the reserve was exhausted.[16]

The $1.7 billion authorization, however, met opposition from Passman in the appropriations committee. On 1 September, he proposed an appropriation of $1.3 billion, feeling that the $300 million in presidential emergency authority and DoD recoupments from previous years would make up any shortfalls. Twelve days later, however, the Senate Appropriations Committee recommended the full $1.7 billion. The conference committee compromised on a $1.6 billion appropriation. On 30 September Congress voted that amount for military assistance, Kennedy's original 22 March request.[17]

Of the total available for FY 1962, just over 50 percent went to a handful of countries—Greece, Iran, Turkey, Republic of China (Taiwan), South Korea, and South Vietnam. MAP underwrote new equipment—166 F-104 and RF-104 jet aircraft, including 94 for future delivery to Greece, Turkey, Taiwan, and Korea; thousands of jeeps and trucks for Iran, Pakistan, Turkey, Taiwan, and Korea; hundreds of tanks, including 135 for Greece and 54 for Korea; Nike surface-to-air missiles for Taiwan and Korea; and ground-to-ground missiles for Greece, Turkey, and Iran. Military assistance planners earmarked FY 1962 money to increase South Vietnamese forces from 170,000 to 200,000 and to develop a special logistics base in Thailand. Altogether 57 nations received grant military aid in FY 1962, ranging from almost $275 million for South Korea to $20,000 for Sudan.[18]

Equipment might be substituted, deferred, or withdrawn from delivery, depending on the situation. At the end of FY 1962 the lag between obligation of

---

*E.O. 10973, 3 November 1961, set the terms for the establishment of the Agency for International Development.

funds for equipment and services and the actual delivery of the items had created a cumulative unexpended balance for grant-aid military assistance, the so-called "pipeline," of $2.784 billion, despite delivering $1.375 billion in assistance by 30 June 1962. MAP could, of course, be adapted and expedited when necessary. To improve mobility of South Vietnamese forces, the FY 1962 program added 5 more helicopters to the 18 already programmed in FY 1961. All were delivered by the end of FY 1962. Conversely, 10 transport or liaison aircraft for Vietnam programmed in FY 1962 would not be delivered until sometime after July 1962.

In April 1962 Comptroller Charles Hitch reported to McNamara that the program was in such disarray that a different approach was needed. McNamara then ordered ISA to revalidate the undelivered balances, and henceforth he took personal interest in expediting MAP deliveries. His efforts would lower the pipeline balance by one-third by FY 1965. Because aircraft, tanks, and wheeled vehicles usually were delivered in installments, however, a backlog persisted.[19]

Latin America

The painful experience with Cuba in 1961 caused the administration to pay new attention to the military assistance program for Latin America. Throughout the previous decade military aid to Latin America had centered on the defense of the hemisphere against external enemies. The focus changed in 1961. Guided by the lessons of the Bay of Pigs, the U.S. government identified the major threat as internal subversion inspired by Cuban revolutionaries.[20]

Accordingly, the administration pressed Congress to repeal the 1954 prohibition against using MAP funds for internal security purposes in Latin America and to increase funding in FY 1962 above the $55 million ceiling. Supplying arms to Latin America was always a sensitive topic, and committee members complained that mere military aid would only create unnecessary armies commanded by "front men" or "stooges of the United States." McNamara offered vigorous testimony at congressional hearings in June 1961, citing the Cuban threat and urging the importance of raising the ceiling on military aid for internal security, though he would later acknowledge that "military programs alone will not solve the problems of instability which arise from the continued economic difficulties in much of Latin America." Asking for $60 million for internal security assistance in addition to the $600 million Congress had appropriated for economic assistance, he deemed it "a small price to pay—10 cents on the dollar—for the maintenance of the stable political conditions necessary to allow economic growth to proceed." Sen. George Aiken (R-Vt.) worried whether arms and materiel given directly to Latin American governments might strengthen the power of dictators or set off wars against neighbors. Admitting the validity of such concerns, McNamara claimed that "the program we are presenting will not in any way contribute to a so-called arms race in Latin America." McNamara's assurance did not allay congressional unease, but it was only in 1963 that Congress imposed a ceiling of $57.5 million for military equipment programmed in a single fiscal year for Latin America, at the same time adding approximately $20 million in defense services annually.[21]

In a genuine effort to help address the larger problem and as a potential bulwark against the penetration of Castro's communism in the Western Hemisphere, in 1961 Kennedy initiated the Alliance for Progress, an ambitious cooperative program for economic and social development. The alliance was formalized by 19 Latin American countries and the United States in a treaty signed at Punta del Este, Uruguay, on 17 August. McNamara told the House Armed Services Committee later "that the military assistance program has reinforced, and has been reinforced by, U.S. efforts under the Alliance for Progress." He emphasized that "the largest part of our military assistance program for Latin America is . . . specifically tailored to help provide communication and transportation equipment and internal security training."[22]

Friction between State and Defense over military assistance to Latin America developed and persisted throughout 1961 and into 1962. A State Department report in April 1962 appeared to blame the military in Latin American nations for Castro's success in making "his influence felt in every country. With the exception of Uruguay, every country is far from stable." An even more pessimistic assessment in August 1962 reflected State's criticism of the military assistance programs, focusing on the "extravagance and irresponsibility" of the military in all the Latin American countries. Lemnitzer, replying for the JCS in August, branded the judgments unfair—they reflected "extremist criticisms and unwarranted assumptions." At the same time, he agreed with the comments of the commander in chief Caribbean (CINCCARIB) that the officers heading missions had not succeeded, as the State critics asserted, in exerting personal influence over Latin military leaders.[23]

The United States could not shake off its bad neighbor image during the Kennedy and Johnson administrations and Latin America remained a source of concern and contention about policy during the 1960s. As a force for promoting internal security and stability in Latin American nations MAP made only limited progress.

The Kitchen Steering Group

As the FY 1962 military assistance bill slowly made its way through congressional committees, the administration realized that MAP policy and organization required reexamination. In May 1961 presidential assistant McGeorge Bundy called for a more thorough review of military assistance than the Marshall report. At a meeting on 26 May to discuss the report, Deputy Secretary of Defense Gilpatric suggested formation of a group to make "a more specific series of recommendations."[24]

Accordingly, the secretaries of state and defense established on 8 July 1961 an interagency steering group chaired by Deputy Assistant Secretary of State for Politico-Military Affairs Jeffrey C. Kitchen and including representatives from State, OSD, the Joint Staff, BoB, and the White House. The group examined programs in six nations on the periphery of the Sino-Soviet bloc—Greece, Turkey, Iran, Pakistan, South Korea, and Taiwan—that appeared most vulnerable to direct attack. ISA asked the Joint Chiefs on 2 August whether smaller military forces in the designated six nations could achieve the same objectives. The JCS responded on 29 September, recommending against MAP reductions for the six countries in the foreseeable future because their military forces were essential to implementing "a forward strategy."[25]

In December the Kitchen group issued its findings. Consistent with presidential guidance, it favored economic development over military assistance to the six countries since it did not consider direct military aggression against them likely in the next decade. Reducing military assistance would, in turn, enable the administration to devote more resources to its top priority of economic development for nation-building, thus promoting internal reform and raising standards of living. The report further proposed an austere FY 1963 MAP budget that continued "deferring force improvement so far as possible." McNamara disagreed with much of the report, Assistant Secretary of Defense (ISA) Paul Nitze called the conclusions "arrant nonsense," and the Joint Chiefs insisted the proposed reductions were dangerous and destabilizing.[26] William Bundy, OSD's representative in the steering group, agreed with the report in general but had reservations about sharp reductions of funding for Korea and Turkey as well as the huge decrease in deliveries for FY 1962-67 to the six peripheral countries from approximately $5.5 billion to about $3.5 billion. Rear Adm. Harry Smith, the JCS participant in the group, disagreed with the proposed reductions. He concluded the United States was urging its allies to increase their defense contributions while it reduced its own military assistance to nations essential to U.S. strategic interests. The JCS agreed "that this is no time to make, nor to plan, reductions in military aid to the six countries."[27]

Proposals for cuts also met stiff bureaucratic resistance from U.S. ambassadors and other embassy officials reluctant to lose the leverage the program provided them in dealing with their host countries. Others worried that a proposal to reduce funding and shift the savings into economic aid might result in the elimination of MAP. Furthermore, the president warned that Congress was more favorably disposed to supplying military assistance than economic assistance; he asked that DoD "help sell Congress on economic assistance."[28]

The FY 1963 Program

Despite his opposition to the Kitchen group's report, McNamara was sympathetic to reducing MAP-supported military forces as well as military assistance and held his initial FY 1963 budget request to $1.7 billion. Informed in early October of his decision, the Joint Chiefs reminded him that developments in Southeast Asia and the recent Berlin crisis made it imperative that funding be increased to at least $2.2 billion.[29]

Kennedy discussed funding with the chiefs on 3 January 1962. After hearing Lemnitzer's objection to reduction of MAP from $1.7 billion to $1.5 billion, he asked Taylor to telephone BoB Director Bell, who reassured him that a cut of $200 million would not force reductions in planned programs. Probably unsure of the timing or the amount of the proposed reductions, McNamara wanted further study of their full implications.[30]

Influenced by the Kitchen group's report, however, OSD deferred $80-85 million from the FY 1962 budget and cut more than $125 million from the six country programs, thus lowering its FY 1963 MAP budget request to $1.5 billion. The president then scheduled an NSC meeting for 18 January to resolve the funding issue. Prior to the meeting, the Joint Chiefs insisted that "any reduction in military assistance to these six [front-line] countries is strategically unsupportable." They regarded diminution of funding as incompatible with the administration's new emphasis on a conventional military buildup for fighting limited wars on the periphery to check communist aggression. In their eyes, "economic assistance should complement MAP."[31]

At the 18 January NSC meeting, the president pointed to interrelationships between trade policy and military interests by remarking that the United States was spending $3 billion a year overseas to maintain its security but at heavy cost to the nation's economy. Because of the balance of payments deficit, Kennedy continued, the United States "must either do a good job of selling abroad or pull back." He instructed AID Director Fowler Hamilton to undertake reviews of "the military and economic aspects of long range US aid planning" for the six countries and reminded his audience that MAP and AID activities were simultaneously complementary and competitive. He further directed the Joint Chiefs to reconsider their comments on the Kitchen report and recognize that "decreases in military aid would be compensated by increases in economic aid."[32]

In mid-February, however, the chiefs reaffirmed their position as still valid. Given the close connection between economic and military assistance, they argued that any changes to MAP had to take into account the "effect on Free World military posture in the given area." Moreover, from previous experience they doubted Congress would approve "dollar-for-dollar transfers from MAP to AID." They further pointed out that the threat had not changed so neither should the amounts of military aid. Unpersuaded by the chiefs' contentions, on 13 March the president requested a $1.5 billion appropriation for MAP.[33]

Earlier, when McNamara had appeared before a congressional committee late in January 1962 to testify on DoD appropriation requests, he was asked how he could possibly defend less money for military assistance than the previous year in view of the deteriorating situation in Southeast Asia. He explained that DoD could shift funds earmarked for other nations to South Vietnam, which confronted a far more serious direct threat. These shifts in funds would permit an overall reduction in military assistance.[34]

At the secretary's subsequent appearance in mid-March before Passman's subcommittee, the Louisiana congressman took issue with McNamara's accounting, insisting that OSD had padded its request and then used the accumulated unexpended balances and recoupments to spend more than Congress appropriated for programs it had never approved—more than $300 million in FY 1962. Aside from Passman's "usual intensive questioning," there was "obviously considerable apathy" and the hearings were poorly attended.[35]

The Foreign Assistance Act of 1962, approved 1 August 1962, authorized $4.67 billion for FY 1963, $206 million less than requested, although the $1.5 billion MAP request remained intact. The legislation also forbade sales of certain defense articles to "economically developed countries" unless they were unavailable from U.S. commercial sources. It also enjoined the president eventually to terminate military grant aid to nations "having sufficient wealth" to equip and maintain their own military forces.[36]

During subsequent appropriations hearings, however, Passman, arguing that MAP had been overfunded for years, maneuvered to cut the appropriation by $200 million despite well-publicized objections by McNamara and Lemnitzer. In an attempt to counteract Passman's tactics, in late August and again in mid-September Kennedy made strong public statements about the shortsightedness of reducing foreign assistance. McNamara, too, tried to marshal congressional support for his MAP figures through late summer and early fall, but bowed to the inevitable in early October by informing Rep. Gerald Ford that $1.375 billion was DoD's minimum requirement.[37]

In the end, Congress approved a cut of $369 million in foreign aid and reduced MAP to $1.325 billion, or $175 million less than the administration's FY 1963 request. As a result, four of the six key countries suffered reductions, Taiwan and Korea being especially hard hit. Passman's unrelenting campaign to reduce overall MAP funding and the increased costs of support for Southeast Asia forced OSD into a juggling act—a proposed decrease in military aid to four of the six key countries to permit increasing assistance to Thailand and South Vietnam. The Joint Chiefs protested that this would retard force modernization and leave the affected nations unable to meet the communist threat.[38]

McNamara shifted the FY 1963 MAP funds to meet the rising Vietnam costs and increased military assistance to Thailand while attempting to address the chiefs' concern. South Vietnam's extra $122.9 million bought patrol boats and various types of landing craft, 18 helicopters, 23 propeller fighter-bombers, plus additional ammunition as well as construction funding, and Thailand's additional $32.8 million went for 9 transport aircraft, 8 helicopters, and construction projects. To offset South Vietnam's extra money, South Korea, the Republic of China, and Turkey took reductions of $198.2 million, mainly from eliminating aircraft deliveries and ship programs. Korea had to defer 223 tanks and 73 howitzers.[39]

Troubles at AID

In late May 1962 AID Director Hamilton submitted his response to the president's request of 18 January for a review of U.S. aid planning. Hamilton sought closer coordination between military and economic aid to make both more effective. The resulting synergy, he concluded, would identify opportunities to enhance the overall foreign assistance effort. Meshing the budget planning and programming cycles of AID and DoD would also facilitate interagency coordination. Kennedy responded by issuing NSAM No. 159 on 31 May, which generally endorsed Hamilton's course and charged him with implementing the new procedures.[40]

This task proved beyond Hamilton. He ran afoul of Passman, who used AID's failure to show positive results to browbeat administrators and pare economic aid requests. Hamilton never fully recovered from his awkward start, and AID suffered from comparison with McNamara's streamlined administration of MAP and ISA's energetic performance. For example, McNamara took a personal interest in reducing the unacceptable and embarrassing two-year backlog in MAP deliveries. He also directed ISA to initiate procedures with AID to ensure that the agency acted on DoD proposals within 7-to-14 days.[41]

Kennedy also grew dissatisfied with the "apparent lack of control and coordination" in matters of foreign aid and the inability of AID and other agencies to advance U.S. interests overseas. Under pressure from OSD, State, and the White House, Hamilton, who, according to Deputy Special Assistant for National Security Affairs Carl Kaysen, "never really did achieve a clear understanding of what he was trying to do," resigned as director of AID in November 1962. Budget Director Bell succeeded him in December. A highly regarded manager, Bell's experience in BoB and his stature among congressmen made him an excellent choice.[42]

On leaving, Hamilton recommended that the president "create a permanent advisory group of private citizens on foreign assistance" to study AID and find ways to revive public and congressional support for the administration's faltering foreign assistance programs. On 6 December, the president established the Committee to Strengthen the Security of the Free World; to garner bipartisan support for the foreign aid program he named as chairman a prominent Republican businessman, retired General Lucius D. Clay.[43]

The Clay Committee

At the 22 January 1963 NSC meeting the president again emphasized that foreign assistance offered first and foremost a way of improving the security of the United States. The Clay Committee would review the existing AID program for the purpose of ensuring that U.S. assistance would be in the national interest. The committee met from 24 to 28 January and 25 to 27 February. Aside from a few private sessions, its meetings were informal "hearings," with representatives from the executive branch discussing their respective economic or military assistance programs. From the outset, Clay believed that the "rich NATO nations" had to share the defense burden with the United States, particularly for aid to Greece and Turkey. Committee members affirmed that military and economic assistance programs were essential to U.S. national security but should be reduced because they were "too diffuse" and trying "to do too much in too many countries." Members were skeptical about the value of military assistance to Latin American nations. Although generally more critical of economic aid, they believed, as did McNamara, that annual military aid could be cut gradually from $1.5 billion to $1 billion over the next several years.[44]

OSD objected to the Clay proposal to force the NATO members to share MAP expenses for Greece and Turkey. It also pointed out that military assistance to Africa and Latin America, which the committee would eliminate, consisted primarily of military training programs and was clearly "worthwhile in terms of return per dollar spent." McNamara affirmed his support for increased assistance to Latin American nations to continue civic action and internal security initiatives.[45]

William Bundy's comments of 8 March on the committee's draft report restated McNamara's concerns and proposed that aid to Latin America be "reduced to a minimum" rather than eliminated. Bundy also opposed the proposal to incorporate military assistance to South Vietnam into the regular DoD budget because it would undercut the administration's policy of "merely assisting" the Vietnamese. McNamara worried that the committee's position that in two years MAP basic needs could be met by a $1 billion appropriation would be interpreted by opponents as an endorsement for that amount when such a figure was really not feasible until FY 1968 at the earliest. The secretary insisted that for FY 1964 the "*rock-bottom* figure" was $1.325 billion and reduction beyond that level would create "serious damage in key areas."[46]

The committee did acquiesce in a revision of the draft report that softened the tone but did not alter the substance. Still both Bundy and Bell expected it to recommend no major cuts, and the former thought the committee might prove helpful to DoD "in this year's Congressional fight." But during a background briefing before the report's release, Clay gave reporters the impression that MAP might be cut $500 million.[47]

The Clay Committee report, issued 20 March 1963, reaffirmed the great importance of foreign assistance to national security while noting concern that it was either "over-extended in resources and under-compensated in results" or poorly administered. It also observed that Americans resented the burden of paying for foreign aid while "other prospering industrialized nations" did not shoulder their fair share. The report singled out MAP, particularly direct military aid, for praise because "dollar for dollar" it contributed more to the security of the free world than other similar DoD expenditures. Nevertheless, the committee concluded that military assistance appropriations could be reduced to $1 billion "in a few years." Although the report noted McNamara's caveat that OSD could not attain that goal until FY 1968, it also pointed out that several nations had military forces far in excess of their requirements.[48]

The committee suggested MAP and AID funding might be reduced by $500 million, but the president ultimately decided against any cutback in MAP. Passman interpreted the findings, Clay remarked, "as a recommendation for a drastic cut in the President's program. Which it was not." Passman's initial reaction was to call for foreign assistance to be chopped in half "to show the world that we are no longer going to be suckers." He was hardly alone; many newspapers also focused on Clay's recommendation to reduce foreign assistance.[49] This set the stage for a prolonged and nasty battle between McNamara and Passman.

The Shift to Military Sales

From early on McNamara, an ardent booster of export sales of weapons and military equipment, pushed DoD "to promote sales of U.S. manufactured military equipment in every way possible." To encourage export sales, the 1961 Foreign Assistance Act authorized use of MAP funds to extend liberal credit terms to foreign governments, which in turn stimulated demand for military arms and equipment.

McNamara testified in March 1962 that military sales were replacing grant aid "to the greatest extent possible." The aggressive military export sales program had as a major goal offsetting the balance of payment deficits incurred from stationing U.S. forces overseas. To this end, McNamara directed that credit sales receive top priority in planning. The $15.5 million allocated for credit assistance in FY 1961 swelled to $142 million in FY 1963 before dropping to $100 million in FY 1964. Funds generated by transaction fees, finance charges, and recoupments were deposited into a revolving account that made financing new credit sales less dependent on MAP-appropriated funds. Military export sales rose steadily from $523.6 million in FY 1961 to $1,527.2 million in FY 1964. For the same years grant aid declined from $1,449.9 million to $793.1 million. Sales deliveries more than doubled, from $474.8 million in FY 1961 to $1,025.5 million in FY 1964, as grant-aid deliveries rose slightly from $709 million to $818.9 million for the same period.[50]

In NSAM No. 242 of 9 May 1963 the president reinforced the call for selling equipment to allies to ease the drain on U.S. gold reserves. McNamara enthusiastically supported this measure and in early July directed DoD "to aggressively pursue" its implementation. To avoid the risk of encouraging developing countries to use grant economic assistance for purchasing military hardware, Rusk counseled a conservative approach to ensure that military sales did not divert funds from economic development or upset regional military balances. He expected that State would provide political guidance on sales and collaborate with DoD in cases where potential competition existed between military grant aid and sales.[51]

On 8 July 1963 McNamara revised DoD policy and delineated in detail the administration of military assistance. ISA assumed responsibility for conducting all MAP activities within DoD, including direction of military aid programs, supervision of military sales, and interdepartmental coordination and planning, using various cost and availability data provided by the service secretaries to develop and review programs. The Joint Chiefs would advise the secretary of defense on strategy, forces, and requirements by country and region, recommending priorities and budgets coordinated with unified commands and MAAGs.[52]

With his realignment of MAP procedures completed, McNamara encouraged an activist ISA to seek out new markets, expand old ones, and sell more and more on favorable credit terms. Military sales surged. Germany, Australia, the United Kingdom, and Italy represented the largest volume of sales. Those four plus Canada, France, Japan, and Switzerland accounted for $1.283 billion, 84 percent of all FY 1964 military exports. That was about to change as credit sales to developing countries accelerated. In mid-1964 Congress provided in the Foreign Assistance Act of 1964 for greater participation by private credit agencies in commercial financing of military sales as well as large-scale use of the Export-Import Bank (Ex-Im Bank) to finance arms sales to developing countries.[53]

Provisions added to the act authorized the president to protect individuals and firms doing business in the United States against credit and political risks related to credit sales of military equipment to friendly foreign governments and international organizations. This would encourage private financing of sales by guaranteeing repayments and help reduce the balance of payments deficit. DoD credit policy adopted in October 1964 envisaged that the Ex-Im Bank or private banks would finance military assistance credit sales to industrialized countries. Military assistance credit authority would also be extended to sales to non-industrialized countries, regarded as less creditworthy, at higher interest rates. Between

FY 1962 and FY 1966, industrialized nations accounted for $207.1 million in credit sales, but developing countries purchased $548.5 million through credit assistance, with the $435.6 million borrowed by Near East and South Asian nations accounting for most of the total.[54]

The FY 1964 Program

In beginning consideration of the FY 1964 MAP budget, McNamara focused DoD's attention again on long-term planning. On 21 January 1963 he met with the Joint Chiefs to discuss the FY 1965-69 five-year guidelines for MAP. He proposed a gradual decrease from $1.5 billion in FY 1965 to $1.2 billion by FY 1969 as opposed to the original straight-line projection of $1.7 billion per annum that the JCS had previously agreed to during preparation of the FY 1963 budget. The chiefs concurred with the new guidelines subject to adjustments they wanted to meet the cutbacks, a reconsideration of certain reductions, an agreement that the guidelines were more targets than ceilings, and an understanding that changing circumstances might require more money. With the secretary's acknowledgement that the figures were not a ceiling but a "realistic objective," in mid-March 1963 General Robert J. Wood, USA, OSD's new director for military assistance, devised a five-year plan to accommodate the reduction to $1.16 billion by FY 1969. Wood assumed that greater contributions by European nations would support NATO, that some less developed nations would manufacture light arms and commercial consumables to supply some of their own military equipment needs, and that the substitution of cheaper weapon systems to meet military requirements would reduce overall MAP grant-aid costs. Based on these computations, McNamara requested $1.405 billion for FY 1964.[55]

As McNamara expected, congressional foes of military assistance used the Clay Committee's $1 billion figure against him. If the committee, the president, and the secretary of defense were all on record that reductions could be made, there were congressmen happy to oblige. McNamara acknowledged the $1 billion figure in his prepared opening statements to the several congressional committees but quickly added that the Clay Committee also approved a gradual reduction just as DoD planned. Still, House Foreign Affairs Committee Chairman Thomas E. Morgan (D-Pa.) asked if the secretary planned to reduce military assistance to countries whose military forces the Clay Committee deemed larger than needed; McNamara responded, "Yes, sir."[56]

Passman's appropriations subcommittee once again bedeviled McNamara during his mid-May testimony. Passman's hectoring started with a reminder to McNamara that the president had previously reduced the foreign aid request by $400 million and that Clay had "indicated further reductions could be made." Over the next day-and-a-half Passman doggedly continued to insist that earlier reductions had not damaged MAP, and McNamara just as determinedly rejected the chairman's observations. In a series of contentious exchanges, Passman charged that in the past OSD had used unspent funds to pay for new programs not authorized by Congress. McNamara gave as good as he got, but Passman remained determined to eliminate "fat" from MAP, "the most wasteful part of the foreign aid program," which would work better stripped to "the bare essentials." He was in a position to make good his threats.[57]

Testifying before the Senate Foreign Relations Committee on 13 June, McNamara tried to deflect Passman's criticisms by repeatedly stating his preference that Congress cut the regular Defense budget rather than his military aid request. With the exception of sharp questions from Wayne Morse (D-Ore.), the hearing on military assistance was favorable. Rusk and Bell, testifying on the economic aid program, were less fortunate, as senators expressed their intention to cut the foreign assistance request, stop the grant-aid giveaways to Western Europe, make changes in the AID program, and end assistance to underdeveloped countries when, in Morse's words, "so much has to be done in depressed areas in our own United States."[58]

Even as the Senate hearings continued, McNamara wrote to Chairman Morgan advising him that in view of increased costs for more ammunition for Vietnam and for two additional divisions and improved communications equipment for India, any cuts to the FY 1964 request would have serious consequences. Moreover, the initial FY 1964 budget request had underestimated by $50 million the amount required to finance an expanding credit sales program that could make a "significant contribution to [solving] the balance of payments problem." In short, McNamara needed more money at a time when Congress appeared clearly opposed to authorizing his original request. The depth of congressional sentiment against foreign assistance became clear as the House Foreign Affairs Committee in August reduced the overall foreign aid authorization request by another $438 million.[59]

The timing for any reductions was particularly unfortunate at this juncture because of reverses in South Vietnam. On 16 August McNamara agreed to co-sign with Rusk a round-robin letter to each House committee member to head off further reductions in foreign assistance during the floor debate on the authorizing legislation scheduled to begin on 20 August. It did little good. McNamara learned from Representative Ford in early September of Passman's intent to reduce the MAP appropriation to $1 billion. Ford thought he could get a figure of $1.05 billion, and in exchange McNamara guaranteed that, barring further emergencies, he would continue to reduce the program.[60]

In reaction to the looming reduction of approximately 30 percent, on 20 September Wood and William Bundy coordinated a revised FY 1964 program based on funding of $1.05 billion to serve as a basis for discussions with the JCS, unified commanders, and AID as well as a preliminary planning document for the FY

1965 program. The following day McNamara approved the draft with minor exceptions but rejected its use in preparation of the FY 1965 MAP budget, due informally to BoB by 30 September, until Congress took final action on the FY 1964 package.[61]

The authorization process resulted in a compromise between the two houses that provided $1 billion for military assistance, $405 million less than DoD had requested; it severely cut economic assistance programs. On 16 December the new president, Lyndon Johnson, signed the Foreign Assistance Act of 1963, decrying the trend in Congress "to hamstring Executive flexibility" and reduce funds with a "consequent dangerous reduction in our security." The same day he directed the creation under George Ball's chairmanship of the President's Committee to Examine the Foreign Assistance Program and assigned it responsibility for the foreign aid studies that Kennedy had requested in May 1962.* Ten days later Johnson issued NSAM No. 276 requesting that AID and DoD prepare for his review the major changes to their assistance programs resulting from the congressional reductions.[62]

In the House, Passman dominated committee deliberations to make certain the MAP appropriation included no more than the reduced $1 billion authorization. He argued that OSD's practice of using recoupments to start unjustified projects proved the program suffered no lack of funds. The Senate went along, and on 6 January 1964, deaf to presidential entreaties, Congress appropriated $1 billion for MAP.[63]

The following day Bell informed McGeorge Bundy of the distribution of the foreign assistance reductions as required by NSAM 276. DoD had determined to "honor all explicit commitments" and meet the increased needs of Laos and South Vietnam by deferring planned modernization programs and radically slashing small programs of little military significance elsewhere. The force modernization cutbacks fell most heavily on some of the nations bordering communist countries. Shortly after, on 17 January 1964, increased ammunition demands from South Vietnam forced AID to transfer $50 million from economic contingency funds to military assistance accounts.[64]

McNamara was already worrying that the escalating needs in Vietnam foreshadowed more shortages. In testimony of 23 March, he sought $143.1 million in military assistance for South Vietnam in FY 1965 compared to $196 million in FY 1964, a 28 percent reduction, but quickly added his doubts about the sufficiency of that amount and the likelihood that increases for Vietnam would have to come at the expense of other countries or from economic aid.[65]

---

*This initiative died a quiet death when Ball and other committee members were unable to reach a consensus. After listening to committee members and senior congressmen disagree over the program at a White House dinner, the president left the AID organization intact and did not recommend major changes (interv David Bell by Paige E. Mulhollan, 27 Dec 68, pt 1, 25-29, LBJL).

Table 7

Selected Country Programs (MAP), FY 1964
($ millions)

	Unified Commanders Requests	OSD's Original Program	OSD's Revised Program	Final MAP Program
Greece	114.6	103.1	80.0	69.5
Turkey	188.5	183.3	131.3	142.0
Iran	55.3	54.4	40.1	50.2
Pakistan	44.0	48.6	41.5	44.5
Taiwan	135.7	133.8	94.3	82.0
Korea	207.1	205.1	150.4	147.1
Vietnam	179.2	159.1	175.5	219.5
Total NOA	924.4	887.4	713.1	754.8

Source: Poole, *JCS and National Policy 1961-64*, pt III:165; Military Assistance Program FY 1966 Estimates, 27, 29, 33, 35, 41, 47, 49, box 72, Subject files, OSD Hist. "Final program" includes $50.3 million of $55 million added in amendment passed 1 October 1964.

Bell suggested that creating a small reserve fund from amounts listed for force modernization in Greece, Turkey, Taiwan, and Korea, plus possible savings gained by shifting force maintenance accounts to the DoD budget, would be a prudent way to offset anticipated Vietnam increases. He reluctantly accepted the lower figure for Vietnam as a device for McNamara's congressional presentation, but suggested a thorough review of "major MAP-supported objectives and missions" before coming to grips with the actual funding for Vietnam.[66]

The FY 1964 congressional reductions not only left the Military Assistance Program seriously underfunded, but forced OSD to make major adjustments in its military aid plan. For example, Greece would not receive 54 self-propelled howitzers and Turkey would not get the initial increment of medium tanks to fill shortages in its armored units. Cutting half the equipment proposed for Thailand deferred delivery of 120 light tanks and armored cars. Korea did not get the 1,300 jeeps and trucks scheduled and it received 10, not 20, F-5 jet aircraft. The Republic of China would wait longer for tanks to replace its World War II-vintage models. By contrast, Thailand received more aircraft, and South Vietnam got 39 attack and 19 cargo aircraft, 25 helicopters, and more than 30,000 carbines and rifles to outfit an additional 25,000 army troops.[67]

The FY 1965 Program

Planning for the FY 1965 submission, which began in the fall of 1963, occupied the 28 October OSD staff meeting. Responding to the secretary's previous guidance, Wood prepared a $1.310 billion MAP budget for FY 1965. Affected by his experience with the FY 1964 budget, McNamara expressed doubt that Congress would approve such an amount considering its recent fierce attack on the FY 1964 request and the weak public support for the administration's foreign aid program. Asked by Wood what a realistic figure might be, McNamara suggested $1.2 billion, a figure he had arrived at three days earlier. Together with recoupments of $125 million, MAP would have $1.35 billion, but McNamara anticipated that Passman "will come along and chop $300 million out." To preclude that, the secretary decided to submit an austere MAP budget reduced to an absolute minimum. To help accomplish this, he requested preparation of legislation to transfer such military assistance expenses as NATO infrastructure and training outlays to the budgets of the military departments.[68]

After McNamara's decision to reduce MAP to $1.2 billion, ISA revised the program. Its 12 November draft sliced military assistance to key nations, the hardest hit being Korea and Turkey, and struck $40 million from the contingency fund. These cuts enabled McNamara to increase military aid for Vietnam by $20 million.[69]

Transfer of some MAP funding to the Defense budget was one facet of a bolder McNamara move to reorganize the military assistance budget for FY 1965. An initial draft of the plan, forwarded on 22 November 1963 to State, BoB, AID, and the White House for coordination, proposed transferring the part of MAP money "closely related to U.S. forces," i.e., operating in South Vietnam, to the Defense budget, separating the remaining military aid authorization and appropriation legislation from economic aid legislation, and establishing a military sales credit fund. Because military aid was far more comparable to items in the Defense budget than to economic aid, he believed that Congress should consider it in relation to the Defense program as a whole. McNamara proposed also to eliminate Section 622(c) of the Foreign Assistance Act of 1961 that gave the secretary of state "continuous supervision and general direction" over foreign assistance. State balked at this provision, but otherwise concurred with the recommendations, contingent on presidential approval. Bending to State's concerns, the secretary dropped the contentious issue before discussing the plan with Kennedy shortly before the president was assassinated. In early December McNamara informed President Johnson that Kennedy had approved the revisions in principle. He further explained that OSD was "virtually under a mandate from the Senate" to present a substantially modified military assistance bill and that approval of his recommendations could reduce the FY 1965 request.[70]

Johnson approved the revisions on 7 December but enjoined McNamara to conduct the military assistance program "in accordance with the foreign policy guidance of the Secretary of State." McNamara then informed interested committee chairmen in the House and Senate about his proposals. Reaction was mixed. Some like Senator Fulbright, who favored putting military assistance appropriations in the DoD budget, agreed with the ideas; others like Representative Morgan rejected the concept of lumping MAP into the Defense budget and otherwise found the changes so sweeping that they could only be decided "at the highest level of our government."[71]

In early December Johnson consulted with his longtime friend and political mentor, Armed Services Committee Chairman Sen. Richard Russell, and concluded that at most Congress would appropriate $1.2 billion for the FY 1965 program, but "there is no assurance we can obtain anything close to that amount."[72] On 16 December, the president reaffirmed his intention to request $1.2 billion, but within days changed his mind, apparently as part of his "drive for economy," and reduced the figure to $1 billion. Bitter experience with the FY 1964 budget submission and the president's caution seem to have convinced McNamara to ask for the minimum the legislators would support. This would place on Congress the onus for any future failures of military policy attributable to inadequate MAP funding. On 10 January 1964 he informed BoB of his FY 1965 MAP request of $1 billion; in mid-March Johnson forwarded it to Congress.[73]

With the $1 billion ceiling, ISA again revised its plans by dropping the "regional" groupings of countries in favor of categories such as "forward defense," "military base programs," etc., which William Bundy felt would emphasize the close ties between the DoD budget and military assistance programs, delineate precisely the appropriate function of specific military assistance instead of lumping general totals under a region or country, and highlight the programs in direct support of U.S. forces. He aimed to display the importance of the FY 1965 request in a readily understandable format for hearings before congressional committees. In late March, the JCS agreed that the FY 1964 and FY 1965 programs reflected an "acceptable distribution" of resources among the regional groupings and recipient countries. The chiefs objected, however, to assistance to Burma at the expense of Korea and Vietnam. Funding for the FY 1964 ammunition program for Vietnam alone required a substantial increase.[74]

As everyone anticipated, military assistance became a controversial subject throughout 1964, with McNamara shuttling back and forth between the authorization and appropriation committees in the two houses. Testifying before the House Subcommittee on Department of Defense Appropriations in February 1964, he exchanged barbs with Rep. Melvin Laird (R-Wis.) over the extent of the damage done by the congressional reductions to military assistance in the previous session. Laird suggested McNamara ask for more funding or resort to Section 510 emergency financing to meet the unanticipated materiel requirements of Vietnam. McNamara retorted that congressional cuts in the FY 1964 program had forced him to cut assistance to Vietnam.[75]

McNamara concluded his opening statement before Passman's subcommittee in March 1964 with a warning that unless Congress assured MAP of at least $1 billion for the next several years, "the military strength we have helped to build up around the periphery of the Communist Bloc will quickly melt away." He placed the responsibility for OSD's request for $1 billion for FY 1965 squarely on the shoulders of Congress, which had "made it crystal clear to the Executive Branch that it is unwilling to appropriate a larger amount." As suggested by William Bundy, McNamara organized his presentation to Congress into six categories[*] and justified each in some detail. Passman dismissed both format and contents as "just about the same every year." McNamara asked Passman to "support wholeheartedly the $1 billion," even though only 40 minutes before two committee members had told him he would probably not even get that amount. By contrast with Passman, the House Foreign Affairs Committee was supportive of the authorization, and subsequent canvassing of sympathetic members of Congress produced strong support for the $1 billion request.[76]

Press reports of JCS unhappiness with the $1 billion ceiling and of Taylor's warning to Congress that any MAP reduction would force the United States to reduce indigenous forces and make up the shortfalls with more expensive U.S. troops, or concede that it did not have adequate strength to support its national interests, created additional pressure for favorable consideration. McNamara's confrontational defense of the military assistance request made headlines and probably encouraged Congress to pass it or risk appearing to vote against national security. The tactic, however, left the economic assistance package vulnerable to reductions. As McGeorge Bundy told the president, "Bob has done what he quite often does—made the case his own way without checking with everybody else."[77]

While McNamara's maneuver to secure passage of the MAP budget was working, other elements of his legislative package were foundering by mid-January 1964. Such influential members of the House as Morgan, House Speaker John McCormack, Majority Leader Carl Albert, and Carl Vinson opposed separating MAP funding from overall foreign assistance and placing it within the DoD budget. This change, they reasoned, would work against passage of the economic aid package.[78] In late February McCormack reiterated his strong opposition to separating the MAP authorization. Although McNamara continued to favor separate bills and believed that it was an issue for the president to decide, he opted not to press this view. To facilitate committee consideration of the pending

---

[*] They were forward defense, Alliance for Progress security, military base rights, grant-aid phaseout, free world orientations, and U.S. forces and military assistance program administration.

legislation, he eliminated proposals to transfer certain military assistance items to the DoD budget and have separate legislation for credit assistance "until there is a more favorable outlook for affirmative Congressional action."[79]

During Senate Appropriations Committee hearings in mid-July, McNamara declared that anything less than a sustained commitment of $1 billion for MAP would result in reduced capabilities of Allied forces and require a corresponding increase in U.S. military forces overseas. The new chairman of the JCS, General Earle G. Wheeler, testified that the FY 1964 reductions had seriously disrupted the chiefs' carefully planned MAP distributions. Military assistance, he continued, was essential to the counterinsurgency campaign in South Vietnam against growing communist activity, hence reductions to the FY 1965 program "would be a tragic emasculation of a program vital to our national security interests."[80]

The House Foreign Affairs Committee initially went along with the $1 billion authorization as requested, but on 18 May the president asked for an additional $55 million for South Vietnam. The House agreed and on 1 June approved $1.055 billion. The Senate Foreign Relations Committee, acting in early July, reduced the House figure by $10 million. In mid-August, McNamara asked Morgan, who served on the committee of conference, to urge authorization of the amount requested, warning that recent events in Southeast Asia and Africa* might "well require a request for a supplemental appropriation after the first of the year." The Senate-House conference report, issued on 1 October, reinstated the original amount, and on 7 October Congress both authorized and appropriated $1.055 billion in military assistance. The president, crisscrossing the nation in his reelection campaign, signed both bills the same day without fanfare.[81]

McNamara's legislative concessions and OSD pressure on Congress, coupled with demonstrable progress in "tightening up the program" and presidential arm-twisting, resulted, according to Bell, in "the most favorable [foreign assistance legislation] in many years." Perhaps more important, Passman's sponsor, House Appropriations Committee Chairman Clarence Cannon, had died on 12 May 1964 and was replaced by George Mahon, a friend of the president's, who "wouldn't play Passman's game." Under the new leadership foreign aid funds were cut only eight percent, the lowest since the program began, and there were no new restrictions on military aid. Indeed, the legislation strengthened U.S. government guarantees to private individuals and corporations against risks of default on credit sales by friendly governments.[82]

The FY 1965 MAP experienced the usual readjustments. Greece, Korea, and the Republic of China received less ammunition and training and fewer vehicles, communications equipment, and other supplies. Turkey lost helicopters and utility aircraft, small naval vessels, and an air defense missile system. Thailand and

---

*Violence spread in the Katanga province of the Congo during mid-1964 as stability in the new nation collapsed. United Nations forces intervened in June 1964, and the United States sent transport aircraft and a few military personnel to help quell the insurgency.

Vietnam again benefited at the expense of other countries, receiving additional ammunition, aircraft, landing ships, patrol craft, equipment, and supplies as well as training and construction money.[83]

Preparing the FY 1966 Request

Even as the battle over the FY 1965 MAP budget became more heated McNamara was looking ahead. On 4 February 1964 he requested that Wood provide him with projected military assistance dollar guidelines for the FY 1966-70 period. Wood responded that "in the present climate" an NOA of more than $1 billion would be unacceptable to Congress. The JCS in April 1964 crafted their input around a $1 billion ceiling and recommended improved procedures to limit the upward spiral of operational and maintenance costs and special attention to new contingency requirements of grant aid to allies. The chiefs especially sought increases in FY 1966 for Turkey and Korea and considered current dollar guidelines for the other forward defense nations as the minimum.[84]

McNamara also decided to submit again his proposal to separate economic and military aid. At the end of August the new ISA assistant secretary, John McNaughton, revived the issue of separating credit assistance funding from grant aid, a move that had been dropped when Congress refused to approve OSD's entire package of changes. Early in October, McNamara approved McNaughton's suggestion to study proposed strategy and force structures for forward defense countries to help establish an appropriate level of MAP funding in future years. ISA also sought the chiefs' advice on the strategic implications of OSD's proposed FY 1966-70 program. Their 20 October response predicted that military assistance under the $1 billion ceiling would be inadequate and result in widespread shortages of major combat elements, especially naval and air forces in Turkey and Korea as well as naval forces in Taiwan. If current trends continued, force modernization would be almost impossible, and by 1970 much combat equipment would be obsolete, leaving allies incapable of coping with the threat. In such circumstances, planners would have to modify the role of foreign forces, revise objectives, and phase out or eliminate selected programs. Such changes, the JCS insisted, were inconsistent with U.S. strategy and would "cause serious adverse foreign political reaction."[85]

In mid-November, McNaughton, following McNamara's guidance, prepared a $1 billion "normal" MAP budget for FY 1966 and added $191 million for "special" expenses involving Vietnam and Laos for a total of $1.191 billion. On 20 November 1964, McNamara forwarded this preliminary estimate to the Joint Chiefs for review and comment. McNaughton had acknowledged that modernization and replacement of high-maintenance equipment would require a budget of $1.377 billion. The chiefs concluded that the insufficiency of the request to modernize forces in the forward defense countries meant that the combat capabilities of those nations would deteriorate. Nevertheless, ISA believed the $1 billion was sufficient, if austere, for peacetime purposes. Thus OSD requested $1.191 billion and included language to separate economic and military assistance, place MAP as a line item in the Defense budget, and obtain the long-sought-after continuing authorization authority. This last provision would eliminate the need to testify twice annually on military assistance before congressional committees.[86]

At a meeting with OSD, State, AID, and White House staff on 24 November, however, BoB had proposed a lesser figure of $1.136 billion, with additional funding for Vietnam to come from reductions in grant military aid to the forward nations. Wood thought BoB's reductions were an attempt to keep "the *total U.S.* budget below some sacred figure (unstated)." He wanted to hold the line on the original request but feared OSD would compromise at $1.160 or $1.170 billion. OSD agreed to the $1.170 billion, forcing McNaughton to reduce credit assistance for Latin America and decrease funding for Taiwan and India, while increasing it for Brazil and Panama, leaving a net decrease of $21 million. McNamara recommended to Bell on 5 December a revised figure of $1.170 billion for FY 1966.[87]

The chiefs, in the midst of preparing their mid-range Joint Strategic Objectives Plan, which included an assessment of MAP requirements, replied in late December to McNamara's request of 5 December for comment. They considered that $1.170 billion would not meet the growing demands from Vietnam, would create "serious quantitative deficiencies," and would have a negative effect on "qualitative improvement of existing forces." They opposed shifting MAP to military department budgets, advised getting Congress to lift the ceiling on military assistance to Latin America, and again proposed separate legislation for military sales credit assistance funds.[88]

Previously, on 4 December, Bell notified Budget Director Kermit Gordon of a FY 1966 request for $1.170 billion and for two legislative changes: a four-year authorization and separate economic and military assistance bills. A few days later Bell summarized for the president the recent history of foreign aid and the proposed recommendations in the pending FY 1966 request. Outlays for military assistance had substantially declined. Grant-aid to Western Europe, with minor exceptions, had been phased out. Bell wanted the president to "make a major effort" to obtain a multi-year authorization but recommended against seeking separate economic and military assistance bills, despite McNamara's objections. Then on 20 December Gordon, as expected, endorsed the full amount of the MAP request but somewhat unexpectedly cut the overall AID request by $100 million.[89]

Meanwhile, heavier fighting in South Vietnam in the fall of 1964 required more military assistance, compounding OSD's problems, since FY 1965 MAP funding had already been exceeded. The burden to make good the shortfalls again fell on the forward defense countries. The Joint Chiefs opposed additional cuts to these nations in order to support Vietnam and feared "serious political repercussions." Barring dramatic new changes to justify invoking Section 510 of the

Foreign Assistance Act or new legislation, AID officials doubted OSD would choose to use Section 510 authority to draw from U.S. stockpiles or seek to shift some Southeast Asia requirements to the Defense budget because McNamara preferred to control MAP expenditures through his self-imposed $1 billion ceiling. This left a transfer of AID funds to military assistance as a likely alternative.[90]

Bell informed Johnson on 10 December of the need to transfer $50 million from the contingency fund to MAP in order to cover FY 1965 combat requirements in Laos and Vietnam. Shortly afterward General Westmoreland urgently requested another $65 million for the enlarged South Vietnamese military forces. This requirement, plus an unanticipated $35 million increase in associated costs attributable to Southeast Asia, left MAP short $100 million. On 22 December McNaughton recommended that McNamara use either Section 510 authority or submit a supplemental request to cover Westmoreland's needs; otherwise, manipulating the FY 1965 MAP budget to "shave the $125 million off of your Congressional-presentation figures" to meet MACV's latest need would create "political (if not military) mayhem."[91]

McNamara had previously been unwilling to ask Congress for supplemental funding because during his testimony he had opposed a move by some members of the House Foreign Affairs Committee to raise OSD's $1 billion request for FY 1965. After considering a supplemental request or use of Section 510 "drawdown" authority, McNamara reprogrammed MAP accounts and requested $50 million from AID. By decreasing some accounts by $31.2 million he was able to assemble $81.2 million for increases to various recipients, of which more than $53 million went to Vietnam. The ceiling on MAP left funding for the rapidly expanding demands of Vietnam dependent on a fixed budget that would be inadequate to meet overall needs.[92]

By January 1965 the grant-aid portion of the Military Assistance Program had been steadily reduced in accordance with a goal originally announced by President Kennedy. The pace of the reductions, however, had proceeded more rapidly than desired by McNamara or the Joint Chiefs, creating imbalances in the forward defense country programs. Other unexpected new requirements, especially for South Vietnam, constantly forced OSD to juggle MAP funds to pay for the mounting costs of military assistance to Southeast Asia. Congressional cuts in appropriations also forced OSD to adjust its planned programs to compensate for chronically inadequate funding. Modernization of forces in the six forward defense nations sputtered, and progress on streamlining the size of Korean or Turkish forces came to a halt.

Since 1962 growing demands from Vietnam for military assistance had siphoned funds from other areas; that trend seemed likely to persist in the near term. While grant aid declined, there occurred a significant shift to credit and military sales thanks largely to favorable congressional legislation designed to protect U.S.

TABLE 8

Military Assistance Program Comparison of
NOA Request with Actual Funding, FY 1961- FY 1965
($ millions)

FY	NOA Request	Recoup. Estimate	Reapp. Request	Estimated Funding Availability	Actual Approp.	Actual Recoup.	Actual Reapp.	Actual Funding
1961	2,000.0	155.7	25.0	2,180.7	1,800.0	120.6	23.6	1,944.2
1962	1,885.0	100.0[a]	25.0	2,010.0	1,600.0	240.7[b]	14.3	1,855.0
1963	1,500.0	204.6	25.0	1,729.6	1,325.0	250.2[b]	24.2	1,599.4
1964	1,405.0	125.0	25.0	1,555.0	1,000.0	119.6	22.3	1,141.9[c]
1965	1,055.0	85.0	1.6	1,141.6[d]	1,130.0	116.8	22.2	1,269.0

[a] Revised upward in June 1962 to $317.7, which along with FY 63 estimate of $204.6 totaled $522.3.
[b] Of the $522.3 estimated for FY 62 and FY 63, only $490.9 was actually realized.
[c] Excludes $90 million transfer from economic assistance.
[d] Funding availability is short of actual program requirements by $73.4 million.

Source: Statement of General Robert J. Wood, Director, MAP, before Senate Appropriations Cte, 23 Jul 64, fldr Military Assistance FY 1965 Budget, box 31, ASD(C) files, OSD Hist.

---

business investments and minimize risks. Conversely, Congress thwarted OSD plans by reducing budget requests in committee, by including restrictive legislation in the various foreign assistance acts, and by asking tough questions about MAP purpose and content. It also rejected OSD proposals to extend authorizations, separate military assistance from economic aid, and place the program in the overall DoD budget. The success OSD enjoyed with favorable legislation for military sales and credit guarantees was offset somewhat by the larger issues that remained unresolved. OSD and State, for example, had still not agreed on the relationship between AID and MAP. Moreover, the $1 billion ceiling left funding for the rapidly expanding demands of Vietnam dependent on a fixed budget; barring additional funds this threatened to damage the overall program.[93] McNamara had made some progress, but in 1965 the Military Assistance Program still faced a highly uncertain future.

CHAPTER XVII

The Search for Savings

McNamara entered office firm in the conviction that he could bring about greater efficiency and significant savings in running the Department of Defense. It did not take long for him to become aware of the many complex problems in constant interplay he would have to address in order to succeed. Procurement of materiel and supplies represented the biggest and most promising area for yielding large savings. Other possibilities included cutting Defense expenditures abroad, which would have the salutary effect of reducing losses in the international balance of payments account; closing or consolidating excess bases; and improving the weapon system selection and acquisition process. In this last category, the secretary encountered one of the most nettlesome issues of his tenure—the controversy over the TFX fighter plane. McNamara, as was his wont, dealt expeditiously with all of these matters, some of which proved more politically sensitive at every level—departmental, domestic, and international—than he may have anticipated or even realized.

McNamara's active and very public assault on waste, duplication, and inadvisable expenditures of taxpayer monies was a conspicuous and persuasive source of his influence in the early 1960s. His position, as expressed in a public address in April 1963, may have seemed to pander to public opinion, but its substance represented a deeply felt belief in the importance of economical management of the Department of Defense and in his ability to do the job: "Every dollar we spend inefficiently or ineffectively is not only an unnecessary addition to the arms race which threatens all mankind, but an unfair burden on the taxpayer, or an unwise diversion of resources which could be invested elsewhere to serve our national interests at home or abroad."[1]

Balance of Payments

As the world's strongest and wealthiest power, the economic health of the United States affected most of the rest of the world. A chronic balance of payments

(BOP)* problem throughout the Eisenhower, Kennedy, and Johnson administrations constantly threatened to undermine the well-being of the country and the international community. All three presidents devoted much time to finding ways to diminish the U.S. deficit, which had significant domestic and international political as well as economic repercussions. They held frequent meetings with their top advisers—the secretaries of state, treasury, and defense and other officials—sent special messages to Congress, suggested or directed actions to be taken, and followed closely the progress of measures proposed or implemented. The issue occasioned two special presidential messages to Congress by Kennedy—in 1961 and 1963. Kennedy also established a Cabinet Committee on the Balance of Payments, headed by Secretary of the Treasury Dillon, that met frequently and reported regularly to the president on efforts to reduce the persistent deficits.[2]

A host of factors contributed to the problem. As Dillon told President Johnson in December 1963, "the balance of payments problem is many faceted and requires constant attention on many fronts." Much of the concern centered on the outflow of gold from the United States—especially critical because of the role played by the American dollar in foreign exchange and transactions. If the U.S. gold supply fell below the level regarded as minimal—$12 billion—the resulting loss in the dollar's value might have a devastating effect on the world economy and international trade. Key to maintaining a stable equilibrium was the balance of exports vs. imports between the United States and its trading partners. During the 1950s and 1960s this balance was generally favorable to the United States and helped to offset debits in the other accounts. Other factors affecting the deficit were capital investment abroad, U.S. economic assistance to foreign countries, tourism, which alone by 1963 was accounting for as much as $1.5 billion outflow from the United States, and—a prime contributor—Department of Defense spending for goods and services overseas.[3]

Defense expenditures abroad went chiefly for maintenance of U.S. forces, including military housing and other construction, purchases of supplies and services, employment of foreign nationals, and military assistance, and involved thousands of civilian employees stationed overseas as well as service personnel and their families. Direct military expenditures abroad, including military assistance and atomic energy, had grown steadily from 1951 on, reaching a peak of $3.435 billion in 1958 and hovering at about $3 billion for several years thereafter. Europe, particularly the major allies—Britain, France, and Germany—presented the most serious problem, since the largest numbers of U.S. troops were stationed in those countries. Elsewhere, Japan and Canada accounted for additional hundreds of millions in Defense outlays. Expenditure deficits appeared likely to run at contin-

---

*The balance of payments account is a record of all international transactions between countries involving merchandise trade, capital assets, and services.

ued high rates. Since DoD played a large part in the creation of the continuing deficit problem, it had to be a part of the solution.[4]

Late in 1960, at the insistence of Treasury Secretary Robert Anderson, Eisenhower directed measures to cut the DoD deficit, most immediately curtailing the amount of money spent by U.S. troops and their families. On 16 November he ordered a reduction in the number of civilian employees and dependents of military personnel stationed overseas. Secretary of Defense Gates specified on 25 November that the dependent population be reduced from nearly 500,000 to 200,000 by 31 July 1962, at a monthly rate of 15,000, beginning 1 January 1961. He also directed that beginning 1 December only products of U.S. manufacture be purchased, with exceptions for such items as perishable goods.[5]

These sweeping measures encountered objections immediately, and requests for exceptions came from all quarters. MAAG personnel were especially vocal, as they generally had long assignments, and among those ordered home were wives who played a useful social role. The JCS made a case for Berlin personnel, and the Continental Air Defense Command appealed strongly on behalf of its people stationed in Canada. Because of alleged hardship assignments in Okinawa, Guantanamo Bay in Cuba, and Panama, dependents there were excepted. The DoD-directed cuts caused political fallout that had reached the boiling point when McNamara came on the job.[6] The message was clear. The Kennedy administration would have to address what appeared to be an unfair burden on DoD if only to restore morale in the armed forces.

On 19 January 1961, the day before Kennedy took office, the president-elect met with Eisenhower and a circle of their advisers to discuss the most pressing problems he would be facing. Anderson spoke forcefully about the "delicate . . . balance of payments situation," particularly the "gold erosion . . . still going on at a rate which we cannot afford." Eisenhower discussed the effects on morale of putting too much of the burden of alleviating the BOP deficit on the overseas U.S. military and their dependents.[7]

The Kennedy administration early on considered and pursued a host of initiatives to diminish Defense overseas expenditures, including reductions in the number of military and civilians and their dependents abroad; voluntary cuts in spending by these people; increased purchase of U.S. Savings Bonds and greater savings in Soldiers, Sailors, and Airmen Deposits; reductions in units stationed overseas; rotation of units overseas (thereby lessening the number of dependents); transfer of overseas procurement for supplies and services to U.S. sources, subject to certain exceptions; consolidation of organizations and facilities; decrease in military assistance expenditures, including MAAGs; reduction in employment of foreign nationals; and cuts in overseas construction. The measures that seemed to offer the best hope for bringing in revenue were increased military equipment sales and offset payments by Allied countries—particularly Germany, which had the largest number of U.S. troops.

In his State of the Union address on 30 January 1961, Kennedy took notice of the effect of these actions on the military: "Ways will be found to ease our dollar outlays abroad without placing the full burden on the families of men whom we have asked to serve our Flag overseas." He followed this with a special message to Congress on 6 February emphasizing the seriousness of the BOP deficit and proposing measures to deal with it, particularly the gold outflow.[8]

By then DoD had already taken action. On 1 February Deputy Secretary Gilpatric recommended and Kennedy approved rescinding Eisenhower's directive of 16 November 1960 curtailing movement of dependents abroad and substituting a modified plan calling for a smaller reduction in their number. In addition, Gilpatric suggested reducing expenditures by military and civilian personnel, spending less for contractual services, and having host countries share expenses at facilities used for joint training.[9]

Indeed, the several measures contemplated for reducing DoD expenditures abroad were all subsequently put into effect in some degree. Some were constrained by overriding political considerations. The Berlin crisis of 1961, for example, required cancellation of plans to reduce forces in Europe, where there were some 300,000 U.S. military, mostly in Germany. European fears, particularly in Germany, that withdrawals would signal a change in U.S. strategic policy, even a withdrawal from Europe, gave the Kennedy and Johnson administrations pause. Although the United States increased its Army forces in Europe by 45,000 during 1961, the German government feared that withdrawals in 1962 and thereafter would mean at the least a diminution of the U.S. defense posture in Europe. Thus, the political sensitivities of Allied countries, including Japan in the Far East, frequently served to frustrate DoD efforts to reduce its presence abroad and the cost of supporting troops around the world.[10]

DoD could not take steps to put into effect most of the plans it had drafted to alter the status of forces and dependents in Europe until well into 1962, by which time the Berlin crisis had abated. In July McNamara announced a program to reduce DoD expenditures abroad from the $2.6 billion deficit in FY 1961 to $1.6 billion in FY 1963. The proposed measures involved rotating Army units without dependents, reducing Air Force dependents in Europe, cutting back Army strength in Europe, scaling back Air Force strength in a number of countries, and shortening unaccompanied tours of Air Force military personnel to 15 months. The secretary made a special point of detailing limitations on procurement of supplies and services for use abroad to hold such expenditures "to an absolute minimum." The president quickly approved the list.[11]

Reducing overseas forces proved difficult and eventually impossible with the growing involvement of the United States in Vietnam. A projection by the OSD comptroller in March 1963 provided for reducing force deployment in foreign countries from about 629,000 as of June 1962 to 590,000 by 30 June 1968, a modest decrease over a six-year period. More than three-quarters of the decrease would be Army troops. The Army had contributed to the effort to cut back during 1962-63 by rotating four battle groups at three-month intervals to Germany for service in Berlin.[12] But the growth of overseas deployment caused by the increasing commitment to the Vietnam War made this a losing battle.

The best hope of offsetting DoD overseas expenditures lay in persuading Allied countries to agree to share the U.S. troop costs, primarily through purchase of American military equipment. Discussions with Germany, begun in the 1950s, continued, with the United States pressing for greater payments by the Germans. Initially, on 24 October 1961, the two countries signed a memorandum of understanding to create a cooperative logistical system that included cost-sharing in research and development projects, depot supply support and maintenance services, storage facilities, U.S. military equipment sales, and joint use of training areas in Germany. FRG payments were expected to be "sufficient to insure that military transactions of direct benefit to the U.S. balance of payments" would "offset the transactions of U.S. forces in Germany of benefit to the FRG balance of payments." The largest item listed was FRG military procurement in the United States, estimated to amount to $400-450 million for the period January 1961–March 1962.

In November 1961 Gilpatric informed the president that German Defense Minister Strauss had told him that the FRG would place orders for $1.3 billion for 1961-62 of which $1 billion would actually be paid to the United States in those years. Gilpatric anticipated that this would reduce DoD foreign expenditures to less than $2 billion a year. As with most such estimates then and in succeeding years, it proved optimistic. Efforts to make similar arrangements for offsets with France, Italy, the United Kingdom, and Japan for much lesser amounts met with less success. The French stated unacceptable conditions for increasing purchases, but the Italians agreed to purchase $100 million of military equipment from the United States. In September 1962 Germany extended the offset agreement through 1964.[13] In 1963 DoD was still spending abroad at about the same rate as in previous years. Without the German agreement the DoD BOP deficit would have been much greater. Negotiations with other Allied countries for offset agreements achieved little benefit.[14]

Kennedy's frustration over resolving the BOP problem came out at a prolonged White House meeting on 18 April 1963. He "remarked that we seem to be faced with a screwy system, in which we had to squeeze public activities in the spheres of defense and aid in order to let the private activities of tourism and foreign investment go forward untouched. However, that was how life was, and how the system operated." Nevertheless, on 18 July 1963, in a special message to Congress, the president reported overall progress on the balance of payments deficit. He gave DoD good marks for its efforts to diminish overseas expenditures, noting a decline in net outlays from $2.7 billion in 1960 to $1.9 billion in 1962. He also stated that efforts would continue to induce other Allied countries to follow

Germany's example by purchasing U.S. military equipment. McNamara sent frequent reports to the president about progress in redeploying troops from Europe and cutting expenditures abroad, especially with reference to Germany.[15]

In the name of foreign policy interests, Secretary of State Rusk exercised a measure of veto power over DoD proposals to reduce overseas expenditures. Responding to a request from the president, in September 1963 McNamara proposed a number of changes in the disposition of U.S. forces abroad, including reducing U.S. strength in Korea and Europe and in some U.S. military headquarters, returning aircraft to the United States from Europe on an accelerated schedule, rotating USAF fighter squadrons to Europe and Japan, and cutting back on foreign procurement of goods and services, hoping to reduce by $339 million DoD expenditures abroad. Rusk opposed redeployment of aircraft from Europe, cuts in the ground forces in Europe and Korea, and reductions in purchases of foreign oil—particularly from Venezuela. Reiterating previous dissents, he concluded "that our basic national security posture and foreign policy interests would be so seriously jeopardized through their acceptance that I recommend that they not be approved." The president agreed with Rusk and approved only the remaining Defense proposals, which totaled $190 million in estimated savings.[16]

In NSAM 270 on 29 October 1963 Kennedy approved a number of DoD redeployment, reorganization, and reduction actions over the next three years. At the same time, he reaffirmed U.S. intention to retain six division equivalents in Europe as long as required. "The United States," he declared, "will continue to meet its NATO commitment." In December Secretary of the Treasury Dillon informed President Johnson that redeployments did not involve Germany because German purchases of U.S. military equipment were fully offsetting the dollar cost of American troops there. In a followup message Dillon stated that without the German offset it would not be possible to maintain six division equivalents in Germany. The secretary pointed out that the Germans had agreed to place orders in 1963 and 1964 to cover U.S. costs, but they would not commit themselves to make payments for those years. It appeared that Germany would make the payments for 1963, but prospects did not look good for 1964. By late April 1964, however, Dillon could inform the president that progress payments from Germany on military procurement were larger than actual deliveries.[17]

The importance of German offset payments received special attention in May when President Johnson affirmed U.S. retention of six division equivalents in Germany but made clear that if the FRG did not meet its offset commitment the United States would be "forced to reconsider the question of U.S. force levels." Fortunately, German offset payments in 1964 and 1965 were sufficient to balance the cost of U.S. troops in Germany.[18]

When Johnson sent a special message to Congress on 10 February 1965, he had in hand the 1964 BOP results. The overall deficit had been reduced to an estimated $3.0 billion, an improvement over the $3.6 billion deficit in 1962 and $3.3 billion in 1963, thanks to the favorable trade balance of exports over imports. Once again the president directed decreases in U.S. expenditures abroad, including cutting Defense and AID expenditures "to the bone" and increasing the sale of military equipment to foreign customers.[19] Also, gold losses in 1964 had amounted to only $125 million, a marked improvement over the 1963 loss of $461 million. For 1965 Secretary Dillon anticipated a gold loss of at least $500 million. Still, as of early 1965 the U.S. gold holdings totaled $15 billion, more than a third of the free world's holdings, as the president put it. Dillon's gold loss estimate was low, for by June the gold outflow for 1965 had reached $1.1 billion—half of it to France because of de Gaulle's new policy of converting all of his country's dollar holdings into gold.[20]

At mid-1965 BOP prospects seemed promising, depending on the success of proposed measures. Overall, if conditions proved favorable, there was a possibility of reducing the $3.1 billion 1964 deficit by more than one-half. DoD's part would be to reduce expenditures by another $50 million in 1965 and $100 million in 1966.[21] But looming ever larger was the prospect of increased rather than decreased Defense costs overseas as the United States became more deeply involved in Southeast Asia. The engagement in larger-scale hostilities in Vietnam soon effectively foreclosed DoD efforts to play a positive role in cutting the BOP deficit.

The Cost Reduction Program

When President-elect Kennedy introduced his new defense secretary-designate to the press in mid-December 1960, he noted that they agreed on the need for an efficient defense establishment that would make "the wisest possible use . . . of the public moneys devoted to its maintenance."[22] Kennedy's remark provided the genesis for McNamara's cost reduction program. According to Assistant Secretary of Defense for Installations and Logistics (I&L) Thomas Morris, it was "really just an organized management-by-objective approach to giving priority attention to the most important opportunities for economy and efficiency."[23] McNamara had come from the business world and freely admitted borrowing key elements of his cost reduction efforts from the private sector. He was certainly not the first secretary of defense to seek to rein in spending, but his commitment, persistence, and enthusiasm for savings and efficient management of government operations made him the most effective.

The new defense secretary acted quickly upon taking office, circulating his famous "96 trombones," several of which directed I&L to reexamine logistics functions, including procurement, contracting practices, and inventory controls, and to undertake a comprehensive five-year review of all 6,700 domestic and foreign military bases and installations.[24] The directives reflected a belief that the public sector could be as efficient as the private and that waste in DoD could be identified and eliminated. Subsequently, McNamara made use of Kennedy's remarks on the Defense budget to justify cutting back or canceling the development or procurement of several weapon systems, including the nuclear-powered aircraft, the Titan II missile, and the B-70. Cost reduction focused initially on base closings and program reductions, but McNamara had something more in mind—a formalized program to encourage efficient logistic management, especially procurement, that would result in significant DoD savings.[25]

McNamara took a hard look at the procedures for the awarding of $29.3 billion in prime contracts in FY 1962. He focused especially on non-competitive contracts where he anticipated that significant cost savings could accrue from the use of competitive bidding and cost reduction incentives. These procedures would reverse the trend to large, sole-source contracts whose prices, he believed, might be reduced an average of 25 percent, realizing an annual saving of $480 million by FY 1967. The secretary also focused on the cost-plus-fixed-fee (CPFF) contract that gave contractors no incentive to hold down expenditures. In mid-March 1962 the revised Armed Services Procurement Regulation specified the firm fixed-price contract as the most preferred type of DoD procurement agreement, an innovation OSD claimed would save an estimated $100 million in FY 1962 alone. Other contracting reforms, such as the increasing reservation of cost-plus-fixed-fee contracts for basic research involving several unknowns, and the use of cost-plus-incentive-fee contracts for the development and production of weapon systems, were expected to lower final costs even more.[26] Reacting to contractor criticism that his competitive procurement policies threatened their profit margins, the secretary insisted to his staff that DoD should not pay high prices to ensure profits for inefficient producers but should allow efficient ones to make a satisfactory profit.[27]

McNamara also gave great attention to emerging techniques to deal with basic management functions such as inventory control. In early April 1962 he expressed his delight that I&L's initiatives to reduce stockpiles of combat consumables might save large sums annually. Moreover, his concept for a formal cost reduction program began coming into focus. At the mid-May White House Conference on National Economic Issues, McNamara restated his mandate from the president and ticked off DoD savings realized from contract cancellations and reductions and base closings. He explained that more efficient organization—the consolidation of common service activities into single entities, such as the new Defense Supply Agency, and improved procurement policies—promised even greater future savings.[28]

McNamara instituted a broad new plan in a 5 July 1962 memorandum to the president titled "Defense Department Cost Reduction Program," a document that reported DoD progress in cutting logistics costs since January 1961 and identified cost reduction goals for the next five years. The secretary cited Kennedy's initial instructions:

1. Develop the force structure necessary to our military requirements without regard to arbitrary budget ceilings.
2. Procure and operate this force at the lowest possible cost.

He then listed three principles adopted in 1961 that he estimated would save DoD $750 million in FY 1963:

1. Buying only what we need to achieve balanced readiness.
2. Buying at the lowest sound price.
3. Reducing operating costs through integration and standardization.

Applying these standards in FY 1962 to improve inventory control had accounted for reductions of $150 million in procurement of spare parts while transfers of excess stocks between departments accomplished savings of more than $225 million and the sale of surplus stocks deposited an estimated $10 million into the U.S. Treasury. The application of "value engineering" practices by technicians and contractors was reducing "goldplating," the practice of using the most expensive components during production. A small turbine wheel milled from stainless steel, for example, cost $175 while an equally acceptable molded plastic version sold for $2. For the year, the Air Force and Navy reported savings of $64 million achieved through value engineering; DoD wanted to save at least $100 million annually.

Shifting $650 million from sole source to competitive contracts in the 12 months ending 31 March 1962 forecast savings of 25 percent, bearing out McNamara's conviction that competition would result in lower costs. Furthermore, moving away from cost-plus-fixed-fee contracts, DoD switched nearly $1 billion to incentive contracts during FY 1962 at an estimated savings of $100 million. The long-term goal was to save $600 million.[29]

In mid-September 1962 McNamara provided the service secretaries and the DSA and DCA directors with a schedule showing categories and subcategories where DoD might achieve his desired savings of $3 billion in logistics by FY 1967. For FY 1963 the cost reduction goal was $1.152 billion. Applying strong management practices promised major savings—$257 million in operating costs from base closures, $80 million from paperwork reduction and standardization, and $116 million from other improved procedures.[30] I&L established an interservice working group to set specific quantitative targets, either in terms of dollars or percentage improvement for DoD agencies, to prepare formats of progress reports to the secretary, and to recognize civilian and military employees who produced outstanding savings or innovations.[31]

The interservice working group identified specific dollar savings goals for the services and DSA through FY 1965. Curtailing overbuying of initial spare parts could save 5 and eventually 10 percent of the $2 billion cost each year. Increased use of excess stocks in lieu of new procurement would save $690 million by FY

1965. Eliminating goldplating of weapon systems could save DoD $100 million in FY 1964. Increasing competitive contracts from 32.9 percent of total awards in FY 1961 to 39.9 percent by FY 1965 might save $494 million and cutting fixed-fee contracts during the same period from 38 percent of total procurement to 12.3 percent could save a potential $683 million by the end of FY 1965. Overall, the group reported reductions in FY 1962 of $1.207 billion and savings of nearly $4 billion through FY 1965.[32]

On 18 October Morris forwarded the group's findings for McNamara's approval. Five days later Deputy Secretary Gilpatric sent the savings targets to the service secretaries and DSA, expressing pleasure that forecasts in McNamara's July memorandum to the president might be achieved and even exceeded in the next three years.[33]

Morris submitted the first Cost Reduction Progress Report to McNamara on 21 December. It identified "hard savings"—cost reductions "precisely measured and placed under control at time of realization," and "cost avoidance savings," those actions that prevented future increases that would have occurred if previous practices had continued. The latter category, while a legitimate accounting tool, was susceptible to great fluctuations. For example, the shift to competitive and incentive contracts produced anticipated hard savings of $91 million in FY 1963 but for the same categories cost avoidance economies accounted for an estimated $115 million in savings plus another $177 million in anticipated savings—a total of $292 million.

It was important to differentiate, as Morris did, between actions initiated to save money and actual realization. Cost avoidance procedures provided an illustration. By reducing its mobilization pipeline—the time it took to move materiel and personnel from their starting point to their point of use—from the standard 120 days of available supply to fewer days depending on mode of transportation and class of supply, the Army saved $500 million in its FY 1964 budget. This paper adjustment saved no actual money (because the supply already existed), but the Army would avoid having to request $500 million in FY 1964 to maintain a 120-day supply. Furthermore, as a "permanent cost avoidance" DoD would carry $500 million in recurrent savings in future fiscal years.[34]

Credit for such recurrent annual savings became a significant portion of the cost reduction program's overall savings by McNamara's reckoning. Put simply, a savings achieved in one year continued to carry over as a cumulative amount into successive years. For example, accountants would credit the same FY 1963 savings of $1,000 on belt buckles as $2,000 in FY 1964, as $3,000 in FY 1965, and so on. In July 1963 Marine Corps Commandant General Shoup told McNamara that he would save money only the first time but did not see how DoD could take credit for that initial savings year after year. The secretary replied that "we retain the benefit of every saving."[35]

McNamara was pleased with Morris's report; at a 7 January 1963 staff meeting he directed senior DoD officials to give the program their closest attention. He enjoined them to review objectives with an eye to avoiding exaggerated savings, instructed the OSD comptroller to audit the data independently to ensure accuracy, and requested the recently established Logistics Management Institute* to evaluate the savings separately "to be sure they are realistic." He asked the staff not "to kid ourselves" about savings and, where possible, to uncover additional ways to economize.[36]

Yet McNamara's enthusiasm for cost reduction led him to stretch its claims to the limit in his FY 1964 posture statement to Congress, the first time the cost reduction program appeared as a separate entry there. Morris had differentiated between hard savings and cost avoidance, identifying $793 million in real, measurable savings in the FY 1964 budget and another $1 billion in "new cost prevention." McNamara's posture statement lumped them together with their combined enormous savings.[37]

Few congressional committee members asked critical questions about the cost reduction program during the January 1963 hearings. Sen. Paul H. Douglas (D-Ill.), chairman of the Senate Subcommittee on Defense Procurement and himself a well-known economist, observed that the committee had not previously had "sound solid figures" to verify the enormous potential savings to be gained from the shift to competitive contracts. The secretary modestly replied that he was merely "applying the free enterprise system to the Defense procurement."[38]

On the House side, perhaps the most penetrating question came from Rep. Robert Sikes (D-Fla.), who wondered why Defense costs kept rising despite McNamara's efforts to contain them with his impressive program. McNamara agreed the DoD budget had grown in recent years but insisted that savings would come from improved management and administrative efficiency. In April 1963 OSD prepared a lengthy answer to the question for Chairman George Mahon's Subcommittee on DoD Appropriations in which it attributed the increased budget to the administration's goal of creating forces necessary to meet the communist challenge, particularly the limited war threat. Research and developments costs, especially for the exceedingly complex missile and space technology, had also risen rapidly. These increases, OSD pointed out, would have been a great deal more but for the savings realized from the cost reduction program.[39]

Nonetheless, the confusion over rising Defense budgets despite reducing costs through cost avoidance techniques persisted. In December 1963, the DoD deputy comptroller (budget), Joseph Hoover, proposed to reduce DoD's NOA appropriation requests in FY 1964 and FY 1965 by $793 million and $1.082 billion respectively to account for anticipated savings from price competition and decreased use of fixed-price contracts identified in the FY 1963 year-end progress

---

* See Chapter II.

report on cost reduction. Morris insisted, and McNamara agreed, that the proposal was "totally unrealistic" because the savings represented the avoidance of cost overruns that were not traditionally budgeted in advance.[40]

McNamara was a tenacious advocate of the cost reduction program. Previously, at a 21 January 1963 OSD staff meeting, he had reinforced earlier instructions to the service secretaries and military chiefs "personally to take charge of the program in their department" in the interests of greater efficiency and economy. Rising Defense costs and increasing budget deficits put pressure on everyone to reduce costs. "Any of us," he told his senior staff, "could take $3 billion out of the budget without reducing force levels or the efficiency and effectiveness of our military potential, by better management, good judgment, and reduction of unessential expenditures." He formalized that guidance in a DoD directive issued 1 February 1963 that gave I&L responsibility for implementing the cost reduction program throughout the department and made the service secretaries responsible for monitoring and reporting their respective programs and achieving monetary goals. Savings, classified as either hard or cost avoidance type, would result from applying efficient practices and actions.[41]

McNamara followed his own advice and closely monitored the service results. While quick to praise good results, he also demanded that DoD elements meet their assigned goals. In early April, for instance, he expressed disappointment that only the Navy had exceeded the goal of 37 percent set for price-competitive awards and asked the service secretaries to inform him of plans to increase the number of such awards during the remainder of FY 1963. Later that summer he also admonished individual secretaries for failure to achieve desired goals.[42] The secretary's personal interest, his characteristic attention to the smallest detail, and his genuine enthusiasm for the program ensured that cost reduction efforts would retain high visibility within DoD.

On 8 July 1963 McNamara submitted his first annual cost reduction program progress report to the president. The 10-page memorandum claimed that the program had already saved DoD in excess of $1 billion, with almost $4 billion to be realized by FY 1967. Examples of specific savings illustrated each category of the program. Better still, McNamara claimed, DoD had effected these savings without sacrificing national security, indeed had greatly increased the nation's military forces and capabilities. The next day McNamara devoted his weekly staff meeting to the subject. Morris briefed the senior officials on the contents of the 8 July report while McNamara's running commentary identified areas, such as aircraft spare parts, where greater savings could be realized.[43]

The staff meeting served as a dress rehearsal for the secretary's 11 July press conference. Speaking from a podium, McNamara, with occasional assistance from Morris, reviewed a series of large charts that detailed the Cost Reduction Program's results. A handout set forth the accomplishments for the assembled reporters. Questioned about such precise savings, McNamara responded that there was an accuracy in the range of plus or minus five percent and he carried the details in his pocket so he could check periodically with the secretaries to make sure everyone was on target. As for savings resulting from competitive bidding, McNamara insisted that competition forced businessmen to hold costs to a minimum level.[44]

Following the change in administrations, President Johnson, pledging to Congress that the government would "set an example of prudence and economy," became a powerful advocate for the Cost Reduction Program. McNamara, in turn, urged his staff to redouble efforts to improve management and identify savings, particularly for those goals established by the program.[45] On 1 December, Johnson and McNamara each sent letters to 7,500 Defense contractors. The president noted that 55 cents of each Defense dollar went to contractors and called on them to reduce costs significantly either by initiating cost savings programs or by accelerating existing ones. OSD would consider their compliance with his request when making future awards. McNamara's accompanying letter identified his cost reduction objectives and urged contractors to adopt value engineering to insure they bought only what they needed, purchased items at the lowest sound price, and conducted their own operations in the most efficient manner.[46] In support of the president's urging, McNamara directed revision of the Armed Services Procurement Regulation and preparation of guidance informing contractors of the basic DoD requirements for their cost reduction programs. By early March 1964, at least 1,500 contractors, including all major corporations, had pledged their support, a response McNamara deemed to be "fantastic."[47]

Congress generally remained enamored of McNamara's cost-cutting initiatives, although a few members voiced vague doubts about his figures. During McNamara's testimony before the House Committee on Armed Services in January 1964, Chairman Vinson wanted to send every member of Congress a copy of the cost reduction program. Representative Hébert, usually a testy inquisitor, complimented the secretary for implementing previous committee recommendations; on behalf of the minority, William H. Bates (R-Mass.) expressed admiration.[48] Senators were equally lavish with their praise. Richard Russell, chairman of the Senate Armed Services Committee, exclaimed that McNamara's program was without precedent in his 30 years in government. Republicans like Leverett Saltonstall offered similar encomiums.[49] There were also scattered murmurings of disbelief. Rep. Porter Hardy, Jr., confessed to being "a little skeptical" about McNamara's numbers, but hoped that they would stand up to scrutiny.[50] Republican Melvin Laird was more outspoken, likening McNamara's savings to boasting about how much "you would have saved by not buying horses since 1899." McNamara cited several examples of real savings, and soon thereafter Rep. Sikes politely declared the two in "substantial agreement" and McNamara moved ahead with the posture statement.[51]

In January 1964 *Armed Forces Management* questioned McNamara's contention that competitive procurement saved 25 cents on every dollar spent and wondered if accepting the "lowest sound price" made good sense in the long term. In mid-June, the *Wall Street Journal* asserted that Defense auditors were unable to substantiate in any detail a large slice of the claimed cost reductions.[52]

McNamara issued DoD's second annual cost reduction report with the now familiar fanfare at a 7 July 1964 press conference. The $2.5 billion savings realized in FY 1964 far exceeded OSD's original estimate of $1.5 billion, and the revised savings goal of $4.6 billion a year by FY 1968 was $600 million more than the previous target. The secretary again stressed the savings inherent in competitive contracts, adding that DoD was a full year ahead in meeting its goal of reducing cost-plus-fixed-fee contracts to around 12 percent of all contracts. Against a

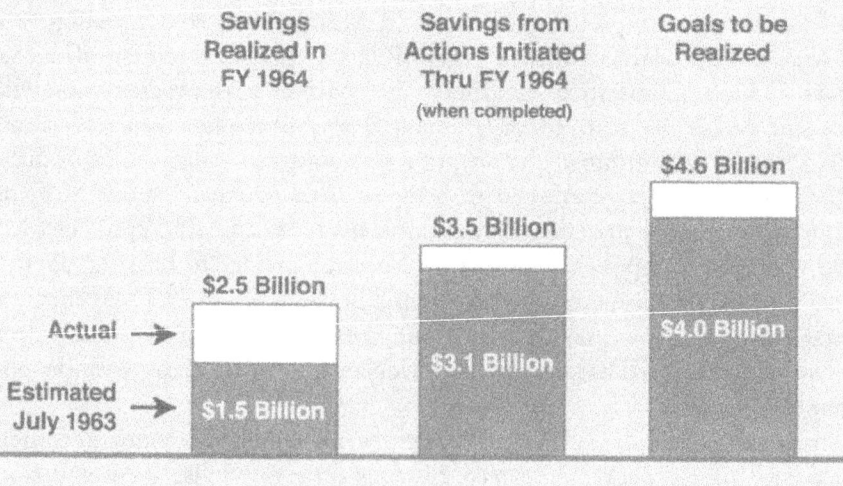

THE SECRETARY OF DEFENSE
7 July 1964

MEMORANDUM FOR THE PRESIDENT
SUBJECT: Department of Defense Cost Reduction Program–Second Annual Progress Report

Two years ago, and again last year, I reported to President Kennedy the steps being taken by the Department of Defense to improve operating efficiency and reduce costs. I have now completed a review of our progress during Fiscal Year 1964 and the prospects for further improvements in the years ahead. I find that both are greater than estimated last year:

1. *Savings of $2.5 billion* were actually realized during FY 1964, compared with our forecast of $1.5 billion.
2. *Savings of $4.6 billion a year by FY 1968 and each year thereafter* have been set as our new long-range goal–an increase of $600 million per year over the previous objective.

STATUS AS OF JUNE 1964

backdrop of wall charts, McNamara, pointer in hand and a microphone around his neck, lectured reporters for nearly an hour on cost reduction accomplishments during FY 1964. When one reporter asked who had verified the savings figures, McNamara explained that OSD had established a separate audit function under the comptroller with 285 auditors. OSD distributed 15,000 copies of the 7 July report, including copies to all members of Congress and their staffs and to more than 7,000 contractors.[53]

Press coverage of the FY 1964 report was generally favorable, but some reporters felt the exact future/dollar savings claimed defied calculation.* Critics questioned whether the secretary's decision to reduce air-to-air and surface-to-air missile procurement for the Air Force and Navy in the interest of savings had in fact hampered readiness.[54] In mid-July McNamara devoted his weekly staff meeting to the cost reduction program. While acknowledging that the military departments had done "a magnificent job" and had far exceeded his expectations, he thought DoD had only "scratched the surface" and urged greater reductions, particularly by eliminating goldplating. It was crucial that the press not "think that this is a numbers racket" and he noted that 285 auditors had questioned and removed about $500 million of the proposed reductions. He expressed annoyance at newspaper reports that "undermine confidence in our savings data," apparently a reference to coverage of his press conference that noted the reductions were not subtracted directly from the DoD budget.[55]

To highlight DoD's Cost Reduction Week (20-25 July 1964), President Johnson spoke at a Pentagon ceremony on 21 July honoring men and women of the Defense Department who had identified significant savings. He lavishly praised McNamara's cost-cutting efforts, and the following day told his cabinet that McNamara's exemplary results had given them all a mark to shoot for and urged them to study and adapt DoD's techniques.[56] He subsequently instructed his recently established 11-member task force, composed of private and public sector representatives, to organize a formal cost reduction program throughout federal agencies and improve standards for interagency cooperation on common problems.[57]

Naturally enough, the task force relied on DoD's model, stressing the need for top-level support and recognition and reward of deserving employees, hallmarks of McNamara's program.[58] Even before the task force issued its 10 November report, in a 31 October speech Johnson publicly accepted its recommendation to establish

---

* The report itself concluded that certain conditions prevented "unqualified audit validation . . . for the first three quarters of FY 1964," and the deputy comptroller for audit policy in the February 1965 quarterly report admitted that, "in most instances, reported goals were not of a nature to permit meaningful audit evaluation at this point in time." Yet the next quarter's audit report in April, prepared by another deputy assistant secretary, stated that although not all costs had been validated, "the savings reported conform to the criteria specified in the above-mentioned directive and instruction." See memo ASD(I&L) for SecDef, 22 Oct 64, w/atchmts A.1 and F, fldr Cost Reduction 1964, box 977, Subject files, OSD Hist; memo ASD(I&L) for SecDef, 16 Feb 65, w/atchmt C, memo ASD(I&L) for SecDef, 20 Apr 65, w/atchmt C: fldr Cost Reduction 1965, box 978, ibid.

government-wide cost reduction programs that he likened to the highly successful DoD Cost Reduction Program. The praise was all the more striking given the president's penchant to keep "a tight lid on the task forces" and complain "about stories even mentioning their existence."[59] Johnson believed the American people would support his expensive Great Society programs only if his administration demonstrated a commitment to efficient management and cost reduction efforts throughout the government.[60]

At this point of the five-year Cost Reduction Program McNamara had not only implemented a highly praised effort in DoD but had seen the president extend the concept throughout the executive branch. Each year the military departments and DoD agencies had exceeded their target goals. Even the defense secretary's harshest critics admitted that his effective management actions had cut operating costs, eliminated much duplication, reduced waste, and curbed Defense spending. McNamara's determined leadership, obvious enthusiasm for the program, and clearly defined program objectives proved the keys to success. It remained to be seen whether the secretary's insistence on more and greater savings and his single-minded approach to achieving his goals would continue to produce such glowing results.

Base Closures

From the beginning, closure of excess DoD bases constituted a major component of McNamara's search for savings. President Kennedy, not convinced of the need for all of DoD's 6,700 bases and other installations and recognizing the political volatility of base closings, wanted, according to Thomas Morris, to act on "this unpopular project in the first 90 days of his administration." In his first State of the Union message on 30 January 1961, Kennedy announced that he had instructed the secretary of defense to consider the elimination of obsolete U.S. military installations at home and abroad. Even as the president spoke, McNamara had already asked Morris for a list of bases for elimination. On 1 March the secretary reported to the president that the previous action by the Eisenhower administration, to close 71 installations, was still under way as of 20 January. Beyond these, he and the service secretaries agreed on closing 73 additional domestic and foreign installations. In his 28 March special message to Congress on the DoD budget, the president announced McNamara's actions and a continuing search to identify additional surplus facilities. With this precedent, in subsequent years OSD published a list of base closures in what became, according to Morris, "a McNamara ritual."[61]

OSD announced officially on 30 March that it intended to shut down 52 facilities in the continental United States and 21 abroad,* most of them small; a

---

*These included 4 air bases in England, 2 in France, 4 in Morocco, and 1 in Italy.

number were inoperative government-owned industrial plants. Nonetheless, the potential savings were large—an estimated $56.8 million in FY 1962 and the elimination of almost 22,000 military and civilian positions. There were, of course, a handful of large installations such as Presque Isle Air Force Base, Maine; Naval Station, New Orleans; Raritan Arsenal, New Jersey; Columbia River Group Pacific Reserve Fleet, Oregon; and two Air Force bases in Texas. These closings represented a severe payroll loss to the respective local communities. To minimize the impact, on 31 March McNamara established the Installations and Relocation Planning Committee, chaired by Morris and comprised of service representatives, to plan phaseout dates for designated bases, assist employees in relocation or reemployment, coordinate with community leaders during the readjustment period, and organize at installations to carry out the policies. The committee gave way to the Office of Economic Adjustments within I&L on 3 May 1961 with the mission of mobilizing federal, state, local, and private resources to assist in converting the closed military bases to other productive uses that would bolster the local economies and offset payroll and job losses.[62]

Newsmen were quick to note that none of the 19 military bases in Georgia, home to the chairmen of the House and Senate Armed Services Committees, were included. Despite such criticism, overall editorial reaction was favorable, and most congressional opposition emanated from more seriously affected areas such as New Jersey and Texas. More to the point, McNamara conducted the reductions as announced with only two exceptions, an air base in Texas and Naval Station, New Orleans, the latter following an appeal to the president by Representative Hébert, of the affected New Orleans district.[63]

A year later, on 31 March 1962, DoD announced that another 97 facilities (11 overseas), including 25 government-owned, contractor-operated plants put up for sale, would close. Most of the installations were old forts, camps, or portions of bases whose elimination would affect about 4,000 employees and save more than $20 million annually. DoD subsequently reported that between 30 March 1961 and 31 May 1962 it had closed, sold, or reduced 269 military installations and eliminated almost 43,000 civilian and military personnel positions at an annual savings of $256.8 million. In July, 80 more facilities were eliminated or consolidated, affecting only 682 workers while realizing maintenance savings of more than $5.4 million annually.[64] As impressive as these figures appeared, the installations represented less than four percent of DoD's total facilities and, with few exceptions, the reductions had been relatively painless. That would not remain so in the future.

Base closure made little news during 1963 until mid-December, when announcement of the closing of almost three dozen more installations, including several in key Democratic strongholds, created shock waves. Moreover, DoD had appointed a board to study possible closure of additional naval shipyards. On 7 December McNamara recommended phasing out 35 military installations, 28 in the United States and 7 overseas, over the next three-and-one-half years. Included were the San Francisco and Philadelphia Navy Yards. Shipyard closings excited special attention and appeals because of their large civilian payrolls. Late that afternoon, the president reviewed the proposal and voiced some hesitancy about the closings. McNamara quickly offered to drop the two navy yards, located in heavily Democratic districts, until the next round of base closings due November 1964, at which time he could make a stronger case to Congress. He dropped them from the first list and substituted the Naval Repair Facility in San Diego, California. Several other large complexes, such as Fort Chaffee, Arkansas, Fifth Army Headquarters in Chicago, Stead Air Force Base, Nevada, and depot facilities in New York and Texas, highlighted the closings. Before the official announcement of the action, scheduled for 12 December, McNamara and other DoD representatives notified key congressional committees and members of Congress from the affected districts of the impending action. As the scale of the actual reductions, 33 installations (26 domestic, 7 foreign), two-thirds of them major, plus the elimination of approximately 16,000 military and civilian positions and closing of six navy yards by October 1966, became known, the affected legislators protested swiftly and vehemently.[65]

At his press conference on 12 December, McNamara denied giving any last-minute reprieves to installations designated for reduction and skirted the shipyard closing issue. He stated that while the Pentagon had under study the usefulness of the existing 12 yards because of acknowledged excess capacity he was unaware of any Navy Survey Board recommendations. As expected, legislators from the hardest hit areas of New York, California, and Illinois denounced the reductions. Chicago Mayor Richard Daley was especially irked because McNamara's decisions transferred Fifth Army Headquarters into a solidly Republican district.[66] The administration claimed mail was running 5 to 1 in favor of the reductions, and on 27 December, at the president's direction, McNamara appointed a board, again headed by Morris, to accelerate the identification of additional unnecessary installations, focusing on naval shipyards. At a 28 January 1964 press conference McNamara promised to visit every yard before making any decision. He also cautioned his audience that "every base we have is in jeopardy in the sense that we don't plan to maintain a single one for which there is not a clear and discernible military requirement." [67]

The next round of cuts came on 24 April 1964 when McNamara announced the closure or consolidation of 63 facilities, including 8 overseas. Most of the affected installations were small, but closure of several major installations such as the Watertown (Mass.) Arsenal and two Army ammunition storage depots, in South Dakota and Nebraska, accounted for slightly more than 26 percent of the personnel reductions and 17 percent of overall savings. The secretary said that it would take another six to nine months for DoD to complete its study of Navy shipyards; he would not forecast when another round of base closings would occur. There was relatively little protest about the latest reductions. "Apparently," in Carl Vinson's words, "they've closed bases that no one is concerned about."[68]

In early October McNamara informed the president of the results of base closures through the end of FY 1964. Some 574 military installations had been closed or consolidated, 32,921 civilian and 52,913 military positions eliminated, and $576.8 million saved annually.[69] The following month he received the special naval yard study, which recommended closing the Brooklyn Navy Yard, phasing out the Portsmouth (N.H.) Navy Yard by FY 1975, and consolidating the Mare Island and San Francisco naval shipyards. Based on "Industrial Capability Factors," the study determined the Philadelphia Navy Yard to be the best shipyard to retain and Portsmouth the best to close. Either the Brooklyn or Boston Navy Yard could be closed, but not both because of the large concentration of naval ships in the northeast. At a 19 November press conference 16 days after Johnson's resounding election victory, McNamara announced 95 actions to reduce, consolidate, or discontinue activities in the United States and overseas. Besides the shipyard closings, the historic Springfield (Mass.) Armory and a large number of Army and Air Force depots and training facilities were closed. The pain of losing more than 63,000 jobs was spread across 33 states and the District of Columbia.[70]

This "most sweeping elimination of bases and installations since World War II" caused an uproar. Although McNamara and Morris had flown to New York City to inform Gov. Nelson Rockefeller and Sen. Robert Kennedy of the decision on the Brooklyn Navy Yard, had met previously with the Maine and New Hampshire congressional delegations to discuss closings in those states, and had ensured advance notification to each affected member of Congress, there was much grumbling. *Time*, for instance, reported that McNamara and his aides received 169 calls from members of Congress the day before he made the announcement. Nonetheless McNamara insisted the decisions were "absolutely, unequivocally, without qualification, irrevocable unless some new evidence is brought to our attention." Politicians vowed to pursue measures to keep open many of the threatened bases. DoD, however, found surprising support in editorial pages that praised McNamara's "rare political courage" or Johnson's determination to promote government efficiency. Furthermore, McNamara blunted the criticism by extending the period for closure of some facilities to several years, assuring affected career employees of continued employment elsewhere in DoD, imposing a hiring freeze to insure job opportunities for displaced employees, and offering job placement and assistance advice.[71]

For the period 1 January 1964–30 September 1966, more than 70 percent of the 103,852 civilian employees affected by base closures and reductions accepted another federal job, most (68.6 percent) in DoD. Retirements and resignations accounted for another 14.4 percent of workers, leaving just over 10 percent subject to separation.[72] The 95 actions announced 19 November 1964 accounted for more than 50 percent of all affected jobs since 1961 and provided almost 46 percent of the savings of all the reductions up to that time.

McNamara's success in closing or disposing of unneeded DoD facilities was a tour de force—a remarkable accomplishment unmatched by any secretary of defense in the ensuing 40 years. He had taken the ax to large, unnecessary, and politically well-connected military installations, a totally thankless task. He had saved the taxpayers much money while maintaining DoD's responsibility for its displaced workers. The release of more than a million acres of land for public and commercial use reaped large savings. The price McNamara paid was the alienation of influential members of Congress and many state and local officials. The pain inflicted on senators and representatives by this experience ensured that in the future Congress would seek to have the final word on closures. Evidence that communities could not only overcome but could benefit from the loss of military installations did not diminish congressional determination not to experience another McNamara-type closure process.

The TFX and Cost Effectiveness

To McNamara, big and costly weapon systems, especially aircraft, offered the likeliest targets for improving the development and procurement process. It seemed apparent that too many of these weapons, duplicating one another in some measure or other, produced the kind of waste and inefficiency that McNamara believed he could root out. One of the most important decisions facing McNamara on taking office concerned new fighter aircraft programs of the Air Force and Navy. This question, inherited from the Eisenhower administration, presented a tangle of issues involving cost, service interest, and political fallout.

What became known as the TFX (tactical fighter, experimental) controversy had its origin in 1959 when the Air Force began looking into development of a variable or sweep-wing structure for a new fighter aircraft, soon designated the TFX. About the same time, the Navy, also in search of a new fighter aircraft, was attracted to the sweep-wing design for a fleet air defense plane to be called the Missileer. The letting of contracts by the two services to aerospace firms to study a new fighter moved Director of Defense Research and Engineering Herbert York to initiate study of joint development of a tactical aircraft common to both services. Meanwhile, throughout 1960 the Air Force aggressively pushed design and initial development of its TFX in hopes of getting recommendations from a source selection board by mid-February 1961. On 11 November 1960 Defense Secretary Gates halted both the Air Force plane and the Navy Missileer, feeling he could not commit the incoming administration to these expensive weapons.[73] Thus, deciding the fate of a new fighter for both the Air Force and Navy became one of McNamara's first major weapon decisions.

In the TFX McNamara immediately saw a unique opportunity to showcase his policy of cost effectiveness by instituting a joint service development program that would produce a common fighter for the Air Force and Navy. Coupled with a new approach to contracting, he believed his approach would save money throughout the life of the weapon system. Unfortunately, the TFX did not materialize as McNamara envisioned; instead it became the most controversial weapon system in DoD history.

McNamara's first step in the new direction came in his instruction to York on 14 February 1961 to oversee a joint service evaluation of the Air Force concept for an advanced tactical fighter. This provided a more specific focus of commonality for DDR&E's study of the fighter than previously. In early March, the Navy expressed grave reservations about the value of commonality, and in mid-March the services submitted their unresolved differences. According to a later Navy account, the Air Force's cost estimates were "grossly more optimistic," but the Navy did not challenge them "in order not to embarrass individuals of another service." York established the Tactical Air Committee to settle the outstanding issues in 60 days. By May the committee had concluded that two aircraft were necessary, a complex, high-performance air superiority aircraft (TFX) for the Air Force and Navy and a smaller, simpler, and cheaper one for close air support, dubbed attack aircraft experimental (VAX).[74]

Early in June, the defense secretary accepted the committee's findings and decided that the Navy would administer VAX, which eventually developed into the A-7 aircraft. More importantly, he determined, on the basis of DDR&E's pricing derived from Air Force cost data, that providing two different air superiority aircraft, one for the Air Force and one for the Navy, would cost approximately $1.5 billion more than using one plane for both services. McNamara therefore directed the Air Force to develop the TFX as a joint service venture, working with the Navy to meet the requirements of both services.[75] As he later explained, his objectives were to provide the services with an advanced tactical aircraft that maximized dependability and minimized costs, goals best accomplished by a multi-service aircraft.[76]

McNamara pushed the TFX process aggressively; his personal interest as well as willingness to make decisions accelerated the program. In early August 1961 he reminded Under Secretary of the Air Force Joseph Charyk to solicit contract proposals for the TFX promptly so that a development contract might be awarded before the new year.[77]

As the Air Force study progressed, the Navy raised concerns about the proposed new aircraft. Could, for instance, the Air Force requirement for an offensive supersonic aircraft be harmonized with the Navy's need for a subsonic fighter for fleet air defense? Navy carrier aircraft needed heavy landing gear to stand up to carrier landings, but this feature would make the Air Force fighter more cumbersome. The Navy insisted on a total aircraft weight of no more than 55,000 pounds while the Air Force's minimum was 65,000 pounds.[78] Both services doubted that the same aircraft could perform the missions they required.

With the services unable to agree on a common aircraft, McNamara made the decision for them. On 1 September he directed the Air Force and Navy to develop a bi-service aircraft capable of executing the Air Force's offensive mission and the Navy's defensive one. To address the Navy's concerns, he ruled on weight and length restrictions, a configuration to accommodate the prototype radar the Navy wanted, and an airframe capable of withstanding carrier landings. Despite these specifications, he demanded that changes to the Air Force model to achieve the Navy mission be held to a minimum. McNamara wanted a request for proposals sent to industry by 1 October and signing of preliminary contracts by 1 February 1962.[79]

As scheduled, on 1 October the joint source Air Force–Navy selection board requested proposals from industry; by mid-December six contractor teams had submitted bids. By 1 February 1962 an evaluation group rated the Boeing and General Dynamics proposals the best and the two companies received letter contracts.[80]

Between April and November 1962, formal selection boards conducted four extensive evaluations of the merits of the Boeing versus General Dynamics proposal. In May after a second evaluation, the Air Force rated the Boeing proposal superior and recommended its acceptance. The Navy also rated it superior but doubted that either proposal could meet naval requirements. McNamara agreed to a 1 June proposal from Air Force Secretary Eugene Zuckert and Navy Secretary Fred Korth that the two companies be allowed three weeks to improve their designs—primarily to correct Navy-stated weight and wing shortcomings.[81] At the end of three weeks, on 20–21 June, the DoD evaluators again stated a preference for the Boeing design. Chief of Naval Operations Anderson indicated that it was an acceptable preliminary design for meeting Navy requirements. Zuckert and Korth considered this third set of findings. On the 29th at McNamara's direction, Zuckert allowed the two contractors another 60 days to establish detailed weapon system designs, address commonality more fully, and provide credible development and production cost projections.[82]

At this point McNamara, increasingly concerned that spiraling cost estimates and rumors surrounding the repeated extensions of the TFX* competition had adversely affected morale at both aircraft companies, took a hand in DoD dealings with them. In a letter drafted by DR&E Director Brown, Deputy Defense Secretary Gilpatric on 13 July informed both Boeing and General Dynamics of the reasons for the extended competition and the conditions the successful bidder would have to meet. Aircraft performance had to satisfy both services with minimum divergence from a common design to protect the inherent savings as well as offer credible cost estimates for development and procurement of the TFX.[83]

---

* In December 1961 the USAF version was designated F-111A and the Navy version F-111B.

Following the submission of a fourth set of design proposals along with cost estimates and development schedules, the Air Force–Navy evaluators on 8 November 1962 completed yet another review. They found that both contractor proposals were satisfactory and could meet stated requirements. However, Boeing's had "a clear and substantial advantage" over that of General Dynamics.[84]

Several days later at a working breakfast held on 13 November, McNamara, Gilpatric, Zuckert, and Charyk tentatively settled instead on General Dynamics, apparently because it offered higher commonality of identical parts—83.8 percent to Boeing's 60.4 percent. Gilpatric believed that Boeing's greater dependence on different parts would prevent it from achieving the promised $1 billion in savings. The same day, McNamara and Gilpatric met with President Kennedy and told him a bi-service TFX could be built. McNamara explained that the Boeing design had operational superiority, but General Dynamics offered the "best chance of hitting program date and cost" and would likely be chosen. The president made no comment. According to Zuckert, who met with McNamara before and after the meeting with the president, this was a tentative conclusion contingent upon Zuckert's review of all pertinent TFX material. On 24 November, OSD announced the selection of General Dynamics as the F-111A/B prime contractor.[85]

The decision came as a shock, not only because civilians had overruled the military's choice but also because the only written justification for selecting General Dynamics was a 21 November 1962 memorandum for the record signed by Zuckert and Korth and approved by McNamara. In the memo they agreed that "inasmuch as either of the proposed aircraft can perform the mission required by both services, and the evaluation of the proposals provides no overriding margin between the competitors, it is necessary to consider other factors in evaluating these aircraft." They went on to judge several novel technical proposals by Boeing as developmentally risky. They thought that the greater commonality and integration promised by the General Dynamics proposal would save $623 million against $397 million for the separate development proposed by Boeing. Finally, they deemed Boeing's cost estimate overly optimistic.[86] In short, as McNamara later stated,* the greater commonality of the General Dynamics design and the company's realistic cost projections were the decisive factors in his decision. He thought Boeing had really proposed two different airplanes and understated costs, leading him to conclude that the company "simply did not appreciate the complexities of developing the TFX."[87] Others agreed that Boeing had underestimated costs, but suspected General Dynamics did too.[88]

Shortly after the announcement, Sen. Henry Jackson of Washington State, home of the Boeing Company, met with McNamara. According to one account, the defense secretary was less than cordial to Jackson, who then turned to Sen.

---

* DoD General Counsel John McNaughton read the secretary's prepared statement to a congressional investigating committee on 13 March 1963.

John McClellan, chairman of the Government Operations Committee and its Permanent Subcommittee on Investigations. On 21 December McClellan wrote to McNamara and asked him to hold up on the TFX contract until his subcommittee conducted hearings on the matter. Gilpatric informed the senator that the decision had been made, the project was far along, delay would not be in the national interest, and an amendment to the original letter contract had been signed. McClellan did not take kindly to this brushoff, and a subsequent meeting with McNamara about the hearings convinced him that the secretary's brisk, no-nonsense style was no more than undisguised arrogance. Already a highly charged issue between McNamara and the military, the TFX now became a political lightning rod as well because McNamara, in Zuckert's words, "bought himself an unnecessary fight."[89]

With McNamara having highlighted the TFX as a centerpiece of his well-publicized economy drive, the congressional hearings examined and at length challenged his notions of efficiency, management, and ethics. In testimony before a subcommittee of the Joint Economic Committee, not the TFX Investigation Committee, on 28 March 1963, he insisted that the TFX undertaking was the most important action to date in reducing the number of U.S. weapon systems. The commonality of the winning proposal underlined that economy and efficiency in DoD could be well served by a multi-service rather than a single-service weapon. The resultant savings from having one aircraft instead of two would probably exceed a billion dollars in TFX development, production, and operation costs.[90] This figure came from a 7 March memorandum prepared by A. W. Blackburn, a former Marine test pilot and aeronautical engineer working in DDR&E, who assumed savings of $400 million in development, $290 million in production, $160 million in inventory stocks over eight years, and another $150 million if procurement reached 1,500 units.[91]

The cost-saving claims notwithstanding, the choice of General Dynamics seemed to some congressmen arguable and arbitrary. A later congressional report in 1970 complained that there was "no paper work, no documentation, and no special staff studies" of key issues and questions raised by the military and characterized McNamara's actions as "capricious, lacking in depth, and without factual substantiation." Even such close supporters as Charyk felt McNamara compounded the TFX's difficulties by appearing to be "making up his mind by himself" and "running roughshod over all these things."[92]

Instead of headlining the prospect of achieving substantial economies, news accounts focused on charges, brought up by the McClellan committee, of conflict of interest, political favoritism, and DoD civilian disregard of military advice. Returning fire, Pentagon spokesman Arthur Sylvester accused unnamed senators of placing their "state self-interest in where the contract goes." An angry McNamara wrote McClellan on 9 March that the fragmentary releases of the hearings had "undermined public confidence in the integrity and judgment" of OSD officials.[93] After filing an affidavit with the committee on 13 March and testifying on the

21st, two days later McNamara again protested the selective release of portions of testimony of witnesses; he was especially incensed over newspaper reports that he wept under Senate questioning.[94]

Among the more damaging charges, McClellan's committee alleged conflict of interest by Gilpatric and improprieties by Korth in the contractor selection process.* An expanded inquiry, launched after the hearings closed, led Korth to resign on 15 October 1963 as a result of his conclusion that "certain of his actions appeared inconsistent" with the high standards of office he had sought to follow. Several days earlier, the *New York Times* had reported that Gilpatric would be leaving government around Christmas. Within days of President Johnson assuming office on 22 November, ugly allegations surfaced that he had received $100,000 to ensure General Dynamics would get the TFX contract. McNamara, however, had never discussed the TFX matter with the then vice president.[95]

Besides these troubling accusations of personal misconduct that shadowed the TFX decision throughout 1963, TFX development itself was not going smoothly, as rising costs seemed to validate congressional skepticism. Contrary to Blackburn's analysis, the Navy's estimated cost of a TFX aircraft had increased dramatically from $4.5 million to $7.75 million between 8 January and 20 March 1963. McNamara deemed realistic cost estimates essential and placed strict limitations on changes leading to higher costs. Glaring overruns threatened the inherent savings he believed existed in joint production and fixed-price-incentive-fee contracts, as well as undermining the credibility of the department's commitment to cost-cutting. In the midst of the hearings, McNamara ordered key staff from DDR&E, the OSD comptroller's office, and the Air Force and Navy to commence monthly meetings once McClellan's investigation concluded.[96]

In mid-January 1964, McNamara requested the latest information on the TFX to include a review of the original versus currently estimated costs. The initially proposed empty weight of the plane was 38,804 pounds, but by mid-December 1963 it stood at about 45,000 pounds. The Navy's reply, delivered on 5 February, warned that the increasing weight of its F-111B mandated major changes in the aircraft to make it acceptable for shipboard use. This would, of course, further reduce commonality. After listening to Navy briefings in early February, Brown, Zuckert, and new Secretary of the Navy Paul Nitze concluded that present weight reduction efforts were encouraging and that development of the F-111B should continue.[97]

Eventually, in May 1964,† General Dynamics received a fixed-price-incentive-fee contract of the type McNamara greatly preferred as a means of placing the burden of performance and cost control on the contractor's shoulders. Since

---

* Gilpatric's law firm had represented General Dynamics, and Korth's banks, which he headed before becoming secretary of the Navy, had made loans to the company.

† Until then the company did the work under the authority of an amendment to the original letter contract in December 1962.

becoming secretary of defense, his own study of several major weapon systems purchased since 1958 had revealed that all came in at least 300 percent over original estimates. A Harvard Business School study published in 1962 supported him; it showed that the average cost increase for 12 major weapon systems was 220 percent.[98]

A fixed-price-incentive-fee contract promised to reduce cost overruns by establishing an upper limit set by the government, usually 30 percent above the target cost. It followed that a fixed-price-incentive-fee contract would force bidders to submit realistic cost figures because the government would no longer compensate them for overruns. Furthermore, the contractor had an incentive to hold down costs to make a higher profit because the firm would still receive the full amount specified in the contract.[99]

Letting the contract resolved only one problem—who would build the plane. A host of others remained. McNamara was willing to trade off lowered performance levels for an acceptable means of reducing weight since he viewed the extra operational advantages desired by the services as unacceptable development risks that would result in cost overruns. By late July 1964, however, modifications to weight and performance had lowered commonality between the Air Force and Navy versions to 78.8 percent. Just as disconcerting, the Air Force, Navy, and contractor were using different assumptions, different methods of calculation, and different starting points when estimating aircraft weight and performance characteristics. Finally, the Navy's design review of 14 August found that most of the several configurations submitted for the F-111B reduced commonality substantially, some to less than 30 percent.[100]

These persistent problems and disagreements led to the creation in August 1964 of a DDR&E ad hoc group to study F-111B problems. It reported on 1 October that the final version might not meet the Navy's specifications chiefly because of weight increases. Research and development cost projections were up at least $100 million over earlier estimates and fewer aircraft than planned were to be ordered, further increasing unit costs.[101] Thus costs and weight for the F-111B continued to rise while commonality continued to fall. No one could tell if these problems were systemic or might be corrected.

On 15 October 1964, about two weeks ahead of schedule, McNamara was on hand to witness the rollout of the first test F-111A at the General Dynamics plant in Fort Worth, Texas.* He reminded the thousands of spectators that this was an aircraft "some believed could never, would never, be built. It will be built." He lauded the plane as uniquely versatile in its performance capability and multi-mission competence. He further praised the program for its technical achievements and noted that joint design and development had saved $1 billion

---

* According to program schedules, the Navy's F-111B was due for rollout around 1 April 1965 and initial flight test around 1 June (*Aviation Daily*, 23 Dec 64).

in costs over two separate weapon systems. On 21 December 1964, 10 days ahead of schedule, the first F-111A test flight occurred and, despite various technical and mechanical problems, deemed insignificant for an aircraft of such complexity, was declared a success. The day was surely McNamara's, but doubts persisted about the aircraft's weight and, more importantly, about steeply rising developmental costs that might force cutbacks in expected production.[102]

In the short run, at least, McNamara had weathered the TFX storm. The McClellan Committee investigation had adjourned its hearings in mid-November 1963 and did not resume in 1964. The F-111A program was slightly ahead of schedule and the F-111B* seemed to be making progress. Success came at a price. McNamara had set a standard for savings that was impossible to achieve. After all, if economy tipped the balance in favor of General Dynamics, then costs had to be carefully controlled and this did not appear to be happening. McNamara was later adamant that the TFX was "an absolutely correct decision." He charged that the military services did not really go along and he could not "monitor underlying day-to-day-change-orders that the two services put in to their versions of the TFX." He faulted Congress for not supporting the project and the Navy for resistance to the F-111 and poor implementation of the concept.[103] One might add that McNamara's perceived dismissive treatment of influential legislators, the public sniping between civilians and the military over the TFX, and conflict of interest charges all contributed to impair the program. Later these festering quarrels would reemerge to discredit the entire TFX effort.

In the years 1961-1965 McNamara pursued his search for savings with genuine conviction, sustained enthusiasm, and dogged determination. Secure in the knowledge that he had full support from Kennedy and Johnson, he acted boldly and purposefully to carry out his initiatives. Thus, four years after taking office, McNamara could point to impressive savings and efficiencies throughout the Department of Defense. He had helped to reduce the balance of payments deficit through many measures, most notably the offset agreements arranged with the West Germans and the closing of dozens of U.S. overseas base facilities. His development and management of the Cost Reduction Program produced large savings, ferreted out waste, streamlined contracting procedures, and became a model for the whole executive branch to emulate. Closing unneeded military bases in the United States met strong opposition despite McNamara's best efforts to ensure that displaced employees received comparable jobs or were retrained for new ones, but the action unquestionably saved much money. Only with the TFX, the showcase for commonality in the development and production of complex weapon systems, did McNamara falter, amid controversy over selection of the contractor, costs that

---

* The first test F-111B had its rollout on 11 May 1965; its first flight followed a week later.

rose beyond initial projections, and criticism of the plane's performance capabilities. On balance, McNamara proved highly successful as a business manager. Among his many management triumphs there can be little doubt that, whatever the disappointments, his search for savings stood at the forefront.

CHAPTER XVIII

Tightening the Budget: FYs 1965 and 1966

By the end of 1963 favorable circumstances helped the Department of Defense embrace cost cutting more fully as a major objective. Most importantly, the international climate had improved since the Kennedy administration's first two years in office. The Berlin crisis, the Bay of Pigs invasion, and the Cuban missile crisis lay behind. The situation in South Vietnam, although of growing concern, did not yet require large resource allocations. The signing of the limited nuclear test ban treaty in August 1963 had appeared, at least to some, to signal a relaxation of tension between the United States and the Soviet Union. Accordingly, large outlays for defense did not seem as desirable or necessary as before. After two years of approving increased budgets, Congress had cut more than $2 billion from the FY 1964 Defense appropriation bill, thereby underscoring its altered perception of national security requirements.* The cut occurred at a time when the Department of Defense foresaw a stabilizing of expenditures after the heavy spending of previous years.[1] Finally, McNamara's cost reduction program, formally inaugurated in July 1962 and reflecting his commitment to efficient management and elimination of unnecessary expenditures, achieved substantial savings in its first year.

Cost cutting gained extra impetus and authority from a succession of well-publicized measures by President Johnson, immediately after assuming office in November 1963, to reduce the size of the FY 1965 budget then nearing completion. In part he was motivated by a desire to slash federal expenditures for the upcoming fiscal year below the politically symbolic ceiling of $100 billion in order to gain support of congressional fiscal conservatives for the Kennedy-proposed tax reduction program stalled in the Senate for months. Because Defense spending accounted for more than half of all expenditures, DoD became the focus of much of the new president's rhetoric and attention.

---

* For congressional action on the FY 1964 appropriation bill, see Chapter VI.

During the 1964 presidential election campaign, when DoD was putting together its FY 1966 budget, Johnson continued to champion the cause of restraint. But the administration's proposals for reduced Defense budgets in FYs 1965 and 1966, which freed up funds for the president's Great Society domestic programs,* left it vulnerable to Republican charges, most prominently from presidential candidate Barry Goldwater, that it was weakening the nation's defenses.

The Kennedy Administration and the FY 1965 Budget

The planning-programming-budgeting system—what came to be called PPBS—that McNamara introduced in 1961 steadily gained wider acceptance by the services. Yet dissatisfaction within OSD about FY 1964 budget procedures prompted changes for FY 1965 aimed at furnishing the secretary of defense more time to evaluate force structure and programs.

Since a flurry of last-minute Program Change Proposals (PCPs) had complicated and delayed the process in the summer of 1962, OSD Comptroller Charles Hitch urged McNamara to advance the timetable for FY 1965 by a few weeks. He recommended that the Joint Chiefs of Staff provide preliminary force structure proposals by 1 May 1963 and that the services and other components submit all major PCPs by 15 June. Earlier deadlines would enable the secretary to complete his own review of the force structure and major PCPs by 15 August, not mid-September as before. McNamara essentially accepted the recommendations but pushed up the date for submission of major PCPs even more—to 1 June. He also wanted the services to submit an updated Five-Year Force Structure and Financial Program (FYFS&FP) on 1 May 1963, although this date, along with others, was allowed to slip.[2]

Another change involved completing the Joint Strategic Objectives Plan (JSOP) sooner in order to integrate it better into the budget process and to allow an earlier updating of the FYFS&FP. Some of the Joint Chiefs, especially the Air Force's General LeMay, feared that McNamara's emphasis on the FYFS&FP might diminish the importance of the JSOP. However, in late 1962 McNamara asked the chiefs to accelerate their work on the next plan, JSOP-68, so that it could help provide guidance for reaching decisions on the FY 1965 force structure. Accordingly, the chiefs submitted several sections of JSOP-68 in December 1962; their JSOP force structure proposals went to McNamara in April 1963. They split on more issues than in the previous year. Major differences continued to involve the required numbers of Air Force strategic missiles, Army divisions, and aircraft carriers, as well as personnel levels for all the services. LeMay wanted far more Minuteman missiles (1,950) in the force by FY 1969 than the others. Chairman

---

* Johnson first publicly used the term "Great Society" in his address at the University of Michigan on 22 May 1964.

Maxwell Taylor and the Army proposed 1,350, the Navy and Marine Corps 1,400. Taylor submitted separate recommendations to McNamara, calling the continental defense program probably the weakest of all and urging additional efforts to develop Nike-X as a high-altitude intercept system.[3]

Considerations other than military ones shaped the Defense budget. More than in the previous year, the reluctance of the administration to exceed the $100 billion mark in federal expenditures acted as a brake on spending. In April 1963, as it launched the annual spring budget preview, the Bureau of the Budget estimated overall expenditures for FY 1965 at $106 billion and suggested reductions of $4.7 billion, including $1.3 billion in space programs, interest on the public debt, and Defense, which might lower the total to $101 billion. Budget Director Kermit Gordon urged department heads to pare down their projected expenditures, emphasizing President Kennedy's intention to apply a substantial portion of additional revenue expected from "the advance of the economy to full employment (anticipated with the enactment of the tax program)" toward eventually eliminating the budget deficit. This meant, Gordon cautioned, a tighter budget than would otherwise be available.[4]

In its preliminary projection, OSD estimated DoD expenditures at $52.69 billion, which included military assistance and civil defense as well as military functions. BoB subsequently arrived at virtually the same figure. Following consultations with McNamara and other cabinet heads, in early August Gordon sent the president the bureau's recommended planning figures. The president approved. BoB set the DoD expenditure target at $52.7 billion, the government-wide target at $102.1 billion. Gordon mentioned possible changes in military programs, including cutbacks in the number of Minuteman missiles and attack carriers and cancellation of the Dynasoar* spacecraft.[5]

While BoB examined overall expenditure targets and individual departmental estimates, McNamara and Hitch met with limited success in accelerating the planning and programming phases. By the fall of 1963 the services had submitted some 300 PCPs. Despite requirements for earlier submissions of key items, slippages continued, deadlines had to be extended, and important target dates, such as that for PCP submissions, which already had been pushed back to 31 August, were not met. On the assumption that the 31 August date would allow it to review and decide all major PCPs by early September, OSD initially had established 21 October as a deadline for submissions of a further updating of the FYFS&FP, but had to let that slide to 30 December. As Hitch later put it, "the calendar defeated us." Program review became "mixed up in a very undesirable way" with the budgeting phase that followed.[6]

---

*Conceived in 1958 in the wake of the Soviet launch of Sputnik, Dynasoar was intended to be a prototype military space plane capable of achieving hypersonic speed but short of orbital velocity. In December 1961 a new plan called for attainment of orbital flights. McNamara increasingly questioned the military missions the project could serve, especially in light of NASA's progress in piloted flight in its Gemini and Apollo programs.

This complicated matters for the services and other DoD components, which had submitted budgets at the beginning of October totaling some $60.9 billion (NOA), including military assistance.[7] At that point the Air Force alone had $3.5 billion of PCPs that OSD had not yet acted on. On 7 October, in forwarding his proposed budget to Secretary Zuckert (it had been due in OSD on 1 October), LeMay pointed out that only a few PCP decisions had been received from OSD. Consequently, many proposals had to be excluded from the basic budget and shown only as addendums. Although he recognized the administrative necessity of submitting a budget, LeMay felt that uncertainties about the proposed program changes and the size of the final budget made it too early to furnish an analysis of future Air Force capabilities.[8]

LeMay had even sharper criticisms. In September the Joint Chiefs and the National Security Council received from OSD early versions of draft presidential memorandums (DPMs) regarding Defense programs in the FY 1965 budget.[9] LeMay believed they really represented "a preview to decisions already reached." More generally, in LeMay's view the tentative decisions in the DPMs reflected "an abandonment of one of the basic tenets of the OSD program system—the merit of reviewing proposals as a package. The draft memoranda, at least as made available, indicate a piecemeal approach to force considerations."[10]

Navy dissatisfaction during the program review centered on McNamara's rejection of its proposal to provide nuclear propulsion for a conventional carrier Congress had authorized in FY 1963. After reviewing the Navy's appeal and discussing the matter with Secretary Korth, Chief of Naval Operations Admiral David McDonald, and others, McNamara reaffirmed his decision on 25 October. He did not accept the Navy's argument that five nuclear-powered task forces were as effective as six conventionally-powered ones. Although nuclear carriers would clearly be more expensive, McNamara contended it was not a matter "of merely trying to hold down costs, but whether any amount of money, large or small, is better spent on nuclear or on conventional ships." Moreover, obtaining congressional approval of additional funds for nuclear construction would most likely result in long delays. Nor did McNamara accept the Navy's fallback position to defer construction of the conventionally-powered carrier, presumably in the hope of securing approval of a nuclear-powered carrier. Deferring construction, he said, might create an impression that construction of new attack carriers was not really required. However, Spurgeon Keeny of the NSC staff argued that if projected expenditures for FY 1965 turned out to be tight, construction of the conventionally-powered carrier should be deferred. Neither the requirement for the conventional carrier nor the urgency of its construction, he believed, had been demonstrated.[11]

The DPM on strategic retaliatory forces recommended a Minuteman force much smaller (McNamara now favored a leveling off at 1,200 missiles) than Le-

May and the other chiefs had advocated. NSC staff member Carl Kaysen, an advocate of smaller strategic forces, thought that the justification for the 1,200-Minuteman force rested on McNamara's belief that the numbers were "the minimum the Services will accept." He believed that a good case could also be made for a force of 950 in FY 1969.[12]

By mid-November OSD and the White House staff began joint consideration of the DPMs. Five of these—land-based tactical air forces, attack carrier forces, airlift and sealift forces, a national underground command center, and research and development—were examined at a meeting on 15 November.[13] The conferees pondered nearly 30 items, reaching decision on some and deferring others, including the fate of the Dynasoar program, to a meeting a week later. Following that, McNamara intended to go over the budget with Kennedy at Hyannis Port on 29 November (the day after Thanksgiving, as had been the administration's practice). He would then prepare a joint memorandum with Gordon setting forth their differences so that the president could make his final decisions by no later than 10 December.[14]

Kennedy's Assassination: Johnson Takes the Reins

In the early afternoon of 22 November, while Defense and White House representatives were engaged in their second budget meeting at the Pentagon, they received word that the president had been shot in Dallas, Texas. McNamara recalled that in the midst of the discussion, his secretary informed him of an urgent telephone call, which he took in his office. It was Attorney General Robert Kennedy telling him that the president had been shot. McNamara returned to the conference room and, "barely controlling my voice, reported the news to the group. Strange as it may sound, we did not disperse: we were in such shock that we simply did not know what to do. So, as best we could, we resumed our deliberations." About 45 minutes later the attorney general called again to report that the president had died. McNamara adjourned the meeting "amid tears and stunned silence."[15]

McNamara then went to the JCS meeting room to inform the Joint Chiefs, who were conferring with a group of West German military officials. After the Germans departed, the secretary and the chiefs agreed to order a worldwide alert of U.S. forces. At Robert Kennedy's request, McNamara and General Taylor accompanied him to Andrews Air Force Base in suburban Maryland to meet Air Force One carrying the body of the dead president, his widow, and new president Lyndon Johnson, who had taken the oath of office aboard the aircraft before leaving Dallas. In the Executive Office Building later that evening Johnson met with McNamara, for whom he had developed great admiration and respect while serving as vice president. Johnson recalled that he told the secretary that "if he ever tried to quit I would send the White House police after him."[16]

Near the top of the list of the most pressing matters facing the new president stood the FY 1965 budget, regarding which Johnson received much advice. Former President Eisenhower, who drove to Washington from his Gettysburg farm the day after the assassination, stressed the importance of a prompt tax cut for the nation's economic health, the need to hold down expenditures for FY 1964, and the projection of even lower expenditures for the following fiscal year. Gordon sent Johnson a memorandum describing BoB's functions and responsibilities and pointing out that, although many tentative decisions had been made on the FY 1965 budget, the president still had time to put his own stamp on it if he were prepared to invest a great deal of time. On Sunday, the 24th, Gordon met with the president and described for him the burden he would take on if he decided to make the budget his own; Johnson said he would do it.[17]

The tragic circumstances that brought Johnson to office made his first weeks predictably hectic. His decision to undertake a major shrinkage of the budget, with so little time left before its presentation to Congress in late January, intensified the pressure on him, demanding innumerable meetings and telephone calls and long hours of study. He later said he "worked as hard on that budget as I have ever worked on anything. . . . I studied almost every line, nearly every page, until I was dreaming about the budget at night."[18]

On the 25th, the day of Kennedy's funeral, Johnson convened a late-evening meeting with his top economic aides, including Gordon and Chairman of the Council of Economic Advisers Walter Heller, to discuss the budget. If it turned out to be the first budget to exceed $100 billion in expenditures, the president believed that congressional approval of the proposed tax reduction would prove difficult. He was worried that the Senate Finance Committee, particularly its powerful chairman, Harry Byrd, might prevent the measure from even reaching the Senate floor. He told the group, "Unless you get that budget down around $100 billion, you won't pee one drop." The next day Gordon reported to the president that prospects were brighter than they looked the previous night for paring expenditures to around $100 billion, in part because McNamara now felt he could reduce Defense spending by an additional $600 million. Nevertheless, the working figure of $101.5 billion they had settled on contained cuts that would "provoke outcries from the wounded agencies and their clienteles."[19]

For Johnson, known as a big spender during his years in Congress, budget trimming now became the order of the day. In addition to providing assurance of continuity following Kennedy's death, the new president strove to impress upon government officials the overriding need for frugality. On the 26th McNamara conveyed to the Joint Chiefs, service secretaries, and other DoD officials Johnson's desire that all presidential appointees continue in office. The best way to honor the memory of President Kennedy and to show loyalty to his successor was "to get back to work." The secretary indicated that the budget ought to be completed by

10 December; no major issues remained for decision.[20] Meeting with the chiefs a few days later, Johnson stressed his commitment to economizing and urged them to take steps to reduce the cost of defense procurement. He asked them to examine again their budget requirements, emphasizing that "unless the Congress is convinced of this Administration's dedication to frugality and thrift, legislation vital to the well-being of the country will not move."[21]

In his public statements, too, Johnson made government economy a central theme. Before a joint session of Congress on the 27th, he urged prompt passage of the civil rights and tax cut bills and promised to administer government expenditures "with the utmost thrift and frugality." The president also visited the Pentagon, where in the building's auditorium he urged his listeners "to protect your country's purse, to safeguard not only her military strength but her financial stability. I count on you and I plead with you to put a premium on sparing instead of spending, to get along with less while you are doing more."[22]

During these first few weeks in office Johnson's goal seemed merely to lower anticipated FY 1965 expenditures to just under $100 billion, which Gordon felt was not difficult to accomplish. Had he lived, Kennedy probably would have done the same. Treasury Secretary Douglas Dillon had reached an understanding with Kennedy that the budget would be under $100 billion, although Dillon thought that $99.5 billion was as low as it could go. "But we all knew," Dillon acknowledged, "there were ways of making budget figures appear somewhat smaller." At DoD some savings resulted from imaginative bookkeeping, which the press noted was nothing new in the federal government. McNamara balked, however, at juggling the figures too much, telling the president and Gordon, "We just can't screw up the integrity of the financial process over here."[23]

The timetable for preparation of the Defense budget suffered only a slight delay; the meeting interrupted by news of Kennedy's death resumed on 27 November. McNamara did not accept BoB's proposals to postpone procurement of 50 Minuteman missiles and effect other savings in that program. On 6 December he submitted to Johnson the final version of the DPM on strategic retaliatory forces and the next day a DPM with his overall recommendations on the budget. In the latter he estimated Defense expenditures at $51.4 billion and new obligational authority for military functions, military assistance, and civil defense at $51.0 billion. At his first news conference, on 7 December, Johnson indicated he had been meeting on the budget that morning with McNamara, who was planning to spend several hundred million dollars less than he had the previous year, partly by reducing civilian employment in DoD. At a separate press conference at the White House McNamara spelled out these plans, which also involved reductions in noncombat military personnel. On 9 December the president made his final budget decisions at a meeting with McNamara, apparently approving all of the DPM's recommendations.[24] The next day the secretary announced one of them—the cancellation of Dynasoar and its replacement by a Gemini-manned orbital laboratory combination, which would save about $100 million during the next 18 months.[25]

Sometime in mid-December Johnson decided to reduce federal expenditures even more. But shaving another $2 billion overall, observed Gordon, required "painful surgery." Contributing to the savings were changes in the Defense budget directed by the White House in late December, including a further lowering of the civilian manpower level and a variety of other adjustments that brought Defense expenditures down from $51.4 billion to $51.2 billion and NOA from $51 billion to $50.88 billion. Yet the president in his public pronouncements remained vague about the eventual size of the budget, suggesting that it would be around $99 billion but also emphasizing how difficult it was to reduce it further.[26]

On 30 December McNamara, Gilpatric, the Joint Chiefs, and Gordon met with the president at the Johnson ranch in Texas for a last look at the Defense budget. Johnson made a special effort to hear out LeMay, who reiterated his concern about the steep decline in procurement of strategic weapons—from $9 billion in FY 1962 to a projected $3 billion in FY 1969—and urged that the Air Force be allowed to reprogram funds to begin development of both a new bomber and an interceptor aircraft. Johnson asked LeMay to submit a formal proposal to McNamara and the JCS, and after it had been "worked over," he wanted to "explore it further inasmuch as he knew many of his old colleagues on the Hill were worried over this trend toward an all-missile force." There followed discussion about BoB's earlier proposal to postpone procurement of 50 Minuteman missiles in FY 1965, which Gordon said he had since withdrawn. LeMay considered the 50 missiles the minimum required, thought that 150 more would be desirable, and noted that he favored an eventual force of 1,400 Minuteman missiles while McNamara wanted only 1,200. The president decided to leave the 50 Minuteman missiles in the budget. Afterwards, in a jovial atmosphere, the president reported that McNamara and the chiefs were "really on the ball this morning." While posing for a picture with LeMay, the president was overheard to say, "I want to see more of the Chiefs than I've been seeing. Not pro forma meetings, either." McNamara told the press the budget still was not final. Expenditures would be about $1 billion less than the previous year; nevertheless the reduced funds would produce "defenses superior to those in any other time in our history in peacetime."[27]

Although the White House had hinted that the final budget would be smaller than at first anticipated, Johnson surprised many observers by the size of the reduction. In his budget message to Congress on 21 January 1964, he announced $97.9 billion in projected expenditures for FY 1965, $900 million less than the estimate for FY 1964. It was only the second budget in nine years to project lower expenditures than the previous year. In the DoD appropriations budget (NOA), the president requested $50.88 billion, including military assistance, about $120 million less than the previous year.[28]

Tightening the Budget: FYs 1965 and 1966   483

In late January the Senate Finance Committee favorably reported out the tax cut bill, after Johnson had instructed Gordon, as a gesture of courtesy, to deliver an advance copy of the budget to Senator Byrd at his Washington apartment. By the end of February, with opposition to the bill dwindling, both the House and Senate approved it. On 26 February, barely six hours after the Senate action, the president signed the tax bill into law,[29] thus capping a remarkably productive first three months in office.

McNamara clearly played a major part in helping the president achieve the sharp scaling down of the proposed FY 1965 budget that led to passage of the tax reduction bill. And his efforts no doubt enhanced Johnson's already favorable opinion of him. Harold Brown recalled a humorous but significant exchange at a budget meeting, probably in December 1964. Since the president could not be expected to know the numbers and designations of various aircraft that McNamara was discussing, the secretary tried to make light of his own mastery of detail by saying, "Well, there are all these names and all these numbers, Mr. President, and I myself can't really identify all the numbers with the aircraft that they are supposed to belong to." McNamara was obviously trying to be polite; everyone knew he could identify all the aircraft. But the president responded, "Yes, we all know you are kind of backward and can't be expected to understand these things." Johnson's riposte, according to Brown, "got a very big laugh and it was the President's way of saying how smart he considered McNamara to be."[30]

McNamara's last-minute trimming also helped launch the Great Society programs. He remembered drawing "a chart to show the President how I anticipated the per cent of GNP devoted to defense should drop between 1964 and 1965 and subsequent years. I pointed out this should permit, by the saving in per cent of GNP going to defense, a financing of both additional public and private goods. And among the public goods to be financed could be programs to meet the pressing problems of our society—programs which would be developed under the term Great Society."[31]

Yet Gordon felt that the president's handling of the FY 1965 budget marked the beginning of a "credibility gap." Some journalists told him that Johnson had deceived the press by emphasizing the difficulty, if not the impossibility, of getting the budget much below $101-102 billion, when in their judgment it was not that difficult. It seemed the president sought "to build up the tension" in order "to make the achievement of getting it below a hundred billion even more dramatic than it would have been in any case." McNamara took a more sympathetic view, acknowledging that the president was ridiculed at the time for some of his gestures to reduce expenditures, such as turning out the White House lights. He considered them "a dramatic indication of his insistence that every part of the government, in every possible way, increase efficiency, reduce expenditures in order that the funds saved could be spent to meet the pressing needs of our society."[32]

The FY 1965 Authorization Bill

Congressional action on the DoD authorization bill for research and development and for procurement proved quicker and less contentious than in the previous two years, despite a larger request. The administration asked for just over $17.185 billion (NOA), a figure enlarged by a wider jurisdiction over research and development authorization that the armed services committees had recently assumed.* Without this the amount would have been lower than the previous year's $15.3 billion.[33]

The election year, with the two major nominating conventions scheduled to take place in the summer, provided an incentive for speedy congressional action. The House leadership wanted the appropriation bills for all departments passed by 5 June to allow Congress to adjourn by 13 July. These target dates meant the Defense authorization bill had to be approved as early in the session as possible. To hasten the process Chairman Carl Vinson asked DoD to submit the authorization request to his House Armed Services Committee as soon as possible, even before the president's annual budget message to Congress when the request was normally transmitted. After McNamara submitted it on 15 January, Vinson announced he would open hearings on 27 January.[34]

Given the intense feeling in Congress about certain Defense budget issues and partisan attacks to be expected during a presidential election year, the outlook for the authorization and appropriation bills in the congressional committees at first seemed uncertain. Prior to the hearings the secretary had customarily paid visits to key members of Congress, including Vinson and Chairman of the Senate Armed Services Committee Richard Russell, who also chaired the Senate Appropriations Defense Subcommittee. McNamara's assistant for legislative affairs, David McGiffert, recommended that the secretary drop in occasionally on McGiffert's breakfast meetings with groups of congressmen, assistant secretaries of defense, and other Defense officials, and that the secretary increase the frequency of his luncheons with members of Congress, including Mendel Rivers, slated to replace Vinson as House Armed Services Committee chairman when the latter retired at the end of the current session.[35] To what extent McNamara heeded this advice has not been determined. If he did, this may have helped to smooth the authorization process.

In January, before hearings began, McNamara dealt forcefully with a charge made by Barry Goldwater, a member of the Senate Armed Services Committee, that U.S. long-range missiles were not dependable. McNamara immediately responded that Goldwater's claim was "completely misleading, politically irrespon-

---

* In PL 88-174, 7 November 1963, Congress amended the DoD authorization procedures by giving the armed services committees responsibility for authorizing funds for all Defense research and development, not just those related to aircraft, missiles, and naval vessels.

sible, and damaging to national security."³⁶ The rebuttal helped keep the issue from being a focus of the upcoming hearings, although it did come up sporadically.

The chief worry in OSD was the likelihood that Congress would cut the authorization request. At a McNamara staff meeting in January, McGiffert remarked that authorizations had declined between FYs 1962 and 1964. He anticipated that what with the president's economy drive, the pending tax bill, and the election in November, congressional "economy-mindedness" would probably continue. Vinson had already said he wanted to cut $390 million—about six percent—from the research and development authorization. McGiffert noted that the recent broadening of the armed services committees' authorization responsibilities made the budget vulnerable to cuts in more programs. On the other hand, McNamara pointed out that past reductions might have stemmed in part from unsatisfactory presentations by DoD officials. In reviewing past testimony regarding areas where cuts had occurred, he found that in certain cases "the witnesses were not prepared, or took positions at variance with the President's budget."³⁷

Another new element entered into the authorization process—hearings by a subcommittee on research and development recently established by the House Armed Services Committee in response to its expanded jurisdiction. Meeting for four days in mid-January 1964, the subcommittee heard testimony from Brown and from military service representatives.³⁸

McNamara's appearances on 27 and 29 January before Vinson's full committee were shorter and calmer than the previous year. The secretary presented his customary posture statement—the classified version consisted of 247 pages, including 54 pages of charts and tables. Committee members showed unusual interest in overseas developments, particularly in Vietnam. However, questioning on missile dependability proved rather mild, which McGiffert interpreted as reluctance by some Republicans to become too closely linked with Goldwater early in the campaign year.³⁹

Testimony from service representatives between 30 January and 7 February was also relatively brief. LeMay made a strong pitch for an additional $52 million to begin work on a manned bomber and $40 million for an interceptor. On 13 February, in what one newspaper called "record time," the committee reported a $16.915 billion authorization bill, $270.5 million less than the administration request. It cut funding for research and development by $362.5 million, including $37 million for the bomber and interceptor. Then it turned around and added $92 million for the two planes. In a dissenting report four committee Democrats objected to the addition as "premature" and "unwarranted" and offered an amendment to remove it.⁴⁰ The amendment lost easily, which McGiffert attributed to "sentimental votes for Vinson, enthusiasm for the bomber, and the relatively small amount of money involved." On 20 February the House passed the authorization bill without change, 336 to 0.⁴¹

The Senate acted with similar dispatch. Although two committees experimented with a new procedure designed to speed subsequent work on the appropriation bill, the experiment had no ostensible effect on consideration of the authorization bill. The Senate Armed Services Committee and the Defense Subcommittee of the Committee on Appropriations, both chaired by Russell, decided to hold joint hearings in February to avoid duplicative testimony and to lighten the burden of attendance by members who served on both committees. McNamara led off the testimony (3-5 February) in poorly attended sessions; only 8 of the 31 members of the two committees attended the final day of his testimony. Goldwater did not participate at all. McGiffert observed that "nothing particularly significant or controversial" had so far come up, but he expected some Republicans to try what they had done during the House hearings, i.e., wait until Air Force representatives testified and attempt "to elicit as much equivocal testimony from them as possible."[42]

When the authorization phase of hearings concluded on 21 February, McNamara sent Russell a letter urging the Armed Services Committee to restore all the research and development funds cut by the House. At the same time he called funding for the follow-on bomber and the interceptor premature. He felt that the Air Force still had not made a case for proceeding with the bomber's development. On 25 February the Armed Services Committee reported a bill of $17.040 billion, $125.5 million more than the House. It removed the money added for the interceptor, but retained $52 million for the bomber. During floor debate on 27 February several senators, including George McGovern, spoke out against the extra money for the advanced bomber, but by a vote of 64 to 20 the Senate rejected McGovern's amendment to delete the funds. It then passed the bill as reported, 80 to 0.[43]

The conference committee, adopting most of the Senate's language on points in dispute, recommended the money for the bomber but eliminated that for the manned interceptor, leaving an amended total of nearly $16.977 billion, $208 million below the original request. All the Republican House conferees refused to sign the report, contending that the final figure should have been closer to the House version, and that the higher amount ran counter to recommendations for steeper cuts made by the House subcommittee on research and development. However, by voice votes the Senate, on 5 March, and the House, on 9 March, approved the conference bill. In signing the bill on 20 March, President Johnson paid tribute to Vinson's role in its passage and to his 50 years of service in Congress. "No man in the history of this republic knows more about the posture of our defense," the president said, "and no man has done more to improve it."[44]

The FY 1965 Appropriation Bill

Despite hopes that Congress would also move quickly on the overall DoD appropriation request of $47.471 billion (NOA),* the measure became bogged down first in the House, then more so in the Senate. The many witnesses appearing before the House Defense Appropriations Subcommittee, chaired by George Mahon, testified over a period of two months, 20 January through 19 March.[45] During his three days of testimony (17-19 February), McNamara read portions of his long statement, devoting the usual attention to a survey of international relations. He told the subcommittee that the Cuban missile crisis had "marked the crest of the latest in the series of crises cycles" precipitated by the Soviet Union since World War II. "We now appear to be on the downward slope of this latest cycle," McNamara observed, "and tensions in our relations with the Soviet Union are easing."

McGiffert described the hearings as "far more political than usual." Gerald Ford and other Republicans pressed McNamara hard on Cuba, Vietnam, and the issue of missile dependability "in an attempt to find some political advantage." Committee members expressed much concern over the unstable situation in Vietnam. In his prepared statement, McNamara noted that the conflict was "a Vietnamese war, and in the final analysis it must be fought and won by the Vietnamese," then stated shortly thereafter that "the survival of an independent government in South Vietnam is so important to the security of all of southeast Asia and to the free world that I can conceive of no alternative other than to take all necessary measures within our capability to prevent a Communist victory." Ford seized on the statement, declaring that he had sensed the administration's reluctance to send U.S. combat forces to Vietnam, an intervention he would support. He didn't "like the use of U.S. forces overseas any better than anybody else," but the United States had "to make some hard choices every once in a while." McNamara answered, "We will make whatever hard choices have to be made." The subject of Vietnam also provoked several testy exchanges between Melvin Laird, among other Republican subcommittee members, and McNamara.[46]

On 17 April the House Appropriations Committee reported out a bill of $46.76 billion, some $711 million less than the administration's request. It pointed out that it had, to a greater degree than in previous years, gone along with the proposed budget. The committee also accepted McNamara's assurances about missile dependability. In another gesture of support, the committee added no funds to provide nuclear propulsion for the previously authorized conventional aircraft carrier because, it said, DoD had not requested the funds and they had not been authorized. The bill also included the additional $52 million earmarked

---

* The bill did not include military construction, civil defense, military assistance, and a pay raise, which were dealt with in separate bills that totaled $3.4 billion (NOA).

for the manned bomber. On 22 April the House approved the appropriation bill, 365 to 0, after voting down three amendments, the most contentious regarding the relative share of repair and conversion work to be done by naval and private shipyards and another that would have added funds for nuclear propulsion for the carrier.[47]

The bill still had a long road ahead. On 12 May OSD submitted a reclama seeking a restoration of approximately $271 million of the $711 million the House had cut. Consideration of the reclama had to wait until the Defense Appropriations Subcommittee held further hearings during a three-day period (25-27 May). Russell then suspended the hearings to devote his time to the debate over the civil rights bill.[48] On 22 June McNamara told his staff the logjam on Capitol Hill was about to be broken and that Russell would reconvene hearings on the appropriation bill, which could be expected to reach the Senate floor by 4 July. There was an even chance, McGiffert observed, that Congress would finish its work by the end of August. He pointed out that, primarily because of the president's efforts, cuts so far amounted to only 1.5 percent of the budget request, less than half the previous year's percentage.[49]

In the last week of June Russell resumed hearings on the appropriation bill, eventually listening to Deputy Secretary of Defense Cyrus Vance's presentation of DoD's reclama on 7 July before concluding the hearings the next day. Following a recess (10-20 July) for the Republican convention, the Senate Appropriations Committee on 24 July reported out a bill of $46.774 billion, an amount slightly above the House bill but still nearly $697 million under the administration's request.[50]

After eight hours of debate on 29 July, the Senate unanimously approved the bill as reported. As in the previous year, proponents of deep cuts failed to carry the day. With Russell arguing in favor of the bill as reported, the Senate rejected three proposed cuts.[51] House and Senate conferees then settled on $46.752 billion, an amount slightly below either version of the bill. On 4 August the House narrowly accepted the Senate's version stipulating that at least 35 percent of shipyard repair and conversion funds be allocated to private yards, despite warnings about the provision's harmful effects from members representing districts with naval shipyards. The House then approved the conference bill, 359 to 0. Later that day the Senate concurred by voice vote. On 19 August the president signed the appropriation bill into law.[52] The following traces the bill's progress:

Administration Request	$47,471,000,000
House Appropriations Committee	46,759,267,000
House	46,759,267,000
Senate Appropriations Committee	46,774,401,000
Senate	46,774,401,000
Conference Committee/Enactment	46,752,051,000

Again Congress had reduced the administration's appropriation request, this time by some $700 million. What made the action noteworthy was that it came amidst Republican charges, similar to those Democrats had directed against the Eisenhower administration during the 1960 presidential campaign, that the Kennedy and Johnson administrations had endangered national security in their pursuit of lowered spending. In the period before the November election, McNamara issued vigorous rebuttals, sometimes personally and occasionally through DoD spokesmen, of claims that the Democratic administrations had failed to inaugurate a single new weapon system and that DoD was planning to reduce the nation's nuclear arsenal over the next decade by 90 percent.[53]

The charges were mistaken, the result in part of excessive partisanship in an election year, but McNamara's sharp criticisms of the state of the nation's defenses inherited from the Eisenhower administration and the trumpeting of achievements under his stewardship were themselves politically tinged. In particular his statement before the Democratic party's platform committee in August, which some felt shattered the nonpartisan tradition of defense policy, so outraged his predecessor, Thomas Gates, that he sent a telegram to Gates attempting to clarify the statement. At the latter's request McNamara made the telegram public, along with assurances that he had the highest regard for Gates and his contributions to the nation's defense. Gates retorted that he was "totally unable to reconcile what you told the platform committee with the tone and content of your dispatch to me."[54]

Largely Goldwater's doing, national defense emerged as a central issue in the 1964 presidential campaign. His attacks on the administration did not resonate on Capitol Hill, where members of Congress may have been more concerned about base closings in their districts.[55] Johnson's landslide victory in the 3 November election—486 to 52 in the electoral vote and a 16 million popular vote plurality—was attributable to several factors, including the president's success in portraying Goldwater as an irresponsible extremist whose policies would increase the chances of nuclear war. McNamara's own statements, while sometimes overblown, may also have helped persuade both Congress and the public that Goldwater's criticisms of national defense lacked substance.

Preparation of the FY 1966 Budget

As the FY 1965 authorization and appropriation bills worked their ways through Congress, DoD began preparation of the FY 1966 budget. Since efforts to advance the FY 1965 timetable had not entirely succeeded, OSD again tried to move up the key submission dates and to streamline procedures. Hitch's deputy, Alain Enthoven, in November 1963 had provided a thorough analysis of the defects in the programming system, including its excessive paperwork and wasted motion that caused delays, staff overload, and diluted effort. In drafting FY 1966 budget schedule instructions for McNamara to circulate, Hitch incorporated some of Enthoven's suggestions and remarked optimistically that he thought an even tighter schedule would resolve most of the difficulties encountered in the current year. A major change called for scheduling force decisions and logistics guidance somewhat earlier to furnish a firmer basis for PCPs and other submissions in the hope of reducing unnecessary work.[56]

Deadlines for the JCS delivery of the Joint Strategic Objectives Plan (JSOP-69) were advanced by a few weeks. This would allow OSD to review force levels and issue changes to the military departments and the Joint Chiefs by 15 May. Not only was the front part of the schedule tighter than before, but the secretary's new guidance memoranda were actually updated versions of the previous year's DPMs, although at this early stage they were not called DPMs in order to make clear that the guidance remained tentative. Each memorandum for the first time would contain a logistics section.[57]

The Joint Chiefs completed the first five parts of JSOP-69 in mid-February 1964, two weeks ahead of schedule. A month later, when Taylor forwarded Part VI (force levels), he noted that the chiefs had split on several of the same issues as the previous year—Minuteman missiles, Army divisions, and Navy aircraft carriers. On Minuteman LeMay still stood alone. He now wanted a force of 1,500, the other chiefs 1,200. With regard to Army divisions, Admiral McDonald, Marine Commandant General Wallace M. Greene, who had replaced Shoup, and Taylor wanted to keep the number at 16. LeMay recommended a reduction to 14 in the next five fiscal years. Army Chief of Staff General Wheeler recommended an increase to 17 in FYs 1966 through 1968 and to 18 in FYs 1969 and 1970. The Navy recommended maintaining the current 15 attack carriers throughout the cycle; Taylor wanted to reduce the number to 14 in the last year; Wheeler recommended a steady reduction to 13. LeMay differed markedly, calling for only 13 carriers in the first year and a decrease of one each subsequent year, leaving 9 carriers in FY 1970.[58] Save for LeMay the positions of the chiefs were not far apart on major force-level issues.

In May McNamara circulated his guidance for preparation of strategic retaliatory force PCPs, noting as a key objective assured destruction of Soviet forces after U.S. absorption of a surprise attack. For this purpose the secretary now believed that the adequacy of a 1,000-missile Minuteman force, rather than the 1,200 previously projected as the ultimate size, was "established beyond a reasonable doubt." He questioned the wisdom of including money in the FY 1966 budget for 100 additional Minuteman missiles, because of uncertainties about the optimum balance between strategic offensive and damage-limiting forces. Regarding the Advanced Manned Strategic Aircraft (AMSA) on which LeMay wished to start development, McNamara sided with the other chiefs in maintaining that a decision on development and procurement be deferred pending review of the program definition phase.[59]

Following a suggestion by Harold Brown, McNamara announced to his staff in March 1964 a change in formulating and presenting the budget. He planned to discuss strategic and defensive forces jointly and the relationship between them; in the past this had not received enough attention. The secretary tasked Brown and Hitch to collaborate in preparing a single draft presidential memorandum on the subject and suggested specific questions they should address.[60]

During BoB's spring preview of the FY 1966 budget, Gordon wanted to emphasize long-range program objectives and asked departments to provide a list of broad program issues and how they affected TOA and expenditures. In early May Vance submitted DoD's five-year program and financial projections and, in a separate letter, a list of 16 sensitive principal force structure issues then under consideration within DoD.[61] That summer the planning and programming phases went a little more smoothly than in previous years. By the time the budgeting phase began in the fall, the services and OSD found their estimates much closer to each other than before. Service budget submissions in early October totaled $50.78 billion. This did not include $3.65 billion for Defense agencies and OSD and $370 million for civil defense, bringing the total to $54.80 billion (NOA), about $6 billion less than the $60.90 billion recommended the previous October for FY 1965.[62]

Despite the tighter deadlines in the FY 1966 budget cycle, some slippages occurred, for which the Joint Chiefs and the military services faulted OSD. The chiefs felt that OSD delays at the outset in providing important requirements studies did not permit timely responses to McNamara's tentative force guidance. Moreover, they thought the 30 days set aside during the summer for preparing PCPs should be doubled. In support of the chief of naval operations and the commandant of the Marine Corps, in late October Secretary of the Navy Nitze suggested changes, including increasing the time for preparation of PCPs. In response, Hitch stated that the current schedule was better than the previous one but that improvement was still needed. "The basic problem," he observed, "is that there is barely sufficient time throughout the year to crowd in all the actions that must be taken." Allowing more time at the beginning would help, as would exercising "better discipline in adhering to the established schedule."[63]

McNamara's consultations with congressional leaders on the budget had usually occurred just before the beginning of hearings each January. For FY 1966, however, he and Vance met with at least two of them, Sens. Mike Mansfield and Leverett Saltonstall, much earlier—at the beginning of October 1964—to learn their views on the budget. Mansfield had no suggestions to make but mentioned that considerable congressional support existed for a manned bomber. While not opposed to the idea, McNamara said that he wanted to be sure of the military requirements for the plane and the cost implications before he undertook a program that might run as high as $10 billion. Moreover, he saw no need for an immediate decision. Saltonstall spoke of congressional interest in a new carrier.

McNamara indicated that he would likely include a nuclear carrier in the FY 1967 budget.[64]

At a meeting on 21 November, McNamara, other OSD officials, BoB representatives, and White House staff members resolved several matters in dispute and left others for later decision, such as a proposal to slow down F-111 aircraft production until a more advanced avionics system became available. They also put off a decision to proceed with the huge new C-5 air transport until Enthoven and Donald F. Hornig, the president's special assistant for science and technology, could review the costs and benefits of alternative approaches.[65]

DoD, BoB, and NSC officials discussed the remaining issues again in the first week of December. By then Hornig had received a report from his Military Aircraft Panel unanimously recommending that the C-5 program not go beyond the program definition phase during FY 1966 and that procurement of sealift capability be accelerated instead. NSC's Keeny supported McNamara on going ahead with the C-5, citing political and military considerations that argued for a prompt decision. Hornig recommended that McNamara put off the decision to initiate the program until the following year, expand the sealift program with roll-on/roll-off ships, and perhaps reduce procurement of C-141 aircraft. In the end McNamara put forward a compromise, which Hornig accepted, to include funds in FY 1966 for the C-5 as well as for four new roll-on/roll-off ships. Meanwhile, OSD and Hornig would join in an intensive study to determine the optimum mix of airlift and sealift forces and their vulnerabilities.[66]

At this late stage of the budgetary process, Alexei Kosygin, who had replaced Nikita Khrushchev as premier of the Soviet Union in October 1964, injected a surprise element. Before the Supreme Soviet on 9 December, Kosygin announced that his government would reduce its defense expenditures in the coming year by 500 million rubles (about $555 million). Almost a year earlier, in December 1963, Khrushchev had announced a four percent reduction in defense expenditures, which he had called a "policy of mutual example" since it came at the same time as a similar downturn in U.S. defense spending. Khrushchev's announcement had prompted Roswell Gilpatric to speculate publicly, after he had departed office, on the possibility that the process would continue, "perhaps not in an unbroken decline in tensions, but at least with a definite trend toward less troubled relations in the military sphere." During the 1964 Geneva disarmament talks the Soviet Union had pressed the United States to agree to a 15 percent mutual reduction in their defense budgets, but the Americans had countered that technical talks first had to establish the comparability of cuts since the two budget systems were quite different.[67]

Kosygin's announcement gained additional significance from his statement that the Soviet government acted after learning of the U.S. intention to reduce its Defense budget. Secretary of State Rusk had passed the information to Foreign Minister Andrei Gromyko after McNamara's press conference remarks to this effect on 10 November 1964. Kosygin's linkage of the U.S. and Soviet planned reductions caused concern at the White House and elsewhere. McGeorge Bundy urged the president to have Press Secretary George Reedy publicize McNamara's remarks. This kind of statement, Bundy added, "not only emphasizes our savings but speaks of your order to him to keep on improving basic military effectiveness. This is the balanced position we have held with success for over a year, and I think there is every reason to be proud of it even if Senator Russell is momentarily troubled by the Soviet announcement." And clarifying the record would stop the "foolish rumors." On 10 December Reedy called attention at a White House press conference to McNamara's remarks and emphasized that there had been "no agreement between the two countries on budget cutting, nor any effort whatsoever at mutuality in this matter."[68]

The Soviet announcement proved only a temporary distraction. On 11 December McNamara met with the president to wrap up the budget. At this point, Keeny felt "few, if any decisions" remained. Still, he considered McNamara's detailed DPM with its final recommendations, like the earlier ones focusing on specific programs, too long and complex to be useful to the president. He therefore highlighted for the president the most important recommendations, where McNamara had identified four issues, including the C-5 transport, that until recently had been in dispute with Gordon and Hornig but on which general agreement had now been reached. The DPM did not mention certain issues no longer in question—reducing the Minuteman force from 1,200 to 1,000 missiles, not proceeding with the advanced bomber and interceptor, and delaying deployment of an ABM system.[69] No record of the discussion at the meeting has been found, but the president apparently accepted the recommendations.

With the budget virtually complete, JCS areas of disagreement with McNamara had become fewer and less pronounced. The official JCS history concluded that the majority of the chiefs moved more toward McNamara's position than he did toward theirs. Yet the new chairman, General Wheeler, who had been appointed in July 1964 when Taylor became ambassador to South Vietnam, told McNamara in November that his views on major issues involving strategic retaliatory forces had changed as a result of the recent studies McNamara had commissioned on viewing strategic retaliatory forces as part of a single offensive-defensive package. For example, he now supported the Air Force position on a new strategic bomber and an interceptor.[70]

On 22 December, at the chiefs' gathering with the president at his Texas ranch, McNamara pointed out that he and they agreed on about 95 percent of the budget items, but the chiefs had their say. Wheeler expressed concern about the proposed reduction of the Minuteman force, especially since it would occur at the same time as the phasing out of the Atlas and Titan missiles. He also urged a speedup in the national fallout shelter program and provision of $200 million for preproduction funding of Nike-X. LeMay reiterated his support for the strategic bomber and interceptor. McNamara replied that he would delay for five months a decision on proceeding with the bomber. When Admiral McDonald spoke of shortages in the Navy shipbuilding program, McNamara agreed to add two naval gunfire support ships. General Harold Johnson, who had succeeded Wheeler as Army chief of staff, indicated that the Army was "doing well" and spoke particularly of the excellent equipment it had in the Far East and Vietnam. Like Wheeler, Johnson favored spending more money on Nike-X.[71]

After the meeting, McNamara told reporters that although he had earlier thought that FY 1966 Defense expenditures would be around $50 billion, the amount would be closer to $49 billion, because DoD had achieved "further economies . . . while continuing to increase our military strength." He also mentioned the president's approval in the FY 1966 budget of $157 million to begin development of the C-5.[72] By meeting with the chiefs and by holding a series of pre-Christmas conferences with cabinet heads at his Texas ranch, the president once more gave the impression of working hard to pare down federal expenditures—this time from estimates as high as $108.5 billion to again below $100 billion.[73]

Since the issue of national defense had worked to his advantage in the 1964 presidential campaign, Johnson understandably continued to give it play. On 18 January 1965, a week before transmitting his annual budget message to Congress, the president—in a departure from past practice—sent Congress a special message on the state of the nation's defenses. A peculiar document according to one journalist, it apparently sought to create an impression of great activity as Johnson took office in his own right. It said little about foreign problems, particularly Vietnam. Parts of the message sounded a triumphal note. The president declared the nation "stronger militarily than at any other time in our peacetime history" and claimed that his administration and Kennedy's had succeeded in their goal of "assuring an indisputable margin of superiority for our defenses." Johnson listed the major advances since 1961: a threefold increase in strategic nuclear forces on alert, a major expansion in tactical nuclear forces, an eightfold growth in special forces, a 45 percent increase in combat-ready Army divisions, 15,000 more Marines, a doubling of airlift capacity, and a 100 percent increase in Air Force tactical firepower to support ground forces. In addition, the United States now had more than 850 land-based ICBMs, 300 nuclear missiles in Polaris submarines, and 900 strategic bombers, half of which could be airborne in 15 minutes.

Johnson briefly described the Defense budget he would soon present to Congress, omitting the NOA amount but estimating defense expenditures at $49 billion, some $2 billion less than in FY 1964. This leveling off, he explained, had occurred because much of the force structure increase had already taken place and savings had materialized from DoD's cost reduction program. "If, over the next several years," the president observed, "we continue to spend approximately the same amount of dollars annually for our national defense that we are spending

TABLE 9

Financial Summary by Program, FY 1961-FY 1966 [a]
($ billions)

	FY 61[b]	FY 62 (Orig)	FY 62 (Final)	FY 63 (Final)	FY 64 (Final)	FY 65 (Est)	FY 66 (Est)
Strategic Offensive Forces	-----	7.6	9.0	8.4	7.3	5.3	4.5
Continental Air & Missile Defense Forces	-----	2.2	2.3	2.0	2.1	1.8	1.8
General Purpose Forces	-----	14.5	17.4	17.6	17.7	18.1	19.0
Airlift/Sealift Forces	-----	.9	1.2	1.4	1.3	1.5	1.6
Reserve and Guard Forces	-----	1.7	1.8	1.8	2.0	2.1	2.0
Research and Development	-----	3.9	4.2	5.1	5.3	5.1	5.4
General Support	-----	11.4	12.1	13.0	13.7	14.3	14.6
Retired Pay	-----	.9	.9	1.0	1.2	1.4	1.5
Military Assistance	-----	1.8	1.8	1.6	1.2	1.2	1.3
Total Obligational Authority	46.1	44.9	50.7	51.9	51.9	50.9	51.7
Less Financing Adjustment	3.0	1.3	1.3	.8	.9	1.1	3.2
New Obligational Authority	43.1	43.7	49.4	51.1	50.9	49.7	48.6
Adjustments to Expenditures	+1.6	+1.0	-1.2	-1.1	+.3	-.4	+.4
Total Expenditures	44.7	44.7	48.2	50.0	51.2	49.3	49.0

[a] As of January 1965. Subsequent tables showed slight changes for some years in figures shown here, as somewhat different program breakdowns came into use. The final figures for FY 1965 and FY 1966 differed from the estimates shown. For FY 1965, TOA came to $51.2 billion, NOA $50.5 billion, and total expenditures $47.4 billion. The actual amounts for FY 1966, largely because of the buildup in the Vietnam War, greatly exceeded the estimates shown here. TOA came to $66.5 billion, NOA $63.5 billion, and total expenditures $55.4 billion. The major change was in General Purpose Forces, where the amount reached $29.5 billion. See SCAS and SSCA, *Hearings: Military Procurement Authorizations for FY 1968*, 90 Cong, 1 sess, 1967, 217-18.

[b] Preparation of the Defense budget by program began with the FY 1963 budget. The OSD comptroller later described by program both the original and final FY 1962 budgets, but not the FY 1961 budget.

Source: SCAS and SSCA, *Hearings: Department of Defense Programs, and Authorization of Appropriations During FY 1966 for Procurement, Research, Development, Test, and Evaluation of Aircraft, Missiles, and Naval Vessels for the Armed Forces*, 89 Cong, 1 sess, 1965, 206.

TABLE 10

Comparison of Active Forces, 1961 and 1965

	Actual June 30, 1961	Actual June 30, 1965
Military personnel (in thousands)		
Army	858	968
Navy	627	671
Marine Corps	177	190
Air Force	820	824
Total	2,482	2,653
Selected military forces		
Strategic retaliatory forces		
Intercontinental ballistic missiles (squadrons)		
Minuteman	-----	16
Titan	-----	6
Atlas	4	-----
Polaris submarines (in commission)	5	29
Strategic bombers (wings)		
B-52	13	14
B-58	1	2
B-47	20	5
Continental air and missile defense forces		
Manned fighter interceptor squadrons	42	39
Interceptor missile squadrons (BOMARC)	7	6
Army air defense missile battalions [a]	49 1/2	23 1/2
General purpose forces		
Army divisions (combat ready)	11	16
Army special forces groups	3	7
Warships (in commission)		
Attack carriers	15	16
Antisubmarine warfare carriers	9	9
Nuclear attack submarines	13	21
Other	328	331
Amphibious assault ships (in commission)	110	135
Carrier air groups (attack and ASW)	28	28
Marine Corps divisions/aircraft wings	3/3	3/3
Air Force tactical forces squadrons	93	117
Airlift and sealift forces		
Airlift aircraft (squadrons)		
C-130 through C-141	16	38
C-118 through C-124	35	19
Troopships, cargo ships, and tankers	101	106
Active aircraft inventory (all programs)		
Army	5,564	6,957
Navy	8,793	8,056
Air Force	16,905	14,875
Commissioned ships in fleet (all programs)	819	880

[a] Decrease from 1961 to 1965 reflects phaseout of Nike-Ajax and transfer of Nike-Hercules battalions to Army National Guard.

Source: *The Budget of the United States, FY 1967*, 76.

today, an ever-larger share of our expanding national wealth will be free to meet other vital needs, both public and private." Pentagon officials later predicted that defense spending could be kept under $50 billion for several years, "barring the unexpected." The FY 1966 budget message to Congress on 25 January, which touched briefly on national defense, disclosed that overall federal expenditures would again come in under $100 billion, at $99.7 billion. The submitted budget requested $48.565 billion (NOA) for Defense, including $1.17 billion for military assistance.[74]

Others in the administration also expressed satisfaction with the state of the nation's defenses. An unnamed high official, perhaps McNamara, was quoted as boasting in private that the United States now had "sufficient nuclear power to survive a surprise attack and in retaliation knock the aggressor right out of the 20th century." But the proposed reductions in the FY 1966 Defense budget, much as in the previous year, created a dilemma for the administration, requiring it to demonstrate that a shrinking budget could actually provide more defense. And in claiming that savings at Defense made money available for Great Society programs, it had to guard against the impression that it was sacrificing the nation's security. On the whole, though, it made a good case. One observer thought that, discounting the "political inflation to its boasts," the administration's claims about creating superior forces were justified, although the forces relied on weapons begun almost entirely during the Eisenhower administration.[75] Some remained skeptical. A *New York Times* editorial in January 1965 warned that reductions in personnel or procurement were a calculated risk, and "it should be understood that the nation cannot buy more defense for significantly fewer dollars; it gets less for less."[76] This warning shortly became moot when large-scale U.S. involvement in the Vietnam War demanded far more men and money.

CHAPTER XIX

Vietnam: Into the Vortex

At the time of President Kennedy's assassination on 22 November 1963 the United States stood at a critical juncture in its policy toward Vietnam. The execution of South Vietnam President Diem earlier in the month had brought to power the military leaders who had carried out the coup against him, but the same troubling military and economic situations remained to be reckoned with. To what extent the coup influenced Kennedy's rethinking and, by some accounts, apparent desire to withdraw U.S. troops cannot be ascertained. Students of the administration's policies and informed participants are much divided on his intentions.[1]

Whatever Kennedy's qualms, there seemed little doubt about the direction of U.S. policy as Johnson and McNamara charted the course. On 23 November, the day after Johnson took the oath of office, both McNamara and Rusk sent him status reports on Vietnam in preparation for a planned meeting with Ambassador Lodge. McNamara emphasized the need for a harmoniously working U.S. country team and for the strongest possible economic assistance to the new government, headed by Duong Van ("Big") Minh. Rusk's report, more comprehensive, declared that the outlook in Vietnam was "hopeful," the new government appeared to have popular support, and the military situation was still serious but should improve, as a single chain of command had replaced Diem's and his brothers' dual chain. Rusk also noted Vietnam's huge financial deficit, labeling it "the major operational problem we face immediately."[2]

With Rusk, McNamara, George Ball, McGeorge Bundy, and John McCone present, Johnson met with Lodge on 24 November. The ambassador presented a rather sanguine report—domestically, politically, and militarily—to the point where he thought North Vietnam "might be interested in arrangements . . . satisfactory to us." McCone then gave a "somewhat more serious" CIA estimate, noting increased Viet Cong activity since 1 November (the date of the recent coup) and growing VC message traffic that might reflect "preparations for further sustained guerrilla pressures." Consequently, McCone could not offer "a particularly optimistic appraisal of the future." The president indicated misgivings about the U.S. role, noting the many critics of Diem's removal and assassination, the growing and more insistent congressional demands for withdrawal, and his own belief that the administration should have supported Diem. He thought it necessary to help the new government perform effectively. Since it was too much to expect "to reform every Asian into our own image," the main objective should be "to get along, win the war."[3]

Johnson concluded his first round of action on Vietnam with the issuance of NSAM 273 on 26 November 1963, which emphasized the importance of persuading the new government to concentrate on the critical problems in the Mekong Delta. He made it clear that "it remains the central object of the United States in South Vietnam to assist the people and Government of that country to win their contest against the externally directed and supported Communist conspiracy." He also asked that planning include "possible increased activity" against North Vietnam and examine the ramifications of pursuing covert military action. At the same time, he restated Kennedy's directive of 2 October for a phased withdrawal of U.S. military personnel.[4]

Whatever the differences in the outlook and temperament of the two men, Johnson made clear that he would continue existing U.S. policies—in Southeast Asia as elsewhere. Even if often an outsider in the formulation of the administration's foreign policy, he had tacitly supported it and in any case recognized the importance of projecting a sense of continuity. Moreover, almost without exception he retained the top advisers who had served Kennedy. In addressing a joint session of Congress on 27 November 1963, Johnson declared that "this nation will keep its commitments from South Vietnam to West Berlin."[5]

McNamara in Saigon–December 1963

For all his seeming determination to stay the course, the new president worried about the conflicting reports he had received from Lodge and McCone. Seeking more information, he asked McNamara and JCS Chairman Taylor to visit South Vietnam on their way home from the December NATO meetings in Paris.[6] McNamara was dispirited by what he found in his two-day (19-20 December) stop in Saigon; since his September visit, the situation had deteriorated to a degree he had not anticipated. As General Krulak, the JCS special assistant for counterinsurgency matters, who accompanied McNamara, pointed out: "Orders are issued, but they are often not carried out—because the chain of authority is still preoccupied with its own political and economic survival, and the supervision is just not there."[7] In brief, McNamara reported, "the situation is very disturbing." Unless current trends were reversed in the next two to three months, the result would be neutralization at best or—even more likely—a communist-controlled state. Not only was the new government run by a committee of generals drifting into disaster but it could obtain little help from Lodge and MACV Commander General Harkins, who disagreed on policy and had little official contact with each other. McNamara attributed Lodge's behavior to his having "operated as a loner all his life."[8]

Not all of McNamara's findings were negative. The U.S. resources and personnel he considered more than adequate and could not "usefully be substantially increased"; he concluded that "we should watch the situation very carefully, running scared, hoping for the best, but preparing for more forceful moves if the situation does not show early signs of improvement."[9] In his press conference the same day, 21 December, a more restrained McNamara attributed much of the current difficulties to the inexperience of the new government and the Viet Cong using this to its advantage. He still envisioned eventual victory for the Minh government: "We have every reason to believe they will be successful. We are determined that they shall be."[10]

As 1963 ended and 1964 began, then, McNamara harbored his own ambivalence toward Vietnam. No one recognized more clearly than he the dismal performance of the Minh government, and yet he appeared able to see a positive outcome to what he had described as an impossible position. On 6 January, the president received proposals from Sen. Mike Mansfield suggesting the neutralization of Vietnam and a peaceful solution in Southeast Asia. Otherwise Mansfield visualized deep U.S. involvement such as had occurred in China and Korea. Johnson asked for comments from his advisers to refute the senator's views.[11] McNamara responded that while the war was a Vietnamese responsibility, "we cannot disengage U.S. prestige to any significant degree." United States support since 1954 made extensive engagement inevitable. But even more important, no matter how serious the situation, "*we can still win*, even on present ground rules."[12]

At the same time, McNamara pointed out that in keeping with Kennedy's October 1963 directive to start pulling out U.S. troops (reaffirmed by Johnson on 26 November), approximately 1,000 had been scheduled for withdrawal by the end of December.* On 27 January McNamara testified before a congressional committee that withdrawal would continue until the end of 1965; thereafter, "there might [only] be a continuing requirement for a limited number of U.S. advisory personnel."[13]

The defense secretary's visit to Vietnam in December 1963 left him repelled by the corruption and incompetence of the government in power and by the ability of the Viet Cong to continue its advances, particularly in the Delta area

---

*The purported December withdrawal amounted to a disingenuous statistical exercise. More than 1,000 men did leave Vietnam but most were part of the regular rotation cycle and included also medical evacuation or administrative returnees. See *Pentagon Papers*, bk 3, IV.B.4, 30.

south of Saigon. He strongly supported a revitalized strategic hamlet program to wean villagers from the Communists. He wanted military assistance directed toward internal reform. In addition, he found attractive what came to be known as OPLAN 34A, a plan for sabotage, propaganda, intelligence, and commando hit-and-run operations against North Vietnam by South Vietnamese troops. NSAM 273 called for planning for such covert activity that would take into account North Vietnamese retaliation and international opposition, as well as "the plausibility of denial." OPLAN 34A at least suggested a sense of movement with possible immediate results; it appealed strongly to the JCS. General LeMay went further and advocated aerial bombardment of North Vietnam openly—"We are swatting flies when we should be going after the manure pile."[14]

Still, the dangers inherent in offensive action inhibited an immediate change of policy. Incursions into Laos or bombing of North Vietnam targets carried too many risks. At the end of 1963 the most that seemed acceptable was a continuation of small CIA-South Vietnamese clandestine actions, even though proponents recognized that they were too meager and that larger-scale operations were needed.[15]

At McNamara's request, on 21 December the president approved the formation of a DoD-State-CIA committee with Krulak as chairman to review and select from the 2,000 proposed covert actions contained in OPLAN 34A. The committee completed its report on 2 January 1964 and the JCS endorsed it although they believed that the covert actions, even if successful, would have no great effect on the progress of the war.[16] McNamara then joined Bundy, Rusk, and McCone in recommending to the president the implementation of OPLAN 34A—progressively escalating pressure by expanding intelligence collection, increasing psychological operations (leaflet drops and radio broadcasts), and intensifying sabotage activities.* Bundy described McNamara as "highly enthusiastic" about the plan, while McCone expected "no great results," and Rusk thought that "98% of the problem is in South Vietnam and not in cross-border operations" but that these operations would convey the message to Hanoi that the United States had no intention of quitting Vietnam.[17] The president approved the plan on 16 January with a starting date of 1 February.[18]

OPLAN 34A would require more cooperative effort among the agencies than in the past. Skeptical of MACV's optimistic reports, McCone told Rusk that the reporting on Vietnamese operations needed change. U.S. field officers "had been grossly misinformed by the [South Vietnamese] province and district chiefs." McNamara also recognized the unreliability of incoming statistical information and demanded a change in the current reporting system.[19]

---

* Covert activities, directed by MACV, included disruption of rear area security within North Vietnam, insertion of agent teams into the North, psychological warfare, and maritime and coastal operations. For an account of sabotage operations against North Vietnam, see Richard H. Shultz, Jr., *The Secret War Against Hanoi*.

On 7 January, McCone proposed "developing a new *covert* method of checking on information on the progress of the war." But McNamara knew that the military would resist change, if only because in accepting a CIA-operated reporting system he would, by implication, be criticizing both the Saigon command and the Joint Chiefs. For this reason, as Michael Forrestal of the NSC staff noted to Bundy, the secretary faced "considerable difficulty in accepting the thought that CIA should take on a separate reporting function." McNamara subsequently informed McCone that although he did not oppose improved covert intelligence collection, the required review of the overall reporting system and its improvement should remain "a joint program" involving all members of the Saigon country team.[20]

The Khanh Coup

Any plans for major changes were put on hold after 30 January 1964, when Maj. Gen. Nguyen Khanh and several other corps commanders in a bloodless coup removed Minh as chairman of the Military Revolutionary Council (MRC). No matter how depressing the action, it should not have come as a surprise to U.S. advisers. McNamara's fact-finding tour in December had confirmed Minh's ineffectiveness. Despite popular support from Buddhists, students, and other opponents of the Diem regime, the MRC had never taken charge of affairs. Moreover, when the generals put an end to the Diem regime, they also swept away what passed for a constitutional system.

The success of the Viet Cong in the Delta in previous months owed much to the leadership vacuum and disarray in Saigon. As McNamara observed only two days before the coup, Minh and his colleagues had retained responsibility for military operations after the November coup while assuming additional responsibility for the political and economic functions of a country under siege: "You can imagine, therefore, that something suffered, and I think that what suffered was the military administration or the administration of military operations, as their attention was forced onto these political and economic problems."[21]

What made Khanh acceptable was his opposition to de Gaulle's proposal on 31 January, the day after the coup, for neutralization of all of Indochina under international guarantees. De Gaulle's initiative touched a raw nerve, already exposed since France had recognized Communist China only several days before and de Gaulle now included it as a participant in the guarantees. Earlier, in his New Year's message to General Minh, President Johnson had specifically referred to neutralization as "another name for a Communist takeover." He made this reference on the advice of McNamara to counteract critical commentary in the press. McNamara was convinced that the Minh government could not survive neutralization, nor could the rest of Southeast Asia.[22]

Khanh's pro-U.S. and anti-neutralization stance made U.S. leaders receptive to his ascendancy, no matter what short-term damage the coup might inflict on the counterinsurgency campaign. Col. Jasper Wilson, I Corps MAAG adviser and confidant of Khanh, assured Lodge that Khanh would be a reliable ally. Lodge found especially attractive Khanh's stated determination to get on with the war. He depicted Khanh as "the most capable general in Vietnam."[23]

McNamara looked for improvement from Khanh. Less than a week after Khanh seized power, McNamara told the Senate Armed Services Committee that "I have spent considerable time with General Khanh during my visits to Vietnam. He has impressed me as a very intelligent, articulate, courageous, aggressive, determined Army commander." The secretary was less effusive in withholding any opinion on Khanh as a chief of state, but given the approving adjectives that both he and Lodge had recited, they clearly sought to make the best of an imperfect situation.[24]

The president and the White House staff, fearing that the neglect of military operations that had followed the 1 November 1963 coup would now recur, directed that Lodge and Harkins be instructed to pressure Khanh to undertake immediate operations against the Viet Cong. In a joint message to Lodge and Harkins on 31 January, Rusk and McNamara so directed, stating "that there must be no opportunity for the Viet Cong to benefit from the events of the past few days—it is essential that he [Khanh] and his government demonstrate to the people of South Vietnam, the people of the United States and the people of the world their unity and strength." To do this required stepping up the pace of military operations "immediately and visibly."[25]

The shakeup produced by the change in government affected the U.S. establishment in Saigon as well. The friction between Lodge and Harkins became more pronounced. Already the dispatch of Lt. Gen. William C. Westmoreland to Vietnam as Harkins's deputy just before the coup suggested, in the words of a *Los Angeles Times* headline, that "Gen. Harkins' Days Numbered." According to the article, Harkins had made the "unpardonable blunder of remaining optimistic about the strategy and program of President Ngo Dinh Diem."[26]

In the White House, Forrestal told Bundy on 4 February 1964 that "if Lodge must remain, the military commander must be changed. The President might publicly load Lodge with full responsibility for the whole U.S. effort in South Vietnam, giving him as deputy the ablest, most modern-minded 3-star general we can find. General Westmoreland might fill the bill." Beyond this, Forrestal recommended that a "Manager for South Vietnam" be appointed in DoD directly under McNamara to deal with under secretaries and assistant secretaries of state as well as with the AID director on equal terms.[27]

Harkins did not depart immediately; his "normal" tour of two years would not end until February and a pro forma retirement at age 60 would not occur until June. McNamara did not want to relieve him until Khanh settled in and until Westmoreland had been in Vietnam long enough to take charge. Forrestal believed that the real reason for McNamara's reluctance was that Taylor and the Joint Chiefs opposed a change at the time.[28] In any event, Westmoreland eventually succeeded Harkins in June 1964 on the latter's retirement, and Maxwell Taylor took over for Lodge as ambassador in Saigon in July.*[29]

Whether responsibility for lack of progress in Vietnam lay more with the military than the civilian U.S. representatives in Saigon was immaterial, Under Secretary of State Ball judged a generation later. Ball felt that Johnson would have served himself better when he became president had he questioned the rationale for continuing the U.S. involvement. "Only a leader supremely sure of himself" could have decided on withdrawal, but Johnson "felt no such certainty." According to Ball, by avoiding the larger question the United States remained at the mercy of events over which it could exercise little control.[30]

Two days after the coup, on 1 February, Lodge confessed that he was disconcerted "at first blush" by Khanh's seizing power just when the Minh government was beginning to make some progress. In a country so short of leaders it seemed a waste to lose what few there were. But he found consolation from the way Khanh catered to American sensibilities, both in his anti-neutralist posture and in providing continuity by keeping Minh on as chief of state. The ambassador's sober evaluation saw no real alternative to Khanh; another coup could bring neutralism or worse in its wake.[31]

Toward Escalation: Spring 1964

As for the direction of the military campaign, the plight in the Delta should have given that area priority. Nothing meant more to administration leaders than retaking the Delta and winning back the countryside.[32] A downturn immediately following Khanh's takeover, having reversed the slight improvement in January, gave all the more reason for the United States to make counterinsurgency the first objective of the new government, but it failed to do so. When Assistant Secretary of State Roger Hilsman left the administration in February 1964, the United States lost a major advocate of counterinsurgency strategy. Only after winning back the countryside, he believed, through careful restructuring of the strategic hamlet program, should South Vietnam begin to attack infiltration bases and training camps in Laos or go after industrial objectives in North Vietnam.[33]

The difficulty with this approach lay essentially in the time required to accomplish its goals. Could the United States afford to wait until South Vietnam had created the political, military, social, and economic conditions necessary to defeat the Communists? Understandably, U.S. leaders wanted quicker solutions, and many wanted to bring the war to North Vietnam as a means of stamping out its

---

* See below, p. 518.

support of the Viet Cong. If North Vietnam suffered enough for its aggression it would pull back and cut its lifeline to the insurgents. A corollary assumption maintained that the insurgents would wither away once aid was withdrawn. In fact, the JCS had made this point before the Khanh coup in some far-ranging recommendations to McNamara on 22 January 1964. Obviously concerned with the continuing deterioration of the South Vietnamese government's ability to pursue reform or prosecute the war in the several months since the Minh ascendancy, the Joint Chiefs proposed a major escalation of the U.S. military role beyond counterinsurgency. Emphasizing that the future of Southeast Asia and, indeed, virtually all of eastern Asia depended on a Communist defeat, the Joint Chiefs declared that "the United States must be prepared to put aside many of the self-imposed restrictions" because "we and the South Vietnamese are fighting the war on the enemy's terms." These restrictions included keeping the war within the boundaries of South Vietnam, avoiding the direct use of U.S. combat forces, and limiting the U.S. role to an advisory one. The chiefs indicated that these self-imposed restrictions conveyed "signals of irresolution" to the enemy. They called for "increasingly bolder actions," specifically the U.S. military commander taking responsibility "for the total US program in Vietnam" and the Vietnamese government turning over to him "temporarily, the actual tactical direction of the war," to include "ground operations in Laos . . . to impede the flow of [enemy] personnel and material southward." He would also command operations against North Vietnam—aerial bombings, commando raids, and seacoast mining. To undertake these operations within South Vietnam and Laos and against North Vietnam would require the overt commitment of additional U.S. combat forces. The chiefs asked McNamara to discuss their recommendations with Rusk.[34]

As it turned out, the timing could not have been worse. The Khanh coup occurred only two days after McNamara sent the proposal to Rusk. Rusk's reply on 5 February was a brief diplomatic non-reply, agreeing in general with the JCS premises but implicitly rejecting the recommended solutions. The focus of counterinsurgency, he wrote, was in South Vietnam, and the war "must be fought and won primarily in the minds of the Vietnamese people." This then meant that the war was "essentially political—an important fact to bear in mind in determining command and control arrangements." While agreeing with the chiefs' statement on the need for an integrated approach to achieve U.S. objectives, he thought any action for this purpose had to be weighed against the expected result as well as balanced against the political and military risks incurred by taking that action. Rusk closed with the bland evasion that State would "always be prepared to consider promptly . . . any courses of action" proposed by DoD and the JCS.[35]

With the uncertainties prevailing in Vietnam and Rusk's courteous but negative reply to the JCS proposals, McNamara deferred strategic decisions until he had visited Vietnam again and determined the progress, if any, being made by the new Khanh government. Harkins and Lodge saw hopeful signs in Khanh's early actions. Nevertheless, Lodge warned that U.S. support remained a critical factor in the survival of any government, and "we should continue [to] render this in the full measure."36

Washington's views about Vietnam derived in good part from the cables sent from Vietnam, which varied in their rendering of events. Rusk publicly labeled the war a "mean, frustrating and difficult struggle" but winnable. On the other hand, William Bundy, scheduled to leave OSD in mid-March to become the assistant secretary of state for Far Eastern affairs, saw a political and military situation that had worsened steadily since November 1963, a view closer to the gloomy appraisal of CIA officers in Vietnam, who considered the increased Viet Cong momentum a consequence of the recent destabilizing coups. Territorial losses in districts previously considered successful areas of counterinsurgency particularly distressed Bundy.37

McNamara heard opposing views on Vietnam policy as he and Taylor, supported by top officials from DoD, State, CIA, and AID, prepared during February and early March for another fact-finding mission to Saigon. From the White House, Forrestal shared the CIA judgment that the strategic hamlet program, including militia training and use of the indigenous Montagnards, had to be revived. The old mix of civil and military counterinsurgency activity suffered from too many Army Special Forces being moved from the central plateau to concentrate on the Laotian border as they took over CIA operations.38

The Joint Chiefs mounted a vigorous counter to this advice in their 2 March response to McNamara's request for their views. They reiterated their recommendations of 22 January for overt military actions against the North Vietnamese as "part of a coordinated diplomatic, military and psychological program" to deter them from supporting the Viet Cong. These actions should occur either with a "sudden blow for shock effect" or in an ascending order of intensity beginning with air strikes and continuing through amphibious raids, sabotage, and harassment of shipping and fishing and then increasing to include military targets in Laos and North Vietnam directly supporting the Viet Cong, airfields and POL facilities in the North, industrial plants in the Hanoi/Haiphong area, and a sea blockade of North Vietnam. The chiefs believed that Communist China would not actively enter the fray. They also observed that even if these intensified operations should cause North Vietnam to terminate its aid, the Viet Cong could still sustain the insurgency for an indeterminate period. They suggested that McNamara use their proposals as a basis for discussion on his visit to Vietnam. The secretary appeared to favor the JCS approach, noting in the margin of their paper: "OK, fuller use of massive U.S. air power in lieu of US g[roun]d forces."39

Terrorist acts against U.S. personnel and their families added to the secretary's concerns. Lodge informed the president on 20 February that "in light of recent terrorism against Americans in Saigon [15 attacks thus far in the month resulting in 5 killed and more than 50 wounded], I believe North Viet Nam should be told secretly that every terrorist act against Americans in South Viet Nam will provoke swift retaliation against North Viet Nam." If U.S. dependents were evacuated, it should be made clear that this was not a frightened response to terrorism, but "clearing the decks for action." The president postponed a decision on evacuation until McNamara had consulted with Lodge, but he directed contingency planning that would speed up pressures against North Vietnam.[40]

With last-minute instructions on 5 March from the president in the form of two letters asking for "the most careful possible assessment of" and "the best possible courses of action for improving" the Vietnamese situation, the McNamara-Taylor mission left for Saigon the same day.[41] The group spent the 6th in Honolulu where Admiral Felt informed them that OPLAN 34A was largely a failure to date; with the exception of the naval blockade, he endorsed the JCS proposals of 22 January and 2 March for a broadened war with increased U.S. military participation and overt strikes against North Vietnam.[42]

After arriving in Saigon on 8 March, McNamara learned that Khanh did not currently favor major military action against North Vietnam, instead wanting first to consolidate his political and military positions in the South. This largely coincided with the president's stance that called for McNamara and Taylor to make Khanh "our boy" and proclaim the fact widely. As Taylor stated, "he [the president] . . . wants to see Khanh in the newspapers with McNamara and Taylor holding up his arms."[43] Consequently, as directed, they toured the provinces and repeatedly were photographed on town-square platforms with each holding up a Khanh arm, as if he were the victor in a boxing match or at a political convention.[44] The *New York Times* described McNamara and Taylor as "shaking hands with wizened old village men, patting childrens' heads, jumping in and out of helicopters and shaking more hands." They intended, McNamara stated, "to emphasize . . . that Khanh has the full and complete support of President Johnson and our whole Government and I want to let his people know this."[45]

The mission returned to Washington on 13 March. The same day McNamara circulated for comment a draft report, much of which William Bundy had prepared almost two weeks earlier, but that was now updated to include McNamara's findings from the trip—three proposed alternative courses of action and 12 specific recommendations. The secretary found current military equipment and concepts sound but believed substantially more performance was required from the Vietnamese military forces and in the economic and civic action areas. He thought the general situation had deteriorated considerably since his visit the previous September, noting Viet Cong control over about 40 percent of the countryside and domination of 22 of the 43 provinces, the apathy and indifference of large segments of the population, and the high (and increasing) rate of desertion among military and paramilitary personnel accompanied by extensive draft dodging, while Viet Cong recruiting was both energetic and effective. And the political control structure between Saigon and the hamlets and villages had virtually ceased to exist since the November coup. The greatest weakness, the secretary declared, was the uncertain viability of the Khanh government. On the other hand, Saigon was now exceptionally receptive to U.S. advice.

Of the possible courses of action, McNamara perceived both neutralization or U.S. withdrawal as catastrophic and constituting major communist victories. He rejected overt attacks against North Vietnam at the time, but one of his dozen specific recommendations was to prepare for such action on a 30-day alert basis. In other major recommendations he advised that the United States declare emphatically that it would support South Vietnam "for as long as it takes to bring the insurgency under control" and that it fully backed the Khanh government. He also called for development of what he termed the Program for National Mobilization, including military and paramilitary forces and a newly created civilian administrative corps. McNamara also proposed to replace many current Vietnamese military aircraft, ground vehicles, and watercraft with better versions. He wanted widespread local publicity for an already approved important program to increase the supply of fertilizers to farmers threefold during the next two years. His final two recommendations would authorize (1) South Vietnamese "hot pursuit" and ground operations along the Laotian and perhaps the Cambodian borders and (2) U.S. preparation for participation on 72 hours' notice in these border control operations and in "retaliatory actions" against North Vietnam.[46] McNamara estimated that enlarging Vietnamese military forces by some 50,000 would cost up to an additional $40 million annually, providing the modern military equipment would require a one-time expenditure of $20 million, and expanding the civil administrative corps would need about $1.5 million the first year.[47]

In coordinating the report with the mission participants and their agencies, McNamara obtained a quick concurrence from all. However, McCone, while agreeing with McNamara's recommendations, deemed them "too little too late" and wanted far more action, including major pressures on Cambodia through border controls, overt U.S. reconnaissance flights over North Vietnam for both intelligence and psychological purposes, and having Khanh negotiate with Chiang Kai-shek to deploy two or three Nationalist Chinese divisions to the southern tip of the Delta in support of the hard-pressed ARVN troops. These and other McCone comments in the "too little too late" vein were not included in McNamara's final report, presumably with the director's agreement, but the president and his staff knew about them from their review of McNamara's draft report to which they were attached.[48]

The JCS had previously, on 22 January and again on 2 March, taken a position calling for stronger action than McNamara advocated in his report; on both occasions they had proposed full-scale U.S. military participation in the war. On 4 March, the day before McNamara left for Vietnam, they had discussed the subject directly with the president, who pointed out the attendant difficulties of such a step—a still traumatized nation recovering from the recent assassination, a Congress and citizenry unprepared for war, and an approaching presidential campaign and election. The president thought that any combat expansion should wait until December when the political arena would have been stabilized "with 4 years and 3 months of permanency ahead." Marine Corps Commandant General Wallace Greene inferred from these comments that "the President . . . was indirectly telling General Taylor that he did not want him to return from SVN with a recommendation that the campaign there be expanded to include NVN."[49] The next morning, 5 March, when Greene asked about this inference, Taylor replied that "his neck and the SecDef's neck were on the chopping block."[50]

The Joint Chiefs met in two sessions on 14 March to consider McNamara's draft report. Greene and LeMay made plain their dissatisfaction both verbally and in writing. The former labeled McNamara's 12 recommendations a continuation of the status quo and stated that if the United States decided to stay in Vietnam it should do so with its full concerted power—"half-measures won't win in South Vietnam." LeMay criticized McNamara's statement that the current war effort was both "sound and adequate" and called for removing the restrictions against hitting Viet Cong sanctuaries in Cambodia and North Vietnam's supply and reinforcement lines through Laos along the Ho Chi Minh Trail.[51]

The Joint Chiefs finally worked out a reply to McNamara on 14 March in which they concurred in the secretary's recommendations but offered some changes. They deemed the proposed program inadequate to turn the tide against the Viet Cong "without positive action being taken against the Hanoi Government at an early date" to deter the latter's aggression and facilitate the counterinsurgency effort. To increase readiness for such actions, they urged the creation of political and military support in the United States and South Vietnam for such purposes. Second, they recommended "hot pursuit" action into Cambodia. Finally, they suggested that McNamara's proposed reaction time for Cambodian and Laotian border control activities and for retaliatory actions against the North be reduced from 72 hours to 24 and for "graduated overt military pressures" against North Vietnam from 30 days to 72 hours.[52] Greene believed that in this fashion Taylor had gotten the chiefs to "recommend essentially the actions involved in his [Taylor's] original position and recommendations,"* thus shifting the burden "from his shoulders to the Joint Chiefs."[53]

McNamara reviewed his proposed report on 16 March in considerable detail with his top staff, the JCS, and the departmental secretaries. He did not accept the JCS proposals for decreasing the reaction times for operations over Cambodia and North Vietnam. Admiral McDonald suggested that dependents in Vietnam be returned and U.S. forces go on wartime footing. "We have been pussyfooting around and need to decide whether to fight," he declared. When McNamara

---

* At the meeting of the JCS and the president on 4 March, Taylor had called for intensifying the counterinsurgency operations within South Vietnam and a progressive campaign of "selective air and naval attacks against North Vietnam" (memcon JCS and Pres, 4 Mar 64, cited in n 43).

noted that officials in Saigon thought such a move bad for morale, McDonald replied that it represented the business-as-usual approach.[54]

McNamara forwarded the report to the president the same day and it underwent scrutiny by the NSC on the 17th. The secretary noted that all involved agencies had concurred in the report and that he had agreed to have the JCS undertake a detailed analysis of their proposed modifications to his 12 recommendations. When the president asked if the report's proposed actions would reverse matters in South Vietnam, McNamara assured him that if Khanh acted energetically, improvement would be apparent within four to six months. Taylor added that the Joint Chiefs "believed the proposed program was acceptable, but it may not be sufficient to save the situation in Vietnam" and could require action against North Vietnam. Johnson addressed the alternatives—putting in more U.S. forces, pulling out entirely, or neutralizing the region—and decided the 12-point program was the only realistic option.[55]

The president approved the report and issued NSAM 288 on 17 March, directing all agencies to proceed with implementation of its provisions. He also released a lengthy public statement containing much of the report's substance but adding that he hoped to continue to withdraw U.S. forces as South Vietnamese replacements were trained. Yet he cautioned that additional personnel would be sent to Vietnam if needed in the future. The president concluded: "It will remain the policy of the United States to furnish assistance and support to South Viet-Nam for as long as it is required to bring Communist aggression and terrorism under control."[56]

It soon became apparent that the immediate acceptance of McNamara's report, quickly followed by the issuance of the secret NSAM 288 and the press release, did not provide the hoped-for solution to the vexing problems of Vietnam. During the period from mid-March through April, the situation worsened greatly. Khanh proved largely incapable of bringing about the planned civilian and military improvements within Vietnam. Although he accepted advice readily and promised much, he lacked the personal capability and experienced people to carry it out. On 4 April, he finally promulgated the long-pending National Mobilization Plan to place the nation on a full wartime footing, but he had no staff with the expertise to implement it. Adding to these woes, he had to cope with growing disputes between the nation's Catholics and Buddhists, as well as equally vicious squabbles among the latter. Viet Cong attacks grew in scope and number as U.S.-Vietnamese discussions about proposed increases to the armed forces dragged on, making little headway despite inability of the ARVN to meet current draft quotas, curb desertions, and replace growing combat losses.[57]

Many officials in Washington believed the U.S. country team also suffered from shortcomings and disarray. They regarded Lodge as an excellent diplomat in his dealings with Khanh, Minh, and other Vietnamese leaders but believed he lacked managerial skills to oversee the numerous programs to capture the hearts and minds of the Vietnamese populace. Nor was there anyone else on hand to take on this role. The deputy chief of mission, David G. Nes, had been appointed with the expectation that he would assume this task, but it did not appear that he had done so. At the same time, the AID program, in the view of Forrestal and others, sorely needed strong direction and additional people.[58] USIA Director Carl Rowan, who visited Vietnam in mid-April with Rusk, informed the president in writing that "the weakest part of the war operation, both on our part and that of the Government of South Viet-Nam, is in the field of information and psychological warfare." Accordingly, he believed that "top priority should be given to a large scale United States program to improve the GVN ability to win the support of the people." He concluded that any effort would fail "unless it has the clear direction of a single individual."[59]

The military element of the country team also received poor marks. Many civilian officials in Washington felt that the U.S. military forces were "fighting" the wrong kind of war, that they had failed to learn from the French, and, like them, were insisting on waging a conventional war against largely invisible insurgents who quickly faded into the general population or into the wooded areas nearby or just across the Laotian and Cambodian borders.[60] Adding to these difficulties was the unpleasant relationship between Lodge and Harkins that McGeorge Bundy termed "childish," but which came to a head not long before both were expected to leave Vietnam.[61]

The difficulty had actually begun with former Ambassador Nolting and Harkins.* In May 1961 President Kennedy had directed that all MAAGs would function under an ambassador's direction, but U.S. forces engaged in military operations in the field were specifically excluded. When Harkins became the MACV head in February 1962 he received specific authority, agreed to by McNamara and Rusk and approved by Kennedy, to meet with and discuss U.S. and Vietnamese military operations directly with South Vietnam's president and other top political and military officials. This resulted in a stormy relationship between Harkins and Nolting that became chillier yet when Lodge became ambassador. He and Harkins failed to keep each other fully informed about pertinent matters and meetings.[62]

On 21 April 1964 Lodge directed all agency heads within the country team, including Harkins, to clear with Deputy Chief of Mission Nes any meeting with Khanh. Harkins immediately protested, pointing to the authority granted him in the February 1962 directive. Lodge on the 23rd then asked Rusk to settle the dispute. A week later, in a letter to Rusk on the objectives and needs of the ambassadorial post in Saigon, in effect spelling these out for his soon-to-be successor, Lodge again made much of the fact that the ambassador lacked authority over U.S. military activities, that the U.S. "military commander has direct access to the chief of state and that the Ambassador does not control all U.S. access to the chief

---

* See Chapter XI.

of state and therefore has no way of assuring that all Americans speak with one voice. Is this special status truly to the advantage of the military? Does it contribute to creating the 'proper political atmosphere'?"[63]

Rusk's reply to Lodge, concurred in by McNamara, was, unsurprisingly, diplomatic. He conceded that Harkins had the authority to discuss military matters with the chief of state (Minh) and the prime minister (Khanh), but this should not conflict with the ambassador's overall supervisory authority to receive advance notice and provide policy guidance. The secretary also suggested that Lodge might amend his directive to except Harkins from reporting to Nes: "I think you can understand that General Harkins would have some sensitivity about appearing to report to the DCM." Moreover, Rusk thought that Lodge-Harkins consultations would undoubtedly be so frequent that "an informal relationship is surely easier and more effective than written communication in almost all cases."[64]

Meanwhile, in the JCS differences between the members continued after receipt of a Joint Staff study recommending certain immediate overt military actions. LeMay and Greene wanted operations "extended and expanded immediately." Taylor, Wheeler, and McDonald found the study contained nothing to justify any change to the president's recent policy statement. In sending the study to McNamara on 14 April, the chiefs maintained their different positions. Given the JCS split views in which the majority did not favor immediate military initiatives, the secretary took no action.[65]

The lack of unanimity over the proper U.S. military role—adviser, covert associate, or overt participant—would continue for several more months. On 16 May the JCS suggested that an interagency working group draft a joint political-military plan of action. They pointed out a week later that to date there had been no consultation with the South Vietnamese government about attacking the North. "The Department of State," the JCS stated, "should take the lead on this but as yet has not." During these same weeks, uncertainty characterized internal discussions among administration "hawks" and "doves" on how and when to involve congressional leaders on the subject of Southeast Asia, on a successor to Lodge, and on the selection of an AID chief in Vietnam to head up the extremely important civic and economic support projects there.[66]

Into this atmosphere of indecision and suspense Khanh dropped a bombshell. Early on 4 May, he told Lodge he was contemplating declaring a state of war and evacuating Saigon, including the government, the diplomatic corps, and its population of two million; replacing "so-called 'politicians'" in the government with technicians; suspending some civil rights; and informing Hanoi that any future interference in South Vietnam's internal affairs would lead to tit-for-tat bombing reprisals. He specifically asked if the United States would undertake bombing attacks, and he added that an American "army corps" of 10,000 Special Forces deployed along the Cambodian-Laotian border would stem the communist incursions. "He thought it was illogical, wasteful, wrong to go on incurring casualties 'just in order to make the agony endure,'" said the ambassador, who concluded his message to the State Department with the commentary:

> This man obviously wants to get on with the job and not sit here indefinitely taking casualties. Who can blame him? His desire to declare a state of war, leaving out specific details such as the plans for evacuating Saigon, seems wholly in line with our desire to get out of a 'business as usual' mentality. He is clearly facing up to all the hard questions and wants us to do it too.[67]

Back in Washington, William Bundy, now at State, discerned "a certain sense of despair and perhaps some trace of panic" in Khanh's remarks and possibly even "some sense of pique" that the United States was pushing too hard for the National Mobilization Plan.[68] Forrestal suggested that Khanh (and Lodge) may have been "somewhat shaken by events of the last few days"—explosive damage to an American naval ship, a terrorist attack that wounded eight U.S. military personnel, and the recent upsurge in other Viet Cong military activity.[69] Rusk also "detect[ed] a trace of despair in Khanh's remarks" and wondered why the general wanted active combat against North Vietnam when he had so recently stated a need to consolidate first his base in the South.[70]

Khanh's remarks provoked similar reactions from the field, confirming Washington's impressions. Admiral Felt labeled them a "temporary (I hope) breakdown under pressures" from both the communists and the United States. Felt saw no need for full-scale war measures, thought that "evacuation of Saigon is desperation talk and should be ignored as a passing mood," and proposed Khanh be given "another pep talk."[71] Harkins had similar views, adding that the solution to Khanh's problems was "effective execution of the National Pacification Plan . . . without recourse to panicky evacuations or unrealistic schemes for governing without 'politicians.'"[72]

At a 6 May meeting the president instructed McNamara to visit South Vietnam after his meeting with German officials in Bonn 9-11 May. McNamara would determine the basis of Khanh's outburst and disabuse him of any possibility of U.S. support to expand the war into North Vietnam or China. McNamara and John McNaughton, who replaced Bundy at ISA, arrived in Saigon on the 12th and were met by Taylor and Forrestal, who had arrived a day earlier.[73] In meetings with Khanh, Minh, Lodge and his country team, and with Harkins, Westmoreland, and the MACV staff, the Washington contingent encountered little of an encouraging nature—either political or military. As Taylor later summed it up, we "returned . . . with no new ideas to translate into programs. . . . We had little to allay the impatience of the President, who had hoped for solid evidence that our policy was indeed on the right track."[74]

Immediately after their return, McNamara and Taylor met with the president on the 14th and with the NSC and an invited bipartisan group of congressional leaders on the 15th and informed them of the dismal prospects for South Vietnam. McNamara reported that conditions had worsened since his mid-March visit, the number of people and the amount of territory under Viet Cong control continued to increase, and the National Mobilization Plan (approved at the beginning of April) could not become operational until September at the earliest and perhaps not before mid- or late 1965. He considered it essential to encourage Khanh in his efforts to increase and improve the military forces, to provide additional financial, logistical, and training support to Khanh, and to provide additional advisory personnel for the civil side of his government. The secretary assured the legislators that U.S. soldiers did not engage in combat but sometimes became exposed to fire during the course of training the South Vietnamese.[75]

The president announced that he intended to seek a supplemental appropriation for increased economic and military assistance but added that "even with increased U.S. aid the prospect in South Vietnam is not bright."[76] A current CIA report echoed this view, stating that "sustained Viet Cong pressure continues to erode GVN authority . . . undercut US/GVN programs and depress South Vietnamese morale. . . . In any case, if the tide of deterioration has not been arrested by the end of the year, the anti-Communist position in South Vietnam is likely to become untenable."[77]

Preparation of numerous policy proposals intensified during the next few days. Johnson on 26 May called for joint meetings of staffs in Washington and Southeast Asia within the week "to review for my final approval a series of plans for effective action" in Southeast Asia.[78] The initial plenary session, held in Honolulu on the morning of 1 June, included more than 50 persons, after which Rusk, McNamara, Taylor, McCone, Lodge, Felt, Westmoreland, Rowan, Forrestal, and others, 16 in number, met in three extended sessions of principals that afternoon and the next day. The remaining 40 participants formed into four working groups, each discussing a pertinent issue. The discussions were varied and far-ranging, as the two-day conference produced support for applying increased pressure and agreement to develop an action program but achieved little consensus on specific recommendations.[79] McGeorge Bundy informed the president that "no one is recommending any major decision today [3 June] or, indeed, in the next few days." He indicated that Rusk and McNamara would not likely push for expanded "military action . . . at least for several weeks, and possibly for quite a lot longer." Bundy also noted that both Lodge and Westmoreland were wary over proposals for "encadrement" or "interlarding"—the placement of U.S. military or civilian personnel at the several levels of South Vietnamese governmental organization; Taylor described it as "extensive incorporation of American officials into the Vietnamese administrative structure," a measure favored by Johnson. Bundy stated that the only major new agreement stemming from the Honolulu meetings concerned the need to centralize authority for public information activities both in Saigon, under Barry Zorthian, already there, and in Washington under Robert J. Manning, assistant secretary of state for public affairs. Bundy anticipated no new startling statements on Vietnam; rather "the political and diplomatic course of action with respect to Laos is probably still the most immediate possible trigger of larger decisions."[80]

The Other Players: Laos and Cambodia

Bundy's reference to Laos concerned the rapidly worsening situation there. He could have also mentioned neutral Cambodia, where the unpredictable Prince Norodom Sihanouk, intimidated by the threat from neighboring China and North Vietnam, sought to appease them by repeatedly confronting the United States. Occasional inadvertent incursions across the Cambodian border by South Vietnamese troops prompted strong verbal attacks by Sihanouk against both South Vietnam and the United States, probably because he believed that North Vietnam would be the ultimate winner.[81]

Laos, where the Communist Pathet Lao remained a plague on Souvanna Phouma's government, posed greater problems. Months before Bundy's observations about Laos, on 25 February 1964 Hilsman sent Rusk a draft memorandum for the president emphasizing that "the recent Communist advances in central Laos highlight the continuing erosion of the situation in Laos." A U.S. response seemed necessary partly to curtail North Vietnamese aid to the Viet Cong and partly to disabuse de Gaulle and Sihanouk about the likelihood of communists taking over Southeast Asia.[82]

These concerns had existed before the president issued NSAM 288 on 17 March. By this time the danger posed by the Pathet Lao to the Plaine des Jarres in Laos placed heavy new pressure on the United States to act. The authorized small-scale "hot pursuit" and intelligence sorties into Laos would not suffice; more was needed to stop the Pathet Lao. The State Department in February had considered recommending dispatch of both an air squadron and a ground unit. The JCS preferred a Marine battalion landing team (BLT) over an Army battle group. William Bundy believed that an air squadron alone would suffice to "provide the right kind of signal for the area as a whole." McNamara held off support of ground intervention. As he advised the president on 25 April, "I see only two ways to prevent an expansion of the influence of the Pathet Lao in Laos: either we must support the Geneva Accords or we must be prepared to introduce U.S. forces into that country. Of the two I much prefer the first."[83] While no direct involvement of U.S. personnel was called for, low-level reconnaissance by U.S. aircraft was. This would mean a step deeper into the war, but OSD planners, more than willing to act,[84] found a receptive hearing in the National Security Council on 29 April, when the CIA estimated that while the Pathet Lao by themselves had only a 50-50 chance of defeating the non-communist forces, they could quickly overrun the entire country if joined by forces from North Vietnam.[85] This confronted the administration with the possibility of a formal partition of Laos if Souvanna should lose power.

Lack of coordination among U.S. agencies also complicated response to the growing crisis. For example, at an 18 May meeting with the JCS McNamara became upset on learning that the CIA had been conducting a "trail-watching operation" in Laos for the past two years, employing 1,200 people in the expensive and unproductive Operation Hardnose. State wanted no publicity about this activity for fear of damaging relations with Souvanna, who had received assurance from North Vietnam that it would stop using the Laotian routes to the South. General Greene noted that even the Defense Intelligence Agency did not know of this operation. He also seemed to relish the discomfort and uncertainty of the president and secretary of defense as they pressed for measures to arrest or reverse the Pathet Lao conquest of the Plaine des Jarres, noting that McNamara was now considering striking targets in North Vietnam, rather than in Laos, even though he had previously opposed this JCS recommendation. Greene observed that "up until now, McNamara has pretty much field-marshaled the entire effort in Southeast Asia, and, with the place starting to fall apart, his whiz-kid-Ford-Motor-Company management techniques apparently aren't paying off."[86]

As an initial response to the Pathet Lao offensive, the United States requested Souvanna's approval to conduct low-level reconnaissance flights for target and other intelligence on communist activity.[87] The loss of an RF-8 to antiaircraft fire on 6 June and of an F-8 fighter escort the next day led to deliberations on 8 June among administration leaders on whether to retaliate and, if so, how. Much discussion centered on whether retaliation would hamper current efforts to reconvene a Geneva Accords meeting, whether such an attack would constitute a breach of the 1962 agreement, and whether to use U.S. F-8 aircraft or unmarked South Vietnamese T-28s. Faced with widely divided views, McNamara told the president he "was even ready to give up Southeast Asia" if the United States continued to talk tough but act weak; it was essential to convey a clear message to Hanoi. The president had some doubts. He did not want to violate the Geneva Accords, even if the communists did. But with the backing of Under Secretary of State Harriman, McNamara managed to obtain the president's reluctant approval to retaliate.[88] On 9 June, eight F-100 planes struck a Pathet Lao antiaircraft installation at Xieng Khouang. Subsequent evaluation revealed that only four of the eight aircraft struck the intended target; the other four hit another nearby fortified target containing the quarters of a Chinese economic and cultural mission.[89]

Whatever the impact of this strike, it had to be weighed against the concern for maintaining Souvanna's neutral stance and his Government of National Union. Souvanna's position was to "make maximum use T-28s" to interdict and destroy

Pathet Lao and Viet Minh supplies but on a basis of "act but don't talk about it." Still, the situation remained fragile, with a general communist sweep in Laos always a possibility.[90]

During the summer and fall of 1964, the administration remained cautious about supporting General Phoumi's ever-optimistic plans for more active military operations in northern Laos. Established policy continued to adhere to the 1962 Geneva Accords as much as possible and to confine escalation largely to air attacks on Viet Cong infiltration routes and facilities in the Laos panhandle. As U.S. armed reconnaissance flights increased, Souvanna continued his support but resisted U.S. efforts in late November to obtain more candor in public statements concerning these operations. He reiterated his position to "let the actions speak for themselves"; after all, this was the position of the North Vietnamese, the 1962 accords notwithstanding.[91] North Vietnamese use of supply routes to the Viet Cong through Laos continued to be a vexing problem.

The Tonkin Gulf Resolution

Meanwhile, in South Vietnam behind every discussion about the state of Khanh's government lay the question of U.S. military intervention and its need for public and, particularly, congressional support. Before soliciting a congressional resolution on the war, the president had his leading political and military advisers meet in Honolulu on 1-2 June, where, as earlier noted, they reaffirmed the U.S. commitment to defend South Vietnam and embraced what amounted to an escalation strategy but remained vague and divided as to what steps should follow. On 5 June McNamara submitted to the president a program to strengthen South Vietnam that included preparation of plans for a strike against North Vietnam. That GVN forces could do the job seemed unlikely. Nor could there be any certainty of the willingness of the American public to take on new burdens. Journalist Charles J. V. Murphy asserted in the May issue of *Fortune* that the Viet Cong was winning the war and that only major U.S. intervention could avert defeat.[92]

The depressing outlook moved the administration to consider in June a congressional resolution to help win public support for greater U.S. involvement in South Vietnam. With the presidential campaign expected to heat up shortly and the civil rights bill still under debate, the question arose whether the resolution should be sought immediately if it could be done without divisive debate. "On balance," McGeorge Bundy advised the president on 10 June, "it appears that we need a Congressional Resolution if and only if we decide that a substantial increase of national attention and international tension is a necessary part of the defense of Southeast Asia in the coming summer."[93] Bundy and his brother did not have in mind a blank check for the president or a dramatic call-up of reserves. Rather, they simply hoped to strengthen the president's hand as commander in chief, using as precedents previous resolutions on the Middle East (1957) and Cuba (1962). Although this would require a presidential message and probably a White Paper, it could send the right message to both friends and enemies in Southeast Asia and elsewhere. But McGeorge Bundy concluded his 10 June memorandum with the opinion that "the risks outweigh the advantages, unless and until we have a firm decision to take more drastic action than we currently plan."[94]

Except for authorization of a direct U.S. military strike against North Vietnam, the president already had adequate freedom of action without a congressional resolution. Continuing difficulties in Vietnam suggested that an emergency requiring direct U.S. military action would come sooner rather than later. In the first six months of 1964 the VC expanded its number of units, increased its terrorist acts, and in general kept up a high rate of successful guerrilla activity. The number of incidents between January and June 1964 totaled 2,100, far exceeding the 1,500 for all of 1963, and while a slight decrease occurred in late May and June, July figures again showed a sharp increase. To justify drastic U.S. actions, more dramatic enemy attacks would have to occur; incidents involving assaults on American dependents or downing of U.S. helicopters might provide the catalyst. So could the establishment of a U.S. naval base at Cam Ranh Bay, currently under consideration, where Marine advisers would conduct amphibious training.[95]

The change in U.S. diplomatic and military leaders in Saigon in the persons of Ambassador Taylor (1 July) and General Westmoreland (20 June) portended an upsurge in operations against the enemy. Lodge's departure to participate in the Republican presidential primary campaign was not unexpected. McGeorge Bundy had drawn up a list on 6 June, less than two weeks before the ambassador submitted his resignation, suggesting possible successors, not excluding himself. Bundy had included McNamara on his list but felt that "he has been trying to think of ways of dealing with this problem for so long that he has gone a little stale. Also, in a curious way, he has rather mechanized the problem so that he misses some of its real political flavor." Taylor was not on the list, but the president announced his appointment at a press conference on 23 June.[96]

Neither Taylor nor Westmoreland, of course, was new to the South Vietnam scene. Westmoreland had been deputy commander since the winter and had overseen a reorganization of MACV during the spring; Taylor, as chairman of the Joint Chiefs of Staff, had played a major role in making Vietnam policy. Bundy noted that the president's directive to Taylor gave him "full control over everything in South Vietnam . . ., something the military never let the Ambassador have before." A well-regarded State Department veteran, U. Alexis Johnson, would serve as deputy ambassador. William H. Sullivan, State's special assistant for Vietnamese affairs and head of the Vietnam Coordinating Committee, temporarily joined Taylor in Saigon in July with the understanding that he would soon become ambassador to Laos (as he did in November). While this "first rate team" could not march into North Vietnam, as Khanh wanted, the administration, Bundy observed, "will be ready to consider new decisions at any time."[97]

Other significant changes occurred between April and July. The president named General Wheeler as the new JCS chairman, and Admiral Ulysses S. Grant Sharp, Jr., replaced Felt as CINCPAC. Forrestal left the NSC staff to succeed Sullivan at State.[98]

It was not long before maritime clashes provided a ready opportunity for new initiatives. In January 1964 MACV had established the Special Operations Group to exercise operational control over the South Vietnamese-conducted OPLAN 34A covert sabotage and intelligence collection actions against North Vietnam. Initially authorized for 1 February–30 May 1964, they had been extended for the June-September period. Distinct from OPLAN 34A missions were DeSoto operations, electronic intelligence and surveillance patrols by U.S. destroyers in the Tonkin Gulf that did not actively support the South Vietnamese forays. The first patrol in 1964 lasted for two weeks in late February and early March, during which time the destroyer USS *Craig* was authorized to go within eight nautical miles of North Vietnam's mainland, well outside the U.S.-recognized three-mile limit. In a second such mission, dispatched on 28 July, the USS *Maddox* also had permission to go within eight miles of the shore. A few nights later, on 30-31 July, several South Vietnamese OPLAN 34A gunboats attacked two islands off the North Vietnamese coast.[99]

On 2 August, while patrolling some 25 to 30 miles off the coast of North Vietnam, the *Maddox* was fired on by three North Vietnamese torpedo boats. The destroyer, along with U.S. Navy carrier aircraft from the USS *Ticonderoga*, struck back and damaged the attacking craft. *Maddox* sustained little damage, but the incident set in motion the Gulf of Tonkin affair. Following the attack the president met with key advisers and decided against immediate retaliation, surmising "that an overeager North Vietnamese boat commander might have been at fault." Instead he directed the Navy to send another destroyer, the USS *Turner Joy*, to join the *Maddox* and continue reconnaissance, to provide the ships with air cover, and to engage in more aggressive action should a repeat attack occur. When Hanoi refused delivery of a stiff note of protest and warning of "grave consequences" if further attacks occurred, it was broadcast to the world.[100]

In a morning telephone conversation on 3 August the president suggested to McNamara that he and Rusk brief selected congressmen about the recent events. McNamara recommended explaining the OPLAN 34A raids because the North Vietnamese undoubtedly connected the destroyer patrol and the attacks. That afternoon McNamara described JCS contingency plans for retaliatory air strikes against North Vietnam for joint committees of the House and Senate and, in general terms, mentioned the South Vietnamese attacks against North Vietnamese territory on 30-31 July. He attempted to disassociate OPLAN 34A from

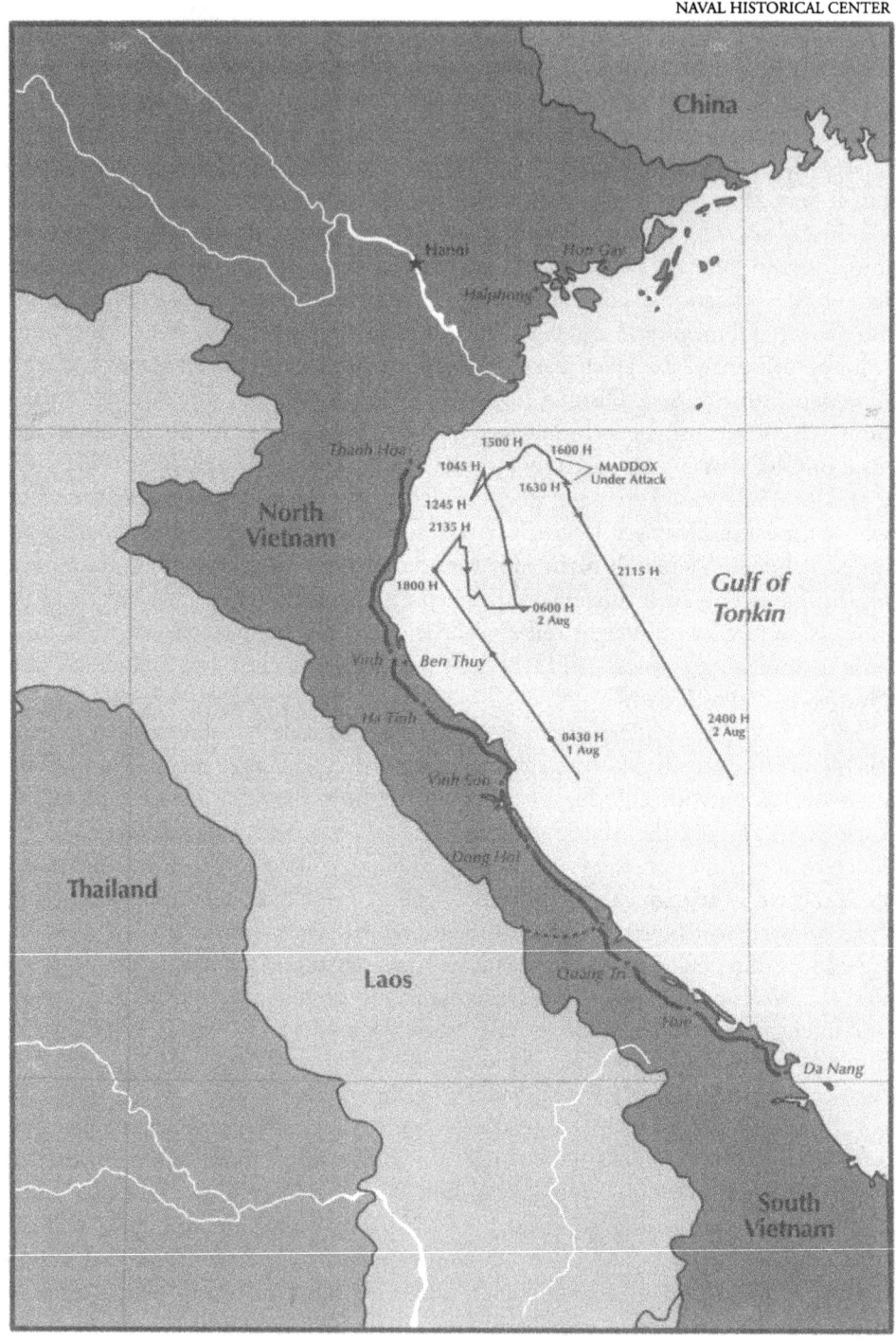

Track of Maddox, 1-2 August 1964

Vietnam: Into the Vortex 521

DeSoto patrols.[101] Unbeknownst to McNamara and members of Congress, the South Vietnamese would carry out another OPLAN 34A raid on the night of 3/4 August.*

Shortly after 8:00 a.m. on 4 August (Washington time) the DIA Indications Center in the Pentagon received a phone report followed almost immediately by a message indicating that deciphered communications revealed the North Vietnamese were preparing for naval action that night, possibly against the DeSoto patrol. McNamara informed the president by phone and met with Vance and Joint Staff officers to discuss possible retaliatory measures in the event of another attack. The attack on *Maddox* on 2 August resulting in the president's determination to retaliate against a repeat North Vietnamese assault no doubt had predisposed Washington to strike back immediately.[102]

Around 11:00 a.m. (11:00 p.m. Tonkin Gulf time) the Pentagon's National Military Command Center received a report that *Maddox* was under attack, and it appeared that the North Vietnamese had struck again. But this time the reported attack, which occurred on a moonless night in heavy seas, was not as clear-cut as the 2 August attack that happened in broad daylight. Flash messages, reports of the engagement, some ambiguous and some conflicting, poured in throughout the day. McNamara repeatedly pressed the Joint Staff and Admiral Sharp in Hawaii for more precise information, but poor communications between the task force in the Tonkin Gulf, CINCPAC in Hawaii, and Washington added to the confusion enveloping the incident. The extraordinary volume of message traffic that overloaded the secure military circuit and communications throughout the hectic day resulted in repeated delays in clarifying events, transmitting orders, and making decisions.[103]

McNamara briefed the NSC around 12:40 p.m. and then, along with Rusk, McCone, Bundy, and Vance, joined the president for lunch. During this meeting the president tentatively approved retaliatory strikes. Meantime, *Maddox* had signaled that evidence of the hostile contact appeared doubtful and needed further evaluation. During the afternoon, McNamara, Vance, and the Joint Chiefs (less Wheeler who was out of town most of the day) reviewed the latest reports from *Maddox* as McNamara tried to clarify through the Joint Staff and Sharp what had happened. Sharp informed McNamara that an initial ambush had been attempted, but he could not be sure that freak radar echoes were not confused with the noise of incoming torpedoes. When the secretary asked if there was a possibility that there had been no attack, Sharp initially replied that there was a "slight possibility," but in later phone calls provided further details supplied by the task force commander that strengthened his belief that an attack had taken place. McNamara, Vance, and the Joint Chiefs studied *Maddox*'s reports, Sharp's updates,

---

* McNamara stated in February 1968 that he did not know of the 3/4 August attacks until after his 6 August 1964 testimony to Congress (SCFR, *Hearings: The Gulf of Tonkin, The 1964 Incidents*, 90 Cong, 2 sess, 20 Feb 68, 15).

and available intelligence, particularly another deciphered North Vietnamese message stating that two "comrades" had been sacrificed, and by late afternoon came to the belief that North Vietnamese torpedo boats had attacked *Maddox*.[104]

By this time the first news reports of the attack had appeared, adding pressure on the administration to confirm the bulletins and act. At the second NSC meeting of the day (the evening of 4 August) the analysis presented by McNamara and his aides provided the administration with all that it needed for the president to order air strikes. The attendees also considered both a draft statement that the president intended to use to inform the American public of the attack and U.S. retaliation and a draft congressional resolution supporting his actions. Despite assurances from Sharp, repeated delays in positioning the carriers for the strike aircraft operations caused more uncertainty about the timing of the air attacks and forced the president to defer his address to the nation until just after 11:30 p.m. The retaliatory air raids struck naval craft at five bases and at a petroleum depot. Code-named "Pierce Arrow," this first U.S. assault on North Vietnam on 5 August destroyed or damaged numerous naval craft and about 10 percent of the nation's petroleum supplies.[105]

On 5 August Johnson asked for passage of a congressional resolution empowering him to take "all necessary action to protect our armed forces and to assist nations covered by the SEATO Treaty." He declared "that the North Vietnamese regime had conducted further deliberate attacks against US naval vessels operating in international waters" and that he had directed retaliation. Testifying in executive session on behalf of the resolution before the Senate committees on foreign relations and armed services on 6 August, McNamara denied any connection between the destroyer patrol and the South Vietnamese attack on the two North Vietnamese islands on 30/31 July. He stressed that the United States did not participate in the South Vietnamese operation, much to the disbelief of Senator Morse, who accused the U.S. Navy of backstopping the South Vietnamese raids and insisted that the United States was implicated in an act of aggression against North Vietnam.

Later that morning, in front of the House Foreign Affairs Committee, McNamara acknowledged the North Vietnamese denied a second attack had occurred. However, he cited testimony from eyewitnesses aboard *Turner Joy* and sonar and radar readings. He stated that "very hard evidence," the deciphered messages* whose

---

* At the time and in 1968 testimony McNamara considered the intercepts unimpeachable evidence that an attack had occurred on 4 August. Subsequent analysis by former NSA and CIA officials concluded that certain of the deciphered messages transmitted on 4 August were actually describing events of 2 August. More recently, additional questions have been raised about NSA's reporting of the second incident, including allegations of errors and misrepresentations in interpreting and conveying the data. See "The 'Phantom Battle' That Led to War," *U.S. News & World Report*, 23 Jul 84, 63-64; *New York Times*, 31 Oct 05; Robert Hanyok, "Skunks, Bogies, Silent Hounds, and the Flying Fish: The Gulf of Tonkin Mystery, 2-4 August 1964," *Cryptologic Quarterly*, Winter 2000/Spring 2001, item 2, Gulf of Tonkin Documents Index, http://www.nsa.gov/vietnam/index (NSA released a partially declassified version on 30 November 2005).

disclosure would "destroy our intelligence sources," confirmed that there was a second attack. Asked if the United States did anything to provoke the attack, McNamara agreed with the assertion that "this came out of a clear sky." He assured members that the DeSoto destroyer patrols were routine, and that, aside from the highly classified intelligence, the administration had kept nothing from them.[106] McNamara deftly and precisely answered each member's questions, without offering any more information than was requested. He and other officials protected the secrecy of U.S. control of 34A covert operations against North Vietnam. The day before McNamara's testimony, the operations had been temporarily suspended.[107]

On 7 August the House adopted the resolution unanimously (416-0); the Senate took similar action, with only two negative votes (88-2). The president signed it into law on 10 August. The joint resolution, which became known as the Tonkin Gulf Resolution, granted Johnson far-reaching discretionary executive authority. Senator Fulbright, chairman of the Foreign Relations Committee, agreed with Kentucky Sen. John Sherman Cooper that the resolution gave the president "advance authority to take whatever action" he deemed necessary on behalf of South Vietnam.[108]

Officials in Washington temporarily suspended 34A activities but did not change 34A policy despite North Vietnamese complaints to the International Control Commission about the maritime raids launched from Da Nang. On 7 August the ICC notified Westmoreland that it would send members to Da Nang to conduct an investigation. He reacted by concealing some of the fast patrol boats used in the covert operations in nearby coves.[109]

On 15 August, anticipating that North Vietnam would likely publicly protest future maritime attacks against its territory and military forces, McNaughton requested that the JCS Office of the Special Assistant for Counterinsurgency and Special Activities (SACSA), which handled the 34A program, develop a plan for publicly acknowledging the covert operations against North Vietnam. After weighing the pros and cons of having General Khanh in Saigon admit to the maritime attacks and leaflet drops, SACSA concluded that "once the door is opened, US political and military officials at all levels must be prepared to field a multitude of queries." This they were not willing to do. Accepting the risk of exposure, in September the president authorized the resumption of the covert 34A operations.[110]

The immediate conjunction of the Tonkin Gulf incidents with a congressional resolution gave rise then and later to suspicion that the second attack was a trumped-up affair by the administration to gain legislative support for a more aggressive Vietnam policy. Ball, the devil's advocate in White House meetings, doubted the existence of any attack. And even the president showed skepticism when, according to Ball, he later remarked, "Hell, those dumb, stupid sailors were just shooting at flying fish."[111] It seems clear that in the brief period 4 and 5 August Washington could not resolve the contradictory evidence and elected to accept the probability of attack. Since 1964 the weight of scholarly opinion, based on extensive review and analysis of the evidence, is that there was no second attack on the DeSoto ships.[112]

The haze surrounding the second incident in particular, combined with rapid introduction of the Tonkin Gulf Resolution, would continue to spawn charges that the administration deliberately misled Congress to secure passage of the measure. Later bitterness over the war and the momentous events that followed the Tonkin Gulf crisis further fueled the conspiracy thesis. But in the absence of any substantiating proof, the charges remain unsupportable. No matter how eager the administration may have been to exploit a real or imagined provocation, there is no evidence that it manufactured the second incident.[113]

Still, in the short run, the Tonkin Gulf Resolution served the administration's objectives well. As the election campaign progressed, the congressional resolution helped protect the president from Senator Goldwater's attacks, permitting Johnson to stress firmness while advocating moderation. Where the Republican candidate seemed to support unlimited involvement in Vietnam, Johnson claimed that he wanted to avoid sending "American boys 9 or 10,000 miles away from home to do what Asian boys ought to be doing for themselves." Indeed, as the campaign progressed, Johnson felt free to move from emphasizing his steadiness over Vietnam to stressing the dangers of the wider war that he claimed Goldwater was espousing.[114]

Crisis in Saigon

Neither the political nor the military situation in the South allowed the administration to implement its plan for more aggressive measures against the North. From his vantage point as information officer in the Saigon embassy, Zorthian recalled "the absolute chaos with the lack of any Vietnamese government structure, the gradual and then the abrupt deterioration of the Vietnamese Army . . . . We couldn't get up in the morning knowing there would be a government in hand." The trouble was not that official Washington was unaware of Saigon's problems but that it simply failed to realize the depth of the government's plight.[115]

Entering August the Khanh regime faced imminent collapse. Khanh spoke boldly of his war leadership, but in reality he had to spend his time trying to cope with student unrest, Buddhist rebellion, and Catholic plotting, all abetted by the ongoing and growing Viet Cong subversion. Following the Gulf of Tonkin incidents, he attempted to remove the popular though ineffectual and disaffected Big Minh from the scene by issuing a provisional constitutional charter that would abolish the office of chief of state and make himself president with sweeping powers. Ensuing riots forced Khanh to offer his resignation on 25 August 1964. The Military Revolutionary Council refused the offer and instead established a triumvirate, with Khanh, Minh, and Lt. Gen. Tran Thien Khiem, the defense minister and one of Khanh's co-conspirators of the January coup, to run the government temporarily. On 13-14 September, an attempted coup by several generals, with little popular or military support and actively opposed by the U.S. embassy, failed and further frayed governmental authority. In the short term these eruptions led to the creation of a shaky civilian government by the beginning of November, complete with a new constitution, a new chief of state, and a new premier, but with Khanh as the military commander in chief whose authority was under pressure from a group of youthful generals, usually referred to as the Young Turks, who sought to assert military control.[116]

Given the chaos in Vietnam and an upcoming election in the United States, few military initiatives occurred during the summer and fall of 1964. The president, as Forrestal noted, wanted "to keep the lid on," and avoid any unhappy surprises that might make unfavorable headlines at home before November. The Joint Chiefs, as usual, were divided. Against the advice of LeMay and Greene, who urged extensive air strikes against North Vietnam, Wheeler and the other JCS members supported Taylor's position "that it was important not to overstrain the currently weakened GVN by drastic action in the immediate future."[117]

The inactivity, however, was one-sided. The Viet Cong insurgency did not let up in this period, and there was no evidence that any U.S. message of determination influenced Hanoi. Rather, Washington's behavior appeared fitful and uncertain, hardly evidence that the United States intended to win a war that its client state could not win on its own. Instead of following up the signal provided by the Tonkin Gulf Resolution, the Johnson administration displayed little more initiative than its South Vietnamese ally.[118]

On 10 September Johnson agreed to the issuance of NSAM No. 314, which provided for the resumption of DeSoto patrol operations but directed that they "be clearly dissociated from 34A maritime operations." The thrust of the memorandum's recommendations for military action was defensive: GVN air and ground movements into the Laotian corridor would be limited and U.S. units would "respond as appropriate" to attacks on them. The administration still hoped that these modest measures, together with political and economic actions, would lift South Vietnamese morale.[119]

The DeSoto patrols were suspended again in September after what was thought to be another enemy attack. On 18 September, a night with weather conditions similar to those of 4 August, the USS *Morton* and USS *Edwards* radioed that they were under attack from four unidentified boats. The destroyers opened fire but there was no response. There had been no visual sightings, only radar. Later, in congressional hearings on the Gulf of Tonkin in 1968, McNamara would testify that lack of credible evidence in this instance had deterred him and the president from taking retaliatory action.[120]

Through October intelligence reports and messages from Taylor reported that conditions continued to deteriorate in South Vietnam as its government became more disarrayed and pressure from the North increased. On 27 October the JCS told McNamara that "strong military actions are required now in order to prevent the collapse of the US position in Southeast Asia." They recommended military actions in ascending order up to the level of U.S. strikes in the South and "forward deployment of US combat units in Southeast Asia." Predictably, LeMay and Greene wanted to go further and undertake "selective air strikes against DRV to include air strikes on infiltration routes." McNamara's position underscoring the higher priority of political and economic over military measures prevailed until election day.[121]

This policy did not help either American or Vietnamese morale. The sense of impotence increased when, just before the U.S. election, on 1 November 1964, the Viet Cong attacked with mortars the air base at Bien Hoa, only a dozen miles from Saigon, killing 4 Americans, wounding 72, and destroying 5 B-57s and damaging another 13. This bold strike impelled Ambassador Taylor and the Joint Chiefs to call for an immediate and powerful response against North Vietnam. But the president resisted; the election was only three days away. As Rusk noted in a message to Taylor, "we are inevitably affected by election timing. Quick retaliation could easily be attacked as [an] election device here."[122] According to Greene, during McNamara's 2 November meeting with the Joint Chiefs, Taylor twice expressed concern that "a major effort in South Vietnam might result in a war with Communist China." McNamara, also worried about China, told the chiefs that "the President being born in Texas is inclined to take some action. He wants to move, but he wants to be God-damned sure of himself before he does so."[123] Several years later, in writing his memoirs, the president ascribed his non-response to the unsteadiness and military weakness of the South Vietnamese government, just being re-formed under civilian leadership, and his fear of Viet Cong attacks against U.S. dependents in Saigon.[124]

Even as the administration rebuffed the military hawks, the deepening gloom over conditions in South Vietnam had forced it to reconsider its options in Vietnam. Weeks earlier, in September, when the president had heard Taylor's pessimistic description of the political confusion in Saigon, he asked "if anyone doubted whether it was worth all this effort." The answer he received then—and probably wanted—held that the United States could not afford to allow Hanoi to succeed. McNamara made a point of noting that "money was no object" in examining courses of action in Southeast Asia. Rusk was convinced that it would be worth any amount to succeed. And the president weighed in with the observation "that it was necessary not to spare the horses." The translation of this political conviction into military action would require, as the Joint Chiefs clearly understood, far more than a tit-for-tat response. Vigorous air strikes offered only one alternative; even the deployment of U.S. ground forces should not be excluded.[125] Consciously or not, the administration seemed to be gearing up to do what it had never wanted to do in the past, take the war out of Vietnamese hands and into its own. This prospect followed inevitably from the premise that South Vietnam could not be allowed to fall to communism. Not only the military chiefs accepted the possible use of U.S. armed forces, but also McGeorge Bundy, who as early as 31 August 1964 suggested to the president that "we should have a hard look at this grim alternative.... It seems to me at least possible that a couple of brigade-size units put in to do specific jobs about six weeks from now might be good medicine everywhere."[126]

Back to the Drawing Board

After deciding not to retaliate for the Bien Hoa attack of 1 November, the next day, just before the national election, Johnson established an NSC Working Group, chaired by William Bundy,* to conduct another in-depth review of U.S. Indochina policy. Using the resources of State, DoD, and CIA, by 17 November the group compiled a 100-page draft and a 20-page summary that then underwent close scrutiny by departmental secretaries or equivalents who constituted themselves the Executive Committee, and by Taylor (back in Washington for about a week, beginning 27 November). The president also reviewed the earlier drafts, before approving a much-altered and shortened version on 3 December 1964.[127]

Its first sentence said it all: "US objectives in South Vietnam (SVN) are unchanged"—stop North Vietnamese support of the Viet Cong and end the latter's insurgency operations, reestablish an independent and secure South Vietnam, and maintain the security of the non-communist countries in the area.[128] In a "*first phase*" 30-day military period, the United States would concentrate on supporting South Vietnamese and Laotian ground and air operations against infiltration and "possibly" conduct air strikes against the North "as reprisal against any major or spectacular Viet Cong action." Beyond the 30-day period, the first-phase actions might be expanded during a designated "*transitional phase*" by deploying large numbers of U.S. aircraft to South Vietnam, possibly initiating air raids a short distance into North Vietnam, and by preparing to remove American dependents from South Vietnam. Thereafter, if South Vietnamese governmental effectiveness improved and if Hanoi failed to negotiate and agree to acceptable terms, "the US is prepared—at a time to be determined—to enter into a *second phase* program, in support of the GVN and RLG, of graduated pressures directed systematically against the DRV" to consist primarily "of progressively more serious air strikes . . . and of appropriate US deployments to handle any contingency."[129]

The same day, in his instructions to Taylor, the president outlined what he regarded as the two major problems: South Vietnamese governmental instability and continued Hanoi support of the Viet Cong; in his view the former far

---

* Other members included John McNaughton; Harold Ford, CIA senior China-Asia officer; Vice Adm. Lloyd M. Mustin, senior operations officer, JCS; and McGeorge Bundy.

outweighed the latter in importance. Consequently, improved SVN governmental performance was essential "before new measures against North Vietnam would be either justified or practicable." He authorized Taylor to initiate planning for the second phase "with the understanding that the USG does not commit itself now to any form of execution of such plans."[130]

The 3 December policy statement and the instructions to the ambassador both addressed diplomatic, political, economic, and civic matters, including even sanitation and hygiene, since any hopes of success rested on obtaining a viable government and winning the backing of the South Vietnamese people. Johnson sent the new policy statement and a copy of his instructions for Taylor to McNamara, Rusk, and McCone on 7 December, along with the injunction that he considered them a "matter of the highest importance" whose substance "should not become public except as I specifically direct."[131]

Despite consideration of plans for more aggressive actions, the latest policy statement represented only a limited change. It still held out some hope of regeneration of an effective South Vietnamese government, negotiations with North Vietnam, and the possibility, if need be, of air strikes. The major difference was the more precise calibration of the sequence of military actions, especially a projected air campaign against the North.

Events in the winter of 1964-65 bore out the improbability of a viable government coming to power in Saigon. The civilian government of Tran Van Huong, installed in late October-early November, lasted only until 20 December, when Khanh and the Armed Forces Council (AFC) abolished the High National Council, the temporary legislative body, pending an election and establishment of a general assembly.[132] Huong stayed on temporarily until 27 January 1965, when Khanh took over direct control of the government and designated a new premier and then another on 16 February.[133] In the course of these maneuverings he completely alienated Taylor, who now viewed him as nothing more than an inveterate schemer. The last straw was Khanh's reported approach to the Viet Cong for the purpose of establishing a neutralist government with himself at its head.[134] At last, after the AFC put down an attempted coup against Khanh on 19-20 February, it voted the next day to send him packing as a roving ambassador abroad. Taylor described the period as "the most topsy-turvy week since I came to this post."[135]

The lack of responsibility by Saigon's ruling elite seems to have slowed rather than accelerated the U.S. takeover of the war. Even when a U.S. officer housing billet in Saigon was bombed on 24 December 1964, killing 2 Americans and wounding 66 Americans and Vietnamese, despite extremely strong recommendations from Taylor, Westmoreland, Sharp, and the JCS for reprisal air strikes against North Vietnamese barracks, Johnson, supported by McNamara and Rusk, rejected the proposal.[136] In a lengthy message of explanation to Taylor on 30 December, the president provided the rationale for his disapproval. Obviously most important was the turmoil and disunity among the Vietnamese people and the lack of a functional government. Nor, he noted, should "we . . . be widening the battle until we get our dependents out of South Vietnam." Additionally he wanted improvement in the apparently weak measures for protection of U.S. barracks and aircraft. Finally, he questioned continued recommendations for air attacks against the North. "I have never felt that this war will be won from the air, and . . . what is much more needed and would be more effective is a larger and stronger use of Rangers and Special Forces and Marines . . . . I am ready to look with great favor on that kind of increased American effort, directed at the guerrillas and aimed to stiffen the aggressiveness of Vietnamese military units . . . . I myself am ready to substantially increase the number of Americans in Vietnam if it is necessary to provide this kind of fighting force against the Viet Cong."[137] It seemed clear that the president, as well as McNamara, Rusk, and McGeorge Bundy, still placed defeat of the insurgents above defeat of North Vietnam as the ultimate solution to the war, and that depended on the establishment of a stable South Vietnamese government.

One week after Johnson's inauguration, McNamara and Bundy, concerned about what they saw as failed U.S. policy in the wake of continuing internal upheaval in the South, warned the president that "our current policy [in Vietnam] can lead only to disastrous defeat." They saw only two alternatives: the first, to use U.S. military power in Southeast Asia to check the communist advance; the second, to pursue negotiations and salvage whatever possible without adding to current U.S. military risks. They opted for the first alternative, noting that "the worst course of action is to continue in this essentially passive role which can only lead to eventual defeat and an invitation to get out in humiliating circumstances." They noted that Rusk disagreed, hoping that current policy, contingent on a strengthened regime in the South, would work out.[138] Rather than have Taylor return to Washington during this tumultuous period in Saigon, the president sent Bundy to survey the scene.*[139]

While the Bundy mission was in South Vietnam, in the early morning of 7 February the Viet Cong carried out four attacks—two against U.S. Army personnel in the Pleiku area that resulted in 7 killed and 109 wounded plus damage to or destruction of a large number of Army aircraft. In an evening meeting (6 February in Washington), supported by the unanimous recommendation of Taylor, Westmoreland, and Bundy (in Saigon) and the NSC members, Johnson authorized air strikes against four targets in North Vietnam—all barracks—and directed the evacuation of all American dependents from South Vietnam.†[140] The next day, the president publicly announced these air strikes along with his order to deploy a

---

*Bundy's party consisted of McNaughton; Leonard Unger, State; Lt. Gen. Andrew Goodpaster, JCS; Chester Cooper, NSC; and Jack A. Rogers, OSD. They left Washington on 2 February and returned on the 7th.

†Only Senator Mansfield, attending the NSC meeting along with House Speaker McCormack, voiced opposition to the reprisal (Johnson, *Vantage Point*, 125).

Hawk air defense battalion to South Vietnam; he ended his public release: "Other reinforcements, in units and individuals, may follow."[141]

That evening (the 7th), Bundy arrived from Vietnam with the mission's findings. The first words delivered the message: "The situation in Vietnam is deteriorating, and without new U.S. action defeat appears inevitable." With the stakes in Vietnam so high, the U.S. investment so large, and no available channel for negotiation, "development and execution of a policy of *sustained reprisal* against North Vietnam" seemed to offer the best "chance of success in Vietnam."[142] On 8 February, with Speaker McCormack and Minority Leader Gerald Ford from the House and Mike Mansfield and Minority Leader Everett Dirksen from the Senate in attendance, the NSC discussed at length possible future actions. At the conclusion, Johnson observed that "it is true that we have real trouble in Vietnam but we are not going to pull out."[143]

The initial reprisal action had little effect, as the Viet Cong struck again on 10 February, attacking U.S. Army barracks at Qui Nhon, killing 23 Americans and wounding 21. After discussions with NSC and congressional members, the president ordered immediate air strikes, again on North Vietnamese barracks, which were carried out on 11 February with a loss of three U.S. naval aircraft.[144]

The Viet Cong attacks of 7 and 10 February against U.S. troops proved to be a turning point for the president and many of his advisers. As he stated during the NSC meeting on 8 February (and later reiterated in his memoirs) he thought the time had come "to deter, destroy and diminish the strength of the North Vietnamese aggressors and to try to convince them to leave South Vietnam alone."[145] This left no doubt about his objective during the NSC's 10 February meeting; Bundy noted "that the President had 'turned the corner' and we were on the track of sustained and continuing operations against the North."[146]

Immediately after the president had finally authorized action against North Vietnam, McNamara asked the Joint Chiefs to ready an eight-week program based on two or three attacks each week. They responded immediately, sending to the secretary on 11 February a plan that consisted primarily of air strikes against North Vietnamese military targets below the 19th parallel but also included proposals for ship bombardment, continued covert operations, DeSoto patrols, and limited ground operations across the Laotian border. It also called for deployment or the readying for deployment of numerous fighter squadrons, a wing of B-52s, a Marine expeditionary brigade, two Army infantry brigades, an aircraft carrier, and supporting units to South Vietnam, Thailand, Guam, or elsewhere in the western Pacific.[147] On 13 February, the president generally approved the JCS plan with modifications as part of a three-pronged program calling for (1) an intensified in-country pacification effort, (2) limited air action against North Vietnamese targets (about once or twice a week), and (3) an approach to the United Nations with the objective of persuading North Vietnam to enter into peace negotiations.[148]

Johnson received reinforcing support from former President Eisenhower with whom he met on 17 February for several hours, along with McNamara, Wheeler, Goodpaster, and Bundy. Eisenhower stated the need to deny Southeast Asia to the communists; however, the South Vietnamese people had to be the critical factor in that effort. American assistance should take many forms—food, medical, morale measures for the civilian population, as well as military operations to include a "campaign of pressure . . . north of the border" to impede infiltration. Should China or the Soviet Union threaten to intervene, messages suggesting the possible use of nuclear weapons could be passed to them, as had occurred in obtaining the Korean War armistice. Eisenhower hoped that the use of U.S. ground troops would not be required, "but if it should be necessary, so be it." He also provided one bit of advice that would be largely ignored in the future. Quoting an old adage that "centralization is the refuge of fear," Eisenhower suggested that the military mission be "very broadly stated" and then rely on the field commander to do the job.[149]

The next day, 18 February, the president approved the first of planned air attacks against North Vietnam—the Rolling Thunder air campaign—by both U.S. and South Vietnamese aircraft. The initial mission, scheduled for the 20th, was canceled because of the attempted coup in Saigon on 19-20 February. Subsequent missions, Rolling Thunder II, III, and IV, were also canceled because of continued concern over the reliability of the Saigon government and military establishment or because of bad weather. Finally, the first Rolling Thunder attack occurred on 2 March 1965 when USAF fighters and light bombers destroyed 75 to 80 percent of an ammunition depot base while South Vietnamese Air Force fighters largely damaged or destroyed most of a naval base at a cost of five USAF and one VNAF aircraft lost to antiaircraft artillery.[150]

Thereafter, until October 1966, this first phase of the Rolling Thunder campaign continued, with the purpose of promoting South Vietnamese morale, reducing the infiltration of men and supplies from the North, and gradually destroying Hanoi's military bases and forces, all in the hope of weakening the enemy's will to fight and initiating peace negotiations, while avoiding a conflict with China and the Soviet Union. Eisenhower's advice notwithstanding, the president and McNamara retained firm control over Rolling Thunder operations; the targets for each mission generally required their personal approval.[151]

"McNamara's War"

From the beginning the United States had intended that military assistance to South Vietnam would consist of providing equipment and advice; success or failure in the conflict would depend on the South Vietnamese themselves. Successive administrations maintained this position, but it gradually eroded as the Viet Cong grew stronger, the South Vietnamese government steadily disintegrated, and its military forces faced problems of inadequate leadership and high rates of desertion. A major change in the U.S. outlook started to occur with the August 1964 Tonkin Gulf incident and the ensuing congressional resolution, which Johnson and his advisers viewed as an endorsement of their long-held belief that the fall of South Vietnam would lead to a communist victory in all of Southeast Asia and possibly beyond. Action to forestall such a catastrophe seemed imperative.

On the occasion of the Tonkin Gulf incident, the president allowed the Navy to conduct a single air attack against a North Vietnamese naval base. Concurrently a sizable buildup of U.S. airpower took place in South Vietnam for the purpose of combating infiltration into the South along the Laotian and Cambodian borders, but attacks against North Vietnam were not allowed. This embargo remained despite Viet Cong assaults against U.S. military forces in November and December 1964. Only after the attacks of 7 and 10 February 1965, which resulted in unacceptable U.S. personnel and weapon losses, did Johnson reluctantly agree to sustained, if limited, air operations against North Vietnam.

Previously, the president, McNamara, Rusk, and other top civilian officials in Washington had opposed any proposal to introduce U.S. ground troops into South Vietnam other than in an advisory role, although they had recognized it as potentially necessary. Even at the time of the Tonkin Gulf incident both Taylor and Westmoreland had opposed such a step. Although after the February 1965 attacks Westmoreland proposed the deployment of ground troops to protect several major U.S. bases,[152] he went along when Taylor on 22 February disagreed, "except possibly for protection of [the] airfield at Danang." Taylor feared that a "white-faced soldier armed, equipped and trained as he is," is not a "suitable guerrilla fighter for Asian forests and jungles." Only with reluctance did Taylor agree to the need for a Marine contingent to defend the Da Nang air base.[153]

Four days later, on 26 February, the president, backed by McNamara, Rusk, the Joint Chiefs, and Eisenhower's recent supportive advice, took the next step and authorized the Marine deployment.[154] On 8 March, two battalion landing teams arrived at Da Nang, followed in four days by a third team and a helicopter unit.[155] Taylor later reflected "how hard it had been to get authority for the initiation of the air campaign against the North and how relatively easy to get the marines ashore. Yet I thought the latter a much more difficult decision and concurred in it reluctantly."[156]

Even though Johnson considered these latest military actions as a consistent evolving policy, they did in fact constitute an escalation of what would soon be an American war. Only U.S. intervention and direction could keep South Vietnam from collapsing. For American policymakers, options other than taking over combat appeared to have evaporated. Limited bombing did not seem to faze either the Viet Cong or the North Vietnamese. And extensive bombing not only made Americans a major target of retaliation but precipitated in turn dispatch of more

Americans to defend those already in the country. The results were precisely what McNamara and Taylor had sought to avoid: the Americanization of the war. U.S. forces in Vietnam grew from 3,164 at the end of 1961 to 23,310 at the start of 1965; deaths from hostile action (including Laos) increased from 11 in 1961 to 147 in 1964. The next year would see the force figure climb to 184,314 and combat fatalities to 1,369.

Until 1965 McNamara appeared to have been of two minds about Vietnam. It was not that he wanted to abandon the effort, although his frustrations with Saigon's leadership tempted him from time to time. Nor did he fail to recognize the importance of the pacification effort. By 1964 McNamara believed that the war had to be won in the villages of the South, not in the bombing of the North. As late as 9 February 1965, immediately after the Pleiku incident, in a report to the president he gave more attention to the work of AID than he did to the military.[157] He remained optimistic throughout 1964 that U.S. support could remain temporary and discriminate. Even as he gave in to the need for selective bombing he still maintained some hope that American advisers could leave by the end of 1965. McNamara was a restraining influence on the Joint Chiefs in the first 15 months of the Johnson presidency.

At the same time he accepted the inevitability of increased involvement in South Vietnam, which required lifting restraints. There were "two paramount reasons," he told the House Foreign Affairs Committee on 11 March 1965, "why we must succeed in helping that country resist the aggression mounted against it by North Vietnam. First, a Communist victory in South Vietnam would immediately open the way for further adventures by the Hanoi regime, and by China, in other neighboring countries . . . . Second, it is vital that the United States prove to the world that the form of aggression being tested in South Vietnam is not the 'wave of the future.'"[158]

As early as April 1964 Senator Morse had referred to the conflict in Vietnam as "McNamara's War." When a reporter asked his reaction, McNamara replied: "This is a war of the United States Government. I am following the President's policy and obviously in close cooperation with the Secretary of State. I must say . . . I don't object to its being called 'McNamara's War.' I think it is a very important war and I am pleased to be identified with it and do whatever I can to win it."[159] Almost a year later, as U.S. ground troops stood poised to enter South Vietnam, McNamara reiterated this view in part. He noted, "Some people have been calling the one [war] in South Vietnam 'McNamara's war.' I don't mind. I strongly support our policy of helping South Vietnam fight off the Communist insurgency. But it's not 'McNamara's war'; it's a Communist war, and a dangerous one, and if we don't meet it now it may endanger us more seriously at a later date."[160] McNamara was correct in that it was not his war; it was a Viet Cong war, a North Vietnamese war, and becoming an American war with South Vietnam more and more a passive partner by 1965. Whatever the depth of his own conviction, he increasingly became the face of a commitment that had passed the point of no return and he pursued the task with characteristic vigor and authority. Some 30 years later, in his memoir of the Vietnam War, McNamara recalled that he delegated many DoD issues to his deputies but "I increasingly made Vietnam my personal responsibility. That was only right: it was the one place where Americans were in a shooting war, albeit as advisers. I felt a very heavy responsibility for it, and I got involved as deeply as I felt I could and be effective. That is what ultimately led people to call Vietnam McNamara's War."[161]

Chapter XX
Conclusion

In his first four years as secretary of defense Robert McNamara had to cope with an unending series of international crises, a wide-ranging reevaluation and transformation of national security policy, and the hands-on management of the Department of Defense colossus—all of this in an unpredictable and menacing world and an increasingly divisive domestic political environment. Some of the problems he encountered were of his own making, the result of his own driving style and sometimes heavyhanded approach. He seemed ever embroiled in controversies with one set of adversaries or another, often at the same time—the Joint Chiefs and the military services, Congress, state and local officials, the press, NATO allies, and, of course, the Soviet Union and the communist bloc. The challenges would have daunted a lesser man. McNamara seemed to relish them.

McNamara's bold management style would not have been possible without the full measure of confidence and support accorded him by the two presidents he served. Both admired and formed a bond of friendship with this member of the administration who was at the same time a star performer and a lightning rod of controversy. Roswell Gilpatric believed that "no cabinet officer in my time has ever been closer to his Chief than McNamara was to John F. Kennedy and Lyndon B. Johnson, both of whom treated him as first among equals. Not only did Bob never take advantage of this unique Presidential trust and confidence; he was careful never to impinge upon, far less usurp, Presidential authority that he could easily have exercised."[1] Johnson had an exalted view of his secretary of defense: "I had a good impression of McNamara from the first day I saw him . . . . And he has exceeded my expectations . . . . When I wake up, the first one I call is McNamara . . . . He is smart, patriotic, works hard . . . . He's like a jackhammer . . . . No human can take what he takes, he drives too hard. He is too perfect."[2] Without certain knowledge that his leaders would stand behind him, the secretary would probably not have undertaken some of his more contentious actions or survived in office as long as he did.

The mastery that McNamara exerted over the Defense Department in his first years in office resulted in no small part from his strong personality and dominating presence. Hyperboles employed by the early critics of his accomplishments reflected the tendency to equate the office with the man. Such labels as "the McNamara Monarchy" and "Master of the Pentagon," and particularly the "McNamara Revolution," identified the institution with its leader as seldom before or since.[3] Eugene Zuckert, who became secretary of the Air Force, later described the striking impact McNamara had on him. "I have never ceased being impressed with the fact that on January 18th [two days before taking office] McNamara had achieved such a grasp of the job at hand and had organized his conclusions so thoroughly that in a meeting with most of the members of his incoming team, he was able to delineate many of the initiatives which would command major attention during the coming months."[4]

From the beginning McNamara had in mind objectives that looked to centralizing in OSD direction of the department, making the military forces more effective, and reducing the costs of operating the military establishment. His cost consciousness doubtless derived in part from his experience as comptroller of the Ford Motor Company and his penchant for statistical analysis. He quickly made his presence felt by calling into question as many activities of the department as he could identify. Within weeks of taking office he set in motion task forces to examine every aspect of the Pentagon's responsibilities. Many of them cut across service lines; their number seemed to increase with each passing day, blossoming to some 140 before McNamara had finished taking the measure of the department. With speed an essential element, deadlines for the reports were short, sometimes only a few weeks.[5]

How much of this "revolution" was a matter of style, of appearance of change rather than a genuine transformation, remains debatable even today. Certainly, some of the changes had been initiated under the Eisenhower administration. McNamara recognized, as did his predecessor, Thomas Gates, that the Department of Defense Reorganization Act of 1958 gave the secretary the power he needed to effect major changes. Gates had set a notable example of the use of such power when in 1960 he established the Joint Strategic Target Planning Staff to develop overall target selection and a single integrated plan for strategic operations.[6]

What distinguished the two administrations was the extent of the new secretary's control of the Defense establishment. McNamara's management approach employed programming (linking military planning and budgeting) and systems analysis (assessing essential cost effectiveness and delving into the hard choices of which funds went into each program) in the service of synergy and efficiency. As McNamara observed in April 1964, he wanted to examine every area in the department, and act on what hitherto had been only a partial recognition that the prime rationale for creation of the Defense Department was to bring about close coordination of the missions involved in land, sea, and air warfare.[7] Administrative changes within OSD, while not extensive, significantly altered not only its composition but its reach. New offices of assistant secretaries and several new Defense agencies served to widen the span of control over DoD exercised by the secretary.[8]

While the three military departments retained the responsibility to arm, supply, and support land, sea, and air forces assigned to unified commands, the secretaries of the departments found their roles much diminished by McNamara's ideas of DoD organization. At the very beginning he declared flatly that "the offices of the service secretaries are anachronisms." He saw no sense in developing a force structure for one service separate from the overall national force structure. The secretaries, he believed, could make only minimal contributions to a coherent program unless they knew what the other services proposed to do. McNamara's emphasis on centralizing management to serve overarching DoD objectives weakened the offices and status of the service secretaries.[9] The secretaries seemed to have only the choice of accepting the downgrading of their offices or resigning.

There was discomfort in Congress with McNamara's changes, particularly having OSD assistant secretaries deal directly with officers and civilians in the military departments, bypassing the secretaries in the process. When Chairman Carl Vinson of the House Armed Services Committee accused McNamara of making the Office of the Secretary of Defense into a fourth service, the secretary responded by saying he was not proposing to change the laws governing DoD. Vinson accepted his argument that the OSD assistant secretaries could not perform their functions without freedom to consult informally with their counterparts in the services.[10]

The Joint Chiefs of Staff also, though not subjected to any organizational changes, recognized that their stature had been diminished. The secretary maintained that he met with the Joint Chiefs faithfully every week and consulted with them on all matters, but the chiefs usually found themselves providing sounding boards for positions he and his OSD staff were advocating. Little of the resentment engendered in the JCS seemed to affect him. Even such a conforming spirit as General Lemnitzer could not conceal his unhappiness with his role as JCS chairman under McNamara. Only the anger of the blunt-spoken General LeMay seemed to impress McNamara, and LeMay could be dismissed as a special case. "It never bothered me that I overruled the majority of the Chiefs," McNamara later asserted. He claimed that all he wanted was the right answer, and if four people proposed the wrong answer and one person the right one, "I supported the one. If I thought all five were wrong, I selected another answer. Initially, that caused a certain amount of resentment and concern."[11]

Lemnitzer's successors as JCS chairman, Maxwell Taylor and Earle Wheeler, had more harmonious and friendly relations with McNamara. They generally, though not always, went along with the secretary's policies and often succeeded in persuading their reluctant JCS colleagues to acquiesce. For sure, some of the chiefs and other military officers regarded Taylor and Wheeler as McNamara's minions, too close to the throne and overly compliant.

Particularly galling to the Joint Chiefs was the secretary's use of civilian experts to second-guess the military strategic planners. Teams of youthful managers were no novelty to the secretary. He had been one of a comparable group of young men who moved from the Army Air Forces after World War II into important management positions at Ford. The 1960s version had their mentor in Charles J. Hitch, who came from the Rand Corporation to the Pentagon in 1961 to become assistant secretary of defense (comptroller). His brightest disciple, Alain Enthoven, became the major figure in the development of systems analysis. Not all the Whiz Kids came from Rand; others—economists, engineers, and lawyers—were drawn from Ivy League universities, industry, and prestigious law firms. Despite their youth, they exuded energy, intelligence, and confidence in their ability to change the ways of the Pentagon.

Understandably, these civilians provided inviting targets for members of the military services, and particularly the Joint Chiefs, who perceived them as intruders on traditional military functions. Some of the Whiz Kids, convinced that objective quantitative analysis counted for more than experience, were, or appeared to be, contemptuous of the military. Enthoven provided an egregious example of this attitude during a visit to U.S. Air Force headquarters in Germany. When a general outlined plans for his briefing, the young economist reportedly interrupted him to say, "General, I don't think you understand. I didn't come for a briefing. I came to tell you what we have decided."[12] Enthoven might not have employed this language in addressing the chairman of the Joint Chiefs of Staff, but Lemnitzer's pique at interference by the Whiz Kids was never difficult to discern.

The Whiz Kids in turn had their own grievances against the Joint Chiefs. Enthoven could scarcely believe that before McNamara no one had responsibility for systematically examining strategy and weapon systems. He found it absurd that the comptroller was not supposed to have anything to do with weapons, forces, and strategy because they were the exclusive territory of the JCS. In retrospect, he was convinced that the JCS "had become a great big political logrolling affair" where officers were assigned to protect the interests of their services without even a pretense of objectivity.[13] (Enthoven overlooked Comptroller Wilfred McNeil's significant role in examining forces and weapons in the Eisenhower administration.)

Service competition and infighting among the chiefs played a key role in neutralizing service and JCS challenges to McNamara and OSD dominance. Disinclination to support the needs of a sister service was common; backbiting all too often accompanied back-scratching. The consequences of this parochialism could and did affect the larger interests of national security. While working to change the system, McNamara took advantage of service rivalries to advance his own programs. LeMay, for example, did not support the Army's Nike-Zeus ABM project and in turn received little support from his colleagues in his fight for the B-70. In such instances the secretary did not have to overrule the chiefs. They defeated themselves.

As the engine to drive the management reforms, particularly the central task of formulating the budget, McNamara instituted PPBS—a planning, programming, and budgeting system intended to remove the duplication, waste, service competition, and uncoordinated appropriation requests that had characterized the planning and budgeting process in the past. The new process would bring together the estimates, requirements, expenditures, and anticipated activities of all the military departments and agencies in the service of coherent national objectives. Its major tool, "systems analysis," represented a quantitative approach to problems that evaluated the cost effectiveness of alternative ways of meeting objectives. A key to the successful operation of the system involved OSD establishing its budget-making authority over the military departments, to which end McNamara lent himself wholeheartedly.

The reasoning behind relating missions and operations more closely to the budget appeared logical. The parochial divide between the services would be bridged by a system that sought to ensure that their individual service missions would serve the common national interest in accordance with a common strategy. Where in the past the Army, Navy, or Air Force might develop programs independently and often in competition with each other, the secretary would now exercise authority to designate a single service to do the work and employ the weapon system. In light of the importance of PPBS in McNamara's Pentagon, the role of Hitch as comptroller and of Enthoven as deputy assistant secretary for systems analysis became conspicuously important to the operation of the department.

The consequent changes reached deep inside the military departments. As the 1963 DoD Annual Report observed, "the organizational structures of all three military departments have been realigned since 1961 to provide better support to the operating forces and more efficient management."[14] The Air Force combined its Air Research and Development Command and part of its Air Force Logistics Command into a single Air Force Systems Command in 1961. In 1962-63 the Army consolidated seven technical services chiefly under the new Army Materiel Command. In 1963 the Navy placed five technical bureaus under the direct supervision of the chief of naval materiel, and command of shore-based installations directly supporting the fleet under the chief of naval operations.

McNamara expected that the organizational reforms and the new budgeting system would produce results quickly: according to his own account he was not disappointed. While efficiency and cost containment as well as centralization of authority constituted the heart of his agenda, they would not come at the expense of national security. And, indeed, he succeeded in enlarging the strength and capabilities of the military establishment while carrying out these far-reaching changes.

Although PPBS proved an effective managerial tool and together with organizational reforms and McNamara's intense efforts at cost reduction actually succeeded in reducing many costs, the secretary found himself presiding over Defense expenditures that grew steadily larger each year, with the exception of FY 1965. Factors and events beyond his control had great impact on the Defense Department, requiring expenditures that offset and eventually exceeded the savings he had achieved. In addition to the rising cost of weapon systems, Defense had to contend with international crises in Berlin, Cuba, and Vietnam that created demands for more men and money.

From the beginning, McNamara dazzled congressional committees with his impressive intellect, his great self-assurance, his capacity to respond in remarkable detail to questions, and his assertive no-nonsense style in disputation. Generally, he appeared before the committees alone, without the usual backup entourage that secretaries had always brought with them. He was, indeed, a one-man band. At the same time, McNamara's institutional changes—employment of PPBS, the cost reduction program, base closures, and OSD control of weapon system choices—prompted close congressional scrutiny and inquiry.

Having dealt successfully with Congress and much of the press in his early years in office, McNamara seemed unprepared for his diminishing influence in subsequent years. In retrospect, he liked to make a point of noting that he never lost a key legislative battle and that time had proven the correctness of his positions, but he came to recognize that his victories left a residue of criticism.[15] Moreover, his record after 1962 did not show him always prevailing. He took the position in 1963, for example, that a billion dollars for military aid was inadequate and unacceptable, yet he failed to secure more in FY 1964. He also failed to recognize that his best efforts could miscarry.

His stand on the Reserves and National Guard quickly brought him into direct conflict with powerful congressional opponents. The secretary held that it was illogical for the two organizations to coexist as inefficiently as they did. Merger made eminent sense, and he proceeded to act on the assumption that reasonable people would recognize the wisdom of his judgment. Clearly, he underestimated the power of vested interests, but he did attempt to court them in Congress from time to time. Reluctantly and belatedly he came to recognize by 1965 that his plans to merge the two would fail because the array of forces against him remained too powerful to overcome. It was not that he misunderstood the reasoning of the partisans of the Reserves and National Guard or failed to recognize their political potency. It was just that, as he viewed it, his logic should have won over even the most obdurate opponents.

McNamara's reputation in Congress suffered from his stubborn stance in favor of the TFX, an aircraft intended to serve both the Air Force and the Navy. His assuredness and determination made enemies much as it did in his contest with the Air Force and Congress over the B-70, where he was more successful. The TFX was produced and found a foreign market, but at an excessively high cost. The Navy eventually canceled its F-111B program after only a handful had been delivered. McNamara countered charges of conflict of interest and of poor judgment in the choice of companies to build the plane by blaming service resistance for undermining the initial plans. He grudgingly admitted that his was a Pyrrhic victory.[16]

Such bitter victories, while impressive, came at a high price—the erosion of congressional confidence and support. He tended too frequently to blame Congress for failing to do its homework. The undertone of condescension could not go unnoticed by congressional leaders, even as McNamara professed deference to the legislative branch and avowed that he strongly believed in its investigative right, declaring that "the record will show that our cooperation exceeds that of any executive department faced with a similar set of circumstances." Sen. Richard Russell observed that "McNamara is entitled to the highest praise for the administration he has brought to the Department of Defense," but "sometimes, I wish he was a little less sensitive about the few areas in which the views of the Congress differ from his and that he did not have to react so defensively and combatively to the exercise of our responsibilities." Adding to the friction, McNamara believed that the armed services and appropriations committees in both houses of Congress were not representative of the electorate: most chairmen were Southerners, the members disproportionately Southerners and reserve officers.[17]

Norman Paul, the OSD assistant for legislative affairs in 1961-62, noted how the initial respect for McNamara's dedication and brilliance wore off over time. Many legislators gained the impression that McNamara was just dictating to them. While they were free to ask all the questions they wanted to, "essentially they were there to critique his program. They felt that they should have been brought in more on the formulation of programs."[18] According to Henry Glass, McNamara's relations with Congress deteriorated over time because "there was a certain talking down" to its members like a professor in the classroom. "At the beginning they were overwhelmed by his knowledge, but he was not well liked, because members of the Congress do not like people who are much smarter than they are, and show it." Glass observed that "he always seemed to have answers. If he didn't have one, he thought it up on the spot."[19]

Gilpatric, who served as McNamara's deputy through January 1964, agreed that "he didn't suffer fools gladly, and he was so clear in his own thinking and his own exposition that he tended to show his disdain for pettifogging questions and tactics" by some congressmen. Moreover, he did not appreciate the importance of winning over congressional staffs. "It was one thing to go up and see Senator Stennis and explain the whole thing to him or to Senator Russell or Margaret Chase Smith, but if you or somebody in your behalf hadn't done the spade work with their staff, you were just wasting your time.... And McNamara didn't think that was an efficient way of operating." In Gilpatric's view, it took McNamara a long time to realize the importance of this kind of "missionary work."[20]

Still, McNamara's self-confidence and stubbornness in defending his decisions won him admiration as well as hostility in Congress. Vinson, a strong foe of his plans to bring the military under more direct control of OSD, nonetheless repeatedly expressed his high regard for the secretary's talents and abilities. On the occasion of Vinson's retirement from Congress in 1964, he proclaimed that McNamara was not "just a good Secretary of Defense, he's the best we've had."[21] Another antagonist, acerbic Representative Hébert, challenged McNamara's authority and judgment frequently but still wanted an autographed photo for his office.[22] The best testimony to McNamara's success during his first four years was that, despite the growing resentment and reservations, Congress on balance approved so much of his agenda.

On the international stage McNamara attained visibility far beyond that of previous secretaries of defense, at times exercising more influence than Secretary of State Rusk. Sometimes he upstaged Rusk by speaking out on foreign policy matters when the latter was silent. Nevertheless, McNamara and Rusk had a mutually supportive and respectful relationship. McNamara's annual posture statements to congressional committees began with a sweeping survey of the international scene and its military significance because he felt the need to fit U.S. military policy into the larger framework of global geopolitics. When this earned McNamara criticism that he was encroaching on State Department prerogatives, he maintained that he acted in concert with the secretary of state, that he expressed his views publicly and privately on such matters because of the military implications inherent in so much of foreign policy. The secretary of state accepted McNamara's casting a large shadow in foreign policy and maintained that "we insisted upon cooperation and worked hard to obtain it." It should be understood, however, that the State Department retained its traditional prerogatives in foreign relations and often succeeded, with the support of the president, in overruling Defense initiatives and positions, including such crucial matters as military redeployments and cuts in overseas forces.[23]

McNamara and his two presidents felt deeply the responsibility imposed on them as custodians of the nation's strategic nuclear forces. They devoted much time and thought to the central problems of strategic policy and the proper role of nuclear forces. Here the questions were legion. How much nuclear force was needed? What was the optimum composition? What was the best mechanism for controlling the use of nuclear weapons? How could their potential use be legitimized? What was their appropriate role in NATO strategy? Could an arms control agreement be reached with the Soviet Union? Could proliferation of nuclear weapons be halted or curtailed? Should there be a shift of emphasis from nuclear to conventional forces? How to defend against nuclear attack? All of these issues were intricately connected and occasioned frequent and intense debate and negotiation. There were few clear-cut resolutions because there could be no definitive answers to the questions. Indeed, the problems proved enduring.

The Cold War warmed dangerously when tension created critical flash points in Berlin, Cuba, Laos, and Vietnam, hardening perception of the Soviet Union as a threat to the United States and world order. Always overshadowing all other considerations in the U.S.-Soviet relationship loomed the ratcheting strategic arms competition. As nuclear weapons and long-range missiles proliferated, the prospect of nuclear war became more chilling and unthinkable.

The frightening thought of such a war spurred McNamara to seek ways to lessen the possibility that it might occur. He sought to limit the number of ICBMs, establish greater controls over U.S. and NATO nuclear forces, and adopt a strategy of greater reliance on conventional military forces. While preparing for war, McNamara aimed always to prevent it. He supported efforts to reach understanding with the Soviet Union on the testing of nuclear weapons. Even as the nuclear competition became more intense, and especially after evidence of nuclear pollution of the atmosphere became more compelling, Kennedy and then Johnson redoubled efforts to contain the competition and succeeded in achieving at least one early success—the Limited Test Ban Treaty in 1963—a crowning achievement of the Kennedy-McNamara years.

While striving to contain the strategic arms competition, the secretary continued to make certain that U.S. "strategic offensive forces are and will continue to be fully capable of carrying out their basic mission under any foreseeable circumstances." In his annual report for FY 1965 he emphasized that "since 1961 the number and megatonnage of nuclear weapons in the alert forces has just about tripled." Missiles continued to replace bombers, but there were still more than 900 manned bombers in the strategic offensive force in 1965.[24]

Primarily in the formulation of NATO strategy, McNamara's approach to the use of nuclear weapons reflected his faith in flexible response and a reliance on the rationality of the communist adversary. Convinced that a nuclear war would be a disaster for both sides, he advanced early in 1962 a counterforce strategy that could withstand the damage from a first nuclear strike with assurance that a secure U.S. retaliatory force would still be able to destroy the enemy's nuclear bases. Knowledge of this capability, he believed, would provide sufficient deterrence against a first strike on the part of the Soviet Union, and would help to remove the strategic nuclear weapon from any future conflict. McNamara at first seemed unable or unwilling to recognize the weaknesses in this position—the reliance on the Soviets' responding in kind, the huge cost, the unlikelihood of effective air defense and civil defense, and the uncertainty whether all enemy prime targets could be destroyed in a counterstrike.

This position accounted for his insensitivity to Europe's fears that the United States and the Soviet Union might reach an understanding that not only would remove the strategic nuclear option from the defense of Western Europe but could also remove the United States from the continent. McNamara remained fixated, as demonstrated by his speeches at Athens and Ann Arbor in May and June 1962, on raising the nuclear threshold as high as possible. The allies were also disconcerted when later that year, clearly in recognition of the prohibitive difficulties counterforce posed, he seemed to abandon it for assured destruction of cities, industrial facilities, and strategic nuclear bases.

The NATO allies were mistaken about McNamara contemplating abandonment of Europe. He recognized the deficiencies of any anti-ballistic missile system and saw his civil defense program rejected by Congress. Moreover, continuing advances in nuclear technology seemed to make the urban and industrial centers of both the United States and the Soviet Union equally vulnerable, thereby providing a mutual deterrent far more effective than any active or passive defense measures could offer.

From the beginning of NATO the United States had exhorted and pressured the European members to build larger and stronger conventional forces. Disinclination and inertia ensured that the Europeans would not meet force goals periodically agreed on. McNamara's proposals to raise the nuclear threshold and place greater emphasis on the conventional forces alarmed and troubled the NATO allies. Building larger conventional forces would not only impose a costly burden on the allies, it would feed their sense of insecurity. If the United States opposed the use of nuclear weapons, would conventional weapons deter a Soviet assault? The nuclear weapon may have been unusable, but flexible response necessarily had to retain a nuclear option.

Although the nuclear option loomed ominously on both sides in the Cuban missile crisis in 1962, the antagonists recoiled from the brink. That military power could be fine-tuned below the nuclear level emerged as a lesson from the crisis. To achieve success required the measured application of force to the degree that it would not yield an unwelcome reaction from the adversary. The key was to display and exercise power in a way that did not "paint the other side into a corner."[25] Such careful calibrations operated on the assumption that the opponent was equally rational. No matter how high the tension in the fall of 1962, the prospect of miscalculation, McNamara was convinced, made the Soviet Union as fearful as the United States of the consequences of a nuclear war, and caused it to remove its missiles from Cuba. He refused to acknowledge that resolution of the Cuban crisis appeared to rest on a deal with the Soviet Union in which the removal of missiles from Cuba would be matched by removal of U.S. missiles from Turkey.

With the Berlin and Cuban crises behind it in 1963, the administration focused its attention on Southeast Asia, where it had long perceived another communist threat. U.S. military involvement in Vietnam had been growing steadily since 1960. When the fateful decision to fight a large-scale war there came in 1965, it may have been influenced by the considerable buildup of the fighting and logistical strength of the U.S. armed forces during this period. Beginning in 1961 McNamara personally directed a substantial increase in ready combat forces and in airlift and sealift capabilities as well as measures to improve command and control of the whole military establishment. The availability of the means may have helped dispose the administration to contemplate with some assurance the extensive use of force in Vietnam to achieve its ends.

Efforts at balancing this great military power with diplomacy to achieve the desired outcome in Vietnam failed badly to meet McNamara's expectations. Vietnam differed greatly from Cuba in most respects. Instead of a short-lived intense crisis it became a long-running open wound that the United States could not stanch. The failure before 1965 to recognize the true nature of the complex circumstances in Vietnam led to a costly involvement that powerfully shook both the domestic and international environments. In the early 1960s McNamara accepted designation of the conflict as "McNamara's War." In retrospect he expressed guilt and contrition for his role and for the country's actions.[26]

While McNamara's behavior in office may have shown the influence of illusion and self-deception, normal human failings, the image of him as deceitful and manipulative seems wide of the mark. Most of the criticism eventually pointed to his management of the Vietnam War. Through most of his years in office, McNamara remained convinced that a far militarily superior United States would prevail in Vietnam. Despite his perception of the incompetence and corruption of successive governments in the course of his frequent visits to South Vietnam, his analyses throughout the years 1961-1965 projected eventual defeat of the communist enemy.

He proved disastrously wrong in his expectations, although it took time for the illusion to be punctured, and only some time after a massive troop buildup had begun. McNamara's opposition to further engagement came later; by then he was trapped by his earlier expectations and his loyalty to the president. For 20 years after he left office he could scarcely bring himself to speak about Vietnam, even as his sense of guilt and remorse grew. Not until 1995 when he published his reflections on the war and his role in it, did he make a public confession of his putative sins. Ironically, the criticisms that this book provoked were as harsh as any directed against him during "McNamara's War." Rather than winning appreciation for candor, his confession unleashed a torrent of angry denunciation from left and right, from those who condemned McNamara for failing to reveal his sentiments when his opposition might have made a difference, to those who charged that his misgivings had fatally damaged the war effort and then tarnished the sacrifice of those who had died for a just cause.

Critics could also point to the missile gap of 1961 as an example of duplicity. McNamara exposed the gap as nonexistent at the time, observing that even if the United States trailed the Soviet Union in the number of ICBMs, there was no "deterrent" gap given the variety of other long-range weapons in America's nuclear arsenal. Yet two years later he could speak of a "destruction" gap that justified his support for a massive buildup of Minuteman and Polaris missiles. His endorsement of rapid growth of nuclear weapons rested on a need to combat the possibility of a future gap as well as to placate uneasy NATO allies, but the action appeared inconsistent or, worse, disingenuous.

While grappling with the great strategic and international questions that increasingly engaged his attention, McNamara also devoted time and his usual energy to important domestic concerns, among the most distressing and troublesome of which were civil rights and racial relations in the military. The call-up of Reserve and National Guard forces during the Berlin crisis of 1961 caused DoD, belatedly, to give serious attention to discrimination against blacks throughout the armed forces and generated pressure on the administration to address the race question. While President Truman by executive order in 1948 had opened the way for full integration of blacks within the military services, it proceeded slowly, since changes in the military did not apply to customs and laws in states that housed many of the bases, and little progress had been made toward removing discriminatory practices in many such places.

McNamara essentially followed the White House's approach that DoD would ensure that all activities within the jurisdiction of the military would be free from any legacy of segregation. In April 1962 a DoD directive required integration of all-black and all-white Reserve units "as rapidly as is consistent with military effectiveness," but excluded the National Guard from its scope on the grounds that it "is an organization of volunteers under the command of the respective Governors." In a report to the president in July 1963 McNamara approved of sanctions against facilities that discriminated against black servicemen but only with the approval of the secretary of the military department concerned.[27]

McNamara resolved his seeming ambivalence as the civil rights movement in the country advanced. After the passage of the Civil Rights Act of 1964, he strongly admonished the secretaries of the services in July "that it is and will be a continuing responsibility of commanders to foster equal treatment for every serviceman" in support of his rights and of the opportunities offered in the Civil Rights Act, which also made it possible to deny funding for federally assisted programs if racial discrimination was not voluntarily eliminated.[28]

In general, Defense's record on civil rights reflected a swelling current of concern and commitment in the country. One reason advanced for avoiding conflict with Southern governors and congressmen over a segregated National Guard in 1961 was fear of the damage federal intrusion might do to unit performance. This argument was stood on its head in 1964 when McNamara stated officially that denial of equality for blacks on or off the base, in the Reserve, or in the National Guard affected their morale and thus damaged military efficiency.[29]

On another front of the civil rights struggle McNamara and DoD also played a prominent part. Five years after President Eisenhower had federalized national guardsmen and sent Army troops to enforce court-ordered integration at a high school in Little Rock, Arkansas, President Kennedy, too, had to call in troops to cope with rioters seeking to deny admission of James H. Meredith to the University of Mississippi in Oxford. When 400 federal marshals could not enforce the ruling of a U.S. Court of Appeals, the president intervened with federal troops.[30]

McNamara participated in the discussions that led to the president's decision on 30 September 1962 to federalize the Mississippi National Guard and to send in federal troops; the secretary was authorized to use military force as necessary to enforce the court order.[31] By the next day the Army had dispatched 20,000 troops to the Oxford area, including elements of two airborne divisions. Troops remained in Oxford in reduced numbers into 1963; all forces left by 25 July of that year.[32]

The number of troops ultimately deployed in Oxford seemed excessive, but the reasoning behind the dispatch of airborne troops was that these elite forces would not only quell the disturbance but that the example set would inhibit future violent challenges to civil rights. The intervention sent the intended message to the nation at large—the federal government would use all its powers to uphold the law of the land.[33] As for McNamara, his active role in support of civil rights earned him, in this arena as in others, powerful enemies as well as friends.

Between 1961 and 1965 Robert McNamara put his mark on the Department of Defense with deeper impression than any secretary in the twentieth century before or after him. He would serve longer and effect more change than any other secretary, but it was the first four years in particular that were so remarkable for their pathbreaking quality. Harold Brown, who served under him for almost seven years as director of research and engineering and secretary of the Air Force, writing years later from the perspective of 1978 when he was himself secretary of defense, felt that McNamara "completely changed (for the better) the way the Defense Department operates. Despite several attempts since then to change it back, that method of operation remains much more as he left it than as he found it . . . . His stamp is on the office much more than that of any of his predecessors or successors. And this is not because his was the longest tenure; what he changed he changed during his first four years."[34]

Even his detractors testified to the quality of his intellect, his management skills, his remarkable dedication to and prodigious capacity for work, and his willing, even aggressive, acceptance of responsibility. His management skills, in particular, evoked near-universal respect and wonderment. McGeorge Bundy, not given to hyperbole, wrote of McNamara that he was "an administrator of truly exceptional force and skill." Assistant Secretary Eugene Fubini, an outstanding scientist, maintained that "management is not a science, it is an art and McNamara was (is) one of the great artists of management." Additionally, he inspired loyalty, admiration, and even affection in his closest associates and assistants in the Office of the Secretary of Defense. "While I consider McNamara to have been the best organized leader of the Defense establishment since General Marshall," his deputy Gilpatric observed, "he is not just a management genius; his qualities of heart and spirit and his generosity and modesty were as effective in attracting the devotion of those under him as his administrative abilities and his system of exercising authority."[35]

At the same time he evoked angry opposition, resentment, and even loathing among contemporaries and later critics. Management guru Peter Drucker pronounced that "the greatest strength of McNamara as a person is that he inspired admiration; his greatest weakness is that he did not inspire trust." John Blandford, a longtime, well-informed, and influential counsel of the House Armed Services Committee, asserted that McNamara "was the wrong man in the wrong job at the wrong time.... He centralized when he should have decentralized. He appeared to ignore professional military advice when he sorely needed sound military advice." Admiral Ulysses Grant Sharp, CINCPAC between 1964 and 1968, found that McNamara "did not seem to understand military strategy" and that he ignored "the recommendations of the Joint Chiefs of Staff and the military commanders in the field." Sharp felt certain that his "negative opinions" and "feelings . . . [were] shared by the large majority of officers who were in high ranking positions during McNamara's tour as Secretary of Defense." Maxwell Taylor attested to this sentiment: "I was probably the only man in uniform who ever said that McNamara was the best Secretary of Defense that had come along. But I believed it."[36]

But even as the military resented and decried McNamara's methods of administering the department and what many considered his arbitrary and contemptuous behavior toward them, they eventually derived important benefits from the relationship. Paradoxical as it may seem, they adopted some of his management techniques, particularly PPBS and systems analysis. Before McNamara left office the military services, adapting to the new era, had trained their own officers in the techniques, permitting them to deal with OSD at a high level of competence. Blandford conceded that McNamara's "greatest contribution . . . to our military structure was to force the military to learn the system [systems analysis]."[37]

Inevitably, the McNamara Pentagon would not remain the same under successive administrations. ISA would lose some of its authority in foreign policy matters and the Joint Chiefs would regain a higher level of authority in their relations with later secretaries. But the impermanence of many of McNamara's reforms did not alter the fact that the Department of Defense and its office of the secretary had experienced lasting change. "When he came in," said John Rubel, deputy director of DDR&E, "we were infinitely troubled.... We didn't see how we could get out of some of our problems—this endless escalation of the arms race, this needless multiplication of strategic weapons. We couldn't see how we were going to get a grip on the enormous programs we were supposed to supervise; we were worried about command control of nuclear weapons; we were worried about response."

Rubel credited McNamara with fundamentally and profoundly "changing the environment," citing "the enormous difference one man can make."[38] Although putting the genie of nuclear weaponry back into the bottle lay beyond McNamara's capacity, the legacy of flexible response and the continuing importance of PPBS and systems analysis remained testimonials to his enduring impact on the Pentagon and the nation's security, despite the dark cloud of the Vietnam War that in the spring of 1965 already threatened to obscure his many accomplishments.

List of Abbreviations

ABM	Anti-Ballistic Missile
ACDA	Arms Control and Disarmament Agency
ACE	Allied Command Europe
AEC	Atomic Energy Commission
AF	Air Force
AFB	Air Force Base
AFC	Armed Forces Council
AFL-CIO	American Federation of Labor-Congress of Industrial Organizations
AFPC	Armed Forces Policy Council
AID	Agency for International Development
AMSA	Advanced Manned Strategic Aircraft
ANF	Atlantic Nuclear Force
ARPA	Advanced Research Projects Agency
ARVN	Army of the Republic of Vietnam
ASD	Assistant Secretary of Defense
ASD(C)	Assistant Secretary of Defense (Comptroller)
ASD(ISA)	Assistant Secretary of Defense (International Security Affairs)
ASD(M)	Assistant Secretary of Defense (Management)
BLT	Battalion Landing Team
BNSP	Basic National Security Policy
BoB	Bureau of the Budget
BOP	Balance of Payments
C	Comptroller
CEF	Cuban Expeditionary Force
CF	Counterforce
CI	Counterinsurgency
CIA	Central Intelligence Agency

CINCCARIB	Commander in Chief, Caribbean
CINCLANT	Commander in Chief, Atlantic
CINCPAC	Commander in Chief, Pacific
CINCSAC	Commander in Chief, Strategic Air Command
CINCSOUTH	Commander in Chief, Southern Command
CIP	Counterinsurgency Plan
CJCS	Chairman, Joint Chiefs of Staff
CM	Chairman's Memorandum
CNO	Chief of Naval Operations
CONAD	Continental Air Defense Command
CPFF	Cost-Plus-Fixed-Fee
CPSVN	Counterinsurgency Plan for South Vietnam
CVA	designation for attack aircraft carrier
DARPA	Defense Advanced Research Projects Agency
DASA	Defense Atomic Support Agency
DASD	Deputy Assistant Secretary of Defense
DCA	Defense Communications Agency
DCM	Deputy Chief of Mission
DDR&E	Director of Defense Research and Engineering
DEFCON	Defense Condition
DIA	Defense Intelligence Agency
DoD	Department of Defense
DPC	Defense Planning Committee
DPM	Draft Presidential Memorandum
DSA	Defense Supply Agency
EDC	European Defense Community
EEC	European Economic Community
ENDC	Eighteen-Nation Disarmament Conference
ER	European Region
ExCom	Executive Committee (NSC)
FAA	Foreign Assistance Act
FCDA	Federal Civil Defense Administration
FEMA	Federal Emergency Management Agency
FM	Financial Management
FRG	Federal Republic of Germany
FY	Fiscal Year
FYFS&FP	Five-Year Force Structure and Financial Program
GDR	German Democratic Republic
GNP	Gross National Product
GRFL	Gerald R. Ford Library
GVN	Government of Vietnam
HCA	House Committee on Appropriations

HCAS	House Committee on Armed Services
HCFA	House Committee on Foreign Affairs
HR	House Resolution
HSCA	House Subcommittee on Appropriations
I&L	Installations and Logistics
ICA	International Cooperation Administration
ICBM	Intercontinental Ballistic Missile
ICC	International Control Commission
IDA	Institute for Defense Analysis
IRBM	Intermediate-Range Ballistic Missile
ISA	International Security Affairs
JCS	Joint Chiefs of Staff
JFKL	John F. Kennedy Library
JSCP	Joint Strategic Capabilities Plan
JSOP	Joint Strategic Objectives Plan
JSTPS	Joint Strategic Targeting Planning Staff
JUSMAAG	Joint United States Military Assistance Advisory Group
LBJL	Lyndon Baines Johnson Library
LC	Library of Congress
MAAG	Military Assistance Advisory Group
MACV	Military Assistance Command Vietnam
MAP	Military Assistance Program
MC	Military Committee
MLF	Multilateral Force
MMRBM	Mobile Medium-Range Ballistic Missile
MRBM	Medium-Range Ballistic Missile
MRC	Military Revolutionary Council
MSP	Mutual Security Program
NAC	North Atlantic Council
NASA	National Aeronautics and Space Administration
NATO	North Atlantic Treaty Organization
NCO	Non-Commissioned Officer
NDUL	National Defense University Library
NESC	Net Evaluation Subcommittee
NHC	Naval Historical Center
NIE	National Intelligence Estimate
NLF	National Liberation Front
NOA	New Obligational Authority
NORAD	North American Air Defense Command
NRO	National Reconnaissance Office
NSA	National Security Agency
NSAM	National Security Action Memorandum

NSC	National Security Council
NSF	National Security File(s)
NSTL	National Strategic Target List
NVN	North Vietnam
OAS	Organization of American States
OASD	Office of the Assistant Secretary of Defense
OCDM	Office of Civil and Defense Mobilization
ODM	Office of Defense Mobilization
OMP	Organizational and Management Planning
OPLAN	Operations Plan
OSD	Office of the Secretary of Defense
OSS	Office of Strategic Services
PACOM	Pacific Command
PCP	Program Change Proposal
PEMA	Procurement of Equipment and Munitions for the Army
PEO	Programs Evaluation Office
PL	Public Law
POF	President's Office Files
POL	Petroleum, Oil, Lubricants
PPBS	Planning-Programming-Budgeting System
PRO	Public Records Office
R&D	Research and Development
R&E	Research and Engineering
RAF	Royal Air Force
RDT&E	Research, Development, Test, and Evaluation
RG	Record Group
RLG	Royal Lao Government
ROK	Republic of Korea
ROTC	Reserve Officer Training Corps
SAC	Strategic Air Command
SACEUR	Supreme Allied Commander, Europe
SACLANT	Supreme Allied Commander, Atlantic
SACSA	Office of the Special Assistant for Counterinsurgency and Special Activities, Joint Chiefs of Staff
SAM	Surface-to-Air Missile
SAMOS	Satellite and Missile Observation System
SCA	Senate Committee on Appropriations
SCFR	Senate Committee on Foreign Relations
SDC	Self Defense Corps
SEAL	Sea-Air-Land Team
SEATO	Southeast Asia Treaty Organization
SG	Special Group

SGA	Special Group (Augmented)
SHAPE	Supreme Headquarters Allied Powers, Europe
SIOP	Single Integrated Operational Plan
SSCA	Senate Subcommittee on Appropriations
STAT	SEABEE Technical Assistance Team
STRAC	Strategic Army Corps
SVN	South Vietnam
TFX	Tactical Fighter Experimental
TOA	Total Obligational Authority
USA	United States Army
USAF	United States Air Force
USAMHI	United States Army Military History Institute
USCINCEUR	United States Commander in Chief, Europe
USG	United States Government
USN	United States Navy
USSOUTHCOM	United States Southern Command
VAX	Attack Aircraft Experimental
VC	Viet Cong
VNAF	Vietnamese Air Force
WSEG	Weapons Systems Evaluation Group

Notes

Where no record group is specified in the citation, archival accessions are part of Record Group (RG) 330, retired records of the Office of the Secretary of Defense. At the time they were consulted, these records were stored at the Washington National Records Center, Suitland, Maryland. Where record group numbers are given in the notes, it should be understood that the records are at the National Archives, College Park, Maryland. Files identified as "OSD Hist" are in the custody of the OSD Historical Office. Readers should consult the bibliography for complete information regarding the location of archival materials and for the publisher and date of publication of printed works.

I. MCNAMARA AND THE NEW FRONTIER

1. George W. Ball, *The Past Has Another Pattern: A Memoir*, 173.
2. Irving L. Janis, *Victims of Groupthink: A Psychological Study of Foreign-Policy Decisions and Fiascoes*, 44.
3. Interv Robert S. McNamara by Maurice Matloff and Roger Trask, 22 May 86, 24, OSD Hist.
4. David Wise, "Scholars of the Nuclear Age—McGeorge Bundy, Walt W. Rostow, and Jerome B. Wiesner," in Lester Tanzer, ed, *The Kennedy Circle*, 40-41.
5. Arthur M. Schlesinger, Jr., *A Thousand Days: John F. Kennedy in the White House*, 60-61.
6. Ibid, 214.
7. Interv Robert S. McNamara by Maurice Matloff and Alfred Goldberg, 3 Apr 86, 6, OSD Hist. His reference in the interview to being "so naive about the ways of Washington" referred specifically to the question of Franklin D. Roosevelt, Jr.'s qualifications for appointment as secretary of the Navy.
8. SCAS, *Hearing: Nomination of Robert S. McNamara*, 87 Cong, 1 sess, 17 Jan 61, 3-4.
9. James M. Roherty, *Decisions of Robert S. McNamara: A Study of the Role of the Secretary of Defense*, 67 (emphasis in original); Roger Hilsman, *To Move a Nation: The Politics of Foreign Policy in the Administration of John F. Kennedy*, 43.
10. Schlesinger, *A Thousand Days*, 129, 132; Theodore C. Sorensen, *Kennedy*, 255.
11. Schlesinger, *A Thousand Days*, 132; McNamara interv, 3 Apr 86, 1.
12. McNamara interv, 3 Apr 86, 4.
13. Ibid, 2-3; Schlesinger, *A Thousand Days*, 132; Sorensen, *Kennedy*, 269; Deborah Shapley, *Promise and Power: The Life and Times of Robert McNamara*, 83-84.
14. McNamara interv, 3 Apr 86, 4; Robert S. McNamara, "Managing the Department of Defense," in Samuel A. Tucker, ed, *A Modern Design for Defense Decision: A McNamara-Hitch-Enthoven Anthology*, 12.

15. Shapley, *Promise and Power*, 83-84; Roger R. Trask and Alfred Goldberg, *The Department of Defense, 1947-1997: Organization and Leaders*, 77.
16. McNamara interv, 3 Apr 86, 2; Schlesinger, *A Thousand Days*, 129.
17. Sorensen, *Kennedy*, 271.
18. Henry Glass, economic advisor to the comptroller between 1961 and 1965, was convinced that McNamara wanted to have Taylor as JCS chairman to get him out of the White House. See interv Henry E. Glass by Maurice Matloff et al, 28 Oct 87, 66, OSD Hist.
19. Sorensen, *Kennedy*, 269-70.
20. Brock Brower, "McNamara Seen Now, Full Length," *Life*, 10 May 68, 86 (quote); Shapley, *Promise and Power*, 89.
21. Brower, "McNamara Seen Now, Full Length," 86.
22. Interv Lyman L. Lemnitzer by Maurice Matloff, 19 Jan 84, 18, OSD Hist.
23. Brower, "McNamara Seen Now, Full Length," 88; OSD Hist, *Department of Defense Key Officials, 1947-2000*, 12, 19.
24. Clark R. Mollenhoff, *The Pentagon: Politics, Profits and Plunder*, 242-43; interv Roswell L. Gilpatric by Maurice Matloff, 14 Nov 83, 6-7, OSD Hist.
25. McNamara interv, 3 Apr 86, 11.
26. Charles J. Hitch and Roland N. McKean, *The Economics of Defense in the Nuclear Age*; Joseph Kraft, "McNamara and His Enemies," *Harper's*, Aug 61, 43.
27. *The Officer*, Mar 61, 12.
28. Memos McNamara for Connally and Zuckert, 9 Jan 61, fldr Reading File, Feb. 1961-Dec. 1960, box 113, McNamara Records, RG 200.
29. Memos McNamara for Stahr and Connally, 16 Jan 61, ibid.
30. Gilpatric interv, 14 Nov 83, 8. After leaving office, Zuckert wrote of the decline in the importance of the service secretaries. See Eugene M. Zuckert, "The Service Secretary: Has He a Useful Role?," *Foreign Affairs*, Apr 66, 458-79.
31. DoD Reorganization Act of 1958, 6 Aug 58, in Alice C. Cole et al, eds, *The Department of Defense: Documents on Establishment and Organization, 1944-1978*, 188-230; DoD Dir 5100.1, 31 Dec 58, ibid, 317; Robert J. Watson, *Into the Missile Age, 1956-1960*, vol IV in *History of the Office of the Secretary of Defense*, 243-91.
32. McNamara interv, 3 Apr 86, 6-7; Schlesinger, *A Thousand Days*, 153; *New York Times*, 26 Jan 61.
33. Schlesinger, *A Thousand Days*, 153-54.
34. Interv McNamara by Maurice Matloff, Alfred Goldberg, and Lawrence Kaplan, 27 Aug 86, 31-32, OSD Hist.
35. *Chicago Sun-Times*, 18 Jan 61; McNamara interv, 27 Aug 86, 31-32; SCAS, *Nomination of Robert S. McNamara*, cited in n 8, 26.
36. *Washington Post*, 7 Jan 61.
37. McNamara interv, 3 Apr 86, 11; Watson, *Into the Missile Age*, 771.
38. Burke memrcd, 10 Jan 61, fldr no 12 (215-250), Case 1448, drawer 5, Sensitive files, Arleigh Burke Papers, NHC; David A. Rosenberg, "Admiral Arleigh Albert Burke," in Robert W. Love, Jr., ed, *The Chiefs of Naval Operations*, 307-09.
39. Lemnitzer interv, 19 Jan 84, 17-18.
40. SCAS, *Nomination of Robert S. McNamara*, 22-23.
41. Ibid, 5-18.
42. Senate, Cte on Govt Opns, Subcte on National Policy Machinery, *Hearings: Organizing for National Security*, 87 Cong, 1 sess, 7 Aug 61, pt 9:1210-12.
43. Inaugural Address, 20 Jan 61, *Public Papers of the Presidents of the United States: John F. Kennedy, 1961*, 2.
44. Annual Message to the Congress on the State of the Union, 30 Jan 61, ibid, 24.
45. HCAS, *Hearings: Military Posture and HR 9751*, 87 Cong, 2 sess, 24 Jan 62, 3162; Annual Message to Congress, 24.
46. HCAS, *Hearings: Military Posture Briefings*, 87 Cong, 1 sess, 23 Feb 61, 637; Stewart Alsop, "Master of the Pentagon," *Saturday Evening Post*, 5 Aug 61, 21.
47. Annual Message to Congress, 23-24.
48. Shapley, *Promise and Power*, 97-99; *Baltimore Sun*, 17, 23 Feb 61. For McNamara's version of these events see his testimony in HCAS, *Military Posture and HR 9751*, 646-47.

49. Edward A. Kolodziej, *The Uncommon Defense and Congress, 1945-1963*, 330-31; Harland B. Moulton, "The McNamara General War Strategy," *Orbis*, Summer 64, 253; William W. Kaufmann, *The McNamara Strategy*, ch 3.
50. *Kennedy Public Papers, 1961*, 232.
51. Interv Alain C. Enthoven by Maurice Matloff, 3 Feb 86, 8-9, OSD Hist. See also Alain C. Enthoven and K. Wayne Smith, *How Much is Enough? Shaping the Defense Program, 1961-1969*, chs 2-3.
52. *Washington Post*, 31 Jan 61.
53. Memo McNamara for SvcSecs et al, 8 Mar 61, fldr SecDef Special Projects 1961-62, box 109, ASD(C) files, OSD Hist (also in fldr Reading File, May 1961-Mar 1961, box 113, McNamara Records, RG 200); *Army, Navy, Air Force Journal*, 15 Apr 61.

II. SHAKEUP IN THE PENTAGON

1. Rcd of mtg, BrigGen George S. Brown, 18 Jan 61, fldr SecDef Staff Meetings Feb-Apr 1961, box 10, AFPC and SecDef Meetings files, Acc 77-0062.
2. Ibid. Just the day before, at his nomination hearing, McNamara disclaimed any wishes to make immediate major changes in Defense organization; see SCAS, *Nomination of Robert S. McNamara*, 23.
3. HCAS, *Military Posture Briefings*, 635.
4. See HSCA, *Hearings: Department of Defense Appropriations for 1963*, 87 Cong, 2 sess, 31 Jan 62, pt 2:149.
5. Sec 202, DoD Reorganization Act of 1958, 6 Aug 58, in Cole et al, *Department of Defense*, 197.
6. Ibid, 197-200; Watson, *Into the Missile Age*, 274-75.
7. Notes on NSC mtg, 5 Jan 61, fldr L-215-71, box 29, Lyman L. Lemnitzer Papers, NDUL.
8. Report on Reorganization of DoD, *Cong Rec*, 9 Feb 61, 107, pt 2:1928-31; *Washington Star*, 5 Dec 60.
9. *Washington Star*, 31 Dec 60.
10. SCAS, *Hearings: Authorization for Military Procurement, Research and Development, Fiscal Year 1969, and Reserve Strength*, 90 Cong, 2 sess, 5 Feb 68, 254.
11. Memo Burke for OP-06, 9 Jun 61, fldr 1 Jun-31 Aug 61, Originator's File, Burke Papers, NHC. Burke commented on the absurdity of setting up "a console type arrangement wherein Defense can push a particular button in order to get a particular response to a given situation."
12. Senate, Cte on Govt Opns, Subcte on National Policy Machinery, *Organizing for National Security*, 7 Aug 61, pt 9:1192.
13. SCAS, *Hearing: Nomination of Roswell L. Gilpatric*, 87 Cong, 1 sess, 17 Jan 61, 3.
14. Ibid, 3-4.
15. McNamara interv, 3 Apr 86, 13.
16. *DoD Annual Report, FY 1961*, 22; memo McNamara for SvcSecs et al, 8 Mar 61, 9, fldr SecDef Special Projects 1961-62, box 109, ASD(C) files, OSD Hist.
17. Cole et al, *Department of Defense*, 239.
18. Ibid.
19. Ernest R. May et al, "History of the Strategic Arms Competition, 1945-1972," II, 588-90, OSD Hist; intervs Marvin Stern by Alfred Goldberg, 28 Feb, 1 Mar 67, OSD Hist.
20. *Army, Navy, Air Force Journal*, 15 Apr 61; DoD Dir 5160.32, 6 Mar 61, in Cole et al, *Department of Defense*, 325-26.
21. *Department of Defense*, 325-26; Watson, *Into the Missile Age*, 386 ff.
22. Memo McNamara for JCS, 8 Feb 61, fldr 310.1, box 44, ISA files, Acc 64A-2382.
23. Joint Chiefs of Staff Decision on JCS 2031/159, 2 Mar 61, encl "A" draft memo for SecDef and appen to encl "A," "Military Intelligence Agency, General Concept," OSD Hist.
24. *New York Times*, 4 Jul 61.
25. DoD Dir 5105.21, 1 Aug 61; *New York Times*, 30 Aug 61.
26. Memo McNamara for CJCS, 21 Jun 63, fldr Reading File, June 20-June 29, 1963, box 118, McNamara Records, RG 200.
27. SSCA, *Hearings: Department of Defense Appropriations for 1963*, 87 Cong, 2 sess, 15 May 62, 684-85.
28. Ibid, 684.
29. Ibid, 686-87.
30. Memo Taylor for DirDIA, 30 Oct 62, memo W.Y.S. [William Y. Smith] for Taylor, 2 Nov 62, fldr Chron File—Oct-Dec 62, box 27, Maxwell D. Taylor Papers, NDUL.

31. DIA, 17 Dec 64, OMP, OASD(A), FY 66 SecDef Backup Book, IV-VII, box 36, ASD(C) files, OSD Hist.
32. Cole et al, *Department of Defense*, 198-99.
33. James E. Hewes, Jr., *From Root to McNamara: Army Organization and Administration, 1900-1963*, 312-13.
34. Memo McNamara for DepSecDef et al, 23 Mar 61, w/atchd Report of Study Committee, 11 Jul 61, "Integrated Management of Common Supply Activities," 1, fldr Defense Supply Agency (Creation of), box 124, ASD(C) files, OSD Hist.
35. Ibid, i-iv; Hewes, *From Root to McNamara*, 313; DoD News Release 885-61, 31 Aug 61, "Secretary McNamara Announces Decision To Establish Defense Supply Agency," OSD Hist.
36. House, Subcte of Cte on Govt Opns, *Hearings: Defense Supply Agency*, 87 Cong, 2 sess, 11 May 62, 107.
37. Hewes, *From Root to McNamara*, 313-14.
38. DoD News Release 885-61, 31 Aug 61, cited in n 35.
39. *DoD Annual Report, FY 1962*, 67, 69.
40. *St. Louis Post-Dispatch*, 4 Dec 61.
41. Memo McNamara for Pres, 12 Sep 61, fldr Reading File, Sept. 1961-Oct. 1961, box 113, McNamara Records, RG 200.
42. HCAS, *Report of Special Subcommittee on Defense Agencies*, 87 Cong, 2 sess, 13 Aug 62, 6597.
43. HCAS, Special Subcte on Defense Agencies, *Hearings*, 87 Cong, 2 sess, 4 Jun 62, 6682.
44. Ibid, 6702.
45. *New York Times*, 8 Jul 62.
46. HCAS, *Report*, cited in n 42, 6617, 6619.
47. Ibid, 6617, 6625, 6634-35, 6921; *Washington Post*, 16 Jul 61; *Baltimore Sun*, 16 Aug 62.
48. SSCA, *DoD Appropriations for 1963*, 1259.
49. House, Cte on Govt Opns, *Defense Supply Agency*, H Rpt 2440, 87 Cong, 2 sess, 20 Sep 62, 14-15.
50. *DoD Annual Report, FY 1963*, 84; *FY 1964*, 96; *FY 1965*, 107.
51. See for example Joint Economic Cte, Subcte on Defense Procurement, *Hearings: Impact of Military Supply and Service Activities on the Economy*, 88 Cong, 1 sess, 28 Mar 63, 20.
52. Harry B. Yoshpe, "Our Missing Shield: The U.S. Civil Defense Program in Historical Perspective," prepared for FEMA, Apr 81, 16, 254-57, 273-74, OSD Hist.
53. Watson, *Into the Missile Age*, 412-13, 418. For a discussion of the Gaither Report, see 136-41.
54. Yoshpe, "Our Missing Shield," 299-314; Schlesinger, *A Thousand Days*, 747-49; Sorensen, *Kennedy*, 613-14; *Kennedy Public Papers, 1961*, 402-03.
55. *Kennedy Public Papers, 1961*, 536-37; Sorenson, *Kennedy*, 614.
56. Interv David O. Cooke by Maurice Matloff and Alfred Goldberg, 23 Oct 89, 23, OSD Hist; Yoshpe, "Our Missing Shield," 362.
57. Memo McNamara for SvcSecs et al, 31 Jul 61, OSD Hist; DoD Dir 5140.1, 31 Aug 61; *Washington Post*, 31 Aug 61; OSD Hist, *Department of Defense Key Officials, 1947-2000*, 30.
58. *DoD Annual Report, FY 1962*, 14; House, Subcte of Cte on Govt Opns, *Hearings: Civil Defense—1961*, 87 Cong, 1 sess, 1 Aug 61, 5-8.
59. Draft memo McNamara for Pres, 6 Oct 61, *Foreign Relations of the United States* (hereafter *FRUS*), *1961-1963*, VIII:158-64; ltr Rusk to Maxwell Taylor, 29 Oct 61, ibid, 190-91.
60. McNamara memo, 25 Nov 61, fldr Reading File, Nov. 1961, box 113, McNamara Records, RG 200; Schlesinger, *A Thousand Days*, 748; memo Johnson (PoliticalAffs) for Rusk w/atchmt A, 29 Nov 61, *FRUS 1961-63*, VIII:219-20.
61. Gilpatric press conf, 14 Dec 61, *Public Statements of Deputy Secretary of Defense Roswell L. Gilpatric, 1961*, 494-95.
62. HSCA, *DoD Appropriations for 1963*, 599, 602.
63. *Washington Post*, 22 Apr 62.
64. Ibid; Schlesinger, *A Thousand Days*, 748; Sorensen, *Kennedy*, 616.
65. *New York Times*, 18 Jun 62; *Washington Post*, 26 Sep 62; *DoD Annual Report, FY 1963*, 321.
66. Sorensen, *Kennedy*, 108; Yoshpe, "Our Missing Shield," 348; *Washington Star*, 1 Feb 63.
67. Ltr Pres to Chairmen Senate and House Appropriations Ctes, 2 Aug 62, *Kennedy Public Papers, 1962*, 601-03; *New York Times*, 30 Jul 62; Yoshpe, "Our Missing Shield," 16.
68. Memo Pittman for SecDef, 4 Aug 62, w/two encl, fldr Reading File, Aug. 10-Aug. 1, 1962, box 115, McNamara Records, RG 200; Yoshpe, "Our Missing Shield," 361-70, 376-77.
69. Yoshpe, "Our Missing Shield," 375.

70. Ibid, 386-91.
71. Ibid, 18; Schlesinger, *A Thousand Days*, 723.
72. *American Foreign Policy: Current Documents, 1961*, 555-58 (quote, 558).
73. Sum Kennedy's remarks to 496th NSC mtg, 18 Jan 62, *FRUS 1961-63*, VIII:238-42 (quote, 240).
74. Memo BrigGen E. G. Lansdale for SecDef and DepSecDef, 17 Jan 61, in DoD, *United States-Vietnam Relations, 1945-1967* (hereafter *Pentagon Papers*), bk 11, 1-12 (quote, 1).
75. Memo for file by Rostow, 30 Jan 61, fldr Mtgs w/Pres, 1/61-6/61, box 317, NSF, JFKL; sum rcd of White House mtg, 28 Jan 61, *FRUS 1961-63*, I:13-15. Rostow noted that Kennedy asked for copies of Mao Tse-tung's and Che Guevara's writings on guerrilla warfare.
76. Watson, *Into the Missile Age*, 646-49; paper by [Saigon] Country Team Staff Cte, 4 Jan 61, *FRUS 1961-63*, I:1-12.
77. Rcd of actions 475th NSC mtg, 1 Feb 61, *FRUS 1961-63*, VIII:20-23 (quote, 22); NSAM 2, 3 Feb 61, *Pentagon Papers*, bk 11, 17.
78. Memo No. 3 Cuba Study Gp to Pres Kennedy, 13 Jan 61, *FRUS 1961-63*, X:603-05 (quote, 605).
79. Msg CAP5416-61 Taylor to Pres, 7 Dec 61, *FRUS 1961-63*, I:724-25; rpt, "Elements of US Strategy to Deal with 'Wars of National Liberation'," 8 Dec 61, fldr CIA Gen 12/61, box 271, NSF, JFKL (quote, 1); ed note, *FRUS 1961-63*, VIII:229-30.
80. NSAM 124, 18 Jan 62, *FRUS 1961-63*, VIII:236-38 (quote, 237).
81. NSAM 165, 16 June 62, ibid, 307, n 3.
82. Maxwell D. Taylor, *Swords and Plowshares*, 200-03, 360-62; NSAM 341, 2 Mar 66, internet copy, LBJL; Charles Maechling, Jr., "Camelot, Robert Kennedy, and Counter-Insurgency—A Memoir," *Virginia Quarterly Review*, Summer 99, 438-58; Arthur M. Schlesinger, Jr., *Robert Kennedy and His Times*, 466-67.
83. JCSM-126-61 Lemnitzer for SecDef, 3 Mar 61, microfiche suppl to *FRUS 1961-63*, vols VII-IX, Doc 232; NSAM 2, 3 Feb 61, cited in n 77; memcon, 6 Feb 61, *FRUS 1961-63*, VIII:27-30; memcon, 23 Feb 61, ibid, 48-54 (quote, 51); memo C. V. Clifton (White House Def Liaison Off) for JCS, 18 Feb 61, fldr DoD Spec Warfare, vol I, Feb-May 1961, box 279, NSF, JFKL.
84. Memo Clifton for JCS, 18 Feb 61, memcon 23 Feb 61, both cited in n 83; Walter S. Poole, *The Joint Chiefs of Staff and National Policy, 1961-1964*, pt I:63; *Kennedy Public Papers, 1961*, 237; "DoD Activities and Events in 1961," OSD Hist; SCAS, *Military Procurement Authorization, FY 1962*, 4 Apr 61, 20-21.
85. *Kennedy Public Papers, 1961*, 401.
86. OASD(C) FAD 431, 18 Jan 62, OSD Hist; memo McNamara for SvcSecs et al, 5 Sep 61, fldr chron file, Jan-Dec 61, box 1, SecDef Spec Asst files, Acc 76-0028; draft memo McNamara for Pres, 6 Oct 61, *FRUS 1961-63*, VIII:158-77 (quote, 175).
87. Memo Clifton for Taylor, 10 Jan 62, fldr DoD Spec Warfare, vol I, Aug 61-Feb 62, box 279, NSF, JFKL; *Newsweek*, 23 Oct 61; *New York Times*, 13 Oct 61.
88. Robert F. Futrell, *The United States Air Force in Southeast Asia: The Advisory Years To 1965*, 79.
89. Ibid, 80-83; NSAM 104, 13 Oct 61, *Pentagon Papers*, bk 11, 328 (quote); memrcd DepSecDef Gilpatric, 11 Oct 61, *FRUS 1961-63*, I:343; Ray L. Bowers, *Tactical Airlift*, 52; FY 65 SecDef Backup Book, III, Tabs A & B, box 33, ASD(C) files, OSD Hist.
90. Edward J. Marolda and Oscar P. Fitzgerald, *From Military Assistance to Combat, 1959-1965*, vol II in *The United States Navy and the Vietnam Conflict*, 102-04, 111-12, 189-91, 218 (quote, 191).
91. Ibid, 112-15, 192-200, 344-55 (quote, 113).
92. Memcon w/Pres, 23 Feb 61, *FRUS 1961-63*, VIII:48-54 (quote, 52); interv LtGen Victor H. Krulak by Benis M. Frank, 20 Jun 70, 188, USMC Hist Div; Robert H. Whitlow, *U.S. Marines in Vietnam: The Advisory and Combat Assistance Era, 1954-1964*, 62.
93. Memo Kennedy for McNamara, 11 Jan 62, *FRUS 1961-63*, VIII:235-36 (quote, 235).
94. Poole, *JCS and National Policy 1961-64*, pt I:69; Krulak interv, 20 Jun 70, 187-88.
95. Memo Kennedy for McNamara, 11 Jan 62, cited in n 93, 235-36 (quote, 236).
96. SSCA, *DoD Appropriations for 1963*, 14 Feb 62, 21; *McNamara Public Statements, 1962*, II:873-75, 883 (quote).
97. Memo Gilpatric for Pres, 1 May 62, fldr RLG Reading File, 1/2-6/30/62, box 2, Gilpatric files, Acc 66A-3529.
98. *New York Times*, 7 Jun 62; NSAM 131, 13 Mar 62, *Pentagon Papers*, bk 12, 457-59; memrcd G. C. Moody, Jr., ExecSec SG(CI), 22 Jan 65, fldr Counter-Insurgency Spec Gp 1964-66, box 15, Komer files, NSF, LBJL; *Washington Post*, 4 Jul 62.

99. NSAM 182, 24 Aug 62, *FRUS 1961-63*, VIII:381; ed note, ibid, 382-83.
100. Memo Pres for McNamara, 15 Jul 63, fldr DoD Spec Warfare, vol I, 1962-63, box 279, NSF, JFKL.
101. Memo Taylor for Pres, 24 Jul 63, fldr DoD Spec Warfare, box 1, C. V. Clifton files, NSF, LBJL; memcon w/Pres, 24 Jul 63, *FRUS 1961-63*, VIII:491-92.
102. Memo Pres for SecState, 26 July 63, fldr DoD Spec Warfare, box 1, Clifton files, NSF, LBJL; memrcd Clifton, 3 Sep 63, fldr DoD Spec Warfare, vol I, 1962-63, box 279, NSF, JFKL; CA-5661, 2 Dec 62, fldr DoD Spec Warfare, box 1, Clifton files, NSF, LBJL.
103. For an account of space activities in the Eisenhower administration, see Watson, *Into the Missile Age*, 383-401.
104. DoD Dir 5160.32, 6 Mar 61, in Cole et al, *Department of Defense*, 325-26.
105. House, Cte on Science and Astronautics, *Hearings: Defense Space Interests*, 87 Cong, 1 sess, 17 Mar 61, 97-98.
106. *DoD Annual Report, FY 1961*, 23, 281; *Washington Post*, 18 Mar 61.
107. *Defense Space Interests*, cited in n 105, 106; *New York Times*, 19 Mar 61.
108. *Defense Space Interests*, 141.
109. House, Cte on Science and Astronautics, *Hearings: Research and Development for Defense*, 87 Cong, 1 sess, 17 Feb 61, 51 (quote); *New York Daily News*, 18 Feb 61.
110. Lemnitzer's protest in a confidential memorandum for McNamara dated 2 March 1961 was leaked to the *Chicago Sun-Times*, 12 Mar 61; Lemnitzer interv, 19 Jan 84, 16, OSD Hist.
111. *Defense Space Interests*, 137-38.
112. Ibid, 15, 38.
113. Jerome B. Wiesner et al, "Report to the President-Elect of the Ad Hoc Committee on Space," 12 Jan 61, published in part in *Defense Space Interests*, 17-23. Gilpatric's figure of "over 90%" appears on p. 37.
114. Memo McNamara for GenCoun, 7 Apr 61, w/clipping from *Washington Post*, 7 Apr 61, fldr Reading File, May 1961-Mar. 1961, box 113, McNamara Records, RG 200.
115. Ltr Pres to Speaker, House of Reps, 28 Mar 61, in House, *Amendments to the Budget for Fiscal Year 1962 . . . .*, H Doc No 125, 87 Cong, 1 sess, 2; *New York Times*, 28 Mar 61; White House Press Release, 28 Mar 61, OSD Hist.
116. *Organizing for National Security*, cited in n 12, pt 9:1197; National Aeronautics and Space Act of 1958, 29 Jul 58, PL 85-579, 72 Stat 426 (Sec 102b); *DoD Annual Report, FY 1961*, 403, *FY 1963*, 321.
117. *Kennedy Public Papers, 1961*, 404-05; Roger D. Launius, *A History of the U.S. Civil Space Program*, 59-66.
118. Memo Col Howard L. Burris for Vice Pres, 1 Mar 63, fldr Colonel Burris 1961-64, box 6, Vice Presidential Security files, NSF, LBJL; *Newport News Times-Herald*, 27 Mar 63; *Omaha World Herald*, 10 Apr 63.
119. Interv Roswell L. Gilpatric by Dennis J. O'Brien, 12 Aug 70, 112, 116-17, JFKL; *New York Herald Tribune*, 8 May 63.
120. *New York Times*, 7 May 63; *Washington Post*, 8 May 63; news conf, 8 May 63, *Kennedy Public Papers, 1963*, 374; *New York Times*, 8, 22 May 63. See also Lawrence Korb, "George Whalen Anderson, Jr.," in Robert W. Love, Jr., ed, *The Chiefs of Naval Operations*, 329-30, and Anderson's recollections of the events surrounding his departure as CNO and subsequent ambassadorial appointment in Anderson intervs with Joseph T. Mason, Jr., 7 Jan and 2 Apr 81, 525-38, 605-10, NHC.
121. Remarks at AFSC Management Conference, 2 May 62, *Gilpatric Public Statements, 1962*, 91, 99.

III. EXPANDING THE FY 1962 BUDGET

1. Watson, *Into the Missile Age*, 757-59.
2. *Public Papers of the Presidents of the United States: Dwight D. Eisenhower, 1960-1961*, 919, 952-53.
3. Watson, *Into the Missile Age*, 757-59.
4. *The Budget of the United States, FY 1962*, 489.
5. Raymond H. Dawson, "Congressional Innovation and Intervention in Defense Policy: Legislative Authorization of Weapons Systems," *American Political Science Review*, Mar 62, 42 (quote), 57; Kolodziej, *Uncommon Defense*, 377-82.
6. Ltr Bell to McNamara, 12 Jan 61, fldr New Frontier—1961-1962 Budget, box 5, ASD(C) files, OSD Hist; rcd of mtg, BrigGen George S. Brown, 18 Jan 61, 3-4, fldr SecDef Staff Meetings, Feb-Apr 61, box 10, AFPC and SecDef Meetings files, Acc 77-0062.
7. HR 4362, 87 Cong, 1 sess, 15 Feb 61; HCAS, *Military Posture Briefings*, 23 Feb 61, 627-29.

8. HSCA, *Hearings: Department of Defense Appropriations for 1962*, 87 Cong, 1 sess, 20 Feb 61, pt 1:1. Part 1 of the hearings, which lasted from 20 February through 1 March, covered overall financial statements and military personnel. Part 2 (1-21 March) covered operations and maintenance.
9. *Kennedy Public Papers, 1961*, 24; ltr Gilpatric to Pres, 3 Feb 61, fldr FY 62 Budget Summary Tables, box 5, ASD(C) files, OSD Hist; LC, Legislative Ref Serv, *United States Defense Policies in 1961*, H Doc 502, 88.
10. Rcd of action 475th NSC mtg, 1 Feb 61, *FRUS 1961-63*, VIII:20-23.
11. HCAS, *Military Posture Briefings*, 634.
12. Rpt, "Strategic Lift Capability for Limited War," 6 Jan 62, FY 63 SecDef Backup Book, III-V, Prog (SA), box 13, ASD(C) files, OSD Hist; OSD sum paper, "Sealift and Airlift," Program Package IV, 28 Jul 61, fldr G-20-23, box 11, ibid; *DoD Annual Report, FY 1961*, 18.
13. Rusk to McNamara, 4 Feb 61, *FRUS 1961-63*, VIII:24-27; ltr McNamara to Pres, 20 Feb 61, w/atchmts, fldr Dept of Defense, General Review of FY 61 and FY 62 Military Programs and Budgets, box 273, NSF, JFKL. McNamara's letter and several of the attachments, except for Annex C containing the views of the Joint Chiefs of Staff, are also in *FRUS 1961-63*, VIII:35-48.
14. Memo McNamara and Bell for Pres, 10 Mar 61, w/atchmts, fldr Dept of Defense, Vol. I-March 1961, box 273, NSF, JFKL. The memo and attachments, except for attached summary tables, are also in *FRUS 1961-63*, VIII:56-65. Comparisons of the BoB and DoD recommendations are in Attachment II, "Proposed Revisions to the FY 1961 and FY 1962 Defense Programs and Budgets Currently in Disagreement."
15. Memo Bundy for Sorensen, 13 Mar 61, *FRUS 1961-63*, VIII:65-66.
16. Attachment II, "Proposed Revisions to the FY 1961 and FY 1962 Defense Programs and Budgets Currently in Disagreement," cited in n 14. Within the Navy, however, the program's rapid expansion raised other funding concerns. Chief of Naval Operations Admiral Arleigh Burke recommended that OSD pay for the program from other parts of the DoD budget, since the submarine-missile combination was a national rather than merely a naval program. Use of Navy funds, he feared, would divert money and personnel from the service's other fleet elements (Enthoven and Smith, *How Much Is Enough?*, 16-17).
17. Watson, *Into the Missile Age*, 363-69, 371; Attachment II, "Proposed Revisions to the FY 1961 and FY 1962 Defense Programs and Budgets Currently in Disagreement," cited in n 14; "Titan II: Objectives of Weapons System," 29 Mar 61 (quote, 6), fldr White Papers 1961-FY 1962 Budget, box 9, ASD(C) files, OSD Hist ; memo McNamara for SvcSecs et al, 17 Mar 61, fldr New Frontier—1961-1962 Budget, box 5, ibid; *Kennedy Public Papers, 1961*, 238. Zuckert recalled that McNamara allowed him to appeal directly to the president on the Titan II issue, "the last time that ever happened." At a luncheon meeting with the president in late March, Zuckert persuaded him to cancel only two instead of four squadrons (interv Eugene M. Zuckert by Lawrence E. McQuade, 18 Apr 64, 20-21, JFKL). The White House luncheon, which included the other service secretaries as well as McNamara and Gilpatric, took place on 24 March (interv Elvis J. Stahr, Jr., by Robert H. Ferrell, 18 Aug 64, 15, JFKL).
18. ODDRE(SW) B-70 chron and paper, 27, 28 Mar 61, fldr White Papers 1961-FY 1962 Budget, box 9, ASD(C) files, OSD Hist; Watson, *Into the Missile Age*, 756; Peter J. Roman, "Strategic Bombers over the Missile Horizon, 1957-1963," *Journal of Strategic Studies*, Mar 95, 204-08.
19. SCAS, *Hearings: Military Procurement Authorization, Fiscal Year 1962*, 87 Cong, 1 sess, 4 Apr 61, 11; interv Roswell L. Gilpatric by Dennis J. O'Brien, 5 May 70, 74, JFKL.
20. Attachment II, "Proposed Revisions to the FY 1961 and FY 1962 Defense Programs and Budgets Currently in Disagreement," cited in n 14; Special Message to Congress on the Defense Budget, 28 Mar 61, *Kennedy Public Papers, 1961*, 238-39.
21. Memo McNamara for SvcSecs et al, 17 Mar 61, cited in n 17.
22. Attachment I, "Agreed Upon Proposed Revisions to the FY 1961 and FY 1962 Defense Programs and Budgets," to memo McNamara and Bell for Pres, 10 Mar 61, cited in n 14; unsignd draft paper, "U.S. Strategic Force Structure: Changes in Strategic Offensive Force Structure Implied by FY 1961 and FY 1962 Budget Proposals," 24 Mar 61, fldr FY 62 Backup General Fact Book I, 1st Set of Amendments, box 9, ASD(C) files, OSD Hist; Special Message to Congress, 28 Mar 61, cited in n 20, 238. In Attachment I to their memo, McNamara and Bell estimated the savings from the accelerated phaseout of the B-47 at only $10.1 million.
23. Paper, "Stopping B-52 Production," 28 Mar 61, fldr White Papers 1961-FY 1962 Budget, box 9, ASD(C) files, OSD Hist.
24. HCA, *Department of Defense Appropriation Bill, 1962*, H Rpt 574, 87 Cong, 1 sess, 23 Jun 61, 7; memo McNamara for Pres, 16 Aug 61, fldr Dept of Defense, General, August 1961, box 273, NSF, JFKL.

25. Paper, "Summary of Central War Defensive Forces," Program Package II, 31 Aug 61, box 11, ASD(C) files, OSD Hist.
26. Watson, *Into the Missile Age*, 380-82, 756.
27. Memo Richard S. Morse (ArmyDirR&D) for Gilpatric, 17 Jan 61, binder Special Report on FY 61-FY 62 Army Budgets, box 6, ASD(C) files, OSD Hist.
28. Poole, *JCS and National Policy 1961-64*, pt I:184.
29. Ibid, 185-86.
30. Attachment II, "Proposed Revisions to the FY 1961 and FY 1962 Defense Programs and Budgets Currently in Disagreement," cited in n 14. No documentation has been found on Kennedy's decision regarding Nike-Zeus, but the decision to continue the program without going into production is inferred from the fact that the president made no mention in his special message to Congress of 28 March, when discussing measures to improve continental defense, of any change in the Nike-Zeus program (*Kennedy Public Papers, 1961*, 235).
31. Memo Hitch for SvcSecs, 20 Mar 61, fldr New Frontier—1961-1962 Budget, box 5, ASD(C) files, OSD Hist; Jon Wayne Fuller, "Congress and the Defense Budget: A Study of the McNamara Years," PhD diss (Princeton Univ, 1972), 378.
32. *Kennedy Public Papers, 1961*, 229-40; ltr McNamara to Bell, 28 Mar 61, fldr New Frontier—1961-1962 Budget, box 5, ASD(C) files, OSD Hist.
33. Ltr Cyrus R. Vance to Vinson, 31 Mar 61, binder FY 1962 Fact Book—Misc, box 5, ASD(C) files, OSD Hist.
34. SCAS, *Military Procurement Authorization, FY 1962*, 62.
35. HSCA, *DoD Appropriations for 1962*, 6 Apr 61, pt 3:16-17.
36. Ibid, 39-40.
37. *Military Procurement Authorization, FY 1962*, 75-76.
38. SSCA, *Hearings: Department of Defense Appropriations for 1962*, 87 Cong, 1 sess, 18 Apr 61, 12-13; HSCA, *DoD Appropriations for 1962*, 19 Apr 61, pt 3:513.
39. Memo McNamara for Pres, 28 Apr 61, fldr Defense 4/61-6/61, box 77, POF, JFKL.
40. Ibid.
41. HCAS, *Hearings: Authorizing Appropriations for Aircraft, Missiles, and Naval Forces for the Armed Forces*, 87 Cong, 1 sess, 2, 3 May 61, 1665-1721; press release, 3 May 61, fldr FY 1962 Budget Revisions, box 7, ASD(C) files, OSD Hist; HCAS, *Authorizing Appropriations for Aircraft, Missiles, and Naval Vessels*, H Rpt 380, 87 Cong, 1 sess, 10 May 61.
42. *Congress and the Nation, 1945-1964*, 311; H Rpt 380, cited in n 41; SCAS, *Authorizing Appropriations for Aircraft, Missiles, and Naval Vessels for the Armed Forces for Fiscal Year 1962*, S Rpt 253, 87 Cong, 1 sess, 11 May 61; Conf Cte, *Authorization for Aircraft, Missiles, and Naval Vessels, Fiscal Year 1962*, H Rpt 462, 87 Cong, 1 sess, 8 Jun 61; *Cong Rec*, 12 Jun 61, 9366-69 (quote 9367); PL 87-53, 21 Jun 61 (75 Stat 94).
43. *Kennedy Public Papers, 1961*, 396-406 (quote, 401).
44. Msg Pres to Speaker, House of Reps, 26 May 61, in House, *Amendments to the Budget Involving Increases for the National Aeronautics and Space Administration, the Small Business Administration, the U.S. Information Agency, the Department of Commerce, and the Department of Defense, Military*, H Doc 179, 87 Cong, 1 sess, 29 May 61, 1; HSCA, *DoD Appropriations for 1962*, 31 May 61, pt 6:175-80.
45. Watson, *Into the Missile Age*, 344, 358-59.
46. Ltr Sorensen to McNamara, 23 Dec 60, fldr New Frontier—1961-1962 Budget, box 5, ASD(C) files, OSD Hist.
47. HSCA, *DoD Appropriations for 1962*, 31 May 61, pt 6:178-79. Regarding the Army's planning in early 1961 for Reserve reorganization, see Karl E. Cocke, "Realignment of the Army's Reserve Components, 1945-1969," U.S. Army Center of Military History, 1977, VIII:3-7.
48. HSCA, *DoD Appropriations for 1962*, 31 May 61, pt 6:203-05 (quote, 205).
49. Ibid, 191.
50. Ltr McNamara to Mahon, 5 Jun 61, fldr Reading File, Aug. 1961-June 1961, box 113, McNamara Records, RG 200.
51. *New York Times*, 24 Jun 61; *Cong Rec*, 27, 28 Jun 61, 10621-43, 10672-99; *Congress and the Nation*, 311.
52. SSCA, *DoD Appropriations for 1962*, 10 Jul 61, 1093-1380 (quote, 1152); DoD News Release 695-61, 10 Jul 61, *McNamara Public Statements, 1961*, II:826; memo McNamara for SecAF, 13 Jul 61, fldr Reading File, Aug. 1961-June 1961, box 113, McNamara Records, RG 200.

53. SSCA, *DoD Appropriations for 1962*, 18 Jul 61, 1542.
54. Memo McNamara for Pres, 15 Jul 61, w/notes of mtg with Eisenhower, 15 Jul 61, fldr Defense 7/61-8/61, box 77, POF, JFKL.
55. Radio and TV Report to the American People on the Berlin Crisis, 25 Jul 61, *Kennedy Public Papers, 1961*, 533-40; Senate, *Amendments to the Budget for the Military Functions of the Department of Defense*, S Doc 39, 87 Cong, 1 sess, 26 Jul 61; memo McNamara for Pres, 18 Jul 61, fldr FY 62 Budget File #2, box 8, ASD(C) files, OSD Hist.
56. SSCA, *DoD Appropriations for 1962*, 26 Jul 61, 1611-39.
57. *Baltimore Sun*, 27 Jul 61; SCAS, *Authorizing Additional Appropriations for Aircraft, Missiles, and Naval Vessels for the Armed Forces*, S Rpt 643, 87 Cong, 1 sess, 27 Jul 61; HCAS, *Authorizing Appropriations for Aircraft, Missiles, and Naval Vessels*, H Rpt 817, 87 Cong, 1 sess, 28 Jul 61; *New York Times*, 29 Jul 61; *Cong Rec*, 28 Jul 61, 12905-16; ibid, 2 Aug 61, 13311-22; *New York Times*, 3 Aug 61; PL 87-118, 3 Aug 61 (75 Stat 243).
58. SSCA, *Department of Defense Appropriation Bill, 1962*, S Rpt 653, 87 Cong, 1 sess, 1 Aug 61, 3; *Cong Rec*, 3 Aug 61, 13470-90 (quote, 13477), 13493-502; *Baltimore Sun*, 4, 5 Aug 61.
59. Conf Cte, H Rpt 873, printed in *Cong Rec*, 9 Aug 61, 14198-200; *New York Times*, 10 Aug 61.
60. *Cong Rec*, 10 Aug 61, 14262-75, 14393-96; *New York Times*, 11 Aug 61; *Congressional Quarterly Almanac, 1961*, 147; PL 87-144, 17 Aug 61 (75 Stat 365).
61. Memo McNamara for Pres, 16 Aug 61, cited in n 24; memo McNamara for Pres, 7 Oct 61, fldr Defense Budget FY 1963—January-October 1961, box 7, NSF, JFKL; DoD News Release 1220-61, 27 Oct 61, *McNamara Public Statements, 1961*, III:1448-49.
62. Fuller, "Congress and the Defense Budget," 379.

IV. THE FY1963 BUDGET: INTRODUCING THE PPBS

1. Frederick C. Mosher, "PPBS: Two Questions," in Senate, Cte on Govt Opns, Subcte on National Security and Internl Opns, *Planning-Programming-Budgeting: Selected Comment*, 90 Cong, 1 sess, 1967, 591; Elmer B. Staats (ComptGen) statement, 26 Mar 68, Subcte on National Security and Internatl Opns, *Hearings: Planning-Programming-Budgeting*, 90 Cong, 2 sess, 1968, pt 3:323. Staats's statement (322-27) contains a good description of the genesis of PPBS; see also Leonard Merwitz and Stephen H. Sosnick, *The Budget's New Clothes: A Critique of Planning-Programming-Budgeting and Benefit-Cost Analysis*, 5-12.
2. Rand Corporation, *The Rand Corporation: The First Fifteen Years*, 20; David Novick, "Origin and History of Program Budgeting," in *Planning-Programming-Budgeting: Selected Comment*, 596.
3. Hitch remarks to Army Management Orientation Course, U.S. Army Management School, Ft. Belvoir, Va, 16 Nov 61, fldr Comptroller, Budget, FY 1961-1963, box 779, Subject files, OSD Hist; Glass interv, 28 Oct 87, 38-39.
4. Maurice Stans test, 31 Jul 61, Senate, Cte on Govt Opns, Subcte on National Policy Machinery, *Organizing for National Security*, pt 1:1108.
5. Robert W. Downey, "An Introduction to the Planning, Programming and Budgeting System in the Department of Defense: An Overview of the Process, Participants and Products," 4, OSD Hist.
6. Richard A. Stubbing with Richard A. Mendel, *The Defense Game*, 133.
7. Maxwell D. Taylor, *The Uncertain Trumpet*, 123-24; Taylor statement, 14 Jun 60, *Organizing for National Security*, pt 1:769-70 (769, quote).
8. Ltr Mahon to McElroy, 18 Aug 59, memo Black for Gates, 17 Nov 59, in Enthoven and Smith, *How Much Is Enough?*, 28-30 (quote, 30). Various germane documents, including an OASD(C) report, "Functional Budget Concept," 28 Nov 60, describing Mahon's efforts in 1959 and again in 1960 to prod DoD into developing budget justification information along functional or program lines, are in fldr Functional Budgeting, box 112, ASD(C) files, OSD Hist.
9. McNamara test, 7 Aug 61, *Organizing for National Security*, pt 1:1194; McNamara interv, 3 Apr 86, 13-14.
10. Hitch biographical sketch and statement, 18 Jan 61, SCAS, *Nominations Hearing on Paul H. Nitze, Charles J. Hitch, Cyrus R. Vance, Arthur Sylvester, and Thomas D. Morris*, 87 Cong, 1 sess, 1961, 12-14; Hitch and McKean, *The Economics of Defense in the Nuclear Age*, 44-59; "Applying an Economist's Yardstick to Defense," *Business Week*, 4 Mar 61, 64; McNamara interv, 3 Apr 86, 14-15; Fred Kaplan, *The Wizards of Armageddon*, 252; Shapley, *Promise and Power*, 99-100.
11. Hitch test, 18 Jan 61, SCAS, *Nominations Hearing*, 15, 18-19.
12. Interv David E. Bell by Robert C. Turner, 11 Jul 64, 76-77, JFKL.

13. For example, see McNamara statement, 19 Jan 62, SCAS, *Hearings: Military Procurement Authorization Fiscal Year 1963*, 87 Cong, 2 sess, 4; rcd of mtg, BrigGen George S. Brown, 18 Jan 61, fldr SecDef Staff Meetings Feb-Apr 1961, box 10, AFPC and SecDef Meetings files, Acc 77-0062.
14. Rcd of action 475th NSC mtg, 1 Feb 61, *FRUS 1961-63*, VIII:20-23; memos McNamara for ASD(C), 1 Feb 61, Hitch for McNamara, 6 Feb 61, fldr FY 1963 Budget—Vol. I, box 17, ASD(C) files, OSD Hist. During Hitch's absence a Rand colleague, David Novick, sat in Hitch's office and unofficially assumed his duties. See Enthoven interv, 3 Feb 86, 7; Glass interv, 28 Oct 87, 5.
15. Draft memo Hitch for SecDef, 3 Mar 61, 4, 6-7, fldr Programming, file #1, box 109, ASD(C) files, OSD Hist; OASD(C) chart, Feb 61, fldr Comptroller (Budget) 1960-69, box 614, Subject files, OSD Hist; "Budget: Where Changes Hit Hardest," *Armed Forces Management*, Nov 61, 98; Hitch memo for staff, 10 Mar 61, fldr Programming, file #1, box 109, ASD(C) files, OSD Hist; DoD organization charts, 10 Mar, 22 Sep 61, fldr DoD Organization Charts, box 503, Subject files, OSD Hist; list of employees in OASD(C), 24 Jul 61, fldr OSD 1961, box 602, ibid; Hitch and McKean, *The Economics of Defense in the Nuclear Age*, 361-405.
16. Kaplan, *Wizards of Armageddon*, 254-55; Enthoven interv, 3 Feb 86, 5.
17. Rosenberg, "Arleigh Albert Burke," 309.
18. Ltr Gilpatric to Rockefeller Public Service Awards, 19 Jun 61, fldr RLG Reading File (30 Dec 60-), box 2, Gilpatric files, Acc 66A-3529; Glass interv, 28 Oct 87, 1-5; *Reader's Digest*, Mar 64, 128.
19. Fuller, "Congress and the Defense Budget," 56-57; Hitch test, 19 Apr 61, HSCA, *DoD Appropriations for 1962*, 540; memo Melvin Anshen for Hitch, 7 Apr 61, fldr FY 1963 Budget—Vol. I, box 17, ASD(C) files, OSD Hist; Hitch address before the National Conference of the Armed Forces Management Association, Washington, DC, 1 Mar 61, 2-3 (quote, 3), fldr Programming, file #1, box 109, ASD(C) files, OSD Hist.
20. Draft memo Hitch for SecDef, 3 Mar 61, cited in n 15, 4, 6-7.
21. Hitch remarks before the graduating class of the Industrial College of the Armed Forces, Washington, DC, 13 Jun 61, 6, fldr OSD Comptroller 1961, box 779, Subject files, OSD Hist; Shapley, *Promise and Power*, 101; Hitch, "Development and Salient Features of the Programming System," in Tucker, *A Modern Design for Defense Decision*, 72.
22. Memos Navy(C) for AsstSecDef(C), 2 Mar 61, Stahr for SecDef, 21 Mar 61, Lyle Garlock (AsstSecAF) for SecDef, 21 Mar 61, fldr FY 1963 Budget (Chron), box 18, ASD(C) files, OSD Hist; Hitch for SvcAsstSecs (FM), 3 Apr 61, fldr Programming, file #1, box 109, ibid.
23. Livesay notes, staff mtg, 17 Apr 61, fldr SecDef Staff Meetings Feb-Apr 1961, box 10, AFPC and SecDef Meetings files, Acc 77-0062. Attached to the notes are a 13-page paper, "A Proposed Programming and Budgeting Process for FY 1963," dated 17 Apr 61, which Hitch distributed at the meeting (also printed in *Army, Navy, Air Force Journal*, 29 Apr 61); a 3-page preliminary "List of Questions Associated with Programming for Fiscal Year 1963 Budget," and a 13-page "List of Program Packages for DoD 5-Year Program Including the FY 1963 Budget."
24. Memo Bell for Pres, 14 Apr 61 (emphasis in original), ltr Bell to SecDef, 27 Apr 61, fldr 110.01 FY 63 1961, box 36, SecDef Subject Decimal files, Acc 65A-3464.
25. Memo Hitch for SvcAsstSecs(FM), 2 May 61, fldr FY 1963 Budget (Chron), box 18, ASD(C) files, OSD Hist.
26. Draft memo Bell for Pres, 8 Jun 61, fldr Budget 1963 (3), box 44, Theodore Sorensen Papers, JFKL.
27. Memo Bell for SecDef, 19 Jun 61, fldr 110.01 FY 63 1961, box 36, SecDef Subject Decimal files, Acc 65A-3464; handwritten memo, "6/20/61 DoD-BoB meeting," nd and ns, and paper, "Bureau of the Budget Baseline Projections (1963 Budget Preview)," 20 Jun 61, ibid; memo Bell for SecDef, nd, w/atchd list of potential reductions, 16 Jun 61, fldr Misc. Budget, box 6, McNamara files, Acc 71A-3470; memo William F. McCandless for DirBoB, 14 Jul 61, w/atchd paper, "1963 NOA Adjustments," 3 Jul 61, fldr Exec Branch Memoranda, box 14, David Bell Papers, JFKL.
28. Hitch test, 24 Jul 61, *Organizing for National Security*, pt 1:1006-07.
29. Memo Hitch for SvcAsstSecs(FM), 13 May 61, fldr FY 1963 Budget—Vol. I, box 17, ASD(C) files, OSD Hist.
30. Memo Hitch for SvcAsstSecs(FM), 19 May 61, ibid.
31. "Applying an Economist's Yardstick to Defense, cited in n 10, 64; Glass interv, 28 Oct 87, 49; Rosenberg, "Arleigh Albert Burke," 309; James R. Schlesinger, "Uses and Abuses of Analysis," in *Planning-Programming-Budgeting: Selected Comment*, 126.

32. Memo Hitch for DDR&E, ASD(I&L), ASD(Manpower), 16 Jun 61, memo McNamara for CJCS, 16 Jun 61, fldr Programming, file #1, box 109, ASD(C) files, OSD Hist; published version of Hitch remarks to Industrial College of the Armed Forces, Washington, DC, 17 Oct 61, 19, fldr OSD Comptroller 1961, box 779, Subject files, OSD Hist.
33. "Budget: Where Changes Hit Hardest, cited in n 15, 96; Hitch, "Development and Salient Features of the Programming System," 73; Hitch test, 25 Jul 62, House, Cte on Govt Opns, Subcte on Military Opns, *Hearings: Systems Development and Management*, 87 Cong, 2 sess, pt 2:528-29.
34. Hitch remarks to Army Management Orientation Course, 16 Nov 61, cited in n 3, 8; Hitch remarks to Industrial College of the Armed Forces, 17 Oct 61, cited in n 32, 15; "Pentagon Profile/Charles J. Hitch: 'To Balance the Teeter-Totter,'" *Armed Forces Management*, Aug 61, 35; Livesay notes, staff mtg, 11 Sep 61, fldr SecDef Staff Meetings Sept-Oct 1961, box 10, AFPC and SecDef Meetings files, Acc 77-0062; *Aviation Daily*, 8 Jan 62.
35. Hitch remarks to Industrial College of the Armed Forces, 17 Oct 61, cited in n 32, 20. Copies of the following program package summaries prepared by the OSD Comptroller are in boxes 9 and 10, ASD(C) files, OSD Hist: (II) Central War Defensive Forces, 31 Aug 61; (III) General Purpose Forces, 4 Sep 61; (IV) Sealift and Airlift, 28 Jul 61; (VI) Research and Development, 25 Aug 61; (VII) Service-wide Support, 8 Sep 61; and (IX) Department of Defense (OSD and DoD Agencies), 8 Sep 61. No program package summaries for Central War Offensive Forces, Reserve and National Guard Forces, and Classified Projects have been found. Information on Reserve and National Guard forces was sent piecemeal to McNamara in the comptroller's summaries for program packages II, III, IV, and VII, and was presented as a whole in Hitch's memo (not in program package summary format) for McNamara, 13 Sep 61. A copy of this memo is in fldr Reserves and National Guard—Package V, box 10, ASD(C) files, OSD Hist.
36. Livesay notes, staff mtg, 11 Sep 61, cited in n 34.
37. Memo McNamara for SvcSecs and CJCS, 22 Sep 61, fldr FY 1963 Budget (Chron), box 18, ASD(C) files, OSD Hist.
38. Poole, *JCS and National Policy 1961-64*, pt I:120-24.
39. Enthoven and Smith, *How Much Is Enough?*, 53-55. Enthoven and Smith (p. 54) mistakenly state that only two DPMs were prepared in 1961, one on strategic nuclear forces and the other on general purpose forces. They do not mention the DPM dated 1 September 1961 that transmitted McNamara's recommendations on airlift and sealift forces for 1963-1967, a copy of which is in a looseleaf notebook entitled FY 63 DPMs, box 116, ASD(C) files, OSD Hist.
40. Documentation on the genesis of the early DPMs is scarce. No copy of the 29 August DPM, the first one, has been found, but it is mentioned in Zuckert's memo for McNamara of 21 September, in fldr Misc. Budget, box 6, McNamara files, Acc 71A-3470, and in Poole, *JCS and National Policy 1961-64*, pt I:123-24. Poole notes that the JCS copy of the 29 August DPM was destroyed.
41. Extracts from draft memo McNamara for Pres, 6 Oct 61, *FRUS 1961-63*, VIII:158-77. For the entire text of the 23 September DPM, see ibid, 138-52. For an extract of the 30 September DPM on Nike-Zeus, see ibid, 153-55. Complete copies of all three DPMs are in a looseleaf notebook entitled FY 63 DPMs, cited in n 39.
42. Extracts from draft memo McNamara for Pres, 6 Oct 61, 159-61, 163-64, 166-68, 175, 177.
43. Hitch test, 24 Jul 61, *Organizing for National Security*, pt 1:1009.
44. *Aviation Week*, 25 Dec 61.
45. Table, Comparison of Service Submissions and Sec Def Guidance, fldr Misc. Budget, box 6, McNamara files, Acc 71A-3470.
46. Memo McNamara for SvcSecs, CJCS, and AdminAsst to SecDef, 7 Nov 61, fldr 110.01 FY 63 General 7-15 Nov 61 (13 May 61), box 37, SecDef Subject Decimal files, Acc 65A-3464.
47. Paper, author unknown, "Summary of Secretary of Defense Actions on Subject/Issue Considerations FY 1963 Budget Review," 4 Jan 62, fldr FY 1963—Index of Issues Sheet & Summary of Actions, box 13, ASD(C) files, OSD Hist; McNamara test, 14 Feb 62, SSCA, *Hearings: Department of Defense Appropriations for 1963*, 87 Cong, 2 sess, 6. The service reclamas and summary sheets showing the service submissions, as well as the secretary of defense's tentative and final decisions, are filed in folders and arranged numerically in boxes 40 and 41, SecDef Subject Decimal files, Acc 65A-3464. An index listing the 560 subject/issues is in fldr Index, box 40, ibid.

48. Air Force comment, signd by Zuckert and LeMay, 26 Nov 61, and summary sheet for Subject/Issue 263: B-70 Development (Air Force), with McNamara's handwritten "no" at the bottom, dated 30 Nov 61, fldr Subject/Issues and Reclamas—Originals—Nos. 251 thru 275 Inclusive, box 40, SecDef Subject Decimal files, Acc 65A-3464.
49. Memo Connally for SecDef, 6 Nov 61, fldr Secretaries and Chiefs Comments-Budget-Issues, box 6, McNamara files, Acc 71A-3470; memo McNamara for ASD(C), 17 Oct 61, fldr 110.01 FY 63 General October 1961 (13 May 61), box 37, SecDef Subject Decimal files, Acc 65A-3464.
50. Memos Zuckert for SecDef, 2, 3 Nov 61, fldr Secretaries and Chiefs Comments-Budget-Issues, box 6, McNamara files, Acc 71A-3470.
51. Memo Stahr for SecDef, 1 Nov 61, ibid.
52. Memo McNamara for SecA, 15 Nov 61, fldr FY 1963 Budget (Chron), box 18, ASD(C) files, OSD Hist.
53. Memo Bell for Pres, 13 Nov 61, fldr Misc. Budget, box 6, McNamara files, Acc 71A-3470.
54. Glass interv, 28 Oct 87, 66.
55. Livesay notes, staff mtg, 20 Nov 61, fldr SecDef Staff Meetings Nov-Dec 1961, box 10, AFPC and SecDef Meetings files, Acc 77-0062.
56. Memrcd Seymour Weiss, 29 Nov 61, *FRUS 1961-63*, VIII:220-21.
57. Richard B. Crossland and James T. Currie, *Twice the Citizen: A History of the United States Army Reserve, 1908-1983*, 154.
58. Memo McNamara for Pres, 7 Dec 61, fldr FY 1963 Budget (Chron), box 18, ASD(C) files, OSD Hist..
59. *New York Times*, 14 Dec 61; Gilpatric press conf, 14 Dec 61, *Gilpatric Public Statements, 1961*, 497-98; *Washington Star*, 10 Jan 62.
60. Glass interv, 28 Oct 87, 29-30.
61. Ltr McNamara to Bell, 7 Dec 61, fldr FY 1963 Budget (Chron), box 18, ASD(C) files, OSD Hist.
62. *New York Times*, 10 Dec 61; Livesay notes, staff mtg, 11 Dec 61, fldr SecDef Staff Meetings Nov-Dec 1961, box 10, AFPC and SecDef Meetings files, Acc 77-0062.
63. *FRUS 1961-63*, VIII:227, n 5; Desmond Ball, *Politics and Force Levels: The Strategic Missile Program of the Kennedy Administration*, 134; *Aviation Daily*, 8 Jan 62.
64. Memo Gilpatric for McNamara, 28 Dec 61, fldr General LeMay's Recommendations, box 6, McNamara files, Acc 71A-3470; memo Kaysen for Pres, 27 Dec 61, fldr Air Force 1961, box 94A, POF, JFKL.
65. Memrcd Gilpatric, 3 Jan 62, *FRUS 1961-63*, VIII:232-34.
66. *New York Times*, 9 Jan 62. A copy of McNamara's briefing notes for the meeting is attached to his memo for the Vice Pres, 9 Jan 62, fldr Reading File, Jan. 1962, box 114, McNamara Records, RG 200.
67. Ltr Bell to McNamara, 9 Jan 62, fldr Defense Budget History—Kennedy Years (FY 62-64), box 124, ASD(C) files, OSD Hist; *Washington Post*, 5 Jan 62.
68. *New York Times*, 5 Feb 62; *Baltimore Sun*, 19 Jan 62.
69. Annual Budget Message to Congress, 18 Jan 62, *Kennedy Public Papers, 1962*, 25-27.
70. Statement to Cabinet members and agency heads, 25 Aug 65, *Johnson Public Papers, 1965*, II:916-17; "Initial Memorandum," in *Planning-Programming-Budgeting: Selected Comment*, 9-13; Thomas C. Schelling, "PPBS and Foreign Affairs," ibid, 112.
71. Hitch, "Decision-Making in Large Organizations," in *Planning-Programming-Budgeting: Selected Comment*, 579; Enthoven statement, 27 Sep 67, ibid, 224.
72. McNamara and Lemnitzer test, 14 Feb 62, cited in n 47, 6, 93.
73. *Planning-Programming-Budgeting: Selected Comment*, 12.
74. Paul R. Schratz, "John B. Connally, 20 January 1961–20 December 1961," in Paolo E. Coletta, ed, *American Secretaries of the Navy*, II:922; *New York Times*, 8 Jul 62.
75. *Aviation Week*, 25 Dec 61.
76. George M. Watson, Jr., *The Office of the Secretary of the Air Force, 1947-1965*, 215-16; Zuckert, "The Service Secretary: Has He a Useful Role?," 463-65.
77. Hitch remarks before the Second Conference on Management Problems of Military RDT&E, Quantico, Va, 8 Jan 62, 3, fldr Programming, file #1, box 109, ASD(C) files, OSD Hist.
78. Glass interv, 28 Oct 87, 45-46.
79. David Halberstam, *The Best and the Brightest*, 72.
80. Brower, "McNamara Seen Now, Full Length," 80.
81. McNamara interv, 3 Apr 86, 15.

V. CONGRESS AND THE FY 1963 BUDGET

1. Kolodziej, *Uncommon Defense*, 417.
2. Glass interv, 28 Oct 87, 13-14.
3. McNamara interv, 3 Apr 86, 9. A copy of the complete, classified statement is in a binder entitled, "FY 63 Posture Statement," box 12, ASD(C) files, OSD Hist.
4. Memo Paul for SecDef, 16 Dec 61, fldr FY 1963 Budget (Chron), box 18, ASD(C) files, OSD Hist.
5. SCAS, *Military Procurement Authorization, FY 1963*, 1-3; HCAS, *Military Posture and HR 9751*, 3159-60.
6. *Military Procurement Authorization, FY 1963*, 2-73 passim; *Military Posture and HR 9751*, 3162-85, 3243-3306 passim.
7. Memo Paul for ASD(C), 18 Dec 61, fldr FY 1963 Budget (Chron), box 18, ASD(C) files, OSD Hist; *Military Procurement Authorization, FY 1963*, 23 Jan 62, 225-28.
8. Glass interv, 28 Oct 87, 25. Backup books I-II and III-V for FY 1963 are in box 13, ASD(C) files, OSD Hist.
9. *Wall Street Journal*, 22 Jan 62; Neal Sanford, *Christian Science Monitor*, 20 Jan 62.
10. Ball, *Politics and Force Levels*, 127-28; *Military Procurement Authorization, FY 1963*, 229-30.
11. *Military Posture and HR 9751*, 3306.
12. Ibid, 3306-07, 3320-22.
13. Ibid, 3697-98, 3796-97.
14. Ibid, 3897-3919. LeMay's comments are on 3909-10.
15. Ibid, 3909-11, 3915.
16. Ibid, 3905-07.
17. SSCA, *DoD Appropriations for 1963*, 27 Feb 62, 185-93 (quote, 188); *St. Louis Post-Dispatch*, 1 Mar 62; *Washington Star*, 1 Mar 62.
18. *Military Posture and HR 9751*, 3963-92; HCAS, *Authorizing Appropriations for Aircraft, Missiles, and Naval Vessels*, H Rpt 1406, 87 Cong, 2 sess, 7 Mar 62, 1-3, 7-9 (emphasis in original).
19. Transc of question and answer period following McNamara's remarks before the Ad Council, 7 Mar 62, *McNamara Public Statements, 1962*, II:924-26; memo Paul for McNamara, 14 Mar 62, fldr B-70—RMcN Statements—Classified, Unclassified Press Conference, box 4, McNamara files, Acc 71A-3470.
20. Sorensen, *Kennedy*, 348.
21. *Kennedy Public Papers, 1962*, 202, 230.
22. Mtg notes, 5 Mar 62, fldr Misc—RS-70, box 3, McNamara files, Acc 71A-3470. The notes are unsigned, but are attached to the following undated handwritten chit: "My notes of yesterday's staff meeting—there are no other copies. SBB [Sidney B. Berry, Jr.]"
23. Memrcd Anderson, 5 Mar 62, fldr 5050/3 SecDef Staff Meeting Jan-May 1962, fldr 5050/3, box 1962-05, Chief of Naval Operations Immediate Office files, NHC.
24. Mtg notes, Sidney B. Berry, Jr., 8 Mar 62, 6, fldr B-70, box 108, ASD(C) files, OSD Hist.
25. Memo Paul for McNamara, 12 Mar 62, fldr B-70—RMcN Statements—Classified, Unclassified Press Conference, box 4, McNamara files, Acc 71A-3470.
26. Vinson statement before House Rules Cte, 13 Mar 62, 19, fldr FY 63 BU—B-70, box 18, ASD(C) files, OSD Hist.
27. Memo Paul for McNamara, 14 Mar 62, cited in n 19; transc, HCAS, *Hearings: Authorization of RS-70*, 14 Mar 62 (exec sess), fldr Strategic Bombers, box 872, Subject files, OSD Hist.
28. *McNamara Public Statements, 1962*, III:976-89; "Text of McNamara's Statement on the B-70 Bombers," *New York Times*, 16 Mar 62 (see also Jack Raymond article).
29. Transc NBC "Today" program, 12 Mar 62, w/atchmt memo Sylvester for McNamara and Hitch, 13 Mar 62, 5, fldr FY 63 Bu—B-70, box 18, ASD(C) files, OSD Hist; *Wall Street Journal*, 14 Mar 62.
30. "B-70 Battle," *Business Week*, 17 Mar 62; *Wall Street Journal*, 14 Mar 62; *New York Times*, 23 Mar 62.
31. Lawrence F. O'Brien, *No Final Victories: A Life in Politics from John F. Kennedy to Watergate*, 118; note McNamara for Pres, 20 Mar 62, w/atchd paper, nd, "Summary of Items Added to the FY '62 Budget by the Congress," fldr Defense 1/62-3/62, box 77, POF, JFKL. In the note McNamara indicated that he was also attaching a brief statement that Kennedy might wish to give Vinson. No copy of this statement has been found.
32. McNamara interv, 3 Apr 86, 24.
33. *New York Times*, 23 Mar 62; *Journal and Register*, 20 Mar 62, 3.

34. Sorensen, *Kennedy*, 348; interv Lawrence F. O'Brien by Michael L. Gillette, 30 Oct 85, 2-3, internet copy, LBJL.
35. For example, see *New York Times*, 23 Mar 62; *Washington Post*, 22 Mar 62; O'Brien, *No Final Victories*, 118.
36. The texts of the letters, both dated 20 March 1962, are printed in *Cong Rec*, 21 Mar 62, 4309-10.
37. Ibid.
38. SCAS, *Authorization of Appropriations for Aircraft, Missiles, and Naval Vessels, FY 1963*, S Rpt 1315, 87 Cong, 2 sess, 2 Apr 62, 1-3; *Baltimore Sun*, 22 Mar 62; *New York Times*, 13 Apr 62; PL 87-436, 27 Apr 62 (76 Stat 55).
39. *Washington Post*, 27 Mar 62; DoD News Release 481-62, 29 Mar 62, *McNamara Public Statements, 1962*, III:1084; *Cong Rec*, 29 Mar 62, 4942.
40. See Russell Baker, *New York Times*, 22 Mar 62; *Wall Street Journal*, 22 Mar 62; *Washington Post*, 22 Mar 62; *Time*, 30 Mar 62, 29. For the views of other colleagues on Vinson's handling of the affair, see *Washington Star*, 24 Apr 62.
41. Rowland Evans, Jr., *Reporter*, 12 Apr 62; O'Brien, *No Final Victories*, 118; Gilpatric notes on talk with Vinson, 19 Aug 63, fldr RLG Reading File, July 1, 1963, box 2, Gilpatric files, Acc 66A-3529.
42. News conf, 21 Mar 62, *Kennedy Public Papers, 1962*, 260; interv McNamara by Louis Cassels (as published in the *Denver Post*, 29 Mar 62), *McNamara Public Statements, 1962*, III:1085.
43. Ltr Zuckert to McNamara, 19 Mar 62, fldr B-70—RMcN Statements—Classified, Unclassified Press Conference, box 4, McNamara files, Acc 71A-3470; Charles J. V. Murphy, "The Education of a Defense Secretary," *Fortune*, May 62, 268. Regarding rumors of LeMay's possible firing, see *New York Times*, 5 Mar 62.
44. HSCA, *DoD Appropriations for 1963*, pt 1:5.
45. Memo Vance, Runge, Ailes for SecDef, 13 Jan 62, w/atchmts, memo McNamara for Pres, 13 Jan 62: fldr 110.01 FY 63 Reserve & National Guard Forces—Package #5, box 38, SecDef Subject Decimal files, Acc 66A-3542.
46. HSCA, *DoD Appropriations for 1963*, pt 2:247, 260; *Cong Rec*, 17 Apr 62, 6324 (Sikes comments).
47. *DoD Appropriations for 1963*, pt 2:58-59; papers, "A Chronology of the Actions of the General Staff Committees on National Guard and Army Reserve Policy" and "A Chronology of the Actions of the Reserve Forces Policy Board In Connection With the Reserve Components Realignment," nd and ns, fldr Backup Book for Hearings on Army Reserve Components Realignment, box 113, ASD(C) files, OSD Hist; memo Ailes for SecDef, 27 Mar 62, fldr 110.01 FY 63 Reserve & National Guard Forces—Package #5, box 38, SecDef Subject Decimal files, Acc 66A-3542. Minutes of the Reserve Forces Policy Board meetings on 1-2 and 25 February 1962 are printed in HCAS, Subcte No. 3, *Hearings: Military Reserve Posture*, 87 Cong, 2 sess, 1962, 6316-20, 6322-35.
48. Memo Ailes for SecDef, 27 Mar 62, cited in n 47, 1-2.
49. *DoD Appropriations for 1963*, 30 Mar 62 (Ailes test), pt 6:112-17, 161-69.
50. H Doc 377, *Amendments to the Budget for the Military Functions of the Department of Defense Redistributing the Funds Requested for the Army Reserve Forces*, 2 Apr 62, 87 Cong, 2 sess; DoD News Release 521-62, 4 Apr 62, OSD Hist.
51. Ltr Truman to Kennedy, 11 Apr 62, fldr Department of Defense (B), General 1962, box 276, NSF, JFKL.
52. SSCA, *DoD Appropriations for 1963*, 1180-81, 1175, 1186, 1209, 1212, 1231-32. For text of the 4 April press release cited in n 50, see ibid, 1169-70.
53. *New York World Telegram*, 6 Mar 62.
54. Livesay notes, staff mtg, 23 Apr 62, 6-7, fldr SecDef Staff Meetings Apr 1962, box 10, AFPC and SecDef Meetings files, Acc 77-0062.
55. HCA, *DoD Appropriation Bill, 1963*, H Rpt 1607, 87 Cong, 2 sess, 13 Apr 62, 3, 8, 23; *Cong Rec*, 17 Apr 62, 6329 (Flood remarks); *New York Times*, 19 Apr 62.
56. Livesay notes, cited in n 54; ltr Gilpatric to Robertson, 1 May 62, in SSCA, *DoD Appropriations for 1963*, 1281-82 (see also 1835-37); Livesay notes, staff mtg, 7 May 62, 8, fldr SecDef Staff Meetings May-Jun 1962, box 10, AFPC and SecDef Meetings files, Acc 77-0062.
57. McNamara statement, w/atchd tables summarizing House actions and DoD reclamas, 15 May 62, SSCA, *DoD Appropriations for 1963*, 1234-81 (quote, 1248-49). Because McNamara arrived a little late for the hearing after attending an urgent White House meeting, Hitch read the first few paragraphs of the statement.
58. Ibid, 1256.

59. Tel Harrison to McNamara, 17 May 62, fldr McNamara—Reserve Component Material 1965, box 89, ASD(C) files, OSD Hist; tel McNamara to Harrison, 17 May 62, *McNamara Public Statements, 1962*, III:1292-93.
60. SCA, *DoD Appropriation Bill, 1963*, S Rpt 1578, 87 Cong, 2 sess, 8 Jun 62; *New York Times*, 9 Jun 62; *Washington Post*, 10 Jun 62.
61. Memo Ailes for SecDef, 15 Jun 62, fldr McNamara—Reserve Component Material 1965, box 89, ASD(C) files, OSD Hist; *New York Times*, 14 Jun 62.
62. Louis Kraar, "The Two Lives of Robert McNamara," *Life*, 30 Nov 62, 102.
63. *McNamara Public Statements, 1962*, IV:1512-17; *Washington News*, 3 Jul 62; DoD News Release 1124-62, 3 Jul 62, OSD Hist; *McNamara Public Statements, 1962*, IV:1550.
64. Text of resolution adopted at the Governors' Conference, 3 Jul 62, *Cong Rec*, 3 Aug 62, A-5968; McNamara interv, 3 Apr 86, 26.
65. Ltr McNamara to Mahon, 20 Jul 62, fldr Reserve and Guard Program, box 6, McNamara files, Acc 71A-3470; ltr McNamara to Robertson, 20 Jul 62, fldr Reading File, July 1962, box 115, McNamara Records, RG 200.
66. Draft ltr prepared by Glass, 28 Jun 62, 7, fldr Army National Guard & Reserve—Realignment, box 113, ASD(C) files, OSD Hist. See too a second draft, dated 2 July and also prepared by Glass. The text of the second letter is virtually identical to the letters sent to Mahon and Robertson on 20 July.
67. Martha Derthick, *The National Guard in Politics*, 153.
68. *Congress and the Nation, 1945-1964*, 316.
69. House, *Department of Defense Appropriations for 1963: Conference Report to Accompany HR 11289*, H Rpt 2036, 87 Cong, 2 sess, 25 Jul 62, 8; PL 85-577, 9 Aug 62 (76 Stat 318).
70. *Cong Rec*, 26 Jul 62, 13859.
71. *Military Reserve Posture*, cited in n 47, 6670-77; *New York Post*, 15 Aug 62.
72. *New York Times*, 5 Dec 62; *Wall Street Journal*, 5 Dec 62; ltr McNamara to Sen Margaret Chase Smith, w/atchmts, 18 Oct 63, fldr Congressional Influence on DoD (Armed Forces Composition), box 93, ASD(C) files, OSD Hist; *McNamara Public Statements, 1962*, IV:1932-62; *DoD Annual Report, FY 1963*, 27-28.
73. Memos Charyk for SecDef, 1 Jun 62, LeMay for SecAF, 26 Jul 62, and Zuckert for SecDef, 4 Aug 62: fldr B-70, box 2, McNamara files, Acc 71A-3470; Poole, *JCS and National Policy 1961-64*, pt I:147; "Office of the Secretary of Defense Analysis of RS-70 Program as Submitted by USAF," 20 Jul 62, w/appens, fldr Analysis of RS-70 Program . . ., box 16, Enthoven Papers, LBJL.
74. Poole, *JCS and National Policy 1961-64*, pt I:148-50.
75. *Washington Post*, 7 Oct 62; *Washington Star*, 17 Oct 62; *Washington Post*, 18 Oct 62; Bernard C. Nalty, "The Quest for an Advanced Manned Strategic Bomber: USAF Plans and Policies, 1961-1966," USAF Hist Div, Aug 66, 10.
76. Poole, *JCS and National Policy 1961-64*, pt I:150-51; DoD News Release 1859-62, 15 Nov 62, OSD Hist; McNamara draft memo for Pres, 20 Nov 62, 1-8, fldr Miscellaneous Memoranda and Reports, box 880, Subject files, OSD Hist.
77. Gilpatric memrcd, 23 Nov 62, *FRUS 1961-63*, VIII:415-16; DoD News Release 1908-62, 25 Nov 62, OSD Hist.
78. Murphy, "The Education of a Defense Secretary," 102.
79. Draft paper, ns, 5 Oct 62, fldr Chron File—1962, box 1, Legislative Affairs files, Acc 67A-4632. The author of the paper was apparently Col. H. M. Hoyler, USMC, director of the plans & coordination staff in the office of the assistant for legislative affairs, who expressed many of the same ideas in similar language in a memo for David McGiffert, assistant to the secretary for legislative affairs, 24 Oct 62, ibid.

VI. THE FY1964 BUDGET

1. See table, Department of Defense Total Obligational Authority (TOA), 1948-1997, in Trask and Goldberg, *The Department of Defense, 1947-1997: Organization and Leaders*, 169.
2. The initial Five-Year Force Structure and Financial Program, dated 15 April 1962, was circulated as an attachment to McNamara memo of 16 April for SvcSecs et al, fldr 110.01(5 YR Force Structure 12 Apr 62), box 20, SecDef Subject Decimal files, Acc 66A-3542. A summary of the program appeared in *Baltimore Sun*, 18 Apr 62. The revised program, dated 7 July 1962, was attached to McNamara memo for SvcSecs et al, 14 Jul 62, fldr FYFSFP, July 1962, box 134, ASD(C) files, OSD Hist.

3. DoD Directive 7045.1, "Program Change Control System," 12 Apr 62; DoD Instruction 7045.2, "Procedures for Program Change Control and Related Progress Reporting," 17 Apr 62. Also serving as guidance was a report prepared by the Programming Office in OASD(C), "Programming System for the Office of the Secretary of Defense," 31 May 62 (rev 25 Jun 62), fldr Financial Mgmt 1962, box 780, Subject files, OSD Hist.
4. Memo McNamara for Pres, 26 Apr 62, fldr Dept of Defense General—April-May 1962, box 274, NSF, JFKL. In the memo McNamara referred to and summarized the president's memo of 17 April expressing these concerns. No copy of the president's memo has been found.
5. Address before the San Francisco section of the Institute of Aerospace Science, Palo Alto, Calif, 5 Sep 62, 8-8a, fldr Comptroller 1962, Budget FY 1962-1964, box 780, Subject files, OSD Hist.
6. Ltrs Bell to McNamara, 3 Apr 62, and McNamara to Bell, 23 May 63, fldr 110.01 (5 YR Force Structure), box 20, SecDef Subject Decimal files, Acc 66A-3542; draft BoB paper, "Revision of 1964 Preview," 13 Jul 62, fldr 110.01 (5 YR Plan) July thru August, ibid.
7. BoB notes on mtg w/McNamara et al regarding DoD 1964 budget preview, ns, 17 Jul 62, fldr NATO, Weapons, Skybolt 3/63 (1), box 227, NSF, JFKL.
8. Memos McNamara for CJCS, 18 Jul 62, and McNamara for SvcSecs, 18 Jul 62, fldr 110.01 (5 YR Plan) July thru August, box 20, SecDef Subject Decimal files, Acc 66A-3542; memo Lemnitzer for SecDef, 31 Aug 62, fldr JCS Views Sep-Nov 1962, box 28, McNamara Records, RG 200. The Navy reply was in memo Korth for SecDef, 31 Aug 62, fldr 110.01 (5 YR Plan) July thru August, box 20, SecDef Subject Decimal files, Acc 66A-3542. The Air Force response was in memo Zuckert for SecDef, 5 Sep 62, fldr 110.01 FY 64, 23 Nov 62 to —, box 7, ibid. The Army response has not been found.
9. Poole, *JCS and National Policy 1961-64*, pt I:242-44; memo Lemnitzer for SecDef, 31 Aug 62, cited in n 8.
10. Memo Bell for Pres, 22 Jun 62, fldr Bureau of the Budget, General 11/61-6/62, box 270, NSF, JFKL. Attached to the memo was a covering note from Bell to Bundy and Kaysen, dated 23 June, in which Bell indicated that the bureau's preliminary recommendations on the FY 1964 budget would be discussed at a meeting on 25 June with the president and others.
11. Memo Bell for Pres, 31 Aug 62, 5, fldr Budget 1964 (1), box 45, Sorensen Papers, JFKL. An earlier but virtually identical draft, dated 22 August, is in fldr 1964 Budget Tables, box 14, Bell Papers, JFKL. A handwritten marginal notation indicates that the draft was discussed on 23 August with Sorensen, Dillon, and Kermit Gordon.
12. Transc White House mtg, 2 Oct 62, printed in Ernest R. May, Timothy Naftali, and Philip D. Zelikow, eds, *The Presidential Recordings: John F. Kennedy: The Great Crises*, 2:321-51 (quotes, 343).
13. Memo Bell for Dillon, 5 Oct 62, w/atchd draft paper, "Possible Reductions in Bureau of the Budget Recommended Expenditures for 1964," fldr Budget 1964 (1), box 45, Sorensen Papers, JFKL. The draft paper has the following handwritten parenthetical notation under the title: "Suggested by Dillon."
14. Memo McNamara for Taylor, 22 Sep 62, w/atchd paper, "Time Schedule for Major Decisions to be Made by SecDef re FY '64 Budget," fldr 110.01 FY 64 Case Date (23 Aug 62) Jan-Sept 62, box 29, SecDef Subject Decimal files, Acc 66A-3542.
15. Memo Hitch for SecDef, 24 Sep 62, fldr FY 1964 Budget (Chron), box 22, ASD(C) files, OSD Hist; Hitch address before Operations Research Society of America, Philadelphia, 7 Nov 62, 14-15, fldr Comptroller, Budget, FY 1962-1964, box 780, Subject files, OSD Hist.
16. The Army and Navy budget submissions were attached to memos Vance for SecDef and Korth for SecDef, both 1 Oct 62, fldr 110.01 FY 64, Case Date (23 Aug 62) October 62, box 29, SecDef Subject Decimal files, Acc 66A-3542. A copy of the Air Force submission has not been found. A tabulation of all three service submissions of 1 October, organized by traditional budget categories, is in fldr FY 1964 Budget (Chron), box 22, ASD(C) files, OSD Hist.
17. Memo McNamara for SvcSecs et al, 24 Oct 62, fldr FY 1964 Budget (Chron), box 22, ASD(C) files, OSD Hist; Pentagon background briefing, 16 Jan 63, 7, fldr Hitch Press Conference—FY 1964 Budget, ibid; memo Hitch for SecDef, 10 Jan 63, w/atchd paper, "Summary of Subject/Issue Considerations," rev 26 Jan 63, fldr 110.01 FY 64 Jan thru April 1963, box 42, SecDef Subject Decimal files, Acc 69A-3131; *New York Times*, 18 Nov 62; UPI wire service dispatch, 20 Nov 62.
18. Livesay notes, staff mtg, 15 Oct 62, 8, fldr SecDef Staff Meetings Sep-Dec 1962, box 11, AFPC and SecDef Meetings files, Acc 77-0062.
19. JCSM-907-62 JCS for SecDef, 20 Nov 62, quoted in ed note, *FRUS 1961-63*, VIII:387-89; memo Taylor for SecDef, 20 Nov 62, ibid, 390-92.

20. Draft memo McNamara for Pres, 21 Nov 62, ibid, 399-401; memo ViceAdm Herbert D. Riley (DirJtStaff) for SecDef, 4 Dec 62, w/atchd table, "Recommendations of the Joint Chiefs of Staff Relative to Forces Supported by FY-64 Military Budget," fldr FY 1964 Budget (Chron), box 22, ASD(C) files, OSD Hist.
21. Memo Kaysen for Bundy, 14 Nov 62, *FRUS 1961-63*, VIII:383-85; memo Wiesner for Pres, 4 Dec 62, fldr Defense Budget FY 1964 Vol. I—Miscellaneous, box 275, NSF, JFKL.
22. Draft memo McNamara for Pres, 20 Nov 62, *FRUS 1961-63*, VIII:392-97; interv Harold Brown by Steven Rifkin, 9 May 64, 18, JFKL.
23. NIE 11-8-62, "Soviet Capabilities for Long Range Attack," 6 Jul 62, *FRUS 1961-63*, VIII:332-33; memo Johnson (DepUSecState) for Rusk, 29 Jul 62, ibid, 350-51 (quote, 351); memo SecState, SecDef, DirCIA, CJCS for Pres, nd, w/atchd rpt, ibid, 350-51, 355-78.
24. Memo Taylor for Pres, 23 Aug 62, ltr Rusk to McNamara, 28 Nov 62: ibid, 380, 417.
25. Poole, *JCS and National Policy 1961-64*, pt I:193-95; memo Legere for Bundy, 26 Nov 62, fldr Defense Budget FY 1964 Vol. I—Miscellaneous, box 275, NSF, JFKL.
26. Brown interv, 9 May 64, 19; memrcd Gilpatric, 23 Nov 62, *FRUS 1961-63*, VIII:415-16; memo Legere for Bundy, 27 Nov 62, fldr Defense Budget FY 1964 Vol. I—Miscellaneous, box 275, NSF, JFKL.
27. Memo McNamara for CJCS, 29 Nov 62, fldr Classified Chron File—July thru Dec 1962, box 45, Enthoven Papers, LBJL; "Adequacy of Overall Budget," Tab D to point paper on FY 1964 budget, nd and ns, bound volume II entitled "Some Controversial Issues during Admiral Anderson's Tenure as CNO," box 1963-35, Chief of Naval Operations Immediate Office files, NHC.
28. Draft memo McNamara for Pres, 3 Dec 62, *FRUS 1961-63*, VIII:428-31.
29. Preliminary recording transc, White House mtg, 5 Dec 62, 10:15-11:57 a.m., 1-2, Miller Center, Univ of Virginia. The OSD Historical Office is grateful to Timothy Naftali and David Coleman of the Miller Center for providing a copy of the preliminary transcript. The transcript is based on tapes 65 and 66, Presidential Recordings, JFKL. While McNamara and other officials used various figures to describe the differences between the service budget submissions and the president's final budget, a detailed tabulation OSD later provided the Senate Appropriations Subcommittee showed a total difference of $12.4798 billion (NOA): $3.7094 billion for the Army, $3.8998 for the Navy, and $4.8706 for the Air Force (SSCA, *Hearings: Department of Defense Appropriations for 1964*, 88 Cong, 1 sess, 1488-89).
30. Preliminary recording transc, White House mtg, 5 Dec 62, 3-4, 7-8.
31. Ibid, 14-15, 18-19.
32. Ibid, 20-28; see Wiesner memo, 4 Dec 62, cited in n 21.
33. Preliminary recording transc, White House mtg, 5 Dec 62, 38-47.
34. *New York Times*, 20 Dec 62; *Washington Post*, 20 Dec 62; question and answer period following address at the Economic Club of New York, 14 Dec 62, and television and radio interview, 17 Dec 62, *Kennedy Public Papers, 1962*, 885, 896-97; *Washington News*, 19 Dec 62.
35. Memcon w/Pres, 27 Dec 62, *FRUS 1961-63*, VIII:446-47. McNamara's handwritten notes on the meeting are in fldr Palm Beach Notes on JCS Views, box 28, McNamara Records, RG 200. A chronology of the Navy's efforts in the fall 1962 to have two nuclear-powered attack submarines added to the budget, as well as discussion of the issue during the 1963 congressional hearings, is in paper, "Request for Addition of 2 Nuclear Attack Submarines," Jun 63, fldr Controversial Issues during GW Anderson's Tour Vol. 2, box 1963-35, Chief of Naval Operations Immediate Office files, NHC.
36. Memcon w/Pres, 27 Dec 62, cited in n 35, 448-50, 453.
37. Ibid, 450-52.
38. Ibid, 452-53; memo MajGen John M. Reynolds (ViceDirJCS) for McNamara, Gilpatric, and JCS, 28 Dec 62, w/atchd policy guidance, fldr 092.3 Nassau (1962 Papers) 1963, box 40, SecDef Subject Decimal files, Acc 69A-3131.
39. Interv George W. Anderson, Jr., by John T. Mason, Jr., 7 Jan 81, 522-23, NHC; memrcd Gilpatric, 2 Jan 63, fldr RLG Reading File—Jan. 1, 1963-June 30, 1963, box 2, Gilpatric files, Acc 66A-3529.
40. *Kennedy Public Papers, 1963*, 27-28, 33, 40. A detailed discussion of the Defense portion of the budget is in *The Budget of the United States, FY 1964*, 61-69.
41. *DoD FY 1964 Budget Highlights*, I-Summary, 1, 26 Feb 63, box 20, ASD(C) files, OSD Hist.
42. *Philadelphia Inquirer*, 18 Jan 63.
43. HCAS, *Authorizing Appropriations for Aircraft, Missiles, and Naval Vessels*, H Rpt 62, 88 Cong, 1 sess, 6 Mar 63, 2-3; ltr McNamara to Pres of Senate, 17 Jan 63, *Cong Rec*, 19 Feb 63, 2363-64; *Baltimore Sun*, 22 Jan 63; SCAS, *Hearings: Military Procurement Authorization, Fiscal Year 1964*, 88 Cong, 1 sess, 19 Feb 63, 2.

44. Charles J. Hitch, "What Tying Dollars to Military Decisions Means to Defense Management," *Armed Forces Management*, Nov 62; *Air Force Times*, 5 Jan 63; Robert E. Hunter, "The Politics of U.S. Defence 1963: Manned Bombers versus Missiles," *World Today*, Mar 63, 98-99; Hunter, "The Politics of U.S. Defence 1963: The Congressional Question," ibid, Apr 63, 156.
45. Memos McGiffert for O'Brien, 14, 21 Jan 63, fldr White House Major Legislative Reports 1963, box 1, Legislative Affairs files, Acc 67A-4632; "Overall Shipbuilding and Conversion Program," Tab A to point paper on FY 1964 budget, cited in n 27.
46. Memo McGiffert for SecDef, 21 Dec 62, w/atchd memrcd, 20 Dec 62, fldr FY 1964 Budget (Chron), box 22, ASD(C) files, OSD Hist.
47. HCAS, *Hearings: Military Posture and HR 2440*, 88 Cong, 1 sess, 30 Jan 63, 233-34, 284; memo McGiffert for O'Brien, 4 Feb 63, fldr White House Major Legislative Reports 1963, box 1, Legislative Affairs files, Acc 67A-4632.
48. *Baltimore Sun*, 5 Feb 63.
49. Memo McGiffert for O'Brien, 11 Feb 63, fldr White House Major Legislative Reports 1963, box 1, Legislative Affairs files, Acc 67A-4632; *Military Posture and HR 2440*, 614-17, 667-69, 724-25; J. F. Shumate (OSD Off of Legis Liaison), rpt on cong hearing, 21 Feb 63, fldr DoD Authorization (FY 64) 1963, box 781, Subject files, OSD Hist.
50. Memo McGiffert for O'Brien, 25 Feb 63, fldr White House Major Legislative Reports 1963, box 1, Legislative Affairs files, Acc 67A-4632; *Military Posture and HR 2440*, 1305-14 (quotes, 1307); *Authorizing Appropriations for Aircraft, Missiles, and Naval Vessels*, cited in n 43, 1-6; *Washington Star*, 9 Mar 63.
51. Memo McGiffert for O'Brien, 18 Mar 63, fldr White House Major Legislative Reports 1963, box 1, Legislative Affairs files, Acc 67A-4632; *Washington Post*, 13, 14 Mar 63; *Baltimore Sun*, 14 Mar 63.
52. Memo McGiffert for SecDef et al, 5 Jan 63, fldr DoD Appros FY 64, box 781, Subject files, OSD Hist; table, "Secretary McNamara's Appearances Before Congressional Committees (Senate), 88 Cong, 1 sess," nd, fldr Foreign Assistance—MAP, AID, etc, box 101, ASD(C) files, OSD Hist; SCAS, *Military Procurement Authorization, FY 1964*, 1-81 passim (quote, 5).
53. *Military Procurement Authorization, FY 1964*, 83-90; for Brown's testimony on 26 February, see 411-85, and for testimony of the service representatives on 27-28 February and on 1 and 4-8 March, 487-1033.
54. SCAS, *Authorizing Appropriations During Fiscal Year 1964 for Procurement, Research, Development, Test, and Evaluation of Aircraft, Missiles, and Naval Vessels for the Armed Forces*, S Rpt 123, 88 Cong, 1 sess, 9 Apr 63, 1-5, 15; *Baltimore Sun*, 12 Apr 63.
55. *Washington Post*, 13 Apr 63; *Baltimore Sun*, 12 Apr 63.
56. Memo McGiffert for O'Brien, 6 May 63, fldr White House Major Legislative Reports 1963, box 1, Legislative Affairs files, Acc 67A-4632; ltr McNamara to Armed Svcs Cte Chairmen, 24 Apr 63, ltr Vinson to McNamara, 29 Apr 63, memo Gilpatric for CJCS, 4 May 63, memo Taylor for SecDef, 8 May 63, w/atchd ltr to Vinson, 8 May 63: fldr 110.01 FY 64 Jan thru April 63, box 42, SecDef Subject Decimal files, Acc 69A-3131.
57. HCAS, *Authorizations for Aircraft, Missiles, and Naval Vessels, Fiscal Year 1964*, H Rpt 289, 88 Cong, 1 sess, 13 May 63, 4; *Aviation Daily*, 13 May 63; *Wall Street Journal*, 15 May 63; PL 88-28, 23 May 63 (77 Stat 48).
58. Maurice H. Stans, *One of the Presidents' Men: Twenty Years with Eisenhower and Nixon*, 102-03; news confs, 6 Mar, 3 Apr 63, *Kennedy Public Papers, 1963*, 238, 307-08; *New York Times*, 8 Mar 63.
59. Memo Pres for SecDef, 3 Apr 63, fldr Department of Defense General 1/63-6/63, box 274, NSF, JFKL; memos Bundy for Yarmolinsky, 5 Apr 63, and Yarmolinsky for Hitch, 6 Apr 63, fldr Interagency Memoranda 1961-1968, box 9, Enthoven Papers, LBJL; memo McNamara for Pres, 17 Apr 63, fldr Department of Defense General 1/63-6/63, box 274, NSF, JFKL. An identical copy of the McNamara memo showing Enthoven as the drafter is in fldr Interagency Memoranda 1961-1968, box 9, Enthoven Papers, LBJL.
60. Memo Gilpatric for Claude Desautels, 23 Mar 63, w/atchd memo Gilpatric for Pres, 23 Mar 63, fldr RLG Reading File—Jan 1, 63-Jun 30, 63, box 2, Gilpatric files, Acc 66A-3529. No DoD analysis was found attached to these documents, but an undated copy of the analysis, entitled "Impact of a $7,756 Million Reduction in FY 1964 NOA," is in fldr $7,756 Million Reduction FY 64 NOA, box 1, ibid.
61. Ltrs Ryan to McNamara, 29 Mar 63, Hitch to Ryan, 11 Apr 63, Melman to Ryan, 3 Jun 63, all in *Cong Rec*, 20 Jun 63, 10611-15; memo Enthoven for DepSecDef, 30 Apr 63, fldr Melman-Nuclear Capabilities, Strategies, etc, box 25, ASD(C) files, OSD Hist.
62. Ltr Melman to McNamara, 10 May 63, ltr Hitch to Melman, 22 May 63: fldr Melman-Nuclear Capabilities, Strategies, etc, box 25, ASD(C) files, OSD Hist. In the margin of Hitch's letter is the handwritten

notation: "Prof. M. came in 7 June—talked with Mr. Hitch, Dr. Enthoven & Mr. Glass." No other record of their discussion has been found.

63. The record of the hearings is in HSCA, *Hearings: Department of Defense Appropriations for 1964*, 88 Cong, 1 sess, pts 1-6. McNamara's testimony, in which he was joined by Taylor, comprises all of pt 1. Testimony by Taylor separately, the Joint Chiefs, certain other OSD personnel, and the service secretaries comprises all of pt 2. Examples of questioning about the Joint Chiefs' role in budget decisions and McNamara's denial or reduction of service requests are in pt 1:342-48 and pt 2:129-31, 300-314, 454, 476-81, 505-24, 548-62. Melman's testimony is in pt 6:891-902.

64. HCA, *Department of Defense Appropriation Bill, 1964*, H Rpt 439, 88 Cong, 1 sess, 21 Jun 63, 3-4; DoD News Release 893-63, 21 Jun 63; memo McGiffert for O'Brien, 24 Jun 63, fldr White House Major Legislative Reports 1963, box 1, Legislative Affairs files, Acc 67A-4632.

65. *Cong Rec*, 25 Jun 63, 10820; *New York Times*, 22 Jun 63; *Cong Rec*, 26 Jun 63, 11105-29; memo McGiffert for O'Brien, 1 Jul 63, fldr White House Major Legislative Reports 1963, box 1, Legislative Affairs files, Acc 67A-4632; *Wall Street Journal*, 27 Jun 63.

66. Memo Brown for McNamara, 27 Jun 63, fldr 110.01 FY 64 May thru August 1963, box 42, SecDef Subject Decimal files, Acc 69A-3131; ltr McNamara to Russell, 12 Jul 63, in SSCA, *DoD Appropriations for 1964*, 1502-06; Gilpatric test, 20 Aug 63, ibid, 1562-63.

67. LtCol S. B. Berry staff mtg notes, 15 Jul 63, fldr SecDef Staff Meetings Apr-Jul 1963, box 11, AFPC and SecDef Meetings files, Acc 77-0062. The information McNamara requested was summarized in memo Hitch for SecDef, 31 Jul 63, fldr 110.01 FY 64 May thru August 1963, box 42, SecDef Subject Decimal files, Acc 69A-3131.

68. Julius Duscha, *Arms, Money, and Politics*, 3; ltr McGovern and Nelson to McNamara, 15 Jul 63, fldr 110.01 1963, box 41, SecDef Subject Decimal files, Acc 69A-3131; *Washington Post*, 3 Aug 63.

69. Ltr McGovern to McGiffert, 7 Aug 63, fldr 110.01 1963, box 41, SecDef Subject Decimal files, Acc 69A-3131.

70. Memo McGiffert for O'Brien, 19 Aug 63, fldr White House Major Legislative Reports 1963, box 1, Legislative Affairs files, Acc 67A-4632.

71. SSCA, *DoD Appropriations for 1964*, 1562-1652 (quotes, 1564, 1624, 1622-23); *Air Force Magazine*, Oct 63.

72. SCA, *Department of Defense Appropriation Bill, 1964*, S Rpt 502, 88 Cong, 1 sess, 17 Sep 63, 1, 62; *Baltimore Sun*, 18 Sep 63; memo McGiffert for McNamara, 17 Sep 63, fldr RLG's Notes on FY 64 Budget, box 1, Gilpatric files, Acc 66A-3529; ltrs McNamara to Russell and to Carl Hayden, both 6 Sep 63, fldr FY 1964 Budget (Chron), box 22, ASD(C) files, OSD Hist.

73. Duscha, *Arms, Money, and Politics*, 6; *Cong Rec*, 24 Sep 63, 16943-72 (quotes, 16956, 16961); *New York Times*, 25 Sep 63.

74. Ltr Gilpatric to Russell, 26 Sep 63, fldr RLG Reading File—July 1, 1963- , box 2, Gilpatric files, Acc 66A-3529.

75. Conf Cte, *Department of Defense Appropriation Bill, 1964*, H Rpt 812, 88 Cong, 1 sess, 7 Oct 63, 1-3; *Washington Post*, 8 Oct 63; *Baltimore Sun*, 9 Oct 63; PL 88-149, 17 Oct 63 (77 Stat 254).

76. *New York Times*, 18 Nov 62; *Congress and the Nation, 1945-1964*, 380.

77. Hunter, "The Politics of U.S. Defence 1963: The Congressional Question," 161; *Business Week*, 31 Aug 63.

78. *Newsweek*, 25 Mar 63; *Atlanta Constitution*, 17 Mar 63.

79. Gilbert C. Fite, *Richard B. Russell, Jr.: Senator from Georgia*, 387-88; *Atlanta Constitution*, 24 Mar 63 (quote); *Baltimore Sun*, 26 Jun 63; *Washington Post*, 28 Jun 63; *Business Week*, 31 Aug 63.

VII. BERLIN: THE WALL

1. Interv Henry Rowen by Alfred Goldberg, 27 Sep 66, 3, OSD Hist.
2. Extract from Khrushchev address, 10 Nov 58, Dept State, *Documents on Germany, 1944-1985* (hereafter *Documents on Germany*), 545; note from Soviet Union to US, 27 Nov 58, ibid, 558-59; Watson, *Into the Missile Age*, 593-97.
3. Schlesinger, *A Thousand Days*, 346.
4. Note from Soviet Union, 27 Nov 58, *Documents on Germany*, 559.
5. Note from US to Soviet Union, 31 Dec 58, ibid, 576.
6. Dulles press conf, 26 Nov 58, *FRUS 1958-60*, VIII:122-23; Watson, *Into the Missile Age*, 596-620.

7. Strobe Talbott, trans, *Khrushchev Remembers*, 458; Adlai Stevenson, rpt of convers w/Menshikov, 14 Dec 60, fldr USSR General 1960, box 125, POF, JFKL.
8. Dept State, Hist Off, "Crisis over Berlin: American Policy Concerning the Soviet Threats to Berlin, November 1958-December 1962," Research Project 614-E, Feb 70, pt V, 1.
9. Aide-memoire Soviet Union to Federal Republic of Germany, 17 Feb 61, *Documents on Germany*, 723-27 (quote, 726).
10. Marc Trachtenberg, *History and Strategy*, 215-16; Jack M. Schick, *The Berlin Crisis, 1958-1962*, 138-41.
11. Schlesinger, *A Thousand Days*, 347-48.
12. *Kennedy Public Papers, 1961*, 19-28; Hillenbrand memcon w/Bowles, Grewe et al, 2 Feb 61, *FRUS 1961-63*, XIV:5-6; msg 1839 Moscow to State, 4 Feb 61, ibid, 6-7.
13. Memcon Pres and Brentano et al, 17 Feb 61, *FRUS 1961-63*, XIV:8-11; memcon Pres and Brandt et al, 13 Mar 61, ibid, 25-30; jt US-West German communiqué, 13 Apr 61, *Documents on Germany*, 727-29.
14. P. H. Johnstone, "Military Policy Making during the Berlin Crisis of 1958-62," IDA, Rpt R-138, Mar 68 (hereafter cited as IDA Rpt R-138), I:145; Gregory W. Pedlow, "Allied Crisis Management for Berlin: The LIVE OAK Organization, 1959-1963," in William W. Epley, ed, *International Cold War Military Records and History*, 87-90.
15. JCSM-33-61 Lemnitzer for SecDef, 26 Jan 61, fldr 381 Germany 1960, box 20, SecDef Subject Decimal files, Acc 64A-2093; ltr Nitze to SecState, 10 Feb 61, ibid.
16. JCSM-476-61 Lemnitzer for SecDef, 12 Jul 61, fldr 092 Germany (Berlin) Jul 61, box 51, ISA files, Acc 64A-2382; memo McNamara for CJCS, 9 Aug 61, ibid; ltr Nitze to John Ausland, 24 Apr 84, Nitze Papers, LC.
17. IDA Rpt R-138, I:145-46; Bundy memo of mtg on Berlin, 17 Jul 61, *FRUS 1961-63*, XIV:211.
18. Dean Acheson, "A Review of North Atlantic Problems for the Future," Mar 61, fldr NATO General, Vol. I, box 220, NSF, JFKL; memo Acheson for Pres, 3 Apr 61, fldr Germany, Berlin-General, box 81, ibid. Trachtenberg, *History and Strategy*, 217, n 175, cites an unpublished paper in the Acheson files by Thomas Schelling, entitled "On the Problem of NATO's Nuclear Strategy" and dated 7 March 1961, which Acheson kept while working on NATO policies.
19. Memo George C. McGhee for McGeorge Bundy, w/atchmt, "The Problem of Berlin," 30 Mar 61 (quote, 11), fldr 092 Germany (Berlin) Jan-Jun 61, box 33, ISA files, Acc 64A-2382.
20. Memo DirISA Coordinating Staff (NSC & Collateral Activities) Robert H. B. Wade for ASecState(RegAffs), 30 Mar 61, ibid; memo DirPolPlngStaff BrigGen James H. Polk for DASD(ISA), 3 Apr 61, ibid.
21. Schlesinger, *A Thousand Days*, 380-82; memcon, 5 Apr 61, *FRUS 1961-63*, XIV:36-37; Poole, *JCS and National Policy 1961-64*, pt II:151-52.
22. JCSM-237-61 Lemnitzer for SecDef, 13 Apr 61, fldr 310.1 (Proj 87), 1/31-15-2-1, box 51, ISA files, Acc 64A-2382; memo William Bundy for SecDef, 21 Apr 61, ibid; JCSM-287-61 Burke for JCS for SecDef, 28 Apr 61, fldr 092 Germany (Berlin) Jan-May 61, box 51, ISA files, Acc 64A-2382; Poole, *JCS and National Policy 1961-64*, pt II:151.
23. IDA Rpt R-138, I:173.
24. Memo McNamara for Pres, 5 May 61, *FRUS 1961-63*, XIV:61-63; memo McNamara for CJCS, 19 May 61, fldr 092 Germany (Berlin) Jan-May 61, box 51, ISA files, Acc 64A-2382; memo McNamara for ASD(ISA), 19 May 61, ibid.
25. JCSM-353-61 LeMay for SecDef, 25 May 61, fldr 092 Germany (Berlin), Jan-May 61, box 51, ISA files, Acc 64A-2382.
26. Poole, *JCS and National Policy 1961-64*, pt II:154-55.
27. Communiqué, Ministerial Session of the North Atlantic Council, Oslo, 8-10 May 1961, *American Foreign Policy: Current Documents, 1961*, 483-85; IDA Rpt R-138, I:187-88.
28. Msg Polto 1646 Finletter (Paris) to State, 3 Jun 61, OSD Hist.
29. Memcon Kennedy and de Gaulle, 31 May 61, 12:30 p.m., *FRUS 1961-63*, XIV:80-83; memcon Pres and de Gaulle, 31 May 61, 2:50 p.m., ibid, 84-86.
30. Documentation regarding the Kennedy-Khrushchev summit conference, 3-4 Jun 61, is in *FRUS 1961-63*, XIV:87-98 (quote, 98); Schlesinger, *A Thousand Days*, 358-67 (quote, 367), 374.
31. Aide-memoire Soviet Union to US, 4 Jun 61, *Documents on Germany*, 729-32; memcon (Akalovsky) Pres and Khrushchev, 4 Jun 61, *FRUS 1961-63*, V:230.
32. Radio and TV Report to American People on Returning from Europe, 6 Jun 61, *Kennedy Public Papers, 1961*, 442.

33. *Documents on Germany*, 733-36, 743.
34. *Kennedy Public Papers, 1961*, 401.
35. IDA Rpt R-138, I:203-04.
36. Rpt by Acheson, 28 Jun 61, *FRUS 1961-63*, XIV:138-59; memrcd disc at NSC mtg, 29 Jun 61, ibid, 160-62.
37. Curtis Cate, *The Ides of August: The Berlin Wall Crisis—1961*, 84-85; interv Abram Chayes by Eugene Gordon, 9 Jul 64, 241-42, JFKL.
38. Harriman's complaint is in Walter Isaacson and Evan Thomas, *The Wise Men: Six Friends and the World They Made: Acheson, Bohlen, Harriman, Kennan, Lovett, and McCloy*, 611.
39. Memrcd cited in n 36; NSAM 58, 30 Jun 61, *FRUS 1961-63*, XIV:162-65; Poole, *JCS and National Policy 1961-64*, pt II:167-68.
40. Schlesinger, *A Thousand Days*, 386-87; memo Schlesinger for Pres, 7 Jul 61, *FRUS 1961-63*, XIV:173-76.
41. Schlesinger, *A Thousand Days*, 388-89; memo Taylor for Pres, 12 Jul 61, *FRUS 1961-63*, XIV:186.
42. Bundy memo of NSC disc, 13 Jul 61, *FRUS 1961-63*, XIV:192-94; Poole, *JCS and National Policy 1961-64*, pt II:170-71.
43. Bundy memo of disc in NSC, 13 Jul 61, cited in n 42; Schlesinger, *A Thousand Days*, 389-90; Bundy memo of mtg, 17 Jul 61, *FRUS 1961-63*, XIV:209-12; Bundy memo of NSC disc, 19 Jul 61, ibid, 219-20.
44. Memo McNamara for CJCS, 14 Jul 61, fldr Reading File, Aug. 1961-June 1961, box 113, McNamara Records, RG 200.
45. Bundy memo of mtg, 17 Jul 61, cited in n 43; NSAM 62, 24 Jul 61, *FRUS 1961-63*, XIV:210; Poole, *JCS and National Policy 1961-64*, pt II:174-76.
46. *Kennedy Public Papers, 1961*, 534, 538-39.
47. Ibid, 535-37.
48. PL 87-117, 1 Aug 61; PL 87-144, 17 Aug 61.
49. Msg 323 Moscow to State, 28 Jul 61, *FRUS 1961-63*, XIV:231-34; Schlesinger, *A Thousand Days*, 392; *Baltimore Sun*, 11 Aug 61.
50. Address by Khrushchev, Moscow, 11 Aug 61, *Current Digest of the Soviet Press*, 6 Sep 61, 9-12.
51. IDA Rpt R-138, II:134-35; memo Pres for SecDef, 14 Aug 61, fldr 370.01, box 51, Miscellaneous Sensitive files, Acc 71A-6489.
52. IDA Rpt R-138, II:195-96; memo McNamara for SecA Stahr, 2 Aug 61, fldr Reading File, Aug.1961-June 1961, box 113, McNamara Records, RG 200.
53. US draft paper for 4-9 Aug Foreign Ministers mtg in Paris, "Military Planning and Preparations Toward a Berlin Crisis," 2 Aug 61, fldr 092 Germany (Berlin), box 51, ISA files, Acc 64A-2382; see memcons Ministerial Consultations on Berlin, 4-9 Aug 61, *FRUS 1961-63*, XIV:269-316.
54. JCSM-476-61 Lemnitzer for SecDef, 12 Jul 61, cited in n 16.
55. Memo McNamara for CJCS, 9 Aug 61, ltr Nitze to Ausland, 24 Apr 84, both cited in n 16.
56. Acheson notes on convers w/Strauss, 1 Aug 61, fldr 092 Germany (Berlin), Jul-Dec 61, box 32, ISA files, Acc 64A-2382.
57. John C. Ausland, *Kennedy, Khrushchev, and the Berlin-Cuba Crisis, 1961-1964*, 10-12.
58. Memcon Ministerial Consultations on Berlin, 5 Aug 61, cited in n 53, 269-70.
59. Ed note, 325, ibid; Ausland, *Kennedy, Khrushchev, and Berlin*, 10, 20-21; Nitze, *From Hiroshima to Glasnost*, 199; *Documents on Germany*, 773-76.
60. Ausland, *Kennedy, Khrushchev, and Berlin*, 21-22. Helmut Trotnow places the initiative with Ulbricht and Secretary of the National Defense Council Erich Honecker, cautiously supported by Khrushchev, in "Who Actually Built the Berlin Wall? The SED Leadership and the 13th of August 1961," in Epley, ed, *International Cold War Military Records and History*, 41 ff.
61. Rusk statement, 13 Aug 61, *Documents on Germany*, 776.
62. Mins mtg Berlin Steering Group, 15 Aug 61, *FRUS 1961-63*, XIV:333-34; memo Col Lawrence Legere for Taylor, 16 Aug 61, 335-37, ibid; Poole, *JCS and National Policy 1961-64*, pt II:190-91.
63. HCAS, *Hearings on Jt Res 505*, 87 Cong, 1 sess, 28 Jul 61, 2475.
64. *McNamara Public Statements, 1961*, III:1103-04.
65. Ltr Brandt to Pres, 16 Aug 61, *FRUS 1961-63*, XIV:345-46.
66. Poole, *JCS and National Policy 1961-64*, pt II:192; Ausland, *Kennedy, Khrushchev, and Berlin*, 23; *New York Times*, 22 Aug 61; John Newhouse, *War and Peace in the Nuclear Age*, 157-58.
67. Memo McNamara for Pres, 24 Aug 61, *FRUS 1961-63*, XIV:369; *Kennedy Public Papers, 1961*, 573. Fears about Clay's propensity to act unilaterally were not fully dispelled in August; they would arise again as new

crises developed in subsequent months (interv Lemnitzer by Walter Poole, 2 Feb 77, cited in Poole, *JCS and National Policy 1961-64*, pt II:193).
68. Rcd of mtg Berlin Steering Group, 17 Aug 61, *FRUS 1961-63*, XIV:347-49; interv William W. Kaufmann by Maurice Matloff, 23 Jul 86, 2, OSD Hist; Schlesinger, *A Thousand Days*, 397; Frank Ninkovich, *Germany and the United States: The Transformation of the German Question Since 1945*, 129; *FRUS 1961-63*, XIV:350, n 1.
69. Ausland, *Kennedy, Khrushchev, and Berlin*, 24. On the problems for the future relating to the issue of dismounting, note the communication of General Freeman (Heidelberg) to General Polk, 5 Nov 63, referring to a letter from Soviet General Yakubovsky of 25 Oct 63 expressing his intentions to enforce existing regulations, which included dismounting for counting (box 174, Lemnitzer Papers, NDUL).
70. *Documents on Germany*, 782; Robert P. Grathwol and Donita M. Moorhus, *American Forces in Berlin, 1945-1994: Cold War Outpost*, 92.
71. Ed note, *FRUS 1961-63*, XIV:704; *New York Herald-Tribune*, 26 Dec 61.
72. Note from Soviet Union to US, 23 Aug 61, *Documents on Germany*, 783-84; note from US to Soviet Union, 26 Aug 61, ibid, 785-86; memo Bundy on mtg of Steering Group, 23 Aug 61, box 2, Miscellaneous Sensitive files, Acc 71A-6489.
73. McGeorge Bundy, *Danger and Survival: Choices About the Bomb in the First Fifty Years*, 384-85.
74. Memo Nitze for SecDef, 24 Aug 61, fldr 092 Germany (Berlin), 1961 Aug 19-31, box 51, ISA files, Acc 64A-2382; Trachtenberg, *History and Strategy*, 222; memo McNamara for SvcSecs, 18 Aug 61, fldr Reading File, Aug. 1961-June 1961, box 113, McNamara Records, RG 200.
75. Msg 632 Gavin (Paris) to State, 3 Aug 61, OSD Hist; msg 982 State to London, 26 Aug 61, *FRUS 1961-63*, XIV:371-73.
76. Ausland, *Kennedy, Khrushchev, and Berlin*, 27.
77. Memo McNamara for Pres, 24 Aug 61, fldr Reading File, Aug. 1961-June 1961, box 113, McNamara Records, RG 200; IDA Rpt R-138, II:135.
78. Poole, *JCS and National Policy 1961-64*, pt II:197-99.
79. Memo Pres for SecDef, 31 Aug 61, box 35, Taylor Papers, NDUL; Poole, *JCS and National Policy 1961-64*, pt II:202-03.
80. *McNamara Public Statements, 1961*, III:1443; *Gilpatric Public Statements, 1961*, 394-95.
81. Ltr Gilpatric to Rusk, 21 Nov 61, w/encl JCSM-799-61 Lemnitzer for SecDef, 15 Nov 61, w/atchmt, ISA paper, "NATO Military Policy in the Berlin Crisis," fldr 092 Germany (Berlin), Jul-Dec 61, box 52, ISA files, Acc 64A-2382.
82. [Nitze] memcon—McNamara, Gilpatric, Nitze, Strauss—at McNamara's home, 7:00 p.m., 26 Nov 61, ibid.
83. Memo McNamara for Pres, 18 Sep 61, fldr 092 Germany (Berlin), 1961 Sep 15-23, box 51, ibid (quote, 3); memrcd Taylor, 18 Sep 61, *FRUS 1961-63*, XIV:428-29.
84. Rowen interv, 27 Sep 66, 2; Kaufmann interv, 23 Jul 86, 1; Nitze, *From Hiroshima to Glasnost*, 203, credits Vice Adm. John M. Lee with the concept if not the name.
85. ISA paper, "Estimate of the Situation #2," 29 Sep 61, fldr 092 Germany (Berlin), 1961 Sep 24-30, box 51, ISA files, Acc 64A-2382; ISA draft paper, "Preferred Sequence of Military Actions in a Berlin Conflict," 12 Oct 61, ibid (fldr Oct 1-14). See ltr ViceAdm John Lee (Ret.) to Steven L. Rearden, 18 May 84, Nitze Papers, LC, on devolution from horse to poodle by way of pony blanket.
86. JCSM-728-61 Lemnitzer for SecDef, 13 Oct 61, fldr 092 Germany (Berlin), 1961 Oct 1-14, box 51, ISA files, Acc 64A-2382; memo Taylor for Nitze, 14 Oct 61, ibid.
87. Memo McNamara for McGeorge Bundy, 18 Oct 61, ibid; msg 553 State to Berlin, 18 Oct 61, *FRUS 1961-63*, XIV:508-09; ltr Pres to SACEUR, 20 Oct 61, w/encl, ibid, 520-23.
88. Memo Seymour Weiss for Kohler and Nitze, 28 Sep 61, fldr 092 Germany (Berlin), 1961 Sep 24-30, box 51, ISA files, Acc 64A-2382 (quote, 2). Emphasis in original.
89. JCSM-666-61 Lemnitzer for SecDef, 22 Sep 61, ibid (fldr Sep 15-23); memo Nitze for McNamara, 28 Sep 61; ltr McNamara to Rusk, 30 Sep 61: ibid (fldr Sep 24-30); memo McNamara for CJCS, 2 Oct 61, ibid (fldr Oct 1-14).
90. Bundy memo of mtg, 20 Oct 61, *FRUS 1961-63*, XIV:519 (emphasis in original).
91. Bundy mins of mtg, 10 Oct 61, ibid, 487-89; memo McNamara for Pres, 10 Oct 61, fldr Reading File, Sept. 1961-Oct. 1961, box 113, McNamara Records, RG 200; msg Polto 28 Finletter (Paris) to State, 23 Oct 61, OSD Hist.

92. *Kennedy Public Papers, 1961*, 601-02.
93. *New York Times*, 18 Oct 61; *Current Digest of the Soviet Press*, 8 Nov 61, 5.
94. See Ausland, *Kennedy, Khrushchev, and Berlin*, 36, for Clay's role from the perspective of a member of the Berlin Task Force.
95. Msg 801 Lightner (Berlin) to State, 23 Oct 61, *FRUS 1961-63*, XIV:524-25; Norstad notes on incidents in Berlin, 26 Oct 61, NAC Briefing file, Norstad Papers, DDEL.
96. Ed note, *FRUS 1961-63*, XIV:544; Ausland, *Kennedy, Khrushchev, and Berlin*, 40-41.
97. Talbott, *Khrushchev Remembers*, 459-60. See ed note, *FRUS 1961-63*, XIV:544.
98. Msg 969 Lightner (Berlin) to State, 8 Nov 61, *FRUS 1961-63*, XIV:565-66; Ausland, *Kennedy, Khrushchev, and Berlin*, 41.
99. Msg 2258 Lyon (Paris) (Stoessel) to State, 26 Oct 61, msg 1001 Dowling (Bonn) to State, 26 Oct 61: OSD Hist.
100. Msg 843 Clay (Berlin) to State, 26 Oct 61, ibid.
101. Msg JCS 2029 to SACEUR, 28 Oct 61, msg 855 Lightner (Berlin) to State, 27 Oct 61: ibid.
102. *Baltimore Sun*, 16 Nov 61; ltr Macmillan to Foreign Secretary, 10 Nov 61, no. 3612, fldr PREM 11/3612, PRO; *New York Post*, 5 Jan 62.
103. Memcon 12 Dec 61, Foreign Ministers mtg, 10-12 Dec 61, *FRUS 1961-63*, XIV:672-78; *American Foreign Policy: Current Documents, 1961*, 505-08; msg Polto 804 USRO (Paris) to State, 18 Dec 61, *FRUS 1961-63*, XIII:341.
104. Memo Pres for Rusk, 9 Mar 62, *FRUS 1961-63*, XV:1-3; memo ASecState(EurAffs) (Kohler) for Rusk, 10 Mar 62, w/encl draft Modus Vivendi, ibid, 4-6.
105. Memo from US to Soviet Union, 15 Feb 62, *Documents on Germany*, 804-05; Ausland, *Kennedy, Khrushchev, and Berlin*, 48-51.
106. Mins NSC mtg, 28 Mar 62, *FRUS 1961-63*, XV:93-94; *American Foreign Policy: Current Documents, 1962*, 691; Ausland, *Kennedy, Khrushchev, and Berlin*, 51.
107. SCFR, *Executive Sessions* (Historical Series), XIV, 87 Cong, 2 sess, 15 May 62, 482-83.
108. *McNamara Public Statements, 1962*, IV:1807, 1812; SCFR, *Executive Sessions* (Hist Series), XIV:803.
109. Ausland, *Kennedy, Khrushchev, and Berlin*, 69.
110. Msg Taylor to Lemnitzer, 8 Nov 63, msg Lemnitzer to Taylor, 12 Nov 63, msg Freeman to Lemnitzer, 14 Nov 63: fldr 30, box 174, Lemnitzer Papers, NDUL.
111. Memo ActgASD(ISA) John T. McNaughton for SecDef, 25 May 64, memo McNamara for CJCS, 27 May 64: fldr Reading File, May 1964, box 120, McNamara Records, RG 200.
112. Soviet-East German Treaty on Friendship, Mutual Assistance, and Cooperation, 12 Jun 64, *Documents on Germany*, 871.
113. Declaration issued by France, UK, and US, 26 Jun 64, ibid, 877-78.
114. Marc Trachtenberg, *A Constructed Peace: The Making of the European Settlement, 1945-1963*, 324, asserts that "the ending of the refugee exodus and even the internal stabilization of the East German state were not [Khrushchev's] most fundamental goals." Khrushchev's greater concern was the control of West Germany's future.

VIII. THE BAY OF PIGS FIASCO

1. Among many excellent accounts of the Bay of Pigs episode, see Trumbull Higgins, *The Perfect Failure: Kennedy, Eisenhower, and the CIA at the Bay of Pigs*; Karl E. Meyer and Tad Szulc, *The Cuban Invasion: The Chronicle of a Disaster*; Haynes Johnson, *The Bay of Pigs: The Leaders' Story of Brigade 2506*; Peter Wyden, *Bay of Pigs: The Untold Story*; Piero Gleijeses, "Ships in the Night: The CIA, the White House and the Bay of Pigs," *Journal of Latin American Studies*, Feb 95, 1-42; Lionel Krisel, "The Bay of Pigs Operation: An Historical Study with Emphasis on Aspects Involving the U.S. Navy," unpub ms, 1974, NHC.
2. US Prohibition of American Exports to Cuba . . ., 19 Oct 60, *American Foreign Policy: Current Documents, 1960*, 240-01; US Determination of the Cuban Sugar Import Quota . . ., 16 Dec 60, ibid, 249.
3. Termination of Diplomatic and Consular Relations Between the United States and Cuba, 3 Jan 61, ibid, 251-52.
4. Memo No. 1 from the Cuba Study Group to President Kennedy: Narrative of the Anti-Castro Cuban Operation Zapata (hereafter Taylor Report), 13 Jun 61, *FRUS 1961-63*, X:576-78; Lyman B. Kirkpatrick,

Jr., "Paramilitary Case Study: The Bay of Pigs," *Naval War College Review*, Nov-Dec 72, 34; Higgins, *The Perfect Failure*, 66; Gleijeses, "Ships in the Night," 5 (n 15).

5. Quoted in Rosenberg, "Arleigh Albert Burke," 311; memo of conf w/Pres, 17 Mar 60, *FRUS 1958-60*, VI:861. See also James G. Blight and Peter Kornbluh, eds, *Politics of Illusion: The Bay of Pigs Reexamined*; interv George H. Decker by Dan H. Ralls, 18 Dec 72, 3, USAMHI.
6. Taylor Report, *FRUS 1961-63*, X:580. Trumbull Higgins noted that CIA officials had introduced Kennedy to leaders of the anti-Castro movement in July 1960: "How much Kennedy learned of the agency's plans for Cuba remains speculative, although it seems to have been a good deal" (*The Perfect Failure*, 59).
7. Taylor Report, *FRUS 1961-63*, X:579; Poole, *JCS and National Policy 1961-64*, pt II:3; Schlesinger, *A Thousand Days*, 238; Johnson, *The Bay of Pigs*, 53-55.
8. Taylor Report, *FRUS 1961-63*, X:578-79; ed note and memrcd pertaining to 3 Jan 61 White House mtg, ibid, 2-4; Taylor, *Swords and Plowshares*, 196; memo McNamara for Kennedy, 24 Jan 61, *FRUS 1961-63*, X:44, ed note. Watson, *Into the Missile Age*, 768, concludes that "when Eisenhower and Gates went out of office, the foundation for the subsequent debacle at the Bay of Pigs had been well laid. As yet, however, there was no irrevocable commitment; it would not have been too late to turn back."
9. Gilpatric interv, 14 Nov 83, 22-23; Richard N. Goodwin, *Remembering America: A Voice from the Sixties*, 173.
10. Richard M. Bissell, Jr., with Jonathan E. Lewis and Frances T. Pudlow, *Reflections of a Cold War Warrior: From Yalta to the Bay of Pigs*, 192. For comments on Bissell's connections with the Kennedy circle see Lucien Vandenbroucke, "Anatomy of a Failure: The Decision to Land at the Bay of Pigs," *Political Science Quarterly*, Fall 84, 481-82; Goodwin, *Remembering America*, 174-75; Evan Thomas, *The Very Best Men: Four Who Dared: The Early Years of the CIA*, 237-72.
11. Sorensen, *Kennedy*, 295-97.
12. *New York Times*, 23 Oct 60; Schlesinger, *A Thousand Days*, 224-26; *Kennedy Public Papers, 1961*, 10-11.
13. Charles J. V. Murphy, "Grenada and the Bay of Pigs: Two Classic Examples of a President in the Role of Commander-in-Chief in a Cold War Situation," *Situation Report* (Publication of the Security and Intelligence Fund), Jan 84, 5.
14. Memcon mtg on Cuba, 22 Jan 61, *FRUS 1961-63*, X:46-52; Rosenberg, "Arleigh Albert Burke," 311; Higgins, *The Perfect Failure*, 62-63.
15. Poole, *JCS and National Policy 1961-64*, pt II:4-6; memcon, 25 Jan 61, *FRUS 1961-63*, X:54-55; memo of disc, 28 Jan 61, ibid, 61-62.
16. JCSM-44-61 Lemnitzer for SecDef, 27 Jan 61, *FRUS 1961-63*, X:57-58; Poole, *JCS and National Policy 1961-64*, pt II:7-8.
17. JCSM-57-61 Lemnitzer for SecDef, 3 Feb 61, *FRUS 1961-63*, X:67-69.
18. Ibid, 69; Poole, *JCS and National Policy 1961-64*, pt II:10-11; Wyden, *Bay of Pigs*, 89.
19. On 7 March 1961 the JCS tentatively approved CINCLANT's Contingency Operation Plan 312-61, identifying the defense of Guantanamo naval base as a prime objective in the event of a military operation. See JCS 2304/30 memo DirJtStaff for JCS, 25 Apr 61, 218, NHC; memcon, 22 Jan 61, cited in n 14, 50.
20. Schlesinger, *A Thousand Days*, 239.
21. Wyden, *Bay of Pigs*, 90; Rosenberg, "Arleigh Albert Burke," 311.
22. Bundy memo of mtg w/Pres, 8 Feb 61, *FRUS 1961-63*, X:90-91. McNamara gave his oral approval to the JCS report on 3 February 1961. See Poole, *JCS and National Policy 1961-64*, pt II:12.
23. JCSM-146-61 Lemnitzer for SecDef, 10 Mar 61, *FRUS 1961-63*, X:119-22; Taylor Report, ibid, 582.
24. Taylor Report, ibid; Goodwin, *Remembering America*, 172-73.
25. Paper prepared in CIA, 11 Mar 61, *FRUS 1961-63*, X:137-42. In an unpublished manuscript in the Allen W. Dulles Papers at Princeton University, Dulles rebutted the charge that intelligence advisers misled the president. He claimed that CIA planners never told Kennedy that the landing of exile troops alone would trigger mass uprisings that would topple Castro. Lucien Vandenbroucke, however, faulted Dulles and his colleagues for lack of candid advice, and for harboring expectation that once engaged the U.S. would not allow the campaign to fail. Bissell in a rejoinder admitted failure of assumptions but not conspiracy to deceive. See Vandenbroucke, "The 'Confessions' of Allen Dulles: New Evidence on the Bay of Pigs," *Diplomatic History*, Fall 84, 367; Bissell, "Response to Lucien S. Vandenbroucke," ibid, 380.
26. Taylor Report, *FRUS 1961-63*, X:583.
27. JCSM-166-61 Lemnitzer for SecDef, 15 Mar 61, ibid, 149-50, 154 (quote, 150).

28. McNamara interv, 22 May 86, 26; Robert S. McNamara, *In Retrospect: The Tragedy and Lessons of Vietnam*, 26; ed note, *FRUS 1961-63*, X:65. McNamara's self-denigration seemed "too much" for Henry Glass; see Glass interv, 4 Nov 87, 33.
29. Nitze interv, 3 Oct 84, 46-47.
30. Psychologist Irving Janis in *Victims of Groupthink: A Psychological Study of Foreign-Policy Decisions and Fiascoes*, 42, cited the Bay of Pigs as a primary case study of the "groupthink" phenomenon. On Fulbright's dissent, see Schlesinger, *A Thousand Days*, 251-52; ed note, *FRUS 1961-63*, X:185.
31. Memo Bundy for Pres, 15 Mar 61, *FRUS 1961-63*, X:158; ed note, ibid, 185.
32. Neustadt and May, *Thinking in Time*, 141, 144-45; Bissell, "Response to Lucien S. Vandenbroucke," cited in n 25, 378 (quote); Bissell, *Reflections of a Cold War Warrior*, 178 (quote).
33. Schlesinger, *A Thousand Days*, 255; memo Schlesinger for Pres Kennedy, 5 Apr 61, *FRUS 1961-63*, X:189.
34. Goodwin, *Remembering America*, 175-76.
35. Gilpatric interv, 14 Nov 83, 22-23.
36. Memo US Army, Navy, AF attachés to Cuba for Hartel, DirWestHemisAffs(ISA), 3 Mar 61, fldr Cuba 1961, box 31, ISA files, Acc 64A-2382.
37. Memo Clyde W. Elliott, DepAsst to SecDef (SpecOps), for Hartel, 21 Mar 61, OSD Hist.
38. Taylor Report, *FRUS 1961-63*, X:585; ed note on first meeting of the Interagency Working Group to coordinate planning for the Zapata Operation on 22 Mar 61, ibid, 167.
39. NSAM 31, 11 Mar 61, ibid, 144.
40. Memo Wayne S. Smith, RegPolAffs(State Bur of Inter-American Affs), for DASD(ISA) Haydn Williams, 21 Mar 61, fldr Cuba 1961, box 31, ISA files, Acc 64A-2382; memo Hartel for Smith, 24 Mar 61, ibid; ed note, *FRUS 1961-63*, X:184.
41. Poole, *JCS and National Policy 1961-64*, pt II:20-21; ed notes, *FRUS 1961-63*, X:185, 159-60.
42. *Kennedy Public Papers, 1961*, 258; Aleksandr Fursenko and Timothy Naftali, *"One Hell of a Gamble": Khrushchev, Castro, and Kennedy, 1958-1964*, 91-92, suggests that Khrushchev believed that his warnings had deterred American military action against Cuba.
43. Taylor Report, *FRUS 1961-63*, X:586-87.
44. Ibid, 586-91; Higgins, *The Perfect Failure*, 130-33.
45. Higgins, *The Perfect Failure*, 132-33. Despite Cuban claims that their security forces had infiltrated the Cuban emigré community, Castro privately lamented to Khrushchev that he knew too little about counter-revolutionary activities, and felt that before the Bay of Pigs invasion the KGB had not provided the intelligence cooperation he had wanted. See Fursenko and Naftali, *"One Hell of a Gamble,"* 97.
46. Taylor Report, *FRUS 1961-63*, X:588-89. For subsequent accounts of events on the scene at the time of the landing, see Grayston L. Lynch, *Decision for Disaster: Betrayal at the Bay of Pigs*; Albert E. Persons, *Bay of Pigs: A Firsthand Account of the Mission by a U.S. Pilot in Support of the Cuban Invasion Force in 1961*; Jack Hawkins, "An Obsession with 'Plausible Deniability' Doomed the 1961 Bay of Pigs Invasion from the Outset," *Military History*, Aug 98.
47. Memrcd, Taylor Report, 3 May 61, *FRUS 1961-63*, X:440.
48. Lemnitzer interv, 19 Jan 84, 22.
49. Murphy, "Cuba: The Record Set Straight," *Fortune*, Sep 61, 94.
50. Hilsman, *To Move a Nation*, 33; Neustadt and May, *Thinking in Time*, 144.
51. Taylor Report, *FRUS 1961-63*, X:596-99.
52. Memrcd, 22 Apr 61, ibid, 318; Taylor, *Swords and Plowshares*, 180.
53. Taylor, *Swords and Plowshares*, 184-85; Taylor Report, *FRUS 1961-63*, X:605.
54. Taylor Report, *FRUS 1961-63*, X:600, 602 (quote), 595 and n 16 (quotes).
55. Lemnitzer's handwritten notes, "Comments to Congressional Leaders," White House, 19 Apr 61, fldr L-214-71, box 29, Lemnitzer Papers, NDUL.
56. Taylor Report, *FRUS 1961-63*, X:583-84; Poole, *JCS and National Policy 1961-64*, pt II:42-43.
57. Luis Aguilar, ed, *Operation Zapata: The "Ultrasensitive" Report and Testimony of the Board of Inquiry on the Bay of Pigs*, 44-45.
58. Taylor, *Swords and Plowshares*, 191-92, 201-03; ed note, *FRUS 1961-63*, VIII:229-30.
59. Aguilar, *Operation Zapata*, 51-52.
60. Taylor Report, *FRUS 1961-63*, X:606.

61. Pres news conf, 21 Apr 61, *Kennedy Public Papers, 1961*, 312; Schlesinger, *A Thousand Days*, 289-90.
62. Higgins, *The Perfect Failure*, 161.
63. McNamara interv, 22 May 86, 23.
64. See Goodwin, *Remembering America*, 125-26; Schlesinger, *A Thousand Days*, 72-73.
65. SCFR, *Executive Sessions* (Hist Series), XIII:pt 1, 19 May 61, 572-73; L. James Binder, *Lemnitzer: A Soldier for His Time*, 257.
66. Decker interv, 18 Dec 72, III:3, 12.
67. Interv Burke by Maurice Matloff, 9 Nov 83, 56-58, OSD Hist.
68. Memo McNamara for Pres, 30 Aug 61, fldr Reading File, Dec. 1960-Nov. 1961, box 113, McNamara Records, RG 200; *New York Times*, 27 May 61; also see Lawrence S. Kaplan and Kathleen A. Kellner, "Lemnitzer: Surviving the French Military Withdrawal," in Robert S. Jordan, ed, *Generals in International Politics: NATO's Supreme Allied Commander, Europe*, 95-96.
69. Lemnitzer interv, 19 Jan 84, 18.
70. *U.S. News & World Report*, 29 May 61; SCFR, *Exec Sess*, 19 May 61, cited in n 65, 574.
71. Murphy, "Cuba: The Record Set Straight," 224, 226; memo McNamara for Pres, 30 Aug 61, cited in n 68.
72. *Time*, 1 Sep 61, 14-15; *Kennedy Public Papers, 1961*, 580; memrcd Col Julian J. Ewell, USA, ExecAsst to Taylor, 14 Sep 61, Taylor Papers, NDUL.
73. Ltr Pres to Luce, 12 Sep 61, Taylor Papers, NDUL.
74. Kirkpatrick, "Paramilitary Case Study: The Bay of Pigs," 39; Michael Warner, "The CIA's Internal Probe of the Bay of Pigs Affair," *Studies in Intelligence*, Winter 98-99, 93-101; *Washington Post*, 23 Feb 98. Robert Pear, "The Pointing of Fingers and the Bay of Pigs," *New York Times*, 30 Dec 87, stated that CIA historian Jack Pfeiffer differed significantly from Kirkpatrick in claiming that the CIA was unfairly burdened with too much of the blame.
75. Schlesinger, *A Thousand Days*, 297; Murphy, "Grenada and the Bay of Pigs," 7; Tad Szulc, "Kennedy's Cold War," *New Republic*, 22 Dec 77; Richard E. Welch, Jr., *Response to Revolution: The United States and the Cuban Revolution, 1959-1961*, 185-93.
76. Taylor, *Swords and Plowshares*, 196-97.
77. NSAM 57, 28 Jun 61, *FRUS 1961-63*, VIII:112-13.
78. Memo McNamara for CJCS, 20 Apr 61, ibid, X:306-07; JCSM-278-61 Wheeler for SecDef, 26 Apr 61, ibid, 373.
79. Memo McNamara for JCS, 1 May 61, ibid, 405-06.
80. Memo McNamara for CJCS, 20 Apr 61, cited in n 78; memo McNamara for ASD(ISA), 22 Apr 61, fldr Cuba 092 1961, box 44, ISA files, Acc 64A-2382; rcd of actions 478th NSC mtg, 22 Apr 61, *FRUS 1961-63*, X:316, n 1.
81. Memo Rostow for Pres, 21 Apr 61, *FRUS 1961-63*, X:310-12. In responding to Rostow's paper Nitze approved the emphasis on building the internal capabilities of Latin American countries, developing contingency plans, and above all the warning "to think again before acting in the old grooves." He believed, however, that public statements telling the world about our approach to the Cuban problem were of "doubtful merit" (memo Nitze for SecDef, 26 Apr 61, fldr 11/60-6/61, box 65, Staff Memoranda—Walt W. Rostow, POF, JFKL).
82. JCSM 414-61 Burke for SecDef, 16 Jun 61, *FRUS 1961-63*, X:606-08; Poole, *JCS and National Policy 1961-64*, pt II:54-55.
83. Rcd of actions 483d NSC mtg, 5 May 61, *FRUS 1961-63*, X:481-83.
84. Memo Bundy for Pres, 5 May 61, ibid, 477; rcd of actions 483d NSC mtg, ibid, 482 (quote); memo McNamara for Yarmolinsky, 5 May 61, ibid, 489; paper for NSC by Interagency Task Force, 4 May 61, ibid, 468-72 (quote, 468).

IX. THE CUBAN MISSILE CRISIS

1. Research into the genesis of the missile crisis benefited from Soviet Premier Mikhail Gorbachev's introduction of *glasnost* in the mid-1980s, which opened opportunities for Soviet and American veterans of the episode not only to enrich their reminiscences, as the Americans did at the Hawk's Cay conference in the Florida Keys in 1987, but also to meet together in Cambridge, Massachusetts, in 1987 and subsequently in Moscow (1989), Antigua (1991), and Havana (1992) to share insights. The resulting literature includes the following: J. Anthony Lukas, "Class Reunion: Kennedy's Men Relive the Cuban Missile Crisis," *New

York Times Magazine, 30 Aug 87, 27 ff; Mark Kramer, "Tactical Nuclear Weapons, Soviet Command Authority, and the Cuban Missile Crisis," Cold War International History *Bulletin*, Fall 93, 40, 45n; John Newhouse, "A Reporter at Large: Socialism or Death," *New Yorker*, Apr 92, 70-77; Raymond L. Garthoff, "The Cuban Missile Crisis: An Overview," in James A. Nathan, ed, *The Cuban Crisis Revisited*, 49-50; James G. Blight et al, "Kramer vs. Kramer," Cold War International History *Bulletin*, Fall 93, 41, 47.

2. Lukas, "Class Reunion," 27; Binder, *Lemnitzer*, 287-88.
3. Senate, Select Cte to Study Govt Opns with Respect to Intell Activities, *Alleged Assassination Plots Involving Foreign Leaders*, Interim Report, S Rpt 94-465, 94 Cong, 1 sess, 20 Nov 75, 141.
4. J2DM-181-61, DepDirIntelJCS RearAdm W. S. Post, Jr., for ASD(ISA), 24 May 61, w/encl, "Assessment of Dr. Ruben de Leon Garcia," fldr Cuba 000.1-092, box 31, ISA files, Acc 64A-2382; memcon DirPolPlngStaff(ISA) Maurice J. Mountain, 22 May 61, ibid; memrcd Asst to SecDef (Spec Ops) Gen Graves B. Erskine, 26 Apr 61, ibid.
5. Memo McNamara for SpecAsst (Yarmolinsky), 5 May 61, *FRUS 1961-63*, X:489; memo Yarmolinsky for SvcSecs et al, 26 May 61, with proposed plan, fldr Cuba 092 Jan 62, box 44, ISA files, Acc 64A-2382.
6. Memo AsstGenCoun Benjamin Forman for Nitze, 4 May 61, fldr Cuba 373.5-1961, box 31, ISA files, Acc 64A-2382; memo USecA Stephen Ailes for ASD(ISA), 1 Jun 61, ibid.
7. Memo McNamara for JCS et al, 10 Jul 61, *FRUS 1961-63*, X:572, n 3; NSAM 54, 26 Jun 61, ibid, 614.
8. Memo Army SpecAsst for Pers Roy K. Davenport for Yarmolinsky, 13 Apr 62, fldr Cuban Volunteers, Cuba Sensitive files, Acc 71A-2896.
9. Ltr Gilpatric to Cardona, 28 Aug 62, ASD(C) files, OSD Hist; DoD News Release 1560-62, 24 Sep 62, OSD Hist.
10. Memo Pres for SecDef, 7 Sep 62, *FRUS 1961-63*, X:1049-50; memo SecDef for Pres, 13 Sep 62, ibid, 1060-62.
11. Memo Pres for SecState, SecDef et al, 30 Nov 61, ibid, X:688; ed note, ibid, 666-67; Schlesinger, *Robert Kennedy*, 477-78.
12. Schlesinger, *Robert Kennedy*, 481-84, 493.
13. Ibid, 472, 481-85, 489 (quote); Thomas Powers, *The Man Who Kept the Secrets: Richard Helms & the CIA*, 141.
14. *Alleged Assassination Plots*, cited in n 3, 141, 146-47; Program Review by Chief of Operations, Operation Mongoose (Lansdale), 18 Jan 62, *FRUS 1961-63*, X:710 ff; memo CIA Off of Current Intel, 3 Jul 62, ibid, 835 ff.
15. *American Foreign Policy: Current Documents, 1962*, 326; msg 1080 EmbCaracas to State, 18 May 61, msg 608 EmbSantiago to State, 20 May 61: OSD Hist; memo CIA Board of Estimates for DCI, 3 Nov 61, *FRUS 1961-63*, X:668-72.
16. Memo McCone on mtg of Special Group, Augmented, 16 Aug 62, *FRUS 1961-63*, X:940-41.
17. Memo DepDir Off of Caribbean & Mexican Affs (Hurtwitch) for ASecState(Inter-AmericanAffs) (Martin), 26 Jul 62, ibid, 885.
18. Memo MSC [Carter] for Dir [CIA], 25 Oct 62, in Mary S. McAuliffe, ed, *CIA Documents on the Cuban Missile Crisis, 1962*, 311-12.
19. Memo DirISA Coordinating Staff (NSC & Collateral Activities) Robert H. B. Wade for BrigGen W. A. Enemark, 28 Sep 61, fldr Cuba 092 1961, box 31, ISA files, Acc 64A-2382.
20. Note William Bundy to Haydn Williams, 24 Nov 61, ibid; memrcd Enemark, 30 Nov 61, ibid.
21. Weapon Systems Evaluation Group, "Historical Analysis of Command and Control Actions in the 1962 Cuban Crisis," 14 Aug 64 (hereafter WSEG Cuba study), 45-47, OSD Hist.
22. Ibid, 46-47; memo SecDef for JCS, 1 May 61, *FRUS 1961-63*, X:405-06; memo Burke for Wheeler, 29 April 61, ibid, 404.
23. WSEG Cuba study, 51-55.
24. Ibid, 56, 59, 61, 70.
25. Ibid, 76-77.
26. Sorensen, *Kennedy*, 667-71; Neustadt and May, *Thinking in Time*, 3.
27. Msg 1205 State to EmbLondon, 30 Aug 62, *FRUS 1961-63*, X:969-71.
28. NSAM 181, 23 Aug 62, ibid, 957-58.
29. Memo Gilpatric for Pres, 1 Sep 62, w/atchmt memo ViceDirJCS MajGen John M. Reynolds for SecDef, 1 Sep 62, *FRUS 1961-63*, X:1010-13.

30. Msg R122322Z CINCLANT to JCS, 12 Sep 62, OSD Hist; Hilsman, *To Move a Nation*, 174-75, 184-86.
31. Memo BrigGen L. A. Hall for DASD(ISA), 5 Oct 62, fldr Cuba Oct 1-7, 1962, box 440, Subject files, OSD Hist.
32. DIA, "Chronology re September 18 Report and Formulation of Hypothesis Concerning Location of MRBM Site," atchmt to memo DirDIA LtGen Joseph F. Carroll for SecDef, 18 Feb 63, fldr Cuba Sep 1962, ibid; SNIE 85-3-62, 19 Sep 62, *FRUS 1961-63*, X:1075.
33. McAuliffe, *CIA Documents on the Cuban Missile Crisis*, 91, and McAuliffe's unofficial comments in "Return to the Brink: Intelligence Perspectives on the Cuban Missile Crisis," SHAFR *Newsletter*, Jun 93, 4-5, which pointed out the extent of the uncertainties behind the CIA's identification of Soviet missiles in Cuba. Sherman Kent, chairman of CIA's Board of National Estimates in 1962, reflected in the spring of 1964 why Special NIE 85-3-62 missed the Soviet deployment of offensive missiles in Cuba in September 1962. He blamed in part the "incredible wrongness of the Soviet decision" as well as the limitations of intelligence analysis; see "A Crucial Estimate Relived," Donald P. Steury, ed, *Sherman Kent and the Board of National Estimates: Collected Essays*, 187.
34. Bundy, *Danger and Survival*, 395, 684; ed notes, 14 Oct 62, *FRUS 1961-63*, XI:29-30; statement issued by the Soviet Union, 11 Sep 62, *American Foreign Policy: Current Documents, 1962*, 370-72.
35. Memo Pres for McNamara, 21 Sep 62, *FRUS 1961-63*, X:1081.
36. Memo Pres for McNamara, 7 Sep 62, ibid, 1049-50; JCSM-713-62 ActgCJCS for SecDef, 12 Sep 62, fldr Cuba 12 Sep 1962, box 444, Subject files, OSD Hist; memo McNamara for Yarmolinsky, 3 Oct 62, fldr Cuba Reconnaissance Photos, Oct. 1962, box 55, McNamara Records, RG 200.
37. Memo McNamara for CJCS (Taylor), 2 Oct 62, *FRUS 1961-63*, XI:6-7.
38. WSEG Cuba study, 68-74.
39. Memo McGeorge Bundy for Gilpatric, 2 Oct 62, fldr Cuba Oct 1-7, 1962, box 440, Subject files, OSD Hist.
40. *Facts on File Yearbook, 1962*, 292; Thomas G. Paterson, "The Historian as Detective: Senator Keating, Missiles In Cuba, and His Mysterious Sources," *Diplomatic History*, Winter 87, 11, 67; Marcus D. Pohlmann, "Constraining Presidents at the Brink: The Cuban Missile Crisis," *Presidential Studies Quarterly*, Spring 89, 339; James Reston, *New York Times*, 12 Oct 62.
41. Dino A. Brugioni, *Eyeball to Eyeball: The Inside Story of the Cuban Missile Crisis*, 206-07; Fursenko and Naftali, "*One Hell of a Gamble*," 221.
42. Ed note, *FRUS 1961-63*, XI:29-30; Bundy, *Danger and Survival*, 395-96, 684-85; Graham T. Allison, *Essence of Decision: Explaining the Cuban Missile Crisis*, 193.
43. Bundy, *Danger and Survival*, 396; NSAM 196, 22 Oct 62, *FRUS 1961-63*, XI:157.
44. NSAM 196, 22 Oct 62, cited in n 43, 157; Sorensen, *Kennedy*, 678-79; Taylor, *Swords and Plowshares*, 266.
45. Taylor, *Swords and Plowshares*, 265-67; off the record mtg on Cuba, 16 Oct 62, *FRUS 1961-63*, XI:55-57, 69. See also May et al, *Presidential Recordings*, 2:435-36.
46. Schlesinger, *Robert Kennedy*, 506-07, has noted that the terms "hawks" and "doves" originated in the missile crisis and were popularized in articles by journalists Charles Bartlett and Stewart Alsop. James Blight et al, "The Cuban Missile Crisis Revisited," *Foreign Affairs*, Fall 87, 173-74, prefer to place McNamara, Bundy, and George Ball among the "owls" (or "persuaders"), a more flexible group between the "invaders" and "traders."
47. McNamara interv, 24 Jul 86, 1; May et al, *Presidential Recordings*, 2:440.
48. Msg JCS 6832 SecJCS M. J. Ingelido to CINCSAC, 21 Oct 62, OSD Hist, authorized CINCLANT "to move alert aircraft from Homestead AFB on 22 October 62 at your discretion. The Secretary of Defense has authorized flying of nuclear weapons in connection with this movement." See also Poole, *JCS and National Policy 1961-64*, pt II:241-43; Taylor, *Swords and Plowshares*, 272-73; memcon Kennedy and Gromyko, 18 Oct 62, *FRUS 1961-63*, XI:110-14.
49. Transc of White House mtg, 16 Oct 62, 11:50 a.m., *FRUS 1961-63*, XI:33-36.
50. "Chronology of JCS Decisions Concerning the Cuban Crisis," 4 Jan 63, entries for 16, 18 Oct 62, fldr JCS Chronology 1963, box 445, Subject files, OSD Hist; JSSC memo 185-62 MajGen J. S. Holtoner, MajGen David W. Gray, RAdm J. D. Wylie for CJCS, 17 Oct 62, fldr Cuba Oct 17, 1962, box 440, ibid.
51. "Chronology of JCS Decisions," cited in n 50, 16 Oct 62; Taylor, *Swords and Plowshares*, 267; rcd of mtg, State Dept, 19 Oct 62, *FRUS 1961-63*, XI:116, 118-20.
52. May et al, *Presidential Recordings*, 2:517-29, 557, 614.

53. Marc Trachtenberg, "White House Tapes and Minutes of the Cuban Missile Crisis: ExCom Meetings October 1962," *International Security*, Summer 85, 167; Schlesinger, *Robert Kennedy*, 507-08.
54. Neustadt and May, *Thinking in Time*, 6.
55. Gilpatric interv, 27 May 70, 51.
56. Quoted in Neustadt and May, *Thinking in Time*, 6; May et al, *Presidential Recordings*, 2:416. McNamara claims that he was the first to propose a quarantine, on 16 October (McNamara interv, 8 Jan 98, 3). The first mention of the blockade by Taylor, at the 16 October morning meeting at the White House, is in *FRUS 1961-63*, XI:35.
57. Nitze interv, 3 Oct 84.
58. HSCA, *DoD Appropriations for 1964*, 6 Feb 63, pt 1:31; Bundy, *Danger and Survival*, 448; *McNamara Public Statements, 1964*, IV:1616-17.
59. Neustadt and May, *Thinking in Time*, 10-11; Allison, *Essence of Decision*, 124 ff; rcd of mtg, State Dept, 19 Oct 62, cited in n 51, 116-22.
60. *Kennedy Public Papers, 1962*, 806-08.
61. Proclamation 3504: Interdiction of Offensive Weapons to Cuba, 23 Oct 62, ibid, 809-11; McCone memo for files, 23 Oct 62, *FRUS 1961-63*, XI:173.
62. Gilpatric paper, 20 Oct 62, fldr Cuba Oct 20, 1962, box 440, Subject files, OSD Hist.
63. Elie Abel, *The Missile Crisis*, 112, 126-31.
64. "Chronology of JCS Decisions," cited in n 50, 23, 24 Oct 62.
65. CIA memo, 25 Oct 62, in McAuliffe, *CIA Documents on the Cuban Missile Crisis, 1962*, 304; Abel, *The Missile Crisis*, 159.
66. "Chronology of JCS Decisions," 25, 27 Oct 62.
67. Allison, *Essence of Decision*, 209-10.
68. Msg JCS 6848 to CINCLANT, 22 Oct 62, 3, memo McNaughton for SecDef, 22 Oct 62: fldr Cuba Oct 22, 1962, box 440, Subject files, OSD Hist. Note the justification of a quarantine by Abram Chayes, legal adviser to the secretary of state, in *The Cuban Missile Crisis: International Crises and the Role of Law*, 66-68.
69. JCSM-328-62 CJCS for SecDef, 26 Oct 62, fldr Cuba Quarantine, box 443, Subject files, OSD Hist.
70. Ibid; memo Rusk for Pres, 10 Nov 62, fldr Cuba Nov 10, 1962, box 441, ibid; paper for CJCS mtg with Pres, 16 Nov 62, *FRUS 1961-63*, XI:474-76.
71. Memo Nitze for CJCS, 25 Oct 62, fldr Cuba Oct 25, 1962, box 440, Subject files, OSD Hist.
72. JCSM-835-62 Taylor for SecDef, 28 Oct 62, fldr Cuba Collection for Security Review, box 444, ibid.
73. McNamara's Law states: "It is impossible to predict with a high degree of confidence what the effects of the use of military force will be because of the risks of accident, miscalculation, misperception, and inadvertence." See Blight et al, "The Cuban Missile Crisis Revisited," 186; McNamara interv, 24 Jul 86, 6.
74. McNamara interv, 24 Jul 86, 5-7.
75. In Anderson's version of the conversation, he claimed to have said in a jocular manner: "Why don't you go back to your quarters and let us handle this?" (interv Anderson by Walter Poole, 7 Nov 78, cited in Poole, *JCS and National Policy 1961-64*, pt II:288, n 78). To Maurice Matloff and Roger Trask, Anderson admitted saying, "Mr. Secretary, if you'll go back to your office, we'll go ahead with our job and run the show as it should be run," but claimed that it was McNamara who introduced John Paul Jones into the exchange (interv 31 May 84, 6, OSD Hist). Gilpatric's recollection was closer to McNamara's version; see Gilpatric interv, 27 May 70, 60-61.
76. Testimony of former participants in the Cuban missile crisis at conferences in Cambridge, Mass., October 1987, and Moscow, January 1989, suggests that the shooting down of the U-2 was an unauthorized act by Soviet generals on the ground. Khrushchev blamed the Cubans directly in Talbott, *Khrushchev Remembers*, 498-99; Kennedy statement in sum rcd 10th ExCom mtg, 28 Oct 62, recounted in Neustadt and May, *Thinking in Time*, 13.
77. Ernest R. May and Philip D. Zelikow, eds, *The Kennedy Tapes: Inside the White House During the Cuban Missile Crisis*, 693.
78. Anatoli I. Gribkov and William Y. Smith, *Operation ANADYR: U.S. and Soviet Generals Recount the Cuban Missile Crisis*, 141-42.
79. *FRUS, 1961-63*, XI:233-41, 257-60.
80. Ibid, 279-83; Robert F. Kennedy, *Thirteen Days: A Memoir of the Cuban Missile Crisis*, 15; Schlesinger, *Robert Kennedy*, 520.

81. Dean Acheson, "Robert Kennedy's Version of the Cuban Missile Affair," *Esquire*, Feb 69.
82. JCSM-844-62 JCS for Pres through SecDef, 28 Oct 62, fldr Cuba Oct 28, 1962, box 444, Subject files, OSD Hist.
83. Sum rcd 7th ExCom mtg, 27 Oct 62, 10:00 a.m., *FRUS 1961-63*, XI:252; sum rcd 10th ExCom mtg, 28 Oct 62, 11:10 a.m., ibid, 284; *Kennedy Public Papers, 1962*, 815.
84. According to Bundy, Rusk's remark, "We are eyeball to eyeball, and I think the other fellow just blinked," may have had its origins in a boyhood game from his Georgia childhood (Bundy, *Danger and Survival*, 405).
85. Sum rcd 10th ExCom mtg, 28 Oct 62, cited in n 83, 283-85.
86. Talbott, *Khrushchev Remembers*, 500; SCFR, *Executive Sessions* (Historical Series), XV, 88 Cong, 1 sess, 11 Jan 63, 16.
87. SCFR, *Exec Sess*, cited in n 86, 15-16; memo Nitze for SpecAsst to Pres, 6 Nov 62, w/atchmt memo McNamara for Nitze, 6 Nov 62, OSD Hist.
88. Poole, *JCS and National Policy 1961-64*, pt II:325.
89. McNamara special briefing on Cuba, 6 Feb 63, *McNamara Public Statements, 1963*, II:968-69.
90. Nitze commentaries in Col Dean notebook on ExCom mtgs of 5-8 Nov 62, Nitze final draft memo, 7 Nov 62: fldr Cuba Nov 9, 1962, box 441, Subject files, OSD Hist; Nitze, *From Hiroshima to Glasnost*, 236.
91. Msg 1189 State to USUN, 3 Nov 62, *FRUS 1961-63*, XI:363-65; memo McNaughton for Nitze, 9 Nov 62, fldr Cuba Nov 9, 1962, box 441, Subject files, OSD Hist.
92. Ltr Pres to Khrushchev, 6 Nov 62, *FRUS 1961-63*, XI:397-400; Nitze final draft memo, cited in n 90.
93. Sum rcd 24th ExCom mtg, 12 Nov 62, *FRUS 1961-63*, XI:432.
94. *Kennedy Public Papers, 1962*, 831; memo for NSC ExCom, 8 Nov 62, memrcd Capt Elmo Zumwalt, 8 Nov 62: fldr Cuba Nov 8, 1962, box 441, Subject files, OSD Hist.
95. Memo Ball for Pres, *FRUS 1961-63*, XI:424-26; memo Nitze for SecDef, 12 Nov 62, 4, fldr Cuba Quarantine, box 443, Subject files, OSD Hist.
96. Msg Khrushchev to Pres, 12 Nov 62, *FRUS 1961-63*, XI:437-41 (quote, 440); ed note, ibid, 443.
97. Sum rcd 25th ExCom mtg, 12 Nov 62, ibid, 441-42; memo Nitze for ExCom, 15 Nov 62 (quote, 3), fldr Cuba untitled, box 445, Subject files, OSD Hist.
98. Ltr Khrushchev to Pres, 14 Nov 62, *FRUS 1961-63*, XI:451-54; ltr (excerpts) Castro to U Thant, 15 Nov 62, *American Foreign Policy: Current Documents, 1962*, 459-60.
99. Msg Pres to Khrushchev, 15 Nov 62, *FRUS 1961-63*, XI:460-62; memo Bundy for ExCom, 16 Nov 62, ibid, 467-68.
100. Memo Hilsman for SecState, 16 Nov 62, OSD Hist; rcd of ExCom mtg, 17 Nov 62, *FRUS 1961-63*, XI:480-81.
101. Msg Khrushchev to Pres, 20 Nov 62, *FRUS 1961-63*, XI:496; *Kennedy Public Papers, 1962*, 830.
102. Sum rcd 26th ExCom mtg, 16 Nov 62, *FRUS 1961-63*, XI:470.
103. Memo JCSM-955-62 Taylor for McNamara, 28 Nov 62, ibid, 538.
104. HCAS, *Hearings on Military Posture*, 88 Cong, 1 sess, 30 Jan 63, 237.
105. *Kennedy Public Papers, 1963*, 151.
106. Msg Khrushchev to Pres, nd [c 28 Sep 62], *FRUS 1961-63*, XV:337-38; memcon Akalovsky, 18 Oct 62, ibid, 371-72.
107. May et al, *Presidential Recordings*, 2:582.
108. Memo McCone for file, 19 Oct 62, *FRUS 1961-63*, XI:108-09.
109. SNIE 11-18-62, 19 Oct 62, ibid, 123; ISA paper, "Cuba and Berlin—Some Hypothetical Questions," 20 Oct 62, 2-3, OSD Hist.
110. "Cuba and Berlin," 2, 5, 6 (emphasis in original).
111. Memo Bundy, 19 Oct 62, sub: The Defense of Berlin if Cuba is Blockaded, OSD Hist.
112. Rcd of mtg No. 1 of Berlin-NATO Subcte, 24 Oct 62, *FRUS 1961-63*, XV:396.
113. Memo ns [Nitze] for Pres, 27 Oct 62, ibid, 401-02.
114. Memo William R. Tyler for SecState, 28 Oct 62, OSD Hist.
115. ISA draft paper, "Re-Examination of Berlin Negotiating Positions," 29 Oct 62, ibid.
116. See James M. Grimwood and Frances Strowd, "History of the Jupiter Missile System," U.S. Army Ordnance Missile Command, 27 Jul 62, cited in Raymond L. Garthoff, *Reflections on the Cuban Missile Crisis*, rev ed, 12; transc of White House mtg, 16 Oct 62, cited in n 49, 37.

117. Neustadt and May, *Thinking in Time*, 12; William Bundy paper, "Generalized Negotiation of Bases as a Possible Face-Saver to the Soviets for Withdrawal of Missiles from Cuba," 21 Oct 62, 1, OSD Hist.
118. Burlatsky comments at Wilson Center Kennan Institute, 9 Sep 88, in "Comparisons Between Khrushchev and Kennedy," mtg rpt, OSD Hist.
119. Off the record mtg on Cuba, 16 Oct 62, cited in n 45, 72; sum rcd 7th ExCom mtg, 27 Oct 62, cited in n 83, 253, 255.
120. Memo (ns) ISA, passed on to Nitze, 21 Oct 62, "The Implications of Withdrawal of Our Ballistic Missiles From Turkey," fldr R&R Unit, Cuban Missile Crisis, Nitze Black Book II, box 2, Cuba Sensitive files, Acc 71A-2896. See also msg Polto 506 Paris to State, 25 Oct 62, *FRUS 1961-63*, XVI:730-33.
121. JCSM-800-62 ViceAdm Herbert D. Riley for SecDef, 21 Oct 62, fldr R&R Unit, Cuban Missile Crisis, box 3, Cuba Sensitive files, Acc 71A-2896; memo W. Houser, Off of DepSecDef, for Taylor, 21 Oct 62, w/atchmt 27 Oct 62, OSD Hist.
122. White House mtg, 22 Oct 62, 11:30 a.m., May et al, *Presidential Recordings*, 3:34, 35, n 29.
123. Lippmann, "Blockade Proclaimed," *Washington Post*, 25 Oct 62; transc White House mtg, 27 Oct 62, 4:00 p.m., in May and Zelikow, *Kennedy Tapes*, 593; ltr Khrushchev to Kennedy, 27 Oct 62, *FRUS 1961-63*, XI:257-60.
124. Sum rcd 7th ExCom mtg, 27 Oct 62, cited in n 83, 252-53; May et al, *Presidential Recordings*, 3:361; Nitze, *From Hiroshima to Glasnost*, 232-33. General Lemnitzer as SACEUR objected vigorously to the removal of Jupiter missiles from Turkey. He had been a prime mover in convincing the Turks "to become targets" and recalled how difficult the negotiations had been (Binder, *Lemnitzer*, 310).
125. May et al, *Presidential Recordings*, 3:428.
126. Taylor, *Swords and Plowshares*, 275-76; sum rcd 8th ExCom mtg, 27 Oct 62, *FRUS 1961-63*, XI:267; McNamara's observation in Lukas, "Class Reunion," 71.
127. Memo R. F. Kennedy for Rusk, 30 Oct 62, *FRUS 1961-63*, XII:270-71; Kennedy, *Thirteen Days*, 108-09; Bundy, *Danger and Survival*, 428-32; Nitze, *From Hiroshima to Glasnost*, 234; Kennedy and Khrushchev msgs, *FRUS 1961-63*, XI:268-69, 279-83.
128. Talbott, *Khrushchev Remembers*, 497-98.
129. Bundy, *Danger and Survival*, 438.
130. Msg 619 EmbAnkara to State, 13 Nov 62, *FRUS 1961-63*, XVI:738-39.
131. Ltr McNamara to Turkish DefMin Sancar, 5 Jan 63, ibid, 743-44; memo McNamara for CJCS, 18 Jan 63, box 55, McNamara Records, RG 200.
132. HSCA, *DoD Appropriations for 1964*, pt 1:57.
133. Interv Robert McNamara by James G. Blight, 21 May 87, 47-48, JFKL. A letter from Rusk to Blight in March 1987 claimed that on the evening of 27 October 1962 Kennedy had instructed Rusk to arrange through Andrew Cordier of Columbia University to have U Thant, UN Secretary General, propose the removal of both the Jupiters in Turkey and the missiles in Cuba when the White House gave him the signal. Only Cordier, Kennedy, and Rusk knew of this plan, which was never executed. See James G. Blight and David A. Welch, *On the Brink: Americans and Soviets Reexamine the Cuban Missile Crisis*, 83-84.
134. Memo Enemark for Sloan, 13 Dec 62, fldr Cuba Dec 11-31, 1962, box 442, Subject files, OSD Hist.
135. Memo McNamara for CJCS, 13 Mar 63, fldr Reading File, Mar. 63, box 117, McNamara Records, RG 200; memo McNamara for CJCS, 12 Sep 63, fldr Reading File, Sept. 1963, box 118, ibid.
136. Memo GenCounA Joseph A. Califano for U. Alexis Johnson, 14 Aug 63, fldr R&R Unit, Cuban Missile Crisis, Rules of Engagement, box 3, Cuba Sensitive files, Acc 71A-2896.
137. Ed note summarizing SNIE 85-2-63, "Reactions to U.S. Low-Level Overflights of Cuba," 21 Feb 63, *FRUS 1961-63*, XI:705-06.
138. Memo Cottrell for ExCom, 25 Jan 63, ibid, 678-81; ltr Rusk to Kennedy, 28 Mar 63, ibid, 738-39.
139. Memo Califano for Vance, 27 May 63, fldr R&R Unit, Cuban Missile Crisis, box 4, Cuba Sensitive files, Acc 71A-2896.
140. NSAM 213, 8 Jan 63, *FRUS 1961-63*, XI:656-57; memo Bundy for Pres, 4 Jan 63, ibid, 648-49; ltr McNamara to Rusk, 30 Jan 63, identifying the secretary of the Army as DoD representative and Yarmolinsky as a point of contact within OSD, fldr Reading File, Jan. 31-Jan. 18, 1963, box 116, McNamara Records, RG 200.
141. Memo Cottrell for ExCom, 24 Jan 63, *FRUS 1961-63*, XI:670-75; sum rcd 38th ExCom mtg, 25 Jan 63, 4:00 p.m., ibid, 687; memo Yarmolinsky for Gilpatric, 18 Apr 63, fldr R&R Unit, Cuban Missile Crisis, box 4, Cuba Sensitive files, Acc 71A-2896.

142. Memrcd Califano, 22 Feb 63, re mtg w/Pres 18 Feb 63, w/atchmt (quote, 4-5), fldr R&R Unit, Cuban Missile Crisis, box 4, Cuba Sensitive files, Acc 71A-2896; William Colby and Peter Forbath, *Honorable Men: My Life in the CIA*, 189-90.
143. Memrcd Taylor, mtg JCS w/Pres 28 Feb 63, *FRUS 1961-63*, XI:711-12; memo McNamara for CJCS, 24 Apr 63, w/atchmt DoD-State paper, fldr R&R Unit, Cuban Missile Crisis, box 4, Cuba Sensitive files, Acc 71A-2896.
144. Memo McNamara for Pres, 7 May 63, fldr Reading File, May 17-May 1, 1963, box 117, McNamara Records, RG 200; *FRUS 1961-63*, XI:802-03.
145. Memo Vance, 18 Feb 63, sub: Cuban Based Communist Subversion in Latin America, OSD Hist.
146. Memo Califano for John H. Crimmins, State Coordinator of Cuban Affairs, 20 May 64, fldr R&R Unit, Cuban Missile Crisis, Project 5A, box 3, Cuba Sensitive files, 71A-2896; CIA Off of Current Intel, no. 1586/64, 4 Jun 64, ibid.
147. Memo of mtg w/Pres, 19 Dec 63, *FRUS 1961-63*, XI:906; paper, "Guantanamo Water Crisis, February 6-21, 1964," NSC Histories, NSF, LBJL; *Johnson Public Papers, 1963-64*, I:271; DoD News Releases 123-64 and 126-64, 10 Feb 64, OSD Hist; WSEG paper, "The Panama Crisis of 1964," 24 Aug 64, OSD Hist; LtCol David W. Miller, SecJtStaff, US Southern Command, "After-Action Report of Panama Disorders, 9-16 January 1964," 13 Feb 64, fldr 092 Panama, box 37, ISA files, Acc 68A-0306; *Johnson Public Papers, 1963-64*, I:436-37.
148. Sum rcd 523d NSC mtg, 5 Mar 64, box 1, NSC Meetings File, NSF, LBJL; *American Foreign Policy: Current Documents, 1964*, 328-29; *McNamara Public Statements, 1965*, II:389.

X. LAOS

1. Memo McNamara for Pres, 24 Jan 61, *FRUS 1961-1963*, XXIV:41-42; Schlesinger, *A Thousand Days*, 163. The thought of going it alone was in Clark Clifford's memorandum on the meeting of 19 January between Eisenhower and Kennedy; see *Pentagon Papers*, bk 2, IV.B.1, 1-2. Fred I. Greenstein and Richard H. Immerman stress the Delphic nature of Eisenhower's advice to Kennedy in "What Did Eisenhower Tell Kennedy about Indochina? The Politics of Misperception," *Journal of American History*, Sep 92, 573-83.
2. Nitze, *From Hiroshima to Glasnost*, 182; Walt W. Rostow, *The Diffusion of Power: An Essay in Recent History*, 116; *Pentagon Papers*, bk 2, IV.B.1, 1-2.
3. Leighton, *Strategy, Money, and the New Look*, 540-41; Watson, *Into the Missile Age*, 640-41.
4. For background on Laos in the 1950s, see Arthur J. Dommen, *Conflict in Laos: The Politics of Neutralization*; Charles A. Stevenson, *The End of Nowhere: American Policy Toward Laos Since 1954*; Martin E. Goldstein, *American Policy Toward Laos*; Bernard Fall, *Anatomy of a Crisis: The Laotian Crisis of 1960-1961*.
5. Goldstein, *American Policy Toward Laos*, 167.
6. Stevenson, *End of Nowhere*, 123; msg 825 Phnom Penh to State, 10 Jan 61, OSD Hist.
7. Memcon w/Pres, BrigGen Andrew Goodpaster, 2 Jan 61, *FRUS 1961-63*, XXIV:1-4; *American Foreign Policy: Current Documents, 1960*, 686.
8. Memo Lemnitzer for SecDef, 14 Jan 61, fldr 092 Laos 1961, box 36, ISA files, Acc 64A-2382; Schlesinger, *A Thousand Days*, 164.
9. Memo McNamara for Pres, 24 Jan 61, cited in n 1; Schlesinger, *A Thousand Days*, 164.
10. Sorensen, *Kennedy*, 640.
11. Memo Nitze for SecDef, 23 Jan 61, w/atchmt, *FRUS 1961-63*, XXIV:26-40 (quote, 29).
12. Ibid (quotes, 26, 27); memo William Bundy for SecState and SecDef, 23 Jan 61, fldr 092 Laos 1961, box 36, ISA files, Acc 64A-2382; Poole, *JCS and National Policy 1961-64*, pt II:75-76.
13. Memcon w/Pres, Goodpaster, 25 Jan 61, 10:15 a.m., *FRUS 1961-63*, XXIV:42-44; Poole, *JCS and National Policy 1961-64*, pt II:79-80.
14. Poole, *JCS and National Policy 1961-64*, pt II:81.
15. Memo George C. McGhee, ChmPolPlngCouncil (State), for Nitze, 15 Feb 61, w/atchmt, fldr Vietnam 370.5-384, box 42, ISA files, Acc 64A-2382.
16. IDA, "Summary of Observations on the U.S. Command Experience in Laos, August 1960-May 1961," first draft, 17 Oct 63, 19, fldr Summary of Observations, First Draft, box 233, Subject files, OSD Hist.
17. Sum rcd mtg 8 Feb 61, *FRUS 1961-63*, XXIV:48-50; msg 022158Z CINCPAC to JCS, 2 Feb 61, OSD Hist.

18. Msg 1508 Bangkok to State, 25 Feb 61; msg 1697 Bangkok to State, 21 Mar 61:ibid.
19. See draft position paper, "Reinvigorating SEATO" (for SEATO Conf, Bangkok, 27-31 Mar 61), 14 Mar 61, fldr South East Asia Laos, box 5, NSC files, Acc 68A-4024; msg Secto 25 Rusk (Bangkok) to State, 28 Mar 61, OSD Hist; communiqué Seventh Ministerial Mtg of Council of SEATO, 30 Mar 61, *American Foreign Policy: Current Documents, 1961*, 940-41.
20. Memcon w/Mikhail Menshikov, 28 Feb 61, *FRUS 1961-63*, XXIV:63-66; circ msg 1265 State to Embs-Asia, 28 Feb 61, OSD Hist; msg 2139 Moscow to State, 10 Mar 61, *FRUS 1961-63*, XXIV:82, n 3; Hilsman, *To Move a Nation*, 130.
21. Circ msg 1323 State to Vientiane, Bangkok, Saigon, et al, 2 Mar 61; msg 1671 Vientiane to State, 11 Mar 61: OSD Hist.
22. Msg 990386 JCS to CINCPAC, 15 Feb 61, msg 990855 DirFE(ISA) L. C. Heinz to CINCPAC, 21 Feb 61: OSD Hist; ltr DASD(ISA) Haydn Williams to USecState for Econ Affs Ball, 6 Feb 61, fldr 320.2 Laos, box 36, ISA files, Acc 64A-2382; see ltr John O. Bell (State) to DASD(ISA) Bundy, 21 Feb 61, fldr 111-130 Laos 1961, ibid.
23. Ltr Williams to Ball, cited in n 22; memo BrigGen C. V. Clifton (White House Def Liaison Off) for SecDef, 28 Mar 61, fldr 092 Laos 1961, box 36, ISA files, Acc 64A-2382.
24. Memo McNamara for Clifton, 30 Mar 61, ibid.
25. Memo LtGen Earle G. Wheeler for SecDef, w/atchmt, 24 Feb 61, ibid; msg PEO 563 ChPEO Laos to CINCPAC, 6 Feb 61, msg PEO 827 ChPEO Laos to CINCPAC, 2 Mar 61: OSD Hist.
26. Ltr Charles E. Gentry, OASD(ISA)(FE), to ICA (Peter Cody), 5 Apr 61, fldr 111-130 Laos 1961, box 36, ISA files, Acc 64A-2382.
27. Memo Rostow for Pres, 28 Feb 61, *FRUS 1961-63*, XXIV:62-63; memo Rostow for Pres, 7 Mar 61, ibid, 71.
28. Memo Landon for Rostow, 7 Mar 61, box 130, NSF, JFKL.
29. Memo Col Thomas Wolfe for Nitze, 7 Mar 61, fldr 092 Laos 1961, box 36, ISA files, Acc 64A-2382.
30. Memo McGhee for SecState, 3 Mar 61, *FRUS 1961-63*, XXIV:68-69; memcon w/Pres (Clifton), 9 Mar 61, ibid, 72, n 1; Poole, *JCS and National Policy 1961-64*, pt II:85-87; IDA, "Historical Analysis of the Laos Incident, August 1960-May 1961, Part II," 1 Oct 63, 129-30, box 233, Subject files, OSD Hist.
31. Memcon DeptState mtg, 12 Mar 61, file 751J-00/3-1261, Central Files, RG 59. Part of this memo appears in *FRUS 1961-63*, XXIV:86-88.
32. Memo Rostow for Pres, 21 Mar 61, memrcd (William Bundy), 21 Mar 61: *FRUS 1961-63*, XXIV:94-96.
33. *Kennedy Public Papers, 1961*, 214; ed note, *FRUS 1961-63*, XXIV:100.
34. Bundy quoted in Montague Kern, Patricia Levering, and Ralph Levering, *The Kennedy Crises: The Press, the Presidency, and Foreign Policy*, 39; aide-memoire from UK to Soviet Union, 23 Mar 61, in *American Foreign Policy: Current Documents, 1961*, 994-95.
35. William Bundy, "History of Vietnam," ch 3, 5-10, William Bundy Papers, LBJL; circ msg 1241 State to EmbsAsia, 21 Mar 61, OSD Hist; memcon Key West, 26 Mar 61, file 751J-00/2-1261, Central Files, RG 59.
36. Memo Wolfe for Williams, 3 Apr 61, fldr 092 Laos 1961, box 36, ISA files, Acc 64A-2382.
37. Communiqué SEATO Council, 30 Mar 61, *American Foreign Policy: Current Documents, 1961*, 940-43.
38. Schlesinger, *A Thousand Days*, 335-36.
39. Memo Wolfe for Col William McCrea, ISA, 13 Mar 61, fldr 092 Laos 1961, box 36, ISA files, Acc 64A-2382.
40. Msg DEF 993225 ActgDirFE(ISA) William McCormick to CINCPAC, 1 Apr 61, fldr 380.1-400, ibid.
41. Memo George Carroll (PolPlngStaff, ISA) for DirPolPlngStaff BrigGen James H. Polk, 5 Apr 61, fldr 092 Laos 1961, ibid.
42. JCSM-222-61 Lemnitzer for SecDef, 11 Apr 61, ibid.
43. Memo Nitze for SecDef, 3 Apr 61, w/atchmt, ibid; memo Polk for ASD(ISA), 3 Apr 61, ibid.
44. Sum rpt of Laos Task Force mtg, 10 Apr 61, fldr Laos, Vol. II, box 130, NSF, JFKL; memo Landon for McGeorge Bundy, 11 Apr 61, ibid; JCSM-232-61 JCS for McNamara, 11 Apr 61, *FRUS 1961-63*, XXIV:121-23.
45. Memo McNamara for CJCS, 10 Mar 61, fldr Reading File, May 1961-Mar. 1961, box 113, McNamara Records, RG 200; memo JCS for SecDef, 11 Apr 61, cited in n 44; JCSM-206-61 JCS for McNamara, 31 Mar 61, w/copy of Trapnell Rpt, 28 Mar 61, fldr 092 Laos 1961, box 36, ISA files, Acc 64A-2382.

46. Ltr Williams to DASecState(FE) John M. Steeves, 14 Apr 61, fldr 092 Laos 1961, box 36, ISA files, Acc 64A-2382.
47. McNamara notes on 481st mtg NSC, 1 May 61, *FRUS 1961-63*, XXIV:162-64; memo David W. Quant (Manpower & Training Div, ODMA), 23 Jun 61, fldr 160-333 Laos 1961, box 36, ISA files, Acc 64A-2382. Quant noted that the PEO was replaced on 19 April by a MAAG established at the request of the Laotian government.
48. Dommen, *Conflict in Laos*, 196-97.
49. Sorensen, *Kennedy*, 644; Schlesinger, *Robert Kennedy*, 702.
50. Bundy, "History of Vietnam," ch 3, 27.
51. Msg 1985 Laos to State, 1 May 61, *FRUS 1961-63*, XXIV:165; Poole, *JCS and National Policy 1961-64*, pt II:98.
52. Schlesinger, *A Thousand Days*, 332-33; Poole, *JCS and National Policy 1961-64*, pt II:88-89; memcon State, 29 Apr 61, *FRUS 1961-63*, XXIV:150-54 (quote, 151).
53. McNamara notes on 481st mtg NSC, 1 May 61, OSD(A), Miscellaneous, Sensitive Files, fldr 381 Laos April-May 1961, Acc 71A-6489; see also n 47 *FRUS* citation for an abridged version.
54. Memo SecDef (McNamara) and DepSecDef (Gilpatric) for Pres, 2 May 61 (quote, 3), fldr Laos, Vol. II, box 130, NSF, JFKL (see also abridged version in *FRUS 1961-63*, XXIV:166-70); ed note, ibid, 169-70; memo SecState and SecDef for Pres, nd, sub: Plan for Possible Intervention in Laos, fldr Vietnam and Laos, box 4, McNamara files, Acc 71A-3470.
55. Msg 1651 Harriman to State, 3 May 61, *FRUS 1961-63*, XXIV:172, n 2; ed note, ibid, 170.
56. Stevenson, *End of Nowhere*, 152.
57. Msg 2012 Vientiane to State, 3 May 61, OSD Hist; msg 1207 State to Vientiane, 3 May 61, *FRUS 1961-63*, XXIV:171-72 (quote, 171); *American Foreign Policy: Current Documents, 1961*, 1000-02, 1004.
58. Gilpatric interv, 14 Nov 83, 30.
59. "Conference on Laos, Geneva, Switzerland, 10 May 61," paper by George A. Carroll, 31 Jul 61 (hereafter Carroll Rpt), fldr 092 Laos 1961, box 36, ISA files, Acc 64A-2382.
60. Ltr Williams to Steeves, 3 May 61, ibid; memo ASD(ISA) for Harriman, 9 May 61, ibid.
61. Carroll Rpt, 1.
62. Ibid, 2-3 (quote, 3); State Dept paper prepared for International Conference on Laos at Geneva, 3 May 61, *FRUS 1961-63*, XXIV:176-83.
63. Carroll Rpt, 5.
64. Ibid, 17.
65. Circ msg 1786 State to Canberra et al, 13 May 61, OSD Hist; Carroll Rpt, 18-19.
66. Msg Secto 146 Rusk (Geneva) to State, 15 May 61, *FRUS 1961-63*, XXIV:197-98; msg Secto 103 Rusk (Geneva) to State, 13 May 61, OSD Hist; msg Secto 118 Rusk (Geneva) to State, 14 May 61, *FRUS 1961-63*, XXIV:193-95 (quote, 194).
67. Harriman paper, nd, *FRUS 1961-63*, XXIV:224-25.
68. Fall, *Anatomy of a Crisis*, 225-26; memcon SovietEmbVienna, 4 Jun 61, *FRUS 1961-63*, XXIV:231-36 (quote, 232).
69. Fall, *Anatomy of a Crisis*, 226; Nitze interv, 3 Oct 84, 3; Carroll Rpt, 19-20. The question of how much control the Soviets had over their clients was recognized but not always appreciated (Schlesinger, *A Thousand Days*, 517).
70. Memo DASecState(FE)(EconAffs) (Avery F. Peterson) for DUSecState for Pol Affs (Johnson), 23 Jun 61, *FRUS 1961-63*, XXIV:256-57.
71. Msg 997728 ViceDirJtStaff RAdm Joseph Wellings to CINCPAC, 17 Jun 61, OSD Hist.
72. Msg 997143 Wellings to CINCPAC, 7 Jun 61, ibid; msg Confe 288 Geneva to State, 27 Jun 61, *FRUS 1961-63*, XXIV:264-66.
73. Msg 2332 Vientiane to State, 28 Jun 61, OSD Hist (summarized in *FRUS 1961-63*, XXIV:265, n 2).
74. Carroll Rpt, 21.
75. Ibid, 21-22; *FRUS 1961-63*, XXIV:273, n 1; msg Confe 287 Geneva to State, 26 Jun 61, ibid, 261-63.
76. Memo Nitze for SecDef, 29 Jun 61, *FRUS 1961-63*, XXIV:273-74.
77. Memo prepared by State for NSC, 28 Jun 61, ibid, 266-72; memcons, 29, 30 Jun 61, ibid, 276-82, 283-86.
78. Memo ASecState(FE) (McConaughy) for USecState (Bowles), 26 Jun 61, ibid, 263-64.
79. Memo WWR (Rostow) for Pres, 26 Jun 61, fldr Laos, Vol. II, box 130, NSF, JFKL.

80. Carroll Rpt, 23-26; memo Carroll for Henry S. Rowen (signd J. M. Lee), 8 Aug 61, fldr 092 Laos 1961, box 36, ISA files, Acc 64A-2382.
81. SCFR, *Executive Sessions* (Historical Series), XIII, 87 Cong, 1 sess, 1961, pt 2:115.
82. Msg 227 State to Belgrade, 30 Aug 61, *FRUS 1961-63*, XXIV:400-01; msg 274 State to Belgrade, 5 Sep 61, ibid, 402-03 (quotes from n 1 and n 2).
83. Ed note, ibid, 358-59.
84. Memrcds Taylor, 25, 30 Aug 61, ibid, 382-85.
85. Memcon [Robert Johnson], 29 Aug 61, ibid, 390-98 (quote 394); NSAM 80, 29 Aug 61, ibid, 399-400.
86. Poole, *JCS and National Policy 1961-64*, pt II:118-19.
87. Sorensen, *Kennedy*, 644.
88. Poole, *JCS and National Policy 1961-64*, pt II:120-21.
89. Ibid, 121-22.
90. Memo ExecSec(State) (Battle) for McGeorge Bundy, 11 Oct 61, *FRUS 1961-63*, XXIV:463-64; memo Heinz for William Bundy, 14 Nov 61, fldr 320.2 Laos 1961, box 36, ISA files, Acc 64A-2382.
91. Memo Williams for SecDef, 5 Oct 61, *FRUS 1961-63*, XXIV:446-49; JCSM-690-61 JCS for McNamara, 5 Oct 61, OSD Hist; memo Taylor for Pres, 26 Sep 61, *FRUS 1961-63*, XXIV:426-29 (quotes).
92. Ltr William Bundy to Johnson, 19 Oct 61, memo William T. McCormick for William Bundy, 16 Oct 61, memo William Leffingwell for William Bundy, 18 Oct 61: fldr 320.2 Laos 1961, box 36, ISA files, Acc 64A-2382.
93. Ltr Johnson to William Bundy, 18 Nov 61, ltr ActgRegDirFE(ICA) James R. Fowler to Heinz, 10 Oct 61: ibid.
94. Msg ChMAAG Laos to CINCPAC, 20 Dec 61, fldr 092 Laos 1961, box 45, ISA files, Acc 65A-3501.
95. Memcon Harriman and Winthrop G. Brown (AmbLaos), 18 Jan 62, ibid; Stevenson, *End of Nowhere*, 167-69.
96. Hilsman, *To Move a Nation*, 137; Stevenson, *End of Nowhere*, 169-70.
97. JCSM-110-62 Lemnitzer for SecDef, 14 Feb 62, fldr 350.5-680 Laos 1962, box 45, ISA files, Acc 65A-3501; SNIE 58-2-62, 11 Apr 62, fldr Special NIEs, box 16, ISA files, Acc 72A-1495; NSAM 149, 19 Apr 62, *FRUS 1961-63*, XXIV:695-96; Sen Doc 73, *A Report of United States Foreign Policy and Operations*, by Sen Allen J. Ellender, 1 Mar 62, 87 Cong, 2 sess, 147.
98. JCSM-376-62 Decker for SecDef, 11 May 62, *FRUS 1961-63*, XXIV:742-44.
99. Memo Hilsman for Harriman, 12 May 62, ibid, 748-54; memrcd Forrestal, 10 May 62, ibid, 734-35; memo Forrestal for Rusk, 24 May 62, ibid, 789; *DoD Annual Report, FY 1962*, 49.
100. Memo Johnson for Rusk, w/atchmts, 1 Jun 62, *FRUS 1961-63*, XXIV:801-09.
101. Memcon Taylor, DeptState [W. H. Sullivan], McNamara, Rusk, Harriman, et al, 2 Jun 62, ibid, 809-13; memo McNamara for Pres, 4 Jun 62, ibid, 815-16 (McNamara did not sign this memo, and apparently it did not go to the White House); memo McNamara for Lemnitzer, 5 Jun 62, ibid, 826-27; memcon DeptState [W. H. Sullivan], Rusk, Harriman, McNamara, Taylor, et al, 12 Jun 62, ibid, 842-44. Lemnitzer's private notes on the latter meeting record that occupation would be advisable only if there were reinforcements available in sufficient numbers to back it up (13 Jun 62, fldr L-204-71, box 29, Lemnitzer Papers, NDUL).
102. Memo Johnson for Rusk, 9 Jun 62, *FRUS 1961-63*, XXIV:832-37 (quote, 834).
103. Ibid, 837, n 1; Stevenson, *End of Nowhere*, 177.
104. Memo Brubeck for Pres [26 Jun 62], *FRUS 1961-63*, XXIV:851-52 (quote, 851); memo Ball for Pres, 28 Jun 62, ibid, 856-60.
105. Declaration and Protocol on the Neutrality of Laos, 23 Jul 62, *American Foreign Policy: Current Documents, 1962*, 1075-83 (quote, 1076); memo Bagley for Taylor, 19 Jul 62, *FRUS 1961-63*, XXIV:864-66; Stevenson, *End of Nowhere*, 178-79; William Colby, with James McCargar, *Lost Victory: A Firsthand Account of America's Sixteen-year Involvement in Vietnam*, 195.
106. Hilsman, *To Move a Nation*, 152. The formal disestablishment of the U.S. Military Assistance Command was 6 October, one day before the deadline; see *DoD Annual Report, FY 1963*, 115, and Colby, *Lost Victory*, 195.
107. JCSM-538-62 Lemnitzer for SecDef, 3 Aug 62, fldr 200-234 Laos 1962, box 45, ISA files, Acc 65A-3501; memo William Bundy for SecDef, 9 Aug 62, ibid.

108. *New York Times*, 23 Apr 63. Sorensen noted that in the spring of 1963 "it was once again necessary for Kennedy to alert the Seventh Fleet and to stage 'war games' in Thailand as a warning against a Communist takeover" (*Kennedy*, 648). See too Colby, *Lost Victory*, 197-98.
109. Msg 868 Laos to State, 10 Dec 64, *FRUS 1964-68*, XXVIII:306-07; *Washington Post*, 24 Dec 64.
110. Colby, *Lost Victory*, 198; Hilsman, *To Move a Nation*, 154-55.
111. Rostow, *Diffusion of Power*, 288-90 (quote, 290).
112. Quoted in Dommen, *Conflict in Laos*, 299.

XI. VIETNAM: RELUCTANT ENGAGEMENT, 1961-1963

1. For a detailed account of the Counterinsurgency Plan see Watson, *Into the Missile Age*, 646-49.
2. IDA, Working Paper No. 3, "The South Vietnam Crisis of 1961: Development of the First Presidential Program," 6 Feb 64, 10-13, OSD Hist; text of Basic CIP for Vietnam, 4 Jan 61, *FRUS 1961-63*, I:1-12.
3. Memo Lansdale for SecDef and DepSecDef, 17 Jan 61, *Pentagon Papers*, bk 11, 1-3.
4. Rostow, *Diffusion of Power*, 264; Bundy, "History of Vietnam," ch 3, 31.
5. Memo Rostow for McGeorge Bundy, 30 Jan 61, *FRUS 1961-63*, I:16-19 (quote, 16); memo Pres for SecState, SecDef, 30 Jan 61, fldr 000.1-091.3 Vietnam 1961, box 42, ISA files, Acc 64A-2382.
6. Memo Lansdale for SecDef and DepSecDef, 17 Jan 61, cited in n 3, 3-4.
7. Hilsman, *To Move a Nation*, 419; notes on mtg between SecState and ASecState(FE), 28 Jan 61, *FRUS 1961-63*, I:19.
8. Cecil B. Currey, *Edward Lansdale: The Unquiet American*, 1-2.
9. Ibid, 2.
10. Memo McGarr for US Amb, 24 Jan 61, fldr 370.5-384 Vietnam 1961, box 43, ISA files, Acc 64A-2382; ltr McGarr to LtGen Williston B. Palmer, 3 Mar 61, *FRUS 1961-63*, I:43-44; memo Lemnitzer for SecDef, 11 Apr 61, ibid, 66-67 (quote, 66).
11. Msg 1329 Saigon to State, 31 Jan 61, *FRUS 1961-63*, I: 25-28. The ambassador did modify some of his criticism as a result of Diem's press conference on 6 February, but only grudgingly; see msg 1351 Saigon to State, 8 Feb 61, ibid, 29-30.
12. Ltr McGarr to DirFE(ISA) (RAdm Luther C. Heinz), 27 Feb 61, fldr 092 Vietnam Jan-Oct 1961, box 42, ISA files, Acc 64A-2382; ltr McGarr to Palmer, 3 Mar 61, cited in n 10.
13. Memo Edward E. Rice (StatePolPlng) for Anderson, 10 Feb 61, fldr 370.5-384 Vietnam 1961, box 43, ISA files, Acc 64A-2382; msg 1115 State to Saigon, 1 Mar 61, *FRUS, 1961-63*, I:40-42.
14. Ltr William Bundy to McGhee, 13 Mar 61, fldr 370.5-384 Vietnam 1961, box 43, ISA files, Acc 64A-2382.
15. Ltr McGarr to Palmer, 3 Mar 61, cited in n 10 (quote, 43).
16. Negotiating the CIP, *Pentagon Papers*, bk 2, IV.B.1, 13-14.
17. Memo Nitze for SecDef, 18 Apr 61, fldr 334-353 Vietnam, box 42, ISA files, Acc 64A-2382; memo William Bundy for DepSecDef, 20 May 61, ibid.
18. Memo Dulles for Pres, 25 Mar 61, fldr Vietnam Jan-Jun 61, box 5, Lansdale files, Acc 63A-1803.
19. Memo Lemnitzer for SecDef, 29 Mar 61, ibid. McNamara passed this to White House via Rostow; see memo Rostow for Pres, 3 Apr 61, w/atchmt, *FRUS 1961-63*, I:61-63.
20. Ed note, *FRUS 1961-63*, I:74.
21. Memo McNamara for DepSecDef, 20 Apr 61, fldr Reading File, May 1961-Mar. 1961, box 113, McNamara Records, RG 200.
22. Memo William Bundy for Nitze, 21 Apr 61, fldr 092 Vietnam Jan-Oct 1961, box 42, ISA files, 64A-2382; draft notes on first mtg of Presidential Task Force on Vietnam, 24 Apr 61, *FRUS 1961-63*, I:77-80; memo McNamara for Pres, 20 Apr 61, fldr Reading File, May 1961-Mar. 1961, box 113, McNamara Records, RG 200.
23. Gilpatric interv, 14 Nov 83, 30.
24. Memo Col E. F. Black for Haydn Williams (ISA), 25 Apr 61, forwarding McGarr's presentation to Vietnam Task Force on 24 Apr, w/atchmt, 15 Nov 60, 1, fldr 370.64 Vietnam 1961, box 43, ISA files, Acc 64A-2382.
25. Memo Gilpatric for Pres, 3 May 61, w/atchmt, *FRUS 1961-63*, I:92-115; Gilpatric interv, 14 Nov 83, 30.
26. Ed note, *FRUS 1961-63*, I:88.
27. *Pentagon Papers*, bk 2, IV.B.1, 35-36; draft memo of second mtg of Vietnam Task Force, 4 May 61, *FRUS 1961-63*, I:115 ff.
28. Bundy, "History of Vietnam," ch 3, 35; *Pentagon Papers*, bk 2, IV.B.1, 36; ltr Lansdale to LtGen S. T. Williams, 10 Oct 64, cited in Newman, *JFK and Vietnam*, 40.

29. Draft rcd of action 480th mtg NSC, 29 Apr 61, in memo ActgExecSec(NSC) Marion W. Boggs for NSC, 9 May 61, fldr Vietnam Task Force, box 5, NSC files, Acc 68A-4024; NSAM 52, 11 May 61, *FRUS 1961-63*, I:132-34 (quote, 133); ltr Pres to Nolting, 27 May 61, *Pentagon Papers*, bk 3, IV.B.3, 20.
30. Annex 2 to Lansdale memo transmitting annexes to a Program of Action for South Vietnam, 8 May 61, *Pentagon Papers*, bk 2, V.B.4, 93-100; msg 1675 Saigon to State, 6 May 61, OSD Hist.
31. Msg Lansdale to MAAG-Vietnam (McGarr), 9 May 61, fldr Vietnam file #1 Jan-Jun 61, box 5, Lansdale files, Acc 63A-1803; rpt Vice Pres, *FRUS 1961-63*, I:152-57; Bundy, "History of Vietnam," ch 3, 35, on the "Churchill of Asia."
32. Ed note, *FRUS 1961-63*, I:179; memo Lansdale for Gilpatric, 26 Jun 61, ibid, 180-81; ltr US Special Financial Group to Presidents Diem and Kennedy, 14 Jul 61, ibid, 221-23; rpt, Joint Action Program (Staley Report), *Pentagon Papers*, bk 11, 182-226.
33. Bundy, "History of Vietnam," ch 4, 4-5.
34. NSAM 65, 11 Aug 61, *Pentagon Papers*, bk 11, 241-44.
35. IDA, Working Paper No. 4, "The South Vietnam Crisis of 1961: Part II, Genesis of the Second Presidential Program," 13 May 66, 1-2, OSD Hist; NIE 14.3/53-61, 15 Aug 61, *Pentagon Papers*, bk 11, vi, 245-46; msg 385 Saigon to State, 20 Sep 61, *FRUS 1961-63*, I:305-06.
36. IDA Working Paper No. 4, 1-2; Diem request in msg 421 Saigon to State, 1 Oct 61, *FRUS 1961-63*, I:316-17; *Kennedy Public Papers, 1961*, 660; Taylor, *Swords and Plowshares*, 225-26.
37. Bundy, "History of Vietnam, "ch 4, 12-13.
38. Taylor, *Swords and Plowshares*, 225-28, 233-34, 236 (quote, 225); Rostow, *Diffusion of Power*, 275.
39. Currey, *Lansdale*, 236-37.
40. Taylor, *Swords and Plowshares*, 238-39 (quote, 238); Currey, *Lansdale*, 237-38; msg Taylor to Pres, 1 Nov 61, *Pentagon Papers*, bk 11, 331-42 (quote, 341).
41. Paper prepared by Taylor, *FRUS 1961-63*, I:479-81 (quote, 480); msg Taylor for Pres, 1 Nov 61, *Pentagon Papers*, cited in n 40; Bowers, *Tactical Airlift*, 45; *New York Times*, 12 Dec 61; Futrell, *The Advisory Years*, 79-82.
42. See Taylor, *Swords and Plowshares*, 242-44; Taylor Rpt, *Pentagon Papers*, bk 2, IV.B.1, 90-103 (quotes, 98, 103).
43. Schlesinger, *A Thousand Days*, 537-38, notes Kennedy's skepticism about the Diem regime but observes too that he "had no choice now but to work within the situation he had inherited"; memo McNamara for Pres, 8 Nov 61, *FRUS 1961-63*, I:559-61 (quote, 560).
44. Memo Rusk and McNamara for Pres, 11 Nov 61, *Pentagon Papers*, bk 11, 359-66 (quote, 360); see also ed note, *FRUS 1961-63*, I:576.
45. List of questions prepared by Pres, 11 Nov 61, *FRUS 1961-63*, I:576-77; notes White House mtg, 11 Nov 61, ibid, 577-78; notes NSC mtg, 15 Nov 61, ibid, 607-10.
46. NSAM 111, ibid, 656-57.
47. Memo Lansdale for Taylor, 2 Nov 61, 2, 4, fldr Asst to SecDef #2 Sep-Dec 61, box 5, Lansdale files, Acc 63A-1803; memo Lansdale for Gilpatric, 30 Nov 61, ibid.
48. NSAM 111, cited in n 46, 657.
49. For details of this controversy see *FRUS 1961-63*, I:665-66, 673-74, 678, 702-03, 720-23, 745-49.
50. For resolution of the controversy see ibid, II:3-4, 35-38, 46-48, 109-12, 171.
51. Msg 906345 SecDef to CINCPAC and ChMAAG, 28 Nov 61, ibid, 679-80.
52. Memo Felt for SecDef, 18 Dec 61, w/encl, sum rcd of conf, 16 Dec 61, fldr Asst to SecDef #2 Sep-Dec 61, box 5, Lansdale files, Acc 63A-1803. See also *FRUS 1961-63*, I:740-44.
53. Robert W. Komer, "Bureaucracy Does Its Thing: Institutional Constraints on U.S.-GVN Performance in Vietnam," R-967-ARPA, Aug 72, Rand rpt prepared for DARPA, 85, OSD Hist; Bundy, "History of Vietnam," ch 4, 54.
54. NSAM 124, 18 Jan 62, *FRUS 1961-63*, II:48-50.
55. Ltr Rusk to McNamara, 16 Jun 62, ltr McNamara to Rusk, 19 Jun 62, ltr Ball to McNamara, 21 Jun 62: fldr Task Force Southeast Asia, box 4, Lansdale files, Acc 63A-1803.
56. Memo McNamara for SecState, 18 Dec 61, *FRUS 1961-63*, I:745; memo McNamara for Pres, 22 Dec 61, ibid, 756.
57. Memo McGeorge Bundy for Pres, 27 Dec 61, ibid, 766; msg 963 Saigon to State, 24 Jan 62, ibid, II:58-59; Hilsman, *To Move a Nation*, 426-27.
58. Msg 2447 ViceDirJtStaff J. H. Wellings to ChMAAG, Vietnam, 4 Dec 61, OSD Hist.

59. Memo McNamara for Pres, 2 Feb 62, *FRUS 1961-63*, II:71-72; memo NSC ExecSec Bromley Smith for SecDef, 5 Feb 62, fldr 384 Vietnam Jan-Jun 1962, box 51, ISA files, Acc 65A-3501.
60. DJSM-1532-61 DirJtStaff for DASD(ISA), 26 Dec 61, w/encl, fldr Vietnam Sep-Dec 61, box 5, Lansdale files, Acc 63A-1803.
61. Paper, "U.S. Military Support for Vietnam," 13 Dec 62, FY 64 SecDef Backup Book, I-II, box 20, ASD(C) files, OSD Hist; status rpt of military actions in South Vietnam, "First Phase of Vietnam Program," 10 Jan 62, fldr Task Force Southeast Asia, box 5, Lansdale files, Acc 63A-1803; memo SecN Korth for SecDef, 16 Nov 62, fldr 370.64 Vietnam, box 51, ISA files, Acc 65A-3501.
62. Ltr Nitze (for McNamara) to Sen Dworshak, 21 Mar 62, fldr 092 Vietnam Jan-Jun 1962, box 51, ISA files, Acc 65A-3501.
63. "First Phase of Vietnam Program," 10 Jan 62, cited in n 61; JCSM-535-62 ActgCJCS for SecDef, 23 Jul 62, fldr 333-370.5 Vietnam, box 51, ISA files, Acc 65A-3501; memo William Bundy for DirJtStaff, 1 Aug 62, ibid.
64. JCSM-617-62 CJCS for SecDef, 13 Aug 62, fldr 123.7-324.5 Vietnam, box 51, ISA files, Acc 65A-3501; memo McNamara for CJCS, 23 Aug 62, ibid; SecDef Honolulu Decisions of July 1962, *Pentagon Papers*, bk 3, IV.B.4, 4; "U.S. Military Support for Vietnam," 13 Dec 62, cited in n 61.
65. *Pentagon Papers*, bk 3, IV.B.2, 4-14; rcd of Sixth SecDef Conference, Camp Smith, Hawaii, 23 Jul 62, *FRUS 1961-63*, II:546-49; memo Dir Vietnam Task Force (Cottrell) to Harriman, 6 Apr 62, ibid, 310-15; Bundy, "History of Vietnam," ch 5, 7.
66. Hilsman, *To Move a Nation*, 431-35 (quote, 431).
67. *Pentagon Papers*, bk 3, IV.B.2, 11-13.
68. Ibid, 3-4.
69. Paper Hilsman, 2 Feb 62, *FRUS 1961-63*, II:73-90; Hilsman, *To Move a Nation*, 438-39; status rpt (MAAG), "South Vietnam Civic Action-Civil Affairs Program," 12 Feb 62, fldr 092 Vietnam Jan-Jun 1962, box 51, ISA files, Acc 65A-3501; memo Heinz for DepSecDef, 24 Aug 62, fldr Vietnam 1962, ibid.
70. *McNamara Public Statements, 1962*, 11 May 62, III:1166-67; paper prepared in DoD, nd, "Visit to Southeast Asia by the Secretary of Defense, 8-11 May 1962," *FRUS 1961-63*, II:379-87; memo Lansdale for Gilpatric, 3 Apr 62, fldr 092 Vietnam Jan-Jun 1962, box 51, ISA files, Acc 65A-3501.
71. CM-917-62 Lemnitzer for SecDef, 28 Aug 62, CM-954-62 Lemnitzer for SecDef, 14 Sep 62: fldr Vietnam 1962, box 51, ISA files, Acc 65A-3501; ltr McGarr to McNamara, 6 Mar 62, w/encl rpt for period 2 Sep 61 to 8 Feb 62 to CINCPAC, 8 Feb 62, fldr 334 Vietnam Jan-Jun 1962, ibid.
72. CM-117-62 Taylor for SecDef, 17 Nov 62, *FRUS 1961-63*, II:736-38 (quotes, 737).
73. Status rpt on SE Asia, 27 Jun 62, ibid, 478-81 (quote, 478).
74. Hilsman, *To Move a Nation*, 440; memo Robert H. Johnson (StatePolPlng) for Cottrell, 11 Sep 62, *FRUS 1961-63*, II:644-48 (quote, 644).
75. Leslie H. Gelb and Richard K. Betts, *The Irony of Vietnam: The System Worked*, 87; Hilsman, *To Move a Nation*, 441-42. Frederick Nolting, *From Trust to Tragedy: The Political Memoirs of Frederick Nolting, Kennedy's Ambassador to Diem's Vietnam*, 54-56, was less judgmental about charges that Nhu padded figures and antagonized villagers.
76. Hilsman, *To Move a Nation*, 441-42.
77. Memo CINCPAC for JCS, 25 Jan 63, w/encl, *FRUS 1961-63*, III:35-49.
78. Memo Heinz for William Bundy, 1 Feb 63, w/encl, 25 Jan 63, fldr 091.1-091.4 Vietnam, box 17, ISA files, Acc 67A-4564.
79. Hilsman, *To Move a Nation*; Neil Sheehan, *A Bright Shining Lie: John Paul Vann and America in Vietnam*; David Halberstam, *The Making of a Quagmire*.
80. See Sheehan, *A Bright Shining Lie*, 264-65; William M. Hammond, *Public Affairs: The Military and the Media, 1962-1968*, 30-32.
81. Sheehan, *A Bright Shining Lie*, 262-63; see also Vann's interv in *U. S. News & World Report*, 16 Sep 63, after his retirement, in which he claimed politics in Saigon handcuffed ARVN troops, and Hammond, *The Military and the Media*, 31-32.
82. CINCPAC, 8 Jan 63, OSD Hist; *Washington Post*, 4 Jan 63. For a full discussion of relations with the press, see Hammond, *The Military and the Media*, 30-38.
83. Colby and Forbath, *Honorable Men*, 204; JCS Team rpt on South Vietnam, Jan 63, *FRUS 1961-63*, III:73-94 (quote, 91).
84. *Kennedy Public Papers, 1963*, 11.

85. NIE 53-63, "Prospects in South Vietnam," 17 Apr 63, *FRUS 1961-63*, III:232-35.
86. Harold P. Ford, *CIA and the Vietnam Policymakers: Three Episodes, 1962-1968*, 14-23.
87. JCSM-152-63 Taylor for SecDef, 21 Feb 63, William Bundy for SecDef, 5 Mar 63, SecDef memo for CJCS, 8 Mar 63, JCSM-114-63 DepDirJtStaff A. H. Manhart for SecDef, 7 Feb 63: fldr Vietnam 1963, box 18, ISA files, Acc 67A-4564.
88. JCSM-38-63 Taylor for SecDef, 15 Jan 63, memo William Bundy for ChStaffAF, 21 Feb 63: ibid.
89. For the role of the American press see Hammond, *The Military and the Media*, 39-65.
90. Ltr Hilsman to William Bundy, 1 May 63, *FRUS 1961-63*, III:260-61; memo William Bundy for SecDef, 15 May 63, fldr 438-452 Vietnam 1963, box 18, Acc 67A-4564; memo McNamara for CJCS, fldr Reading File, May 17-May 1, 1963, 17 May 63, box 118, McNamara Records, RG 200.
91. Memo William Bundy for SecDef, 20 Apr 63, fldr 091.3-091.4 Vietnam, box 17, ISA files, Acc 67A-4564; memo SecDef MilAsst George S. Brown for ASD(ISA), 25 Apr 63, ibid.
92. Hilsman, *To Move a Nation*, 466-67; memrcd of SecDef Conf Honolulu, 6 May 63, *FRUS 1961-63*, III:265-68 (quote, 265).
93. Memo JCS for SecDef, 20 Aug 63 (sum rpt on Eighth SecDef Conf Honolulu, 7 May 63), memo ActgASD(ISA) Henry S. Rowen for SecDef, 30 Aug 63, CM-874-63 Taylor for SecDef, 11 Sep 63: fldr 334-381 Vietnam 1963, box 18, ISA files, Acc 67A-4564.
94. Memo McNamara for Nitze, 8 May 63, *FRUS 1961-63*, III:275-76; memo Heinz for William Bundy, 23 Jul 63, fldr 091.3-091.4 Vietnam, box 17, ISA files, Acc 67A-4564.
95. Taylor, *Swords and Plowshares*, 289; *Pentagon Papers* lists nine victims, while CIA reported eight (*Pentagon Papers*, bk 3, IV.B.5, ii); memo McCone for Gilpatric, 23 Aug 63, fldr 092 Vietnam Jun-Dec 1963, box 18, ISA files, Acc 67A-4564.
96. Hammond, *The Military and the Media*, 39-49; memcon Ball, Nolting, Chalmers B. Wood, George S. Springsteen, 5 Jul 63, fldr 092 Vietnam Jul-Dec 1963, box 18, ISA files, Acc 67A-4564.
97. Msg 299 Saigon to State, 21 Aug 63, *FRUS 1961-63*, III:595-97. See also Hammond, *The Military and the Media*, 55-58.
98. Msgs 324 and 320 Saigon to State, 24 Aug 63, *FRUS 1961-63*, III:611-14.
99. Msg 243 State to Saigon, 24 Aug 63, ibid, 628-29.
100. A note in the Harriman Papers, fldr Vietnam Aug-Nov 63, box 519, LC, identified Hilsman as the author, while Hilsman allocated a share of the responsibility to Harriman and Ball as well as Forrestal and himself (Hilsman, *To Move a Nation*, 487-88). President Johnson in retrospect felt that sending the wire was "a very dangerous thing to do." He blamed Hilsman for the action, and noted that "when I became President, the first man I instructed to be fired was Hilsman" (interv Lyndon B. Johnson by William J. Jorden, 12 Aug 69, LBJL).
101. Hilsman, *To Move a Nation*, 488; Schlesinger, *A Thousand Days*, 991; msg 329 Saigon to State, 24 Aug 63, *FRUS 1961-63*, III:620-21. McNamara, *In Retrospect*, 55, wrote that "the fault lay as much with those who failed to rein him in as it did with Hilsman himself," but Lodge emerges in this account as evasive about his reaction. Taylor, *Swords and Plowshares*, 292-93, blamed anti-Diem activists in the State Department for the 24 August cable's tone.
102. Hilsman, *To Move a Nation*, 490-92; msgs 272, 279 State to Saigon, 29 Aug 63, *FRUS 1961-63*, IV:32-34; msg 0499 CIA Station Saigon to Agency, 31 Aug 63, ibid, 64.
103. Memo of conf w/Pres, 29 Aug 63, *FRUS 1961-63*, IV:26-31; msg 1540 MACV to CJCS, 27 Aug 63, ibid, III:655-57.
104. Hilsman memcon, Dept State, 31 Aug 63, ibid, IV:69-74 (quote, 73); for Krulak's record of the meeting, see *Pentagon Papers*, bk 12, 540-44.
105. Transc of broadcast with Walter Cronkite, CBS-TV News, 2 Sep 63, *Kennedy Public Papers*, 1963, 652. Nhu was reported to be talking with Ho Chi Minh about reuniting Vietnam and expelling Americans from the country. See ltr William H. Sullivan to Hilsman, 3 Oct 63, fldr General 1963, box 519, Harriman Papers, LC; Bundy, "History of Vietnam," ch 9, 13, 19; Hilsman, *To Move a Nation*, 498.
106. Msg 412 Saigon to State, 4 Sep 63, *FRUS 1961-63*, IV:107-08; memcon w/Pres, 6 Sep 63, ibid, 117-21; Hilsman, *To Move a Nation*, 500-01.
107. Krulak's report is in *FRUS 1961-63*, IV:153-60; Mendenhall's report, ibid, 144-45, 243-49; memcon, White House, 10 Sep 63, ibid, 161-67 (quote, 162).
108. Transc of Cronkite broadcast, 2 Sep 63, cited in n 105; transc of broadcast on NBC-TV "Huntley-Brinkley Report," 9 Sep 63, *Kennedy Public Papers, 1963*, 659; memo for DirCIA, 26 Sep 63, *FRUS 1961-63*,

IV:295-98; msg 674 State to Saigon, 1 Nov 63, ibid, 521; see also Fredrik Logevall, *Choosing War: The Lost Chance for Peace and the Escalation of War in Vietnam*, 63.

109. Memo Pres for SecDef, 21 Sep 63, *FRUS 1961-63*, IV:278-79; Hilsman, *To Move a Nation*, 507-08.
110. Memo CJCS and SecDef for Pres, 2 Oct 63, *FRUS 1961-63*, IV:337; msg MAC 2028 Harkins to Taylor, 30 Oct 63, ibid, 479-82; H. R. McMaster, *Dereliction of Duty: Lyndon Johnson, Robert McNamara, the Joint Chiefs of Staff, and the Lies that Led to Vietnam*, 45.
111. Memo CJCS and SecDef for Pres, cited in n 110, 338-42. The McNamara-Taylor mission report was endorsed by the NSC, rcd of action 2472, taken at the 519th NSC mtg, 2 Oct 63, ibid, 353-54.
112. Hilsman, *To Move a Nation*, 514-15; msg 643 Saigon to State, 6 Oct 63, *FRUS 1961-63*, IV:384-85.
113. McNamara-Taylor rpt, 2 Oct 63, *FRUS 1961-63*, IV:339; ed note, ibid, 427; msgs Saigon to State, 28, 29 Oct 63, ibid, 449-52.
114. Hilsman, *To Move a Nation*, 518-20; msg 647 State to Saigon, 25 Oct 63, *FRUS 1961-63*, IV:437-39; msg 805 Saigon to State, 28 Oct 63, ibid, 442-46; msg 854 Saigon to State, 1 Nov 63, ibid, 514-15.
115. Nitze, *From Hiroshima to Glasnost*, 256-57.
116. HCFA, *Hearings: Foreign Assistance Act of 1963*, 88 Cong, 1 sess, 8 Apr 63, 64.
117. Halberstam, *The Best and the Brightest*, 247; Cong Research Serv interview with Kattenburg, 16 Feb 79, in S Rpt 98-185, *The U.S. Government and the Vietnam War: Executive and Legislative Roles and Relationships, Part II, 1961-1964*, CRS study prepared for SCFR, 98 Cong, 2 sess, Dec 84, 161.

XII. FLEXIBLE RESPONSE

1. Taylor, *The Uncertain Trumpet*, 5-6.
2. Nitze, *From Hiroshima to Glasnost*, 251.
3. Ltr Kaysen to Rowen, 16 Jun 61, *FRUS 1961-63*, VIII:102-05; Nitze interv, 9 Oct 84, 35-36; Poole, *JCS and National Policy 1961-64*, pt I:82-83.
4. Draft BNSP, 5 Dec 61, *FRUS 1961-63*, VIII:222-24; ed notes, ibid, 243-47, 281-82.
5. JCSM-277-62 Lemnitzer for SecDef, 12 Apr 62, ibid, 260-62; memo WYS(mith) for Taylor, 20 Apr 62, fldr T-230-69, box 40, Taylor Papers, NDUL; ltr Taylor to Rostow, 23 Apr 62, *FRUS 1961-63*, VIII:272-74.
6. Memo WYS(mith) for Taylor, 1 Aug 62, fldr T-230-69, box 40, Taylor Papers, NDUL.
7. Memo ExecSecNSC for Holders of NSC 5906, 17 Jan 63, CJCS files, RG 218; ed note, *FRUS 1961-63*, VIII:455; Poole, *JCS and National Policy 1961-64*, pt I:16; memo Gilpatric for Taylor, 4 Apr 63, fldr T-253, box 40, Taylor Papers, NDUL.
8. Memo Rostow for Rusk, w/atchmt, 23 Jul 63, *FRUS 1961-63*, VIII:489-90.
9. Memo CM-381-65 Wheeler for LeMay et al, 14 Jan 65, box 116, Wheeler files, RG 218.
10. Watson, *Into the Missile Age*, 314-16.
11. "Chronology of Two-Year Dispute on 'Missile Gap,'" *New York Times*, 9 Feb 61; *Kennedy Public Papers, 1961*, 24.
12. "Missile Gap" chron, cited in n 11; McNamara, *In Retrospect*, 21.
13. *Kennedy Public Papers, 1961*, 67-68; "Missile Gap" chron.
14. Lemnitzer interv, 19 Jan 84, 4; Gilpatric interv, 14 Nov 83, 18.
15. HCAS, *Military Posture Briefings*, 23 Feb 61 (McNamara test), 646-47; HSCA, *DoD Appros for 1962*, 6 Apr 61 (McNamara test), pt 3:60.
16. "Missile Gap" chron.
17. OSD paper, "The Problem of Measuring the 'Missile Gap,'" 14 Feb 61, fldr Missile Gap-1961, box 45, ASD(C) files, OSD Hist.
18. NIE 11-5-60, 3 May 60, *FRUS 1958-60*, III: 404-05 (ed note); NIE 11-8-60, 1 Aug 60, ibid, 437-42; NIE 11-4-60, 1 Dec 60, *FRUS 1961-63*, VIII:47, n c(4).
19. NIE 11-8-61, Annex C, 7 Jun 61, *FRUS 1961-63*, VIII:83.
20. NIE 11-8/1-61, 21 Sep 61, ibid, 132; Walter A. McDougall, *The Heavens and the Earth: A Political History of the Space Age*, 329.
21. McNamara interv, 22 May 86, 1-2; Edgar M. Bottome, *The Missile Gap: A Study of the Formulation of Military and Political Policy*, 160-64.

22. Kevin C. Ruffner, ed, *CORONA: America's First Satellite Program*, xiii; Bissell, *Reflections of a Cold Warrior*, 135-38; Gerald K. Haines, *The National Reconnaissance Office: Its Origins, Creation, & Early Years*, 145-47. For the "500" figure, see Watson, *Into the Missile Age*, 351.
23. Haines, *NRO*, 149-53.
24. DoD Dir 5160.32, 6 Mar 61, in Cole et al, *Department of Defense*, 325-26; Haines, *NRO*, 153; Ruffner, *CORONA*, 152.
25. Ruffner, *CORONA*, 152.
26. Gilpatric address, 21 Oct 61, *Gilpatric Public Statements, 1961*, 395.
27. NIE 11-4-60, cited in n 18.
28. Memrcd DepDirER(ISA) S. K. Eaton, 3 Feb 61, fldr 334 NATO, box 45, ISA files, Acc 64A-2382; Policy Directive, NATO and the Atlantic Nations, 20 Apr 61, *FRUS 1961-63*, XIII:285-91.
29. Memrcd Capt C. N. Shane, USN, 24 Feb 61, fldr 334 NATO, box 45, ISA files, 64A-2382; JCSM-190-61 Lemnitzer for SecDef, 28 Mar 61, fldr 334 NATO, box 46, ibid.
30. *FRUS 1961-63*, XIII:285-91 (quotes, 286-87).
31. *Kennedy Public Papers, 1961*, 254-56; statement Lemnitzer at Mil Cte mtg, 10 Apr 61, 2, fldr 334 NATO Apr 1-15, 1961, box 17, ISA files, Acc 64A-2382; Polto 1619, Paris to State, 28 May 61, OSD Hist; memcon, NATO Defense Strategy and Planning, 15 Jun 61, fldr 334 NATO Jun 1-15, 1961, box 21, ISA files, Acc 64A-2382; Poole, *JCS and National Policy 1961-64*, pt III:8.
32. Poole, *JCS and National Policy 1961-64*, pt III:5-6; JCSM-190-61, cited in n 29.
33. Memcon, sub: Visit of Minister of Defense Strauss to SHAPE, 12 Jun 61, 5, fldr Germany Jan-Jun 61, box 33, ISA files, Acc 64A-2382.
34. Memrcd Eaton on 15 Jun 61 Nitze mtg w/Stikker, 27 Jun 61, fldr 334 NATO Jun 1-30, 1961, box 17, ibid.
35. Memo Ruffner for JCS, 31 Oct 61, ibid.
36. Memo Nitze for SvcSecs et al, 19 Dec 61, w/atchd McNamara remarks at NATO Ministerial mtg, 14 Dec 61, fldr 334 NATO Ministerial mtg, box 46, ibid.
37. Interv William W. Kaufmann by Alfred Goldberg, 14 May 66, 7, OSD Hist.
38. Memo McGeorge Bundy for McNamara, 1 May 62, fldr 334 NATO 1961, box 54, ISA files, Acc 64A-2382.
39. Interv William W. Kaufmann by Lawrence Kaplan and Maurice Matloff, 14 Jul 86, 19, OSD Hist.
40. McNamara Athens address excerpts, 5 May 62, *FRUS 1961-63*, VIII:275-81.
41. Ibid, 275.
42. Memo William Bundy for SvcSecs et al, 10 May 62, w/atchd McNamara Athens address (full text), 5 May 62, 7-8, Policy Planning Staff files, Lot 69D-121, RG 59.
43. Ibid, 10-12.
44. McNamara Athens address, 5 May 62, cited in n 40, 278-79.
45. McNamara Athens address, cited in n 42, 24-25.
46. Poole, *JCS and National Policy 1961-64*, pt III:70-72.
47. David N. Schwartz, *NATO's Nuclear Dilemmas*, 165.
48. Kaufmann interv, 14 May 66, 7; Kaufmann interv, 14 Jul 86, 19.
49. *McNamara Public Statements, 1962*, III:1505-09 (quote, 1505). See also excerpted text in *American Foreign Policy: Current Documents, 1962*, 548-51.
50. McNamara remarks, Ann Arbor, cited in n 49, 1508-09.
51. Watson, *Into the Missile Age*, 474-75; Alfred Goldberg, "A Brief Survey of the Evolution of Ideas about Counterforce," 5-21, OSD Hist.
52. Stern interv, 28 Feb-1 Mar 67, 7-8.
53. Kaufmann interv, 14 May 66, 6-7, 10; Kaufmann interv, 14 Jul 86, 16-17; Henry S. Rowen, "Formulating Strategic Doctrine," *Report of Commission on the Organization of the Government for the Conduct of Foreign Policy*, Jun 75, vol 4, 230.
54. JCSM-170-61 Lemnitzer for SecDef, 17 Mar 61, *FRUS 1961-63*, VIII:72-74; JCSM-252-61 Lemnitzer for SecDef, 18 Apr 61, ibid, 76-78.
55. CM-190-61 Lemnitzer for SecDef, 18 Apr 61, ibid, 74-75.
56. Poole, *JCS and National Policy 1961-64*, pt I:87-92; ed note, *FRUS 1961-63*, VIII:125.
57. Draft memo McNamara for Pres, 23 Sep 61, *FRUS 1961-63*, VIII:138-52 (quote, 142).

58. Thomas S. Power, with Albert A. Arnhym, *Design for Survival*, 83, 119-20; Steven L. Rearden, "U.S. Strategic Bombardment Doctrine Since 1945," in R. Cargill Hall, ed, *Case Studies in Strategic Bombardment*, 428; interv Maxwell Taylor by Alfred Goldberg, 14 Jun 66, 1, 2, OSD Hist.
59. Memo Gilpatric for McNamara, 28 Dec 61, OSD Hist; SCAS, Preparedness Investigating Subcte, LeMay test in exec sess, 17 Jul 62; interv Curtis LeMay by Alfred Goldberg, 12 Oct 66, 4-5, OSD Hist.
60. Enthoven interv, 3 Feb 86, 24-25.
61. Interv Paul Nitze by Alfred Goldberg, 15 Jun 66, 5, OSD Hist; Nitze, *From Hiroshima to Glasnost*, 246.
62. Taylor interv, 14 Jun 66, 2, 5; JCSM-252-61, cited in n 54, 77.
63. Schwartz, *NATO's Nuclear Dilemmas*, 145-46; Enthoven and Smith, *How Much Is Enough?*, 124-29.
64. Memo McNamara for Lemnitzer, 23 May 62, *FRUS 1961-63*, VIII:294-98 (quote, 295-96).
65. JCSM-952-62 Lemnitzer for SecDef, 7 Dec 62, ibid, 436-38.
66. Pierre Gallois, "U.S. Strategy and the Defense of Europe," *Orbis*, Summer 63, 247; Gallois, *The Balance of Terror: Strategy for the Nuclear Age*; André Beaufre, *Deterrence and Strategy*; Jane E. Stromseth, *The Origins of Flexible Response: NATO's Debate over Strategy in the 1960s*, 48.
67. McNamara reply to press query about Ann Arbor address, 23 Jun 62, *McNamara Public Statements, 1962*, IV:1511.
68. Harold Macmillan, *At the End of the Day, 1961-1963*, 334-35.
69. Dean Acheson, "Our Atlantic Alliance," 5 Dec 62, *Vital Speeches of the Day*, 1 Jan 63, 163.
70. Schwartz, *NATO's Nuclear Dilemmas*, 168-69.
71. Goldberg, "A Brief Survey of the Evolution of Ideas about Counterforce," 29-30.
72. McNamara interv, 22 May 86, 3-5.
73. Watson, *Into the Missile Age*, 475-77; memo of disc at 387th NSC mtg, 20 Nov 58, *FRUS 1958-60*, III:147-52; ed note, ibid, 382.
74. Watson, *Into the Missile Age*, 490-95, 790.
75. Lemnitzer interv, 19 Jan 84, 47; memo Bell for McGeorge Bundy, McNamara, 30 Jan 61, w/atchd draft disc notes for 1 Feb NSC mtg, 2, fldr NSC Meetings, 1961, box 313, NSF, JFKL.
76. Ltr McNamara to Pres, 20 Feb 61, w/atchmt "Memorandum on Review of FY 1961 and FY 1962 Military Programs and Budgets," *FRUS 1961-63*, VIII:35-48; Stern interv, 28 Feb-1 Mar 67, 7-8.
77. Poole, *JCS and National Policy 1961-64*, pt I:81-84, 96 (quote, 83).
78. Memo Hitch for SecDef, 22 Dec 61, sub: Review of the Hickey Study, OSD Hist; *FRUS 1961-63*, VIII:196, n 5; Enthoven and Smith, *How Much Is Enough?*, 172-73.
79. Stern interv, 28 Feb-1 Mar 67, 9; memo Hitch for SecDef, 22 Dec 61, cited in n 78; Enthoven and Smith, *How Much Is Enough?*, 172-73.
80. Memo McNamara for Pres, 24 Aug 61, fldr Reading File, Aug. 1961-June 1961, box 113, McNamara Records, RG 200.
81. Ibid; memo McNamara for Pres, 17 Nov 61, ibid. Memo WYS(mith) for Taylor, 15 Mar 62, Taylor Papers, NDUL, noted that the Partridge recommendations on the question of devolution of authority in case of nuclear attack would be managed informally within OSD.
82. HCAS, Special Subcte on Defense Agencies, *Hearings*, 87 Cong, 2 sess, 28 Jun 62, 6960.
83. Rowen, "Formulating Strategic Doctrine," cited in n 53, 231; Enthoven quoted in Gregg Herken, *Counsels of War*, 170.
84. Draft memo McNamara for Pres, 6 Dec 63, *FRUS 1961-63*, VIII:545-64 (quote, 549).
85. Ibid, 550.
86. HCAS, *Hearings: Military Posture*, 88 Cong, 2 sess, 27 Jan 64, 6920.
87. Poole, *JCS and National Policy 1961-64*, pt I:105-08.
88. Draft memo McNamara for Pres, 6 Dec 63, cited in n 84, 559.
89. Draft memo McNamara for Pres, 14 Nov 63, *FRUS 1961-63*, VIII:526-33 (quotes, 528-29).
90. HCAS, *Hearings: Military Posture*, 89 Cong, 1 sess, 18 Feb 65, 256.
91. Interv Glenn A. Kent by Alfred Goldberg, 11-12 May 66, 4, OSD Hist; memo McNamara for CJCS, 9 Jan 64, fldr Reading File, Jan. 17-Jan. 2, 1964, box 119, McNamara Records, RG 200; SCAS and SSCA, *Hearings: Military Procurement Authorizations, FY 1966*, 89 Cong, 1 sess, 24 Feb 65, 43-46.
92. SCAS, *Hearings: Status of U.S. Strategic Power*, 90 Cong, 2 sess, 23 Apr 68, 138.
93. Robert S. McNamara, *The Essence of Security*, x.
94. Ibid, 53.

95. McNamara address to Economic Club of New York, 18 Nov 63, *McNamara Public Statements, 1963*, IV:2553.
96. McNamara, *In Retrospect*, 345. McNamara had used the same language in "The Military Role of Nuclear Weapons," *Foreign Affairs*, Fall 83, 79.

XIII. THE LIMITED NUCLEAR TEST BAN TREATY

1. SCFR, *Hearings: Nuclear Test Ban Treaty*, 88 Cong, 1 sess, 13 Aug 63, 120; Sorensen, *Kennedy*, 740.
2. Bundy, *Danger and Survival*, 461; Schlesinger, *A Thousand Days*, 910; Radio and TV Address, 26 Jul 63, *Kennedy Public Papers, 1963*, 601-06 (quote, 602).
3. Schlesinger, *A Thousand Days*, 911.
4. General Research Corp, "Arms Control of Ballistic Missile Defense," Dec 68, vol I, ACDA/ST-145 I, 10, box 1269, Subject files, OSD Hist; Poole, *JCS and National Policy 1961-64*, pt I:399-400, 406.
5. For a summary of arms control activity between 1956 and 1960, see Watson, *Into the Missile Age*, 729-30. On the test ban debate in particular, see Arthur T. Hadley, *The Nation's Safety and Arms Control*, 50-60; Robert A. Divine, *Blowing on the Wind: The Nuclear Test Ban Debate, 1954-1960*.
6. Statement by Pres, 29 Dec 59, *Eisenhower Public Papers, 1959*, 883.
7. Bundy, *Danger and Survival*, 328-29, 334; Schlesinger, *A Thousand Days*, 452.
8. Inaugural Address, 20 Jan 61, *Kennedy Public Papers, 1961*, 2.
9. News conf, 25 Jan 61, ibid, 8.
10. Rusk, *As I Saw It*, 251; Nitze interv, 3 Oct 84, 7, 10-11; Nitze, *From Hiroshima to Glasnost*, 182; Watson, *Into the Missile Age*, 727-28.
11. HCFA, *Hearings: To Establish a United States Arms Control Agency*, 87 Cong, 1 sess, 24 Aug 61, 2-3 (McCloy test).
12. For the announcement of Foster's appointment, see the president's remarks, 26 Sep 61, *Kennedy Public Papers, 1961*, 627. See also Glenn T. Seaborg, *Kennedy, Khrushchev, and the Test Ban*, 95. Foster was deputy secretary of defense from September 1951 to January 1953.
13. Poole, *JCS and National Policy 1961-64*, pt I:300-01.
14. Ltr Eisenhower to McCloy, 29 Jun 61, in HCFA, *To Establish a United States Arms Control Agency*, 31-32.
15. Ibid, 25 Aug 61, 78-79, 83.
16. Nitze, *From Hiroshima to Glasnost*, 188; Poole, *JCS and National Policy 1961-64*, pt I:302-05.
17. ACDA, "A Chronology of Disarmament Developments, 1961," nd [1961], 3, box 1270a, Subject files, OSD Hist; "The Nuclear Test-Ban Treaty: Gateway to Peace," Dept State Pub 7254, Aug 61, 5-6.
18. Memo McCloy for Pres, 8 Mar 61, *FRUS 1961-63*, VII:14-17.
19. "The Nuclear Test-Ban Treaty: Gateway to Peace," 6-11; Seaborg, *Kennedy, Khrushchev, and the Test Ban*, 41-43; memcon, 4 Jun 61, *FRUS 1961-63*, VII:87. On the West's rationale for 20 visits, see ed note, ibid, 10-11.
20. Memcon, 4 Jun 61, cited in n 19, 87.
21. Lippmann, "The Test Ban," *New York Herald Tribune*, 20 Jun 61.
22. *Washington Star*, 30 Jan 61.
23. "JCS Positions and Statements on Disarmament, January 1961-November 1969," Hist Div, Jt Secretariat, 17 Jan 79, 2-3, box 1267, Subject files, OSD Hist; JCSM-182-61 CJCS for SecDef, 23 Mar 61, *FRUS 1961-63*, VII:21-27.
24. Memo Black for Bonesteel, 19 Apr 61, fldr Col Black Reading File, 8/1/60, box 4, OSD Admin sec files, Acc 65A-3078.
25. Seaborg, *Kennedy, Khrushchev, and the Test Ban*, 43. See, too, ed note, *FRUS 1961-63*, VII:10-14, which quotes Seaborg's journal entry for a White House meeting on 4 March where the same topic was discussed. Nitze referred there to DoD concerns over "loopholes" in the composition of the Control Commission and inspection certification methods "that might negate the purposes of the treaty."
26. "JCS Positions and Statements on Disarmament," cited in n 23, 2; ltr McNamara to McCloy, 28 Jul 61, *FRUS 1961-63*, VII:116-24; ltr Brown to Wiesner, 3 Aug 61, Doc CK3100242766, Declassified Documents Reference System, Internet.

27. Seaborg, *Kennedy, Khrushchev, and the Test Ban*, 69; ltr JFK to Macmillan, 16 May 61, fldr Arms Control and Disarmament Agency General 4/61-5/61, box 255, NSF, JFKL; U.S. aide-memoire delivered to Soviet Ministry of For Affs, 17 Jun 61, excerpts in *American Foreign Policy: Current Documents, 1961*, 1137.
28. *American Foreign Policy: Current Documents, 1961*, 1137-39; Seaborg, *Kennedy, Khrushchev, and the Test Ban*, 74-75. The 11-member Ad Hoc Panel on Nuclear Testing began meeting in July.
29. Seaborg, *Kennedy, Khrushchev, and the Test Ban*, 75; McGeorge Bundy mins 490th NSC mtg, 8 Aug 61, *FRUS 1961-63*, VII:134-35.
30. Ltr McNamara to McCloy, 28 Jul 61, memo JCSM-517-61 CJCS for SecDef, 2 Aug 61, memo Taylor for Pres, 7 Aug 61, Bundy mins 490th NSC mtg, 8 Aug 61: *FRUS 1961-63*, VII:116-24, 125-27, 133-34, 136.
31. Memo Bundy for Pres, 8 Aug 61, fldr Panofsky Panel, 8/4/61-9/5/61, Panofsky file, Disarmament 1961, box 302, NSF, JFKL; memo Pres for Taylor, 7 Aug 61, *FRUS 1961-63*, VII:127n.
32. Seaborg, *Kennedy, Khrushchev, and the Test Ban*, 84; Sorensen, *Kennedy*, 619.
33. Msg 323 EmbMoscow to State, 28 Jul 61, *FRUS 1961-63*, VII:110-13 (see also "A Chronology of Disarmament Developments, 1961," cited in n 17, 5); Seaborg, *Kennedy, Khrushchev, and the Test Ban*, 74, 83-84; interv Lemnitzer by Walter Poole, 31 Mar 77, in Poole, *JCS and National Policy 1961-64*, pt I:370; interv John T. McNaughton by George Bunn, 21 Nov 64, 1-2, JFKL; ltr Seaborg to Pres, 7 Oct 61, *FRUS 1961-63*, VII:192-93.
34. Sorensen, *Kennedy*, 619; Seaborg, *Kennedy, Khrushchev, and the Test Ban*, 82.
35. White House statement on Soviet resumption of nuclear weapons tests, 30 Aug 61, *Kennedy Public Papers, 1961*, 580-81; Seaborg, *Kennedy, Khrushchev, and the Test Ban*, 86 (Seaborg gives the date as 2 September); Kennedy-Macmillan jt statement, 3 Sep 61, *Kennedy Public Papers, 1961*, 587.
36. Seaborg, *Kennedy, Khrushchev, and the Test Ban*, 85.
37. Statement by Pres, 5 Sep 61, *Kennedy Public Papers, 1961*, 589-90; Schlesinger, *A Thousand Days*, 482.
38. Poole, *JCS and National Policy 1961-64*, pt I:368; Nitze, *From Hiroshima to Glasnost*, 190; Seaborg, *Kennedy, Khrushchev, and the Test Ban*, 86.
39. "Implications of 50-100 MT Weapons," 12 Jan 62, fldr White Papers 1962 FY 1963 Budget, box 12, ASD(C) files, OSD Hist.
40. "A Chronology of Disarmament Developments, 1961," 9; "Implications of 50-100 MT Weapons," cited in n 39.
41. Statement by Pres, 2 Nov 61, *Kennedy Public Papers, 1961*, 692-93; Poole, *JCS and National Policy 1961-64*, pt I:370-71.
42. Poole, *JCS and National Policy 1961-64*, pt I:371.
43. Bethe lecture, 5 Jan 62, memo Spurgeon Keeney, Jr, for Carl Kaysen, 18 Jan 62, ltr Pres to Sen Clinton Anderson, 22 Jan 62: fldr Nuclear Testing, Bethe Incident 3/62-7/62, box 376, NSF, JFKL.
44. Seaborg, *Kennedy, Khrushchev, and the Test Ban*, 132-35.
45. Ibid, 136-37. JCS discomfort was reinforced by the Twining Committee's report. Initiated by General LeMay on 28 November 1961, the committee was tasked to analyze the military implications of Soviet weapons tests. See Twining Committee rpt to ChStaffAF, 5 Jan 62, "Military Implications of 1961 Soviet Nuclear Tests," fldr Nuclear Weapons, Twining Committee Report, box 302, NSF, JFKL.
46. Radio and TV Address, 2 Mar 62, *Kennedy Public Papers, 1962*, 186-92; ACDA, "A Chronology of Disarmament Developments, 1962," 13 Jun 63, 3, box 1270a, Subject files, OSD Hist; *New York Times*, 26 Apr 62; *New York Journal-American*, 21 Apr 62; Seaborg, *Kennedy, Khrushchev, and the Test Ban*, ch 11.
47. Memo Bundy for Pres, 18 Apr 62, fldr 499th Mtg Nuclear Atmospheric Test 1962, box 313, NSF, JFKL.
48. Poole, *JCS and National Policy 1961-64*, pt I:378-79; Lemnitzer notes on White House mtg, 20 Jun 62, fldr L-214-71, box 29, Lemnitzer Papers, NDUL.
49. Seaborg, *Kennedy, Khrushchev, and the Test Ban*, 158.
50. Memo DirACDA for Pres, 3 Mar 62, fldr Eighteen-Nation Disarmament Cte 2/62-11/62, box 100, POF, JFKL.
51. Lemnitzer notes on White House mtg, 6 Mar 62, fldr L-214-71, box 29, Lemnitzer Papers, NDUL; see also memrcd Lemnitzer, 6 Mar 62, *FRUS 1961-63*, VII:362-65.
52. "A Chronology of Disarmament Developments, 1962," cited in n 46, 5; memo Foster for Pres, 9 Mar 62, fldr Eighteen-Nation Disarmament Cte, box 100, POF, JFKL; news release, 18 Apr 62, fldr Disarmament—Nuclear Test Ban Negotiations 4/62-8/63, box 100, POF, JFKL.
53. Poole, *JCS and National Policy 1961-64*, pt I:318-19, 322-23.

54. Ibid, 323-24.
55. Memo ASD(ISA) for CJCS, nd [early Nov 62], ibid, 324 (emphasis in original).
56. "A Chronology of Disarmament Developments, 1962," 7-8.
57. Herbert F. York, *Making Weapons, Talking Peace: A Physicist's Odyssey from Hiroshima to Geneva*, 220-21; "VI. Project VELA," nd, fldr White Papers 1962 FY 1963 Budget, 6-7, box 12, ASD(C) files, OSD Hist.
58. *Documents on Disarmament, 1962*, II:633-35; memo Bundy for Pres, 26 Jul 62, fldr Nuclear Testing 1962-63, box 104, POF, JFKL.
59. Seaborg, *Kennedy, Khrushchev, and the Test Ban*, 162-63; on the Dean contretemp, see ed note, *FRUS 1961-63*, VII:487-88.
60. Report of the Inspection Study Group, nd [Jul 62], *FRUS 1961-63*, VII:524-27; ltr Foster to Bundy, 31 Aug 62, fldr Arms Control and Disarmament Agency, box 257, NSF, JFKL.
61. Seaborg, *Kennedy, Khrushchev, and the Test Ban*, 164-68; memo of White House mtg, 1 Aug 62, *FRUS 1961-63*, VII:527-30; Lemnitzer notes on White House mtg, 1 Aug 62, fldr L-214-71, box 29, Lemnitzer Papers, NDUL.
62. News conf, 1 Aug 62, *Kennedy Public Papers, 1962*, 591; *Documents on Disarmament, 1962*, II:791-804; ed note, *FRUS 1961-63*, VII:560.
63. Seaborg, *Kennedy, Khrushchev, and the Test Ban*, 168-70.
64. Ibid, 164-65; memo of White House mtg, 1 Aug 62, cited in n 61.
65. *Documents on Disarmament, 1962*, II:804-07, 791-92.
66. "A Chronology of Disarmament Developments, 1962," 12; news conf, 29 Aug 62, *Kennedy Public Papers, 1962*, 649; *Documents on Disarmament, 1962*, II:820-32.
67. Memo Wiesner for Pres, 20 Aug 62, *FRUS 1961-63*, VII:553; statement by Pres, 4 Nov 62, *Kennedy Public Papers, 1962*, 822.
68. "A Chronology of Disarmament Developments, 1962," 15; Seaborg, *Kennedy, Khrushchev, and the Test Ban*, 177-79; ltr Khrushchev to Pres, 19 Dec 62, *FRUS 1961-63*, VI:234-37.
69. Ltr Pres to Khrushchev, 28 Dec 62, *FRUS 1961-63*, VI:238-40; ltr Dean to Foster, 23 Feb 63 (quote, 3), fldr ACDA Disarmament 3/7/63-3/31/63, box 258, NSF, JFKL; Seaborg, *Kennedy, Khrushchev, and the Test Ban*, 178-81. Seaborg suggests Dean may have been vaguer in his reply to Khrushchev than he later maintained and that the differing accounts may well have been a case of genuine misunderstanding.
70. Ed note, *FRUS 1961-63*, VII:625; memo W. O. Anderson for Guthrie, 27 Jun 63, box 560, Harriman Papers, LC (according to Anderson, the Soviet Union had posed the "three" figure as early as July 1960); ACDA, "A Chronology of Disarmament Developments, 1963," 14 Aug 64, 1, box 1270a, Subject files, OSD Hist.
71. Ltr Pres to Khrushchev, 28 Dec 62, cited in n 69, 238-39; ACDA, "U.S. Position Regarding a Nuclear Test Ban Treaty," 9 Feb 63, fldr Disarmament Subject, Basic Doc #2, box 367, NSF, JFKL; ed note, *FRUS 1961-63*, VII:644-46; "A Chronology of Disarmament Developments, 1963," cited in n 70, 1; statement by Pres on postponing underground testing in Nevada, 26 Jan 63, *Kennedy Public Papers, 1963*, 104; Seaborg, *Kennedy, Khrushchev, and the Test Ban*, 187.
72. Memo Bundy for Pres, 21 Jan 63, fldr 508th NSC Mtg, box 314, NSF, JFKL; Seaborg, *Kennedy, Khrushchev, and the Test Ban*, 181; ltr Pres to Macmillan, 10 Jan 63, fldr 508th NSC Mtg, box 314, NSF, JFKL; Pres remarks to NSC, 22 Jan 63, *FRUS 1961-63*, VIII:462.
73. *Baltimore Sun*, 1 Feb 63; *Los Angeles Times*, 22 Feb 63; Seaborg, *Kennedy, Khrushchev, and the Test Ban*, 187.
74. Memo Taylor for SecDef, 16 Feb 63, w/appen, 9 Feb 63, fldr Disarmament Subject, Basic Doc #2, box 367, NSF, JFKL.
75. Memo ActgDirACDA Adrian Fisher for Pres, 17 Feb 63, w/memo Fisher for Members Cte of Principals, 17 Feb 63 (quote, 9), ibid.
76. Memo Taylor for SecDef, 21 Mar 63, fldr ACDA Disarmament 3/7/63-3/31/63, box 258, NSF, JFKL; memo McNamara for Pres, 12 Feb 63, sub: US-USSR military balance with and without a test ban, fldr 95 USP Test Ban Treaty Basic, box 3, Atomic Energy files, Acc 69A-2243.
77. Memo McNamara for Pres, 12 Feb 63, sub: Diffusion of nuclear weapons with and without a test ban agreement, fldr 95 USP Test Ban Treaty Basic, box 3, Atomic Energy files, Acc 69A-2243.
78. Seaborg, *Kennedy, Khrushchev, and the Test Ban*, 190-91 (Harriman quote, 191).
79. News conf, 8 May 63, *Kennedy Public Papers, 1963*, 377-78; *Washington Post*, 10 May 63; *Christian Science Monitor*, 22 May 63.

80. News conf, 22 May 63, *Kennedy Public Papers, 1963*, 424; NSAM 239, 6 May 63, *FRUS 1961-63*, VII:692.
81. JCSM-449-63 CJCS for SecDef, 13 Jun 63, memo McNamara for Foster, 14 Jun 63, both in fldr Reading File, June 1-June 19, 1963, box 118, McNamara Records, RG 200 (McNamara enclosed a copy of JCSM-449-63 with the latter memo); memcon McNamara w/ LeMay, 24 Jun 63, ibid.
82. Memo McNamara for Taylor, Seaborg, Brown, Wiesner, 26 Jun 63, ibid; memcon, 14 Jun 63, *FRUS 1961-63*, VII:720-22; Poole, *JCS and National Policy 1961-64*, pt I:397-98.
83. Memcon, 14 Jun 63, cited in n 82, 721.
84. Norman Cousins, "Notes on a 1963 Visit with Khrushchev," *Saturday Review*, 7 Nov 64; Seaborg, *Kennedy, Khrushchev, and the Test Ban*, 179-80, 207-09, 212-13 (on Cousins' "unofficial liaison" role, see also Milton S. Katz, *Ban the Bomb*, 81, 83-84); memo Thompson for Rusk, 24 Apr 63, *FRUS 1961-63*, VII:687; on the Kennedy-Macmillan-Khrushchev correspondence during this period, see ibid, 663-718 passim.
85. Commencement address at American Univ, 10 Jun 63, *Kennedy Public Papers, 1963*, 460-64; Sorensen, *Kennedy*, 730-31.
86. CIA Information Report, 11 Jun 63, fldr Disarmament—Nuclear Test Ban Negotiations, 7/63 Meeting in Moscow, box 100, POF, JFKL; Seaborg, *Kennedy, Khrushchev, and the Test Ban*, 217-18; Newhouse, *War and Peace in the Nuclear Age*, 193.
87. Schlesinger, *A Thousand Days*, 903; McNaughton interv, 21 Nov 64, 6.
88. See Seaborg, *Kennedy, Khrushchev, and the Test Ban*, 227-31.
89. Msg Secto 20, Rusk for Foster and Harriman, 28 Jun 63, OSD Hist (emphasis in original); instructions for Harriman, 5 Jul 63, *FRUS 1961-63*, VII:769.
90. Instructions for Harriman, 10 Jul 63, *FRUS 1961-63*, VII:787; memo Foster for Pres, 12 Jul 63, w/cover memo for members of Cte of Principals, 12 Jul 63, citing DepSecDef letter to ACDA, 23 May 63, fldr Disarmament Subject, Basic Documents #3, 5/63-6/63, box 367, NSF, JFKL.
91. Memcon, George Rathjens, 8 Jul 63, fldr Disarmament Subject, Basic Documents #3, 5/63-7/63, box 367, NSF, JFKL (see also *FRUS 1961-63*, VII:772-76).
92. *FRUS 1961-63*, VII:772-76 (quote, 776, n 6); "Action Taken on Agenda Items" at 8 Jul 63 mtg of Cte of Principals, OSD Hist.
93. Memcon Harriman w/McNamara, 8 Jul 63, *FRUS 1961-63*, VII:776-77.
94. McNaughton interv, 21 Nov 64, 9; biog sketch of Lord Hailsham, in fldr JFK-LBJ, Trips and Missions, Test Ban Treaty Background (2), box 560, Harriman Papers, LC.
95. Memrcd Kaysen, 10 Jul 63, *FRUS 1961-63*, VII:789-90; memcon McNaughton, 1 Jul 63, fldr Disarmament Subject, Test Ban Inspections, box 370, NSF, JFKL; McNaughton interv, 21 Nov 64, 7.
96. McNaughton interv, 21 Nov 64, 9, 11; msgs Pres to Macmillan, 16 Jul 63, Macmillan to Pres, 18 Jul 63 (quotes, 2, 4, 6), Pres to Macmillan, 19 Jul 63: fldr ACDA Disarmament—Nuclear Test Ban, box 264, NSF, JFKL; memo Rostow for Pres, 23 Jul 63, w/atchd Rostow memo, 22 Jul 63, fldr Disarmament—Nuclear Test Ban Negotiations, 7/63 Meeting in Moscow, box 100, POF, JFKL. Marc Trachtenberg has observed in *A Constructed Peace*, 390-91, that with respect to France and Germany the test ban treaty involved "a whole web of understandings" of larger political significance beyond the issue of arms control. On the implications for the Sino-Soviet relationship, see memo Edward D. Rice for Harriman, 5 Jul 63, fldr JFK-LBJ, Trips and Missions, Test Ban Treaty Background (2), box 560, Harriman Papers, LC; memo William H. Sullivan for Harriman, 10 Jul 63, ibid; Gordon Chang, "JFK, China, and the Bomb," *Journal of American History*, Spring 88, 310. Chang suggests that contrary to Kennedy's ostensible purpose of enhancing peace and stability, the administration sought to exploit the test ban negotiations to aggravate tensions between the Soviet Union and China and sharpen the Sino-Soviet split.
97. McNaughton interv, 21 Nov 64, 11 (quote); Livesay notes, staff mtg, 29 Jul 63, fldr SecDef Staff Meetings Apr-Jul 1963, box 11, AFPC and SecDef Meetings files, Acc 77-0062; communiqué, 25 Jul 63, *American Foreign Policy: Current Documents, 1963*, 977-78; memcon Bromley Smith w/Pres, 23 Jul 63, *FRUS 1961-63*, VII:835.
98. McNaughton interv, 21 Nov 64, 13-16 (quote, 15); Seaborg, *Kennedy, Khrushchev, and the Test Ban*, 244-47.
99. Seaborg, *Kennedy, Khrushchev, and the Test Ban*, 242.
100. Treaty Banning Nuclear Weapon Tests in the Atmosphere, in Outer Space and Under Water, 5 Aug 63, *American Foreign Policy: Current Documents, 1963*, 1032-34.

101. Memcon Smith w/Pres, 23 Jul 63, cited in n 97, 835; communiqué, 5 Aug 63, *Documents on Disarmament, 1963*, 294-95.
102. Special msg to Senate, 8 Aug 63, *Kennedy Public Papers, 1963*, 622-23.
103. Tel transc, Pres and Rusk, 24 Jul 63, Item 23C1, Telephone Recordings, JFKL.
104. Memcon Smith w/Pres, 23 Jul 63, cited in n 97, 835; SCAS, Preparedness Investigating Subcte, *Hearings: Military Aspects and Implications of Nuclear Test Ban Proposals and Related Matters*, 88 Cong, 1 sess, 26 Jun 63, 306 (Anderson test), 356 (LeMay test).
105. Ibid, 16 Aug 63, 719 (LeMay), 12 Aug 63, 558 (Teller); tel transc, Pres and Fulbright, 23 Aug 63, Item 26B5, Telephone Recordings, JFKL.
106. SCAS, Preparedness Investigating Subcte, *Investigation of the Preparedness Program*, Interim Rpt on Military Implications of the Proposed Limited Nuclear Test Ban Treaty, 88 Cong, 1 sess, 9 Sep 63, 11-12.
107. *Hearings: Nuclear Test Ban Treaty*, cited in n 1, 21 Aug 63, 577-78.
108. Ibid, 13 Aug 63, 108-09.
109. Draft memo JCS for SecDef, nd, fldr ACDA Disarmament—Test Ban Safeguards, box 266, NSF, JFKL; Poole, *JCS and National Policy 1961-64*, pt I:399-400; tel transc, Pres and Mansfield, 12 Aug 63, Item 25C1, Telephone Recordings, JFKL.
110. Ltr Taylor to Sen Richard Russell, 23 Aug 63, w/encl criteria to ensure safeguards, copy in OSD Hist; tel transc, Pres and Fulbright, 23 Aug 63, Item 26C1, Telephone Recordings, JFKL.
111. Goldwater exchange with LeMay at Stennis subcte hearing, cited in n 104, 16 Aug 63, 733; Taylor, *Swords and Plowshares*, 287; Taylor interv, 18 Oct 83, 32.
112. Ed note, *FRUS 1961-63*, VII:886.
113. See Macmillan, *At the End of the Day*, 484; Sorensen, *Kennedy*, 740.
114. Hilsman, *To Move a Nation*, 581; Seaborg, *Kennedy, Khrushchev, and the Test Ban*, 297-301; Jerome B. Wiesner, "The Glory and Tragedy of the Partial Test Ban," *New York Times*, 11 Apr 88.
115. Carl Kaysen, "The Limited Test Ban Treaty of 1963," in Douglas Brinkley and Richard T. Griffiths, eds, *John F. Kennedy and Europe*, 112.
116. Ivo Daalder, "The Limited Test Ban Treaty," in Albert Carnesale and Richard N. Haass, eds, *Superpower Arms Control: Setting the Record Straight*, 35.

XIV. NATO RELATIONS: TRANSATLANTIC DIFFERENCES

1. See Richard J. Barnet and Marcus Raskin, *The Decline of NATO and the Search for a New Policy in Europe*; Ronald Steel, *The End of Alliance: America and the Future of Europe*, 215-16.
2. See Rowen, "Formulating Strategic Doctrine," *Rpt of Commission on Organization of Government for the Conduct of Foreign Policy*, vol 4, App K, pt 3:225, n 7.
3. Memo McNamara for ASD(ISA), 1 Feb 61, fldr Reading File, Feb. 1961-Dec. 1960, box 113, McNamara Records, RG 200.
4. Ltr Norstad to Acheson, 20 Apr 61, Norstad Papers, DDEL.
5. *Kennedy Public Papers, 1961*, 254.
6. Memo Gilpatric for SvcSecs et al, 29 Apr 61, fldr 334 NATO Apr 16-19, 1961, box 17, ISA files, Acc
7. CM-301-61 Lemnitzer for SecDef, w/encl A, 3 Aug 61, fldr 320.2 Jan-Aug, 1961, box 46, ISA files, Acc 64A-2382. For similar views see memos Lemnitzer for SecDef, 28 Mar, 15 Jun 61, ibid.
8. App A, "Current Comparison of Conventional Capabilities," ibid.
9. Msg ALO 327 Norstad to McNamara and Lemnitzer, 3 Apr 61, 4, ltr Norstad to Acheson, 20 Apr 61: Norstad Papers, DDEL; memo Lemnitzer for SecDef, 28 Mar 61, cited in n 7.
10. Ltr Rowen to Acheson, 3 Mar 61, w/encl, fldr 334 NATO, box 17, ISA files, Acc 64A-2382.
11. Memo DirER(ISA) MajGen F. H. Miller for Nitze, 10 Mar 61, fldr 334 NATO Jan-Jun 1961, box 46, ibid; memo DirPolPlngStaff(ISA) James H. Polk for Nitze, 15 Jun 61, fldr 334 NATO Jun 1-15, 1961, box 17, ibid.
12. Memo Nitze for SecDef, 28 Feb 61, fldr 334 NATO Feb 61, box 46, ibid; *Baltimore Sun*, 8 Mar 61.
13. Memcon Spaak, McNamara, et al, 20 Feb 61, fldr 334 NATO Feb 61, box 46, ISA files, Acc 64A-2382.
14. Memrcd DepDirER(ISA) Eaton, 3 Feb 61, ibid.
15. JCSM-407-61 Lemnitzer for SecDef, 15 Jun 61, fldr 320.2 Jan-Aug, 1961, box 46, ibid; ltr Norstad to Acheson, 20 Apr 61, cited in n 4.

16. Msg Polto 1463 Paris to State, 19 Apr 61, OSD Hist.
17. *Kennedy Public Papers, 1961*, 254.
18. Taylor, *Swords and Plowshares*, 209.
19. Memo Nitze for ASD(AE), 9 Jun 61, memo W. M. Shankle [for ASD(AE) Herbert B. Loper] for ASD(ISA), 13 Jun 61: fldr 334 NATO Jun 1-15, 1961, box 17, ISA files, Acc 64A-2382.
20. Memcon Stikker, Rusk, Acheson, et al, 14 Jun 61, ibid (excerpted version in *FRUS 1961-63*, XIII:316-21).
21. Memo Gilpatric for SpecAsst to Pres for NatSecAff, 15 Jun 61, fldr 334 NATO Jun 1-15, 1961, box 17, ISA files, Acc 64A-2382; memo McGeorge Bundy for SecDef, 1 May 61, fldr 334 NATO May 16-31, ibid.
22. Memo Bundy for SecDef, 1 May 61, cited in n 21.
23. Memo SecDef for SpecAsst to Pres for NatSecAff, 2 Jun 61, w/atchd memo William Bundy for SecDef, 1 Jun 61, fldr 334 NATO Jun 1-16, 1961, ibid.
24. JCSM-306-61 Burke for SecDef, 5 May 61, fldr 330 1/1/81-15-2-1, box 45, ISA files, Acc 64A-2382.
25. Memo J. L. Throckmorton, 1 Aug 61, w/encl, "Security of the North Atlantic Area: A Supporting Study to 'A United States Military Program,'" 4-5, fldr 091.3 Jul-Dec 61, box 44, ibid. For MC 70, see Watson, *Into the Missile Age*, 504-06.
26. Memo McNamara for CJCS, 2 Jun 61, fldr Jun 1-15, 1961, box 17, ISA files, Acc 64A-2382; CM-275-61 Lemnitzer for SecDef, 14 Jul 61, w/encl, fldr 334 NATO 2/81-15-2-1, box 46, ibid; Report of the Chairman's NATO Working Group (Rowny report), 1 Sep 61, 4, 6-7, ibid.
27. Rowny rpt, cited in n 26, Annex C to App I, "Estimated Cost of NATO Forces FY 61-66"; CM-350-61 Lemnitzer for SecDef, 5 Sep 61, 3, fldr 334 NATO, box 46, ISA files, Acc 64A-2382.
28. Rowny rpt, 12; Poole, *JCS and National Policy 1961-64*, pt III:15.
29. ISA paper for mtg, "Recommended Allied Force Contributions," 18 Jul 61, fldr 320.2, box 46, ISA files, Acc 64A-2382.
30. Msg Topol 365 State to NATO Mission, 16 Sep 61, *FRUS 1961-63*, XIII:329-32; Poole, *JCS and National Policy 1961-64*, pt III:17-18.
31. Memo Nitze for SvcSecs et al, 19 Dec 61, w/atchd McNamara remarks, 14 Dec 61 (quote, 4), fldr NATO 1961-65, box 99, ASD(C) files, OSD Hist.
32. Stikker quoted in Poole, *JCS and National Policy 1961-64*, pt III:21; msg 1108 Brussels to State, 19 Dec 61, memcons Rusk and Stikker, 5 Feb 62, Pres and Stikker, 6 Feb 62: *FRUS 1961-63*, XIII:345, 359-62.
33. Memo DepDirER(ISA) Col Edward A. Bailey, 3 Jul 62, I-2, I-4, IIA-1, IIAF-1, II-N-1, fldr 334 NATO, box 54, ISA files, Acc 64A-2382; *DoD Annual Report, FY 1962*, 17-18.
34. Memo DepDirER(ISA) R. M. Miner for Col L. J. Legere, Off MilRep Pres, 12 Feb 62, fldr 320.2 Jan-May, 1962, box 46, ISA files, Acc 64A-2382.
35. Memo McNamara for Pres, 9 Nov 62, fldr Reading File, Nov. 30-Nov. 1, 1962, box 116, McNamara Records, RG 200.
36. "Increases in NATO Country Force Capabilities, 1962-1963," ER(ISA) paper, 27 Nov 63, FY 65 SecDef Backup Book, I-II, ASD(C) files, OSD Hist.
37. Draft memo McNamara for Pres, 24 May 63, fldr Reading File, May 31-May 18, 1963, box 117, McNamara Records, RG 200.
38. Memo McNamara for CJCS, 8 Aug 63, fldr Reading File, Aug. 1963, box 118, ibid.
39. Memo McNamara for SvcSecs et al, 21 Dec 63 (quote, 14), fldr NATO 1961-65, box 99, ASD(C) files, OSD Hist.
40. See table on net expenditures for the Bundeswehr in Catherine M. Kelleher, *Germany & the Politics of Nuclear Weapons*, 98; memo Nitze for McNamara, 16 Mar 63, fldr Reading File, Mar. 1963, box 117, McNamara Records, RG 200; memo McNamara for CJCS, 19 Mar 63, ibid.
41. "French Defense Effort and Economic Capabilities," background paper D. D. Duff, ER(ISA), for NATO Ministerial mtg, Ottawa, 22-24 May 63, fldr NATO Ministerial Mtgs—France 1963-64, box 1, ISA files, Acc 67A-4736.
42. Memo Nitze for SvcSecs et al, 24 May 63, w/atchmts, McNamara remarks, ibid; NATO: Facts (1976), 58; Stromseth, *Origins of Flexible Response*, 54; memcon Rusk, Couve de Mourville, Bohlen, Alphand, 8 Oct 63, fldr France—General, box 73, NSF, JFKL.
43. "Draft Administrative History of DoD, 1963-69," 23, OSD Hist; Poole, *JCS and National Policy 1961-64*, pt III:135.
44. CM-222-64 Col Bernard Rogers, ExecSec to CJCS, for DirJtStaff, 30 Oct 64, w/atchmt, memo Llewelyn Thompson, 29 Oct 64, fldr 092.3, box 68, RG 218.

45. Memrcd B. K. Yount, ER(ISA), 3 Nov 60, fldr Baudet Mission France 1960-63, ISA files, Acc 67A-4736; msg 5102 Paris to State, 21 May 61, ibid, on Baudet's plan for a visit to Washington to follow up November 1960 discussions on reciprocal purchases of military equipment. For an analysis of Franco-American relations within the European context, see Erin R. Mahan, *Kennedy, de Gaulle, and Western Europe*.
46. Memo William R. Tyler for SecState, 25 Jul 61, memo Bundy for SecDef, 9 Aug 61: ibid; Agreement on Military Procurement, 20 Dec 61, TIAS 4914 (12 UST 3132).
47. "United States Pershing Missile Offer," ISA background paper for Messmer visit, 29-30 Nov 61, nd, ER(ISA) memo on "Offer of Pershing to France," 3 May 61, memo Yount, 19 May 61: fldr Baudet Mission France 1960-63, ISA files, Acc 67A-4736.
48. Memo DepAsst(Mutual Security) W. K. McNown for ASD(ISA), 8 Aug 61, note Rowen to Nitze, 7 Nov 61, w/atchmt, memo Miller for Nitze, 3 Nov 61: ibid.
49. Memo Miller for Rowen, Williams, Bundy, 13 Nov 61, ibid; Wilfred L. Kohl, *French Nuclear Diplomacy*, 217.
50. Msg 01340 Eaton to USCINCEUR, 22 Jan 63, fldr SERGEANT-PERSHING-MACE (France), ISA files, Acc 67A-4736. For text of de Gaulle's remarks at the 14 January press conference, see *American Foreign Policy: Current Documents, 1963*, 378-80, 441-43.
51. Memo DepSecDef for McGeorge Bundy, 22 Apr 63, w/atchmt, ltr Pres to Sen John Pastore, ChJtCte on Atomic Energy, 1 May 63, ltr ChMAAG(France) H. G. Sparrow to Eaton, 19 Jul 63, ltr Eaton to Sparrow, 3 Aug 63: fldr SERGEANT-PERSHING-MACE (France), ISA files, Acc 67A-4736.
52. Kohl, *French Nuclear Diplomacy*, 219.
53. Ibid, 215, 217; msg 2542 Paris to State, 14 Nov 61, *FRUS 1961-63*, XIII:678, n 1.
54. Msg 2542 Paris to State, cited in n 53; msg 3090 State to Paris, 29 Nov 61, *FRUS 1961-63*, XIII:678-79; ltr Gavin to Pres, 9 Mar 62, ibid, 687-88; msg 4920 State to Paris, 14 Mar 62, ibid, 688.
55. Msg 3090 State to Paris, 29 Nov 61, ibid, 678-79; Sorensen, *Kennedy*, 572-73; *American Foreign Policy: Current Documents, 1963*, 378-80.
56. "Nuclear Submarine Cooperation with France," background paper D. D. Duff, ER(ISA), for NATO Ministerial mtg, Ottawa, 22-24 May 63, fldr NATO Ministerial Mtgs—France 1963-64, box 1, ISA files, Acc 67A-4736.
57. *American Foreign Policy: Current Documents, 1963*, 378-80.
58. Kelleher, *Germany & the Politics of Nuclear Weapons*, 184-86. U.S. and British worries about Strauss's nuclear ambitions were reflected in ltr McNamara to Strauss, 5 Dec 61, fldr Reading File, Dec. 1963, box 113, McNamara Records, RG 200.
59. Kelleher, *Germany & the Politics of Nuclear Weapons*, 186-87.
60. Memrcd Goodpaster, 13 Dec 62, fldr 334 NATO Ministerial Mtgs, box 55, ISA files, Acc 67A-4736.
61. Memo Frank K. Sloan (ISA) for SvcSecs et al, 18 Dec 62, w/atchd McNamara remarks at 14 Dec 62 NATO Ministerial mtg, ibid; memcon State, 17 Dec 62, fldr 334-350.5 Germany 1962, box 41, ISA files, Acc 65A-3501.
62. Ltr McNamara to Rusk, 25 Feb 63, fldr Reading File, Feb. 1963, box 117, McNamara Records, RG 200.
63. Memo Hitch for SecDef, 26 Feb 63, memo McNamara for SecA, 28 Feb 63: ibid. See also Chapter XVII.
64. Memo Gilpatric for Pres, 22 Apr 63, fldr SERGEANT-PERSHING-MACE (France), ISA files, Acc 67A-4736; *DoD Annual Report, FY 1964*, 188-89.
65. Memo McGeorge Bundy for SecDef, 1 May 62, fldr Reading File, May 17-May 1, 1962, box 114, McNamara Records, RG 200.
66. Msg 3550 Paris to State, 22 Jan 62, OSD Hist.
67. The Skybolt controversy generated a wealth of analysis and literature on both sides of the Atlantic, including an in-house study commissioned by President Kennedy that describes in detail the U.S. side of the story. At Kennedy's request, Columbia University Professor Richard E. Neustadt wrote, "Skybolt and Nassau: American Policy-Making and Anglo-American Relations." Completed on 15 November 1963 and given to the president just before his death, it was not declassified until 1992 and was subsequently published in Neustadt, *Report to JFK: The Skybolt Crisis in Perspective*, 19-122. Neustadt incorporated the study's findings in other works, most notably his *Alliance Politics*. He enjoyed virtually unlimited access to U.S. records and interviewed high-level U.S. and British officials. However, he did not interview Macmillan, and the Macmillan government refused him access to British records. Among monographs that deal with the British role, see David Nunnerley, *President Kennedy and Britain*, 127-61; Ian Clark, *Nuclear Diplomacy and the Special Relationship: Britain's Deterrent and America, 1957-1962*, 240-96, 338-421; John Baylis, *Ambi-

guity and Deterrence: British Nuclear Strategy, 1945-1964, 290-326; Donette Murray, *Kennedy, Macmillan and Nuclear Weapons*, 31-104; and Nigel J. Ashton, *Kennedy, Macmillan and the Cold War: The Irony of Interdependence*, 152-92.

68. Interv Gilpatric by O'Brien, 30 Jun 70, 88, JFKL.
69. Enthoven and Smith, *How Much Is Enough?*, 251-53.
70. For Skybolt's early history, see Watson, *Into the Missile Age*, 373-74, 562-64, and Ronald D. Landa, "The Origins of the Skybolt Controversy in the Eisenhower Administration," in Roger G. Miller, ed, *Seeing Off the Bear: Anglo-American Air Power Cooperation During the Cold War*, 117-31.
71. McNamara interv, 3 Apr 86, 25; memo USecAF Joseph Charyk for ChStaffAF, 23 Feb 61, fldr SecAF/Defense, box 47, Thomas White Papers, LC; memo Vance for SvcSecs et al, 30 Mar 61, w/atchmt DDR&E White Paper, "Skybolt," 27 Mar 61, fldr White Papers, box 108, ASD(C) files, OSD Hist.
72. Policy Directive, "NATO and the Atlantic Nations," 20 Apr 61, *FRUS 1961-63*, XIII:289.
73. "Preliminary Report of the DOD Committee on Strategic Weapons," 31 Oct 61, 16, fldr GAM 87-Skybolt, box 2, DDR&E Skybolt files, Acc 68A-1575; memo Hitch for SecDef, 9 Nov 61, fldr UK 471.94 1960-1961 Papers, box 9, SecDef Subject Decimal files, Acc 66A-3542.
74. Memo Zuckert for SecDef, 21 Oct 61, w/atchd paper, "GAM-87A System Package Program: Interim Revision I," 2 Oct 61, fldr UK 471.94 (27 Apr 62) 1960-1961 Papers, box 9, SecDef Subject Decimal files, Acc 66A-3542; memo McNamara for SecAF, 1 Dec 61, fldr GAM 87-Skybolt, box 2, DDR&E Skybolt files, Acc 68A-1575; Neustadt, *Report to JFK*, 29.
75. Memo Rubel for SecDef, nd, fldr UK 471.94 (27 April 62) 1960-1961 Papers, box 9, SecDef Subject Decimal files, Acc 66A-3542. The memo was attached to a note from S. E. Clements (ISA) to McNamara's military assistant, Brig. Gen. George S. Brown, dated 21 March 1961. The note was stamped, "SECDEF HAS SEEN."
76. Memcons Watkinson w/McNamara, Watkinson w/Gilpatric, both 21 Mar 61, fldr UK 400.112 Complementarity, box 9, SecDef Subject Decimal files, Acc 66A-3542; memcon Watkinson and McNamara, 11 Dec 61 (afternoon), fldr Official Chron File 1961-62, box CL 1, Paul Nitze Papers, LC; Henry Brandon, "Skybolt: The Full Inside Story of How a Missile Nearly Split the West," *Sunday Times Weekly Review*, 8 Dec 63, 29-30.
77. Paper, "White House Brief: Anglo-U.S. Discussions," 6 Feb 61, fldr UK Skybolt Polaris 11 Dec. 59-29 Jan. 61, box 1, ISA United Kingdom files, Acc 67A-4738; memo Wiesner for Pres, 25 Apr 62, fldr NATO, Weapons, Skybolt 3/63-Folder 1 of 2, box 227, NSF, JFKL.
78. Memo Gilpatric for Zuckert, 21 May 62, fldr RLG Reading File-1/2/62 thru 6/30/62, box 2, Gilpatric files, Acc 66A-3529; memo McNamara for SecAF, 25 May 62, fldr GAM 87-Skybolt, box 2, DDR&E Skybolt files, Acc 68A-1575; BoB draft paper, "1964 Budget Preview: Department of Defense—Military Functions," 13 Jul 62, fldr FY 1964 Budget Bureau Proposals July-Sept 1962, box 20, McNamara Records, RG 200; memo Brown for SecDef, 21 Aug 62, w/atchmts, fldr Skybolt-Studies and AF Press Release of Test 8/21/62, box 23, ibid; Neustadt, *Report to JFK*, 30-31; interv with Harold Brown by Steven Rivkin, 9 Jul 64, 13-14, JFKL.
79. Draft memo, "Format A," nd, and ER(ISA) paper, "U.K. Participation in Skybolt Program," 15 Aug 62, both atchd to memo Brown for SecDef, 21 Aug 62, cited in n 78.
80. Paper, "Record of Conversations Regarding Skybolt: Selected Excerpts," nd, fldr Skybolt (1 of 3), box 21, McNamara Records, RG 200; interv Peter Thorneycroft by David Nunnerley, 18 Jun 69, 12-13 (quote, 13), fldr Transcripts-Redmayne-Thorneycroft, box 1, David Nunnerley Papers, JFKL. The paper suggests that the McNamara-Thorneycroft conversation regarding Skybolt took place on 12 September at SAC headquarters, Omaha, Nebraska.
81. Memo Bell for Bundy, 26 Oct 62, fldr NATO, Weapons, Skybolt 3/63 (1), box 227, NSF, JFKL.
82. Memo, State Dept, "Implications for the United Kingdom of Decision to Abandon Skybolt," 31 Oct 62, *FRUS 1961-63*, XIII:1083-85; memo Nitze for SecDef, 3 Nov 62, w/atchmts, fldr UK 471.94 (27 Apr 62) November 1962, box 9, SecDef Subject Decimal files, Acc 66A-3542.
83. Marginal handwritten notes on memo Nitze for SecDef, 3 Nov 62, cited in n 82.
84. Neustadt, *Report to JFK*, 35-37; McNamara notes of conversations relating to Skybolt, 9 Nov 62, fldr NATO, Weapons, Skybolt 3/63 (1), box 227, NSF, JFKL; Neustadt memcons w/McNamara, 30 May 63, 3, and 29 Jun 63, 3, fldr Memcons-U.S., box 21, Richard Neustadt Papers, JFKL. An excerpt of the McNamara notes is in *FRUS 1961-63*, XIII:1085-86.
85. McNamara notes, 9 Nov 62, cited in n 84.

86. Draft memo McNamara for Pres, 21 Nov 63, *FRUS 1961-63*, VIII:398-414; memrcd Gilpatric, 23 Nov 62, ibid, 415; Neustadt, *Report to JFK*, 41; ltr Rusk to McNamara, 24 Nov 62, *FRUS 1961-63*, XIII:1086-87.

87. Handwritten note Weymouth for Eaton and Barringer, 26 Nov 62, fldr UK Skybolt-21 Mar 61-30 Nov 62, box 1, ISA United Kingdom files, Acc 67A-4738; Neustadt, *Report to JFK*, 65 (quote); msg DEF 922514 to London, personal for Bruce from McNamara, 6 Dec 62, fldr UK Skybolt-Dec 3-Dec 31, 1962, box 1, ISA United Kingdom files, Acc 67A-4738.

88. *Aviation Week*, 26 Nov 62; *Daily Express* (London), 28 Nov 62; *St. Louis Post-Dispatch*, 6 Dec 62; comments Covington on GAM-87 GL-1 Missile #20032 (fifth launch), 30 Nov 62, fldr GAM 87-Skybolt, box 2, DDR&E Skybolt files, Acc 68A-1575.

89. Telcon Ball and McNamara, 10 Dec 62, 7:25 pm, fldr Britain 12/3/62-11/8/63, box 1, George Ball Papers, JFKL; Ball, *Past Has Another Pattern*, 264 (quote); memcon Neustadt w/Ball, 24 May 63, 1 (quote), fldr Memcons-U.S., box 21, Neustadt Papers, JFKL. Ball's published account differs in some respects with the record of the telephone conversation. Moreover, McNamara's references to Skybolt went beyond the test flights. He also spoke of the press speculation about Skybolt's future and mentioned that the U.S. government was "taking a very hard look at all of our programs" in preparing the next fiscal year's Defense budget, which included Skybolt, "one of our bigger programs." Skybolt was "very expensive," he said, "and, technically, extremely complex." Moreover, "costs have climbed sharply." McNamara indicated that he and Thorneycroft later in the day would "review the current status of the Skybolt program and its prospects for the future. As I have said previously, no decision has been reached by our government on the program for fiscal year 1964" (*McNamara Public Statements, 1962*, IV:1966). According to still another source, the State Department the night before had urged McNamara to delete from the statement all references to Skybolt, not just comments about the flight tests, and to delay any public comment about Skybolt until after the meeting with Thorneycroft; see memo Lennartson for Gilpatric, 12 Dec 62, fldr Skybolt, box 5, Legislative Affairs files, Acc 67A-4632.

90. Lord Harlech [David Ormsby Gore], "Suez SNAFU, Skybolt SABU," *Foreign Policy*, Spring 71, 49.

91. Memcon Neustadt w/McNamara, 30 May 63, 4, fldr Memcons-U.S., box 21, Neustadt Papers, JFKL; Neustadt, *Report to JFK*, 67-69; Bundy memcon, 10 Dec 62, *FRUS 1961-63*, vols. XIII, XIV, XV Microfiche Supplement, Doc 27.

92. Aide-memoire, 11 Dec 62, fldr UK 471.96 (27 Apr 62) December 1962, box 9, SecDef Subject Decimal files, Acc 66A-3542; Rubel notes of McNamara-Thorneycroft mtg, 11 Dec 62, fldr 12/62 Skybolt-Nassau (1), box 19, Neustadt Papers, JFKL; Rubel paper, "Skybolt Notes," Jun 91, 11, fldr Skybolt, box 869, Subject files, OSD Hist (emphasis in original).

93. Memcon Neustadt w/McNamara, 30 May 63, cited in n 91; Clark, *Nuclear Diplomacy and the Special Relationship*, 352-57.

94. See, for example, Neustadt, *Report to JFK*, 48-55; Schlesinger, *A Thousand Days*, 859-60. When the British, according to their 30-year rule, opened the records regarding Skybolt to the public in the early 1990s, Neustadt discovered that his earlier conclusions about British passivity had been mistaken (Neustadt, *Report to JFK*, 124-27).

95. Macmillan, *At the End of the Day*, 358; memo of understanding between Pres and Prime Min, 21 Dec 62, fldr GAM 87-Skybolt 1963-64, box 2, DDR&E Skybolt files, Acc 68A-1575; *Baltimore Sun*, 1 Jan 63; see also msg 4 Delegation to Heads of Government Mtg in Nassau to EmbParis, w/text of ltr to de Gaulle, 20 Dec 62, *FRUS 1961-1963*, XIII:1112-14; jt statement, Kennedy and Macmillan, 21 Dec 62, *American Foreign Policy: Current Documents, 1962*, 635-37; Alistair Horne, *Harold Macmillan*, II:439.

96. Interv David Ormsby Gore by Neustadt, 5 May 64, 19, JFKL; Gilpatric interv, 30 Jun 70, 89; ltr McNamara to LeMay, 5 Jan 63, fldr Reading File, Jan. 17-Jan. 1, 1963, box 116, McNamara Records, RG 200.

97. Memcon Neustadt w/Pres, 27 Apr 63, 1, memcon Neustadt w/McNamara, 29 Jun 63, 1: fldr Memcons-U.S., box 21, Neustadt Papers, JFKL.

98. Lord Harlech, "Suez SNAFU, Skybolt SABU," 48.

99. Memcon Neustadt w/Pres, 27 Apr 63, 1, cited in n 97.

XV. MLF: A NOTION TOO FAR

1. For the genesis of the MLF during the Eisenhower years see Watson, *Into the Missile Age*, 550-61; draft ms, Ronald D. Landa, "Preparing for the Long Haul: The Office of the Secretary of Defense and the Defense of Europe, 1953-1961," ch XI ("Birth of the Multilateral Force (MLF)"), OSD Hist; Pascaline Wi-

nand, *Eisenhower, Kennedy, and the United States of Europe*, 214-15. On the limited deployment of the Thor and Jupiter, see Watson, *Into the Missile Age*, 539-43. The terms "IRBMs" and "MRBMs" were used interchangeably in the late fifties. Watson notes that at Norstad's suggestion OSD adopted the MRBM nomenclature in January 1960, perhaps to distinguish the new delivery vehicles from the much criticized earlier ones.

2. Landa, "MLF," 15-17; Schwartz, *NATO's Nuclear Dilemmas*, 78.
3. Watson, *Into the Missile Age*, 554-60, and Landa, "MLF," 18-38, treat these deliberations, involving Eisenhower, the JCS, the AEC, and the civilian leadership at State and Defense, at length.
4. Msg Polto A-234 USRO to State, 17 Dec 60, w/encl text of Herter statement, *FRUS 1958-60*, VII, pt 1:674-82.
5. Memcon SecDef, Lemnitzer et al, 21 Apr 61, ltr Norstad to Gilpatric, 2 May 61: Norstad Papers, DDEL; memrcd Eaton, 20 Apr 61, fldr 2/81 15-2-1, Jan-Jun 61, box 46, ISA files, Acc 64A-2382; John D. Steinbruner, *The Cybernetic Theory of Decision: New Dimensions of Political Analysis*, 228.
6. Memcon Spaak, McNamara, Gilpatric, USAmbNATO W. Randolph Burgess, Nitze et al, 20 Feb 61, fldr 334 NATO—Feb 1961, ISA files, Acc 64A-2382.
7. Landa, "MLF," 44; Winand, *Eisenhower, Kennedy, and the United States of Europe*, 224-25; memcon Richard Neustadt w/Weiss, 29 May 63, fldr Memcons—U.S., box 21, Neustadt Papers, JFKL.
8. Memcon 20 Feb 61, cited in n 6; memrcd Eaton, 20 Apr 61, memcon SecDef, Lemnitzer et al, 21 Apr 61: both cited in n 5; Landa, "MLF," 42-43; Pagedas, *A Troubled Partnership*, 85.
9. *Kennedy Public Papers, 1961*, 67, 72 (quote), 385.
10. Winand, *Eisenhower, Kennedy, and the United States of Europe*, 229.
11. Memo Eaton for Nitze, 30 May 61, fldr 092 Germany, box 33, ISA files, Acc 64A-2382.
12. On the delicate political considerations involving the European governments, see msg 2054 Paris to State, 16 Oct 61, *FRUS 1961-63*, XIII:333; ltr Rusk to McNamara, 29 Oct 61, ibid, 333-35; Winand, *Eisenhower, Kennedy, and the United States of Europe*, 226-29.
13. Rcd of mtg Pres and Stikker, 16 Jun 61, *FRUS 1961-63*, XIII:322.
14. Policy Directive, 20 Apr 61, ibid, 285-91; memo Acheson for SecDef, 19 Jul 61, 4 (quote), box 216, Norstad Papers, DDEL.
15. Ltr Walter Stoessel, PolAd SACEUR, to Russell Fessenden, DirER, State, 17 Nov 61, ltr Norstad to Pres, 20 Dec 61, w/encl list of SHAPE's questions, 20 Dec 61: Norstad Papers, DDEL.
16. Kennedy's circumspection regarding the MLF is discussed throughout the chapter. A collection of participants' characterizations of the president's attitude toward the MLF is in Winand, *Eisenhower, Kennedy, and the United States of Europe*, 223-24.
17. Msg JCS 997069 to CINCAL, other commands, 6 Jun 61, OSD Hist.
18. Memrcd Eaton, mtg Nitze and Stikker (15 Jun 61), 27 Jun 61, OSD Hist.
19. Ltr McNamara to Rusk, 5 Dec 61, fldr Reading File, Dec. 1961, box 54, McNamara Records, RG 200; msg Polto A-270 USRO to State, 16 Dec 61, OSD Hist. It was this list of questions that prompted the SHAPE submittal that Norstad sent on to the White House. See note 15.
20. Memcon McNamara and Watkinson, Paris (15 Dec 61), 5 Jan 62, fldr 12/61 NATO Mtg, box 4, McNamara files, 71A-3470; Alastair Buchan, "The Multilateral Force: An Historical Perspective," *Adelphi Papers*, No 13 (Oct 64), 5-6.
21. Memo Kaysen for Bundy, 22 Feb 62, fldr Multilateral Force, General, Vol I, 1/61-12/62, box 216, NSF, JFKL.
22. Memo ASecState Foy Kohler for Nitze, 31 Jan 62, w/encl, fldr 333, Jan 62, box 54, ISA files, Acc 64A-2382.
23. "Pentagon Presses MRBM Development," *Aviation Daily*, 26 Feb 62.
24. Msg Norstad to CJCS, 20 Feb 62, OSD Hist; msg Topol 1579 State to Missions to NATO and Eur Reg Orgs, 16 Apr 62, *FRUS 1961-63*, XIII:380-83; Norstad's angry comment in msg to Lemnitzer, 18 Apr 62, MRBM (Channels) file, personal NATO (NAC), Norstad Papers, DDEL. Steinbruner, *Cybernetic Theory*, 226, and Winand, *Eisenhower, Kennedy, and the United States of Europe*, 232, identify Henry Owen as the primary author of the 16 April paper.
25. Minutes of mtg Kennedy, McNamara, Rusk, Bundy, 16 Apr 62, *FRUS 1961-63*, XIII:377-80 (quote, 379); NSAM 147, 18 Apr 62, NATO Nuclear Program, ibid, 384-87; memrcd Taylor, 19 Apr 62, fldr SPCOL-159-88, Taylor Papers, NDUL (quote).

26. Memrcd Taylor, 19 Apr 62, cited in n 25.
27. Memo McNamara for CJCS, 3 Apr 62, fldr Reading File, Apr. 18-Apr. 1, 1962, box 114, McNamara Records, RG 200.
28. Remarks by McNamara at NATO Ministerial mtg, 5 May 62 (quote, 24), Policy Planning Staff files, Lot 69D-121, RG 59.
29. Memo McNamara for CJCS, 16 May 62, fldr Reading File, May 17-May 1, 1962, box 114, McNamara Records, RG 200; memo Legere for Taylor, 1 Jun 62, fldr Multilateral Force, General, Vol I, 1/61-12/62, box 216, NSF, JFKL; memo Taylor for Pres, 13 Jun 62, fldr SPCOL-S-34-89, Taylor Papers, NDUL.
30. Msg Norstad to CJCS, 18 May 62, memo BrigGen Robert Richardson for Norstad, 20 Jun 62, w/encl: Norstad Papers, DDEL.
31. Memo Taylor for Pres, 13 Jun 62, cited in n 29; instructions for Finletter, nd, *FRUS 1961-63*, XIII: 408-11; msg Secto 12, US del at NAC Ministerial mtg (Paris) to State, 20 Jun 62, ibid, 411-13; memcon Rusk and Adenauer, 22 Jun 62, ibid, 419-22 (quote, 421).
32. Msg Polto 1711 USRO to State, 22 Jun 62, OSD Hist; memcon Kissinger with Stikker (26 Jun 62), 13 Jul 62, fldr T-094-69, box 37, Taylor Papers, NDUL; "Initial Reactions to 15 June 1962 MRBM Paper presented by Amb Finletter," Stoessel comments, memo for file, 19 Jun 62, ibid.
33. Memcon Neustadt w/Pres, 27 Apr 63, fldr Memcons-U.S., box 21, Neustadt Papers, JFKL.
34. Memo Richardson for Norstad, 20 Jun 62, cited in n 30.
35. Memcon Neustadt w/Rowen, 1 Jul 63, fldr Memcons-U.S., box 21, Neustadt Papers, JFKL.
36. *Kennedy Public Papers, 1962*, 538; Winand, *Eisenhower, Kennedy, and the United States of Europe*, 235-36.
37. Memcon Neustadt w/Weiss, 29 May 63, fldr Memcons-U.S., box 21, Neustadt Papers, JFKL; msg Topol 344 State to Paris, 15 Sep 62, OSD Hist; Steinbruner, *Cybernetic Theory*, 228-33; DoD study, "NATO Multilateral Sea-Based MRBM Force," nd [c 15 Sep 62], fldr SPCOL-S-074-88, box 37, Taylor Papers, NDUL; OSD comments on "NATO Multilateral Sea-Based MRBM Force," nd, ibid.
38. Memo Legere for Taylor, 6 Jul 62, fldr T094-69, box 37, ibid.
39. Memo Richardson for Norstad, 6 Sep 62, MRBM file, Norstad Papers, DDEL; memo Legere for Bundy, 19 Nov 62, fldr Multilateral Force, General, Vol I, 1/61-12/62, box 216, NSF, JFKL; memo Rusk and McNamara for Pres, undated [16 Jul 62], *FRUS 1961-63*, XIII:430-34.
40. Msg LNI 4388 Norstad to SecDef, 2 Nov 62, Norstad Papers, DDEL.
41. Steinbruner, *Cybernetic Theory*, 233-34; ed note, *FRUS 1961-63*, XIII:446-47; memrcd ER(ISA) James C. Cross, 20 Nov 62, fldr 337, Jan 62 NATO Min Mtgs, box 55, ISA files, Acc 64A-2382; Lemnitzer notes on DoD-State mtg, 30 Nov 62, fldr L-216-71, box 29, Lemnitzer Papers, NDUL.
42. Memrcd Cross, 20 Nov 62, cited in n 41.
43. The MLF does not appear in the NATO Council's communiqué of 15 December 1962 (*NATO Final Communiqués, 1949-1974*, 147-49); news reports on the "veto" subject in *Baltimore Sun* and *Washington Star*, 14 Dec 62; on McNamara's conviction that the Europeans would balk at the "preconditions," see Steinbruner, *Cybernetic Theory*, 234.
44. Statement by Kennedy and Macmillan, 21 Dec 62, *American Foreign Policy: Current Documents, 1962*, 636.
45. On de Gaulle's summary rejection of the U.S. offer, see his 14 January 1963 press conference, excerpted in *American Foreign Policy: Current Documents, 1963*, 378-80; see also Winand, *Eisenhower, Kennedy, and the United States of Europe*, 320-24.
46. Neustadt, *Report to JFK*, 98. See, too, Winand, *Eisenhower, Kennedy, and the United States of Europe*, 319-20; Murray, *Kennedy, Macmillan and Nuclear Weapons*, 101-04; Buchan, "The Multilateral Force: An Historical Perspective," 7. Buchan noted that the final communiqué reflected "two soliloquies rather than an understanding."
47. Memo, ns, "The Multilateral Force," 27 Dec 62, fldr Multilateral Force, General, Vol II, Merchant, box 217, NSF, JFKL; memo Kitchen for Rusk, 4 Jan 63, *FRUS 1961-63*, XIII:1123-28; NSAM 215 to SecState and SecDef, 12 Jan 63, cited in Poole, *JCS and National Policy 1961-1964*, pt III:94; memo McNamara for CJCS, 12 Jan 63, fldr Reading File, Jan. 17-Jan. 1, 1963, box 116, McNamara Records, RG 200; memo McNamara for SecAF, 12 Jan 63, ibid; TV and radio interv, 17 Dec 62, *Kennedy Public Papers, 1962*, 903; McNaughton interv, 14 Nov 64, 6.
48. Paper, "Outline of NATO Multilateral Strategic Retaliatory Force," 19 Jan 63, fldr Reading File, Jan. 31-Jan. 18, 1963, box 116, McNamara Records, RG 200; Poole, *JCS and National Policy 1961-1964*, pt III:94-95.
49. Msg 1436 State to Bonn, 21 Dec 62, *FRUS 1961-63*, XIII:467-68; msg 1569 State to Bonn, 10 Jan 63, ibid, 468-71; msg Polto cir 27 Paris to State, 11 Jan 63, ibid, 471-74.

50. Memo McNamara for SecN et al, 29 Jan 63, fldr Reading File Jan. 31-Jan. 18, 1963, box 116, McNamara Records, RG 200; memo Pres for members of MLF Negotiating Del, 21 Feb 63, *FRUS 1961-63*, XIII:509-11 (quote, 509); memo for MLF Negotiating Team, 15 Feb 63, fldr Multilateral Force, General, Vol II, Merchant, box 217, NSF, JFKL. The latter appears to have come out of the White House, and contains Kennedy's marginal notes; it was signed, however, by Merchant.
51. Memcon mtg w/Pres, 18 Feb 63, *FRUS 1961-63*, XIII:502-06 (quote, 502); McNaughton interv, 14 Nov 64, 7; draft memcon Neustadt w/McNamara, 29 Jun 63, 12-13, fldr Memcons-U.S., box 21, Neustadt Papers, JFKL.
52. Memo Bundy for Pres, 15 Jun 63, *FRUS 1961-63*, XIII:592-95 (quotes, 594); memcons Neustadt w/Rusk, 27 Aug 63, McNamara, 29 Jun 63, Nitze (draft), 11, 19 Jun 63, fldr Memcons-U.S., box 21, Neustadt Papers, JFKL.
53. Memcons Neustadt w/Ball, 2 Jul 63, McNamara (draft), 29 Jun 63, 12-13, fldr Memcons-U.S., box 21, Neustadt Papers, JFKL; Steinbruner, *Cybernetic Theory*, 250-51, 319.
54. McNaughton interv, 14 Nov 64, 5-8; sum rcd 41st NSC ExCom mtg, 12 Feb 63, *FRUS 1961-63*, XIII:494-502; draft White Paper, 15 Feb 63, fldr Multilateral Force, General, Vol III, Merchant, box 217, NSF, JFKL; memo Bundy for SecState and SecDef, 11 Mar 63, *FRUS 1961-63*, XIII:524.
55. Memo Pres for Taylor and Anderson, 21 Feb 63, fldr Multilateral Force, General, Vol II, Merchant, box 216, NSF, JFKL; memo Lemnitzer for Gilpatric, 14 Feb 63, fldr SPCOL-TS-004-89, box 143, Lemnitzer Papers, NDUL; memo SpecAsst(CJCS) A. J. Goodpaster for Nitze, 20 Apr 63, w/atchmt, fldr SPCOL-TS-005-89, box 40, ibid; memo Lemnitzer for Taylor, 12 Jun 63, fldr 31 1963, Vol 1, box 174, ibid.
56. Memo Kohler for Bruce, 8 Feb 63, fldr JFK-LBJ Trips and Missions—Test Ban Treaty Background, box 560, Harriman Papers, LC; memrcd Bundy, mtg in Cabinet Room, 21 Feb 63, *FRUS 1961-63*, XIII:507-08; McNaughton interv, 14 Nov 64, 7 (also see *FRUS 1961-63*, XIII:561-64); sum rcd 41st NSC ExCom mtg, 12 Feb 63, cited in n 54, 497. On the "unanimity" principle, which represented a significant change in the U.S. position, see memo Pres for members of MLF Negotiating Del, 21 Feb 63, cited in n 50, 510.
57. Memo Merchant for Rusk, 20 Mar 63, *FRUS 1961-63*, XIII:529-37; msg 4851 State to London, 14 Mar 63, ibid, 527-28; USIA briefing item, 7 Mar 63, "Initial West European Assessment of US Multilateral Force Proposals," fldr Multilateral Force, General, box 218, NSF, JFKL.
58. Memo Merchant for Rusk, 20 Mar 63, cited in n 57, 532-33; Baylis, *Ambiguity and Deterrence*, 328-30; msg 4851 State to London, 14 Mar 63, cited in n 57, 528. Murray, *Kennedy, Macmillan and Nuclear Weapons*, devotes ch 7 to the subject of British antipathy toward the MLF (Thorneycroft "nonsense" quote on p. 124).
59. Memo Merchant for Rusk, 20 Mar 63, cited in n 57, 536-37; memo mtg at White House, 22 Mar 63, *FRUS 1961-63*, XIII:537-42; msg 236 State to Bonn, 29 Mar 63, w/encl ltr Kennedy to Adenauer, 29 Mar 63, ibid, 542-46 (a similar letter was drafted for Fanfani); memo McNamara for Ricketts, 9 Apr 63, fldr Reading File, Apr. 17-Apr. 5, 1963, box 55, McNamara Records, RG 200; McNaughton interv, 14 Nov 64, 6-8; msg 2673 State to Bonn, 2 May 63, w/encl ltr Adenauer to Kennedy, 30 Apr 63, *FRUS 1961-63*, XIII:565-66. Winand, *Eisenhower, Kennedy, and the United States of Europe*, 345, discusses an interesting sidelight to Tyler's call on Fanfani.
60. Ltr Adenauer to Kennedy, 30 Apr 63, cited in n 59, 566; McNaughton interv, 14 Nov 64, 7; communiqué NAC mtg, 22-24 May 63, *American Foreign Policy: Current Documents, 1963*, 408-09.
61. Memo McNamara for CJCS, 28 Jun 63, w/atchmt ltr McNamara to DefMin Giulio Andreotti, 24 Jun 63, fldr Reading File, June 20-June 29, 1963, box 118, McNamara Records, RG 200; memo Bundy for Pres, 15 Jun 63, cited in n 52, 592-95; McNaughton interv, 14 Nov 64, 7; memcon Neustadt w/Taylor and Maj William Smith, 3 Jul 63, fldr Memcons-U.S., box 21, Neustadt Papers, JFKL. For an extensive examination of the MLF see McGeorge Bundy, "The Multilateral Force: Where it came from, what it is, and what it is not," 24 Jun 63, McGeorge Bundy file, NSF, LBJL.
62. *Kennedy Public Papers, 1963*, 518; ltr McNamara to Merchant, 28 Jun 63, fldr Reading File, June 20-June 29, 1963, box 118, McNamara Records, RG 200; Steinbruner, *Cybernetic Theory*, 283 (Bowie similarly compared their plight to Sisyphus's in his interview with Neustadt; see memcon, 1 Jul 63, fldr memcons--U.S., box 21, Neustadt Papers, JFKL).
63. NSAM 253, 13 Jul 63, *FRUS 1961-63*, XIII:604; msg Topol 292 State to USRO, 11 Sep 63, ibid, 608-10; memo McNamara for Pres, 26 Aug 63, fldr Reading File, Aug. 1963, box 118, McNamara Records, RG 200; Winand, *Eisenhower, Kennedy, and the United States of Europe*, 350; memcon White House mtg on MLF, 4 Oct 63, *FRUS 1961-63*, XIII:613-14.

64. Murray, *Kennedy, Macmillan and Nuclear Weapons*, 141-43 (quote, 143). Neustadt described Kennedy as not so much equivocal as "erratic" in his handling of the MLF.
65. Memrcd Rostow, 18 Dec 63, box 173, S/MF files, Lot 66D-182, RG 59; paper, Dept State, 6 Dec 63, *FRUS 1961-63*, XIII:635-39 (quote, 639).
66. Philip Geyelin, *Lyndon B. Johnson and the World*, 7, 15.
67. Memo McNamara for SecN, 31 Jan 64, fldr Reading File, Jan. 31-Jan. 18, 1964, box 119, McNamara Records, RG 200; *Johnson Public Papers, 1963-64*, I:496; memo of disc, 10 Apr 64, *FRUS 1964-68*, XIII:35-37 (quotes, 35). See, too, memo David Klein for Bundy, 7 Apr 64, fldr NATO, General—Vol 1, box 35, Agency File, NSF, LBJL. On the misreading, or embellishment, of Johnson's position, see Geyelin, *Johnson and the World*, 160.
68. Ltr SecDef and ChAEC to Pres, 18 May 64, *American Foreign Policy: Current Documents, 1964*, 471-73 (an unsigned letter dated 15 May was found at the Johnson Library); memo McNamara for CJCS, 15 Jul 64, fldr Reading File, July 1964, box 120, McNamara Records, RG 200; ltr McNamara to Mahon, 28 Aug 64, ibid.
69. "Status Report on the Multilateral Force," 19 Aug 64, fldr 1-11, Office of MLF Affairs, ISA files, Acc 64A-2382; memo Bundy for Pres, 15 Jun 63, cited in n 52, 593; London *Times*, 7 Jul 64 (cited in Boulton, "NATO and the MLF," 275); msg Bundy to de Zulueta, w/encl msg Kennedy to Macmillan, 10 May 63, *FRUS 1961-63*, XIII:573.
70. Jt communiqué issued by Johnson and Erhard, 12 Jun 64, *American Foreign Policy: Current Documents, 1964*, 537 (see also communiqué issued by McNamara and German Defense Minister von Hassel, 14 Nov 64, excerpts, ibid, 552-53); ltr McNamara to von Hassel, 29 Jun 64, fldr Reading File, July 1964, box 120, McNamara Records, RG 200; memo NSO for Gen Lemnitzer, 9 Jul 64, fldr SPCOL S-351-89, Taylor Papers, NDUL; note Col K. B. Langdon, U.K.N.M.R., to SACEUR re MLF, 7 Jul 64, w/encl paper, "Presentation of British Technical Study: Introductory Statement by Shuckburgh," 2 Jul 64, fldr SPCOL-S-349a-89, ibid. For accounts of the genesis and evolution of the ANF, see Andrew J. Pierre, *Nuclear Politics: The British Experience with an Independent Strategic Force, 1939-1970*, 276-78; Boulton, "NATO and the MLF," 286-92; Steinbruner, *Cybernetic Theory*, 289, 294-97.
71. Steinbruner, *Cybernetic Theory*, 286; Seaborg, *Stemming the Tide*, 124-25; memo Bundy for Pres, 8 Nov 64, *FRUS 1964-68*, XIII:103-07 (quotes, 105).
72. Memo Bundy for Pres, 8 Nov 64, cited in n 71, 104-06; memo Klein for Bundy, 10 Oct 64 (quote, 4), fldr Multilateral Force, General—Vol 2, box 23, Subject File, NSF, LBJL.
73. Steinbruner, *Cybernetic Theory*, 292-93. Steinbruner here depicts Bundy as friendlier toward the MLF and its partisans than the record indicates, perhaps equating indulgence (as McNamara, too, showed at times) with support.
74. The British ambassador to NATO insisted the proposal was presented "in a constructive spirit," offering cost benefits and other advantages compared with a force of seaborne Polaris missiles. See Shuckburgh introductory statement to British technical study, cited in n 70.
75. Msg Bundy for Bruce and Neustadt, 29 Nov 64, fldr Multilateral Force, General—Vol 2, box 23, Subject File, NSF, LBJL; ed note, *FRUS 1964-68*, XIII:120; memo Bundy for Ball, 25 Nov 64, ibid, 121.
76. Memo Neustadt for Pres, 5 Dec 64, fldr December 1-10, 1964, box 5, McGeorge Bundy files, NSF, LBJL; memo (ns) for Pres, 4 Dec 64, ibid; memo Bundy for Pres, 6 Dec 64, ibid; memo Bundy for Pres, 6 Dec 64, *FRUS 1964-68*, XIII:134-37 (quote, 137).
77. Geyelin, *Johnson and the World*, 160, 168-69; Steinbruner, *Cybernetic Theory*, 304-07.
78. Jt US-UK Communiqué, Washington, 8 Dec 64, *American Foreign Policy: Current Documents, 1964*, 615-16; NSAM 322, 17 Dec 64, *FRUS 1964-68*, XIII:165-67; communiqué NAC mtg, 15-17 Dec 64, *NATO Final Communiqués, 1949-1974*, 158-60. See also *FRUS 1964-68*, XIII:168-69. The president's instructions to embassies to avoid discussions of NATO and the MLF were carried out literally in Brussels that December, as the ambassador canceled a widely publicized presentation on the origins of NATO that Fulbright lecturer at the University of Louvain Lawrence Kaplan was scheduled to give to members of the diplomatic community at the American Cultural Center in Brussels.
79. James Reston, "President Urges Full U.S. Effort to Reunify NATO," *New York Times*, 21 Dec 64; interv Harlan Cleveland by Paige Mulhollan, 13 Aug 69, 37-38, LBJL; *Johnson Public Papers, 1965*, I:58; Steinbruner, *Cybernetic Theory*, 309-10. Steinbruner suggests that the president's actions in the aftermath of the Wilson visit were not intended to kill the project outright but to thwart a conceivable belated Anglo-Ger-

man accord, which would have left France as the odd man out and put Johnson in an untenable position given his and Kennedy's past support for the venture.

80. Winand, *Eisenhower, Kennedy, and the United States of Europe,* 356 (the date and year of the Johnson-Reston contact are incorrectly cited); memo McNamara for Bundy, 12 Mar 65, fldr Reading File, Mar. 1965, box 122, McNamara Records, RG 200; memo McNamara for Ball, 7 Apr 65, ibid; Boulton, "NATO and the MLF," 293-94.
81. Paper (ns but probably Bundy), "The Case for a Fresh Start on Atlantic Nuclear Defense," 18 Oct 65, fldr Vol 16, box 5, McGeorge Bundy file, NSF, LBJL; memo Leddy for Rusk, 8 Nov 65, *FRUS 1964-68*, XIII:261-62; memo Bundy for Pres, 25 Nov 65, fldr Vol 17, box 5, McGeorge Bundy file, NSF, LBJL; memcon Pres, Erhard, 20 Dec 65, *FRUS 1964-68*, XIII:289-92; jt statement, 21 Dec 65, *Johnson Public Papers, 1965,* II:1165-67.
82. Buchan, "The Multilateral Force: An Historical Perspective," 13.
83. Steinbruner, *Cybernetic Theory,* 172, 153; Buchan, "The Multilateral Force: An Historical Perspective," 13.
84. Steinbruner's application of cybernetics and behavioral psychology to decisionmaking seems overdrawn in the use of syndromes and paradigms to account for McNamara's and others' motives and actions; nonetheless, his analysis is indispensable to comprehending McNamara's seeming inconsistency (see *Cybernetic Theory,* 316-19). McNamara adviser William Kaufmann offered another angle: "He used to make fun of it in front of Rusk at the pre-NATO meetings . . . . He sort of went along with it finally, when he thought Kennedy was somehow or other committed to it . . . . The minute that it became clear that Erhard and LBJ didn't really give a damn about MLF, he pounced on that thing" (Kaufmann interv, 14 Jul 86, 35).
85. McNamara interv, 22 May 86, 21-22.
86. Bundy, *Danger and Survival,* 496.

XVI. THE EMBATTLED MILITARY ASSISTANCE PROGRAM

1. For an account of foreign aid in the Eisenhower administration, see Watson, *Into the Missile Age,* 657-82.
2. "Selected Problems of Military Assistance," nd [likely Nov-Dec 60], fldr Transition Memoranda, Topical Memoranda (2), box 17, Neustadt Papers, JFKL; "Report Prepared by the Policy Planning Council," nd [drafted 19 Jan 61], *FRUS 1961-63,* IX:189-90.
3. Diane B. Kunz, *Butter and Guns: America's Cold War Economic Diplomacy,* 117; NSAM 22, 20 Feb 61, *FRUS 1961-63,* IX:199.
4. Memcon, 25 Feb 61, *FRUS 1961-63,* IX:201-03.
5. Memrcd L. E. Harrison, 26 Feb 61, fldr 091.3--Jan-Jun 1961, box 44, ISA files, Acc 64A-2382; memcon, 25 Feb 61, cited in n 4.
6. Memo SecDef for SecState, 7 Mar 61, fldr RLG Reading File 30 Dec 60, box 2, Gilpatric files, Acc 66A-3529; ed note, *FRUS 1961-63,* IX:220; *Kennedy Public Papers, 1961,* 210-11, 207-08.
7. Ltr Rusk to McNamara, 15 Mar 61, *FRUS 1961-63,* IX:211; ed note, ibid, 240-41.
8. Poole, *JCS and National Policy 1961-64,* pt III:153.
9. Rpt prepared by Charles Burton Marshall, 17 May 61, *FRUS 1961-63,* IX:242; memo ActgSecState (Bowles) and SecDef for Pres, 18 May 61, fldr 62 MAP Misc, box 4, McNamara files, Acc 71A-3470.
10. Memo ActgSecState and SecDef for Pres, 18 May 61, cited in n 9; memo Rusk for Pres, 10 Mar 61, *FRUS 1961-63,* IX:210; Special Message to Congress on Urgent National Needs, 25 May 62, *Kennedy Public Papers, 1961,* 400; Poole, *JCS and National Policy 1961-64,* pt III:154.
11. HCFA, *Hearings: The International Development and Security Act,* 87 Cong, 1 sess, 8 Jun 61, pt 1:72-74, 82.
12. "Notes on NSC Meeting," 13 Jun 61, fldr National Security Council (III), box 4, Vice Presidential Security File, LBJL; interv Lawrence F. O'Brien by Michael L. Gillette, 18 Sep 85, I, 77, internet copy, LBJL.
13. HSCA, *Hearings: Foreign Operations Appropriations for 1962,* 87 Cong, 1 sess, 29 Jun 61, pt 1:98-99, 107 (quote).
14. Conf Cte, *Foreign Assistance Act of 1961,* H Rpt 1088, 87 Cong, 1 sess, 30 Aug 61, 12-15, 54-56; ed note, *FRUS 1961-63,* IX:260; PL 87-195, 4 Sep 61; HCFA, *Mutual Security Act of 1961,* H Rpt 851, 87 Cong, 1 sess, 4 Aug 61, 2, 54.
15. PL 87-195, 22; ed note, *FRUS 1961-63,* IX:261.
16. PL 87-195, 5-6, 13-14.
17. HCA, *Foreign Assistance and Related Agencies Appropriation Bill, 1962,* H Rpt 1107, 87 Cong, 1 sess, 1 Sep 61, 8; SCA, *Foreign Assistance and Related Agencies Appropriation Bill, 1962,* S Rpt 991, 87 Cong, 1 sess, 13

Sep 61, 7; Conf Cte, *Foreign Assistance and Related Agencies Appropriation Bill, 1962*, H Rpt 1270, 87 Cong, 1 sess, 26 Sep 61, 6; PL 87-329, 30 Sep 61.

18. Programming Div, ODMA, "Priority Listing FY 62 MAP Supplemental," 24 May 61, fldr FY 62 Bu--SecDef House Statement May 31—Further Amendments to Budget, box 8, ASD(C) files, OSD Hist; memo ActgSecState and SecDef for Pres, 18 May 61, cited in n 9; NSAM 52, 11 May 61, *FRUS 1961-63*, I:133; "Military Assistance Facts," 1 Mar 62, 29, box 78, Subject files, OSD Hist; MAP FY 1963 Estimates, 8-9, 11-12, 125, 147, 165, 181, Military Assistance binders, Subject files, OSD Hist; MAP FY 1962 Estimates, 10-11, 186, 190, ibid.

19. MAP FY 1963 Estimates, 7, 198-99; HCFA, *Hearings: Foreign Assistance Act of 1964*, 88 Cong, 2 sess, 25 Mar 64, pt 1:85-86; memos ASD(C) for SecDef, 6 Apr 62, SecDef for ASD(ISA), 9 Apr 62, fldr Reading File, Apr. 18-Apr. 1, 1962, box 114, McNamara Records, RG 200.

20. ISA papers, "Internal Security in Latin America," 25 Apr 61, "U.S. Guarantees Against External Aggression in Latin America," 26 Apr 61, fldr 092 Intl Affairs Jan 62, box 44, ISA files, Acc 64A-2382. See also memo DirISA Coordinating Staff (NSC & Collateral Activities) Robert H. B. Wade for DirWestHemis Affs(ISA), 27 Jul 61, fldr Cuba 000.1-092, 11 Jul 61-Jan 62, box 31, ibid.

21. *Hearings: International Development and Security Act*, cited in n 11, 73, 89; SCFR, *Hearings: International Development and Security*, 87 Cong, 1 sess, 14 Jun 61, pt 2:670; SCFR, *Hearings: Foreign Assistance Act of 1963*, 88 Cong, 1 sess, 13 Jun 63, 175; HCAS, *Hearings on Military Posture and HR 9637*, 88 Cong, 2 sess, 27 Jan 64, 6911.

22. The Charter of Punta del Este, Establishing an Alliance for Progress, 17 Aug 61, *American Foreign Policy: Current Documents, 1961*, 395-407; *Hearings on Military Posture and HR 9637*, 6910-12.

23. "Report of the Washington Assessment Team on Internal Situation in South America," Apr 62, fldr 109 Latin America, box 4, McNamara files, Acc 71A-3470; circ msg 230 State to LA posts, 10 Aug 62, *FRUS 1961-63*, XII:227-28; CM-894-62 JCS for SecDef, 16 Aug 62, fldr 89 Latin America, box 4, McNamara files, Acc 71A-3470.

24. Memrcd Kenneth R. Hansen, 19 May 61, fldr Budget-Miscellaneous, box 44, Sorensen Papers, JFKL; memcon, 26 May 61, *FRUS 1961-63*, IX:255.

25. Poole, *JCS and National Policy 1961-64*, pt III:154; briefing William Bundy for SecDef, 7 Aug 61, fldr L-208-71, box 29, Lemnitzer Papers, NDU; JCSM-677-61 CJCS for SecDef, 29 Sep 61, fldr 091.3 1961 Jul-Dec, box 44, ISA files, Acc 64A-2382; memo Kitchen for SecState and SecDef, 12 Dec 61, w/Tab A, "Steering Group Report," fldr NSC Meetings 1962, 1/18/62, box 313, NSF, JFKL.

26. Memo Kitchen for SecState and SecDef, 12 Dec 61, w/Tab A, cited in n 25 (quote, 40); Poole, *JCS and National Policy 1961-64*, pt III:156-57.

27. Tab A, "Steering Group Report," 9, and Tab C, memo Smith for Kitchen, 30 Nov 61, atchmts to memo Kitchen for SecState and SecDef, 12 Dec 61, cited in n 25.

28. Memrcd Komer, 23 Oct 61, *FRUS 1961-63*, IX:271-72; Kennedy's remarks in rcd of action 508th NSC mtg, 22 Jan 63, *FRUS 1961-63*, VIII:460.

29. JCSM-769-61 CJCS for SecDef, 7 Nov 61, fldr Secs & Chiefs Comments-Budget Issues, box 17, McNamara Records, RG 200.

30. Gilpatric memrcd, Pres mtg w/JCS, 3 Jan 62, *FRUS 1961-63*, VIII:232-34; memo Taylor for DepSecDef, 5 Jan 62, w/atchmt, nd, fldr T-141-69, box 29, Taylor Papers, NDU.

31. Memo Bromley Smith for NSC, 15 Jan 62, w/atchd draft NSC rcd of action; "Guidelines for the Military Aid Program," 13 Jan 62; "Position of the JCS on Draft NSC Record of Action Dated 13 January 1962," 18 Jan 62 (quotes, 3, 4); memo Komer for Pres, 17 Jan 62: fldr NSC Meetings 1962, 1/18/62 (4), box 313, NSF, JFKL.

32. "Summary of the President's Remarks to the NSC—January 18, 1962," 18 Jan 62, ibid (3); NSC rcd of action, nd, *FRUS 1961-63*, IX:284-85.

33. JCSM-122-62 CJCS for SecDef, 17 Feb 62, fldr Reading File, Feb. 1962, box 114, McNamara Records, RG 200; Special Message to the Congress on Foreign Aid, 13 Mar 62, *Kennedy Public Papers, 1962*, 216. The actual figure was $1.7 billion (TOA) because of recoupments and sales. See memo McNamara for William Bundy, 7 Dec 61, fldr Reading File, Dec. 1961, box 113, McNamara Records, RG 200.

34. HSCA, *DoD Appropriations for 1963*, 1 Feb 62, pt 2:207-08.

35. HSCA, *Hearings: Foreign Operations Appropriations for 1963*, 87 Cong, 2 sess, 16 Mar 62, pt 1:380-81; Livesay notes, staff mtg, 23 Apr 62, fldr SecDef Staff Meetings Apr. 1962, box 10, AFPC and SecDef Meetings files, Acc 77-0062.

36. *Philadelphia Inquirer*, 2 Aug 62; PL 87-565, 1 Aug 62; memo SecDef for SvcSecs et al, 8 Sep 62, fldr Reading File, Sept. 17-Sept. 4, 1962, box 115, McNamara Records, RG 200.
37. *New York Times*, 30 Sep 62; *Kennedy Public Papers, 1962*, 651-52; *American Foreign Policy: Current Documents, 1962*, 1469; ltr McNamara to Hayden, 25 Sep 62, fldr Reading File, Sept. 17-Sept. 4, 1962, box 115, McNamara Records, RG 200; ltr William Bundy to Ford, 3 Oct 62, fldr Foreign Aid Appropriation FY 1963, box H-4, Committee Files, Ford Congressional Papers, GRFL.
38. PL 87-872, 23 Oct 62; Poole, *JCS and National Policy 1961-64*, pt III:161-63.
39. MAP FY 1964 Estimates, 5-8, Military Assistance binders, Subject files, OSD Hist.
40. Memo Hamilton for Pres, 25 May 62, *FRUS 1961-63*, IX:302-04; Schlesinger, *A Thousand Days*, 594-95; NSAM 159, 31 May 62, *FRUS 1961-63*, IX: 307-08.
41. Interv David Bell by William T. Dentzer, 2 Jan 65, 130, JFKL; memo SecDef for SvcSecs et al, 31 May 62, fldr Reading File, May 31-May 18, 1962, box 114, McNamara Records, RG 200.
42. Memo Pres for SecState, SecDef, and DirAID, 23 Jun 62, *FRUS 1961-63*, IX:316; memo SecState for Pres, 11 Jul 62, ibid, 322; memo Kaysen for Pres, 16 Nov 62, ibid, 335-36.
43. Ed note, ibid, 352; Bell interv, 2 Jan 65, 148.
44. Rcd of action 508th NSC mtg, 22 Jan 63, *FRUS 1961-63*, VIII:460; memo Bell for Pres, 4 Mar 63, fldr 091.3 MAP Jan & Table 36, box 38, SecDef Subject Decimal files, Acc 69A-3131; memo William Bundy for SecDef, 28 Jan 63, ibid; Jean Edward Smith, *Lucius D. Clay: An American Life*, 671-72.
45. Memo William Bundy for SecDef, 23 Feb 63, memo Bundy for Bell, 4 Mar 63, fldr 091.3 MAP Jan & Table 36, box 38, SecDef Subject Decimal files, Acc 69A-3131; memo Kaysen for Dungan, 5 Mar 63, *FRUS 1961-63*, IX:344.
46. Memo William Bundy for Clay, 8 Mar 63 (quote, 2), fldr 091.3 MAP Jan & Table 36, box 38, SecDef Subject Decimal files, Acc 69A-3131; memo McNamara for Clay, 8 Mar 63 (quote, 3), ibid (emphasis in original).
47. Note William Bundy to McNamara, 5 Mar 63, ibid; Schlesinger, *A Thousand Days*, 598-99; Smith, *Clay*, 672-73; Bell interv, 2 Jan 65, 137.
48. Rpt to Pres from Committee to Strengthen the Security of the Free World, "The Scope and Distribution of United States Military and Economic Assistance Programs," 20 Mar 63, 1-2, 5, 7, 19-20, fldr Foreign Assistance-MAP, AID, etc, box 101, ASD(C) files, OSD Hist.
49. Livesay notes, staff mtg, 18 Mar 63, fldr SecDef Staff Meetings Jan-Mar 1963, box 11, AFPC and SecDef Meetings files, Acc 77-0062; Smith, *Clay*, 673; *New York Times*, 21 Mar 63; Steven A. Hildreth, "Perceptions of U.S. Security Assistance, 1959-1983: The Public Record," in Ernest Graves and Steven A. Hildreth, eds, *U.S. Security Assistance: The Political Process*, 54.
50. HCFA, *Hearings: Foreign Assistance Act of 1962*, 87 Cong, 2 sess, 15 Mar 62, pt 1:69; memo McNamara for Nitze, 18 Sep 62, fldr Reading File, 29 Sept.-18 Sept., 1962, box 115, McNamara Records, RG 200; "Military Sales Credit Financing," 23 Dec 64, fldr SecDef Backup Book, FY 1966 Budget, vols I-III, box 36, ASD(C) files, OSD Hist.
51. Ltr McNamara to Rusk, 9 Jul 63, *FRUS 1961-63*, IX:382; ltr Rusk to McNamara, 26 Jul 63, ibid, 383.
52. DoD Directive 5132.3, 8 Jul 63.
53. "International Sales and Logistics Program," 23 Dec 64, SecDef Backup Book, FY 1966 Budget, vols I-III, box 36, ASD(C) files, OSD Hist; DoD News Release 692-67, 27 Jul 67, OSD Hist.
54. "Military Sales Credit Financing," 23 Dec 64, cited in n 50; "Military Assistance and Foreign Sales Facts," May 67, box 63, Subject files, OSD Hist.
55. Poole, *JCS and National Policy 1961-64*, pt III:161, citing JCSM-584-62; JCSM-173-63 CJCS for SecDef, 6 Mar 63, fldr 091.3 MAP Feb 1963, box 38, SecDef Subject Decimal files, Acc 69A-3131; Livesay notes, staff mtg, 18 Mar 63, cited in n 49; HCFA, *Hearings: Foreign Assistance Act of 1963*, 88 Cong, 1 sess, 8 Apr 63, pt 1:55.
56. *Hearings: Foreign Assistance Act of 1963*, 160-61, 56, 70.
57. HSCA, *Hearings: Foreign Operations Appropriations for 1964*, 88 Cong, 1 sess, 15 May 63, pt 2:85, 95.
58. *Washington Post*, 14 Jun 63; OffLegisLiaison (Dillender), "Report on Congressional Hearing," 17 Jun 63, OSD Hist; Dillender memo, "Report on Congressional Hearing," 18 Jun 63, ibid.
59. Ltr McNamara to Morgan, 17 Jun 63, fldr 091.3 MAP May thru July 1963, box 37, SecDef Subject Decimal files, Acc 69A-3131; memo ISA for SecDef, 16 Aug 63, w/atchmt, fldr 091.3 MAP Aug thru 15 Sep 63, box 36, ibid; ltr Rusk and McNamara to House members, 19 Aug 63, in *McNamara Public Statements, 1963*, V:2273-74.

Notes to Pages 436–41   613

60. Memo SecDef for SecA, 8 Aug 63, fldr Reading File, Aug. 1963, box 118, McNamara Records, RG 200; memo ISA for SecDef, 16 Aug 63, w/atchmt, cited in n 59; memrcd McGiffert, "Meeting with Congressman Ford, September 5," 6 Sep 63, fldr 091.3 MAP Aug thru 15 Sep 63, box 36, SecDef Subject Decimal files, Acc 69A-3131.
61. Memo William Bundy for Wood, 20 Sep 63, memo Wood for SecDef, 20 Sep 63, w/McNamara's marginalia: fldr 091.3 MAP 16 Sep thru Oct 1963, box 35, SecDef Subject Decimal files, Acc 69A-3131.
62. Conf Cte, *Conference Report on Foreign Assistance Act of 1963*, H Rpt 1006, 88 Cong, 1 sess, 6 Dec 63, 16-17; *Johnson Public Papers, 1963-64*, I:58; PL 88-205, 16 Dec 63; ed note, *FRUS 1961-63*, IX:391-92; NASM 276, 26 Dec 63, ibid, 392.
63. HCA, *Foreign Aid and Related Agencies Appropriation Bill*, 1964, H Rpt 1040, 88 Cong, 1 sess, 14 Dec 63, 36, 39, 45; PL 88-258, 6 Jan 64.
64. Memo Bell for McGeorge Bundy, 7 Jan 64, memo Komer for Pres, 17 Jan 64, *FRUS 1964-68*, IX:4, 5.
65. McNamara statement before HSCA (Foreign Operations), 23 Mar 64, fldr Military Assistance FY 1965 Budget, box 31, ASD(C) files, OSD Hist. An expurgated version appears in HSCA, *Hearings: Foreign Operations Appropriations for 1965*, 88 Cong, 2 sess, 23 Mar 64, pt 1:313-14.
66. Ltrs Bell to McNamara, 22 Jan 64, 5 Feb 64 (quote, 2), fldr 091.3 MAP (22 Jan 64) 1964, box 34, SecDef Subject Decimal files, Acc 69A-7425; ltr McNamara to Bell, 24 Jan 64, fldr Reading File, Jan. 31-Jan. 18, 1964, box 119, McNamara Records, RG 200.
67. SecDef Backup Book, FY 1965 Budget, vol I, Tab H, "Effect of Reductions in FY 1964 MAP," box 32, ASD(C) files, OSD Hist; MAP FY 1963 Estimates, 194; MAP FY 1964 Estimates, 183, 201; MAP FY 1966 Estimates, 45, 49.
68. Livesay notes, staff mtg, 28 Oct 63 (quote, 5), fldr SecDef Staff Meetings Aug-Dec 1963, box 11, AFPC and SecDef Meetings files, Acc 77-0062; memo SecDef for ASD(C), ASD(ISA), GenCoun, 1 Nov 63, ibid; ltr McNamara to Bell, 14 Nov 63, Reading File, Nov. 1963, box 119, McNamara Records, RG 200.
69. Memo ISA (Peter Solbert) for SecDef, 12 Nov 63, fldr Reading File, Nov. 1963, box 119, McNamara Records, RG 200. The amount was subsequently increased to $383.5 million.
70. Memo William Bundy for ActgSecState et al, 22 Nov 63, w/atchmt, draft ltr McNamara to Russell, 22 Nov 63, fldr Defense Budget (1), box 45, Sorensen Papers, JFKL; ltr Ball to Bundy, 30 Nov 63, ibid; memo SecDef for Pres, 3 Dec 63, fldr 091.3 MAP (4 Sep 63) December 1963, box 35, SecDef Subject Decimal files, Acc 69A-3131.
71. Memo Pres for SecDef, 7 Dec 63, fldr 091.3 MAP (4 Sep 63) December 1963, box 35, SecDef Subject Decimal files, Acc 69A-3131; ltr McNamara to Cannon, 13 Dec 63, OSD Hist; ltrs Fulbright to McNamara, Morgan to McNamara, 20 Dec 63, fldr 091.3 MAP (4 Sep 63) December 1963, box 35, SecDef Subject Decimal files, Acc 69A-3131.
72. Cited in Poole, *JCS and National Policy 1961-64*, pt III:167.
73. Memo DepSecDef for ActgASD(ISA), 16 Dec 63, fldr RLG Reading File, July 1, 1963- , box 2, Gilpatric Files, Acc 66A-3529; memrcd Gilpatric, 26 Dec 63, sub: Last minute changes in proposed DoD budget for FY 65, fldr 110.01 1963, box 41, SecDef Subject Decimal files, Acc 69A-3131; SecDef staff mtg notes, 20 Jan 64 (quote, 1), fldr SecDef Staff Meetings Jan-Aug 1964, box 11, AFPC and SecDef Meetings files, Acc 77-0062. The 10 January 1964 date appears in HSCA, *Hearings: Foreign Operations Appropriations for 1965*, 24 Mar 64, pt 1:371; Special Message to Congress on Foreign Aid, 19 Mar 64, *Johnson Public Papers, 1963-64*, I:394.
74. Memo Wood for SecDef, 4 Feb 64, fldr 091.3 MAP Jan thru March 1964, box 34, SecDef Subject Decimal files, Acc 69A-7425; memo William Bundy for SecDef, 8 Feb 64 (quote, 1), ibid; JCSM 271-64 CJCS for SecDef, 31 Mar 64 (quote, 4), fldr 091.3 MAP (22 Jan 64) 1964, ibid.
75. HSCA, *Hearings: DoD Appropriations for 1965*, 88 Cong, 2 sess, 18 Feb 64, pt 4:104-06, 109.
76. SecDef statement before HSCA, 23 Mar 64, 30, cited in n 65; memo Bundy for SecDef, 8 Feb 64, cited in n 74; *Hearings: Foreign Operations Appropriations for 1965*, 23 Mar 64 (quotes, 326, 359); "Notes of Discussions of the MAP with Members of Congress," 5 May 64, fldr Reading File, May 1964, box 120, McNamara Records, RG 200.
77. *New York Times*, 25 Mar 64; *Baltimore Sun*, 26 Mar 64; memo McGiffert for O'Brien, 30 Mar 64, fldr White House Major Legislative Reports 1964, box 1, Legislative Affairs files, Acc 67A-4632; memo McGeorge Bundy for Pres, 2 Apr 64, *FRUS 1964-68*, IX:13-14.
78. Note William Bundy to SecDef, 16 Jan 64, memo Bundy for Ball, 22 Jan 64, fldr 091.3 MAP Jan thru March 1964, box 34, SecDef Subject Decimal files, Acc 69A-7425.

79. Memo William Bundy for SecDef, 24 Feb 64, w/McNamara marginalia, ibid; memo SecDef for CJCS, 16 May 64, fldr Reading File, May 1964, box 120, McNamara Records, RG 200.
80. SecDef statement before SCA, 22 Jul 64, 29-30, fldr Military Assistance FY 1965 Budget, box 31, ASD(C) files, OSD Hist; CJCS statement before SCA, 22 Jul 64 (quote, 9), ibid.
81. Special Message to Congress, 18 May 64, *Johnson Public Papers, 1963-64*, I:692; HCFA, *Report on Foreign Assistance Act of 1964*, H Rpt 1443, 88 Cong, 2 sess, 1 Jun 64, 22-23; SCFA, *Report on Foreign Assistance Act of 1964 to Accompany HR 11380*, S Rpt 1188, as summarized in *USC: Congressional and Administrative News*, 88 Cong, 2 sess (1964), vol 2, 3849; ltr McNamara to Morgan, 15 Aug 64, fldr Reading File, July 1964, box 120, McNamara Records, RG 200; Conf Cte, *Report on Foreign Assistance Act of 1964*, H Rpt 1925, 88 Cong, 2 sess, 1 Oct 64, 6; *New York Times*, 8 Oct 64; PL 88-634, 7 Oct 64; PL 88-633, 7 Oct 64.
82. Memo Bell for Pres, 7 Oct 64, *FRUS 1964-68*, IX:28-29; interv Lawrence F. O'Brien by Michael L. Gillette, 11 Feb 86, VI, 14, internet copy, LBJL; PL 88-633, 7 Oct 64.
83. MAP FY 1966 Estimates, 14-15.
84. Memo Wood for SecDef, 4 Feb 64, cited in n 74; JCSM-324-64 CJCS for SecDef, 14 Apr 64, fldr 091.3 MAP (22 Jan 64) 1964, box 34, SecDef Subject Decimal files, Acc 69A-7425.
85. Memo McNaughton for SecDef, 31 Aug 64, memo McNaughton for SecDef, 2 Oct 64, w/McNamara marginalia, JCSM-888-64 CJCS for SecDef, 20 Oct 64 (quote, 3): ibid.
86. Memo ISA for SecDef, 19 Nov 64 (quote, 1), fldr Defense Budget—FY 1966, box 16, Agency File, NSF, LBJL; memo SecDef for CJCS, 20 Nov 64, fldr Reading File, Nov. 1964, box 121, McNamara Records, RG 200; memo Solbert for Califano, 19 Nov 64, fldr 091.3 MAP FY66 (19 Nov 64) 1964, box 34, SecDef Subject Decimal files, Acc 69A-7425.
87. Memrcd Wood, 25 Nov 64, BoB mtg on FY 1966 MAP Budget, 24 Nov 64, fldr MAP General—1964, 1965, 1966—Jan-Feb-Mar, box 40, Komer files, NSF, LBJL (emphasis in original); memo McNaughton for SecDef, 2 Dec 64, fldr 091.3 MAP FY 66 (19 Nov 64) 1964, box 34, SecDef Subject Decimal files, Acc 69A-7425; memo McNamara for Bell, 5 Dec 64, fldr Reading File, Dec. 1964, box 121, McNamara Records, RG 200.
88. JCSM-1082-64 CJCS for SecDef, 29 Dec 64 (quote, 3), fldr 091.3 MAP FY 66 (19 Nov 64), box 34, SecDef Subject Decimal files, Acc 69A-7425.
89. Ltr Bell to Gordon, 4 Dec 61, *FRUS 1964-68*, IX:61-62; memo Bell for Pres, 9 Dec 64, ibid, 76; memo Komer for McGeorge Bundy, 15 Dec 64, fldr Defense Budget—FY 1966, box 16, Agency File, NSF, LBJL; memo Gordon for Pres, 20 Dec 64, fldr FI4/FG Budget—Appropriations (Federal Government) (1966 Budget), box 43, WH Confidential File, LBJL.
90. Memo Chenery for Bell, 17 Oct 64, *FRUS 1964-68*, IX:32-33; Poole, *JCS and National Policy 1961-64*, pt III:169-70; memo Bell for SecState, 11 Jan 65, *FRUS 1964-68*, IX:88. On McNamara's fiscal tactics see memo McNaughton for SecDef, 22 Dec 64, fldr 091.3 MAP (May thru 1964), box 34, SecDef Subject Decimal files, Acc 69A-7425; memo Bell for SecDef, 11 Nov 64, *FRUS 1964-68*, IX:41.
91. Memo Bell for Pres, 10 Dec 64, *FRUS 1964-68*, IX:81; memo McNaughton for SecDef, 22 Dec 64, cited in n 90.
92. Memo Bell for Rusk, 30 Dec 64, *FRUS 1964-68*, IX:86-87; ltr Vance to Bell, 31 Dec 64, fldr Chron File, December 1964, box 1, Cyrus Vance files, Acc 69A-2317.
93. Memo Komer for McGeorge Bundy, 15 Dec 64, cited in n 89.

XVII. THE SEARCH FOR SAVINGS

1. *McNamara Public Statements, 1963*, IV:1594.
2. Memos Pres for Dillon, 7 Jun 62, Dillon for Pres, 14 Jun 62, Pres for Dillon, 22 Jun 62: fldr Balance of Payments-Misc, box 1, Gilpatric files, Acc 66A-3529. See also Thomas Zoumanis, "Plugging the Dike: The Kennedy Administration Confronts the Balance of Payments Crisis with Europe," in Brinkley and Griffiths, eds, *John F. Kennedy and Europe*, 169-88.
3. Memo Dillon for Pres, 2 Dec 63, *FRUS 1961-63*, IX:104; memcon White House mtg, 25 May 63, ibid, XIII:770; ltr Dillon to Rusk, 19 Mar 63, ibid, IX:169; memcon, 24 Jun 63, ibid, 171.
4. Census Bur, *Historical Statistics of the United States: Colonial Times to 1970*, pt 2, 864; *Kennedy Public Papers, 1961*, 65. For an account of the Eisenhower administration's handling of the BOP problem, see Watson, *Into the Missile Age*, 747-50.

5. Memcon w/Pres, 9 Nov 60, *FRUS 1958-60*, IV:130-32; *Eisenhower Public Papers, 1960-61*, 862; msg JCS 533004 to CINCAL et al, 25 Nov 60, OSD Hist; msg DA536518 CivAffsDA to HICOMRY Okinawa, 161945Z Dec 60, ibid.
6. Msg X346 CINCONAD to SecDef, 29 Nov 60, msg ECJAJ9-6302 USCINCEUR to OSD, 30 Nov 60, msg DA541376 CJCS to Norstad and Palmer, 19 Jan 61, msg DA536518 CivAffsDA to HICOMRY Okinawa, 161945Z Dec 60, 4: OSD Hist.
7. Memrcd [Wilton B. Persons], 19 Jan 61, *FRUS 1961-63*, IX:1-2.
8. *Kennedy Public Papers, 1961*, 21, 57-60, 65.
9. Ltr Gilpatric to Pres, 1 Feb 61, fldr RLG Reading File (30 Dec 60), box 2, Gilpatric files, Acc 66A-3529; news conf, 1 Feb 61, *Kennedy Public Papers, 1961*, 31.
10. Memo McNamara for Pres, 4 Jun 63, *FRUS 1961-63*, IX:65; ltr Rusk to McNamara, 7 Jun 63, ibid, 66; memo Rusk for Pres, [18] Sep 63, ibid, 90; memcon White House mtg, 24 Sep 63, ibid, 186-87.
11. Memo McNamara for SvcSecs et al, 10 Jul 62, w/atchmt "Revised Project Eight," 9 Jul 62, 1, fldr Balance of Payments 1963, box 14, Francis Bator Papers, LBJL; memo McNamara for SvcSecs et al, 16 Jul 62, fldr Balance of Payments-Misc, box 1, Gilpatric files, Acc 66A-3529; NSAM 171, 16 Jul 62, *FRUS 1961-63*, IX:25-26; *McNamara Public Statements, 1962*, IV:1574-76.
12. *Annual Report of Secretary of the Army, FY 1963*, in *DoD Annual Report, FY 1963*, 114; OASD Comptr table, "Military Departments' Planned Deployment in Foreign Countries End FYs 1963-1968," 1 Mar 63, fldr SecDef Staff Meetings Jan-Mar 1963, box 11, AFPC and SecDef Meetings files, Acc 77-0062.
13. Ltr Rusk to Dillon, 1 Feb 61, *FRUS 1961-63*, IX:106-07; memcon White House mtg, 13 Apr 61, ibid, 115-16; ed note, ibid, 132-33; memo Tyler for Ball, 9 Oct 61, ibid, 130; memo Gilpatric for Sorensen, 27 Nov 61, w/encl memo Gilpatric for Pres, 27 Nov 61, 4, fldr RLG Reading File (1 July 61-), box 2, Gilpatric files, Acc 66A-3529; memo Dillon for Pres, 9 Oct 62, *FRUS 1961-63*, IX:36.
14. Livesay notes, staff mtg, 22 Jul 63, 2, fldr SecDef Staff Meetings Apr-Jul 1963, box 11, AFPC and SecDef Meetings files, Acc 77-0062; ltr Dillon to Rusk, 8 Mar 63, *FRUS 1961-63*, IX:165-66.
15. Memrcd mtg w/Pres, 18 Apr 63, *FRUS 1961-63*, IX:61; *Kennedy Public Papers, 1963*, 578; draft memo McNamara for Pres, 19 Sep 63, *FRUS 1961-63*, IX:94-97; memo Gilpatric for Nitze, 24 Sep 63, fldr RLG Reading File, July 1, 1963- , box 2, Gilpatric files, Acc 66A-3529.
16. Draft memo McNamara for Pres, 19 Sep 63, fldr Reading File, Sept. 1963, box 118, McNamara Records, RG 200; memrcd, 23 Sep 63, *FRUS 1961-63*, IX:97; memo Rusk for Pres, nd [c 20-22 Sep 63], ibid, 89-93 (quote, 90).
17. *FRUS 1961-63*, IX:98-100 (quotes, 100); memo Dillon for Pres, 2 Dec 63, ibid, 104; memo Dillon for Pres, 18 Dec 63, fldr F04-1 Balance of Payments (1963-1964), box 49, WH Confidential File, LBJL; memo Dillon for Pres, 24 Apr 64, *FRUS 1964-68*, VIII:5.
18. Memo Bundy for Rusk, Fowler, McNamara, 8 May 64, *FRUS 1964-68*, VIII:12; memrcd, 20 Sep 65, ibid, 185; ltr McNamara to Rusk, 19 Apr 65, fldr Reading File, April 1965, box 122, McNamara Records, RG 200.
19. *Johnson Public Papers, 1965*, 10 Feb 65, I:170-77.
20. Ibid, 173; Cabinet Cte on Balance of Payments rpt to Pres, nd [c 2 Feb 65], *FRUS 1964-68*, VIII:86; memo Dillon for Pres, 4 Jan 65, ibid, 71-73; Cabinet Cte on Balance of Payments rpt to Pres, 7 Jun 65, ibid, 161.
21. Rpt to Pres, 7 Jun 65, cited in n 20, 160, 165.
22. Pres and SecDef jt press conf, 13 Dec 60, *McNamara Public Statements, 1961*, I:1.
23. Interv Thomas D. Morris by Alfred Goldberg and Maurice Matloff, 6 Apr 87, 24, OSD Hist.
24. Memo Boatman for Blaisdell et al, 14 Mar 61, w/atchmt "Projects within the Department of Defense Assigned 8 March 1961," fldr SecDef Special Projects 1961-62, box 109, ASD(C) files, OSD Hist.
25. HSCA, *DoD Appropriations for 1962*, 6 Apr 61, pt 3:63-64, 122-23.
26. *DoD Annual Report, FY 1962*, 43-44.
27. Memrcd Claude Ricketts, SecDef staff mtg, 2 Apr 62, fldr 5050 Meetings, Conferences, Conventions & Visits Jan-Jun 1962, box 1962-04, CNO Immediate Office Files, NHC.
28. Ibid; DoD News Release 839-62, 22 May 62, OSD Hist.
29. Memo SecDef for Pres, 5 Jul 62, fldr Reading File, July 24-July 2, 1962, box 115, McNamara Records, RG 200.

30. Memo SecDef for SvcSecs and DirsDSA, DCA, 14 Sep 62, w/encl "Summary of DoD's Procurement & Logistics Cost Reduction Program," fldr $3 Billion Savings—Cost Reduction Program, box 112, ASD(C) files, OSD Hist.
31. Memo Morris for Altizer, 14 Sep 62, ibid; memo Morris for AsstSecA et al, 14 Sep 62, ibid.
32. Memo Morris for SecDef, 18 Oct 62, w/encl "Cost Reduction Summary Procurement and Logistics," ibid.
33. Memo Morris for SecDef, 18 Oct 62, memo Morris for AsstSvcSecs, DSA, DCA, 20 Oct 62, memo DepSecDef for SvcSecs and DDSA, 23 Oct 62: ibid.
34. Memo Morris for SecDef, 21 Dec 62, w/encl 5, "Status of Cost Reduction Actions for FY 1963 as of 12/31/62," ibid.
35. Livesay notes, staff mtg, 9 Jul 63, fldr SecDef Staff Meetings Apr-Jul 1963, box 11, AFPC and SecDef Meetings files, Acc 77-0062.
36. Livesay notes, staff mtg, 7 Jan 63, fldr SecDef Staff Meetings Jan-Mar 1963, ibid.
37. Memo Morris for SecDef, DepSecDef, 29 Dec 62, fldr $3 Billion Savings—Cost Reduction Program, box 112, ASD(C) files, OSD Hist; draft text for posture statement on Cost Reduction Program, 31 Dec 62, ibid; McNamara statement before House Subcte on DoD Approps, 6 Feb 63, 137, and Table 5, 157, fldr FY 64 Defense Budget, box 1, SecDef Posture Statements, OSD Hist.
38. Subcte on Defense Procurement of the Joint Economic Cte, *Hearings: Impact of Military Supply and Service Activities on the Economy*, 88 Cong, 1 sess, 28 Mar 63, 25.
39. HSCA, *DoD Appropriations for 1964*, 13 Feb 63, pt 1:470; draft position paper, nd [Apr 63], fldr $3 Billion Savings—Cost Reduction Program, box 112, ASD(C) files, OSD Hist.
40. Memo Morris for SecDef, 5 Dec 63, w/atchmt, fldr Cost Reduction Program (FY 1965 Budget), box 34, ibid.
41. Livesay notes, staff mtg, 21 Jan 63, fldr SecDef Staff Meetings Jan-Mar 1963, box 11, Acc 77-0062. DoD Directive 5010.6, 1 Feb 63, and DoD Instruction 7720.6, issued 7 March, established uniform reporting procedures and formats.
42. Memo SecDef for SvcSecs and DDSA, 8 Apr 63, fldr Reading File, Apr. 17-Apr. 5, 1963, box 117, McNamara Records, RG 200; memo SecDef for SecAF, 9 Aug 63, fldr Reading File, Aug. 1963, box 118, ibid.
43. Memo SecDef for Pres, 8 Jul 63, fldr July 1, 1963 Cost Reduction Program Memorandum to the President, box 112, ASD(C) files, OSD Hist; Livesay notes, staff mtg, 9 Jul 63, cited in n 35.
44. News conf, 11 Jul 63, *McNamara Public Statements, 1963*, V:2054-70.
45. Memo SecDef for SvcSecs et al, 7 Dec 63, fldr Cost Reduction Program (FY 1965 Budget), box 34, ASD(C) files, OSD Hist.
46. Ltr Pres to Defense Contractors, 1 Dec 63, *Johnson Public Papers, 1963-64*, I:16; ltr McNamara to Defense Contractors, 1 Dec 63, *McNamara Public Statements, 1963*, VI:2679.
47. Memo SecDef for SvcSecs et al, 7 Dec 63, cited in n 45; *Newsweek*, 9 Mar 64.
48. HCAS, *Military Posture and HR 9637*, 29 Jan 64, 7106-08.
49. SCAS and SSCA, *Hearings: Military Procurement Authorizations, FY 1965*, 88 Cong, 2 sess, 4 Feb 64, 229-30.
50. *Military Posture and HR 9637*, 7107-08.
51. HSCA, *DoD Appropriations for 1965*, 17 Feb 64, pt 4:271, 273-74.
52. *Armed Forces Management*, Jan 64, 8; *Wall Street Journal*, 11 Jun 64.
53. News conf, 7 Jul 64, *McNamara Public Statements, 1964*, III:1350, 1358, 1360-62; *Baltimore Sun*, 8 Jul 64.
54. *Baltimore Sun*, 8 Jul 64.
55. Livesay notes, staff mtg, 13 Jul 64, fldr SecDef Staff Meetings May-Jul 1964, box 11, AFPC and SecDef Meetings files, Acc 77-0062; *New York Times*, 8 Jul 64; *Wall Street Journal*, 8 Jul 64.
56. Memo DirBoB Gordon for Cabinet Members, 24 Jul 64, w/encl "Remarks by the President to the Cabinet," 22 Jul 64, fldr Cost Reduction Program (FY 1966 Budget), box 39, ASD(C) files, OSD Hist; *Johnson Public Papers, 1963-64*, II:874-75.
57. Ltr Lawton to Pres, 10 Nov 64, w/atchmt President's Task Force on Cost Reduction, "Report to the President," 10 Nov 64, 1, 3, fldr 1964 Task Force on Cost Reduction, LBJL.
58. Ibid, 4, 5.
59. *Johnson Public Papers, 1963-64*, II:1548-49; *Washington Post*, 12 Nov 64.
60. Pres statement on "The Great Society," 19 Nov 64, *Johnson Public Papers, 1963-64*, II:1604.

61. Thomas D. Morris, "Taking Charge in Washington," *Harvard Business Review*, Jul-Aug 84, 3; Annual Message to the Congress on the State of the Union, 30 Jan 61, Special Message to the Congress on the Defense Budget, 28 Mar 61, *Kennedy Public Papers, 1961*, 24, 239-40; memo SecDef for Pres, 1 Mar 61, fldr 88, box 4, McNamara files, Acc 71A-3470; Morris interv, 6 Apr 87, 10.
62. Memos SecDef for Pres, 1 Mar 61, SecDef for SvcSecs, 31 Mar 61, fldr 88, box 4, McNamara files, Acc 71A-3470; DoD News Release 269-61, 30 Mar 61, OSD Hist; "Draft Administrative History of DoD, 1963-69," vol 5, 1921, ibid.
63. *Wall Street Journal*, 31 Mar 61; "Base Closing," nd [post-Sep 66], Notebook Management Decisions 1961-1966, box 27, SecDef files, OSD Hist; HSCA, *Hearings: DoD Appropriations for 1963*, 2 Feb 62, 238; *New York Herald Tribune*, 18 Jun 61.
64. *Washington Post*, 31 Mar, 11 Jul 62; "Base Closings," nd, in notebook, Management Decisions 1961-1966, box 27, SecDef files, OSD Hist. See also fldr Excess Installations 1962, box 989, Subject files, OSD Hist.
65. Memo SecDef for Pres, 7 Dec 63, fldr Defense Department, vol I [2 of 2] 11/63, box 11, Agency File, NSF, LBJL; telcon Pres w/McNamara, 7 Dec 63, 5:03 p.m., fldr December 1963, Chron File, box 1, JFK Series, transc of telephone conversations, LBJL; *New York Times*, 12 Dec 63; DoD News Release 393-63, 22 Mar 63, OSD Hist.
66. *McNamara Public Statements, 1963*, VI:2727, 2729, 2734-36; "Base Closing," cited in n 63; *Chicago Tribune*, 13 Dec 63.
67. White House press release, 27 Dec 63, in *McNamara Public Statements, 1964*, I:240-41.
68. DoD News Release 337-64, 24 Apr 64, fldr Closing of Installations 1964, box 989, Subject files, OSD Hist; *McNamara Public Statements, 1964*, III:1198-99, 1211; *Washington Post*, 25 Apr 64.
69. DoD News Release 730-64, 10 Oct 64, w/atchd memo SecDef for Pres, 8 Oct 64, fldr Closing of Installations 1964, box 989, Subject files, OSD Hist.
70. DoD News Release 822-64, 19 Nov 64, ibid; summary paper on "Study of Naval Requirements for Shipyard Capacity," nd, fldr Cost Reduction Program (FY 1966 Budget), box 39, ASD(C) files, OSD Hist. McNamara disclaimed any connection between the election and the timing of his announcement (*McNamara Public Statements, 1964*, IV:1779).
71. *Time*, 27 Nov 64, 29; interv Morris, 6 Apr 87, 15; *McNamara Public Statements, 1964*, IV:1780, 1782; see 20 Nov 64 columns and editorials in *Washington Evening Star, New York Times, Washington Post, New York Herald Tribune*, and *Baltimore Sun*; ASD(M), "DoD Program for Placement of Employees Affected by Base Closures and Consolidations," nd, fldr SecDef Backup Book, FY 1966 Budget, vols IV-VII, box 36, ASD(C) files, OSD Hist.
72. ASD(M), "Job Opportunity Program," 30 Nov 66, SecDef Backup Book, FY 1968 Budget, bk II, vols III-V, box 60, ASD(C) files, OSD Hist.
73. Michael H. Gorn, "The TFX: Conceptual Phase to F-111B Termination, 1958-1968," 4-5, 11-12, box 879, Subject files, OSD Hist; Robert J. Art, *The TFX Decision: McNamara and the Military*, 25-26.
74. "History of the TFX Development," 10 Jan 63, SecDef Backup Book, FY 1964 Budget, vol V, Tab E, box 20, ASD(C) files, OSD Hist; Senate, Cte on Govt Opns, Permanent Subcte on Investigations, *Hearings: TFX Contract Investigation (Second Series)*, 91 Cong, 2 sess, 24 Mar 70, pt 1:12; memo AIR-506 (Spangenberg) for AIR-09 (Adm Fawkes), 13 Mar 67, George Spangenberg oral hist, exhibit VF-6, internet copy, www.georgespangenberg.com/exhibitindex.htm; Art, *The TFX Decision*, 38.
75. Memo SecDef for SvcSecs, 7 Jun 61, fldr Reading File, June-August 1961, box 113, McNamara Records, RG 200; memo AIR-506 for AIR-09, cited in n 74; Senate, Cte on Govt Opns, Permanent Subcte on Investigations, *Hearings: TFX Contract Investigation*, 88 Cong, 1 sess (hereafter *TFX: Hearings*), 28 Jun 63, pt 6:1386-88; *TFX Contract Investigation*, S Rpt 91-1496, 91 Cong, 2 sess, 18 Dec 70 (hereafter *TFX Report*), 6.
76. *TFX: Hearings*, pt 2:429.
77. See, for example, memos SecDef for SecAF, 7 Jul 61, 3 Aug 61, SecDef for USecAF, 10 Aug 61, fldr Reading File, June-August 1961, box 113, McNamara Records, RG 200.
78. Gorn, "TFX," cited in n 73, 13-15; Art, *The TFX Decision*, 48.
79. Gorn, "TFX," 17-18; memo SecDef for SecAF, SecN, 1 Sep 61, *TFX: Hearings*, pt 2:333-34.
80. "History of the TFX Development," 10 Jan 63, box 20, ASD(C) files, OSD Hist.
81. Memo SecAF, SecN for SecDef, 1 Jun 62, *TFX: Hearings*, pt 6:1399; memo SecDef for SecAF, SecN, 9 Jun 62, fldr Reading File, 21 June-1 June 1962, box 115, McNamara Records, RG 200; "History of the TFX Development," 10 Jan 63, cited in n 80.

82. *TFX: Hearings*, pt 6:1599; memo SecAF for Ch, Source Selection Board, 29 Jun 62, memrcd LtGen D. C. Strother, nd [c 22 Jun 62]: ibid, 1400, 1401.
83. Memo DDR&E for SecDef, 11 Jul 62, ltr Gilpatric to Lewis, 13 Jul 62: *TFX: Hearings*, pt 5:1194-95.
84. Memo SecAF, SecN et al for CNO, ChStaffAF, 8 Nov 62, ibid, pt 6:1473-75.
85. Richard Austin Smith, "The $7-Billion Contract that Changed the Rules," pt II, *Fortune*, Apr 63, 199; *TFX Report*, 23 (quote); interv Eugene M. Zuckert by Lawrence E. McQuade, 11 Jul 64, 100, JFKL; "History of the TFX Development," 4; DoD News Release 1907-62, 24 Nov 62, OSD Hist.
86. Memrcd SecN, SecAF, SecDef, 21 Nov 62, *TFX: Hearings*, pt 2:350-53 (quote, 351).
87. Gorn, "TFX," 29; Smith, "The $7-Billion Contract," 111, 191; *TFX: Hearings*, pt 2:381, 385 (quote).
88. Interv Joseph V. Charyk by James C. Hasdorff, 15 Jan, 24 Apr 74, 24, AF Hist Support Off. The Evaluation Group estimated Boeing was 21 percent low and General Dynamics 18 percent (see *TFX: Hearings*, pt 1:146).
89. Shapley, *Promise and Power*, 210-11; ltr McClellan to McNamara, 21 Dec 62, fldr Misc Congressional Inquiries 1962, box 92, ASD(C) files; ltr Gilpatric to McClellan, 26 Dec 62, *TFX: Hearings*, pt 5:1146-47; interv Zuckert, 11 Jul 64, 103; interv Zuckert by George M. Watson, Jr., 3, 4, 5, 9 Dec 86, 133-34, AF Hist Support Off.
90. *TFX Report*, 30; *Hearings: Impact of Military Supply and Service Activities on the Economy*, cited in n 38, 1 2-13.
91. Memrcd A. W. Blackburn, 7 Mar 63, sub: Cost savings and effectiveness improvements offered by TFX, fldr TFX, box 108, ASD(C) files, OSD Hist. Only six days earlier, however, Blackburn had informed his boss, Harold Brown, that there was no supportable basis for McNamara's choice of General Dynamics in operational, technical, management, or cost considerations (memrcd Blackburn for DDR&E, 1 Mar 63, *TFX: Hearings*, pt 5:1207).
92. *TFX Report*, 50; interv Charyk, 15 Jan, 24 Apr 74, 25.
93. *Washington Post*, 9 Mar 63; DoD News Release 333-63, 12 Mar 63, OSD Hist; *Baltimore Sun*, 13 Mar 63.
94. Ltr McNamara to McClellan, 23 Mar 63, w/encl, *Washington Star*, 23 Mar 63, memcon McNamara w/ Jackson, 23 Mar 63, McNamara notes of conversation with Sen McClellan, 23 Mar 63: fldr Reading File, March 1963, box 117, McNamara Records, RG 200.
95. "Statement for Secretary McNamara," 16 Oct 63, 1, fldr Reading File, October 1963, box 118, McNamara Records, RG 200; memrcd McNamara, 2 Dec 63, fldr Reading File, December 1964, box 121, ibid; *New York Times*, 4 Oct 63.
96. Memrcd McNamara, 29 Mar 63, fldr Memos for the Record, box 1, McNamara files, Acc 71A-3470.
97. Memo SecDef for DDR&E, SecN, SecAF, 18 Jan 64, memo ChBurNavWeapons for CNO, 5 Feb 64, memo DDR&E, SecAF, SecN for SecDef, 15 Feb 64: *Hearings: TFX Contract Investigation (Second Series)*, pt 2:400, 401-02, 435-37.
98. News conf, 28 Feb 63, *McNamara Public Statements, 1963*, III:1428; Art, *The TFX Decision*, 86, 89.
99. Memo SecDef for Pres, 8 Jul 63, *McNamara Public Statements, 1963*, V:2077-78.
100. Gorn, "TFX," 38; memo SecN for SecAF, 31 Jul 64, memo G. A. Spangenberg for R, 14 Aug 64: *Hearings: TFX Contract Investigation (Second Series)*, pt 2:462-63, 453, 455.
101. Memo Leonard Sullivan, Jr. for DDR&E, 1 Oct 64, *Hearings: TFX Contract Investigation (Second Series)*, pt 3:479-81.
102. Gorn, "TFX," 39-40; DoD News Release 744-64, 15 Oct 64, OSD Hist; *McNamara Public Statements, 1964*, IV:1656; *New York Times*, 22 Dec 64.
103. Interv McNamara by Alfred Goldberg, Lawrence Kaplan, and Edward Drea, 8 Jan 98, 9-10, OSD Hist; interv McNamara by Walt W. Rostow, 8 Jan 75, 59-61, LBJL.

XVIII. TIGHTENING THE BUDGET: FYS 1965 AND 1966

1. Gilpatric remarks at UPI Conf, Chicago, 19 Oct 63, *Gilpatric Public Statements, 1963*, 398.
2. Memo Hitch for McNamara, 24 Sep 62, fldr FY 1964 Budget (Chron file), box 22, ASD(C) files, OSD Hist; memo McNamara for SvcSecs et al, 4 Dec 62, fldr Budget Guidance and Planning Memoranda 1962-1967, box 9, Enthoven Papers, LBJL; memo McNamara for SvcSecs et al, 18 Mar 63, fldr Programming 1963, box 782, Subject files, OSD Hist; memo Gilpatric for SvcSecs et al, 10 Apr 63, fldr FY 1965 Budget (Chron), box 30, ASD(C) files, OSD Hist. The FYFS&FP of 7 January 1963 was not updated until 1 June 1963; a bound copy of each is in box 134, ASD(C) files, OSD Hist.

3. Poole, *JCS and National Policy 1961-64*, pt I:37-38, 41, 43-44, 160; JCSM-300-63 and CM-524-63 Taylor for SecDef, 13, 17 Apr 63, fldr JCS Views-FY 1965 Program April 1963, box 32, McNamara Records, RG 200.
4. Troika statement, "Estimates of Revenues and Expenditures, Fiscal Years 1965-1967," 5 Apr 63, w/atchd summary table, "Preliminary Budget Projections," 2 Apr 63, fldr Budget-1965, box 45, Sorensen Papers, JFKL; ltr Gordon to McNamara, 20 Apr 63, fldr Interagency Memoranda 1961-1968, box 9, Enthoven Papers, LBJL; ltr McNamara to Gordon, 23 May 63, w/atchd table, "Expenditures by Program—FY 1964-1968," fldr FY 1965 Budget (Chron), box 30, ASD(C) files, OSD Hist.
5. BoB paper, "1965 Budget Preview Discussions: Department of Defense," nd [stamped as received in OSD on 16 Jul 63], fldr 110.01 FY 65 Jan thru Jul 1963, box 44, SecDef Subject Decimal files, Acc 69A-3131; Enthoven memrcd, 17 Jul 63, fldr Interagency Memoranda 1961-1968, box 9, Enthoven Papers, LBJL; memo Gordon for Pres, 8 Aug 63, w/atchmts, "1965 Budget Preview: Expenditures" and "List of Possible Further Reductions for 1965," both 5 Aug 63, fldr Budget 1965 Proposed Planning Figures Background & Detail, box 45, Sorensen Papers, JFKL.
6. Memo McNamara for SvcSecs et al, 26 Aug 63, memo Gilpatric for SvcSecs et al, 27 Sep 63, fldr FY 1965 Budget (Chron), box 22, ASD(C) files, OSD Hist; Hitch address to the American Society of Military Comptrollers, 24 Mar 64, fldr Comptroller 1964, box 783, Subject files, OSD Hist. A copy of the revised and updated FYFS&FP, dated 10 January 1964, is in box 134, ASD(C) files, OSD Hist.
7. Tables of services' budget submissions, SCAS and SSCA, *Hearings: Military Procurement Authorizations, FY 1965* [hereafter *Hearings: Military Procurement Authorizations*], 88 Cong, 2 sess, 1964, 82-83. A table, dated 20 November 1963, showing the amounts the services proposed and the secretary of defense recommended for specific programs for FY 1965 and other fiscal years, is in fldr Back-up for Discussion w/President, box 4, McNamara files, Acc 71A-3470. Handwritten notations indicate that the total difference for FY 1965 between the two amounts was $9 billion (TOA) as of that date.
8. Memo Zuckert for McNamara, 5 Oct 63, fldr 110.01 FY 65 Oct thru- 1963, box 43, SecDef Subject Decimal files, Acc 69A-3131; memo LeMay for SecAF, 7 Oct 63, ibid. In a covering memo of 15 October for McNamara forwarding the Air Force budget and LeMay's memo, Zuckert said that he shared LeMay's "concern about the framework within which the military departments' budgets have been developed this year" (ibid).
9. The DPM on strategic retaliatory forces, dated 31 August 1963, was sent to the Joint Chiefs on 2 September (Poole, *JCS and National Policy 1961-64*, pt I:161-62). OSD transmitted nine other DPMs to the NSC on 28 September, which covered airlift and sealift forces, the Air Force tactical aircraft program, attack carrier (CVA) forces, anti-submarine warfare, amphibious assault forces, naval mine warfare, fleet air defense, underway replenishment forces, and block obsolescence (memo Enthoven for Bundy, 28 Sep 63, w/atchd list, fldr 031.1 WH Draft Memos 1963, box 5, SecDef Subject Decimal files, Acc 69A-3131). Copies of early versions of the DPMs are in ibid, box 5, and in box 117, ASD(C) files, OSD Hist.
10. Memo LeMay for SecAF, 7 Oct 63, cited in n 8; Poole, *JCS and National Policy 1961-64*, pt I:162. During testimony before the Defense Subcommittee of the House Appropriations Committee on 25 February 1964, LeMay made similar criticisms of the budget planning procedures (HSCA, *Hearings: Department of Defense Appropriations for 1965*, 88 Cong, 2 sess, 1964, pt 4:509-11). Hitch, in a letter to Subcommittee Chairman Mahon on 16 March, responded to the criticisms (fldr FY 1965 Budget (Chron), box 30, ASD(C) files, OSD Hist).
11. Memo McNamara for SecNav, 25 Oct 63, fldr Nuclear Powered Ships vs Conventional Powered Ships, box 1, McNamara files, Acc 71A-3470; memo Keeny for McGeorge Bundy, 15 Nov 63, *FRUS 1961-63*, Microfiche Supplement: Vols VII, VIII, IX, Doc 304.
12. Memo Kaysen for McGeorge Bundy, 25 Oct 63, *FRUS 1961-63*, Microfiche Supplement: Vols VII, VIII, IX, Doc 302.
13. Memo McNamara for McGeorge Bundy, Gordon, and Wiesner, 13 Nov 63, fldr 031.1 WH Draft Memos 1963, box 5, SecDef Subject Decimal files, Acc 69A-3131.
14. Joseph S. Hoover (OASD(Comptr)) memrcd, 16 Nov 63, fldr Defense Budget-1965 Sec. 2, box 15, Agency File, NSF, LBJL. For Keeny's views on the last four DPMs, see memo Keeny for McGeorge Bundy, 22 Nov 63, *FRUS 1961-63*, VIII:534-37.
15. Interv McNamara by Robert Dallek, 26 Mar 93, internet copy, 6, LBJL; McNamara, *In Retrospect*, 89-90. For Gilpatric's recollection and those of BoB officials at the meeting, see interv Gilpatric by Ted Gittinger, 2 Nov 82, internet copy, 6-7, LBJL; interv Elmer B. Staats by T. H. Baker, 9 Dec 71, 7, LBJL; and interv Kermit

Gordon by David G. McComb, 9 Jan 69, 23-24, ibid. Deborah Shapley's account draws on the recollections of her father, Willis Shapley, another BoB official in attendance (*Promise and Power*, 271-72).

16. Shapley, *Promise and Power*, 274-75; Johnson, *Vantage Point*, 20, 36.
17. Johnson, *Vantage Point*, 31-32; Gordon interv, 9 Jan 69, 24-25.
18. Gordon interv, 9 Jan 69, 24-26; Johnson, *Vantage Point*, 36.
19. Memo Gordon for Pres, 25 Nov 63, fldr Budget-1965, box 45, Sorensen Papers, JFKL; memo Gordon for Pres, 26 Nov 63, fldr FI 4/FG 115 11/22/63- , box 26, WH Confidential File, LBJL; Staats interv, 9 Dec 71, 8-9; Irving Bernstein, *Guns or Butter: The Presidency of Lyndon Johnson*, 31-32; Dallek, *Flawed Giant*, 71-72.
20. Livesay notes, staff mtg, 26 Nov 63, fldr SecDef Meetings Aug-Dec 1963, box 11, AFPC and SecDef Meetings files, Acc 77-0062.
21. C. V. Clifton and Tazewell Shepard memo of conf with Pres, 29 Nov 63, fldr White House 1963, box 153, LeMay Papers, LC.
22. *Johnson Public Papers, 1963-64*, I:8-10, 15-16, 43-45.
23. Interv Gordon by McComb, 21 Mar 69, 3-4, LBJL; Charles J. V. Murphy, "The Desperate Drive to Cut Defense Spending," *Fortune*, Jan 64, 188; interv Douglas Dillon by Paige Mulhollan, 29 Jun 69, 10, LBJL; telcon between Johnson, Gordon, and McNamara, 10 Dec 63, 11:50 am, Tape K6312.06, PNO 17, Telephone Conversations, LBJL.
24. Hoover memrcd, 30 Nov 63, fldr FY 1965 Budget (Chron), box 30, ASD(C) files, OSD Hist; memo Keeny for McGeorge Bundy, 30 Nov 63, *FRUS 1961-63*, Microfiche Supplement, Vols VII, VIII, IX, Doc 307; memo Gordon for Pres, 9 Dec 63, ibid, Doc 309; draft memo McNamara for Pres, 6 Dec 63, *FRUS 1961-63*, VIII:545-64; draft memo McNamara for Pres, 7 Dec 63, fldr Budget Memos to the President, box 4, McNamara files, Acc 71A-3470; news conf, 7 Dec 63, *Johnson Public Papers, 1963-64*, I:34-38; press conf and news release, 7 Dec 63, *McNamara Public Statements, 1963*, VI:2680-87; *Washington Post*, 10 Dec 63.
25. McNamara news briefing and DoD news release, 10 Dec 63, *McNamara Public Statements, 1963*, VI:2696-2711. According to McNamara's memo of conversation, Senators Jackson and Magnuson of Washington met with the president on 10 December to ask him to reconsider the Dynasoar cancellation because it would lay off 4,000 people at Seattle's Boeing plant. Jackson offered to make a deal with the president, promising not to complain about the Dynasoar cancellation if the administration closed the Navy yards in Boston and Philadelphia (fldr Memos for the Record, box 1, McNamara files, Acc 71A-3470).
26. Bernstein, *Guns or Butter*, 34; Gordon interv, 21 Mar 69, 3-4; Gilpatric memrcd, 26 Dec 63, fldr 110.01 FY 65 Oct thru- 1963, box 43, SecDef Subject Decimal files, Acc 69A-3131; news conf, 18 Dec 63, *Johnson Public Papers, 1963-64*, I:65-71.
27. Memo of conf w/Pres, 30 Dec 63, *FRUS 1961-63*, VIII:587-96; *New York Times*, 31 Dec 63; McNamara and Salinger press conf, Austin, Tex, 30 Dec 63, *McNamara Public Statements, 1963*, VI:2798-2806 (quote, 2799). In a memorandum of 26 December for McNamara, Gilpatric summarized the points that McDonald and LeMay intended to raise at the meeting and enclosed a memorandum regarding the Army's points (fldr RLG Reading File, July 1, 1963- , box 2, Gilpatric files, Acc 66A-3529). McNamara's handwritten notes regarding the meeting are in fldr Back-up for Discussion w/President, box 4, McNamara files, Acc 71A-3470. Another account of the meeting is a debriefing paper prepared by I. C. Kidd, 31 Dec 63, fldr 7100/2 1965 Budget, box 1964-16, CNO Immediate Office files, NHC. McNamara transmitted the final budget estimates in a letter to Gordon, 10 Jan 64 (fldr FY 1965 Budget (Chron), box 30, ASD(C) files, OSD Hist).
28. Annual Budget Message to Congress, 21 Jan 64, *Johnson Public Papers, 1963-64*, I:175-87; *The Budget of the United States, FY 1965*, 71-81.
29. Bernstein, *Guns or Butter*, 37-38.
30. Interv Harold Brown by Dorothy Pierce, 17 Jan 69, 11, LBJL.
31. McNamara interv, 8 Jan 75, 22.
32. Gordon interv, 21 Mar 69, 6; McNamara interv, 8 Jan 75, 22.
33. Vinson remarks, 27 Jan 64, HCAS, *Hearings: Military Posture and HR 9637* [hereafter *Hearings: Military Posture*], 88 Cong, 2 sess, 6892.
34. Ibid, 6893; *Baltimore Sun*, 16 Jan 64; *Washington Post*, 16 Jan 64.
35. Memo McGiffert for SecDef, 11 Jan 64, fldr 110.01 FY 65 Jan thru Mar 1964, box 35, SecDef Subject Decimal files, Acc 69A-7425; *New York Times*, 15 Feb 64. In handwritten notes in the margins of McGiffert's memo, McNamara accepted all the suggestions, subject to limitations on his time in seeing large numbers of House members during the upcoming week.

36. "Goldwater View Belittles ICBMs," *New York Times*, 10 Jan 64; press statement, 9 Jan 64, *McNamara Public Statements, 1964*, I:1; "McNamara Says Goldwater Errs," *New York Times*, 10 Jan 64.
37. Livesay notes, staff mtg, 20 Jan 64, fldr SecDef Staff Meetings Jan-Apr 1964, box 11, AFPC and SecDef Staff Meetings files, Acc 77-0062.
38. Brown's testimony, 17 January, is in *Hearings: Military Posture*, 7549-7647; for the military service representatives' testimony, 20-22 January, see ibid, 7647-7906.
39. Memo McGiffert for O'Brien, 3 Feb 64, fldr White House Major Legislation Reports 1964, box 1, Legislative Affairs files, Acc 67A-4632. A compilation of testimony before Congress on the Defense authorization and appropriation bills for FY 1965 is in James H. McBride and John I. H. Eales, *Military Posture: Fourteen Issues before Congress, 1964*. The issues included reliability and dependability of missiles, MMRBM, the follow-on bomber, the ABM, nuclear test ban safeguards, employment of the TFX aircraft, air and sealift, nuclear power for ships, anti-submarine warfare, Army air support, counter-insurgency (COIN) aircraft, nuclear strategy, basic advanced weapons research and development, and the balance of power.
40. *Hearings: Military Posture*, 7474-79; *Washington Star*, 9 Feb 64; HCAS, *Authorizing Defense Procurement and Research and Development*, H Rpt 1138, 88 Cong, 2 sess, 13 Feb 64, pt 1:1-2. For the dissenting views, see 17 Feb 64, ibid, pt 2:1-6.
41. Memo McGiffert for O'Brien, 24 Feb 64, fldr White House Major Legislation Reports 1964, box 1, Legislative Affairs files, Acc 67A-4632; *Cong Rec*, 20 Feb 64, 3068-3100.
42. Memo McGiffert for O'Brien, 10 Feb 64, fldr White House Major Legislation Reports 1964, box 1, Legislative Affairs files, Acc 67A-4632.
43. Ltr McNamara to Russell, 21 Feb 64, *Hearings: Military Procurement Authorizations*, 885-97; memo McNamara for Taylor, 6 Feb 64, *FRUS 1964-68*, X:22-24 (quote, 24); SCAS, *Authorizing Appropriations During Fiscal Year 1965 for Procurement of Aircraft, Missiles, and Naval Vessels, and Research, Development, Test, and Evaluation for the Armed Forces*, S Rpt 876, 88 Cong, 2 sess, 25 Feb 64, 1-2; *New York Times*, 26, 28 Feb 64; *Cong Rec*, 26, 27 Feb 64, 3602-03, 3678-3701.
44. HCAS, *Authorizing Defense Procurement and Research and Development for Fiscal Year 1965*, H Rpt 1213, 88 Cong, 2 sess, 5 Mar 64, 1-5; memo McGiffert for O'Brien, 9 Mar 64, fldr White House Major Legislation Reports 1964, box 1, Legislative Affairs files, Acc 67A-4632; PL 88-288, 20 Mar 64; Pres remarks, 20 Mar 64, *Johnson Public Papers, 1963-64*, I:402-03.
45. The proceedings were published in five parts in HSCA, *Hearings: DoD Appropriations for 1965*, cited in n 10.
46. Memo McGiffert for O'Brien, 24 Feb 64, cited in n 41; HSCA, *DoD Appropriations for 1965*, pt 4:1-12, 97-117 (quotes, 5, 11-12, 117). On 24 February Hitch and Assistant Secretary of Defense (Manpower) Norman Paul also testified before the subcommittee; see ibid, pt 4:375-438.
47. HCA, *Department of Defense Appropriation Bill, 1965*, H Rpt 1329, 88 Cong, 2 sess, 17 Apr 64, 3, 9, 37, 44; memo McGiffert for O'Brien, 20 Apr 64, fldr White House Major Legislation Reports 1964, box 1, Legislative Affairs files, Acc 67A-4632; *Cong Rec*, 21 Apr 64, 8260-70, 8283-98, 22 Apr 64, 8494-8538; McGiffert memrcd, 23 Apr 64, fldr 110.01 FY 65 Apr thru Oct 1964, box 35, SecDef Subject Decimal files, Acc 69A-7425.
48. Ltr Vance to Russell, 12 May 64, fldr FY 1965 Budget (Chron), box 30, ASD(C) files, OSD Hist; Hitch written statement, 25 May 64, SSCA, *Hearings: Department of Defense Appropriations for 1965*, 88 Cong, 2 sess, 25 May 64, pt 2:1-61 (Army test 25-27 May 64, ibid, 62-193).
49. Livesay notes, staff mtg, 22 Jun 64, fldr SecDef Staff Meetings May-July 1964, box 11, AFPC and SecDef Meetings files, Acc 77-0062.
50. SSCA, *DoD Appropriations for 1965*, pt 2:195-561, 741-837; SCA, *Department of Defense Appropriation Bill, 1965*, S Rpt 1238, 88 Cong, 2 sess, 24 Jul 64, 4; memo McGiffert for O'Brien, 27 Jul 64, fldr White House Major Legislation Reports 1964, box 1, Legislative Affairs files, Acc 67A-4632.
51. *Cong Rec*, 29 Jul 64, 16778-830; *Baltimore Sun*, 30 Jul 64; *Congress and the Nation, 1945-1964*, 329.
52. HCA, *Department of Defense Appropriation Bill, 1965*, H Rpt 1642, 88 Cong, 2 sess, 31 Jul 64, 1-4; memo McGiffert for O'Brien, 3 Aug 64, fldr White House Major Legislation Reports 1964, box 1, Legislative Affairs files, Acc 67A-4632; *Cong Rec*, 4 Aug 64, 17308-16; *New York Times*, 5 Aug 64; PL 88-446, 19 Aug 64.
53. DoD news releases, 18 Apr, 29 Jun, 11 Aug, 7 Oct, 19 Oct 64, *McNamara Public Statements, 1964*, III: 1194-97, 1343-45, IV:1565-66, 1640-42, 1658-60.
54. McNamara statement before the Democratic Party Committee on Resolutions and Platform, Washington, DC, 17 Aug 64, ibid, IV:1567-79; McNamara ltr to Gates, 31 Aug 64, w/DoD press statement, 18 Sep 64, ibid, 1606-10; Mark S. Watson, *Baltimore Sun*, 24 Aug 64; Shapley, *Promise and Power*, 287.

55. *Congress and the Nation, 1945-1964*, 327-28.
56. Memo Enthoven for Hitch, 26 Nov 63, fldr Budget Guidance and Planning Memoranda 1962-1967, box 9, Enthoven Papers, LBJL; memo Hitch for McNamara, 13 Dec 63, w/atchd draft instructions, fldr FY 1966 Budget, box 41, ASD(C) files, OSD Hist. In a memo of the same date as the latter, McNamara circulated the draft instructions to DoD components for comment (ibid). He sent the final instructions, in slightly amended form, to the service secretaries and others on 21 December (fldr 110.01 FY 1966, box 5, SecDef Subject Decimal files, Acc 69A-7425).
57. Memo Enthoven for Systems Analysis Staff, 15 Jan 64, memo Hitch for DDR&E et al, 20 Feb 64: fldr FY 1966 Budget, box 41, ASD(C) files, OSD Hist.
58. JSOP-69 (Parts I-V), atchd to CM-1181-64 Taylor for SecDef, 14 Feb 64, fldr JSOP-'69-'71, box 41, McNamara Records, RG 200; JCSM-219-64 and CM-1272-64 Taylor for SecDef, 16, 20 Mar 64, *FRUS 1964-68*, X:57-64; Poole, *JCS and National Policy 1961-64*, pt I:168, 278, 288. Parts I and II of JSOP-69 are printed in *FRUS 1964-68*, X:26-41.
59. Memo McNamara for Nitze, Zuckert, and Taylor, 16 May 64, *FRUS 1964-68*, X:84-89.
60. Memo Brown for SecDef, 29 Nov 63, w/atchmts, fldr 031.1 WH Draft Memos 1963, box 5, SecDef Subject Decimal files, Acc 69A-3131; Livesay notes, staff mtg, 2 Mar 64, fldr SecDef Staff Meetings Jan-Apr 1964, box 11, AFPC and SecDef Meetings files, Acc 77-0062; memo McNamara for DDR&E and ASD(C), 2 Mar 64, ibid. McNamara's handwritten notes on the points he intended to raise at the 2 March staff meeting are in fldr FY 66 Budget, box 41, McNamara Records, RG 200. Vance carried out McNamara's instruction with a detailed memorandum of 12 March to the service secretaries and other officials; see fldr Chron File, March 1964, box 1, Vance files, Acc 69A-2317.
61. Ltr Gordon to McNamara, 7 Apr 64, fldr FY 1965 Budget (Chron), box 30, ASD(C) files, OSD Hist; ltr Vance to Gordon, 8 May 64, fldr Classified Chron File-Jan thru Dec 1964, box 46, Enthoven Papers, LBJL; ltr Vance to Gordon, 8 May 64, fldr Chron File, May 1964, box 1, Vance files, Acc 69A-2317.
62. Table, OASD(C), "Summary of 1 October 1964 Service Submissions: Fiscal Year 1966 Budget Estimates," 14 Oct 64, fldr FY 1966 Budget, box 41, ASD(C) files, OSD Hist.
63. JCSM-1000-64 Wheeler for SecDef, 30 Nov 64, memo Hitch for SecN, 18 Nov 64: fldr 110.01 Projects (9 Jan 64) CY 64, 5-Yr Plan Nov 1964, box 37, SecDef Subject Decimal files, Acc 69A-7425. In the 18 November memo Hitch summarized and replied to a memorandum of 28 October from Secretary of the Navy Nitze, which has not been found.
64. Vance memos of conv, both 1 Oct 64, fldr Memos for the Record, box 1, McNamara files, Acc 71A-3470. Although the conversations took place on 1 October, the memos were dated 3 October.
65. Hoover memrcd, 23 Nov 64, fldr 110.01 (Budget) August thru- , box 35, SecDef Subject Decimal files, Acc 69A-7425.
66. Memo Keeny for McGeorge Bundy, 5 Dec 64, fldr DoD-Budget Review-December 5, 1964, box 14, Agency File, NSF, LBJL; ltr Hornig to McNamara, 7 Dec 64, Enthoven memrcd, 7 Dec 64: fldr Budget Guidance and Planning Memoranda 1962-1967, box 9, Enthoven Papers, LBJL. According to Keeny's memo, the meeting was scheduled for 5 December, a Saturday. However, no record of a meeting that day has been found. Hornig's letter to McNamara and Enthoven's memo for the record, both dated 7 December, suggest that the meeting may have been postponed to Monday, 7 December.
67. *New York Times*, 10 Dec 64; *Baltimore Sun*, 10 Dec 64; Roswell L. Gilpatric, "Our Defense Needs: The Long View," *Foreign Affairs*, Apr 64, 369-71.
68. Memo Bundy for Pres, 9 Dec 64, fldr FI 4/FG 115 11/22/63- , box 26, WH Confidential File, LBJL; *New York Herald Tribune*, 10 Dec 64.
69. Memo Keeny for Bundy, 5 Dec 64, cited in n 66; memo McNamara for Pres, nd [another copy is dated 10 Dec], memo Bundy and Keeny for Pres, 10 Dec 64: *FRUS 1964-68*, X:187-91.
70. Poole, *JCS and National Policy 1961-64*, pt I:181; CM-267-64 Wheeler for McNamara, 23 Nov 64, *FRUS 1961-64*, X:176-79.
71. Clifton memrcd, 22 Dec 64, *FRUS 1964-68*, X:199-201. Prior to the meeting the chiefs and Chairman Wheeler, in response to McNamara's request, sent him brief memos summarizing the matters they intended to raise with the president. Wheeler's comments are in CM-316-64 of 17 December from Goodpaster, his assistant, for McNamara (fldr 110.01 FY 1966, box 5, SecDef Subject Decimal files, Acc 69A-7425). Memos for McNamara from LeMay and from Director of Navy Program Planning Vice Adm. Horacio Rivero, on behalf of Admiral McDonald, both dated 17 December, and from Army Chief of Staff General Harold Johnson, dated 18 December, are in fldr 110.01 Projects (9 Jan 64) CY 64 5-Yr Plan Nov 1964, box 37, ibid.

72. News conf, 22 Dec 64, *McNamara Public Statements, 1964*, IV:1834-48 (quote, 1835). On 5 December McNamara, after meeting with the president, had announced that in all likelihood defense expenditures would not exceed $50 billion in the next budget and that new obligational authority would fall to a little under $49 billion, which was substantially lower than in any recent years (ibid, 1802-03).
73. *Washington Star*, 23 Dec 64.
74. *Washington Post*, 19 Jan 65; *Wall Street Journal*, 26 Jan 65; *Johnson Public Papers, 1965*, I:62-71, 82-99; *The Budget of the United States, FY 1966*, 68-79.
75. *New York Times*, 31 Jan 65.
76. Ibid, 19 Jan 65.

XIX. VIETNAM: INTO THE VORTEX

1. Whether Kennedy would have withdrawn U.S. troops from Vietnam had he lived has been a subject of much debate and speculation. There is consensus that he would have taken no action until he won reelection in 1964. Stanley Karnow, *Vietnam: A History*, and Robert Dallek, *An Unfinished Life: John F. Kennedy, 1917-1963*, conclude that Kennedy would have withdrawn the troops after the election. Two other studies, by Guenter Lewy, *America in Vietnam*, and John M. Newman, *JFK and Vietnam: Deception, Intrigue, and the Struggle for Power*, take opposite sides on the issue: Lewy believes Kennedy would have followed the same course as Johnson, and Newman maintains that Kennedy had begun plans early in 1963 to end U.S. involvement even at the cost of defeat. There can be, of course, no definitive answer. For the musings of top Kennedy aides Theodore Sorensen and Arthur Schlesinger, Jr., in the context of the U.S. search 40 years later for an exit strategy from an entangling engagement in Iraq, see Sorensen and Schlesinger, "What Would J.F.K. Have Done?," *New York Times*, 4 Dec 2005.
2. Memo SecDef for Pres, 23 Nov 63, *FRUS 1961-63*, IV:627-28; DeptState Situation Rpt, 23 Nov 63, ibid, 629-30 (quotes).
3. Memrcd McCone, 24 Nov mtg, 25 Nov 63, ibid, 635-37.
4. NSAM 273, 26 Nov 63, ibid, 637-40.
5. *Johnson Public Papers, 1963-64*, I:8-10 (quote, 8).
6. News conf, 7 Dec 63, ibid, 34; memo of telcon, Rusk and McNamara, 7 Dec 63, *FRUS 1961-63*, IV:690.
7. Rpt JCS SpecAsst(CI) (Krulak), 21 Dec 63, *FRUS 1961-63*, IV:721-27 (quote, 721).
8. Memo SecDef for Pres, 21 Dec 63, ibid, 732-35.
9. Ibid, 735.
10. *McNamara Public Statements, 1963*, VI:2792.
11. Memo Mansfield for Pres, 6 Jan 64, *FRUS 1964-68*, I:2-3; memo McGeorge Bundy for Pres, 9 Jan 64, ibid, 8-9.
12. Memo SecDef for Pres, 7 Jan 64, ibid, 12-13.
13. Ed note, *FRUS 1961-63*, IV:652; HCAS, *Military Posture and HR 9637*, 27 Jan 64, 6904.
14. NSAM 273, cited in n 4, 639; *The Joint Chiefs of Staff and the War in Vietnam, 1960-1968*, pt I:ch 7, 38-39, ch 8, 18-19. The LeMay statement is quoted in Hilsman, *To Move a Nation*, 526-27.
15. Memo SecDef for Pres, 21 Dec 63, cited in n 8, 734.
16. *JCS and the War in Vietnam, 1960-68*, pt I:ch 8, 20-21.
17. Memo McGeorge Bundy for Pres, 7 Jan 64, *FRUS 1964-68*, I:4-5.
18. *JCS and the War in Vietnam, 1960-68*, pt I:ch 8, 21.
19. Ltr McCone to SecState, 7 Jan 64, *FRUS 1964-68*, I:5-6; Rand Rpt, "An Analysis of Large-Scale VC Operations," fldr VN092 Jul-Dec 63, box 18, ISA files, Acc 67A-4564.
20. Ltr McCone to SecState, 7 Jan 64, cited in n 19, 6; memo Forrestal for McGeorge Bundy, 8 Jan 64, *FRUS 1964-68*, I:7-8; ltr McNamara to McCone, 16 Jan 64, fldr Vietnam 1964 (Jan 7-May 13), box 30, SecDef files, OSD Hist.
21. Press briefing, 28 Jan 64, *McNamara Public Statements, 1964*, I:246.
22. *New York Times*, 28 Jan, 1 Feb 64; New Year's msg to Minh, 1 Jan 64, *Johnson Public Papers, 1963-64*, I:106; memo SecDef for Pres, 21 Dec 63, *FRUS 1961-63*, IV:734.
23. Msg 1431 Saigon to State, 29 Jan 64, *FRUS 1964-68*, I:37-39 (quote, 39).
24. SCAS and SSCA, *Military Procurement Authorizations, FY 1965*, 3 Feb 64, 63.
25. Msg Rusk and McNamara to Lodge and Harkins, 31 Jan 64, *FRUS 1964-68*, I:47-48.
26. S. L. A. Marshall, "Gen. Harkins' Days Numbered," *Los Angeles Times*, 26 Jan 64.

27. Memo Forrestal for McGeorge Bundy, 4 Feb 64, *FRUS 1964-68*, I:59-60.
28. Memo Forrestal for McGeorge Bundy, 30 Mar 64, ibid, 199-201.
29. See Johnson remarks at swearing in of Taylor, 2 Jul 64, *Johnson Public Papers, 1963-64*, II:841-42.
30. Ball, *Past Has Another Pattern*, 375-76.
31. Msg 1467 Saigon to State, 1 Feb 64, *FRUS 1964-68*, I:54-55.
32. See Saigon msg A-455, Cmdr's Personal Mil Assessment of the 4th Qtr CY 63, Jan 64, box 237, Subject files, OSD Hist. The full date of the message is not given on this copy.
33. Hilsman, *To Move a Nation*, 536.
34. A condensed version of memo JCS for SecDef, 22 Jan 64, is in ed note, *FRUS 1964-68*, I:35. The complete memo JCSM-46-64 is in *Pentagon Papers* (Gravel ed), III:496-99.
35. Ltr Rusk to McNamara, 5 Feb 64, *FRUS 1964-68*, I:63.
36. Msgs COMUSMACV to CINCPAC, 13 Feb 64, 1533 Saigon to State, 14 Feb 64, box 237, Subject files, OSD Hist.
37. Rusk's description appeared in the *New York Times*, 4 Mar 64; memo McGeorge Bundy for Rusk, McNamara, et al, 18 Feb 64, w/encl, 13 Feb 64, OSD Hist; William Bundy, "History of Vietnam," chs 12, 16. The president announced William Bundy's new appointment on 29 February 1964 (*Johnson Public Papers, 1963-64*, I:322).
38. Memo Forrestal for McNamara, 14 Feb 64, *FRUS 1964-68*, I:77-79.
39. Memo McNamara for CJCS, 21 Feb 64, ibid, 97-99; JCSM-174-64 CJCS for SecDef, 2 Mar 64, ibid, 112-18 (quote, 116); McNamara's marginal note, ibid, 118, n 9.
40. Msg 1583 Saigon to State, 20 Feb 64, memrcd Forrestal, 20 Feb 64, ibid, 93-95.
41. Ltr Pres to SecDef, 5 Mar 64, ibid, 131-33; *New York Times*, 6 Mar 64.
42. *JCS and the War in Vietnam, 1960-68*, pt I:ch 9, 11.
43. Msg 1740 Saigon to State, 13 Mar 64, *FRUS 1964-68*, I:141; memcon (Taylor), JCS and Pres, 4 Mar 64, ibid, 129.
44. Taylor, *Swords and Plowshares*, 310.
45. *New York Times*, 10 Mar 64.
46. Memo SecDef for Pres, 16 Mar 64, *FRUS 1964-68*, I:153-67 (quotes 166, 167).
47. Ibid, 161-64.
48. Ibid, 164, n 18.
49. Memcon JCS and Pres, 4 Mar 64, cited in n 43; notes on JCS conf w/Pres, 4 Mar 64, Binder vol 1, Wallace Greene Papers, MC Hist & Mus Div.
50. Notes on JCS mtg, 5 Mar 64, Binder vol 1, Greene Papers.
51. *JCS and the War in Vietnam, 1960-68*, pt I:ch 9, 18-20; memo JCSM-222-64 CJCS for SecDef, 14 Mar 64, *FRUS 1964-68*, I:149-50 and n 3.
52. JCSM-222-64 CJCS for SecDef, 14 Mar 64, cited in n 51.
53. Notes on JCS mtg w/SecDef, 14 Mar 64, Binder vol 1, Greene Papers.
54. Livesay notes, staff mtg, 16 Mar 64, fldr SecDef Staff Mtgs Jan-Apr 1964, box 11, AFPC and SecDef Meetings files, Acc 77-0062.
55. Memo SecDef for Pres, 16 Mar 64, *FRUS 1964-68*, I:153-67; sum rcd 524th mtg NSC, 17 Mar 64, ibid, 170-72 (quote, 171).
56. Sum rcd 524th mtg NSC, ibid, 170-72; NSAM 288, 17 Mar 64, ibid, 172-73; White House statement, 17 Mar 64, *Johnson Public Papers, 1963-64*, I:387-88.
57. *JCS and the War in Vietnam, 1960-68*, pt I:ch 9, 24-25; msg 2203 Lodge to Rusk and McNamara, 14 May 64, *FRUS 1964-68*, I:315-16.
58. Memos Forrestal for McGeorge Bundy, 30 Mar, 26 May 64, *FRUS 1964-68*, I:199-201, 385-89.
59. Memo Rowan for Pres, 21 Apr 64, ibid, 254-55.
60. Memrcd White House staff mtg, 30 Mar 64, ibid, 196-99.
61. Ibid, 298, n 1.
62. Memo Forrestal for Bundy, 30 Mar 64, ibid, 199-201; McNamara notes for rpt to Pres, 14 May 64, ibid, 322-27.
63. Ibid, 298, n 2; ltr Lodge to Rusk, 30 Apr 64, ibid, 279-80.
64. Ltr Rusk to Lodge, 7 May 64, ibid, 298-99, n 1.
65. *JCS and the War in Vietnam, 1960-68*, pt I:ch 9, 22-23.

66. Ibid, 34-36 (quote, 36); memo Forrestal for McGeorge Bundy, 31 Mar 64, w/atchmt, *FRUS 1964-68*, I:206-13; ltr Bundy to Lodge, 4 Apr 64, ibid, 225-29; memos Forrestal for Bundy, 16, 28 Apr 64, ibid, 242-43, 271-72.
67. Msg 2108 Saigon to State, 4 May 64, ibid, 284-87 (quotes, 287).
68. Memo William Bundy for Rusk, 4 May 64, ibid, 287-88.
69. Memo Forrestal for McGeorge Bundy, 5 May 64, ibid, 289-90.
70. Msg 1838 State to Saigon, 5 May 64, ibid, 291-93.
71. Msg 070745Z Felt to Taylor, 6 May 64, ibid, 295-96.
72. *JCS and the War in Vietnam, 1960-68*, pt I:ch 10, 2-3.
73. Memrcd William Colby, Pres mtg on Vietnam, 6 May 64, document CK310011145, http://www.galenet.com/servelet/DDRS; ed note, *FRUS 1964-1968*, I:304.
74. Taylor, *Swords and Plowshares*, 311-12.
75. McNamara notes for rpt to Pres, 14 May 64, cited in n 62; sum rcd 532d mtg NSC, 15 May 64, *FRUS 1964-68*, I:328-32.
76. Sum rcd 532d mtg NSC, ibid (quote, 332).
77. Memo by CIA, 15 May 64, ibid, 336.
78. Msg Pres to Lodge, 26 May 64, ibid, 393-94.
79. Sum rcd Honolulu mtg, 1 Jun 64, ibid, 412-33; McMaster, *Dereliction of Duty*, 100.
80. Memo McGeorge Bundy for Pres, 3 Jun 64, ibid, 440-41; Taylor, *Swords and Plowshares*, 313.
81. William Bundy, "History of Vietnam," ch 12, 32-33.
82. Draft memo for Pres, 25 Feb 64, *FRUS 1964-68*, XXVIII:14-17, sent on 26 Feb to Vientiane (msg 664), Bangkok (msg 1438), and Saigon (msg 1319).
83. Memo ASecState (Hilsman) for Rusk, 28 Feb 64, ibid, 21-23; memo Bundy for SecDef, 28 Feb 64, fldr Reading File, Feb. 1964, box 119, McNamara Records, RG 200; memo SecDef for Pres, 25 Apr 64, *FRUS 1964-68*, XXVIII:69-70 (quote, 70).
84. Memo Forrestal for Pres, 29 Apr 64, *FRUS 1964-68*, I:275.
85. Sum rcd 529th mtg NSC, 29 Apr 64, ibid, 276-77.
86. Memo William Bundy for Harriman, 29 Apr 64, memrcd Colby, 29 Apr 64, ibid, XXVIII:76-80; notes on JCS mtgs w/SecDef, 17 Apr, 18 May 64, Binder vol 1, Greene Papers.
87. Msg 1011 State to Vientiane, 17 May 64, *FRUS 1964-68*, XXVIII:88-90.
88. Sum rcd 533d mtg NSC, 6 Jun 64, memrcd Forrestal, 7 Jun 64, memo of conf w/Pres, 8 Jun 64: ibid, 141-42, 147-48, 152-60 (quote, 159).
89. Memo McGeorge Bundy for Pres, 12 Jun 64, ibid, 184 and n 2, 3.
90. Sum rcd White House mtg, 10 Jun 64, msg 1587 Vientiane to State, 11 Jun 64: ibid, 170-74, 181-83 (quote, 182).
91. Msg DEF9535 OSD to CINCPAC, 7 Oct 64, JCSM-897-64 ActgCJCS for SecDef, 22 Oct 64, msg 868 Vientiane to State, 10 Dec 64: ibid, 280, 288-89, 306-07 (quote, 306).
92. Memos McGeorge Bundy for Pres, 3 Jun 64, William Bundy for Rusk, 3 Jun 64, ibid, I:440-46; paper prepared for Pres by SecDef, 5 Jun 64, ibid, 463; Charles J. V. Murphy, "Vietnam Hangs on U.S. Determination," *Fortune*, May 64; *Pentagon Papers*, bk 3, IV.C.1, 76-81.
93. McGeorge Bundy draft memo, 10 Jun 64, *FRUS 1964-68*, I:493-96 (quote, 496); memos Bundy for Pres, 10 Jun 64, Bundy for Rusk and McNamara, w/atchmts, 15 Jun 64, ibid, 496-97, 500-16.
94. Memos Bundy for Pres, 10 Jun 64, Bundy for Rusk and McNamara, 15 Jun 64, w/atchmt 3 drafted by William Bundy, ibid, 497, 514.
95. Rpt, "Viet Cong Activity—January Through June 1964," fldr vol. 3, box 1, NSC Meetings, NSF, LBJL; draft memo SpecAsst W. H. Sullivan, 13 Jun 64, *FRUS 1964-68*, I:500-07.
96. Memo Bundy for Pres, 6 Jun 64, *FRUS 1964-68*, I:472-73; press conf, 23 Jun 64, *Johnson Public Papers, 1963-64*, I:802.
97. Memo Bundy for Pres, 25 Jun 64, *FRUS 1964-68*, I:530-31.
98. See *FRUS 1964-68*, I:xxiv, xxvii, xxviii.
99. Msg 328 Rusk to Taylor, 2 Aug 64, ibid, 592; Marolda and Fitzgerald, *From Military Assistance to Combat*, 393-97, 410. The United States armed, equipped, supplied, and trained the South Vietnamese units involved in OPLAN 34A.

100. Johnson, *Vantage Point*, 112-13; Vietnam Information Grp, "Presidential Decisions: The Gulf of Tonkin Attacks of August 1964," 1 Nov 68, iii, 11-12, doc CK3100511725, http://www.galenet.com/servlet/DDRS.
101. Telcon McNamara and Pres, 3 Aug 64, 10:30 a.m., no. 4633, pgm no. 10, tape WH 6408.03, LBJL. No record of the 3 August meeting has been found (ed note, *FRUS 1964-68*, I:600). This account is drawn from telcon McNamara and Pres, 3 Aug 64, 1:21 p.m., no. 4369, pgm no. 16, tape WH 6408.03, LBJL; SecDef test on Tonkin Gulf Resolution before SCFR and SCAS (excerpts), 6 Aug 64, 496, 504, 506, fldr Vietnam 1964, box 30, SecDef files, OSD Hist; "Chronology of Secretary of Defense McNamara's Activities Vietnam PT Boat Crisis," 6 Aug 64, fldr Vietnam PT Operations Aug. 1964, box 347, Subject files, OSD Hist; SecDef statement to SCFR, 20 Feb 68, master copy, 30, fldr Tonkin, box 347, Subject files, OSD Hist.
102. Msg USM 626J to Golf/Eleven/Alpha, 041140Z Aug 64, fldr Presidential Decisions—Gulf of Tonkin Attacks of August 1964, vol I, Tab 9 [2 of 2], box 38, NSC Histories, NSF, LBJL; ed notes, *FRUS 1964-68*, I:604-05; DDR&E, WSEG, "Command and Control of the Tonkin Gulf Incident 4-5 August 1964," Critical Incident Report No. 7, 26 Feb 65, 7, fldr Command and Control of the Tonkin Gulf Incident 4-5 August 1964, 7, box 239, Subject files, OSD Hist; telcon McNamara and Alfred Goldberg, 23 Mar 05, OSD Hist.
103. Statement McNamara to SCFR, 20 Feb 68, cited in n 101, 23; memo McGeorge Bundy for Pres, Chronology of the Gulf of Tonkin, 4 Sep 64, doc CK3100341000, http://www.galenet.com/servlet/DDRS.
104. Rcd of telcon, McNamara and Sharp, 4 Aug 64, fldr Gulf of Tonkin (Misc), box 228, Country File, Vietnam, NSF, LBJL; ed note, *FRUS 1964-68*, I:607-10; msg to Quebec/India [routing designator] 041646Z Aug 64, fldr Presidential Decisions—Gulf of Tonkin Attacks of August 1964, cited in n 102; statement McNamara to SCFR, 20 Feb 68, cited in n 101; "Presidential Decisions: The Gulf of Tonkin Attacks," cited in n 100, 23-24. The most thorough examination of the event is found in Edwin E. Moïse, *The Tonkin Gulf and the Escalation of the Vietnam War*.
105. Sum notes 538th mtg NSC, 4 Aug 64, *FRUS 1964-68*, I:611-13; ed note, ibid, 626; Radio and TV Report to American People, 4 Aug 64, *Johnson Public Papers, 1963-64*, II:927-28; "Command and Control of the Tonkin Gulf Incident," cited in n 102, 31-33.
106. Special Message to Congress, 5 Aug 64, *Johnson Public Papers, 1963-64*, II:930-31; SecDef test before SCFR and SCAS (excerpts), 6 Aug 64, cited in n 101, 504-07; SecDef test before HCFA (Exec Sess) (excerpts), 6 Aug 64, 524-27, fldr Vietnam 1964, box 30, SecDef files, OSD Hist.
107. Memo ActgSpecAssist SACSA for CJCS, 5 Aug 64, fldr Vietnam (Jul-Aug 64), box 43, Wheeler files, RG 218.
108. Special Message to Congress, 5 Aug 64, cited in n 106; ed note, *FRUS 1964-68*, I:664; *Cong Rec*, 7 Aug 64, 110, pt 14:18409 (Fulbright quote).
109. *Baltimore Sun*, 3 Aug 64; *New York Herald Tribune* (ed), 3 Aug 64; COMUSMACV to CINCPAC et al, OPLAN 34A Operations, 070519Z, atchmt to memo DirJtStaff for CJCS, 8 Aug 64, fldr Vietnam (Jul-Aug 64), box 43, Wheeler files, RG 218. The message also states that some boats were relocated because of threat of an air attack; other sources identify the new location as Cam Ranh Bay. The ICC, with members from Poland, Canada, and India, supervised the provisions of the 1954 Geneva Accords.
110. Memo A. R. Brownfield (DepSACSA) for CJCS, 15 Aug 64, w/atchmt, fldr Vietnam (Jul-Aug 64), box 43, Wheeler files, RG 218. For the role of SACSA in 34A, see Shultz, *Secret War Against Hanoi*.
111. Ball, *Past Has Another Pattern*, 379.
112. The literature on the Tonkin Gulf incident is extensive. See for instance: Johnson, *Vantage Point*; McNamara, *In Retrospect*; *FRUS 1964-1968*, vol I; SCFR, *Hearings: The Gulf of Tonkin, The 1964 Incidents*, 90 Cong, 2 sess, 20 Feb 68; Marolda and Fitzgerald, *From Military Assistance to Combat*; Moïse, *Tonkin Gulf and the Escalation of the Vietnam War*; Ezra Y. Siff, *Why the Senate Slept: The Gulf of Tonkin Resolution and the Beginning of America's Vietnam War*; Joseph C. Goulden, *Truth Is The First Casualty: The Gulf of Tonkin Affair—Illusion and Reality*; John Prados, "Essay: 40th Anniversary of the Gulf of Tonkin Incident," National Security Archive, 4 Aug 04, internet copy; Edward Drea, "Received Information Indicating Attack: The Gulf of Tonkin Incident 40 Years Later," *MHQ: The Quarterly Journal of Military History*, Summer 04. Moise is the most convincing that a second attack did not occur. Marolda's position has evolved based on subsequent analysis and additional information. In 2005 he concluded that no attack had occurred on 4 August; see Edward J. Marolda, "Summary of the Tonkin Gulf Crisis of August 1964," 13 Jul 05, Frequently Asked Questions: Tonkin Gulf Crisis, August 1964, http://www.history.navy.mil/faqs/faq120-1.htm. Former Secretary of Defense Melvin Laird has said, "From all I was able to determine when I read the dispatches five years later as secretary of defense, there was no second attack. There was confusion, hysteria, and miscom-

munication on a dark night" (Melvin R. Laird, "Iraq: Learning the Lessons of Vietnam," *Foreign Affairs*, Nov-Dec 05, 31).
113. Gelb and Betts, *Irony of Vietnam*, 104.
114. Johnson remarks at Akron Univ, 21 Oct 64, *Johnson Public Papers, 1963-64*, II:1387-94 (quote, 1391); Brian VanDeMark, *Into the Quagmire: Lyndon Johnson and the Escalation of the Vietnam War*, 19.
115. Ted Gittinger, ed, *The Johnson Years: A Vietnam Roundtable*, 23-24.
116. *FRUS 1964-68*, I, contains numerous documents covering this period. A good summary of them and the uncertainties of the time is in *JCS and the War in Vietnam, 1960-68*, pt I:chs 12, 13.
117. Interv Forrestal by Paige Mulhollan, 3 Nov 69, in VanDeMark, *Into the Quagmire*, 20; memo of White House mtg, 9 Sep 64, *FRUS 1964-68*, I:749-50 (quote, 750).
118. Gelb and Betts, *Irony of Vietnam*, 105; *JCS and the War in Vietnam, 1960-68*, pt I:ch 12, 5.
119. Memo McGeorge Bundy for Pres, 8 Sep 64, *FRUS 1964-68*, I:746-49; NSAM 314, 10 Sep 64, ibid, 758-60.
120. Memrcd McGeorge Bundy, 20 Sep 64, *FRUS 1964-68*, I:778-81; Chester L. Cooper, *The Lost Crusade: America in Vietnam*, 241-42; George McT. Kahin, *Intervention: How America Became Involved in Vietnam*, 237.
121. CM-124-64 Wheeler for SecDef, 9 Sep 64, *Pentagon Papers* (Gravel ed), III:564; memo JCSM-902-64 Wheeler for SecDef, 27 Oct 64, *FRUS 1964-1968*, I:847-57; memo McNamara for Wheeler, 29 Oct 64, fldr Reading File, Oct. 31-20, 1964, box 121, McNamara Records, RG 200; *JCS and the War in Vietnam, 1960-68*, pt I:ch 12, 37, 40, 44-45.
122. Figures for the losses at Bien Hoa vary slightly among several sources: *FRUS 1964-68*, I:873, n 2; *Pentagon Papers*, bk 3, IV.C.3, 4; *JCS and the War in Vietnam, 1960-68*, pt I:ch 13, 10. For exchanges between State and Saigon, see msgs 1357 and 1360 Saigon to State, 1451 Wheeler to Sharp, 978 and 979 State to Saigon, all 1 Nov 64, *FRUS 1964-68*, I:873-79 (quote, 878).
123. Memrcd, sum JCS mtg w/SecDef, 2 Nov 64, Greene Papers.
124. Johnson, *Vantage Point*, 121.
125. Memo of White House mtg, 9 Sep 64, cited in n 117, 749-55 (quotes, 752, 753).
126. Memo Bundy for Pres, 31 Aug 64, *FRUS 1964-68*, I:723-24.
127. Ed notes, ibid, 886-88, 964-65, 974; memrcd, White House mtg, 19 Nov 64, ibid, 914-16; NSC wkg gp paper, 21 Nov 64, ibid, 916-29; notes on White House mtg, 1 Dec 64, ibid, 965-69; ExCom paper, 2 Dec 64, ibid, 969-74.
128. ExCom paper, cited in n 127 (quote, 969).
129. Ibid (quotes, 970).
130. Instructions Pres to Taylor, 3 Dec 64, *FRUS 1964-68*, I:974-78.
131. Memo Pres for SecState, SecDef, DirCIA, 7 Dec 64, ibid, 984, 969-78; McNamara, *In Retrospect*, 163.
132. Msgs 1351 Saigon to State, 31 Oct 64, 1416 Saigon to State, 6 Nov 64, 1870 Saigon to State, 20 Dec 64: *FRUS 1964-68*, I:860-61, 890-92, 1014-16.
133. Memo DepDir(I&R)(Denney) for Rusk, 27 Jan 65, ibid, II:91-93; msgs 2322 Saigon to State, 27 Jan 65, 2617 Saigon to State, 16 Feb 65, ibid, 93-95, 281-82.
134. Taylor, *Swords and Plowshares*, 330-31; msg 2382 Saigon to State, 3 Feb 65, *FRUS 1964-68*, II:124-26; memcon McGeorge Bundy group w/Taylor and Emb staff, 4 Feb 65, ibid, 133-38.
135. Taylor, *Swords and Plowshares*, 336-37; DeptState Situation Rpt, 20 Feb 65, *FRUS 1964-68*, II:339-41; msg 2720 Saigon to State, 23 Feb 65, ibid, 349-50 (quote, 349).
136. Msgs 1941 Saigon to State, 25 Dec 64, 1975 Saigon to State, 28 Dec 64, JCS 5458 Wheeler to Westmoreland, 28 Dec 64, 1365 State to Saigon, 29 Dec 64, *FRUS 1964-68*, I:1043-44, 1049-53.
137. Msg CAP 64375 Pres to Taylor, 30 Dec 64, ibid, 1057-59.
138. Memo Bundy for Pres, 27 Jan 65, ibid, II:95-97.
139. Msg 1549 State to Saigon, 27 Jan 65, ibid, 98-99.
140. Sum notes 545th mtg NSC, 6 Feb 65, memrcd Colby, 6 Feb 65, memrcd Vance, 7 Feb 65: ibid, 155-57, 158-60, 160-68.
141. Statement on dependent withdrawal, 7 Feb 65, *Johnson Public Papers, 1965*, I:153; White House statement on retaliatory attacks, 7 Feb 65, ibid, 153-54n.
142. Memo Bundy for Pres, 7 Feb 65, *FRUS 1964-68*, II:174-81 (quote, 175); Annex A, paper prep by Bundy Mission members, 7 Feb 65, ibid, 181-85 (quotes, 181).
143. Sum notes 547th mtg NSC, 8 Feb 65, ibid, 188-92 (quote, 192).
144. *JCS and the War in Vietnam, 1960-68*, pt II:ch 17, 21-22; ed note, *FRUS 1964-68*, II:212. The JCS history put the number wounded in the Qui Nhon attack at 22, but subsequent sources cite 21.

145. Sum notes 547th mtg NSC, cited in n 143 (quote, 191); Johnson, *Vantage Point*, 129.
146. McCone memrcd, 10 Feb 65, *FRUS 1964-68*, II:220-25 (quote, 223).
147. JCSM-100-65 CJCS for McNamara, 11 Feb 65, ibid, 240-43; *JCS and the War in Vietnam, 1960-68*, pt II: ch 18, 5-11.
148. Msg 1718 State to Saigon, 13 Feb 65, *FRUS 1964-68*, II:263-65.
149. Goodpaster memrcd of mtg w/Pres, 17 Feb 65, ibid, 298-308.
150. Msg 2654 Saigon to State, 19 Feb 65, ibid, 328; Jacob Van Staaveren, *Gradual Failure: The Air War Over North Vietnam, 1965-1966*, 81-85.
151. Van Staaveren, *Gradual Failure*, 3-7, 323-24.
152. *JCS and the War in Vietnam, 1960-68*, pt II:ch 19, 1-2.
153. Msg 473 Taylor to JCS, 22 Feb 65, *FRUS 1964-68*, II:347-49.
154. Msgs 1840 State to Saigon, 26 Feb 65, JCS 736-65 Wheeler to Sharp and Westmoreland, 27 Feb 65: ibid, 376, 380-81.
155. Ed note, ibid, 413.
156. Taylor, *Swords and Plowshares*, 338.
157. Memo SecDef for Pres, 9 Feb 65, fldr Vietnam 1965 (Jan 14-May 10), box 32, Subject files, OSD Hist.
158. HCFA, *Hearings: Foreign Assistance Act of 1965*, 89 Cong, 1 sess, 11 Mar 65, pt 4:628.
159. *Baltimore Sun*, 26 Apr 64.
160. *New York Times*, 11 Apr 65.
161. McNamara, *In Retrospect*, 41.

XX. CONCLUSION

1. Ltr Gilpatric to Thomas Morris, 16 Jan 78, w/atchmt, 2, OSD Hist.
2. Doris Kearns, *Lyndon Johnson and the American Dream*, 177.
3. Hanson Baldwin, "The McNamara Monarchy," *Saturday Evening Post*, 9 Mar 63; Stewart Alsop, "Master of the Pentagon," ibid, 5 Aug 61; Theodore H. White, "Revolution in the Pentagon," *Look*, 23 Apr 63.
4. Ltr Zuckert to Thomas Morris, 15 Feb 78, w/atchmt, 6, OSD Hist.
5. Memo McNamara for SvcSecs et al, 8 Mar 61, fldr Reading File, Dec. 60-Dec. 61, box 113, McNamara Records, RG 200.
6. Watson, *Into the Missile Age*, ch 15.
7. "McNamara Defines His Job," *New York Times Magazine*, 26 Apr 64.
8. Cole et al, *Department of Defense*, 239.
9. McNamara interv, 27 Aug 86, 21-22.
10. Ltrs Vinson to McNamara, 23 May 61, McNamara to Vinson, 25 May 61, Vinson to McNamara, 5 Jun 61, in *Army, Navy, Air Force Journal*, 10 Jun 61.
11. McNamara interv, 3 Apr 86, 17, 18.
12. Quoted in Henry L. Trewitt, *McNamara*, 13.
13. Enthoven interv, 3 Feb 86, 5.
14. *DoD Annual Report, FY 1963*, 32.
15. McNamara interv, 3 Apr 86, 22; McNamara interv, 8 Jan 75, 15.
16. McNamara interv, 8 Jan 98, 9-10.
17. Gilpatric interv, 30 Jun 70, 91-92; press conf, 5 Feb 62, *McNamara Public Statements, 1962*, II:725; McNamara interv, 8 Jan 75, 13-14; *Cong Rec*, Senate, 21 Mar 67, 75.
18. Interv Norman Paul by Dorothy Pierce McSweeney, 21 Feb 69, 36-38, LBJL.
19. Glass interv, 28 Oct 87, 23-24, 27.
20. Gilpatric interv, 30 Jun 70, 91-92.
21. *Washington Post*, 1 Jan 65.
22. McNamara interv, 3 Apr 86, 27.
23. Ibid, 9-10, 20-21; Rusk, *As I Saw It*, 521; memrcd McGeorge Bundy, 23 Sep 63, *FRUS 1961-63*, IX: 97-98; Nitze interv, 3 Oct 84, 32.
24. *DoD Annual Report, FY 1965*, 13-14.
25. Quoted in James A. Nathan, "Force, Statecraft, and American Foreign Policy," *Polity*, Winter 95, 241.
26. McNamara, *In Retrospect*.

27. Interv Adam Yarmolinsky by Alfred Goldberg and Ronald Landa, 14 May 93, 26, OSD Hist; Yarmolinsky paper, "Gays, Blacks, the Military and the Community," 25 Jun 93, 2-3, ibid; Morris J. MacGregor, Jr., *Integration of the Armed Forces, 1940-1965*, 520; *New York Times*, 21 Apr 62; memo McNamara for Pres, 24 Jul 63, in Morris J. MacGregor and Bernard C. Nalty, eds, *Blacks in the United States Armed Forces: Basic Documents*, XIII:169-70.
28. Memo McNamara for SvcSecs, 10 Jul 64, in DoD News Release 510-64, 13 Jul 64, *McNamara Public Statements, 1964*, III:1380-81.
29. Ibid. McNamara underscored the linkage between integration and enhanced military effectiveness.
30. Sorensen, *Kennedy*, 486-87.
31. Pres rpt to nation on situation at Univ of Mississippi, 30 Sep 62, *Kennedy Public Papers, 1962*, 726-28; McNamara interv, 27 Aug 86, 3-4.
32. *Washington Post*, 3 Oct 62; Schlesinger, *A Thousand Days*, 948; msg Howze to Wheeler, 4 Oct 62, fldr XVIII Airborne Corps Messages, 1-7 Oct 62, box 12, Records of Oxford, Miss. Operations, 1961-63, RG 319; CGUSCONARC/CINCARSTRIKE to RUCAC/CGUSARMYTHREE et al, 23 Jul 63, fldr Dept of the Army (CONARC) II, Messages Sent (Jan-Jul 63), box 10, ibid.
33. Sorensen, *Kennedy*, 487-88.
34. Ltr Brown to Thomas Morris, 23 May 78, OSD Hist.
35. McGeorge Bundy, *The Strength of Government*, 37; ltr Fubini to Thomas Morris, 6 Jan 78, OSD Hist; ltr Gilpatric to Morris, 16 Jan 78, w/atchmt, 3, ibid.
36. Ltrs Drucker to Morris, 6 Feb 78, Blandford to Morris, 8 Mar 78, Sharp to Morris, 9 Apr 78, OSD Hist; Taylor interv, 18 Oct 83, 18.
37. Ltr Blandford to Morris, cited in n 36.
38. White, "Revolution in the Pentagon," 46.

Notes on Sources and Selected Bibliography

The most important records used in research for this volume were retired files in Record Group (RG) 330, Records of the Office of the Secretary of Defense, at the Washington National Records Center, Suitland, Maryland. The Records Center has since transferred some of these files to the National Archives at College Park, Maryland. Eventually the remainder will be sent there.

Key among the RG 330 materials are the annual subject-decimal files of the secretary and deputy secretary of defense, plus other collections of Robert McNamara files that span his entire tenure. In 1992 a large collection of McNamara files in RG 330, designated Accession 71A-4401 and comprising 203 boxes, was transferred from Suitland to College Park. McNamara deeded the collection to the National Archives, where it became part of RG 200, Donated Records. Although most of the research took place while the collection was at Suitland, citations are to its new box numbers and new name at College Park—McNamara Records.

McNamara himself made few records. He kept no diaries and prepared typewritten memoranda, which are scattered throughout the files, of only a few of the many meetings he attended. Nor did he have a secretary listen in on telephone conversations to take notes, as did some officials like George Ball at the Department of State. His personal imprint, however, is evident in occasional handwritten summaries on lined notepads enumerating a paper's major points, in "to do" lists, and in marginal notations on memoranda he received. The notepad jottings—often undated, lacking context, and extremely sketchy—are generally of less value than the marginal notations.

A particularly useful source in RG 330 are notes of McNamara's weekly Monday morning staff meetings, prepared usually by R. Eugene Livesay. Attendees included the service secretaries, the chairman and the Joint Chiefs of Staff, the deputy secretary and assistant secretaries of defense, and McNamara's special assistants. As a rule meetings dealt with organizational, management, legislative, and budgetary matters, and sometimes featured a special briefing on a weapon system or an issue of current concern. Seldom did they delve into broad policy or strategic issues. McNamara discontinued the meetings held during the Truman and Eisenhower years of the Joint Secretaries and the Staff Council and only briefly in 1961 held Armed Forces Policy Council meetings. In effect his staff meetings replaced the meetings of these former bodies. Notes of the staff meetings are in Accession 77-0062, which also holds records of the earlier meetings of the Joint Secretaries, Staff Council, and Armed Forces Policy Council. In previous volumes of the OSD History Series this accession was called either AFPC Meeting files or OASD(C)(A) files. Here it is called AFPC and SecDef Meetings files. Also of utility are notebooks in the OSD Historical Office containing handwritten notes made by McNamara's military assistant, Sidney B. Berry, Jr., not only of certain of the staff meetings, but also of several meetings the secretary held separately with the Joint Chiefs and of meetings during his visits to Southeast Asia in September-October and December 1963 and March 1964.

No complete record of McNamara's appointments has been found. The OSD Historical Office has fragments of an appointment book, but the irregular, scattered entries diminish its usefulness and reliability. Much of McNamara's high-level meeting schedule can be gleaned from Roswell L. Gilpatric's appointment books at the Kennedy Library and from the appointment books of Secretary of State Dean Rusk at the Lyndon Baines Johnson Library and of Presidents Kennedy and Johnson at the respective presidential libraries.

In RG 330 the files of the assistant secretary of defense for international security affairs, both the annual collections of general files and the more specialized regional or country files, proved extremely helpful. Of limited value were the files of deputy secretaries Gilpatric and Cyrus R. Vance, which consist essentially of chronologically arranged outgoing correspondence, and the files of special assistants and other assistant secretaries.

A notable exception are the files retired by the assistant secretary of defense (comptroller). Two accessions, on loan from the Suitland Records Center to the OSD Historical Office, were essential in the writing of the budget chapters. Accessions 71A-2684 and 73A-497, which together span the years 1947 to 1970, represent material gathered by Henry Glass during his service in the comptroller's office and as special assistant to the secretary and deputy secretary. Previous volumes in the series cited them as the files of the Assistant to the Secretary and the Deputy Secretary of Defense. Here they are called Assistant Secretary of Defense (Comptroller) files, or more simply ASD(C) files. Upon completion of Volume VII the office will return them to the Records Center for eventual transfer to the National Archives. Also useful regarding the budget are the files of the assistant for legislative affairs (Accession 67A-4632), which contain OSD's weekly reports, 1962-1964, to Lawrence F. O'Brien, the president's special assistant.

The authors took advantage of the OSD Historical Office's extensive subject files of newspaper and journal clippings, a collection of miscellaneous material on the Vietnam War, congressional publications, and other reference material, as well as a partial collection of the secretary of defense's telegraphic cables.

Next in importance to OSD records were the holdings of the Kennedy and Johnson libraries, especially the national security files. Collections of the papers of OSD officials at these repositories include those of Gilpatric and Adam Yarmolinsky at the Kennedy Library and Alain C. Enthoven at the Johnson Library. The William Bundy papers at the Johnson Library consist only of his lengthy draft manuscript on the Vietnam War. The Johnson Library also has an unprocessed collection of Harold Brown papers, which library officials indicate contains mostly speeches and awards. Among the personal papers of OSD officials in other repositories are those of Paul H. Nitze at the Library of Congress.

Joint Chiefs of Staff material includes the papers of Air Force Chiefs of Staff Thomas D. White and Curtis E. LeMay at the Library of Congress, the extremely rich papers of Chief of Naval Operations Arleigh A. Burke (his tenure lasted only through 1 August 1961) at the Naval Historical Center, and the retired records of the Joint Chiefs of Staff (RG 218) at College Park, including Earle G. Wheeler's files as chairman. The papers of Lyman L. Lemnitzer and Maxwell D. Taylor, Wheeler's predecessors, are at the National Defense University Library. Taylor's papers include material from his service as the president's military representative, 1961-62, and as ambassador to South Vietnam, 1964-65. The Naval Historical Center has the papers of Burke's successors, George W. Anderson and David L. McDonald, but neither is organized for research. Much good documentation for their tenures is in the Chief of Naval Operations Immediate Office Files (Double Zero Files), which are processed and for which a detailed finding aid is available. The U.S. Marine Corps History and Museums Division has Wallace M. Greene's notes as commandant, many of them handwritten, of meetings beginning in 1964 that President Johnson held with McNamara and the JCS regarding Southeast Asia. Papers at the Hoover Institution of Greene's predecessor, David M. Shoup, and of Edward G. Lansdale yielded nothing of use.

The primary published documentary collections used were *Public Papers of the Presidents of the United States*, the OSD Historical Office's limited edition volumes of *Public Statements of Secretary of Defense Robert S. McNamara*, and the Department of State's indispensable *Foreign Relations of the United States* series. The authors also utilized the growing number of published transcripts of White House meetings and telephone conversations and in some cases consulted audio tapes for which transcripts have so far not been made. They made use, too, of documentary collections on the internet, particularly declassified documents at www.galenet.com.

Supplementing the memoir literature were oral history interviews conducted by the OSD Historical Office, the military services, and the Kennedy and Johnson libraries. Especially helpful were interviews the presidential libraries undertook during the 1960s and early 1970s when events were still relatively fresh in participants' memories, as well as Richard Neustadt's interviews conducted at President

Kennedy's request in the wake of the 1962 Skybolt crisis and Alfred Goldberg's interviews in the late sixties with U.S. officials regarding strategic questions.

Doctoral dissertations, as well as unpublished studies and research reports produced within the Department of Defense and elsewhere, proved valuable. Note should be made of the seven-volume draft administrative history of the Department of Defense, 1963-69, and the JCS Historical Division's volumes on the Joint Chiefs of Staff and national policy, and the Joint Chiefs and the war in Vietnam.

Some records used in the preparation of this volume remain classified. The select bibliography that follows includes records, publications, and other materials cited in the notes.

OFFICIAL RECORDS AND PERSONAL PAPERS

Dwight D. Eisenhower Library, Abilene, Kans.
    Lauris Norstad Papers
Gerald R. Ford Library, Ann Arbor, Mich.
    Gerald R. Ford Congressional Papers
Lyndon Baines Johnson Library, Austin, Tex.
    Francis M. Bator Papers
    William P. Bundy Papers
    Alain C. Enthoven Papers
    National Security File (NSF)
        Agency File
        McGeorge Bundy Files
        Country File
        Country File, Vietnam
        C. V. Clifton Files
        Robert W. Komer Files
        National Security Council Histories
        National Security Council Meetings File
        Subject File
    Recordings and Transcripts of Conversations and Meetings
    Vice Presidential Security Files
    White House Central Files
        Confidential File
        Subject File
John F. Kennedy Library, Boston, Mass.
    George W. Ball Papers
    David E. Bell Papers
    Roswell L. Gilpatric Papers
    Kermit Gordon Papers
    National Security Files (NSF)
    Richard E. Neustadt Papers
    David Nunnerley Papers
    President's Office Files (POF)
    Presidential Recordings
        Meeting Recordings
        Telephone Recordings
    Arthur M. Schlesinger, Jr. Papers
    Theodore C. Sorensen Papers
Library of Congress, Washington, D.C.
    W. Averell Harriman Papers

634   Bibliography

    Curtis E. LeMay Papers
    Paul H. Nitze Papers
    Thomas D. White Papers
Marine Corps History and Museums Division, Washington, D.C.
    Wallace M. Greene, Jr. Papers
National Archives, College Park, Md.
    General Records of the Department of State (RG 59)
        Central Files
        Lot Files
            66 D 182, S/MF (Special Assistant to the Secretary of State for Multilateral Force Negotiations) Files
            69 D121, S/P (Policy Planning Council) Files
    Donated Records (RG 200)
        Robert S. McNamara Records
    Records of the Joint Chiefs of Staff (RG 218)
        Chairman, Joint Chiefs of Staff Files
        Earle G. Wheeler Files
    Records of the Army Staff (RG 319)
        Records of Oxford, Mississippi Operations
National Defense University Library, Washington, D.C.
    Lyman L. Lemnitzer Papers
    Maxwell D. Taylor Papers
Naval Historical Center, Washington, D.C.
    Arleigh M. Burke Papers
        Bumpy Road Files
            Originator's Files
            Sensitive Files
    Chief of Naval Operations Immediate Office Files (Double Zero Files)
Historical Office, Office of the Secretary of Defense, Arlington, Va.
    Assistant Secretary of Defense (Comptroller) Files
    Sidney B. Berry, Jr. Notebooks
    Biographical Files
    Secretary of Defense Cable Files
    Subject Files
Public Record Office, Kew, London, England
    Prime Minister's Office Files (PREM 11)
Washington National Records Center, Suitland, Md.
    Records of the Office of the Secretary of Defense (RG 330)
        64A-2093   SecDef Subject Decimal Files, 1960
        64A-2382   ISA Files, 1961
        65A-3078   Administrative Secretary Files, 1955-61
        65A-3464   SecDef Subject Decimal Files, 1961
        65A-3501   ISA Files, 1962
        66A-3529   Roswell Gilpatric Files, 1961-64
        66A-3542   SecDef Subject Decimal Files, 1962
        67A-4564   ISA Files, 1963
        67A-4632   Legislative Affairs Files, 1961-64
        67A-4736   ISA Files, 1957-63
        67A-4738   ISA United Kingdom Files, 1957-62
        67A-4801   Legislative Affairs Files, 1961-64
        68A-0306   ISA Files, 1964
        68A-1575   DDR&E Skybolt Files, 1959-64
        68A-4024   National Security Council Files, 1947-65
        69A-2243   Atomic Energy Files, 1958-63
        69A-2317   Cyrus Vance Files, 1964-67

```
69A-3131   SecDef Subject Decimal Files, 1963
69A-7425   SecDef Subject Decimal Files, 1964
71A-2170   Norman Paul Files, 1962-65
71A-2896   Cuba Sensitive Files, 1961-64
71A-3470   Robert McNamara Files, 1961-68
71A-6489   Miscellaneous Sensitive Files, 1951-66
76-0028    SecDef Special Assistant Files, 1958-73
77-0062    AFPC and SecDef Meetings Files, 1950-72
```

INTERVIEWS

Air Force Historical Support Office, Bolling Air Force Base, Washington, D.C.
    Charyk, Joseph V. Interviewed by James C. Hasdorff. Washington, D.C., 15 January, 24 April 1974.
    Zuckert, Eugene M. Interviewed by George M. Watson, Jr. Washington, D.C., 3, 4, 5, 9 December 1986.

Lyndon Baines Johnson Library, Austin, Tex.
    Brown, Harold. Interviewed by Dorothy Pierce. Washington, D.C., 17 January 1969.
    Cleveland, Harlan. Interviewed by Paige E. Mulhollan. Washington, D.C., 13 August 1969.
    Dillon, C. Douglas. Interviewed by Paige E. Mulhollan. New York, 29 June 1969.
    Gilpatric, Roswell L. Interviewed by Ted Gittinger. New York, 2 November 1982 (Internet copy).
    Gordon, Kermit. Interviewed by David G. McComb. Washington, D.C., 9 January 1969.
    Johnson, Lyndon B. Interviewed by William J. Jorden. LBJ Ranch, Tex., 12 August 1969.
    McNamara, Robert S. Interviewed by Walt W. Rostow. Washington, D.C., 8 January 1975.
    _____. Interviewed by Robert Dallek. Washington, D.C., 26 March 1993 (Internet copy).
    O'Brien, Lawrence F. Interviewed by Michael L. Gillette. New York, 18 September, 30 October 1985, 11 February 1986 (Internet copies).
    Paul, Norman. Interviewed by Dorothy Pierce McSweeny. Washington, D.C., 21 February 1969.
    Staats, Elmer B. Interviewed by T. H. Baker. Washington, D.C., 9 December 1971.

John F. Kennedy Library, Boston, Mass.
    Bell, David E. Interviewed by Robert C. Turner. Washington, D.C., 11 July 1964.
    _____. Interviewed by William T. Dentzer. Washington, D.C., 2 January 1965.
    Brown, Harold. Interviewed by Steven Rifkin. Washington, D.C., 9 July 1964.
    Chayes, Abram. Interviewed by Eugene Gordon. Washington, D.C., 9 July 1964.
    Gilpatric, Roswell L. Interviewed by Dennis J. O'Brien. New York, 5, 27 May, 12 August 1970.
    McNamara, Robert S. Interviewed by James G. Blight. Washington, D.C., 21 May 1987.
    McNaughton, John T. Interviewed by Lawrence E. McQuade. Washington, D.C., 14 November 1964.
    _____. Interviewed by George Bunn. Washington, D.C., 21 November 1964.
    Ormsby Gore, David. Interviewed by Richard Neustadt. Boston, 5 May 1964.
    Stahr, Elvis J., Jr. Interviewed by Robert H. Ferrell. Bloomington, Ind., 18 August 1964.
    Zuckert, Eugene M. Interviewed by Lawrence E. McQuade. Washington, D.C., 18 April, 11 July 1964.

Marine Corps History and Museums Division, Washington, D.C.
    Krulak, Victor H. Interviewed by Benis M. Frank. San Diego, Calif., 20 June 1970.

Naval Historical Center, Washington, D.C.
    Anderson, George W. Interviewed by John T. Mason, Jr. Washington, D.C., 7 January, 2 April 1981.

Historical Office, Office of the Secretary of Defense, Arlington, Va.
    Anderson, George W. Interviewed by Maurice Matloff and Roger R. Trask. Washington, D.C., 7 August 1984.
    Cooke, David O. Interviewed by Maurice Matloff and Alfred Goldberg. Washington, D.C., 23 October 1989.

Enthoven, Alain C. Interviewed by Maurice Matloff. Stanford, Calif., 3 February 1986.
Gilpatric, Roswell L. Interviewed by Maurice Matloff. Washington, D.C., 14 November 1983.
Glass, Henry. Interviewed by Maurice Matloff, Lawrence Kaplan, Alfred Goldberg, and Robert J. Watson. Washington, D.C., 28 October 1987.
Harriman, W. Averell. Interviewed by Alfred Goldberg and Doris Condit. Washington, D.C., 29 May 1975.
Kaufmann, William W. Interviewed by Alfred Goldberg. Washington, D.C., 14 May 1966.
———. Interviewed by Lawrence Kaplan and Maurice Matloff. Washington, D.C., 14 July 1986.
———. Interviewed by Maurice Matloff. Washington, D.C., 23 July 1986.
Kent, Glenn A. Interviewed by Alfred Goldberg. Washington, D.C., 11-12 May 1966.
LeMay, Curtis E. Interviewed by Alfred Goldberg. Newport Beach, Calif., 12 October 1966.
Lemnitzer, Lyman L. Interviewed by Maurice Matloff. Washington, D.C., 19 January 1984.
McNamara, Robert S. Interviewed by Maurice Matloff and Alfred Goldberg. Washington, D.C., 3 April 1986.
———. Interviewed by Maurice Matloff and Roger Trask. Washington, D.C., 22 May 1986.
———. Interviewed by Alfred Goldberg, Lawrence Kaplan, and Edward Drea. Washington, D.C., 8 January 1998.
Morris, Thomas D. Interviewed by Alfred Goldberg and Maurice Matloff. Washington, D.C., 6 April 1987.
Nitze, Paul H. Interviewed by Alfred Goldberg. Washington, D.C., 15 June 1966.
———. Interviewed by Maurice Matloff and Roger Trask. Arlington, Va., 3 October 1984.
Rowen, Henry. Interviewed by Alfred Goldberg. Washington, D.C., 27 September 1966.
Stern, Marvin. Interviewed by Alfred Goldberg. Santa Monica, Calif., 28 February, 1 March 1967.
Taylor, Maxwell D. Interviewed by Alfred Goldberg. Washington, D.C., 14 June 1966.
———. Interviewed by Maurice Matloff. Washington, D.C., 18 October 1983.
Yarmolinsky, Adam. Interviewed by Alfred Goldberg and Ronald Landa. Washington, D.C., 14 May 1993.
United States Army Military History Institute, Carlisle Barracks, Pa.
Decker, George H., Jr. Interviewed by Dan H. Ralls. Washington, D.C., 18 December 1972.

PUBLISHED SOURCES

U.S. CONGRESS: GENERAL

Congressional Record. 1961-1965.

U.S. CONGRESS: HOUSE HEARINGS

Committee on Appropriations. Subcommittee. *Department of Defense Appropriations for 1962.* 87 Cong, 1 Sess, 1961.
———. *Department of Defense Appropriations for 1963.* 87 Cong, 2 Sess, 1962.
———. *Department of Defense Appropriations for 1964.* 88 Cong, 1 Sess, 1963.
———. *Department of Defense Appropriations for 1965.* 88 Cong, 2 Sess, 1964.
———. *Foreign Operations Appropriations for 1962.* 87 Cong, 1 Sess, 1961.
———. *Foreign Operations Appropriations for 1963.* 87 Cong, 2 Sess, 1962.
———. *Foreign Operations Appropriations for 1964.* 88 Cong, 1 Sess, 1963.
———. *Foreign Operations Appropriations for 1965.* 88 Cong, 2 Sess, 1964.
Committee on Armed Services. *Authorizing Appropriations for Aircraft, Missiles, and Naval Vessels for the Armed Forces.* 87 Cong, 1 Sess, 1961.
———. *Military Posture Briefings.* 87 Cong, 1 Sess, 1961.
———. *Military Posture and H.R. 9751.* 87 Cong, 2 Sess, 1962.
———. *Military Posture and H.R. 2440.* 88 Cong, 1 Sess, 1963.

Bibliography   637

———. *Military Posture and H.R. 9637.* 88 Cong, 2 Sess, 1964.
———. *Military Posture and H.R. 4016.* 89 Cong, 1 Sess, 1965.
———. *House Joint Resolution 505, to Authorize the President to Order Units and Members in the Ready Reserve to Active Duty for Not More Than 12 Months and for Other Purposes; and H.R. 8353, to Authorize Additional Appropriations for Aircraft, Missiles, and Naval Vessels for the Armed Forces, and for Other Purposes.* 87 Cong, 1 Sess, 1961.
———. Subcommittee No. 3. *Military Reserve Posture.* 87 Cong, 2 Sess, 1962.
———. Special Subcommittee on Defense Agencies. *Hearings.* 87 Cong, 2 Sess, 1962.
Committee on Foreign Affairs. *To Establish a United States Arms Control Agency.* 87 Cong, 1 Sess, 1961.
———. *The International Development and Security Act.* 87 Cong, 1 Sess, 1961.
———. *Foreign Assistance Act of 1962.* 87 Cong, 1 Sess, 1961.
———. *Foreign Assistance Act of 1963.* 87 Cong, 2 Sess, 1962.
———. *Foreign Assistance Act of 1964.* 88 Cong, 1 Sess, 1963.
———. *Foreign Assistance Act of 1965.* 88 Cong, 2 Sess, 1964.
Committee on Government Operations. Subcommittee. *Civil Defense—1961.* 87 Cong, 1 Sess, 1961.
———. *Defense Supply Agency.* 87 Cong, 2 Sess, 1962.
———. Subcommittee on Military Operations. *Systems Development and Management.* 87 Cong, 2 Sess, 1962.
Committee on Science and Astronautics. *Defense Space Interests.* 87 Cong, 1 Sess, 1961.
———. *Research and Development for Defense.* 87 Cong, 1 Sess, 1961.

U.S. CONGRESS: HOUSE DOCUMENTS AND REPORTS

Amendments to the Budget Involving Increases for the National Aeronautics and Space Administration, the Small Business Administration, the U.S. Information Agency, the Department of Commerce, and the Department of Defense, Military. 87 Cong, 1 Sess, 1961. H. Doc 179.
Amendments to the Budget for the Military Functions of the Department of Defense Redistributing the Funds Requested for the Army Reserve Forces. 87 Cong, 1 Sess, 1962. H. Doc. 377.
Committee on Appropriations. *Department of Defense Appropriation Bill, 1962,* 87 Cong, 1 Sess, 1961. H. Rpt. 574.
———. *Department of Defense Appropriation Bill, 1963.* 87 Cong, 2 Sess, 1962. H. Rpt. 1607.
———. *Department of Defense Appropriation Bill, 1964.* 88 Cong, 1 Sess, 1963. H. Rpt. 439.
———. *Department of Defense Appropriation Bill, 1964.* 88 Cong, 1 Sess, 1963. H. Rpt. 812.
———. *Department of Defense Appropriation Bill, 1965.* 88 Cong, 2 Sess, 1964. H. Rpt. 1329.
———. *Department of Defense Appropriation Bill, 1965.* 88 Cong, 2 Sess, 1964. H. Rpt. 1642.
———. *Department of Defense Appropriations for 1963: Conference Report to Accompany HR 11289.* 87 Cong, 2 Sess, 1962. H. Rpt. 2036.
———. *Foreign Assistance Act of 1961.* 87 Cong, 1 Sess, 1961. H. Rpt. 1088.
———. *Foreign Assistance and Related Agencies Appropriation Bill, 1962.* 87 Cong, 1 Sess, 1961. H. Rpt. 1107.
———. *Foreign Assistance Act of 1963.* 88 Cong, 1 Sess, 1963. H. Rpt. 1006.
———. *Foreign Aid and Related Agencies Appropriation Bill, 1964.* 88 Cong, 1 Sess, 1963. H. Rpt. 1040.
———. *Foreign Assistance Act of 1964.* 88 Cong, 2 Sess, 1964. H. Rpt. 1925.
Committee on Armed Services. *Report of Special Subcommittee on Defense Agencies.* 87 Cong, 2 Sess, 1962.
———. *Authorizing Appropriations for Aircraft, Missiles, and Naval Vessels.* 87 Cong, 1 Sess, 1961. H. Rpt. 380.
———. *Authorizing Appropriations for Aircraft, Missiles, and Naval Vessels.* 87 Cong, 1 Sess, 1961. H. Rpt. 817.
———. *Authorization for Aircraft, Missiles, and Naval Vessels, Fiscal Year 1962.* 87 Cong, 1 Sess, 1961. H. Rpt. 462.

638 Bibliography

————. *Authorizing Appropriations for Aircraft, Missiles, and Naval Vessels.* 87 Cong, 2 Sess, 1962. H. Rpt. 1406.
————. *Authorizing Appropriations for Aircraft, Missiles, and Naval Vessels.* 88 Cong, 1 Sess, 1963. H. Rpt. 62.
————. *Authorizations for Aircraft, Missiles, and Naval Vessels, Fiscal Year 1964.* 88 Cong, 1 Sess, 1963. H. Rpt. 289.
————. *Authorizing Defense Procurement and Research and Development.* 88 Cong, 1 Sess, 1964. H. Rpt. 1138.
————. *Authorizing Defense Procurement and Research and Development for Fiscal Year 1965.* 88 Cong, 2 Sess, 1964. H. Rpt. 1213.
Committee on Foreign Affairs. *Mutual Security Act of 1961.* 87 Cong, 1 Sess, 1961. H. Rpt. 651.
————. *Foreign Assistance Act of 1964.* 88 Cong, 2 Sess, 1964. H. Rpt. 1443.
Committee on Government Operations. *Defense Supply Agency.* 87 Cong, 2 Sess, 1962. H. Rpt. 2440.
Library of Congress, Legislative Reference Service. *United States Defense Policies in 1961.* 87 Cong, 2 Sess, 1962. H. Doc. 502.

U.S. Congress: Senate Hearings

Committee on Appropriations. *Foreign Assistance and Related Agencies Appropriations for 1962.* 87 Cong, 1 Sess, 1961.
————. Subcommittee. *Department of Defense Appropriations for 1962.* 87 Cong, 1 Sess, 1961.
————. ————. *Department of Defense Appropriations for 1963.* 87 Cong, 2 Sess, 1962.
————. ————. *Department of Defense Appropriations for 1964.* 88 Cong, 1 Sess, 1963.
Committee on Armed Services. *Nomination of Robert S. McNamara.* 87 Cong, 1 Sess, 1961.
————. *Nominations Hearing on Paul H. Nitze, Charles J. Hitch, Cyrus R. Vance, Arthur Sylvester, and Thomas D. Morris.* 87 Cong, 1 Sess, 1961.
————. *Nomination of Roswell L. Gilpatric.* 87 Cong, 1 Sess, 1961.
————. *Military Procurement Authorization Fiscal Year 1962.* 87 Cong, 1 Sess, 1961.
————. *Military Procurement Authorization Fiscal Year 1963.* 87 Cong, 2 Sess, 1962.
————. *Military Procurement Authorization Fiscal Year 1964.* 88 Cong, 1 Sess, 1963.
————. *Authorization for Military Procurement, Research and Development, Fiscal Year 1969, and Reserve Strength.* 90 Cong, 2 Sess, 1968.
————. *Status of U.S. Strategic Power.* 90 Cong, 2 Sess, 1968.
————. Preparedness Investigating Subcommittee. *Military Aspects and Implications of Nuclear Test Ban Proposals and Related Matters.* 88 Cong, 1 Sess, 1963.
Committee on Armed Services and Subcommittee of the Committee on Appropriations. *Military Procurement Authorizations, Fiscal Year 1965.* 88 Cong, 2 Sess, 1964.
————. *Military Procurement Authorizations, Fiscal Year 1966.* 89 Cong, 1 Sess, 1965.
Committee on Foreign Relations. *International Development and Security.* 87 Cong, 1 Sess, 1961.
————. *Foreign Assistance Act of 1963.* 88 Cong, 1 Sess, 1963.
————. *Nuclear Test Ban Treaty.* 88 Cong, 1 Sess, 1963.
————. *The Gulf of Tonkin, The 1964 Incidents.* 90 Cong, 2 Sess, 1968.
————. *Executive Sessions of the Senate Foreign Relations Committee* (Historical Series).
Vol. XIII. *Eighty-Seventh Congress, First Session, 1961.* 2 parts. 1984.
Vol. XIV. *Eighty-Seventh Congress, Second Session, 1962.* 1986.
Committee on Government Operations. Subcommittee on National Policy Machinery. *Organizing for National Security: State, Defense, and the National Security Council.* Part IX. 87 Cong, 1 Sess, 1961.
————. Permanent Subcommittee on Investigation. *TFX Contract Negotiations.* 88 Cong, 1 Sess, 1963-64.
————. ————. *TFX Contract Investigations* (Second Series). 91 Cong, 2 Sess, 1970.
————. Subcommittee on National Security and International Operations. *Planning—Programming—Budgeting.* 90 Cong, 2 Sess, 1968.

U.S. Congress: Senate Documents and Reports

Amendments to the Budget for the Military Functions of the Department of Defense. 87 Cong, 1 Sess, 1961. S. Doc. 39.
Committee on Appropriations. *Foreign Assistance and Related Agencies Appropriation Bill, 1962.* 87 Cong, 1 Sess, 1961. S. Rpt. 991.
_____. *Department of Defense Appropriation Bill, 1962.* 87 Cong, 1 Sess, 1961. S. Rpt. 653.
_____. *Department of Defense Appropriation Bill, 1963.* 87 Cong, 2 Sess, 1962. S. Rpt. 1578.
_____. *Department of Defense Appropriation Bill, 1964.* 88 Cong, 1 Sess, 1963. S. Rpt. 502.
_____. *Department of Defense Appropriation Bill, 1965.* 88 Cong, 2 Sess, 1964. S. Rpt. 1238.
Committee on Armed Services. *Authorizing Additional Appropriations for Aircraft, Missiles, and Naval Vessels for the Armed Forces.* 87 Cong, 1 Sess, 1961. S. Rpt. 643.
_____. *Authorizing Appropriations for Aircraft, Missiles, and Naval Vessels for the Armed Forces for Fiscal Year 1962.* 87 Cong, 1 Sess, 1961. S. Rpt. 253.
_____. *Authorization of Appropriations for Aircraft, Missiles, and Naval Vessels, Fiscal Year 1963.* 87 Cong, 2 Sess, 1962. S. Rpt. 1315.
_____. *Authorizing Appropriations During Fiscal Year 1964 for Procurement, Research, Development, Test, and Evaluation of Aircraft, Missiles, and Naval Vessels for the Armed Forces.* 88 Cong, 1 Sess, 1963. S. Rpt. 123.
_____. *Authorizing Appropriations During Fiscal Year 1965 for Procurement of Aircraft, Missiles, and Naval Vessels, and Research, Development, Test, and Evaluation for the Armed Forces.* 88 Cong, 2 Sess, 1964. S. Rpt. 876.
_____. Preparedness Investigating Subcommittee. *Investigation of the Preparedness Program: Interim Report on Military Implications of the Proposed Limited Nuclear Test Ban Treaty.* 88 Cong, 1 Sess, 1963. Committee Print. Committee on Government Operations. Permanent Subcommittee on Investigations. *TFX Contract Investigations.* 91 Cong, 2 Sess, 1970. S. Rpt. 91-1496.
_____. Select Committee to Study Government Operations. *Alleged Assassination Plots Involving Foreign Leaders.* 94 Cong, 1 Sess, 1975. Interim Report. S. Rpt. 94-465.
_____. *Report of United States Foreign Policy and Operations, by Senator Allen J. Ellender on His Visit to Japan, Taiwan, and Southeast Asia.* 87 Cong, 2 Sess, 1962. S. Doc. 73.
_____. Subcommittee on National Policy Machinery. *Organizing for National Security.* 87 Cong, 1 Sess, 1961.
_____. Subcommittee on National Security and International Operations. *Planning—Programming—Budgeting: Selected Comment.* 90 Cong, 1 Sess, 1967.

U.S. Congress: Joint Hearings

Joint Economic Committee. Subcommittee on Defense Procurement. *Impact of Military and Related Civilian Supply and Service Activities on the Economy.* 88 Cong, 1 Sess, 1963.

Executive Branch: Documents and Reports

The Budget of the United States Government for the Fiscal Year Ending June 30, 1961.
The Budget of the United States Government for the Fiscal Year Ending June 30, 1962.
The Budget of the United States Government for the Fiscal Year Ending June 30, 1963.
The Budget of the United States Government for the Fiscal Year Ending June 30, 1964.
The Budget of the United States Government for the Fiscal Year Ending June 30, 1965.
The Budget of the United States Government for the Fiscal Year Ending June 30, 1966.
Cole, Alice C., Alfred Goldberg, Samuel A. Tucker, and Rudolph A. Winnacker, eds. *The Department of Defense: Documents on Establishment and Organization, 1944-1978.* Washington, D.C.: Historical Office, Office of the Secretary of Defense, 1978.
General Services Administration, National Archives and Records Service, Office of the Federal Register. *Public Papers of the Presidents of the United States: Dwight D. Eisenhower, 1953-61.* 8 vols. 1958-1961.

640   Bibliography

———. *Public Papers of the Presidents of the United States: John F. Kennedy, 1961-1963.* 3 vols. 1962-1964.
———. *Public Papers of the Presidents of the United States: Lyndon B. Johnson, 1963-1969.* 10 vols. 1963-1970.
U.S. Arms Control and Disarmament Agency. *Documents on Disarmament, 1962.* 1963.
U.S. Bureau of the Census. *Historical Statistics of the United States: Colonial Times to 1970.* Washington, D.C.: U.S. Government Printing Office, 1975.
U.S. Department of Defense. *Annual Report for Fiscal Year 1961, Including the Reports of the Secretary of Defense, Secretary of the Army, Secretary of the Navy, Secretary of the Air Force.* 1962.
———. *Annual Report for Fiscal Year 1962, Including the Reports of the Secretary of Defense, Secretary of the Army, Secretary of the Navy, Secretary of the Air Force.* 1963.
———. *Annual Report for Fiscal Year 1963, Including the Reports of the Secretary of Defense, Secretary of the Army, Secretary of the Navy, Secretary of the Air Force.* 1964.
———. *Annual Report for Fiscal Year 1964, Including the Reports of the Secretary of Defense, Secretary of the Army, Secretary of the Navy, Secretary of the Air Force.* 1966.
———. *United States-Vietnam Relations, 1945-1967. (Pentagon Papers.)* 12 vols. 1971.
———. OSD Historical Office. *Department of Defense Key Officials, 1947-2000.* 2000.
———. ———, comp. *Public Statements of Secretary of Defense Robert S. McNamara, 1961-68.* 39 vols.
———. ———, comp. *Public Statements of Deputy Secretary of Defense Roswell L. Gilpatric, 1961-64.* 4 vols.
———. ———, comp. *Public Statements of Deputy Secretary of Defense Cyrus A. Vance, 1964-67.* 4 vols.
U.S. Department of State. *American Foreign Policy: Current Documents, 1960.* Washington, D.C.: U.S. Government Printing Office, 1964.
———. *American Foreign Policy: Current Documents, 1961.* Washington, D.C.: U.S. Government Printing Office, 1965.
———. *American Foreign Policy: Current Documents, 1962.* Washington, D.C.: U.S. Government Printing Office, 1966.
———. *American Foreign Policy: Current Documents, 1963.* Washington, D.C.: U.S. Government Printing Office, 1967.
———. *American Foreign Policy: Current Documents, 1964.* Washington, D.C.: U.S. Government Printing Office, 1967.
———. *Documents on Germany, 1944-1985.* Publication 9446, nd.
———. *Foreign Relations of the United States, 1958-1960.* Vol. VIII: Berlin Crisis, 1958-1959. Washington, D.C.: U.S. Government Printing Office, 1993.
———. *Foreign Relations of the United States, 1961-1963.* 25 vols., some with microfiche supplements. Washington, D.C.: U.S. Government Printing Office, 1988-2002.
———. *Foreign Relations of the United States, 1964-68.* 22 vols. to date. Washington, D.C.: U.S. Government Printing Office, 1992- .
———. *The Nuclear Test Ban Treaty: Gateway to Peace.* Publication 7254. August 1961.

OTHER DOCUMENTARY COLLECTIONS

Aguilar, Luis, ed. *Operation Zapata: The "Ultrasensitive" Report and Testimony of the Board of Inquiry on the Bay of Pigs.* Frederick, Md.: University Publications of America, 1981.
Beschloss, Michael R., ed. *Taking Charge: The Johnson White House Tapes, 1963-1964.* New York: Simon & Schuster, 1997.
Jackson, Henry M., ed. *The National Security Council: Jackson Subcommittee Papers on Policy-Making at the Presidential Level.* New York: Praeger, 1965.
MacGregor, Morris J., and Bernard C. Nalty, eds. *Blacks in the United States Armed Forces: Basic Documents.* 13 vols. Washington, D.C.: Scholarly Resources, 1977.
May, Ernest R., and Philip D. Zelikow, eds. *The Kennedy Tapes: Inside the White House During the Cuban Missile Crisis.* Cambridge, Mass.: Harvard University Press, 1997.

McAuliffe, Mary S., ed. *CIA Documents on the Cuban Missile Crisis, 1962.* Washington, D.C.: History Staff, Central Intelligence Agency, 1992.
Naftali, Timothy, Ernest May, and Philip Zelikow, eds. *The Presidential Recordings: John F. Kennedy: The Great Crises.* New York: W. W. Norton, 2001.
    Vol. I: July 30-August 1962, edited by Timothy Naftali.
    Vol. II: September-October 21, 1962, edited by Timothy Naftali and Philip Zelikow.
    Vol. III: October 22-28, 1962, edited by Philip Zelikow and Ernest May.
North Atlantic Treaty Organization. *Facts About NATO.* Paris: NATO Information Service, nd.
———. *Texts of Final Communiqués, 1949-1974.* Brussels, nd.
The Pentagon Papers: The Defense Department History of United States Decisionmaking on Vietnam. (Senator Gravel Edition.) 4 vols. Boston: Beacon, 1971.

Memoirs

Ball, George W. *The Past Has Another Pattern: A Memoir.* New York: W. W. Norton, 1982.
Bissell, Richard M., Jr., with Jonathan E. Lewis and Frances T. Pudlow. *Reflections of a Cold Warrior: From Yalta to the Bay of Pigs.* New Haven, Conn.: Yale University Press, 1996.
Brugioni, Dino A. *Eyeball to Eyeball: The Inside Story of the Cuban Missile Crisis.* New York: Random House, 1991.
Bundy, McGeorge. *Danger and Survival: Choices About the Bomb in the First Fifty Years.* New York: Random House, 1988.
Colby, William, and Peter Forbath. *Honorable Men: My Life in the CIA.* New York: Simon and Schuster, 1978.
Colby, William, with James McCargar. *Lost Victory: A Firsthand Account of America's Sixteen-year Involvement in Vietnam.* Chicago: Contemporary Books, 1989.
Cooper, Chester L. *The Lost Crusade: America in Vietnam.* New York: Dodd, Mead, 1970.
Goodwin, Richard N. *Remembering America: A Voice From the Sixties.* Boston: Little, Brown, 1988.
Gribkov, Anatoli I., and William Y. Smith. *Operation ANADYR: U.S. and Soviet Generals Recount the Cuban Missile Crisis.* Chicago: Edition q, 1994.
Harlech, Lord [David Ormsby Gore]. "Suez SNAFU, Skybolt SABU." *Foreign Policy*, 2 (Spring 1971): 38-50.
Hilsman, Roger. *To Move a Nation: The Politics of Foreign Policy in the Administration of John F. Kennedy.* New York: Doubleday, 1967.
Johnson, Lyndon Baines. *The Vantage Point: Perspectives of the Presidency, 1963-1969.* New York: Holt, Rinehart and Winston, 1971.
Kennedy, Robert F. *Thirteen Days: A Memoir of the Cuban Missile Crisis.* New York: W. W. Norton, 1969.
Khrushchev, Nikita S. *Khrushchev Remembers.* Trans. from the Russian by Strobe Talbott. Boston: Little, Brown, 1972.
Macmillan, Harold. *At the End of the Day, 1961-1963.* London: Macmillan, 1973.
Maechling, Charles, Jr. "Camelot, Robert Kennedy, and Counter-Insurgency—A Memoir." *Virginia Quarterly Review*, 75 (Summer 1999):438-58.
McNamara, Robert S. *The Essence of Security: Reflections in Office.* New York: Harper & Row, 1968.
———, with Brian VanDeMark. *In Retrospect: The Tragedy and Lessons of Vietnam.* New York: Random House, 1995.
Nitze, Paul H., with Ann M. Smith and Steven L. Rearden. *From Hiroshima to Glasnost: At the Center of Decision.* New York: Grove Weidenfeld, 1989.
Nolting, Frederick. *From Trust to Tragedy: The Political Memoirs of Frederick Nolting, Kennedy's Ambassador to Diem's Vietnam.* New York: Praeger, 1988.
O'Brien, Lawrence F. *No Final Victories: A Life in Politics from John F. Kennedy to Watergate.* Garden City, N.Y.: Doubleday, 1974.
Persons, Albert E. *Bay of Pigs: A Firsthand Account of the Mission by a U.S. Pilot in Support of the Cuban Invasion Force in 1961.* Jefferson, N.C.: McFarland, 1990.
Power, Thomas S., with Albert A. Arnhym. *Design for Survival.* New York: Coward-McCann, 1965.

Rostow, Walt W. *The Diffusion of Power: An Essay in Recent History*. New York: Macmillan, 1972.
Rusk, Dean. *As I Saw It: As Told to Richard Rusk*. Edited by Daniel S. Papp. New York: W. W. Norton, 1990.
Seaborg, Glenn T., with Benjamin S. Loeb. *Kennedy, Khrushchev, and the Test Ban*. Berkeley: University of California Press, 1981.
_____. *Stemming the Tide: Arms Control and the Johnson Years*. Lexington, Mass.: Lexington Books, 1987.
Stans, Maurice H. *One of the President's Men: Twenty Years with Eisenhower and Nixon*. Washington, D.C.: Brassey's, 1995.
Taylor, Maxwell D. *Swords and Plowshares*. New York: W. W. Norton, 1972.
_____. *The Uncertain Trumpet*. New York: Harper and Brothers, 1959.
York, Herbert F. *Making Weapons, Talking Peace: A Physicist's Odyssey from Hiroshima to Geneva*. New York: Basic Books, 1987.

Books

Abel, Elie. *The Missile Crisis*. Philadelphia: Lippincott, 1966.
Allison, Graham T. *Essence of Decision: Explaining the Cuban Missile Crisis*. Boston: Little, Brown, 1971.
Art, Robert J. *The TFX Decision: McNamara and the Military*. Boston: Little, Brown, 1968.
Ashton, Nigel J. *Kennedy, Macmillan and the Cold War: The Irony of Interdependence*. New York: Palgrave Macmillan, 2002.
Ausland, John C. *Kennedy, Khrushchev, and the Berlin-Cuba Crisis, 1961-1964*. Oslo: Scandinavian University Press, 1996.
Ball, Desmond. *Politics and Force Levels: The Strategic Missile Program of the Kennedy Administration*. Berkeley: University of California Press, 1990.
Barnet, Richard J., and Marcus Raskin. *The Decline of NATO and the Search for a New Policy in Europe*. New York: Random House, 1965.
Bayliss, John. *Ambiguity and Deterrence: British Nuclear Strategy, 1945-1964*. Oxford: Clarendon, 1995.
Beaufre, André. *Deterrence and Strategy*. Trans. from the French by R. H. Barry. New York: Praeger, 1965.
Bernstein, Irving. *Guns or Butter: The Presidency of Lyndon Johnson*. New York: Oxford University Press, 1996.
Binder, L. James. *Lemnitzer: A Soldier for His Time*. Washington, D.C.: Brassey's, 1997.
Bird, Kai. *The Color of Truth: McGeorge Bundy and William Bundy: Brothers in Arms*. New York: Simon & Schuster, 1998.
Blight, James G., and Peter Kornbluh, eds. *Politics of Illusion: The Bay of Pigs Reexamined*. Boulder, Colo.: Lynne Rienner, 1998.
_____, and David A. Welch. *On the Brink: Americans and Soviets Reexamine the Cuban Missile Crisis*. New York: Farrar, Straus and Giroux, 1989.
Bottome, Edgar M. *The Missile Gap: A Study of the Formulation of Military and Political Policy*. Rutherford, N.J.: Farleigh Dickinson Press, 1971.
Bowers, Ray L. *Tactical Airlift*. Washington, D.C.: Office of Air Force History, U.S. Air Force, 1983.
Brinkley, Douglas. *Dean Acheson: The Cold War Years, 1953-1971*. New Haven, Conn.: Yale University Press, 1992.
Bundy, McGeorge. *The Strength of Government*. Cambridge, Mass.: Harvard University Press, 1968.
Cate, Curtis. *The Ides of August: The Berlin Wall Crisis—1961*. New York: M. Evans, 1978.
Catudal, Honoré M. *Kennedy and the Berlin Wall Crisis: A Case Study in U.S. Decision Making*. Berlin: Berlin-Verlag, 1980.
Chayes, Abram. *The Cuban Missile Crisis*. New York: Oxford University Press, 1974.
Clark, Ian. *Nuclear Diplomacy and the Special Relationship: Britain's Deterrent and America, 1957-1962*. Oxford: Clarendon, 1994.
Congress and the Nation, 1945-1964. Washington, D.C.: Congressional Quarterly Service, 1965.

Crossland, Richard B., and James T. Currie. *Twice the Citizen: A History of the United States Army Reserve, 1908-1983.* Washington, D.C.: Office of the Chief, Army Reserve, 1984.
Currey, Cecil B. *Edward Lansdale: The Unquiet American.* Boston: Houghton Mifflin, 1988.
Dallek, Robert. *Flawed Giant: Lyndon Johnson and His Times, 1961-1973.* New York: Oxford University Press, 1998.
———. *An Unfinished Life: John F. Kennedy, 1917-1963.* Boston: Little, Brown, 2003.
Derthick, Martha. *The National Guard in Politics.* Cambridge, Mass.: Harvard University Press, 1965.
Divine, Robert A. *Blowing on the Wind: The Nuclear Test Ban Debate, 1954-1960.* New York: Oxford University Press, 1978.
Dommen, Arthur J. *Conflict in Laos: The Politics of Neutralization.* Rev. ed. New York: Praeger, 1971.
Duscha, Julius. *Arms, Money, and Politics.* New York: Ives Washburn, 1965.
Enthoven, Alain C., and K. Wayne Smith. *How Much Is Enough? Shaping the Defense Program, 1961-1969.* New York: Harper & Row, 1971.
Facts on File Yearbook, 1962. New York: Facts on File, 1963.
Fall, Bernard. *Anatomy of a Crisis: The Laotian Crisis of 1960-1961.* Garden City, N.Y.: Doubleday, 1967.
Fite, Gilbert C. *Richard B. Russell, Jr.: Senator from Georgia.* Chapel Hill: University of North Carolina Press, 1991.
Ford, Harold P. *CIA and the Vietnam Policymakers: Three Episodes, 1962-1968.* Washington, D.C.: History Staff, Center for the Study of Intelligence, Central Intelligence Agency, 1998.
Freedman, Lawrence. *Kennedy's Wars: Berlin, Cuba, Laos, and Vietnam.* New York: Oxford University Press, 2000.
Fursenko, Aleksandr, and Timothy Naftali. *"One Hell of a Gamble": Khrushchev, Castro, and Kennedy, 1958-1964.* New York: W. W. Norton, 1997.
Futrell, Robert F. *The United States Air Force in Southeast Asia: The Advisory Years to 1965.* Washington, D.C.: Office of Air Force History, United States Air Force, 1981.
Gallois, Pierre. *The Balance of Terror: Strategy for the Nuclear Age.* Trans. from the French by Richard Howard. Boston: Houghton Mifflin, 1961.
Garthoff, Raymond L. *Reflections on the Cuban Missile Crisis.* Washington, D.C.: Brookings Institution, 1989.
Gelb, Leslie H., and Richard K. Betts. *The Irony of Vietnam: The System Worked.* Washington, D.C.: Brookings Institution, 1979.
Geyelin, Philip. *Lyndon B. Johnson and the World.* New York: Praeger, 1966.
Gibbons, William Conrad. *The U.S. Government and the Vietnam War: Executive and Legislative Roles and Relationships.* Part II: 1961-1964. Washington, D.C.: U.S. Government Printing Office, 1985.
Gittinger, Ted, ed. *The Johnson Years: A Vietnam Roundtable.* Austin, Tex.: Lyndon B. Johnson School of Public Affairs and Lyndon Baines Johnson Library, 1993.
Goldstein, Martin E. *American Policy Toward Laos.* Rutherford, N.J.: Fairleigh Dickinson University Press, 1973.
Goulden, Joseph C. *Truth Is the First Casualty: The Gulf of Tonkin Affair—Illusion and Reality.* Chicago: Rand McNally, 1969.
Grathwol, Robert P., and Donita M. Moorhus. *American Forces in Berlin: Cold War Outpost, 1945-1994.* Washington, D.C.: Cold War Project, Legacy Resources Management Program, Department of Defense, 1994.
Hadley, Arthur T. *The Nation's Safety and Arms Control.* New York: Viking, 1961.
Haines, Gerald K. *The National Reconnaissance Office: Its Origins, Creation, & Early Years.* Washington, D.C.: Historical Office, National Reconnaissance Office, 1996.
Halberstam, David. *The Best and the Brightest.* New York: Ballantine, 1969.
———. *The Making of a Quagmire.* New York: Random House, 1965.
Hammond, William M. *Public Affairs: The Military and the Media, 1962-1968.* Washington, D.C.: Center of Military History, U.S. Army, 1988.
Herken, Gregg. *Counsels of War.* Expanded ed. New York: Oxford University Press, 1987.

Hewes, James E., Jr. *From Root to McNamara: Army Organization and Administration, 1900-1963*. Washington, D.C.: Center of Military History, U.S. Army, 1975.

Higgins, Trumbull. *The Perfect Failure: Kennedy, Eisenhower, and the CIA at the Bay of Pigs*. New York: W. W. Norton, 1987.

Hitch, Charles J., and Roland N. McKean. *The Economics of Defense in the Nuclear Age*. Cambridge, Mass.: Harvard University Press, 1960.

Horne, Alistair. *Harold Macmillan*. 2 vols. New York: Viking, 1989.

Isaacson, Walter, and Evan Thomas. *The Wise Men: Six Friends and the World They Made; Acheson, Bohlen, Harriman, Kennan, Lovett, and McCloy*. New York: Simon and Schuster, 1986.

Janis, Irving L. *Victims of Groupthink: A Psychological Study of Foreign-Policy Decisions and Fiascoes*. Boston: Houghton Mifflin, 1972.

Johnson, Haynes. *The Bay of Pigs: The Leaders' Story of Brigade 2506*. New York: W. W. Norton, 1964.

The Joint Chiefs of Staff and the War in Vietnam, 1960-1968. Washington, D.C.: Historical Division, Joint Secretariat, Joint Chiefs of Staff, 1970.

Kahin, George McTurnan. *Intervention: How America Became Involved in Vietnam*. Garden City, N.Y.: Anchor Press/Doubleday, 1987.

Kaplan, Fred. *The Wizards of Armageddon*. New York: Simon and Schuster, 1983.

Karnow, Stanley. *Vietnam: A History*. Rev. ed. New York: Viking, 1991.

Katz, Milton S. *Ban the Bomb: A History of SANE, the Committee for a Sane Nuclear Policy, 1957-1985*. Westport, Conn.: Greenwood, 1986.

Kaufmann, William W. *The McNamara Strategy*. New York: Harper & Row, 1964.

Kearns, Doris. *Lyndon Johnson and the American Dream*. New York: Harper & Row, 1976.

Kelleher, Catherine M. *Germany & the Politics of Nuclear Weapons*. New York: Columbia University Press, 1975.

Kern, Montague, Patricia Levering, and Ralph Levering. *The Kennedy Crises: The Press, the Presidency, and Foreign Policy*. Chapel Hill: University of North Carolina Press, 1983.

Kohl, Wilfred L. *French Nuclear Diplomacy*. Princeton, N.J.: Princeton University Press, 1971.

Kolodziej, Edward A. *The Uncommon Defense and Congress, 1945-1963*. Columbus: Ohio State University Press, 1966.

Kunz, Diane B. *Butter and Guns: America's Cold War Economic Diplomacy*. New York: Free Press, 1997.

Launius, Roger D. *NASA: A History of the U.S. Civil Space Program*. Malabar, Fla.: Krieger, 1994.

Leighton, Richard M. *Strategy, Money, and the New Look, 1953-1956*. Vol. III in *History of the Office of the Secretary of Defense*. Washington, D.C.: Office of the Secretary of Defense, 2001.

Lewy, Guenter. *America in Vietnam*. New York: Oxford University Press, 1978.

Logevall, Fredrik. *Choosing War: The Lost Chance for Peace and the Escalation of War in Vietnam*. Berkeley: University of California Press, 1999.

Lynch, Grayston L. *Decision for Disaster: Betrayal at the Bay of Pigs*. Washington, D.C.: Brassey's, 1998.

MacGregor, Morris J., Jr. *Integration of the Armed Forces, 1940-1965*. Washington, D.C.: Center of Military History, U.S. Army, 1981.

Mahan, Erin R. *Kennedy, de Gaulle, and Western Europe*. New York: Palgrave Macmillan, 2002.

Marolda, Edward J., and Oscar P. Fitzgerald. *From Military Assistance to Combat, 1959-1965*. Vol. II in *The United States Navy and the Vietnam Conflict*. Washington, D.C.: Naval Historical Center, Department of the Navy, 1986.

McBride, James H., and John I. H. Eales. *Military Posture: Fourteen Issues Before Congress, 1964*. Washington D.C.: Center for Strategic Studies, Georgetown University, 1964.

McDougall, Walter A. *The Heavens and the Earth: A Political History of the Space Age*. New York: Basic Books, 1985.

McMaster, H. R. *Dereliction of Duty: Lyndon Johnson, Robert McNamara, the Joint Chiefs of Staff, and the Lies that Led to Vietnam*. New York: HarperCollins, 1997.

Merwitz, Leonard, and Stephen H. Sosnick. *The Budget's New Clothes: A Critique of Planning-Programming-Budgeting and Benefit-Cost Analysis*. Chicago: Markham, 1971.

Meyer, Karl E., and Tad Szulc. *The Cuban Invasion: The Chronicle of a Disaster*. New York: Praeger, 1962.

Moïse, Edwin E. *The Tonkin Gulf and the Escalation of the Vietnam War.* Chapel Hill: University of North Carolina Press, 1996.
Mollenhoff, Clark R. *The Pentagon: Politics, Profits and Plunder.* New York: Putnam, 1967.
Murray, Donette. *Kennedy, Macmillan and Nuclear Weapons.* New York: St. Martin's, 2000.
Neustadt, Richard E. *Alliance Politics.* New York: Columbia University Press, 1970.
_____. *Report to JFK: The Skybolt Crisis in Perspective.* Ithaca, N.Y.: Cornell University Press, 1999.
_____, and Ernest R. May. *Thinking in Time: The Uses of History for Decision-Makers.* New York: Free Press, 1986.
Newhouse, John. *War and Peace in the Nuclear Age.* New York: Knopf, 1989.
Newman, John M. *JFK and Vietnam: Deception, Intrigues, and the Struggle for Power.* New York: Warner, 1992.
Ninkovich, Frank. *Germany and the United States: The Transformation of the German Question Since 1945.* Boston: Twayne, 1988.
Nunnerley, David. *President Kennedy and Britain.* London: Bodley Head, 1972.
Pagedas, Constantine A. *Anglo-American Strategic Relations and the French Problem, 1960-1963: A Troubled Partnership.* London: Frank Cass, 2000.
Pierre, Andrew J. *Nuclear Politics: The British Experience with an Independent Strategic Force, 1939-1970.* London: Oxford University Press, 1972.
Poole, Walter S. *The Joint Chiefs of Staff and National Policy, 1961-1964.* Vol. VIII in *The History of the Joint Chiefs of Staff.* Washington, D.C.: Historical Division, Joint Secretariat, Joint Chiefs of Staff, 1983.
Powers, Thomas. *The Man Who Kept the Secrets: Richard Helms & the CIA.* New York: Knopf, 1979.
Rand Corporation. *The Rand Corporation: The First Fifteen Years.* Santa Monica, Calif., 1963.
Roherty, James M. *Decisions of Robert S. McNamara: A Study of the Role of the Secretary of Defense.* Coral Gables, Fla.: University of Miami Press, 1970.
Ruffner, Kevin C., ed. *CORONA: America's First Satellite Program.* Washington, D.C.: History Staff, Center for the Study of Intelligence, Central Intelligence Agency, 1995.
Schick, Jack M. *The Berlin Crisis, 1958-1962.* Philadelphia: University of Pennsylvania Press, 1971.
Schlesinger, Arthur M., Jr. *Robert Kennedy and His Times.* Boston: Houghton Mifflin, 1978.
_____. *A Thousand Days: John F. Kennedy in the White House.* Boston: Houghton Mifflin, 1965.
Schwartz, David N. *NATO's Nuclear Dilemmas.* Washington, D.C.: Brookings Institution, 1983.
Shapley, Deborah. *Promise and Power: The Life and Times of Robert McNamara.* Boston: Little, Brown, 1993.
Sheehan, Neil. *A Bright Shining Lie: John Paul Vann and America in Vietnam.* New York: Random House, 1988.
Shultz, Richard H., Jr. *The Secret War Against Hanoi: Kennedy's and Johnson's Use of Spies, Saboteurs, and Covert Warriors in North Vietnam.* New York: HarperCollins, 1999.
Siff, Edgar Y. *Why the Senate Slept: The Gulf of Tonkin Resolution and the Beginning of America's Vietnam War.* Westport, Conn.: Praeger, 1999.
Smith, Jean Edward. *Lucius D. Clay: An American Life.* New York: H. Holt, 1990.
Sorensen, Theodore C. *Kennedy.* New York: Harper & Row, 1965.
Steel, Ronald. *The End of Alliance: America and the Future of Europe.* New York: Dell, 1964.
Steinbruner, John D. *The Cybernetic Theory of Decision: New Dimensions of Political Analysis.* Princeton, N.J.: Princeton University Press, 1974.
Steury, Donald P., ed. *Sherman Kent and the Board of National Estimates: Collected Essays.* Washington, D.C.: History Staff, Center for the Study of Intelligence, Central Intelligence Agency, 1994.
Stevenson, Charles A. *The End of Nowhere: American Policy Toward Laos Since 1954.* Boston: Beacon, 1972.
Stromseth, Jane E. *Origins of Flexible Response: NATO's Debate Over Strategy in the 1960's.* New York: St. Martin's, 1988.
Stubbing, Richard A., with Richard A. Mendel. *The Defense Game: An Insider Explores the Astonishing Realities of America's Defense Establishment.* New York: Harper & Row, 1986.

Thomas, Evan. *The Very Best Men: Four Who Dared: The Early Years of the CIA.* New York: Simon and Schuster, 1995.
Trachtenberg, Marc. *A Constructed Peace: The Making of the European Settlement, 1945-1963.* Princeton, N.J.: Princeton University Press, 1999
———. *History and Strategy.* Princeton, N.J.: Princeton University Press, 1991.
Trask, Roger R., and Alfred Goldberg. *The Department of Defense, 1947-1997: Organization and Leaders.* Washington, D.C.: Historical Office, Office of the Secretary of Defense, 1997.
Trewhitt, Henry L. *McNamara.* New York: Harper & Row, 1971.
VanDeMark, Brian. *Into the Quagmire: Lyndon Johnson and the Escalation of the Vietnam War.* New York: Oxford University Press, 1991.
Van Staaveren, Jacob. *Gradual Failure: The Air War Over North Vietnam, 1965-1966.* Washington, D.C.: Air Force History and Museums Division, 2002.
Watson, George M., Jr. *The History of the Office of the Secretary of the Air Force, 1947-1965.* Washington, D.C.: Office of Air Force History, 1989.
Watson, Robert J. *Into the Missile Age, 1956-1960.* Vol. IV in *History of the Office of the Secretary of Defense.* Washington, D.C.: Office of the Secretary of Defense, 1997.
Welch, Richard E., Jr. *Response to Revolution: The United States and the Cuban Revolution, 1959-1961.* Chapel Hill: University of North Carolina Press, 1985.
Whitlow, Robert H. *U.S. Marines in Vietnam: The Advisory and Combat Assistance Era, 1954-1964.* Washington, D.C.: History and Museums Division, Headquarters, U.S. Marine Corps, 1977.
Winand, Pascaline. *Eisenhower, Kennedy, and the United States of Europe.* New York: St. Martin's, 1993.
Wyden, Peter. *Bay of Pigs: The Untold Story.* New York: Simon and Schuster, 1979.

ARTICLES

Acheson, Dean. "Robert Kennedy's Version of the Cuban Missile Affair." *Esquire,* 62 (February 1969):76 ff.
Alsop, Stewart. "Master of the Pentagon." *Saturday Evening Post,* 234 (5 August 1961):20-21, 45-46.
Baldwin, Hanson W. "The McNamara Monarchy." *Saturday Evening Post,* 236 (9 March 1963):8, 11.
Bissell, Richard M. "Reply to Lucien S. Vandenbroucke's the 'Confessions' of Allen Dulles: New Evidence on the Bay of Pigs." *Diplomatic History,* 8 (Fall 1984):377-80.
Blight, James G., Bruce J. Allyn, and David A. Webb. "Kramer vs. Kramer: Or How Can You Have Revisionism in the Absence of Orthodoxy?" Cold War International History Project *Bulletin* (Fall 1993):41 ff.
———, Joseph S. Nye, Jr., and David A. Welch. "The Cuban Missile Crisis Revisited." *Foreign Affairs,* 66 (Fall 1987):170-88.
Boulton, J. W. "NATO and the MLF." *Journal of Contemporary History,* 7 (July-October 1972): 275-94.
Brower, Brock. "McNamara Seen Now, Full Length." *Life,* 64 (10 May 68):86 ff.
Buchan, Alistair. "The Multilateral Force: An Historical Perspective." *Adelphi Papers,* No. 13 (October 1964):3-14.
Chang, Gordon. "JFK, China, and the Bomb." *Journal of American History,* 85 (Spring 1988): 287-310.
Daalder, Ivo. "The Limited Test Ban Treaty." In *Superpower Arms Control: Setting the Record Straight,* edited by Albert Carnesale and Richard E. Haas, 9-39. Cambridge, Mass.: Ballinger, 1987.
Dawson, Raymond H. "Congressional Innovation and Intervention in Defense Policy: Legislative Authorization of Weapons Systems." *American Political Science Review,* 56 (March 1962):42-57.
Drea, Edward. "Received Information Indicating Attack: The Gulf of Tonkin Incident 40 Years Later." *MHQ: The Quarterly Journal of Military History,* 16 (Summer 2004):74-83.
Gallois, Pierre. "U.S. Strategy and the Defense of Europe." *Orbis,* 7 (Summer 1963):226-49.
Garthoff, Raymond L. "The Cuban Missile Crisis: An Overview." In *The Cuban Missile Crisis Revisited,* edited by James A. Nathan, 41-54. New York: St. Martin's, 1992.
Gilpatric, Roswell L. "Our Defense Needs: The Long View." *Foreign Affairs,* 42 (April 1964): 366-78.

Gleijeses, Piero. "Ships in the Night: The CIA, the White House and the Bay of Pigs." *Journal of Latin American Studies*, 26 (February 1995):1-42.
Greenstein, Fred I., and Richard H. Immerman. "What Did Eisenhower Tell Kennedy About Indochina? The Politics of Misperception." *Journal of American History*, 79 (September 1992): 568-87.
Hawkins, Jack. "An Obsession with 'Plausible Deniability' Doomed the 1961 Bay of Pigs Invasion from the Outset." *Military History*, 15 (August 1998):12 ff.
Hildreth, Steven A. "Perceptions of U.S. Security Assistance, 1959-1983: The Public Record." In *U.S. Security Assistance: The Political Process*, edited by Ernest Graves and Steven A. Hildreth, 41-99. Lexington, Mass.: D.C. Heath, 1985.
Hunter, Robert E. "The Politics of U.S. Defence, 1963: The Congressional Question." *World Today*, 19 (April 1963):155-66.
──────. "The Politics of U.S. Defence, 1963: Manned Bombers versus Missiles." *World Today*, 19 (March 1963):98-107.
Kaplan, Lawrence S. "The MLF Debate." In *John F. Kennedy and Europe*, edited by Douglas Brinkley and Richard T. Griffiths, 51-65. Baton Rouge: Louisiana State University Press, 1999.
──────, and Kathleen A. Kellner. "Lemnitzer: Surviving the French Military Withdrawal." In *Generals in International Politics: NATO's Supreme Allied Commander, Europe*, edited by Robert S. Jordan, 93-121. Lexington: University Press of Kentucky, 1987.
Kaysen, Carl. "The Limited Test Ban Treaty of 1963." In *John F. Kennedy and Europe*, edited by Douglas Brinkley and Richard T. Griffiths, 95-115. Baton Rouge: Louisiana State University Press, 1999.
Kirkpatrick, Lyman B., Jr. "Paramilitary Case Study: The Bay of Pigs." *Naval War College Review*, 25 (November-December 1972):32-42.
Korb, Lawrence. "George Whalen Anderson, Jr.: 1 August 1961-1 August 1963." In *The Chiefs of Naval Operations*, 321-30, edited by Robert William Love, Jr. Annapolis, Md.: Naval Institute Press, 1980.
Kraar, Louis. "The Two Lives of Robert McNamara." *Life*, 53 (30 November 1962):94-102.
Kraft, Joseph. "McNamara and His Enemies." *Harper's*, 223 (August 1961):41-48.
Kramer, Mark. "Tactical Nuclear Weapons, Soviet Command Authority, and the Cuban Missile Crisis." Cold War International History Project *Bulletin* (Fall 1993):40 ff.
Landa, Ronald D. "The Origins of the Skybolt Controversy in the Eisenhower Administration." In *Seeing Off the Bear: Anglo-American Air Power Cooperation During the Cold War*, Proceedings of the Joint Meeting of the Royal Air Force Historical Society and the Air Force Historical Foundation, edited by Roger G. Miller, 117-31. Washington, D.C.: Air Force History and Museums Program, United States Air Force, 1995.
Lukas, J. Anthony. "Class Reunion: Kennedy's Men Relive the Cuban Missile Crisis." *New York Times Magazine* (30 August 1987):22 ff.
McAuliffe, Mary S. "Return to the Brink: Intelligence Perspectives on the Cuban Missile Crisis." SHAFR *Newsletter*, 24 (June 1993):4-8.
McNamara, Robert S. "Managing the Department of Defense." In *A Modern Design for Defense Decision: A McNamara-Hitch-Enthoven Anthology*, edited by Samuel A. Tucker, 11-19. Washington, D.C.: Industrial College of the Armed Forces, 1966.
──────. "The Military Role of Nuclear Weapons: Perceptions and Misperceptions." *Foreign Affairs*, 62 (Fall 1983):59-80.
Morris, Thomas D. "Taking Charge in Washington." *Harvard Business Review*, 84 (July-August 1984):24-40.
Moulton, Harland B. "The McNamara General War Strategy." *Orbis*, 8 (Summer 1964):238-54.
Murphy, Charles J. V. "Cuba: The Record Set Straight." *Fortune*, 64 (September 1961):92 ff.
──────. "The Desperate Drive to Cut Defense Spending." *Fortune*, 69 (January 1964):95 ff.
──────. "The Education of a Defense Secretary." *Fortune*, 65 (May 1962):102 ff.
──────. "Grenada and the Bay of Pigs: Two Classic Examples of a President in the Role of Commander-in-Chief in a Cold War Situation." *Situation Report* [Security and Intelligence Fund], 4 (January 1984):1-7.

———. "Vietnam Hangs on U.S. Determination." *Fortune*, 69 (May 1964):159 ff.
Nathan, James A. "Force, Statecraft, and American Foreign Policy." *Polity*, 28 (Winter 1995): 237-59.
Newhouse, John. "A Reporter at Large: Socialism or Death." *New Yorker*, 68 (April 1992):52-83.
Paterson, Thomas G. "The Historian as Detective: Senator Keating, Missiles in Cuba, and His Mysterious Sources." *Diplomatic History*, 11 (Winter 1987):61-70.
Pedlow, Gregory W. "Allied Crisis Management for Berlin: The Live Oak Organization, 1959-1963." In *International Cold War Military Records and History: Proceedings of the International Conference*, edited by William W. Epley, 87-116. Washington, D.C.: Office of the Secretary of Defense, 1996.
Pohlmann, Marcus D. "Constraining Presidents at the Brink: The Cuban Missile Crisis." *Presidential Studies Quarterly*, 19 (Spring 1989):337-46.
Rearden, Steven L. "U.S. Strategic Bombardment Doctrine Since 1945." In *Case Studies in Strategic Bombardment*, edited by R. Cargill Hall, 383-467. Washington, D.C.: Air Force History and Museums Program, 1998.
Roman, Peter J. "Strategic Bombers over the Missile Horizon, 1957-1963." *Journal of Strategic Studies*, 18 (March 1995):198-236.
Rosenberg, David Alan. "Arleigh Albert Burke: Chief of Naval Operations, 1955-1961." In *The Chiefs of Naval Operations*, edited by Robert William Love, 263-319. Annapolis, Md.: Naval Institute Press, 1980.
Rowen, Henry S. "The Evolution of Strategic Nuclear Doctrine." In *Strategic Thought in the Nuclear Age*, edited by Laurence Martin, 131-56. Baltimore, Md.: Johns Hopkins University Press, 1979.
Schratz, Paul R. "John B. Connally, 20 January 1961—20 December 1961." *In American Secretaries of the Navy*, edited by Paolo E. Coletta, vol. II, 911-23. Annapolis, Md.: Naval Institute Press, 1980.
Smith, Richard Austin. "The $7-Billion Contract That Changed the Rules." Part II. *Fortune*, 67 (April 1963):110 ff.
Trachtenberg, Marc. "White House Tapes and Minutes of the Cuban Missile Crisis: EXCOM Meetings October 1962." *International Security*, 10 (Summer 1985):164-203.
Trotnow, Helmut. "Who Actually Built the Berlin Wall? The SED Leadership and the 13th of August 1961." In *International Cold War Military Records and History: Proceedings of the International Conference*, edited by William W. Epley, 41-48. Washington, D.C.: Office of the Secretary of Defense, 1996.
Vandenbroucke, Lucien S. "Anatomy of a Failure: The Decision to Land at the Bay of Pigs." *Political Science Quarterly*, 99 (Fall 1984):471-91.
———. "The 'Confessions' of Allen Dulles: New Evidence on the Bay of Pigs." *Diplomatic History*, 8 (Fall 1984):365-75.
Warner, Michael. "The CIA's Internal Probe of the Bay of Pigs Affair." *Studies in Intelligence* (Winter 1998-99):93-101.
White, Theodore H. "Revolution in the Pentagon." *Look*, 27 (23 April 1963):31-49.
Wise, David. "Scholars of the Nuclear Age—McGeorge Bundy, Walt W. Rostow, and Jerome B. Wiesner." In *The Kennedy Circle*, edited by Lester Tanzer, 29-57. Washington, D.C.: Luce, 1961.
Zoumanis, Thomas. "Plugging the Dike: The Kennedy Administration Confronts the Balance of Payments Crisis with Europe." In *John F. Kennedy and Europe*, edited by Douglas Brinkley and Richard T. Griffiths, 169-88. Baton Rouge: Louisiana State University Press, 1999.
Zuckert, Eugene. "The Service Secretary: Has He a Useful Role?" *Foreign Affairs*, 44 (April 1966): 458-79.

DISSERTATIONS AND UNPUBLISHED STUDIES

Cocke, Karl E. "Realignment of the Army's Reserve Components, 1945-1969." Washington, D.C.: U.S. Army Center of Military History, 1977.
Cole, Alice C., et al. "History of Strategic Arms Competition, 1945-1972: Chronology." 3 vols. Washington, D.C.: Historical Office, Office of the Secretary of Defense, 1974.

Downey, Robert W. "An Introduction to the Planning, Programming and Budgeting System in the Department of Defense: An Overview of the Process, Participants, and Products." 1985.

"Draft Administrative History of the Department of Defense, 1963-1969." [Compiled in late 1968 and early 1969 by the Office of the Assistant Secretary of Defense (Administration), with contributions by various DoD components, in response to a request from the White House.]

Fuller, Jon Wayne. "Congress and the Defense Budget: A Study of the McNamara Years." Ph. D. Dissertation, Princeton University, 1972.

Goldberg, Alfred. "A Brief Survey of the Evolution of Ideas About Counterforce." Memorandum RM-5431-PR. Santa Monica, Calif.: Rand, October 1967.

Gorn, Michael H. "The TFX: Conceptual Phase to F-111B Termination, 1958-1968." Andrews Air Force Base, Md.: Office of History, Air Force Systems Command, nd.

Johnstone, P. H. "Military Policy Making During the Berlin Crisis of 1958-1962." 2 vols. Report R-138. Washington, D.C.: Institute for Defense Analysis, March 1968.

Krisel, Lionel. "The Bay of Pigs: An Historical Study with Emphasis on Aspects Involving the U.S. Navy." Washington, D.C.: Naval Historical Center, 1974.

Landa, Ronald D. "Preparing for the Long Haul: The Office of the Secretary of Defense and the Defense of Europe, 1953-1961." Draft manuscript, Historical Office, Office of the Secretary of Defense, nd.

May, Ernest R., John D. Steinbruner, and Thomas W. Wolfe. "History of the Strategic Arms Competition, 1945-1972." 2 parts. Washington, D.C.: Historical Office, Office of the Secretary of Defense, 1981.

Nalty, Bernard C. "The Quest for an Advanced Manned Strategic Bomber: USAF Plans and Policies, 1961-1966." Washington, D.C.: USAF Historical Division Liaison Office, August 1966.

U.S. Department of State, Historical Office. "Crisis Over Berlin: American Policy Concerning the Soviet Threats to Berlin, November 1958-December 1962." Research Project 614-E. February 1970.

Yoshpe, Harry B. "Our Missing Shield: The U.S. Civil Defense Program in Historical Perspective." Washington, D.C.: Federal Emergency Management Agency, 1981.

Index

Acheson, Dean, 2, 6, 314, 381; and Berlin, 147-49, 151-53, 155, 161, 164, 170; and Cuban missile crisis, 206, 214; and MLF, 389, 391, 393, 398; and NATO, 303-04, 359, 361, 362, 363, 389, 391
Acheson-Lilienthal report, 324
Adenauer, Konrad, 146, 156, 210, 359, 361, 373, 392, 404n, 410-12
Advanced Manned Strategic Aircraft (AMSA), 486, 490
Advanced Research Projects Agency (ARPA), 337
Agency for International Development, 36-37, 252, 256, 424-25, 429, 431-33, 436-37, 439, 444-46, 453, 506, 511-12, 533
Aiken, Sen. George, 351, 426
Ailes, Stephen B., 34, 108-10
Air America, 256
Air Force, U.S., 7-8, 16-18, 21-25, 28, 35, 38-40, 50, 72-74, 539, 541; and balance of payments, 450, 452; and base closures, 464-65; and Bay of Pigs, 176; and Berlin, 154, 161; and cost reduction program, 455, 461; and counterinsurgency, 38-40; and flexible response, 295, 301-02, 309, 311-12, 316-17, 319-20; and FY 1962 budget, 53-55, 59-63, 67, 70; and FY 1963 budget, 82-83, 85-87, 90, 93, 95, 100, 103, 106, 115-16; and FY 1964 budget, 120, 122-23, 125-28, 137; and FY 1965 budget, 476, 478, 482; and FY 1966 budget, 490, 493-94, 496; and multilateral force, 404; and Skybolt, 376-77; and space development, 44-47, 49; and TFX, 466-69, 471-72, 540; and Vietnam, 531
aircraft carriers, 85, 467, 478, 487, 490, 491-92
airlift, 12, 68, 70, 80, 83, 85, 92, 129, 368, 495, 496
Albert, Rep. Carl, 441
Algeria, 363, 367

Alliance for Progress, 195, 199, 227, 427, 441n
Alsop, Joseph, 152, 400
Alsop, Stewart, 12
Amery, Julian, 378
Anderson, Admiral George W., Jr., 47-48, 86, 91, 102, 125, 128-29, 132, 203, 212, 352, 407, 468
Anderson, Robert, 449
Anderson, Maj. Rudolph, 222
Ann Arbor address, 295, 308-09, 313, 315, 373, 384, 396, 398
anti-ballistic missile (ABM), 34, 35, 60, 61, 69, 123-25, 128, 309, 315, 320, 321, 348, 493, 544
Ap Bac, battle of, 281-82
Apollo, 477n
Arends, Rep. Leslie C., 115, 133
Argentina, 211
Armed Services Procurement Regulation, 454, 459
arms control and disarmament, 2, 18, 323-56. *See also* limited nuclear test ban treaty
Arms Control and Disarmament Agency (ACDA), 325-26, 336, 338, 342-45, 348, 356
Army, U.S., 7-8, 16-18, 21-25, 28, 33-35, 44-46, 73-74, 539, 547; and balance of payments, 450-51; and base closures, 464-65; and Bay of Pigs, 173, 182; and Berlin, 143, 151, 153-54, 161; and cost reduction program, 456; and Cuban missile crisis, 224; and counterinsurgency, 38-41; and flexible response, 293-95, 316; and FY 1962 budget, 54-55, 60-63, 65-66, 68; and FY 1963 budget, 81-82, 86-89, 91, 93, 107-09, 112-14; and FY 1964 budget, 120, 122-26, 128, 137; and FY 1965 budget, 476-77; and FY 1966 budget, 490, 494, 496; and NATO, 368; and Vietnam, 506, 512, 515, 529-30

650

assured destruction, 34, 295, 319-22
Athens address, 295, 305-09, 313, 315, 373, 384, 396-99
Atlantic Nuclear Force (ANF), 414-16, 418
Atlantic, Supreme Allied Commander (SACLANT), 211, 366, 391, 393
Atlantic Command, Commander in Chief (CINCLANT), 186, 193, 200, 202, 211, 213
Atlas, 53, 54, 59, 335, 493
Atomic Energy Act, 1958 Amendments to, 372, 375
Atomic Energy Commission, 32, 62, 138, 328-29, 331, 335, 345
Ausland, John, 168
Australia, 251, 434

B-26, 173, 175, 179, 183, 237
B-47, 60, 62, 348, 404, 496
B-52, 54, 60, 63, 64, 66, 68, 69, 83, 104, 213, 376, 496, 526, 530
B-58, 54, 60, 63, 64, 66, 68, 69, 496
B-59 (Soviet submarine), 212
B-70, 15, 59-60, 62, 63, 64, 69, 70, 71, 85, 86, 90, 104, 312, 454, 539, 541
Badger (Soviet bomber), 348
balance of payments (BOP), 142, 368, 370, 422, 429, 434, 436, 447-53, 473
Ball, George W., 1, 437; and Cuban missile crisis, 206, 206n, 216; and MLF, 385, 388-89, 400, 401n, 405-06, 408, 413, 416, 418; and NATO, 382; and Vietnam, 286, 498, 504, 523
Baruch Plan, 324
base closures, 447, 453, 462-66, 540
Basic National Security Policy (BNSP), 295-98, 313
Bates, Rep. William H., 99-100, 459
Baudet, Philippe, 370
Bay of Pigs invasion. See Cuba
Belgium, 360, 363, 365, 367, 414
Bell, David E., 317, 379; and FY 1962 budget, 56-58, 60; and FY 1963 budget, 75, 78-79, 87-89, 91; and FY 1964 budget, 119-20, 127; and military assistance, 422, 429, 431-32, 436-37, 438, 442, 444-45
Berle, Adolf A., 178, 182
Berlin, 15, 30, 32-33, 121, 143-71, 232, 250, 270, 294, 353, 388, 449; and Cuban missile crisis, 203, 207, 208, 218-20; and FY 1962 budget, 64, 67-70; and FY 1963 budget, 82, 84, 86-87, 88, 91, 99
Berlin Task Force, 147, 160, 162, 164
Bethe, Hans, 334, 442
Bien Hoa, 526-27
Bissell, Richard M., Jr., 36n, 173-74, 178-79, 180-81, 184, 188, 196, 301

Black, Col. E. F., 329
Blackburn, A. W., 470-71
Blandford, John, 548
Blomeyer-Bartenstein, Horst, 374
Blue Streak, 376, 378
Boeing, 468-69
Bohlen, Charles, 399
Boston Navy Yard, 465
Boun Oum, Prince, 229, 245, 247-48, 253
Bowie, Robert, 385, 387, 389, 398n, 400, 405
Bowie Report, 387
Bowles, Chester, 180
Boyle, Brig. Gen. Andrew J., 252
Brandt, Willy, 146, 156, 158
Brazil, 211, 227, 444
Bridges, Sen. Styles, 19
Brooklyn Navy Yard, 465
Brown, Harold, 7-8, 483, 485, 491, 547; and FY 1964 budget, 131-33, 137, 139; and MLF, 400; and Nike-Zeus, 124; and nuclear testing, 330, 333, 343, 353; and Skybolt, 379; and TFX, 468, 471
Brown, Winthrop G., 247-48
Bucharest, 211
Buchan, Alastair, 419-20
budget, 12, 13-14, 296, 317, 540; FY 1961, 47, 53, 56, 57, 75; FY 1962, 14, 30-31, 38, 46, 52-71, 75, 82, 97, 143, 145, 153-54, 170, 308, 376, 421-27; FY 1963, 31-32, 33, 47, 72-95, 96-117, 308, 377, 424, 428-31, 435; FY 1964, 33, 47, 115, 116, 118-42, 379, 432-38, 440, 442, 456, 475; FY 1965, 34, 436-37, 439-43, 457, 478, 480-89, 540; FY 1966, 34, 443-45, 489; FY 1967, 492
Budget, Bureau of the, 56-62, 73, 75, 78-79, 82, 85, 87, 89, 119-21, 127, 317, 379, 422, 428-29, 431, 437, 439-40, 444, 477, 480-83, 492
Bundy, McGeorge, 6, 58, 87, 493, 547; and Bay of Pigs, 178, 180, 185; and Berlin Wall, 152, 160; and counterinsurgency, 36-37; and Cuban missile crisis, 198, 202, 204, 206, 209, 219, 222-23; and Laos, 238; and military assistance, 427, 437, 441; and MLF, 399-400, 402, 404, 406, 411-15, 416-20; and NATO, 363, 379-82; and nuclear test ban, 323, 325, 331, 335, 338-39; and Vietnam, 275, 291, 498, 501, 503, 511, 514-15, 517-18, 521, 527, 529, 530-31
Bundy, William P., 180, 220; and Bay of Pigs, 182, 200; and Laos, 252; and military assistance, 422, 428, 432, 436, 440-41; and NATO, 363, 370; and Vietnam, 265, 269-70, 274, 283-84, 288, 506-07, 513, 515, 517, 527
Burchinal, Maj. Gen. David A., 312
Burke, Admiral Arleigh, 10-11, 61, 76, 78, 80, 173, 177-78, 183, 186-87, 189-90, 242

Burlatsky, Fedor, 220
Burma, 37, 236, 240, 440
Byrd, Sen. Harry F., 480, 483

C-5, 492, 494
C-130, 58, 129
C-141, 58, 492
Cabell, General Charles P., 184, 302
Cambodia, 37, 228n, 229, 231, 236, 240, 255, 283, 508, 509, 515
Cameroon, 37
Canada, 240, 360, 365, 409, 434, 448, 449
Cannon, Rep. Clarence, 31, 131, 442
Capehart, Sen. Homer E., 204
Caribbean, Commander in Chief (CINCCARIB), 427
Carroll, George, 244-45, 248-49
Carroll, Lt. Gen. Joseph F., 23
Carter, Lt. Gen. Marshall, 199
Case, Sen. Francis, 190
Castro, Fidel, 3, 13, 172-75, 183-84, 193-200, 202-03, 215-19, 223-27, 427
Central Intelligence Agency: and Bay of Pigs, 172-92; and Berlin, 67; and counterinsurgency, 36-37; and Cuban missile crisis, 196, 198-99, 202, 210, 225-26; and Defense Intelligence Agency, 24; and Laos, 232, 236-37, 241-42, 253, 256-57; and limited nuclear test ban treaty, 331, 346, 348; and missile gap, 300-02; and Vietnam, 266-67, 282-83, 286-87, 289, 498, 501-02, 506, 514-16, 522n, 527
Charyk, Joseph V., 8, 106, 301, 467, 469-70
Chavez, Sen. Dennis, 62
Chiang Kai-shek, 508
Chile, 199
China, Communist, 145, 515; and Laos, 241, 242, 243, 244, 246, 250-51; and nuclear test ban treaty, 328, 329, 342, 343, 347, 349, 350; and Vietnam, 272, 506, 513, 526, 531, 533. *See also* Taiwan
Christmas Island, 333, 334, 335
civil defense, 18, 29-35, 51, 65, 69, 70, 85, 92, 96n, 125, 130, 320, 321, 477, 481, 543, 544
Civil Guard, 262-63, 266, 273-74, 276-77
civil rights legislation, 138, 481, 488, 491, 546
Clarke, General Bruce, 165
Clay, General Lucius, 158-59, 165-68, 170, 432-33, 435
Clay Committee, 431-33, 435
Cleveland, Harlan, 418
Clifford, Clark, 4, 17n
Colby, William E., 225, 257, 282, 289, 291
Colombia, 37, 38
Committee of Principals, 325-26, 329, 336, 344-45, 348

Committee on the Defense Establishment. *See* Symington Committee
comptroller, assistant secretary of defense, 8, 13, 538-39; and cost reduction program, 457; and flexible response, 308, 310; and FY 1962 budget, 63; and FY 1963 budget, 74-77, 81, 85, 89, 95; and FY 1964 budget, 119, 122, 132; and FY 1965 budget, 476; and FY 1966 budget, 489-92; and military assistance, 426; and Skybolt, 377, 379; and TFX, 471
Conference on Cessation of Nuclear Weapons Tests, 327. *See also* limited nuclear test ban treaty
Congo, 38, 193, 442n
Connally, John B., Jr., 8-9, 86, 93
Continental Air Defense Command (CONAD), 449
continental defense, 14, 18, 53, 74, 92, 477, 495
contracts, awarding of, 454-59, 466-73
controlled response, 295, 310, 311, 314, 317, 322. *See also* flexible response
conventional forces, 3, 12, 52, 65, 87, 129, 143, 146, 149, 152-53, 161-62, 170-71, 304, 305, 308, 314, 324, 359, 369, 396, 429, 543. *See also* limited warfare
Cooper, Chester, 529n
Cooper, Sen. John Sherman, 523
cost reduction, 98, 140, 453-62, 475, 494, 540
Cottrell, Sterling J., 224
Council of Economic Advisers, 82, 121, 480
counter-cities, 294, 295, 320
counterforce, 294, 295, 306, 309, 310, 312, 313, 319, 320, 321
counterinsurgency, 35-43, 52, 62, 129, 233, 248, 262-67, 271, 272, 275-80, 281, 291, 292, 294
Cousins, Norman, 346
Craig, U.S.S., 519
Craig, Brig. Gen. William H., 251-52
Cuba: Bay of Pigs invasion, 1, 13, 15, 20, 22, 24, 30, 36, 172-94, 195, 196, 197, 198, 199, 224, 227, 239, 241, 242, 243, 257, 267, 269, 301, 426, 475; exiles, 196-97 (*see also* Bay of Pigs invasion); missile crisis, 48, 115, 121, 128, 135, 168-69, 195-227, 340, 356, 374, 401, 475, 487, 544; and Operation Mongoose, 194, 198-99, 225
Cuban Revolutionary Council, 196
Cuba Study Group, 36, 186-88, 192, 194
Cuban Task Force, 225

Daley, Richard, 464
Da Nang, 532
Dean, Arthur H., 2, 332, 338, 341

Decker, General George H., 61, 87, 89, 91, 162, 173, 189, 242
Defense Atomic Support Agency, 20
Defense Communications Agency, 17, 20, 455
Defense Intelligence Agency, 15, 17, 19, 22-24, 49, 202, 215, 226, 516, 521
Defense Reorganization Act of 1958, 5, 8, 16, 17, 24, 25, 28-29, 536
defense research and engineering, director of (DDR&E), 7, 8, 15, 44, 61, 81, 86, 131, 309, 318, 330, 343, 353, 378-79, 400, 466-68, 470-72, 491, 548
Defense Special Missile and Astronautic Center, 24
Defense Supply Agency, 20, 24-29, 454-56
defoliation program, 276, 291
de Gaulle, Charles, 150, 156, 210, 314, 350, 453; and MLF, 400, 403, 404n, 406, 409, 414, 417; and NATO, 368, 370-74; and Vietnam, 288, 502, 515
Denmark, 367
Dennison, Admiral Robert, 176, 193, 206
dependents abroad, 448-50
DeSoto patrols, 519, 521, 523, 525
Development Loan Fund (DLF), 423, 425
Dillon, C. Douglas, 121, 206n, 207, 389, 448, 452-53, 481
directives, DoD, 22, 23, 44, 45, 46, 458
Dirksen, Sen. Everett M., 130, 354, 530
Disarmament Administration, 327. *See also* Arms Control and Disarmament Agency
Dixon, John W., 76
Dobrynin, Anatoly, 201-02, 217, 222-23
Dodd, Sen. Thomas J., 342
Dominic, Operation, 335, 337
Dominican Republic, 226
domino principle, 288
Douglas, James, 10, 76
Douglas, Sen. Paul H., 457
Douglas-Home, Alec, 351, 414, 415
Dowling, Walter C., 159, 165-66
Draft Presidential Memorandums (DPMs), 83-85, 86, 116, 121, 122, 123, 295, 478, 479, 481, 490
Drucker, Peter, 548
Dulles, Allen W., 36, 67, 173-76, 178, 180, 182, 186, 188, 196, 198, 242, 266, 331
Dulles, John Foster, 144
Duong Van Minh, General, 271, 498, 502, 504, 505, 510, 512-13, 524
Durbrow, Elbridge, 263-65
Dworshak, Sen. Henry, 276
Dynasoar, 69, 104, 477, 479, 481

East Germany. *See* German Democratic Republic
Ecuador, 37, 38
Edwards, U.S.S., 525
Egypt, 202
Eighteen-Nation Disarmament Committee (ENDC), 334, 335, 336, 337, 339, 340-41
Eisenhower, Dwight D., 52, 67, 73, 145, 189, 260, 293, 296, 359, 377, 480, 546; and balance of payments, 448-49; and Castro regime, 172-75; and Defense Reorganization Act of 1958, 16; and FY 1962 budget, 53-54; and FY 1964 budget, 135; and Laos, 228-29, 231; and missile gap, 299; and nuclear test ban, 324-26, 327n, 331, 342; and SIOP, 316; and Vietnam, 263, 267, 531-32
elections: 1960, 2-3, 9, 13, 144, 175, 293, 298-99, 357, 377; 1964, 121, 476, 484, 489, 524, 526
Ellender, Sen. Allen J., 253
Ellsberg, Daniel, 308
Engle, Sen. Clair, 63
Enthoven, Alain C., 8, 14, 76, 84, 136, 308, 317, 538-39; and assured destruction, 319, 321; and counterforce strategy, 309-10, 312-13; and FY 1966 budget, 489-90, 492
Erhard, Ludwig, 414, 416, 419
Europe, Supreme Allied Commander (SACEUR), 155, 164, 190, 222, 304, 358-60, 363, 369, 375, 386-88, 391, 393-95, 397, 401, 404, 407
Europe, U.S. Commander in Chief (USCINCEUR), 146, 155, 161, 363
Executive Committee (ExCom), 204-10, 213-17, 219-21
Export-Import Bank, 423n, 434

F-5, 438
F-8, 516
F-100, 516
F-101, 284
F-102, 85
F-104G, 223
F-106, 85
F-111, 469, 471-73, 492, 541
Fanfani, Amintore, 410
Farm Gate, 39, 272
Federal Civil Defense Administration, 30
Felt, Admiral Harry, 262, 282-83, 290, 507, 513-14, 519
Finletter, Thomas K., 17n, 150, 304, 362, 392-94, 396-98, 413, 418-19
Fisk, James B., 325
Fitzgerald, Desmond, 225
Five-Year Force Structure and Financial Program (FYFS&FP), 119, 120, 476-77

flexible response, 13, 52, 143, 170-71, 293-322, 358, 360, 369, 543, 549
Flood, Rep. Daniel J., 66
Foertsch, General Friedrich, 373
Food for Peace program, 138
Ford, Rep. Gerald R., 108-09, 136, 430, 436, 487, 530
Ford, Harold P., 283, 527n
Ford, Henry, II, 4
foreign aid, 422, 424-25, 430, 431, 436, 437, 442, 445-46
Foreign Assistance Act of 1961, 424, 433, 439, 444-45
Foreign Assistance Act of 1962, 430
Foreign Assistance Act of 1964, 434
Forrestal, Michael, 37, 281, 286, 502-04, 506, 513-14, 519, 525
Fort Chaffee, Ark., 464
Foster, John S., 330, 352
Foster, William C., 326, 336, 341, 348
France, 304, 307, 309, 314, 357, 362, 373, 384; base closures in, 462n; and Berlin, 146, 150, 155, 156; *force de frappe*, 314, 370-73; and Indochina, 228-29, 231, 502; and MLF, 385, 389, 391, 403, 404n, 406, 408, 414, 417; military assistance and sales to, 421, 434; and NATO requirements, 360, 365-70; and nuclear test ban, 342, 349-50; and U.S. balance of payments, 448, 451, 453
Frankel, Rear Adm. Samuel B., 23
Freeman, General Paul, 169
Fubini, Eugene, 547
Fulbright, Sen. J. William, 130, 180, 351, 354, 440, 523

Gaither panel, 30
Garcia, Reuben de Leon, 196
Gates, Thomas S., 5, 10-11, 17, 35, 76, 392, 449, 536; and creation of DCA, 20; and Laos, 231; and McNamara, 489; and missile gap, 300; and MLF, 387-88; and SIOP, 316; and Skybolt, 376; and TFX, 466; and Vietnam, 262
Gavin, James, 372
Gemini, 477n, 481-82
general counsel, DoD, 7, 19, 28
General Dynamics, 468-73
Geneva Accords (1954), 228-29, 235, 246, 260, 268
Geneva Conference on Laos (1961), 243-47
Geneva Conference on Laos (1962), 254-56, 268
Geneva Foreign Ministers Conference (1959), 144, 324-25
German Democratic Republic (GDR), 143, 144, 145, 149, 150-51, 154, 156-57, 163-64, 168, 169-70, 360

Germany, Federal Republic of (FRG), 38, 42, 357, 358, 434; and Berlin crisis, 143-71; and flexible response, 304, 314-15, 384; and MLF, 385, 386, 389, 390, 391, 392, 394, 396, 403, 408, 410, 412, 414, 416, 418, 419, 420; and NATO requirements, 360-61, 362-70; and nuclear aspirations, 373-75 (*see also* MLF); and U.S. balance of payments, 448, 449, 450, 451, 452
Geyelin, Philip, 413
Gilpatric, Roswell, L., 7, 10, 14, 17n, 19, 48, 61, 76-77, 81, 86-87, 89-90, 106, 110, 120, 129, 136, 326, 450-51, 456, 482, 492; and B-70, 59; and Bay of Pigs, 180-81; and Berlin Wall, 67, 150-51; and centralization of power in OSD, 49; and civil defense program, 32; and counterinsurgency, 37, 41; and Cuban missile crisis, 197-98, 201, 206n, 208, 210, 212; and FY 1964 budget, 139-40; and Laos, 242, 244, 251; and Lansdale, 267-68; and McNamara, 535, 541-42, 548; and military assistance, 423n, 427; and NATO, 363, 375-76; and National Reconnaissance Office, 302; and nuclear testing, 333-34; and nuclear weapons policy, 162, 296-97, 299; and Skybolt, 378-79, 383-84; and space research, 45-46; and TFX, 468-71; and Vietnam, 264, 286
Glass, Henry E., 76-77, 80, 88-89, 94, 97, 99, 132, 136, 541
Goldberg, Arthur J., 9
Goldwater, Sen. Barry, 68, 352, 354, 476, 484-86, 489, 524
Goodpaster, Lt. Gen. Andrew J., 374, 529n, 531
Goodwin, Richard, 178, 180
Gordon, Kermit, 444, 477, 480-83, 491, 493
Gore, Sen. Albert, 190
Goulart, Joao, 227n
Gray, Brig. Gen. David W., 176-77
Gray report, 176
Great Britain, 357, 362, 421, 434; base closures in, 462n; and Berlin, 146, 148, 155, 156, 163-64; and flexible response, 314; and Geneva Conference, 231, 238, 240, 243, 246-47; and MLF, 386, 392, 402-05, 406, 409, 410-11, 412, 414-15, 416-18; and NATO requirements, 360-61, 362-70; and nuclear test ban, 332, 339-40, 349-51; and Skybolt, 375-84, 402-03; and U.S. balance of payments, 448, 451
Great Society, 462, 476, 483, 497
Greece, 252, 367, 398, 425, 428, 432, 438, 442
Greene, General Wallace M., 490, 509, 512, 516, 525-26
Gromyko, Andrei, 164, 167, 206, 218, 348, 350-51, 492
Grozny, 214

Guantanamo, 173, 177, 203, 206, 207, 210, 213, 215, 449
Guatamala, 37, 173, 174, 175, 178

Hailsham, Viscount Quinton, 349
Halberstam, David, 281, 291
Hamilton, Fowler, 17n, 37, 429, 431
Hardy, Rep. Porter, Jr., 27, 459
Hare, Raymond, 221
Harkins, General Paul D., 274-75, 277, 279-80, 282-84, 286, 289, 291, 500, 503-05, 511-13
Harriman, W. Averell, 2, 37, 278, 289; and Berlin Wall, 145, 152; and Laos, 239, 241, 243-44, 246-48, 252-53, 256, 516; and NATO, 361; and nuclear test ban, 344, 347-50, 352-53; and Vietnam, 275, 286, 290
Harrison, Maj. Gen. William H., Jr., 111
Hartel, Brig. Gen. Frederick O., 182
Hawk, 530
Hayward, Vice Adm. John T., 46
health and medical, assistant secretary of defense for, 20
Hébert, Rep. F. Edward, 96, 103, 106, 110, 114, 132-33, 459, 463, 542
Heller, Walter, W., 121, 480
Helms, Richard, 181, 198
Herter, Christian A., Jr., 144n, 228, 387, 389
Hickenlooper, Sen. Bourke B., 351
Hickey, Lt. Gen. Thomas F., 316-18
Hickey reports, 295, 316-18
Hilsman, Roger: and assessment of McNamara, 4; and Bay of Pigs, 185; and Laos, 256-58, 515; and nuclear test ban treaty, 355; and Vietnam, 275, 278, 280-81, 284, 286, 288-90, 292, 504
Hitch, Charles J., 8, 13, 89, 95, 136, 310, 538-39; and FY 1962 budget, 63; and FY 1964 budget, 119-22, 131; and FY 1965 budget, 476-77; and FY 1966 budget, 490-91; and military assistance, 426; and PPBS, 74-75, 77, 79-81, 92; and SIOP, 317-18; and Skybolt, 377, 379
Ho Chi Minh, 228, 244
Ho Chi Minh Trail, 244, 249, 256, 257, 260, 509
Hoelscher, Leonard W., 65n
Honest John, 371
Hoover Commission (1955), 24n
Hoover, Joseph S., 85, 457
Hornig, Donald F., 492-93
hot line, 346
Hound Dog, 127, 381, 383
House Appropriations Committee, 30-31, 56-57, 62-63, 66, 74, 96-97, 103-04, 107, 109-10, 130-31, 136-37, 414, 424-25, 430, 435-37, 440, 442, 457, 487-88

House Armed Services Committee, 10, 12, 13, 29, 47, 55, 62-64, 68, 97-106, 110, 114, 131-35, 321, 427, 459, 463-64, 484-86, 537, 548
House Foreign Affairs Committee, 424, 435-36, 441-42, 445, 522, 533
House Government Operations Committee, 26-29
House Science and Astronautics Committee, 44-45
Humphrey, Sen. Hubert H., 331, 351
Hyannis Port, Mass., 88, 116, 125, 156, 381, 479

IL-28, 207, 215-18
India, 238, 240, 436, 444
Indonesia, 202, 251
installations and logistics (I&L), assistant secretary of defense for, 20, 453-55, 457-58, 461n, 462-63
intercontinental ballistic missiles (ICBMs), 53, 61, 63, 299, 300, 301, 302, 312, 368, 373, 394, 398, 415, 494, 496, 543, 545. *See also* Minuteman
Interdepartmental Committee on Cuba, 224
intermediate-range ballistic missiles (IRBMs), 202, 207, 218, 220, 401
International Control Commission (ICC), 238-40, 243, 245, 248-49, 255-56, 284, 523
International Cooperation Administration, 232n, 252, 266, 421-23, 425
international security affairs (ISA), assistant secretary of defense for, 7, 548; and Bay of Pigs, 180, 182, 192; and Berlin, 143, 146, 148; and Cuban missile crisis, 200, 219-20; and flexible response, 296-97, 308; and FY 1964 budget, 124; and Laos, 234, 236, 238-40, 244, 248-49, 251-52; and military assistance, 422-23, 426, 428, 431, 434, 439-40, 443-44; and multilateral force, 388-89, 393, 398n, 400, 405, 414; and NATO, 360-61, 363, 365, 368, 370, 379, 381; and Vietnam, 284, 513
Iran, 37, 38, 425, 428, 438
Iraq, 202
Italy, 220n, 221, 363, 368, 398, 402, 411, 434, 451, 462n

Jackson, Sen. Henry M., 6, 68, 103, 342, 352, 469
Japan, 147, 434, 448, 451, 452
Johnson, General Harold K., 494
Johnson, Vice President and President Lyndon B., 9, 38, 92, 142, 158-59, 176, 208, 226, 227, 268-69, 277, 287, 367, 448, 452-53, 471, 479, 489, 535, 543; and cost reduction, 459, 461-

62, 465, 473, 475, 476; and FY 1965 budget, 480, 481-83, 486; and FY 1966 budget, 493-97; and Gulf of Tonkin incident, 519-24, 532; and Joint Strategic Capabilities Plan (JSCP-65), 320; and military assistance, 437, 439-40, 442, 445; and multilateral force, 412-13, 414-19; and NSAMs, 415, 417-18, 437, 499, 510, 515, 525; and OPLAN 34A, 501, 519, 523, 525; and Vietnam, 268-69, 277, 287, 498-99, 502, 504, 507-10, 513-14, 516, 517, 525, 526-31, 532, 533

Johnson, U. Alexis, 37, 198, 200, 250, 252, 255, 518

Johnston Island, 207, 335

Joint Atomic Energy Committee, 333, 415

Joint Chiefs of Staff, U.S., 5-7, 9-10, 14, 17-18, 21-22, 35, 50, 535, 537-38, 548; and balance of payments, 449; and Bay of Pigs, 173-80, 183-85, 187-90, 192-93; and Berlin, 148-53, 155, 158, 163, 166-67, 170; and counterinsurgency, 37-38, 41-42; and Cuban missile crisis, 195-96, 200-03, 206-07, 209, 211, 214, 218, 221, 223-25; and Defense Intelligence Agency, 22-24; and Defense Supply Agency, 26-28; and flexible response, 295-98, 304, 310-13, 315-18, 320; and FY 1962 budget, 56-58, 67-68; and FY 1963 budget, 73, 76, 80, 82-87, 90, 92, 94, 98, 102-03, 115-16; and FY 1964 budget, 120, 122-23, 125-26, 128-29, 132, 134, 136, 139; and FY 1965 budget, 476, 479-80, 482; and FY 1966 budget, 490-91, 493; and Laos, 231, 233-35, 237, 239-43, 248, 250-55, 258; and limited nuclear test ban treaty, 323, 325-27, 342-43, 345, 347, 352-56; and military assistance, 421, 423, 427-30, 434-36, 440-45; and multilateral force, 387-88, 393-95, 397, 401-02, 404, 407, 414; and NATO, 360-65, 367, 369, 374, 380-81; and Skybolt, 380-81; and space development, 45-46; and Vietnam, 262, 264, 266-68, 272-76, 279, 281-84, 289, 292, 499, 501-02, 504-10, 512, 515-16, 519, 521, 523, 525-26, 528, 530, 532-33

Joint Economic Committee, 470

Joint Strategic Objectives Plan: JSOP-67, 120, 317; JSOP-68, 476; JSOP-69, 490

Joint Strategic Target Planning Staff, 17, 316

Joint Study Group on Foreign Intelligence Activities, 22

Jones, Col. David C., 100

Jungle Jim (4400th Combat Crew Training Squadron), 39, 272

Jupiter, 213-14, 220-23, 386, 394, 404n

Kattenburg, Paul, 287, 291-92

Kaufmann, William W., 159, 305, 308, 310

Kaysen, Carl, 90, 123, 152, 347, 355, 393, 431, 479

Keating, Sen. Kenneth B., 204

Keenan, Joseph, 9-10

Keeny, Spurgeon, 478, 492-93

Kelleher, Philip W., 104-05

Kennan, George F., 8, 249

Kennedy, President John F., 1-2, 4-5, 6, 9, 17-19, 40, 47, 48, 191-92, 197, 317, 404n, 413, 418, 469, 473, 481, 535, 547; and Acheson, 147, 151-52, 153, 164, 303, 359, 389; assassination, 290, 479-80, 498; and balance of payments, 422, 429, 434, 449-52; and base closures, 462-65; and Bay of Pigs, 173-80, 183-86, 188-91, 241, 243, 269; and Berlin crisis, 64, 68, 145-47, 150, 152-64, 218, 219, 249; and civil defense, 30, 32-34; and cost reduction program, 453-55; and counterinsurgency, 35-42, 52, 224-25, 263-64, 268, 294; and Cuban missile crisis, 201, 204-10, 213, 215-18, 220-22; and FY 1962 budget, 52, 58-60, 61, 62-65, 68, 69, 145; and FY 1963 budget, 78, 82, 84, 88, 89-91, 96; and FY 1964 budget, 119, 120-21, 125-29, 135; and FY 1965 budget, 477, 479; guidance to McNamara, 12-13, 36, 38, 57, 75, 454-55, 462; and Joint Chiefs of Staff, 38, 90-91, 128-29, 176-77, 189, 196, 203, 206, 221, 233, 250, 335, 353-54, 407, 429-30; and Khrushchev, 144-45, 150-51, 160, 209, 213-14, 216-18, 222, 246, 249, 328, 330-32, 341, 346-47, 349-50, 355; and Laos, 228, 231, 232-33, 235, 236-38, 241-43, 246, 248-50, 258-59, 269; and limited nuclear test ban treaty, 323, 325, 328-36, 338-42, 346-47, 353-55, 543; and military assistance, 422-25, 428-32, 437, 439, 445; and multilateral force, 390-91, 395, 397-99, 401, 405-08, 410-15; and NATO, 303-04, 359, 362, 364, 367, 372, 376-78, 381, 383-84, 389-91, 403-04; and NSAMs, 42, 201, 269, 273, 395, 431, 434, 452; and nuclear strategy, 293, 296-97, 305-06, 322; and overthrow of Castro, 192-95, 198, 200, 203, 224-25; and Reserve forces, 65-66, 89, 109, 112, 151; and strategic weapons, 94-95, 119, 299; and Vietnam, 39, 260, 262-63, 267-73, 282, 286, 288-89, 499-500, 511

Kennedy, Robert F., 4-5, 241-42, 479; and Bay of Pigs, 175, 186; and civil defense, 32; and counterinsurgency, 37; and Cuba, 196, 198, 201; and Cuban missile crisis, 206, 207-08, 214, 217, 222-24

Kent, Brig. Gen. Glenn A., 321

Khrushchev, Nikita, 13, 64, 164, 195, 298, 492; and Berlin, 143-44, 150-51, 153-54, 165-69, 218-20; and Berlin Wall, 156, 158, 160, 162; and Cuban missile crisis, 201-02, 208-09, 213-

17, 227; and Laos, 234, 246, 249; and nuclear test ban, 328, 330-32, 341-42, 344, 346-47, 349-50, 353; and U.S. missiles in Turkey, 221-23; and wars of national liberation, 35, 145, 421
Killian, James R., 22
Kirkpatrick, Lyman B., Jr., 191
Kissinger, Henry A., 398
Kitchen, Jeffrey C., 406n, 428
Kitchen Group report, 427-29
Klein, David, 416
Kohler, Foy, D., 147, 161, 407
Komer, Robert W., 275
Konev, Marshal Ivan, 159n, 165, 167
Kong Le, 252, 257-58
Korea. *See* South Korea
Korean War, 96, 118, 128, 168, 233
Korth, Fred H., 48, 98, 468, 471, 478
Kosygin, Alexei, 492-93
Krulak, Lt. Gen. Victor H., 40-41, 286-88, 499, 501
Kuznetsov, Vasily, 216, 340-41

Laird, Rep. Melvin R., 440, 459, 487
Landon, Kenneth P., 236
Lange, Halvard, 389
Lansdale, Brig. Gen. Edward G., 35-36, 180, 196, 198-99, 233, 262-65, 267-68, 270-71, 279, 291-92
Laos, 37, 38, 52, 143, 173, 228-59, 260, 267, 268, 269, 270, 275, 294, 501, 504, 505, 515-17, 533; MAP assistance to, 437, 443, 445
Lawrence Livermore Radiation Laboratory, 6, 8, 330, 342, 352
Leddy, John M., 419
Lee, Rear Adm. John M., 388-89, 400-02, 405
Legere, Col. Lawrence, 397, 400
legislative affairs, assistant to the secretary of defense for, 97-98, 131, 484, 487, 541
LeMay, General Curtis E., 47-48, 67, 100, 127-28, 139, 384, 476, 537; and assured destruction, 320; and counterinsurgency, 39; and Cuban missile crisis, 203; and FY 1963 budget, 83, 86, 90, 101-03; and FY 1965 budget, 478, 482, 485; and FY 1966 budget, 490, 493; and Laos, 242; and Nike-Zeus, 125, 539; and nuclear test ban, 345, 352, 354; and RS-70, 106, 115; and SIOP, 311; and Vietnam, 501, 509, 512, 525-26
Lemnitzer, General Lyman L., 6-7, 10, 14, 17, 45, 56, 83, 85, 93, 98, 115, 120, 254, 313, 326, 334n, 393n, 394-95, 401, 427, 430; and Bay of Pigs, 36, 173, 175-76, 185, 187-90; and Berlin, 67, 155, 158-59, 169; and counterinsurgency, 37; and Cuba, 198; and Laos, 233, 236-37, 240-41, 243, 250; and McNamara, 11, 537-38; and missile gap, 299; and NATO, 303-04, 311, 361-62, 407; and Nike-Zeus, 61; and nuclear test ban, 330, 333, 335-36, 339; and SIOP, 316; and Vietnam, 279, 292
Leva, Marx, 17n
Lightner, E. Allan, Jr., 165
limited nuclear test ban treaty, 139, 141, 323-56, 475, 543
limited warfare, 62, 68, 74, 233, 304, 310, 429
Lincoln Laboratories, 27
Lippmann, Walter, 221, 328
LIVE OAK, 146, 160
Lodge, Henry Cabot, 285-90, 498-500, 503-07, 510-14, 518
logistics, 18, 27, 123, 451, 455
Logistics Management Institute, 27, 457
Lovett, Robert A., 3-4, 206
Luce, Henry, 191
Luxembourg, 409

Mace, 370
Macmillan, Harold, 148, 156, 167, 238, 314, 414; and MLF, 409, 412; and nuclear test ban, 330, 332, 334, 339-40, 342, 346, 349-50, 355; and Skybolt, 376, 380, 383, 403-04
Maddox, U.S.S., 519, 521, 522
Mahon, Rep. George H., 31, 56, 63, 66, 74, 104, 107, 109, 112-13, 136-37, 414, 442, 457, 487
Malinovsky, Marshal Rodion, 220
Manning, Robert J., 515
manpower, assistant secretary of defense for, 9, 20, 110
Mansfield, Sen. Mike, 491, 500, 529n, 530
Mao Tse-tung, 145, 263
Marine Corps, U.S.: and Bay of Pigs, 177; and cost reduction program, 456; and counterinsurgency, 38, 40; and FY 1962 budget, 55, 65, 68; and FY 1963 budget, 91; and FY 1964 budget, 125, 128-29; and FY 1965 budget, 477; and FY 1966 budget, 490-91, 494, 496; and Laos, 237; and Vietnam, 509, 515, 518, 529-30, 532
Marshall, Charles Burton, 423, 427
Marshall, George C., 6, 548
massive retaliation, 3, 13, 52, 84, 155, 295, 304, 309, 315, 317, 358
May, Ernest R., 213
McClellan, Sen. John L., 141, 470-71
McCloy, John J., 2, 154, 204, 217, 325-27, 329, 347
McCone, John A., 37, 198, 201, 206n, 207, 283, 286, 348, 498-99, 501-02, 508, 514, 528
McCormack, Rep. John W., 104, 441, 529n, 530

McCullough, Hugh, 76
McDonald, Admiral David L., 478, 490, 494, 509-10, 512
McElroy, Neil H., 60, 299
McGarr, Lt. Gen. Lionel C., 264-67, 272, 275, 278-79
McGhee, George C., 265
McGiffert, David, 131-33, 138-39, 484-88
McGovern, Sen. George, 138-41, 486
McGowan, Maj. Gen. Donald W., 109-10
McNamara, Lt. Gen. Andrew T., 26-27
McNamara, Robert S., 13, 19, 25, 47-48, 78-80, 95, 97-98, 119-20, 126, 135, 197, 226, 258, 294, 297, 320, 476-77, 546-47; and Anderson, Admiral George W., Jr., 47-48, 102, 125, 128, 212; Ann Arbor speech, 308-09, 313-15, 373, 384, 396, 398, 544; appointment as secretary of defense, 1, 4-6, 10-11; Athens speech, 305-09, 313-15, 373, 384, 396-99, 544; and base closures, 462-66, 473; and Bay of Pigs, 175-80, 183-84, 188-90; and Berlin crisis, 67, 84, 91, 99, 147-49, 152-53, 155, 158-62, 164-65, 168, 170, 219, 250, 305; and Bureau of the Budget, 79, 119-20, 481, 492; and civil defense, 30-34, 320, 544; congressional relations, 27, 96, 99, 101, 103-04, 114, 116-17, 131, 133, 137, 141, 433, 436, 439-40, 459, 464-66, 469-71, 473, 484-85, 491-92, 537, 540-42; congressional testimony, 11-12, 28-29, 31, 56, 62-64, 66, 97-100, 103, 107, 131-33, 136, 209, 218, 223, 249, 320-21, 353, 424, 426-27, 430, 435-36, 440-42, 445, 456, 459, 470, 485-87, 500, 503, 519, 522-23, 533; and cost effectiveness, 140, 361, 447, 449-50, 452, 467, 536; cost reduction program, 453-62, 473, 475, 540; and counterinsurgency, 35-36, 38, 41-42, 224, 275, 291-92; and critics, 10-11, 17, 27, 28, 93, 136, 190, 314, 365, 382, 459, 469-70, 489, 516, 518, 536-37, 541, 545, 548; and Cuban missile crisis, 115, 132, 135, 168, 201, 204, 205n, 206-13, 218-19, 222-23, 319, 379, 487, 544; and DoD reorganization, 2-4, 5, 8, 10, 14-16, 18-30, 49-50, 57-58, 65n, 536-37, 539, 547-48; and flexible response, 13, 155, 170, 214, 227, 293, 295-98, 303, 305-07, 314-16, 322, 543-44; and FY 1962 budget, 52, 56-64, 66-70; and FY 1963 budget, 75, 77, 79, 81-82, 85-87, 89-91, 94, 96-100, 102-03, 107; and FY 1964 budget, 118-22, 125-29, 131-34, 136-39; and FY 1965 budget, 476-84, 485-89, 497; and FY 1966 budget, 490-91, 493-94; and Gulf of Tonkin incident, 519-23; and Harkins, General Paul D., 275, 284, 289, 500, 503-04, 511, 513; and influence of Thomas S. Gates, Jr., 5, 10, 17, 20, 536; and Joint Chiefs of Staff (JCS), 7-8, 10-11, 115; and Laos, 231-32, 235-40, 242-43, 248-50, 253-55, 259, 515-16; and LeMay, General Curtis E., 47, 67, 102-03, 106, 125, 127-28, 345, 354, 476, 482, 490, 493-94, 509, 537; and limited nuclear test ban treaty, 323, 325, 329-30, 332-39, 343-45, 348, 353-56; management philosophy, 49, 63, 74, 78, 119, 447, 453, 455-56, 458-61, 471-72, 474, 535-37, 547; and military assistance, 422-23, 426-45, 446; and missile gap, 3, 12-13, 299-301, 545-46; and multilateral force, 388-89, 391-92, 393, 395-402, 404, 406-07, 410-20; and NATO, 305-08, 315, 322, 359, 361, 363-69, 374-75, 380-81, 391-92, 396, 398, 543-44; and nuclear strategy, 20, 297, 305-21, 542-43; and overseas meetings, 274, 277, 281, 284, 288-89, 305-08, 369, 375, 381, 383, 396, 402, 418, 499-500, 502, 507, 513, 514, 517; and overthrow of Castro, 192-93, 195, 198, 200, 203, 224-25; personality, 1-5, 7, 11, 46, 48, 94, 141, 291, 382, 470, 535, 540-42, 547-48; and personnel selection, 6-10, 19, 74-75; and planning-programming-budgeting system (PPBS), 72, 77-78, 92-93, 95, 476, 539-40; and posture statement, 97-98, 132, 297, 457, 485; and reorganization of Reserves and National Guard, 88-89, 107-08, 110-14, 116, 161, 540; and RS-70, 102-06, 110-11, 115-16, 119n, 132, 136-37; and Rusk, Secretary of State Dean, 6, 273, 287, 290-91, 325, 339, 345, 374, 380-82, 395, 400-01, 404, 406n, 408, 413, 422-23, 436, 498, 505, 511-12, 542; and Skybolt, 118, 120, 123, 136, 314, 376-84, 402, 404; and space program, 22, 43-44, 46-47, 481-82; and strategic nuclear weapons, 13, 59-61, 69, 94-95, 123-25, 127, 149, 161-62, 164, 168, 209, 227, 293, 301-02, 318-21, 348, 356, 368, 478-79, 482, 490; and tactical fighter experimental (TFX), 141, 447, 466-74, 540-41; and Vietnam, 1, 242, 263-68, 270-77, 279, 281, 283-92, 430-31, 437, 439, 487, 498-514, 517-20, 526, 528-34, 545; and Whiz Kids, 4, 7-8, 76, 116, 291, 516, 538
McNaughton, John T., 216, 347, 349-50, 407-08, 410n, 411, 414, 418, 443-45, 469n, 513, 523, 527n, 529n
McNeil, Wilfred J., 74-75, 77, 538
Meany, George, 9
medium-range ballistic missiles (MRBMs): in Cuba, 201, 202, 204, 205, 207; and NATO, 297, 306, 357, 360, 361, 363, 366, 374, 381, 387, 390-91, 393-403, 408
Melman, Seymour, 136, 138-39
Mendenhall, Joseph, 288
Menshikov, Mikhail, 145, 234
Merchant, Livingston, 405, 407-11
Mercury, 43

Meredith, James H., 547
Michaelis, Rear Adm. Frederick, 400
MIGs, 167, 202, 207
Mikoyan, Anastas I., 215
military assistance, 51, 54, 80, 83, 85, 92, 119-20, 125, 129-30, 241, 252, 253, 277, 281, 283, 291, 421-46, 448, 449, 477, 481, 482, 501
Military Assistance Advisory Group (MAAG): and balance of payments, 449; and counterinsurgency, 38-39, 41; and Laos, 237, 240-41, 252-53, 256; and military sales, 434; and NATO, 371; and Vietnam, 264-66, 268, 270, 274, 278-79, 290, 503, 511
Military Assistance Command, Vietnam (MACV), 274-76, 281-82, 286, 290-91, 500-01, 511, 513, 518-19
Military Assistance Program (MAP), 235, 241, 281, 284, 421-46. *See also* military assistance
Military Revolutionary Council, 502, 524
Millpond, 237
Minuteman, 15, 83, 300, 312, 317, 377, 381, 415, 416, 496, 546; and FY 1962 budget, 53, 54, 59, 60, 62, 63; and FY 1963 budget, 87, 90; and FY 1964 budget, 121-28, 134; and FY 1965 budget, 476, 478-79, 481, 482; and FY 1966 budget, 490, 493
Miro Cardona, Jose, 196-97
missile gap, 3, 12-13, 127, 295, 298-99, 545
Missileer, 466
mobile medium-range ballistic missiles, 121, 139, 140
Mollenhoff, Clark, 7
Mongoose, Operation, 194, 198-99, 225
Monnet, Jean, 386
Morgan, Rep. Thomas E., 435-36, 440-42
Morocco, 462n
Morris, Thomas, 453, 456-58, 462-64
Morse, Richard S., 45
Morse, Sen. Wayne, 436, 522, 533
Morton, U.S.S., 525
multilateral force (MLF), 297, 306, 308, 377, 381, 382, 383, 384, 385-420
Murphy, Charles J. V., 185, 190-91, 517
Murrow, Edward R., 182, 332
Mustin, Vice Adm. Lloyd M., 527n
Mutual Security Program (MSP), 422, 424

Nassau Conference, 372, 383-84, 402, 403, 404, 405, 406, 409, 416
National Aeronautics and Space Act of 1958, 43
National Aeronautics and Space Administration, 43, 45-47
National Guard, 18, 51, 65-66, 70, 78, 83, 88-89, 96, 99, 107-14, 116, 130-31, 143, 151, 161, 170, 495, 540, 546-47

National Intelligence Estimates (NIEs), 124, 181, 283
National Liberation Front (NLF), 262
National Military Command Center, 521
National Reconnaissance Office (NRO), 302
National Security Agency, 20, 22-23, 522n
National Security Council (NSC): and Bay of Pigs, 173, 192-94; and Berlin, 152-54, 163-64; and counterinsurgency, 36-37; and Cuban missile crisis, 196, 200-01, 204; and Defense Intelligence Agency, 22; and flexible response, 296-97, 317; and FY 1962 budget, 57; and FY 1963 budget, 75; and FY 1965 budget, 478-79; and FY 1966 budget, 492-93; and Laos, 242; and limited nuclear test ban treaty, 326, 331; and military assistance, 429, 432; and multilateral force, 391; and NATO, 372; and Vietnam, 273, 281, 502, 510, 514-15, 521-22, 529-30
Navy, U.S., 7-9, 16-18, 21-25, 28, 35, 44, 46, 48, 50, 73-74, 539; and base closures, 464-65; and Bay of Pigs, 173; and Berlin, 161; and cost reduction program, 455, 458, 461; and counterinsurgency, 38, 40; and Cuban missile crisis, 200, 203, 206, 211-15; and flexible response, 293, 295, 316; and FY 1962 budget, 53-55; and FY 1963 budget, 81-82, 85-86, 91, 93, 98, 102; and FY 1964 budget, 120, 122-23, 125-26, 128, 131, 137; and FY 1965 budget, 476-78; and FY 1966 budget, 490-91, 454, 496; and multilateral force, 391, 400, 407, 412; and TFX, 466-69, 471-72, 540-41; and Vietnam, 519-22, 532
Nehru, Jawaharlal, 238
Nelson, Sen. Gaylord, 138
Nes, David G., 511-12
Net Evaluation Subcommittee (NESC), 298, 316
Netherlands, 360, 365, 414
Neustadt, Richard, 296, 398n, 403, 406n, 412, 416
Nevada underground testing, 341-42
New Frontier, 1-2, 413
New Orleans Naval Station, 463
New Zealand, 9
Ngo Dinh Diem, 244, 257, 260, 262-66, 268-71, 273, 277-80, 282, 285-86, 288-90, 292, 498-99, 503
Ngo Dinh Nhu, 280, 285-88
Nguyen Dinh Thuan, 286
Nguyen Khanh, Maj. Gen., 502-05, 507-08, 510-14, 517, 519, 523-25, 528
Nhu, Madame, 285
Nike-Ajax, 496
Nike-Hercules, 371, 496
Nike-X, 124, 320, 321, 477, 493

Nike-Zeus, 31, 45, 60, 61, 62, 63, 70, 71, 85, 87, 90, 121, 122, 124, 125, 127, 128, 134, 141, 320, 539
Nitze, Paul H., 7-8, 149, 221, 296, 312, 371, 398, 428, 471, 491; and ACDA, 325-26; and Acheson report, 303-04; and Bay of Pigs, 178, 180, 192-93; and Berlin, 146-47, 161-63; and Cuban missile crisis, 206, 208-09, 211, 214, 216-17, 219; and Laos, 228, 240, 244, 246, 248; and MLF, 388, 392, 406, 414; and NATO, 361-62, 380-81, 383; and Nike-Zeus, 124; and nuclear test ban, 333, 339, 342; and Vietnam, 276, 291
Nixon, Richard M., 175
no-cities doctrine, 295, 310, 319, 322
Nolting, Frederick, 265, 268, 274, 279-80, 283, 285, 287, 290, 511
Norstad, General Lauris, 221, 304, 388-89, 397-98, 403; and Berlin, 146-47, 149, 155, 160-61, 163-64, 169-70; and MLF, 394-95, 400-01; and NATO, 358-62, 371-72, 375, 386, 391, 393
North Atlantic Treaty Organization (NATO), 2, 234, 357-84, 535, 542-44, 546; and balance of payments, 452; and Berlin, 144, 146-50, 155, 160-64, 166-67, 171, 219; and flexible response, 3, 294, 297, 303-10, 313-15, 322; and Jupiter missiles in Turkey, 221-23; and limited nuclear test ban treaty, 324, 342, 347-48; and military assistance, 432, 435, 439; and multilateral force, 395-420
North Vietnam. *See* Vietnam, Democratic Republic of
Norway, 363
NSAM 65, 269
NSAM 109, 163
NSAM 111, 273-74
NSAM 147, 395
NSAM 159, 431
NSAM 181, 201
NSAM 182, 42
NSAM 242, 434
NSAM 270, 452
NSAM 273, 499, 501
NSAM 276, 437
NSAM 288, 510, 515
NSAM 314, 525
NSAM 318, 415-16
NSAM 322, 417-19
NSC 5096/1, 297
NSC Counter-Guerrilla Warfare Task Force, 36
nuclear-powered aircraft, 62
nuclear proliferation, 306, 328, 342, 344, 355, 373, 420
nuclear sharing, 392, 408, 414, 419. *See also* multilateral force (MLF)

nuclear warfare, 3, 13, 14, 15, 34, 155, 168, 170-71, 209, 243, 259, 293, 294, 305-22, 340, 355, 357, 361-62, 374, 544
nuclear weapons, 303, 306-08, 331-34; stockpiles, 138, 155, 162, 324, 329, 353, 386; testing, 324-25, 327-35, 341-44

O'Brien, Lawrence F., 102, 104, 106
Office of Civil and Defense Mobilization, 30-31, 96n
Office of Defense Mobilization, 30
Office of Emergency Planning, 30
Office of Organizational and Management Planning. *See* Vance Task Force
Office of the Secretary of Defense (OSD), 14, 17-18, 20-23, 28, 31, 44-45, 47, 49, 51, 536-42, 547-49; and base closures, 462; and Bay of Pigs, 180, 182; and Berlin, 146, 148-49, 158, 162-64, 170; and cost reduction program, 454, 457-62; and Cuban missile crisis, 198, 224, 247; and flexible response, 295, 302-03, 310, 312, 315, 317, 319, 322; and FY 1962 budget, 70; and FY 1963 budget, 89, 93-95, 100, 107, 110, 112, 116; and FY 1964 budget, 119, 121-23, 131, 136-38; and FY 1965 budget, 476-79, 485; and FY 1966 budget, 489-92; and Laos, 233, 237, 252, 254; and limited nuclear test ban treaty, 326, 337; and military assistance, 429-31, 433, 435-39, 441-46; and multilateral force, 388, 393-94; and NATO, 367-68, 371, 376, 378; and Planning-Programming-Budgeting System (PPBS), 74-77, 80, 84-85, 93, 95; and TFX, 469-71; and Vietnam, 274, 513
offset payments, 451, 452, 473
O'Hara, Rep. James G., 326-27
Okinawa, 38, 449
on-site inspection, 334, 337-40, 344, 347, 351
OPLAN 34A, 501, 519, 521, 523, 525
OPLAN 312-62, 200, 201
OPLAN 314-61, 200
Organization of American States (OAS), 182, 193, 195, 199, 209-10, 227
Ormsby Gore, David, 380, 382, 384
Owen, Henry D., 385, 389-90, 400, 406, 418

Pacific Command, United States (PACOM), 274, 282
Pacific, Commander in Chief (CINCPAC), 36, 233, 235, 239, 247, 256, 262-63, 265, 274, 279, 282-84, 290, 519, 521-22, 548
Pakistan, 231, 425, 428, 438
Panama, 38, 39, 40, 226, 444, 449
Panofsky, Wolfgang K. H., 330-31
Partridge, General Earle E., 20, 318

Partridge Committee report, 20, 295, 318
Passman, Rep. Otto E., 424-25, 430-31, 433, 435-37, 439, 441
Pastore, Sen. John O., 351
Pathet Lao, 229-59, 515-17
Paul, Norman S., 97-98, 103, 541
Pershing, 370, 371, 375, 389, 415, 416
Peurifoy, John E., 252
Philadelphia Navy Yard, 464, 465
Philippines, 234
Phoumi Nosovan, General, 229, 233-37, 239-40, 243, 247-48, 252-53, 255, 517
"Pierce Arrow," 522
Pittman, Steuart L., 31-34
Planning-Programming-Budgeting System (PPBS), 3, 14, 72-95, 476, 539, 540, 548-49
Pleiku, 529
Poland, 240, 360
Polaris, 12, 83, 300, 312, 317, 335, 494, 496, 546; and FY 1962 budget, 54, 57, 58, 59, 60, 62; and FY 1964 budget, 124, 125, 127, 134; and NATO use, 308, 361, 363, 366, 372, 377, 380, 381, 382-84, 386-89, 392, 393, 394, 403, 404
Portsmouth (N.H.) Navy Yard, 465
Portugal, 48, 409
posture statement, 76, 97, 98, 457, 485
Power, General Thomas S., 211, 312, 317
Presque Isle Air Force Base, Maine, 463
Procurement of Equipment and Munitions for the Army (PEMA), 126
program change proposals (PCPs), 119, 121, 122, 476-78, 490, 491
Programs Evaluation Office, 229, 236-37, 240-41
Proxmire, Sen. William, 68, 140
public affairs, assistant secretary of defense for, 103, 470

Quinn, Maj. Gen. William W., 23

Ramsey, Henry C., 36n
RAND Corporation, 6, 8, 10, 13, 27, 72, 76-77, 309
Randolph, Sen. Jennings, 140
Raritan (N.J.) Arsenal, 463
Reedy, George, 493
research and development, 14, 38, 44, 57, 80, 83, 92, 130, 139, 457, 484, 485, 486, 495. *See also* Advanced Research Projects Agency; defense research and engineering, director of
Reserve forces, 18, 51, 65-66, 70, 78, 83, 88-89, 92, 96, 107-14, 116, 130-31, 143, 151, 161, 170, 270, 495, 540

Reston, James, 400, 418
RF-8, 516
Richardson, John, 289
Ricketts, Admiral Claude V., 400, 410, 411, 413n
Rickover, Admiral Hyman, 400, 407
Riley, Rep. John J., 66
Rivers, Rep. L. Mendel, 484
Roa, Raul, 183
Robertson, Sen. A. Willis, 68, 96, 101, 109, 110-13, 135
Rockefeller, Nelson D., 30, 342, 465
Rockefeller report, 7
Rogers, Jack A., 529n
roles and missions, 42, 45-47, 74, 78, 81, 468, 537
Rolling Thunder, 531
Rosson, Maj. Gen. William B., 41
Rostow, Walt W., 1, 36n, 152, 193, 236, 248, 258, 270-71, 280, 290, 297-98, 385, 389, 398, 400, 413, 418
Rowan, Carl T., 511, 514
Rowen, Henry S., 143, 296-97, 305, 308, 310, 360, 371, 398
Rowny, Brig. Gen. Edward L., 364
Rowny report, 364
RS-70, 47, 70, 96, 100-03, 105-07, 110-11, 113, 115-16, 119, 121, 122, 131-32, 134, 136-37, 141
Rubel, John H., 378, 381, 383, 548-49
Ruffner, General Clark, 304
Runge, Carlisle P., 110
Rusk, Dean, 5-6, 36, 97, 146, 180, 187, 198, 201, 413, 436, 452, 492; and Bay of Pigs, 175-78, 184-85; and Berlin, 152-53, 157, 160, 164, 167; and BNSP, 297-98; and counterinsurgency, 42; and Cuban missile crisis, 206; and Laos, 232, 237, 239, 243, 245-46, 248; and McNamara, 325, 542; and military assistance, 422-23, 434; and MLF, 388, 395, 398, 400-02, 404, 406n, 408-09, 412, 416, 419; and NATO, 303, 363, 365, 372, 374; and Nike-Zeus, 124-25; and nuclear test ban, 338-39, 345-47, 351-53; and Skybolt, 380-83; and Vietnam, 266, 273, 286-87, 289-91, 498, 501, 503, 505-06, 511-15, 519, 521, 526, 528-29, 532
Russell, Sen. Richard B., 10, 98-99, 103, 133-34, 137-41, 342, 352, 440, 459, 484, 486, 488, 493, 541
Ryan, Rep. William F., 136

Saltonstall, Sen. Leverett, 11, 29, 63, 99, 109, 113, 140, 351, 459, 491
SAMOS, 301, 310

San Francisco Navy Yard, 464
San Marcos, U.S.S., 176
Sarit Thanarat, 255
Schaetzel, Robert J., 389, 400, 406
Schlesinger, Arthur M., Jr., 2, 5, 34, 152, 177, 181-82, 191, 323, 347
Schriever, General Bernard A., 44-45
SEABEEs (construction battalions), U.S. Navy, 40
Seaborg, Glenn T., 330-32, 335, 339, 344-45, 350, 355, 413n
sealift, 12, 68, 70, 80, 83, 85, 92, 129, 495, 496
SEALs (Sea-Air-Land teams), U.S. Navy, 40
Self Defense Corps (SDC), 273-74, 276-79
Senate Appropriations Committee, 23, 29, 41, 56-57, 62-63, 67-68, 96, 101, 107, 109-11, 135, 137-39, 141, 425, 442, 446n, 486, 488, 495n
Senate Armed Services Committee, 6, 10, 11, 33, 55, 62, 68, 97-99, 103, 105-06, 133-35, 141, 167, 190, 352-54, 440, 458, 463, 484, 486, 495n, 503, 522
Senate Finance Committee, 480, 483
Senate Foreign Relations Committee, 130, 167, 180, 249, 352-54, 424, 436, 442, 522-23
Senate Government Operations Committee, 470, 473
Senate Government Operations Committee, (Jackson) Subcommittee on National Policy Machinery, 6, 11
Senate Preparedness Committee, 69, 141
Senior Interdepartmental Group, 38
Sergeant, 371
Sharp, Admiral Ulysses S., Jr., 519, 521-22, 528, 548
Sheehan, Neil, 281, 282
Shoup, General David M., 40, 91, 128, 177-78, 456, 490
Shriver, Robert Sargent, Jr., 4
Sihanouk, Prince Norodom, 231, 255, 515
Sikes, Rep. Robert L. F., 107, 457, 459
Single Integrated Operational Plan (SIOP), 20, 297, 311, 316, 317, 319, 321
single manager system, 25-27
Skybolt, 59, 83, 118, 119, 121, 123, 125, 131, 132, 136, 314, 375-84, 402, 403, 404
Smathers, Sen. George A., 198
Smith, Maj. Gen. Dale, 345
Smith, General Frederic H., Jr., 90, 100
Smith, Gerard, 385, 389, 400-02, 405, 408, 413, 418
Smith, Rear Adm. Harry, 428
Smith, Sen. Margaret Chase, 9, 97-98, 133, 541
Smith, Col. William Y., 297
Sorensen, Theodore, 6, 65, 87, 104, 121, 152, 174, 201-02, 206n, 208, 232, 241, 331, 372, 390
Souphanouvong, Prince, 229, 247, 255
Southeast Asia Treaty Organization (SEATO), 228-29, 231-34, 236, 238, 241-44, 247-48, 250-51, 254, 256, 275, 522
South Korea, 147, 425, 428, 431, 438, 439, 440, 442, 443, 452
South Vietnam. *See* Vietnam, Republic of
Souvanna Phouma, Prince, 229, 231, 234-35, 239, 244-45, 247-51, 253, 255-57, 515-17
Soviet Union, 35, 172, 421; anti-ballistic missile defense, 124, 125, 134; and Berlin, 143-71, 218-23; and Cuban missile crisis, 194, 195, 201-23; and Laos, 232-49 passim; military budget, 492-93; and missile gap, 3, 298-302; and NATO, 358-62, 364, 365; and nuclear test ban, 323-56; and space competition, 3, 43, 47; and U.S. strategic planning, 293, 294, 305, 307, 308, 310, 311, 315, 321, 322; and Vietnam, 236, 531
Spaak, Paul-Henri, 361-62, 365, 388-89, 391
space development, 43-47, 65, 121, 477
Sparkman, Sen. John, 323
Special Air Warfare Center, 39
Special Forces, 38-40, 42, 268, 506, 512, 529. *See also* counterinsurgency
Special Group (Augmented), 187, 194, 198, 201
Special Group (Counterinsurgency), 37-38, 40, 275
Special National Intelligence Estimates (SNIEs), 202, 219
special operations, assistant to the secretary of defense for, 22
Special Warfare Center, 38, 39, 41
Springfield (Mass.) Armory, 465
Sputnik, 3, 43, 298, 358, 369, 370, 386, 477n
Staats, Elmer B., 120
Stahr, Elvis J., Jr., 8, 16, 28, 46, 86-87, 93
Staley, Eugene, 269
Stans, Maurice H., 135
State, Department of, 5, 8; and Bay of Pigs, 173, 180-82, 185, 187, 192; and Berlin, 146-49, 152, 158, 162, 165, 167, 170; and counterinsurgency, 35-37, 42; and Cuban missile crisis, 196, 199-201, 211, 224-26; and flexible response, 296-97, 313; and FY 1962 budget, 58; and Laos, 231-32, 235, 237, 240, 244-45, 247, 249-50, 252, 254-56; and limited nuclear test ban treaty, 325-26, 328, 341, 349; and military assistance, 421-23, 427-28, 431, 439, 444, 446; and multilateral force, 387-90, 392-95, 397, 400-02, 405, 406n, 410, 412-13, 418, 420; and NATO, 359-63, 370, 373-75, 377, 379-84; and Planning-Programming-Budget-

ing System (PPBS), 92; and posture statements, 97, 542; and Vietnam, 264-67, 274, 278, 281, 286-88, 290, 501, 506, 512-13, 515-16, 518, 527
Stead Air Force Base, Nev., 464
Steinbruner, John, 411, 419-20
Stennis, Sen. John, 99, 352, 541
Stern, Marvin, 309-10
Stevenson, Adlai, 185, 210
Stikker, Dirk, 160, 167, 304, 362-63, 365, 391-94, 397-98
Strategic Air Command, Commander in Chief (CINCSAC), 211n, 213, 310, 312, 316-18
Strategic Army Corps (STRAC), 233
"strategic hamlet" program, 277-80, 281, 283
Strauss, Franz Josef, 155-56, 162, 304, 361, 373, 392-93, 451
Sudan, 425
Sullivan, William H., 518-19
Sweden, 333
Switzerland, 434
Sylvester, Arthur, 103, 470
Symington, Sen. W. Stuart, 17-18, 68, 98-99, 342
Symington Committee, 7, 17-19, 30, 49
systems analysis, 61, 72, 77, 536, 549. *See also* Planning-Programming-Budgeting System (PPBS)

T-6, 237
T-28, 516
T-33, 284
T-34, 225
Tactical Air Command (TAC), 213
Taiwan (Republic of China), 425, 428, 431, 438, 442, 443, 444
Tartar, 370
tax reduction, 120-21, 127, 475, 480, 481, 483, 485
Taylor, General Maxwell D., 6, 22, 73, 88, 115-16, 129, 190-92, 198, 293, 295, 297, 320, 322, 331, 477, 479, 490, 493; and Bay of Pigs, 174, 178, 182, 186-87, 194; and Berlin, 152, 163; and counterinsurgency, 37, 42; and Cuban missile crisis, 196, 206, 207-08, 221-22; and flexible response, 311-12; and FY 1964 budget, 136, 139; and Laos, 250; and McNamara, 537-38, 548; and military assistance, 429, 441; and MLF, 400, 402, 407, 411; and NATO, 362, 372, 395, 397-98; and Nike-Zeus, 124-25; and nuclear test ban, 323, 345, 348, 353-54; and Skybolt, 123, 381; and Taylor-Rostow mission, 270-74; and Vietnam, 275-76, 279, 282, 286-89, 291-92, 499, 504, 506-07, 509, 510, 512-14, 518, 525-29, 532-33
Teller, Edward, 342, 352-53

Ten-Nation Committee on Disarmament, 324, 334
TFX, 48, 141, 447, 466-74, 540-41
Thailand, 37, 275; and Laos, 231, 232, 233, 234, 236, 237, 241, 242, 243, 245, 249, 250, 253, 254, 255, 256, 257; military assistance to, 425, 430-31, 438, 442-43; and Vietnam, 530
Thant, U, 217
Third World, 13
Thomas, Rep. Albert, 30
Thompson, Llewellyn, 166, 206n, 220, 234, 238, 346
Thompson, Robert, 275, 277-78
Thor, 223, 386, 394
Thorneycroft, Peter, 379-84, 409
Thornton, Charles (Tex), 4
Thresher, U.S.S., 134
Thurmond, Sen. Strom, 62, 134, 352
Ticonderoga, U.S.S., 519
Titan, 15, 53, 54, 59, 62, 83, 454, 493, 496
Tonkin Gulf incident, 519-24, 525, 532
Tonkin Gulf Resolution, 517-18, 522-24, 525
Tran Thien Khiem, Lt. Gen., 524
Tran Van Huong, 528
Trapnell, Lt. Gen. Thomas, J., 240, 264
Treasury, Department of, 4, 36, 82, 121, 140, 481
Trinidad, Operation, 174-75, 179, 181, 187
Trudeau, Lt. Gen. Arthur G., 45-46
Truman, Harry S., 109, 546
Turkey: and Cuban missile crisis, 195, 207, 208, 210, 213-14, 218, 220-23, 402; military assistance to, 367, 425, 428, 431, 432, 438, 439, 442, 443
Turner Joy, U.S.S., 519, 522
Twining, General Nathan F., 387, 393n
Tyler, William R., 406n, 410

U-2, 174, 201, 202, 204, 211, 213, 215, 222, 226, 301, 324
Ulbricht, Walter, 151, 156-57, 165
Unger, Leonard, 529n
United Nations, 183-85, 204, 209-10, 215, 217, 333
United Nations Disarmament Commission, 324-26, 332
United States Information Agency (USIA), 36, 182, 224, 237, 267, 325n, 332, 408, 510
United States Intelligence Board, 23
U.S. Seventh Army, 161, 164
U.S. Sixth Fleet, 161, 412
University of Mississippi, integration of, 547

Van Fleet, Lt. Gen. James, 252
Van Zandt, Rep. James E., 210
Vance, Cyrus R., 7, 19, 25, 46, 112, 114, 224-26, 488, 491, 521
Vance Committee, 25-26
Vance Task Force, 19-20, 22
Vandiver, Ernest S., 10
Vanguard, 73
Vann, Lt. Col. John Paul, 281-82
VAX, 467
V-bomber, 376, 377, 381, 404
VELA, 337-39, 343
Venezuela, 37, 199, 211, 452
Vienna Summit Conference (1961), 150-51, 246, 328, 331, 341
Viet Cong, 262-73, 276-77, 280-81, 283-85, 287-88, 498, 500, 502-03, 505-07, 509, 513-15, 517-18, 524-33
Vietnam, 1, 52, 191, 228, 229, 244, 294, 353, 450, 453, 487, 494, 495, 540, 543, 544-45
Vietnam, Democratic Republic of (North Vietnam), 229; and Laos, 232, 237, 241, 242, 244, 245, 249, 251, 253, 254, 255, 256, 257, 258; and South Vietnam, 260, 262, 263, 264, 265, 266, 272, 276, 278, 290, 498-534 passim; and Tonkin Gulf incident, 519-24; U.S. air strikes against, 525-33
Vietnam, Republic of (South Vietnam), 229; and Buddhist rebellion, 283, 285-86; counterinsurgency activities in, 35-36, 37, 38-40; and crisis in Laos, 231, 232, 233, 236, 242, 243, 244, 245, 249, 250, 251, 254, 255, 256, 257, 259; and defoliation program, 276, 291; deployment of U.S. Marines to, 532; and Diem assassination, 290; during Johnson administration, 498-534; during Kennedy administration, 260-92; Gilpatric task force on, 267-68; and Khanh coup, 502-04; military assistance to, 425, 426, 430, 431, 432, 436, 437, 438, 439, 440, 441, 442, 443, 444, 445, 446; Staley report on, 269; and strategic hamlet program, 277-80, 281, 283; visits to by U.S. officials (McGeorge Bundy) 529-30, (Vice President Johnson) 268-69, (Lansdale) 262-63, (McNamara) 288-89, 499-501, 507-08, 513-14, (Taylor-Rostow mission) 270-74
Vietnam Task Force, 267-68, 275, 278
Vinson, Rep. Carl, 10, 12, 29, 459, 465; and FY 1962 budget, 56, 63-64; and FY 1963 budget, 96, 98-99, 101-06; and FY 1964 budget, 131-34, 141; and FY 1965 authorization bill, 484-86; and McNamara, 537, 542; and military assistance, 441
Vo Nguyen Giap, General, 244

von Braun, Werner, 45
von Brentano, Heinrich, 146
von Hassel, Kai-Uwe, 415

Ward, Rear Adm. N. G., 411
Warren, Maj. Gen. Frederick M., 109-10
Warsaw Pact, 199, 201, 214, 313, 324, 347, 360, 364
Washington Ambassadorial Steering Group, 156, 160
Watertown (Mass.) Arsenal, 464
Watkinson, Harold, 378-79, 392
Watson, Maj. Gen. Albert, III, 165
Weapons Systems Evaluation Group (WSEG), 321
Webb, James E., 47
Weiss, Seymour, 162, 400
West Germany. See Germany, Federal Republic of
Westmoreland, General William C., 445, 503-04, 513-14, 518, 523, 528-29, 532
Wheeler, General Earl G., 132, 139, 224, 519; and Bay of Pigs, 177; and counterinsurgency, 42; and FY 1964 budget, 126, 128; and FY 1966 budget, 490, 493; and McNamara, 537-38; and military assistance, 442; and Vietnam, 282-83, 512, 521, 525, 531
White, General Thomas D., 44, 61, 176, 243
Whiz Kids, 4, 7-8, 76, 116, 190, 291, 538
Wiesner, Jerome B., 46, 123-27, 152, 330, 355, 378
Wilson, Charles E., 8, 11
Wilson, Harold, 415-19
Wilson, Col. Jasper, 503
Wolfe, Col. Thomas, 239
Wood, General Robert J., 435-36, 439, 443
World War II, 2, 3, 4, 74, 174, 179, 294, 358, 421, 425, 465, 487, 538

Yarmolinsky, Adam, 31, 308
York, Herbert F., 8, 15, 61, 337, 466-67
Yoshpe, Harry, 34
Yugoslavia, 249

Zapata, Operation, 179, 181, 187, 188, 198
Zelikow, Philip D., 213
Zorthian, Barry, 515, 524
Zuckerman, Solly, 349
Zuckert, Eugene M., 8, 14, 67, 86, 93-94, 100, 106, 115, 468-71, 478, 536

www.ingramcontent.com/pod-product-compliance
Lightning Source LLC
Chambersburg PA
CBHW080921100426
42812CB00007B/2338